Looking for ways to integrate the Web into your curriculum?

ClassZone℠

www.mcdougallittell.com

ClassZone, McDougal Littell's textbook-companion Web site, is the solution! Online teaching support for you and engaging, interactive content for your students!

Access *Auf Deutsch!* ClassZone site to find:

- Links correlated to the textbook for relevant Internet exploration
- Online flipcards for vocabulary practice
- Self-scoring quizzes to check understanding of concepts
- Writing center promotes and reinforces student's writing skills
- Internet research tutorial to help students conduct research
- Teacher center for classroom ideas (accessible to teachers only)

Log on to ClassZone at www.mcdougallittell.com

With the purchase of *Auf Deutsch!*, you have immediate access to ClassZone.

Teacher Access Code

MCDFJWXEKHERT

Use this code to create your own user name and password. Then, access both teacher only and student resources.

Student Access Code

MCDCVQ9ZSA9R3

Give this code to your class. Each student creates a unique username and password to access resources for students.

www.mcdougallittell.com

Auf Deutsch!

Auf Deutsch!

3 DREI

LIDA DAVES-SCHNEIDER
Chino Valley (CA) Unified School District

KARL SCHNEIDER
Chino Valley (CA) Unified School District

DANIELA DOSCH FRITZ

STEPHEN L. NEWTON
University of California, Berkeley

Chief Academic and Series Developer
ROBERT DI DONATO
Miami University, Oxford, Ohio

McDougal Littell
A HOUGHTON MIFFLIN COMPANY
Evanston, Illinois • Boston • Dallas

Auf Deutsch!
3 Drei
Teacher's Edition

C, 2

2004 Impression

This book is printed on acid-free paper.

2 3 4 5 6 7 8 9   QVK   09 08 07 06 05

ISBN 0-618-02966-4

Cover photographs *Clockwise from top:* © BAV/Helga Lade Fotoagentur; © Siegfried Layda/Corbis Images; © M. Listri/Corbis Images; © Peter Weber/Tony Stone Images.

Illustrations were created by Wolfgang Horsch, Manfred von Papan, Eldon Doty, Anica Gibson, Carol Faulkner, and maps by Lori Heckelman.

Internet: www.mcdougallittell.com

CONTENTS

ENGAGING STORY LINKS LANGUAGE TO LIFE

Auf Deutsch! is an integrated program of print, *Fokus Deutsch Video Series*, audio, and technology. This exciting, three-level German program for middle school and high school:

- **Integrates technology** through videos that immerse students in authentic language and culture.
- **Presents language clearly**, concisely, and in context for more accurate communication.
- **Encourages retention** with language, culture, and study strategies.
- **Adapts to varied learning styles** and ability levels.

INTRODUCE YOUR STUDENTS TO THE RICHNESS OF GERMAN LANGUAGE AND CULTURE

Fokus Deutsch Video Series **helps students communicate in meaningful contexts as they learn about and develop an understanding of German-speaking cultures.**

Motivating dialogues, **with embedded vocabulary and structures, present language in real-life contexts to develop students' understanding and help them express themselves.**

KAPITEL 29

VIDEOTHEK

Heute ist die Bundesrepublik Deutschland eine grosse Wirtschaftsmacht. Aber wie ist das passiert? Und wie sieht das heutige Arbeitsleben aus?

I: Wirtschaft im Wandel

In dieser Folge sehen Sie, in welcher Lage sich die deutsche Wirtschaft nach dem Zweiten Weltkrieg befand, und wie sie heute aussieht.

A Was bedeutet für Sie das Wort Wirtschaft? Machen Sie eine kleine Liste mit Wörtern und Begriffen, die Sie mit Wirtschaft assoziieren. Was hat Wirtschaft mit Ihrem Leben zu tun?

B Wirtschaft und Menschen durch die Jahre. Welcher Satz passt zu welchem Bild?

1. Die Familien müssen umziehen, um eine Arbeitsstelle zu finden.
2. Viele Roboter werden in den Fabriken eingesetzt.
3. Viele Familien kaufen sich zum ersten Mal Konsumgüter wie Kühlschränke, Fernseher oder Autos.
4. Die Berufe wandeln sich immer schneller. Neue Kommunikationstechniken und Computer verändern die Arbeit und auch das Leben vieler Deutscher.
5. Die meisten Deutschen arbeiten zu dieser Zeit in der Industrie.

A. *Answers will vary.*

1955 wurde der millionste Volkswagen hergestellt.

B. **1.** a   **2.** c   **3.** b   **4.** d   **5.** e

WORTSCHATZ ZUM VIDEO

schuften	to toil
sich abrackern	to slave away
das Atelier	(artist's) studio; small office
das Wirtschaftswunder	German economic miracle
verharren	to persevere
die EDV-Erfahrung	data processing experience
anrechnen	to count; to take into account
die Früchte	fruits

a.   b.   c.

d.   e.

C Persönliche Geschichten. Was machen diese Menschen beruflich?

Gürkan   Erika   Anja   Bob

1. Diese Person malt und geht oft in Museen.
2. Diese Person arbeitet selbstständig und führt gemeinsam mit zwei anderen ein Reisebüro.
3. Diese Person arbeitet an einem Deutschkurs mit Hilfe einer Assistentin.
4. Diese Person lehrt Deutsch am Goethe-Institut.

II: Eine Arbeitsvermittlerin

In dieser Folge lernen Sie Monika Schneider kennen. Sie ist Arbeitsvermittlerin und sucht Stellen für Arbeitslose und Arbeitsuchende.

A Arbeitgeber und Arbeitnehmer. Monika unterstützt Arbeitnehmer, eine Arbeit zu finden. Dabei hilft sie auch den Arbeitgebern, die Arbeiter brauchen. Lesen Sie die folgenden Sätze, und sagen Sie, welche Person der Satz beschreibt, Frau Schneider, Herrn Weinart, Herrn Kloss oder Herrn Lebendig.

1. _____ ist Elektromeister von Beruf.
2. _____ ist Apotheker, und sucht eine Mitarbeiterin.
3. _____ arbeitet beim Arbeitsamt.
4. _____ möchte nicht in eine andere Stadt ziehen.
5. _____ sucht einen Groß- und Außenhandelskaufmann.

B Ostdeutsche Perspektiven. Anja erzählt von den Problemen der Arbeitslosigkeit in der ehemaligen DDR. Stimmen die folgenden Sätze?

1. Arbeitslosigkeit ist heute das größte Problem in Deutschland.
2. Viele Leute wollen alle fünf Jahre in einer neuen Firma arbeiten.
3. Die Arbeitslosigkeit unter Leuten, die in der ehemaligen DDR gearbeitet haben, ist nicht wesentlich schlimmer als unter denen, die in der BRD gearbeitet haben.
4. Die Jahre, die ihre Eltern in der DDR gearbeitet haben, werden nicht angerechnet. Deswegen bekommen sie nicht viel Geld.

B. 1. Das stimmt. 2. Das stimmt nicht. 3. Das stimmt nicht. 4. Das stimmt.

Gürkan.
C. 1. Erika 2. Gürkan 3. Bob 4. Anja

Monika Schneider spricht mit Herrn Weinart.
A. 1. Herr Weinart 2. Herr Kloss 3. Frau Schneider 4. Herr Weinart 5. Herr Lebendig

KULTURSPIEGEL

In den neuen Bundesländern sind die wirtschaftlichen Problemen viel größer als in den alten. Nach der Wende schaffte man viele Arbeitsplätze ab. Viele ältere Leute gingen in den Vorruhestand, aber junge Leute, die vor der Wende einen garantierten Arbeitsplatz zu erwarten hatten, haben viel Angst vor Arbeitslosigkeit.

Authentic cultural and *historical footage unveil the interrelationships between language and culture and encourage students to make comparisons between the German-speaking world and their own.*

Personal testimonials explore topics that affect German-speaking people today such as everyday life, family life, and the world of work.

T 9

BALANCE PROFICIENCY AND GRAMMAR TO MAXIMIZE COMMUNICATION

Auf Deutsch! **is a proficiency-driven program supported by clear vocabulary and grammar instruction to better prepare students for comprehensive recognition and confident production.**

Activities in **Auf Deutsch!** *flow from receptive to productive.*

VOKABELN

die Arbeitslosenzahl	*number of unemployed*
die Berufserfahrung	*work experience*
die Entwicklung	*development*
die Rente	*pension*
die Steuer	*tax*
die Wirtschaft	*economy*
der Arbeitsvermittler /	*employment agent*
die Arbeitsvermittlerin	
der Betrieb	*business operation*
der Rentner / die	*pensioner*
Rentnerin	
der Termin	*appointment*
das Unternehmen	*business enterprise*
auf•bauen	*to build; to set up*
ein•setzen	*to put in place*
erfordern	*to require*
erhalten	*to receive*
erlernen	*to learn*
her•stellen	*to manufacture; to produce*
steigern	*to raise*
zwingen	*to force*
gering	*small, negligible*
künftig	*future*

Was kann die Gesellschaft tun, um die wirtschaftliche Lage zu verbessern?

unentbehrlich   *essential(ly), indispensable*

Sie wissen schon
die Kenntnis, die Stelle, der Arbeitsplatz, der Beruf, der Bewerber / die Bewerberin, einen Beruf aus•üben, (mit etwas) einverstanden sein, selbstständig, zufrieden/unzufrieden, ungefähr

Aktivitäten

A Definitionen. Welche Wörter aus dem Kasten auf Seite 101 passen zu den folgenden Definitionen?

1. Zahl der arbeitslosen Menschen
2. eine Person, die Stellen für Arbeitslose sucht
3. organisieren, gestalten, strukturieren
4. jemand, der sich um eine Arbeitsstelle bewirbt
5. jemandem einer Sache zustimmen, akzeptieren
6. bekommen
7. das Kennen einer Sache, das Wissen von etwas
8. Einkommen vom Staat, wenn man alt ist

---

die Kenntnis		einverstanden sein
die Arbeitsvermittlerin	erhalten	die Rente
der Bewerber	aufbauen	die Arbeitslosenzahl

B Arbeitswelt. Ergänzen Sie die Sätze.

1. Auszubildende arbeiten bei einer Firma und lernen, wie man einen Beruf _____.
2. Die neuen Umstände in der Arbeitswelt _____, dass man sehr flexibel sein muss.
3. Wer eine neue Karriere haben will, muss natürlich auch einen neuen Beruf _____.
4. In Deutschland werden viele Autos _____.
5. Immer mehr Maschinen werden in der Industrie _____.
6. Viele Menschen sind _____, Jobs zu nehmen, die ihnen nicht besonders gut gefallen.

erfordern
hergestel
erlernen
eingeset
gezwungen
ausü

See answers below.

C Anders gesagt. Setzen Sie für die kursiv gedruckten Wörter Synonyme aus der Wortliste auf Seite 100 ein.

1. Wir sind *darüber einig*, dass Arbeiter mehr Urlaub haben sollen.
2. Die Stadt Heidelberg hat *etwa* 150 000 Einwohner.
3. Die Zahl der Arbeiter, die in der Schwerindustrie arbeiten, wird immer *kleiner*.
4. Gute Ratschläge sind oft *nötig*.
5. Renate ist in ihrer neuen Stelle sehr *unglücklich*.
6. Klaus arbeitet lieber *ohne Hilfe*.

KULTURSPIE

Viele junge Deutsche fangen Karriere als Lehrlinge an. Sie ihren neuen Beruf sowohl in als auch am Arbeitsplatz. Drei lang belegen Lehrlinge Kurse Berufsschule und machen zus Lehre in einer Fabrik oder in Büro. Abiturienten können die Lehrperiode um bis zu zwei verkürzen.

D Wie stellen Sie sich Ihre künftige Karriere vor? Was möchten Sie werden? Warum? Was müssen Sie tun, um diesen Beruf ausüben zu können?

MODELL: Ich möchte Mechanikerin werden, weil ich gern mit Werkzeugen und Autos arbeite. Ich möchte in einer Autowerkstatt arbeiten, wo ich diesen Beruf erlernen kann.

Kulturspiegel provides cultural notes that connect to the video, readings, and activities.

T10

Grammar lessons present concepts clearly and concisely and follow-up with numerous practice activities.

Sprachspiegel are language notes that compare German to English to give students a frame of reference for better understanding.

STRUKTUREN

REVIEW OF COMPARATIVES
COMPARING PEOPLE AND THINGS

To say someone or something is (not) the same as someone or something else, use the expression **(nicht) so . . . wie.**

Ein Beruf ist **so gut wie** der andere.	*One occupation is as good as the other.*
Ein Krankenpfleger verdient **nicht so viel wie** ein Arzt.	*A nurse doesn't earn as much as a doctor.*

Note that the phrase **(nicht) so . . . wie** uses the positive form of adjectives and adverbs—the form that normally appears in vocabulary lists and dictionaries.

The comparative form of adjectives and adverbs includes the ending **-er.** Most one-syllable words with the vowel **a, o,** or **u** also add an umlaut in the comparative.

POSITIVE	COMPARATIVE	POSITIVE	COMPARATIVE
schnell	schneller	groß	größer
alt	älter	klug	klüger

A small number of one-syllable words with these vowels do not add the umlaut: **klar → klarer** and **rot → roter** (although some speakers do say **röter**).

A number of adjectives and adverbs in German have irregular forms in the comparative.

POSITIVE	COMPARATIVE	POSITIVE	COMPARATIVE
gern	lieber	hoch	höher
gut	besser	viel	mehr

Ich arbeite **gern** im Büro, aber ich arbeite **lieber** zu Hause.	*I like working in the office, but I prefer working at home.*

German also uses the comparative form of adjectives and adverbs with the word **als** to make comparisons of inequality. Note that in German the nouns or pronouns in comparison—those that both precede and follow **als**—share the same case. This rule is also true in English, although speakers frequently use object forms (*me, him, her, us*) after the word *than.*

Er arbeitet **fleißiger als** ich.	*He works harder than I (do).*
Ich kann **schneller** laufen **als** er.	*I can run faster than he (can).*
Sie hat ihm **mehr** Hilfe gegeben **als** mir.	*She gave him more help than (she gave) me.*

Note that the phrase beginning with **wie** or **als** stands outside the clause it refers to.

Ich habe **nicht so viel** gelernt **wie du.**	*I didn't study as much as you (did).*

Remember that comparatives take the same endings as other attributive adjectives when they stand before a noun.

Ausgebildete Menschen haben **bessere** Chancen im Berufsleben.	*Educated people have better opportunities in professional life.*

German uses the word **immer** plus the comparative form of an adjective or adverb to show progression, whereas English uses the comparative form twice, or the words *more and more* plus the positive form of an adjective or adverb.

Es wird **immer kälter.**	*It's getting colder and colder.*
Sie singen **immer schöner.**	*They sing more and more beautifully.*

The German expression **je (mehr) . . . je/desto/umso (mehr)** is equivalent to the English *the (more) . . . the (more) . . .* Notice that one of three different words can begin the second part of the German expression. Both German and English use comparative forms of adjectives or adverbs in these expressions.

Je mehr man arbeitet, **desto mehr** man verdient.	*The more one works, the more one earns.*

Übungen

A Zurück nach Aachen. Guy, der Student aus Kamerun, kommt nach einigen Jahren wieder nach Aachen. Die Stadt hat sich inzwischen sehr verändert. Was sagt er? Ergänzen Sie die Adjektive oder Adverbien im Komparativ.

1. Die Stadt ist jetzt _____. (groß)
2. Die Preise sind _____. (hoch)
3. Die Wohnungen sind _____. (teuer)
4. Die neuen Kurse sind _____. (interessant)
5. Das neue Universitätsgebäude ist _____ als die alten. (schön)
6. Ich finde es sehr schön in Deutschland, aber ich wohne _____ in Kamerun. (gern)

A. 1. größer 2. höher 3. teurer 4. interessanter 5. schöner 6. lieber

SPRACHSPIEGEL

German forms the comparative of all adjectives and adverbs with **-er,** whereas English forms many comparatives with *-er,* but others with the word *more.*

Er ist **intelligenter** als ich.
He is more intelligent than I (am).

Sie schreibt **interessantere** Berichte als du.
She writes more interesting reports than you (do).

Sie arbeiten **fleißiger** als wir.
They work harder than we (do).

Guy trifft alte Freunde in Aachen. Einige sind schon länger in Deutschland als er.

Auf Deutsch!

T11

PRESENT LANGUAGE CLEARLY, CONCISELY, AND IN CONTEXT

Auf Deutsch! supports teachers and students alike with the listening, speaking, reading, writing, and cultural strategies necessary to build confident communicators.

KAPITEL 29

PERSPEKTIVEN

WORTSCHATZ ZUM HÖRTEXT

der Blechblas-instrumentenbauer	*maker of brass (musical) instruments*
die Gesellenprüfung	*examination to become a journeyman*
die Meisterprüfung	*examination to become master craftsman*
absolvieren	*to pass; to complete*

A. 1. ja   2. nein   3. ja   4. ja   5. nein   6. ja

KULTURSPIEGEL

Mackenbach liegt im südwestlichen Teil von Rheinland-Pfalz. Diese Gegend ist als Musikantenland bekannt. Im neunzehnten Jahrhundert zwangen schlechte wirtschaftliche Bedingungen die Menschen in dieser Gegend, alternative Berufe zu finden. Viele wurden Musikanten, zogen in Gruppen durch ganz Europa und gaben Konzerte. Manche dieser Musikanten kamen auch nach Amerika.

B. 1. Das hat der deutsche Komponist Paul Hindemith gesagt.   2. Über der Haustür von Horst Molter.   3. In Kaiserslautern hat Horst Molter seine Lehre als Blechbasinstrumentenbauer gemacht.   4. Horst Molter wanderte 1956 nach Amerika aus.   5. Er hat neun Jahre in New York gearbeitet.   6. 1965 kam er zurück nach Deutschland.   7. In Frankfurt hat er seine Meisterprüfung absolviert.   8. Das Geschäft in Mackenbach hat er seit 1974.

HÖREN SIE ZU!
EINE AHNUNG VON TUTEN UND BLASEN

A Horst Molter. Sie hören einen Text über einen Mann mit einem seltenen Beruf. Was für Informationen hören Sie im Text? Beantworten Sie die Fragen mit „ja" oder „nein".

Hören Sie
1. ein Zitat des Komponisten Paul Hindemith?
2. Information über Mackenbach?
3. die Namen der Städte, in denen Horst Molter gelebt hat?
4. Information über seine Ausbildung?
5. etwas über amerikanische Komponisten?
6. etwas über Kunden von Horst Molter?

B Was wissen Sie jetzt über Horst Molter? Hören Sie den Text noch einmal, und beantworten Sie dann die Fragen.

1. Wer hat gesagt, „Musik machen ist besser als Musik hören"?
2. Wo hängt eine Miniaturtrompete?
3. Was hat Horst Molter in Kaiserslautern gemacht?
4. Wann ist er nach Amerika ausgewandert?
5. Wo hat er in Amerika gearbeitet?
6. Wann kam er zurück nach Deutschland?
7. Was hat er in Frankfurt gemacht?
8. Seit wann hat er ein Geschäft in Mackenbach?

LESEN SIE!

Zum Thema

A Was macht man in jedem Beruf? Verbinden Sie die Berufe mit den Beschreibungen auf Seite 109.

MODELL: mit Steinen und Mörtel arbeiten →
Ein Maurer arbeitet mit Steinen und Mörtel.

Friseurin	Clown	Tischlerin	Bäcker
Schriftstellerin	Metzger	Stierkämpferin	Lehrer
Schauspieler	Melker	Straßenbahnschaffner	Lacher

1. Kühe melken
2. Häuser oder Möbel bauen
3. in Spanien: Stier kämpfen
4. in einer Schule lehren
5. Bücher schreiben
6. Brot und Brötchen backen
7. Theater spielen
8. im Zirkus arbeiten
9. Haare schneiden
10. auf Bitte lachen
11. Fahrausweise kontrollieren
12. Fleisch verkaufen

A. 1. Melker 2. Tischlerin 3. Stierkämpferin
4. Lehrer 5. Schriftstellerin 6. Bäcker
7. Schauspieler 8. Clown 9. Friseurin
10. Lacher 11. Straßenbahnschaffner
12. Metzger

B Berufe. Arbeiten Sie in Dreiergruppen. Wählen Sie sechs Berufe aus der Liste. Beschreiben Sie jeden der sechs Berufe aus der Liste und beantworten Sie dabei folgende Fragen:

1. Wo arbeitet jemand, der diesen Beruf ausübt?
2. Wie würden Sie die Arbeitswoche dieser Person beschreiben?
3. Ist die Arbeit körperlich oder eher geistig?
4. Verdient man gewöhnlich viel oder wenig in diesem Beruf?
5. Stellen Sie sich vor: Was will diese Person in der Freizeit machen? Was will sie nicht machen?

B. Answers will vary.

Der Lacher

Wenn ich nach meinem Beruf gefragt werde, befällt mich Verlegenheit: ich werde rot, stammele, ich, der ich sonst als ein sicherer Mensch bekannt bin. Ich beneide die Leute, die sagen können: ich bin Maurer. Friseuren, Buchhaltern und Schriftstellern neide ich die Einfachheit ihrer Bekenntnisse,
5 denn alle diese Berufe erklären sich aus sich selbst und erfordern keine längeren Erklärungen. Ich aber bin gezwungen, auf solche Fragen zu antworten: Ich bin Lacher. Ein solches Bekenntnis erfordert weitere, da ich auch die zweite Frage „Leben Sie davon?" wahrheitsgemäß mit „Ja" beantworten muß. Ich lebe tatsächlich von meinem Lachen, und ich lebe
10 gut, denn mein Lachen ist – kommerziell ausgedrückt – gefragt. Ich bin ein guter, bin ein gelernter Lacher, kein anderer lacht so wie ich, keiner beherrscht so die Nuancen meiner Kunst. Lange Zeit habe ich mich – um lästigen Erklärungen zu entgehen – als Schauspieler bezeichnet, doch sind meine mimischen und sprecherischen Fähigkeiten so gering, daß mir
15 diese Bezeichnung als nicht der Wahrheit gemäß erschien: ich liebe die Wahrheit, und die Wahrheit ist: ich bin Lacher. Ich bin weder Clown noch Komiker, ich erheitere die Menschen nicht, sondern stelle Heiterkeit dar: ich lache wie ein römischer Imperator oder wie ein sensibler Abiturient, das Lachen des 17. Jahrhunderts ist mir so geläufig wie das des 19., und wenn
20 es sein muß, lache ich alle Jahrhunderte, alle Gesellschaftsklassen, alle Altersklassen durch: ich hab's einfach gelernt, so wie man lernt, Schuhe zu besohlen. Das Lachen Amerikas ruht in meiner Brust, das Lachen Afrikas, weißes, rotes, gelbes Lachen – und gegen ein entsprechendes Honorar lasse ich es klingen, so wie die Regie es vorschreibt.
25 Ich bin unentbehrlich geworden, ich lache auf Schallplatten, lache auf Band, und die Hörspielregisseure behandeln mich rücksichtsvoll. Ich lache schwermütig, gemäßigt, hysterisch – lache wie ein Straßenbahnschaffner oder wie ein Lehrling der Lebensmittelbranche; das Lachen am Morgen, das Lachen am Abend, nächtliches Lachen

WORTSCHATZ ZUM LESEN

die Verlegenheit	embarrassment
beneiden	to envy
lästig	troublesome, tiresome
gemäß	suitable
die Heiterkeit	amusement
geläufig	familiar, fluent
der Schubkasten	drawer
vorziehen	to prefer
der Ernst	seriousness
verlernen	to forget (lit. unlearn)
verschlossen	reserved, closed

SIND SIE WORTSCHLAU?

The endings **-heit** and **-keit** change adjectives to feminine nouns.

heiter → die Heiterkeit, -en
verlegen → die Verlegenheit, -en

Wortschatz zum Lesen features point-of-use vocabulary lists to aid reading comprehension.

Sind Sie wortschlau? offers tips for learning and expanding vocabulary in German.

T13

Ensure smooth-sailing with planning guide and strategies

The comprehensive Teacher's Edition, resource materials, and classroom management suggestions provide the support you need to organize and streamline classroom instruction.

Time-saving lesson plans present sequenced teaching suggestions and ideas.

DAY 1

Note: (1) Please see TE, pp. 96E–96J, for other suggestions not referenced in these plans. (2) Not all homework options need be assigned.

CHAPTER OPENER
- Quick Start Review: Vocabulary (TE, p. 96E). 5 MIN
- Follow the Teaching Suggestions for discussing the German economy (TE, p. 96E). 4 MIN

VIDEOTHEK
- Do *Akt. A*, p. 98, as a class. Write lists on the board (TE, p. 96F). 6 MIN
- Follow the suggestions for viewing *Folge I: Wirtschaft im Wandel* and then have students do *Akt. B*, p. 98, in pairs (TE, p. 96F). 16 MIN
- Follow the Teaching Suggestions for a discussion (TE, p. 96F), then view *Folge II: Eine Arbeitsvermittlerin.* 11 MIN
- Do *Akt. A*, p. 99, silently, then check answers with partners (TE, p. 96F). 8 MIN

Homework Options:
- *Arbeitsheft*, p. 68, *Videothek, Akt. C*
- *Videothek, Akt. C*, p. 99

DAY 2

VIDEOTHEK
- Quick Start Review 1: Subjunctive (TE, p. 96E). 5 MIN
- Read the *Kulturspiegel*, p. 99, as a class and then do *Akt. B*, p. 99, individually. Check answers as a class and engage students in a discussion (TE, p. 96F). 8 MIN

VOKABELN
- Present the vocabulary on p. 100. 7 MIN
- Do *Akt. A*, pp. 100–101, silently, then check their answers with a partner. Conclude with the follow-up activity in the Teaching Suggestions (TE, p. 96G). 15 MIN
- Do the warm-up activity for *Akt. B*, p. 101, then do the activity as a class (TE, p. 96G). 8 MIN
- Do *Akt. C*, p. 101, silently, then check answers as a class. 7 MIN

Homework Options:
- *Vokabeln, Akt. D*, p. 101
- *Arbeitsheft*, p. 71, *Vokabeln, Akt. C*

DAY 3

VOKABELN
- Quick Start Review 1: Ordinal numbers (TE, p. 96F). 6 MIN
- Discuss *Akt. D*, p. 101, as a class (TE, p. 96G). 6 MIN

STRUKTUREN
- Present comparatives on pp. 102–103 using OHT 29.G1. 8 MIN
- Do *Übung A*, p. 103, silently, then check answers as a class. Do follow-up activity in the Teaching Suggestions (TE, p. 96H). 10 MIN
- Do *Übung B*, p. 104, in small groups, including the variation in the Teaching Suggestions. Have them share the answers with the class (TE, p. 96H). 12 MIN
- *Arbeitsheft*, p. 73, *Strukturen, Akt. D.* 8 MIN

Homework Options:
- *Übung C*, p. 104
- *Arbeitsheft*, p. 74, *Strukturen, Akt. F–H*

DAY 4

STRUKTUREN
- Quick Start Review 1: Genitive (TE, p. 96G). 5 MIN
- Present the superlatives on pp. 104–105 using OHT 29.2–29.G1. Follow the Teaching Suggestions (TE, p. 96H). 8 MIN
- *Arbeitsheft*, p. 75, audio *Akt. I.* 8 MIN
- Do *Übung A*, p. 105, with a partner and then check their answers as a class. 8 MIN
- Do *Übung B*, p. 106. Follow the Teaching Suggestions (TE, p. 96H). 12 MIN
- Present verbs as adjectives, participial constructions, and extended modifiers on pp. 106–107. 9 MIN

Homework Options:
- *Übung C*, p. 106
- *Übung A*, p. 107
- *Arbeitsheft*, pp. 75–76, *Strukturen, Akt. J–K*

Block scheduling lesson plans offer options for pacing and variety.

DAY 1

Note: (1) Please see TE, pp. 96E–96J, for other suggestions not referenced in these plans. (2) Not all homework options need be assigned.

CHAPTER OPENER
- Quick Start Review: Vocabulary (TE, p. 96E). 5 MIN
- Discuss the German economy (TE, p. 96E). 4 MIN

VIDEOTHEK
- View *Folge I* 11 MIN
- Do *Akt. A–B,* p. 98 (TE, p. 96F). 11 MIN
- View *Folge II.* 11 MIN
- Do *Akt. A–B,* p. 99 (TE, p. 96F). 16 MIN
- Block Schedule activity: Change of Pace (TE, p. 96F). 10 MIN

VOKABELN
- Present vocabulary on p. 100. 7 MIN
- Do *Akt. A,* pp. 100–101. 15 MIN

Homework Options:
- *Arbeitsheft,* p. 68, *Videothek, Akt. C* and p. 71, *Vokabeln, Akt. C–D*
- *Videothek, Akt. C,* p. 99
- *Vokabeln, Akt. D,* p. 101

DAY 2

VOKABELN
- Quick Start Review 1: Ordinal numbers (TE, p. 96F). 5 MIN
- Discuss *Akt. D,* p. 101, as a class (TE, p. 96G). 6 MIN
- Do *Akt. B,* p. 101, as a class (TE, p. 96G). 8 MIN
- Do *Akt. C,* p. 101, silently. 7 MIN
- Block Schedule activity: Change of Pace (TE, p. 96G). 10 MIN

STRUKTUREN
- Present comparatives on pp. 102–103. 8 MIN
- Do *Übung A,* p. 103, silently (TE, p. 96H). 10 MIN
- Do *Übung B,* p. 104, in small groups (TE, p. 96H). 12 MIN
- *Arbeitsheft,* p. 78, audio *Akt. A–C.* 16 MIN
- Present superlatives on pp. 104–105 (TE, p. 96H). 8 MIN

Homework Options:
- *Übung C,* p. 104
- *Arbeitsheft,* pp. 74–76, *Strukturen, Akt. F–H, J–K*
- *Übung C,* p. 106

DAY 3

STRUKTUREN
- Quick Start Review 1: Genitive (TE, p. 96G). 5 MIN
- *Arbeitsheft,* p. 75, audio *Akt. I.* 6 MIN
- Do *Übung A,* p. 105, in pairs. 7 MIN
- Do *Übung B,* p. 106 (TE, p. 96H). 7 MIN
- Present verbs as modifiers on pp. 106–107. 8 MIN
- Do *Übung B,* p. 107, in pairs. 8 MIN
- Block Schedule activity: Expansion (TE, p. 96H). 8 MIN

PERSPEKTIVEN
- *Arbeitsheft,* p. 77, *Akt. A–B.* 6 MIN
- Do *Hören Sie zu!, Akt. A,* p. 108 (TE, p. 96I). 10 MIN
- Do *Hören Sie zu!, Akt. B,* p. 108 (TE, p. 96I). 8 MIN
- Do *Zum Thema, Akt. A,* p. 109, in small groups. 7 MIN
- Introduce the text on pp. 111–112 and read it in groups (TE, p. 96I). 10 MIN

Homework Options:
- *Übung A,* p. 107
- *Arbeitsheft,* p. 76, *Akt. L–M*
- *Perspektiven, Zum Thema, Akt. B,* p. 109, individually

DAY 4

PERSPEKTIVEN
- Quick Start Review 1: Subjunctive (TE, p. 96H). 4 MIN
- Discuss *Zum Text, Akt. A,* p. 113, as a class. Follow the Teaching Suggestions (TE, p. 96I). 6 MIN
- Do *Zum Text, Akt. B,* p. 113, in small groups. 6 MIN
- Discuss *Zur Interpretation,* p. 113, as a class (TE, p. 96I). 5 MIN
- *Interaktion,* p. 113. 14 MIN
- Begin *Schreiben Sie!* by discussing the assignment, *Tipp zum Schreiben,* and *Schreibmodell.* 5 MIN
- *Vor dem Schreiben,* p. 113. Begin *Beim Schreiben,* p. 113. 10 MIN
- Block Schedule activity: Fun Break (TE, p. 96J). 10 MIN
- *Beim Schreiben,* p. 113. 30 MIN

Homework Options:
- *Arbeitsheft,* pp. 78–80, *Perspektiven, Akt. D–F*

DAY 5

PERSPEKTIVEN
- Quick Start Review 2: Vocabulary (TE, p. 96I). 5 MIN
- Do the first step in *Nach dem Schreiben,* p. 113. 10 MIN
- Conduct the interviews (step 2 from *Nach dem Schreiben*). 10 MIN
- Do step 3 from *Nach dem Schreiben.* 10 MIN
- Have students do the fourth step in *Nach dem Schreiben* and begin the fifth step, p. 114. 10 MIN
- Block Schedule activity: Peer Teaching (TE, p. 96J). 10 MIN
- Questions and review. 5 MIN
- *Prüfung, Kapitel 29.* 30 MIN

Homework Options:
- Finish the final draft of the report

SUPPORT STUDENTS' VARIED LEARNING STYLES AND ABILITY LEVELS

The Teacher's Edition and ancillaries offer strategies that address multiple intelligences, different ability levels, and different needs.

Quick Start Reviews set up short student-directed activities that review and reinforce previously learned vocabulary and grammar concepts.

Teaching All Students features numerous creative ideas to address varied learning styles and abilities.

KAPITEL 29 — TEACHING SUGGESTIONS

Chapter Opener, pp. 96–97
PROGRAM RESOURCES
- Overhead Transparency 29.1

Quick Start Review
Vocabulary
Ergänzen Sie die Sätze.
WÖRTER: Diplomarbeit, Mittelalter, Ruf, Kommilitonen, Rechtswissenschaft, Geisteswissenschaften
1. Sprachen gehören zu den _____.
2. Am Ende des Studiums müssen viele eine _____ schreiben.
3. Im _____ wurden die Bücher mit der Hand und bei Kerzenlicht geschrieben.
4. Die Naturwissenschaften an der Universität Göttingen haben einen guten _____.
5. Studenten, die das gleiche Fach zur gleichen Zeit studieren nennt man _____.
6. Wenn man Richter oder Anwalt werden will, studiert man _____.
Answers: 1. Geisteswissenschaften
2. Diplomarbeit   3. Mittelalter
4. Ruf   5. Kommilitonen
6. Rechtswissenschaft

TEACHING SUGGESTIONS
Ask students to name some German products they know, such as cars, electronics, or appliances. Find out what they know about the economic situation in the European union. What do they think of the economic situation in the U.S.?

TEACHING ALL STUDENTS
Multiple Intelligences Intrapersonal: Have students write a short paragraph

describing their dreams for the future. Where do they see themselves 5 years from now? If they could pick any profession, what would they choose? Encourage them to use the subjunctive in their descriptions.

Videothek, pp. 98–99
PROGRAM RESOURCES
- Videocassette, *Folge 29*
- *Arbeitsheft*, pp. 67–69
- Audio Program, Cassette 3A/CD 3
- Audioscript, pp. 29–31

Quick Start Review 1
Subjunctive
Ergänzen Sie die Sätze.
MODELL: Er lernt seine Vokabeln nicht. Ich wünschte, . . . →
Ich wünschte, er würde seine Vokabeln lernen.
1. Ich kann nicht einschlafen. Ich wünschte, . . .
2. Er redet nicht mit mir. Ich wünschte, . . .
3. Er kommt nicht mit zur Party. Ich wünschte, . . .
4. Das Essen ist nicht gut. Ich wünschte, . . .
5. Es regnet den ganzen Tag. Ich wünschte, . . .
6. Meine Geschwister helfen mir nie bei der Wäsche. Ich wünschte, . . .
Answers: 1. Ich wünschte, ich könnte einschlafen.   2. Ich wünschte, er redete mit mir (würde mit mir reden).
3. Ich wünschte, er käme mit zur Party.
4. Ich wünschte, das Essen wäre besser.   5. Ich wünschte, es regnete

nicht den ganzen Tag (es würde nicht den ganzen Tag regnen).   6. Ich wünschte, meine Geschwister würden mir bei der Wäsche helfen.

Quick Start Review 2
Vocabulary
Ergänzen Sie die Verben in den Sätzen.
VERBEN: quatschen, zugenommen, gewöhnen, übersetzen, verlangen, beleidigen
1. Es ist nicht immer leicht, von einer Sprache in die andere zu _____.
2. Die Zahl der Studenten an deutschen Universitäten hat stark _____.
3. Lehrer ärgern sich normalerweise, wenn Schüler im Unterricht zu viel _____.
4. Studenten aus anderen Ländern müssen sich an ihre neue Umgebung erst _____.
5. Es ist nicht sehr klug, seine Lehrer zu _____.
6. Manche Lehrer _____ mehr von den Schülern als andere.
Answers: 1. übersetzen
2. zugenommen   3. quatschen
4. gewöhnen   5. beleidigen
6. verlangen

TEACHING SUGGESTIONS
- *Folge I: Wirtschaft im Wandel,* pp. 98–99

This episode gives an overview of economic changes that have occurred in Germany over the last 100 years. Play the episode without sound and ask students to identify the products they see. Remind them to review the *Wortschatz zum Video* and have them

96E   TEACHING SUGGESTIONS: KAPITEL 29

> **Classroom Community** provides paired, group, and cooperative learning activities to help build a community of German speakers in your classroom.

watch the episode a second time. They should take notes as they watch.

• *Aktivität A,* p. 98

Have students brainstorm their answers on a personal level, as well as on a statewide or nationwide level. Have them think about the local economic situation.

• *Aktivität B,* p. 98

Ask students to come up with one representative sentence for each time period portrayed in the video. Keep track of these sentences on the board and establish a time line together.

• *Folge III: Eine Arbeitsvermittlerin,* p. 99

Discuss the problem of unemployment before viewing this section. Ask questions like *Wie sucht man Arbeit? An wen kann man sich wenden, wenn man lange Zeit arbeitslos ist? Ist es schwer, einen guten Arbeitsplatz zu finden?*

• *Aktivität A,* p. 99

Ask students to name 1–2 typical activities that belong to each of the professions mentioned. For example, *Ein Apotheker: er/sie verkauft Arzneimittel; er/sie hilft Kunden...*

• *Aktivität B,* p. 99

Read the *Kulturspiegel* before doing the activity. Follow-up: Have students create some more statements capturing the differences between the old and new German states.

TEACHING ALL STUDENTS

Extra Help Have students look at a map of Germany and name the new and old German states. Try to find

some statistics on what products are produced where. Point out states that have been hit very hard by unemployment since reunification in 1990. Information is available from the Goethe Institute (www.goethe.de).

LANGUAGE NOTE

Keep in mind that German comparative forms never use *mehr* and superlatives never use *meist/am meisten.* For example, *Der Artikel in der **Frankfurter Rundschau** war interessanter als der im **Spiegel**. Peters Artikel war der interessanteste in der letzten Schülerzeitung.*

CLASSROOM COMMUNITY

Paired Activity Have students work in pairs to invent a story about a former GDR citizen who has lost his or her job because of the changes taking place since reunification. Students should explain the reasons for the job loss and try to imagine how the person might deal with the new situation. Some possible subjects might be *ein 55-jähriger Geschichtslehrer, ein 40-jähriger Journalist für die Zeitung **Neues Deutschland,** or ein 35-jähriger Arbeiter in einer Kinderkleiderfabrik.*

INTERDISCIPLINARY CONNECTION

Have students compare statistics for unemployment in the U.S. and in Germany.

BLOCK SCHEDULE

Change of Pace Have students work in pairs to role-play the visit of an unemployed person to the employment specialist (*Arbeitsvermittlerin*), Monika Schneider.

Vokabeln, pp. 100–101

PROGRAM RESOURCES

• *Arbeitsheft,* pp. 70–71
• Audio Program, Cassette 3A/CD 3
• Audioscript, pp. 31–32

Quick Start Review 1
⊙ Ordinal numbers
Schreiben Sie die Zahlen als Wörter.
1. Wir wohnen im _____ (3.) Stock.
2. Das ist schon das _____ (2.) Mal, dass er zu spät kommt.
3. Er hat am _____ (5.) April Geburtstag.
4. Heute ist der _____ (9.) September 1999.
5. Wir haben Theaterkarten für die _____ (13.) Reihe.
6. Fahren Sie die Hauptstraße entlang und biegen Sie nach der Tankstelle in die _____ (1.) Straße rechts ein. Unser Haus ist das _____ (2.) auf der linken Seite.

Answers: 1. dritten 2. zweite
3. fünften 4. neunte 5. dreizehnte
6. erste, zweite

Quick Start Review 2
⊙ Prepositions
Ergänzen Sie die richtige Präposition und die Artikel.
1. Er arbeitet oft noch sehr spät _____ _____ Firma.
2. Leg den Schlüssel bitte _____ _____ Auto.
3. _____ _____ Cafeteria gibt es heute Steak zum Mittagessen.
4. _____ _____ letzten Zeit war er oft müde.

PROGRAM COMPONENTS TAILORED TO YOUR STUDENTS' NEEDS

Arbeitsheft
(Workbook/Laboratory Manual)
Provides supplementary activities in vocabulary and grammar plus additional practice in reading, writing, pronunciation, speaking, and global listening comprehension. The Teacher's Edition contains overprinted answers for easy grading.

Assessment Program
Includes Chapter Tests (Forms A & B), 5-skill exams provided in two forms for easy classroom management. For additional assessment support, there are review tests and a final exam for each level.

High School Distance Learning Guide
Contains useful information on implementing a distance learning course and how to incorporate the *Fokus Deutsch Video Series* and *Auf Deutsch!* textbooks in that environment.

Overhead Transparencies
Support the language and cultural objectives for each chapter and stimulate communication, role-playing, and critical thinking. Overhead Transparencies include:
- **Map Transparencies** that give students a sense of where German is spoken throughout the world
- **Chapter Opener Transparencies**, an easy way to present and discuss the new chapter
- **Vocabulary Transparencies** that offer teachers another option for introducing new vocabulary
- **Grammar Transparencies** that help students see how the language works (also available as PowerPoint® slides)

INTEGRATED TECHNOLOGY

Fokus Deutsch Video Series
Consists of 36 fifteen-minute
episodes integrated with 12
fifteen-minute review episodes
keyed to the chapters of all
three levels of *Auf Deutsch!*
These episodes help all
students use the language
while following a series of
story lines that illustrate
various aspects of life and
culture in the German-
speaking world.

The *Fokus Deutsch Video
Series* is a co-production of
WGBH/Boston, Inter Nationes,
and the Goethe-Institut, with
funding from the Annenberg/CPB
Project. For more information
call 800-LEARNER (532-7637).

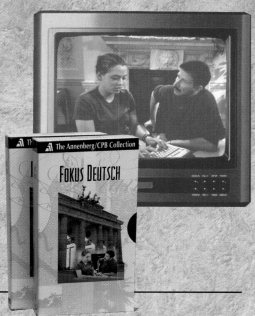

Audio Program
(audiocassette/CD)
Correlates to the listening
comprehension activities in the
Pupil's Edition, *Arbeitsheft*, and
tests. Packaged with the Audio
Program, the Audioscript
contains the complete recording
script of the Audio Program.

**Teacher's Resource
CD-ROM**
Contains visuals from all three
levels for use in creating
overhead transparencies and
PowerPoint® slides for
classroom use. The CD-ROM
also includes the complete
Assessment Program for creating
tests that meet your classroom's
needs.

ClassZone is the on-line text
companion for *Auf Deutsch!*
that provides instant access to
Internet activities and
resources. Access *ClassZone* at
www.mcdougallittell.com

COMMUNICATION	VOCABULARY	GRAMMAR	CULTURE	STRATEGIES

EINFÜHRUNG (Introduction) p. 1

COMMUNICATION	VOCABULARY	GRAMMAR	CULTURE	STRATEGIES
Communicate with the teacher in the classroom Identify objects in the classroom Count and identify numbers Use time expressions: days of the week, telling time Say when you plan to do something	The alphabet Cardinal numbers *Sprachspiegel:* spelling out numbers Days of the week Classroom objects	*So geht's!:* the letter ß *So geht's!:* der, die, das	The relationship of German and English *So geht's!:* the 24-hour clock Where German is spoken	**Listening:** Listen for cognates Listen for directions from the teacher **Speaking:** Pronounce German Ask questions and request clarification **Connecting Cultures:** Identify German and English cognates Learn where German is spoken around the world

KAPITEL 1 · ARBEITLOS (Unemployed) p. 10   Introduction of the Koslowski family and video story

COMMUNICATION	VOCABULARY	GRAMMAR	CULTURE	STRATEGIES
Identify family members Say what someone's name is Describe people	*Bist du wortschlau?:* compound words Family members *So geht's!:* compounds with *Lieblings-* Adjectives	*So geht's!:* possession Personal pronouns *So geht's!:* du, ihr, Sie The verbs *heißen* and *sein* Nouns: gender, articles, and plurals *Bist du wortschlau?:* using a pronoun in place of a noun Pronouns and articles *Sprachspiegel:* similarities between German and English noun plurals	Rheinhausen, Germany *Kulturspiegel:* hand signal for wishing someone good luck *So geht's!:* how to ask where someone is from	**Listening:** Use visual clues to guess content Listen for who says what **Speaking:** Describe a person **Reading:** Read a letter for the gist Identify cognates Locate specific information in a text **Writing:** Describe a character from the video **Connecting Cultures:** Find important information about a German city

COMMUNICATION	VOCABULARY	GRAMMAR	CULTURE	STRATEGIES

KAPITEL 2 • KEIN GELD (No money) p. 30   Marion learns that her family may move to Cologne

COMMUNICATION	VOCABULARY	GRAMMAR	CULTURE	STRATEGIES
Describe the color of objects Express one's favorite color Talk about leisure-time activities Express possession of things	Colors *Sprachspiegel:* color words that are cognates in German and English Hobbies, sports, and leisure-time activities	Infinitives Present tense of several regular verbs and *haben* *Sprachspiegel: du* and *thou* *So geht's!:* possessive adjectives Nominative and accusative cases *So geht's!:* masculine nouns with special accusative forms *So geht's!: es gibt* *Sprachspiegel:* word order	Free-time activities in Germany *Kulturspiegel: Abitur* and *Abifete*	**Listening:** Listen to get the gist Sort and categorize details **Speaking:** Persuade someone to come along **Reading:** Scan for information Find cognates and anglicisms **Writing:** Tell interesting things about yourself Ask interesting questions of someone else **Connecting Cultures:** Connect and compare leisure activities in your community with those in German-speaking countries Connect and compare high school celebrations in your community with the *Abitur/Abifete* in German-speaking areas

COMMUNICATION	VOCABULARY	GRAMMAR	CULTURE	STRATEGIES

KAPITEL 3 · WIE GEHT ES PAPA? (How's Dad?) p. 50

Herr Koslowski waits to hear about a job and the family wonders what will happen

COMMUNICATION	VOCABULARY	GRAMMAR	CULTURE	STRATEGIES
Describe a room or a dwelling Say what is in a room Say what you do or like to do Say what you don't do or don't like to do	Rooms in a house Furniture and furnishings Months of the year	Present tense of stem-changing verbs **So geht's!:** *gern* and *nicht gern*	**Kulturspiegel:** answering the phone in German-speaking countries Concepts of *Heim* and *Heimat* How Beethoven, Maria Theresa, and Martin Luther lived Typical living quarters in German-speaking countries **Kulturspiegel:** *WC*	**Listening:** Learn words from context **Speaking:** Make negative statements Describe a house **Reading:** Scan for information Visualize the information in a text **Writing:** Organize information Write to a penpal **Connecting Cultures:** Compare apartments in Cologne and Boston

WIEDERHOLUNG I (Review 1) p. 70

COMMUNICATION	VOCABULARY	GRAMMAR	CULTURE	STRATEGIES
Describe a person Describe a home	Hobbies, leisure-time activities Family members Adjectives	Present tense of *heißen, sein,* and *haben* Present tense of several regular verbs Nominative case pronouns	Create a family tree	

COMMUNICATION	VOCABULARY	GRAMMAR	CULTURE	STRATEGIES

KAPITEL 4 • DER UMZUG NACH KÖLN (The move to Cologne) p. 76 Marion's family moves to Cologne, but she stays in Rheinhausen with the Mertens family

COMMUNICATION	VOCABULARY	GRAMMAR	CULTURE	STRATEGIES
Say where and how you live Talk about how you would like to live and why Describe life in the city and country Ask questions Talk about the dates of events	Types of buildings and their locations Types of businesses *Bist du wortschlau?:* wohnen vs. leben	*So geht's!:* indefinite pronoun *man* *So geht's!:* use of *lieber* to indicate preferences Yes/No questions *W*-Questions Ordinal numbers *Sprachspiegel:* ordinal numbers and their use in dates *Sprachspiegel:* months in English and German	*So geht's!:* room measurements How people live in Germany *Kulturspiegel:* shops and businesses *Kulturspiegel:* German tennis player Steffi Graf Cologne, Germany *Kulturspiegel: Hochschule* How people lived in the Stone Age	**Listening:** Listen for words you know **Speaking:** Say what you like or prefer **Reading:** Activate prior knowledge Scan for information **Writing:** Organize information **Connecting Cultures:** Compare city and country lifestyles

KAPITEL 5 • DAS KARNEVALSFEST (Celebrating Carnival) p. 96 • The Koslowski's throw a block party and umbrellas save the day

COMMUNICATION	VOCABULARY	GRAMMAR	CULTURE	STRATEGIES
Talk about holidays and celebrations Talk about the months and seasons Describe the weather	Holidays Seasons Weather	Personal pronouns in the accusative case *So geht's!:* accusative prepositions; masculine definite and indefinite articles and *kein* in the accusative case Attributive adjectives *Sprachspiegel:* adjective endings in English	Carnival *Fasching* in the *Steiermark*	**Listening:** Listen for specific information **Speaking:** Express holiday greetings **Reading:** Read and interpret poetry **Writing:** Write a poem **Connecting Cultures:** Compare holiday traditions

COMMUNICATION	VOCABULARY	GRAMMAR	CULTURE	STRATEGIES

KAPITEL 6 • DER UNFALL (The accident) p. 116 Marion is in an accident; her parents rush to her side in the hospital

COMMUNICATION	VOCABULARY	GRAMMAR	CULTURE	STRATEGIES
Talk about your body Talk about symptoms, hospitals, and doctors Say what you can and want to do Say what you are obliged or permitted to do	Parts of the body *So geht's!:* using an infinitive as a noun; the contraction *zum* *Bist du wortschlau?:* compound nouns with *Schmerzen* Health and health care	*So geht's!:* a *wenn*-clause as a short answer to a question *Können* and *wollen* in the present tense *Sprachspiegel:* false cognates *Müssen, dürfen,* and *sollen* in the present tense *So geht's!: müssen* and *dürfen* with *nicht*	*Kulturspiegel:* good luck charms in Germany Fitness, health concerns, and lifestyles in German-speaking countries	**Listening:** Listen to learn how to say something **Speaking:** Say what your symptoms are Make short answers **Reading:** Read for helpful information **Writing:** Write to share helpful information **Connecting Cultures:** Compare good luck charms from your culture and German-speaking cultures

WIEDERHOLUNG 2 (Review 2) p. 136

COMMUNICATION	VOCABULARY	GRAMMAR	CULTURE	STRATEGIES
Describe where and how you live Talk about holidays, the seasons, and the weather Talk about hospitals, illness, symptoms, and health Describe your body	Buildings and their locations Holidays Dates Health and health care Body parts	Prepositions, personal pronouns, and adjective endings in the accusative case *Müssen, sollen, wollen,* and *dürfen* in the present tense	Cologne, Germany A celebration during the time of Neanderthal man	

COMMUNICATION	VOCABULARY	GRAMMAR	CULTURE	STRATEGIES

KAPITEL 7 • DER URLAUB (Vacation) p. 142 Marion is recuperating from her accident. She and her mother prepare for a vacation

COMMUNICATION	VOCABULARY	GRAMMAR	CULTURE	STRATEGIES
Talk about what you wear Make travel plans Say what someone should do	Clothing Modes of transportation Travel-related vocabulary	*So geht's!:* gender of nouns referring to males and females *So geht's!: möchte* Two-part verbs in the present tense *Sprachspiegel:* two-part verbs in German and English Imperatives (*Sie, ihr,* and *du*) *So geht's!: bitte, doch,* and *mal* with imperatives	*Kulturspiegel:* closed doors in German-speaking countries Tourist attractions in Zurich and Vienna The island of *Hiddensee*	**Listening:** Listen for peoples' preferences Listen for important details **Speaking:** Make plans with other people **Reading:** Compare what's not in a text with what is in a text **Writing:** Write yourself a to-do list **Connecting Cultures:** Compare vacation plans

KAPITEL 8 • AUF DER INSEL RÜGEN (On the island of *Rügen*) Marion and her mother arrive in *Sellin* on the island of *Rügen*

COMMUNICATION	VOCABULARY	GRAMMAR	CULTURE	STRATEGIES
Make reservations for overnight accommodations Talk about things you do when you're on vacation Talk about things you've done in the past	Types of overnight accommodations Rooms and features within a hotel Sports and other leisure-time activities	The present perfect tense *So geht's!:* English equivalents of the German present perfect tense *Sprachspiegel:* the present perfect tense in English and German Simple past tense of *sein, haben,* and *wissen* *So geht's!:* simple past tense vs. the present perfect tense in German *So geht's!: dass-*clauses after *wissen*	*Kulturspiegel:* thermal waters of health resorts *Die Kur* More about *Hiddensee*	**Listening:** Listen for who said what in the video Sort out details **Speaking:** Ask for and provide information **Reading:** Scan for content clues **Writing:** Write to yourself: keep a diary **Connecting Cultures:** Compare German and American vacations

COMMUNICATION	VOCABULARY	GRAMMAR	CULTURE	STRATEGIES

KAPITEL 9 · ABENTEUER UND LIEBE (Adventure and love) p. 182 Marion and Michael go sailing and get lost in the fog

COMMUNICATION	VOCABULARY	GRAMMAR	CULTURE	STRATEGIES
Summarize a story Talk about cities and countries in Europe Talk about geographical features Say where you've been Talk about things that have happened	Countries of Europe Geographical features *Bist du wortschlau?:* use of *-er* to form geographical feature names	*So geht's!:* the feminine definite article in the dative case *So geht's!:* the plural definite article in the dative case *So geht's!:* use of *noch nicht* Forming past participles Present perfect tense: *sein* as the auxiliary verb *Sprachspiegel:* past participles in English *So geht's!: haben* as the auxiliary if the main verb takes a direct object Simple past tense of *wollen, sollen, können, müssen,* and *dürfen*	*Die Hanse* and *die Hansekogge*	**Listening:** Listen to a summary to verify details Listen to options and make a preference decision **Speaking:** Ask questions about someone's life **Reading:** Read to find out about a person's life **Writing:** Write an adventure story Turn a narrative into a drama or dialogue **Connecting Cultures:** *Die Hanse:* explore a historical period *Der Störtebeker:* learn about a historical figure

WIEDERHOLUNG 3 (Review 3) p. 202

COMMUNICATION	VOCABULARY	GRAMMAR	CULTURE	STRATEGIES
Talk about clothes and weather conditions Make travel arrangements Talk about Europe	Weather and clothing Modes of transportation and travel-related vocabulary Overnight accommodations Rooms and features within a hotel Countries in Europe Geographical features	Imperative Simple past tense Present perfect tense	Painter Caspar David Friedrich	

COMMUNICATION	VOCABULARY	GRAMMAR	CULTURE	STRATEGIES

KAPITEL 10 • DIE WESPE (The Wasp) p. 208 An article Michael writes for the school newspaper lands him in trouble

COMMUNICATION	VOCABULARY	GRAMMAR	CULTURE	STRATEGIES
Talk about school and school subjects Discuss things you feel strongly about	School rooms School-related vocabulary *Bist du wortschlau?:* arbeiten vs. lernen Words used to express emotions and opinions	Dative case *So geht's!:* dative case endings on der- and ein-words in the dative case *So geht's!:* wem *So geht's!:* masculine nouns with special forms in the dative case	A typical school day	**Listening:** Listen to form an opinion **Speaking:** Confront people and solve problems **Reading:** Read to determine an opinion React to a poem **Writing:** Make a schedule with detailed plans **Connecting Cultures:** Compare relationships of authority

KAPITEL 11 • EIN LIEBESDRAMA (A romantic crisis) p. 228 Michael's friend, Silke, finds a letter and photos from Marion

COMMUNICATION	VOCABULARY	GRAMMAR	CULTURE	STRATEGIES
Talk about school subjects Talk about school systems	School subjects *So geht's!:* omission of article with school subjects The German school system	Prepositions that take dative or accusative cases *So geht's!:* idioms with an, auf, and in *So geht's!:* wo and wohin *So geht's!:* common contractions	The German school system Views of various high school students about what they will do after they graduate	**Listening:** Listen to a story Hear about what's going on at school **Speaking:** Draw comparisons Resolve conflicts **Reading:** Read poetry **Writing:** Write your own version of an existing poem Describe a problem and how you resolved it **Connecting Cultures:** Compare the German school system with your school system

COMMUNICATION	VOCABULARY	GRAMMAR	CULTURE	STRATEGIES

KAPITEL 12 • SILKE (Silke) p. 248
Marion tells the story of Michael, Silke, and herself in fairy-tale style. Marion's own story takes a twist

COMMUNICATION	VOCABULARY	GRAMMAR	CULTURE	STRATEGIES
Talk about fairy tales Say who and what you know and what you can do	Fairy tale characters Typical fairy-tale vocabulary *So geht's!:* use of simple past tense for storytelling	Verbs *können, kennen,* and *wissen* *So geht's!: ob* and indirect questions Dative case prepositions *So geht's!:* the idioms *zu Hause* and *nach Hause*	*Die Gebrüder Grimm*	**Listening:** Listen to a fairy tale **Speaking:** Talk about fairy tale theater Express opinions **Reading:** Read a fairy tale **Writing:** Write a fairy tale **Connecting Cultures:** Learn about fairy tales in a historical context

WIEDERHOLUNG 4 (Review 4) p. 268

COMMUNICATION	VOCABULARY	GRAMMAR	CULTURE	STRATEGIES
Talk about school	School subjects and school-related vocabulary	Pronouns and nouns in the dative and accusative cases Prepositions that take either accusative or dative cases *Können, kennen,* and *wissen* *Legen, stellen, hängen,* and *stecken* Dative prepositions	The German school system After the *Abitur* *So geht's!:* the grading system in German schools and universities	

COMMUNICATION	VOCABULARY	GRAMMAR	CULTURE	STRATEGIES

EINFÜHRUNG (Introduction) p. 1

COMMUNICATION	VOCABULARY	GRAMMAR	CULTURE	STRATEGIES
Describe a person Ask questions	Classroom objects Nationalities Leisure-time activities Parts of the body Clothing	Questions Accusative and dative cases Imperatives	Holiday celebrations The German school system	**Speaking:** Ask questions Tell about yourself **Reading:** Find information in a chart **Connecting Cultures:** Compare the German school system with your system

KAPITEL 13 · DER AZUBI (The apprentice) p. 10 Michael now lives in Hamburg and has an apprenticeship with a shipping company

COMMUNICATION	VOCABULARY	GRAMMAR	CULTURE	STRATEGIES
Talk about the work-place Talk about professions	Work-related vocabulary Professions ***Bist du wortschlau?:*** the feminine forms of profession nouns	***So geht's!:*** the reflexive pronoun *sich* Review: sentence structure—subject, verb, direct object, and indirect object Review: definite and indefinite articles and *kein* in the nominative, accusative, and dative cases Review: *du-, ihr-,* and *Sie*-imperatives The *wir*-imperative ***So geht's!:*** imperative forms of *sein* ***So geht's!:*** use of *bitte, doch, mal* in imperatives	Job opportunities in the German-speaking countries The *Haribo* company	**Listening:** Listen for specific information **Speaking:** Discuss a text **Reading:** Think about what you expect to find in a text Determine themes in a text Look for structures in a text **Writing:** Write an advertisement **Connecting Cultures:** Compare job opportunities in German-speaking countries and North America

| COMMUNICATION | VOCABULARY | GRAMMAR | CULTURE | STRATEGIES |

KAPITEL 14 • DER TRICK (The trick) p. 30 While Michael is taking a tour of one of his company's ships, the ship departs from the dock

COMMUNICATION	VOCABULARY	GRAMMAR	CULTURE	STRATEGIES
Talk about the past Ask someone questions about himself or herself	Resume-related vocabulary Job-search vocabulary	Review: the present perfect tense **So geht's!:** *sein* as the auxiliary verb in the present perfect tense for verbs of motion **Sprachspiegel:** English equivalents of the German present perfect tense	Young Germans' thoughts about the employment situation in Europe Novelist Wolfgang Koeppen's thoughts on the Statue of Liberty; his life	**Listening:** Listen for details **Speaking:** Say what you're interested in doing **Reading:** Find information in a help-wanted ad Read about someone's life **Writing:** Write a *Lebenslauf* Write a travel report **Connecting Cultures:** Describe and compare famous statues Experience reactions to a different country

KAPITEL 15 • ZU VIEL SALZ (Too much salt) p. 50 Michael's boss invites him and other friends over for dinner

COMMUNICATION	VOCABULARY	GRAMMAR	CULTURE	STRATEGIES
Talk about food Talk about restaurants	Food and beverages Types of restaurants	Review: nominative, accusative, and dative case pronouns **So geht's!:** *wer, wen, wem* Definite articles and *ein*-words in the genitive case **Sprachspiegel:** contrast word order in German and English statements showing possession; use of *-s'* with proper names in German **So geht's!:** *kein* and possessive adjectives are *ein*-words	**Kulturspiegel:** salt and pepper not typically included in table settings in German-speaking countries Typical German restaurants A recipe for *Schwarzwälder Kirschtorte*	**Listening:** Listen for preferences **Speaking:** Order food **Reading:** Read a recipe Read a short story Speculate about the content of a piece **Writing:** Write an invitation **Connecting Cultures:** Compare how a German family handled an awkward situation with how you might handle it

COMMUNICATION	VOCABULARY	GRAMMAR	CULTURE	STRATEGIES

WIEDERHOLUNG 5 (Review 5) p. 70

COMMUNICATION	VOCABULARY	GRAMMAR	CULTURE	STRATEGIES
Say what people should bring to a party Ask questions about a classmate's *Lebenslauf*	Work-related vocabulary Food and beverages	Present perfect tense *Sie*- and *du*-imperatives Genitive case Dative, accusative, and reflexive pronouns	The fast food culture in Germany The creation of *Erbswurst*	

KAPITEL 16 · AM WOCHENENDE (On the weekend) p. 76   The Schäfer and the Cornelius families go about their typical weekend routines

COMMUNICATION	VOCABULARY	GRAMMAR	CULTURE	STRATEGIES
Talk about weekend activites Talk about shopping Talk about breakfast	Weekend chores and activities Types of stores Breakfast foods	*Der*-words The expression *Was für* (*ein*) Review: two-way prepositions Reviews: *stellen, legen, setzen, hängen, stehen, liegen, sitzen*	***Kulturspiegel:*** typical breakfast in German-speaking countries and North America Typical weekend activities in the German-speaking countries *Ein Biomarkt* in Bergisch-Gladbach ***Kulturspiegel:*** Heinrich Böll	**Listening:** Listen for specific words and phrases **Speaking:** Talk and ask about specifics **Reading:** Read for information Read for tone Read a short story **Writing:** Describe a physical scene Visualize and draw a scene before you write about it **Connecting Cultures:** Compare German and North American breakfasts

COMMUNICATION	VOCABULARY	GRAMMAR	CULTURE	STRATEGIES

KAPITEL 17 • NACH THÜRINGEN? (To Thuringia?) p. 96   The Cornelius family ponders Mr. Cornelius's job transfer to Thuringia

COMMUNICATION	VOCABULARY	GRAMMAR	CULTURE	STRATEGIES
Talk about the *Bundes-länder* and their *Hauptsstädte* Talk about legends, festivals, and customs Talk about the future	Festivals, legends, and customs **Bist du wortschlau?:** the German word *Herbst* is a cognate of English word "harvest"	The future tense **So geht's!:** position of future tense auxiliary *werden* in a dependent clause **Sprachspiegel:** the similar use of future tense in German and English Nominative, accusative, and dative case endings on adjectives that follow *der-* and *ein-*words **So geht's!:** lack of endings on predicate adjectives	**Kulturspiegel:** Germany's three city-states **Kulturspiegel:** comparison of German *Erntedankfest* and North American Thanksgiving History of the *Hamburger Dom* **Kulturspiegel:** Siegfried Lenz A German view of American culture	**Listening:** Listen for specific information **Speaking:** Describe where you feel at home **Reading:** Read about a German tradition Read about stereotypes **Writing:** Write a brochure of travel tips Analyze eye-catching brochures **Connecting Cultures:** Describe your culture Discuss stereotypes

KAPITEL 18 • DIE LÖSUNG (The solution) p. 116   Mr. and Mrs. Cornelius resolve their conflict about Mr. Cornelius's job transfer.

COMMUNICATION	VOCABULARY	GRAMMAR	CULTURE	STRATEGIES
Talk about German reunification Talk about the geography of Austria and Switzerland	German reunification Nationalities around the globe	**So geht's!:** feminine forms of several nationalities Genitive case prepositions **So geht's!:** use of dative case with *wegen* and *trotz* Negation with *kein* and *nicht* **So geht's!:** *noch nicht, noch kein, nicht mehr,* and *kein . . . mehr*	**Kulturspiegel:** reorganization of East German *Bezirke* into West German *Länder* **Kulturspiegel:** Switzerland's cantons	**Listening:** Listen for problem-solving ideas **Speaking:** Talk about how you live **Reading:** Read for tone Read Germans' thoughts on Berlin **Writing:** Write a fictitious person's memoir **Connecting Cultures:** Talk about your cultural identity

COMMUNICATION	VOCABULARY	GRAMMAR	CULTURE	STRATEGIES

WIEDERHOLUNG 6 (Review 6) p. 136

COMMUNICATION	VOCABULARY	GRAMMAR	CULTURE	STRATEGIES
Talk about life in the former *DDR* Say where things go and are located in a room	Weekend chores and activities Nationalities	Future tense Genitive case prepositions *Stellen, hängen, stecken,* and *legen* Negation	Well-known sites in Germany History, famous landmarks, and well-known citizens of Thuringia	

KAPITEL 19 · DER SPAGHETTI-PROFESSOR (The spaghetti professor) p. 142 Klara Cornelius, a student at the university of Munich, tries to register for a particular course

COMMUNICATION	VOCABULARY	GRAMMAR	CULTURE	STRATEGIES
Talk about university life Talk about groceries Talk about setting the table	University life More foods Table-setting vocabulary	*So geht's!:* how to say the quantity of something Reflexive verbs and pronouns Comparatives and superlatives *So geht's!: so . . . wie, nicht so . . . wie,* and *als* *Sprachspiegel:* comparison of comparative and superlative forms in German with archaic English forms	*Kulturspiegel:* the Euro *Kulturspiegel:* BAföG *Kulturspiegel: Numerus clausus*	**Listening:** Listen to a personal history **Speaking:** Talk about the future **Reading:** Read about future possibilities **Writing:** Present information in a flyer **Connecting Cultures:** Learn about a German student's life

COMMUNICATION	VOCABULARY	GRAMMAR	CULTURE	STRATEGIES

KAPITEL 20 • DER UMWELTSÜNDER (The litterbug) p. 162 Klara and her friend Markus catch someone polluting the environment

COMMUNICATION	VOCABULARY	GRAMMAR	CULTURE	STRATEGIES
Talk about the environment Talk about German reunification Talk about problems facing society	Environmental protection vocabulary Vocabulary related to problems facing Germany and the world today	Use of the subjunctive to express polite requests The subjunctive of *haben, sein, werden,* and the modals Relative clauses and pronouns ***So geht's!:*** relative pronouns that differ from the definite article forms ***So geht's!:*** position of a preposition in a relative clause	German Reunification ***Kulturspiegel:*** full employment in the former *DDR* ***Kulturspiegel:*** comparison of citizenship laws in the U.S. and Germany ***Kulturspiegel:*** author Hilde Domin Recycling in Germany	**Listening:** Listen to ways of saving the environment **Speaking:** Act out a poem **Reading:** Read a poem **Writing:** Write a poem **Connecting Cultures:** Compare recycling practices in Germany and North America

KAPITEL 21 • DIE FALSCHEN KLAMOTTEN (The wrong clothes) p. 182 Markus's brother, Thomas, and his cousin, Laura Stumpf, go to a disco

COMMUNICATION	VOCABULARY	GRAMMAR	CULTURE	STRATEGIES
Talk about clothes and fashion Talk about media, newspapers, and television	Clothing and fashion The media, reporting, and advertising	Passive voice ***So geht's!:*** use of *von* and *durch* to express the agent in a passive sentence ***So geht's!:*** review of formation of past participles Alternative to the passive: *es* as dummy subject, *man,* and *sich lassen* ***So geht's!:*** modal auxiliaries in the passive voice	Fashion German television	**Listening:** Listen to descriptions of dress **Speaking:** Prepare and carry out a survey **Reading:** Read opinions about name brand clothing **Writing:** Write a newspaper article **Connecting Cultures:** Compare clothing fashions and trends in Germany and in your area

COMMUNICATION	VOCABULARY	GRAMMAR	CULTURE	STRATEGIES

WIEDERHOLUNG 7 (Review 7) p. 202

COMMUNICATION	VOCABULARY	GRAMMAR	CULTURE	STRATEGIES
Talk about newspapers and magazines Talk about advertising	University life Food and beverages Problems facing today's society Clothing and fashion The media, reporting, and advertising	Reflexive verbs and pronouns Comparatives and superlatives Modals in the subjunctive Relative clauses Passive voice	Informational radio programming	

KAPITEL 22 • EIN NEUES GEMÄLDE (A new painting) p. 208 Laura's family buys a new painting

COMMUNICATION	VOCABULARY	GRAMMAR	CULTURE	STRATEGIES
Talk about shopping Give directions about how to get somewhere	Places to shop Travel directions Modes of transportation	The simple past tense of regular and irregular verbs *So geht's!:* use of simple past versus the present perfect tense with *haben, sein, wissen,* and the modals *Als, wenn, wann* *Sprachspiegel:* similarities between *als* and "as" *So geht's!:* use of *als* in making comparisons	*Sprachspiegel:* similarities between Berlin dialect and English Artist Gabriele Münter Friedensreich Hundertwasser *Kulturspiegel:* Johann Strauss, *Wienerschnitzel,* and *Salzburger Nockerl*	**Listening:** Listen to information about a museum **Speaking:** Describe a building **Reading:** Read an artist's opinion about art and society **Writing:** Write a script for a tour **Connecting Cultures:** Speculate about life in early 20th century Berlin, Munich, and Texas

| COMMUNICATION | VOCABULARY | GRAMMAR | CULTURE | STRATEGIES |

KAPITEL 23 • DER HAUSMANN (The stay-at-home dad) p. 228 Heiner Sander, who is on parental leave, takes the baby along to his soccer game

COMMUNICATION	VOCABULARY	GRAMMAR	CULTURE	STRATEGIES
Talk about equal rights in the family Talk about sports	Equality in the family Sports	Use of the subjunctive to express wishes, hypothetical situations and conditions contrary to fact **So geht's!:** the expression *an deiner Stelle* Past subjunctive to express what might have been **So geht's!:** omission of *wenn* in past subjunctive clauses	**Kulturspiegel:** *Erziehungsurlaub* and *Erziehungsgeld* Male and female roles in the family in German-speaking countries	**Listening:** Listen to a telephone conversation **Speaking:** Discuss men's and women's expectations **Reading:** Read a poem **Writing:** Write a dialogue **Connecting Cultures:** Compare family life in German-speaking countries and North America

KAPITEL 24 • DAS AU PAIR (The au pair) p. 248 Inéz, an au pair from Mexico, faces the challenge of adjusting to life in Germany

COMMUNICATION	VOCABULARY	GRAMMAR	CULTURE	STRATEGIES
Talk about traveling Talk about customs in Germany	Travel vocabulary German customs and lifestyles	The past perfect tense Infinitive clauses with *zu*	Views of Germany from U.S. and Turkish students	**Listening:** Listen to an interview with people of other cultures living in Germany **Speaking:** Plan an exchange **Reading:** Read about a student exchange program **Writing:** Write about another culture **Connecting Cultures:** Contrast parental discipline in German, North American, and Turkish families

COMMUNICATION	VOCABULARY	GRAMMAR	CULTURE	STRATEGIES

WIEDERHOLUNG 8 (Review 8) p. 268

COMMUNICATION	VOCABULARY	GRAMMAR	CULTURE	STRATEGIES
Talk about summer plans	Places to shop Sports Travel vocabulary	The simple past tense The past perfect tense Subjunctive: present and past Infinitive clauses with *zu*	The Pergamon Museum	

EINFÜHRUNG (Introduction) p. 1

COMMUNICATION	VOCABULARY	GRAMMAR	CULTURE	STRATEGIES
Talk about school Talk about what you like to do in your free time	School and university Leisure time Classroom phrases	Review: nominative and accusative cases Review: infinitives and the present tense Review: two-part verbs ***Kurz notiert:*** special masculine nouns; *es gibt;* English equivalents to German present tense; German verbs consisting of two verbs	University life in Germany Important cities in the German-speaking countries Customs and holidays in the German-speaking countries	**Speaking:** Introduce yourself to someone Describe a vacation Contradict someone **Writing:** Write about a vacation

COMMUNICATION	VOCABULARY	GRAMMAR	CULTURE	STRATEGIES

KAPITEL 25 • MITEINANDER (Together) p. 10 Susanne Dyrchs and several other Germans express their views on "family"

COMMUNICATION	VOCABULARY	GRAMMAR	CULTURE	STRATEGIES
Talk about the family	Family relationships	Review: the simple past tense Coordinating conjunctions *aber, denn, sondern,* and *und* Subordinating conjunctions *als, dass, weil,* and *wenn* Review: negation with *kein* and *nicht* ***Sprachspiegel:*** strong, weak, and mixed verbs ***Kurz notiert:*** punctuation with *und* and *oder;* meaning of *als* and *wenn;* phrases for negation	Family life in the German-speaking countries Felix Mendelssohn-Bartholdy	**Listening:** Listen for specific information **Speaking:** Describe a famous person **Reading:** Read and interpret a poem **Writing:** Write a short biographical sketch **Connecting Cultures:** Compare the concept of "family" in Germany and North America

KAPITEL 26 • JUGEND (Youth) p. 30 Susanne Dyrchs and three other German young people talk about their interests

COMMUNICATION	VOCABULARY	GRAMMAR	CULTURE	STRATEGIES
Talk about the interests of German youth	Youth Political activism	Review: accusative and dative cases Review: genitive case Review: prepositions—accusative, dative, and accusative/dative ***Sprachspiegel:*** position of noun modifiers in genitive case ***Kurz notiert:*** special masculine nouns; *wer, wen,* and *wem;* idiomatic phrases *nach Hause* and *zu Hause*	Life goals of young people in Germany	**Listening:** Listen to a text about young people in Germany **Speaking:** Talk about getting along with adults **Reading:** Read about a teenager's call to a help line **Writing:** Create a flyer **Connecting Cultures:** Compare interests of young people in Germany and North America

COMMUNICATION	VOCABULARY	GRAMMAR	CULTURE	STRATEGIES

KAPITEL 27 • SCHULALLTAG (A typical school day) p. 50
The history of a *Gymnasium* in Bremen is presented; and several German speakers talk about their schools

Talk about school	School	Review: *der-* and *ein-* words Review: adjective endings Indefinite numerals and the interrogative pronoun *was für (ein)* ***Kurz notiert:*** use of accusative case in expressions of time	The German school system Albert Einstein ***Kulturspiegel:*** mandatory education in Germany	**Listening:** Listen to a biography of a famous scientist **Speaking:** Discuss ways of improving your school **Reading:** Read and interpret a short story by Heinrich Spoerl **Writing:** Write a proposal **Connecting Cultures:** Discuss opinions about playing pranks

WIEDERHOLUNG 9 (Review 9) p. 70

Talk about family life, young people and their interests, the roles of men and women in the family, and the role of the family in today's society	Family Young people and activism	Simple past tense Negation Pronouns in the accusative and dative cases Prepositions Adjective endings		

COMMUNICATION	VOCABULARY	GRAMMAR	CULTURE	STRATEGIES

KAPITEL 28 • UNIVERSITÄT (University) p. 76

The university in Heidelberg is presented; Susanne Dyrchs talks about her future plans, German university students talk about their studies; profile of a student from Cameroon

COMMUNICATION	VOCABULARY	GRAMMAR	CULTURE	STRATEGIES
Talk about courses of study	University	Subjunctive **Sprachspiegel:** *wäre* and "were" **Kurz notiert:** the expression *an deiner Stelle; wollte* and *wünschte;* the expression *(doch) nur; als ob*	Favorite courses of study at the university level in Germany	**Listening:** Listen to a text about Cameroon **Speaking:** Role-play characters from the short story **Reading:** Read and interpret a short story by Günter Anders **Writing:** Give a friend advice about a problem **Connecting Cultures:** Compare favorite university level courses of study in Germany and North America

KAPITEL 29 • ARBEIT UND WIRTSCHAFT (Work and the economy) p. 96

Brief history of the German economy is presented; German speakers discuss their working life

COMMUNICATION	VOCABULARY	GRAMMAR	CULTURE	STRATEGIES
Talk about professions and work	Work	Review: comparatives and superlatives Verbs as adjectives Participial constructions Extended modifiers **Sprachspiegel:** German and English comparative forms **Sind Sie wortschlau?:** suffixes *-heit* and *-keit*	Working in Germany Germany's economy **Kulturspiegel:** difficulties in Germany since reunification; the German apprenticeship system; Mackenbach in Rheinland-Pfalz; Heinrich Böll	**Listening:** Listen to a short biographical sketch **Speaking:** Play a guessing game **Reading:** Read a short piece by Heinrich Böll about a person with an unusual profession **Writing:** Prepare a questionnaire **Connecting Cultures:** Contrast working situations in Germany and North America

| COMMUNICATION | VOCABULARY | GRAMMAR | CULTURE | STRATEGIES |

KAPITEL 30 • FRAUEN UND MÄNNER (Women and men) p. 116 Historical and present-day
perspectives of women's issues are presented

COMMUNICATION	VOCABULARY	GRAMMAR	CULTURE	STRATEGIES
Talk about women's rights	Women's rights and related issues	Indirect discourse Indirect questions Review: Imperatives *Sprachspiegel:* English subjunctive forms *Kurz notiert:* use of subjunctive II in speaking	*Kulturspiegel:* support for working women in the former GDR; women in German politics today	**Listening:** Listen to an advertisement for a women's bookstore **Speaking:** Role-play a conversation between an adult and a child **Reading:** Read a conversation **Writing:** Imagine and report the thoughts of people from the past **Connecting Cultures:** Compare the position of women in German and North American cultures

WIEDERHOLUNG 10 (Review 10) p. 136

COMMUNICATION	VOCABULARY	GRAMMAR	CULTURE	STRATEGIES
Talk about university-level studies Talk about women's rights and issues	University, work, and women's rights and related issues	Subjunctive *Wenn* clause and *würde* + infinitive Superlatives Indirect discourse	Studying and working in Germany Women's rights in Germany	

COMMUNICATION	VOCABULARY	GRAMMAR	CULTURE	STRATEGIES

KAPITEL 31 • FREIZEIT (Leisure time) p. 142

German speakers talk about what they do in their free time; the history behind Berlin's *Kleingärten*

COMMUNICATION	VOCABULARY	GRAMMAR	CULTURE	STRATEGIES
Talk about leisure-time activities Discuss separating work and free time	Leisure-time activities and hobbies Enrichment courses	Modal verbs *Da-* and *wo*-compounds ***Sprachspiegel:*** the difference between *können* and *dürfen* in German and "can" and "may" in English ***Kurz notiert:*** subjunctive II and simple past-tense forms of *sollen, wollen,* and *können*	Favorite leisure-time activities of Germans; ability of Germans to separate their leisure-time and work *Kleingärten* in Berlin	**Listening:** Listen to a radio broadcast **Speaking:** Talk about animals **Reading:** Short story by Elke Heidenreich **Writing:** Write a public service announcement **Connecting Cultures:** Compare attitudes of German speakers and North Americans toward leisure-time and work

KAPITEL 32 • FERIEN UND URLAUB (Holidays and vacation) p. 162

Several German speakers relate their favorite vacation destinations and activities; a historical overview of how Germans vacation

COMMUNICATION	VOCABULARY	GRAMMAR	CULTURE	STRATEGIES
Discuss vacation activities	Vacation and travel	Review: the present perfect tense Modal verbs in the present perfect tense ***Sind Sie wortschlau?:*** past participles of verbs with the same stem form ***Kurz notiert:*** verbs that take *sein* in the present perfect tense	Vacation activities of German speakers	**Listening:** Listen to a text about a travel club **Speaking:** Talk about places you like to go **Reading:** Short story by Wolfgang Hildesheimer **Writing:** Design a travel brochure **Connecting Cultures:** Compare vacations of Germans with vacations of North Americans

COMMUNICATION	VOCABULARY	GRAMMAR	CULTURE	STRATEGIES

KAPITEL 33 • GESUNDHEIT UND KRANKHEIT (Health and illness) p. 182 The *Kurort, Bad Ems,* is featured; several German speakers talk about what they do to stay healthy

COMMUNICATION	VOCABULARY	GRAMMAR	CULTURE	STRATEGIES
Talk about health-related issues	Health care	Review: reflexive verbs and pronouns Review: two-way prepositions Verbs with two-way prepositions *Kurz notiert:* verbs that are reflexive in German but not in English	Germans' health and fitness regimes *Bad Ems,* Germany Germany's system of socialized health care	**Listening:** Listen to an introduction by a *Kurort* director **Speaking:** Discuss ways to maintain good health **Reading:** Read a magazine article **Writing:** Design a personal fitness plan and chart **Connecting Cultures:** Compare fitness regimes in Germany and North America

WIEDERHOLUNG 11 (Review 11) p. 202

COMMUNICATION	VOCABULARY	GRAMMAR	CULTURE
Talk about what you do to stay healthy Discuss your favorite leisure-time activities	Work and leisure time Vacation Fitness and health care	Modal verbs in the present and simple past tenses Reflexive verbs and pronouns Present perfect tense Two-way prepositions	Views of people from German-speaking areas about work, vacations, and maintaining their health

COMMUNICATION	VOCABULARY	GRAMMAR	CULTURE	STRATEGIES

KAPITEL 34 • MULTI-KULTI? (Multicultural?) p. 208 People of other cultures living in Germany today are interviewed; young Germans and Austrians express their views on the diversity of their countries' societies

COMMUNICATION	VOCABULARY	GRAMMAR	CULTURE	STRATEGIES
Talk about stereotypical characteristics of Germans Talk about foreigners in Germany	Stereotypes of Germans Immigration	Review: relative clauses Review: infinitive clauses with *zu* *Kurz notiert: da* and *wo* + a preposition beginning with a vowel	*Kulturspiegel:* statistics on foreigners in Germany; political asylum in Germany; university student exchange programs; *DAAD*	**Listening:** Listen to an interview with two students in Würzburg **Speaking:** Talk about people of other cultures that you know **Reading:** Read a piece by a foreigner living in Germany **Writing:** Make a catalog of the multicultural ethnic heritage of your home town **Connecting Cultures:** Learn about foreigners living in Germany

KAPITEL 35 • DER UMWELT ZULIEBE (For the sake of the environment) p. 228 Environmental problems in Germany are presented

COMMUNICATION	VOCABULARY	GRAMMAR	CULTURE	STRATEGIES
Talk about protecting the environment	Environmental protection	Review: the passive voice Review: the future tense *Kurz notiert:* position of conjugated verb in dependent clause	*Kulturspiegel:* Germany's dying forests; overuse of automobiles	**Listening:** Listen to a text about three young environmental researchers **Speaking:** Retell a short story **Reading:** Read a short story by Achim Bröger and Bernd Küsters **Writing:** Design a poster **Connecting Cultures:** Compare environmental problems in Germany and North America

COMMUNICATION	VOCABULARY	GRAMMAR	CULTURE	STRATEGIES

KAPITEL 36 • FOKUS AUF KULTUR (Focus on culture) p. 248 Performers at the GRIPS Theater perform a scene from a musical; excerpts from several German films are shown

Talk about the theater and film	Theater and film	Review: the past perfect tense Review: alternatives to the passive Word order with verbs *Kurz notiert:* comparison of the past perfect tense in German and English; position of *nicht*	Theater and movies in Germany *Kulturspiegel:* emigration of German and Austrian filmmakers to the U.S.	**Listening:** Listen to a short description of the play *Biedermann und die Brandstifter* **Speaking:** Perform a text **Reading:** Read and perform a text **Writing:** Write summaries of movies and a top ten list **Connecting Cultures:** Learn about German theater and movies

WIEDERHOLUNG 12 (Review 12) p. 268

Talk about movies	Stereotypical characteristics of Germans, environmental protection, and movies	Relative clauses Infinitive clauses with *zu* Uses of *werden* Passive voice	*Kulturspiegel:* Georg Heym	

Auf Deutsch!

Auf Deutsch!

3 DREI

LIDA DAVES-SCHNEIDER
Chino Valley (CA) Unified School District

KARL SCHNEIDER
Chino Valley (CA) Unified School District

DANIELA DOSCH FRITZ

STEPHEN L. NEWTON
University of California, Berkeley

Chief Academic and Series Developer
ROBERT DI DONATO
Miami University, Oxford, Ohio

McDougal Littell
A HOUGHTON MIFFLIN COMPANY
Evanston, Illinois • Boston • Dallas

Auf Deutsch!
3 Drei

This book is printed on acid-free paper.

1 2 3 4 5 6 7 8 9   WVK   06 05 04 03 02 01 00

ISBN 0-618-02963-X

Cover photographs *Clockwise from top:* © BAV/Helga Lade Fotoagentur; © Siegfried Layda/Corbis Images; © M. Listri/Corbis Images; © Peter Weber/Tony Stone Images.

Internet: www.mcdougallittell.com

CONTENTS

KAPITEL 27

SCHULALLTAG 50

We learn about the history of a very old Gymnasium in Bremen, as well as what a typical school day in Germany is like today.

WIEDERHOLUNG 9
70

KAPITEL 28

UNIVERSITÄT 76

We learn about the history of the University of Heidelberg. Then we learn about life in a German university from the point of view of a student from Cameroon.

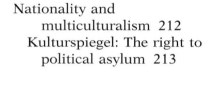

PREFACE

Welcome to *Auf Deutsch! 3 Drei,* the third part of the textbook program that is integrated with the *Fokus Deutsch* video program. *Fokus Deutsch* brings German language and culture to life with a video series that spans three levels of instruction. Whether you have used *Auf Deutsch!* Level 1 and 2, or are just starting with *Auf Deutsch!* Level 3, you will find that the approach offers a seamless transition for using the textbook and the video series. The textbook features a uniquely clear and user-friendly organization, with a chapter structure similar to both Level 1 and 2, while the video series begins a new format. Of course, Level 3 can also follow any beginning German program. Overall, the self-contained modules of the *Fokus Deutsch* video series maximize flexibility for your German course.

THE AUF DEUTSCH! PROGRAM

FOKUS DEUTSCH AND AUF DEUTSCH!

Fokus Deutsch is a video-based course for German language and culture consisting of three levels that span the introductory and intermediate stages of learning. Each level of the video series consists of twelve fifteen-minute episodes and four fifteen-minute reviews. A total of twelve hours of video across the three levels of the series brings the richness of German language and culture to beginning and intermediate learners.

The video episodes of *Fokus Deutsch* Level 1 follow the lives of the fictional Koslowski family: Marion, her brother Lars, and their parents, Vera and Heinz. Level 2 presents a number of mini-dramas that offer insights into the lives of other speakers of German. Level 3 offers cultural, historical, and personal perspectives on themes of interest to teachers as well as students. This intermediate course can follow any beginning level program.

THE CONCEPT OF THE VIDEO SERIES

The *Fokus Deutsch* video series integrates mini-dramas, authentic cultural and historical footage, and personal testimonials to provide students with an in-depth view of German language, society, culture, and history. The *Fokus Deutsch* series develops a simple concept: A young German student (Marion Koslowski) comes to the United States to help an American professor (Dr. Robert Di Donato) develop a contemporary German language course that focuses on historical and cultural studies. Together through the videos, they teach German language and culture as they present a variety of issues important to German-speaking people today and offer insights into the historical contexts of these topics.

A CULTURAL APPROACH

Together, *Fokus Deutsch* and *Auf Deutsch!* teach language while covering a wide array of cultural and historical topics from many different perspectives. Video topics range from everyday life, family, work, and daily routines to political and social issues that affect German-speaking people today. Themes also include the worlds of art, theater, and film. In Levels 1 and 2, Professor Di Donato and Marion introduce the topics, which unfold within the context of the mini-dramas and through commentaries of speakers of German from Austria, Switzerland, and Germany. Cultural footage, interspersed throughout, provides actual views of life in various geographical locations and authentic treatment of topics such as the **Abitur** and **Karneval**. Level 3 picks up the topics introduced in Levels 1 and 2 and explores them from a documentary perspective through historical and contemporary cultural footage. This approach to language learning enables viewers (1) to gain a wide variety of insights into the culture, society, and history of speakers of German; (2) to explore topics from multiple perspectives; and (3) to learn gradually to understand and communicate in German.

Auf Deutsch!, used in conjunction with *Fokus Deutsch*, enables students to focus on the following "Five Cs of Foreign Language Education" outlined in *Standards for Foreign Language Learning: Preparing for the 21st Century* (1996; National Standards in Foreign Language Education Project, a collaboration of ACTFL, AATG, AATF, and AATSP). *Communication* and *Cultures:* With the *Auf Deutsch!* approach, students communicate in German in meaningful contexts as they learn about and develop an understanding of German-speaking cultures. *Connections:* The videos, readings, activities, and exercises all encourage students to connect their German language study with other disciplines and with their personal lives. *Comparisons: Auf Deutsch!* helps students realize the interrelationships between language and culture and compare the German-speaking world with their own. *Community: Auf Deutsch!* offers many opportunities for students to relate to communities of German-speaking peoples through a variety of interactive resources, including the Internet.

USING FOKUS DEUTSCH WITH AUF DEUTSCH!

Auf Deutsch! offers several options for using the materials in a traditional classroom setting. For example, teachers may:

- use both the **Auf Deutsch!** textbook and **Fokus Deutsch** video series in the class, assign most of the material in the **Arbeitsheft** for homework, and follow up with selected activities and discussions in class.

- use only the **Auf Deutsch!** textbook in class and have students view the video episodes at home, in the media center, or in the language laboratory.

Fokus Deutsch is also designed as a complete credit telecourse for the distant ("at-home") learner. Telecourse students can watch each episode and complete all sections of the **Auf Deutsch!** textbook and **Arbeitsheft**.

In all cases, students should watch each episode from beginning to end without interruption. They can replay and review selected segments once they are familiar with the content of an episode. The Teacher's Manual provides more detailed suggestions for using the **Auf Deutsch!** textbook program with the **Fokus Deutsch** video series.

THE VIDEO SERIES

The **Fokus Deutsch** video series consists of 36 fifteen-minute episodes. A video review follows every third episode. The videos are time-coded for easier classroom use.

STRUCTURE OF LEVEL 3

Whereas Levels 1 and 2 of **Fokus Deutsch** rely primarily on the story lines of various mini-dramas, Level 3 develops from documentary footage. The documentaries present a cultural or social topic in its historical as well as its contemporary contexts. Each episode—usually four to five minutes in length—contains two perspectives: The historical view presents a retrospective survey, whereas the contemporary view usually focuses on one particular aspect of the topic. Thus, for example, the episode **"Urlaub gestern und heute"** explores the Germans' love of vacation and its historical development. Viewers then experience the excitement of a virtual **"Abenteuerurlaub"** (adventure vacation).

Professor Di Donato guides learners through Level 3. He usually introduces the cultural footage and then offers comments that provide a transition from historical to contemporary viewpoints. Finally, he summarizes the topic at the end of the episode and often poses a question to provoke thought. For example, he might ask viewers to ponder the differences and similarities between going to school in a German-speaking country and in their own country. Throughout Level 3 native speakers comment on the topics at hand, either by elaborating on specific aspects and thereby providing further cultural information, or by addressing the topic from a personal perspective.

CAST OF CHARACTERS

CHARACTERS IN THE FRAMEWORK OF *FOKUS DEUTSCH*

Robert Di Donato, an American professor of German, continues his role from Levels 1 and 2 of presenting German language and culture to students through a video-based program.

Susanne Dyrchs, who plays the role of Marion Koslowski in Levels 1 and 2, speaks as herself in Level 3 and offers commentary on various contemporary issues and topics.

PERSONS IN THE LEVEL 3 DOCUMENTARIES

The people who appear throughout the Level 3 documentaries play themselves. They exemplify and personalize the topics.

Meta Heyn narrates her family history to her granddaughter. The family album simultaneously tells the history of the Heyn family and reveals German life through two world wars and reconstruction.

Sybilla Heyn looks at photos with her grandmother, Meta Heyn.

Sabine and **Peter Schenk** discuss why they decided to marry and have children. Each had different reasons for wanting to marry. They discuss what family means to them.

Nora Bausch talks about being single and what her life is like as a single person.

Ulla, 19 years old, talks about what she wants to do after she finishes her **Abitur.**

Ramona, an apprentice in a floral shop in Erfurt, tells why she wants to be a florist.

Kristian, whose family originally came from Croatia, works as an apprentice in a bank in Frankfurt. He talks about how he sees his future.

Karolin attends a **Gesamtschule** (similar to an American high school) about forty kilometers from Frankfurt. She takes viewers through a typical school day, which includes her classes and extracurricular activities.

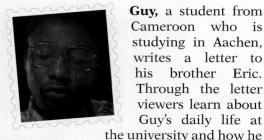

Guy, a student from Cameroon who is studying in Aachen, writes a letter to his brother Eric. Through the letter viewers learn about Guy's daily life at the university and how he feels as a foreign student in Germany.

Monika Schneider works as a representative of the employment bureau in Cologne. She assists unemployed workers in their search for a job. Viewers meet Monika Schneider as she is interviewing a client, Herr Weinert.

Julia works in a feminist bookstore, where she combines her political activities with her job. Julia compares her situation today with that of her mother, grandmother, and great-grandmother.

Christa Piper lives in Saarbrücken and works to resolve women's issues in the workplace.

Frau Vogtlander, acting director of the **Volks-hochschule** (similar to a community college) in Potsdam, describes the types of courses adults can take at the school in their free time.

Birgit wants to go on an adventure vacation. She goes "canyoning" and afterward describes her experiences.

Sven Schuder goes to the doctor for preventative health care. His exam is covered by the health care system, which is interested in making sure that people lead healthy lives.

Ergün Çevik takes viewers on a tour of things German from the perspective of a Turk living in Germany. He presents stereotypical ideas of German culture and calls them into question.

Bärbel Barmbeck shows viewers her specially built, environmentally friendly house. Not only does the house save energy, but the family tries to protect the environment through their various domestic activities.

Volker Ludwig talks about the "Grips," a children's theater in Berlin, and describes a performance of the musical **"Linie 1."**

THE TEXTBOOKS: A GUIDED TOUR

Three *Auf Deutsch!* textbooks correspond to the three levels of the *Fokus Deutsch* video series. Each textbook contains twelve regular chapters and four review chapters. Each chapter corresponds to one episode of the video series. Review chapters—in which students review the video story line, vocabulary, and grammatical structures—follow every third regular chapter. Level 3, like Levels 1 and 2, begins with an introductory chapter, **Einführung.**

ORGANIZATION OF *LEVEL 3*

Auf Deutsch! features a uniquely clear and user-friendly organization. Each regular chapter consists of the following self-contained teaching modules that maximize flexibility in designing a German course.

KAPITEL 30

FRAUEN UND MÄNNER

Heute steht jegliche Berufsmöglichkeit offen.

Wie geht es den Frauen von heute? Leben sie immer noch in einer Männerwelt?

In diesem Kapitel
- lernen Sie Julia, eine Buchhändlerin in einem Frauenbuchladen, kennen.
- diskutieren Sie über das Thema Gleichberechtigung.
- lernen Sie Christa Piper, eine Frauenbeauftragte in Saarbrücken, kennen.

Sie werden auch
- lernen, wie man die indirekte Rede gebraucht.
- lernen, wie man indirekte Fragen stellt.
- die Formen des Imperativs wiederholen.
- eine Geschichte über Emanzipation lesen.
- die Gedanken und Gefühle von drei Frauen beschreiben.

Vor 1900 durften nur Männer höhere Schulen besuchen.

116 hundertsechzehn

hundertsiebzehn 117

CHAPTER OPENER

Chapter learning goals prepare learners for what is to come in the chapter and in the accompanying video episode. The photos illustrate both historical and contemporary aspects of the chapter themes.

VIDEOTHEK

Pre- and post-viewing activities coordinate directly with the video episode to help students gain a thorough comprehension of what they see and hear.

VOKABELN

A section of thematic vocabulary linked to the two video episodes offers abundant activities for vocabulary development.

STRUKTUREN

Three sections, each introducing a single grammar point through clear and concise explanations, offer a wide range of practice, from controlled and form-focused exercises to open-ended and creative activities.

KAPITEL 34 — VIDEOTHEK

Was heißt für Sie „deutsch"? In diesem Kapitel sehen Sie, was ausländische Einwohner von Deutschland und den Deutschen halten und wie Deutsche und Österreicher auf ihre ausländischen Mitbürger reagieren.

Ergün Çevik,

I: Typisch deutsch?

In dieser Folge lernen Sie Ergün Çevik kennen, der schon lange in Deutschland lebt.

A Ergün erwähnt drei Eigenschaften, die ihm einfallen: Sauberkeit, Ordnung und Pünktlichkeit.

SCHRITT 1: Welche dieser drei Eigenschaften werden in den folgenden Aussagen dargestellt?

1. „Bei Rot stehen, bei Grün gehen."
2. „Wenn du eine Verabredung mit einem Deutschen hast, verspäte dich nie länger als fünf Minuten."
3. „Samstag ist in Deutschland Putztag."
4. „Damit sich alle an die Regeln halten, ist alles beschildert."
5. „Ein Terminkalender ist in Deutschland eine sehr wichtige Sache."
6. „Für mich zeigt sich in einem Schrebergarten die deutsche Seele."

SCHRITT 2: Wie finden Sie die „Regeln", die Ergün beschreibt? Gibt es solche Regeln auch bei Ihnen? Erklären Sie Ihre Antwort.

B Verkehrsschilder. Verbinden Sie jede Beschreibung auf Seite 211 mit dem richtigen Verkehrsschild.

WORTSCHATZ ZUM VIDEO

der Putztag — cleaning day
der Schrebergarten — small allotted garden
der Fahrplan — transit schedule
die Aufführung — performance
die Passkontrolle — passport control
die Flitterwochen — honeymoon

FOKUS INTERNET

For more information on the cultures represented in Germany, visit the *Auf Deutsch!* Web Site at

---

KAPITEL 34 — VOKABELN

die Essgewohnheit — eating habit
die Genauigkeit — accuracy; exactness
die Nichtakzeptanz — nonacceptance
die Ordnung — order
die Pünktlichkeit — promptness; punctuality
die Regel — rule
die Sauberkeit — cleanliness
die Verabredung — appointment; date
die Verachtung — contempt
der Auswanderer / die Auswanderin — emigrant
der Einwanderer / die Einwanderin — immigrant
das Asyl — political asylum
das Bedürfnis — necessity

an•nehmen — to accept, take on
beachten — to observe
bei•tragen zu — to contribute to
darstellen — to depict, portray; to present
duzen — to address someone with **du**
einfallen — to come to (an appointment)
einhalten — to keep (an appointment)
siezen — to address someone with **Sie**
vereinbaren — to arrange
verfolgen — to persecute
sich verspäten — to be late

Sie wissen schon
die Ausländerfeindlichkeit, der Ausländer, der Schritt, beeinflussen, unbedingt

deutlich — clear(ly)
inzwischen — in the meantime
rechtlich — legally
unmittelbar — direct(ly)
unweigerlich — inevitable; inevitably

Das Essen in Deutschland ist multikultureller geworden.

Aktivitäten

A Ausländer in der Bundesrepublik. Ergänzen Sie die Sätze mit Wörtern aus dem Kasten.

Die fünfziger Jahre waren eine Zeit des Wohlstands in Deutschland. 1950 gab es wenige ____ in der Bundesrepublik, aber ____ ist die Zahl der ausländischen Arbeiter in Deutschland enorm gestiegen. Die deutsche Wirtschaft brauchte dringend Arbeitskräfte. Viele junge Männer, besonders Türken und Griechen, kamen nach Deutschland, um zu arbeiten. Sie haben Arbeiten

Asyl · rechtlich · Ausländer · inzwischen · Verachtung · ____gen · beeinflusst · ____folgt

---

KAPITEL 33 — STRUKTUREN

REVIEW OF REFLEXIVE VERBS AND PRONOUNS
DOING SOMETHING FOR ONESELF

As you recall, some verbs have reflexive pronouns that refer back to the subject. Note the objects in the following sentences.

Ich ziehe **mich** an.   *I'm getting dressed.*
Ich ziehe **mir** eine Jacke an.   *I'm putting on a jacket.*

Reflexive pronouns occur in the accusative or dative case. The only distinctly different case forms are **mich/mir** and **dich/dir**. All other reflexive pronouns are identical in the accusative and dative cases.

	SINGULAR			PLURAL			
ACCUSATIVE		DATIVE		ACCUSATIVE		DATIVE	
mich	myself	mir		uns	ourselves	uns	
dich	yourself	dir		euch	yourselves	euch	
sich	yourself	sich		sich	yourselves	sich	
sich	herself	sich		sich	themselves	sich	
sich	himself						
sich	itself						

Note that the verbs **legen** and **setzen** require accusative reflexive pronouns to describe the process of lying or sitting down.

Ich lege **mich** ins Bett.   *I'm going to lie down in bed.*
(I'm going to put myself to bed.)

Du hast **dich** an den Tisch **gesetzt**.   *You sat down at the table.*
(You seated yourself at the table.)

If a sentence with a reflexive verb contains a direct object, the reflexive pronoun will be in the dative case.

KURZ NOTIERT

Some German verbs are always reflexive, although their English counterparts may not be.

sich erinnern an (+ acc.) — to remember
sich interessieren für — to be interested in
sich unterhalten — to have a conversation
sich überlegen — to decide
sich aufregen — to get excited
sich entspannen — to relax
sich freuen auf (+ acc.) — to look forward to
sich freuen über (+ acc.) — to be glad about
sich vorstellen — to imagine; to introduce
sich schminken — to put on makeup

PERSPEKTIVEN

The chapter culminates in four-skills development through this final section, which includes the following features.

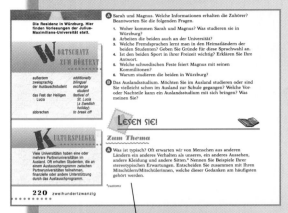

HÖREN SIE ZU! develops listening comprehension skills as it features testimonials, interviews, narratives, and other types of listening passages, along with follow-up comprehension exercises.

LESEN SIE! exposes students to a wide variety of German texts, including author-written passages, as well as authentic literary and non-literary reading selections.

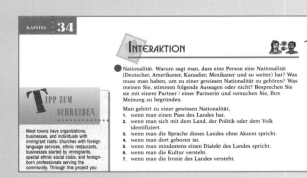

INTERAKTION, a combination of role-playing, partner, and group activities, gives students a chance to integrate what they've learned in real communication with others.

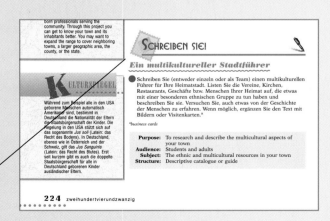

SCHREIBEN SIE! guides students carefully through the pre-writing, writing, and editing processes and facilitates their use of chapter vocabulary and grammatical structures in a personalized context.

OTHER FEATURES

Many other features round out the chapters of *Auf Deutsch!* The linguistic notes in **Sprachspiegel** offer practical insights into the similarities between German and English. **Tipp zum Hören, Tipp zum Lesen,** and **Tipp zum Schreiben** tips aid students in developing listening, reading, and writing skills.

SIND SIE WORTSCHLAU? Vocabulary notes offer tips for learning and expanding vocabulary in German.

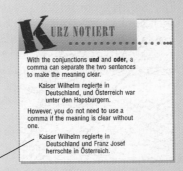

KURZ NOTIERT Grammar notes provide brief but essential information for understanding language structures and/or for carrying out a particular activity.

KULTURSPIEGEL Cultural notes provide information pertaining to concepts presented in the videos, readings, or activities.

FOKUS INTERNET Cues direct students to the *Auf Deutsch!* Web Site where they can connect to sites on the World Wide Web and explore cultural concepts more fully.

WORTSCHATZ ZUM VIDEO / WORTSCHATZ ZUM HÖRTEXT / WORTSCHATZ ZUM LESEN Brief vocabulary lists aid viewing, listening, and reading comprehension.

PROGRAM COMPONENTS

BOOKS, VIDEOS, AND ORDERING INFORMATION

The 36 *Fokus Deutsch* videos, as well as the complete program of textbooks and supplementary materials for *Auf Deutsch!*, are available through the publishers. To order videos, call the Annenberg/CPB Foundation at 1-800-LEARNER. To order copies of the textbooks and supplements, contact your McDougal Littell representative.

The following descriptions of components apply to all three levels of *Auf Deutsch!*

PUPIL'S EDITION

The *Auf Deutsch!* Level 3 textbook correlates to the third level of the video series and contains viewing activities, vocabulary activities, grammar explanations and exercises, cultural and historical readings, listening comprehension activities, and reading and writing activities.

ARBEITSHEFT (WORKBOOK)

A combined Workbook and Laboratory Manual accompanies the Pupil's Edition for each level. Each chapter is divided into sections that mirror the sections in the main textbook, and each section, as appropriate, may contain both laboratory and workbook exercises. All sections provide practice in global listening comprehension, pronunciation, speaking, reading, and writing.

AUDIO PROGRAM

Each set of audio CDs or Cassettes provides thirty minutes of material correlated with the listening comprehension sections in the Pupil's Edition. In addition, the Audio Program provides another six hours of additional listening material correlated with the listening portions of the **Arbeitsheft** (Workbook).

WORLD WIDE WEB

Correlated with the **Fokus Internet** feature in the Pupil's Edition, this feature allows students to explore interesting links by connecting to the *Auf Deutsch!* Web Site (www.mcdougallittell.com). Available in 2000, this site also includes engaging web-based activities.

TEACHER'S EDITION

The Teacher's Edition is identical to the corresponding Pupil's Edition, except that it contains an interleaf with a planning guide, listening scripts, pacing guides for 50- and 90-minute classes, and teaching suggestions for each chapter.

AUDIO SCRIPT

Packaged with the Instructor's Audio Program, the Audio Script contains the complete recording script of the Audio Program.

Teacher's Resource CD-ROM
The Teacher's Resource CD-ROM contains visuals—from all three levels of the main textbooks and videos—for use in creating overhead transparencies, Power Point™ slides for classroom use, and the complete Assessment Program in Microsoft Word 97 format. The Assessment Program consists of chapter quizzes, review tests, and a final exam.

Assessment Program
The *Auf Deutsch!* Assessment Program contains 12 chapter tests, 4 review tests, and a final exam. It is also available on the *Auf Deutsch!* Teacher's Resource CD-ROM.

Overhead Transparencies
A collection of Overhead Transparencies from the textbook contains visuals from the vocabulary sections as well as the grammar presentations.

High School Distance Learning Guide
The High School Distance Learning Guide contains useful information on implementing a distance learning course and how to incorporate the *Fokus Deutsch* video series and the print materials in that environment.

ACKNOWLEDGMENTS

A project of this magnitude takes on a life of its own. So many people have helped with the video series and print materials that it is impossible to acknowledge the work and contributions of all of them in detail. Here are some of the highlights.

MEMBERS OF THE ADVISORY BOARD, THE ANNENBERG/CPB PROJECT AND WGBH

Robert Di Donato, Chief Academic and Series Developer
Professor of German
Miami University of Ohio

Keith Anderson
Professor Emeritus and Acting Director of International Studies
St. Olaf College

Thomas Keith Cothrun
Past President, American Association of Teachers of German
Las Cruces High School

Richard Kalfus
German Instructor and Foreign Language Administrator
Community College District, St. Louis, Missouri

Beverly Harris-Schenz
Vice Provost for Faculty Affairs and Associate
  Professor of German
University of Pittsburgh

Marlies Stueart
Wellesley High School

Dr. Claudia Hahn-Raabe
Deputy Director and Director of the Language
  Program
Goethe-Institut

Jürgen Keil
Director
Goethe-Institut

Manfred von Hoesslin
Former Director of the Language Department
Goethe-Institut

REVIEWERS AND FOCUS GROUP PARTICIPANTS

Karen Alms, Laguna Hills High School, CA
John Austin, Georgia State University, GA
Helga Bister-Broosen, University of North Carolina
  at Chapel Hill, NC
Marty Christopher, Woodward High School, OK
Donald Clark, Johns Hopkins University, MD
Sharon Di Fino, University of Florida, FL
Judy Graunke, Temple High School, CA
Ingeborg Henderson, University of California,
  Davis, CA
Richard Kalfus, St. Louis Community College,
  Meramec, MO

David Kleinbeck, Midland College, TX
Alene Moyer, Georgetown University, DC
Margaret L. Peo, Victor J. Andrew High School,
  Orland Park, IL
Barbara Pflanz, University of the Redlands, CA
Monica Polley, Wilmette Junior High, Wilmette, IL
Donna Van Handle, Mount Holyoke College, MA
Morris Vos, Western Illinois University, IL

The authors of *Auf Deutsch!* would also like to extend very special thanks to the following organizations and individuals:

- The Annenberg/CPB Project (Washington, DC), especially to Pete Neal and Lynn Smith for their support across the board.

- WGBH Educational Foundation, especially to Michele Korf for her guidance in shaping the series, to Project Director Christine Herbes-Sommers for her tireless work on the project and for her wonderfully creative ideas, and to Producer-Director Fred Barzyk for his creative leadership.

- The Goethe-Institut, especially Claudia Hahn-Raabe for her stewardship in developing the series, and to Jürgen Keil in Boston for his creative and intellectual support and for sharing the use of Boston's beautiful Goethe-Institut building.

- InterNationes, especially to Rüdiger van den Boom and Beate Raabe.

Deutschland und Luxemburg
Einwohner
Deutschland (1998): 82,0 Mio.
Luxemburg (1998): 418 000
Maßstab 2,0 cm = 100 km

DÄNEMARK

OSTSEE

NORDSEE

Flensburg

Helgoland

Hiddensee

Rügen
Sellin

Kiel

Stralsund

SCHLESWIG-
HOLSTEIN

Rostock
Greifswald

MECKLENBURG-

Ostfriesische Inseln

Cuxhaven

Lübeck

Güstrow

VORPOMMERN

Neubrandenburg

Bremerhaven

HAMBURG

Hamburg

Schwerin

Emden

Leer

BREMEN

Lüneburg

Prenzlau

Oldenburg

Bremen

BRANDENBURG

Havel

POLEN

NIEDERSACHSEN

LÜNEBURGER
HEIDE

DIE NIEDERLANDE

Osnabrück

Kirchlinteln

Wolfsburg

BERLIN

Berlin

Oder

Brandenburg

Potsdam

Frankfurt

Oder

Bielefeld

Hannover

Braunschweig

Magdeburg

Eisenhüttenstadt

Münster

TEUTOBURGER WALD

Hameln

Bad
Harzburg

SACHSEN-

Dessau

Wittenberg

Cottbus

NORDRHEIN-WESTFALEN

Essen

Dortmund

Paderborn

Brocken

Wernigerode

Neiße

Duisburg

Ruhr

HARZ

ANHALT

Rheinhausen

Wuppertal

Göttingen

Eisleben

Halle

Leipzig

Görlitz

Krefeld

Kassel

THÜRINGEN

Wengelsdorf

SACHSEN

Dresden

Düsseldorf

Köln

Rhein

Erfurt

Weimar

Meißen

Aachen

Marburg

Eisenach

Kosmar

Chemnitz

Bonn

Gießen

Fulda

Gera

Zwickau

BELGIEN

Limburg

HESSEN

THÜRINGER WALD

Suhl

ERZGEBIRGE

Koblenz

Mosel

RHÖN

Wiesbaden

Frankfurt

Main

EIFEL

RHEINLAND-

Mainz

Bayreuth

TSCHECHIEN

LUXEMBURG

HUNSRÜCK

PFALZ

Würzburg

FRÄNKISCHE ALB

Luxemburg

Trier

Worms

SAARLAND

Ludwigshafen

Mannheim

Nürnberg

BÖHMER WALD

Saarbrücken

Kaiserslautern

Rothenburg
ob der Tauber

BAYERN

Heidelberg

BAYERISCHER
WALD

BADEN-
WÜRTTEMBERG

Regensburg

Karlsruhe

Rhein

Stuttgart

Straubing

Passau

VOGESEN

Neckar

SCHWÄBISCHE ALB

Donau

Isar

SCHWARZWALD

Tübingen

Ulm

Augsburg

Inn

FRANKREICH

Rottweil

München

Tegernsee

Chiemsee

Freiburg

BAYERISCHE ALPEN

Berchtesgaden

Weil am Rhein

Friedrichshafen

Garmisch-
Partenkirchen

Konstanz

Lindau

ÖSTERREICH

Bodensee

Zugspitze

DIE SCHWEIZ

ISLAND
Reykjavik

NORWEGEN
SCHWEDEN
FINNLAND
Helsinki
Oslo
Stockholm
ESTLAND
Tallinn
LETTLAND
Riga
OSTSEE
LITAUEN
Wilna
Minsk
(ZU RUSSLAND)
WEISSRUSSLAND

Nordirland
Schottland
NORDSEE
DÄNEMARK
Kopenhagen
Berlin
Warschau
Kiew

ATLANTISCHER
OZEAN
IRLAND
Dublin
England
Wales
GROSSBRITANNIEN
London
Der Ärmelkanal
DIE NIEDERLANDE
Den Haag
Brüssel
BELGIEN
DEUTSCHLAND
POLEN

Paris
Luxemburg
LUXEMBURG
LIECHTENSTEIN
TSCHECHIEN
Prag
DIE SLOWAKEI
MOLDAWIEN
Kischinew
Wien
Budapest
ÖSTERREICH
UNGARN
RUMÄNIEN

FRANKREICH
Bern
DIE SCHWEIZ
SLOWENIEN
Mailand
Venedig
Ljubljana
Zagreb
Belgrad
Bukarest
SERBIEN UND
MONTENEGRO
Sarajevo
BULGARIEN

KROATIEN
BOSNIEN UND
HERZEGOWINA
ADRIATISCHES
MEER
Skopje
Sofia

ANDORRA
MONACO
Korsika
VATIKANSTADT
Rom
Tirana
ALBANIEN
MAKEDONIEN

PORTUGAL
Lissabon
Madrid
SPANIEN
Mallorca
Sardinien
ITALIEN
TYRRHENISCHES
MEER
GRIECHENLAND
IONISCHES
MEER
Athen

Straße von
Gibraltar
Algier
Tunis
Sizilien
MALTA
KRETA

Rabat
TUNESIEN
MITTELMEER

MAROKKO
ALGERIEN
Tripolis
LIBYEN

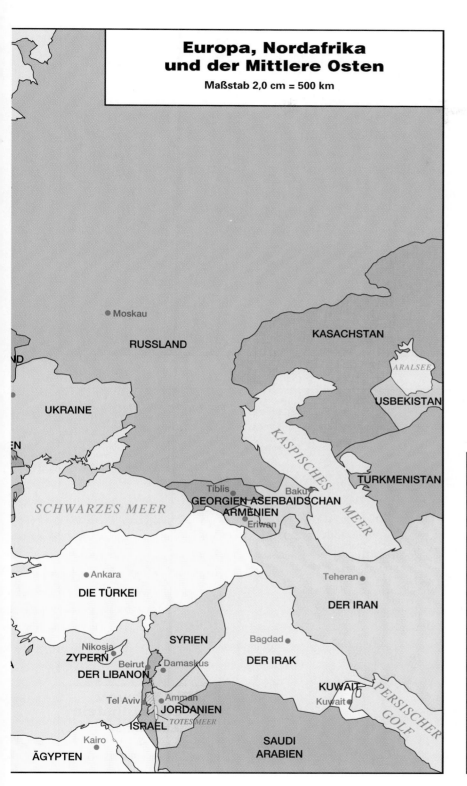

Europa, Nordafrika und der Mittlere Osten

Maßstab 2,0 cm = 500 km

Moskau

KASACHSTAN

RUSSLAND

ARALSEE

ND

UKRAINE

USBEKISTAN

KASPISCHES

TURKMENISTAN

Tiblis

Baku

GEORGIEN ASERBAIDSCHAN

ARMENIEN

SCHWARZES MEER

Eriwan

MEER

Ankara

Teheran

DIE TÜRKEI

DER IRAN

Nikosia

SYRIEN

Bagdad

ZYPERN

Beirut

Damaskus

DER IRAK

DER LIBANON

KUWAIT

PERSISCHER

Tel Aviv

Amman

Kuwait

JORDANIEN

GOLF

ISRAEL

TOTES MEER

Kairo

SAUDI

ÄGYPTEN

ARABIEN

EU-LÄNDER (1998)	EINWOHNER (1998)
Belgien	10,2 Mio.
Dänemark	5,3 Mio.
Deutschland	82,0 Mio.
Finnland	5,1 Mio.
Frankreich	58,5 Mio.
Griechenland	10,5 Mio.
Großbritannien	58,9 Mio.
Irland	3,6 Mio.
Italien	57,5 Mio.
Luxemburg	0,4 Mio.
Niederlande	15,6 Mio.
Österreich	8,0 Mio.
Portugal	9,9 Mio.
Schweden	8,9 Mio.
Spanien	39,3 Mio.
Gesamtbevölkerungszahl	373,7 Mio.
Mio. = Millionen	

Österreich

Einwohner (1998): 8 Mio.
Maßstab 1,5 cm = 50 km

TSCHECHIEN

DEUTSCHLAND

Gmünd
Horn
Krems
Donau
WIEN
Linz
Sankt Pölten
Wien
OBERÖSTERREICH
Melk
Baden
Amstetten
Eisenstadt
Gmunden
NIEDERÖSTERREICH
Neusiedler See
Salzburg
Bad Ischl
Wiener Neustadt
Bodensee
Salzkammergut
Mariazell
Bregenz
Hallstatt
Liezen
BURGENLAND
Kufstein
Sankt Johann in Tirol
Bruck an der Mur
VORARLBERG
Reutte
Wörgl
STEIERMARK
Oberwart
Feldkirch
Innsbruck
Bischofshofen
Enns
Arlberg
Kitzbühel
Zell am See
Sankt Georgen
Güssing
Landeck
Bruck
TIROL
SALZBURG
Radstadt
Mauterndorf
Osttirol
(zu Tirol)
DIE SCHWEIZ
Vintschgau
Lienz
Spittal an der Drau
Graz
Mur
Meran
Feldkirchen
UNGARN
SÜDTIROL
Drau
KÄRNTEN
Klagenfurt
Bozen
Villach
Wörther See
ITALIEN
SLOWENIEN

SCHAFFHAUSEN
Schaffhausen
DEUTSCHLAND
Rhein
Kreuzlingen
BASEL
(STADT)
Rhein
THURGAU
Bodensee
Basel
Liestal
Winterthur
Frauenfeld
FRANKREICH
Baden
ZÜRICH
St. Gallen
St. Margrethen
BASEL
(LAND)
AARGAU
Zürich
Herisau
AUSSER-RHODEN
Delemont
Aarau
APPENZELL
Appenzell
JURA
SOLOTHURN
Reuss
INNER-RHODEN
ÖSTERREICH
Solothurn
Zürichsee
Vaduz
Biel
LUZERN
Zug
SANKT
LIECHTENSTEIN
Neuchâtel
ZUG
Einsiedeln
GALLEN
NEUENBURG
Bern
Luzern
SCHWYZ
Glarus
Chur
BERNER
Stans
Schwyz
GLARUS
Fribourg
OBERLAND
Sarnen
NIDW
Altdorf
Braunwald
Klosters
Thun
UNTERWALDEN
OBW
Engelberg
Davos
BERN
Brienz
URI
WAADT
Thuner See
Interlaken
Andermatt
Disentis
GRAUBÜNDEN
Lausanne
Jungfrau
Grindelwald
St. Moritz
Montreux
Jungfraujoch
Gstaad
Brig
Genfer See
TESSIN
Genf
Sion
Bellinzona
GENF
Rhône
WALLIS
Locarno
Zermatt
Lugano
Matterhorn
Langensee
ITALIEN

NIDW = NIDWALDEN
OBW = OBWALDEN

**Die Schweiz
und Liechtenstein**
Einwohner

Schweiz (1998): 7,1 Mio.
Liechtenstein (1998): 30 000
Maßstab 2,0 cm = 50 km

PLANNING GUIDE
CLASSROOM MANAGEMENT

OBJECTIVES

Communication
- Practice greetings, p. 2.
- Review school-related vocabulary, p. 2.

Grammar
- Review the nominative and accusative cases, p. 3.
- Review infinitives and the present tense, pp. 4–5.
- Review two-part verbs, p. 7.

Culture
- Learn about cities in German-speaking countries, p. 8.

PROGRAM RESOURCES

 Print
- *Arbeitsheft* (Workbook), pp. 1–4
- *Arbeitsheft* (Workbook), Teacher's Edition, pp. 1–4

 Audiovisual
- Overhead Transparencies E.1–E.2
- Audio Program, Cassette 1A/CD 1

 Technology
- Annenberg *Fokus Deutsch* Video Series, *Einführung*
- www.mcdougallittell.com

PACING GUIDE
50-MINUTE SCHEDULE

DAY 1

Note: (1) Please see TE, pp. 1C–1F, for other suggestions not referenced in these plans. (2) Not all homework options need be assigned.

Chapter Opener
- Quick Start Review: Introductions (TE p. 1C). 5 MIN
- Discuss the photo, p. 1 (TE, p. 1C). 4 MIN

VOKABELN
- Quick Start Review: Plural of nouns (TE, p. 1C). 5 MIN
- Do *Akt. A*, p. 2, in pairs, then introduce partners to the class (TE, p. 1C). 10 MIN
- In groups, have students write German definitions for the words in the box on p. 2. Share the definitions with the class. 9 MIN
- Do *Akt. B*, p. 2, as a class. Ask comprehension questions (TE, p. 1C). 8 MIN
- Do *Akt. C*, p. 2, silently, then check answers as a class (TE, p. 1D). 8 MIN

Homework Options:
- *Arbeitsheft*, p. 1, *Vokabeln*, *Akt. A–B*

DAY 2

STRUKTUREN
- Quick Start Review 1: Dates (TE, p. 1D). 6 MIN
- Review the nominative and accusative cases on p. 3. 8 MIN
- Have students do *Übung A*, pp. 3–4 silently, then check their answers with a partner (TE, p. 1D). 10 MIN
- Have students do *Übung B*, p. 4, then share their answers with the class. 9 MIN
- Review infinitives and the present tense on pp. 4–5. 7 MIN
- Have students do *Übung A*, p. 6, alone, creating at least 6 sentences (TE, p. 1E). 10 MIN

Homework Options:
- *Arbeitsheft*, pp. 2–3, *Strukturen*, *Akt. A–D*

PACING GUIDE
50-MINUTE SCHEDULE

DAY 3

STRUKTUREN

- Quick Start Review 2: Vocabulary (TE, p. 1D). 5 MIN
- Do *Übung B*, p. 6, then follow the Teaching Suggestions for a follow-up activity (TE, p. 1E). 15 MIN
- Classroom Community: Group Activity (TE, p. 1E). 8 MIN
- Review two-part verbs on p. 7. 6 MIN
- Have students do *Übung A*, pp. 7–8, silently and then check their answers as a class (TE, p. 1E). 8 MIN
- Have students do *Übung B*, p. 8, with a partner, then follow the Teaching Suggestions for a follow-up activity (TE, p. 1E). 8 MIN

Homework Options:

- *Arbeitsheft*, p. 3, *Strukturen, Akt. E*

DAY 4

PERSPEKTIVEN

- Quick Start Review: Two-part verbs (TE, p. 1E). 6 MIN
- Have students do *Akt. A*, p. 8, silently and then check their answers with a partner. Follow the Teaching Suggestions for a follow-up activity (TE, p. 1E). 12 MIN
- Do *Akt. B*, p. 8, in pairs. Follow the Teaching Suggestions for a follow-up activity (TE, p. 1E). 20 MIN
- Classroom Community: Paired Activity (TE, p. 1E). 12 MIN

Homework Options:

- *Arbeitsheft*, p. 4, *Perspektiven, Akt. A–B*

PACING GUIDE
90-MINUTE SCHEDULE

DAY 1

Note: (1) Please see TE, pp. 1C–1D, for other suggestions not referenced in these plans. (2) Not all homework options need be assigned.

Chapter Opener

- Quick Start Review: Introductions (TE p. 1C). 7 MIN
- Discuss the photo, p. 1 (TE, p. 1C). 5 MIN

VOKABELN

- Quick Start Review: Plural of nouns (TE, p. 1C). 7 MIN
- Do *Akt. A*, p. 2, (TE, p. 1C). 10 MIN
- Have students write definitions in German for the words on p. 2. 12 MIN
- Do *Akt. B–C*, p. 2. Ask questions (TE, p. 1C). 17 MIN

STRUKTUREN

- Review the cases on p. 3. 10 MIN
- Do *Übungen A–B*, pp. 3–4, silently, then check answers (TE, pp. 1D–1E). 22 MIN

Homework Options:

- *Arbeitsheft*, p. 1, *Akt. A–B*

DAY 2

STRUKTUREN

- Quick Start Review: Dates (TE, p. 1D). 7 MIN
- Review infinitives and the present tense on pp. 4–5. 10 MIN
- Have students do *Übung A*, p. 6, alone, creating at least 6 sentences (TE, p. 1E). 10 MIN
- *Übung B*, p. 6. 10 MIN
- Block Schedule activity: Change of Pace (TE, p. 1E). 10 MIN
- Review two-part verbs on p. 7. 10 MIN
- *Übungen A–B, A*, pp. 7–8, check answers (TE, p. 1E). 6 MIN

PERSPEKTIVEN

- Do *Akt. A*, p. 8. Do follow-up activity (TE, p. 1E). 12 MIN
- Do *Akt. B*, p. 8, in pairs. Do follow-up activity (TE, p. 1E). 15 MIN

Homework Options:

- *Arbeitsheft*, pp. 2–3, *Strukturen, Akt. A–D*

The *Einführung* for **Auf Deutsch! 3** touches on several topics of grammar, culture, and vocabulary items. It is not meant to be comprehensive but does offer a review of several important points with which students should already be familiar.

Use the format of the activities to construct your own as needed. For example, you might target a semantic field such as clothing, shopping, or food for practice by creating activities resembling those in the *Vokabeln* activities, p. 2. Or you might focus on culture to construct an activity like *Aktivität B* in the *Perspektiven* section, p. 8, that concerns well-known people from the German-speaking world.

Chapter Opener, p. 1

PROGRAM RESOURCES

• Overhead Transparencies E.1–E.2

Quick Start Review

Questions
Bilden Sie Fragen zu den Antworten. Fragen Sie nach dem unterstrichenen Objekt.
1. Ich lerne *seit drei Jahren* Deutsch.
2. Meine Lieblingsfarbe ist *grün*.
3. Ich möchte *Journalist* werden.
4. *1989* ist die Berliner Mauer gefallen.
5. Ein Berliner kostet *1.50DM*.
6. Das Brandenburger Tor steht *in Berlin*.

Answers: 1. Seit wann lernen Sie Deutsch? 2. Welche ist Ihre Lieblingsfarbe? 3. Was möchten Sie werden?/Welchen Beruf möchten Sie lernen? 4. Wann ist die Berliner Mauer gefallen? 5. Wie viel kostet ein Berliner? 6. Wo steht das Brandenburger Tor?

TEACHING SUGGESTIONS

• Photo, p. 1

As a class, have students describe the student pictured in the photo. How old is she? What color is her hair? her eyes? What is she doing? What do you think she is thinking? Expansion: Have students work in pairs to write a paragraph in which they imagine who this student is, where she lives in the German-speaking world, and anything else they care to imagine about her life, her family, or her school.

TEACHING ALL STUDENTS

Extra Help Draw a short, simple family tree on the board for a real or imagined person and point out to students the various relationships. Then, ask one or more students to draw on the board their own family trees and to describe them to the class in German: *Das ist mein Vater. Er heißt Jack. Das ist meine Mutter. Sie heißt Jill. Ich habe zwei Geschwister: Johnny, mein Bruder, und Julie, meine Schwester. usw.*

CLASSROOM COMMUNITY

Group Activity Have students work in groups of 5–6 students. One student gives the first line of a story that starts with the description of a person. For example, *Es gibt einen Mann, der in der Schweiz wohnt.* The next student makes up the next sentence of the story. Students go around the circle, each adding a sentence, until their story reaches a conclusion.

Vokabeln, p. 2

PROGRAM RESOURCES

• Overhead Transparencies E.1–E.2
• *Arbeitsheft*, p. 1
• Audio Program, Cassette 1A/CD 1

Quick Start Review

Plural of nouns
Setzen Sie die Substantive in den Plural und ändern Sie die Verbformen.
1. Diese Burg ist sehr alt.
2. Dieser Gast ist sehr unhöflich.
3. Der Schlüssel hängt in der Rezeption an der Wand.
4. Das Formular muss bis morgen bei uns sein.
5. Der Aufzug in den zweiten Stock ist fast immer voll.
6. Die Ferienwohnung kostet 120 DM pro Nacht.

Answers: 1. Diese Burgen sind sehr alt. 2. Diese Gäste sind sehr unhöflich. 3. Die Schlüssel hängen in der Rezeption an der Wand. 4. Die Formulare müssen bis morgen bei uns sein. 5. Die Aufzüge in den zweiten Stock sind fast immer voll. 6. Die Ferienwohnungen kosten 120 DM pro Nacht.

TEACHING SUGGESTIONS

• *Aktivität A*, p. 2

Expansion: Have students ask each other questions such as *Was hast du im Sommer gemacht? Warst du schon mal in Deutschland? Was hast du heute Morgen gemacht?*

• *Aktivität B*, p. 2

Warm-up: Have students go over the vocabulary in the box. Instead of having students translate the vocabulary items, ask them to use each one in a sentence.

• *Aktivität C*, p. 2

Expansion: Write the following expressions on the board or on an OHT and discuss with the students.

Ich habe noch eine Frage dazu.
Entschuldigung, ich habe das nicht ganz verstanden.
Könnten Sie bitte langsamer sprechen.
Was war denn falsch?
Was haben Sie gerade gesagt? Was hast du gerade gesagt?
Würden Sie bitte den letzten Satz noch einmal wiederholen.
Ist das richtig, was ich hier geschrieben habe?
Was bedeutet dieses Wort?

TEACHING ALL STUDENTS

Multiple Intelligences Intrapersonal: Have students work with a partner and write a detailed description of their classroom. They should describe all the furniture and technical equipment. They should use colors, numbers, and various descriptive adjectives. Have students read their descriptions to the class.

Extra Help Before doing each activity in this section, review necessary vocabulary. With books closed, have students brainstorm a list of vocabulary pertinent to the subject of the activity. Write their suggestions on the board. Expansion: Have students group the vocabulary by gender. Have them also give past participles of all verbs.

CLASSROOM COMMUNITY

Group Activity Give students a minute to find a classmate whose birthday is in the same month as theirs. Whoever finds a classmate sharing a birth-month first scores a point. Keep track of students' points on the board. Continue the activity by asking more questions and keeping score of responses. Possible questions might be *Wer hat im selben Monat Geburtstag wie Sie? Wer hat am Wochenende den gleichen Film gesehen wie Sie? Wer hat die gleiche Hausnummer wie Sie? Wer treibt dieselbe Sportart wie Sie? Wer hat die gleiche Schuhgröße wie Sie? usw.*

BLOCK SCHEDULE

Peer Teaching Divide students into small groups. Have them choose a vocabulary topic such as clothes, hobbies, or school life. Have them write a list of all the words they can think of in this field. Have them post their lists on the classroom wall and give them time to look over each other's work.

Strukturen, pp. 3–8

PROGRAM RESOURCES

• *Arbeitsheft*, pp. 2–3
• Audio Program, Cassette 1A/CD 1

Quick Start Review 1

♻ Dates
Bilden Sie Sätze.
1. am / acht / März / können / dich / ich / besuchen / in München
2. der / Februar / zwölft / haben / heute / wir
3. mein / am / acht / Mai / Geburtstag / ist
4. man / dürfen / nicht / durch den Park / fahren / mit dem Motorrad
5. er / wohnen / in Düsseldorf / seit / der / erst / September

6. an Weihnachten / fliegen / sie / zu / ihre Schwester / nach Boston

Answers: 1. Am achten März kann ich dich in München besuchen.   2. Wir haben heute den zwölften Februar. 3. Mein Geburtstag ist am achten Mai. 4. Man darf nicht mit dem Motorrad durch den Park fahren.   5. Er wohnt seit dem ersten September in Düsseldorf.   6. An Weihnachten fliegt sie nach Boston zu ihrer Schwester.

Quick Start Review 2

♻ Vocabulary
Verbinden Sie die Sätze.
1. Ich schlage vor,
2. Klaus wollte heute Mittag bei mir
3. Wie viele Bücher hast du dir
4. Wir sind jetzt 25
5. Würdest du lieber ein Zimmer mieten
6. Aufräumen hat mir
a. vorbeikommen.
b. Schüler in unserer Klasse.
c. oder im Studentenwohnheim wohnen?
d. noch nie Spaß gemacht.
e. ausgeliehen?
f. dass wir mit dem Rad zum Schwimmbad fahren.

Answers: 1. f   2. a   3. e   4. b
5. c   6. d

TEACHING SUGGESTIONS

• *Übung A*, pp. 3–4

Review the nominative and accusative cases. Point out weak nouns as well as the use of the accusative after the expression *es gibt*. Personalize this exercise by asking the students about their own daily routines.

- *Übung B*, p. 4

Ask additional questions, such as *Wer macht das Frühstück? Wer gießt die Blumen? Wer kauft die Lebensmittel ein?*

- *Übung A*, p. 6

Personalize this exercise by asking the students about trips they have taken.

- *Übung B*, p. 6

Follow-up: Have students write a description of some problems they had on a trip such as losing a suitcase, forgetting something, or losing directions. Have them then write an outline for a skit and ask them to narrate it for the class or with a partner.

- *Übung A*, pp. 7–8

Follow up: Have students form their own sentences with each of the verbs used in the activity.

- *Übung B*, p. 8

Expansion: Have students form imperatives for each of the sentences. Possible answers: (MODELL) *Ruf uns bitte an!*
1. *Sei bitte pünktlich!* 2. *Hör uns bitte zu!* 3. *Stell uns bitte deine Freunde vor!* 4. *Bring bitte zurück, was du von uns leihst!*

TEACHING ALL STUDENTS

Extra Help Have students make a list of verb prefixes and of verbs using that prefix. Write them on the board or on an OHT. Have students discuss the possible meanings of the prefixes.
MODELL: *ab-: abfahren, abnehmen, abholen*
an-: ankommen, anfangen, anrufen, angreifen
auf-: aufhören, aufgeben, aufstehen

CLASSROOM COMMUNITY

Dictation Do the following dictation with the class. Provide students with the correct version of the dictation on the board or an OHT. Have them exchange their writings to correct each other. *Köln ist eine Großstadt. Es ist die viertgrößte Stadt Deutschlands und hat über eine Million Einwohner. Die Römer haben die Stadt gegründet. Der berühmte Kölner Dom ist schon 750 Jahre alt. In Köln gibt es viele Museen, einen Zoo und eine Universität.*

BLOCK SCHEDULE

Change of Pace Have students write a letter or an e-mail to a student in Germany. They should introduce themselves, explain where they live, which school they attend, and why they study German. Try to find a class of the same age as your students at a school in Germany with whom to exchange e-mails or letters. A good starting point for contacts is www.schulweb.de

Perspektiven, p. 8

PROGRAM RESOURCES

- *Arbeitsheft*, p. 4
- Audio Program, Cassette 1A/CD 1
- www.mcdougallittell.com

Quick Start Review
Two-part verbs
Beantworten Sie die Fragen.
MODELL: *Wann sollen wir abfahren? (um halb zehn) →*
Wir fahren um halb zehn ab.
1. Wann sollen wir aufstehen? (um neun)
2. Wo müssen wir umsteigen? (Bahnhof Zoo)

3. Wen sollen wir einladen? (Nachbarn und Freunde)
4. Wann wird er zurückkommen? (am Sonntag)
5. Was sollen wir bestellen? (Wiener Schnitzel)
6. Wann werden wir umziehen? (am ersten Mai)
Answers: 1. Wir stehen um neun auf.
2. Wir steigen am Bahnhof Zoo um.
3. Wir laden Nachbarn und Freunde ein.
4. Wir kommen am Sonntag zurück.
5. Wir bestellen Wiener Schnitzel.
6. Wir ziehen am ersten Mai um.

TEACHING SUGGESTIONS

- *Aktivität A*, p. 8

Follow-up: Have students tell what else they know about the cities mentioned in the activity. Ask also *Was wissen Sie über Österreich? Was wissen Sie über die Schweiz?*

- *Aktivität B*, p. 8

Ask which of the cultural details in this activity are new to the students. Discuss *Karneval,* the school system, German reunification, and the European Union. Find out what interests students and let the discussion run its course.

TEACHING ALL STUDENTS

Challenge Have students write a definition of one of the vocabulary items on p. 9. Call on different students to read their definition. The class must find the word in the vocabulary list that matches the definition.

CLASSROOM COMMUNITY

Paired Activity Have students interview a partner to learn as much as possible about that person's personality. They should focus not just on hobbies and interests, but try to elicit some unusual information such as *Was ist deine Lieblingsfarbe? Was ist dein Lieblingsfilm? Nimmst du im Supermarkt an der Kasse Papier- oder Plastiktüten?* Have students write their list of questions before they start.

BLOCK SCHEDULE

Fun Break Have students play a round of Scrabble in German. They could either play together on the board writing in the letters, or play in smaller groups.

PROJECTS

Have students pick a German cultural event (*Fasching, Karneval, Oktoberfest*) or some other tradition (*Maibaum, Nikolaus am 6. Dezember, St. Martin am 11. November*). Have them research how it is celebrated in various German-speaking countries. One student could report on *Fasching* in Switzerland and another on *Karneval* in Cologne. Have students write a report on their findings.

RUBRIC   **A** = 13–15 pts.   **B** = 10–12 pts.
C = 7–9 pts.   **D** = 4–6 pts.   **F** <4 pts.

Writing Criteria	Scale				
Grammar, vocabulary	1	2	3	4	5
Organization	1	2	3	4	5
Creativity, presentation	1	2	3	4	5

EINFÜHRUNG

In diesem Kapitel

- werden Sie Ihre Mitschüler/Mitschülerinnen kennen lernen.
- werden Sie nützliche Grundvokabeln und Ausdrücke wiederholen.

Sie werden auch

- die Formen des Nominativs und des Akkusativs wiederholen.
- Verben im Präsens gebrauchen.
- den Gebrauch von trennbaren Verben wiederholen.
- besprechen, was Sie bereits über Kultur und Alltag in den deutschsprachigen Ländern wissen.

Studenten und Studentinnen bei einer Vorlesung an der Uni.

VOKABELN

„Darf ich vorstellen?"

A Begrüßungen. Suchen Sie sich drei von Ihren Mitschülern/Mitschülerinnen aus und stellen Sie sich ihnen vor. Hier sind mögliche Fragen, damit Sie sich besser kennen lernen können.

A. *Answers will vary.*

1. Wie heißt du?
2. Was ist dein Lieblingsfach?
3. Welche Kurse belegst du dieses Semester?
4. Warum belegst du Deutsch?
5. Was machst du gern in deiner Freizeit?

B Tanja und ihre Freundin Sabine wollen nach dem Abitur an einer Universität studieren. Die beiden schmieden Plane. Ergänzen Sie die Lücken mit den Wörtern im Kasten.

Hauptfach
Studium
Studentenwohnheim
fertig
Vorlesungen
Studiengebühren
belegen

Tanja überlegt gemeinsam mit ihrer Freundin Sabine, was sie als _____[1] studieren soll. Obwohl Tanjas Lieblingsfach Mathematik ist, interessiert sie sich auch für Architektur. Sabine mag Sprachen und will Französisch als Hauptfach studieren. Als Nebenfach will sie _____[2] in Englisch _____.[3] Beide Freundinnen möchten mit ihrem _____[4] schnell _____[5] sein. Obwohl Studenten in Deutschland keine _____[6] bezahlen müssen, sprechen die beiden Freundinnen davon, dass sie nach dem Abitur für ein paar Monate Geld verdienen wollen. Außerdem diskutieren sie darüber, ob sie in einem _____[7] wohnen möchten oder sich lieber eine Wohnung mit einer Freundin teilen sollen.

B. 1. Hauptfach 2. Kurse 3. belegen 4. Studium 5. fertig
6. Studiengebühren 7. Studentenwohnheim

C Im Klassenzimmer. Ordnen Sie jedem Ausdruck links eine passende Situation rechts zu.

1. „Ich stimme damit überein."
2. „Was meinen Sie damit?"
3. „Was halten Sie davon?"
4. „Das steht auf Seite . . . "
5. „Können Sie das bitte wiederholen?"
6. „Ich schlage vor, . . . "

C. 1. e 2. d 3. f 4. c 5. a 6. b

a. Sie haben den Lehrer / die Lehrerin nicht gehört. *Oder:* Sie möchten etwas noch einmal hören.
b. Sie wollen einen Vorschlag machen.
c. Sie möchten sagen, wo etwas im Text steht.
d. Sie möchten wissen, warum jemand etwas sagt oder glaubt.
e. Sie möchten sagen, dass Sie gleicher Meinung sind.
f. Sie möchten jemanden fragen, welche Meinung er/sie zu einem bestimmten Thema hat.

Der Professor hält einen Vortrag.

STRUKTUREN

REVIEW OF THE NOMINATIVE AND ACCUSATIVE CASES
MARKING SUBJECTS AND DIRECT OBJECTS

In English, subjects tend to come right before the verb and direct objects right after the verb. In German, subjects may come before or after the verb. In the following example, subjects appear in blue and direct objects in red.

Marion besucht den Professor.	*Marion visits the professor.*
Wen besucht sie?	*Whom does she visit?*
Der Professor serviert einen Kuchen.	*The professor serves a cake.*
Was serviert er?	*What does he serve?*

Notice that in the preceding examples the forms of the definite article show the function of the noun within the sentence.

In German, subjects are in the nominative case, direct objects in the accusative case. Feminine nouns are identified by the articles **die/eine,** masculine nouns by **der/ein,** neuter nouns by **das/ein,** and all plural nouns by **die.**

The forms of the accusative case are exactly the same as those of the nominative case, with the following exception: The masculine articles **der** and **ein** become **den** and **einen.**

NOMINATIVE	ACCUSATIVE
der Mann	**den** Mann
ein Mann	**einen** Mann

Übungen

A Das Semester fängt schon an! Klara beschreibt, was sie morgens macht. Ergänzen Sie die Lücken mit der richtigen Form des Artikels im Nominativ oder im Akkusativ.

KURZ NOTIERT

Some masculine nouns take an **-n** or **-en** ending in the accusative case.

der Herr → den Herr**n**
ein Herr → einen Herr**n**
der Student → den Student**en**
ein Student → einen Student**en**

The following are some common **-n** or **-en** masculine nouns.

der Junge, der Nachbar, der Mensch, der Kollege, der Name, der Neffe, der Patient, der Polizist, der Präsident, der Soldat, der Student

KURZ NOTIERT

A singular or plural noun in the accusative case always follows the expression **es gibt.**

Gibt es **einen neuen** Schüler in der Klasse?
Is there a new student in class?

Es gibt **viele Jugendliche,** die sportlich interessiert sind.
There are a lot of young people interested in sports.

Klara steht vor dem schwarzen Brett.

A. 1. der 2. den 3. die 4. eine 5. das
6. die 7. den 8. den

B. *Answers will vary. The questions are:* 1. Wer spült bei euch das Geschirr? 2. Wer wäscht bei euch die Wäsche? 3. Wer mäht bei euch den Rasen? 4. Wer deckt bei euch den Tisch? 5. Wer räumt bei euch das Schlafzimmer auf?

Um halb sieben klingelt _____¹ Wecker (der). Ich sehe auf _____² Wecker (der) und mache ihn aus. Ich stehe nur langsam auf. Ich gehe in _____³ Küche (die) und mache mir _____⁴ Tasse (eine) Tee. Während _____⁵ Teewasser (das) kocht, gehe ich unter _____⁶ Dusche (die) und dusche mich schnell. Ich mache _____⁷ Kleiderschrank (der) auf, aber ich weiß nicht, ob ich am ersten Tag _____⁸ blauen oder dunkelbraunen Rock (der) tragen soll. Es ist zu früh am Morgen, um solche Entscheidungen zu treffen!

B Hausarbeit. Wie ist die Rollenverteilung in Ihrer Familie? Bilden Sie Fragen, und stellen Sie diese Fragen einem Partner / einer Partnerin.

MODELL: Abendessen kochen →
     A: Wer kocht bei euch das Abendessen?
     B: Mein Vater kocht das Abendessen.

1. Geschirr spülen
2. Wäsche waschen
3. Rasen mähen
4. Tisch decken
5. Schlafzimmer aufräumen

REVIEW OF INFINITIVES AND THE PRESENT TENSE
TALKING ABOUT DOING THINGS

The verbs **brauchen** and **arbeiten** are two examples of regular verbs. To form the present tense, drop the **-en** from the infinitive and add the present-tense personal endings.

Verbs with stems that end in **-t** or **-d** insert an **-e** before the endings for the forms for **du** and **sie/er/es.**

INFINITIVE: **brauchen** *to need*
STEM: **brauch-**

ich	brauche	wir	brauchen
du	brauchst	ihr	braucht
Sie	brauchen	Sie	brauchen
sie/er/es	braucht	sie	brauchen

INFINITIVE: **arbeiten** *to work*
STEM: **arbeit-**

ich	arbeite	wir	arbeiten
du	arbeitest	ihr	arbeitet
Sie	arbeiten	Sie	arbeiten
sie/er/es	arbeitet	sie	arbeiten

The verb **haben** has irregular forms for **du** and **sie/er/es.**

INFINITIVE: **haben** *to have*	
STEM: **hab-**	
ich hab**e**	wir hab**en**
du **hast**	ihr hab**t**
Sie hab**en**	Sie hab**en**
sie/er/es **hat**	sie hab**en**

Some German verbs have stem-vowel changes in the forms for **du** and **sie/er/es.**

VERBS WITH STEM-VOWEL CHANGE a → ä

INFINITIVE: **schlafen** *to sleep*	
STEM: **schlaf-**	
ich schlafe	wir schlafen
du schl**ä**fst	ihr schlaft
Sie schlafen	Sie schlafen
sie/er/es schl**ä**ft	sie schlafen

Also: fahren: du fährst, sie/er/es fährt
laufen: du läufst, sie/er/es läuft

VERBS WITH STEM-VOWEL CHANGE e → ie

INFINITIVE: **lesen** *to read*	
STEM: **les-**	
ich lese	wir lesen
du l**ie**st	ihr lest
Sie lesen	Sie lesen
sie/er/es l**ie**st	sie lesen

Also: sehen: du siehst, sie/er/es sieht

VERBS WITH STEM-VOWEL CHANGE e → i

INFINITIVE: **essen** *to eat*	
STEM: **ess-**	
ich esse	wir essen
du **i**sst	ihr esst
Sie essen	Sie essen
sie/er/es **i**sst	sie essen

Also: sprechen: du sprichst, sie/er/es spricht
geben: du gibst, sie/er/es gibt
nehmen: du nimmst, sie/er/es nimmt
vergessen: du vergisst, sie/er/es vergisst

Das Deutsche Museum in München.

Birgit steigt in den Zug ein.

KURZ NOTIERT

German has one present tense, which is equivalent to all three forms of the present tense in English.

Ich **arbeite.**
{ *I work.* (simple)
I do work. (emphatic)
I am working.
(progressive)

Übungen

A Urlaub in München. Sie reisen mit Freunden nach München. Bilden Sie Sätze, um Ihren Urlaub zu beschreiben.

MODELL: Wir übernachten heute Abend im Hotel „Bayerischer Hof".

ich	übernachten	nächste	an der Isar
wir	liegen	Woche	in der Sonne
meine	genießen	am Montag	im Englischen
Freundin	ändern	am Freitag	Garten
mein	besuchen	heute	in einer
Freund	fotografieren	ein paar Tage	Jugendherberge
meine	machen	jeden Tag	das Deutsche
Freunde	reservieren	abends	Museum
	verbringen	morgen früh	das warme Wetter
		heute Abend	im Hotel
			„Bayerischer
			Hof"
			Aufnahmen
			eine
			Stadtrundfahrt
			ein Picknick

A. *Answers will vary. Possible answers are:* Nächste Woche reservieren wir in einer Jugendherberge. Wir verbringen jeden Tag im Englischen Garten. Meine Freundin liegt jeden Tag in der Sonne. Wir machen heute Abend ein Picknick. Wir machen am Montag eine Stadtrundfahrt. Ich mache jeden Tag Aufnahmen. Wir besuchen am Freitag das Deutsche Museum. Wir genießen jeden Tag das warme Wetter. Mein Freund fotografiert morgen früh an der Isar.

B Birgits Reise. Birgit macht Urlaub in Österreich. Beschreiben Sie die Reise.

MODELL: nach Österreich fahren →
Sie fährt nach Österreich.

1. viel Gepäck haben
2. eine Broschüre lesen
3. ihr Portemonnaie vergessen
4. eine alte Schulfreundin in Wien treffen
5. in die Oper gehen
6. müde werden
7. ins Hotel gehen
8. morgens sehr lange schlafen

B. 1. Sie hat viel Gepäck.
2. Sie liest eine Broschüre.
3. Sie vergisst ihr Portemonnaie.
4. Sie trifft eine alte Schulfreundin in Wien. **5.** Sie geht in die Oper.
6. Sie wird müde. **7.** Sie geht ins Hotel. **8.** Sie schläft morgens sehr lange.

REVIEW OF TWO-PART VERBS
MORE ON DOING THINGS

German has a number of two-part verbs that consist of a prefix, such as an adverb or preposition, plus the infinitive. The prefixes slightly or significantly alter the meaning of the basic verb. Such two-part verbs appear as a single word in the infinitive form. However, when the verb is conjugated, the prefix goes at the end of the clause or sentence.

Susanne **will** ihre Schwestern **anrufen.**	*Susanne wants to call her sister (on the phone).*
Susanne **ruft** ihre Schwester **an.**	*Susanne calls her sister (on the phone).*

In the present perfect tense, the past participle of a two-part verb appears as one word with **-ge-** separating the prefix from the verb form.

Susanne **hat** ihre Schwester schon **angerufen.**	*Susanne already called her sister.*

The following are some common two-part verbs.

aufhören	*to stop*	mitkommen	*to come along*
aufpassen	*to watch out*	umziehen	*to move*
aufstehen	*to get up*	vorbeikommen	*to come by*
aussehen	*to look, appear*	vorhaben	*to plan, intend*
einladen	*to invite*	zurückkommen	*to come back*

To help you identify two-part verbs, a dot separates the prefix from the infinitive in the chapter vocabulary lists in this book: **an•rufen.** The vocabulary list at the end of the book identifies two-part verbs in this way: **anrufen (ruft an).**

A. 1. Klaus steht sehr früh auf. 2. Zwei Freunde kommen mit. 3. Sie kommen am Bahnhof an. 4. Sie steigen in den Zug ein. 5. Die Reise fängt schon an. 6. Der Kurort sieht sehr schön aus. 7. Sie gehen im Wald spazieren. 8. Klaus ruht sich gut aus. 9. Am Freitag fahren sie nach Hause zurück.

Übungen

A Klaus geht zur Kur. Schreiben Sie vollständige Sätze.

MODELL: Klaus / eine Erholungsreise / vorhaben →
Klaus hat eine Erholungsreise vor.

1. Klaus / sehr früh / aufstehen
2. zwei Freunde / mitkommen
3. sie (*pl.*) / am Bahnhof / ankommen
4. sie (*pl.*) / in den Zug / einsteigen
5. die Reise / schon / anfangen
6. der Kurort / sehr schön / aussehen

Bad Ems – ein berühmter deutscher Kurort.

URZ NOTIERT

The verb **spazieren gehen** (*to go for a walk*) is made up from two verbs: **spazieren** (*to walk*) and **gehen** (*to go*). In the present tense, the second part (**gehen**) is conjugated:

Sie **geht** spazieren.
She is going for a walk.

When used with a modal, the entire verb appears at the end of the sentence:

Sie will **spazieren gehen.**
She wants to go for a walk.

In the present perfect tense, the past participle of the second part of the verb is used:

Sie ist spazieren **gegangen.**
She has gone for a walk.

The verb **kennen lernen** (*to get to know*) also follows these patterns.

A. 1. e 2. f 3. d 4. c 5. a 6. g 7. b

7. sie (*pl.*) / im Wald / spazieren gehen
8. Klaus / sich gut / ausruhen
9. am Freitag / sie (*pl.*) / nach Hause / zurückfahren

B Vorwürfe.[a] In den Ferien haben Sie in einem anderen Staat gearbeitet. Sie sind jetzt wieder zu Hause und Ihre Eltern machen Ihnen viele Vorwürfe. Widersprechen Sie ihren Vorwürfen im Perfekt.

MODELL: Du rufst uns nie an! →
Ich habe euch doch angerufen.

1. Du kommst nie pünktlich an!
2. Du hörst uns nie zu!
3. Du stellst uns deine Freunde nie vor!
4. Du bringst nie zurück, was du von uns leihst!

[a]*Accusations*

B. 1. Ich bin doch pünktlich angekommen.   2. Ich habe euch doch zugehört.   3. Ich habe euch meine Freunde doch vorgestellt.   4. Ich habe euch doch zurückgebracht, was ich von euch geliehen habe.

PERSPEKTIVEN

A Wo ist das? Welche Beschreibung passt zu welcher Stadt?

1. Köln
2. Berlin
3. Zürich
4. Hamburg
5. München
6. Wien
7. Frankfurt

a. Stadt an der Isar, die für das Oktoberfest berühmt ist
b. Internationales Finanzzentrum und Sitz der Europäischen Zentralbank
c. Stadt an der Elbe mit einem großen Hafen
d. berühmte Handelsstadt in der Schweiz
e. Stadt am Rhein, die von den Römern gegründet wurde
f. Stadt, die seit der Wiedervereinigung wieder die Hauptstadt Deutschlands ist
g. Stadt, die einmal die Hauptstadt der Doppelmonarchie Österreich-Ungarn war

B Wie gut kennen Sie Europa? Was stimmt? Was stimmt nicht? Wenn ein Satz nicht stimmt, korrigieren Sie ihn mit der richtigen Information.

1. In Köln feiert man Karneval.
2. Das Abitur ist eine Art von Schule, ähnlich wie die amerikanische „High-School".
3. In der Drogerie kann man Rezepte abholen.
4. Nach der Wende wurde Bonn die neue Bundeshauptstadt.
5. Nach der Wende wurden viele Deutsche im Osten arbeitslos.
6. Deutschland, Österreich und die Schweiz sind Mitglieder der Europäischen Union.

B. *Answers will vary. Possible answers are:* 1. Das stimmt.   2. Das stimmt nicht. Das Abitur ist ein Schulabschluss. Es ist die Prüfung am Ende des Gymnasiums.   3. Das stimmt nicht. Medikamente holt man in einer Apotheke.   4. Das stimmt nicht. Bonn war die Bundeshauptstadt vor der Wende. Nach der Wende wurde Berlin zur neuen Bundeshauptstadt.   5. Das stimmt.   6. Das stimmt nicht. Die Schweiz ist kein Mitgliedsland der Europäischen Union.

Blick vom Rheinufer auf den Kölner Dom, ein Meisterwerk deutscher Gotik.

WORTSCHATZ

Substantive	Nouns
die **Gebühr**, -en	fee
die **Wäsche**	laundry
der **Kurort**, -e	health spa, resort
das **Geschirr**	dishes
das **Geschirr spülen**	to wash or do the dishes

Verben	Verbs
aus•sehen (sieht aus), sah aus, ausgesehen	to appear
bei•stehen, stand bei beigestanden	to support
ein•laden (lädt ein), lud ein, eingeladen	to invite
genießen, genoss, genossen	to enjoy
halten (hält), hielt, gehalten	to hold
halten von	to have an opinion of
leihen, lieh, geliehen	to borrow
meinen	to think; to mean
übereinstimmen (mit etwas)	to agree (*with something*)
übernachten	to spend the night
wiederholen	to repeat

Adjektive und Adverbien	Adjectives and adverbs
fertig	finished
immer	always

Sie wissen schon	You already know
die **Freizeit**	free time
die **Vorlesung**, -en	lecture
die **Zwischenprüfung**, -en	mid-diploma exam

der **Kurs**, -e	(*academic*) course
der **Rasen**	lawn
den **Rasen mähen**	to mow the lawn
der **Schüler**, - / die **Schülerin**, -nen	student (*not in a university*)
der **Student** (**-en** *masc.*) / die **Studentin**, -nen	student (*at a university*)
der **Vortrag**, ¨e	lecture; talk
einen **Vortrag halten**	to give a talk
das **Hauptfach**, ¨er	minor subject
das **Nebenfach**, ¨er	minor subject
das **Semester**, -	semester
das **Studentenwohnheim**, -e	dormitory
das **Studium**, *pl.* **Studien**	course of study (*at a university*)
an•rufen, rief an, angerufen	to call on the phone
auf•hören	to stop
auf•passen	to watch out, pay attention
auf•räumen	to clean up, organize
belegen	to take (*a course*)
brauchen	to need
mit•kommen, kam mit, ist mitgekommen	to come along
verbringen, verbrachte, verbracht	to spend (*time*)
vorbei•kommen, kam vorbei, ist vorbeigekommen	to drop by
vor•schlagen (schlägt vor), schlug vor, vorgeschlagen	to suggest
zurück•kommen, kam zurück, ist zurückgekommen	to come back
bald	soon

PLANNING GUIDE • CLASSROOM MANAGEMENT

OBJECTIVES

Communication
- Talk about family life, pp. 14–15.

Grammar
- Review the simple past tense, pp. 16–18.
- Use coordinating and subordinating conjunctions, pp. 19–20.
- Review negation, pp. 20–21.

Culture
- Learn about Felix Mendelssohn-Bartholdy, p. 22.

Recycling
- Reuse relationship terms, pp. 12–13.

STRATEGIES

Listening Strategies
- Listen for changes in tense, p. 22.

Speaking Strategies
- Connect and contrast ideas, pp. 19–20.
- Negate positive statements, pp. 20–21.
- Describe a famous person, p. 28.

Reading Strategies
- Analyze a poem, pp. 25–27.

Writing Strategies
- Write a biography of an older family member, pp. 27–28.

Connecting Cultures Strategies
- Compare a German and an American family, pp. 12–13.

PROGRAM RESOURCES

Print
- *Arbeitsheft* (Workbook), pp. 5–18
- *Arbeitsheft* (Workbook), Teacher's Edition, pp. 5–18

Audiovisual
- Overhead Transparencies 25.1–25.G1
- Audio Program, Cassette 1A, 7A/CD 1, 9
- Audioscript, pp. 1–7

Technology
- Annenberg *Fokus Deutsch* Video Series, *Folge 25*
- www.mcdougallittell.com

Assessment Program Options
- *Prüfung, Kapitel 25,* Assessment Program, pp. 3–12
- Audio Program, Cassette 8A/CD 10
- Audioscript, p. 107
- Teacher's Resource CD-ROM

DAY 1

Note: (1) Please see TE, pp. 10E–10J, for other suggestions not referenced in these plans. (2) Not all homework options need be assigned.

CHAPTER OPENER

- Quick Start Review: Verb meanings (TE, p. 10E). 5 MIN
- Use the photos on pp. 10–11 as the basis for a class discussion (TE, p. 10E). 10 MIN

VIDEOTHEK

- Play *Folge I: Eine Familiengeschichte.* Have students do *Akt. A,* p. 11, silently. Check answers as a class, then use the Teaching Suggestions for a follow-up activity (TE, p. 10F). 15 MIN
- Do *Akt. B–C,* p. 12, without viewing the episode a second time. Then play the episode again and allow students to check their answers and make corrections. Discuss answers as a class. 20 MIN

Homework Options:

- *Videothek, Akt. D,* p. 12

DAY 2

VIDEOTHEK

- Quick Start Review 1: Family (TE, p. 10E). 5 MIN
- Discuss the answers to *Akt. D,* pp. 12–13 (TE, p. 10F). 5 MIN
- Play *Folge II: Lebensstile* after dividing the class into 2 groups. Do *Akt. A,* p. 13 (TE, p. 10F). 16 MIN
- Do *Akt. B,* p. 13, then follow the Teaching Suggestions for the expansion activity. If necessary, play this portion of the episode again (TE, p. 10F). 6 MIN
- Do *Akt. C,* p. 13, in small groups. End with a class discussion of the opinions of the different groups (TE, p. 10F). 10 MIN
- *Arbeitsheft,* p. 6, audio *Akt. C.* 8 MIN

Homework Options:

- *Arbeitsheft,* p. 6, *Videothek, Akt. B*

DAY 3

VOKABELN

- Quick Start Review 1: *Haben, sein* (TE, p. 10G). 5 MIN
- Present the *Vokabeln* on p. 14. 8 MIN
- Use the photo on p. 14 as the basis for a class discussion (TE, p. 10G). 5 MIN
- Do *Akt. A,* p. 14, silently, then have students check their answers in pairs after reviewing the new vocabulary, including the past-tense forms of the verbs (TE, p. 10G). 14 MIN
- Do *Akt. B,* p. 15, as a quiz show (TE, p. 10G). 8 MIN
- Do *Akt. C,* p. 15, as a whole-class activity (TE, p. 10G). 10 MIN

Homework Options:

- *Arbeitsheft,* p. 9, *Vokabeln, Akt. D–E*

DAY 4

VOKABELN

- Quick Start Review 2: Articles, possessive adjectives (TE, p. 10G). 4 MIN
- *Arbeitsheft,* p. 8, audio *Akt. B.* 7 MIN

STRUKTUREN

- Review the simple past tense on pp. 16–17 using OHT 25.G1 (TE, p. 10H). 6 MIN
- Do *Übung A,* p. 18, silently. Check answers as a class and discuss the meaning of each sentence (TE, p. 10H). 10 MIN
- Do *Übung B,* p. 18, in pairs, including the expansion activity in the Teaching Suggestions (TE, p. 10H). 18 MIN
- Begin *Übung C,* p. 18 (TE, p. 10H). 5 MIN

Homework Options:

- Finish *Übung C,* p. 18
- *Arbeitsheft,* pp. 10–11, *Strukturen, Akt. B–C*

STRUKTUREN

- Quick Start Review 1: Simple past of modals (TE, p. 10G). 5 MIN
- Review conjunctions on p. 19 (TE, p. 10H). 9 MIN
- Do *Übung A,* p. 19, as a class and discuss the meaning of each new sentence. 10 MIN
- Have students do *Übung B,* p. 20, silently and then check their answers with a partner. 10 MIN
- Follow the Teaching Suggestions for *Übung C,* p. 20 (TE, p. 10H). 16 MIN

Homework Options:

- *Arbeitsheft,* p. 13, *Strukturen, Akt. H–I*

STRUKTUREN

- Quick Start Review 2: Opposites (TE, p. 10H). 5 MIN
- Review negation on pp. 20–21. 8 MIN
- Do *Übung A,* p. 21, silently, then check answers as a class (TE, p. 10H). 10 MIN
- Do *Übung B,* p. 21, as a class, writing answers on the board (TE, p. 10H). 7 MIN

PERSPEKTIVEN

- Discuss *Tipp zum Hören,* p. 22 (TE, p. 10I). Play the recording and encourage students to take notes. Have students work in small groups to come up with as many descriptions as possible for *Hören Sie zu!, Akt. B,* p. 22. Follow up by drawing a family tree on the board. 14 MIN
- Do *Hören Sie zu!, Akt. A,* p. 22, as a class after doing *Akt. B.* 6 MIN

Homework Options:

- *Arbeitsheft,* p. 14, *Strukturen, Akt. L–M*
- *Arbeitsheft,* pp. 16–17, *Perspektiven, Akt. F–H*

PERSPEKTIVEN

- Quick Start Review 1: *Können, kennen, wissen* (TE, p. 10I). 4 MIN
- Follow the Teaching Suggestions for *Zum Thema, Akt. A,* p. 23 (TE, p. 10I). 5 MIN
- Discuss *Zum Thema, Akt. B,* p. 23, as a class (TE, p. 10I). 6 MIN
- Do *Zum Text* p. 24, as a class. 5 MIN
- Have students discuss *Zur Interpretation, Akt. A–B,* p. 24, in small groups. End with a brief class discussion (TE, p. 10I). 11 MIN
- Do *Interaktion,* p. 28 (TE, p. 10I). 10 MIN
- Begin *Schreiben Sie!* pp. 25–27, by discussing the assignment, *Tipp zum Schreiben,* and *Schreibmodell* (TE, p. 10J). 5 MIN
- Begin *Vor dem Schreiben,* p. 27. 4 MIN

Homework Options:

- Finish *Vor dem Schreiben* and do *Beim Schreiben,* p. 28.

PERSPEKTIVEN

- Quick Start Review 2: Accusative and dative verbs (TE, p. 10I). 4 MIN
- Do *Nach dem Schreiben,* p. 28, and begin the final drafts of their *Biografie.* 11 MIN
- Questions and review. 5 MIN
- *Prüfung, Kapitel 25.* 30 MIN

Homework Options:

- Finish the final draft of the *Biografie*
- *Arbeitsheft,* pp. 17–18, *Perspektiven, Akt. I*

DAY 1

Note: (1) Please see TE, pp. 10E–10J, for other suggestions not referenced in these plans. (2) Not all homework options need be assigned.

CHAPTER OPENER

- Quick Start Review: Verb meanings (TE, p. 10E). 5 MIN
- Discuss the photo on pp. 10–11 (TE, p. 10E). 6 MIN
- Multiple Intelligences: Verbal (TE, p. 10E). 9 MIN

VIDEOTHEK

- Play *Folge 1*. Do *Akt. A*, p. 12. Check answers, then do follow-up activity (TE, p. 10F). 14 MIN
- Do *Akt. B–C*, p. 12. Play the episode again. Discuss. 16 MIN
- Block Schedule activity: Fun Break (TE, p. 10F). 10 MIN
- *Akt. D*, pp. 12–13 (TE, p. 10F). 14 MIN
- Play *Folge II* after dividing the class into groups. Do *Akt. A*, p. 13. 16 MIN

Homework Options:

- *Videothek, Akt. B*, p. 13
- *Arbeitsheft*, p. 6

DAY 2

VIDEOTHEK

- Quick Start Review 1: Family (TE, p. 10E). 5 MIN
- Do *Akt. C*, p. 13, in small groups. Discuss the groups' opinions (TE, p. 10F). 12 MIN

VOKABELN

- Present *Vokabeln* on p. 14. 8 MIN
- Discuss the photo on p. 14 (TE, p. 10G). 5 MIN
- Do *Akt. A*, p. 14. (TE, p. 10G). 14 MIN
- Do *Akt. B*, p. 15, as a quiz show (TE, p. 10G). 8 MIN
- Block Schedule activity: Survey (TE, p. 10G). 10 MIN
- Do *Akt. C*, p. 15, as a class activity (TE, p. 10G). 12 MIN

STRUKTUREN

- Review the simple past tense on pp. 16–17 (TE, p. 10H). 6 MIN
- Do *Übung A*, p. 18 (TE, p. 10H). 10 MIN

Homework Options:

- *Arbeitsheft*, p. 9, *Vokabeln, Akt. D–E*
- *Arbeitsheft*, pp. 10–11, *Akt. B–C*

DAY 3

STRUKTUREN

- Quick Start Review 1: Simple past of modals (TE, p. 10G). 5 MIN
- Do *Übung B*, p. 18, in pairs (TE, p. 10H). 10 MIN
- Block Schedule activity: Expansion (TE, p. 10I). 10 MIN
- Review conjunctions on p. 19 (TE, p. 10H). 8 MIN
- Do *Übung A*, p. 19, as a class. 10 MIN
- Do *Übung B*, p. 20, silently, then check answers with a partner. 10 MIN
- *Übung C*, p. 20 (TE, p. 10H). 14 MIN
- Review negation on pp. 20–21. 8 MIN
- Do *Übung A*, p. 21, then check answers as a class (TE, p. 10H). 9 MIN
- Do *Übung B*, p. 21; write answers on the board (TE, p. 10H). 6 MIN

Homework Options:

- *Strukturen, Übung C*, p. 18 TE, p. 10H
- *Arbeitsheft*, p. 13, *Strukturen, Akt. H–I*
- *Arbeitsheft*, p. 14, *Akt. L–M*

DAY 4

PERSPEKTIVEN

- Quick Start Review 1: *Können, kennen, wissen* (TE, p. 10I). 4 MIN
- Discuss the *Tipp zum Hören*, p. 22 (TE, p. 10I).
- Do *Hören Sie zu! Akt. B*, p. 22. Draw a family tree on the board. 14 MIN
- Do *Hören Sie zu! Akt. A*, p. 22, as a class after doing *Akt. B*. 6 MIN
- *Zum Thema, Akt. A*, p. 23. 5 MIN
- *Akt. B*, p. 23. 6 MIN
- Do *Zum Text*, p. 24, as a class. 5 MIN
- Discuss *Zur Interpretation, Akt. A–B*, p. 24, in small groups. (TE, p. 10I). 9 MIN
- *Interaktion*, p. 28 (TE, p. 10I). 10 MIN
- Begin *Schreiben Sie!*, pp. 25, by discussing the *Tipp zum Schreiben* and *Schreibmodell* (TE, p. 10I). 5 MIN
- *Vor dem Schreiben* and *Beim Schreiben*, p. 27–28. 26 MIN

Homework Options:

- Finish first draft of the *Biografie*
- *Arbeitsheft*, pp. 16–17, *Akt. F–G*

DAY 5

PERSPEKTIVEN

- Quick Start Review 2: Accusative and dative verbs (TE, p. 10I). 6 MIN
- *Nach dem Schreiben*, p. 28. 16 MIN
- Begin final draft of the *Biografie*. 16 MIN
- Block Schedule activity: Change of pace (TE, p. 10J). 16 MIN
- Questions and review. 6 MIN
- *Prüfung, Kapitel 25*. 30 MIN

Homework Options:

- Finish final draft of the *Biografie*
- *Arbeitsheft*, pp. 17–18, *Perspektiven, Akt. H–I*

Chapter Opener, pp. 10–11

PROGRAM RESOURCES

• Overhead Transparency 25.1

Quick Start Review

♻ Verb meanings
Ergänzen Sie die richtigen Verben.
WÖRTER: aufpassen, aufstehen, einladen, mitkommen, umziehen, zurückkommen

1. Klaus, willst du ins Kino _____?
2. Wann wird Peter aus dem Urlaub _____?
3. Karin muss heute Mittag auf ihre kleine Schwester _____.
4. Um wie viel Uhr musst du morgens _____?
5. Wir werden euch zu unserer Silvesterparty _____.
6. Mayers wollen im Sommer in ein großes Haus _____.

Answers: 1. mitkommen
2. zurückkommen   3. aufpassen
4. aufstehen   5. einladen   6. umziehen

TEACHING SUGGESTIONS

• Photo, p. 10

Have students look at the photo and speculate on who each person in the picture is; what the adults do for a living; what their ages, hobbies and interests are, and so forth.

• Photos, p. 11

Have students compare 2 photos and speculate about aspects of family life that have changed in the past 100 years. Pay attention to the number of family members, their clothes, their posture, what their roles in the family might be, and so on.

TEACHING ALL STUDENTS

Multiple Intelligences Verbal: Give students a short summary of the life of someone you knew personally or whose life you are very familiar with who was born before 1940 (perhaps a grandparent). Encourage students to take notes and have them save their questions until you are finished. Bring in photographs or memorabilia, if possible. Finally, ask each student in turn to recall 1 piece of information you have shared.

CLASSROOM COMMUNITY

Group Activity Have students work in groups and exchange information on the lives of a grandparent or some other older adult they know. When, where, how, and under what circumstances did he or she live? Have each group select 2 members to present their stories to the class.

CULTURE HIGHLIGHTS

Are there any students whose grandparents or other relative once lived in Germany? Assign a special project to those students. Have them find out about one or more of their lives. Have them share what they learn with the class and bring in photos, maps, or other memorabilia to enhance their presentations.

Videothek, pp. 12–13

PROGRAM RESOURCES

• Videocassette, *Folge 25*
• *Arbeitsheft*, pp. 5–7
• Audio Program, Cassette 1A/CD 1
• Audioscript, pp. 1–2

Quick Start Review 1

♻ Family
Ergänzen Sie die Substantive in den folgenden Sätzen.
WÖRTER: Geschwister, Großmutter, Onkel, Cousine, Neffe, Schwester

1. Susanne hat nur eine _____.
2. Brüder und Schwestern nennt man auch _____.
3. Die Mutter Ihrer Mutter ist Ihre _____.
4. Der Bruder meines Vaters ist mein _____.
5. Die Tochter meiner Tante ist unsere _____.
6. Der Sohn Ihrer Schwester ist Ihr _____.

Answers: 1. Schwester
2. Geschwister   3. Großmutter
4. Onkel   5. Cousine   6. Neffe

Quick Start Review 2

♻ Sentence structure
Bilden Sie Sätze.

1. du / nicht brauchen / die dicke Jacke / heute
2. haben / ihr / die Hausaufgaben / schon / gemacht / für morgen?
3. wie lange / du / schlafen / samstags?
4. meine Tante / lesen / deutsche Zeitungen / immer / online
5. meine Schwester / essen / Gemüse / gar kein

Answers: 1. Du brauchst die dicke Jacke heute nicht.   2. Habt ihr die Hausaufgaben für morgen schon gemacht?   3. Wie lange schläfst du samstags?   4. Meine Tante liest deutsche Zeitungen immer online.   5. Meine Schwester isst gar kein Gemüse.

TEACHING SUGGESTIONS

• *Aktivität A*, p. 12

Follow-up: Go over the *Sprachspiegel*, p. 12, and point out that the word *Familie* always precedes the family's name when addressing a letter. Have students introduce families they know. For example, *Neben uns wohnt Familie Walker. Sie haben zwei Kinder, Kelsey und Brian. Sie haben auch eine Katze und ein Aquarium mit Goldfischen.*

• *Aktivität B*, p. 12

Expansion: Have students turn the statements into questions. One student asks: *Wer hat früher in Dresden gewohnt?* And another answers *Ihre Oma hat früher in Dresden gewohnt.*

• *Aktivität C*, p. 12

Ask students to volunteer information about their grandparents or older relatives: where they live, how old they are, what they do, how often the students see them, and so on.

• *Aktivität D*, pp. 12–13

Variation: Have students restate sentences 1–4 in the negative.
Answers: 1. Sybillas Mutter hat nicht Jura studiert. 2. Sybillas Eltern haben nicht beide Karriere gemacht. (oder) Sybillas Mutter hat keine Karriere gemacht. 3. Sybillas Vater hat sich nicht um seine Tochter und den Haushalt gekümmert. 4. Die Familie hatte lange Zeit kein Auto und kein eigenes Haus.

• *Aktivität A*, p. 13

Divide students into 2 groups. While watching the video, have one group focus on Sabine, and the other on Peter. Have them jot down as many details as possible.

• *Aktivität B*, p. 13

Expansion: Have students write a list of possible advantages to living alone.

• *Aktivität C*, p. 13

Ask students about their goals and future plans. Have them tell each other what kind of lifestyle they would prefer. Ask *Wie möchten Sie leben? Möchten Sie heiraten? Möchten Sie Kinder haben? Was ist Ihnen wichtig im Leben?*

TEACHING ALL STUDENTS

Extra Help Ask either/or and yes/no questions to aid comprehension. Ask *Verstehen sich Sybilla und Meta Heyn gut? Sieht die Großmutter ihre Enkelin häufig? Lebt Sybilla gerne allein? War Meta Heyn berufstätig? War Sybillas Mutter berufstätig?*

CLASSROOM COMMUNITY

Dictation Dictate the following text to the class. Have them exchange papers with a partner and try to correct their partner's paper. They then return their papers. Display the text on an OHT and have them do a final correction of their own paper.
Meine Großmutter hatte sieben Geschwister. Sie waren drei Mädchen und vier Jungen. Meine Großmutter war das älteste Mädchen. Sie musste für ihre kleinen Geschwister sorgen. Als sie zwölf Jahre alt war, erwartete ihre Mutter wieder ein Kind. Als meine Großmutter das hörte, musste sie weinen.

LANGUAGE NOTE

Remind students of the difference between the verb *heiraten* (to marry) and *verheiratet sein* meaning *being married* (as opposed to being single, divorced, or widowed). Offer these examples: *Er heiratet im Mai! Ich will nie heiraten. Als er geheiratet hat, hat ihm sein Onkel ein Auto geschenkt. Seit Mait is er verheiratet. Bist du ledig oder verheiratet? Ich bin sehr glücklich verheiratet und verstehe Leute nicht, die nicht heiraten wollen.*

BLOCK SCHEDULE

Fun Break Have students bring in magazines and newspapers and make a collage of family life and how it is portrayed in the media. Ask them to write German captions for the various scenes in their collage.

INTERDISCIPLINARY CONNECTION

Sociology/History Have students research population statistics in Germany before and after unification. How many children were born each year before and after? How many children does the average family have? What are the reasons for population changes after unification?

Vokabeln, pp. 14–15

PROGRAM RESOURCES

• *Arbeitsheft*, pp. 8–9
• Audio Program, Cassette 1A/CD 1
• Audioscript, pp. 2–3

Quick Start Review 1

♻ *Haben, sein*

Ergänzen Sie die richtigen Formen der Verben *haben* oder *sein* im Präsens.

1. _____ dein Vater berufstätig?
2. Wie viele Geschwister _____ du?
3. Wir _____ heute einen tollen Video angesehen.
4. In welchem Jahr _____ du geboren?
5. Ein Lehrer zu seinen Schülern: _____ ihr auch alle wach?
6. Sie _____ am ersten Januar Geburtstag.

Answers: 1. Ist 2. hast 3. haben 4. bist 5. seid 6. hat

Quick Start Review 2

♻ Articles, possessive adjectives

Ergänzen Sie die Formen.

1. Wiederholen Sie bitte _____ (der) Satz!
2. Bitte, ich suche _____ (der) Bahnhof.
3. Sie hat _____ (ihr) Mann verlassen.
4. Siehst du _____ (die) Frau dort vor dem Videoladen?
5. Vergiss _____ (dein) Mantel nicht!
6. Ich verstehe _____ (dein) Frage nicht.

Answers: 1. den 2. den 3. ihren 4. die 5. deinen 6. deine

. . . .

TEACHING SUGGESTIONS

• Photo, p. 14

Have students tell what they have learned about the family in the photo shown in the video. List their answers on the board.

• *Aktivität A,* p. 14

Go over the new vocabulary, especially the past-tense forms of the verbs. This activity may be assigned as homework.

• *Aktivität B,* p. 15

Do this activity as a quiz show by dividing the class into groups of 5. The teacher as MC reads out the cue. The team that gives the correct answer first scores a point.

• *Aktivität C,* p. 15

Have students comment on the opinions given in the video. With whom do they agree or disagree and why? Have them respond to the question *Was bedeutet „Familie" für Sie?* Have one or several students list the students' answers on the board. Use this list as a basis for discussion.

TEACHING ALL STUDENTS

Multiple Intelligences Kinesthetic: Divide students into groups of 4–5. Have each group write a short skit about family dinner. Have them perform their skits and have the other students take notes on the family members' roles and behavior.

CLASSROOM COMMUNITY

Paired Activity Assign each student a noun or word from the *Wortschatz,* p. 29. Have each "noun" find a "verb" and create a logical sentence.

CULTURE HIGHLIGHTS

Show students the video episode again where Sybilla Heyn visits her grandmother. This time, they should focus on any features that strike them as particularly German (for example, clothes, gestures, furniture). Draw up a list of the features they mention and discuss how and why they differ from their, if any, American equivalents.

BLOCK SCHEDULE

Survey Have students conduct a survey in their class about family structure. Remind students that they can answer for an imaginary family if they wish. As a class, create a list of multiple-choice questions and write them on an OHT or on the board. For example, *Wie viele Personen leben in Ihrer Familie? Wer verdient Geld? Wer sorgt für den Haushalt?* Have students answer the questions individually in writing. Then ask for a show of hands as you ask each question aloud. Assign students to tally the results, then summarize the survey for the class.

Strukturen, pp. 16–21

PROGRAM RESOURCES

• Overhead Transparency 25.G1
• *Arbeitsheft,* pp. 10–14
• Audio Program, Cassette 1A/CD 1
• Audioscript, pp. 3–5

. . . .

Quick Start Review 1

♻ Simple past of modals

Ergänzen Sie die richtigen Formen im Präteritum.

1. Herr Fiechel _____ (müssen) eine neue Stelle finden, weil seine Firma ihm gekündigt hatte.
2. Gerd _____ (können) die Formen des Präsens noch nicht, weil er erst seit zwei Wochen Deutsch lernte.

3. Als ich klein war, _____ (dürfen) ich nicht fernsehen.
4. Wir _____ (wollen) um 21.00 Uhr zu Hause sein, aber dann kam der Bus nicht.
5. Als meine Großmutter jung war, _____ (müssen) sie viel zu Hause helfen.

Answers: 1. musste   2. konnte   3. durfte   4. wollten   5. musste

Quick Start Review 2

♻ Opposites

WÖRTER: froh, jung, langweilig, lustig, nett
Ergänzen Sie die Lücken mit den Gegenteilen.

1. Die Englischstunde heute war nicht interessant, sondern _____.
2. Meine Oma war nicht alt, als sie nach Amerika kam, sondern sehr _____.
3. Unser neuer Chef ist mir unsympatisch, der alte war so _____.
4. Gestern war ich traurig, aber heute bin ich _____.
5. Peter ist immer so ernst, aber sein Bruder ist sehr _____.

Answers: 1. langweilig   2. jung   3. nett   4. froh   5. lustig

TEACHING SUGGESTIONS

• Simple past tense, pp. 16–18

Explain the simple past tense by using OHT 25.G1 or the board to contrast strong and weak verbs, vowel changes versus tense markers. Go over the *Sprachspiegel*, p. 17, and point out similarities to English cognates that undergo vowel changes. For example, *singen, sang* / sing, sang; *rennen, ran* / run, ran.

• *Übung A,* p. 18

Additional practice: Have students give the present-tense form of each verb in the box.

• *Übung B,* p. 18

Expansion: Have students work in pairs to invent Meta Heyn's answers to Sybilla's questions.

• *Übung C,* p. 18

Expansion: After doing all 3 activities on p. 18, ask students to summarize the lives of Meta and Sybilla Heyn orally or in writing. Ask *Wie alt war Meta Heyn, als sie geheiratet hat? Was machten die beiden Frauen beruflich, Wie unterscheidet sich ihr Leben? Was haben sie gemeinsam?*

• Conjunctions, pp. 19–20

Go over *Kurz notiert,* p. 20, and have students explain the choice of conjunctions in the following sentences. *Als er in Berlin war, rief er mich an. Wenn er in Berlin ist, ruft er mich an. Als ich krank war, hatte ich zu nichts Lust. Wenn ich krank bin, habe ich zu nichts Lust.*

• *Übung C,* p. 20

Have students work in pairs and interview each other. Have the interviewees check off the conjunctions as they use them. Partners should help each other position the verbs correctly. When the interviews are done, choose several students to introduce their partners to the class.

• *Übung A,* p. 21

Remind students that *nicht* may negate either an individual sentence element or an entire sentence. If it negates an individual element, it precedes that element. If *nicht* negates the entire sentence it usually follows the subject, the verb, and all objects.
Sie geben uns das Geld nicht. (*nicht* negates the entire sentence)
Wir gehen nicht aus. Ich habe den Hamburger nicht bestellt. (*nicht* precedes the second part of the verbs)
Ich möchte nicht allein in der Nacht nach Hause fahren. Das Geld liegt nicht auf dem Tisch. (*nicht* precedes modifiers of manner and place)
Ich kann am Sonntag nicht mitkommen. (*nicht* follows many time expressions)

• *Übung B,* p. 21

Variation: Have students work in pairs to say what they like or dislike, using negations and conjunctions at the same time: *Karin mag Hamburger, aber Peter mag kein Fastfood. Ken möchte keine Familie haben, aber Petra will heiraten.*

TEACHING ALL STUDENTS

Extra Help Go over *Kurz notiert,* p. 20, and help students understand the differences in meaning in the following examples: *Als es Frühling wurde, freute ich mich über die Blumen. Wenn es Frühling wird, freue ich mich über die Blumen. Als meine Oma krank war, war ich traurig. Wenn meine Oma krank ist, bin ich traurig.* Try to find other examples with the class.

CLASSROOM COMMUNITY

Challenge Divide the class into 2 groups and have each group come up with 10 statements about things and activities they like. For example, *ich* *lerne gern Deutsch, ich esse gern Schokoladeneis, ich stehe gern früh auf.* Then have the groups exchange their lists and try to negate the statements.

BLOCK SCHEDULE

Expansion Have students look in the Appendix at the list of principal parts of irregular verbs, pp. R4–R5, then write a list of as many cognates as they can identify.

Perspektiven, pp. 22–29

PROGRAM RESOURCES

- *Arbeitsheft,* pp. 15–18
- Audio Program, Cassette 1A, 7A/CD 1, 9
- Audioscript, pp. 5–7
- www.mcdougallittell.com

Quick Start Review 1

Können, kennen, wissen
Ergänzen Sie die Sätze mit der richtigen Form von *können, kennen* oder *wissen.*

1. Beate _____ gut Rad fahren.
2. _____ du den neuen Film von Wim Wenders?
3. Ich _____ noch nicht, wann ich heute Abend nach Hause komme.
4. Peter _____ nicht, ob er die Prüfung bestanden hat.
5. _____ du mir bei meinen Hausaufgaben helfen?
6. _____ du, wie man „inches" in Zentimeter umrechnet?

Answers: 1. kann   2. Kennst   3. weiß   4. weiß   5. Kannst   6. Weißt

Quick Start Review 2

Accusative and dative verbs
Ergänzen Sie mit den richtigen Formen der Artikel.

1. Leg deinen Pullover in _____ (der) Schrank und nicht auf _____ (das) Bett!
2. Liegt der Schlüssel nicht auf _____ (der) Tisch?
3. Stell dein Glas nicht auf _____ (der) Schreibtisch!
4. Wirf die Bücher bitte nicht auf _____ (der) Boden!
5. Setzt euch bitte an _____ (der) Tisch, das Essen ist fertig.

Answers: 1. den, das   2. dem   3. den   4. den   5. den

TEACHING SUGGESTIONS

- *Hören Sie zu!, p. 22*

Go over *Tipp zum Hören,* p. 22, and remind students to pay attention to the tense forms in the audio text. Encourage them to take notes as they listen and to be ready to tell how changes from the past to the present tense affect their reactions to what they hear.

- *Aktivität B, p. 22*

Expansion: Have students draw a family tree of the Mendelssohn family. After students have done their individual trees, draw one together on the board.

- *Lesen Sie!, p. 23*

Give students time to familiarize themselves with the *Wortschatz zum Lesen,* p. 23, before they read the poem. Also practice the pronunciation of certain words. Then, since poetry benefits from oral recitation, ask for student volunteers to read the poem aloud.

- *Zum Thema, Aktivität A, p. 23*

Have small groups discuss *Schritt 1* and then share their interpretations

with the class. Then have the whole class do *Schritt 2.* Contrast the title with the alternate form *Meine Großmutter hat kein Gesicht.* How does capitalization change the meaning?

- *Zum Thema, Aktivität B, p. 23*

Is the change from simple past tense to present tense comparable to the changes you heard in the listening passage on Felix Mendelssohn-Bartholdy? Remind the students that present and past are interconnected and that the present tense can extend into the past (memories) as well as into the future.

- *Zum Text, p. 24*

Fill in the table as a group on an OHT or on the board. Ask *Welche Kleidungsstücke der Großmutter werden genannt? Welche Möbel werden genannt? Welche Gegenstände/Dinge werden genannt? Welche Körperteile kommen vor? Welche Verben beschreiben, was die Großmutter tut? usw.*

- *Zur Interpretation, Aktivität A, p. 24*

Expand with additional questions about the speaker. Ask *Hat er/sie die Großmutter gern gehabt oder nicht? Warum?*

- *Zur Interpretation, Aktivität B, p. 24*

Encourage students to find alternative titles for the poem.

- *Interaktion, p. 25*

Follow the steps in *Schritt 1* to describe a person of your choice.
MODELL: *Substantive: Professor, Physik, Nobelpreis; Verben: lehren, revolutionieren, auswandern*

Er wurde 1879 in Ulm geboren und hat in der Schweiz Physik gelehrt. Während der Nazizeit ist er in die Vereinigten Staaten ausgewandert und 1940 Amerikaner geworden. Mit seiner Theorie hat er die moderne Physik revolutioniert. Er hat den Nobelpreis bekommen und später in Princeton gelehrt. Er trug seine grauen Haare lang und hatte auch einen Schnurrbart. Wer war er? (Albert Einstein)

- *Tipp zum Schreiben,* p. 25

Have students collect examples of short biographical sketches. Have each student bring in at least 3. Then have the class create categories of information contained in the samples and summarize the sample in a chart.

- *Schreibmodell,* pp. 26–27

Have students read the text silently, then ask for volunteers to read it aloud. Point out the 4 sections.

TEACHING ALL STUDENTS

Multiple Intelligences Intrapersonal: Have students list in their notebooks things they remember about someone who has died or moved away. They can share their writings if they wish.

CLASSROOM COMMUNITY

Paired Activity Have students underline all simple past verb forms in the biographical sketches they wrote. Then have them exchange their writings with a partner who will check whether these forms are correct.

LANGUAGE NOTE

It is more common in Northern Germany than in Southern Germany to use the simple past when telling a story that happened in the immediate past. Contrast these examples.
Ich bin um 4.30 Uhr aufgestanden, habe schnell gefrühstückt und bin zur Straßenbahn gelaufen. Da habe ich sie gerade noch von hinten um die Ecke fahren sehen. Ich hatte sie verpasst!
Ich stand um 4.30 Uhr auf, frühstückte schnell und lief zur Straßenbahn. Da sah ich sie gerade noch von hinten um die Ecke fahren. Ich hatte sie verpasst!

BLOCK SCHEDULE

Change of Pace Have students post their biographical sketches on the classroom wall. Allow time for everybody to review the sketches. Then have the class discuss what students found impressive or instructive about someone else's writing style.

PORTFOLIO

Have students research a famous German, Austrian, or Swiss composer of their choice. Have them write a short biography of the composer and bring in a recording of his/her work (often available through the public library). Also, the Goethe Institutes have excellent Web sites for researching German subjects (www.goethe.de).

RUBRIC **A** = 13–15 pts. **B** = 10–12 pts. **C** = 7–9 pts. **D** = 4–6 pts. **F** = <4 pts.

Writing Criteria	Scale				
Organization	1	2	3	4	5
Vocabulary use	1	2	3	4	5
Creativity	1	2	3	4	5

PROJECT

Find an older, retired German speaker who can come to the class and talk about family life in his/her childhood. (Start by asking students if they know such a person.) Before the person arrives, students can work in groups to develop questions to ask the person after his/her presentation. Encourage them to create questions that will build on what the person is likely to say.

RUBRIC **A** = 13–15 pts. **B** = 10–12 pts. **C** = 7–9 pts. **D** = 4–6 pts. **F** = <4 pts.

Speaking Criteria	Scale				
Vocabulary use	1	2	3	4	5
Grammatical accuracy	1	2	3	4	5
Creativity of questions	1	2	3	4	5

25 MITEINANDER

In diesem Kapitel

- lernen Sie deutsche Familien kennen.
- erfahren Sie, wie sich das Ideal der Familie geändert hat.
- besprechen Sie, was für Sie eine Familie bedeutet.

Sie werden auch

- über die Vergangenheit erzählen.
- Komplexe Sätze und Satzverbindungen gebrauchen.
- Gegensätze ausdrücken.
- das Imperfekt, Konjunktionen und **nicht/kein** wiederholen.
- eine kurze Biografie schreiben.

Susanne Dyrchs mit
ihrer Familie.

Eine deutsche Familie
von damals.

Familienfoto mit Kindern, Eltern
und Großeltern.

VIDEOTHEK

Susanne mit ihrer Großmutter.

Das Konzept „Familie" hat sich über die Jahre geändert. In diesem Kapitel sehen Sie „Familie" aus persönlicher und historischer Sicht.

A. 2. Mutter   **3.** Oma   **6.** Schwester, and **9.** Vater

I: Eine Familiengeschichte

In dieser Folge erfahren wir etwas über Familie. Zuerst beschreibt Susanne Dyrchs ihre Familie.

A Welche Familienmitglieder erwähnt Susanne?

1. Bruder
2. Mutter
3. Oma
4. Onkel
5. Opa
6. Schwester
7. Tante
8. Urgroßeltern
9. Vater

B Wen in Susannes Familie beschreiben diese Sätze? Verbinden Sie die Satzteile.

a. ihr Vater   b. ihre Mutter   c. ihre Oma   d. ihre Familie

1. _____ hat früher in Dresden gewohnt.
2. _____ ist Professor/Professorin für Jura.
3. _____ ist Richter/Richterin.
4. _____ kocht dreimal die Woche für die Familie.
5. _____ wohnt etwas außerhalb von Köln, in einem Vorort.
6. _____ wohnt in Köln.

B. **1.** c   **2.** a   **3.** b
4. c   **5.** d   **6.** c

C In dieser Folge erfahren wir auch etwas über die Familie Heyn. Meta erzählt ihrer Enkelin Sybilla die Geschichte der Familie Heyn. Wen beschreiben diese Sätze? Meta, Sybilla oder beide Frauen?

1. Sie hat in einer WG gewohnt.
2. Sie heiratete mit 22 Jahren und hatte drei Kinder.
3. Sie musste ihren Beruf aufgeben.
4. Sie löste die Verlobung zu ihrem Freund.
5. Sie wohnt jetzt allein.

C. **1.** Sybilla   **2.** Meta
3. Meta   **4.** Sybilla
5. beide Frauen

D Sybilla und ihre Familie: als sie Kind war und heute. Verbessern Sie die falschen Informationen.

MODELL: Sybilla ist die Tochter von Meta Heyn. →
Sybilla ist die Tochter von Meta Heyns Sohn Karl.
oder: Sybilla ist die Enkelin von Meta Heyn.

SPRACHSPIEGEL

In English, the word *family* follows the family's name:

> the Dyrchs family;

but in German, the word **Familie** precedes the family's name:

> die Familie Dyrchs.

The word **Familie** may also be omitted:

> die Meiers.

WORTSCHATZ ZUM VIDEO

sich entscheiden	to decide
der Vorort	suburb
die Vergangenheit	past
das Jahrhundert	century
die Macht	power
aus	over with, finished
eng	close
spüren	to feel
der Begriff	expression
zu jemandem halten	to stick with someone

1. Sybillas Mutter studierte Jura.
2. Sybillas Eltern machten beide Karriere.
3. Sybillas Vater kümmerte sich um seine Tochter und den Haushalt.
4. Erst nach einer langen Zeit bekam die Familie ein Auto und ein eigenes Haus.
5. Sybilla wuchs in einer untypischen deutschen Großfamilie auf.
6. Erst in den siebziger Jahren änderten sich die Ideale von Ehe und Familie.
7. Sybilla teilte sich mit einer Freundin eine Wohnung.
8. Heute wohnt Sybilla mit ihrem Mann zusammen.

II: Lebensstile

In dieser Folge hören wir die Meinungen von drei Menschen über Familie und Ehe.

A Sabine und Peter Schenk

SCHRITT 1: Sehen Sie sich das Video an, und beantworten Sie die Fragen.

1. Wie lange sind sie schon verheiratet?
2. Wie viele Kinder wünschen sich die Schenks?
3. Was bedeutet für Peter Ehe? Wie sieht Sabine das?
4. Was erwarten die beiden voneinander?

SCHRITT 2: Und Sie? Was bedeutet für Sie Heiraten? Was erwarten Sie von einem Ehepartner / einer Ehepartnerin?

B Nora Bausch. Nora lebt allein und möchte nicht heiraten. Was sagt sie?

1. Wie lange hat sie schon allein gewohnt?
2. Fühlt sie sich als Single „allein"? Warum oder warum nicht?
3. Warum möchte sie nicht heiraten?

C Diskussion. In diesem Video haben Sie sehr verschiedene Lebensstile gesehen: eine traditionelle Familie, eine moderne Ehe und eine Frau, die lieber allein lebt. Wie stellen Sie sich Ihr Leben vor? Möchten Sie heiraten, oder wohnen Sie lieber allein? Was sind die Vor- und Nachteile davon?

Großmutter und Enkelin.

D. 1. Sybillas Vater studierte Jura. 2. Sybillas Vater machte Karriere. 3. Sybillas Mutter kümmerte sich um ihre Tochter und den Haushalt. 4. Die Familie hatte bald ein Auto und ein eigenes Haus. 5. Sybilla wuchs in einer typisch deutschen Kleinfamilie auf. 6. In den sechziger Jahren änderten sich die Ideale von Ehe und Familie. 7. Sybilla teilte sich mit Freunden eine Wohnung. 8. Heute wohnt Sybilla allein.

See answers below.

Nora Bausch.

A. Schritt 1: 1. Sabine und Peter Schenk sind seit fünf Jahren verheiratet. 2. Die Schenks wünschen sich mindestens zwei Kinder. 3. Die Ehe bedeutet für Peter Verantwortung. Für Sabine ist Heiraten etwas sehr Romantisches. 4. Sabine erwartet von ihrem Ehepartner, dass er sich um die Familie kümmert. Peter erwartet von seiner Ehefrau, dass sie zu ihm hält. Schritt 2: *Answers will vary.*

B. 1. Nora Bausch wohnt schon seit zwei Jahren allein. 2. Sie fühlt sich als Single nicht allein, weil sie viele Freunde hat. 3. Nora möchte nicht heiraten, weil ihre Freiheit ihr wichtig ist.

C. *Answers will vary.*

VOKABELN

die Jugend	youth	befreundet	friends with someone
die Trennung	separation	damals	at that time, earlier
die Umstellung	adjustment		
die Unabhängigkeit	independence	ehelich	marital
die Veränderung	change	geboren	born
die Verlobung	engagement	getrennt	separated
der/die Erwachsene (decl. adj.)	adult	unabhängig	independent
		verheiratet	married
der Vertrag	contract	verliebt	in love
das Ehepaar	married couple	verlobt	engaged

auf•wachsen	to grow up
betreffen	to concern, affect
beweisen	to prove
ernähren	to nourish
erreichen	to achieve
erwarten von	to expect from
respektieren	to respect
nah stehen	to be close to
überleben	to survive

Sie wissen schon

aufgeben, die Ehe, die Scheidung, der Familienstand, der Haushalt, die Eltern, aufgeben, heiraten, sorgen für, verdienen, berufstätig, eigen, ledig/single

Famile, Ehe, Partnerschaft – wie trennt man die Rollen in der Familie?

Aktivitäten

A Welches Wort passt? Ergänzen Sie die Sätze mit Vokabeln aus der Liste.

verdienten
verheiratet
aufwachsen
befreundet
heiratete
eigene
überlebten
Umstellung
Verlobung

1. Wir waren froh, dass wir den Krieg _____.
2. Sybilla löste ihre _____ und zog in eine WG.
3. Wenn ich das Wort Familie höre, denke ich an meine _____ Familie.
4. Sie war _____ und bekam drei Kinder.
5. Die Männer _____ das Geld.
6. Mit 22 Jahren _____ Meta Franz Heyn.
7. Peter und Sabine waren acht Jahre _____, bevor sie verheiratet waren.
8. Die Schenks finden, Kinder sollen in einer Familie _____.
9. Am Anfang ist es eine große _____, allein zu leben.

A. 1. überlebten   2. Verlobung   3. eigene
4. verheiratet   5. verdienten   6. heiratete
7. befreundet   8. aufwachsen   9. Umstellung

B Familie und Beruf. Wie kann man das anders sagen?

1. Es war schön *damals* in der WG.
2. Sie *gab* ihren Beruf *auf* und bekam drei Kinder.
3. Ihre Enkelin *wuchs* in einer typisch deutschen Kleinfamilie *auf*.
4. Wir waren vorher acht Jahre *befreundet* und irgendwann wollten wir denn einfach heiraten.
5. Ich *erwarte von* meinem Ehepartner, dass er sich um seine Familie kümmert.
6. Am Anfang war es schon eine große *Umstellung,* alleine zu leben.
7. Die Hausfrau *sorgte für* den Haushalt.

a. Sie machte nicht mehr Karriere, sondern sie blieb mit ihren drei Kindern zu Hause.
b. Während dieser Periode meines Lebens fand ich die WG schön.
c. Wir waren acht Jahre Freunde, bevor wir uns entschieden, Mann und Frau zu werden.
d. Die Hausfrau machte alle Hausarbeit: Sie kochte, putzte, nähte . . .
e. Ihre Enkelin verbrachte ihre Kindheit in einer typisch deutschen Kleinfamilie.
f. Am Anfang musste sie sich an die neue Situation anpassen.
g. Mein Ehepartner soll sich um seine Familie kümmern. Ich halte das für selbstverständlich.

C Meinungen. Was bedeutet „Familie"? Im Video hören Sie verschiedene Meinungen zum Thema „Familie". Mit welchen Meinungen sind Sie einverstanden? Mit welchen nicht? Warum?

ANETT: Wenn ich das Wort „Familie" höre, denke ich an meine eigene Familie. Die bedeutet mir sehr viel. Ich lebe mit meinen Eltern zusammen, und ich habe auch eine große Schwester.

DANIELA: Ich finde Familie ist das, womit jeder glücklich ist. Und jeder muss es selbst definieren. Für mich sind's eben Kinder und ein Hund. Für andere ist es vielleicht eine Person oder nur die Person alleine.

STEFAN: Ich hoffe sehr, dass die traditionelle Familie überleben wird, weil in der modernen Familie vielleicht beide Eltern arbeiten und die Kinder sind meistens alleine. Das führt doch nur zu Scheidungen in meiner Meinung.

SABINE: Für mich ist Heiraten etwas ganz Romantisches. Ich wollte eigentlich schon immer heiraten.

NORA: Single heißt ja nicht, dass ich alleine bin. Ich habe ja haufenweise Freunde. Seit ich alleine lebe, unternehme ich viel mehr als früher, treffe mich mit Freunden, gehe ins Kino, ins Theater.

Daniela.

STRUKTUREN

REVIEW OF THE SIMPLE PAST TENSE
TELLING ABOUT PAST EVENTS

Remember, that to relate connected events that happened in the past—such as a story, narrative, or anecdote—use the simple past tense.

Strong verbs

Strong verbs form the simple past tense by changing their stem-vowels and adding special past-tense endings. No ending is added in the first- and third-person singular.

INFINITIVE: **bleiben** *to stay*	
STEM: **blieb-**	
ich blieb	wir blieb**en**
du blieb**st**	ihr blieb**t**
Sie blieb**en**	Sie blieb**en**
sie blieb	
er blieb	sie blieb**en**
es blieb	

The stem vowels of most strong verbs change according to one of the following patterns.

	VOWEL CHANGE	INFINITIVE	PAST-TENSE STEM	
1.	**ei → ie**	bl**ei**ben	bl**ie**b	*to stay*
2.	**ei → i**	b**ei**ßen	b**i**ss	*to bite*
3.	**ie → o**	fl**ie**gen	fl**o**g	*to fly*
4.	**i → a**	s**i**ngen	s**a**ng	*to sing*
5.	**o → a**	k**o**mmen	k**a**m	*to come*
6.	**e → a**	n**e**hmen	n**a**hm	*to take*
7.	**a → ie**	schl**a**fen	schl**ie**f	*to sleep*
8.	**a → u**	aufw**a**chsen	w**u**chs auf	*to grow up*

Some strong verbs undergo a change of consonants as well as vowels in the simple past tense. (See the appendix for a list of the simple past-tense forms of many common strong verbs.)

gehen, ging	*to go*	treffen, traf	*to meet*
reiten, ritt	*to ride*	tun, tat	*to do*
sein, war	*to be*	werden, wurde	*to become*
stehen, stand	*to stand*	ziehen, zog	*to move, pull*

Weak verbs

As you recall, weak verbs form the simple past tense by adding the tense marker **-t-** to the verb stem and then the past-tense endings.

Weak verbs with stems that end in **-t** or **-d** insert an **-e-** before the past-tense marker **-t-** plus endings.

INFINITIVE: **brauchen** *to need*	
STEM: **brauch-**	
ich brauch**te**	wir brauch**ten**
du brauch**test**	ihr brauch**tet**
Sie brauch**ten**	Sie brauch**ten**
sie brauch**te**	
er brauch**te**	sie brauch**ten**
es brauch**te**	

INFINITIVE: **heiraten** *to marry*	
STEM: **heirat-**	
ich heirat**ete**	wir heirat**eten**
du heirat**etest**	ihr heirat**etet**
Sie heirat**eten**	Sie heirat**eten**
sie heirat**ete**	
er heirat**ete**	sie heirat**eten**
es heirat**ete**	

Mixed verbs

Like weak verbs, mixed verbs (also called irregular weak verbs) take the past-tense marker **-t-**; like strong verbs, they have a stem change. The following are the most common mixed verbs in German. Four of the modal verbs fall into this category.*

brennen, brannte	*to burn*
bringen, brachte	*to bring*
denken, dachte	*to think*
haben, hatte	*to have*
kennen, kannte	*to know, be familiar with*
nennen, nannte	*to name*
rennen, rannte	*to run*
wissen, wusste	*to know*
dürfen, durfte	*to be permitted*
können, konnte	*to be able to, can*
mögen, mochte	*to like to, care to*
müssen, musste	*to have to, must*

SPRACHSPIEGEL

German and English have three main types of verbs: strong, weak, and mixed. Notice the similarities in the simple past-tense forms.

GERMAN	ENGLISH
STRONG VERBS	
sprechen, sprach	*speak, spoke*
stehen, stand	*stand, stood*
sein, war	*be, was*
WEAK VERBS	
lachen, lachte	*laugh, laughed*
leben, lebte	*live, lived*
MIXED VERBS	
bringen, brachte	*bring, brought*
können, konnte	*can, was able to*

*Note that **sollen/sollte** and **wollen/wollte** are weak verbs.

Übungen

A Verben im Imperfekt.[a] Wie war es damals in der Familie? Ergänzen Sie die Sätze. Benutzen Sie jedes Verb nur einmal.

1. Der Vater _____ alle wichtigen Entscheidungen.[b]
2. Meta Heyns Mann wollte, dass sie zu Hause _____.
3. Meta _____ ihren Beruf _____ und _____ drei Kinder.
4. Im Krieg _____ viele Frauen ihre Männer.
5. Meta Heyns Enkelin Sybilla _____ in einer typischen Kleinfamilie _____.
6. Als Frau _____ Sybilla mit der Tradition.
7. Sie löste ihre Verlobung und _____ mit Freunden in eine WG.

[a]*simple past tense*   [b] Entscheidungen treffen . . . *to make decisions*

zog wuchs... bekam
blieb ...auf
verloren
brach ...auf
gab ...auf traf

A. 1. traf   2. blieb   3. gab . . . auf, bekam
4. verloren   5. wuchs . . . auf   6. brach   7. zog

B Sybilla stellt ihrer Großmutter viele Fragen. Bilden Sie die Fragen im Imperfekt.

MODELL: Wie geht es der Familie? → Wie ging es der Familie?

1. Warum bleiben die Frauen zu Hause?
2. Wo schlafen die Kinder?
3. Welche Lieder singen sie?
4. Reiten die Kinder gern?
5. Wann werden die Söhne Soldaten?
6. Was tun die deutschen Familien?
7. Wann wird die wirtschaftliche Situation besser?
8. Wo steht das Familienhaus?
9. Wann ziehen viele Familien aus der Stadt?

B. 1. Warum blieben die Frauen zu Hause?
2. Wo schliefen die Kinder?   3. Welche Lieder sangen sie?   4. Ritten die Kinder gern?
5. Wann wurden die Söhne Soldaten?   6. Was taten die deutschen Familien?   7. Wann wurde die wirtschaftliche Situation besser?   8. Wo stand das Familienhaus?   9. Wann zogen viele Familien aus der Stadt?

C Damals und heute. Bilden Sie Sätze im Imperfekt.

MODELL: die Familie / leben / damals / in einer festen Ordnung →
Die Familie lebte damals in einer festen Ordnung.

1. Meta / heiraten / Franz Heyn
2. die traditionelle Frau / sorgen / für Haus und Familie
3. dein Großvater / wollen, / dass ich daheim blieb
4. der Vater / verdienen / das Geld für die Familie
5. Meta Heyn / sollen / sich um den Haushalt kümmern
6. dennoch / lernen / sie, *sg.* / einen Beruf
7. der Krieg / trennen / die Familie Heyn
8. nach dem Krieg / suchen / viele Frauen / ihre Männer
9. Metas Sohn Karl / studieren / Jura
10. die Ideale von Familie / ändern / sich in den sechziger Jahren
11. Sybilla / lösen / ihre Verlobung
12. Meta / denken / oft an ihre Familie
13. die Frauen / wissen / nicht, wo ihre Männer waren
14. der Krieg / bringen / viele Veränderungen im Familienleben

C. 1. Meta heiratete Franz Heyn.   2. Die traditionelle Frau sorgte für Haus und Familie.
3. Dein Großvater wollte, dass ich daheim blieb.
4. Der Vater verdiente das Geld für die Familie.
5. Meta Heyn sollte sich um den Haushalt kümmern.   6. Dennoch lernte sie einen Beruf.
7. Der Krieg trennte die Familie Heyn.   8. Nach dem Krieg suchten viele Frauen ihre Männer.
9. Metas Sohn Karl studierte Jura.   10. Die Ideale von Familie änderten sich in den sechziger Jahren.   11. Sybilla löste ihre Verlobung.
12. Meta dachte oft an ihre Familie.   13. Die Frauen wussten nicht, wo ihre Männer waren.
14. Der Krieg brachte viele Veränderungen im Familienleben.

CONJUNCTIONS
CONNECTING WORDS, SENTENCES, AND IDEAS

German has two types of conjunctions: coordinating and subordinating. Coordinating conjunctions join words, phrases, and complete sentences. The most common ones are **aber, denn, sondern,** and **und.**

> Stefan denkt oft an die Ehe, **und** eines Tages will er eine Frau und Kinder haben.

> *Stefan often thinks of marriage, and one day he wants to have a wife and children.*

Subordinating conjunctions join two dependent clauses or ideas. The most common ones are **als, dass, weil,** and **wenn.** Subordinating conjuctions may appear before the first or second clause.

> **Wenn** ich an „Familie" denke, denke ich meistens an Kinder und einen Hund.

> *When I think about "family," I usually think about children and a dog.*

Note that the conjugated verb appears at the end of clauses that begin with a subordinating conjunction. Note also that when a sentence begins with a subordinating conjunction, the second clause begins with the verb.

Übungen

A Kommentare über Ehe, Kinder und Lebensstil. Verbinden Sie die Satzteile.

1. Die Nationalsozialisten kamen an die Macht, aber _____
2. Frauen suchten ihre Männer, und _____
3. Ich lebe mit meinen Eltern zusammen und _____
4. Ich erwarte von meinem Ehepartner, dass _____
5. Wir waren froh, dass _____
6. Beide Frauen leben heute allein, aber _____
7. Es war schön damals in der WG, aber _____
8. Als wir noch klein waren, _____
9. Ich möchte eine Zeit lang Single bleiben, weil _____

a. das Familienleben in Deutschland ging weiter.
b. er sich um seine Familie kümmert.
c. hat Großmutter immer auf uns aufgepasst.
d. heute bin ich lieber alleine.
e. mir meine Freiheit wichtig ist.
f. sie fühlen sich eng miteinander verbunden.
g. sie sind mir sehr wichtig.
h. Väter suchten ihre Familien.
i. wir den Krieg überlebt hatten.

A. 1. a 2. h 3. g 4. b 5. i 6. f
7. d 8. c 9. e

B. 1. Viele Frauen mussten außer Haus arbeiten, weil die Männer Soldaten waren.   **2.** Meta heiratete Franz Heyn, als sie 22 Jahre alt war.   **3.** Stefan hofft, dass die traditionelle Familie überleben wird.   **4.** Wir waren einige Zeit befreundet, und irgendwann wollten wir heiraten.   **5.** Meine Schwester ist verheiratet, aber mein Bruder und ich sind Singles.   **6.** Sabine wollte schon immer heiraten, denn Heiraten ist für sie sehr romantisch.   **7.** Susanne wohnt nicht in der Stadt, sondern ihre Familie hat ein Haus in einem Vorort.   **8.** Wenn die Großmutter zu Besuch kommt, kocht sie für Familie Dyrchs.

B Familien. Verbinden Sie die beiden Sätze mit der angegebenen Konjunktion. Achten Sie auf Wortstellung.

MODELL: Ich denke an meine eigene Familie. (wenn) Ich höre das Wort „Familie". →
Ich denke an meine eigene Familie, wenn ich das Wort „Familie" höre.

1. Viele Frauen mussten außer Haus arbeiten. (weil) Die Männer waren Soldaten.
2. Meta heiratete Franz Heyn. (als) Sie war 22 Jahre alt.
3. Stefan hofft. (dass) Die traditionelle Familie wird überleben.
4. Wir waren einige Zeit befreundet. (und) Irgendwann wollten wir heiraten.
5. Meine Schwester ist verheiratet. (aber) Mein Bruder und ich sind Singles.
6. Sabine wollte schon immer heiraten. (denn) Heiraten ist für sie sehr romantisch.
7. Susanne wohnt nicht in der Stadt. (sondern) Ihre Familie hat ein Haus in einem Vorort.
8. (wenn) Die Großmutter kommt zu Besuch. Sie kocht für Familie Dyrchs.

C. *Answers will vary.*

C Wie war Ihre frühe Kindheit? Beantworten Sie die folgenden Fragen. Benutzen Sie einige oder alle dieser Konjunktionen: **aber, denn, sondern, und, als, dass, weil** und **wenn.**

MODELL: Meine Tante und Onkel wohnten in Seattle, aber meine Familie wohnte in Boston.

1. Wo wohnten Ihre Familienmitglieder (Ihre Mutter [Stiefmutter, Großmutter, Tante], Ihr Vater [Stiefvater, Großvater, Onkel])?
2. Was machten Ihre Familienmitglieder von Beruf?
3. Blieb Ihre Mutter (Stiefmutter, Großmutter, Tante) zu Hause, oder machte sie Karriere?
4. Als Sie Kind waren, gingen Sie gern in die Grundschule?
5. Wer passte auf Sie als Baby auf? Warum?

REVIEW OF NEGATION
NEGATING WORDS, SENTENCES, AND CONCEPTS

German, as you recall from your previous study, has two words for negation: **kein** and **nicht. Kein** is equivalent to English *no, not a,* or *not any;* **nicht** is equivalent to English *not.*

Use **kein** to negate nouns that would otherwise be preceded by an indefinite article or no article.

Ich habe **keine** Ahnung.	*I have no idea.*
Ich trinke **keinen** Tee.	*I don't drink tea.*
Ich brauche **keinen** Tisch.	*I don't need a/any table.*

Use **nicht** to negate an entire sentence or just part of it. To negate a specific part of the sentence, place **nicht** before that particular noun, adjective, adverb, or prepositional phrase.

Das ist **nicht** mein Mann.	*That is not my husband.*
Dein Cousin ist **nicht** verheiratet.	*Your cousin is not married.*
Das Leben war damals **nicht** sehr einfach.	*Life wasn't very simple in those days.*

To negate the entire sentence or idea, place **nicht** at the end of the sentence or just before the nonconjugated verb.

Viele Frauen fanden ihre Männer **nicht.**	*Many women did not find their husbands.*
Metas Bruder hat den Krieg **nicht** überlebt.	*Meta's brother did not survive the war.*

Übungen

A Das stimmt aber nicht! Verneinen Sie die Informationen mit **nicht** oder **kein.**

MODELL: Familie Dyrchs wohnt in der Stadt. →
Familie Dyrchs wohnt nicht in der Stadt.

1. Nora fühlt sich einsam.
2. Anja kam pünktlich zum Essen.
3. Susanne hat einen Bruder.
4. Mein Vater war geduldig.
5. Meine Großmutter hatte einen Hund.
6. Meine Mutter hat ein neues Auto.
7. Wir kennen die Nachbarn gut.

B Nein, das ist nicht so gewesen. Ein neugieriger Freund stellt Sabine Fragen über ihre Familie. Sabine antwortet auf alle Fragen negativ. Geben Sie ihre Antworten.

MODELL: Bist du in Rheinhausen geboren? →
Nein, ich bin nicht in Rheinhausen geboren.

1. Bist du auf Rügen aufgewachsen?
2. Hattest du eine langweilige Kindheit?
3. Musste deine Familie nach Köln umziehen?
4. War dein Vater Ingenieur?
5. Hat deine Mutter bei der Post gearbeitet?

KURZ NOTIERT

The phrase **noch kein / noch nicht** occurs primarily in negative answers to questions with **schon.**

Habt ihr **schon** ein Auto?
—Nein, wir haben **noch kein** Auto.
Do you already have a car?
—*No, we don't have a car yet.*

Kennst du **schon** diesen Film?
—Nein, ich kenne ihn **noch nicht.**
Do you already know this film?
—*No, I'm not yet familiar with it.*

The phase **kein . . . mehr / nicht mehr** occurs often in negative answers to questions with **noch.**

Wo finde ich die Zettel?
—Es gibt **keine Zettel mehr.**
Where do I find the slips?
—*There aren't any more slips.*

Willst du **noch** nach Neuseeland fahren?
—Nein, das ist **nicht mehr** mein Wunsch.
Do you still want to go to New Zealand?
—*No, that's no longer my wish.*

A. **1.** Nora fühlt sich nicht einsam. **2.** Anja kam nicht pünktlich zum Essen. **3.** Susanne hat keinen Bruder. **4.** Mein Vater war nicht geduldig. **5.** Meine Großmutter hatte keinen Hund. **6.** Meine Mutter hatte kein neues Auto. **7.** Wir kennen die Nachbarn nicht gut.

B. **1.** Nein, ich bin nicht auf Rügen aufgewachsen. **2.** Nein, ich hatte keine langweilige Kindheit. **3.** Nein, meine Familie musste nicht nach Köln umziehen. **4.** Nein, mein Vater war kein Ingenieur. **5.** Nein, meine Mutter hat nicht bei der Post gearbeitet.

PERSPEKTIVEN

WORTSCHATZ ZUM HÖRTEXT

außergewöhnlich	unusual
prahlen	to boast
jüdisch	Jewish
das Mitglied	member
der Philosoph	philosopher
der Dichter	poet
das Vorbild	model
berühmt	famous
das Schauspiel	play
der Klavierlehrer	piano teacher
verursachen	to cause

TIPP ZUM HÖREN

In the biography, you will hear Felix Mendelssohn-Bartholdy talk about his family. In a biography in German, the sentences are usually in the simple past tense, but in some instances the present tense is used. That is the case in this biography. What is the effect of this change from one tense to another?

HÖREN SIE ZU!
DIE FAMILIE MENDELSSOHN

A Sie hören jetzt biographische Information über die Familie Mendelssohn. Sagen Sie, wie die Familienmitglieder miteinander verwandt sind.

1. Felix sagt . . .
   a. Menachem ist mein _____.
   b. Fanny ist meine _____.
   c. Dorothea ist meine _____.
   d. Moses ist mein _____.
2. Menachem sagt . . .
   a. Felix ist mein _____.
   b. Fanny ist meine _____.
   c. Moses ist mein _____.
3. Fanny sagt . . .
   a. Felix ist mein _____.
   b. Lea ist meine _____.
   c. Friedrich ist mein _____.

A. 1. a. Urgroßvater b. Schwester c. Tante d. Großvater
2. a. Urenkel b. Urenkelin c. Sohn
3. a. Bruder b. Mutter c. Onkel

B Wie waren sie verwandt? Wofür war jeder/jede bekannt? Kombinieren Sie!

MODELL: Menachem war (Fannys Urgroßvater / Abrahams Großvater / ?). Er war Schreiber.

Menachem	Großvater	Autor/Autorin und
Moses	Vater	Theoretiker/Theoretikerin
Dorothea	Urgroßvater	Schrifsteller/Schriftstellerin
Fanny	Mutter	Komponist/Komponistin
Lea	Sohn	Philosoph/Philosophin
Friedrich	Onkel	Klavierlehrer/Klavierlehrerin
Felix	Tante	Beruf unbekannt
Abraham	Schwester	
	Bruder	
	Tochter	

B. *Answers will vary. Possible answers are:* **Menachem** war Fannys und Felix' Urgroßvater / Abrahams Großvater / Moses' Vater. Er war Schreiber. **Moses** war Menachems Sohn / Abrahams Vater / Fannys und Felix' Großvater. Er war Philosoph. **Dorothea** war Moses' Tochter / Abrahams Schwester / Felix' und Fannys Tante. Ihr Beruf ist unbekannt, aber sie war berühmt für ihren literarischen Salon. **Fanny** war Felix' Schwester / Leas und Abrahams Tochter. Sie war Komponistin. **Lea** war Felix' und Fannys Mutter. Sie war Klavierlehrerin. **Friedrich** war Fannys und Felix' Onkel. Er war Autor und Theoretiker. **Felix** war Fannys Bruder / Leas und Abrahams Sohn. Er war Komponist. *Abraham* war Felix' und Fannys Vater / Moses' Sohn. Sein Beruf ist unbekannt.

LESEN SIE!

Zum Thema

A Zum Titel

SCHRITT 1: Was bedeutet der Titel vielleicht?

1. Die Großmutter hat keine Persönlichkeit.
2. Die Großmutter hat etwas Schreckliches getan und hat Ansehen[a] verloren.
3. Der Erzähler / Die Erzählerin kennt die Großmutter nicht sehr gut.
4. Die Großmutter wurde in Wirklichkeit ohne Gesicht geboren.

[a]*respect*

SCHRITT 2: Warum ist das Verb in diesem Titel im Imperfekt?

1. Die Großmutter hat sich sehr geändert. In der Vergangenheit war sie ganz anders als heute.
2. Die Großmutter lebt nicht mehr.

B In diesem Gedicht porträtiert die Dichterin ihre Großmutter. Am Anfang des Gedichts sind alle Verben im Imperfekt, aber am Ende sind sie im Präsens.

1. Wovon handeln die meisten Zeilen des Gedichts?
2. Wovon handeln die letzten vier Zeilen?
3. Suchen Sie das erste Verb im Präsens. Was bedeutet dieser Tempuswechsel zwischen Präsens und Imperfekt?

meine grossmutter hatte kein gesicht

meine grossmutter hatte kein gesicht
aber ein gebiss in der schürzentasche
einen einsteckkamm auf der kommode
graue haare in der bürste
und auf dem nachttisch ein feines haarnetz
sie hatte keine arme aber finger
die heisse teegläser auf den tisch stellten 5
und dauernd die wachstuchdecke glattstrichen
einen körper hatte sie überhaupt nicht
aber eine stimme die ist immer noch
unheimlich stark und flüstert
und hetzt und fieselt mir sachen ins ohr 10
die darf ich nie jemand erzählen

Annemarie Zornack (1932–   )

KULTURSPIEGEL

Die deutsche Schriftstellerin Annemarie Zornack wurde 1932 in Aschersleben geboren. Nach dem Zweiten Weltkrieg kam sie nach Kiel, wo sie heute noch lebt.

WORTSCHATZ ZUM LESEN

das Gesicht	*face*
das Gebiss	*dentures*
die Schürzentasche	*apron pocket*
die Bürste	*hairbrush*
dauernd	*constantly*
die Wachstuchdecke	*oilcloth tablecloth*
glattstreichen	*to stroke smooth*
unheimlich	*strangely*
flüstern	*to whisper*
hetzen	*to hurry*

WAS: ein Gebiss, WO: in der Schürzentasche; WAS: einen Einsteckkamm, WO: auf der Kommode; WAS: Haare, WIE: grau, WO: in der Bürste; WAS: ein Haarnetz, WIE: fein, WO: auf dem Nachttisch; WAS: Finger; WAS SIE DAMIT MACHTE: heiße Teegläser auf den Tisch stellen, die Wachstuchdecke glattstreichen; WAS: eine Stimme, WIE: unheimlich stark, WAS SIE DAMIT MACHTE: flüstert, hetzt, fieselt Sachen ins Ohr.

Zum Text

● Was hatte die Großmutter? Was können Sie darüber sagen? Füllen Sie die Tabelle aus.

MODELL:

WAS	WIE	WO	WAS SIE DAMIT MACHTE
ein Gebiss ein Haarnetz	fein	in der Schürzentasche auf dem Nachttisch	

Zur Interpretation

A. Answers will vary. Possible answers are:
1. Nein, das ist nicht möglich.   2. Die Zeilen nennen die Körperteile der Großmutter, an die sich die Dichterin erinnert und die für sie, als sie ein Kind war, eine Bedeutung hatten. Sie hat ihre Großmutter nur zum Teil wahrgenommen.
3. Die Enkelin beschreibt die Großmutter. Sie beschreibt sie nicht sehr positiv. Vor allem ihre Stimme ist unangenehm: Sie fieselt und hetzt.
4. Die Enkelin hat ihr Großmutter wohl nicht sehr gern gehabt. Und obwohl die Großmutter schon tot ist, scheint ihre Stimme die Enkelin zu bedrohen.

A Was meinen Sie dazu?

1. Ist es möglich, dass die Großmutter wirklich kein Gesicht, keine Arme und keinen Körper hatte?
2. Was bedeuten die folgenden Zeilen: meine großmutter hatte kein gesicht / sie hatte keine arme aber finger / einen körper hatte sie überhaupt nicht?
3. Wer beschreibt die Großmutter? Welche Bemerkungen macht diese Person über die Großmutter?
4. Was können Sie über diese Person sagen?

B Kontraste. Das Bindewort (die Konjunktion) *aber* hat eine wichtige Funktion: es stellt einen Kontrast her.

1. Suchen Sie das Wort *aber* im Gedicht. Wie oft kommt es im Gedicht vor?
2. Welche Eigenschaften sind in jedem Fall um das Wort *aber* gruppiert? Welche Gemeinsamkeiten gibt es in jeder Gruppe? Welche Unterschiede?
3. Warum kann sich diese Person noch gut an viele kleinere Eigenschaften der Großmutter erinnern, aber gar nicht an ihr Gesicht?

B. 1. Das Wort *aber* kommt drei Mal in dem Gedicht vor.
2. In allen drei Fällen beschreibt das Wort *aber* einen Widerspruch. Eigentlich ist es unmöglich, dass man Finger hat, aber keine Arme oder eine Stimme, aber keinen Körper. Ein Gebiss kann man nicht gebrauchen, wenn man kein Gesicht hat. Der Unterschied zwischen den drei Beispielen ist, dass die Arme ein Körperteil sind, während die Stimme etwas ist, was ein Körperteil produziert, und das Gebiss in der Schürzentasche ist eine Prothese, ein Ersatzteil.
3. Answers will vary. Possible answers are: Vielleicht hatte die Person als Kind Angst vor ihrer Großmutter und erinnert sich deshalb nur an Dinge an ihr, die sie nicht gemocht hat. Als die Person noch klein war, sah sie nur Dinge in ihrem Blickfeld, das heißt Hände, Kommode, Tischdecke, Schürzentasche, usw.

FOKUS INTERNET

For more information, visit the *Auf Deutsch!* Web Site at www.mcdougallittell.com.

INTERAKTION

● Ein Spiel: Wen beschreiben wir?   *Answers will vary.*

SCHRITT 1:

1. Arbeiten Sie mit einem Partner / einer Partnerin. Denken Sie an eine berühmte Person, die Sie beide beschreiben möchten. Vielleicht möchten Sie eine Politikerin, einen Rockstar, eine Sportlerin oder einen Schauspieler beschreiben?
2. Notieren Sie zusammen drei bis fünf Substantive und drei bis fünf Verben, die Sie mit dieser Person verbinden, zum Beispiel körperliche oder persönliche Eigenschaften, konkrete Gegenstände.[a] Schreiben Sie dann gemeinsam ein kurzes Porträt der Person (drei bis fünf Sätze).
3. Teilen Sie die Sätze der Beschreibung zwischen Ihnen und Ihrem Partner / Ihrer Partnerin auf, um sie der Klasse vorzulesen.

SCHRITT 2: Lesen Sie Ihre Beschreibung der Klasse vor.

SCHRITT 3: Nach dem kurzen Vortrag, darf die Klasse Ihnen Fragen stellen, um herauszufinden, wer die Person ist. Beantworten Sie die Fragen. Wer die Person kennt, nennt ihren Namen.

[a]*objects*

SCHREIBEN SIE!

Texts will vary.

Eine kurze Biografie

● Nehmen Sie das Foto eines älteren Familienmitglieds (oder das Foto einer bekannten Person aus einer Illustrierten) und schreiben Sie die Lebensgeschichte dieser Person.

Purpose:	To write about someone's life
Audience:	A classmate; readers seeking biographical information about a person
Subject:	An older family member or a celebrity
Structure:	Illustrated biographical sketch

TIPP ZUM SCHREIBEN

Short illustrated biographical sketches are printed on the dust cover of new novels, in the liner notes for CDs, and in encyclopedias. These sketches are factual and concise, yet packed with vital data, pointing out all the significant events and accomplishments in that person's life.

Schreibmodell

The city and state are separated by a slash mark. Prose is written in the simple past tense.

The writer uses several paragraphs to illustrate the most important stages of the person's life. In German, paragraphs are not indented.

By using conjunctions and relative pronouns the writer creates more complex sentences and adds variety.

Helen aus Indiana

Meine Großmutter Helen Guy wurde am 1. August 1913 in Whiting/Indiana geboren. Als Tochter von Immigranten aus der Slowakei war ihre Muttersprache Slowakisch; erst im Kindergarten lernte Helen Englisch. Helens Vater arbeitete in einer Ölraffinerie, Helens Mutter war Hausfrau.

Als Helen neun Jahre alt war, starb ihr Vater bei einem Motorradunfall. Auf einmal waren sie und ihre vier jüngeren Schwestern Halbwaisen[a] und die Familie hatte kein Einkommen mehr. Mit siebzehn Jahren musste Helen deshalb die Schule abbrechen, um Geld für die Familie zu verdienen. 1931 verliebte sich meine Großmutter in einen jungen Mann aus Kentucky, Joseph, der in Whiting Arbeit gefunden hatte, und die beiden heirateten. Helen und Joseph bauten ein Haus und hatten vier Kinder miteinander, zwei Töchter und zwei Söhne. Mein Vater, der 1950 geboren wurde, war der Jüngste.

[a]persons who have lost one parent

1971, als ihre Kinder schon erwachsen waren, wurde Helen auf einmal sehr krank. Die Ärzte kannten die Krankheit nicht, für die es keine Behandlung gab und an der sie beinahe starb. Erst viele Jahre später wurde festgestellt, dass sie eines der allerersten Opfer der „Legionärskrankheit" gewesen war und eine damals tödliche Krankheit überlebt hatte.

Heute ist meine Großmutter Witwe, aber sie ist noch sehr aktiv und versucht, jeden Tag eine Meile spazieren zu gehen. Und für die Familie kocht sie noch immer die slowakischen Spezialitäten aus ihrer Kindheit.

> The concluding paragraph brings the reader up to date on the subject of the sketch.

Schreibstrategien

Vor dem Schreiben

To prepare for writing this biographical sketch, follow these steps:

- Read several biographical sketches and decide what information is essential, what provides interesting detail, and what could be left out.

- Choose a person in your family or a celebrity whose life history makes an interesting story. Quickly jot down all interesting facts and memories you have of this person.

- Write a loose outline for the biographical sketch, giving each major life stage of your subject a separate entry or section.

- Determine what you know and what you'd like to know about this person, and make a list of questions that need to be answered.

- Ask others who know your subject to help fill in information gaps. If possible, contact your subject, ask your questions directly, and take good notes.

- Locate a picture of your subject to illustrate the biography.

TIPP ZUM SCHREIBEN

To write a biographical sketch you will need to use the past tense. If you are not sure how to form the simple past tense, review pages 16–17 of this chapter and consult Appendix A, 11. *Principal Parts of Irregular Verbs*, and 13. *Conjugation of Verbs*.

Ein echter Sportler

Mein Onkel Jeff wurde am (Juni 7.) 1965 in Tyler/Texas geboren. In der Schule hatte Jeff immer sehr schlechte Noten, aber im Sport war er ein Star. Im Finalspiel der Football-Liga ~~gewann~~ *gewann* er mit dem letzten Touchdown die Meisterschaft. Wegen seines sportlichen Talents gab ihm Texas A&M ein Stipendium. Jeff studierte Betriebswirtschaft aber seine Noten waren manchmal so schlecht, dass er (bekam) fast Spielverbot. Aber dann verbesserte er seine Noten und durfte weiter spielen. 1987 ~~erhielt~~ *erhielt* er sein B.A. Diplom. Heute arbeitet mein Onkel als Verkaufsmanager für eine deutsche Firma. In seiner Freizeit arbeitet er als Coach und Trainer für die Little League.

Beim Schreiben

- As you prepare to write, remind yourself who your audience is so you can shape your prose and set the right tone.

- Determine how long your sketch should be in advance, and stick to your plan. Write your draft double-spaced, leaving room for changes and corrections.

- Vary the way you begin sentences to add flavor and interest to your writing.

- Check your outline frequently. Some detail may be informative and entertaining, but it may make the biographical sketch stray from its purpose. Follow your outline.

- Once you have completed your first draft, read it critically before showing it to others. Give yourself time to edit and make changes.

Nach dem Schreiben

- Ask another student to peer edit a copy of your sketch. Keep your original copy for yourself. (You will be a peer editor for another student as well.)

- Peer editors make corrections in grammar and word choice, and provide positive feedback on successful passages. Peer editors also read critically and point out problems in the prose. Suggestions for improvement are helpful.

- Once you get back the edited copy, read your peer editor's comments and suggestions. Read through your sketch again, and start revising your first draft.

- After you complete each paragraph, stop and read the changes you have made. Is this the tone and style you wanted? You may choose to include or ignore suggested changes in your final draft.

- Double-check your facts. Are the names, dates, places, and occurrences accurate and in the right chronological order?

Stimmt alles?

- Read your revision a last time for accuracy in spelling, grammar, and style.

- Prepare a clean copy of your finished sketch, leaving space for the picture. Position this illustration on the page, and make sure your name is on the page.

WORTSCHATZ

Substantive	Nouns
die **Fürsorge, -n**	support
die **Jugend**	youth
die **Kusine, -n**	(female) cousin
die **Schwägerin, -nen**	sister-in-law
die **Schwiegermutter, ⸚**	mother-in-law
die **Trennung, -en**	separation
die **Umstellung, -en**	adjustment
die **Unabhängigkeit**	independence
die **Veränderung, -en**	change
die **Verlobung, -en**	engagement
der/die **Erwachsene, -n** (*decl. adj.*)	adult
der **Schwager, -**	brother-in-law
der **Schwiegervater, ⸚**	father-in-law
der **Stiefbruder, ⸚**	stepbrother
der **Vertrag, ⸚e**	contract
der **Vetter, -n**	(male) cousin
das **Ehepaar, -e**	married couple
die **Urenkel** (*pl.*)	great-grandchildren
die **Urgroßeltern** (*pl.*)	great-grandparents

Verben	Verbs
auf•wachsen (wächst auf), wuchs auf, ist aufgewachsen	to grow up
aus•prägen	to mark, impress
betreffen, betraf, betroffen	to concern, affect
beweisen, bewies, bewiesen	to prove
ernähren	to nourish
erreichen	to achieve
erwarten von	to expect from
regeln	to regulate
respektieren	to respect
jemandem nah stehen, nah gestanden	to be close to someone
überleben	to survive

Adjektive und Adverbien	Adjectives and adverbs
befreundet	friends with someone

damals	at that time
ehelich	marital
getrennt	separated
männlich	masculine, male
unabhängig	independent(ly)
verheiratet	married
verliebt	in love
verlobt	engaged
weiblich	feminine, female

Sie wissen schon	You already know
die **Ehe, -n**	marriage
die **Enkelin, -nen**	granddaughter
die **Mutter, ⸚**	mother
die **Nichte, -n**	niece
die **Scheidung, -en**	divorce
die **Tante, -n**	aunt
die **Tochter, ⸚**	daughter
der **Bruder, ⸚**	brother
der **Enkel, -**	grandson
der **Familienstand**	marital status
der **Haushalt, -e**	household
der **Neffe** (**-n** *masc.*)	nephew
der **Onkel, -**	uncle
der **Sohn, ⸚e**	son
der **Vater, ⸚**	father
die **Eltern** (*pl.*)	parents
die **Geschwister** (*pl.*)	siblings
die **Großeltern** (*pl.*)	grandparents
auf•geben (gibt auf), gab auf, aufgegeben	to give up
heiraten	to marry
sorgen für	to care for
verdienen	to earn
berufstätig	employed
eigen	own
geboren	born
ledig/single	single, unmarried

KAPITEL 26 JUGEND
pages 30–49

PLANNING GUIDE • CLASSROOM MANAGEMENT

OBJECTIVES

Communication
- Discuss changes for youth in the last 50 years, p. 33.
- Learn about young people in the former East Germany, p. 33.
- Discuss the attitudes of today's youth, p. 35.

Grammar
- Review the accusative and dative, pp. 36–38.
- Review the genitive case, p. 38.
- Review use of accusative versus dative after prepositions, pp. 41–43.

Culture
- Learn about the youth movements of the 1960s and 1970s, p. 32.
- Learn about the future goals of young Germans, pp. 33, 35.
- Read about the effects of unification on German youth, p. 33.

Recycling
- Review use of nominative, accusative, and dative cases, pp. 36–40.

STRATEGIES

Listening Strategies
- Listen to identify speakers, p. 32.
- Listen for statistical information, p. 44.
- Listen for key information in subordinate clauses, p. 44.

Speaking Strategies
- Discuss attitudes of today's youth, p. 35.
- Describe personal interests, p. 43.

Reading Strategies
- Analyze a story about a crisis, pp. 45–47.

Writing Strategies
- Write a flyer for a citizen action program, pp. 47–48.

Connecting Cultures Strategies
- Compare historical events in Europe and North America, p. 33.

PROGRAM RESOURCES

Print
- *Arbeitsheft* (Workbook), pp. 19–32
- *Arbeitsheft* (Workbook), Teacher's Edition, pp. 19–32

Audiovisual
- Overhead Transparencies 26.1–26.G1
- Audio Program, Cassette 1B, 7A/CD 1, 9
- Audioscript, pp. 8–13

Technology
- Annenberg *Fokus Deutsch* Video Series, *Folge* 26
- www.mcdougallittell.com

Assessment Program Options
- *Prüfung, Kapitel 26,* Assessment Program, pp. 13–21
- Audio Program, Cassette 8A/CD 10
- Audioscript, p. 107
- Teacher's Resource CD-ROM

DAY 1

Note: (1) Please see TE, pp. 30E–30J, for other suggestions not referenced in these plans. (2) Not all homework options need be assigned.

CHAPTER OPENER

- Quick Start Review: Vocabulary review (TE, p. 30E). 5 MIN
- Follow the Teaching Suggestions for using the photos on pp. 30–31 as the basis for a class discussion (TE, p. 30E). 4 MIN

VIDEOTHEK

- Play *Folge I: Jugend in Bewegung,* then have students do *Akt. A,* p. 32, silently. Play the episode again to check answers. (TE, p. 30F). 11 MIN
- Do *Akt. B,* p. 32 as a class. 5 MIN
- Discuss *Akt. C,* p. 33 (top), as a class (TE, p. 30F). 10 MIN
- *Arbeitsheft,* p. 19, audio *Akt. B.* 5 MIN
- Have students read through *Akt. A,* p. 33, then play *Folge II: Drei Jugendporträts* while they mark their answers. Follow the Teaching Suggestions for a variation (TE, p. 30F). 10 MIN

Homework Options:

- *Arbeitsheft,* p. 19, Videothek, *Akt. A–B*

DAY 2

VIDEOTHEK

- Quick Start Review 1: Question words (TE, p. 30E). 5 MIN
- Play the second episode again and have students do *Akt. B,* p. 33, silently (TE, p. 30F). 7 MIN
- *Arbeitsheft,* p. 21, audio *Akt. D.* 7 MIN
- Have students discuss *Akt. C,* p. 33, in pairs, then have them share their discussions with the class (TE, p. 30F). 15 MIN

VOKABELN

- Present the vocabulary on p. 34 using OHT 26.G1. 8 MIN
- Do *Akt. A,* pp. 34–35, silently, then check answers as a class (TE, p. 30G). 8 MIN

Homework Options:

- *Arbeitsheft,* p. 23, Vokabeln, *Akt. C–D*

DAY 3

VOKABELN

- Quick Start Review 1: Simple past (TE, p. 30F). 6 MIN
- Do *Akt. B,* p. 35, alone and then check answers with a partner. 10 MIN
- *Arbeitsheft,* p. 22, audio *Akt. B.* 14 MIN
- Do *Akt. C,* p. 35, in groups. End with a class discussion (TE, p. 30G). 20 MIN

Homework Options:

- *Arbeitsheft,* p. 23, Vokabeln, *Akt. E*

DAY 4

VOKABELN

- Quick Start Review 2: *Wenn* or *als*? (TE, p. 30G). 4 MIN
- *Arbeitsheft,* p. 22, audio *Akt. A.* 5 MIN

STRUKTUREN

- Follow the Teaching Suggestions for presenting the accusative and dative cases on pp. 36–37. (TE, p. 30H). 10 MIN
- Do *Übung A,* p. 37, silently, then check answers as a class. Follow the Teaching Suggestions for a follow-up activity (TE, p. 30H). 11 MIN
- Do *Übung B,* p. 38, then follow the Teaching Suggestions for a follow-up activity (TE, p. 30H). 8 MIN
- Have students do *Übung C,* p. 38, in small groups. (TE, p. 30H). 7 MIN
- *Arbeitsheft,* p. 25, *Akt. C.* 5 MIN

Homework Options:

- *Übung D,* p. 38
- *Arbeitsheft,* pp. 25–26, Strukturen, *Akt. D–F*

PACING GUIDE • SAMPLE LESSON PLAN, 50-MINUTE SCHEDULE

DAY 5

STRUKTUREN

- Quick Start Review 1: *Wo*-compounds (TE, p. 30H). 4 MIN
- Review the genitive case on pp. 38–40. 12 MIN
- Have students do *Übung A,* p. 40, silently, then check their answers as a class. 8 MIN
- Have students do *Übung B,* p. 40, in small groups, then share with the class the statements they create. 12 MIN
- Follow the Teaching Suggestions to present accusative, dative, and accusative/dative prepositions on pp. 41–42. (TE, p. 30H). 8 MIN
- Have students do *Übung A,* p. 42, silently, then check their answers with a partner. 6 MIN

Homework Options:

- *Arbeitsheft*, p. 26, *Strukturen, Akt. G*
- *Arbeitsheft*, p. 28, *Strukturen, Akt. K*

DAY 6

STRUKTUREN

- Quick Start Review 2: Reflexive pronouns (TE, p. 30H). 5 MIN
- Have students do *Übung B,* p. 43, with a partner, then check their answers as a class (TE, p. 30H). 10 MIN
- Have students do *Übung C,* p. 43, in pairs, then share what they learn with the class. 15 MIN

PERSPEKTIVEN

- Follow the Teaching Suggestions for the first *Hören Sie zu!* recording, then do *Akt. A,* p. 44, as a class (TE, p. 30I). 8 MIN
- Play the second *Hören Sie zu!* recording and do *Akt. A–B,* pp. 44–45, as a class (TE, p. 30I). 12 MIN

Homework Options:

- Read *Lesen Sie!,* pp. 45–46
- *Arbeitsheft,* pp. 29–30, *Perspektiven, Akt. C–D*

DAY 7

PERSPEKTIVEN

- Quick Start Review 1: Subordinating conjunction *dass* (TE, p. 30I). 5 MIN
- Have students read the text, then do *Zum Text,* pp. 46–47, in pairs, after briefly reviewing and discussing the text as a class (TE, p. 30J). 19 MIN
- Begin *Schreiben Sie!,* pp. 47–48, by discussing the assignment, *Tipp zum Schreiben,* and *Schreibmodell* (TE, p. 30J). 10 MIN
- Do *Vor dem Schreiben,* p. 48, and begin *Beim Schreiben,* p. 48. 16 MIN

Homework Options:

- Finish *Beim Schreiben,* p. 48, and complete the first draft of the flyer
- *Arbeitsheft,* p. 31, *Perspektiven, Akt. F*

DAY 8

PERSPEKTIVEN

- Quick Start Review 2: Simple past (TE, p. 30I). 5 MIN
- Do *Nach dem Schreiben,* p. 48, and begin the final draft of the flyer. 10 MIN
- Questions and review. 5 MIN
- *Prüfung, Kapitel 26.* 30 MIN

Homework Options:

- Finish the final draft of the flyer
- *Arbeitsheft,* p. 32, *Perspektiven, Akt. G*

DAY 1

Note: (1) Please see TE, pp. 30E–30J, for other suggestions not referenced in these plans. (2) Not all homework options need be assigned.

CHAPTER OPENER

- Quick Start Review: Vocabulary review (TE, p. 30E). 5 MIN
- Discuss the photos on pp. 30–31 (TE, p. 30E). 7 MIN

VIDEOTHEK

- Play *Folge I*, then do *Akt. A*, p. 32, silently. Check answers with video. (TE, p. 30F). 15 MIN
- *Akt. B*, p. 32. 5 MIN
- Discuss *Akt. C*, p. 33 (top), as a class (TE, p. 30F). 10 MIN
- *Arbeitsheft*, p. 19, audio *Akt. B*. 5 MIN
- Read *Akt. A*, p. 33, then play *Folge II*. Do variation (TE, p. 30F). 12 MIN
- Block Schedule activity: Research (TE, p. 30F). 10 MIN
- *Arbeitsheft*, p. 21, audio *Akt. D*. 6 MIN
- Discuss *Akt. C*, p. 33, in pairs, then with class (TE, p. 30F). 15 MIN

Homework Options:

- *Arbeitsheft*, p. 19, *Videothek, Akt. A–B*

DAY 2

VOKABELN

- Quick Start Review 1: Simple past (TE, p. 30F). 5 MIN
- Present vocabulary on p. 34. 8 MIN
- Do *Akt. A*, pp. 34–35, silently and then check answers as a class (TE, p. 30G). 8 MIN
- Do *Akt. B*, p. 35, alone, then check answers with a partner. 10 MIN
- *Arbeitsheft*, p. 22, audio *Akt. B*. 14 MIN
- Do *Akt. C*, p. 35, in groups (TE, p. 30G). 13 MIN
- Block Schedule activity: Fun Break (TE, p. 30G). 10 MIN

STRUKTUREN

- Present the accusative and dative cases on pp. 36–37. (TE, p. 30H). 10 MIN
- Do *Übung A*, p. 37, silently, then check answers as a class. Do follow-up activity (TE, p. 30H). 12 MIN

Homework Options:

- *Arbeitsheft*, p. 23, *Vokabeln, Akt. C–E*
- *Übung D*, p. 38
- *Arbeitsheft*, p. 25, *Akt. D–E*

DAY 3

STRUKTUREN

- Quick Start Review 1: *Wo*-compounds (TE, p. 30H). 5 MIN
- Do *Übung B*, p. 38, and follow-up activity (TE, p. 30H). 8 MIN
- Do *Übung C*, p. 38, in small groups. (TE, p. 30H). 7 MIN
- Review the genitive case on pp. 38–40. 12 MIN
- Do *Übung A*, p. 40, silently, then check answers as a class. 8 MIN
- Do *Übung B*, p. 40, in small groups, then share with the class. 12 MIN
- Block Schedule activity: Retention (TE, p. 30H). 10 MIN
- Present prepositions on pp. 41–42. (TE, p. 30H). 8 MIN
- Do *Übung A*, p. 42, silently, then check answers with a partner. 6 MIN
- Do *Übung C*, p. 43, in pairs, then share with the class. 14 MIN

Homework Options:

- *Arbeitsheft*, p. 26, *Akt. F–G*
- *Übung B*, p. 43
- *Arbeitsheft*, p. 28, *Akt., K*

DAY 4

PERSPEKTIVEN

- Quick Start Review 1: Subordinating conjunction *dass* (TE, p. 30H). 4 MIN
- Do the first *Hören Sie zu!* activity, p. 44, as a class (TE, p. 30I). 8 MIN
- Play the second *Hören Sie zu!* recording, then do *Akt. A–B*, pp. 44–45 (TE, 30I). 12 MIN
- *Zum Thema*, p. 45 (TE, p. 30I). 4 MIN
- Have students read the text on pp. 45–46 in small groups. 10 MIN
- Do *Zum Text*, pp. 46–47, in pairs (TE, p. 30J). 12 MIN
- *Zur Interpretation* activity, p. 48 (TE, p. 30J). 8 MIN
- Block Schedule activity: Expansion (TE, p. 30J). 10 MIN
- Begin *Schreiben Sie!*, pp. 47–48, (TE, p. 30J). 6 MIN
- Do *Vor dem Schreiben*, p. 48, and begin *Beim Schreiben*, p. 48. 16 MIN

Homework Options:

- Finish *Beim Schreiben*, p. 48, and first draft of flyer

DAY 5

PERSPEKTIVEN

- Quick Start Review 2 (TE, p. 30I). 5 MIN
- *Arbeitsheft*, p. 29, audio *Akt. A–B*. 15 MIN
- *Arbeitsheft*, p. 31, audio *Akt. E*. 10 MIN
- Do *Nach dem Schreiben*, p. 48, and begin the final draft of the flyer. 15 MIN
- Block Schedule activity: Research (TE, p. 30J). 10 MIN
- Questions and review. 5 MIN
- *Prüfung, Kapitel 26*. 30 MIN

Homework Options:

- Finish the final draft of the flyer
- *Arbeitsheft*, pp. 31–32, *Perspektiven, Akt. F–G*

Chapter Opener, pp. 30–31

PROGRAM RESOURCES

• Overhead Transparency 26.1

Quick Start Review

♻ Vocabulary review
Verbinden Sie die Definitionen mit den richtigen Wörtern.

    a. _____ beweisen
    b. _____ aufwachsen
    c. _____ getrennt
    d. _____ damals
    e. _____ verheiratet
    f. _____ der Vertrag
    g. _____ ernähren

    1. der Kontrakt
    2. nicht zusammen
    3. mit Essen versorgen
    4. zeigen, dass etwas so ist, wie Sie glaubten
    5. nicht mehr ledig sein
    6. größer und älter werden
    7. in jener Zeit

Answers: a. 4   b. 6   c. 2   d. 7   e. 5   f. 1   g. 3

TEACHING SUGGESTIONS

• Photos, pp. 30–31

Have students compare the 2 smaller photos and speculate about the life choices of the people depicted. Ask *Was ist ihnen wichtig? Welchen Effekt haben ihre Ideale auf ihre Lebensstile?*

TEACHING ALL STUDENTS

Multiple Intelligences Intrapersonal: Give students 5 minutes to write in German about an issue that they feel strongly about. You may want to list a few controversial issues on the board (*Umweltschutz, Frieden, Menschenrechte*). Follow up by asking students to tell what issues they chose and why this issue is so important.

CLASSROOM COMMUNITY

Paired Activity Have students work in pairs to create a short dialogue between a youth from the 1960s and one of his/her parents. Then have 2–3 pairs perform their dialogues for the class.

CULTURE HIGHLIGHTS

Give the students some background information on the *Studentenbewegung* in Germany in the 1950s and 1960s. During this period, thousands of students all over Germany took part in demonstrations calling for reforms in the educational system, and against France's war in Algeria, nuclear armament in Germany, and U.S. involvement in Vietnam.

INTERDISCIPLINARY CONNECTION

History Have students ask their history teachers or family members about the student protests during the 1960s in North America, such as those at U.C. Berkeley, Kent State University, and the 1968 Democratic Convention in Chicago. Have students report back to the class and discuss with the class how these events might have influenced the protests in Germany.

Videothek, pp. 32–33

PROGRAM RESOURCES

• Videocassette, *Folge 26*
• *Arbeitsheft*, pp. 19–21
• Audio Program, Cassette 1B/CD 1
• Audioscript, pp. 8–9

Quick Start Review 1

♻ Question words
Ergänzen Sie die Fragewörter in den folgenden Sätzen.
FRAGEWÖRTER: Warum, Wen, Welche, Wie, Wer

    1. _____ sahen die Ziele und Hoffnungen der Jugend damals aus?
    2. _____ sagt das im Video, Susanne, Erika oder Stefan?
    3. _____ Hoffnungen haben Sie für die Zukunft?
    4. _____ finden Sie diese Person besonders interessant?
    5. _____ möchten Sie am liebsten kennen lernen?

Answers: 1. Wie   2. Wer   3. Welche   4. Warum   5. Wen

Quick Start Review 2

♻ Infinitive clauses with *zu*
Bilden Sie Sätze.

    1. Es ist ihr nicht wichtig / viel Geld verdienen
    2. Er hat sich entschlossen / eine große Familie haben
    3. Es ist interessant / sich mit anderen über Zukunftsträume unterhalten
    4. Sie wird versuchen / optimistisch bleiben
    5. Es ist schön / Leute kennen lernen
    6. Sie hoffen / ein eigenes Haus und einen Sportwagen kaufen können

Answers: 1. Es ist ihr nicht wichtig, viel Geld zu verdienen.   2. Er hat sich entschlossen, eine große Familie zu haben.   3. Es ist interessant, sich mit anderen über Zukunftsträume zu unterhalten. 4. Sie wird versuchen, optimistisch zu bleiben. 5. Es ist schön, Leute kennen zu lernen. 6. Sie hoffen, ein eigenes Haus und einen Sportwagen kaufen zu können.

....

TEACHING SUGGESTIONS

• *Aktivität A, p. 32*

Expansion: Create associograms for each decade by writing key words and phrases on the board. Begin with the activity answers, then add further associations as suggested by students.

• *Aktivität C, p. 33 (top)*

Expansion: Have students make a timeline of the historical events described in the video. Then have students work with a partner to identify parallel events in North America that they can add to their timelines. *Rosa Parks' Busfahrt (1955), der Vietnam-Krieg (1961–1975), Generalstreik in Berkeley (1964), Demonstrationen auf dem Parteikonvent der Demokraten in Chicago (1968), Höhepunkt der amerikanischen Aufrüstung (1983), der Golfkrieg (1991).*

• *Aktivität A, p. 33*

Variation: Have students answer each question using *dass* and a subordinate clause. For example, *Es stimmt nicht, dass Ulla Psychologie studieren möchte.*

• *Aktivität C, p. 33 (bottom)*

Warm-up: Model a formal introduction for the class. Integrate the following vocabulary into your presentation and write it on the board: *Darf ich (mich)*

vorstellen? Es freut mich, Sie kennen zu lernen. Angenehm. Then have students introduce themselves to 2 other people in the class using the new vocabulary.

TEACHING ALL STUDENTS

Challenge After students have completed *Aktivitäten A–C, p. 33,* ask them to write the names Ulla, Ramona, and Kristian next to each other on a sheet of paper. Give them 2 minutes to jot down as many facts as they can remember about each of the 3 young people, then call on students to describe the lives of Ulla, Ramona, and Kristian.

CLASSROOM COMMUNITY

Paired Activity As an expansion of *Aktivität C, p. 33,* have students work in pairs to create a dialogue of themselves meeting with Ulla, Ramona, or Kristian. Select a few pairs to perform their dialogues for the class.

CULTURE HIGHLIGHTS

Have students read the *Kulturspiegel,* p. 33, then ask *Wie veränderte sich das Leben für Jugendliche im Osten nach der Wiedervereinigung? Was waren die Vorteile und Nachteile dieser Veränderungen?*

BLOCK SCHEDULE

Research Write *Fünfziger, Sechziger, Siebziger, Achtziger,* and *Neunziger* on the board. Have students brainstorm for associations with the various decades and create associograms around each one.

Vokabeln, pp. 34–35

PROGRAM RESOURCES

• *Arbeitsheft,* pp. 22–23
• Audio Program, Cassette 1B/CD 1
• Audioscript, pp. 9–10

....

Quick Start Review 1

Simple past
Schreiben Sie die Sätze ins Imperfekt um.

1. Die Frau der fünfziger Jahre sorgt für Haus und Familie.
2. Der Vater trifft alle wichtigen Entscheidungen.
3. In den sechziger Jahren singen viele Liedermacher über die Ungerechtigkeit.
4. Die Ideale der Familie werden anders.
5. Studenten in der BRD und den USA protestieren gegen den Vietnam-Krieg.

Answers: 1. Die Frau der fünfziger Jahre sorgte für Haus und Familie. 2. Der Vater traf alle wichtigen Entscheidungen. 3. In den sechziger Jahren sangen viele Liedermacher über die Ungerechtigkeit. 4. Die Ideale der Familie wurden anders. 5. Studenten in der BRD und den USA protestierten gegen den Vietnam-Krieg.

Quick Start Review 2

Wenn or *als*?
Ergänzen Sie die Sätze mit *wenn* oder *als.*

1. _____ ich ein Teenager war, hörten alle Diskomusik.
2. Es machte immer viel Spaß, _____ wir am Wochenende tanzen gingen.

3. Einmal, _____ ich mit meinen Freunden ausgehen wollte, klingelte das Telefon.
4. _____ ich ans Telefon ging, stolperte ich mit meinen hohen Absätzen über das Kabel.
5. _____ ich diese blöden Schuhe nicht getragen hätte, wäre ich nicht gefallen.

Answers: 1. Als 2. wenn 3. als 4. Als 5. Wenn

TEACHING SUGGESTIONS

• Photos, pp. 34–35

Have students choose 1 of the 2 photos and give them a few minutes to describe it in a short paragraph. Encourage them to speculate about the people in the photos.

• *Aktivität A,* pp. 34–35

Expansion: Have students write a definition of one of the vocabulary items on p. 34 on a slip of paper. Call on students to read their definition. The class must find the word in the vocabulary list that matches the definition.

• *Aktivität C,* p. 35

Have the class make up a list of adjectives to describe people, their goals, their attitudes, and their values. Have students describe the 3 characters in the video (or fellow students) with words from the list.

TEACHING ALL STUDENTS

Multiple Intelligences Naturalist: Introduce terms such as *die Umwelt, umweltfreundlich, der Umweltschutz,* and *die Umweltverschmutzung.* Have students take notes during a walk around their neighborhood on the impact of their community on the environment. Ask *Wie können wir in unserer Stadt die Umwelt besser schützen?* Have students report their findings to the class.

CLASSROOM COMMUNITY

Challenge Have students work with a partner to make a list of words they know related to the vocabulary items on p. 34. Then give them a few more minutes to expand their lists with the use of a dictionary or the vocabulary section in the back of *Auf Deutsch!* Have students share their findings with the class.

CULTURE HIGHLIGHTS

Distribute this *Umfrage* to the class. *Was sind bei Ihnen die wichtigsten Lebensziele? Ordnen Sie die Ziele von 1 bis 5 nach Ihren Prioritäten.*

_____ *Erfolg im Beruf*
_____ *Selbstverwirklichung*
_____ *gute Freunde haben*
_____ *Unabhängigkeit*
_____ *die eigene Familie*
_____ *modische Kleidung*

Before having students indicate their preferences, give examples of the *Lebensziele* in German. For example, *Unabhängigkeit: Ich brauche kein Geld mehr von meinen Eltern. Ich verdiene gut und kann davon leben.* Once students have filled out the *Umfrage,* read through the *Kulturspiegel* and compare students' rankings with those of German youths. Finally, brainstorm other important *Lebensziele* not included in the *Umfrage.*

BLOCK SCHEDULE

Fun Break Prepare note cards with a vocabulary word on each card. Give each student one card. Students must now communicate the meaning of the word on the card to the class in 1 of 3 ways: (1) Pictionary: the student expresses the meaning of the word through a drawing, (2) Charades: the student expresses the meaning of the word through gestures and miming, or (3) Definition: the student gives a definition orally. Do this activity in teams, or individually within small groups.

Strukturen, pp. 36–43

PROGRAM RESOURCES

• Overhead Transparencies 26.2–26.G1
• *Arbeitsheft,* pp. 24–28
• Audio Program, Cassette 1B/CD 1
• Audioscript, pp. 10–12

Quick Start Review 1

♻ *Wo*-compounds
Bilden Sie Fragen mit *wo*-Verbindungen.
MODELL: Ich reagiere auf die Nachricht. → *Worauf reagierst du?*

1. Ich interessiere mich für Kunst.
2. Ich denke oft an die Zukunft.
3. Ich träume immer von meiner Kindheit.
4. Ich engagiere mich für Politik.
5. Ich freue mich auf eine tolle Reise.
6. Ich fahre meistens mit der U-Bahn.

Answers: 1. Wofür interessierst du dich? 2. Woran denkst du oft? 3. Wovon träumst du immer?

4. Wofür engagierst du dich?
5. Worauf freust du dich? 6. Womit fährst du meistens?

Quick Start Review 2

♻ Reflexive pronouns
Ergänzen Sie die Reflexivpronomen.

1. Klara und Markus treffen _____ vor der Uni.
2. Er engagiert _____ für Umweltschutz.
3. Klara möchte _____ gegen falsche Hoffnungen wehren.
4. Interessiert ihr _____ für solche progressiven Ideen?
5. Du ärgerst _____ so über die heutige Jugend.
6. Ich ziehe _____ meine Lederjacke an.
7. Auf der Demonstration haben wir _____ verletzt.
8. Sie haben _____ die ganze Woche nicht entspannen können.

Answers: 1. sich 2. sich 3. sich
4. euch 5. dich 6. mir 7. uns
8. sich

TEACHING SUGGESTIONS

• Review of the accusative and dative cases, pp. 36–37

Write the example sentences on the board and ask students to identify the subject and the accusative and dative objects in each sentence.

• *Übung A*, p. 37

Follow-up: Have students respond to the questions in the negative and then give alternate answers. For example, *Haben Sie den Film zusammen mit Peter gesehen? Nein, ich habe den Film mit meinem Bruder gesehen.*

• *Übung B*, p. 38

Follow-up: Ask questions concerning the content of the exercise. For example, *Welchen Film hat Peter nicht gesehen? Mit wem will Maria nicht ausgehen? Warum nicht?*

• *Übung C*, p. 38

Remind students of the similarity of the question words to the masculine definite articles and the masculine pronouns: *wer – der – er; wen – den – ihn; wem – dem – ihm.*

• Review of accusative, dative, and accusative/dative prepositions, pp. 41–43

Point out that the phenomenon of two-way prepositions is connected to the distinction between direction and location as well as the transitivity or the intransitivity of positional verbs (*setzen, stellen, legen* vs. *sitzen, stehen, liegen*). Also point out the principal parts of transitive verbs are regular, while those of intransitive verbs are irregular.

• *Übung B*, p. 43

Point out that certain verbs are always accompanied by certain prepositions, for example, *reagieren auf, sich wehren gegen, sich freuen auf, führen zu, sich interessieren für,* and *suchen nach.*

TEACHING ALL STUDENTS

Multiple Intelligences Visual: Place objects you have described to students in various places around the room, for example, under a chair, on a cabinet, or between 2 desks. Have students look for the objects and write sentences describing their location. Then move the objects and have students write sentences describing what you did.

CLASSROOM COMMUNITY

Paired Activity Have students work in pairs to formulate as many definitions of familial relations as they can using the genitive case. For example, *der Onkel: Der Onkel ist der Bruder meines Vaters (oder meiner Mutter). Der Onkel ist auch der Mann meiner Tante.* Then have students exchange partners and quiz each other. For example, *Wer ist der Bruder meines Vaters?*

BLOCK SCHEDULE

Retention Tell how the famous composer Johann Strauß *der Jüngere* wrote a composition to help a teacher-friend explain dative prepositions. Originally entitled *Der Walzer der Dativpräpositionen*, the piece would later be known as *An der schönen blauen Donau*. Play a recording of the Blue Danube Waltz and have students sing the dative prepositions: *aus, außer, bei, mit – nach, seit – von, zu . . .*

Perspektiven, pp. 44–48

PROGRAM RESOURCES

• *Arbeitsheft*, pp. 29–32
• Audio Program, Cassette 1B, 7A/ CD 1, 9
• Audioscript, pp. 12–13
• www.mcdougallittell.com

Quick Start Review 1

♻ Subordinating conjunction *dass*
Bilden Sie Sätze mit der Konjunktion *dass.*

MODELL: Er sagte: „Ich komme aus Leipzig." → *Er sagte, dass er aus Leipzig kommt.*

1. Sie sagte: „Meine Eltern sind sehr autoritär."
2. Der Mann berichtet: „Acht Prozent der Kinder haben Angst."
3. Wir erzählten: „Bei uns ist der Erziehungsstil viel progressiver."
4. Katrins Mutter meinte: „Ich kann die Jugend von heute nicht verstehen."
5. Habt ihr gesagt: „Wir werden strenge Eltern sein."?
6. Du erzählst immer: „Damals war es ganz anders."

Answers: 1. Sie sagte, dass ihre Eltern sehr autoritär sind.   2. Der Mann berichtet, dass acht Prozent der Kinder Angst haben.   3. Wir erzählten, dass bei uns der Erziehungsstil viel progressiver ist.   4. Katrins Mutter meinte, dass sie die Jugend von heute nicht verstehen kann.   5. Habt ihr gesagt, dass ihr strenge Eltern sein werdet?   6. Du erzählst immer, dass es damals ganz anders war.

Quick Start Review 2

♻ Simple past
Wählen Sie die passende Form im Imperfekt.

1. Zum Frühstück _____ wir Brötchen mit Butter und Marmelade.
   a. aßen   b. saßen
   c. gegessen   d. isst
2. Ich _____ Kaffee mit Milch.
   a. traf   b. trankst
   c. trank   d. trinke
3. Mein Vater _____ die Zeitung.
   a. lag   b. lasse
   c. las   d. liest

4. Dann _____ er ein paar Eier.
   a. koch   b. kochen
   c. kocht   d. kochte
5. Das Geschirr _____ ich in die Küche.
   a. breche   b. brachte
   c. bringt   d. brachtet
6. Um drei Uhr _____ sie in die Stadt.
   a. fuhren   b. führen
   c. für   d. fährt
7. Sie _____ bei dem großen Kaufhaus an.
   a. kämmen   b. kämen
   c. kamen   d. kommen
8. Du _____ schon da.
   a. wurdest   b. warst
   c. war   d. wirst
9. An dem Tag _____ du in der Frauenabteilung.
   a. arbeitest   b. arbeite
   c. arbeitetet   d. arbeitetest
10. Ihr _____ zusammen ins Restaurant.
   a. ginst   b. gingt
   c. gegangen   d. gähnt

Answers: 1. a   2. c   3. c   4. d   5. b   6. a   7. c   8. b   9. d   10. b

....

TEACHING SUGGESTIONS

• *Hören Sie zu!,* p. 44

Read through the introductory passage with students before listening to the report. Also have them look over *Wortschatz.* Have them listen as they consider these questions: *Sind die Eltern heute so streng wie damals? Was war damals anders als heute? Was durften Kinder damals machen? Was nicht? Was dürfen Kinder heute*

machen? Was nicht? Have them jot down ideas and then collect responses on the board under the headings *Erziehungsstile: Damals / Heute.* As a follow up, compare the students' responses with the information presented in the report.

• *Aktivität A,* p. 44

Have students conduct a survey by asking each other the following questions: *Hältst du deine Eltern für gute Freunde? Hast du manchmal Angst vor deinen Eltern? Sind deine Eltern sehr streng?* Collect the results and compare them to the results in the report.

• *Aktivität B,* pp. 44–45

The results of the survey from *Culture Highlights,* (TE, p. 30G) could be included in the table. Discuss differences among cultures and have students guess at their causes.

• *Lesen Sie!,* pp. 45–47

Have students first review the *Wortschatz zum Lesen* on p. 47 before reading the text. Make sure they avoid using their dictionaries, only looking up words that are absolutely necessary for their comprehension of the text.

• *Zum Thema,* p. 45

Read through the introductory paragraph and discuss the questions. Students may respond more readily to general questions than to personal ones in a class discussion. Elicit responses concerning *gewöhnliche Ängste und Probleme* and *mögliche Lösungen* and list them on the board.

Preview the text with students. Explain the context of the reading and have students read the first paragraph to themselves. Ask them to give the gist of what they have read and, if possible, a detail or two.

• *Zum Text,* p. 47

Review the text as a class as needed, before students work in pairs. Have students support their answers with passages from the text.

• *Schreiben Sie!,* p. 47

Have students brainstorm for points that would help gain support for the plan to establish a youth center. Have students argue the legitimacy of their ideas.

• *Schreibmodell,* p. 48

Have students skim the text, then ask them *Was werden die Jugendlichen im Jugendzentrum alles machen können? Wann findet der Diskussionsabend statt?*

• *Tipp zum Schreiben,* p. 48

Give students time to collect the vocabulary they need for their flyers. Offer help and make suggestions.

• *Nach dem Schreiben,* p. 48

Have students post their flyers in the classroom and critique one another's work. Ask *Ist das Flugblatt wirkungsvoll? Warum? Warum nicht? Wie könnte man es verbessern? usw.*

TEACHING ALL STUDENTS

Multiple Intelligences Intrapersonal: In *Notgroschen für das Sorgentelefon,* Rolf has a diary. In class or as homework, have students write brief diary entries for a few days. Suggest that they write about their relationships with friends, parents, and teachers, or about the difficulties they face as teenagers.

CLASSROOM COMMUNITY

Group Activity Role-play a city council or town meeting. Divide the class into board members (or town meeting members), young representatives of the initiative, and local citizens. Have the young representatives present their proposal and engage in a debate with the board members. The local citizens can join in the discussion on either side. To enliven the debate, you can distribute note cards with brief descriptions of the players. For example, *Sie sind ein alter Knacker, der keine Jugendlichen mag,* or *Sie sind ein junger, sehr idealistischer Aktivist.*

LANGUAGE NOTE

Point out the use of the comparative in the *Schreibmodell: ruhigere Straßen, angenehmeres Alltagsleben.* Remind students that adjective endings are added on to the comparative *-er.*

INTERDISCIPLINARY CONNECTION

Have students obtain information from their social studies teachers about city council or town meeting protocol where they live and about the process necessary to establish such a youth center in their community.

BLOCK SCHEDULE

Expansion Ask students *Warum führt man ein Tagebuch?* and collect answers

on the board. Then have students scan *"Notgroschen für das Sorgentelefon"* for references to Rolf's *Tagebuch.* Discuss these references and have students begin the assignment in class of re-creating Rolf's *Tagebuch,* complete with sketches and reflections. They can complete it as homework.

Research There are countless *Jugendzentren* in German-speaking countries and many of them have active Web sites. Have students search using the keyword *Jugendzentrum* and gather information (*was? wann? wo?*) on the types of activities and events offered by at least 3 youth centers. Such information is most often found on a page entitled *Aktuelles* or *Veranstaltungen.* Have students report back to class with their findings.

PORTFOLIO

Grade the students' flyers using the following rubric.

RUBIC **A** = 13–15 pts. **B** = 10–12 pts.
C = 7–9 pts. **D** = 4–6 pts. **F** = <4 pts.

Writing Criteria	Scale				
Vocabulary use	1	2	3	4	5
Grammatical accuracy	1	2	3	4	5
Layout, graphics	1	2	3	4	5

PROJECT

Have students choose a famous person from a German-speaking country, research his or her youth, and give oral presentations on what they learn.

KAPITEL 26

JUGEND

In diesem Kapitel

- sehen Sie, wie sich die Vorstellungen der Jugendlichen in den letzten Jahrzehnten geändert haben.
- erfahren Sie, wie deutsche Jugendliche von heute ihre Zukunft planen.

Sie werden auch

- über Jugendliche und Politik diskutieren.
- die Kasusformen des Nominativs, Akkusativs und Dativs wiederholen.
- wiederholen, wie man den Genitiv benutzt.
- den Gebrauch von Präpositionen wiederholen.
- eine Geschichte über einen deutschen Jugendlichen lesen.
- ein Flugblatt schreiben.

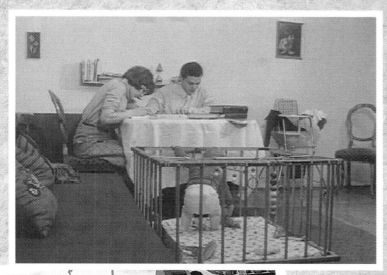

Die Ideale der fünfziger Jahre:
Ausbildung, Familie und Beruf.

Schweizer Gymnasiasten
am Rheinufer in Basel.

Jetzt können Jugendliche zwischen
verschiedenen Lebensstilen wählen.

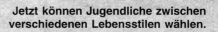

VIDEOTHEK

Die Jugendbewegungen der sechziger und siebziger Jahre haben zu neuen Möglichkeiten und Lebensstilen geführt. Was waren die Ziele und Hoffnungen der Jugend damals und wie sieht die Zukunft für junge Leute von heute aus?

I: Jugend in Bewegung

In dieser Folge hören Sie, wie sich das Bild der Jugendlichen in den letzten fünfzig Jahren geändert hat.

A Die letzten fünf Jahrzehnte werden durch bestimmte Ereignisse charakterisiert. Schauen Sie sich das Video an. Welches Ereignis passt zu welchem Jahrzehnt?

Studentenprotest in den sechziger Jahren.

die fünfziger Jahre   die siebziger Jahre
        die sechziger Jahre
die neunziger Jahre   die achtziger Jahre

1. Die wichtigen Themen sind Frieden, soziale Gerechtigkeit und Umweltschutz.
2. Der Rock 'n' Roll ist Ausdruck des Protests gegen die Ideale der Eltern.
3. Die Demonstrationen waren am Anfang friedlich.
4. Der Protest ist leiser geworden, dafür die Musik etwas lauter.
5. Junge Leute fangen an, ihre eigene Kultur zu schaffen.
6. Musik und lange Haare sind Zeichen des Protests.
7. Es gibt große Techno-Parties für Jugendliche aus ganz Europa.

WORTSCHATZ ZUM VIDEO

über einen Kamm scheren	to treat everyone alike
der Wandel	change
die fünfziger Jahre	the Fifties
träg	lazy; sluggish
das Bestehende	the prevailing situation
auf Tour	on the road
schick	chic; stylish
sich selbst verwirklichen	to develop one's personality; to fulfill oneself

B Wer sagt das im Video, Susanne, Erika oder Stefan?

1. Viele Jugendliche sind desillusioniert.
2. Es gibt unterschiedliche Typen von Jugendlichen.
3. Man ist politisch nicht sehr interessiert.
4. Alles wird jetzt in Frage gestellt.
5. Diese Person ist in der SPD, bei den Jungsozialisten.
6. Diese Person beschreibt die deutsche Jugend als „sehr, sehr gute junge Leute".

C Ereignisse. Sie haben ein bisschen über die Ereignisse in den letzten Jahrzehnten in deutschsprachigen Ländern gelernt. Welche dieser Ereignisse hat man auch in Ihrem Land erlebt? Wie waren die Ereignisse in Europa und in Nordamerika ähnlich? Wie waren sie anders? *C. Answers will vary.*

Ulla.

II: Drei Jugendporträts

In dieser Folge lernen Sie drei Jugendliche kennen. Welche Hoffnungen haben sie für die Zukunft?

A Was stimmt? Was stimmt nicht? Wenn ein Satz nicht stimmt, geben Sie die richtige Information.

MODELL: Ulla möchte Psychologie studieren. →
Das stimmt nicht. Ulla möchte Meeresbiologie studieren.

1. Ulla ist Studentin an der Uni.   See answers below.
2. Ramona lernt Floristin.
3. Kristian ist in Kroatien geboren.
4. Ramona wohnt in München, in Süddeutschland.
5. Kristian ist mit seiner Ausbildung fertig.
6. Ulla findet, das Wichtigste ist einfach leben.
7. Kristian will seine privaten Ziele sofort verwirklichen.
8. Ramona möchte beides haben, Karriere und Familie.

Kristian.

B. 1. Ramona   2. Kristian   3. Ulla

B Zukunftsträume. Wer ist das, Ulla, Kristian oder Ramona?

1. Diese Person möchte eine große Familie, also viele Kinder, haben. Erfolg ist dieser Person sehr wichtig, aber nicht unbedingt wegen des Geldes.
2. Diese Person ist sehr optimistisch, will sich ein eigenes Haus und ein großes, schickes Auto kaufen, und vielleicht auch eine Familie haben.
3. Diese Person will sich selbst verwirklichen und studieren. Das Leben ist viel wichtiger als das Geld.

Ramona.

C Eine neue Bekanntschaft. Stellen Sie sich vor, Sie können Ulla, Kristian oder Ramona kennen lernen. Wen möchten Sie am liebsten kennen lernen? Warum finden Sie diese Person besonders interessant? Wie stellen Sie sich das Treffen vor? Was unternehmen Sie zusammen? *C. Answers will vary.*

KULTURSPIEGEL

Mit der Wiedervereinigung veränderte sich das Leben für Jugendliche im Osten wie Ramona Baum. Die staatlichen Jugendorganisationen, wie zum Beispiel die Freie Deutsche Jugend (FDJ), verschwanden. Auch wegen Veränderungen in der Regierung und in der Wirtschaft hatten junge Leute nicht mehr die Garantie eines zukünftigen Jobs. Während viele junge Leute sich über ihr neues Leben freuten, hatten sie auch Angst vor den Unsicherheiten der Zukunft.

VOKABELN

die Auseinandersetzung	*dispute, argument*
die Bewegung	*movement*
die Gerechtigkeit	*justice*
die Identität	*identity*
die Suche	*search*
die Zukunft	*future*
der Einfluss	*influence*
der Frieden	*peace*
der/die Jugendliche (*decl. adj.*)	*young person, teenager*
der Lebensstil	*lifestyle*
der Staatsbürger / die Staatsbürgerin	*citizen*
der Wandel	*change*
das Ideal	*ideal*
das Jahrzehnt	*decade*
das Ziel	*goal, aim*
an•passen (+ *dat.*)	*to conform to*
begeistern	*to inspire; to make enthusiastic*
diskutieren über (+ *acc.*)	*to discuss*
sich engagieren für	*to get involved in*
führen zu	*to lead to*
gestalten	*to shape*
reagieren auf (+ *acc.*)	*to react to*
teil•nehmen an (+ *dat.*)	*to take part in*
um•gehen: mit etwas umgehen	*to deal with, handle*

Jugendliche bei einer Diskussion.

wählen	*to choose; to elect; to vote*
sich wehren gegen	*to defend oneself against*
angepasst	*conformist*
ehrgeizig	*ambitious(ly)*
friedlich	*peaceful(ly)*
gewalttätig	*violent(ly)*
leise	*soft(ly), quiet(ly)*
unterschiedlich	*various*
vergangen	*past; preceding*

Sie wissen schon
der Erfolg, erleben

Aktivitäten

A Bedeutungen. Welche Wörter aus der Vokabelliste passen zu den folgenden Bedeutungen?

1. junge Menschen
2. die erst kommende Zeit, zum Beispiel morgen, nächste Woche, nächstes Jahr, . . .

A. **1.** Jugendliche **2.** die Zukunft **3.** der Staatsbürger **4.** ehrgeizig **5.** sich engagieren für **6.** angepasst **7.** begeistern **8.** friedlich **9.** der Erfolg **10.** Wandel

3. Mitglied des Staates: Man darf einen Pass dieses Landes haben.
4. ambitiös
5. starkes, persönliches Interesse für etwas haben
6. konformistisch
7. erfreuen, entflammen
8. freundschaftlich, wohlwollend
9. positives Resultat nach viel Arbeit
10. Justiz

B Welches Wort passt? Ergänzen Sie die Sätze mit Hilfe der Wortliste.

anpassen
Auseinandersetzungen
engagiert
Jahrzehnt
vergangenen
Suche
friedlich

B. 1. Suche 2. engagiert 3. Auseinandersetzungen 4. anpassen 5. Jahrzehnt 6. friedlich 7. vergangenen

1. Die _____ nach Identität ist für die Jugend ein wichtiger Teil des Lebens.
2. In den sechziger Jahren haben sich viele Jugendliche für Politik _____.
3. Damals gab es viele gewalttätige _____ auf den Straßen.
4. Nicht alle jungen Leute waren Radikale; es gab auch viele, die sich den Idealen der Eltern _____ wollten.
5. Die fünfziger Jahre waren das _____ des Rock 'n' Roll.
6. Die Studenten wollten, dass alle Menschen _____ zusammenlebten.
7. In den _____ Jahren hat sich das Bild über die Jugendlichen stark geändert.

C Arbeiten Sie in Gruppen. Jede Gruppe wählt eine der folgenden Thesen. Die Hälfte der Gruppe sucht jetzt nach Argumenten, die die These stützen, die andere Hälfte sucht nach Argumenten dagegen. Diskutieren Sie anschließend alle gemeinsam die These mit Hilfe der gefundenen Pro- und Contra-Argumente.

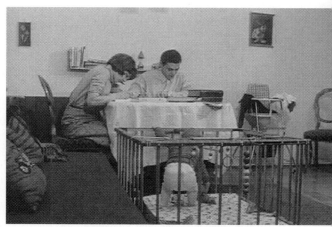

Eine junge Familie in den fünfziger Jahren.

C. *Answers will vary.*

• man soll alles tun, um die Umwelt zu schützen
• die heutige Jugend denkt nicht an die Zukunft
• Jugendliche können keinen Einfluss auf die Welt üben
• Erfolg heißt viel Geld haben

STRUKTUREN

REVIEW OF THE ACCUSATIVE AND DATIVE CASES
MARKING DIRECT AND INDIRECT OBJECTS

In German, the accusative case marks the direct object of a sentence; the direct object tells who or what is immediately affected by the action.

Ich kenne **diesen Mann** nicht.	*I don't know this man.*
Er macht **das Fenster** auf.	*He's opening the window.*

The dative case identifies the indirect object, which tells who benefits from or receives the result of the action.

Ich gebe **meiner Schwester** einen Rat.	*I'm giving my sister some advice.*
Frau Stumpf hat **mir** Abendessen gekocht.	*Frau Stumpf cooked dinner for me.*

Here are the forms of the definite and indefinite articles in the nominative, accusative, and dative cases.

KURZ NOTIERT

Some masculine nouns take special endings in the accusative and dative cases. Three common ones are:

der Herr → den/dem Herr**n**
ein Herr → einen/einem Herr**n**

der Nachbar → den Nachbar**n**
ein Nachbar → einen/einem Nachbar**n**

der Student → den/dem Student**en**
ein Student → einen/einem Student**en**

der Tourist → den/dem Tourist**en**
ein Tourist → einen/einem Tourist**en**

		SINGULAR			PLURAL
		FEMININE	MASCULINE	NEUTER	ALL GENDERS
NOMINATIVE		**die** Frau	**der** Mann	**das** Kind	**die** Kinder
		eine Frau	**ein** Mann	**ein** Kind	**keine** Kinder
ACCUSATIVE		**die** Frau	**den** Mann	**das** Kind	**die** Kinder
		eine Frau	**einen** Mann	**ein** Kind	**keine** Kinder
DATIVE		**der** Frau	**dem** Mann	**dem** Kind	**den** Kinder**n**
		einer Frau	**einem** Mann	**einem** Kind	**keinen** Kinder**n**

A personal pronoun can also stand as the subject, direct object, or indirect object of a sentence.

Hat der Vater seiner Tochter den Mantel gegeben?	*Did the father give his daughter the coat?*
Ja, **er** hat **ihn ihr** gegeben.	*Yes, he gave it to her.*

Remember, the indirect object usually precedes the direct object, unless the direct object is a pronoun.

Also recall that a pronoun must agree in gender, case, and number with the noun it replaces. The forms of the personal pronouns in the nominative, accusative, and dative cases are as follows.

NOMINATIVE	ACCUSATIVE	DATIVE
SUBJECT	DIRECT OBJECT	INDIRECT OBJECT
ich *I*	mich *me*	mir *(to/for) me*
du *you*	dich *you*	dir *(to/for) you*
Sie *you*	Sie *you*	Ihnen *(to/for) you*
sie *she*	sie *her*	ihr *(to/for) her*
er *he*	ihn *him*	ihm *(to/for) him*
es *it*	es *it*	ihm *(to/for) it*
wir *we*	uns *us*	uns *(to/for) us*
ihr *you*	euch *you*	euch *(to/for) you*
Sie *you*	Sie *you*	Ihnen *(to/for) you*
sie *they*	sie *them*	ihnen *(to/for) them*

A number of German verbs frequently have both an accusative and a dative object. Such verbs include **erklären, erzählen, geben, schenken, schicken, schreiben, wünschen,** and **zeigen** among others.

| Der Lehrer erklärt dem Studenten die Antwort. | *The teacher is explaining the answer to the student.* |
| Ich erzähle meinem Freund eine Geschichte. | *I'm telling my friend a story.* |

A small number of verbs have only dative objects. Some of these are **danken, gefallen, gehören, helfen,** and **schmecken.**

| Könnten Sie **mir** helfen? | *Could you help me?* |
| Dieser Pulli gefällt **mir** nicht. | *I don't like this sweater.* |

Übungen

A So viele Fragen. Akkusativ oder Dativ? Ergänzen Sie die Fragen mit der richtigen Form des bestimmten Artikels.ᵃ

A. **1.** den **2.** den **3.** dem **4.** das **5.** den **6.** die **7.** der

1. Haben Sie _____ Film mit Peter gesehen?
2. Haben Sie _____ Kindern ein Eis gekauft?
3. Haben Sie _____ Mann einen guten Rat gegeben?
4. Könnten Sie bitte _____ Fenster aufmachen?
5. Möchten Sie _____ neuen Mitarbeitern die Situation erklären?
6. Kennen Sie _____ Frau von nebenan?
7. Möchten Sie _____ Lehrerin Blumen schenken?

ᵃ*definite article*

B. 1. ihn **2.** er **3.** es **4.** ihm **5.** sie **6.** ihn

C. 1. Wem hat Jutta ein Geschenk gekauft?
2. Wer hat das Abendessen gekocht? **3.** Wer war sehr froh? **4.** Wem habt ihr mit dem Essen geholfen? **5.** Wen hast du eingeladen?

URZ NOTIERT

As you recall, the German interrogative pronoun for *who/whom* has three forms: **wer** (nominative), **wen** (accusative), and **wem** (dative).

Wer ist dieser Junge?
Who is that boy?
Wen rufen Sie an?
Whom are you calling?
Wem erzählst du den Witz?
Whom are you telling the joke to?

Even though English speakers frequently use *who* instead of *whom*, German requires the correct form for each case.

D. 1. mir, ihm, uns **2.** dir, ihr, einer Studentin **3.** mir, uns Schülern, den Kindern **4.** Herrn Lenz, den Studentinnen, dem Studenten **5.** der Lehrerin, dem Direktor, den Nachbarn

B Eine Verabredung. Ergänzen Sie das Gespräch zwischen Peter und Maria mit dem richtigen Pronomen.

MARIA: Hast du den Film „Jenseits der Stille" gesehen?
PETER: Nein, ich habe _____¹ noch nicht gesehen. Wo läuft _____²?
MARIA: In dem kleinen Kino nebenan. Kennst du _____³?
PETER: Ja, ich gehe oft dahin. Vielleicht kann Jens auch mitkommen.
MARIA: Naja, ich will nicht mit _____⁴ ausgehen. Er hat meine neuen CDs ausgeliehen, und ich habe _____⁵ noch nicht zurückbekommen.
PETER: Also kannst du _____⁶ heute Abend fragen, wenn wir uns treffen!

C Was sagt Ihr Freund über ein Familienfest? Was fragen Sie ihn, um alles richtig zu verstehen? Stellen Sie Fragen mit der richtigen Form von **wer.**

MODELL: *Meine Schwester Jutta* ist zu Besuch gekommen. →
Wer ist zu Besuch gekommen?

1. Jutta hat *meiner Mutter* ein Geschenk gekauft.
2. *Jens* hat das Abendessen gekocht.
3. *Meine Tante und ich* waren sehr froh.
4. Wir haben *ihm* mit dem Essen geholfen.
5. Ich habe *meine Freundin* eingeladen.

D In der Schule / auf der Uni. Ergänzen Sie die Sätze mit der richtigen Form der Wörter in Klammern.

1. Das Essen in der Mensa schmeckt _____ nicht. (ich, er, wir)
2. Dieses Buch gehört _____. (du, sie [*sg.*], eine Studentin)
3. Die Lehrer haben _____ immer geholfen. (ich, wir Schüler, die Kinder)
4. Die neue Bibliothek gefällt _____ sehr. (Herr Lenz, die Studentinnen, der Student)
5. Wir haben _____ herzlich gedankt. (die Lehrerin, der Direktor, die Nachbar)

REVIEW OF THE GENITIVE CASE
SHOWING RELATIONSHIPS AND POSSESSION

You have learned to use the preposition **von** to talk about relationships and possessions.

Die Freunde **von** meinem Sohn waren besonders nett.
My son's friends were particularly nice.

In more formal writing, the genitive case indicates family or personal relationships, ownership, and characteristics of persons, objects, or ideas.

FAMILY RELATIONSHIP
Die Eltern **des Jungen** waren böse.
The boy's parents were angry.

OWNERSHIP
Die Schultasche **des Jungen** war schwarz.
The boy's school bag was black.

CHARACTERISTICS OF PERSONS/OBJECTS/IDEAS
Die Laune **des Jungen** war schlecht.
The boy's mood was bad.

The following table shows the forms of the definite article and the endings for **der-** and **ein-**words in the genitive case.

	SINGULAR		PLURAL
FEMININE	MASCULINE	NEUTER	ALL GENDERS
der Mutter dies**er** Mutter mein**er** Mutter	**des** Vaters dies**es** Vaters mein**es** Vaters	**des** Kindes dies**es** Kindes mein**es** Kindes	**der** Kinder dies**er** Kinder mein**er** Kinder

Note that most masculine and neuter nouns add **-s** in the genitive case. Masculine and neuter nouns of just one syllable add **-es.** Also, masculine nouns that add **-n** or **-en** in the dative and accusative also add **-n** or **-en** in the genitive case.

Der Vater beantwortet die Fragen **des Polizisten.**
The father answers the policeman's questions.

Das Leben **eines Studenten** kann schwierig sein.
A student's life can be difficult.

Furthermore, as you already know, the genitive case follows certain prepositions: **wegen** (*because of*), **außerhalb** (*outside of*), **innerhalb** (*inside of*), **trotz** (*in spite of*), and **während** (*during, in the time of*). Notice that the English equivalents frequently contain the preposition *of.*

Wegen **des Telefongesprächs** war Rolf erleichtert.
Während **seiner Reise** schrieb Rolf in sein Tagebuch.

Rolf was at ease because of the phone call.
During his trip Rolf wrote in his diary.

In German, the noun in the genitive case usually follows the noun it modifies, whereas the opposite is true in English.

die Rolle des Mannes
the husband's role

The genitive form occasionally comes first in antiquated German constructions.

Wo ist des Deutschen Vaterland?
Where is the German's homeland?

A. 1. Das Bild der Jugendlichen hat sich stark verändert. **2.** Der Protest der Studenten war am Anfang friedlich. **3.** Die Ziele der Demonstration waren Frieden und Umweltschutz. **4.** Der Unterrichtsstil des Lehrers war damals sehr streng. **5.** Die Rede des Kanzlers war sehr wichtig.

B. 1. Die fünfziger Jahre waren das Jahrzehnt des Rock 'n' Rolls. **2.** Die sechziger Jahre waren das Jahrzehnt des Wandels, der Hippies und des Vietnam-Kriegs. **3.** Die siebziger Jahre waren das Jahrzehnt der Disko und der Inflation. **4.** Die achtziger Jahre waren das Jahrzehnt des Wandels und der Glasnost. **5.** Die neunziger Jahre waren das Jahrzehnt des Wandels und der Techno-Partys.

In conversational German, the dative frequently replaces the genitive after these prepositions.

A small number of verbs also takes the genitive case: **bedürfen** (*to have need of*) and **gedenken** (*to recall, remember*) among others.

Er bedarf **meiner Hilfe.**	*He has need of my help.*
Ich gedenke oft **des schönen Tages** in Basel.	*I often recall the nice day in Basel.*

Übungen

A Protest und Politik. Schreiben Sie die Sätze neu. Benutzen Sie den Genitiv und nicht Dativ.

MODELL: Die Geschichte von dem alten Gymnasium war interessant. →
Die Geschichte des alten Gymnasiums war interessant.

1. Das Bild über die Jugendlichen hat sich stark verändert.
2. Der Protest von den Studenten war am Anfang friedlich.
3. Die Ziele von der Demonstration waren Frieden und Umweltschutz.
4. Der Unterrichtsstil von dem Lehrer war damals sehr streng.
5. Die Rede von dem Kanzler war sehr wichtig.

B Unser Jahrhundert. Was assoziieren Sie mit den vergangenen Jahrzehnten?

MODELL: Die fünfziger Jahre waren das Jahrzehnt des Rock 'n' Rolls.

der Rock 'n' Roll   die Disko
die Inflation   der Wandel
die Techno-Partys   die Glasnost
der Vietnam-Krieg   die Hippies

1. die fünfziger Jahre
2. die sechziger Jahre
3. die siebziger Jahre
4. die achtziger Jahre
5. die neunziger Jahre

REVIEW OF ACCUSATIVE, ACCUSATIVE/ DATIVE, AND DATIVE PREPOSITIONS
COMBINING WORDS AND CONNECTING IDEAS

Different prepositions require nouns in different cases, sometimes depending on the meaning of the sentence. The following group of nouns requires only the accusative case: **durch** (*through*), **für** (*for*), **gegen** (*against*), **ohne** (*without*), **um/herum** (*around*).

> Ramona geht **durch** den Blumenladen.
> Viele Jugendliche engagieren sich **für** die Umwelt.
> Sie demonstrieren **gegen** die Umweltverschmutzung.
> **Ohne** eine Ausbildung bekommt man schlechte Arbeit.
> Die Demonstranten marschieren **um** die Altstadt (**herum**).

Another group of prepositions takes the accusative case to indicate motion, and the dative case to indicate location: **an** (*to; at*); **auf** (*to; on*); **hinter** (*behind*); **in** (*in; into*); **neben** (*beside, next to*); **über** (*over, above*); **unter** (*under, beneath, below*); **vor** (*before; in front of*); and **zwischen** (*between*).

ACCUSATIVE	DATIVE
Ich gehe **auf die Bank.**	Ich arbeite **auf der Bank.**
Er stellt die Vase **auf den Tisch.**	Die Vase steht **auf dem Tisch.**
Er parkt das Auto **vor das Hotel.**	Das Auto steht **vor dem Hotel.**

Many verbs also combine with the prepositions **an, auf,** and **über,** such as **denken an** (*to think about*), **sich freuen auf** (*to look forward to*), and **diskutieren über** (*to talk about*). The prepositions in these three verbal expressions take the accusative case.

> Er denkt oft **an sie.** — *He often thinks about her.*
> Sie freut sich **auf ihre Reise.** — *She's looking forward to her trip.*
> Wir haben **über die Umwelt** gesprochen. — *We discussed the environment.*

However, these same prepositions take the dative case with certain other verbs in other expressions.

> Wir nehmen **an einer Demo** teil. — *We're taking part in a demonstration.*
> Sie ist **an dieser Tat** schuld. — *She's guilty of this deed.*
> Ich erkenne ihn **an seiner Stimme.** — *I recognize him by his voice.*

KURZ NOTIERT

Recall these two idiomatic expressions with dative prepositions: **nach Hause,** which occurs with verbs of motion such as **fahren, gehen,** and **kommen;** and **zu Hause,** which occurs with verbs of location such as **arbeiten, bleiben,** and **sein.**

Er fährt morgen **nach Hause.**
He's driving home tomorrow.
Er bleibt den ganzen Tag **zu Hause.**
He'll stay home the entire day.

Do not confuse these verb/preposition combinations with two-part verbs, in which the preposition is part of the infinitive (**anrufen, aufgeben**) but goes at the end of a sentence when the verb is in the main clause: **Er ruft mich oft an.**

The following group of prepositions always takes the dative case: **aus** (*from; out of*); **außer** (*besides, except for*); **bei** (*with; at the home of; next to; near*); **gegenüber** (*across*); **mit** (*with; along with; by means of*); **nach** (*to a place; after*); **seit** (*since; for an amount of time*); **von** (*of; from*); **zu** (*to; for an occasion*)

> **Außer dem neuen Schüler** nimmt die ganze Klasse an der Demonstration teil.
> Wohnen Jugendliche in Deutschland meistens **bei den Eltern**?

Übungen

A Drei Jugendporträts. Ergänzen Sie die Sätze.

Ramona bei der Arbeit.

A. **1.** einem Dorf; sie; der Natur **2.** einer Bank; der Schulzeit; der U-Bahn; ihn **3.** ihrer Mutter; die Zukunft

1. Ramona wohnt in _____ (ein Dorf) nicht weit von Erfurt. Sie lernt Floristin. Das ist für _____ (sie) ein Beruf, der Freude bringt und sehr kreativ ist, weil sie viel mit _____ (die Natur) zu tun hat.
2. Kristian arbeitet auf _____ (eine Bank). Nach _____ (die Schulzeit) hat er dort eine Lehre bekommen. Er fährt jeden Tag mit _____ (die U-Bahn) zur Arbeit. Für _____ (er) sind Geld, Haus und Familie sehr wichtig.
3. Ulla wohnt bei _____ (ihre Mutter). Ulla ist optimistisch und freut sich auf _____ (die Zukunft).

B Jugendliche heute und damals. Ergänzen Sie die Sätze mit der richtigen Präposition.

1. Die Studenten marschieren _____ die Straßen.
2. Die Friedensbewegung protestierte _____ den Krieg.
3. Viele Jugendliche wollen sich nicht _____ Politik engagieren.
4. Wie haben die Demonstranten _____ die Nachricht reagiert?
5. Man muss sich _____ falsche Hoffnungen wehren.
6. Ich freue mich _____ eine bessere Zukunft.
7. Im Klassenzimmer diskutieren wir _____ alles Mögliche.
8. Die Situation damals hatte _____ einer Krise geführt.
9. Die Suche _____ Identität ist für junge Leute sehr wichtig.
10. Ramonas Dorf liegt _____ der Stadt Erfurt.
11. _____ Kristian interessieren sich die drei Jugendlichen nicht für Geld.

Jugendliche müssen große Entscheidungen treffen!

B. 1. über   2. gegen   3. für   4. auf   5. gegen
6. auf   7. über   8. zu   9. nach   10. bei
11. Außer

C Und Sie? Was ist Ihnen und Ihren Mitschülern/Mitschülerinnen wichtig? Finden Sie einen Partner / eine Partnerin, und stellen Sie ihm/ihr die folgenden Fragen. Berichten Sie der Klasse, was Ihr Partner / Ihre Partnerin sagt.

C. *Answers will vary.*

1. Wofür interessierst du dich?
2. Worauf freust du dich?
3. Wovon träumst du?
4. Woran denkst du oft?
5. Woran denkst du nicht oft?
6. Wofür engagierst du dich am liebsten?

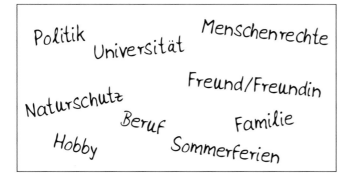

Politik   Universität   Menschenrechte
Freund/Freundin
Naturschutz   Beruf   Familie
Hobby   Sommerferien

FOKUS INTERNET

For more information, visit the **Auf Deutsch!** Web Site at
www.mcdougallittell.com.

PERSPEKTIVEN

HÖREN SIE ZU!
NEUER ERZIEHUNGSSTIL IN ÖSTERREICH

Eltern haben sich auch in den vergangenen Jahrzehnten geändert. Sind die Eltern von heute so streng wie damals? Wie werden die Kinder erzogen? Hören Sie diesen kurzen Bericht, und beantworten Sie dann diese Fragen.

● Was sagen Kinder in Österreich über ihre Eltern? Verbinden Sie die richtigen Satzteile.

1. Die Tendenz führt
2. Ein Drittel sagen, dass
3. Ein Viertel sagen, dass
4. Acht Prozent sagen, dass
5. Die Hälfte sagen, dass

a. die Eltern gute Freunde sind.
b. sie Angst haben.
c. sie tun müssen, was die Eltern sagen.
d. die Eltern sehr streng sind.
e. zu einem weniger autoritären Erziehungsstil.

WORTSCHATZ ZUM HÖRTEXT

der Erziehungsstil	style of parenting
die Forschung	research
berichten	to report
die Befragten	people being asked

1. e 2. d 3. c 4. b 5. a

TIPP ZUM HÖREN

In reportage, subordinate clauses frequently tell what others have said or written.

Die Jugendlichen sagen, dass ihre Eltern nicht mehr so autoritär sind.

Listen for introductory clauses with verbs such as **sagen, berichten, erzählen, fragen,** and so forth, since they often signal subordinate clauses with key information.

LANDESKUNDE IN KÜRZE
JUGENDLICHE IM OSTEN UND IM WESTEN

Sie hören einen Text über deutsche Jugendliche im Osten und im Westen.

Ⓐ Die erste gesamtdeutsche Jugendstudie. Beantworten Sie die folgenden Fragen.

1. Woher kommen die befragten Schüler und Schülerinnen?
2. Wie alt sind die befragten Schüler und Schülerinnen?
3. Die Wissenschaftler haben 1990 diese Studie durchgeführt. Was ist an diesem Datum wichtig? Was können wir von den Ergebnissen lernen?

Ⓑ Prioritäten. Welches Prozent? Machen Sie sich eine Tabelle wie auf Seite 45, und füllen Sie sie aus.

A. 1. Die befragten Schüler und Schülerinnen kommen aus Nordrhein-Westfalen und aus der Region Halle-Leipzig.   2. Die Schüler und Schülerinnen sind zwischen sieben und siebzehn Jahren alt.   3. *Answers will vary. Possible answers are:* Wichtig an dem Datum der Studie ist, dass sie ein Jahr nach der deutschen Wiedervereinigung durchgeführt wurde. Sie zeigt, dass es zwischen den Jugendlichen im Osten und im Westen mehr Gemeinsamkeiten als Unterschiede gibt.

	PROZENTANTEIL IM WESTEN	PROZENTANTEIL IM OSTEN
gute Freunde haben		
Erfolg im Beruf		
die eigene Familie		
Unabhängigkeit		
Selbstverwirklichung		
modische Kleidung		

B. gute Freunde haben: IM WESTEN 76 %; IM OSTEN 67 % Erfolg im Beruf: IM WESTEN 60 %; IM OSTEN 62 % die eigene Familie: IM WESTEN 49 %; IM OSTEN 58 % Unabhängigkeit: IM WESTEN 44 %; IM OSTEN 45 % Selbstverwirklichung: IM WESTEN 31 %; IM OSTEN 32 % modische Kleidung: IM WESTEN 31 %; IM OSTEN 31 %

LESEN SIE!

Zum Thema

Answers will vary.

● Viele junge Menschen zweifeln oft an sich selbst und haben Angst vor Veränderungen und Herausforderungen. Waren Sie selbst schon einmal verzweifelt? Wie haben Sie das Problem gelöst und wie wurden Sie wieder optimistisch? Sie lesen jetzt die Geschichte von einem Schüler, dessen Eltern seine schlechten Noten in der Schule wiederholt mit Hausarrest bestraften.

WORTSCHATZ ZUM LESEN

der Käfig	*cage*
der Versager	*failure*
der Knast (*slang*)	*clink, can*
das Gefängnis	*prison*
der Streich	*trick, prank*
trippeln	*to dance around*
stumm	*silent*
jemanden in die Pfanne hauen	*to be very critical of someone*
der Riss	*crack*

Notgroschen für das Sorgentelefon

„Das ist das Ende", flüsterte Rolf. „He, Rolf", riefen die Freunde aus der Klasse, „kommst du mit ins Schwimmbad?" – Rolf hob den Kopf und schwieg. Er fühlte sich schrecklich – wie in einem Käfig aus
5 dickem Glas. Da war Lars. Er sprang fröhlich auf sein Fahrrad. Lars blickte zu Rolf und wartete auf eine Antwort. Aber Rolf war mit seinen Gedanken weit weg. Dachte er überhaupt an etwas? Nein. Die Wörter flogen ihm weg. Er fühlte sich schlecht: wie
10 ein schwarzer Rabe auf einem schwarzen Baum in der Wüste. Das Bild hatte er in sein Tagebuch gemalt. Vor ein paar Tagen. Er hatte vier Wochen Hausarrest. Für eine Vier in Erdkunde. „Was wollt ihr eigentlich", weinte Rolf, „eine Vier ist doch
15 ausreichend." „Uns reicht das nicht", schimpften die Eltern. – Lars fuhr mit seinem Fahrrad weg. „Er ist mein bester Freund", dachte Rolf. „Aber ich werde ihn auch verlieren."

In seiner Schultasche war das Unglück: eine Vier in Mathematik. „Es muß eine Zwei werden", hatte
20 der Vater gesagt. „Ich habe stundenlang mit dir geübt." Doch dann, bei der Arbeit kam die Panik. Wieder flogen die Gedanken davon. „Du bist besser geworden", hatte der Mathematiklehrer gesagt, „nur ein halber Punkt fehlt, dann wäre es eine Drei
25 Minus." Rolf hörte schon die Worte seiner Eltern. Der Vater: „Du bist einfach miserabel." Die Mutter: „Aus dir wird nie etwas!" Rolf glaubte selbst, daß er ein Versager war. „Kein Wunder, daß du keine Freunde hast", sagten die Eltern. Die wollten ja nur sein
30 Bestes.

Und jetzt saß er auf einer Bank gleich neben der Eisdiele. Er rechnete aus: eine Vier in Mathe, das sind mindestens drei Wochen Knast. Rolf haßte sein Zimmer, es war sein Gefängnis. Bis auf sechs
35 Groschen hatte er sein letztes Taschengeld ausgegeben. Da sah er das kleine gelbe Telefonhäuschen. Manchmal, zu Hause, kam er auf die merkwürdigsten Ideen. Telefonstreiche nannte er

40 das. Er wählte einfach irgendeine Nummer und lauschte der Stimme am anderen Ende, dann legte er wieder auf.

Rolf stand nun in dem Häuschen und wollte wieder Stimmen hören. Eine Nummer für das 45 Sorgentelefon starrte ihn an. Rolf stutzte. Sorgentelefon? „Mal sehen, was die für Sorgen haben", kicherte er, nahm den Hörer in die Hand und wählte. Es klingelte zweimal, eine männliche Stimme meldete sich: „Sorgentelefon für Kinder und 50 Jugendliche." Rolf fiel vor Schreck der Hörer aus der Hand. „Eigentlich", dachte er „müßten meine Eltern da anrufen, die haben ja Sorgen mit ihrem Kind."

Ungefähr eine halbe Stunde trippelte Rolf vor dem gelben Häuschen hin und her, diesem 55 Sorgentelefon wollte er unbedingt einen Streich spielen. Er wählte erneut. Zweimal klingelte es, dann war sie wieder da, diese Stimme. „Nicht unsympathisch", dachte Rolf und sagte kein Wort. „Hallo, wer bist du, melde dich", sagte die Stimme. 60 „Nee", sagte Rolf. „Dann eben nicht", war die Antwort am anderen Ende, und plötzlich fragte die fremde Stimme: „Wie geht es dir?" Er blieb stumm, eine ganze Weile. Die Stimme am anderen Ende blieb auch stumm. Meist wurde dann der Hörer wütend 65 aufgeknallt. Nein, der Mann am anderen Ende blieb ruhig und wartete. „Hallo", hörte er ihn sagen, „willst du dich mit mir unterhalten?" Rolf schluckte einmal und noch einmal, und dann murmelte er muffig: „Warum sollte ich?" „Ja, warum eigentlich", 70 antwortete die Stimme am anderen Ende, „dann leg doch einfach den Hörer wieder auf."

Aber Rolf legte den Hörer nicht wieder auf. Irgendwas hinderte ihn, dem Typ am anderen Ende einfach abzuhängen. „Weißt du, mit wem du sprichst?" fragte Rolf. „Woher soll ich das wissen, du 75 hast dich ja nicht vorgestellt." – Rolf machte eine Pause, und dann wollte er witzig sein: „Du redest mit dem größten Idioten von . . . " stotterte er. – Schweigen. „Nee", sagte die fremde Stimme am anderen Ende der Leitung, „das Spiel mach' ich nicht 80 mit. Du kannst dich ja gerne in die Pfanne hauen, aber mich überzeugst du nicht so schnell davon, daß du ein Idiot bist. Wer hat dir denn diesen Floh ins Ohr gesetzt?"

Rolf verschlug es den Atem. „ . . . Ich muß jetzt 85 Schluß machen", stammelte er. „Okay", antwortete die Stimme, „wenn du Lust hast, kannst du ja mal wieder anrufen." – „Geht nicht", sagte Rolf. „Ich verreise für ungefähr vierzehn Tage", und – peng – knallte er den Hörer auf. Schweißgebadet verließ er 90 die Telefonzelle. „Sorgentelefon . . . ", flüsterte Rolf, „daß ich nicht lache, war der nun nett oder nur ein bißchen doof?"

Die „Reise" dauerte genau siebzehn Tage. Die Eltern hatten den Stubenarrest verschärft. Rolf 95 schrieb in dieser Zeit lange Briefe in sein Tagebuch, und kein einziges Mal stand darin: Ich hasse mich. Irgendwie ahnte er, daß er doch nicht ganz allein auf der Welt war, daß es sogar für ihn noch Freunde gab. Den Telefonstreich wollte er wiederholen. Seit 100 diesem Gespräch, das spürte Rolf ganz deutlich, hatte das Glas von seinem Käfig, in dem er sich oft gefangen fühlte, Risse und Sprünge bekommen.

Zum Text

1. Das stimmt. **2.** Das stimmt. **3.** Das stimmt.
4. Das stimmt nicht. **5.** Das stimmt. **6.** Das
stimmt nicht. **7.** Das stimmt.

A Was wissen Sie über Rolf? Was stimmt? Was stimmt nicht?

1. Für jede schlechte Note muss Rolf mit mehr Hausarrest rechnen.
2. Um seine Einsamkeit zu überwinden, ruft er manchmal sogar fremde Leute an.
3. Rolf ist erstaunt, dass der Mann beim Sorgentelefon mit ihm sprechen will.
4. Der Mann am Sorgentelefon glaubt Rolf alles, was er sagt.
5. Rolf legt auf, weil er nichts mehr hören will.
6. Während der siebzehn Tage Hausarrest wird Rolfs negatives Selbstbildnis[a] noch schlimmer.
7. Im Endeffekt meint Rolf, dass es noch Hoffnung für ihn gibt.

[a]*self-portrait*

B Warum hält Rolf so wenig von sich selbst? Welche Personen und Ereignisse tragen zu Rolfs negativem Selbstbildnis bei? Welche Gefahren gibt es für einsame Teenager mit schlechtem Selbstwertgefühl? Wie könnte jemand wie Rolf ein positiveres Selbstbildnis entwickeln?

Answers will vary.

SCHREIBEN SIE!

Ein Flugblatt

Texts will vary.

● Schreiben Sie ein Flugblatt, mit dem Sie für die Gründung eines neuen Jugendzentrums in ihrer Stadt werben wollen.

Purpose:	To gain support for a citizen action program
Audience:	Adult residents and students of your hometown
Subject:	Plans for a new youth center in town
Structure:	Handbill or flyer

Schreibmodell

> **„Aktion Jugendzentrum"**
> *sucht Ihre Unterstützung*
> *für einen Treffpunkt für die Jugendlichen*
> *von Eschenbach*
>
> **„Aktion Jugendzentrum" möchte einen**
> **Jugendtreffpunkt mit Platz für**
>
> • Studios, Werkstätten und AGs für Kunst, Tanz, Theater und Musik
> • Sport- und Fitnessprogramme
> • Computerspiele, Flipper, Tischfußball, Billard und Tischtennis
>
> **Was hat Eschenbach davon?**
>
> • ruhigere Straßen, angenehmeres Alltagsleben
> • Förderung gesunder Lebensstile und kooperativer Gemeinschaftsarbeit
> • Aktivierung des sozialen Jugendprogramms der Gemeinde
>
> **Wir laden Sie ein zum Diskussionsabend**
> **Dienstag, 27.11.   19.30 Uhr**
> **Stadtbibliothek   Günter-Grass-Str. 37**
> **Weitere Infos: Rufnummer (07502) 55 539 79**

The writer immediately identifies the name of the group.

The writer describes the goals and the benefits.

This section describes the benefits to the town.

Note that the genitive case is used twice in this item.

Factual information is given: the type of meeting, date, time, and place, and a phone number.

TIPP ZUM SCHREIBEN

In many towns there is no place for teenagers to go after school—no safe, inexpensive place to meet, get exercise, play games, pursue hobbies, or just hang out. A center specially suited to the interests and needs of young people can be a great solution to their problems and the concerns of their communities. However, youth centers are expensive and require strong public support to succeed. How could you express the center's benefits in terms that would be convincing to both young people and adults? How would you try to raise support for your plan?

Schreibstrategien

Vor dem Schreiben

- Consider what kind of youth programs already exist in your area (in schools, churches, social organizations, sports groups, scouting groups, etc.) and how popular and effective they are. Which kids participate? Which kids do not? Why not?

- Jot down all the things your ideal youth center would offer: after school, evenings, weekends, and vacation recreational programs, classes, clubs, crafts, arts, sports, outings, social activities, and support. Write down your ideas for the ideal facilities: the site, building, rooms, equipment, entertainment, and personnel.

- How would the community benefit from your youth center? Make notes of your ideas.

Beim Schreiben

- Keep your lists (youth center offerings, facilities, benefits) in front of you and refer to them often.

- Decide what your most important message is and how you want to highlight it for maximum attention. Use short, information-packed phrases and sentences.

- Focus on your most important points and decide whether details add or detract from the effectiveness of your handbill.

Nach dem Schreiben

- Read your draft critically and then share it with a peer editor to get reactions, suggestions, and advice.

- Revise your flyer, taking all suggestions for changes and corrections into consideration.

- Consider whether illustrations and attractive graphic design will enhance your message or not, and if so, include them.

Stimmt alles?

- Hold up the latest version of the handbill and check it for legibility and attractiveness; if either is a problem, fix the layout and the particulars of the design.

- Print or publish your finished text, complete with illustrations.

Ein neues Jugendzentrum!

Wir fordern neue Ideen und neue Aktivitäten. Wir brauchen Ihre Hilfe!

Was wir für der Zukunft sehen wollen:

- Ein Grundstück und Pläne für das neue Jugendzentrum
- einen Platz für alle Jugendlichen nach der Schule, am Wochenende und in der Ferien
- eine tolle Auswahl von Clubs, Vereinen, Werken, Sport und Spaß

Wir brauchen Ihre Stimme und Ihre Unterstützung. Kommen Sie zu uns an den Tag der Offenen Tür, Montag 11.05. um 6.30 in die Aula das Heine-Gymnasium, Schulstraße 25.

WORTSCHATZ

Substantive	Nouns
die **Art, -en**	type, sort
die **Auseinandersetzung, -en**	dispute, argument
die **Bescheidenheit**	modesty
die **Bewegung, -en**	movement
die **Gerechtigkeit, -en**	justice
die **Identität, -en**	identity
die **Suche, -n**	search
die **Zukunft, ⸚e**	future
der **Ausdruck, ⸚e**	expression
der **Einfluss, ⸚e**	influence
der **Frieden**	peace
der **Gymnasiast (-en** *masc.***) / die Gymnasiastin, -nen**	student at a *Gymnasium*
der/die **Jugendliche** (*decl. adj.*)	young person, teenager
der **Kunde (-n** *masc.***) / die Kundin, -nen**	customer
der **Lebensstil, -e**	lifestyle
der **Schutz**	protection
der **Staatsbürger, - / die Staatsbürgerin, -nen**	citizen
der **Wandel**	change
der **Wohlstand**	prosperity
das **Geschäft, -e**	business; store
das **Ideal, -e**	ideal
das **Jahrzehnt, -e**	decade
das **Wissen**	knowledge
das **Zeichen, -**	sign; token
das **Ziel, -e**	goal, aim

Verben	Verbs
an•passen	to conform
begeistern	to inspire
bewegen	to set into motion
denken an (+ *acc.*)	to think about
diskutieren über (+ *acc.*)	to discuss; to talk about

sich engagieren für	to get involved in
sich erinnern an (+ *acc.*)	to remember
erkämpfen	to gain by struggle
führen zu	to lead to
gestalten	to shape
reagieren auf (+ *acc.*)	to react to
teil•nehmen an (+ *dat.*) **(nimmt teil), nahm teil, teilgenommen**	to take part in
mit etwas um•gehen: ging um, ist umgegangen	to deal with, handle
vermitteln	to convey, impart
verwirklichen	to realize; to fulfill oneself
wählen	to choose; to elect
sich wehren gegen	to defend oneself against

Adjektive und Adverbien	Adjectives and adverbs
andererseits	on the other hand
angepasst	conformist
dafür	instead; in return; for it/them
ehrgeizig	ambitious(ly)
freudig	joyful(ly); happy (happily)
friedlich	peaceful(ly)
gewalttätig	violent(ly)
leise	quiet(ly)
tabu	taboo
unterschiedlich	various
vergangen	past; preceding

Sie wissen schon	You already know
der **Erfolg, -e**	success
erleben	to experience

PLANNING GUIDE • CLASSROOM MANAGEMENT

OBJECTIVES

Communication
- Talk about schools of yesterday and today, pp. 52–53.
- Talk about the German school system, pp. 45–55.

Grammar
- Learn more about *der-* and *ein-*words, pp. 56–57.
- Learn about attributive adjectives, pp. 58–59.
- Use indefinite numerals and the interrogative *was für* (*ein*), p. 61.

Culture
- Learn about the history of a school in Bremen, p. 52.
- Learn about different types of schools in Germany, p. 53.
- Learn about school reform efforts in Germany, p. 68.

Recycling
- Review *der-* and *ein-*words, pp. 56–57.
- Review adjectives, pp. 58–60.

STRATEGIES

Listening Strategies
- Listen for information about Albert Einstein, p. 62.

Speaking Strategies
- Discuss school field trips, p. 53.
- Discuss practical jokes, p. 65.

Reading Strategies
- Read a short story, p. 63.

Writing Strategies
- Describe a typical day, p. 53.
- Write a newspaper ad, p. 60.
- Write a short biography, p. 62.
- Write a proposal for school reform, pp. 65–68.

Connecting Cultures Strategies
- Compare the American and German school systems, p. 55.

PROGRAM RESOURCES

Print
- *Arbeitsheft* (Workbook), pp. 33–46
- *Arbeitsheft* (Workbook), Teacher's Edition, pp. 33–46

Audiovisual
- Overhead Transparencies 27.1–27.G3
- Audio Program, Cassette 2A, 7A/CD 2, 9
- Audioscript, pp. 14–19

Technology
- Annenberg *Fokus Deutsch* Video Series, *Folge 27*
- www.mcdougallittell.com

Assessment Program Options
- *Prüfung, Kapitel* 27, Assessment Program, pp. 22–31
- Audio Program, Cassette 8A/CD 10
- Audioscript, p. 108
- Teacher's Resource CD-ROM

DAY 1

Note: (1) Please see TE, pp. 50E–50J, for other suggestions not referenced in these plans. (2) Not all homework options need be assigned.

CHAPTER OPENER
- Quick Start Review: Dative or accusative? (TE, p. 50E). 5 MIN
- Use the photos on pp. 50–51 as a basis for class discussion (TE, p. 50E). 4 MIN

VIDEOTHEK
- Follow the Teaching Suggestions for *Folge I: Geschichte eines Gymnasiums* (TE, p. 50E). 12 MIN
- Do *Akt. A*, p. 52, *Schritt 1*, then *Schritt 2* (TE, p. 50F). 12 MIN
- Do *Akt. B*, pp. 52–53, in pairs, then discuss the activities as a class (TE, p. 50F). 7 MIN
- Do *Akt. C*, p. 53, in pairs (TE, p. 50F). 10 MIN

Homework Options:
- *Arbeitsheft*, p. 34, *Videothek, Akt. E*

DAY 2

VIDEOTHEK
- Quick Start Review 1: Genitive case (TE, p. 50E). 5 MIN
- *Arbeitsheft*, p. 34, audio *Akt. D*. 5 MIN
- Have students create the table needed to do *Akt. A*, p. 53, before watching *Folge II: Der Schulalltag.* Have them fill out the table as they watch. End with a class discussion. 12 MIN
- Do *Akt. B*, p. 53, *Schritt 1*, as a whole-class activity on the board. 5 MIN
- Do *Akt. B*, p. 53, *Schritt 2*, in pairs. Conclude by having several students tell about their partner's school day. 16 MIN
- *Arbeitsheft*, p. 35, *Akt. F.* 7 MIN

Homework Options:
- *Arbeitsheft*, p. 35, *Videothek, Akt. F*

DAY 3

VOKABELN
- Quick Start Review 1: Vocabulary (TE, p. 50F). 5 MIN
- Present the vocabulary on p. 54 using OHT 27.2. 8 MIN
- Follow Teaching Suggestions for *Akt. A*, p. 54 (TE, p. 50G). 9 MIN
- Warm up for *Akt. B*, pp. 54–55 (TE, p. 50G). After doing the activity silently, have students check their answers with a partner. 15 MIN
- Do *Akt. C*, p. 55, following the Teaching Suggestions for the expansion activity (TE, p. 50G). 13 MIN

Homework Options:
- *Arbeitsheft*, pp. 36–37, *Vokabeln, Akt. D–F*

DAY 4

VOKABELN
- Quick Start Review 2: Genitive vs. dative (TE, p. 50F). 4 MIN
- *Akt. D,* p. 55. 10 MIN

STRUKTUREN
- Present *der-* and *ein-* words on pp. 56–57 using OHT 27.G1. 10 MIN
- *Arbeitsheft*, p. 39, audio *Akt. A*. 5 MIN
- Follow the Teaching Suggestions for the warm-up activity for *Übung A*, p. 57 (TE, p. 50H). Have students do *Übung A*, p. 57, silently, then check their answers as a class. 12 MIN
- Do *Übung B*, pp. 57–58, as a class, then follow the Teaching Suggestions for an expansion activity (TE, p. 50H). 9 MIN

Homework Options:
- *Arbeitsheft*, pp. 39–40, *Strukturen, Akt. E–F*

DAY 5

STRUKTUREN

- Quick Start Review 1: Simple past (TE, p. 50G). 4 MIN
- Follow the Teaching Suggestions for presenting the adjectives on pp. 58–59. Use OHT 27.G2–27.G3. (TE, p. 50H). 12 MIN
- Do *Übung A,* p. 60 (TE, p. 50H). 8 MIN
- Do *Akt. B,* p. 60. Follow the Teaching Suggestions for a variation (TE, p. 50H). 8 MIN
- Present the indefinite numerals and *was für (ein)* on p. 61. 7 MIN
- Have students do the exercise on p. 61 silently, then discuss their answers as a class. Follow the Teaching Suggestions for a follow-up activity (TE, p. 50I). 11 MIN

Homework Options:

- *Übung C,* p. 60
- *Arbeitsheft,* pp. 39–41, Strukturen, Akt. H–J

DAY 6

STRUKTUREN

- Quick Start Review 2: Conjunctions (TE, p. 50H). 5 MIN
- Have several students share the ads they created for *Übung C,* p. 60. 6 MIN
- *Arbeitsheft,* p. 45, audio Akt. I. 9 MIN

PERSPEKTIVEN

- While doing *Hören Sie zu!,* Akt. A, p. 62 (TE, p. 50I), have students fill in what they can for *Akt. B,* p. 62. 15 MIN
- Play the recording again and have students complete *Akt. B,* p. 62. Have them read their notes in small groups as a preparation for *Akt. C,* p. 62. 15 MIN

Homework Options:

- *Hören Sie zu!, Akt. C,* p. 62
- *Arbeitsheft,* pp. 45–46, Perspektiven, Akt. C–E

DAY 7

PERSPEKTIVEN

- Quick Start Review 1: Verbs with prepositions (TE, p. 50I). 4 MIN
- Have students share their biographies from *Akt. C* in pairs. 6 MIN
- Discuss *Zum Thema,* p. 68A, as a class. 3 MIN
- Read *Der Stift* as a class, then do *Zum Text, Akt. A,* p. 68 (TE, p. 50I). 15 MIN
- Do *Zum Text, Akt. B,* p. 68, as a class. 7 MIN
- Do *Interaktion,* p. 68, in pairs, then have them share their conclusions with the class. 10 MIN
- Begin *Schreiben Sie!* by discussing the assignment, *Tipp zum Schreiben,* and *Schreibmodell.* 5 MIN

Homework Options:

- Do *Vor dem Schreiben* and *Beim Schreiben* and complete the first draft of the proposal

DAY 8

PERSPEKTIVEN

- Quick Start Review 2: Strong verbs (TE, p. 50I). 4 MIN
- Do *Nach dem Schreiben,* p. 68, and begin writing the final draft of the proposal (TE, p. 50I). 11 MIN
- Questions and review. 5 MIN
- *Prüfung, Kapitel 27.* 30 MIN

Homework Options:

- Finish the final draft of the proposal, if necessary
- *Arbeitsheft,* p. 46, Perspektiven, Akt. F

DAY 1

Note: (1) Please see TE, pp. 50E–50J, for other suggestions not referenced in these plans. (2) Not all homework options need be assigned.

CHAPTER OPENER

- Quick Start Review: Dative or accusative? (TE, p. 50E). 5 MIN
- Discuss the photos on pp. 50–51 (TE, p. 50E). 4 MIN

VIDEOTHEK

- *Folge I* (TE, p. 50E). 12 MIN
- *Akt. A–B,* pp. 52–53, in pairs (TE, p. 50F). 19 MIN
- *Akt. C,* p. 53 (TE, p. 50F). 9 MIN
- Block Schedule activity: Change of Pace (TE, p. 50F). 10 MIN
- Do *Akt. A,* p. 53, then watch *Folge II.* Have students fill out the table as they watch. (TE, p. 50F). 12 MIN
- Do *Akt. B,* p. 53, *Schritt 1,* as a whole-class activity on the board. 5 MIN
- Do *Akt. B,* p. 53, *Schritt 2,* in pairs. 14 MIN

Homework Options:

- *Arbeitsheft,* p. 34, *Videothek, Akt. E*

DAY 2

VIDEOTHEK

- Quick Start Review 1: Genitive case (TE, p. 50E). 5 MIN
- *Arbeitsheft,* audio *Akt. F, Schritt 1,* p. 37. 7 MIN

VOKABELN

- Present vocabulary on p. 54 using OHT 27.2. 8 MIN
- *Akt. A,* p. 54 (TE, p. 50G). 9 MIN
- Warm up for *Akt. B,* pp. 54–55 (TE, p. 50G). Do the activity silently, then check answers with a partner. 15 MIN
- Block Schedule activity: Change of pace (TE, p. 50G). 10 MIN
- Do *Akt. C,* p. 55, and expansion activity (TE, p. 50G). 13 MIN
- *Akt. D,* p. 55. 7 MIN

STRUKTUREN

- Present *der-* and *ein-* words on pp. 56–57 using OHT 27.G1. 10 MIN
- *Arbeitsheft,* audio *Akt. A.* p. 38. 6 MIN

Homework Options:

- *Arbeitsheft,* p. 35, *Videothek, Akt. F*
- *Arbeitsheft,* pp. 39–40, *Strukturen, Akt. E–F*

DAY 3

STRUKTUREN

- Quick Start Review 1: Simple past (TE, p. 50G). 7 MIN
- Do warm-up activity for *Übung A,* p. 57 (TE, p. 50H). Do *Übung A,* p. 57, silently, then check answers as a class. 15 MIN
- Do *Übung B,* pp. 57–58, as a class, then do the expansion activity (TE, p. 50H). 9 MIN
- Present the adjectives on pp. 58–59. Use OHT 27.G2–27.G3. (TE, p. 50H). 12 MIN
- *Übung A,* p. 60 (TE, p. 50H). 8 MIN
- Block Schedule activity: Recycle (TE, p. 50I). 10 MIN
- Present the indefinite numerals and *was für (ein)* on p. 61. 7 MIN
- Do the exercise on p. 61, silently, then discuss answers as a class. Do follow-up activity (TE, p. 50I). 12 MIN
- *Arbeitsheft, Akt. I,* p. 41. 10 MIN

Homework Options:

- *Übung C,* p. 60
- *Arbeitsheft,* p. 41, *Strukturen, Akt. J*

DAY 4

PERSPEKTIVEN

- Quick Start Review 1: Verbs with prepositions (TE, p. 50I). 4 MIN
- Have students share biographies from *Akt. C* in pairs. 6 MIN
- Do *Hören Sie zu!, Akt. C,* p. 62, silently, then share biographies in small groups. 10 MIN
- Do *Vokabeln,* Portfolio activity (TE, p. 50G). 10 MIN
- Discuss *Zum Thema,* p. 63, as a class. 6 MIN
- Read *Der Stift* as a class, then do *Zum Text, Akt. A,* p. 68 (TE, p. 50I). 17 MIN
- Do *Akt. B,* p. 68, as a class. 12 MIN
- Do *Interaktion,* p. 68, in pairs, then share conclusions. 15 MIN
- Begin *Schreiben Sie!* 10 MIN

Homework Options:

- Do *Vor dem Schreiben* and *Beim Schreiben* and complete the first draft of *Antrag*
- *Arbeitsheft,* p. 45, *Perspektiven, Akt. C–D*

DAY 5

PERSPEKTIVEN

- Quick Start Review 2: Strong verbs (TE, p. 50I). 5 MIN
- Do *Nach dem Schreiben,* p. 68, and begin writing the final draft of the proposal (TE p. 50I). 20 MIN
- Block Schedule activity: Fun Break (TE, p. 50J). 15 MIN
- *Arbeitsheft,* p. 46, *Perspektiven, Akt. E–F.* 15 MIN
- Questions and review. 5 MIN
- *Prüfung, Kapitel 27.* 30 MIN

Homework Options:

- Finish the final draft of the proposal, if necessary

PACING GUIDE • SAMPLE LESSON PLAN, 90-MINUTE SCHEDULE

Chapter Opener, pp. 50–51

PROGRAM RESOURCES

• Overhead Transparency 27.1

Quick Start Review

Dative or accusative?
Ergänzen Sie die Sätze.

1. Möchtest du dein_____ Oma Blumen mitbringen?
2. Für wen ist _____ Geschenk?
3. Kennen Sie _____ Mann von Frau Lichtenstern?
4. Kannst du _____ Kindern bei _____ Hausaufgaben helfen?
5. Kannst du mein_____ Freunden auf der Karte zeigen, wo wir wohnen?

Answers: 1. deiner   2. das   3. den
4. den, den   5. meinen

TEACHING SUGGESTIONS

• Photo, p. 50

Have students state their impressions of the students in the photo. Ask *Sehen sie froh aus? Wie sind sie angezogen? Wann wurde das Photo gemacht – am ersten Schultag? am letzten Schultag?*

• Photos, p. 51

Have students look at the 2 photos, then ask *Sieht es in Ihrem Klassenzimmer so ähnlich aus oder ganz anders? Was machen die Schüler gerade? Was macht die Lehrerin?*

TEACHING ALL STUDENTS

Multiple Intelligences Verbal: Help students refresh their memories about the German school system. Ask *Wie viele Jahre gehen deutsche Schüler*

aufs Gymnasium? (9 Jahre: 5. bis 13. Klasse) Wie viele Jahre geht man zur Realschule? (6 Jahre: 5. bis 10. Klasse) Welche Schule ist der amerikanischen High School ähnlich? (Die Gesamtschule, denn sie integriert Hauptschule, Realschule und Gymnasium). Next, list the following terms on the board or an OHT: *die Gesamtschule, die Realschule, das Gymnasium, unterrichten, lehren, sich beschäftigen mit.* Have students write sentences using each word and then read them aloud in turn. Discuss and correct the content of the sentences.

CLASSROOM COMMUNITY

Dictation Have students do the following dictation. *Früher gab es an den Schulen andere Methoden. Die Lehrer haben mehr geredet und die Schüler haben mehr geschrieben. Es gab keine modernen Medien. Videos oder Computer kannte man noch nicht. Die Schüler haben auch nicht in Gruppen gearbeitet. Man hat geglaubt, dass die Schüler am besten von den Lehrern lernen. Vielleicht haben Schüler heute mehr Spaß beim Lernen.*

Videothek, pp. 52–53

PROGRAM RESOURCES

• Videocassette, *Folge 27*
• *Arbeitsheft*, pp. 33–35
• Audio Program, Cassette 2A/CD 2
• Audioscript, pp. 14–15

Quick Start Review 1

Genitive case
Ergänzen Sie die richtigen Artikel im Genitiv.

1. Wegen _____ Regens konnten wir heute nicht an den Strand fahren.
2. Die Sportler aus unserer Klasse spielen während _____ großen Pause immer Basketball.
3. Innerhalb _____ Stadt darf man nicht so schnell fahren.
4. Wir sind trotz _____ vielen Verkehrs noch rechtzeitig angekommen.
5. Herr Schmitt mag es nicht, wenn die Schüler während _____ Unterrichts essen.

Answers: 1. des   2. der   3. der
4. des   5. des

Quick Start Review 2

Accusative/dative prepositions
Ergänzen Sie die richtigen Artikel.

1. Leg bitte die Bücher auf _____ Schreibtisch!
2. Wo sind sie denn? Sie liegen noch (in) _____ Auto.
3. Hast du meinen Schlüssel gesehen? Ich glaube, er liegt auf _____ Tisch im Esszimmer.
4. Kannst du das Auto vor _____ Garage parken?
5. Wo steht es? Es steht jetzt auf _____ Straße.

Answers: 1. den   2. im   3. dem   4. der   5. der

TEACHING SUGGESTIONS

• *Folge I: Geschichte eines Gymnasiums,* pp. 52–53

Have students review the *Wortschatz zum Video* before they watch the episode. Explain that this is a video about the history of a *Gymnasium* in Bremen, in northern Germany, and that it portrays a chronology of events. Encourage them to take notes while they watch. Afterward, ask them to single out one event that they find most interesting. Also, have students look at the photo *"Die Schule ist besetzt"* and ask *Warum haben die Schüler protestiert? Wann war das?*

• *Aktivität A,* p. 52

Go over the key vocabulary in the activity and explain key concepts as needed. For example, *Es gibt verschiedene Unterrichtsmethoden – nur der Lehrer spricht, die Schüler hören zu, oder die Schüler arbeiten in Gruppen, der Lehrer hat die Rolle eines Moderators. Welche sind Ihre Hauptfächer? Welche sind Ihre Nebenfächer?*

• *Aktivität B,* pp. 52–53

Which of the activities mentioned in the video and the activity do students find attractive and why? Ask *Welche der Reisen oder welches der Projekte gefällt Ihnen besonders gut? Warum?*

• *Aktivität C,* p. 53

Have students work in pairs to elicit each other's fondest memories of elementary or middle school. Have them take notes and then share their partner's story with the class.

• *Aktivität A,* p. 53

Do this as a whole-class activity. Have 2 students keep track of the class's answers at the board. After completing the activity, have students compare Susanne and Karolin or Susanne, Karolin, and themselves. Encourage them to use connectors such as *aber*

and *und,* as well as subordinating conjunctions. You might introduce the expression *während: Während wir in der Schule Deutsch lernen, lernt Karolin Französisch.*

TEACHING ALL STUDENTS

Multiple Intelligences Intrapersonal: Have students review *Folge II: Der Schulalltag.* Allow them 8 minutes to write down or comment on anything they feel strongly about. Ask *Stimmen Sie den Sprechern zu? Stimmen Sie ihnen nicht zu? Wer von den Sprechern ist Ihnen sympatisch?*

CLASSROOM COMMUNITY

Group Activity Game: After students have completed *Aktivität A,* p. 52, ask them to refer to the dates in the box and write a description of an event that they associate with one of the dates. Then have them read their descriptions aloud and let the class guess the date of the event.

INTERDISCIPLINARY CONNECTION

History Have students focus on the dates given in the box below *Aktivität A,* p. 52. Ask them to come up with events in U.S. history corresponding to each of these dates or time frames. Have them draw a time line showing the chronology of parallel events in Germany and in the U.S.

BLOCK SCHEDULE

Change of Pace Have students work in groups of 4 to plan a class trip related to their German studies. They could visit a German store (butcher, baker) in the area or a community college where German is being taught. Have them

write a list of questions in German they would ask during their visit.

Vokabeln, pp. 54–55

PROGRAM RESOURCES
• Overhead Transparency 27.2
• *Arbeitsheft,* pp. 36–37
• Audio Program, Cassette 2A/CD 2
• Audioscript, pp. 15–16

Quick Start Review 1

♻ Vocabulary
Bilden Sie Sätze, achten Sie auf die richtigen Verbformen.

1. viele / engagieren sich / Jugendliche / für / den Frieden
2. diskutierte / in den 60er Jahren / und / Frieden / die Jugendbewegung / über / Gerechtigkeit
3. zwischen / Eltern / gibt / Auseinandersetzungen / und / Jugendlichen / es / oft
4. führen zu / Wohlstand / nicht / mehr Gerechtigkeit / immer
5. die Suche / bewegt / Jugendliche / nach / Identität / viele

Answers: 1. Viele Jugendliche engagieren sich für den Frieden. 2. In den 60er Jahren diskutierte die Jugendbewegung über Frieden und Gerechtigkeit. 3. Zwischen Eltern und Jugendlichen gibt es oft Auseinandersetzungen. 4. Wohlstand führt nicht immer zu mehr Gerechtigkeit. 5. Viele Jugendliche bewegt die Suche nach Identität.

Quick Start Review 2

♻ Genitive versus dative
Schreiben Sie die Sätze neu mit dem Genitiv.

MODELL: Das ist die Mutter von dem Jungen, der neu bei uns in der Klasse ist. → *Das ist die Mutter des Jungen, der neu bei uns in der Klasse ist.*

1. Kennst du den Autor von dem spannenden Kriminalroman?
2. Die Freunde von meiner Schwester sind besonders nett.
3. Die Reparatur von meinem Auto war sehr teuer.
4. Die Großmutter kümmert sich um den Haushalt von ihrer Tochter.
5. Das ist der Hund von unserem Nachbarn.

Answers: 1. des spannenden Kriminalromans   2. meiner Schwester   3. meines Autos   4. ihrer Tochter   5. unseres Nachbarn

．．．．．．．．．．．．．．．．．．．．．．．．．．

TEACHING SUGGESTIONS

• Photo, p. 54

Have students make up a funny conversation between the 2 groups of German students shown in the photo.

• *Aktivität A,* p. 54

Have students do this activity as a game show. Divide them into 2 teams. Then have one student (the host) read the cues. Whichever team guesses the correct answer first scores a point.

• *Aktivität B,* pp. 54–55

Warm-up: Have students form easy questions using the words in the box on page 55. For example, *Was findest du langweilig?* (*Mathematik*) *Was machst du häufig?* (*Hausaufgaben*)

• *Aktivität C,* p. 55

Expansion: Have each student write a definition for one of the vocabulary items on p. 54 on a slip of paper. Have them read their definitions aloud and let the class guess which vocabulary item it defines.

TEACHING ALL STUDENTS

Multiple Intelligences

Musical/Rhythmic: Have students develop mnemonic devices, such as rhymes, raps, or songs, to help them remember some of the verbs and nouns on p. 54. Have them share their techniques with the class.

CLASSROOM COMMUNITY

Paired Activity Have students read *Kulturspiegel,* p. 55, in pairs and help each other with unfamiliar vocabulary. Then have each pair create 2 questions about the German school system for the whole class to answer.

INTERDISCIPLINARY CONNECTION

History/Mathematics/Chemistry/Music
Have students interview different teachers to find out how their disciplines were taught 50 years ago. What has changed? What have we learned? What do they think was better then? Which approaches are better now?

BLOCK SCHEDULE

Change of Pace Have students describe one item they see in the classroom in great detail. For example, *Ich sehe eine schwarze Tafel mit weißen und grauen Kreideflecken. Auf dem Regal an der Wand sehe ich zwei rote Bücher und ein gelb-schwarzes Lexikon.*

PORTFOLIO

Have students describe a typical school day for a friend in Germany. The description should not just list the names of the classes, but also describe at least 2 things that happened between classes (*In der Pause haben wir über den neuen Star Wars Film geredet*), one very funny incident during class, and a particularly boring period. Try to find an English class at a German *Gymnasium* or *Gesamtschule* on the Internet and share your descriptions with students via e-mail.

RUBRIC   **A** = 13–15 pts.   **B** = 10–12 pts.   **C** = 7–9 pts.   **D** = 4–6 pts.   **F** = <4 pts.

Writing Criteria	Scale				
Creativity	1	2	3	4	5
Vocabulary	1	2	3	4	5
Organization	1	2	3	4	5

Strukturen, pp. 56–61

PROGRAM RESOURCES

• Overhead Transparencies 27.G1–27.G3
• *Arbeitsheft,* pp. 38–41
• Audio Program, Cassette 2A/CD 2
• Audioscript, pp. 16–18

．．．．．．．．．．．．．．．．．．．．．．．．．．

Quick Start Review 1

♻ Simple past
Ergänzen Sie die richtigen Verben in den Sätzen.
WÖRTER: *mussten, traf, blieb, zogen an, brachten, ging*

1. Mein Vater ＿＿＿ alle wichtigen Entscheidungen in unserer Familie.

2. Meine Eltern _____ sich früher in der Schule stellen, ehe sie mit dem Lehrer reden durften.
3. Die 60er Jahre _____ viele Veränderungen in das deutsche Schulsystem.
4. Meine Mutter und ihre Freundinnen _____ für die Schule immer Röcke _____.
5. Mein Opa _____ nie gerne lang auf, er _____ immer früh ins Bett.

Answers: 1. traf   2. mussten
3. brachten   4. zogen an   5. blieb, ging

Quick Start Review 2

♺ Conjunctions
Verbinden Sie die Sätze mit *aber, denn, oder* oder *und.*
1. Karin verdient nicht viel. Ihre Arbeit macht ihr Spaß.
2. Sie ist in der Küche. Sie ist im Garten.
3. Er geht heute früh schlafen. Er ist krank.
4. Emil wohnt in Paris. Er spricht kein Französisch.
5. Sie ist intelligent. Sie ist optimistisch.

Answers: 1. Karin verdient nicht viel, aber die Arbeit macht ihr Spaß.   2. Sie ist in der Küche oder sie ist im Garten.
3. Er geht heute früh schlafen, denn er ist krank.   4. Emil wohnt in Paris, aber er spricht kein Französisch.   5. Sie ist intelligent und sie ist optimistisch.

TEACHING SUGGESTIONS

• *Der-* and *ein*-words, pp. 56–57
Describe the 3 categories of adjective endings: *der*-words, *ein*-words, and unpreceded adjectives. Explain that gender inflections are either on the article or on the adjective (*der große Fisch* vs. *ein großer Fisch*). Review the possessive adjectives by asking questions about family relationships: *Meine Großeltern wohnen in Frankfurt und wo wohnen Ihre? Seine Großeltern wohnen in Florida und wo wohnen Ihre? usw.*

• *Übung A,* p. 57

Warm-up: Ask *Welche Musikgruppen gefallen Ihnen? Welche Sportarten machen die Schüler in unserer Klasse? Treiben alle Schüler Sport? Welche Schüler spielen ein Musikinstrument? Welche Fächer gibt es an jeder Schule? Welche Fächer gibt es nicht an allen Schulen? usw.*

• *Übung B,* pp. 57–58

Expansion: Have students talk about their own lives and families using statements similar to the ones here. Encourage one student to start the discussion, then pick someone else and so on until everyone in the class has spoken.

• Adjectives, pp. 58–60

Guide students through the following steps before working on *Aktivitäten A–C.*
EXAMPLE A: *Sie hat einen sehr gut_____ Roman geschrieben.*
1. Notice that the adjective *gut-* is preceded by an *ein*-word with an ending showing gender, number, and case of the noun *Roman* (i.e., masculine, singular, and accusative).
2. Look at the chart on page 58. The ending for an adjective modifying a masculine, singular, accusative noun is *-en.*

Answer: Sie hat einen sehr gut<u>en</u> Roman geschrieben.
EXAMPLE B: *Wir haben heute frisch_____ Äpfel!*
1. Notice that the adjective *frisch-* is not preceded by a *der-* or an *ein-* word. Therefore it must take an ending that shows the gender, number, and case of the noun it modifies.
2. Refer to the chart on page 59. Since *Äpfel* is plural and in the accusative case, the ending is *-e.*

Answer: Wir haben heute frisch<u>e</u> Äpfel!

• *Übung A,* p. 60

Have students describe each other's clothing orally before you start this exercise. For example, *Jan trägt eine grüne Hose und ein weißes T-Shirt. Lisas Jacke ist rot und sie hat heute blaue Schuhe an.*

• *Übung B,* p. 60

Variation: After finishing the activity, have students change the *der*-words to *ein*-words (or omit them if possible).
Answers: 1. Meine Großmutter hat ein altes Buch geschrieben.   2. Ein kleiner Junge ist mein Neffe.   3. Nette ältere Frauen sind meine Tanten.   4. Meine Schwester liest einen berühmten Roman von Thomas Mann.   5. Junge Familienmitglieder interessieren sich für Politik.   6. Teure Sachen gefallen meiner Familie nicht.   7. Meine Eltern haben einer neuen Lehrerin ein Geschenk gekauft.

- *Übung C*, p. 60

Encourage students to write amusing ads. For example: *Kreativer Opernsänger mit 3 Haustieren (Schlange, Iguana, Katze) sucht 3 nette, tierliebende Mitbewohner für eine 4-Zimmer-Wohnung.*

- *Übung A*, p. 61

Follow-up: Write all the indefinite numerals on the board. Assign each student one of the indefinite numerals. Have them create a sentence for their numeral.

TEACHING ALL STUDENTS

Multiple Intelligences Visual: Have students watch *Folge II: Der Schulalltag* again. Have students pay attention to details that differ from an American school. Encourage them to take notes while watching.

CLASSROOM COMMUNITY

Paired Activity Have students work in pairs and write a short dialogue between a grandparent and grandchild discussing each other's school experiences.

BLOCK SCHEDULE

Recycle Have students write a short paragraph about 3 animals of their choice, using at least 6 adjectives. The animals might talk to each other as in fairy tales or fables.

Perspektiven, pp. 62–68

PROGRAM RESOURCES

- Overhead Transparencies 27.G1–27.G3
- *Arbeitsheft*, pp. 42–46

- Audio Program, Cassette 2A, 7A/ CD 2, 9
- Audioscript, pp. 18–19
- www.mcdougallittell.com

....

Quick Start Review 1

♻ Verbs with prepositions
Verbinden Sie die folgenden Satzteile.
1. Ich engagiere mich
2. An Demonstrationen
3. Ich interessiere mich
4. Ich denke sehr oft
5. Wir freuen uns schon
a. auf unseren nächsten Urlaub.
b. sehr für Astronomie.
c. nicht gerne für politische Ziele.
d. nehme ich nicht gerne teil.
e. an dich.

Answers: 1. c   2. d   3. b   4. e   5. a

Quick Start Review 2

♻ Strong verbs
Setzen Sie die Sätze ins Imperfekt.
1. Er reitet durch den Wald.
2. Er geht in Berlin immer in die Oper.
3. Es wird im Januar sehr kalt.
4. Mein Hals tut mir weh!
5. Mein Bruder singt mir am Abend gerne Lieder vor.
6. Dieser Baum wächst in einem Jahr fast einen halben Meter.
7. Die Katze läuft über die Straße.

Answers: 1. ritt   2. ging   3. wurde
4. tat   5. sang   6. wuchs   7. lief

....

TEACHING SUGGESTIONS

- *Hören Sie zu!*, p. 62

Remind students to look over the *Wortschatz* before they listen to the recording. Encourage them to take notes.

- *Aktivität A*, p. 62

Follow-up: Ask *Wofür hat sich Albert Einstein interessiert? Was hat ihm keinen Spaß gemacht? Weshalb bestand er sein zweites Examen nicht? Kennen Sie andere Künstler/ Wissenschaftler, die nicht gut in der Schule waren oder nicht gern zur Schule gingen?* (z.B. *Thomas A. Edison*)

- *Zum Thema*, p. 63

Remind students that Germans traditionally play practical jokes on each other on April Fool's Day. Do students remember any stories they have read about students playing practical jokes on their teachers?

- *Zum Text, Aktivität A*, p. 64

Follow-up: Ask *Welches Fach hat der Lehrer unterrichtet? Warum können die Schüler nicht schlafen, als die Unterrichtsstunde vorbei ist? Warum will der Lehrer nicht, dass die Schüler Hausaufgaben machen? usw.*

- *Schreiben Sie!*, p. 65–66

Go over *Kulturspiegel*, p. 68, before students start the writing assignment.

- *Tipp zum Schreiben*, p. 68

Have students research plans for school reform in their school district and in their home state.

- *Vor dem Schreiben*, p. 67

Have students make separate lists of nouns and verbs that they want to include in their proposal.

- *Nach dem Schreiben*, p. 68

Have students collect copies of their proposals and put them in a newsletter. Optional: Exchange proposals with another class of German students at the school for comment and discussion.

TEACHING ALL STUDENTS

Extra Help Have students choose a noun from the *Wortschatz,* p. 69, and write down a definition on a slip of paper. Have them read their definitions aloud and have the class guess which word they are defining.

CLASSROOM COMMUNITY

Group Activity Have students reread *Der Stift* in small groups. Then have them comment on teacher/student behavior in the story and how that represents a former time. Which aspects of the story would have to be changed in order to make it more contemporary?

BLOCK SCHEDULE

Fun Break Have students make up the biography of a famous figure in science, literature, or sports without using his or her name. Divide the class into small groups and have each person in the group read to the others without revealing the subject's identity. The other members of the group have to guess the identity.

PROJECT

Have students research some alternative educational philosophies, such as those of Maria Montessori or Rudolf Steiner (Waldorf Schools). In addition to using the library or the Internet, they could interview a teacher at a local alternative school. Their written report should be no longer than 2 pages.

RUBRIC **A** = 13–15 pts. **B** = 10–12 pts.
C = 7–9 pts. **D** = 4–6 pts. **F** = <4 pts.

Writing Criteria	Scale				
Organization	1	2	3	4	5
Grammar, spelling	1	2	3	4	5
Presentation	1	2	3	4	5

27 SCHULALLTAG

In diesem Kapitel

- lernen Sie einiges über die Geschichte eines alten Gymnasiums in Bremen.
- erleben Sie den Schultag einer deutschen Schülerin von heute.

Sie werden auch

- darüber sprechen, wie Schulen und Gymnasien damals waren, und wie sie heute sind.
- wiederholen, wie man zwischen **der** und **ein** Wörtern unterscheidet.
- Adjektivendungen wiederholen.
- lernen, wie man unbestimmte Zahlwörter wie **einige, mehrere** und **viele** gebraucht.
- eine Geschichte über das Schulleben am Anfang des zwanzigsten Jahrhunderts lesen.
- einen Antrag auf Schulreform schreiben.

Schüler im neunzehnten Jahrhundert.

Schule in der Vergangenheit und in der Gegenwart – was ist anders?

Szene in einem Klassenzimmer von heute.

VIDEOTHEK

„Die Schule ist besetzt!"

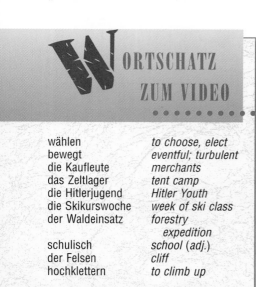

WORTSCHATZ ZUM VIDEO

wählen	to choose, elect
bewegt	eventful; turbulent
die Kaufleute	merchants
das Zeltlager	tent camp
die Hitlerjugend	Hitler Youth
die Skikurswoche	week of ski class
der Waldeinsatz	forestry expedition
schulisch	school (adj.)
der Felsen	cliff
hochklettern	to climb up

Schule macht Spaß—aber nicht immer! Der Schulalltag hat sich stark geändert. Was hat man aus den alten Zeiten behalten, und was ist jetzt anders?

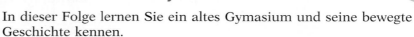

I: Geschichte eines Gymnasiums

In dieser Folge lernen Sie ein altes Gymasium und seine bewegte Geschichte kennen.

Ⓐ Was passiert?

SCHRITT 1: Schauen Sie sich das Video an, und bringen Sie die folgenden Sätze in die richtige Reihenfolge.

a. Die Schüler und Schülerinnen protestierten, und die Schulen wurden reformiert.
b. Die Schule stand trotz weitgehender Zerstörung in Bremen, noch immer.
c. Es gab neue Fächer, wie zum Beispiel Biologie, Chemie und Physik.
d. Die Schüler und Schülerinnen können mitbestimmen und Hauptfächer selbst auswählen.
e. Sport wurde zu dieser Zeit zum Hauptfach.
f. Das Gymnasium wurde für die Söhne der reichen Kaufleute in Bremen gegründet.
g. Die Unterrichtsmethoden waren trotz der Demokratisierung in Deutschland streng.

SCHRITT 2: Wann ist das passiert? Verbinden Sie die Sätze oben mit dem richtigen Datum im Kasten.

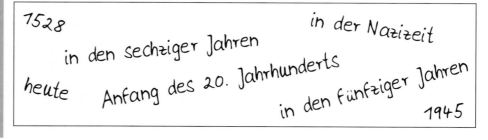

1528   in den sechziger Jahren   in der Nazizeit
heute   Anfang des 20. Jahrhunderts   in den fünfziger Jahren   1945

Ⓑ Schulzeiterinnerungen. Auf Seite 53 lesen Sie Erinnerungen von Daniela, Dirk, Anett und Erika. Ordnen Sie die Sätze den Personen zu. Wer erinnert sich an was?

1. Wir sind mit dem Bus nach Budapest gefahren. Wir haben die Stadt erobert.
2. Wir sind im März eine Woche auf Skikurs gefahren. Das ist meine beste Erinnerung.
3. Wir sind in die Berge gefahren. Der Lehrer hat uns gesagt, dass wir nicht auf einen Felsen klettern dürfen. Aber wir haben ihn und seinen Freund hoch auf dem Felsen gesehen.
4. Wir haben in der achten Klasse einen Waldeinsatz gemacht. Wir haben zwei Wochen lang im Wald gelebt, haben Waldarbeit gemacht und viel über die Umwelt gelernt.

C Schulreise oder Alltag? Die schönsten Erinnerungen aus der Schulzeit waren alles Erlebnisse, die diese Personen auf einer Schulreise gemacht hatten. Finden Sie einen Partner / eine Partnerin, und stellen Sie einander folgende Fragen.

1. Ist es besonders schön auch für dich, mit den Schulkameraden zu reisen oder Klassenausflüge zu machen?
2. Wohin bist du gefahren?
3. Was hast du dort gemacht?
4. Wie war das anders als der Alltag in der Schule?
5. War die Schulreise viel schöner als der Alltag in der Schule? Warum?
6. Was ist deine schönste Erinnerung an die Schule?

II: Der Schulalltag

A Was wissen Sie über Susannes und Karolins Schulalltag? Machen Sie sich eine Tabelle wie die folgende, und füllen Sie sie aus.

Karolin mit Sammy.

C. *Answers will vary.*

KULTURSPIEGEL

Karolin ist Schülerin auf einer Gesamtschule, eine Schule, die Aspekte eines Gymnasiums, einer Realschule und einer Hauptschule verbindet. Schüler und Schülerinnen besuchen die Gesamtschule von der fünften bis zum Ende der zehnten Klasse. Dann können sie entweder den Hauptschulabschluss bekommen, oder sie können ihre Schulausbildung bis zum Abitur weiterführen.

	SUSANNE	KAROLIN
1. Um wie viel Uhr beginnt die Schule?		
2. Wie viele Stunden gibt es am Tag Unterricht?		
3. Wie kommen sie zur Schule?		
4. Welches sind ihre Lieblingsfächer?		
5. Welches Fach ist für sie langweilig?		

A. SUSANNE: **1.** etwa um acht Uhr **2.** sechs bis acht Stunden **3.** mit dem Bus **4.** Deutsch, Biologie, Philosophie; KAROLIN: **1.** um acht Uhr **2.** fast immer sechs Stunden **3.** mit dem Schulbus **4.** Französisch **5.** Mathematik

B Schulablauf

SCHRITT 1: Karolins Schulalltag. Beschreiben Sie einen typischen Schultag von Karolin. Welche Fächer hat sie? Was macht sie nachmittags? Was macht sie in der Freizeit?

1. Zuerst . . .　2. Dann . . .　3. Danach . . .　4. Zuletzt . . .

SCHRITT 2: Ihr Schultag. Beschreiben Sie jetzt den typischen Schultag für Sie selbst. Welche Pflichtfächer[a] haben Sie? Welche Wahlfächer haben Sie? Warum belegen Sie gerade diese Wahlfächer?

Karolins Schulablauf.

[a]*required courses*

B. Schritt 1: *Answers will vary. Possible answers are:* **1.** Zuerst fährt sie mit dem Schulbus zur Schule. **2.** Dann hat sie sechs Stunden Unterricht. Zuerst hat sie Mathe, später Französisch. **3.** Nachmittags singt sie in der Schulband oder malt mit dem Kunstkurs. **4.** Zu Hause macht sie eine Stunde Hausaufgaben. Schritt 2: *Answers will vary.*

VOKABELN

die Gegenwart	present time
die Unsicherheit	insecurity, uncertainty
die Unterrichtsmethode	teaching method
die Vergangenheit	past
die Wirkung	result; effect
die Wissenschaft	science
der Alptraum	nightmare
der Ratschlag	advice
der Wettbewerb	competition
das Pflichtfach	required course
das Wahlfach	optional course, elective
sich begegnen	to meet
besetzen	to occupy
erobern	to conquer
gründen	to found
legen: Wert legen auf	to value something;
(+ acc.)	to consider important
mit•bestimmen	to have a say
rechnen	to calculate
sich unterscheiden von	to differ from
sich verändern	to change
vertreten	to appear; to represent
(sich) vor•bereiten (auf)	to prepare (for)
zerstören	to destroy
auswendig (lernen)	(to learn) by heart;
	(to memorize)

Gymnasiasten und Gymnasiastinnen genießen ihre Freizeit.

bewegt	eventful; turbulent
eher	rather; sooner
fast	almost, nearly
gegen	approximately
häufig	often, frequent(ly)
weitgehend	extensive(ly), far-reaching

Sie wissen schon

die Gesamtschule, die Nähe, die Realschule, das Dorf, das Fach, das Gymnasium, sich beschäftigen mit, bestehen, lehren, unterrichten, verbieten, verlassen, langweilig, streng

Die Nacht vor einer großen Prüfung!

A Bedeutungen. Welche Wörter aus der Wortliste passen zu den Bedeutungen unten?

1. eine sehr kleine Stadt
2. ein schrecklicher Traum
3. nicht weit weg
4. ein Fach, das alle Schüler belegen müssen
5. um eine ungefähre Zeit
6. sehr oft
7. treffen
8. jemandem sagen, dass sie oder er etwas nicht machen darf

B Vokabelarbeit. Ergänzen Sie die Sätze auf Seite 55 mit den Wörtern in dem Kasten.

A. 1. das Dorf 2. der Alptraum 3. die Nähe 4. das Pflichtfach
5. gegen 6. häufig 7. sich begegnen 8. verbieten

---

rechnen   häufig   bewegte   unterscheiden

Vergangenheit   Nähe   gegen

langweilig   fast   Alptraum

---

1. In der _____ waren die Unterrichtsmethoden streng, aber heute gibt es mehr Eigeninitiative und Kreativität.
2. Damals hat Schule keinen Spaß gemacht; für manche Schüler war es ein _____.
3. Karolin wohnt in der _____ von Frankfurt.
4. Mathe kann ein sehr interessantes Fach sein, aber Karolin findet es _____.
5. Schüler und Schülerinnen sollen _____ in die Bibliothek gehen, wenn sie gute Noten bekommen wollen.
6. Die Schulen in Österreich und Deutschland _____ sich sehr von den Schulen in Nordamerika.
7. In Deutschland beginnt die Schule normalerweise _____ acht Uhr.
8. Das alte Gymnasium in Bremen hat eine _____ Geschichte.
9. Im Kindergarten in Nordamerika lernen viele schon lesen, schreiben und _____.
10. Viele deutsche Städte wurden im Zweiten Weltkrieg _____ total zerstört.

C Alles über die Schule. Lesen Sie die Sätze links, und suchen Sie die passende Definition für die kursiv gedruckten Wörter aus der rechten Spalte.

1. Heute können die Schüler *mitbestimmen* und zum Beispiel ihre Hauptfächer selber wählen.
2. Trotz der Demokratisierung blieben die Unterrichtsmethoden *streng*.
3. Schule in Deutschland: Spaß oder *Alptraum*?
4. In Bremen wurde 1528 das alte Gymnasium *gegründet*.
5. Die Gesellschaft *veränderte sich*, und die Schulen wurden reformiert.
6. Meine Klassenlehrerin *unterrichtet* uns in Mathematik und Deutsch.
7. Nach dem Krieg war Bremen weitgehend *zerstört*.
8. In Kursen wie Deutsch und Philospohie bin ich *häufig* zu finden.

D Das Schulsystem. Sie besuchen Freunde in Deutschland, die wissen wollen, wie die Schulen in Nordamerika sind. Wie viele Fächer hat man? Wie lange muss man Hausaufgaben machen? Beschreiben Sie ihnen den Schulalltag eines Schülers / einer Schülerin.

a. lehren
b. oft
c. genau, sehr korrekt, strikt
d. an wichtigen Entscheidungen teilnehmen
e. anders werden
f. ruinieren
g. instituieren, etablieren
h. ein schlechter Traum

KULTURSPIEGEL

Die Schulpflicht in Deutschland besteht vom sechsten bis zum achtzehnten Lebensjahr. Nach vier Jahren Grundschule wählen Schüler und Schülerinnen zwischen Hauptschule, Realschule, Gesamtschule oder Gymnasium. Die Hauptschulen dienen als Übergang zu einer Lehre. Die Gymnasien vermitteln eine vertiefte Bildung, und bereiten auf das Studium an einer Hochschule (wie zum Beispiel Universität oder Fachhochschule) vor.

B. 1. Vergangenheit 2. Alptraum 3. Nähe
4. langweilig 5. häufig 6. unterscheiden
7. gegen 8. bewegte 9. rechnen 10. fast

C. 1. d 2. c 3. h 4. g 5. e 6. a
7. f 8. b

D. *Answers will vary.*

STRUKTUREN

DER- AND EIN-WORDS
REFERRING TO SPECIFIC OR GENERAL PERSONS OR THINGS

The forms of **der**-words closely resemble those of the definite article, **die, der, das.** The most common **der**-words are the following.

alle (*pl.*)	*all*	welcher	*which*
dieser	*this, that*	mancher	*some*
jeder (*sg.*)	*every, each*	solcher	*such*
jener	(*the one*) *that*		

Note that **jeder** occurs only in the singular, **alle** only in the plural.

Jeder Schüler hielt den Atem an.   *Every pupil held his breath.*
Der Professor versuchte mit **allen**   *The professor tried all the keys*
    Schlüsseln die Tür zu öffnen.   *to open the door.*

Welcher is a question word.

Zu **welcher** Stunde kamen   *What time did the boys get out*
    die Jungen aus dem   *of the classroom?*
    Klassenzimmer heraus?

Here are all the forms of **dieser.** Notice the similarity between the endings and the forms of **die, der, das.**

	SINGULAR			PLURAL
	FEMININE	MASCULINE	NEUTER	ALL GENDERS
NOMINATIVE	dies**e** Frau	dies**er** Mann	dies**es** Kind	dies**e** Kinder
ACCUSATIVE	dies**e** Frau	dies**en** Mann	dies**es** Kind	dies**e** Kinder
DATIVE	dies**er** Frau	dies**em** Mann	dies**em** Kind	dies**en** Kinder**n**
GENITIVE	dies**er** Frau	dies**es** Mann**es**	dies**es** Kind**es**	dies**er** Kinder

As always, the dative plural of the noun also takes a special ending, **-n.**

Ein-words, as you might have guessed, follow the same pattern as the indefinite article **ein.** The most common **ein**-words are the possessive adjectives and the negative article **kein.** Here are all the forms for **mein.**

	SINGULAR			PLURAL
	FEMININE	MASCULINE	NEUTER	ALL GENDERS
NOMINATIVE	mein**e** Frau	mein Mann	mein Kind	mein**e** Kinder
ACCUSATIVE	mein**e** Frau	mein**en** Mann	mein Kind	mein**e** Kinder
DATIVE	mein**er** Frau	mein**em** Mann	mein**em** Kind	mein**en** Kinder**n**
GENITIVE	mein**er** Frau	mein**es** Mann**es**	mein**es** Kind**es**	mein**er** Kinder

KURZ NOTIERT

You will recall the possessive adjectives:

mein	*my*
dein	(*sg. inform.*) *your*
Ihr	(*sg. form.*) *your*
ihr	*her*
sein	*his*
sein	*its*
unser	*our*
euer	(*pl. inform.*) *your*
Ihr	(*pl. form.*) *your*
ihr	*their*

The possessive adjective **euer** drops the last **-e-** before adding a case ending: **euer Sohn,** but **euren/eurem Sohn, eures Sohnes, eure Söhne, euren Söhnen, eurer Söhne.**

Übungen

A Schüler und Schülerinnen. Ergänzen Sie die richtige Form der Wörter in Klammern.

1. Susanne sagt, ihr Schulalltag ist wie der Schulalltag von _____ (jeder) Schüler.
2. Sie interessiert sich sehr für Biologie und Deutsch. _____ (Solcher) Fächer machen ihr Spaß.
3. Normalerweise muss man _____ (jeder) Abend Hausaufgaben machen.
4. _____ (Jeder) Schüler ist anders.
5. _____ (Mancher) Studenten haben gute Erinnerungen an die Schule.
6. _____ (Welcher) Fach gefällt Ihnen am besten?
7. _____ (Welcher) Kurs belegen Sie jetzt?

B Meinungen. Junge Leute reden über ihr Leben und ihre Familien. Ergänzen Sie das Gespräch auf Seite 58.

A. **1.** jedem **2.** Solche **3.** jeden **4.** Jeder **5.** Manche **6.** Welches **7.** Welchen

KURZ NOTIERT

German uses the accusative case in expressions that refer to specific time. You already know the greetings **guten Morgen** and **guten Abend.** In context, the accusative forms of the definite article or **der**-words often occur with nouns relating to time.

Ich arbeite **jeden Donnerstag. Dieses Wochenende** fahre ich aufs Land.
Ich wohne **den ganzen Sommer** im Dorf.

KAI: _____[1] (Mein) Alltag ist ziemlich anstrengend. Ich habe immer viel zu tun. _____[2] (Mein) Freunde sagen mir, ich sollte weniger arbeiten. Ich lege Wert auf _____[3] (ihr) Meinung.

JULIA: In _____[4] (unser) Familie ist das Leben sehr friedlich. Wenn ich mit _____[5] (mein) Eltern rede, verstehen wir einander. Wie ist es in _____[6] (euer) Familie?

WOLF: Die Eltern brauchen auch _____[7] (ihr) Freizeit. Man kann sich nicht immer nur um die Kinder kümmern! Ich habe _____[8] (mein) Vater gesagt, er sollte ab und zu Urlaub machen.

HAIKE: Ich möchte _____[9] (kein) Kinder haben. In _____[10] (mein) Zukunft sehe ich nur Beruf und Freunde.

ADJECTIVES
DESCRIBING PEOPLE, OBJECTS, PLACES, AND IDEAS

You have learned to recognize and use both predicate and attributive adjectives. Predicate adjectives follow nouns and have no endings, whereas attributive adjectives precede nouns and do take endings.

Attributive adjectives that follow articles or **der-** or **ein-**words take one of two endings: **-e** or **-en.** Here are all the forms for adjectives that follow the definite article or a **der-**word.

	SINGULAR			PLURAL
	FEMININE	MASCULINE	NEUTER	ALL GENDERS
NOM.	die lieb**e** Mutter	der alt**e** Pfarrer	das klein**e** Kind	die streng**en** Lehrer
ACC.	die lieb**e** Mutter	den alt**en** Pfarrer	das klein**e** Kind	die streng**en** Lehrer
DAT.	der lieb**en** Mutter	dem alt**en** Pfarrer	dem klein**en** Kind	den streng**en** Lehrern
GEN.	der lieb**en** Mutter	des alt**en** Pfarrer**s**	des klein**en** Kind**es**	der streng**en** Lehrer

Adjectives that end in **-el** or **-er,** such as **dunkel** and **teuer,** drop the **-e** before adding the endings.

Wer hat das **teure** Gemälde gekauft?

Who bought the expensive painting?

The adjective **hoch** becomes **hoh-** before adding an adjective ending.

> Jutta ist auf den **hohen** Berg geklettert.
>
> *Jutta climbed up the high mountain.*

When adjectives follow each other, all take the same endings.

> Wo sind die **schönen alten** Fotos?
>
> *Where are the nice old photos?*
>
> Dieses **kleine blaue** Auto gehört Stefan.
>
> *This little blue car belongs to Stefan.*

Adjectives that follow **ein-**words have the same pattern of endings as those that follow **der-**words, with three exceptions.

	MASCULINE	NEUTER
NOM. ACC.	**ein kleiner** Junge	**ein schweres** Examen **ein schweres** Examen

Attributive adjectives that do not follow articles or **der-** or **ein-**words must have endings that show the gender, number, and case of the nouns they modify. Note that these endings are very similar to the forms of the missing definite articles **die, der, das,** with two exceptions: masculine and neuter singular in the genitive case.

	SINGULAR			PLURAL
	FEMININE	MASCULINE	NEUTER	ALL GENDERS
NOM.	klein**e** Stadt	streng**er** Lehrer	klar**es** Wasser	schwer**e** Examen
ACC.	klein**e** Stadt	streng**en** Lehrer	klar**es** Wasser	schwer**e** Examen
DAT.	klein**er** Stadt	streng**em** Lehrer	klar**em** Wasser	schwer**en** Examen
GEN.	klein**er** Stadt	streng**en** Lehrer**s**	klar**en** Wasser**s**	schwer**er** Examen

Attributive adjectives that do not follow articles or **der-** or **ein-**words often appear in telegraphic-style messages, on signs, and in ads.

> Gesucht: **strenger Lehrer** für Nachhilfe in Englisch
>
> *Wanted: strict teacher for coaching in English*

Übungen

A Meine Schulerlebnisse

SCHRITT 1: Ergänzen Sie die Sätze mit den Wörtern aus dem Kasten.

kreativer hohen
bewegte
typischen
kleinen guten
interessantes
besseren

1. Meine Schule hat eine _____ Geschichte.
2. Biologie ist für mich ein sehr _____ Fach.
3. Ich wohne in einem _____ Dorf, und wir machen Ausflüge in die Natur.
4. Auf unserer Klassenreise durften wir nicht auf einen _____ Felsen klettern.
5. Ich träume von einer _____ Zukunft.
6. Mein Lehrer hat mir einen _____ Ratschlag gegeben.
7. In einer _____ Gesamtschule wie meiner gibt es viele Wahlfächer.
8. Für manche Jugendlichen ist ein _____ Beruf sehr wichtig.

SCHRITT 2: Machen Sie die Sätze interessanter! Wählen Sie fünf Sätze, und fügen Sie andere Adjektive hinzu!

A. Schritt 1: 1. bewegte **2.** interessantes **3.** kleinen **4.** hohen **5.** besseren **6.** guten **7.** typischen **8.** kreativer
Schritt 2: *Answers will vary.*

B Über meine Familie. Ergänzen Sie die Sätze mit den Adjektiven in Klammern.

1. Meine Großmutter hat dieses _____ (alt) Buch geschrieben.
2. Der _____ (klein) Junge da ist mein Neffe.
3. Die _____ _____ (nett älter) Frauen sind meine Tanten.
4. Meine Schwester liest den _____ (berühmt) Roman[a] von Thomas Mann.
5. Manche _____ (jung) Familienmitglieder engagieren sich für Politik.
6. Solche _____ (teurer) Sachen gefallen meiner Familie nicht.
7. Meine Eltern haben der _____ (neu) Lehrerin ein Geschenk gekauft.

[a]*novel*

B. 1. alte **2.** kleine **3.** netten älteren **4.** berühmten **5.** jungen **6.** teuren **7.** neuen

C Eine Kleinanzeige. Sie haben eine neue Wohnung und brauchen mindestens einen Mitbewohner / eine Mitbewohnerin. Wie würden Sie sich selbst beschreiben? Wie viele Mitbewohner/Mitbewohnerinnen suchen Sie? Welche Eigenschaften sollten sie haben? Gebrauchen Sie die Wörter im Kasten. Schreiben Sie eine Anzeige, in der Sie das alles sehr kurz ausdrücken.

C. *Answers will vary.*

faul gutgelaunt aktiv
sauber kreativ nett
interessant ? berufstätig

MODELL: Netter, kreativer Student mit vielen Interessen sucht drei interessante, berufstätige Mitbewohner für eine große Wohnung.

INDEFINITE NUMERALS AND THE INTERROGATIVE PRONOUN WAS FÜR (EIN)
TALKING ABOUT AMOUNTS AND ASKING ABOUT THINGS

The following indefinite numerals may precede nouns with or without other adjectives: **einige** (*a few*), **mehrere** (*several*), **viele** (*many*), and **wenige** (*few*). These words take the same endings as other plural attributive adjectives that do not follow **der-** or **ein-**words.

> Die Jungen verbrachten **viele** lange Stunden mit Professor Heimbach.
> *The boys spent many long hours with Professor Heimbach.*

Do not confuse **alle** with this category of indefinite numerals. **Alle** takes the endings of a plural **der-**word; adjectives that follow **alle** take the plural ending **-en.**

> Die Jungen haben **alle** möglichen Ausreden probiert.
> *The boys tried all possible excuses.*

The expression **was für** asks the question *what kind(s) of.* Remember, **für** does not function as a preposition in this construction and, therefore, does not influence the case endings of the noun expression that follows. Rather, the case of **ein** plus the noun depends on whether it functions as the subject, direct object, indirect object, or object of a preposition within the sentence.

> Was für **ein Lehrer** ist dieser Herr?
> *What kind of a teacher is this gentleman?*

Übungen

Eine Reise nach Bremen. Sie sind gerade von einer Reise nach Bremen zurückgekommen. Ihre Freunde haben viele Fragen. Beantworten Sie die Fragen mit den Wörtern in Klammern.

MODELL: Was für eine Stadt ist Bremen? (alt, hochinteressant) →
          Bremen ist eine alte, hochinteressante Stadt.

1. Was für Tage hast du in Bremen verbracht? (viele schöne)
2. Was für Gebäude hast du gesehen? (einige interessant)
3. Was für Deutsche hast du kennen gelernt? (mehrere jung)
4. Was für Postkarten hast du gekauft? (wenig alt)
5. Was für Musik hast du gehört? (neu, deutsch)

1. Ich habe viele schöne Tage in Bremen verbracht.   2. Ich habe einige interessante Gebäude gesehen.   3. Ich habe mehrere junge Deutsche kennen gelernt.   4. Ich habe wenige alte Postkarten gekauft.   5. Ich habe neue deutsche Musik gehört.

Die Stadt Bremen wurde im Zweiten Weltkrieg weitgehend zerstört.

PERSPEKTIVEN

A. 1. Das stimmt. **2.** Das stimmt nicht. **3.** Das stimmt. **4.** Das stimmt. **5.** Das stimmt. **6.** Das stimmt. **7.** Das stimmt nicht.

B. GEBURTSDATUM: 14. März 1879; GEBURTSORT: Ulm; BERUF DES VATERS: Kaufmann; WOHNORTE: Ulm, München, Padua, Mailand, Schweiz

Der berühmte Wissenschaftler Albert Einstein.

HÖREN SIE ZU!
EINSTEINS FRÜHE JAHRE

Sie hören eine kurze Biografie des Wissenschaftlers Albert Einstein.

A Schule und Ausbildung. Welche Probleme hatte Albert Einstein? Was stimmt? Was stimmt nicht?

Albert Einstein . . .
1. lernte spät sprechen.
2. zeigte kein Interesse an Mathematik und Physik.
3. war nicht gut diszipliniert.
4. verließ mit fünfzehn Jahren das Gymnasium.
5. konnte keine klassischen Fremdsprachen lernen.
6. besuchte die Vorlesungen nicht.
7. bestand sein zweites Examen nicht.

B Kindheit und Familie. Hören Sie gut zu, und machen Sie sich Notizen.

GEBURTSDATUM:		
GEBURTSORT:		
BERUF DES VATERS:		
WOHNORTE:		

C Die frühen Jahre Albert Einsteins. Schreiben Sie mit Hilfe Ihrer angekreuzten Sätze in Aktivität A und Ihrer Notizen in Aktivität B eine kurze Biografie des jungen Albert Einsteins.

C. *Text of biographies will vary.*

WORTSCHATZ ZUM HÖRTEXT

Mailand	Milan
das Musterkind	model child
geistig zurückgeblieben	mentally challenged
die Aufnahmeprüfung	entrance exam
die Vertretung	stand-in
fehlen	to be missing

Lesen Sie!

Zum Thema

● Haben Sie schon einmal jemandem einen Streich gespielt? Erzählen Sie Ihren Mitschülern/Mitschülerinnen davon.

Answers will vary.

Sie lesen jetzt eine Kurzgeschichte von Heinrich Spoerl. Die Geschichte handelt von Schülern, die ihrem Englischlehrer einen Streich spielen. Wer zeigt es am Ende wem?

Der Stift

Eine Türklinke besteht aus zwei Teilen, einem positiven und einem negativen. Sie stecken ineinander, der kleine wichtige Stift hält sie zusammen. Ohne ihn zerfällt die Herrlichkeit.

Auch die Türklinke an der Obertertia ist nach diesem bewährten
5   Grundsatz konstruiert.

Als der Lehrer für Englisch um zwölf in die Klasse kam und mit der ihm gewohnten konzentrierten Energie die Tür hinter sich schloß, behielt er den negativen Teil der Klinke in der Hand. Der positive Teil flog draußen klirrend auf den Gang.

10   Mit dem negativen Teil kann man keine Tür öffnen. Die Tür hat nur ein viereckiges Loch. Der negative Teil desgleichen.

Die Klasse hat den Atem angehalten und bricht jetzt in unbändige Freude aus. Sie weiß, was kommt. Nämlich römisch eins: Eine ausführliche Untersuchung, welcher schuldbeladene Schüler den Stift
15   herausgezogen hat. Und römisch zwei: Technische Versuche, wie man ohne die Klinke die Tür öffnen kann. Damit wird die Stunde herumgehen.

Aber es kam nichts. Weder römisch eins noch römisch zwei. Professor Heimbach war ein viel zu erfahrener Pädagoge, um sich ausgerechnet
20   mit seiner Obertertia auf kriminalistische Untersuchungen und technische Probleme einzulassen. Er wußte, was man erwartete, und tat das Gegenteil.

„Wir werden schon mal wieder herauskommen", meinte er gleichgültig. „Mathiesen, fang mal an. Kapitel siebzehn, zweiter Absatz."
25   Mathiesen fing an, bekam eine drei minus. Dann ging es weiter; die Stunde lief wie jede andere. Die Sache mit dem Stift war verpufft.

Aber die Jungens waren doch noch schlauer. Wenigstens einer von ihnen. Auf einmal steht der Klostermann auf und sagt, er muß raus.

WORTSCHATZ ZUM LESEN

die Türklinke	door handle
der Stift	pin
zerfallen	to fall apart
die Obertertia	fifth year of German secondary school; approx. equivalent to 9th grade
der Gang	hallway
schuldbeladen	burdened with guilt
sich einlassen auf	to get involved in
verpufft	fizzled
der Pflaumenkuchen	plum cake
widerlegen	to dispute
feixen	to smirk
die Anstalt	institution
die Insassen	occupants; inmates
Klassenhiebe	punishment by the class

KULTURSPIEGEL

Heinrich Spoerl wurde 1887 in Düsseldorf geboren, wo er 1919–1937 als Rechtsanwalt arbeitete. Seine Romane waren sehr populär und wurden alle verfilmt.

„Wir gehen nachher alle."

30 Er muß aber trotzdem.

„Setzt dich hin!"

Der lange Klostermann steht immer noch; er behauptet, er habe Pflaumenkuchen gegessen und so weiter.

Professor Heimbach steht vor einem Problem. Pflaumenkuchen kann
35 man nicht widerlegen. Wer will die Folgen auf sich nehmen?

Der Professor gibt nach? Er stochert mit seinen Hausschlüsseln in dem viereckigen Loch an der Tür herum. Aber keiner läßt sich hineinklemmen.

„Gebt mal eure Schlüssel her." Merkwürdig, niemand hat einen
40 Schlüssel. Sie krabbeln geschäftig in ihren Hosentaschen und feixen.

Unvorsichtigerweise feixt auch der Pflaumenkuchenmann. Professor Heimbach ist Menschenkenner. Wer Pflaumenkuchen gegessen hat und so weiter, der feixt nicht.

„Klostermann, ich kann dir nicht helfen. Setz dich ruhig hin. Die
45 Rechnung kannst du dem schicken, der den Stift auf dem Gewissen hat. – Kebben, laß das Grinsen und fahr fort."

Also wieder nichts.

Langsam, viel zu langsam, wird es ein Uhr. Es schellt. Die Anstalt schüttet ihre Insassen auf die Straße. Die Obertertia wird nicht erlöst. Sie
50 liegt im dritten Stock am toten Ende eines langen Ganges.

Professor Heimbach schließt den Unterricht und bleibt auf dem Katheder. Die Jungens packen ihre Bücher. „Wann können wir gehen?"
– „Ich weiß nicht. Wir müssen eben warten."

Warten ist nichts für Jungens. Außerdem haben sie Hunger. Der dicke
55 Schrader hat noch ein Butterbrot und kaut mit vollen Backen; die andern kauen betreten an ihren Bleistiften.

„Können wir nicht vielleicht unsere Hausarbeiten machen?"

„Nein! Erstens werden Hausarbeiten, wie der Name sagt, zu Hause gemacht. Und zweitens habt ihr fünf Stunden hinter euch und müßt eure
60 zarte Gesundheit schonen. Ruht euch aus; meinethalben könnt ihr schlafen."

Schlafen in den Bänken hat man genügend geübt. Es ist wundervoll. Aber es geht nur, wenn es verboten ist. Jetzt, wo es empfohlen wird, macht es keinen Spaß und funktioniert nicht.

65 Eine öde Langeweile kriecht durch das Zimmer. Die Jungen dösen. Der Professor hat es besser: er korrigiert Hefte.

Kurz nach zwei kamen die Putzfrauen, die Obertertia konnte nach Hause, und der lange Klostermann, der das mit dem Stift gemacht hatte und sehr stolz darauf war, bekam Klassenhiebe.

Heinrich Spoerl (1887–1955)

Zum Text

A Was haben Sie gelesen? Ergänzen Sie die Sätze.

1. Die Türklinke ging kaputt, weil
   a. sie verrostet war.
   b. ein Junge sie auseinander genommen hatte.
2. Der Professor hat
   a. eine Gliederung[a] mit der Funktion einer Türklinke an die Tafel geschrieben.
   b. die Jungen zum Vorlesen aufgefordert.
3. Der Schüler Klostermann
   a. hatte Pflaumenkuchen gegessen.
   b. hatte keinen Pflaumenkuchen gegessen.
4. Als der Schultag zu Ende ging,
   a. konnten die Jungen sofort das Klassenzimmer verlassen.
   b. mussten die Jungen eine Weile sitzen bleiben.

[a]outline

B Ein Rollenspiel. Führen Sie mit Ihren Mitschülern/Mitschülerinnen die Geschichte von Professor Heimbach und seinen Schülern auf. Machen Sie dabei aber die Türklinke Ihres Klassenzimmers nicht kaputt!

A. 1. b 2. b 3. b 4. b

For more information, visit the *Auf Deutsch!* Web Site at www.mcdougallittell.com.

B. *Answers will vary.*

INTERAKTION

● Eine Diskussion. Was halten Sie von Streichen? Wie unterscheiden Sie „gute Streiche" von „bösen Streichen"? Geben Sie Beispiele jeder Art an.

Answers will vary.

SCHREIBEN SIE!

Ein Antrag

● Stellen Sie sich vor, dass an Ihrer Schule über eine Schulreform diskutiert wird. Sie sind eingeladen, als Vertreter/Vertreterin ihrer Jahrgangstufe der Sonderkommission zur Schulreform beizutreten. Die Kommission sammelt Ideen und Vorschläge für die ideale Schule der Zukunft. Schreiben Sie einen Antrag, in dem Sie Ihre

Texts will vary.

KULTURSPIEGEL

In Deutschland wird immer wieder über eine Schulreform diskutiert. Schüler klagen zum Beispiel über altmodischen Unterricht, der nicht auf moderne Jobs vorbereitet. Lehrer wollen mehr Freiheiten, wie sie ihren Unterricht gestalten können. Gesucht werden kreative Modelle, die auf der Tradition des deutschen Schulsystems aufbauen und gleichzeitig auf das technische Zeitalter der Zukunft vorbereiten.

TIPP ZUM SCHREIBEN

You may want to talk with friends or acquaintances who attend other schools about their schools. Their schools may offer courses and facilities that you think would be advantageous to your school.

Vorstellungen für eine ideale Schule formulieren. Schreiben Sie Vorschläge zu mindestens vier der folgenden Themen.

Schüler	Kreativität	Technik
Lehrer	Pflichtfächer	Bewertung
Verwaltung	Wahlfächer	Abschluss
Schularten	Berufliche	Unterrichtsfreie
Schuljahr	Ausbildung	Zeit
Schultag	Praktikum	Klassenfahrten
Schulpflicht	Alternative	Wettbewerb
Behindertenbildung	Bildungswege	Gemeinschaftsdienst
kooperatives Lernen	Projekte	Klassenzimmer

Purpose:	To present a model for schools of the future
Audience:	Educators, students, parents, administrators
Subject:	School reform: the ideal school of the future
Structure:	Proposal

Schreibmodell

The report has many adjectives. Make note of their endings.

In the opening paragraph, the writer analyzes why change is needed.

To create a more gender-neutral tone, the writer has chosen to use a fairly new spelling convention for titles, adding a capitalized feminine plural ending to the masculine forms: **SchülerInnen, LehrerInnen.**

> ### Ideen für eine moderne Schule
> von Inge Schmitt
>
> In der Zeitung lesen wir über die rapiden Fortschritte in der Technik, über eine multikulturelle Gesellschaft und die wachsende Notwendigkeit, unser Wissen und unsere Informationen mit allen Ländern der Welt zu teilen. Die ideale Schule der Zukunft muss mit der modernen Welt Schritt halten können. Im Namen meiner MitschülerInnen möchte ich folgende Verbesserungen vorschlagen.
>
> Computer und neue Medien:
> Die ideale Schule hat einen modernen Computerraum und E-mail Adressen für alle SchülerInnen. Nicht alle unserer MitschülerInnen haben zu Hause einen Computer mit Internetanschluss, an dem sie den Umgang mit den neuen Medien lernen können. Das Internet soll auch im Unterricht eingesetzt werden.

To help orient the reader to what's coming, the writer uses a short topical header for each suggestion.

> Fremdsprachen und SchülerInnenaustausch: Die ideale Schule der Zukunft bietet mehr Fremdsprachen an als nur Englisch, Französisch oder Latein. Heutzutage sprechen die meisten Menschen auf der Welt Chinesisch und Spanisch. Das Fremdsprachenangebot der idealen Schule muss deshalb erweitert werden. Außerdem soll jede Klasse an einem SchülerInnenaustausch mit einem fremden Land teilnehmen. Klassenfahrten sollen auch ins Ausland gehen.

Schreibstrategien

Vor dem Schreiben

- Draw a line to divide a sheet of paper into two vertical columns. In the left column write down all the things you really like about your school. In the right column write down all the aspects that you don't like and feel need to be changed. Try to think of as many items as you can (minimum of four for each column). If necessary, refer to the list of **Themen** on p. 66 to help you.

- Now look at the list of things needing change in the right-hand column. Circle the four that you feel are the most important to change in order to improve your school. Rank these four in their order of importance, with 1 being the most important and 4 the least important. On the back of the same sheet, write these items in their order of importance, leaving plenty of room between each for notes.

- Think about each of these problems individually, and jot down how you would improve on each of them. Make sure you have concrete suggestions for improvement, not just a list of complaints.

Beim Schreiben

- Write your draft double-spaced, leaving room for changes and corrections. Remember who your audience is and what the purpose of this proposal is. This will help you set the right tone.

- Keep your list of likes and dislikes about your school in front of you. If more ideas come to you as you write, jot them down for future reference.

- State the purpose of your paper in a brief opening paragraph. You may want to mention problems that need to be fixed, your charge as student representative, or some other approach, but you need to establish your reason for writing for the reader.

Die ideale Schule:
viel Kreativität und wenige
Autorität
von Christopher Thomas

Die ideale Schule der Zukunft
soll einen guten Platz für alle
Schülerinnen und Schüler sein.
Aber in unserer Schule wird
nicht das unterrichtet, was viele
Schülerinnen und Schüler
interessiert. Sportunterricht ist
leider immer wichtiger als der
Unterricht in die kreativen
Fächer. Ich mache folgenden
Vorschläge:

Wie alles andere Fähigkeiten
Kreativität kommt nicht von
allein: Sie muss geübt und
aufgebaut werden. Aber es gibt
an unserer Schule zu wenige
Unterricht in Musik, Kunst,
Tanz und Theater. Die neuen
Medien sind sehr wichtig.
Schüler und Schülerinnen sollen
lernen, mit der Videokamera
und dem World Wide Web zu
arbeiten. Es gibt viele neue
Berufe mit den neue Medien.
Kreative Fächer sollen deshalb
Pflichtfächer sein. Aber
braucht unsere Schule auch
talentierte Lehrerinnen und
Lehrer, die sich für ihre
Schülerinnen und Schüler
interessieren und keine
autoritären „Supermächte".

Neuer Absatz?

- Next, write out your suggestions for improving the schools of the future in individual paragraphs. You don't need to write more than three or four sentences for each suggestion, and in many cases, one well-crafted sentence may be enough. Make a heading for each paragraph. Proceed in the descending order of importance you established earlier.

- You may choose to compare and contrast existing conditions with your suggestions for improvement, or you may simply explain your suggestions in greater detail.

- After you have created a full set of suggestions, finish your proposal with a concluding statement that ties all the topics together.

Nach dem Schreiben

- Read your proposal critically, marking problems in grammar, word choice, and tone. Trade papers with a peer editor. Try to make comments that are both practical (spelling corrections) and philosophical (an additional idea about one of the items).

- Finally, read your introductory paragraph and summary paragraph one last time and make sure you've done what you say you've done.

Stimmt alles?

- Create a second draft that reflects the suggestions for improvement of your peer editor and yourself.

- Read the improved version once, then think about it for a minute; then read it again. Are you satisfied with its tone, structure, and content?

- Give the proposal a title that matches its tone and content.

WORTSCHATZ

Substantive	Nouns
die **Freude, -n**	pleasure, joy
die **Gegenwart**	present time
die **Grundlage, -n**	foundation, basis
die **Überlastung, -en**	burden, overload
die **Unsicherheit, -en**	insecurity, uncertainty
die **Unterrichtsmethode, -n**	teaching method
die **Vergangenheit**	past
die **Wirkung, -en**	result; effect
die **Wissenschaft, -en**	science
der **Alltag**	everyday life
der **Alptraum, ¨e**	nightmare
der **Handel**	trade
der **Ratschlag, ¨e**	advice
der **Stil, -e**	style
der **Wettbewerb, -e**	competition
das **Jahrhundert, -e**	century
das **Pflichtfach, ¨er**	required course
das **Wahlfach, ¨er**	elective, optional course

Verben	Verbs
sich begegnen	to meet
besetzen	to occupy
erobern	to conquer
gründen	to found
Wert legen auf (+ *acc.*)	to value something
mit•bestimmen	to have a say
rechnen	to calculate
sich unterscheiden von, unterschied, unterschieden	to differ from
sich verändern	to change
vertreten (vertritt), vertrat, vertreten	to appear; to represent
(sich) vor•bereiten	to prepare
weihen (+ *dat.*)	to dedicate
zerstören	to destroy

Adjektive und Adverbien	Adjectives and adverbs
auswendig (lernen)	(to learn) by heart; to memorize
bewegt	eventful; turbulent
eher	rather; sooner
fast	almost, nearly
gegen	approximately
häufig	often, frequent(ly)
prima	great, excellent
weitgehend	extensive(ly)

Sie wissen schon	You already know
die **Gesamtschule, -n**	comprehensive school
die **Nähe**	vicinity
die **Realschule, -n**	vocational school
das **Dorf, ¨er**	small town
das **Fach, ¨er**	school subject
das **Gymnasium,** *pl.* **Gymnasien**	college preparatory high school
sich beschäftigen mit	to be occupied with
bestehen, bestand, bestanden	to pass (a test)
lehren	to teach
statt•finden, fand statt, stattgefunden	to take place
unterrichten	to teach
verbieten, verbot, verboten	to forbid, prohibit
verlassen, verließ, verlassen	to leave
beschädigt	damaged
langweilig	boring
lustig	fun(ny), cheerful(ly)
streng	strict(ly)

PLANNING GUIDE
CLASSROOM MANAGEMENT

OBJECTIVES

Communication
- Talk about young peoples' expectations for the future, p. 70.
- Discuss gender roles in the past and present, p. 72.
- Recount post-war changes in the German school system, p. 70.
- Imagine a wedding celebration, p. 75.

Grammar
- Review the simple past, p. 72.
- Review negation, pp. 72–73.
- Review pronouns, p. 73
- Review cases, p. 73.

Culture
- Learn about Bremen, p. 73.
- Listen to a department store's ad for wedding gifts, p. 74.

PROGRAM RESOURCES

Print
- *Arbeitsheft* (Workbook), pp. 47–50
- *Arbeitsheft* (Workbook), Teacher's Edition, pp. 47–50

Audiovisual
- Overhead Transparencies 25.G1, 26.G1, and 27.G1–27.G3
- Audio Program, Cassette 2A/CD 2
- Audioscript, pp. 20–21

Technology
- Annenberg *Fokus Deutsch* Video Series, *Wiederholung 9*
- www.mcdougallittell.com

Assessment Program Options
- *Prüfung, Wiederholung 9*, Assessment Program, pp. 108–109
- Audio Program, Cassette 8A/CD 10
- Audioscript, p. 108
- Teacher's Resource CD-ROM

PACING GUIDE
50-MINUTE SCHEDULE

DAY 1

Note: (1) Please see TE, pp. 70C–70D, for other suggestions not referenced in these plans. (2) Not all homework options need be assigned.

VIDEOTHEK
- Quick Start Review: Adjectives (TE, p. 70C). 5 MIN
- Play video episode, then do *Akt. A,* p. 70. Discuss (TE, p. 70C). 10 MIN
- Do *Akt. B,* p. 70 in small groups. 8 MIN
- Do *Akt. C,* p. 70, as a whole-class activity. 8 MIN

VOKABELN
- Do *Akt. A,* p. 71, silently, then check answers with a partner. 9 MIN
- Do *Akt. B,* pp. 71–72, as a whole-class activity. 8 MIN

Homework Options:
- *Videothek, Akt. D,* p. 70
- *Arbeitsheft,* p. 48, *Vokabeln, Akt. B*

DAY 2

VOKABELN
- Quick Start Review: Indefinite numerals (TE, p. 70C). 5 MIN
- In small groups, briefly discuss answers to *Akt. D,* p. 70. 5 MIN
- Do *Akt. C,* p. 72, silently, then (with a partner) write a sentence using each of the words in the right-hand column. 10 MIN
- Follow the Teaching Suggestions for *Akt. D,* p. 72 (TE, p. 70C). 8 MIN
- Follow the Teaching Suggestions for *Akt. E,* p. 72. Follow-up with a class discussion. 10 MIN

STRUKTUREN
- Do *Übung A,* p. 72, silently, then compare answers with a partner. 12 MIN

Homework Options:
- *Arbeitsheft,* p. 50, *Strukturen, Akt. D*
- *Übung C,* p. 73

PACING GUIDE
50-MINUTE SCHEDULE

DAY 3

STRUKTUREN

- Quick Start Review: Negation (TE, p. 70D). 5 MIN
- *Übung B*, pp. 72–73. Include the follow-up activity in the Teaching Suggestions (TE, p. 70D). 9 MIN
- Do *Übung D*, p. 73, in pairs, then discuss the answers as a class. 12 MIN

PERSPEKTIVEN

- Follow the Teaching Suggestions for a warm-up activity, then play the entire recording while students do *Akt. A*, p. 74, silently (TE, p. 70D). 10 MIN
- Do *Akt. D*, p. 75, in pairs (TE, p, 70D). 14 MIN

Homework Options:

- *Arbeitsheft*, p. 49, *Strukturen, Akt. C*
- *Übung C, E*, p. 73

DAY 4

PERSPEKTIVEN

- Quick Start Review: Simple past (TE, p. 70D). 6 MIN
- Play the recording again and do *Akt. B*, p. 74, as a class. 9 MIN
- Questions and review. 5 MIN
- *Prüfung, Wiederholung 9.* 30 MIN

Homework Options:

- *Perspektiven, Akt. C*, p. 75

PACING GUIDE
90-MINUTE SCHEDULE

DAY 1

Note: (1) Please see TE, pp. 70C–70D, for other suggestions not referenced in these plans. (2) Not all homework options need be assigned.

VIDEOTHEK

- Quick Start Review: Adjectives (TE, p. 70C). 5 MIN
- Play video episode, then do *Akt. A*, p. 70. Discuss (TE, p. 70C). 10 MIN
- Do *Akt. B*, p. 70. 8 MIN
- Do *Akt. C*, p. 70, as a class, then discuss. 8 MIN

VOKABELN

- Do *Akt. A*, p. 71. 9 MIN
- Do *Akt. B*, pp. 71–72, as a class. 8 MIN
- Do *Akt. C*, p. 72, silently; then write a sentence with a partner. 10 MIN
- *Akt. D–E*, p. 72 (TE, p. 70C). 18 MIN

Homework Options:

- *Videothek, Akt. D*, p. 70
- *Übung C*, p. 73
- *Arbeitsheft*, p. 48, *Akt. B*
- *Arbeitsheft*, p. 50, *Akt. D*

DAY 2

STRUKTUREN

- Quick Start Review: Negation (TE, p. 70D). 4 MIN
- *Übung B*, pp. 72–73. 5 MIN
- Do *Übung D*, p. 73, in pairs, then discuss answers as a class. 12 MIN

PERSPEKTIVEN

- Block Schedule activity: Change of Pace (TE, p. 70D). 10 MIN
- Follow Teaching Suggestions for warm-up, then play the entire recording while students do *Akt. A*, p. 74, silently (TE, p. 70D). 10 MIN
- Play the recording again, and do *Akt. B*, p. 74, as a class. 9 MIN
- Do *Akt. D*, p. 75, in pairs (TE, p. 70D). 14 MIN
- *Prüfung, Wiederholung 9.* 30 MIN

Homework Options:

- *Übung E*, p. 73
- *Arbeitsheft*, p. 49, *Strukturen, Akt. C*
- *Perspektiven, Akt. C*, p. 75

Videothek, p. 70

PROGRAM RESOURCES

- Videocassette, *Wiederholung 9*
- *Arbeitsheft*, p. 47
- Audio Program, Cassette 2A/CD 2
- Audioscript, p. 20

Quick Start Review

♻ Adjectives

Ergänzen Sie mit dem Adjektiv *grün*.

MODELL: Ich suche eine _____ Hose. →
Ich suche eine grüne Hose.

1. Gehört Ihnen dieser _____ Mantel?
2. Kannst du mir fünf _____ Pflanzen bringen?
3. Die Bücher mit dem _____ Punkt sind reduziert.
4. In dem _____ Kleid mit dem gelben Schal siehst du gut aus.
5. Wem gehört das _____ Auto vor meiner Garage?

Answers: 1. grüne 2. grüne
3. grünen 4. grünen 5. grüne

TEACHING SUGGESTIONS

- *Aktivität A, p. 70*

Have students take notes while watching the video. Have them pay attention to the birthdates of the 2 women. Keep track of students' answers at the board. Have 2 columns: *Was ist anders?* and *Was ist ähnlich?* Then discuss the reasons that might have led to the different lives of grandmother and granddaughter.

TEACHING ALL STUDENTS

Multiple Intelligences Kinesthetic: Have students act out the following

words: *heiraten, friedlich, zerstören, der Wettbewerb, auswendig lernen.*

CLASSROOM COMMUNITY

Dictation Write the following sentences on the board, or an OHT, leaving blanks in place of the italicized words. Have students write the missing words as you read the complete sentences.
1. Die Schüler und die Schülerinnen *protestierten,* und die Schulen wurden *reformiert.*   2. Die *Unterrichtsmethoden* waren früher sehr streng.   3. Später konnten die Schüler *mitbestimmen* und viele Fächer selbst auswählen.

BLOCK SCHEDULE

Process Time Have students work in groups to re-enact scenes from the video, such as Meta and Sybilla Heyn looking at the photo album, or the 3 young people talking about their plans and dreams for the future.

Vokabeln, pp. 71–72

PROGRAM RESOURCES

- *Arbeitsheft*, p. 48
- Audio Program, Cassette 2A/CD 2
- Audioscript, p. 20

Quick Start Review

♻ Indefinite numerals

Ergänzen Sie mit den richtigen Endungen.

1. In Berlin habe ich viele jung___ Leute getroffen, und alle jung___ Leute waren sehr nett.
2. Ich habe im Urlaub mehrere gut___ Bücher gelesen.
3. Kannst du mir einige deiner schön___ CDs ausleihen?
4. Alle schön___ Sachen sind leider schon weg!

5. Ich habe in Prag einige interessant___ Gebäude gesehen.

Answers: 1. junge, jungen 2. gute 3. schönen 4. schönen 5. interessante

TEACHING SUGGESTIONS

- *Aktivität D, p. 72*

Divide students in groups and have them create 2 lists: one of changes in lifestyle in the post-war era for men and one for women. Have groups share their results. Record and post them as a reference for *Aktivität E.*

TEACHING ALL STUDENTS

Extra Help Before doing each activity in the *Vokabeln* section, have students activate their memory of vocabulary. With books closed, have the whole class brainstorm vocabulary related to the topic of the activity.

CLASSROOM COMMUNITY

Storytelling Have students bring in photos of one or more of their grandparents or other older members of their family or community. Have them introduce the family member to the class and describe his or her role in the family or the student's life. They should try to include one particularly noteworthy event in the person's life.

BLOCK SCHEDULE

Research Divide students into groups. Using the Internet or the public library, have them find out what percentage of women with small children work in Germany. How does this compare to the U.S.? Does the German school system support the two-career family?

Strukturen, pp. 72–73

PROGRAM RESOURCES

- Overhead Transparencies 25.G1, 26.G1, and 27.G1–27.G3
- *Arbeitsheft*, pp. 49–50
- Audio Program, Cassette 2A/CD 2
- Audioscript, p. 21

Quick Start Review

♻ Negation

Antworten Sie negativ: *noch nicht* oder *nicht mehr*?

MODELL: Ist er schon gegangen? → *Nein, noch nicht.*

1. Wohnt sie noch in Barcelona?
2. Bist du schon fertig?
3. Hast du ihm schon geschrieben?
4. Ist der Film schon aus?
5. Hast du das Buch schon gelesen?

Answers: 1. Nein, nicht mehr.
2. Nein, noch nicht.   2. Nein, noch nicht.   3. Nein, noch nicht.   4. Nein, noch nicht.   5. Nein, noch nicht.

TEACHING SUGGESTIONS

- *Übung B, pp. 72–73*

Follow-up: Have students do the activity again in pairs, adding *schon* to each cue.
MODELL: Bist du schon aufgestanden? → *Nein, ich stehe in fünf Minuten auf.*

TEACHING ALL STUDENTS

Multiple Intelligences
Musical/Rhythmic: Have students come up with their own rhythmical ideas remembering the prepositions and the cases they go with. Suggest putting them in alphabetical order and finding a melody to support the string of syllables.

BLOCK SCHEDULE

Peer Teaching Have students work in groups of 3 to review the *Strukturen* sections of chapters 25–27.

Perspektiven, pp. 74–75

PROGRAM RESOURCES

- Audio Program, Cassette 2A/CD 2
- www.mcdougallittell.com

Quick Start Review

♻ Simple past

Setzen Sie die Sätze ins Imperfekt.

1. Wir kennen ihn nicht.
2. Er läuft nicht so schnell.
3. Sie ruft mich später an.
4. Sie kommt immer zu spät.
5. Er hat nie Zeit.

Answers: 1. kannten   2. lief   3. rief
4. kam   5. hatte

TEACHING SUGGESTIONS

- *Aktivität A, p. 74*

Warm-up: Discuss wedding preparations and wedding gifts. What kinds of gifts are commonly given in this country? Now read through the list of words in the activity and check comprehension.

- *Aktivität D, p. 75*

Variation: have students plan an actual party for their German class. A specific German holiday might be coming up or they could simply celebrate German Studies with some language-learning games designed by students.

TEACHING ALL STUDENTS

Multiple Intelligences Intrapersonal: Have students write a journal entry in which they imagine their own wedding or the wedding of a close friend.

CULTURE HIGHLIGHTS

Explain that Otto von Bismarck introduced the civil ceremony for marriages. In Germany, a religious wedding ceremony can only be held after a civil ceremony has already taken place at the *Standesamt*. Civil ceremonies are often informal. Not every couple chooses to have a religious ceremony.

BLOCK SCHEDULE

Change of Pace After having done the listening activities in the *Perspektiven* section, ask students to make up an ad for another type of service, such as a shopping, catering (*Partyservice*), or animal-sitting service and read it to the class.

PROJECT

Have students research how weddings are celebrated in Germany. Ideally, they could interview someone who has gotten married in Germany or who has attended a wedding there. Otherwise, they should do their research on the Internet, in the local library, or by contacting the local consulate.

RUBRIC   **A** = 13–15 pts.   **B** = 10–12 pts.
C = 7–9 pts.   **D** = 4–6 pts.   **F** = <4 pts.

Writing Criteria	Scale				
Grammar	1	2	3	4	5
Originality	1	2	3	4	5
Accuracy of Sources	1	2	3	4	5

VIDEOTHEK

A. *Possible answers are:* Meta und Sybilla leben heute beide allein. Aber Meta Heyn ist erst Single, seit ihr Mann gestorben ist. Sie hat mit 22 Jahren geheiratet und hat drei Kinder bekommen. Sybilla Heyn war nie verheiratet. Ihre Verlobung hat sie gelöst und ist mit Freunden in eine gemeinsame Wohnung gezogen. Als junge Frau fand sie das Leben in der WG schön, aber jetzt lebt sie lieber allein.

A Eine Familiengeschichte. Hier sehen Sie Meta und Sybilla Heyn, Großmutter und Enkelin. Beide wohnen jetzt allein, aber sie haben bisher ganz anders gelebt. Vergleichen Sie das Familienleben und den Alltag der beiden Frauen. Was ist anders, und was ist ähnlich? Warum haben beide so unterschiedlich gelebt?

B Die Familie damals. Als Meta Heyn jung war, lebte die deutsche Familie in einer festen Ordnung. Beschreiben Sie die typische Familie aus dieser Zeit. Welche Rolle hat der Vater gespielt? Welche Rolle hat die Mutter gespielt? Wie lebten damals die Söhne und die Töchter?

C Jugend. Was wünschen sich Ulla, Kristian und Ramona vom Leben? Wollen alle ein traditionelles Familienleben? Oder wollen sie alle arbeiten und Karriere machen? Welche Berufswünsche haben sie? Was machen sie heute, damit sich ihre Träume verwirklichen?

See answers below.

Meta und Sybilla Heyn.

B. *Answers will vary.*

Eine Familie in der Zeit vor dem Zweiten Weltkrieg.

	ULLA	KRISTIAN	RAMONA
BERUFSWÜNSCHE			
FAMILIENWÜNSCHE			
WAS SIE HEUTE MACHEN			

Ulla.

Kristian.

Ramona.

C. *Possible answers are:*
ULLA: BERUFSWÜNSCHE: möchte Meeresbiologin werden und anderen Menschen ihr Wissen vermitteln. FAMILIENWÜNSCHE: will erst studieren und dann noch mal über Kinder nachdenken. WAS SIE HEUTE MACHEN: geht noch zur Schule. Sie macht das Abitur. KRISTIAN: BERUFSWÜNSCHE: wird Bankkaufmann; er möchte in zehn Jahren so viel Geld verdienen, dass er sich ein Haus und ein schickes Auto kaufen kann. FAMILIENWÜNSCHE: möchte Ehefrau und Kind haben. WAS SIE HEUTE MACHEN: Er ist im zweiten Lehrjahr, macht eine Lehre als Bankkaufmann. RAMONA: BERUFSWÜNSCHE: wird Floristin und möchte gern ein eigenes Geschäft leiten; sie ist ehrgeizig, aber Geld ist für sie nicht so wichtig. FAMILIENWÜNSCHE: möchte eine große Familie mit vielen Kindern haben. WAS SIE HEUTE MACHEN: hat gerade ihre Lehre als Floristin angefangen.

D Schulalltag. Beschreiben Sie Karolins Schulalltag und den Schulalltag von früher. Diskutieren Sie darüber, wie sich der Schulalltag in Deutschland seit dem Zweiten Weltrieg verändert hat.

D. *Answers will vary.*

Karolins Klassenzimmer.

Ein Klassenzimmer von damals.

VOKABELN

A Familie. Ergänzen Sie die Sätze mit den Wörtern aus dem Kasten.

1. Das Familienleben von heute ist ziemlich anders als das von _____.
2. Meine Eltern blieben ihr ganzes Leben zusammen. Sie hatten eine sehr glückliche _____.
3. Die Entscheidungen der Eltern _____ natürlich auch die Kinder.
4. Meine Mutter ist in Deutschland _____, aber sie lebt jetzt in den USA.
5. Früher wollte ich _____, aber jetzt finde ich es schön, allein zu wohnen.
6. Nach einer _____ wohnen die Kinder oft bei der Mutter.
7. Meine Großeltern haben sich schon als Kinder ineinander _____.

B Jugendliche. Ergänzen Sie die Sätze 1–8 mit der richtigen Deklination der Wörter im Kasten.

heiraten
aufgewachsen
Scheidung   verliebt
damals betreffen
unabhängig Ehe

die Art   anpassen   das Zeichen
der Wandel   friedlich
teilnehmen
die Suche   unterschiedlich

1. Jetzt können junge Leute zwischen _____ Lebensstilen wählen.
2. Es gibt viele _____ von Jugendlichen: Manche engagieren sich für Politik, andere für Sport.
3. Im Klassenzimmer sollte man immer an den Gesprächen _____.
4. Die sechziger Jahre waren das Jahrzehnt des großen _____ in Europa und Amerika.
5. Der Rock 'n' Roll ist ein _____ der fünfziger Jahre.

A. **1.** damals **2.** Ehe **3.** betreffen **4.** aufgewachsen **5.** heiraten **6.** Scheidung **7.** verliebt

B. **1.** unterschiedlichen **2.** Arten **3.** teilnehmen **4.** Wandels **5.** Zeichen **6.** friedlich **7.** Die Suche **8.** anpassen

6. Das Recht, sich _____ gegen den Staat versammeln zu können, ist sehr wichtig.

7. _____ nach Identität ist auch für ältere Menschen sehr wichtig.

8. Nicht alle Menschen sind radikal, viele wollen sich einfach nur _____.

C Synonyme. Was passt zusammen?

1. zehn Jahrzehnte
2. heute
3. eine gute Idee
4. toll
5. ruinieren, kaputt machen
6. eine kleine Stadt
7. uninteressant
8. wichtig finden
9. zu viel Arbeit
10. neu oder anders machen

a. zerstören
b. prima
c. verändern
d. langweilig
e. auf etwas Wert legen
f. das Jahrhundert
g. die Gegenwart
h. die Überlastung
i. ein Ratschlag
j. ein Dorf

D Mann und Frau. Vergleichen Sie die Rolle des Mannes und die Rolle der Frau während des Zweiten Weltkriegs. Was hat sich für Männer und Frauen geändert? Wie stellen Sie sich das Familienleben von damals vor?

E Lebensstile. Wie hat sich die Situation der Familie in der heutigen Gesellschaft verändert? Beschreiben Sie die Rolle der Frau und die Rolle des Mannes. Wie sind diese Rollen anders als früher? Warum ist alles so anders geworden?

STRUKTUREN

A Nicht jetzt, sondern damals. Schreiben Sie die Sätze im Imperfekt.

MODELL: Meine Eltern kommen aus Europa. →
Meine Eltern kamen aus Europa.

1. Mein Großvater wächst in Deutschland auf.
2. Seine Mutter steht ihm immer sehr nah.
3. Er denkt oft an die alten Zeiten.
4. Sie nehmen nie an Demos teil.
5. Sie wählen einen neuen Präsidenten.
6. Die Bomben zerstören die Stadt.
7. Er muss sein Dorf verlassen.

B Alles erledigt? Sie hatten heute keine Zeit, alles zu erledigen. Beantworten Sie die Sätze als Negation.

MODELL: Hast du das Auto gewaschen? →
Nein, ich habe das Auto nicht gewaschen.

1. Bist du früh aufgestanden?
2. Bist du in die Stadt gefahren?

3. Hast du das Video gesehen?
4. Bist du auf die Post gegangen?
5. Hast du Briefmarken gekauft?
6. Hast du Hausaufgaben gemacht?
7. Hast du den Roman gelesen?
8. Hast du einen Tagebucheintrag geschrieben?

C Kenntnisse und Fähigkeiten. Beantworten Sie die Fragen mit Pronomen.

MODELL: Kennen Sie Sigrid Unslet? →
Ja, ich kenne sie.
oder: Nein, ich kenne sie nicht.

1. Kennen Sie Gerhard Schroeder?
2. Haben Sie die Zeitung von heute gelesen?
3. Kennen Sie den Roman „Der Zauberberg"?
4. Haben Sie das Deutschbuch schon durchgelesen?
5. Haben Sie Ihre Hausaufgaben für heute gemacht?
6. Haben Sie Ihrer Mutter die Blumen gegeben?
7. Haben Sie ihren Mitstudenten geholfen?
8. Schmeckt Ihnen scharfe Currywurst?

C. 1. Ja, ich kenne ihn. *oder:* Nein, ich kenne ihn nicht. **2.** Ja, ich habe sie gelesen. *oder:* Nein, ich habe sie nicht gelesen. **3.** Ja, ich kenne ihn. *oder:* Nein, ich kenne ihn nicht. **4.** Ja, ich habe es schon durchgelesen. *oder:* Nein, ich habe es noch nicht durchgelesen. **5.** Ja, ich habe sie gemacht. *oder:* Nein, ich habe sie nicht gemacht. **6.** Ja, ich habe sie ihr gegeben. *oder:* Nein, ich habe sie ihr nicht gegeben. **7.** Ja, ich habe ihnen geholfen. *oder:* Nein, ich habe ihnen nicht geholfen. **8.** Ja, sie schmeckt mir. *oder:* Nein, sie schmeckt mir nicht.

D Karins Geschichte. Ergänzen Sie die Lücken mit den richtigen Formen der Wörter in Klammern. Achten Sie auf die Präpositionen.

Karin wohnt bei _____¹ (ihre Mutter) in _____² (ein Dorf) nicht weit von _____³ (die Stadt) Hannover. Jeden Morgen geht sie auf _____⁴ (die Bank). Sie arbeitet auf _____⁵ (die Bank) als Kundenberaterin. Sie findet diesen Beruf toll, weil sie viel Kontakt mit _____⁶ (andere Menschen) hat. Öfters, wenn Karin durch _____⁷ (die Innenstadt) von Hannover geht, trifft sie ihre Kunden und Kundinnen. Die Bank steht neben _____⁸ (ein Hotel), das im neunzehnten Jahrhundert erbaut wurde. Das Hotel hat ein kleines Café. Karin geht in _____⁹ (das Café), wenn sie eine Tasse Tee trinken will. Sie denkt oft an _____¹⁰ (die Zukunft) und träumt von _____¹¹ (ein Leben), das sehr positiv sein wird.

D. 1. ihrer Mutter **2.** einem Dorf **3.** der Stadt **4.** die Bank **5.** der Bank **6.** anderen Menschen **7.** die Innenstadt **8.** einem Hotel **9.** das Café **10.** die Zukunft **11.** einem Leben

E Bremen – eine Stadt stellt sich vor. Lesen Sie diese Beschreibung des Schnoorviertels in Bremen, und ergänzen Sie die fehlenden Adjektivendungen.

Das Schnoorviertel, auf gut___¹ Hochdeutsch „Schnurviertel", ist der ältest___² Teil der Stadt Bremen und wurde im Zweit___³ Weltkrieg kaum zerstört. Dieser historisch___⁴ Bezirkᵃ besteht aus vielen klein___⁵ Häusern, die fast wie eine Schnurᵇ sehr dicht nebeneinander stehen. Die erst___⁶ Siedlerᶜ des Schnoorviertels waren Fischer und andere arm___⁷ Leute. Aber dann kamen die reich___⁸ Kaufleute, die den Bezirk schön fanden. Heute stehen viele schön___⁹ Cafés und einige historisch___¹⁰ Gaststätten da, wo früher die Fischer ihre Häuser gebaut hatten.

ᵃdistrict ᵇstring ᶜsettlers

E. 1. gutem **2.** älteste **3.** Zweiten **4.** historische **5.** kleinen **6.** ersten **7.** arme **8.** reichen **9.** schöne **10.** historische

Das Schnoorviertel in Bremen.

PERSPEKTIVEN

Eine deutsche Hochzeit findet statt.

Sie hören jetzt eine Werbung für den Hochzeits-Service eines großen Kaufhauses in Deutschland.

A Welche Geschenke werden in der Werbung erwähnt? Ja oder nein?

1. Bettwäsche?
2. Eierkocher?
3. Gläser?
4. Kaffeemaschinen?
5. Porzellan?[a]
6. Tischdecke?
7. Toaster?
8. Vasen?

[a]*porcelain, china*

A. 1. nein **2.** ja **3.** ja **4.** ja **5.** ja **6.** ja **7.** ja **8.** nein

B Was wissen Sie von diesem Service? Hören Sie noch einmal zu. Was stimmt? Was stimmt nicht?

1. Ohne den Service könnte man dreizehn Kaffeemaschinen bekommen.
2. Mit dem Service können Sie Gläser und Porzellan koordinieren.
3. Wunschgeschenke werden in eine Hochzeitsliste eingetragen.
4. Das Brautpaar nimmt die Hochzeitsliste mit nach Hause.
5. Den Hochzeits-Service findet man auf der dritten Etage.[a]

[a]*floor*

B. 1. Das stimmt nicht. **2.** Das stimmt. **3.** Das stimmt. **4.** Das stimmt nicht. **5.** Das stimmt.

C Beschreiben Sie eine Hochzeit, die Sie einmal besucht haben, oder wie Sie sich eine vorstellen. Wo fand die Hochzeit statt? Wer war da? Wie war die Zeremonie? Wie waren die Hochzeitsgäste angezogen? Die Wörter im Kasten stehen Ihnen zur Hilfe.

C. *Answers will vary.*

---

das Brautpaar   die Gäste   die Unterhaltung

die Dekorationen   der Ort

Kleidung

die Zeremonie

das Fest   das Essen und Trinken   traditionell

D Partnerarbeit. Arbeiten Sie in einer Kleingruppe, und planen Sie eine Hochzeit oder ein anderes Fest. Was müssen Sie organisieren? Wann und wo findet das Fest statt? Wie viele Gäste laden Sie ein? Wen laden Sie ein? Was wird es zum Essen geben? Wie sollen die Gäste sich anziehen—Jeans, lange Kleider und Anzüge? Oder vielleicht planen Sie ein Kostümfest? Soll es Musik geben? Was noch?

D. *Answers will vary.*

28 UNIVERSITÄT

pages 76–95

PLANNING GUIDE • CLASSROOM MANAGEMENT

OBJECTIVES

Communication
- Talk about courses of study, pp. 78–79.
- Talk about university life, pp. 80–81.
- Act out a scene from a short story, p. 93.

Grammar
- Review the subjunctive, pp. 82–83.
- Review the present subjunctive of weak and strong verbs, pp. 84–86.
- Review the past subjunctive for unreal events, pp. 86–87.

Culture
- Learn about foreign students in Germany, pp. 78–79.
- Meet a student from Cameroon studying in Germany, p. 79.
- Learn about subject preferences of German students, p. 81.

Recycling
- Review the subjunctive mood, pp. 82–83.

STRATEGIES

Listening Strategies
- Speculate about the speaker in a listening text, p. 88.

Speaking Strategies
- Describe reactions to hypothetical situations, p. 86.

Reading Strategies
- Read a letter, p. 89.
- Read a short story, pp. 91–92.

Writing Strategies
- Write a letter, p. 89.
- Give advice in an e-mail message, p. 94.

Connecting Cultures Strategies
- Think about study abroad, p. 79.
- Compare American and Austrian school systems, p. 81.

PROGRAM RESOURCES

 Print
- *Arbeitsheft* (Workbook), pp. 51–66
- *Arbeitsheft* (Workbook), Teacher's Edition, pp. 51–66

 Audiovisual
- Overhead Transparencies 28.1–28.G4
- Audio Program, Cassette 2B, 7A/CD 3, 9
- Audioscript, pp. 23–28

 Technology
- Annenberg *Fokus Deutsch* Video Series, *Folge 28*
- www.mcdougallittell.com

 Assessment Program Options
- *Prüfung, Kapitel 28,* Assessment Program, pp. 42–51
- Audio Program, Cassette 8A/CD 10
- Audioscript, p. 109
- Teacher's Resource CD-ROM

DAY 1

Note: (1) Please see TE, pp. 76E–76J, for other suggestions not referenced in these plans. (2) Not all homework options need be assigned.

CHAPTER OPENER
- Quick Start Review: Vocabulary (TE, p. 76E). 5 MIN
- Discuss the photos on pp. 76–77 (TE, p. 76E). 5 MIN

VIDEOTHEK
- Review the *Wortschatz zum Video,* p. 78, then read through the academic subjects named in *Akt. A,* p. 78. Play the entire *Folge I: Geschichte einer Universität.* Have students do the activity as they watch the video (TE, p. 76E). 15 MIN
- Have students do *Akt. B,* p. 78, silently, then check their answers as a class. Follow the Teaching Suggestions for a follow-up activity (TE, p. 76F). 8 MIN
- *Arbeitsheft,* p. 51, audio *Akt. B.* 7 MIN
- Play *Folge II: Ein Student aus Kamerun* while students do *Akt. A, Schritt 1,* p. 79. 10 MIN

Homework Options:
- *Arbeitsheft,* p. 53, *Videothek, Akt. G*

DAY 2

VIDEOTHEK
- Quick Start Review 1: *Der-* and *ein-*words (TE, p. 76E). 5 MIN
- Discuss answers to *Akt. A, Schritt 1,* p. 79, then do *Schritt 2* as a class. 10 MIN
- Do *Akt. B,* p. 79, in small groups, then end with a class discussion of the answers. 10 MIN
- Do *Akt. C,* p. 79, as a class, then use the Teaching Suggestions for a follow-up activity (TE, p. 76F). 12 MIN
- *Arbeitsheft,* p. 52, audio *Akt. C–D.* 13 MIN

Homework Options:
- *Arbeitsheft,* p. 53, *Videothek, Akt. H*

DAY 3

VOKABELN
- Quick Start Review 1: Vocabulary (TE, p. 76F). 5 MIN
- Use the photo on p. 80 as a starting point for introducing vocabulary (TE, p. 76G). Present the vocabulary on p. 80. 12 MIN
- Do *Akt. A,* p. 80, silently, then check answers as a class. 11 MIN
- Do *Akt. B,* p. 81, in pairs (TE, p. 76G). 10 MIN
- *Arbeitsheft,* p. 54, audio *Akt. A.* 5 MIN
- Discuss *Akt. C,* p. 81, as a class (TE, p. 76G). 7 MIN

Homework Options:
- *Vokabeln, Akt. D,* p. 81
- *Arbeitsheft,* p. 55, *Vokabeln, Akt. C–E*

DAY 4

VOKABELN
- Quick Start Review 2: Adjectives and vocabulary (TE, p. 76F). 4 MIN
- Do the follow-up activity in the Teaching Suggestions for *Akt. D,* p. 81 (TE, p. 76G). 8 MIN

STRUKTUREN
- Present the subjunctive of polite requests and unreal situations on pp. 82–83 using OHT 28.2–28.G2. Follow the Teaching Suggestions (TE, p. 76H). 10 MIN
- Have students do *Übung A,* pp. 83–84 alone and then discuss it as a class, encouraging them to create their own variations (TE, p. 76H). 9 MIN
- Do *Übung B,* p. 84, silently, then check their answers with a partner. Follow the Teaching Suggestions for a warm-up activity (TE, p. 76H). 9 MIN
- Do *Übung C,* p. 84, as a class, then follow the Teaching Suggestions for the expansion activity (TE, p. 76H). 10 MIN

Homework Options:
- *Arbeitsheft,* pp. 56–59, *Strukturen, Akt. D–G*

DAY 5

STRUKTUREN

- Quick Start Review 1: Simple past of strong and mixed verbs (TE, p. 76G). 4 MIN
- Present the subjunctive of weak and strong verbs on pp. 84–85 using OHT 28.G3. 8 MIN
- *Übung A*, p. 85. Follow the Teaching Suggestions for a variation (TE, p. 76H). 7 MIN
- Do *Übung C*, p. 86, in pairs. Have 1 or 2 pairs role-play their situations for the class (TE, p. 76H). 10 MIN
- Review the past subjunctive on pp. 86–87 using OHT 28.G4. 8 MIN
- Do *Übung A*, p. 87, as a class, then follow the Teaching Suggestions for the expansion activity (TE, p. 76H). 7 MIN
- *Arbeitsheft*, p. 56, audio *Akt. A.* 6 MIN

Homework Options:

- *Strukturen, Übung B,* pp. 85–86
- *Arbeitsheft*, pp. 59–60, *Strukturen, Akt. I, K*

DAY 6

STRUKTUREN

- Quick Start Review 2: Personal pronouns (TE, p. 76G). 5 MIN
- Have students do *Übung B*, p. 87, alone, then check their answers with a partner. 8 MIN

PERSPEKTIVEN

- Have students read through *Wortschatz zum Hören* and the questions in *Hören Sie zu! Akt. A,* p. 88, before playing the recording. Encourage students to take notes. 12 MIN
- Do *Hören Sie zu!, Akt. A,* p. 88, in small groups (TE, p. 76I). 10 MIN
- Do *Hören Sie zu!, Akt. B,* p. 88, in the same small groups. Conclude with a class discussion (TE, p. 76I). 10 MIN
- Discuss *Zum Thema, Akt. A,* p. 89, as a class. 5 MIN

Homework Options:

- *Hören Sie zu!, Akt. C,* p. 89
- *Arbeitsheft*, pp. 61–63, *Frau Holle*
- *Arbeitsheft*, pp. 63–64, *Perspektiven, Akt. C–D*

DAY 7

PERSPEKTIVEN

- Quick Start Review 1: *Kennen, können* oder *wissen*? (TE, p. 76I). 5 MIN
- Do *Zum Thema, Akt. B,* p. 89, as a class. Follow up with the questions in the Teaching Suggestions (TE, p. 76I). 6 MIN
- Do *Zum Thema, Akt. C,* p. 90, as a class. Take a poll of which ending students select. 6 MIN
- Do *Zum Text, Akt. A,* p. 91, as a class, then move directly to *Zum Text, Akt. B,* p. 91 (TE, p. 76I). 12 MIN
- Have students do *Zur Interpretation, Akt. A,* p. 91, in pairs. Discuss (TE, p. 76I). 10 MIN
- Have students role-play 2–3 scenes listed in the *Interaktion*, p. 92. 6 MIN
- Begin *Schreiben Sie!* by discussing the assignment, *Tipp zum Schreiben*, p. 92, and *Schreibmodell.* 5 MIN

Homework Options:

- Do *Vor dem Schreiben* and *Beim Schreiben*, pp. 93–94 and complete the first draft of the e-mail
- *Arbeitsheft*, p. 64, *Perspektiven, Akt. E*

DAY 8

PERSPEKTIVEN

- Quick Start Review 2: *Legen/stellen/liegen/stellen* (TE, p. 76I). 5 MIN
- Do *Nach dem Schreiben* and begin writing the final draft of the e-mail. 10 MIN
- Questions and review. 5 MIN
- *Prüfung, Kapitel 28.* 30 MIN

Homework Options:

- Complete final draft of the e-mail
- *Arbeitsheft*, pp. 64–65, *Perspektiven, Akt. F–H*

DAY 1

Note: (1) Please see TE, pp. 76E–76J, for other suggestions not referenced in these plans. (2) Not all homework options need be assigned.

CHAPTER OPENER

- Quick Start Review: Vocabulary (TE, p. 76E). 5 MIN
- Discuss the photos on pp. 76–77 (TE, p. 76E). 5 MIN

VIDEOTHEK

- Play *Folge I* while students do *Akt. A*, p. 78. (TE, p. 76E). 18 MIN
- Do *Akt. B*, p. 78, silently, then check answers as a class. (TE, p. 76F). 9 MIN
- Block Schedule activity: Expansion (TE, p. 76F). 10 MIN
- Play *Folge II* while students do *Akt. A, Schritt 1*, p. 79. Discuss the answers, then do *Schritt 2* as a class. 20 MIN
- Do *Akt. B*, p. 79, in small groups. 10 MIN
- *Arbeitsheft*, pp. 51–52, audio *Akt. C–D*. 13 MIN

Homework Options:

- *Arbeitsheft*, p. 53, *Videothek, Akt. G–H*

DAY 2

VIDEOTHEK

- Quick Start Review 1: *Der-* and *ein-* words (TE, p. 76E). 5 MIN
- Do *Akt. C*, p. 79, as a class (TE, p. 76F). 11 MIN

VOKABELN

- Use the photo on p. 80 to introduce vocabulary (TE, p. 76G). 12 MIN
- Do *Akt. A*, p. 80. 11 MIN
- Do *Akt. B*, p. 81 (TE, p. 76G). 10 MIN
- Block Schedule activity: Time Saver (TE, p. 76G). 10 MIN
- *Arbeitsheft*, p. 54, audio *Akt. A*. 5 MIN
- Discuss *Akt. C*, p. 81, as a class (TE, p. 76G). 7 MIN

STRUKTUREN

- Present the subjunctive pp. 82–83 using OHT 28.2–28.G2. 10 MIN
- Do *Übung A*, pp. 83–84, then discuss it as a class (TE, p. 76H). 9 MIN

Homework Options:

- *Akt. D*, p. 81
- *Arbeitsheft*, p. 55, *Vokabeln, Akt. C–E*
- *Arbeitsheft*, pp. 56–57, *Akt. D–E*

DAY 3

STRUKTUREN

- Quick Start Review 1: Simple past of strong and mixed verbs (TE, p. 76G). 5 MIN
- Do *Übung B–C*, p. 84, (TE, p. 76H). 16 MIN
- Present the subjunctive on pp. 84–85 using OHT 28.G3. 11 MIN
- Do *Übung A*, p. 85 and *Übung C*, p. 86. (TE, p. 76H). 16 MIN
- Block Schedule activity: Peer Teaching (TE, p. 76H). 10 MIN
- Present the subjunctive on pp. 86–87 using OHT 28.G4. 8 MIN
- Do *Übung A*, p. 87 (TE, p. 76H). 7 MIN
- *Arbeitsheft*, p. 56, audio *Akt. A*. 5 MIN

PERSPEKTIVEN

- Do *Akt. A*, p. 88 (TE, p. 76I). 12 MIN

Homework Options:

- *Übung B*, pp. 85–86
- *Arbeitsheft*, pp. 58–59, *Strukturen, Akt. F–G* and pp. 59–60, *Strukturen, Akt. I, K*

DAY 4

PERSPEKTIVEN

- Quick Start Review 1: *Kennen, können* oder *wissen*? (TE, p. 76I). 5 MIN
- Do *Akt. A–B*, p. 88, in small groups. Discuss (TE, p. 76I). 19 MIN
- Discuss *Zum Thema, Akt. A–B*, p. 89, as a class. (TE, p. 76I). 11 MIN
- Do *Akt. C*, p. 90, as a class. 6 MIN
- Block Schedule activity: Fun Break (TE, p. 76J). 10 MIN
- Do *Zum Text, Akt. A–B*, p. 91, (TE, p. 76I). 13 MIN
- Do *Zur Interpretation, Akt. A*, p. 91, in pairs. Discuss. 10 MIN
- Have students role play 2–3 scenes listed in the *Interaktion*, p. 92. 10 MIN
- Begin *Schreiben Sie!* p. 92. 6 MIN

Homework Options:

- *Akt. C*, p. 89
- Do *Vor dem Schreiben* and *Beim Schreiben*, pp. 93–94, and complete the first draft of the e-mail
- Read *Frau Holle* in the *Arbeitsheft*, pp. 61–63
- *Arbeitsheft*, pp. 63–64, *Akt. C–E*

DAY 5

PERSPEKTIVEN

- Quick Start Review 2: *Legen/stellen, liegen/stehen* (TE, p. 76I). 6 MIN
- *Arbeitsheft*, p. 65, audio *Akt. A and B*. 14 MIN
- Do *Nach dem Schreiben*, p. 94, and begin writing the final draft of the e-mail. 20 MIN
- Do the *Strukturen* Portfolio activity described in the Teaching Suggestions (TE, p. 76H). 15 MIN
- Questions and review. 5 MIN
- *Prüfung, Kapitel 28*. 30 MIN

Homework Options:

- Complete final draft of the e-mail
- *Arbeitsheft*, pp. 64–65, *Perspektiven, Akt. F–G*

Chapter Opener, pp. 76–77

PROGRAM RESOURCES

• Overhead Transparency 28.1

Quick Start Review

♻ Vocabulary
Ergänzen Sie die Vokabeln in den Sätzen.

VOKABELN: erinnern, Unterrichtsmethoden, Gesamtschule, Gymnasium, demonstrierten, Jahrhundert

1. Im 19. _____ lernten die Schüler lesen, schreiben, rechnen und Philosophie.
2. Damals waren die _____ sehr streng in Deutschland.
3. In den 60er Jahren _____ die Studenten in Deutschland.
4. Die _____ ist der amerikanischen High School ähnlich.
5. An einem _____ lernt man normalerweise zwei Sprachen.
6. Schüler _____ sich am liebsten an Schulausflüge.

Answers: 1. Jahrhundert
2. Unterrichtsmethoden
3. demonstrierten   4. Gesamtschule
5. Gymnasium   6. erinnern

TEACHING SUGGESTIONS

• Photos, pp. 76–77

Point out the bridge over the river Neckar and the castle in the photos. Have students find Heidelberg on a map. Ask if anyone would like to study overseas. Ask if students know of any other university cities?

TEACHING ALL STUDENTS

Multiple Intelligences Verbal: Introduce the topic of university life. Go over the structures to be covered in this chapter and introduce each with an example.

CLASSROOM COMMUNITY

Paired Activity Have students discuss their own academic plans in pairs. Students could then introduce their discussion partner to the class.

Videothek, pp. 78–79

PROGRAM RESOURCES

• Videocassette, *Folge 28*
• *Arbeitsheft,* pp. 51–53
• Audio Program, Cassette 2B/CD 3
• Audioscript, pp. 23–24

Quick Start Review 1

♻ *Der-* and *ein-*words
Ergänzen Sie die richtige Form der Wörter in Klammern.

1. _____ (Manch-) Schüler haben gute Erinnerungen an die Schule.
2. _____ (Jed-) Schüler ist anders.
3. _____ (Manch-) Schüler lernen besser beim Schreiben, andere beim Sprechen.
4. An einem Gymnasium hat man _____ (jed-) Tag verschiedene Fachlehrer.
5. Wissen Sie schon, _____ (welch-) Fach Sie studieren wollen?
6. Ich weiß noch nicht, an _____ (welch-) Tag die Abiturfeier stattfinden wird.

Answers: 1. Manche   2. Jeder
3. Manche   4. jeden   5. welches
6. welchem

Quick Start Review 2

♻ Adjectives
Ergänzen Sie die richtigen Adjektivendungen in den Sätzen.

1. Ich esse nicht gerne scharf_____ Würste.
2. Hier habe ich einen süß_____, saftig_____ Apfel für dich!
3. Bei Meiers gibt es zum Abendessen immer frisch_____ Salat.
4. Das rot_____ Eis ist Erdbeereis.
5. Ich hätte gern ein Schnitzel mit Pommes frites und frisch_____ Gemüse.
6. Haben Sie frisch_____ Eier?

Answers: 1. scharfe   2. süßen, saftigen   3. frischen   4. rote
5. frischem   6. frische

TEACHING SUGGESTIONS

• *Aktivität A,* p. 78

This video presents the history of university education in Germany by focusing on Heidelberg. As a warm-up, ask students *Welche Fächer gehören zu den Geisteswissenschaften? Welche Fächer gehören zu den Naturwissenschaften? In welchen Bereich gehören Dolmetschen und Übersetzen?* Have students review the vocabulary in the *Wortschatz zum Video,* p. 78, and read through the subjects in the activity before viewing the video. Encourage students to take notes as they watch the video. After viewing, ask them to single out one historical fact about the university in Heidelberg that they find most interesting.

- *Aktivität B, p. 78*

Follow-up: Have students describe their impressions of the people in the video. Then ask *Haben sie gerne studiert? War das eine positive Erfahrung?*

- *Aktivität C, p. 79*

Have students work in pairs to make up a schedule for a typical day for Sabine at the university in Cologne.

TEACHING ALL STUDENTS

Multiple Intelligences Kinesthetic: Have students name their favorite subjects and a profession related to that subject. Have them then act out an activity typical of the profession.

CLASSROOM COMMUNITY

Dictation Do the following dictation activity. Have students correct each other's dictations. Afterwards, hand out the correct paragraph or put it on an OHT. *Guy kommt aus Kamerun. Er wohnt in Aachen in einem Studentenwohnheim. Am Anfang war es nicht leicht, Freunde zu finden. Jetzt hat Guy einen Freund, der auch Maschinenbau studiert. Er fühlt sich wohl in Aachen. Das Essen in der Mensa ist gut und preiswert. Manchmal trifft sich Guy auch mit Landsleuten in einem Restaurant.*

BLOCK SCHEDULE

Expansion After students have completed *Aktivitäten A–C*, have them role-play an interview with someone who has studied at a German university. They can use the questions and the vocabulary in the activities as a basis for structuring their interviews.

PORTFOLIO

Ask students to research another university of their choice in Germany, Austria, or Switzerland. They should include information on the size of the town where the university is located, the size of student population, and any subjects or professors for which the university is noted.

RUBRIC **A** = 13–15 pts. **B** = 10–12 pts.
C = 7–9 pts. **D** = 4–6 pts. **F** = < 4 pts.

Writing Criteria	Scale				
Organization	1	2	3	4	5
Grammar and vocabulary	1	2	3	4	5
Content	1	2	3	4	5

Vokabeln, pp. 80–81

PROGRAM RESOURCES

- *Arbeitsheft,* pp. 54–55
- Audio Program, Cassette 2B/CD 3
- Audioscript, pp. 24–25

Quick Start Review 1
Vocabulary
Ergänzen Sie die Verben in den Sätzen.
1. Erika _____ _____ auf eine Prüfung _____. (sich vorbereiten)
2. Ernst _____ _____ gern mit naturwissenschaftlichen Themen. (sich beschäftigen)
3. Meine Eltern _____ _____ _____ gute Noten. (Wert legen auf)
4. Unsere Stadt hat _____ in den letzten fünf Jahren sehr _____. (sich verändern)
5. Ich bin Frau Schmitt schon lange nicht mehr _____. (begegnen)

Früher habe ich sie immer im Bus getroffen.
6. Das Studium in den USA _____ _____ von dem Studium in Deutschland. (sich unterscheiden)

Answers: 1. Erika bereitet sich auf eine Prüfung vor.   2. Ernst beschäftigt sich gern mit naturwissenschaftlichen Themen.   3. Meine Eltern legen Wert auf gute Noten.   4. Unsere Stadt hat sich in den letzten fünf Jahren sehr verändert.   5. Ich bin Frau Schmitt schon lange nicht mehr begegnet.
6. Das Studium in den USA unterscheidet sich von dem Studium in Deutschland.

Quick Start Review 2
Adjectives and vocabulary
Sagen Sie es anders.
MODELL: Ich habe eine nette, junge Frau *getroffen.* (begegnen) →
Ich bin einer netten jungen Frau begegnet.
1. Sie kommt *ohne ihren Mann.* (mit)
2. Ich *mag* deinen neuen Freund. (gefallen)
3. Wir haben im Unterricht über einen interessanten *Komponisten* gesprochen. (Buch)
4. Wir sind gestern unserem Lehrer in der Stadt *begegnet.* (treffen)
5. Wir *beschäftigen* uns in Biologie mit seltenen Pflanzen. (kennen lernen)

Answers: 1. Sie kommt mit ihrem Mann.   2. Dein neuer Freund gefällt mir.   3. Wir haben im Unterricht über ein interessantes Buch gesprochen.

4. Wir haben unseren Lehrer in der Stadt getroffen.   5. Wir lernen in Biologie seltene Pflanzen kennen.

TEACHING SUGGESTIONS

• Photo, p. 80

Ask students to imagine the answers to these questions: *Was studieren die Leute auf dem Bild? Was könnten ihre Hauptfächer sein? Sind alle Leute auf dem Bild Studenten?*

• Aktivität B, p. 81

Follow-up: Have students work on pronunciation in pairs. Have them read to each other, try to improve their pronunciation, and then read aloud for the teacher who will check pronunciation and intonation.

• Aktivität C, p. 81

Explain to students that the Austrian/German *Diplom* is the equivalent of an American masters degree. Ask *Was sind die Vorteile des amerikanischen Systems? Was sind die Nachteile des deutschen Systems?* (*Der B.A./B.S. Abschluss erlaubt mehr Flexibilität. Man spezialisiert sich nicht von Anfang an.*) usw.

• Aktivität D, p. 81

Have students do this activity in writing and post their finished paragraphs on a classroom wall. Follow-up: Provide time for everybody to read their fellow students' writings and ask each other questions.

TEACHING ALL STUDENTS

Multiple Intelligences

Logical/Mathematical: Have students read *Kulturspiegel*, p. 81. Ask them to research the favorite majors of undergraduates in their home state. Have them depict their findings in a graph or in columns. Expansion: Do a survey of the German class and prepare a chart showing everyone's favorite subjects.

CLASSROOM COMMUNITY

TPR Call out a vocabulary word or phrase from p. 80. With books closed, have students work in pairs to mime the meaning.

INTERDISCIPLINARY CONNECTION

Science: Have students interview their math or science teacher and find out about any famous German mathematicians or scientists. Have them report back to the class in German.

BLOCK SCHEDULE

Time Saver Have students see how many German words they can form using the letters of their first and last names. Have students share their results with the class.

PROJECT

Have students go through German newspapers and magazines looking for subjunctive forms. They should find at least 3 or 4 examples. Have them cut out or copy these examples and paste them on a sheet of paper. They should illustrate them if possible. These collages can be put up in the classroom in order to create an "art gallery" of expressions in the subjunctive.

LANGUAGE NOTE

It is important to know and recognize the subjunctive forms of strong verbs especially in written German. In the everyday language (*Alltagssprache*) subjunctive forms that have an archaic feel to them are not used at all, for example *schwämme, führe, trüge*. The *würde* paraphrase is used instead. It is safe to use the subjunctive forms of verbs which are frequently used and don't sound funny or archaic, for example *gäbe, käme, ginge, bliebe*.

Strukturen, pp. 82–87

PROGRAM RESOURCES

• Overhead Transparencies 28.2–28.G4
• *Arbeitsheft*, pp. 59–60
• Audio Program, Cassette 2B/CD 3
• Audioscript, pp. 26–27

Quick Start Review 1

Simple past of strong and mixed verbs
Schreiben Sie die Sätze im Imperfekt.

1. Er bringt mir eine deutsche Zeitung mit.
2. Ich weiß nicht, was „Guten Morgen" auf Französisch heißt.
3. Das Feuer brennt im Kamin und der Truthahn brutzelt im Backofen.
4. Er ruft mich nach der Prüfung an.
5. Wir kennen uns schon von Anfang an.
6. Sie singt sehr gut.

Answers: 1. brachte   2. wusste
3. brannte, brutzelte   4. rief
5. kannten   6. sang

Quick Start Review 2

Personal pronouns
Schreiben Sie die Sätze zu Ende.
MODELL: Ich schreibe dir und *du schreibst mir.*

1. Er liebt sie und _____ _____ _____.

2. Wir helfen euch und _____ _____ _____.

3. Ich mag dich und _____ _____ _____.

4. Ihr ärgert uns und _____ _____ _____.

5. Sie freut sich auf ihn und _____ _____ _____ _____ _____.

6. Sie lobt ihn und _____ _____ _____.

Answers: 1. sie liebt ihn   2. ihr helft uns   3. du magst mich   4. wir ärgern euch   5. er freut sich auf sie   6. er lobt sie

....

TEACHING SUGGESTIONS

- The subjunctive used to express polite requests and unreal situations, pp. 82–83

Have students brainstorm situations that require polite formulas. Point out to students that English also uses the subjunctive for polite requests. The subjunctive mood expresses what is unreal, uncertain, hypothetical, possible, or indefinite.

- *Sprachspiegel*, p. 83

Go over *Sprachspiegel*. Point out that the verb form *were* in English is used to express a past-time situation in the indicative mood (*They were sick yesterday*) and to express a present-time situation in the subjunctive mood (*If they were here now, we could tell them all the details*).

- *Übung A*, pp. 83–84

Have students come up with their own variations of this activity. Give them cues such as *Vokabeln lernen, Sport*

treiben, zum Zahnarzt gehen, Gemüse essen, CDs kaufen, im Internet surfen, usw.

- *Übung B*, p. 84

Warm-up: Ask *Was würden Sie machen, wenn Sie 1.000 Dollar gewinnen würden? Wo würden Sie studieren, wenn Sie sich eine Universität aussuchen könnten und dort ein Stipendium bekämen?*

- *Übung C*, p. 84

Expansion: Have students formulate polite requests having to do with their immediate classroom surroundings. Start off the process by saying *Können Sie mir bitte die Tafel abwischen?* Pick a student to continue and go through the whole class as quickly as possible.

- Present subjunctive of weak and strong verbs, pp. 84–85

Have students find all the verbs in the box on p. 80 and give their present subjunctive forms.

- *Übung A*, p. 85

Variation: Have students work in pairs. The first student states an enviable position. The second student responds in the subjunctive, saying that he/she would like to do the same. For example: First student: *Ich bekomme immer gute Noten.* Second student: *Ich wünschte, ich bekäme auch gute Noten.*

- *Übung C*, p. 86

Select 1 or 2 groups to role-play their situations.

- *Übung A*, p. 87

Expansion: Have students remember 3 situations in the past week that they would like to have changed if they

could have. For example: *Wenn ich doch nur für Mathe mehr gelernt hätte!*

TEACHING ALL STUDENTS

Extra Help Help students to restate the following sentences, first in the present- and then in the past-time subjunctive. Explain their different meanings. MODELL: Wenn das Wetter schön ist, fahren wir an den Strand. → *Wenn das Wetter schön wäre, würden wir an den Strand fahren. Wenn das Wetter schön gewesen wäre, wären wir an den Strand gefahren.*
Wenn meine Katze hungrig ist, miaut sie. Wenn ich reich bin, schenke ich dir Geld. Wenn er vorsichtiger fährt, hat er keinen Unfall.

CLASSROOM COMMUNITY

Challenge Have students imagine that their classroom is empty and ask them how they would furnish and decorate it, if it were up to them. Ask *Wie würden Sie die Wände anmalen? Was würden Sie mit dem Fußboden machen? Was würden Sie ans Fenster stellen? usw.*

BLOCK SCHEDULE

Peer Teaching Have students look at the cartoon on p. 86 (*Würden Sie bitte meine Katze retten?*) and have them come up with 3 different reasons why this request will not be fulfilled by the man wearing the cap.

PORTFOLIO

Have students write a journal entry answering one of the following questions: *Wenn ich nicht hier wäre, wo wäre ich? Wenn ich nicht ich wäre, wer möchte ich gern sein?* or *Wenn ich nicht in dieser Zeit leben würde, wann würde ich gern leben?*

RUBRIC **A** = 13–15 pts. **B** = 10–12 pts.
C = 7–9 pts. **D** = 4–6 pts. **F** = < 4 pts.

Writing Criteria	Scale				
Use of subjunctive	1	2	3	4	5
Logic	1	2	3	4	5
Vocabulary	1	2	3	4	5

Perspektiven, pp. 88–94

PROGRAM RESOURCES

- *Arbeitsheft*, pp. 61–66
- Audio Program, Cassette 2B, 7A/ CD 3, 9
- Audioscript, p. 28
- www.mcdougallittell.com

Quick Start Review 1

♻ *Kennen, können oder wissen?*
Ergänzen Sie die Sätze mit dem richtigen Verb.

1. Silke _____ die Eltern von Ruth nicht.
2. _____ du, wo wir uns morgen früh treffen?
3. Er _____ sehr gut segeln.
4. Wir _____ morgen leider nicht mitkommen.
5. Ich _____ noch nicht, ob ich mitkommen kann.
6. Ihr _____ euch morgen bei meiner Party kennen lernen.

Answers: 1. kennt 2. Weißt
3. kann 4. können 5. weiß
6. könnt

Quick Start Review 2

♻ *Legen/stellen, liegen/stehen*
Ergänzen Sie die Sätze. Benutzen Sie die *du*-Form (Singular) für die Imperativsätze.

1. _____ bitte die Bücher auf meinen Schreibtisch!
2. Wo _____ denn die Flasche mit dem Orangensaft?
3. _____ die Gläser bitte nicht an den Rand des Tisches!
4. Peter _____ noch im Bett.
5. Warum _____ du am Fenster und schaust auf die Straße?
6. Meine Pullover _____ ganz unten im Kleiderschrank.

Answers: 1. Leg 2. steht 3. Stell
4. liegt 5. stehst 6. liegen

TEACHING SUGGESTIONS

- *Aktivität A,* p. 88

Have students read through the *Wortschatz zum Hörtext* and the questions in the activity before playing the recording.
Follow-up: have students look up Cameroon on a map, in an encyclopedia, or on a World Picture Atlas (CD format). What additional information can they find?

- *Aktivität B,* p. 88

Have students create an outline for the organization of the audio text.

- *Aktivität A,* p. 89

Ask students to guess the meaning of the word *Flaschenpost*. Explain that *Freiheitspost* could be a pun on the concept, evoking a slightly different connotation.

- *Aktivität B,* p. 89

Ask students further *Warum schreiben andere Menschen keine Briefe? Glauben Sie, dass E-Mail das Briefeschreiben ganz ersetzen wird?*

- *Aktivität B,* p. 90

Ask *Welche Handlungen stehen auf den beiden Seiten der Liste? Kann man Pflicht und Liebe immer trennen?*

- *Aktivität C,* p. 90

Take a poll of which ending students select.

- *Zur Interpretation,* p. 91

Have students reflect on the title again. What does it imply? Ask *Warum hat der Autor diesen Titel gewählt? Könnten Sie sich einen anderen Titel vorstellen?*

- *Tipp zum Schreiben,* p. 92

Have students decide on their friend's problem first (it might be helpful to pick a situation they can sympathize with), then try to imagine themselves in their imaginary friend's position. How would they feel if they were abroad at a new school and didn't know many people?

- *Schreibmodell,* p. 93

Have students read *Schreibmodell* and then explain why Tom is not happy in Weimar, what Max's advice for Tom is, and whether they would have advised Max differently?

- *Vor dem Schreiben,* p. 93

Encourage students to choose a city or university they have heard about before.

TEACHING ALL STUDENTS

Extra Help *Wenn ich ein Vöglein wär' und auch zwei Flügel hätt', flög ich zu dir, da's aber nicht kann sein, da's aber nicht kann sein, bleib' ich allhier.*
—Volkslied
Write the words of the folksong above as a handout or OHT. Read or sing it for the students. Have them identity each verb form in the song. Ask *Welche Verben sind im Konjunktiv? Welche im Indikativ? Wer singt dieses Lied?*

CLASSROOM COMMUNITY

Paired Activity Have students work in pairs. Tell them to imagine that a friend has returned after only 2 months of a junior year abroad because he/she felt terribly lonely and overwhelmed in Frankfurt am Main. Have half of the pairs create some thoughtful questions they could ask to find out what happened. Have the other pairs brainstorm a more detailed explanation of why the student left. Then have each pair join with another and create and act out a skit.

BLOCK SCHEDULE

Fun Break Have students imagine that they will spend a year at a German Gymnasium. The first week does not go smoothly. Have them write a humorous letter or e-mail home recounting events of the first days. They should focus on everyday life: food, the family they are staying with, transportation, fellow students at the Gymnasium, and teachers.

UNIVERSITÄT

In diesem Kapitel

- erfahren Sie einiges über die Geschichte der Universität Heidelberg.
- lernen Sie einen Studenten aus Kamerun kennen.
- sprechen Sie darüber, wie sich das Studium über die Jahre hindurch verändert hat.

Sie werden auch

- höfliche Bitten und Wünsche mit dem Konjunktiv ausdrücken.
- die Gegenwartsformen und die Vergangenheitsformen des Konjunktivs lernen.
- eine Geschichte über einen interessanten Briefwechsel lesen.
- nachforschen, wie man im Ausland studieren kann.
- eine E-Mail schreiben.

Die heutige Stadt Heidelberg.

Heidelberg – eine der bekanntesten Universitätsstädte Deutschlands.

Heidelberg im Mittelalter.

VIDEOTHEK

In diesem Kapitel sehen Sie, wie Bildung und Studium in den deutschsprachigen Ländern damals waren und wie sie heute sind.

Die Uni Heidelberg hat eine lange Geschichte.

I: Geschichte einer Universität

A Studienfächer

Wann konnte man diese Fächer an der Universität in Heidelberg studieren?

A. Seit dem vierzehnten Jahrhundert: 3, 5, 8, 9   Seit dem neunzehnten Jahrhundert: 1, 2, 6   Seit den sechziger Jahren: 4, 7

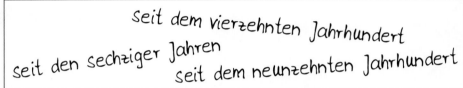

seit dem vierzehnten Jahrhundert
seit den sechziger Jahren
seit dem neunzehnten Jahrhundert

1. Physik	4. Dolmetschen	7. Übersetzen
2. Geisteswissenschaften	5. Philosophie	8. Medizin
3. Rechtswissenschaft	6. Chemie	9. Theologie

B Persönliche Geschichten. Verbinden Sie jede Person mit dem richtigen Satzteil.

Klaus   Sabine
Daniela   Susanne   Anja

1. _____ hat Germanistik und Musikwissenschaft in Greifswald studiert.
2. _____ hat Mathematik in Münster studiert. Das war ein sehr positives Erlebnis.
3. _____ studiert in Köln und lernt viele Ausländer an der Uni kennen.
4. _____ hat in Österreich studiert.
5. _____ hat das Abitur noch nicht gemacht. Diese Person will vielleicht Politologie in Köln studieren.

WORTSCHATZ ZUM VIDEO

der Bunsenbrenner	*Bunsen burner*
das Krebsfor-schungszentrum	*cancer research center*
verfestigen	*to strengthen*
die Landesleute	*compatriots; countrymen*
die Sport-wissenschaft	*sports science*
bewaldet	*forested*

B. 1. Anja   2. Klaus   3. Sabine   4. Daniela
5. Susanne

II: Ein Student aus Kamerun

In dieser Folge erfahren Sie, was ein ausländischer Student von Deutschland und den Deutschen hält. **A. Schritt 1: 1.** Das stimmt nicht. Er schreibt in dem Brief an seinen Bruder Eric, dass in Deutschland alles sehr teuer ist. **2.** Das stimmt. **3.** Das stimmt. **4.** Das stimmt nicht. Sie treffen sich in der Mensa. **5.** Das stimmt. **6.** Das stimmt nicht. Aachen gefällt ihm gut. **7.** Das stimmt.

A Auslandsstudium

SCHRITT 1: Guy in Aachen. Was stimmt? Was stimmt nicht?

1. Guy findet die Lebenshaltungskosten in Deutschland billig.
2. Guy wohnt in einem Studentenwohnheim.
3. Guy und Robert studieren Maschinenbau.
4. Guy trifft sich mit Landsleuten im Restaurant.
5. Das Essen in der Mensa ist preiswert.
6. Guy ist in Aachen unzufrieden.
7. Guy hat viele gute Freunde in Aachen.

SCHRITT 2: Und Sie? Was meinen Sie zu den folgenden Fragen?

1. Stellen Sie sich vor, Sie studieren in Heidelberg. Würden Sie auch mit Ihren Landsleuten sprechen wollen? Oder wollten Sie nur Deutsche kennenlernen? Warum?
2. Gibt es ausländische Schüler und Schülerinnen an Ihrer Schule? Woher kommen sie?

B Sabines Studium. Susannes Schwester, Sabine, studiert an der Uni in Köln.
See answers below.

1. Welches Fach hat Sabine zuerst in Köln studiert?
2. Warum hat sie ihr Studienfach nach zwei Jahren gewechselt?
3. Welches Fach beziehungsweise welche Fächer studiert sie jetzt?
4. Möchten Sie nach der High School weiterstudieren? Warum oder warum nicht?
5. Wenn Sie weiterstudieren wollen, wissen Sie schon, was Sie als Hauptfach studieren wollen?

C Alltagsleben an der Universität. Sabine erzählt von ihrem Alltag an der Uni.
See answers below.

1. Was macht sie?
2. Vergleichen Sie Ihren mit Sabines Alltag. Was ist ähnlich? Was ist anders?
3. Möchten Sie an einer deutschen oder österreichischen Uni studieren? Warum oder warum nicht?

B. 1. Sie hat zuerst Jura studiert. **2.** Sie hat festgestellt, dass Jura nicht ihre Berufung ist. **3.** Jetzt studiert sie Sportwissenschaft und Wirtschaftswissenschaft. **4.** *Answers will vary.* **5.** *Answers will vary.*

C. 1. Zuerst hat Sabine zum Beispiel Kurse in Schwimmen und Anatomie. Mittags geht sie in die Mensa und trifft sich mit Freunden. **2.** *Answers will vary.* **3.** *Answers will vary.*

Guy schreibt einen Brief an seinen Bruder Eric.

Schritt 2: *Answers will vary.*

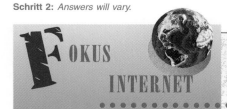

For more information on international students in Germany, visit the *Auf Deutsch!* Web Site at www.mcdougallittell.com.

Sabine Dyrchs.

VOKABELN

die Diplomarbeit	*thesis work*
die Erfahrung	*experience*
die Germanistik	*German studies*
die Jura	*law*
die Medizin	*medicine*
die Rechtswissenschaft	*jurisprudence*
der Begriff	*concept, idea*
der Kommilitone / die Kommilitonin	*classmate*
der Ruf	*reputation*
die Geisteswissenschaften (*pl.*)	*humanities*
auf•nehmen	*to start, take up*
sich befinden	*to be located*
entstehen	*to arise; to develop, evolve*
schaffen	*to make; accomplish*
um•wechseln	*to change*
sich unterhalten über (+ *acc.*)	*to converse; to entertain*
sich wundern über (+ *acc.*)	*to be surprised at*
zu•nehmen	*to increase*
allmählich	*gradual(ly)*
beliebt	*popular; famous*

Studieren, lesen, sich mit Freunden unterhalten – das Leben an der Uni.

gemeinsam	*together; common*
heutig	*today's*
riesengroß	*enormous*

Sie wissen schon

die Bemerkung, die Bildung, die Chemie, die Geschichte, die Physik, der Maschinenbau, bekommen, sich fürchten vor (+ *dat.*), sich gewöhnen an (+ *acc.*), merkwürdig

Aktivitäten

A. 1. die Diplomarbeit **2.** sich fürchten vor **3.** sich befinden **4.** die Erfahrung **5.** merkwürdig **6.** schaffen **7.** gemeinsam **8.** sich wundern **9.** riesengroß

A Definitionen. Welche Wörter aus der Vokabelliste passen zu den folgenden Definitionen?

1. schriftliche Arbeit, mit der ein Diplom erworben wird
2. Angst vor etwas haben
3. an einem bestimmten Ort sein
4. das Erlebnis
5. eigenartig, seltsam
6. machen, arbeiten
7. miteinander, zusammen
8. überrascht sein
9. sehr groß

B Studium und Fächer. Ergänzen Sie die Sätze.

> Ruf
>
> Jura beliebt gewöhnt
>
> Geisteswissenschaften
>
> Fürchten nimmt . . . zu heutigen

1. Philosophie, Literatur und Sprachwissenschaft gehören zu den _____.
2. Die Universität Heidelberg hat überall in der Welt einen sehr guten _____.
3. Wenn man Richter oder Richterin werden möchte, muss man _____ studieren.
4. Die Zahl der Studenten an deutschen Universitäten _____ jedes Jahr _____.
5. Die Professoren, die bei den Studenten besonders _____ sind, haben großen Erfolg.
6. Die _____ Universitäten sind sehr anders als die von damals.
7. Viele Studenten _____ sich vor Prüfungen.
8. Andere haben sich schon daran _____, ständig geprüft zu werden.

C Studium in Österreich und in Ihrem Land. Lesen Sie Danielas Beschreibung vom Studienablauf in Österreich, und beantworten Sie dann die Fragen.

„Der Studienablauf in Österreich teilt sich in zwei Abschnitte. Der erste Studienabschnitt dauert zwei Jahre, dann hat man die erste Diplomprüfung. Dann kommen wieder zwei Jahre, man hat die zweite Diplomprüfung, plus man muss eine Diplomarbeit schreiben und dann ist das Studium beendet."

1. Wie finden Sie den österreichischen Studienablauf?
2. Ist der österreichische Studienablauf so wie der in Ihrem Land?
3. Wie ist das Studium in Ihrem Land? Beschreiben Sie es.

D Ihre Freunde/Freundinnen oder Familienmitglieder. Sie haben erfahren, welche Studienfächer verschiedene Personen in verschiedenen Städten studieren oder schon studiert haben. Erklären Sie jetzt, was drei von Ihren Freunden/Freundinnen oder Familienmitgliedern studieren oder studiert haben. An welchen Universitäten und/oder in welchen Städten?

KULTURSPIEGEL

Was wollen junge Deutsche an der Uni studieren? Das beliebteste Studienfach bei Männern und Frauen ist Wirtschaftswissenschaften. An zweiter Stelle liegt Rechtswissenschaft (Frauen) und Maschinenbau (Männer). Geisteswissenschaften wie Germanistik werden von nur drei Prozent der Frauen als Studienfach erwünscht.

B. 1. Geisteswissenschaften 2. Ruf 3. Jura
4. nimmt . . . zu 5. beliebt 6. heutigen
7. fürchten 8. gewöhnt

C. *Answers will vary.*

FOKUS INTERNET

To learn more about school and education in German-speaking countries, visit the *Auf Deutsch!* Web Site at www.mcdougallittell.com.

D. *Answers will vary.*

STRUKTUREN

REVIEW OF SUBJUNCTIVE

EXPRESSING UNREAL SITUATIONS AND POLITE REQUESTS

The indicative mood describes facts: actual events, situations, conditions, or states of existence.

Sie **ist** glücklich.	*She's happy.*
Er **kann** kochen.	*He knows how to cook.*
Wir **wussten** das.	*We knew that.*

The subjunctive mood does not describe actual facts, but possibilities or unreal situations that often depend on some unrealized condition.

Sie **wäre** glücklich, wenn . . .	*She would be happy, if . . .*
Wenn er kochen **könnte,** . . .	*If he knew how to cook, . . .*
Wenn wir nur **wüssten,** dass . . .	*If we only knew that . . .*

Subjunctive forms, especially those of **haben, sein,** and the modal verbs (**dürfen, können, mögen, müssen, sollen,** and **wollen**), also express polite requests or invitations.

Hättest du Zeit, mir zu helfen?	*Would you have time to help me?*
Könnten Sie mir helfen?	*Could you help me?*

There are two ways to express the subjunctive in German: 1) with the subjunctive form of the verb, particularly of verbs such as **haben, sein,** the modal verbs, and **wissen**; or 2) with the subjunctive form of **würde** plus the infinitive of the main verb, which resembles the construction of modal verb plus infinitive. The **würde**-construction works well with virtually all infinitives other than those of the previously mentioned verbs.

Könnten Sie das bitte **wiederholen**?	*Could you please repeat that?*
Würden Sie das bitte **wiederholen**?	*Would you please repeat that?*

The subjunctive stem of a verb derives from the past-tense form plus **-e.** The stem also adds an umlaut to **a, o,** or **u.** The exceptions are **sollen** and **wollen,** which do not add the umlaut and so have identical past-tense and subjunctive forms. The forms for **haben, sein, können,** and **wissen** are as follows.

INFINITIVE: SUBJUNCTIVE STEM:	**haben** **hätte**	**sein** **wäre**	**können** **könnte**	**wissen** **wüsste**
SINGULAR				
ich	hätte	wäre	könnte	wüsste
du	hätte**st**	wäre**st**	könnte**st**	wüsste**st**
Sie	hätte**n**	wäre**n**	könnte**n**	wüsste**n**
sie/er/es	hätte	wäre	könnte	wüsste
PLURAL				
wir	hätte**n**	wäre**n**	könnte**n**	wüsste**n**
ihr	hätte**t**	wäre**t**	könnte**t**	wüsste**t**
Sie	hätte**n**	wäre**n**	könnte**n**	wüsste**n**
sie	hätte**n**	wäre**n**	könnte**n**	wüsste**n**

SPRACHSPIEGEL

Note the similarity between German **wäre** and English *were.* As in English, the subjunctive stem derives from the simple past-tense form. German, however, adds special subjunctive endings to this stem. The umlaut of the vowel is also a characteristic sign of the subjunctive, as in the forms **wäre, hätte, könnte, müsste, dürfte, möchte** (from **mögen**), and **wüsste.**

The subjunctive forms of **werden (würde)** are as follows. Use these forms much in the same way you use the word *would* in English.

INFINITIVE: **werden** SUBJUNCTIVE STEM: **würde**		
SINGULAR		PLURAL
ich würde		wir würde**n**
du würde**st**		ihr würde**t**
Sie würde**n**		Sie würde**n**
sie/er/es würde		sie würde**n**

Das **würde** ich nicht **machen.**   *I wouldn't do that.*

Übungen

A Guter Rat ist teuer. Ihre Freunde haben Probleme. Geben Sie ihnen einen Rat mit Hilfe des Ausdrucks **an deiner Stelle** und des Konjunktivs.

MODELL: Ich fahre zu schnell. →
          An deiner Stelle würde ich nicht zu schnell fahren.

A. 1. An deiner Stelle würde ich nicht zu viel Cola trinken.   2. An deiner Stelle würde ich nicht jeden Tag Pizza essen.   3. An deiner Stelle würde ich nicht um Mittag aufstehen. 4. An deiner Stelle würde ich weniger Hausaufgaben verlangen.   5. An deiner Stelle würde ich mich nicht vor Prüfungen fürchten.   6. An deiner Stelle würde ich nicht viel fern sehen.

B. 1. Wenn Jutta Geld hätte, würde sie Urlaub machen. **2.** Wenn Kai und Anja nett wären, würden sie mehr Freunde haben. **3.** Wenn die Schäfers Zeit hätten, würden sie ein großes Abendessen planen. **4.** Wenn Jens fleißig wäre, würde er Erfolg im Leben haben. **5.** Wenn Heiner Arbeit hätte, würde er Geld verdienen.

C. 1. Könntest du mir helfen? **2.** Dürfte ich das Fenster aufmachen? **3.** Könntet ihr mehr Platz machen? **4.** Könntest du mich anrufen? **5.** Hättest du gern, dass ich hier bliebe? **6.** Dürften wir heute Abend ins Kino? **7.** Würdest du mit uns in die Stadt fahren wollen? **8.** Müssten wir das jetzt machen?

1. Ich trinke zu viel Cola.
2. Ich esse jeden Tag Pizza.
3. Ich stehe um Mittag auf.
4. Ich verlange weniger Hausaufgaben.
5. Ich fürchte mich vor Prüfungen.
6. Ich sehe viel fern.

B Wenn das so wäre. Sagen Sie, was diese Leute machen würden, wenn ihr Leben anders wäre.

MODELL: Klaus möchte ein großes Haus kaufen, aber er ist nicht reich. →
Wenn Klaus reich wäre, würde er ein großes Haus kaufen.

1. Jutta möchte Urlaub machen, aber sie hat kein Geld.
2. Kai und Anja möchten mehr Freunde haben, aber sie sind nicht nett.
3. Die Schäfers möchten ein großes Abendessen planen, aber sie haben keine Zeit.
4. Jens möchte Erfolg im Leben haben, aber er ist nicht fleißig.
5. Heiner will Geld verdienen, aber er hat keine Arbeit.

C So ein höflicher Mensch! Schreiben Sie die folgenden Sätze höflicher mit Hilfe des Konjunktivs.

MODELL: Kannst du mir ein Abendessen kochen? →
Könntest du mir ein Abendessen kochen?

1. Kannst du mir helfen?
2. Darf ich das Fenster aufmachen?
3. Könnt ihr mehr Platz machen?
4. Kannst du mich anrufen?
5. Hast du gern, dass ich hier bleibe?
6. Dürfen wir heute Abend ins Kino?
7. Wirst du mit uns in die Stadt fahren wollen?
8. Müssen wir das jetzt machen?

REVIEW OF PRESENT SUBJUNCTIVE OF WEAK AND STRONG VERBS
MORE ON EXPRESSING UNREAL EVENTS

The present subjunctive forms of weak verbs—those that follow regular conjugation patterns—are identical to the simple past forms.

INFINITIVE	SIMPLE PAST	SUBJUNCTIVE
wünschen	wünschte	wünschte
arbeiten	arbeitete	arbeitete

The subjunctive stem of strong verbs—those verbs that have stem changes in the past tense—consists of the simple past stem plus **-e** and an umlaut if the stem vowel is **a, o,** or **u.**

INFINITIVE	SIMPLE PAST	SUBJUNCTIVE
fahren	fuhr	führe
bleiben	blieb	bliebe
gehen	ging	ginge
kommen	kam	käme

To use strong verbs in the present subjunctive, simply add the appropriate endings to the subjunctive stem, as in the following example.

INFINITIVE: **kommen**	
SUBJUNCTIVE STEM: **käme**	
SINGULAR	PLURAL
ich käme	wir kämen
du kämest	ihr kämet
Sie kämen	Sie kämen
sie/er/es käme	sie kämen

Es wäre schön, wenn sie zu uns zu Besuch **kämen.**

It would be nice if they would come visit us.

KURZ NOTIERT

Expressions with the subjunctive **wollte** or **wünschte** introduce clauses that also require the subjunctive forms of verbs or use of the **würde**-construction.

Ich wollte, du **kämest mit.**
I want you to come along.

Wir wünschten, er **würde** fleißiger **arbeiten.**
We wish he would work harder.

Übungen

Ⓐ Wünsche. Was einer hat, möchte der andere auch haben! Bilden Sie Sätze mit Hilfe des Ausdrucks . . . **wünschte.**

MODELL: Alex arbeitet in einem Buchladen. (Tanja) →
Tanja wünschte, sie arbeitete auch in einem Buchladen.

1. Helga arbeitet nur drei Tage in der Woche. (meine Freunde)
2. Frau Schmidt spielt sehr gut Tennis. (Sabine)
3. Karsten verdient sehr viel Geld. (wir)
4. Lars lernt schnell. (ich)
5. Erika studiert an der Uni Heidelberg. (Patrick)

A. **1.** Meine Freunde wünschten, sie arbeiteten auch nur drei Tage in der Woche. **2.** Sabine wünschte, sie spielte auch sehr gut Tennis. **3.** Wir wünschten, wir verdienten auch sehr viel Geld. **4.** Ich wünschte, ich lernte auch schnell. **5.** Patrick wünschte, er studierte auch an der Uni Heidelberg.

KURZ NOTIERT

The expression **(doch) nur** is commonly used when expressing wishes in the subjunctive.

Wenn er doch nur mit uns kommen könnte.
If only he could come with us.

B. 1. Wenn (doch) nur das Essen fertig wäre.
2. Wenn meine Freunde (doch) nur pünktlich wären. 3. Wenn Jens (doch) nur kommen könnte. 4. Wenn ich die Einladung (doch) nur finden könnte. 5. Wenn meine kleine Schwester (doch) nur in ihrem Zimmer bliebe. 6. Wenn es (doch) nur nicht regnete. 7. Wenn es (doch) nur gute Musik gäbe.

C. *Answers will vary.*

Würden Sie bitte meine Katze retten?

B Ein Fest. Sie haben ein großes Fest geplant, aber alles geht schief.[a] Was sagen Sie? Verwenden Sie dabei den Ausdruck **(doch) nur.**

> MODELL: Du hast keine Zeit mehr. →
> Wenn ich (doch) nur mehr Zeit hätte.

1. Das Essen ist nicht fertig.
2. Deine Freunde kommen nicht pünktlich.
3. Jens darf nicht kommen.
4. Du kannst die Einladungen nicht finden.
5. Deine kleine Schwester bleibt nicht in ihrem Zimmer.
6. Es regnet.
7. Es gibt keine gute Musik.

[a]*wrong*

C Partnerarbeit. Arbeiten Sie mit einem Partner / einer Partnerin und fragen Sie einander, was Sie in den folgenden Situationen tun würden oder wie sie sich fühlen würden.

> MODELL: Du lädst deine Freunde zu einer Party ein, aber kein Mensch kommt. Was würdest du tun? →
> Ich würde weinen. Ich würde sehr böse sein, . . .

1. Eine alte Dame bittet um deine Hilfe, ihre Katze von einem hohen Baum zu holen. Die Katze sieht sehr böse aus!
2. Du hast eine Brieftasche gefunden. In der Brieftasche findest du einen Ausweis mit Namen und Telefonnummer und auch viel Geld.
3. Du spielst Trompete. Dein bester Freund / Deine beste Freundin spielt auch Trompete. Ihr möchtet beide ins Schulorchester und spielt der Dirigentin vor. Das Orchester braucht aber nur einen Trompeter / eine Trompeterin. Du wirst genommen.

REVIEW OF PAST SUBJUNCTIVE
TALKING ABOUT UNREAL EVENTS IN THE PAST

The past subjunctive describes unreal or hypothetical events or situations that might have occurred or existed in the past but did not. Often such statements take the form of wishful thinking, looking back on what might have been.

Wenn er nur seine Hausaufgaben **gemacht hätte.**	*If only he had done his homework.*
Wenn du nur zu Hause **geblieben wärest.**	*If only you had stayed at home.*

The subjunctive has only one way of expressing the past: the subjunctive form of the auxiliary verb **haben** or **sein** with the past participle of the main verb. Note that this construction is very similar to the past perfect tense, which uses the past-tense forms of the auxiliary verbs with past participles. Remember, verbs that can take direct objects use the auxiliary **haben;** verbs that do not take objects use **sein.** This rule applies to the past subjunctive as well as to the perfect tenses of the indicative.

INFINITIVE	PAST PERFECT	PAST SUBJUNCTIVE
kaufen	hatte gekauft	hätte gekauft
nehmen	hatte genommen	hätte genommen
sein	war gewesen	wäre gewesen
gehen	war gegangen	wäre gegangen

Übungen

A Wenn nur! Das Schülerleben ist manchmal schwer. Bilden Sie Sätze im Konjunktiv der Vergangenheit.

MODELL: Ich habe das Referat nicht geschrieben. →
           Wenn ich das Referat nur geschrieben hätte.

1. Ich habe keine gute Note in Mathe bekommen.
2. Du hast zu viele Kurse belegt.
3. Wir haben die Bücher nicht gelesen.
4. Ich habe den Text nicht übersetzt.
5. Er hat den Bunsenbrenner nicht ausgemacht.
6. Ihr habt euch nicht mit den anderen Schülern unterhalten.

B Unter anderen Umständen. Verbinden Sie die Sätze mit Hilfe des Konjunktivs der Vergangenheit.

MODELL: Ich habe keine Einladung bekommen. Ich bin nicht zu
           deiner Party gegangen. →
           Wenn ich eine Einladung bekommen hätte, wäre ich zu
           deiner Party gegangen.

1. Ich habe keine Zeit gehabt. Ich bin nicht in die Bibliothek gegangen.
2. Wir haben keine Urlaubstage gehabt. Wir sind nicht in die Schweiz gereist.
3. Du hast meine Katze nicht gerettet. Ich bin sehr traurig gewesen.
4. Ihr habt uns den Witz[a] nicht erzählt. Wir sind sehr enttäuscht[b] gewesen.
5. Sie hat uns zugehört. Sie ist nicht in den Bus eingestiegen.

[a]joke   [b]disappointed

KURZ NOTIERT

To express an *as if* situation, use the words **als ob** plus a subjunctive verb at the end of the clause.

Sie tut so, **als ob** sie nichts davon **wüsste.**
She acts as if she knew nothing about it.

You can also omit the word **ob** and place the conjugated verb immediately after **als.**

Sie tun so, **als hätten** sie das selbst gemacht.
They act as if they had done it themselves.

Guy unterhält sich mit Freunden in der Mensa.

A. 1. Wenn ich nur eine gute Note in Mathe bekommen hätte.   2. Wenn ich nur nicht so viele Kurse belegt hätte.   3. Wenn wir die Bücher nur gelesen hätten.   4. Wenn ich den Text nur übersetzt hätte.   5. Wenn er den Bunsenbrenner nur ausgemacht hätte.   6. Wenn ihr euch nur mit den anderen Schülern unterhalten hättet.

B. 1. Wenn ich Zeit gehabt hätte, wäre ich in die Bibliothek gegangen.   2. Wenn wir Urlaubstage gehabt hätten, wären wir in die Schweiz gereist.   3. Wenn du meine Katze gerettet hättest, wäre ich nicht traurig gewesen.   4. Wenn ihr uns den Witz erzählt hättet, wären wir nicht enttäuscht gewesen.   5. Wenn sie uns nicht zugehört hätte, wäre sie in den Zug eingestiegen.

PERSPEKTIVEN

HÖREN SIE ZU!
ENTDECKEN SIE KAMERUN!

WORTSCHATZ ZUM HÖRTEXT

sorgen für	to provide for
die Abwechslung	variety
überragen	to tower over
der Vergnügungspark	theme park
dünn	thinly
besiedelt	populated
beeindruckend	impressive
freilebend	free-roaming
einheimisch	local
herrscht kein	there's no
Mangel	shortage
die Garnele	shrimp
der	entertainment
Unterhaltungskünstler	artist
der Zugang	access

A. 1. Die Stadt Yaoundé ist auf sieben Hügeln erbaut.   2. Die Höhenlage macht das Klima angenehm.   3. In Ostkamerun kann man die Nachtigallfälle des Flusses Sanga sehen.
4. Auf der Speisekarte stehen oft französische und libanesische Küchen.   5. Im Süden isst man gern Garnelen.   6. Unterhaltungskünstler kann man vor allem während der Festtage sehen.
7. Man kann in Kamerun angeln, baden, Tennis, Golf und Fußball spielen.

B. Answers will vary.

Die Hofmusikanten des Sultans.

A Was haben Sie über Kamerun gelernt? Hören Sie gut zu, und beantworten Sie die Fragen.

1. Auf wie vielen Hügeln ist die Stadt Yaoundé erbaut?
2. Was macht das Klima in Yaoundé so angenehm?
3. Was kann man in Ostkamerun sehen?
4. Was für Küchen stehen auf der Speisekarte?
5. Was isst man gern in Südkamerun?
6. Wann kann man die Unterhaltungskünstler sehen?
7. Welche Sportarten kann man in Kamerun betreiben?

B Hörerkreis. Hören Sie den Text noch einmal an, und stellen Sie sich vor, Sie hören ihn im Radio. Wie werden die Informationen organisiert? Warum? Beschreiben Sie kurz die Hörer/Hörerinnen, für die dieser Hörtext wohl geschrieben wurde. Was für Berufe würden solche Personen ausüben? Wofür würden sie sich interessieren? Was würden sie gern im Urlaub machen und warum? Spekulieren Sie.

C Briefwechsel. Guy schreibt gern Briefe an seine Familie zu Hause in Kamerun. Hier ist der Brief, den er seinem Bruder Eric geschrieben hat. Stellen Sie sich vor, Sie wären Eric. Schreiben Sie einen kurzen Brief an Guy. Wie ist alles zu Hause in Kamerun? Was haben Sie in den letzten Wochen gemacht? Nehmen Sie einige Informationen aus dem Hörtext für den Brief.

C. Letters will vary.

Cher Eric,

du wunderst dich darüber, wie viel Geld ich als Student in Deutschland habe. Aber hier ist alles teuer. Zum Beispiel zahle ich jeden Monat 250 Mark für mein kleines Zimmer, das ich im Studentenwohnheim bekommen habe. Hier sind die Zimmer billiger und ich habe jetzt mehr Kontakt zu deutschen Kommilitonen.

   Aachen ist eine viel ruhigere Stadt als die Städte in Kamerun. Eigentlich gefällt es mir in Aachen sehr gut. Nach den Vorlesungen gehe ich manchmal abends noch aus und treffe mich mit anderen Studenten. Auch wegen der guten Freunde, die ich hier gefunden habe, fühle ich mich wohl, aber manchmal sehne ich mich doch nach den warmen Abenden in Kamerun.

Alles Gute,
dein Guy

LESEN SIE!

Zum Thema

A Zum Titel. Bevor Sie die folgende Kurzgeschichte von Günther Anders lesen, schauen Sie sich den Titel an. Was bedeutet „Die Freiheitspost"? Wovon handelt wohl die Geschichte?

A. Answers will vary.

B Briefe. Aus welchen Gründen schreiben sich Menschen Briefe? Warum schreiben Sie Briefe oder E-Mails an Freunde oder Verwandte? Machen Sie eine Liste von typischen Gründen.

B. Answers will vary.

Ein alter Hafen in Deutschland.

C. *Answers will vary.*

C Was passiert? Lesen Sie jetzt die Geschichte bis zum Satz „Und er sah, dass es mit ihm zu Ende ging." Wie geht die Geschichte wohl weiter? Was meinen Sie?

- Er versucht, zurück in seine Heimatstadt zu gehen.
- Die Mutter kommt zu ihm in den fernen Hafen.
- Er überwindet seine Krankheit und lebt weiter.
- Er stirbt und die Geschichte ist zu Ende.
- Jetzt sind Sie dran. Was meinen Sie?

Die Freiheitspost

Als Dil, der Matrose, seinen Heimathafen verließ, um für ein Jahrzehnt alle Meere der Welt zu durchkreuzen, versprach er seiner alten Mutter, ihr von jedem noch so entfernten Ort aus ein Lebenszeichen zu geben. Zwei Jahre hindurch erhielt sie jeden Monat eine Karte; und je nach der Jahreszeit mahnte sie ihr Sohn, die Boote zu teeren, das Gartengitter zu 5 streichen oder den Birnbaum zu stützen. Zwei Jahre lang erhielt sie regelmäßig seine Nachrichten, und es war ihr, als sei er in ihrer Nähe. Nach zwei Jahren erkrankte Dil in einem fernen Hafen. Und er sah, dass es mit ihm zu Ende ging.

„Wozu muss meine Mutter wissen", sprach er zu seinem Kapitän, „dass 10 es mit mir zu Ende geht?" Und er ließ sich einen Packen Postkarten bringen und begann in den Stunden, die ihm noch blieben, die Karten zu schreiben, die seine Mutter in den nächsten acht Jahren empfangen

WORTSCHATZ ZUM LESEN

der Matrose	sailor
entfernt	removed; distant
das Lebenszeichen	sign of life
mahnen	to remind
teeren	to tar
das Gartengitter	garden fence
streichen	to paint
der Birnbaum	pear tree
stützen	to support; to prop up
empfangen	to receive
die Abwesenheit	absence
abnehmen	to decrease
gleichfalls	likewise
nachkommen	to comply with
die Pflicht	duty

15 sollte. Jede zeigte ein anderes Datum, jede einen anderen Hafennamen, und auf jeder schrieb er, wie gut es ihm ging und dass er ihre Karten erhalten habe und dass sie die Boote teeren solle oder den Birnbaum stützen, je nach Jahreszeit. Als er seine Korrespondenz für die nächsten acht Jahre erledigt hatte, übergab er den Packen seinem Kapitän, bat ihn, acht Jahre hindurch jeden Monat eine der Karten abzusenden, und
20 starb.

Drei Jahre lang erhielt seine Mutter regelmäßig die Nachrichten ihres Sohnes. Und sie war glücklich, dass die Zeit seiner Abwesenheit abnahm, und sie war stolz auf ihn und lebte von Postempfang zu Postempfang. Nach fünf Jahren seiner Abwesenheit legte sie sich hin und starb
25 gleichfalls.

Der Kapitän aber, der nicht ahnte, dass die Mutter seines toten Matrosen gestorben war, kam seiner Pflicht mit vollkommener Regelmäßigkeit nach. Und sandte jeden Monat die Post des längst Gestorbenen an die Tote. So liefen die Nachrichten weiter von
30 niemandem an niemanden. Die Boote hatten weiter geteert, der Birnbaum weiter gestützt zu werden. Aber niemand teerte. Und niemand stützte.

Günther Anders

Zum Text

A Wer machte was? Dil, Dils Mutter oder der Kapitän?

Wer
1. wollte alle Meere der Welt durchkreuzen?
2. sollte den Birnbaum stützen?
3. schrieb regelmäßig Briefe?
4. erkrankte in einem fernen Hafen?
5. lebte von Postempfang zu Postempfang?
6. hatte die Pflicht, Postkarten acht Jahre hindurch zu senden?

B Pflicht und Liebe. Was meinen Sie? Was macht Dil aus Liebe? Was macht er aus Pflicht? Suchen Sie Beispiele im Text, und machen Sie zwei Listen.

Zur Interpretation

● Dil. Beantworten Sie die Fragen.

1. Was für ein Mensch ist Dil? Warum, glauben Sie, wollte er so lange von zu Hause weg sein?

A. 1. Dil 2. Dils Mutter 3. Dil 4. Dil 5. Dils Mutter 6. der Kapitän

B. *Possible answers are:* PFLICHT: Dil sendet aus jedem Hafen ein Lebenszeichen, weil er es seiner Mutter versprochen hat. LIEBE: Als Dil merkt, dass er sterben wird, schreibt er Postkarten an seine Mutter, weil er sie nicht traurig machen will.

Answers will vary.

2. Warum mahnte der Sohn seine Mutter, die Boote zu teeren und den Birnbaum zu stützen? Was halten Sie von diesen Mahnungen?
3. Warum hat der Kapitän die Postkarten regelmäßig geschickt? Hätten Sie das auch gemacht?
4. Stimmen Sie überein, dass es gute und schlechte Lügen gibt? Was wäre eine „gute" Lüge?
5. Ist diese Geschichte heute noch möglich? Können Sie sich vorstellen, dass der Kapitän E-Mails an die Mutter schickt? Warum (nicht)?

INTERAKTION

Dialogues will vary.

● Rollenspiel. Arbeiten Sie mit einem Partner / einer Partnerin. Spielen Sie folgende Szenen zur Geschichte „Die Freiheitspost" nach.

1. Dil und seine Mutter verabschieden sich.
2. Dils Mutter zeigt einer Freundin die Postkarten, die sie von ihrem Sohn bekommt.
3. Dil bittet seinen Kapitän, die Postkarten an seine Mutter regelmäßig zu schicken.
4. Der Kapitän erzählt einem Matrosen, was er für Dil macht.

SCHREIBEN SIE!

Texts will vary.

Ratschläge per E-Mail

TIPP ZUM SCHREIBEN

You have a great deal of creative freedom in this assignment. You must make up what your friend's problems are that he/she has written to you about and you must also come up with solutions to those problems. To solve a problem, explain what you would do in your friend's position.

● Sie haben eine E-Mail von einem Freund / einer Freundin erhalten, der/die eben begonnen hat, in einer fremden Stadt zu studieren. In der E-Mail wird deutlich, dass es Ihrem Freund / Ihrer Freundin nicht gut geht. Der Freund / Die Freundin bittet Sie um Ihren Rat. Schreiben Sie eine E-Mail zurück, in der Sie sagen, was Sie an seiner/ihrer Stelle tun würden oder getan hätten.

Purpose:	Acknowledging receipt of a message and giving advice
Audience:	An unhappy friend
Subject:	What you would do or would have done
Structure:	E-mail reply

Schreibmodell

The writer confirms getting an e-mail from his friend.

> **An:** tom.andrews@uni-weimar.de
> **Betreff:** Antwort: Heimweh in Weimar
>
> Grüß dich, Tom! Habe mich richtig gefreut, von dir zu hören. Tut mir Leid, dass du so unglücklich in Weimar bist. Ich wünschte ich könnte dir helfen.

The writer uses a combination of **du**-form imperatives and statements in the subjunctive to give advice and make suggestions.

> Wenn du doch nur nicht so viel lernen würdest! An deiner Stelle würde ich öfter ins Kino gehen und mir einen lustigen Film ansehen. Oder treib doch zur Abwechslung Sport. An der Uni gibt es bestimmt eine Fußballmannschaft. Wenn du einmal etwas anderes tätest als nur in die Bibliothek zu gehen, wärest du nicht so alleine. Durchhalten, Junge, du lernst bald neue Freunde kennen und alles wird besser.

The subjunctive is used to make polite requests.

> Ich hätte eine Bitte, könntest du mir ein T-Shirt der Universität schicken? Du weißt ja, für meine Sammlung.
> Grüße, dein Max

Schreibstrategien

Vor dem Schreiben

• Before you start to write your e-mail, you need to create a fictional problem for your friend. Then you can give advice and make suggestions for improving his/her situation. Write out your answers to the following questions and be prepared to turn them in with your e-mail message.

Zur Person: Wie heißt der Freund / die Freundin, der/die Ihnen die E-Mail geschickt hat? Woher kennen Sie einander? Wie ist Ihr Freund / Ihre Freundin: freundlich, schüchtern, lustig, seriös, fleißig, faul? Worüber sprechen Sie normalerweise miteinander? Was für Probleme diskutieren Sie?

Zur Situation: An welcher Universität studiert Ihr Freund / Ihre Freundin? Kennt er/sie sich in der neuen Stadt aus oder nicht? Was für eine Hochschule oder Universität ist es? Warum hat Ihr Freund / Ihre Freundin diese Uni gewählt? Über welche Probleme schreibt Ihr Freund / Ihre Freundin? Was hat er/sie schon getan, um die Probleme zu lösen?

TIPP ZUM SCHREIBEN

E-mail addresses in Germany often use the suffix **.de.** In Switzerland, the suffix is **.ch,** and in Austria it is **.au.**

An: mausi529@baystate.edu
Betreff: Antwort: Ich will weg von hier!

Liebe Marianne! Ich habe mir ~~mich~~ so gefreut, deine E-Mail zu bekommen, aber dann habe ich ~~es~~ sie gelesen! O jeh! Es ist gar nicht nett, dass du so unglücklich bist.
Aufgeben und heimkommen? Das ist nicht die Marianne, ~~dass~~ die ich kenne! Du bist erst ein paar Wochen da. An deiner Stelle würde ich eine Weile warten! Tut mir Leid, dass die Studenten unfreundlich sind. Aber dann mußt du selbst freundlicher sein! An deiner Stelle würde ich (machen) eine Fete. Lade alle Leute im Heim ein. Alle kennen dich dann nachher. Jetzt aufhören und heimkommen wäre das Schlimmste, was du machen ~~kannst~~ könntest! Lass dir Zeit, und es wird bestimmt besser.
Mit vielen lieben Grüßen,
Deine Jennifer

- Now that you have established the facts and you know what the problems are, start planning your response. Make notes about what advice you will give your friend about each of his/her problems and complaints. These questions will help guide you in your planning.

  Womit hat Ihr Freund / Ihre Freundin die meisten Probleme und worüber beschwert er/sie sich? Wie ist der Tonfall Ihrer Antwort: mitleidig,[a] gleichgültig,[b] ärgerlich, neutral oder . . . ? Was für einen Rat wollen Sie ihm/ihr geben, welche Vorschläge wollen Sie machen?

[a]*sympathetic* [b]*indifferent*

Beim Schreiben

- Start your reply with a standard greeting: **Lieber . . . / Liebe . . . ,** or **Grüß dich, . . .**

- Address the problems one by one. Make suggestions, give advice, and explain what you'd do or would have done.

- Write a concluding sentence or two, then end with a standard closing and signature.

Nach dem Schreiben

- Read through your e-mail, correcting any mistakes as you read.

- Trade papers with a peer editor. Read your partner's paper once, checking for problems in spelling, grammar, and word choice; make improvements. Read it a second time: Are the solutions clear and logical? If not, suggest changes.

- Write a second draft, making corrections and incorporating suggestions you feel will improve your e-mail. Proofread your second draft.

Stimmt alles?

- Make sure your message includes an e-mail address for your friend and subject after the word **Betreff.**[a]

- Write or type the final draft of your e-mail. Attach the background information on your friend to the message, and hand both in.

[a]*re*

KAPITEL 28
WORTSCHATZ

Substantive	Nouns
die **Berufung, -en**	vocation
die **Diplomarbeit, -en**	thesis work
die **Erfahrung, -en**	experience
die **Germanistik**	German studies
die **Jura**	law
die **Medizin**	medicine
die **Rechtswissenschaft**	jurisprudence
der **Abschnitt, -e**	cut; segment
der **Begriff, -e**	concept, idea
der **Kommilitone, (-n** *masc.*) / die **Kommilitonin, -nen**	classmate
der **Kreis, -e**	circle
der **Ruf, -e**	reputation
der **Stoff, -e**	material
das **Mittelalter**	Middle Ages
die **Geisteswissenschaften** (*pl.*)	humanities

Verben	Verbs
auf•nehmen (nimmt auf) nahm auf, aufgenommen	to start, take up
sich befinden, befand, befunden	to be located
dolmetschen	to interpret (*languages*)
entstehen, entstand, ist entstanden	to arise; to evolve
prüfen	to test
quatschen	to talk, gossip
schaffen, schuf, geschaffen	to make
sich sehnen nach	to long for
übersetzen	to translate
um•wechseln	to change
sich unterhalten über (+ *acc.*) **(unterhält)** unterhielt, unterhalten	to converse; entertain

sich wundern über (+ *acc.*)	to be surprised at
zu•nehmen (nimmt zu) nahm zu, zugenommen	to increase

Adjektive und Adverbien	Adjectives and adverbs
allmählich	gradual(ly)
beliebt	popular; famous
beziehungweise	respective(ly)
eigenartig	unique(ly)
gemeinsam	common; together
heutig	today's
riesengroß	enormous

Sie wissen schon	You already know
die **Bemerkung, -en**	observation, remark, comment
die **Bildung**	education
die **Chemie**	chemistry
die **Geschichte, -n**	history; story
die **Physik**	physics
der **Maschinenbau**	mechanical engineering
bekommen, bekam, bekommen	to receive
beleidigen	to insult
sich fürchten vor (+ *dat.*)	to be afraid of
sich gewöhnen an (+ *acc.*)	to get used to
verlangen	to demand
merkwürdig	remarkable; peculiar, odd
ruhig	peaceful(ly)

KAPITEL 29 · ARBEIT UND WIRTSCHAFT

pages 96–115

PLANNING GUIDE • CLASSROOM MANAGEMENT

OBJECTIVES

Communication
- Discuss career goals, pp. 101, 113.
- Describe high and low points of one's past, p. 106.

Grammar
- Review comparatives, pp. 102–103.
- Review superlatives, pp. 104–105.
- Learn about verbs as adjectives, participial constructions, and extended modifiers, pp. 106–107.

Culture
- Learn about the changing German economy, pp. 98–99.
- Meet an employment specialist, p. 99.
- Learn about the economic situation in the former East Germany, p. 99.
- Read about the apprenticeship system in Germany, p. 101.
- Learn about Mackenbach, p. 108.
- Learn about Heinrich Böll, p. 112.

Recycling
- Review comparatives, pp. 102–104.
- Review superlatives, pp. 104–106.

STRATEGIES

Listening Strategies
- Listen to a story about a musical instrument maker, p. 108.

Speaking Strategies
- Interview a partner about free-time activities, p. 107.
- Discuss people and their work, p. 113.

Reading Strategies
- Read a short story about an extraordinary career, pp. 111–112.

Writing Strategies
- Develop a public opinion questionnaire, p. 114.

Connecting Cultures Strategies
- Learn about musical connections between southwestern Germany and the U.S., p. 108.

PROGRAM RESOURCES

Print
- *Arbeitsheft* (Workbook), pp. 67–80
- *Arbeitsheft* (Workbook), Teacher's Edition, pp. 67–80

Audiovisual
- Overhead Transparencies 29.1–29.G1
- Audio Program, Cassette 3A, 7A/CD 3, 9
- Audioscript, pp. 29–35

Technology
- Annenberg *Fokus Deutsch* Video Series, *Folge 29*
- www.mcdougallittell.com

Assessment Program Options
- *Prüfung, Kapitel 29*, Assessment Program, pp. 52–61
- Audio Program, Cassette 8A/CD 10
- Audioscript, pp. 109–110
- Teacher's Resource CD-ROM

DAY 1

Note: (1) Please see TE, pp. 96E–96J, for other suggestions not referenced in these plans. (2) Not all homework options need be assigned.

CHAPTER OPENER

- Quick Start Review: Vocabulary (TE, p. 96E). 5 MIN
- Follow the Teaching Suggestions for discussing the German economy (TE, p. 96E). 4 MIN

VIDEOTHEK

- Do *Akt. A,* p. 98, as a class. Write lists on the board (TE, p. 96F). 6 MIN
- Follow the suggestions for viewing *Folge I: Wirtschaft im Wandel* and then have students do *Akt. B,* p. 98, in pairs (TE, p. 96F). 16 MIN
- Follow the Teaching Suggestions for a discussion (TE, p. 96F), then view *Folge II: Eine Arbeitsvermittlerin.* 11 MIN
- Do *Akt. A,* p. 99, silently, then check answers with partners (TE, p. 96F). 8 MIN

Homework Options:

- *Arbeitsheft,* p. 68, *Videothek, Akt. C*
- *Videothek, Akt. C,* p. 99

DAY 2

VIDEOTHEK

- Quick Start Review 1: Subjunctive (TE, p. 96E). 5 MIN
- Read the *Kulturspiegel,* p. 99, as a class and then do *Akt. B,* p. 99, individually. Check answers as a class and engage students in a discussion (TE, p. 96F). 8 MIN

VOKABELN

- Present the vocabulary on p. 100. 7 MIN
- Do *Akt. A,* pp. 100–101, silently, then check their answers with a partner. Conclude with the follow-up activity in the Teaching Suggestions (TE, p. 96G). 15 MIN
- Do the warm-up activity for *Akt. B,* p. 101, then do the activity as a class (TE, p. 96G). 8 MIN
- Do *Akt. C,* p. 101, silently, then check answers as a class. 7 MIN

Homework Options:

- *Vokabeln, Akt. D,* p. 101
- *Arbeitsheft,* p. 71, *Vokabeln, Akt. C*

DAY 3

VOKABELN

- Quick Start Review 1: Ordinal numbers (TE, p. 96F). 6 MIN
- Discuss *Akt. D,* p. 101, as a class (TE, p. 96G). 6 MIN

STRUKTUREN

- Present comparatives on pp. 102–103 using OHT 29.G1. 8 MIN
- Do *Übung A,* p. 103, silently, then check answers as a class. Do follow-up activity in the Teaching Suggestions (TE, p. 96H). 10 MIN
- Do *Übung B,* p. 104, in small groups, including the variation in the Teaching Suggestions. Have them share the answers with the class (TE, p. 96H). 12 MIN
- *Arbeitsheft,* p. 73, *Strukturen, Akt. D.* 8 MIN

Homework Options:

- *Übung C,* p. 104
- *Arbeitsheft,* p. 74, *Strukturen, Akt. F–H*

DAY 4

STRUKTUREN

- Quick Start Review 1: Genitive (TE, p. 96G). 5 MIN
- Present the superlatives on pp. 104–105 using OHT 29.2–29.G1. Follow the Teaching Suggestions (TE, p. 96H). 8 MIN
- *Arbeitsheft,* p. 75, audio *Akt. I.* 8 MIN
- Do *Übung A,* p. 105, with a partner and then check their answers as a class. 8 MIN
- Do *Übung B,* p. 106. Follow the Teaching Suggestions (TE, p. 96H). 12 MIN
- Present verbs as adjectives, participial constructions, and extended modifiers on pp. 106–107. 9 MIN

Homework Options:

- *Übung C,* p. 106
- *Übung A,* p. 107
- *Arbeitsheft,* pp. 75–76, *Strukturen, Akt. J–K*

PACING GUIDE • SAMPLE LESSON PLAN, 50-MINUTE SCHEDULE

STRUKTUREN

- Quick Start Review 2: *Der-* and *ein-*words (TE, p. 96H). 5 MIN
- Do *Übung B,* p. 107, in pairs. 10 MIN

PERSPEKTIVEN

- Have students read through the *Wortschatz zum Hörtext, Kulturspiegel,* and the statements in *Hören Sie zu!, Akt. A,* p. 108, before listening to the recording (TE, p. 96I). 5 MIN
- Have students do *Hören Sie zu!, Akt. A,* p. 108, as they listen. Encourage them to jot down other information as well (TE, p. 96I). 10 MIN
- Have students listen to the text again and do *Hören Sie zu!, Akt. B,* p. 108, with a partner (TE, p. 96I). 10 MIN
- Do *Zum Thema, Akt. A,* p. 109, in small groups. 7 MIN
- Introduce the text on pp. 111–112 (TE, p. 96I). 3 MIN

Homework Options:

- *Zum Thema, Akt. B,* p. 109 (individually)
- Read the text on pp. 111–112 (This must be assigned as out-of-class work.)
- *Arbeitsheft,* p. 76, *Strukturen, Akt. L–M*

PERSPEKTIVEN

- Quick Start Review 1: Subjunctive (TE, p. 96H). 4 MIN
- Discuss *Zum Text, Akt. A,* p. 113, as a class. Follow the Teaching Suggestions (TE, p. 96I). 6 MIN
- Do *Zum Text, Akt. B,* p. 113, in small groups. 6 MIN
- Discuss *Zur Interpretation,* p. 113, as a class (TE, p. 96I). 5 MIN
- Do *Interaktion,* p. 113. 14 MIN
- Begin *Schreiben Sie!* by discussing the assignment, *Tipp zum Schreiben,* and *Schreibmodell.* 5 MIN
- Do *Vor dem Schreiben* and begin *Beim Schreiben,* p. 113. 10 MIN

Homework Options:

- Complete the first part of *Beim Schreiben,* p. 113
- *Arbeitsheft,* pp. 78–80, *Perspektiven, Akt. D–F*

PERSPEKTIVEN

- Quick Start Review 2: Vocabulary (TE, p. 96I). 4 MIN
- Have students complete the second part of *Beim Schreiben,* p. 113. 15 MIN
- Do the first step in *Nach dem Schreiben,* p. 113. 10 MIN
- Conduct the interviews (the second step in *Nach dem Schreiben,* p. 114). 10 MIN
- Do the third step in *Nach dem Schreiben.* 11 MIN

Homework Options:

- Complete the first draft of the report

PERSPEKTIVEN

- Use *Vokabeln* Quick Start Review 2: Prepositions, as a review activity (TE, pp. 96F–96G). 5 MIN
- Have students do the fourth step in *Nach dem Schreiben,* p. 114, and begin the fifth step. 10 MIN
- Questions and review. 5 MIN
- *Prüfung, Kapitel 29.* 30 MIN

Homework Options:

- Finish the final draft of the report

PACING GUIDE • SAMPLE LESSON PLAN, 50-MINUTE SCHEDULE

DAY 1

Note: (1) Please see TE, pp. 96E–96J, for other suggestions not referenced in these plans. (2) Not all homework options need be assigned.

CHAPTER OPENER
- Quick Start Review: Vocabulary (TE, p. 96E). 5 MIN
- Discuss the German economy (TE, p. 96E). 4 MIN

VIDEOTHEK
- View *Folge I.* 11 MIN
- Do *Akt. A–B*, p. 98 (TE, p. 96F). 11 MIN
- View *Folge II.* 11 MIN
- Do *Akt. A–B*, p. 99 (TE, p. 96F). 16 MIN
- Block Schedule activity: Change of Pace (TE, p. 96F). 10 MIN

VOKABELN
- Present vocabulary on p. 100. 7 MIN
- Do *Akt. A*, pp. 100–101. 15 MIN

Homework Options:
- *Arbeitsheft*, p. 68, *Videothek, Akt. C* and p. 71, *Vokabeln, Akt. C–D*
- *Videothek, Akt. C*, p. 99
- *Vokabeln, Akt. D*, p. 101

DAY 2

VOKABELN
- Quick Start Review 1: Ordinal numbers (TE, p. 96F). 5 MIN
- Discuss *Akt. D*, p. 101, as a class (TE, p. 96G). 6 MIN
- Do *Akt. B*, p. 101, as a class (TE, p. 96G). 8 MIN
- Do *Akt. C*, p. 101, silently. 7 MIN
- Block Schedule activity: Change of Pace (TE, p. 96G). 10 MIN

STRUKTUREN
- Present comparatives on pp. 102–103. 8 MIN
- Do *Übung A*, p. 103, silently (TE, p. 96H). 10 MIN
- Do *Übung B*, p. 104, in small groups (TE, p. 96H). 12 MIN
- *Arbeitsheft*, p. 78, audio *Akt. A–C*. 16 MIN
- Present superlatives on pp. 104–105 (TE, p. 96H). 8 MIN

Homework Options:
- *Übung C*, p. 104
- *Arbeitsheft*, pp. 74–76, *Strukturen, Akt. F–H, J–K*
- *Übung C*, p. 106

DAY 3

STRUKTUREN
- Quick Start Review 1: Genitive (TE, p. 96G). 5 MIN
- *Arbeitsheft*, p. 75, audio *Akt. I*. 6 MIN
- Do *Übung A*, p. 105, in pairs. 7 MIN
- Do *Übung B*, p. 106 (TE, p. 96H). 7 MIN
- Present verbs as modifiers on pp. 106–107. 8 MIN
- Do *Übung B*, p. 107, in pairs. 8 MIN
- Block Schedule activity: Expansion (TE, p. 96H). 8 MIN

PERSPEKTIVEN
- *Arbeitsheft*, p. 77, *Akt. A–B*. 6 MIN
- Do *Hören Sie zu!*, *Akt. A*, p. 108 (TE, p. 96I). 10 MIN
- Do *Hören Sie zu!*, *Akt. B*, p. 108 (TE, p. 96I). 8 MIN
- Do *Zum Thema, Akt. A*, p. 109, in small groups. 7 MIN
- Introduce the text on pp. 111–112 and read it in groups (TE, p. 96I). 10 MIN

Homework Options:
- *Übung A*, p. 107
- *Arbeitsheft*, p. 76, *Akt. L–M*
- *Perspektiven, Zum Thema, Akt. B*, p. 109, individually

DAY 4

PERSPEKTIVEN
- Quick Start Review 1: Subjunctive (TE, p. 96H). 4 MIN
- Discuss *Zum Text, Akt. A*, p. 113, as a class. Follow the Teaching Suggestions (TE, p. 96I). 6 MIN
- Do *Zum Text, Akt. B*, p. 113, in small groups. 6 MIN
- Discuss *Zur Interpretation*, p. 113, as a class (TE, p. 96I). 5 MIN
- *Interaktion*, p. 113. 14 MIN
- Begin *Schreiben Sie!* by discussing the assignment, *Tipp zum Schreiben*, and *Schreibmodell*. 5 MIN
- *Vor dem Schreiben*, p. 113. Begin *Beim Schreiben*, p. 113. 10 MIN
- Block Schedule activity: Fun Break (TE, p. 96J). 10 MIN
- *Beim Schreiben*, p. 113. 30 MIN

Homework Options:
- *Arbeitsheft*, pp. 78–80, *Perspektiven, Akt. D–F*

DAY 5

PERSPEKTIVEN
- Quick Start Review 2: Vocabulary (TE, p. 96I). 5 MIN
- Do the first step in *Nach dem Schreiben*, p. 113. 10 MIN
- Conduct the interviews (step 2 from *Nach dem Schreiben*). 10 MIN
- Do step 3 from *Nach dem Schreiben*. 10 MIN
- Have students do the fourth step in *Nach dem Schreiben* and begin the fifth step, p. 114. 10 MIN
- Block Schedule activity: Peer Teaching (TE, p. 96J). 10 MIN
- Questions and review. 5 MIN
- *Prüfung, Kapitel 29*. 30 MIN

Homework Options:
- Finish the final draft of the report

Chapter Opener, pp. 96–97

PROGRAM RESOURCES

• Overhead Transparency 29.1

Quick Start Review

♻ Vocabulary
Ergänzen Sie die Sätze.
WÖRTER: Diplomarbeit, Mittelalter, Ruf, Kommilitonen, Rechtswissenschaft, Geisteswissenschaften

1. Sprachen gehören zu den _____.
2. Am Ende des Studiums müssen viele eine _____ schreiben.
3. Im _____ wurden die Bücher mit der Hand und bei Kerzenlicht geschrieben.
4. Die Naturwissenschaften an der Universität Göttingen haben einen guten _____.
5. Studenten, die das gleiche Fach zur gleichen Zeit studieren nennt man _____.
6. Wenn man Richter oder Anwalt werden will, studiert man _____.

Answers: 1. Geisteswissenschaften
2. Diplomarbeit   3. Mittelalter
4. Ruf   5. Kommilitonen
6. Rechtswissenschaft

TEACHING SUGGESTIONS

Ask students to name some German products they know, such as cars, electronics, or appliances. Find out what they know about the economic situation in the European union. What do they think of the economic situation in the U.S.?

TEACHING ALL STUDENTS

Multiple Intelligences Intrapersonal: Have students write a short paragraph describing their dreams for the future. Where do they see themselves 5 years from now? If they could pick any profession, what would they choose? Encourage them to use the subjunctive in their descriptions.

Videothek, pp. 98–99

PROGRAM RESOURCES

• Videocassette, *Folge 29*
• *Arbeitsheft,* pp. 67–69
• Audio Program, Cassette 3A/CD 3
• Audioscript, pp. 29–31

Quick Start Review 1

♻ Subjunctive
Ergänzen Sie die Sätze.
MODELL: Er lernt seine Vokabeln nicht.
Ich wünschte, . . . →
Ich wünschte, er würde seine Vokabeln lernen.

1. Ich kann nicht einschlafen. Ich wünschte, . . .
2. Er redet nicht mit mir. Ich wünschte, . . .
3. Er kommt nicht mit zur Party. Ich wünschte, . . .
4. Das Essen ist nicht gut. Ich wünschte, . . .
5. Es regnet den ganzen Tag. Ich wünschte, . . .
6. Meine Geschwister helfen mir nie bei der Wäsche. Ich wünschte, . . .

Answers: 1. Ich wünschte, ich könnte einschlafen.   2. Ich wünschte, er redete mit mir (würde mit mir reden).
3. Ich wünschte, er käme mit zur Party.
4. Ich wünschte, das Essen wäre besser.   5. Ich wünschte, es regnete nicht den ganzen Tag (es würde nicht den ganzen Tag regnen).   6. Ich wünschte, meine Geschwister würden mir bei der Wäsche helfen.

Quick Start Review 2

♻ Vocabulary
Ergänzen Sie die Verben in den Sätzen.
VERBEN: quatschen, zugenommen, gewöhnen, übersetzen, verlangen, beleidigen

1. Es ist nicht immer leicht, von einer Sprache in die andere zu _____.
2. Die Zahl der Studenten an deutschen Universitäten hat stark _____.
3. Lehrer ärgern sich normalerweise, wenn Schüler im Unterricht zu viel _____.
4. Studenten aus anderen Ländern müssen sich an ihre neue Umgebung erst _____.
5. Es ist nicht sehr klug, seine Lehrer zu _____.
6. Manche Lehrer _____ mehr von den Schülern als andere.

Answers: 1. übersetzen
2. zugenommen   3. quatschen
4. gewöhnen   5. beleidigen
6. verlangen

TEACHING SUGGESTIONS

• *Folge I: Wirtschaft im Wandel,* pp. 98–99

This episode gives an overview of economic changes that have occurred in Germany over the last 100 years. Play the episode without sound and ask students to identify the products they see. Remind them to review the *Wortschatz zum Video* and have them watch the episode a second time. They should take notes as they watch.

- *Aktivität A,* p. 98

Have students brainstorm their answers on a personal level, as well as on a statewide or nationwide level. Have them think about the local economic situation.

- *Aktivität B,* p. 98

Ask students to come up with one representative sentence for each time period portrayed in the video. Keep track of these sentences on the board and establish a time line together.

- *Folge II: Eine Arbeitsvermittlerin,* p. 99

Discuss the problem of unemployment before viewing this section. Ask questions like *Wie sucht man Arbeit? An wen kann man sich wenden, wenn man lange Zeit arbeitslos ist? Ist es schwer, einen guten Arbeitsplatz zu finden?*

- *Aktivität A,* p. 99

Ask students to name 1–2 typical activities that belong to each of the professions mentioned. For example, *Ein Apotheker: er/sie verkauft Arzneimittel; er/sie hilft Kunden. . .*

- *Aktivität B,* p. 99

Read the *Kulturspiegel* before doing the activity. Follow-up: Have students create some more statements capturing the differences between the old and new German states.

TEACHING ALL STUDENTS

Extra Help Have students look at a map of Germany and name the new and old German states. Try to find

some statistics on what products are produced where. Point out states that have been hit very hard by unemployment since reunification in 1990. Information is available from the Goethe Institute (www.goethe.de).

LANGUAGE NOTE

Keep in mind that German comparative forms never use *mehr* and superlatives never use *meist/am meisten.* For example, *Der Artikel in der **Frankfurter Rundschau** war interessanter als der im **Spiegel**. Peters Artikel war der interessanteste in der letzten Schülerzeitung.*

CLASSROOM COMMUNITY

Paired Activity Have students work in pairs to invent a story about a former GDR citizen who has lost his or her job because of the changes taking place since reunification. Students should explain the reasons for the job loss and try to imagine how the person might deal with the new situation. Some possible subjects might be *ein 55-jähriger Geschichtslehrer, ein 40-jähriger Journalist für die Zeitung **Neues Deutschland**,* or *ein 35-jähriger Arbeiter in einer Kinderkleiderfabrik.*

INTERDISCIPLINARY CONNECTION

Have students compare statistics for unemployment in the U.S. and in Germany.

BLOCK SCHEDULE

Change of Pace Have students work in pairs to role-play the visit of an unemployed person to the employment specialist (*Arbeitsvermittlerin*), Monika Schneider.

Vokabeln, pp. 100–101

PROGRAM RESOURCES

- *Arbeitsheft,* pp. 70–71
- Audio Program, Cassette 3A/CD 3
- Audioscript, pp. 31–32

Quick Start Review 1
♻ Ordinal numbers
Schreiben Sie die Zahlen als Wörter.

1. Wir wohnen im _____ (3.) Stock.
2. Das ist schon das _____ (2.) Mal, dass er zu spät kommt.
3. Er hat am _____ (5.) April Geburtstag.
4. Heute ist der _____ (9.) September 1999.
5. Wir haben Theaterkarten für die _____ (13.) Reihe.
6. Fahren Sie die Hauptstraße entlang und biegen Sie nach der Tankstelle in die _____ (1.) Straße rechts ein. Unser Haus ist das _____ (2.) auf der linken Seite.

Answers: 1. dritten 2. zweite
3. fünften 4. neunte 5. dreizehnte
6. erste, zweite

Quick Start Review 2
♻ Prepositions
Ergänzen Sie die richtige Präposition und die Artikel.

1. Er arbeitet oft noch sehr spät _____ _____ Firma.
2. Leg den Schlüssel bitte _____ _____ Auto.
3. _____ _____ Cafeteria gibt es heute Steak zum Mittagessen.
4. _____ _____ letzten Zeit war er oft müde.

5. Hast du noch eine Münze _____ _____ Tasche?

6. _____ _____ letzten Jahren ist er Weihnachten immer nach Mexiko geflogen.

Answers: 1. in der   2. in das   3. In der   4. In der   5. in der   6. In den

TEACHING SUGGESTIONS

• *Aktivität A*, p. 100

Follow-up: Ask students to write a definition of one of the vocabulary items on p. 100 on a slip of paper. Call on students to give the definition they have written. The class must find the word in the vocabulary list that matches the definition.

• *Aktivität B*, p. 101

Warm-up: Have students find the infinitive forms of the past participles in the box. Encourage them to form sentences with the verbs.

• *Aktivität D*, p. 101

Write on the board all the professions mentioned, then have students brainstorm a list of skills and activities associated with each profession.

TEACHING ALL STUDENTS

Multiple Intelligences Verbal: Have students choose 2 verbs from the list on p. 100 and form hypothetical statements about the economy. For example, *Wenn wir die Produktion steigerten, müssten wir mehr Arbeiter einstellen. Wenn wir die Firma schneller aufbauen könnten, könnten wir unsere Produkte eher auf den Markt bringen.*

CLASSROOM COMMUNITY

Dictation Dictate the following sentences. Project the text on an OHT or write it on the board after you are done. Have students exchange papers with a partner and correct their work. *Der Fall der Mauer hat viele ostdeutsche Bürger gezwungen, sich eine neue Arbeit zu suchen. Junge Leute sind in den Westen gegangen. Viele Betriebe mussten schließen. Ostdeutsche Waren wollte niemand mehr herstellen. Die Arbeitslosenzahl ist sehr schnell gestiegen.*

CULTURE HIGHLIGHTS

Have students read the *Kulturspiegel*, p. 101, and remind them of the video episode in *Kapitel 26* about Kristian and Ramona. (Kristian was an *Auszubildende* preparing to be a banker and Ramona was a *Lehrling* working to become a florist.) Ask students to comment on how job training works in this country.

BLOCK SCHEDULE

Change of Pace Bring in some German newspapers and magazines. Have students cut them up to make a collage of people at work. Ask them to arrange their findings in groups of professions that might be linked together (white collar, blue collar, health, computers).

PORTFOLIO

Have students interview someone who works in the profession they would like to learn. How does the person like the work? What is a typical day like? Would the person choose the same profession again? Have students write a short report for the class and present it both orally and on a poster.

RUBRIC   **A** = 13–15 pts.   **B** = 10–12 pts.   **C** = 7–9 pts.   **D** = 4–6 pts.   **F** = <4 pts.

Writing Criteria	Scale				
Organization and presentation	1	2	3	4	5
Grammar and vocabulary	1	2	3	4	5
Content	1	2	3	4	5

Strukturen, pp. 102–107

PROGRAM RESOURCES

• Overhead Transparencies 29.2–29.G1
• *Arbeitsheft*, pp. 72–76
• Audio Program, Cassette 3A/CD 3
• Audioscript, pp. 32–34

Quick Start Review 1

Genitive

Ergänzen Sie die Endungen.

1. Er wohnt in der schönsten Gegend unser_____ Stadt.
2. Das ist das Auto mein_____ Kollegen.
3. Die Tochter mein_____ Bruders wohnt jetzt in Bilbao.
4. Das muss der Zahn ein_____ großen Tieres gewesen sein.
5. Das ist das Ergebnis ein_____ langen Arbeitstages.
6. Die Zufriedenheit unser_____ Kunden ist das Wichtigste für uns.
7. Die Haare mein_____ Mutter sind jetzt weiß.

Answers: 1. unserer   2. meines   3. meines   4. eines   5. eines   6. unserer   7. meiner

Quick Start Review 2

♻ *Der-* and *ein-*words

Ergänzen Sie die Personalpronomen.

1. Mein_____ Mann gefallen rote Kleider nicht.
2. Sie hilft ihr_____ älteren Schwester sehr gerne.
3. Er hat sein_____ Lehrer nicht geantwortet. Er blieb einfach stumm.
4. Wir fahren morgen mit mein_____ Nichte und mein_____ Neffen aufs Land.
5. Kannst du dein_____ Schwester deinen Regenschirm geben?
6. Mein_____ Mutter gehören drei Häuser.

Answers: 1. Meinem 2. ihrer
3. seinem 4. meiner, meinem
5. deiner 6. Meiner

- -

TEACHING SUGGESTIONS

- Comparatives, pp. 102–104

Remind students that after expressions like *so gut wie* or *besser als,* the noun phrase that follows is in the nominative case.

- *Übung A,* p. 103

Follow-up: Have students give the 3 forms of each adjective in the activity: the base form, the comparative, and the superlative.

- *Übung B,* p. 104

Variation: Ask students to write a sentence using the opposite of the adjectives highlighted in the activity. For example, **Jüngere** *Leute haben Angst, dass sie keine Lehrstellen finden werden.*

- *Übung C,* p. 104

Variation: Have students disagree with the statements, for example, *Nein, heute ist es nicht so heiß wie gestern. Nein, ich finde das Benzin billiger als letztes Jahr.*

- Superlatives, pp. 104–105

Introduce superlatives by asking questions like *Wo gibt es hier in der Stadt den besten Kaffee? Wo ist der schönste Park? Wo ist das beste Kino? Was ist der beste Videoladen?*

- *Übung B,* p. 106

Follow-up: Have each student make up 2 more questions similar to those in the activity and write them on a slip of paper. Place all the slips in a box or a hat and have each student draw a slip and answer the questions on it.

CLASSROOM COMMUNITY

Group Activity Divide students into groups of 4. Have each group choose 6 words belonging to a certain vocabulary set, for example, animals, groceries, clothes, or household items. Have groups exchange their sets of 6 words and then create sentences for each item using the superlative.
MODELL: Elefant, Katze, Hund, Pferd, Igel, Gazelle → *Der Elefant ist das größte Tier. Die Gazelle ist das schnellste Tier. Der Hund ist am gehorsamsten. Der Igel ist am langsamsten.*

BLOCK SCHEDULE

Expansion Have students choose a group of adjectives or nouns and rank them according to temperature, speed, size, or some other criterion. For example, *kalt, kühl, angenehm, warm, heiß, kochend,* or *Fahrrad, Motorrad, Auto, Schnellzug, Flugzeug.* Each group might let the others guess what their ranking criterion was.

Perspektiven, pp. 108–114A

PROGRAM RESOURCES

- *Arbeitsheft,* pp. 77–80
- Audio Program, Cassette 3A, 7A/ CD 3, 9
- Audioscript, pp. 34–35
- www.mcdougallittell.com

- -

Quick Start Review 1

♻ Subjunctive

Setzen Sie die Sätze in den Konjunktiv.
MODELL: Wenn das Wetter schön ist, komme ich mit. → *Wenn das Wetter schön wäre, würde ich mitkommen (käme ich mit).*

1. Wenn ich reich bin, fliege ich nach Hawaii.
2. Wenn du mitkommst, freue ich mich.
3. Wenn ich Zeit habe, sehe ich mir den neuen Film an.
4. Wenn ich Deutsch kann, bewerbe ich mich beim deutschen Fernsehen.
5. Wenn ich Urlaub habe, besuche ich dich.
6. Wenn es nicht so lange dauert, komme ich mit.

Answers: 1. Wenn ich reich wäre, würde ich nach Hawaii fliegen (flöge). 2. Wenn du mitkommen würdest, würde ich mich freuen. 3. Wenn ich Zeit hätte, würde ich mir den neuen

Film ansehen (sähe ich mir den neuen Film an). 4. Wenn ich Deutsch könnte, würde ich mich beim deutschen Fernsehen bewerben. 5. Wenn ich Urlaub hätte, würde ich dich besuchen. 6. Wenn es nicht so lange dauern würde, käme ich mit (würde ich mitkommen).

Quick Start Review 2

♻ Vocabulary

Bilden Sie Sätze.

1. mit / ich / unterhalte / ihm / gerne / mich
2. sehne / nach / mich / im Dezember / ich / immer / der Sonne
3. du / mit / hast / dieser Bemerkung / Herrn Schmidt / beleidigt
4. Heidelberg / schon / die Stadt / entstanden / im Mittelalter / ist
5. muss / jedes Jahr / ich / an den Winter / gewöhnen / wieder / mich
6. befinden / wir / am Anfang / eines neuen Jahrtausends / uns

Answers: 1. Ich unterhalte mich gerne mit ihm. 2. Ich sehne mich im Dezember immer nach der Sonne. 3. Du hast Herrn Schmidt mit dieser Bemerkung beleidigt. 4. Die Stadt Heidelberg ist schon im Mittelalter entstanden. 5. Jedes Jahr muss ich mich wieder an den Winter gewöhnen. 6. Wir befinden uns am Anfang eines neuen Jahrtausends.

TEACHING SUGGESTIONS

• *Hören Sie zu!*, p. 108

Before listening to the recording, have students read through the *Wortschatz* *zum Hörtext*, the *Kulturspiegel*, and *Aktivität A.* Have them find Rhineland-Palatinate on a map. Mackenbach is in the vicinity of Kaiserslautern.

• *Aktivität A*, p. 108

Follow-up: Have students look up Paul Hindemith in an encyclopedia or on the Internet.

• *Aktivität B*, p. 108

Follow-up: Have students write their own summary of Horst Molter's story.

• *Lesen Sie!*, p. 109

Have students first review the *Wortschatz zum Lesen* before reading the text. Make sure they use dictionaries only to look up words that are absolutely necessary for their comprehension of the text.

• *Zum Thema, Aktivität A*, p. 110

Warm-up: Have students look at the numbered list of activities (while keeping the list of professions covered up) and then think of professions to match these activities.

• *Der Lacher*, pp. 111–112

Preview the text by having students look at the title, *Der Lacher.* What might the title mean in the context of this chapter on professions? Then have students read the first paragraph silently. The narrator's profession is revealed. Ask students to use details from the paragraph to describe the narrator's profession.

• *Zum Text, Aktivität A*, p. 113

Ask *Wer findet die Geschichte lustig und weshalb? Wer findet die Geschichte traurig oder gar nicht lustig?*

Es gibt Leute, die behaupten: Man soll sein Hobby nicht zum Beruf machen. Dann macht es keinen Spaß mehr. Fallen Ihnen Beispiele ein, die die Meinung bestätigen? Gibt es Gegenbeispiele?

• *Zur Interpretation*, p. 113

Ask *Was würden Sie dem Lacher raten, wenn Sie persönlich mit ihm sprechen könnten?*

• *Tipp zum Schreiben*, p. 114

Have students choose a general topic, such as *Braucht man wirklich einen Hochschulabschluss?* Have them develop questions related to this theme, for example, *Welche Berufe kann man ohne Hochschulabschluss ausüben? In welchen Bereichen sollte man zuerst praktische Erfahrung sammeln und dann später studieren?* Have them brainstorm as a class before they break up into groups to work on their surveys.

TEACHING ALL STUDENTS

Multiple Intelligences Verbal: Have students imagine a scene in the short story they read about. The main character, *Der Lacher,* receives a request to perform for a certain audience. Who is the audience, what are they asking him to do, what is the occasion? Then the scene could be acted out.

CLASSROOM COMMUNITY

Challenge Ask students to find definitions for the following words: *Arbeitsvermittler, Arbeitgeber, Arbeitnehmer, Sozialleistung, Berufserfahrung.* They should write a short description of each word, including an example. Suggest they think in terms of explaining it to a child.

BLOCK SCHEDULE

Peer Teaching Have students review the subjunctive pairs and explain to each other how they form present-tense and past-tense subjunctive statements. Have the pairs then talk about each other giving a few examples, *Das ist Peter und er würde am liebsten den ganzen Tag Fußball spielen, wenn er könnte. Weil er aber später Medizin studieren möchte, lernt er auch Mathe und Biologie.*

Fun Break Have students jot down 3 things they like and 3 things they do not like. It is up to each student to choose between more profound and trivial details. Have students introduce their dislikes and likes to the class quickly by going round in a circle. *Ich mag gerne Schokolade, aber noch nicht am frühen Morgen. Heiße Schokolade trinke ich nicht gerne. Ich mag viel lieber Milch.*

PORTFOLIO

Have students review the first video episode, *Wirtschaft im Wandel,* and develop a time line for the events mentioned. Have them do their own research and draw a parallel time line for events in their own country.

RUBRIC **A** = 13–15 pts. **B** = 10–12 pts. **C** = 7–9 pts. **D** = 4–6 pts. **F** = <4 pts.

Writing Criteria		Scale			
Historical accuracy and content	1	2	3	4	5
Grammar and spelling	1	2	3	4	5
Presentation	1	2	3	4	5

ARBEIT UND WIRTSCHAFT

In diesem Kapitel

- erfahren Sie, wie sich die deutsche Wirtschaft nach dem Zweiten Weltkrieg entwickelt hat.

- lernen Sie Monika Schneider, eine Arbeitsvermittlerin in Köln, kennen.

- lernen Sie, wie junge Deutsche und Schweizer das Arbeitsleben von heute sehen.

Sie werden auch

- wiederholen, wie man den Komparativ gebraucht.

- die Formen des Superlativs wiederholen.

- lernen, wie Verben als Adjektive gebraucht werden können.

- eine Geschichte über eine seltsame Karriere lesen.

- einen Fragebogen für eine Umfrage schreiben.

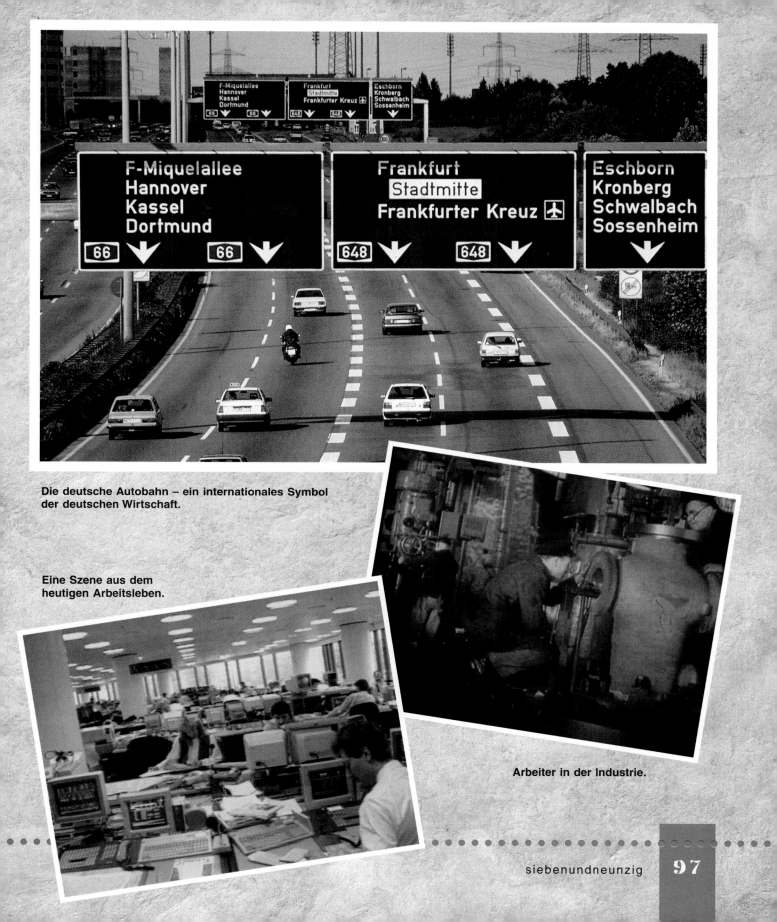

F-Miquelallee
Hannover
Kassel
Dortmund
66 ↓   66 ↓

Frankfurt
Stadtmitte
Frankfurter Kreuz ✈
648 ↓   648 ↓

Eschborn
Kronberg
Schwalbach
Sossenheim
↓

Die deutsche Autobahn – ein internationales Symbol der deutschen Wirtschaft.

Eine Szene aus dem heutigen Arbeitsleben.

Arbeiter in der Industrie.

VIDEOTHEK

Heute ist die Bundesrepublik Deutschland eine grosse Wirtschaftsmacht. Aber wie ist das passiert? Und wie sieht das heutige Arbeitsleben aus?

I: Wirtschaft im Wandel

In dieser Folge sehen Sie, in welcher Lage sich die deutsche Wirtschaft nach dem Zweiten Weltkrieg befand, und wie sie heute aussieht.

A Was bedeutet für Sie das Wort Wirtschaft? Machen Sie eine kleine Liste mit Wörtern und Begriffen, die Sie mit Wirtschaft assoziieren. Was hat Wirtschaft mit Ihrem Leben zu tun?

B Wirtschaft und Menschen durch die Jahre. Welcher Satz passt zu welchem Bild?

1. Die Familien müssen umziehen, um eine Arbeitsstelle zu finden.
2. Viele Roboter werden in den Fabriken eingesetzt.
3. Viele Familien kaufen sich zum ersten Mal Konsumgüter wie Kühlschränke, Fernseher oder Autos.
4. Die Berufe wandeln sich immer schneller. Neue Kommunikationstechniken und Computer verändern die Arbeit und auch das Leben vieler Deutscher.
5. Die meisten Deutschen arbeiten zu dieser Zeit in der Industrie.

A. Answers will vary.

1955 wurde der millionste Volkswagen hergestellt.

B. 1. a   2. c   3. b   4. d   5. e

WORTSCHATZ ZUM VIDEO

schuften	to toil
sich abrackern	to slave away
das Atelier	(artist's) studio; small office
das Wirtschaftswunder	German economic miracle
verharren	to persevere
die EDV-Erfahrung	data processing experience
anrechnen	to count; to take into account
die Früchte	fruits

a.

b.

c.

d.

e.

C Persönliche Geschichten. Was machen diese Menschen beruflich?

Gürkan   Erika   Anja   Bob

1. Diese Person malt und geht oft in Museen.
2. Diese Person arbeitet selbstständig und führt gemeinsam mit zwei anderen ein Reisebüro.
3. Diese Person arbeitet an einem Deutschkurs mit Hilfe einer Assistentin.
4. Diese Person lehrt Deutsch am Goethe-Institut.

II: Eine Arbeitsvermittlerin

In dieser Folge lernen Sie Monika Schneider kennen. Sie ist Arbeitsvermittlerin und sucht Stellen für Arbeitslose und Arbeitssuchende.

A Arbeitgeber und Arbeitnehmer. Monika unterstützt Arbeitnehmer, eine Arbeit zu finden. Dabei hilft sie auch den Arbeitgebern, die Arbeiter brauchen. Lesen Sie die folgenden Sätze, und sagen Sie, welche Person der Satz beschreibt, Frau Schneider, Herrn Weinart, Herrn Kloss oder Herrn Lebendig.

1. _____ ist Elektromeister von Beruf.
2. _____ ist Apotheker, und sucht eine Mitarbeiterin.
3. _____ arbeitet beim Arbeitsamt.
4. _____ möchte nicht in eine andere Stadt ziehen.
5. _____ sucht einen Groß- und Außenhandelskaufmann.

B Ostdeutsche Perspektiven. Anja erzählt von den Problemen der Arbeitslosigkeit in der ehemaligen DDR. Stimmen die folgenden Sätze?

1. Arbeitslosigkeit ist heute das größte Problem in Deutschland.
2. Viele Leute wollen alle fünf Jahre in einer neuen Firma arbeiten.
3. Die Arbeitslosigkeit unter Leuten, die in der ehemaligen DDR gearbeitet haben, ist nicht wesentlich schlimmer als unter denen, die in der BRD gearbeitet haben.
4. Die Jahre, die ihre Eltern in der DDR gearbeitet haben, werden nicht angerechnet. Deswegen bekommen sie nicht viel Geld.

B. **1.** Das stimmt.   **2.** Das stimmt nicht.   **3.** Das stimmt nicht.   **4.** Das stimmt.

Gürkan.

C. **1.** Erika   **2.** Gürkan   **3.** Bob   **4.** Anja

Monika Schneider spricht mit Herrn Weinart.

A. **1.** Herr Weinart   **2.** Herr Kloss   **3.** Frau Schneider   **4.** Herr Weinart   **5.** Herr Lebendig

KULTURSPIEGEL

In den neuen Bundesländern sind die wirtschaftlichen Probleme viel größer als in den alten. Nach der Wende schaffte man viele Arbeitsplätze ab. Viele ältere Leute gingen in den Vorruhestand, aber junge Leute, die vor der Wende einen garantierten Arbeitsplatz zu erwarten hatten, haben viel Angst vor Arbeitslosigkeit.

VOKABELN

die Arbeitslosenzahl	*number of unemployed*
die Berufserfahrung	*work experience*
die Entwicklung	*development*
die Rente	*pension*
die Steuer	*tax*
die Wirtschaft	*economy*
der Arbeitsvermittler / die Arbeitsvermittlerin	*employment agent*
der Betrieb	*business operation*
der Rentner / die Rentnerin	*pensioner*
der Termin	*appointment*
das Unternehmen	*business enterprise*
auf•bauen	*to build; to set up*
ein•setzen	*to put in place*
erfordern	*to require*
erhalten	*to receive*
erlernen	*to learn*
her•stellen	*to manufacture; to produce*
steigern	*to raise*
zwingen	*to force*
gering	*small, negligible*
künftig	*future*

Was kann die Gesellschaft tun, um die wirtschaftliche Lage zu verbessern?

unentbehrlich	*essential(ly), indispensable*

Sie wissen schon
die Kenntnis, die Stelle, der Arbeitsplatz, der Beruf, der Bewerber / die Bewerberin, einen Beruf aus•üben, (mit etwas) einverstanden sein, selbstständig, zufrieden/unzufrieden, ungefähr

Aktivitäten

A. 1. die Arbeitslosenzahl   2. die Arbeitsvermittlerin   3. aufbauen   4. der Bewerber   5. einverstanden sein   6. erhalten   7. die Kenntnis   8. die Rente

A Definitionen. Welche Wörter aus dem Kasten auf Seite 101 passen zu den folgenden Definitionen?

1. Zahl der arbeitslosen Menschen
2. eine Person, die Stellen für Arbeitslose sucht
3. organisieren, gestalten, strukturieren
4. jemand, der sich um eine Arbeitsstelle bewirbt
5. jemandem einer Sache zustimmen, akzeptieren
6. bekommen
7. das Kennen einer Sache, das Wissen von etwas
8. Einkommen vom Staat, wenn man alt ist

die Kenntnis

einverstanden sein

die Arbeitsvermittlerin

erhalten

die Rente

der Bewerber

aufbauen

die Arbeitslosenzahl

B. 1. ausübt **2.** erfordern **3.** erlernen
4. hergestellt **5.** eingesetzt **6.** gezwungen

B Arbeitswelt. Ergänzen Sie die Sätze.

1. Auszubildende arbeiten bei einer Firma und lernen, wie man einen Beruf _____.
2. Die neuen Umstände in der Arbeitswelt _____, dass man sehr flexibel sein muss.
3. Wer eine neue Karriere haben will, muss natürlich auch einen neuen Beruf _____.
4. In Deutschland werden viele Autos _____.
5. Immer mehr Maschinen werden in der Industrie _____.
6. Viele Menschen sind _____, Jobs zu nehmen, die ihnen nicht besonders gut gefallen.

C Anders gesagt. Setzen Sie für die kursiv gedruckten Wörter Synonyme aus der Wortliste auf Seite 100 ein.

1. Wir sind *darüber einig*, dass Arbeiter mehr Urlaub haben sollen.
2. Die Stadt Heidelberg hat *etwa* 150 000 Einwohner.
3. Die Zahl der Arbeiter, die in der Schwerindustrie arbeiten, wird immer *kleiner*.
4. Gute Ratschläge sind oft *nötig*.
5. Renate ist in ihrer neuen Stelle sehr *unglücklich*.
6. Klaus arbeitet lieber *ohne Hilfe*.

D Wie stellen Sie sich Ihre künftige Karriere vor? Was möchten Sie werden? Warum? Was müssen Sie tun, um diesen Beruf ausüben zu können?

MODELL: Ich möchte Mechanikerin werden, weil ich gern mit Werkzeugen und Autos arbeite. Ich möchte in einer Autowerkstatt arbeiten, wo ich diesen Beruf erlernen kann.

erfordern

hergestellt

erlernen

eingesetzt

gezwungen ausübt

See answers below.

KULTURSPIEGEL

Viele junge Deutsche fangen ihre Karriere als Lehrlinge an. Sie erlernen ihren neuen Beruf sowohl in der Klasse als auch am Arbeitsplatz. Drei Jahre lang belegen Lehrlinge Kurse in einer Berufschule und machen zusätzlich ihre Lehre in einer Fabrik oder in einem Büro. Abiturienten können diese Lehrperiode um bis zu sechs Monate verkürzen.

C. 1. einverstanden **2.** ungefähr **3.** geringer
4. unentbehrlich **5.** unzufrieden
6. selbstständig

D. *Answers will vary.*

STRUKTUREN

REVIEW OF COMPARATIVES
COMPARING PEOPLE AND THINGS

To say someone or something is (not) the same as someone or something else, use the expression **(nicht) so . . . wie.**

Ein Beruf ist **so gut wie** der andere.	*One occupation is as good as the other.*
Ein Krankenpfleger verdient **nicht so viel wie** ein Arzt.	*A nurse doesn't earn as much as a doctor.*

Note that the phrase **(nicht) so . . . wie** uses the positive form of adjectives and adverbs—the form that normally appears in vocabulary lists and dictionaries.

The comparative form of adjectives and adverbs includes the ending **-er.** Most one-syllable words with the vowel **a, o,** or **u** also add an umlaut in the comparative.

POSITIVE	COMPARATIVE	POSITIVE	COMPARATIVE
schnell	schneller	groß	größer
alt	älter	klug	klüger

A small number of one-syllable words with these vowels do not add the umlaut: **klar** → **klarer** and **rot** → **roter** (although some speakers do say **röter**).

A number of adjectives and adverbs in German have irregular forms in the comparative.

POSITIVE	COMPARATIVE	POSITIVE	COMPARATIVE
gern	lieber	hoch	höher
gut	besser	viel	mehr

Ich arbeite **gern** im Büro, aber ich arbeite **lieber** zu Hause.	*I like working in the office, but I prefer working at home.*

German also uses the comparative form of adjectives and adverbs with the word **als** to make comparisons of inequality. Note that in German the nouns or pronouns in comparison—those that both precede and follow **als**—share the same case. This rule is also true in English, although speakers frequently use object forms (*me, him, her, us*) after the word *than.*

Er arbeitet **fleißiger als** <u>ich</u>.	*He works harder than I (do).*
Ich kann **schneller** laufen **als** <u>er</u>.	*I can run faster than he (can).*
Sie hat <u>ihm</u> **mehr** Hilfe gegeben **als** <u>mir</u>.	*She gave him more help than (she gave) me.*

Note that the phrase beginning with **wie** or **als** stands outside the clause it refers to.

Ich habe **nicht so viel** gelernt **wie du.**	*I didn't study as much as you (did).*

Remember that comparatives take the same endings as other attributive adjectives when they stand before a noun.

Ausgebildete Menschen haben **bessere** Chancen im Berufsleben.	*Educated people have better opportunities in professional life.*

German uses the word **immer** plus the comparative form of an adjective or adverb to show progression, whereas English uses the comparative form twice, or the words *more and more* plus the positive form of an adjective or adverb.

Es wird **immer kälter.**	*It's getting colder and colder.*
Sie singen **immer schöner.**	*They sing more and more beautifully.*

The German expression **je (mehr) . . . je/desto/umso (mehr)** is equivalent to the English *the (more) . . . the (more) . . .* Notice that one of three different words can begin the second part of the German expression. Both German and English use comparative forms of adjectives or adverbs in these expressions.

Je mehr man arbeitet, **desto mehr** man verdient.	*The more one works, the more one earns.*

SPRACHSPIEGEL

German forms the comparative of all adjectives and adverbs with **-er**, whereas English forms many comparatives with *-er*, but others with the word *more*.

Er ist **intelligenter** als ich.
He is more intelligent than I (am).

Sie schreibt **interessantere** Berichte als du.
She writes more interesting reports than you (do).

Sie arbeiten **fleißiger** als wir.
They work harder than we (do).

Übungen

A Zurück nach Aachen. Guy, der Student aus Kamerun, kommt nach einigen Jahren wieder nach Aachen. Die Stadt hat sich inzwischen sehr verändert. Was sagt er? Ergänzen Sie die Adjektive oder Adverbien im Komparativ.

1. Die Stadt ist jetzt _____. (groß)
2. Die Preise sind _____. (hoch)
3. Die Wohnungen sind _____. (teuer)
4. Die neuen Kurse sind _____. (interessant)
5. Das neue Universitätsgebäude ist _____ als die alten. (schön)
6. Ich finde es sehr schön in Deutschland, aber ich wohne _____ in Kamerun. (gern)

A. 1. größer 2. höher 3. teurer
4. interessanter 5. schöner 6. lieber

Guy trifft alte Freunde in Aachen. Einige sind schon länger in Deutschland als er.

Frau Schneider hilft Herrn Weinart, einen neuen Job zu finden.

B. 1. größeren **2.** besseren **3.** höheren
4. weiteren **5.** Kürzere

C. 1. Ja, das Benzin wird immer teurer. **2.** Ja, in der Schweiz werden die Steuern immer höher. **3.** Ja, die Sozialleistungen werden immer geringer. **4.** Ja, Berufserfahrung wird immer wichtiger. **5.** Ja, bei unserer Firma werden die Arbeitszeiten auch immer länger. **6.** Ja, ein neues Auto wird immer mehr Geld kosten.

B Die heutige Arbeitslage. Drücken Sie die Sätze mit den Komparativformen der Adjektive aus.

MODELL: **Alte** Leute haben Angst, dass sie ihre Stellen verlieren werden. →
Ältere Leute haben Angst, dass sie ihre Stellen verlieren werden.

1. In den **großen** Städten hat man mehr Berufsmöglichkeiten.
2. Es kann schwer sein, einen **guten** Job zu finden.
3. Ökonomen versuchen, die **hohen** Arbeitslosenzahlen in den vergangenen Jahren zu erklären.
4. Im **weiten** Sinn ist die Arbeitslosigkeit ein Problem für alle Menschen in unserer Gesellschaft.
5. **Kurze** Arbeitszeiten wären wohl eine attraktive Lösung.

C Ja, das Leben wird immer schwerer. Sie sind mit den folgenden Bemerkungen einverstanden. Drücken Sie Ihre Zustimmung im Komparativ aus.

MODELL: Heute ist das Wetter sehr heiß. →
Ja, das Wetter wird immer heißer.

1. Im Moment ist Benzin ziemlich teuer.
2. In der Schweiz sind die Steuern sehr hoch.
3. Die Sozialleistungen sind gering.
4. Berufserfahrung ist sehr wichtig.
5. Bei unserer Firma sind die Arbeitszeiten ziemlich lang.
6. Ein neues Auto kostet viel Geld.

REVIEW OF SUPERLATIVES
EXPRESSING THE HIGHEST DEGREE

German forms the superlative of adjectives and adverbs by adding **-st-** to the positive form; **-est-** is added if that form ends in **-d, -t,** or **-z.** If the comparative form has an umlaut, so does the superlative form. Note that unlike German, in which all adjectives and adverbs form the comparative and superlative in the same way, English sometimes adds the words *more* and *most* instead of the endings **-er** and **-(e)st.**

POSITIVE	COMPARATIVE	SUPERLATIVE	ENGLISH
alt	älter	ältest-	*old, older, oldest*
schön	schöner	schönst-	*beautiful, more beautiful, most beautiful*

You can use the superlative in two different ways in German: as an attributive adjective (**die älteste Stadt**) or in a prepositional phrase with **am (am ältesten).** Note that either way, an ending must be added to the superlative form.

When the superlative form stands before a noun, it takes the same endings as other attributive adjectives.

Sie ist die **klügste** Frau, die ich kenne. *She's the smartest woman I know.*

In German as in English, the noun following a superlative adjective may be understood rather than actually stated, depending on the context of the sentence.

Welches Zimmer möchten Sie? *Which room would you like?*
—Ich nehme **das billigste.** *—I'll take the cheapest (one).*

In a prepositional phrase with **am,** the superlative takes the dative case ending **-en.** This construction stands alone and describes a person, place, thing, or idea in terms of the highest degree of some characteristic.

Welcher Fluss ist **am längsten**? *Which river is the longest?*

Adverbs take this form as well.

Dieses Auto fährt **am schnellsten.** *This car goes the fastest.*
Am liebsten spiele ich Karten. *I like to play cards the best.*

Words that have irregular comparative forms usually also have irregular superlative forms.

POSITIVE	COMPARATIVE	SUPERLATIVE
gern	lieber	liebst-, am liebsten
gut	besser	best-, am besten
hoch	höher	höchst-, am höchsten
viel	mehr	meist-, am meisten

„Spieglein, Spieglein, an der Wand, wer ist die Schönste im ganzen Land?"

A. 1. älteste 2. interessantesten 3. größte
4. besten 5. teuersten 6. höchsten, niedrigsten

Übungen

A Heidelberg. Stellen Sie sich vor, Sie studieren in Heidelberg. Ein Freund kommt zu Besuch. Erklären Sie ihm, wo alles am besten ist. Benutzen Sie die Superlativformen der Adjektive.

MODELL: Die **schönen** Restaurants sind in der Altstadt. →
Die schönsten Restaurants sind in der Altstadt.

1. Das **alte** Gebäude ist das Schloss.
2. Die **interessanten** Museen sind an der Hauptstraße.
3. Die **große** Buchhandlung steht neben der Universitätsbibliothek.
4. Die **guten** Buchhandlungen sind nicht weit von der Uni.
5. In den **teuren** Läden kann man natürlich sehr schöne Sachen kaufen.
6. Die **hohen** Preise findest du im Supermarkt, die **niedrigen** auf dem Markt.

Eine Cafészene in der Heidelberger Altstadt.

B. *Answers will vary.*

C. *Answers will vary.*

B Starke Erlebnisse. Arbeiten Sie mit einem Partner / einer Partnerin, und stellen Sie einander die folgenden Fragen.

1. Was ist deine beste Erinnerung an die Grundschule?
2. Was war deine größte Verlegenheit?
3. Was war dein dümmster Fehler?
4. Was war deine klügste Entscheidung?
5. Was war die längste Reise, die du je gemacht hast? (Meine Reise nach . . . / in . . . war . . .)
6. Was hast du da am besten gefunden? am schlimmsten?

C Heimat. Was ist bei Ihnen am (schönsten)? Beschreiben Sie Ihre Stadt oder Ihre Heimat im Superlativ.

MODELL: Bei uns sind die Wälder am schönsten, die Leute am interessantesten, das Essen am besten, . . .

VERBS AS ADJECTIVES; PARTICIPIAL CONSTRUCTIONS; EXTENDED MODIFIERS
MORE ON DESCRIBING PEOPLE AND THINGS

Two verb forms can function as adjectives: the present and past participles of virtually any verb.

To form the present participle, simply add **-d** to the infinitive; this form corresponds with the *-ing* form of the verb in English. When participles stand before nouns, they add the same endings as other attributive adjectives.

—Ich höre einen **lachenden** Mann.
—*I hear a laughing man.*

—Wo ist der **lachende** Mann?
—*Where is the laughing man?*

You already know how to form the past participles of verbs. To use them as attributive adjectives, simply add the appropriate endings.

Diese **hergestellten** Waren kommen aus China.
These manufactured goods come from China.

Niemand kann seine **übertriebene** Beschreibung glauben.
No one can believe his exaggerated description.

Extended modifiers are more common, and often lengthier, in German than in English. These descriptive expressions generally include a participial phrase that comes between the article and the noun. Because these constructions usually occur in written language, you should learn to recognize them, even though you need not use them in your own writing.

Die ständig steigende Arbeitslosenzahl ist ein großes Problem in Deutschland.	*The ever-increasing number of unemployed is a big problem in Germany.*
Die nach dem Zweiten Weltkrieg wieder aufgebaute deutsche Wirtschaft wurde als Wunder bezeichnet.	*The German economy, which was rebuilt after World War II, was described as a miracle.*

Notice that the English equivalent of the second example includes a relative clause. To aid your comprehension, you can also rephrase the German sentence with a relative clause. Just move the noun from the end of the expression up to follow the article, then create a relative clause with the information that separated the two elements.

Die Wirtschaft, die nach dem Zweiten Weltkrieg wieder aufgebaut wurde, wurde als Wunder bezeichnet.

Übungen

A Wirtschaft und Arbeit. Ergänzen Sie die Sätze mit den Adjektivenformen der Partizipien Präsens und Perfekt.

1. Die _____ (folgen) Sätze handeln von Wirtschaft und Arbeit.
2. Die _____ (zunehmen) Arbeitslosenzahl wird zu _____ (dringen) Problemen in der Gesellschaft führen.
3. Gibt es eine _____ (passen) Lösung zur _____ (steigen) Arbeitslosigkeit?
4. In den _____ (vergehen) Jahrzehnten hat sich das Arbeitsleben stark verändert.
5. Die neu _____ (einsetzen) Maschinen kosten viel Geld.
6. Niemand will einen _____ (gebrauchen) Computer kaufen.
7. Das _____ (fordern) Ziel ist im Moment nicht zu erreichen.

A. 1. folgenden 2. zunehmende, dringenden
3. passende, steigenden 4. vergangenen
5. eingesetzten 6. gebrauchten 7. geforderte

B Interview. Ab und zu muss man auch Freizeit haben. Arbeiten Sie mit einem Partner / einer Partnerin und stellen Sie einander die folgenden Fragen.

1. Was ist deine liebste Freizeitbeschäftigung?
2. Welche Aktivitäten findest du anstrengend? Warum?
3. Was sind die Vorteile einer kürzeren Arbeitszeit? Was sind die Nachteile?
4. Findest du, dass die Meinungen über das heutige Arbeitsleben übertrieben sind?

B. *Answers will vary.*

PERSPEKTIVEN

WORTSCHATZ ZUM HÖRTEXT

der Blechblas-instrumentenbauer	maker of brass (musical) instruments
die Gesellenprüfung	examination to become a journeyman
die Meisterprüfung	examination to become master craftsman
absolvieren	to pass; to complete

A. 1. ja   2. nein   3. ja   4. ja   5. nein   6. ja

KULTURSPIEGEL

Mackenbach liegt im südwestlichen Teil von Rheinland-Pfalz. Diese Gegend ist als Musikantenland bekannt. Im neunzehnten Jahrhundert zwangen schlechte wirtschaftliche Bedingungen die Menschen in dieser Gegend, alternative Berufe zu finden. Viele wurden Musikanten, zogen in Gruppen durch ganz Europa und gaben Konzerte. Manche dieser Musikanten kamen auch nach Amerika.

B. 1. Das hat der deutsche Komponist Paul Hindemith gesagt.   2. Über der Haustür von Horst Molter.   3. In Kaiserslautern hat Horst Molter seine Lehre als Blechblasinstrumentenbauer gemacht.   4. Horst Molter wanderte 1956 nach Amerika aus.   5. Er hat neun Jahre in New York gearbeitet.   6. 1965 kam er zurück nach Deutschland.   7. In Frankfurt hat er seine Meisterprüfung absolviert.   8. Das Geschäft in Mackenbach hat er seit 1974.

HÖREN SIE ZU!
EINE AHNUNG VON TUTEN UND BLASEN

A Horst Molter. Sie hören einen Text über einen Mann mit einem seltenen Beruf. Was für Informationen hören Sie im Text? Beantworten Sie die Fragen mit „ja" oder „nein".

Hören Sie
1. ein Zitat des Komponisten Paul Hindemith?
2. Information über Mackenbach?
3. die Namen der Städte, in denen Horst Molter gelebt hat?
4. Information über seine Ausbildung?
5. etwas über amerikanische Komponisten?
6. etwas über Kunden von Horst Molter?

B Was wissen Sie jetzt über Horst Molter? Hören Sie den Text noch einmal, und beantworten Sie dann die Fragen.

1. Wer hat gesagt, „Musik machen ist besser als Musik hören"?
2. Wo hängt eine Miniaturtrompete?
3. Was hat Horst Molter in Kaiserslautern gemacht?
4. Wann ist er nach Amerika ausgewandert?
5. Wo hat er in Amerika gearbeitet?
6. Wann kam er zurück nach Deutschland?
7. Was hat er in Frankfurt gemacht?
8. Seit wann hat er ein Geschäft in Mackenbach?

LESEN SIE!

Zum Thema

A Was macht man in jedem Beruf? Verbinden Sie die Berufe mit den Beschreibungen auf Seite 109.

MODELL: mit Steinen und Mörtel arbeiten →
Ein Maurer arbeitet mit Steinen und Mörtel.

Friseurin	Clown	Tischlerin	Bäcker
Schriftstellerin	Metzger	Stierkämpferin	Lehrer
Schauspieler	Melker	Straßenbahnschaffner	Lacher

1. Kühe melken
2. Häuser oder Möbel bauen
3. in Spanien: Stier kämpfen
4. in einer Schule lehren
5. Bücher schreiben
6. Brot und Brötchen backen
7. Theater spielen
8. im Zirkus arbeiten
9. Haare schneiden
10. auf Bitte lachen
11. Fahrausweise kontrollieren
12. Fleisch verkaufen

A. 1. Melker 2. Tischlerin 3. Stierkämpferin
4. Lehrer 5. Schriftstellerin 6. Bäcker
7. Schauspieler 8. Clown 9. Friseurin
10. Lacher 11. Straßenbahnschaffner
12. Metzger

B Berufe. Arbeiten Sie in Dreiergruppen. Wählen Sie sechs Berufe aus der Liste. Beschreiben Sie jeden der sechs Berufe aus der Liste und beantworten Sie dabei folgende Fragen:

B. *Answers will vary.*

1. Wo arbeitet jemand, der diesen Beruf ausübt?
2. Wie würden Sie die Arbeitswoche dieser Person beschreiben?
3. Ist die Arbeit körperlich oder eher geistig?
4. Verdient man gewöhnlich viel oder wenig in diesem Beruf?
5. Stellen Sie sich vor: Was will diese Person in der Freizeit machen? Was will sie nicht machen?

Der Lacher

Wenn ich nach meinem Beruf gefragt werde, befällt mich Verlegenheit: ich werde rot, stammele, ich, der ich sonst als ein sicherer Mensch bekannt bin. Ich beneide die Leute, die sagen können: ich bin Maurer. Friseuren, Buchhaltern und Schriftstellern neide ich die Einfachheit ihrer Bekenntnisse,
5   denn alle diese Berufe erklären sich aus sich selbst und erfordern keine längeren Erklärungen. Ich aber bin gezwungen, auf solche Fragen zu antworten: Ich bin Lacher. Ein solches Bekenntnis erfordert weitere, da ich auch die zweite Frage „Leben Sie davon?" wahrheitsgemäß mit „Ja" beantworten muß. Ich lebe tatsächlich von meinem Lachen, und ich lebe
10 gut, denn mein Lachen ist – kommerziell ausgedrückt – gefragt. Ich bin ein guter, bin ein gelernter Lacher, kein anderer lacht so wie ich, keiner beherrscht so die Nuancen meiner Kunst. Lange Zeit habe ich mich – um lästigen Erklärungen zu entgehen – als Schauspieler bezeichnet, doch sind meine mimischen und sprecherischen Fähigkeiten so gering, daß mir
15 diese Bezeichnung als nicht der Wahrheit gemäß erschien: ich liebe die Wahrheit, und die Wahrheit ist: ich bin Lacher. Ich bin weder Clown noch Komiker, ich erheitere die Menschen nicht, sondern stelle Heiterkeit dar: ich lache wie ein römischer Imperator oder wie ein sensibler Abiturient, das Lachen des 17. Jahrhunderts ist mir so geläufig wie das des 19., und wenn
20 es sein muß, lache ich alle Jahrhunderte, alle Gesellschaftsklassen, alle Altersklassen durch: ich hab's einfach gelernt, so wie man lernt, Schuhe zu besohlen. Das Lachen Amerikas ruht in meiner Brust, das Lachen Afrikas, weißes, rotes, gelbes Lachen – und gegen ein entsprechendes Honorar lasse ich es klingen, so wie die Regie es vorschreibt.
25   Ich bin unentbehrlich geworden, ich lache auf Schallplatten, lache auf Band, und die Hörspielregisseure behandeln mich rücksichtsvoll. Ich lache schwermütig, gemäßigt, hysterisch – lache wie ein Straßenbahnschaffner oder wie ein Lehrling der Lebensmittelbranche; das Lachen am Morgen, das Lachen am Abend, nächtliches Lachen

ORTSCHATZ ZUM LESEN

die Verlegenheit	embarrassment
beneiden	to envy
lästig	troublesome, tiresome
gemäß	suitable
die Heiterkeit	amusement
geläufig	familiar, fluent
der Schubkasten	drawer
vorziehen	to prefer
der Ernst	seriousness
verlernen	to forget (lit. unlearn)
verschlossen	reserved, closed

IND SIE WORTSCHLAU?

The endings **-heit** and **-keit** change adjectives to feminine nouns.

heiter → die Heiterkeit, -en
verlegen → die Verlegenheit, -en

KULTURSPIEGEL

Heinrich Böll war einer der größten deutschen Schriftsteller der Nachkriegszeit. 1971 erhielt er den Nobelpreis. Er war ein prominenter Vertreter der „Gruppe 47", eine Gruppe von deutschen Autoren, die sich nicht nur für die Literatur, sondern auch sehr viel für die Politik engagierte.

FOKUS INTERNET

For more information visit the **Auf Deutsch!** Web Site at
www.mcdougallittell.com.

und das Lachen der Dämmerstunde, kurzum: wo immer und wie immer gelacht werden muß: ich mache es schon. 30

Man wird mir glauben, daß ein solcher Beruf anstrengend ist, zumal ich – das ist meine Spezialität – auch das ansteckende Lachen beherrsche; so bin ich unentbehrlich geworden auch für Komiker dritten und vierten Ranges, die mit Recht um ihre Pointen zittern, und ich sitze 35 fast jeden Abend in den Varietés herum als eine subtilere Art Claqueur, um an schwachen Stellen des Programms ansteckend zu lachen. Es muß Maßarbeit sein: mein herzhaftes, wildes Lachen darf nicht zu früh, darf auch nicht zu spät, es muß im richtigen Augenblick kommen – dann platze ich programmgemäß aus, die ganze Zuhörerschaft brüllt mit, und 40 die Pointe ist gerettet.

Ich aber schleiche dann erschöpft zur Garderobe, ziehe meinen Mantel über, glücklich darüber, daß ich endlich Feierabend habe. Zu Hause liegen meist Telegramme für mich „Brauchen dringend Ihr Lachen. Aufnahme Dienstag", und ich hocke wenige Stunden später in 45 einem überheizten D-Zug und beklage mein Geschick.

Jeder wird begreifen, daß ich nach Feierabend oder im Urlaub wenig Neigung zum Lachen verspüre: der Melker ist froh, wenn er die Kuh, der Maurer glücklich, wenn er den Mörtel vergessen darf, und die Tischler haben zu Hause meistens Türen, die nicht funktionieren, oder 50 Schubkästen, die sich nur mit Mühe öffnen lassen. Zuckerbäcker lieben saure Gurken, Metzger Marzipan, und der Bäcker zieht die Wurst dem Brot vor; Stierkämpfer lieben den Umgang mit Tauben, Boxer werden blaß, wenn ihre Kinder Nasenbluten haben: ich verstehe das alles, denn ich lache nach Feierabend nie. Ich bin ein todernster Mensch, und die 55 Leute halten mich – vielleicht mit Recht – für einen Pessimisten.

In den ersten Jahren unserer Ehe sagte meine Frau oft zu mir: „Lach doch mal!", aber inzwischen ist ihr klargeworden, daß ich diesen Wunsch nicht erfüllen kann. Ich bin glücklich, wenn ich meine angestrengten Gesichtsmuskeln, wenn ich mein strapaziertes Gemüt durch tiefen Ernst 60 entspannen darf. Ja, auch das Lachen anderer macht mich nervös, weil es mich zu sehr an meinen Beruf erinnert. So führen wir eine stille, eine friedliche Ehe, weil auch meine Frau das Lachen verlernt hat: hin und wieder ertappe ich sie bei einem Lächeln, und dann lächele auch ich. Wir sprechen leise miteinander, denn ich hasse den Lärm der Varietés, 65 hasse den Lärm, der in den Aufnahmeräumen herrschen kann. Menschen, die mich nicht kennen, halten mich für verschlossen. Vielleicht bin ich es, weil ich zu oft meinen Mund zum Lachen öffnen muß.

Mit unbewegter Miene gehe ich durch mein eigenes Leben, erlaube mir nur hin und wieder ein sanftes Lächeln, und ich denke oft darüber 70 nach, ob ich wohl je gelacht habe. Ich glaube: nein. Meine Geschwister wissen zu berichten, daß ich immer ein ernster Junge gewesen sei.

So lache ich auf vielfältige Weise, aber mein eigenes Lachen kenne ich nicht.

Heinrich Böll (1917–1985)

Zum Text

A „Der Lacher". Wenn Sie den Titel der Geschichte lesen, erwarten Sie eine lustige Geschichte? Warum (nicht)? Finden Sie diesen Titel ironisch?

B Was meint der Lacher? Beantworten Sie die Fragen.

1. Warum beneidet der Lacher Leute in anderen Berufen?
2. Warum ist es schwer, seinen eigenen Beruf zu erklären?
3. Wie beschreibt der Lacher seinen Beruf? Wie lacht er? Wo? Wann?
4. Was sagt er über den Feierabend in anderen Berufen?
5. Was sagt er über seinen eigenen Feierabend?

Zur Interpretation

● Menschen und ihre Arbeit. Warum kennt der Lacher sein eigenes Lachen nicht? Was, glauben Sie, sagt der Autor dieser Geschichte über die Beziehung von Menschen zu ihren Berufen?

INTERAKTION

● Welcher Beruf?

SCHRITT 1: Arbeiten Sie mit einem Partner / einer Partnerin. Fragen Sie ihn/sie, was er/sie für einen Beruf ausüben will. Bitten Sie ihn/sie, den Beruf zu beschreiben. Wenn nötig, machen Sie sich Notizen.

SCHRITT 2: Beschreiben Sie der Klasse den Beruf, den Ihr Partner / Ihre Partnerin ausüben will. Sagen Sie aber nicht, wie der Beruf heißt. Die Klasse soll den Beruf erraten.

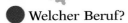

SCHREIBEN SIE!

Eine Umfrage unter Jugendlichen

● Bilden Sie Zweier- oder Dreiergruppen. Entwerfen Sie in der Gruppe eine Umfrage mit etwa zehn Fragen zum Thema „Beruf und Karriere". Mögliche Themen finden Sie in dem Tipp zum Schreiben.

A. *Answers will vary.*

B. *Possible answers are:* **1.** Er beneidet Menschen in anderen Berufen, weil sie ihre Berufe leicht erklären können oder die Berufe sich aus sich selbst erklären. **2.** Es ist schwer, den Beruf des Lachers zu erklären, weil man diesen Beruf nicht erlernen kann, und weil man sich schwer vorstellen kann, dass man mit seinem Lachen Geld verdient. **3.** Der Lacher stellt Heiterkeit dar. Er lacht wie verschiedene Menschen in verschiedenen Jahrhunderten, aus allen Gesellschaftsschichten und Altersklassen. Er lacht wie Menschen aus unterschiedlichen Kulturen und zu unterschiedlichen Tageszeiten. Er lacht auf Schallplatte, auf Band, im Radio und im Varieté, wenn ein Witz schwach ist. **4.** Er sagt über den Feierabend in anderen Berufen, dass die Menschen, die diese Berufe haben, nach Feierabend vergessen wollen, womit sie den ganzen Tag gearbeitet haben. **5.** Dem Lacher geht es auch so, nach Feierabend will er nicht mehr lachen, weil er das schon den ganzen Tag bei der Arbeit getan hat.

Answers will vary.

Answers will vary.

TIPP ZUM SCHREIBEN

Mögliche Themen: Braucht man wirklich einen Hochschulabschluss? • Die Rolle von Fremdsprachen im Berufsleben • Was ist wichtiger an der Arbeit: Geld oder Spaß? • Traditionelle Männerberufe: Bleiben sie so? • Die Technik in der Berufswelt der Zukunft • Einen Beruf fürs Leben, oder viele? • Wollt ihr eine Karriere oder nur einen Job? • Arbeitnehmer oder Arbeitgeber: Was willst du werden? • Handwerker: Ein Beruf mit Zukunft?

Texts will vary.

Jedes Mitglied Ihres Teams soll dann drei bis fünf Personen aus Ihrem Deutschkurs interviewen. Zum Schluss soll das Team die Ergebnisse in einem Bericht zusammenfassen und analysieren.

Purpose: To create a questionnaire, survey students, and report the results
Audience: Your classmates
Subject: Attitudes and opinions about work and professions
Structure: Public opinion questionnaire and report

Schreibmodell

Karriere oder Job?

Eine Umfrage von Paul Smith, Anna Thomas und Cathy Johnson

Fragebogen

1. Mädchen _____   Junge _____

2. Alter: _____ Jahre

3. In welcher Klasse bist du? _____

4. Wenn du mit der Schule fertig bist, möchtest du lieber studieren oder sofort arbeiten gehen? _____

5. Wenn du sofort arbeiten gehen willst, was für eine Arbeit möchtest du dir suchen? _____

6. Wenn du studieren willst, was möchtest du eventuell werden?

   _____

7. Willst du Karriere machen? _____

8. Was sind für dich die drei wichtigsten Gründe, eine Arbeitsstelle anzunehmen? _____

   _____

Since the survey is aimed at classmates, the writer uses the **du**-form.

To ask for the *most important* reasons, the writer uses the superlative form of **wichtig: wichtigste-**.

Can you guess the meaning of **Befragten**?

Bericht zur Umfrage – Karriere oder Job?

Wir haben 9 Personen interviewt – 5 Mädchen, 4 Jungen. Zwei der Befragten sind sechzehn Jahre alt und sind in der elften Klasse. Sieben sind siebzehn Jahre alt und in der zwölften Klasse. Sechs Schüler wollen nach der Schule auf ein College gehen. Fünf davon hoffen nach dem Studium Karriere zu machen. Ein Schüler will eine Ausbildung als Koch machen und später eine Karriere als Chefkoch in einen teuren Restaurant in einer Großstadt haben. Die zwei anderen wollen sich einen Job suchen und gleich Geld verdienen. Zur Zeit denken sie nicht daran, Karriere zu machen.

An erster/zweiter/dritter Stelle (*in first/second/third place*) is a typical expression used in reporting the results of a survey.

Für die meisten Befragten, ist die Bezahlung einer Arbeit am wichtigsten. Am zweithäufigsten wurde insgesamt gesagt, dass die Arbeit interessant sein soll, außer für drei Befragte, die Karriere in Politik und Betriebswirtschaft machen wollen: Für sie steht Prestige an zweiter Stelle.

Meist- is the superlative form of **viel**. **Mehr** is the comparative.

Es gibt bei den Antworten keine Unterschiede zwischen Mädchen und Jungen. Wir schließen Folgendes aus den Antworten: Die meisten wissen schon, ob sie Karriere machen wollen. Für die meisten ist eine gesicherte finanzielle Zukunft wichtig.

Schreibstrategien

Vor dem Schreiben

- With your group, select one of the topics in the **Tipp zum Schreiben** on page 111 and brainstorm a list of vocabulary and phrases that you might use in forming your questions. For example, **deiner Meinung nach** (*in your opinion*), **möchtest du . . .** (*would you like to . . .*), **glaubst du . . .** (*do you think . . .*).

Beim Schreiben

- Next, each member of the group should compose a set of ten or more questions. As you write your questions, remind yourself of the central topic and try to phrase questions that will provide the most useful information.

- Meet with your group to read through everyone's questions and select ten or so questions that will produce the most useful answers. Include at least one question from each member of the group. Prepare the draft questionnaire.

Nach dem Schreiben

- As a group, exchange draft questionnaires with another group for peer editing. Are the questions clear, thought-provoking, and answerable in German? It may be necessary to rephrase questions. Revise the questionnaire according to the feedback you receive.

TIPP ZUM SCHREIBEN

The type of questions used in a questionnaire often determine its outcome, so be sure your questions will produce the information you are looking for. Yes/no questions ("Do you . . .") only allow for yes/no answers. Information questions ("When/Where/How/How often/Why do you . . .") focus on specific types of information and are more open-ended. Craft your questions carefully to get the information you want.

Umfrage: Braucht man Fremdsprachen im Beruf?

Fragebogen

1. Welche Fremdsprache hast du in ~~die~~ der Schule gelernt? _____

2. Willst du studieren? Welche⁽ˢ⁾ Fach? _____

3. Glaubst du, dass man ohne Kenntnisse von einer Fremdsprache gute Arbeit finden kann? Warum?

   _____

4. Was meinst du, für welche Berufe |man|braucht| wahrscheinlich eine Fremdsprache? _____

5. Willst du im Ausland arbeiten? _____

Bericht

Wir haben 10 Jungen und Mädchen gefragt. Die meisten ~~wissen~~ können mindestens eine Fremdsprache und wollen nach der Schule studieren. Die meisten Schülerinnen und Schüler (nämlich sechs) glauben, dass sie ohne eine Fremdsprache eine gute Stelle finden werden. Die anderen vier meinen, dass man (kann) ohne gute Fremdsprachenkenntnisse nicht beruflich weiter kommen. Die wenigsten, nur drei, wollen ins Ausland gehen und dort arbeiten.

- Interview three to five of your German classmates. Be sure to tell the interviewee the topic of your survey. Allowing the interviewee to read your questions and think a little about the topic of your survey will result in a better interview.

- Ask the questions personally and record the answers as you go. You may wish to fill out a questionnaire for each person you interview.

- As a group, organize the data you have collected in useful categories (gender, age, grade level, future plans, etc.) and see if any trends are clear.

- Write a report summarizing your data and giving your analysis of it.

- Exchange reports with another group and provide each other with feedback.

Stimmt alles?

- As a group, prepare the final report, taking your peer editing group's comments and suggestions into consideration.

- Add a blank copy of your questionnaire to the report. You may also wish to include the questionnaires you filled out during the interview process as part of the final report.

- Create a title page and a table of contents (**Inhalt**) and hand in your report.

WORTSCHATZ

Substantive	Nouns
die **Arbeitslosenzahl, -en**	number of unemployed
die **Bedingung, -en**	condition
die **Berufserfahrung, -en**	work experience
die **Entwicklung, -en**	development
die **Erklärung, -en**	explanation
die **Fähigkeit, -en**	capability
die **Miene, -n**	demeanor; facial expression
die **Möglichkeit, -en**	possibility
die **Mühe, -n**	trouble
die **Rente, -n**	pension
die **Sozialleistung, -en**	social support
die **Steuer, -n**	tax
die **Verlegenheit, -en**	embarrassment
die **Wirtschaft**	economy
der **Arbeitsvermittler, -** / die **Arbeitsvermittlerin, -nen**	employment agent
der **Aufschwung, ⸚e**	upswing
der **Betrieb, -e**	business operation
der **Elektromeister, -** / die **Elektromeisterin, -nen**	electrician
der **Feierabend**	time off (work)
der **Rentner, -** / die **Rentnerin, -nen**	pensioner
der **Sinn, -e**	sense
der **Termin, -e**	appointment
der **Wiederaufbau**	reconstruction
das **Berufsfeld, -er**	career field
das **Unternehmen, -**	business enterprise

Verben	Verbs
auf•bauen	to build; to set up
beginnen, begann, begonnen	to begin
begreifen, begriff, begriffen	to understand, grasp
bestimmen	to determine
ein•setzen	to put in place

erfordern	to require
erhalten (erhält), erhielt, erhalten	to receive
erlernen	to learn
her•stellen	to produce
steigern	to increase; to raise
(sich) überlegen	to consider
übertreiben, übertrieb, übertrieben	to exaggerate
verbinden, verband, verbunden	to unite
zwingen, zwang, gezwungen	to force

Adjektive und Adverbien	Adjectives and adverbs
gering	small, negligible
kritisch	critical(ly)
künftig	future
rücksichtsvoll	considerate
sicherlich	surely
unentbehrlich	essential
(un)zufrieden	(un)satisfied

Sie wissen schon	You already know
die **Kenntnis, -se**	knowledge
die **Stelle, -n**	place; position
der **Arbeitsplatz, ⸚e**	workplace
der **Beruf, -e**	job; occupation, profession
der **Bewerber, -** / die **Bewerberin, -nen**	job applicant
einen **Beruf aus•üben**	to practice a profession
(mit etwas) einverstanden sein	to be in agreement
selbstständig	independent(ly)
ungefähr	approximate(ly)

PLANNING GUIDE • CLASSROOM MANAGEMENT

OBJECTIVES

Communication
- Discuss the history of women, p. 118.
- Discuss male and female roles in the family, p. 119.
- Engage in a discussion of gender rights and discrimination, p. 133.

Grammar
- Use the subjunctive in indirect discourse, pp. 122–123.
- Report what other people ask, pp. 124–125.
- Review the imperative, pp. 125–127.

Culture
- Learn about the position of women in the former DDR, pp. 118–119.
- Meet a social service worker helping women to settle issues in the workplace, p. 119.
- Get to know the owner of a women's bookstore in Germany, pp. 128–129.

Recycling
- Review imperatives, pp. 125–127.

STRATEGIES

Listening Strategies
- Listen to a text about a women's bookstore, pp. 128–129.
- Listen to speakers' views on women's rights, p. 118.

Speaking Strategies
- Discuss how women can improve their lives, p. 129.
- Debate issues of male/female equality, p. 133.

Reading Strategies
- Read a short story on attitudes toward gender roles, pp. 131–132.

Writing Strategies
- Report in writing on someone else's thoughts and feelings, p. 133.

Connecting Cultures Strategies
- Compare the role of women in politics in Germany and in the U.S., p. 121.

PROGRAM RESOURCES

 Print
- *Arbeitsheft* (Workbook), pp. 81–96
- *Arbeitsheft* (Workbook), Teacher's Edition, pp. 81–96

 Audiovisual
- Overhead Transparencies 30.1–30.G1
- Audio Program, Cassette 3B, 7B/CD 4, 9
- Audioscript, pp. 36–42

 Technology
- Annenberg *Fokus Deutsch* Video Series, *Folge 30*
- www.mcdougallittell.com

 Assessment Program Options
- *Prüfung, Kapitel 30,* Assessment Program, pp. 62–73
- Audio Program, Cassette 8A/CD 10
- Audioscript, p. 10
- Teacher's Resource CD-ROM

DAY 1

Note: (1) Please see TE, pp. 116E–116J, for other suggestions not referenced in these plans. (2) Not all homework options need be assigned.

CHAPTER OPENER

- Quick Start Review: Vocabulary (TE, p. 116E). 5 MIN
- Use the photos on pp. 116–117 as a basis for class discussion (TE, p. 116E). 5 MIN

VIDEOTHEK

- Follow the Teaching Suggestions for the warm-up activity for *Akt. A,* p. 118 (TE, p. 116F). 2 MIN
- Play *Folge I: Die Frauenbewegung,* and do *Akt. A,* p. 118, as a class. 12 MIN
- Do *Akt. B,* p. 118, silently, then discuss answers and opinions in pairs. 6 MIN
- After reading the *Kulturspiegel* on p. 119, do *Akt. C,* pp. 118–119, in pairs. 12 MIN
- *Arbeitsheft,* p. 81, audio *Akt. B.* 8 MIN

Homework Options:

- *Arbeitsheft,* pp. 83–84, *Videothek, Akt. E–F*

DAY 2

VIDEOTHEK

- Quick Start Review 1: Superlatives (TE, p. 116E). 6 MIN
- Have students read the statements in *Akt. A, Schritt 1,* p. 119, before playing *Folge II: Im Auftrag der Frauen.* Then have them do *Schritt 1* individually and *Schritt 2* in pairs (TE, p. 116F). 12 MIN
- Do *Akt. B,* p. 119, and conclude with the follow-up activity in the Teaching Suggestions (TE, p. 116F). 12 MIN
- *Arbeitsheft,* p. 83, audio *Akt. D.* 8 MIN

VOKABELN

- Follow the Teaching Suggestions for using the photo on p. 120 (TE, p. 116G). Present the vocabulary words on p. 120. 12 MIN

Homework Options:

- *Arbeitsheft,* p. 84, *Videothek, Akt. G*
- *Arbeitsheft,* p. 86, *Vokabeln, Akt. D–E*

DAY 3

VOKABELN

- Quick Start Review 1: Comparisons (TE, p. 116F). 5 MIN
- Have students do *Akt. A,* pp. 120–121, in pairs, then follow the Teaching Suggestions for a follow-up activity (TE, p. 116G). 8 MIN
- Do *Akt. B,* p. 121, silently. Follow the Teaching Suggestions to discuss the sentences that were created (TE, p. 116G). 12 MIN
- Discuss *Akt. C,* p. 121, as a class (TE, p. 116G). 5 MIN
- *Arbeitsheft,* p. 85, audio *Akt. B.* 8 MIN

STRUKTUREN

- Present indirect discourse on pp. 122–123 using OHT 30.G1. 12 MIN

Homework Options:

- *Arbeitsheft,* p. 96, *Vokabeln, Akt. F*
- *Übung A,* p. 123
- *Arbeitsheft,* p. 86 *Strukturen, Akt. E–F*

DAY 4

STRUKTUREN

- Quick Start Review 1: Extended modifiers (TE, p. 116G). 5 MIN
- *Arbeitsheft,* p. 87, audio *Akt. A.* 6 MIN
- Discuss the answers to *Übung A,* p. 123 (TE, p. 116H). 4 MIN
- Do *Übung B,* p. 124, as a class. 5 MIN
- Follow the Teaching Suggestions for *Übung C,* p. 124 (TE, p. 116H). 10 MIN
- Present indirect questions on pp. 124–125 (TE, p. 116H). 8 MIN
- Do the warm-up activity in the Teaching Suggestions (TE, p. 116H), then do *Übung A,* p. 125, silently. Check answers as a class. 12 MIN

Homework Options:

- *Arbeitsheft,* p. 91, *Strukturen, Akt. H*

DAY 5

STRUKTUREN

- Quick Start Review 2: Subjunctive II (TE, p. 116H). 4 MIN
- Do *Übung B*, p. 125, in pairs, then discuss the answers as a class. Have students think of more questions the police officer might have asked. 10 MIN
- Present the imperative on pp. 125–127. 10 MIN
- *Arbeitsheft*, p. 92, audio *Akt. I*. 6 MIN
- Have students do *Übung A, Schritte 1–2*, p. 127, in pairs, taking turns giving the commands (TE, p. 116H). 12 MIN
- Do *Übung B*, p. 127, silently and then check answers as a class. 8 MIN

Homework Options:

- *Arbeitsheft*, p. 92, *Strukturen, Akt. J–K*

DAY 6

PERSPEKTIVEN

- As a review of pertinent vocabulary, do Vocabulary Quick Start Review 2: Vocabulary (TE, p. 116G). 5 MIN
- Do *Akt. A*, p. 128, in small groups. Follow the Teaching Suggestions for a follow-up (TE, p. 116I). 5 MIN
- Read through *Akt. B*, pp. 128–129, as a class and then listen once to the audio text. Have the students answer the questions as they listen and then discuss the answers as a class (TE, p. 116I). 12 MIN
- *Arbeitsheft*, p. 93, audio *Akt. A*. 10 MIN
- Do *Akt. C*, p. 129, in small groups, then share ideas with the class. 10 MIN
- *Zum Thema*, p. 129 (TE, p. 116I). 8 MIN

Homework Options:

- *Zum Text, Akt. D*, p. 131
- *Arbeitsheft*, p. 94, *Perspektiven, Akt. B*
- *Arbeitsheft*, pp. 95–96, *Perspektiven, Akt. F–G*

DAY 7

PERSPEKTIVEN

- Quick Start Review 1: Superlatives (TE, p. 116H). 4 MIN
- Do *Zum Text, Akt. A*, p. 131, as a class (TE, p. 116I). 5 MIN
- Have students do *Zum Text, Akt. B*, p. 131, in small groups (TE, p. 116I). 5 MIN
- Discuss *Zum Text, Akt. C*, p. 131, as a class. 6 MIN
- Have students discuss *Zur Interpretation*, p. 131, in pairs and then share some ideas with the class (TE, p. 116I). 8 MIN
- Do *Interaktion*, p. 132, in small groups (TE, p. 116I). 12 MIN
- Begin *Schreiben Sie!* by discussing the assignment, *Tipp zum Schreiben*, and *Schreibmodell* (TE, p. 116I). 5 MIN
- Do *Vor dem Schreiben* and begin *Beim Schreiben*, p. 134, if possible. 5 MIN

Homework Options:

- Finish *Beim Schreiben*, p. 134, and write the first draft of the photo captions

DAY 8

PERSPEKTIVEN

- Quick Start Review 2: Vocabulary (TE, p. 116I). 4 MIN
- Do *Nach dem Schreiben* in pairs and begin writing the final draft of the photo captions. 11 MIN
- Questions and review. 5 MIN
- *Prüfung, Kapitel 30*. 30 MIN

Homework Options:

- *Arbeitsheft*, p. 96, *Perspektiven, Akt. H*
- Complete the final draft of the photo captions

DAY 1

Note: (1) Please see TE, pp. 116E–116J, for other suggestions not referenced in these plans. (2) Not all homework options need be assigned.

CHAPTER OPENER

- Quick Start Review: Vocabulary (TE, p. 116E). 5 MIN
- Discuss photos on pp. 116–117 (TE, p. 116E). 5 MIN

VIDEOTHEK

- Play *Folge I* then have students do *Akt. A*, p. 118, as a class. 14 MIN
- Do *Akt. B–C*, pp. 118–119, silently (TE, p. 116F). 18 MIN
- Block Schedule activity: Change of Pace (TE, p. 116F). 10 MIN
- Play *Folge II* and then do *Akt. A–B*, p. 119 (TE, p. 116F). 24 MIN
- *Arbeitsheft*, pp. 81–83, audio *Akt. B, D*. 14 MIN

Homework Options:

- *Arbeitsheft*, p. 83–84, *Videothek, Akt. E–G*

DAY 2

VIDEOTHEK

- Quick Start Review 2: Present perfect (TE, p. 116E). 5 MIN
- *Arbeitsheft*, p. 81, audio *Akt. A*. 8 MIN

VOKABELN

- Discuss the photo and present the vocabulary words on p. 120 (TE, p. 116G). 12 MIN
- Do *Akt. A*, pp. 120–121, in pairs (TE, p. 116G). 9 MIN
- Do *Akt. B*, p. 121, silently. (TE, p. 116G). 13 MIN
- Discuss *Akt. C*, p. 121, as a class (TE, p. 116G). 6 MIN
- Block Schedule activity: Expansion (TE, p. 116G). 10 MIN

STRUKTUREN

- Present indirect discourse on pp. 122–123 using OHT 30.G1. 10 MIN
- Do *Übung A*, p. 123, silently and then check answers with a partner. 10 MIN
- Do *Übung B*, p. 124, as a class. 7 MIN

Homework Options:

- *Arbeitsheft*, p. 86, *Vokabeln, Akt. F*
- *Arbeitsheft*, pp. 89–90, *Akt. E–F*

DAY 3

STRUKTUREN

- Quick Start Review 1: Extended Modifiers (TE, pp. 116–116H). 5 MIN
- *Übung C*, p. 124 (TE, p. 116H). 10 MIN
- Present indirect questions on pp. 124–125. 8 MIN
- Do the warm-up activity (TE, p. 116H), then do *Übung A*, p. 125, silently. 12 MIN
- Do *Übung B*, p. 125, in pairs (TE, p. 116H). 10 MIN
- Block Schedule activity: Recycle (TE, p. 116H). 10 MIN
- Present the imperative on pp. 125–127. 10 MIN
- *Arbeitsheft*, p. 92, audio *Akt. I*. 5 MIN
- Have students do *Übung A–B*, p. 127 (TE, p. 116H). 20 MIN

Homework Options:

- *Arbeitsheft*, pp. 91–92, *Strukturen, Akt. H, J–K*

DAY 4

PERSPEKTIVEN

- Quick Start Review 1: Superlatives (TE, p. 116H–116I). 5 MIN
- Do *Akt. A–B*, p. 128, (TE, p. 116I). 11 MIN
- *Arbeitsheft*, p. 93, audio *Akt. A*. 8 MIN
- Do *Akt. C*, p. 129, in small groups. 9 MIN
- *Zum Thema*, p. 129 (TE, p. 116I). 8 MIN
- Block Schedule activity: Fun Break (TE, p. 116I). 10 MIN
- Do *Zum Text, Akt. A–C*, p. 131, as a class. 15 MIN
- Discuss *Zur Interpretation*, pp. 131–132, in pairs (TE, p. 116I). 8 MIN
- Do *Interaktion*, p. 132 (TE, p. 116I). 6 MIN
- Begin *Schreiben Sie!*, p. 132 (TE, p. 116I). 5 MIN
- Do *Vor dem Schreiben*, and begin *Beim Schreiben* p. 134. 5 MIN

Homework Options:

- Finish *Beim Schreiben*, p. 134 and write first draft of photo captions
- *Zum Text, Akt. D*, p. 131
- *Arbeitsheft*, pp. 94–95, *Perspektiven, Akt. B, F–G*

DAY 5

PERSPEKTIVEN

- Quick Start Review 2: Vocabulary (TE, p. 116I). 6 MIN
- Do *Interaktion*, p. 132, in small groups (TE, p. 116I). 10 MIN
- *Arbeitsheft*, p. 93, audio *Akt. A*. Discuss the meaning of the text by asking comprehension questions. 15 MIN
- Do *Nach dem Schreiben*, p. 134, in pairs and begin writing the final draft of the photo captions. 14 MIN
- Block Schedule activity: Variety (TE, p. 116J). 10 MIN
- Questions and review. 5 MIN
- *Prüfung, Kapitel 30*. 30 MIN

Homework Options:

- *Arbeitsheft*, p. 96, *Perspektiven, Akt. H*
- Complete the final draft of the photo captions

Chapter Opener, pp. 116–117

PROGRAM RESOURCES

- Overhead Transparency 30.1

Quick Start Review

♻ Vocabulary

Bilden Sie Sätze.

1. für / Stellen / viele / es / gibt / mehrere / Bewerber
2. in Deutschland / nach / der Vereinigung / gestiegen / der Arbeitslosen / die Zahl / ist
3. Berufsfelder / studiert / heute / man / an der Universität / eher / ein / Fach / nur / als
4. die niedrigen Sozialleistungen / viele Rentner in den USA / zwingen / zu arbeiten / weiter
5. ein Arbeitsvermittler / Arbeitslosen / wieder / hilft / zu finden / eine Stelle
6. braucht / heute / für viele Stellen / nicht nur / ein Studium / sondern auch / Berufserfahrung

Answers: 1. Für viele Stellen gibt es mehrere Bewerber.   2. In Deutschland ist die Zahl der Arbeitslosen nach der Vereinigung gestiegen.   3. Heute studiert man eher Berufsfelder an der Universität als nur ein Fach.   4. Die niedrigen Sozialleistungen zwingen viele Rentner in den USA, weiter zu arbeiten. 5. Ein Arbeitsvermittler hilft Arbeitslosen wieder eine Stelle zu finden.   6. Für viele Stellen braucht man heute nicht nur ein Studium, sondern auch Berufserfahrung.

TEACHING SUGGESTIONS

- Photos, pp. 116–117

Have students look at the photos and discuss their own opinions about *Gleichberechtigung.* Have students make comments using the questions posed in the captions: *Wie geht es den Frauen von heute? Leben sie immer noch in einer Männerwelt?*

TEACHING ALL STUDENTS

Multiple Intelligences Intrapersonal: Have students write a short journal entry concerning an instance in their lives when they have witnessed gender bias or discrimination against women or men. Have them share their writing with the class if they like.

CLASSROOM COMMUNITY

Paired Activity Introduce the topic of gender equality. Who does what in the family? How are parental roles divided? How have women faced discrimination? Have students work in pairs to answer these questions. Then have the pairs report back to the class.

Videothek, pp. 118–119

PROGRAM RESOURCES

- Videocassette, *Folge 30*
- *Arbeitsheft,* pp. 81–84
- Audio Program, Cassette 3B/CD 4
- Audioscript, pp. 36–42

Quick Start Review 1

♻ Superlatives

Ergänzen Sie die richtigen Formen des Superlativs.

WÖRTER: hoch, gern, gut, schnell

1. In der Schweiz sind die Berge am _____.
2. Bei meiner Oma schmeckt der Kuchen am _____.
3. Ich gehe am _____ mit meiner Schwester einkaufen, denn sie weiß, was mir gefällt.
4. Oliver ist immer am _____ beim 800-Meter-Lauf.
5. In der Bäckerei Pfister gibt es die _____ Brötchen.
6. Mein Bruder baut die _____ Legotürme.

Answers: 1. höchsten   2. besten 3. liebsten   4. schnellsten   5. besten 6. höchsten

Quick Start Review 2

♻ Present perfect

Setzen Sie die Sätze ins Perfekt.

1. Wir wandern zwei Stunden lang.
2. Er steht um acht Uhr auf.
3. Esst ihr schon?
4. Wo verbringt ihr euren Urlaub?
5. Er studiert in Berlin.
6. Er fährt nach Jena.

Answers: 1. Wir sind zwei Stunden lang gewandert.   2. Er ist um acht Uhr aufgestanden.   3. Habt ihr schon gegessen?   4. Wo habt ihr euren Urlaub verbracht?   5. Er hat in Berlin studiert.   6. Er ist nach Jena gefahren.

TEACHING SUGGESTIONS

- *Folge I: Die Frauenbewegung,* pp. 118–119

Remind students to review the *Wortschatz zum Video* before they watch. Encourage them to take notes during the video. Ask them to single out one event that they find most interesting in the video and be prepared to tell why.

- *Aktivität A,* p. 118

Warm-up: Have students look at the photos of the 3 women: Sophie, Bertha, and Anna. Ask *Woran sieht man, dass die Fotos nicht aus unserer Zeit sind? Welche Jahre würden Sie den Fotos zuordnen, ohne das Video zu kennen?*

- *Aktivität B,* p. 118

Have students do the activity individually, then discuss their opinions in pairs. Ask them to find examples for the statements in *Schritt 1.* Ask *Was bedeutet das: Die Diskriminierung ist heute subtiler geworden? Können Sie Beispiele dafür finden, dass Frauen in der gleichen Position härter kämpfen müssen als Männer?*

- *Aktivität A,* p. 119

Schritt 1: Have students read the statements before playing the recording, then have them do this activity individually.
Schritt 2: Have student pairs act out another conversation between Frau Meisel and Frau Piper.

- *Aktivität B,* p. 119

Follow-up: Ask students what they thought of the discussion between Gürkan and Grace.

TEACHING ALL STUDENTS

Extra Help The comparative is used when someone wants to express something discreetly or politely. For example, *Ein älterer Herr kam herein. Eine jüngere Frau mit Sonnenbrille begrüßte sie. Herr Meier zu seinem*

Chef: „Wir haben hier ein kleineres Problem." Have students discuss these examples and ask them to point out what is left unsaid by being polite. Ask them to think of some other examples.

CLASSROOM COMMUNITY

Group Activity Do a quick writing activity. Ask *Was fällt Ihnen ein, wenn Sie das Wort „Frauen" hören? Was fällt Ihnen ein, wenn Sie das Wort „Männer" hören?* Have students quickly write down the first 10 things that come to their minds. Read out their responses anonymously and follow up with a discussion.

INTERDISCIPLINARY CONNECTION

Literature/English: Ask for volunteers to discuss a novel or a story they have read that fits in with the topic of gender history and discrimination. Suggest they ask their English teacher to recommend something. Have them prepare a short report for the class and draw some parallels to the theme of this chapter.

BLOCK SCHEDULE

Change of Pace Have students bring in various magazines. Have them work in groups to create collages showing how women are portrayed in the media. Encourage them to find captions for the photos they choose, then decide on a title for their collage and display it.

PORTFOLIO

Ask students to research the biography of a female scientist. They might ask their science teacher for suggestions. Have them write a short paper, present it to the class, and illustrate it.

RUBRIC **A** = 13–15 pts. **B** = 10–12 pts.
C = 7–9 pts. **D** = 4–6 pts. **F** < 4 pts.

Writing Criteria		Scale			
Content and organization	1	2	3	4	5
Grammar and spelling	1	2	3	4	5
Presentation	1	2	3	4	5

Vokabeln, pp. 120–121

PROGRAM RESOURCES

- *Arbeitsheft,* pp. 85–86
- Audio Program, Cassette 3B/CD 4
- Audioscript, pp. 37–38

....

Quick Start Review 1
Comparisons
Sagen Sie das Gegenteil.
MODELL: Deutsch ist schwieriger als Englisch. → *Nein, Deutsch ist nicht so schwierig wie Englisch.*

1. Spanisch ist leichter als Französisch.
2. Cola schmeckt besser als Orangensaft.
3. Mathematik macht mehr Spaß als Sport.
4. Auf Hawaii ist es schöner als auf Tahiti.
5. Unser neuer Chef ist netter als der alte.
6. Dieser Winter ist kälter als der letzte.

Answers: 1. Nein, Spanisch ist nicht so leicht wie Französisch. 2. Nein, Cola schmeckt nicht so gut wie Orangensaft. 3. Nein, Mathematik macht nicht so viel Spaß wie Sport. 4. Nein, auf Hawaii ist es nicht so schön wie auf Tahiti. 5. Nein, der neue Chef ist nicht so nett wie der alte. 6. Nein, dieser Winter ist nicht so kalt wie der letzte.

Quick Start Review 2

♻ Vocabulary

Ergänzen Sie die Verben.

VERBEN: verbunden, hergestellt, erfordert, ausüben, gestiegen

1. Der wirtschaftliche Aufschwung ist mit viel Arbeit _____.
2. Am Anfang des Studiums wissen viele Studenten noch nicht, welchen Beruf sie später _____ wollen.
3. Das neue Unternehmen _____ viel Einsatz und Energie von allen Arbeitnehmern.
4. Die Arbeitslosenzahl ist im Winter wieder _____.
5. In unserer Firma wird ein neues Produkt _____.

Answers: 1. verbunden   2. ausüben
3. erfordert   4. gestiegen
5. hergestellt

TEACHING SUGGESTIONS

• Photo, p. 120

Ask *Wer sind die Leute auf dem Bild? Worüber könnten sie reden?*

• *Aktivität A,* pp. 120–121

Follow-up: Have each student write a definition of one of the vocabulary items on p. 120 on a slip of paper. Call on students to give the definition they have written. The class must find the word in the vocabulary list that matches the definition.

• *Aktivität B,* p. 121

Follow-up: Ask students what they know about women's rights in other countries. Discuss attitudes toward women in other cultures. As a further follow-up, have students choose a particular country and investigate this issue, then report their findings to the class.

• *Aktivität C,* p. 121

Divide the class into groups and have each work on a different time period: pre-World War II, the '50s and '60s, or the present. Have students read *Kulturspiegel,* p. 121. Ask *In welchen leitenden Positionen sind Frauen in der Politik vertreten? Sind sie in der Wirtschaft in leitenden Positionen vertreten? Gibt es typische Frauen- oder Männerberufe?*

TEACHING ALL STUDENTS

Multiple Intelligences Intrapersonal: Write the following words on the board or an OHT: *die Emanzipation, die Frauenbewegung, die Kinderkrippe, die Redefreiheit, die Gedankenfreiheit, das Wahlrecht.* Ask students to pick 2 of these words and jot down on a piece of paper what comes to mind when they hear them. Collect their papers and read some of their associations to the class. Follow up with a discussion.

CLASSROOM COMMUNITY

Dictation Dictate the following text to the class. Then write it on the board or an OHT. Have students exchange papers with a partner to correct it. *Schon im 19. Jahrhundert haben sich Frauen organisiert, um zusammen für ihre Rechte zu kämpfen. Erst 1919 hatten Frauen in den USA das Wahlrecht, davor durften nur Männer wählen. Obwohl Frauen in der Gesellschaft oft eine Mehrheit bilden, sind sie in leitenden Positionen immer noch eine Minderheit.*

BLOCK SCHEDULE

Expansion Have students make up simple crossword puzzles with the verbs in the box on p. 120, creating sentences with blanks as cues. Tell them that crossword and word search puzzles use capital letters: therefore, *ß* becomes *SS* and takes 2 spaces.

Strukturen, pp. 122–127

PROGRAM RESOURCES

• Overhead Transparency 30.G1
• *Arbeitsheft,* pp. 87–92
• Audio Program, Cassette 3B/CD 4
• Audioscript, pp. 38–40

Quick Start Review 1

♻ Extended modifiers

Ergänzen Sie die Sätze mit den Adjektivformen der Partizipien Präsens oder Perfekt.

1. Die im Erdbeben _____ (zerstören) Kirche wurde wieder aufgebaut.
2. Die _____ (folgen) Sätze sind kompliziert.
3. Ich habe das vor vier Wochen _____ (bestellen) Auto immer noch nicht bekommen.
4. Vor dem Firmengebäude laufen die _____ (streiken) Arbeiter auf und ab.
5. Das _____ (stehlen) Geld wurde in einer Tasche auf der Autobahn gefunden.
6. Die ständig _____ (wachsen) Zahl der Einwohner in unserer Stadt treibt auch die Preise für Häuser und Wohnungen hoch.

Answers: 1. zerstörte 2. folgenden 3. bestellte 4. streikenden 5. gestohlene 6. wachsende

Quick Start Review 2
♻ Subjunctive II
Ergänzen Sie die Sätze mit einer Konjunktivform in der Vergangenheit (Wenn ich du wäre, . . .).
MODELL: früher aufstehen →
Wenn ich du wäre, wäre ich früher aufgestanden.
1. nicht so schnell fahren
2. wärmere Kleider anziehen
3. nicht so viel reden
4. nicht so viele Sorgen machen
5. zu Hause bleiben
6. nicht so viel Geld ausgeben

Answers: 1. . . . , wäre ich nicht so schnell gefahren. 2. . . . , hätte ich wärmere Kleider angezogen. 3. . . . , hätte ich nicht so viel geredet. 4. . . . , hätte ich mir nicht so viele Sorgen gemacht. 5. . . . , wäre ich zu Hause geblieben. 6. . . . , hätte ich nicht so viel Geld ausgegeben.

....

TEACHING SUGGESTIONS

• *Übung A,* p. 123

Follow-up: Encourage students to come up with their own statements on women's rights. Collect their statements and then transfer them into indirect discourse.

• *Übung C,* p. 124

Have students work individually, then exchange their papers with a neighbor and correct them together.

• Indirect questions, pp. 124–125

Point out that *ob* means *if* in cases where *if* can be replaced with *whether.*

This must not be confused with the conditional *if,* which is *wenn* in German.

• *Übung A,* p. 125

Warm-up: Have students change the following sentences to the indicative.
1. Er sagt, er könne uns nicht helfen.
2. Sie schreibt, sie wolle nicht mehr mit diesen Leuten reden.
3. Christa fragte ihren Lehrer, ob er ihren Test schon gelesen habe.

Answers: 1. Er sagt: Ich kann euch nicht helfen. 2. Sie schreibt: Ich will nicht mehr mit diesen Leuten reden. 3. Christa fragt ihren Lehrer: Haben Sie meinen Test schon gelesen?

• *Übung B,* p. 125

Discuss answers as a class. Have students think of other questions the police officer might have asked.

• *Übung A,* p. 127

Have students take turns giving the commands.
Follow-up: Have students act as tourist guides in their own town. Which places, sights, and restaurants would they recommend to visitors? Have them use imperatives.

TEACHING ALL STUDENTS

Extra Help Ask students to report on Sabine's, Susanne's, and Daniela's statements using indirect discourse. Have them use *Aktivität B,* p. 118, as a starting point. You might want to show this video episode again.

CLASSROOM COMMUNITY

Group Activity Ask students to give commands to each other and then to

carry out these commands. For example, *Gib mir bitte den Bleistift, der auf deinem Tisch liegt. Öffne bitte das Fenster! Ruf mich heute Nachmittag an!*

LANGUAGE NOTE

Have students read the *Kurz notiert* box, p. 123, and add that German actually has 3 different ways of expressing indirect discourse: (1) with the indicative: *Er sagt, er kann nicht alle Probleme lösen;* (2) using subjunctive II: *Er sagt, er könnte nicht alle Probleme lösen;* and (3) using Subjunctive I: *Er sagt, er könne nicht alle Probleme lösen.*

BLOCK SCHEDULE

Recycle Have students invent a few other scenes that might take place in Christa Piper's office (she is the social service worker who helps women settle issues or problems in the workplace). Have students create dialogues in groups and read them aloud.

Perspektiven, pp. 128–129

PROGRAM RESOURCES
• *Arbeitsheft,* pp. 99–102
• Audio Program, Cassette 3B, 7B/ CD 4, 9
• Audioscript, p. 110
• www.mcdougallittell.com

....

Quick Start Review 1
♻ Superlatives
Ergänzen Sie die Sätze mit den richtigen Superlativformen.
1. Was machst du in deiner Freizeit am _____ (gern)?
2. Welches ist der _____ (gut) Computer von den dreien?

3. Wer von euch hat die _____ (viel) Fehler in der Prüfung?
4. Wo gibt es die _____ (hoch) Berge?
5. In den _____ (groß) Städten ist die Lebensqualität nicht die beste.
6. Das _____ (teuer) Fleisch ist nicht immer auch das beste.

Answers: 1. liebsten 2. beste
3. meisten 4. höchsten 5. größten
6. teuerste

Quick Start Review 2

♻ Vocabulary
Ergänzen Sie die Sätze mit den Wörtern.

WÖRTER: unentbehrlich, rücksichtsvoll, selbständig, zufrieden, gering, ungefähr

1. Wenn unsere Kunden _____ sind, dann haben wir unsere Sache gut gemacht.
2. Herr Schmidt ist immer hilfsbereit und _____. Ich mag ihn sehr.
3. Schüler müssen lernen _____ zu arbeiten.
4. Meine Sekretärin ist _____ in unserer Firma.
5. Er ist _____ zwei Meter groß.
6. Ich kann die Stelle nicht annehmen. Das Gehalt ist zu _____.

Answers: 1. zufrieden
2. rücksichtsvoll 3. selbständig
4. unentbehrlich 5. ungefähr
6. gering

· ·

TEACHING SUGGESTIONS

• *Hören Sie zu!, Aktivität A*, p. 128

Follow-up: Ask *Kennen Sie einen Frauenbuchladen? Würden Sie in einen Frauenbuchladen gehen?*

• *Aktivität B*, pp. 128–129

Remind students to look over the *Wortschatz* and the activity questions before they listen to the recording. Encourage them to take notes while they listen.

Follow-up: Have students work with a partner to summarize the main goals of the bookstore. Have them turn their summary into an advertisement for the bookstore.

• *Emanzipation*, pp. 129–131

Have students first review the *Wortschatz zum Lesen* on p. 130 before reading the text. Make sure they use their dictionaries minimally, only looking up words that are absolutely necessary for their comprehension of the text.

• *Zum Thema*, p. 129

Have students read the text silently, then give the gist of the text and a few details about it. Since this text is in dialogue form, it could be dramatized. Have students read the text aloud in pairs. Then ask them to list the topics covered by the father and son regarding *Gleichberechtigung*.

• *Zum Text, Aktivität A*, p. 131

Have students think of examples for the topics they heard in the dialogue.

• *Zum Text, Aktivität B*, p. 131

Follow-up: Have students act out the dialogue between Charly's mother and father.

• *Zur Interpretation*, pp. 131–132

Point out to students that the father might not even be so sure of his opinions on women's rights. He says a lot between the lines. What could he be afraid of?

• *Interaktion*, p. 132

Follow-up: Discuss this thesis with the students: *Es ist jetzt an der Zeit, dass wir über die Rolle des Mannes diskutieren. Die Erwartungen an Männer sind zu hoch.*

• *Schreiben Sie!*, p. 132

Have students jot down thoughts without regard to grammar or indirect speech. Have them write down 3 nouns and 3 verbs for each photo.

• *Tipp zum Schreiben*, p. 132

Have students write down direct quotations first, that is, transform their notes from the brainstorming activity into complete sentences. Then they can rewrite their sentences using subjunctive I forms.

TEACHING ALL STUDENTS

Multiple Intelligences Kinesthetic: Ask for students to volunteer to mimic different facial expressions. Have the other students describe these expressions. For example, *Er sieht so aus, als ob er müde wäre. Sie sieht so aus, als ob sie Bauchweh hätte. Er sieht so aus, als ob er sich langweilte.*

CLASSROOM COMMUNITY

Group Activity The Past and the Present: Have students work on a poster portraying the lives of women in the past and women in the present. They should try to capture the different expectations and roles for women at the beginning and at the end of the 20th century.

BLOCK SCHEDULE

Fun Break Have students play "Simon Says," to review the imperative forms. Use both singular and plural forms. For example, *Simon sagt: Hebt alle euren rechten Arm hoch! Macht euer Deutschbuch zu!*

Variety Encourage students to discuss cultural differences in the roles of women in different countries or cultures. It is better not to force the discussion in a certain direction, but instead to give students the opportunity to have a natural conversation about something in which they are interested.

PROJECT

Have students research German actresses or female directors. They might also want to report on the plot of a movie if it ties in with the overall theme of gender roles. You might want to recommend certain films. German movies and movie scripts can be borrowed at Goethe Institute libraries. They can also be mailed to high school teachers who have an account.

RUBRIC A = 13–15 pts. B = 10–12 pts.
C = 7–9 pts. D = 4–6 pts. F < 4 pts.

Writing Criteria	Scale				
Grammar and vocabulary	1	2	3	4	5
Content	1	2	3	4	5
Organization	1	2	3	4	5

KAPITEL 30

FRAUEN UND MÄNNER

In diesem Kapitel

- lernen Sie Julia, eine Buchhändlerin in einem Frauenbuchladen, kennen.

- diskutieren Sie über das Thema Gleichberechtigung.

- lernen Sie Christa Piper, eine Frauenbeauftragte in Saarbrücken, kennen.

Sie werden auch

- lernen, wie man die indirekte Rede gebraucht.

- lernen, wie man indirekte Fragen stellt.

- die Formen des Imperativs wiederholen.

- eine Geschichte über Emanzipation lesen.

- die Gedanken und Gefühle von drei Frauen beschreiben.

Vor 1900 durften nur Männer höhere Schulen besuchen.

Heute steht jegliche
Berufsmöglichkeit offen.

Wie geht es den Frauen von heute? Leben
sie immer noch in einer Männerwelt?

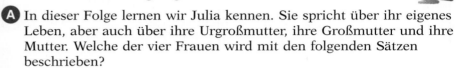

VIDEOTHEK

Frauen mussten für ihre Gleichberechtigung in der Gesellschaft und im Beruf hart kämpfen.

I: Die Frauenbewegung

A In dieser Folge lernen wir Julia kennen. Sie spricht über ihr eigenes Leben, aber auch über ihre Urgroßmutter, ihre Großmutter und ihre Mutter. Welche der vier Frauen wird mit den folgenden Sätzen beschrieben?

Julia, eine Buchhändlerin.
A. 1. Sophie **2.** Sophie **3.** Anna **4.** Julia
5. Sophie **6.** Bertha **7.** Julia

Sophie.   **Bertha.**   **Anna.**

1. Sie war gesetzlich[a] nicht gleichberechtigt.
2. Sie konnte nicht wählen.
3. Sie hat sich sehr stark in der Frauenbewegung engagiert.
4. Sie ist Buchhändlerin geworden.
5. Sie ist Köchin geworden.
6. Sie war die erste, die wählen durfte.
7. Sie konnte Frauenbewegung und Beruf kombinieren.

[a]*legally*

WORTSCHATZ ZUM VIDEO

die Frauenrechtlerin	*worker for women's rights*
wesentlich	*essential(ly)*
die Quotierungsfrage	*question of quotas*
die PR-Abteilung	*PR department*
die Öffentlich-keitsarbeit	*public relations work*
ärztliche Behandlung	*medical treatment*
unter einen Hut bringen	*to reconcile*
die Frauenbeauftragte	*commissioner for women's issues*
die Brotverdienerin	*breadwinner*

B Persönliche Geschichten. Susanne, Sabine und Daniela beschreiben, was Frauen heute in der Arbeitswelt erleben.

SCHRITT 1: Wer behandelt die folgenden Themen: Susanne, Sabine oder Daniela?

1. Die Diskriminierung ist subtiler geworden.
2. Frauen müssen härter kämpfen als ein Mann in der gleichen Position.
3. Eine Frau kommt heute vielleicht etwas einfacher an eine Stelle, aber es gibt nachher Probleme.

SCHRITT 2: Was meinen Sie dazu? Mit welchen der obigen Meinungen stimmen Sie überein? Warum?

B. Schritt 1: 1. Daniela **2.** Susanne
3. Sabine
Schritt 2: *Answers will vary.*

C Frauen in der DDR. Anja und Claudia besprechen die Situation der Frau in der ehemaligen DDR und wie es damals war.

SCHRITT 1: Wer sagt das? Anja oder Claudia?

1. „Es ist so ein bisschen eine Männerwelt."
2. „Einerseits war die Rolle der Frau und das Leben einer Frau in der DDR leichter und respektvoller als jetzt."
3. „Jetzt ist es etwas schwieriger."
4. „Die Kinder waren im Kindergarten und in der Krippe."
5. „Für mich als Frau, ich war früher sehr selbstständig erzogen, sehr emanzipiert."

SCHRITT 2: Heute und damals. Sie haben die Meinungen von zwei Frauen aus den neuen Bundesländern gehört. Was ist seit der Wiedervereinigung besser geworden? Was ist schlimmer?

II: Im Auftrag der Frauen

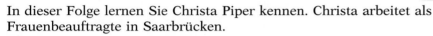

In dieser Folge lernen Sie Christa Piper kennen. Christa arbeitet als Frauenbeauftragte in Saarbrücken.

A Ein Gespräch mit der Frauenbeauftragten. Frau Meisel kommt zu Frau Piper und bittet um Hilfe, weil sie Probleme mit der Arbeit hat.

SCHRITT 1: Stimmt das oder stimmt das nicht?

1. Sie ist verheiratet und hat zwei Kinder.
2. Sie ist allein stehende Mutter mit zwei Kindern.
3. Sie arbeitet nicht und sucht eine Arbeitsstelle.
4. Sie arbeitet ganztags.
5. Die Kinder sind nachmittags oft allein zu Hause.

SCHRITT 2: Welche Lösung schlägt Frau Piper vor? Glauben Sie, dass eine solche Lösung immer möglich ist? Welchen Rat würden Sie Frau Meisel geben?

B Diskussion. Grace und Gürkan diskutieren über das Thema Gleichberechtigung.

SCHRITT 1: Wer äußert folgende Meinungen – Grace oder Gürkan? Wie finden Sie diese Sätze?

1. Frauen sind einfach süß.
2. Frauen und Männer können beide Mittelpunkte sein.
3. Frauen müssen überall in der Politik vertreten sein.
4. Es ist schwieriger für eine Frau, Karriere und Kinder zu haben.
5. Vielleicht könnte der Mann zu Hause bleiben und ein bisschen mehr in der Küche tun.
6. Ich würde gern zu Hause mit den Kindern bleiben.

SCHRITT 2: Partnerarbeit. Arbeiten Sie mit einem Partner / einer Partnerin und führen Sie das Gespräch zwischen Grace und Gürkan weiter.

KULTURSPIEGEL

Nach der Wende gab es für Frauen in der ehemaligen DDR neue Sorgen um die Zukunft. Heute stellen Frauen etwa zwei Drittel der Arbeitslosen in den neuen Bundesländern. Die staatlich organisierten Kinderkrippen, die nach der Wende abgeschafft wurden, hatten es einfacher gemacht, Familie und Beruf unter einen Hut zu bringen.

See answers below.

Christa Piper spricht mit Frau Meisel.

C. Schritt 1: 1. Claudia 2. Anja 3. Claudia 4. Anja 5. Claudia
Schritt 2: *Answers will vary.*

A. Schritt 1: 1. Das stimmt nicht. 2. Das stimmt. 3. Das stimmt nicht. 4. Das stimmt. 5. Das stimmt.
Schritt 2: Frau Piper schlägt vor, dass Frau Meisel eine Stunde später zur Arbeit geht und dass ihre Kinder den ganzen Tag betreut werden. *Answers to other questions will vary.*

B. Schritt 1: 1. Gürkan 2. Grace 3. Gürkan 4. Grace 5. Grace 6. Gürkan
Schritt 2: *Dialogues will vary.*

VOKABELN

die Emanzipation	*emancipation*
die Frauenbewegung	*women's movement*
die Gedankenfreiheit	*freedom of thought*
die Kinderkrippe	*daycare center*
die Minderheit	*minority*
die Redefreiheit	*freedom of speech*
die Schwierigkeit	*difficulty*
der/die Abgeordnete (*decl. adj.*)	*delegate; member of parliament*
das Menschenrecht	*human right*
das Wahlrecht	*right to vote, suffrage*
behandeln	*to treat*
benachteiligen	*to place at a disadvantage*
beschimpfen	*to insult*
beschuldigen	*to accuse*
besitzen	*to possess, own*
betrachten	*to consider, regard*
betreuen	*to look after*
emanzipieren	*to emancipate*
gestatten	*to allow*
kämpfen	*to struggle; to fight*
sich kümmern um	*to concern oneself with*
leiten	*to lead*
sich organisieren	*to organize oneself*
unterdrücken	*to suppress*
wollen: auf etwas hinaus wollen	*to imply something; to have a certain goal*

Frauen in der Politik engagieren sich für die völlige Gleichberechtigung.

allein erziehend	*single parenting*
gleichberechtigt sein	*to have equal rights*
gleichgestellt sein	*to be at an equal level*
jedenfalls	*in any case*

Sie wissen schon
die Gleichberechtigung

Aktivitäten

A. 1. gleichberechtigt sein   2. die Kinderkrippe
3. die Schwierigkeit   4. die Frauenbewegung
5. der Abgeordnete   6. unterdrücken
7. betreuen   8. die Redefreiheit
9. gleichgestellt   10. benachteiligen

A Definitionen. Welche Worter aus dem Wortkasten auf Seite 121 passen zu den Definitionen unten?

1. die gleichen Rechte haben
2. wo die Kinder berufstätiger Eltern oder allein erziehender Mütter betreut werden
3. das Problem
4. organisierte Form des Kampfes um die Gleichberechtigung der Frau
5. eine Person im Parlament, vom Volk gewählt
6. jemanden beherrschen, jemandem keine Freiheit lassen

7. sorgen für
8. das Recht, eine Meinung zu haben und sie zu äußern
9. rechtlich auf dem gleichen Niveau sein
10. diskriminieren

die Kinderkrippe   der Abgeordnete

   die Frauenbewegung   gleichberechtigt sein

betreuen   gleichgestellt sein   benachteiligen

   die Redefreiheit   die Schwierigkeit
          unterdrücken

KULTURSPIEGEL

Die Gleichberechtigung der Frauen wird im deutschen Grundgesetz ausdrücklich festgelegt. Die Politikerin Rita Süßmuth (CDU) war 1988–98 Präsidentin des deutschen Bundestags. Nach den Wahlen 1998 stellten Frauen 31 Prozent der Abgeordneten im Parlament. In welchen leitenden Positionen sind Frauen in Ihrem Land vertreten?

B Die Frauenbewegung. Ergänzen Sie die Sätze mit den Wörtern aus dem Kasten.

1. Erst 1919 hatten Frauen in den USA das _____, zuvor durften nur Männer wählen.
2. Obwohl Frauen in der Gesellschaft oft eine Mehrheit bilden, sind sie in den leitenden Positionen immer noch eine _____.
3. Frauen haben oft _____, Familie und Arbeit unter einen Hut zu bekommen.
4. Männer können auch zu Hause bleiben und sich um die Kinder _____.
5. Schon im neunzehnten Jahrhundert haben sich Frauen _____, um zusammen für ihre Rechte zu kämpfen.
6. Jede Bürgerin soll das Recht _____, den gleichen Lohn zu erhalten wie Männer.
7. Grace meint, Frauen werden immer noch unfair _____.

gekämpft   kümmern

       Wahlrecht

Minderheit   besitzen

organisiert   behandelt

B. **1.** Wahlrecht   **2.** Minderheit   **3.** gekämpft
4. kümmern   **5.** organisiert   **6.** besitzen
7. behandelt

Die Frauenbewegung in den USA.

C Was wissen Sie von der Frauenbewegung in Ihrem Land? Wer waren die ersten Frauenrechtlerinnen? Was haben sie gemacht? Wie ist die Situation heute?

C. *Answers will vary.*

STRUKTUREN

INDIRECT DISCOURSE
REPORTING WHAT OTHERS SAY

You have already learned to use the subjunctive to express wishes and to make polite requests. The forms you learned—**würde, wäre, käme, arbeitete**—are those known as Subjunctive II, because their stems derive from the simple past tense or the *second* principle part of the verb (**sein, war, ist gewesen**).

Another set of subjunctive forms, Subjunctive I, derives from the infinitive or the *first* principle part of the verb. To create Subjunctive I, simply add subjunctive endings to the stem, the infinitive without the final **-n.** Compare the Subjunctive I and Subjunctive II forms of **kommen.**

SPRACHSPIEGEL

Like German, English also has two contrasting subjunctive forms, one based on the past tense, the other on the infinitive.

If only we weren't running late.
It's important that we be on time.

INFINITIVE: **kommen** SUBJUNCTIVE I STEM: **komme**		INFINITIVE: **kommen** SUBJUNCTIVE II STEM: **käme**	
SINGULAR	PLURAL	SINGULAR	PLURAL
ich komme	wir komme**n**	ich käme	wir käme**n**
du komme**st**	ihr komme**t**	du käme**st**	ihr käme**t**
Sie komme**n**	Sie komme**n**	Sie käme**n**	Sie käme**n**
sie/er/es komme	sie komme**n**	sie/er/es käme	sie käme**n**

Notice that most Subjunctive I forms are identical with those of the indicative mood. However, Subjunctive I primarily occurs in the third-person singular, and this form clearly distinguishes itself: **er/sie/es komme** as opposed to the indicative **er/sie/es kommt.**

Because **sein** is such an irregular verb, all Subjunctive I forms differ from those of the indicative.

INFINITIVE: **sein** SUBJUNCTIVE I STEM: **sei**	
SINGULAR	PLURAL
ich sei	wir sei**en**
du sei**est**	Ihr sei**et**
Sie sei**en**	Sie sei**en**
sie/er/es sei	sie sei**en**

The most common use of Subjunctive I is indirect discourse or reporting what other people say.

DIRECT DISCOURSE	INDIRECT DISCOURSE
Julia sagt, „Ich **bin** Buchhändlerin."	Julia sagt, sie **sei** Buchhändlerin.
Christa sagt, „Ich **kann** nicht alle Probleme lösen."	Christa sagt, sie **könne** nicht alle Probleme lösen.

Like Subjunctive II, Subjunctive I has one way of expressing the past. As you might have guessed, you use the Subjunctive I form of the appropriate auxiliary verb, **haben** or **sein,** with the past participle of the main verb.

> Julia sagt, „Meine Mutter hat so was wie Gleichberechtigung erlebt."
>
> Julia sagt, ihre Mutter **habe** so was wie Gleichberechtigung erlebt.

Whenever the Subjunctive I form is identical to that of the present or present-perfect tense of the indicative mood, substitute the Subjunctive II form.

> Christa Piper sagt: „Zu mir **kommen** Frauen mit ihren Problemen."

SUBJUNCTIVE I: Christa Piper sagt, zu ihr **kommen** Frauen mit ihren Problemen.

SUBJUNCTIVE II: Christa Piper sagt, zu ihr **kämen** Frauen mit ihren Problemen.

> Susanne meint: „Die Frauen **haben** für ihre Rechte gekämpft."

SUBJUNCTIVE I: Susanne meint, die Frauen **haben** für ihre Rechte gekämpft.

SUBJUNCTIVE II: Susanne meint, die Frauen **hätten** für ihre Rechte gekämpft.

Übungen

A Grace und Gürkan. Was sagen die beiden? Setzen Sie das Gespräch in die indirekte Rede.

MODELL: Grace sagt: „Ich bin politisch engagiert." →
Grace sagt, sie sei politisch engagiert.

1. Gürkan meint: „Frauen sind süß."
2. Grace sagt: „Ich bin total für Gleichberechtigung."
3. Grace sagt: „Die Welt hat zwei Mittelpunkte."
4. Gürkan sagt: „Ich verstehe die Frage nicht."
5. Gürkan meint: „Ich sehe keine Diskriminierung."
6. Grace meint: „Eine Frau soll nicht als süß betrachtet werden."
7. Grace sagt: „Ich habe Gürkan gar nicht beschuldigt."

KURZ NOTIERT

Particularly in speech, many speakers substitute Subjunctive II forms for Subjunctive I.

> Claudia sagt, sie **könnte** nicht alle Probleme lösen.
> Julia sagt, ihre Mutter **hätte** erst so was wie Gleichberechtigung erlebt.

The Subjunctive I forms are more typical of written language, particularly newspaper reporting. Use of the subjunctive often indicates that the writer makes no claims regarding the accuracy of the statement, but is merely reporting it.

A. 1. Gürkan meint, Frauen seien süß. 2. Grace sagt, sie sei total für Gleichberechtigung. 3. Grace sagt, die Welt habe zwei Mittelpunkte. 4. Gürkan sagt, er verstehe die Frage nicht. 5. Gürkan meint, er sehe keine Diskriminierung. 6. Grace meint, eine Frau solle nicht als süß betrachtet werden. 7. Grace sagt, sie habe Gürkan nicht beschuldigt.

Grace und Gürkan diskutieren über Gleichberechtigung.

B. 1. sei 2. solle 3. versuche 4. könne
5. werde

Julias Mutter Anna.

Susannes Mutter.

C. Julia sagt, Anna sei 1944 geboren. Sie habe sich sehr stark für die Frauenbewegung engagiert. Die Frauenbewegung habe die Gleichberechtigung in allen Bereichen verlangt, aber in der Praxis sei die völlige Gleichberechtigung noch nicht verwirklicht. Susanne sagt, für Frauen sei es damals schwieriger gewesen. Ihre Mutter habe auch Schwierigkeiten im Beruf gehabt. Sie sei Richterin geworden und anfangs habe man sie nicht ernst genommen. Sie habe schon härter kämpfen müssen als ein Mann in der Position.

B Ein Zentrum für Frauen. Die Stadt Saarbrücken braucht ein neues Frauenbildungszentrum. Ergänzen Sie die Sätze aus einem Zeitungsartikel mit dem Konjunktiv I.[a]

1. Gestern Abend wurde im Rathaus viel über das neue Zentrum diskutiert. Viele glauben, das alte Zentrum _____ viel zu klein. (sein)
2. Andere meinten, man _____ es einfach renovieren. (sollen)
3. Daraufhin wurde gesagt, dass man das schon seit fünf Jahren _____. (versuchen)
4. Die Stadt _____ nicht länger warten. (können)
5. Das Problem _____ immer schlimmer. (werden)

[a]*subjunctive I*

C Mütter und Töchter. Die Personen im Video beschreiben die Frauenbewegung aus der Perspektive ihrer eigenen Familien. Schreiben Sie die Sätze in der indirekten Rede. Benutzen Sie den Konjunktiv I der Vergangenheit.

JULIA: Anna ist 1944 geboren. Sie hat sich sehr stark für die Frauenbewegung engagiert. Die Frauenbewegung hat Gleichberechtigung in allen Bereichen verlangt, aber in der Praxis ist die völlige Gleichberechtigung noch nicht verwirklicht.

SUSANNE: Für Frauen damals ist es schwieriger gewesen. Meine Mutter hat auch Schwierigkeiten im Beruf gehabt. Sie ist Richterin geworden und anfangs hat man sie nicht ernst genommen. Sie hat schon härter kämpfen müssen als ein Mann in der Position.

INDIRECT QUESTIONS
REPORTING WHAT OTHER PEOPLE ASK

To report what someone asks when that person poses a yes/no question, use the word **ob** (*whether*) and place the verb in either Subjunctive I or II at the end of the clause.

DIRECT QUESTION

Julia fragt Karsten: „**Hast** du den neuen Film gesehen?"
Gürkan fragt sich, „**Ist** eine Lösung möglich?"

INDIRECT QUESTION

Julia fragt Karsten, **ob** er den neuen Film gesehen **habe/hätte.**
Gürkan fragt sich, **ob** eine Lösung möglich **sei/wäre.**

To report what someone asks when the question begins with **wer, was, warum, wann, wo,** or some other question word, simply begin with that word and place the conjugated verb at the end of the clause.

Grace fragt Gürkan, „**Was kann** man gegen Diskriminierung **tun**?"
Grace fragt Gürkan, **was** man gegen Diskriminierung **tun
könne/könnte.**

Übungen

A Meinungen zur Gleichberechtigung. Die Leute im Video stellen sich
viele Fragen. Schreiben Sie die Fragen in der indirekten Rede.

> MODELL: Der Professor fragt Daniela: „Hast du offene
> Diskriminierung persönlich erlebt?" →
> Der Professor fragt Daniela, ob sie offene Diskriminierung
> persönlich erlebt habe.

1. Der Professor fragt Susanne: „Wie ist die Situation für Frauen
   heute?"
2. Grace fragt Gürkan: „Warum gibt es keine Bundeskanzlerin?"
3. Grace fragt Anja: „Was hast du nach der Wende gemacht?"
4. Anja fragt Claudia: „Wie ist deine Tochter aufgewachsen?"
5. Christa fragt Frau Meisel: „Wie kann ich Ihnen helfen?"
6. Christa fragt Herrn Bauer: „Könnte Frau Meisel eine Stunde später
   anfangen?"

A. 1. Der Professor fragt Susanne, wie die Situation für Frauen heute sei. 2. Grace fragt Gürkan, warum es keine Bundeskanzlerin gebe. 3. Grace fragt Anja, was sie nach der Wende gemacht habe. 4. Anja fragt Claudia, wie ihre Tochter aufgewachsen sei. 5. Christa fragt Frau Meisel, wie sie ihr helfen könne. 6. Christa fragt Herrn Bauer, ob Frau Meisel eine Stunde später anfangen könnte.

B Sie sind Polizist/Polizistin geworden. Sie haben gerade Ihre erste
Befragung mit einem Angeklagten gehabt, und Ihr Chef will wissen,
was Sie ihn alles gefragt haben.

> MODELL: Sind Sie gestern Abend zu Hause gewesen? →
> Ich habe ihn gefragt, ob er gestern Abend zu Hause
> gewesen sei.

1. Was haben Sie gestern Abend gemacht?
2. Haben Sie mit jemandem telefoniert?
3. Sind Sie früh ins Bett gegangen?
4. Wohnen Sie bei dieser Adresse?
5. Gehen Sie abends ins Theater?
6. Sind Sie gestern in diesem Theater gewesen?
7. Haben Sie diesen Mann gesehen?

B. 1. Ich habe ihn gefragt, was er gestern Abend gemacht habe. 2. Ich habe ihn gefragt, ob er mit jemandem telefoniert habe. 3. Ich habe ihn gefragt, ob er früh ins Bett gegangen sei. 4. Ich habe ihn gefragt, ob er bei dieser Adresse wohne. 5. Ich habe ihn gefragt, ob er abends ins Theater gehe. 6. Ich habe ihn gefragt, ob er gestern im Theater gewesen sei. 7. Ich habe ihn gefragt, ob er diesen Mann gesehen habe.

REVIEW OF IMPERATIVES
MAKING DIRECT REQUESTS

You have now learned to use all three moods in German: the *indicative*
for talking or writing about facts; the *subjunctive* for expressing polite
requests, unreal situations, wishful thinking, or indirect speech; and the
imperative for making direct requests.

As you recall, the imperative occurs only in all the second-person forms and the first-person plural. To form the **du**-imperative, simply begin the sentence with the conjugated verb without the **-st** ending and without the pronoun.

Du kommst nicht mit.   **Komm** mit!
Du arbeitest zu viel.   **Arbeite** nicht so viel!

Verbs that have the stem-vowel change from **e** to **i** or **ie** also have this change in the **du**-imperative. All other stem-changing verbs retain the vowel of the infinitive in the **du**-imperative.

Du gibst mir die Antwort nicht. **Gib** mir die Antwort!
Du liest die Zeitung nicht. **Lies** die Zeitung!
but: Du schläfst zu lang. **Schlaf** nicht so lang!

To form the **ihr**-imperative, simply use the conjugated verb form at the beginning of the sentence without the pronoun.

Ihr schlaft zu lang. **Schlaft** nicht so lang!
Ihr versprecht mir das nicht. **Versprecht** mir das!

The **ihr**-imperative commonly occurs in commands and exhortations directed at people or society in general.

Rettet den Regenwald! *Save the rainforest!*
Stoppt die Gewalt! *Stop the violence!*

The **Sie**-imperative *does* include the pronoun. Just switch the present-tense form of the verb and pronoun to issue imperative sentences.

Sie sagen mir nicht die Wahrheit. Sagen Sie mir die Wahrheit!
Sie machen das Fenster nicht zu. Machen Sie das Fenster zu!

To offer suggestions to one or more persons and include yourself, use the **wir**-imperative (*let's . . .*). As with the **Sie**-form, include the pronoun but switch its position with the verb to make an imperative rather than an indicative sentence.

Notice that the **Sie**- and **wir**-imperatives match the construction of yes/no questions. Only the punctuation differs and the intonation in speech.

Wir gehen jetzt ins Kino. Gehen wir ins Kino.
Wir machen das zusammen. Machen wir das zusammen!

Kommen Sie mit? Bitte, kommen Sie mit!
Bleiben wir hier? Ja, bleiben wir hier!

As you recall, the particles **doch, mal,** or **doch mal** soften imperative sentences.

Gehen wir doch jetzt. *Why don't we go now?*
Schreibt mal. *Write sometime.*

To request that somebody allow someone else to do something, use the imperative form of the verb **lassen.**

Lass sie das machen.   *Let her do that.*
Lassen Sie ihn fragen.   *Let him ask.*

The verb **sein** has special forms in the imperative.

Sei lieb zu mir!   *Be nice to me.*
Seid pünktlich!   *Be on time.*
Seien Sie bitte etwas höflicher!   *Please be more polite.*
Seien wir nett zueinander!   *Let's be nice to each other.*

Übungen

A Sehenswürdigkeiten

SCHRITT 1: Stellen Sie sich vor, Sie wohnen in Saarbrücken. Raten Sie Ihrem Freund, der Sie besucht, was er alles in der Stadt machen könnte.

MODELL: ins Stadtzentrum gehen →
Geh (doch) mal ins Stadtzentrum.

1. einen Einkaufsbummel am Schlossplatz machen
2. Postkarten kaufen
3. einen Reisebrief schreiben
4. einen Stadtführer lesen
5. ein Theaterstück im Landestheater ansehen
6. nach Frankreich fahren
7. das Saarland-Museum besuchen

SCHRITT 2: Ihr Freund hat seine Freundin mitgebracht. Jetzt raten Sie den beiden, was sie in Saarbrücken machen könnten.

MODELL: ins Stadtzentrum gehen →
Geht (doch) mal ins Stadtzentrum.

B Ein Gespräch mit der Frauenbeauftragten. Sie haben Probleme und brauchen Hilfe von Frau Piper. Weil alles für Sie im Moment so stressig ist, sind Sie nicht besonders höflich. Bilden Sie Sätze im Imperativ.

MODELL: Frau Piper, könnten Sie mir bitte helfen? →
Helfen Sie mir bitte.

1. Könnten Sie mir bitte zuhören?
2. Könnten Sie mir bitte einen Rat geben?
3. Könnten Sie meinen Chef anrufen?
4. Könnten Sie ihm erklären, dass ich zwei kleine Kinder habe?
5. Könnten Sie mir bitte eine Lösung vorschlagen?

Saarbrücken, Hauptstadt des Saarlandes.

A. Schritt 1: 1. Mach (doch mal) einen Einkaufsbummel am Schlossplatz. **2.** Kauf (doch mal) Postkarten. **3.** Schreib (doch mal) einen Reisebrief. **4.** Lies (doch mal) einen Reiseführer. **5.** Schau (doch mal) ein Theaterstück im Landestheater an. **6.** Fahr (doch mal) nach Frankreich. **7.** Besuch (doch mal) das Saarland-Museum.
Schritt 2: 1. Macht (doch mal) einen Einkaufsbummel am Schlossplatz. **2.** Kauft (doch mal) Postkarten. **3.** Schreibt (doch mal) einen Reisebrief. **4.** Lest (doch mal) einen Reiseführer. **5.** Schaut (doch mal) ein Theaterstück im Landestheater an. **6.** Fahrt (doch mal) nach Frankreich. **7.** Besucht (doch mal) das Saarland-Museum.

B. 1. Hören Sie mir bitte zu. **2.** Geben Sie mir bitte einen Rat. **3.** Rufen Sie meinen Chef an. **4.** Erklären Sie ihm, dass ich zwei kleine Kinder habe. **5.** Schlagen Sie mir bitte eine Lösung vor.

PERSPEKTIVEN

HÖREN SIE ZU!
EIN FLUGBLATT AUS EINEM FRAUENBUCHLADEN

A. *Answers will vary.*

A Was meinen Sie? Diskutieren Sie mit Ihren Mitschülern/Mitschülerinnen über das Thema „Frauenbuchladen", bevor Sie den Text hören. Beantworten Sie die folgenden Fragen.

1. Was erwarten Sie von einem Frauenbuchladen?
2. Wofür interessieren sich wohl die Mitarbeiterinnen eines Frauenbuchladen?
3. Welchen Ton oder Stil erwarten Sie in einem Flugblatt über dieses Thema?

B. **1.** b   **2.** b   **3.** a, b und c   **4.** b und c
5. a, b und c

WORTSCHATZ ZUM HÖRTEXT

verändern	to alter, change
überzeugen	to convince
das Verhalten	behavior
die Gleichgültigkeit	indifference
schuld sein	to be at fault
die Schweigsamkeit	silence
unterstützen	to support
der Bruchteil	fraction
das Gesamtvermögen	total wealth
die Leistung	(job) performance
die Mehrfachbelastung	multiple burden
ausliefern	to hand over
die Gewalt mit sprachlichen Mitteln	verbal abuse

B Ergänzen Sie die Sätze 1–5. Passen Sie auf, manchmal gibt es mehr als eine richtige Ergänzung.

1. Der Buchladen will darüber informieren,
   a. wie Frauen Männer im Berufsleben unterdrücken können.
   b. wie Frauen ihre private und berufliche Unterdrückung verändern können.
2. Der Buchladen stellt die Frage,
   a. warum Frauen in östlichen Ländern sich nicht selbstverwirklichen wollen.
   b. warum Frauen in westlichen Ländern, trotz unbegrenzter Möglichkeiten, sich nicht verwirklichen wollen.
3. Der Buchladen gibt zu,
   a. dass sich die Mitarbeiterinnen seit Jahren über die Behandlung von Frauen beklagt haben.
   b. dass die Mitarbeiterinnen kritisiert haben, was „frau" sich so alles gefallen lassen muss.
   c. dass die Mitarbeiterinnen jetzt davon überzeugt sind, dass Frauen an diesem ungerechten Verhalten ihnen gegenüber oft selbst schuld sind.
4. Der Buchladen ermutigt, nicht zu vergessen,
   a. dass Frauen einen großen Teil des Gesamtvermögens in Deutschland besitzen.
   b. dass sogar Mädchen im Durchschnitt acht Mark weniger Taschengeld bekommen als Jungen.
   c. dass auch Lehrerinnen und Erzieherinnen ihre Mädchen und Jungen nicht gleich erziehen oder erzogen haben.

5. Der Buchladen kritisiert,
   a. dass Frauen noch viel zu oft in schlecht bezahlten Berufen arbeiten und weniger verdienen als Männer.
   b. dass die meisten Frauen nicht erkennen, dass sie durch Sprache „machtlos" gemacht werden.
   c. dass Frauen mitmachen müssen, weil sie nonverbal dazu gezwungen werden.

C Vorschläge. Das Flugblatt ist etwas kritisch Frauen gegenüber. Hören Sie den Text noch einmal, und machen Sie sich Notizen. Was können Frauen tun, um ihr Berufs- und Privatleben zu verbessern? Arbeiten Sie in einer Kleingruppe, und schreiben Sie eine Liste von positiven Vorschlägen.

C. *Answers will vary.*

MODELL: Frauen müssen ihre Unterdrückung im Berufs- und Privatleben erkennen!

LESEN SIE!

Answers will vary.

Zum Thema

Assoziationen. Beschreiben Sie die Menschen, die Sie in einem positiven oder negativen Sinn mit jedem Begriff in dem Kasten rechts assoziieren.

MODELL: Emanzipation →

* Frauen, die für ihre Gleichberechtigung in der Gesellschaft und auch für ihre Gleichstellung im Beruf kämpfen
* Männer, die diese Frauen unterstützen wollen
* Männer und Frauen, die den Kampf um weibliche Gleichberechtigung kritisieren und lächerlich machen wollen

> Emanzipation
> Gleichberechtigung
> Demokratie Redefreiheit
> Unterdrückung
> Gleichstellung
> Organisation
> Solidarität

Emanzipation

Vater schlägt einen Nagel in die Wand.

SOHN: Papa! Charly hat gesagt, seine Mutter hat gesagt . . .
VATER: Ach, sieh mal an, hat die auch mal was zu
5 sagen?
SOHN: Wieso?
VATER: Na, bisher habe ich dich noch nie von der Mutter deines Freundes reden hören.
SOHN: Na ja, ich sehe sie ja auch nicht oft. Sie ist ja
10 immer in der Küche beschäftigt. Wie Mama.
VATER: Das ist auch der beste Platz für eine Frau.

SOHN: Aber Charly hat gesagt, seine Mutter hat gesagt, daß sie genug davon hat.
15 Und daß es Zeit wird, daß die Frauen den Männern einmal zeigen, daß sie auch ihren Mann stehen können!
Papa, was meint sie damit?
VATER: Womit?
SOHN: Na, daß Frauen ihren Mann stehen sollen –
20 wenn sie doch Frauen sind?
VATER: Wahrscheinlich hat sie was von Emanzipation gehört.

SOHN: Und was heißt das?

25 VATER: Mein Gott, wie soll ich dir das erklären? Also, paß auf: Die Frauen wollen plötzlich gleichberechtigt sein – das heißt, sie wollen den Männern gleichgestellt sein.

SOHN: Und warum?

VATER: Sie fühlen sich unterdrückt.

30 SOHN: Ja, das hat Charly auch gesagt, daß seine Mutter gesagt hat, sie lasse sich nicht weiter unterdrücken von den Männern.

VATER: Na siehst du!

SOHN: Papa, aber warum unterdrücken die Männer
35 Frauen?

VATER: Aber das tun sie doch gar nicht.

SOHN: Und warum sagt es dann Charlys Mutter?

VATER: Das versuche ich dir doch gerade zu erklären. Irgendeine Frau hat damit angefangen, sich
40 unterdrückt zu fühlen, und nun glauben es die anderen auch und organisieren sich.

SOHN: Und was heißt organisieren? Klauen?

VATER: Mein Gott, nein, hör mir doch zu: sich organisieren heißt, sich zusammentun, eine
45 Gruppe bilden, um sich stark zu fühlen.

SOHN: Und warum muß sich Charlys Mutter stark fühlen?

VATER: Das weiß ich doch nicht. Vielleicht will sie etwas erreichen bei Charlys Vater.

50 SOHN: Und das kann sie nur organisiert?

VATER: Sicher glaubt sie das. Sonst würde sie es ja nicht tun. Das darf man nicht so ernst nehmen.

SOHN: Warum nicht? Wenn es doch die Frauen ernst
55 nehmen?

VATER: Aber das sind doch nur wenige. Gott sei Dank. Eine vernünftige Frau kommt überhaupt nicht auf eine solche Idee.

SOHN: Ist Mama vernünftig?

60 VATER: Aber sicher. Deine Mutter ist viel zu klug, um diesen Unsinn mitzumachen.
Frag sie doch mal.

SOHN: Hab ich schon.

VATER: Na, und was hat sie gesagt?

65 SOHN: Daß sie das alles gar nicht so dumm findet.

VATER: So, hat sie das gesagt? Aber das ist doch etwas anderes.

SOHN: Weil Mama vernünftig ist?

70 VATER: Nein, herrgottnochmal, mußt du dich in deinem Alter mit solchen Fragen beschäftigen?
Mama macht sich nur Gedanken darüber – allein, und ohne nun auf die Barrikaden zu gehen.

75 SOHN: Papa, was heißt: Barrikaden?

Der Vater ist erleichtert, weil er hofft, abgelenkt zu haben.

VATER: Auf die Barrikaden gehen heißt – naja, das ist so eine Redewendung, verstehst du, wenn
80 man lauthals seine Meinung vertritt, ohne eine andere gelten zu lassen.

SOHN: Aber Charly hat gesagt, seine Mutter hat gesagt, daß hier die Frauen überhaupt keine Meinung haben dürfen.

85 VATER: Aber das ist doch Unsinn. Wir leben doch in einer Demokratie. Da kann jeder seine Meinung haben.

SOHN: Auch sagen?

VATER: Natürlich. In einer Demokratie hat man auch
90 Redefreiheit.

SOHN: Und wir leben in einer Demokratie?

VATER: Das sag ich doch.

SOHN: Also können auch Frauen hier ihre Meinung sagen?

95 VATER: Ja. Worauf willst du jetzt wieder hinaus?

SOHN: Naja, wenn das so ist, daß auch Frauen ihre Meinung sagen können, und Charlys Mutter tut das, warum darf sie dann nicht arbeiten gehen?

100 VATER: Wie bitte?
Was hat denn das damit zu tun?

SOHN: Charly hat gesagt, seine Mutter hat gesagt, daß sie gerne wieder arbeiten gehen möchte – und Charlys Vater hat es ihr
105 verboten.

VATER: Das war auch richtig.
Frauen gehören ins Haus, wenn sie verheiratet sind und Kinder haben.

SOHN: Also dürfen Frauen eine Meinung haben und
110 sie auch sagen – aber sie dürfen es dann nicht tun?

VATER: Natürlich nicht. Wo kämen wir da hin, wenn jeder das täte, was er wollte?

SOHN: Also darf Mama auch nicht einfach tun, wozu sie Lust hat?

15

VATER: Nein. Ich kann auch nicht immer tun, wozu ich Lust habe! Schließlich muß ich das Geld verdienen, um dich und Mama zu ernähren.

SOHN: Kann Mama sich nicht selbst ernähren?

20 VATER: Nicht so gut wie ich, weil Mama weniger verdienen würde, weil sie nicht einen Beruf gelernt hat wie ich. Deshalb verdiene ich das Geld, und Mama macht die Arbeit im Hause.

SOHN: Kriegt sie denn Geld dafür von dir?

125 VATER: Nein, natürlich nicht so direkt, indirekt aber doch.

SOHN: Und wenn sie was braucht, muß sie dich fragen.

VATER: Ja.

130 SOHN: Weil – wenn sie was kaufen will, braucht sie Geld.

VATER: Ja.

SOHN: Und wenn sie damit in ein Geschäft geht, kann sie auch etwas dafür verlangen.

135 VATER: Jaaa.

SOHN: Papa – hast du Mama auch gekauft?

Ingeburg Kanstein

Zum Text

A Vater und Sohn haben in ihrem Gespräch viele Themen erwähnt. Welche Themen der folgenden Liste wurden angesprochen und welche nicht?

Emanzipation, Gleichberechtigung, Gleichstellung, Menschenrechte, Gedankenfreiheit, Unterdrückung, Benachteiligung, Organisationen, Barrikaden, Gewalt, Demokratie, Redefreiheit, Bevormundung,[a] Rassismus, Solidarität, Antisemitismus, Gleichbehandlung, Engagement,[b] Eigeninitiative

[a]patronage [b]commitment

B Das Gespräch. Was hat Charlys Mutter wirklich gesagt? Schreiben Sie in der direkten Rede.

MODELL: Charlys Mutter sagt, „Ich habe genug davon!"

C Die Rolle der Frau. Was ist die Meinung des Vaters im Text über die Rolle der Frau in der Familie und der Gesellschaft? Machen Sie eine Liste mit Zitaten, die seine Meinung am besten ausdrücken.

D Ein Dialog. Schreiben Sie einen Dialog zwischen Charlys Mutter und dem Vater. Lassen Sie die beiden Partner über Emanzipation, Gleichberechtigung in der Ehe, Gleichstellung und Meinungsfreiheit diskutieren. D. *Dialogues will vary.*

Zur Interpretation

Was sagen der Vater und der Sohn und was meinen sie? Wie interpretieren Sie den Unterschied? Diskutieren Sie die folgenden Zeilen mit Ihren Mitschülern/Mitschülerinnen, und suchen Sie weitere Textbeispiele. *Answers will vary.*

WORTSCHATZ ZUM LESEN

bisher	up to now
plötzlich	suddenly
klauen	to steal
vernünftig	rational; reasonable
der Unsinn	craziness
erleichtert	relieved
die Redewendung	figure of speech
lauthals	at the top of one's voice

A. angesprochene Themen: Emanzipation, Gleichberechtigung, Gleichstellung, Unterdrückung, Organisation, Barrikaden, Demokratie, Redefreiheit

B. Charlys Mutter sagt: „Ich habe genug davon." „Es wird Zeit, dass die Frauen den Männern einmal zeigen, dass sie auch ihren Mann stehen können." „Ich lasse mich nicht weiter unterdrücken von den Männern." „Die Frauen dürfen hier überhaupt keine Meinung haben." „Ich möchte gerne wieder arbeiten gehen."

C. *Possible answers are:* Die Küche ist der beste Platz für eine Frau. Eine vernünftige Frau kommt nicht auf die Idee, sich zu organisieren und auf die Barrikaden zu gehen. Frauen gehören ins Haus, wenn sie verheiratet sind und Kinder haben. Frauen bekommen für ihre Arbeit im Haus kein Geld. Sie müssen ihre Männer fragen, wenn sie Geld brauchen.

MODELL: SOHN: Charly hat gesagt, seine Mutter hat gesagt . . .
VATER: . . . hat die auch mal was zu sagen?

Interpretation: Der Sohn zitiert die Mutter seines Freundes. Der Vater impliziert, dass die Mutter sonst nicht viel sagt, oder dass sie nicht sehr intelligent ist.

SOHN: Ja, das hat Charly auch gesagt, dass seine Mutter gesagt hat, sie lasse sich nicht weiter unterdrücken von den Männern.
VATER: Na siehst du!
SOHN: Papa, aber warum unterdrücken die Männer Frauen?

INTERAKTION

Answers will vary.

● Eine Debatte. Arbeiten Sie in Gruppen. Stimmt die These unten, oder stimmt sie nicht? Die Hälfte der Gruppe sucht nach Argumenten, die die These stützen, die andere Hälfte sucht nach Argumenten dagegen. Diskutieren Sie anschließend alle gemeinsam die These mit Hilfe der gefundenen Pro- und Contra-Argumente.

Frauen sind gleichberechtigt. Das Thema Frauengleichberechtigung ist nicht mehr aktuell.

SCHREIBEN SIE!

Was denken sie wohl?

Texts will vary.

● Sehen Sie sich diese drei historischen Fotos an, die die Rollen und Aufgaben von Frauen in der Vergangenheit darstellen. Versetzen Sie sich in die Rolle von diesen Frauen. Lesen Sie ihre Gedanken: Was haben sie in diesen Situationen wohl gefühlt, gedacht und gesagt? Berichten Sie die Gedanken und Aussagen jeder dieser Frauen mit mindestens drei Sätzen in der indirekten Rede.

Purpose:	To report what someone else felt, said, or thought
Audience:	Students of history and gender studies
Subject:	Women of the past
Structure:	Photo captions

Schreibmodell

1

2

3

Subjunctive I is used to report what the woman is thinking.

The writer lets the reader know which woman he/she is referring to.

Bild 1. Die Frau, die hinter der Tischlampe steht, denkt wohl, sie müsse jetzt einer anderen Frau helfen.

Bild 2. Sie überlegt wohl, sie habe so viele Kinder und zu wenig Hilfe im Haushalt.

Bild 3. Die vierte Frau von vorne links, die eine Brille trägt, fragt sich wohl, ob sie etwas vergessen habe.

Here the writer reports what the woman asks herself. Subjunctive is used for such indirect questions.

Schreibstrategien

Vor dem Schreiben

- Think about the photos on page 133, considering the historical conditions and circumstances under which the women lived.

- Make a rough sketch of each photo on a blank sheet of paper. Number each sketch with the number of the photo.

- Working with a partner, label every object in the photos to the best of your ability. If it is helpful, invent names for the people.

- After labelling all objects and people, write below or next to each sketch verbs that describe the actions and activities depicted.

- Review the nouns and verbs you've used and think of additional descriptive words (adjectives or adverbs) that would provide more information. Write them down next to the appropriate noun or verb.

- Continuing to work with your partner, pretend each of you is the central person in each photo and that the time in the photo is the present. Together, generate as many present-tense first person "I" statements as you can for each photo. Write the sentences down.

Beim Schreiben

- Now working on your own, write at least three sentences in indirect discourse for each photo. You can report random, disconnected thoughts one by one, or you may write a short connected paragraph of continuing thoughts. Remember that you are reporting what you believe these women might have felt, thought, or said. Label the statements or paragraph for each photo with the number that appears next to the photo in the book.

- Check over what you have written. Be sure you have not written actual quotations, but rather indirect statements of what the women said in present or past subjunctive.

- Finally, write a suitable title for each photograph on your sketch.

Nach dem Schreiben

- Check over what you've written for accuracy and appropriateness. Trade statements or paragraphs with a classmate. Give your partner feedback on his/her statements.

Stimmt alles?

- Prepare a final draft of your titles and indirect statements, writing or typing them on a separate piece of paper. Be sure it is clear which statements go with which picture. Put the paper(s) with the statements together with your photo sketches and sentences.

- Be sure your name is on your work and hand it in.

Bild 1. Das Mädchen, daß vor dem Tisch auf dem Boden sitzt, denkt wohl, sie spielt lieber Klavier.

Bild 2. Sie sagt die den Kinder, sie brauchte ihre Hilfe.

Bild 3. Die Frau, die rechts neben dem Mann sitzt, denke wohl, sie macht diese Arbeit nicht gern.

WORTSCHATZ

Substantive	Nouns
die **Emanzipation**	emancipation
die **Frauenbewegung, -en**	women's movement
die **Gedankenfreiheit**	freedom of thought
die **Kinderkrippe, -n**	daycare center
die **Minderheit, -en**	minority
die **Redefreiheit**	freedom of speech
die **Reihe, -n**	row; series
der **Richter, -** / die **Richterin, -nen**	judge
die **Schwierigkeit, -en**	difficulty
der/die **Abgeordnete** (*decl. adj.*)	delegate; member of parliament
der/die **Angeklagte** (*decl. adj.*)	defendant
der **Beitrag, ̈e**	contribution
der **Hintergrund, ̈e**	background
das **Menschenrecht, -e**	human right
das **Wahlrecht**	right to vote, suffrage

Verben	Verbs
behandeln	to treat
behüten	to protect
benachteiligen	to place at a disadvantage
beschimpfen	to insult
beschuldigen	to accuse
besitzen, besaß, besessen	to possess, own
betrachten	to consider; regard
betreuen	to look after

emanzipieren	to emancipate
erreichen	to reach
gelten lassen (lässt gelten), ließ gelten, gelten lassen	to approve of something; to agree
gestatten	to allow
kämpfen	to struggle; to fight
sich kümmern um	to concern oneself with
leiten	to lead
lösen	to loosen
sich organisieren	to organize oneself
unterdrücken	to suppress
wollen: auf etwas hinaus wollen	to imply something; to have a certain goal

Adjektive und Adverbien	Adjectives and adverbs
allein erziehend	single parenting
anfangs	at first
gleichberechtigt sein	to have equal rights
gleichgestellt sein	to be at an equal level
jedenfalls	in any case
obwohl	although

Sie wissen schon	You already know
die **Gleichberechtigung**	equality

PLANNING GUIDE
CLASSROOM MANAGEMENT

OBJECTIVES

Communication
- Talk about political rights for women, p. 139.

Grammar
- Review subjunctive forms, pp. 139–140.
- Use the comparative, p. 140.
- Review indirect discourse, pp. 140–141.

Culture
- Learn about Heidelberg, p. 137.
- Learn about foreign students in Germany, p. 137.
- Read a short story, p. 141.

PROGRAM RESOURCES

Print
- *Arbeitsheft* (Workbook), pp. 97–100
- *Arbeitsheft* (Workbook), Teacher's Edition, pp. 97–100

Audiovisual
- Overhead Transparencies 28.1, 28.G1–28.3, 29.G1, and 30.G1
- Audio Program, Cassette 3B/CD 4
- Audioscript, pp. 43–45

Technology
- Annenberg *Fokus Deutsch* Video Series, *Wiederholung 10*
- www.mcdougallittell.com

Assessment Program Options
- *Prüfung, Wiederholung 10*, Assessment Program, pp. 74–83
- Audio Program, Cassette 8A/CD 10
- Audioscript, p. 11
- Teacher's Resource CD-ROM

PACING GUIDE
50-MINUTE SCHEDULE

 DAY 1

 DAY 2

DAY 1

Note: (1) Please see TE, pp. 136C–136D, for other suggestions not referenced in these plans. (2) Not all homework options need be assigned.

VIDEOTHEK
- Quick Start Review: Vocabulary (TE, p. 136C). 5 MIN
- Do *Akt. A*, p. 136, silently, then discuss answers as a class (TE, p. 136C). 17 MIN
- Read through *Akt. B*, p. 137, and play the episode. Discuss (TE, p. 136C). 10 MIN
- Watch the episode and discuss answers to *Akt. C*, p. 137, in groups. 6 MIN
- Do *Akt. D*, p. 137, *Schritt 1*, then discuss. 3 MIN

VOKABELN
- *Akt. A*, p. 138, and follow-up activity (TE, p. 136D). 9 MIN

Homework Options:
- *Videothek, Akt. D, Schritt 2*, p. 137
- *Arbeitsheft*, p. 98, *Vokabeln, Akt. C*

DAY 2

VOKABELN
- Quick Start Review: Indirect discourse (TE, p. 136C). 5 MIN
- Have students do *Akt. B*, p. 138, silently, then check answers with a partner. Follow the Teaching Suggestions for a follow-up (TE, p. 136C). 13 MIN
- Have students do *Akt. C*, p. 139, in pairs (TE, p. 136C). 10 MIN
- Have students choose one statement to explain and share their results to *Akt. C*, p. 139. 7 MIN

STRUKTUREN
- Follow the Teaching Suggestions for a warm-up activity for *Übung A*, p. 139 (TE, p. 136D). 5 MIN
- *Übung A*, p. 139. 10 MIN

Homework Options:
- *Übung E*, pp. 140–141
- *Arbeitsheft*, p. 100, *Strukturen, Akt. D*

PACING GUIDE
50-MINUTE SCHEDULE

DAY 3

STRUKTUREN

- Quick Start Review: Imperatives (TE, p. 136D). 6 MIN
- *Übung B,* p. 140. Have students share their answers. Follow the Teaching Suggestions for the expansion activity (TE, p. 136D). 10 MIN
- Do the warm-up activity (TE, p. 136D), then do *Übung C,* p. 140, in pairs. 10 MIN
- Do *Übung D,* p. 140, as a class. 10 MIN

PERSPEKTIVEN

- Follow the Teaching Suggestions for *Akt. A,* p. 141 (TE, p. 136D). 14 MIN

Homework Options:

- *Arbeitsheft,* p. 100, *Strukturen, Akt. B–C*

DAY 4

PERSPEKTIVEN

- Quick Start Review: Vocabulary (TE, p. 136D). 5 MIN
- Have students do *Akt. B,* p. 141, in small groups and then compare lists with the class (TE, p. 136D). 10 MIN
- Questions and review. 5 MIN
- *Prüfung, Wiederholung 10.* 30 MIN

Homework Options:

- Finish *Perspektiven, Akt. A,* p. 141

PACING GUIDE
90-MINUTE SCHEDULE

DAY 1

Note: (1) Please see TE, pp. 136C–136D, for other suggestions not referenced in these plans. (2) Not all homework options need be assigned.

VIDEOTHEK

- Quick Start Review: Vocabulary (TE, p. 136C). 5 MIN
- Do *Akt. A–C,* p. 136 (TE, p. 136C). 28 MIN
- Do *Akt. D, Schritt 1,* p. 137, as a class. 7 MIN

VOKABELN

- Block Schedule activity: Recycle (TE, p. 136C). 10 MIN
- *Akt. A–C,* pp. 138–139 (TE, p. 136C). 25 MIN

STRUKTUREN

- Do *Übung A,* p. 139 (TE, p. 136D). 15 MIN

Homework Options:

- *Videothek, Akt. D, Schritt 2,* p. 137
- *Arbeitsheft,* p. 98, *Vokabeln, Akt. C* and p. 100, *Strukturen, Akt. B–C*

DAY 2

STRUKTUREN

- Quick Start Review: Imperatives (TE, p. 136D). 5 MIN
- Do *Übung B,* p. 140, and the expansion activity (TE, p. 136D). 10 MIN
- Do *Übung C,* p. 140, in pairs, including the warmup (TE, p. 136D). 9 MIN
- *Übung D,* p. 140 (TE, p. 136C). 10 MIN
- Block Schedule activity: Peer Teaching (TE, p. 136D). 10 MIN

PERSPEKTIVEN

- Do *Akt. A,* p. 141 (TE, p. 136D). 11 MIN
- Questions and review. 5 MIN
- *Prüfung, Wiederholung 10.* 30 MIN

Homework Options:

- *Übung E,* pp. 140–141
- *Arbeitsheft,* p. 100, *Strukturen, Akt. D*
- *Perspektiven, Akt. A,* p. 141

TEACHING SUGGESTIONS

Videothek, pp. 136–137

PROGRAM RESOURCES

- Videocassette, *Wiederholung 10*
- Overhead Transparency 28.1
- *Arbeitsheft*, p. 97
- Audio Program, Cassette 3B/CD 4
- Audioscript, p. 43

Quick Start Review

♻ Vocabulary

Welches dieser Wörter passen zu den Definitionen?

WÖRTER: a. das Wahlrecht
b. gleichberechtigt sein   c. für jemanden sorgen   d. die Minderheit
  1. die gleichen Rechte haben
  2. sich kümmern um
  3. das Recht, wählen zu können
  4. eine kleinere Zahl als die Mehrheit

Answers: 1. b   2. c   3. a   4. d

TEACHING SUGGESTIONS

- *Aktivität B*, p. 137

Ask *Was hat Ihnen an Heidelberg am besten gefallen? War jemand schon mal in Heidelberg? in einer anderen deutschen Universitätsstadt?*

TEACHING ALL STUDENTS

Multiple Intelligences Intrapersonal: After watching the 2 video segments in each chapter (28, 29, and 30) have students choose the 3 they liked best and write a 5-sentence summary of each.

CLASSROOM COMMUNITY

Dictation Read the following text. Have students write down only the verbs they hear. Can they summarize the text? *Grace fragt Gürkan, warum es keine Bundeskanzlerin gebe. Gürkan*

antwortet, dass das ja in den nächsten Jahren passieren könne. Grace und Gürkan haben unterschiedliche Vorstellungen von der Rolle der Frau in der Gesellschaft. Es ist nicht ganz leicht zu verstehen, was Gürkan wirklich meint, wenn er sagt, für ihn seien Frauen einfach süß.

BLOCK SCHEDULE

Process Time Have students work in groups to re-enact video scenes.

PROJECT

Have students research summer work or study opportunities in Germany and give a report for the class.

RUBRIC   A = 13–15 pts.   B = 10–12 pts.
C = 7–9 pts.   D = 4–6 pts.   F < 4 pts.

Writing Criteria	Scale				
Content	1	2	3	4	5
Presentation	1	2	3	4	5
Grammar and vocabulary	1	2	3	4	5

Vokabeln, pp. 138–139

PROGRAM RESOURCES

- *Arbeitsheft*, p. 98
- Audio Program, Cassette 3B/CD 4
- Audioscript, pp. 43–44

Quick Start Review

♻ Indirect discourse

Setzen Sie die Sätze in die indirekte Rede. (Konjunktiv I Formen).
  1. Er sagte: Ich komme nicht mit.
  2. Sie antwortete: Dann bleibe ich auch da.
  3. Der Lehrer erklärte: Die halbe Klasse ist krank und wir schreiben keinen Test.

  4. Sie sagte: Ich muss noch arbeiten.
  5. Er sagte: Ich habe kein Interesse daran.

Answers: 1. Er sagte, er käme nicht mit.   2. Sie antwortete, dann bleibe sie auch da.   3. Der Lehrer erklärte, die halbe Klasse sei krank und sie schrieben keinen Test.   4. Sie sagte, sie müsse noch arbeiten.   5. Er sagte, er habe kein Interesse daran.

TEACHING SUGGESTIONS

- *Aktivität C*, p. 139

Follow-up: Have students write similar statements reflecting their own situations. Male students could try to write from their mothers' perspectives.

TEACHING ALL STUDENTS

Extra Help Before doing the activities in the *Vokabeln* section, have the class brainstorm vocabulary related to each activity with books closed.

CLASSROOM COMMUNITY

Group Activity Find out what students remember about the following subjects from the video: *die Universität Heidelberg, Monika Schneider, Guy, Christa Piper, Julia.*

BLOCK SCHEDULE

Recycle Vocabulary Game: Have students consult the vocabulary lists on pp. 80, 100, and 120, choose 2 vocabulary items, and write their definitions on slips of paper. Students exchange slips with a partner, who must supply the word that is defined.

Strukturen, pp. 139–141

PROGRAM RESOURCES

- Overhead Transparencies 28.G1–28.G3, 29.G1, and 30.G1
- *Arbeitsheft*, pp. 99–100
- Audio Program, Cassette 3B/CD 4
- Audioscript, pp. 44–45

Quick Start Review

♻ Imperatives

Machen Sie Imperative aus den folgenden Sätzen in die indirekten Rede.

MODELL: Hans sagt, Peter solle ihm die Tasche geben. → *Peter, gib mir die Tasche.*

1. Karin sagt, Petra solle sie anrufen.
2. Herr Schmidt sagt, morgen sollten alle Schüler Geld mitbringen.
3. Helge sagt, Karin solle doch bitte mitkommen.
4. Mutter sagt, Kerstin solle die Tür schließen.
5. Mein Freund sagt, ich solle mehr lernen.

Answers: 1. Petra, ruf mich an! 2. Bringt morgen alle Geld mit! 3. Karin, komm doch bitte mit! 4. Kerstin, schließ die Tür! 5. Lern mehr!

TEACHING SUGGESTIONS

- *Übung C, p. 140*

Warm-up: Have students think of pairs of nouns (*Orangensaft-Apfelsaft, Deutsch-Spanisch*). Have them compare the nouns in various ways: *Orangensaft schmeckt besser als Apfelsaft. Ich kann wenger Deutsch als Spanisch.*

TEACHING ALL STUDENTS

Multiple Intelligences Kinesthetic: Have students act out the following:

Gehen Sie,

1. als ob Sie sehr müde wären
2. als ob Sie sehr alt wären
3. als ob Sie etwas Schweres trügen
4. als ob Sie ein Seiltänzer wären
5. als ob Sie durch Wasser laufen müssten

The student who understands the commands scores a point.

CLASSROOM COMMUNITY

Group Activity Write the following sentences on the board: *Das hättest du viel früher tun sollen. Jetzt ist es zu spät. Wenn ich das vorher gewusst hätte, wäre ich nicht mitgekommen. Was für eine tolle Überraschung! Das hätte ich nicht gedacht!* After writing each sentence, have students guess the kind of situation in which these statements could have been made.

BLOCK SCHEDULE

Peer Teaching Have students work together in groups or pairs to review the *Strukturen* explanations and *Übungen* in Chapters 28–30.

Perspektiven, p. 141

PROGRAM RESOURCES

- Audio Program, Cassette 3B/CD 4
- www.mcdougallittell.com

Quick Start Review

♻ Vocabulary

Ergänzen Sie die Sätze.

WÖRTER: allein erziehende, beschuldigen, Beitrag, Angeklagte, lösen, Abgeordneten

1. Warum musst du mich immer _____?
2. Die Grünen haben viele Frauen unter ihren _____ im Parlament.
3. _____ _____ Eltern müssen sich um vieles kümmern.
4. Hast du eine Idee, wie wir das Problem _____ könnten?

Answers: 1. beschuldigen 2. Abgeordneten 3. Allein erziehende 4. lösen

TEACHING SUGGESTIONS

- *Aktivität A, p. 141*

Read this story aloud while students' books are closed. Have them identify the main idea and some details. Then have them read the story and summarize it in chain fashion, each student adding 1–2 more details.

- *Aktivität B, p. 141*

This short story, or fable, is based on an ancient piece of wisdom: *Wer spart, hat in der Not auch was zu knabbern.* Have students make up their own *Weisheiten.*

TEACHING ALL STUDENTS

Multiple Intelligences Intrapersonal: Have students write a short paragraph about the topics presented in the last 3 chapters. What did they enjoy, what did they find superfluous? Do they feel that they learned a lot about Germany?

CLASSROOM COMMUNITY

Paired Activity Have students quiz each other on the vocabulary lists in Chapters 28–30. Have them list the words they found difficult to learn and write definitions for them.

BLOCK SCHEDULE

Change of Pace Collect various items (pencils, books, erasers, calculators). Put everything in a bag and have students grab something blindly, then speculate what they are holding. For example, *Es könnte ein Bleistift sein oder auch ein Füller.*

VIDEOTHEK

A Studium, Arbeit, Gleichberechtigung. Können Sie sich erinnern, wer was sagt?

a. Stefan

b. Erika

c. Gürkan

d. Julia

e. Guy

f. Anja

A. 1. d   2. e   3. b   4. f   5. c   6. a

1. „Obwohl die Frauenbewegung viel erreicht hat, ist diese Forderung noch nicht Wirklichkeit geworden."
2. „Merkwürdig ist, dass man hier beim Essen nur mit Menschen redet, die man kennt."
3. „Jeden Morgen fahre ich mit dem Auto in mein Atelier und male den ganzen Tag lang."
4. „Viele meiner Verwandten sind arbeitslos und sie haben ihre Arbeit verloren, nachdem die Mauer gefallen ist."
5. „Also Frauen, die sind einfach süß für mich. Das ist der Mittelpunkt von eigentlich allen Männern."
6. „Besonders in der Schweiz sind die Leute alarmiert. Die Schweizer haben die Tendenz, alles zu übertreiben."

B. 1. Die Universität Heidelberg wurde im vierzehnten Jahrhundert gegründet. **2.** Heidelberg liegt am Neckar. **3.** Max Weber, Robert Wilhelm Bunsen, Karl Jaspers **4.** Robert Wilhelm Bunsen hat den Bunsenbrenner erfunden. **5.** *Answers will vary.*

B Geschichte einer Universität. Was wissen Sie über Heidelberg?

1. In welchem Jahrhundert wurde die Universität Heidelberg gegründet?
2. An welchem Fluss ist die Stadt Heidelberg zu finden?
3. Können Sie einige berühmte Leute nennen, die in Heidelberg gelehrt haben?
4. Was hat Robert Bunsen erfunden?
5. In den sechziger Jahren gab es viele Proteste in Heidelberg. Stichworte waren „demokratisieren", „Modernisierung" und „Reform". Denken Sie an diese Stichworte und erklären Sie, warum sie sehr wichtig für die Universitäten und die Gesellschaft in Deutschland waren.

Die Universitätsstadt Heidelberg.

C Ein Student aus Kamerun. Erinnern Sie sich an die Geschichte von Guy und sein Studium in Aachen. Ergänzen Sie die Fragen. **C.** *Answers will vary.*

1. Guy isst in der Mensa, weil . . .
2. Guy studiert . . .
3. Aachen ist anders als die Städte in Kamerun, weil . . .
4. Guy ist glücklich in Deutschland, weil . . .
5. Guy vermisst das Leben in Kamerun, weil . . .

D Hilfe für Arbeitslose

SCHRITT 1: Wer ist Monika Schneider? Sie haben Monika schon kennen gelernt. Was wissen Sie noch über sie?

1. Was macht Monika beruflich?
2. Was macht sie an einem typischen Tag?
3. Warum sitzt sie nicht den ganzen Tag in ihrem Büro?

Guy mit Robert in der Mensa.

SCHRITT 2: Anzeigen. Wer braucht Hilfe?

1. Herr Kloos sucht eine Apothekenhelferin. Schreiben Sie eine Anzeige für eine Apothekenhelferin.
2. Herr Lebendig sucht einen Groß- und Außenhandelskaufmann. Schreiben Sie eine Anzeige für einen Groß- und Außenhandelskaufmann.

Monika fährt mit der Straßenbahn zur Arbeit.

D. Schritt 1: *Possible answers are:* **1.** Monika Schneider ist Arbeitsvermittlerin von Beruf. **2.** Sie spricht mit Arbeitsuchenden. Außerdem besucht sie Arbeitgeber, die eine freie Stelle gemeldet haben. **3.** Frau Schneider sitzt nicht den ganzen Tag im Büro, weil sie sich zum Beispiel die angebotenen Arbeitsplätze selber anschaut und mit den Arbeitgebern spricht, um genau zu erfahren, was der Bewerber können muss. Außerdem bringt Frau Schneider Arbeitgebern auch die Unterlagen der Bewerber.
Schritt 2: *Texts for ads will vary.*

VOKABELN

A Definitionen. Welche Definition passt zu welchem Ausdruck?

1. die Erfahrung
2. der Kreis
3. der Begriff
4. umwechseln
5. sich befinden
6. sich gewöhnen an
7. allmählich
8. merkwürdig
9. gemeinsam

a. ungewöhnlich
b. eine Idee oder ein Ausdruck
c. ändern
d. ein Erlebnis, eine Kenntnis
e. eine Gruppe von Personen, die ähnliche Ziele haben
f. an einer Stelle oder einem Ort sein
g. zusammen
h. etwas nicht mehr als fremd oder unheimlich betrachten
i. schrittweise

B Was passt? Ergänzen Sie die Sätze mit den richtigen Formen der Wörter im Kasten.

> die Entwicklung   überlegen   zwingen
> gering   der Termin   unentbehrlich
> selbstständig   bestimmen   die Fähigkeit

1. Studenten, die im Studentenwohnheim wohnen, fühlen sich öfter _____ als die Studenten, die immer noch bei den Eltern leben.
2. Nachdem Monika Schneider eine Arbeitsstelle gefunden hat, ruft sie den Arbeitssuchenden an, um einen _____ zu machen.
3. Susanne _____, ob sie in den USA oder England studieren soll.
4. Die sozialen _____ haben es möglich gemacht, dass junge Leute jetzt zwischen verschiedenen Lebensstilen wählen können.
5. Eine gute Ausbildung ist für den heutigen Arbeitsmarkt _____.
6. Arbeitssuchende müssen heute verschiedene Talente und _____ haben.
7. Frauen im neunzehnten Jahrhundert wurden _____, zu Hause zu bleiben und sich um die Kinder zu kümmern.
8. Die Zahl der Frauen in leitenden Positionen bleibt immer noch _____.
9. Vor 1900 hatten Arbeiter fast keine Möglichkeit, ihre Arbeitsbedingungen zu _____.

C Partnerarbeit. Führen Sie die folgenden Meinungen zum Thema „Gleichberechtigung" weiter. Die Wörter im Kasten stehen Ihnen zur Verfügung.

C. *Discussions will vary.*

> JULIA: „Für mich ist heute vieles selbstverständlich, was früher nicht selbstverständlich war, also zum Beispiel überhaupt nicht für meine Urgroßmutter, für meine Oma nicht und für meine Mutter auch noch nicht."
>
> SUSANNE: „Ja, ich glaube, für meine Mutter war es damals schwieriger. Noch schwieriger als für die Frauen heute, denn das sollte nicht heißen, dass es jetzt für die Frauen wahnsinnig toll ist und gleichberechtigt heutzutage, ist es immer noch nicht so."
>
> CHRISTA PIPER: „Natürlich kann ich nicht alle Probleme lösen. Es geht darum, bessere Rahmenbedingungen für Frauen herzustellen. Dazu brauchen wir die Gemeinsamkeit und Solidarität von Frauen und Männern."

---

die Emanzipation   der Beitrag   benachteiligen

betreuen   kämpfen

das Menschenrecht   die Frauenbewegung

die Schwierigkeit   alleinerziehend   behandeln

gleichgestellt   unterdrücken

STRUKTUREN

A Mark hat viele Wünsche. Ergänzen Sie seine Wunschsätze mit den Verben in Klammern. Benutzen Sie den Konjunktiv.

A. **1.** wäre **2.** könnte **3.** hätte **4.** ließen **5.** führen **6.** gäbe

1. Wenn ich nur reich _____! (sein)
2. Wenn ich nur in Heidelberg studieren _____! (können)
3. Wenn ich nur mehr Zeit _____! (haben)
4. Wenn meine Eltern mir nur mehr Freizeit _____! (lassen)
5. Wenn wir nur nicht jeden Sommer nach Österreich _____! (fahren)
6. Wenn mein Vater mir nur mehr Taschengeld _____! (geben)

B. 1. Wenn du genug Geld hättest, würdest du dir eine Flugkarte kaufen. **2.** Wenn ich genug Geld hätte, würde ich in einem teuren Hotel übernachten. **3.** Wenn das Wetter schön wäre, würden wir an die Küste fahren. **4.** Wenn ihr genug Energie hättet, würdet ihr eine lange Wanderung mit mir machen. **5.** Wenn meine Freunde Spanisch könnten, würden sie viele neue Freunde treffen.

C. 1. Welcher Lohn ist höher? **2.** Welche Stelle ist besser? **3.** Welcher Arbeitsplatz ist sicherer? **4.** Welche Arbeitszeit ist kürzer? **5.** Welche Arbeit ist anstrengender? **6.** In welcher Firma gibt es bessere Aufstiegsmöglichkeiten?

Ein Gespräch mit Herrn Weinart.

D. 1. In Konstanz war das Wetter am schönsten. **2.** In Halle waren die Hotels am billigsten. **3.** In Berlin waren die Menschen am freundlichsten. **4.** In Hamburg waren die Nächte am kältesten. **5.** In Bayern waren die Berge am höchsten. **6.** In Düsseldorf war das Bier am besten. **7.** In Köln redeten die Menschen am schnellsten. **8.** Ich wohne am liebsten hier.

E. 1. Michael sagte, er gehe nach Hause. **2.** Er fragte Claudia, ob sie mitkomme. **3.** Claudia antwortete, sie wolle ihr Buch zu Ende lesen. **4.** Michael fragte sie, was für ein Buch sie lese. **5.** Claudia sagte, das Buch heiße „Das andere Geschlecht" und sei sehr interessant.

B Susanne spricht mit ihren Freunden und träumt von einer Reise nach Spanien. Gebrauchen Sie **wenn** und die **würde**-Konstruktion, um neue Sätze zu bilden.

MODELL: Wir haben eine Woche frei. Wir machen die Reise. →
Wenn wir eine Woche frei hätten, würden wir die Reise machen.

1. Du hast genug Geld. Du kaufst dir eine Flugkarte.
2. Ich habe genug Geld. Ich übernachte in einem teuren Hotel.
3. Das Wetter ist schön. Wir fahren an die Küste.
4. Ihr habt genug Energie. Ihr macht lange Wanderungen mit mir.
5. Meine Freunde können Spanisch. Sie werden viele neue Freunde finden.

C Beim Vorstellungsgespräch. Frau Schneider hat zwei neue Stellen für Herrn Weinart gefunden. Er möchte die beiden Stellen vergleichen. Bilden Sie Fragen mit dem Komparativ.

MODELL: FRAU SCHNEIDER: Beide Firmen sind ziemlich groß. →
HERR WEINART: Welche Firma ist größer?

1. Der Lohn ist hoch.
2. Die Stelle ist gut.
3. Der Arbeitsplatz ist sicher.
4. Die Arbeitszeit ist kurz.
5. Die Arbeit ist anstrengend.
6. In dieser Firma gibt es gute Aufstiegsmöglichkeiten.

D Reisebericht. Sie sind gerade von einer Reise nach Deutschland zurückgekommen. Sagen Sie, wo alles am schönsten oder am besten war.

MODELL: Die Läden in München waren teuer. →
In München waren die Läden am teuersten.

1. Das Wetter in Konstanz war schön.
2. Die Hotels in Halle waren billig.
3. Die Menschen in Berlin waren freundlich.
4. Die Nächte in Hamburg waren kalt.
5. Die Berge in Bayern waren hoch.
6. Das Bier in Düsseldorf war gut.
7. Die Menschen in Köln redeten schnell.
8. Ich wohne gern hier.

E In der Frauenbuchhandlung. Claudia und Michael verbringen den Nachmittag in der Buchhandlung. Michael muss jetzt nach Hause gehen. Setzen Sie das Gespräch zwischen Michael und Claudia in die indirekte Rede.

MODELL: Claudia sagte, „Ich habe viel Zeit zu lesen.“ →
Claudia sagte, sie habe viel Zeit zu lesen.

1. Michael sagte, „Ich gehe nach Hause.“
   Michael sagte, _____.
2. Er fragte Claudia, „Kommst du mit?“
   Er fragte Claudia, ob _____.
3. Claudia antwortete, „Ich will mein Buch
   zu Ende lesen.“
   Claudia antwortete, _____.
4. Michael fragte sie, „Was für ein Buch
   liest du?“
   Michael fragte sie, _____.
5. Claudia sagte, „Das Buch heißt „Das andere
   Geschlecht“ und ist sehr interessant.“
   Claudia sagte, _____.

A. Stories will vary.

PERSPEKTIVEN

A Sie lesen jetzt eine Kurzgeschichte von Franz Josef Bogner. Wovon
handelt wohl die Geschichte? Welche Jahreszeit ist es? Sehen Sie sich
dann das Bild an, und schreiben Sie eine kleine Geschichte über diese
Szene.

WORTSCHATZ ZUM LESEN

das Vertrauen	*trust*
das Sparkonto	*savings account*
die Weisheit	*wisdom*
der Vorrat	*reserve; provision*
aufzehren	*to eat up*
umkommen	*to perish*
verdauen	*to digest*
der Umkreis	*surroundings*
knabbern	*to nibble*

Es war einmal eine Maus, die hatte volles Vertrauen zu der
Wirtschaftspolitik ihres Landes und ein Sparkonto bei der Mäusebau- und
Bodenbank. Außerdem hatte ihre Großmutter – eine Frau, die mit vier
Beinen im Leben gestanden – ihr die alte Weisheit mit auf den Weg
5 gegeben – „Spare in der Zeit, so hast du nach dem Tod!“
   Einmal folgte einem verregneten Sommer ein langer, strenger Winter,
die ältesten Mäuse erinnerten sich nicht, jemals einen solch strengen
Winter erlebt zu haben (die ältesten Mäuse sind so furchtbar
alt nun auch wieder nicht, dafür aber sehr vergesslich). Die
10 Vorräte waren bald aufgezehrt, über die Mäusetiere brach
eine schreckliche Hungersnot herein und viele kamen um.
   Doch: in der Not frisst halt die Maus Papier auch ohne
Butterbrot! Und als sie eben den allerletzten Schnippel des
Sparbuchs verdaut hatte – da hielt der Lenz seinen Einzug mit
15 warmen Sonnenstrahlen und grünen Grasspitzen, und
Mäusenahrung lag auf allen Straßen. Die kluge Maus aber
war in weitem Umkreis die einzige, die diesen Winter überlebt
hatte.
   Wer spart, hat in der Not auch was zu knabbern.

Franz Josef Bogner

Die kluge Maus.

B Eine tüchtige Maus. Sind Sie auch so? Sparen Sie, oder
geben Sie Ihr ganzes Geld aus? Haben Sie ein Sparkonto? Warum
spart man Geld? Machen Sie eine Liste von den Gründen. Hier sind
einige Vorschläge.

B. Lists will vary.

1. für das Studium
2. um sich ein Auto zu kaufen
3. damit man den Ruhestand genießen kann

PLANNING GUIDE • CLASSROOM MANAGEMENT

OBJECTIVES

Communication
- Talk about leisure-time activities, p. 146.
- Ask for and give advice, p. 154.

Grammar
- Use modal verbs to express abilities, likes, intentions, and desires, pp. 148–149.
- Use modal verbs to express permission or obligation, pp. 151–152.
- Use *da-* and *wo-*compounds, pp. 152–153.

Culture
- Learn about leisure-time activities in Germany, pp. 144–145.
- Learn about Elke Heidenreich, p. 160.
- Learn about the euro, p. 159.

Recycling
- Review modal verbs, pp. 148–152.
- Consider various academic subjects, p. 145.

STRATEGIES

Listening Strategies
- Listen to a radio call-in show, p. 154.

Speaking Strategies
- Talk about organized leisure-time activities, p. 145.
- Discuss the relationship between work and play, p. 147.
- Talk about one's talents, p. 150.
- Discuss the ideal house pet, p. 160.

Reading Strategies
- Read a story told from an animal's perspective, pp. 155–157.

Writing Strategies
- Write a radio ad, p. 158.

Connecting Cultures Strategies
- Compare the daily lives of German and North American students, p. 152.

PROGRAM RESOURCES

Print
- *Arbeitsheft* (Workbook), pp. 101–114
- *Arbeitsheft* (Workbook), Teacher's Edition, pp. 101–114

Audiovisual
- Overhead Transparencies 31.1–31.G2
- Audio Program, Cassette 4A, 7B/CD 5, 9
- Audioscript, pp. 46–52

Technology
- Annenberg *Fokus Deutsch* Video Series, *Folge 31*
- www.mcdougallittell.com

Assessment Program Options
- *Prüfung, Kapitel 31,* Assessment Program, pp. 84–93
- Audio Program, Cassette 8B/CD 10
- Audioscript, p. 111
- Teacher's Resource CD-ROM

Note: (1) Please see TE, pp. 142E–142J, for other suggestions not referenced in these plans. (2) Not all homework options need be assigned.

CHAPTER OPENER

- Quick Start Review: Comparative and superlative (TE, p. 142E). 5 MIN
- Use the photos on pp. 142–143 as a basis for class discussion (TE, p. 142E). 3 MIN

VIDEOTHEK

- After reviewing the *Wortschatz zum Video,* have students watch *Folge I: Ein grünes Hobby.* 9 MIN
- Have students do *Akt. A,* p. 144, silently, then check their answers as a class. Discuss. (TE, p. 142F). 9 MIN
- Have students do *Akt. B,* p. 145, with a partner. Do the follow-up activity in the Teaching Suggestions (TE, p. 142F). 9 MIN Watch *Folge II:*
- *Weiterbilden in der Freizeit.* 5 MIN Do *Akt. A–B,* p. 145, as a
- class (TE, p. 142F). 10 MIN

Homework Options:

- *Arbeitsheft,* p. 103,
- *Videothek, Akt. H*

VIDEOTHEK

- Quick Start Review 1: Vocabulary (TE, p. 142E). 6 MIN
- Do the warm-up activity in the Teaching Suggestions for *Akt. C,* p. 145. Have students do the activity in small groups. End with a brief class discussion (TE, p. 142F). 12 MIN
- *Arbeitsheft,* p. 102, audio *Akt. C.* 7 MIN

VOKABELN

- Present the vocabulary on p. 146. 9 MIN
- Do the warm-up activity in the Teaching Suggestions for *Akt. A,* pp. 146–147 (TE, p. 142G). 6 MIN
- Do *Akt. A,* pp. 146–147, silently, then check answers as a class. Conclude by asking comprehension questions about the statements they created. 10 MIN

Homework Options:

- *Arbeitsheft,* p. 105, *Vokabeln, Akt. C*

VOKABELN

- Quick Start Review 1: Indirect questions (TE, p. 142F). 6 MIN
- Have students do *Akt. B,* p. 147, silently, then compare answers with a partner. Conclude with the follow-up activity in the Teaching Suggestions (TE, p. 142G). 15 MIN
- *Arbeitsheft,* p. 104, audio *Akt. B.* 7 MIN
- Have students do *Akt. C,* p. 147, with a partner. 8 MIN
- Do the expansion for *Akt. C,* p. 147, in the Teaching Suggestions (TE, p. 142G). 14 MIN

Homework Options:

- *Arbeitsheft,* p. 105, *Vokabeln, Akt. D–E*

VOKABELN

- Quick Start Review 2: Vocabulary review (TE, p. 142F). 4 MIN
- *Arbeitsheft,* p. 104, audio *Akt. A.* 6 MIN

STRUKTUREN

- Present modal verbs I on pp. 148–149 using OHT 31.G1 (TE, p. 142H). 8 MIN
- Do *Übung A,* p. 150, silently, then check the answers as a class. End with the follow-up activity in the Teaching Suggestions (TE, p. 142H). 12 MIN
- Have students do *Übung B,* p. 150, silently, then compare answers with a partner. 9 MIN
- *Übung C,* p. 150. Conclude with the follow-up expansion activity in the Teaching Suggestions (TE, p. 142H). 11 MIN

Homework Options:

- *Arbeitsheft,* p. 108, *Strukturen, Akt. F–G*

PACING GUIDE • SAMPLE LESSON PLAN, 50-MINUTE SCHEDULE

STRUKTUREN

- Quick Start Review 1: School and university subjects (TE, p. 142G). 4 MIN
- Present modal verbs II on p. 151 using OHT 31.G2. 6 MIN
- Do *Übung A,* p. 152, as a class. 7 MIN
- Do *Übung B,* p. 152, silently, then check the answers as a class. Do the follow-up activity in the Teaching Suggestions (TE, p. 142H). 10 MIN
- Present *da-* and *wo-*compounds on pp. 152–153. Follow the Teaching Suggestions (TE, p. 142H). 10 MIN
- *Arbeitsheft,* p. 109, audio *Akt. I.* 5 MIN
- Follow the Teaching Suggestions for *Übung A,* p. 153 (TE, p. 142H). 8 MIN

Homework Options:

- *Arbeitsheft,* p. 109, *Strukturen, Akt. J–K*

STRUKTUREN

- Quick Start Review 2: Verbs with prepositions (TE, p. 142H). 5 MIN
- Do *Übung B,* p. 153, silently, then check answers with a partner. 12 MIN

PERSPEKTIVEN

- Have students review the *Wortschatz zum Hörtext* and the questions in *Hören Sie zu!, Akt. A,* p. 154, before listening to the recording. Have students do the activity in pairs and discuss their answers as a class, listening to the recording again as necessary. 15 MIN
- Do *Hören Sie zu!, Akt. B,* p. 154, as a class (TE, p. 142I). 8 MIN
- Do *Zum Thema* on p. 155 as a class, after introducing the names for some uncommon animals (TE, p. 142I). 6 MIN
- Begin reading *Die erste Begegnung* on pp. 155–157 (TE, p. 142I). 4 MIN

Homework Options:

- Finish reading *Die erste Begegnung,* pp. 155–157
- Brainstorm ideas and vocabulary for *Zum Text,* pp. 157–158, item 4

PERSPEKTIVEN

- Quick Start Review 1: *Du* and *ihr* imperatives (TE, p. 142I). 4 MIN
- Do *Zum Text,* p. 157, in small groups and then conclude with a class comparison of ideas (TE, p. 142I). 14 MIN
- Do *Zur Interpretation,* p. 158, as a class (TE, p. 142I). 5 MIN
- Have students do *Interaktion,* p. 158, and share their thoughts with the class (TE, p. 142I). 14 MIN
- Begin *Schreiben Sie!* by discussing the assignment, *Tipp zum Schreiben,* and *Schreibmodell.* 5 MIN
- Do *Vor dem Schreiben* and then begin *Beim Schreiben,* pp. 159–160 (TE, p. 142J). 8 MIN

Homework Options:

- Finish the first draft of the radio ad
- *Arbeitsheft,* pp. 111–113, *Perspektiven, Akt. C–E*

PERSPEKTIVEN

- Quick Start Review 2: *Sie* and *wir* imperatives (TE, p. 142I). 5 MIN
- Do *Nach dem Schreiben* on p. 160 (TE, p. 142J) and begin writing the final draft of the radio ad. 10 MIN
- Questions and review. 5 MIN
- *Prüfung, Kapitel 31.* 30 MIN

Homework Options:

- Finish the final draft of the radio ad and record it
- *Arbeitsheft,* p. 114, *Perspektiven, Akt. F–G*

DAY 1

Note: (1) Please see TE, pp. 142E–142J, for other suggestions not referenced in these plans. (2) Not all homework options need be assigned.

CHAPTER OPENER

- Quick Start Review: Comparative and superlative (TE, p. 142E). 5 MIN
- Discuss the photos on pp. 142–143 (TE, p. 142E). 5 MIN

VIDEOTHEK

- Watch *Folge I* (TE, p. 142F). 10 MIN
- Do *Akt. A,* p. 144. 10 MIN
- Do *Akt. B,* p. 145, with a partner (TE, p. 142F). 10 MIN
- Have students watch *Folge II.* Do *Akt. A–B,* p. 145, as a class (TE, p. 142F). 19 MIN
- Block Schedule activity: Research (TE, p. 142F). 10 MIN
- Do *Akt. C,* p. 145 in small groups (TE, p. 142F). 13 MIN
- *Arbeitsheft,* p. 102, audio *Akt. C.* 8 MIN

Homework Options:

- *Arbeitsheft,* p. 103, *Videothek, Akt. H*

DAY 2

VOKABELN

- Quick Start Review 2: Vocabulary (TE, p. 142F). 8 MIN
- Present the vocabulary on p. 146. 10 MIN
- Do the warm-up, then *Akt. A,* pp. 146–147 (TE, p. 142G). 16 MIN
- Do *Akt. B,* p. 147, silently, then compare answers with a partner (TE, p. 142G). 14 MIN
- Block Schedule activity: Change of Pace (TE, p. 142G). 12 MIN
- Do *Akt. C,* p. 147, with a partner, then the expansion for *Akt. C,* p. 147 (TE, p. 142G). 14 MIN

STRUKTUREN

- Present modal verbs I on pp. 148–149 (TE, p. 142H). 8 MIN
- Do *Übung A,* p. 150, silently, then check answers (TE, p. 142H). 8 MIN

Homework Options:

- *Arbeitsheft,* p. 108, *Akt. F–G*

DAY 3

STRUKTUREN

- Quick Start Review 1: School and university subjects (TE, p. 142G). 5 MIN
- Have students do *Übung B,* p. 150, silently, then compare answers with a partner. 8 MIN
- *Übung C,* p. 150 (TE, p. 142H). 8 MIN
- Present modal verbs II on p. 151. 7 MIN
- Do *Übung A,* p. 152, as a class. 7 MIN
- Do *Übung B,* p. 152, silently, then check answers (TE, p. 142H). 10 MIN
- Block Schedule activity: Fun Break (TE, p. 142I). 10 MIN
- Present *da-* and *wo-* compounds on pp. 152–153 (TE, p. 142H). 10 MIN
- *Arbeitsheft,* p. 109, audio *Akt. I.* 5 MIN
- *Übung A,* p. 153 (TE, p. 142H). 8 MIN
- Do *Übung B,* p. 153, silently, then check their answers with a partner. 12 MIN

Homework Options:

- *Arbeitsheft,* p. 109, *Strukturen, Akt. J–K*

DAY 4

PERSPEKTIVEN

- Quick Start Review 1: *Du* and *ihr* imperatives (TE, p. 142I). 4 MIN
- Review the *Wortschatz* and *Hören Sie zu!, Akt. A,* p. 154, before listening. Do the activity in pairs and discuss. 10 MIN
- Do *Hören Sie zu!, Akt. B,* p. 154 (TE, p. 142I). 8 MIN
- Do *Zum Thema* on p. 155 (TE, p. 142I). 6 MIN
- Read *Die erste Begegnung,* pp. 155–157, in groups (TE, p. 142I). 13 MIN
- Block Schedule activity: Fun Break (TE, p. 142J). 10 MIN
- Do *Zum Text, Zur Interpretation,* and *Interaktion,* pp. 157–158 (TE, p. 142I). 33 MIN
- Begin *Schreiben Sie!* by discussing the assignment, *Tipp zum Schreiben,* and *Schreibmodell.* 6 MIN

Homework Options:

- Finish the first draft of the radio ad
- *Arbeitsheft,* pp. 111–113, *Akt. C–E*

DAY 5

PERSPEKTIVEN

- Quick Start Review 2: *Sie* and *wir* imperatives (TE, p. 142I). 5 MIN
- Do *Nach dem Schreiben,* p. 160, and write the final draft of the radio ad. 20 MIN
- Have students record their radio ads and play them for the class. 20 MIN
- Block Schedule activity: Research (TE, p. 142J). 10 MIN
- Questions and review. 5 MIN
- *Prüfung, Kapitel 31.* 30 MIN

Homework Options:

- *Arbeitsheft,* p. 114, *Perspektiven, Akt. F–G*

KAPITEL 31 : TEACHING SUGGESTIONS

Chapter Opener, p. 142

PROGRAM RESOURCES

- Overhead Transparency 31.1

Quick Start Review

♻ Comparative and superlative
Ergänzen Sie die Adjektive oder
Adverbien im Komparativ (K) oder
Superlativ (S).

1. Die Rosen in unserem Garten
   sind viel _____. (schön – K)
2. Wie heißt der _____ Stadtpark in
   Deutschland? (groß – S)
3. Am _____ liege ich einfach auf
   dem Rasen in der Sonne.
   (gern – S)
4. Euer Zaun ist viel _____ als unser
   Zaun. (hoch – K)
5. Das schwarzweiße Foto ist am
   _____. (alt – S)
6. Je _____ Blumen es im Garten
   gibt, desto _____ riecht es.
   (viel – K, gut – K)
7. Im Sommer essen sie _____ im
   Garten als im Frühling. (oft – K)

Answers: 1. schöner 2. größte
3. liebsten 4. höher 5. ältesten
6. mehr, besser 7. öfter

TEACHING SUGGESTIONS

- Introduce the concept of *Freizeit* and
  the other topics addressed in this
  chapter. Have each student interview
  3 other students to find out what
  they do in their free time. Have them
  report their findings to the class or
  conduct a class poll.

- Photos, pp. 142–143

Look over the photos and ask *Wie alt
ist das linke Foto? Warum wissen Sie
das? Warum nennt man den Stadtpark
in Berlin-Kreuzberg eine „grüne
Lunge"? Was machen die Leute wohl
in einer Laubenkolonie?*

TEACHING ALL STUDENTS

Multiple Intelligences Naturalist:
Instruct students to spend some time
in a garden or park and write down
their observations in German.
Encourage them to describe the
vegetation (colors, textures, smells)
and the feelings they experience.

CLASSROOM COMMUNITY

Dictation Compose a paragraph based
on one of the 3 photos and read it to
the class as a dictation. Make it a short
narrative about 1 of the people seen in
the photos. You might leave it open
ended and have students come up with
their own endings.

CULTURE HIGHLIGHTS

Explain the phenomenon of the
Schrebergarten and have students
speculate about its function in German
society.

Videothek, pp. 144–145

PROGRAM RESOURCES

- Videocassette, *Folge 31*
- *Arbeitsheft,* pp. 101–103
- Audio Program, Cassette 4A/CD 5
- Audioscript, pp. 46–48

Quick Start Review 1

♻ Vocabulary review
Verbinden Sie die Definitionen mit den
richtigen Wörtern.

1. _____ die Kinderkrippe
2. _____ das Menschenrecht
3. _____ gestatten
4. _____ leiten
5. _____ die Minderheit
6. _____ unterdrücken
7. _____ der Angeklagte
8. _____ emanzipieren
a. führen
b. zurückhalten; durch Gewalt und
   Terror benachteiligen
c. sich von der Kontrolle anderer
   Menschen befreien
d. erlauben
e. Ort, wo kleine Jungen und
   Mädchen betreut werden
f. eine Person, die beschuldigt
   wird
g. kleinerer Teil einer bestimmten
   Anzahl von Personen
h. z.B. die Meinungsfreiheit, die
   Redefreiheit *usw.*

Answers: 1. e 2. h 3. d 4. a 5. g
6. b 7. f 8. c

Quick Start Review 2

♻ Indirect discourse
Setzen Sie die Sätze in die indirekte
Rede.
MODELL: Susanne sagt: „Ich mag
Gartenarbeit nicht." →
*Susanne sagt, sie möge Gartenarbeit
nicht.*

1. Dirk sagt: „Ich gehe gern in die
   Stadt."
2. Erika sagt: „Die Freizeit ist als
   Künstler etwas schwierig."
3. Susanne sagt: „Wir haben einen
   schönen Garten."
4. Dirk sagt: „In meiner Freizeit
   versuche ich rauszukommen aus
   dem Haus."
5. Erika sagt: „Man hat bei der
   Arbeit nie ein gutes Gefühl."

Answers: 1. Dirk sagt, er gehe gern in die Stadt.   2. Erika sagt, die Freizeit sei als Künstler etwas schwierig. 3. Susanne sagt, sie hätten einen schönen Garten.   4. Dirk sagt, in seiner Freizeit versuche er rauszukommen aus dem Haus. 5. Erika sagt, man habe bei der Arbeit nie ein gutes Gefühl.

TEACHING SUGGESTIONS

• *Aktivität A,* p. 144

Follow-up: Ask students if the idea of *"ein kleiner Garten mit einer Laube mitten in der Stadt"* is old-fashioned or if there is room for such a notion today. How do American city dwellers get back to nature?

• *Aktivität B,* p. 145

Follow-up: Ask students *Mit welcher Meinung identifizieren Sie sich am besten?* Have students talk about their choices with a partner.

• *Aktivität A,* p. 145

Follow-up: List the courses mentioned on the board under the headings *DDR-Zeiten* and *Jetzt.* Discuss the reasons for such differences. Lead a similar discussion with the categories *Frauenkurse* and *Männerkurse.*

• *Aktivität C,* p. 145

Warm-up: Have students define what *organisierte Freizeitaktivitäten* means. Ask *Was muss man alles organisieren? Warum?* Follow-up: Have them list the advantages and disadvantages of using free time to pursue educational interests.

TEACHING ALL STUDENTS

Extra Help Watch an episode of the video again, this time pausing it occasionally to allow students to summarize the content. Have them jot down 3–4 new vocabulary items they hear and share them with the class. The class should then brainstorm possible definitions.

CLASSROOM COMMUNITY

Group Activity Divide students into small groups and have each group imagine an organized *Freizeitaktivität* that they could sponsor. Have them decide when and where the activity will take place, what it will cost, and so forth. Have them create a poster that advertises their activity and includes all relevant information.

INTERDISCIPLINARY CONNECTION

Art Have students taking an art class describe the types of activities they do there. Ask students to bring in examples of their work and talk about their inception and meaning.

BLOCK SCHEDULE

Research Search the Internet using the keyword *Volkshochschule* and print out the course listings for a few of the schools. Distribute copies to students and have them choose several classes that interest them and present their choices to class.

Vokabeln, pp. 146–147

PROGRAM RESOURCES

• *Arbeitsheft,* pp. 104–105

• Audio Program, Cassette 4A/CD 5
• Audioscript, pp. 48–49

Quick Start Review 1

Indirect questions

Ergänzen Sie die indirekten Fragen mit *ob, was* oder *wo.*

1. Ich habe den Angeklagten gefragt, _____ er gestern Abend gemacht habe.
2. Ich habe ihn dann gefragt, _____ er mit jemandem telefoniert habe.
3. Zunächst habe ich gefragt, _____ er einen Mann namens Stefan Schmarotzer kenne.
4. Ich fragte dann, _____ er von halb acht bis zehn Uhr gewesen sei.
5. Dann fragte ich, _____ er diese Pistole je gesehen habe.
6. Zuletzt fragte ich ihn, _____ er nun zu sagen habe.

Answers: 1. was   2. ob   3. ob 4. wo   5. ob   6. was

Quick Start Review 2

Vocabulary

Ersetzen Sie die kursiv gedruckten Wörter mit den folgenden Synonymen.

SYNONYME: erhalten, gering, ungefähr, Feierabend, steigen, sicherlich, herstellen, begreifen

1. Ich komme *ganz bestimmt.*
2. Der Unterschied dazwischen ist *sehr klein.*
3. Er hat fünfhundert Mark dafür *bekommen.*
4. Es ist endlich fünf Uhr. Jetzt erstmal *keine Arbeit mehr.*
5. Das kann ich einfach nicht *verstehen.*

6. Solche schönen Autos können sie in den USA nicht *produzieren*.
7. Sie hat *etwa* 10.000 DM auf der Bank.
8. Hoffentlich wird die Arbeitslosenzahl nicht *höher werden*.

Answers: 1. sicherlich 2. gering 3. erhalten 4. Feierabend 5. begreifen 6. herstellen 7. ungefähr 8. steigen

TEACHING SUGGESTIONS

• *Aktivität A*, pp. 146–147

Warm-up: Ask students to make 2 columns on a sheet of paper with the headings *Freizeit* and *Arbeit*. Give students 2 minutes to write down as many terms and expressions as they can that fit each category. When the 2 minutes are up, have students compare their lists with those of another student.

• *Aktivität B*, p. 147

Follow-up: Ask students to choose a word from the vocabulary list, p. 146, and to write a definition of it on a slip of paper. Call on students to read their definitions aloud. The class then identifies the word that matches the definition.

• *Aktivität C*, p. 147

Expansion: Have students form groups of 3. Each group invents 3 short skits illustrating the situations described by Susanne, Dirk, and Erika. Supply them with the following prompts: *Susanne spricht mit ihren Eltern im Garten über die Gartenarbeit. Beim Einkaufsbummel trifft Dirk in der Stadt zwei Freunde von seinem Gymnasium. Erika unterhält sich über die Arbeit mit zwei Freundinnen, die als Geschäftsfrau und Lehrerin arbeiten.* Select a few groups to perform their skits for the class.

CLASSROOM COMMUNITY

Dictation As a follow-up to *Aktivität A*, pp. 146–147, have students work in pairs and take turns dictating the paragraphs to each other. Have them check their own work.

CULTURE HIGHLIGHTS

Inform students that Germans on average work 200 fewer hours per year than Americans and often receive 6 weeks of paid vacation. Have them compare these figures with what they know about their parents' working schedules.

BLOCK SCHEDULE

Change of Pace Have each student fold a piece of paper into 8 horizontal strips. Each student will then write the first sentence of a story, starting above the first fold, but writing the last 2–4 words of the sentence below it. Have students fold the top over so that only the last few words are showing and pass the paper on to the student next to them. Students then read the ends of the sentences on the papers they receive and write a continuation of the story, again recording the last few words below the next fold. Repeat this process until the eighth sentence has been written. Finally, have each student unfold the paper and read the story out loud. Alternately, collect the completed stories and read them out loud to the class, deciphering difficult handwriting and adjusting the grammar as you go.

Strukturen, pp. 148–153

PROGRAM RESOURCES

• Overhead Transparencies 31.G1–31.G2
• *Arbeitsheft,* pp. 112–116
• Audio Program, Cassette 4A/CD 5
• Audioscript, pp. 49–52

Quick Start Review 1

School and university subjects Verbinden Sie die Definitionen mit den richtigen Schul- und Universitätsfächern.

1. _____ Informatik
2. _____ Landeskunde
3. _____ Kunstgeschichte
4. _____ Musikwissenschaft
5. _____ Meeresbiologie
6. _____ Latein
7. _____ Philosophie
8. _____ Physik
9. _____ Chemie
10. _____ Maschinenbau

a. Beschäftigt sich mit den Fragen nach dem Sinn des Lebens
b. Studium der Elemente und deren Eigenschaften
c. Fach, in dem man lernt, mechanische Geräte zu bauen
d. Studium der Kunstentwicklungen im Wandel der Zeit
e. Beschäftigt sich mit Computern und deren Programmierungen
f. Naturwissenschaft, die die Gesetze der Materie erforscht
g. Sprache der Römer und des Vatikans

h. Studium der Tiere und Pflanzen der Ozeane

i. Beschäftigt sich mit der Entwicklung der musikalischen Formen

j. Studium von der Geographie und den Kulturen

Answers: 1. e   2. j   3. d   4. i   5. h
6. g   7. a   8. f   9. b   10. c

Quick Start Review 2

Verbs with prepositions
Ergänzen Sie die Sätze mit den passenden Präpositionen.

1. Heinrich wunderte sich _____ die brillante Farbe der Blume.
2. Jetzt kann er _____ nichts Anderes denken.
3. Renate nahm gern _____ dem Fremdsprachenkurs teil.
4. Sie konnte sich _____ aber nicht die Aussprache des neuen Lehrers gewöhnen.
5. Das kleine Mädchen fürchtet sich nicht _____ dem großen Monster.
6. Sie interessiert sich sogar _____ Filme wie *Nosferatu* und *Frankenstein.*
7. Sie beschäftigen sich die ganze Woche _____ den Vorbereitungen.
8. Heute kümmern sie sich _____ die Zimmerreservierungen.

Answers: 1. über   2. an   3. an
4. an   5. vor   6. für   7. mit   8. um

TEACHING SUGGESTIONS

• Modal verbs I, pp. 148–150

Point out that several modal verbs have cognates in English with forms and functions that are similar to those of the German modals.

• *Übung A,* p. 150

Follow-up: Ask students to make comments on their high school or childhood experiences using modal verbs. For example, *Ich möchte nächstes Jahr einen Malkurs belegen. Als kleines Kind wollte ich nie ins Bett gehen.*

• *Übung C,* p. 150

Expansion: Have students take the items from the *Was ich lernen soll* column and write sentences explaining their motivations. For example, *Ich soll Informatik lernen, weil ich später als Computerprogrammierer arbeiten will.*

• *Übung B,* p. 152

Follow-up: Ask content-based questions such as *Wer musste in Fabriken arbeiten? Wo durften die Kinder nicht spielen?* Then ask a few *Interpretationsfragen.* For example, *Warum mussten die Leute in die Stadt ziehen und in Fabriken arbeiten? Warum musste man um die Jahrhundertwende nicht mehr immer am Arbeitsplatz sein?* Discuss possible explanations.

• *Da-* and *wo*-compounds, pp. 152–153

Have students write on the board all the prepositions they know. Explain how the *da-* and *wo*-compounds are formed and used. Point out that certain prepositions such as *ohne, außer,* and *seit* do not form *da-* or *wo*-compounds.

• *Übung A,* p. 153

As a warm-up, have students scan each sentence in the *Übung* and locate its main verb. List the infinitive form of these verbs with their prepositions on the board. After doing the *Übung,* add a few more common verbs with prepositions to the list (*sich freuen auf, warten auf, denken an, reden über/von*) and have students formulate statements using verbs from the list to which other students react. For example, *Ich interessiere mich für Autos. Ich interessiere mich nicht dafür.*

TEACHING ALL STUDENTS

Extra Help Go over the present- and past-tense conjugations of the modal verbs on pp. 149 and 151. Point out that the first- and third-person singular forms of a modal verb are always the same. Remind them again of the stem change for *können, mögen, müssen,* and *dürfen* in the present tense.

CLASSROOM COMMUNITY

Paired Activity Give students 2 minutes to reflect on the responsibilities and the privileges they had as children. Then have them interview a partner and ask *Was musstest du als kleines Kind machen? Was durftest du (nicht) machen?* They should also ask about how things have changed: *Was musst du jetzt machen? Was darfst du (nicht) machen?* Have the interviewers take notes and report on what their partners say to the class.

LANGUAGE NOTE

Bring an excerpt of Shakespeare's writing to class and have students look for evidence of connections between English and German. Explain that English belongs to the Germanic family of languages and that texts written in Middle and Old English bear a striking resemblance to German.

BLOCK SCHEDULE

Fun Break Explain the following personality types to the class: *der Angsthase, der Unzufriedene, der Milchbub, der Angeber, der Träumer, der Paranoiker.* Have students formulate statements in the first person characteristic of these various types. Encourage them to use modal verbs. For example, *Ich will keinen Gruselfilm sehen. Ich darf mich nicht verletzen. Ich möchte lieber nicht Fallschirmspringen gehen. (Angsthase)* Have students then read their statements aloud and the class guess which personality type they are representing.

Perspektiven, pp. 154–160

PROGRAM RESOURCES

- *Arbeitsheft,* pp. 110–114
- Audio Program, Cassette 4A, 7B/ CD 5, 9
- Audioscript, p. 52
- www.mcdougallittell.com

Quick Start Review 1

♻ *Du* and *ihr* imperatives
Bilden Sie Sätze im *du-* und *ihr-* Imperativ.
1. an das Rockkonzert denken
2. auf keinen Fall diese Veranstaltung verpassen
3. um 19 Uhr 30 kommen
4. dabei sein

Answers: 1. Denk (Denkt) an das Rockkonzert.   2. Verpass (Verpasst) auf keinen Fall diese Veranstaltung. 3. Komm (Kommt) um 19 Uhr 30. 4. Sei (Seid) dabei.

Quick Start Review 2

♻ *Sie* and *wir* imperatives
Bilden Sie Sätze im *Sie-* und *wir-* Imperativ.
1. doch hingehen
2. zum Konzert fahren
3. einen Werbespot schreiben
4. kreativ sein

Answers: 1. Gehen Sie (Gehen wir) doch hin.   2. Fahren Sie (Fahren wir) zum Konzert.   3. Schreiben Sie (Schreiben wir) einen Werbespot. 4. Seien Sie (Seien wir) kreativ.

TEACHING SUGGESTIONS

- *Hören Sie zu!, Aktivität B,* p. 154

Follow-up: Form a panel of 4–5 student "experts" and have them answer the "pet" questions posed by the rest of the class.

- *Zum Thema,* p. 155

Introduce the uncommon animals listed in the box by giving first-person descriptions of them and then having students guess which animal is being described. For example *Ich bin klein und grün, und ich sage „quak, quak". Wer bin ich?*

- *Die erste Begegnung* pp. 155–157

Have students review the *Wortschatz zum Lesen* before reading the text. Make sure they use their dictionaries only to look up words that are absolutely necessary to comprehend the text. Preview the text with the students by having them read the first paragraph silently. Ask students to respond to *wer, was, wie, wo* questions on the content and to speculate what

the title *"Die erste Begegnung"* might mean.

- *Zum Text,* p. 157

Have students read the *Tipp zum Schreiben* before doing question 4. Provide an example of how a cat might describe something it cannot call by name, for example, *Ich liege so bequem auf dem schönen, weichen Ding im großen Zimmer. Manchmal sitzen meine Menschen mit mir darauf.* You may want to assign question 4 as homework.

- *Zur Interpretation,* p. 158

Have students think of adjectives to describe the personality of a typical cat and write them on the board. Ask them to name some well-known cats like Garfield and to describe their personalities.

- *Interaktion,* p. 158

Follow-up: Break students into groups according to their favorite animal. Have 2 students facilitate a debate between the various groups and another 2 record the best argumentative points on the board.

- *Schreiben Sie!,* pp. 158–160

Record the ad from the *Schreibmodell* or devise one of your own. Introduce this writing activity by playing your recording for the class. Listen twice and have students take notes. Follow up with *was, wann, wo, wie viel* questions. You may want to have students write their ads in pairs. Before pairing them up, ask which students have cassette recorders with microphones. Each pair will need access to one.

- *Schreibmodell,* p. 159

Review the devices discussed in the *Tipp zum Schreiben* (comedy, action, drama, music, special effects) and have students analyze the *Schreibmodell* and identify examples of their implementation. Encourage students to use these or other devices in their ads.

- *Vor dem Schreiben,* p. 159

Ask students to present a list of ideas for their ads to you, the *Produzent des Radioprogramms.* You can then either give them the green light and have them start the production of their ad or send them back to try again.

- *Nach dem Schreiben,* p. 160

Go over the student model with corrections before peer editing begins. Encourage students to ask for your help editing only after they have corrected as much as they can on their own.

TEACHING ALL STUDENTS

Multiple Intelligences

Musical/Rhythmic: Before students record their ads, point out how important musicality and rhythm are to the effectiveness of spoken advertisements. Illustrate the difference between a monotone and a highly modulated performance of a text. When the recordings are presented to the class, have students pay attention to the musicality of the voices.

CLASSROOM COMMUNITY

Group Activity You can use *Fragen Sie Professor Cato!,* p. 154, as a model. Each student can become an "expert" in a field. Either have students choose fields or assign them. Each student must write his or her field on a name tag. Give students 4 minutes to look at the different fields chosen and to formulate at least 5 questions related to at least 3 different fields. Then have students move around the classroom and ask their questions. Follow up with the "experts" reporting on their most ingenious solutions or on the questions that stumped them.

CULTURE HIGHLIGHTS

Inform students of the widespread use of English in German advertising. Discuss examples from German magazines and, if possible, German radio. (Many German, Austrian, and Swiss radio stations can be accessed over the Internet. Search for *Radio* with the search engine *Yahoo Germany* or use *Alta Vista* and set the language to German.)

BLOCK SCHEDULE

Fun Break Have students choose 3 passages from *"Die erste Begegnung"* and draw illustrations to accompany them in small groups. Remind students to include captions.

Research Distribute German-language magazines to students and give them 5 minutes to find as many English words (not cognates) as they can. Write the words they find on the board and try to divide them into categories.

PORTFOLIO

Have students listen to the final versions of the recorded advertisements and evaluate them with the aid of the rubric in the next column. Provide a handout containing the rubric as well as prompts for other relevant information and suggestions. For example, *Namen der Autoren. Wie könnten die Autoren dieser Reklame sie verbessern? Was war besonders gut an dieser Reklame?* After collecting each student's packet of evaluations, redistribute them to the authors of the ads and have them sum up their classmates' reactions to their work.

RUBRIC **A** = 13–15 pts. **B** = 10–12 pts. **C** = 7–9 pts. **D** = 4–6 pts. **F** < 4 pts.

Ad Criteria	Scale				
Clarity and pronunciation	1	2	3	4	5
Creativity	1	2	3	4	5
Musicality	1	2	3	4	5

PROJECT

Have students find an ad, preferably in a German-language magazine or newspaper, and analyze it. The analysis can be written or presented to the class orally. To prepare the class for this assignment, present a few ads of your own and discuss the techniques and strategies used in them. Consider questions such as *Was wird in dieser Werbung verkauft? Was für Assoziationen möchte die Werbeagentur durch diese Werbung wachrufen? Wer sind die Konsumenten, auf die die Werbung abzielt? Welche Techniken werden in der Werbung benutzt? Berücksichtigen Sie Farbe, Blickwinkel, Text, Kontext.* In a follow-up discussion, consider the differences between German-language ads and ads in this country.

KAPITEL 31 FREIZEIT

Szene aus einem Kleingarten von früher.

In diesem Kapitel

- erfahren Sie, wie Deutsche früher ihre Freizeit verbrachten.
- erfahren Sie, was junge Deutsche von heute in ihrer Freizeit machen.
- diskutieren Sie die Vor- und Nachteile organisierter Freizeitaktivitäten.

Sie werden auch

- den Gebrauch der Modalverben wiederholen.
- lernen, wie man Verbindungen mit **da-** und **wo-** benutzt.
- eine Geschichte über einen schlauen Kater lesen.
- einen Werbespot für das Radio schreiben.

**Winterspaß.
Jugendliche bei einem
Spaziergang im
Schnee.**

**Viele Berliner verbringen gern ihre
Freizeit in einer Laubenkolonie.**

In diesem Kapitel sehen Sie, wie sich die Idee von „Freizeit" entwickelt hat. Was heißt für Sie Freizeit? Machen Sie eine Liste von Wörtern, die Sie mit dem Begriff „Freizeit" assoziieren.

I: Ein grünes Hobby

In dieser Folge sehen Sie eine kurze Geschichte über die Stadt Berlin und ihre Einwohner, die ein kleines Stück Natur in der wachsenden Metropole suchten.

A Freizeit damals und jetzt. Was passt? Welcher Satz beschreibt welches Bild?

a.   b.   c.

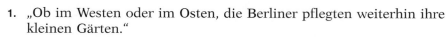

d.   e.   f.

1. „Ob im Westen oder im Osten, die Berliner pflegten weiterhin ihre kleinen Gärten."
2. „Die Kinder mussten zwischen den Gebäuden in den Höfen spielen."
3. „Schon damals war es vor allem für Kinder ungesund und gefährlich, in der Stadt zu wohnen."
4. „Berlin in den zwanziger Jahren – eine Weltstadt mit vielen Menschen und viel Verkehr."
5. „Was braucht der Berliner, . . . ? Einen kleinen Garten mit einer Laube mitten in der Stadt."
6. „Der Kleingarten gab den Arbeiterfamilien damals ein kleines Stück Natur und Erholung mitten in der Stadt."

In den Kleingärten gab es Platz für Kinderspiele.

WORTSCHATZ ZUM VIDEO

eingereicht	submitted
der Verleger	publisher
die Laubenkolonie	garden colony
der Malkurs	painting class
erschwinglich	affordable
der Grad	grade; degree
stur	stubborn

A. 1. d 2. e 3. c 4. f 5. a 6. b

B Persönliche Meinungen. Wer sagt das, Klaus, Daniela, Bob, Dirk, Susanne oder Grace?

B. 1. Grace 2. Daniela 3. Dirk 4. Klaus 5. Bob 6. Susanne

1. „Je mehr Feiertage, desto besser."
2. „Ich sitze gern am Computer und surfe im Internet."
3. „In meiner Freizeit versuche ich vor allem rauszukommen aus dem Haus."
4. „Mein Hauptinteresse ist die Musik."
5. „Ich interessiere mich sehr für Theater und Museen."
6. „Besonders im Sommer gehen wir gern am See grillen."

II: Weiterbilden in der Freizeit

In dieser Folge erfahren Sie, dass Freizeit nicht immer faulenzen sein muss. Viele benutzen ihre Freizeit, um etwas Neues zu lernen. Was könnte man in der Freizeit lernen? Wo kann man das machen?

A Volkshochschule in Potsdam. Beantworten Sie die Fragen.

1. Was für Kurse gab es an der Volkshochschule zu DDR-Zeiten? Welche gibt es heute? Warum? Was meinen Sie?
2. Unter den Teilnehmern sind meistens mehr Frauen als Männer. Das gilt vor allem für kreative Kurse wie den Malkurs. Warum belegen mehr Frauen als Männer diese Kurse? Was meinen Sie? Welche Kurse möchten Männer Ihrer Meinung nach belegen?

B Beliebte Kurse. Die folgenden Kurse sind einige der beliebtesten, die an der Volkshochschule angeboten werden. Warum ist das so? Was sagen die Teilnehmer über die Kurse? Welcher Kurs interessiert Sie besonders? Warum?

1. Malen   2. Fremdsprachen lernen   3. Informatik

C Freizeitaktivitäten

C. Answers will vary.

SCHRITT 1: Was sagen Daniela und Stefan zum Thema „organisierte Freizeitaktivitäten"? Mit welcher Meinung stimmen Sie überein? Warum?

DANIELA: Ich bin für organisierte Freizeitaktivitäten zu einem bestimmten Grad. Wenn es nicht zu organisiert ist.

STEFAN: Ich bin völlig gegen organisierte Freizeitaktivitäten. Ich finde, das ist sehr unoriginell, und die Leute sind ein bisschen blöd und stur.

SCHRITT 2: Welche Sportarten sind „organisiert"? Diskutieren Sie die Vor- und Nachteile organisierter Freizeitaktivitäten. Warum treibt man solche Sportarten?

FOKUS INTERNET

To learn more about leisure time in German-speaking countries, visit the **Auf Deutsch!** Web Site at www.mcdougallittell.com.

Frau Vogtländer, Leiterin der Potsdamer Volkshochschule.

B. Answers will vary.

Teilnehmer an einem Malkurs in Potsdam.

A. 1. Zu DDR-Zeiten gab es an der Volkshochschule Potsdam vor allem Kurse in Maschinenschreiben und Fremdsprachen. Heute gibt es dort auch viele künstlerische Kurse wie Malen, Töpfern und Gitarrenspiel. Answers to "Warum" will vary.
2. Answers will vary.

VOKABELN

die Anregung	*stimulation*
die Erholung	*rest; recuperation*
die Gartenarbeit	*gardening*
der Hof	*yard; courtyard*
der Kleingarten	*small garden*
der Nachweis	*proof*
das Gefühl	*feeling*
das Hobby	*hobby*
an•fassen	*to touch; to grasp*
an•regen	*to stimulate*
bedenken	*to consider*
bummeln	*to stroll; to idle*
sich entspannen	*to relax*
sich langweilen	*to be bored*
pflegen	*to look after*
teilen	*to divide; to share*
weiter•bilden	*to continue one's education*
draußen	*outside*
hauptsächlich	*primarily*
im Freien	*in the open air; outdoors*

Viele Jugendliche engagieren sich sehr für Sport.

preisgünstig	*fairly priced*
unersetzlich	*irreplaceable*

Sie wissen schon
die Freizeit, der Feiertag, anfangen, belegen, gefallen, sich interessieren für, unternehmen, verbringen

---

bummeln
Erholung
Gefühl
belegen
entspannen
Hobby
Feiertagen
interessieren

Aktivitäten

A. 1: 1. Feiertagen 2. Erholung 3. Gefühl
4. entspannen; 2: 5. bummeln 6. belegen
7. Hobby 8. interessieren

A Wie stellt man sich die Freizeit vor? Ergänzen Sie die Sätze mit den Wörtern im Kasten.

1. An großen _____[1] hat man oft Familie zu Besuch, oder man geht in die Kirche. Viele finden diese Zeiten des Jahres besonders anstrengend. Für solche Leute bedeutet Ostern oder Chanukka keine _____,[2] sondern Stress und Mühe. Sie bekommen immer das _____,[3] dass sie an diesen Tagen einfach zu viel zu tun haben. Nur wenn die Gäste nach Hause gegangen sind, kann sich der Gastgeber / die Gastgeberin endlich _____.[4]

2. In der Freizeit kann man mehr machen, als einfach zu Hause sitzen oder in der Stadt _____.[5] Die Volkshochschule hat ein weites Angebot von Kursen, die man in der Freizeit _____[6] kann. Man kann zum Beispiel Spanisch lernen oder lernen, wie man mit einem Computer umgeht. Töpfern ist ein _____,[7] das immer

beliebter wird. Wenn Sie sich für solche Beschäftigungen _____,[8] und Ihre Mitmenschen kennen lernen möchten, sollten Sie sich unbedingt bei der Volkshochschule anmelden.

B Definitionen. Lesen Sie die Sätze links, und suchen Sie dann aus der rechten Spalte die passenden Definitionen für die kursiv gedruckten Wörter.

B. 1. c 2. h 3. f 4. d 5. a 6. g 7. i
8. b 9. e

1. In meiner Freizeit *beschäftige* ich *mich* im Wesentlichen mit Musik.
2. Meine Freizeit ist sehr *unterschiedlich*.
3. Die Kinder mussten zwischen den Gebäuden und in den *Höfen* spielen.
4. Der *Kleingarten* hat gerade in Berlin eine lange Tradition.
5. Der Kleingarten gab den Arbeiterfamilien ein kleines Stück Natur und *Erholung* mitten in der Stadt.
6. Nach dem Zweiten Weltkrieg war Berlin eine *geteilte* Stadt.
7. Die haben Spaß daran und können *sich* richtig *entspannen*.
8. Die Volkshochschule kann ihre Kurse recht *preisgünstig* anbieten
9. Ich denke, dass es ganz gut ist, eine Prüfung hier abzulegen und dann den *Nachweis* zu haben, dass man mit so einem Gerät umgehen kann.

a. eine Chance, wieder gesund zu werden
b. nicht teuer, billig
c. sich auf etwas konzentrieren
d. kleiner Garten in der Stadt
e. etwas zu zeigen, wie eine Note oder ein Zertifikat
f. Platz, der von Mauern, Zäunen oder Gebäuden umgeben ist
g. in zwei Teilen zerlegt
h. nicht gleich, verschieden
i. relaxen

C Freizeit und Arbeit

SCHRITT 1: Kann man eigentlich Freizeit und Arbeit verbinden? Lesen Sie die folgenden Meinungen.

SUSANNE: Ja, also erstmal zum Thema Gartenarbeit. Die mag ich überhaupt nicht, obwohl wir eigentlich einen schönen großen Garten haben, mit vielen Bäumen und all so was, und vielen Blumen, und meine Eltern machen das eher.

DIRK: In meiner Freizeit versuche ich vor allem rauszukommen aus dem Haus weg oder von der Schularbeit, dass ich dann einfach mal rauskomme, dass ich dann in die Stadt gehe, ein bisschen rumbummeln und in die Geschäfte gehen, ein bisschen einkaufen, so was.

ERIKA: Die Freizeit ist etwas schwierig, wenn man ein Künstler ist. Man hat immer das Gefühl, heute habe ich nicht genug gearbeitet. Man hat nie das Gefühl, jetzt ist es fünf Uhr, die Arbeitszeit ist vorbei, jetzt fängt der Abend an. Ich mache gerne, was ich mache, und darum ist die Freizeit nicht so ein Problem.

Dirk.

C. *Answers will vary.*

SCHRITT 2: Was meinen Sie? Arbeiten Sie mit einem Partner / einer Partnerin, und diskutieren Sie über die folgenden Fragen.

1. Wer versucht, sich in der Freizeit eher zu entspannen, und nicht zu arbeiten?
2. Wer findet, dass Arbeit auch Spass machen kann?
3. Was ist für Sie der Unterschied zwischen Arbeit und Freizeit?
4. Wie kann man Arbeit und Freizeit verbinden?

STRUKTUREN

REVIEW OF MODAL VERBS I
EXPRESSING ABILITIES, LIKES, INTENTIONS, AND DESIRES

As you know, modal verbs describe different attitudes with regard to activities, states, or conditions; and they commonly occur in both the present and simple past tenses.

Können expresses knowledge or ability.

Sabine **kann** sehr gut Englisch.	*Sabine knows English very well.*
Alle Kinder **konnten** Fußball **spielen.**	*All children could (were able to) play soccer.*

Mögen expresses liking. The indicative forms of this verb usually occur without a main verb and refer to people or things rather than to activities. You are already familiar with the subjunctive form **möchte,** which commonly expresses likes and dislikes with regard to activities.

Stefan **mag** das Gemälde nicht.	*Stefan doesn't like the painting.*
Ich **möchte** gern den ganzen Tag **malen.**	*I would really like to paint the entire day.*

Sollen expresses intention or obligation.

Die Maschine **soll** in einigen Minuten **ankommen.**	*The plane is supposed to arrive in a few minutes.*
Wir **sollten** eine längere Reise **machen.**	*We should (were supposed to) take a longer trip.*

Note the two different meanings of the second sentence. Because the past-tense and Subjunctive II forms of **sollen** are the same, the broader context in which this sentence appears would determine its meaning.

Wollen expresses intention, wish, or desire.

Viele **wollen** Deutsch **lernen.**	*Many people want to learn German.*
Ich **wollte** nicht im Garten **arbeiten.**	*I wouldn't (didn't) want to work in the garden.*

Just as with **sollen, wollen** has identical forms in the simple past and Subjuntive II.

The present-tense forms of these four modal verbs are as follows.

INFINITIVE:	können	mögen	sollen	wollen
SINGULAR				
ich	kann	mag	soll	will
du	kannst	magst	sollst	willst
Sie	können	mögen	sollen	wollen
sie/er/es	kann	mag	soll	will
PLURAL				
wir	können	mögen	sollen	wollen
ihr	könnt	mögt	sollt	wollt
Sie	können	mögen	sollen	wollen
sie	können	mögen	sollen	wollen

The simple past-tense forms for these four verbs are as follows. Note that **können** and **mögen** drop the umlaut, and **mögen** also has a stem change.

INFINITIVE:	können	mögen	sollen	wollen
SINGULAR				
ich	konnte	mochte	sollte	wollte
du	konntest	mochtest	solltest	wolltest
Sie	konnten	mochten	sollten	wollten
sie/er/es	konnte	mochte	sollte	wollte
PLURAL				
wir	konnten	mochten	sollten	wollten
ihr	konntet	mochtet	solltet	wolltet
Sie	konnten	mochten	sollten	wollten
sie	konnten	mochten	sollten	wollten

KURZ NOTIERT

As the examples point out, the Subjunctive II forms of **sollen** and **wollen** are identical to the simple past-tense forms. However, remember to distinguish between the Subjunctive II forms of **können** that retain the umlaut (**könnte**) and the simple-past forms that drop the umlaut (**konnte**).

Du **könntest** ihm wenigstens helfen.
You could at least help him.
Du **konntest** ihm nicht helfen.
You weren't able to help him.

A. 1. kann 2. wollen 3. soll 4. konnte
5. mochten 6. sollen

Übungen

A Weiterbilden. Ergänzen Sie die Sätze mit den richtigen Formen der Modalverben im Präsens oder im Imperfekt.[a]

1. An der Volkshochschule _____ man unterschiedliche Kurse belegen. (können)
2. Für Erwachsene, die ein neues Hobby lernen _____, sind solche Kurse geeignet. (wollen)
3. Der Malkurs _____ besonders interessant sein. (sollen)
4. Früher _____ man an der Volkshochschule nur Maschinenschreiben oder Fremdsprachen lernen. (können)
5. Damals _____ die Teilnehmer nur traditionelle Fächer lernen. (mögen)
6. Die Teilnehmer _____ selber entscheiden, welche Kurse wichtig sind. (sollen)

[a]*simple past tense*

B. 1. kann 2. mag 3. sollte 4. wollten
5. Wollt, möchtet 6. wolltest 7. wollte

B Gartenarbeit bei Familie Dyrchs. Susannes Mutter braucht Hilfe im Garten. Ergänzen Sie die Sätze.

FRAU DYRCHS: Ich _____[1] nicht alles im Garten allein machen.

SUSANNE: Aber, Mutti, du weißt doch, ich _____[2] nicht im Garten arbeiten.

FRAU DYRCHS: Eine Tochter _____[3] ihren Eltern helfen, wenn sie sonst nichts zu tun hat. Mach dir keine Sorgen – die Arbeit geht schnell.

SUSANNE: Früher _____[4] wir Kinder euch im Garten helfen, aber wir haben es zu stressig gefunden.

FRAU DYRCHS: _____[5] ihr also jetzt nur faulenzen am Wochenende? Oder gibt es eine andere Beschäftigung, die du lieber _____[6]?

SUSANNE: Ich habe total vergessen! Ich _____[7] heute mit Sabine ins Kino gehen! Tschüss!

Susanne.

C. *Answers will vary.*

C Talente und Pläne

SCHRITT 1: Was können Sie schon sehr gut machen? Was wollen Sie noch lernen? Was sollen Sie noch lernen, um bessere Berufschancen zu haben? Machen Sie drei Listen.

WAS ICH GUT KANN	WAS ICH LERNEN WILL	WAS ICH LERNEN SOLL
malen	töpfern	Informatik
Deutsch sprechen	musizieren	Mathe

SCHRITT 2: Finden Sie jetzt einen Partner / eine Partnerin, und fragen Sie einander, welche Talente und Pläne Sie haben.

REVIEW OF MODAL VERBS II
EXPRESSING PERMISSION OR OBLIGATION

You have just reviewed four modal verbs: **können, mögen, sollen,** and **wollen;** the two others are **dürfen** and **müssen. Dürfen** expresses permission to do something.

Das Kind **darf** im Hof **spielen.**	*The child is allowed to play in the courtyard.*

In the present tense, the negated form of **dürfen** is often equivalent to English *must not* in the sense of *not allowed/permitted.*

Das Kind **darf nicht** im Hof **spielen.**	*The child must not play in the courtyard.*

Müssen expresses obligation. In positive sentences, **müssen** is equivalent to English *must* or *to have to.*

Wir **mussten** früh nach Hause **kommen.**	*We had to come home early.*

However, **müssen nicht** only means *not to have to.*

Er **muss** morgen **nicht arbeiten.**	*He doesn't have to work tomorrow.*

The present- and simple past-tense forms of **dürfen** and **müssen** are as follows.

		PRESENT TENSE			SIMPLE PAST TENSE	
		SINGULAR				
ich		darf	muss		durfte	musste
du		darfst	musst		durftest	musstest
Sie		dürfen	müssen		durften	mussten
sie/er/es		darf	muss		durfte	musste
		PLURAL				
wir		dürfen	müssen		durften	mussten
ihr		dürft	müsst		durftet	musstet
Sie		dürfen	müssen		durften	mussten
sie		dürfen	müssen		durften	mussten

Notice that both **müssen** and **dürfen** drop the umlaut in all forms of the past tense.

SPRACHSPIEGEL

In German, the distinction between the modal verbs **können** and **dürfen** is greater than that between the English verbs *can* and *may.* Whereas many English speakers ask *can I?* when seeking permission, as opposed to the more correct *may I?*, German speakers usually ask **darf ich?** or the more polite subjunctive form **dürfte ich?**.

KURZ NOTIERT

Modal verbs often occur without a main verb, when motion or a sense of direction is clear.

Ich **muss** ins Fitness-Center.
I have to go to the gym.
Wir **müssen** los!
We have to go!

A. 1. muss 2. darf 3. Dürfen 4. müssen 5. Müsst 6. darf

B. 1. mussten 2. mussten 3. durften 4. mussten 5. durften 6. musste

Berlin im neunzehnten Jahrhundert.

SPRACHSPIEGEL

English once used the words *there* and *where* in a similar manner. This is still true in legal language, in phrases such as *in witness thereof* and in words such as *thereto, therefore,* and *whereof*. In the Shakespearean exclamation, *wherefore art thou, Romeo?,* Juliet is not asking for her lover's location, but rather *why (for what reason)* he is who he is.

Übungen

A Schüler in Europa und Nordamerika. Ergänzen Sie die Sätze mit den richtigen Formen der Modalverben im Präsens.

1. Dirk _____ seine Hausaufgaben machen. (müssen)
2. Er _____ nicht in die Stadt gehen und bummeln. (dürfen)
3. _____ Schüler in Nordamerika zu Hause zu Mittag essen? (dürfen)
4. In Deutschland _____ Schüler auch am Samstag in die Schule gehen. (müssen)
5. _____ ihr auch so viel Schularbeit machen? (müssen)
6. Im Gymnasium _____ man zwischen verschiedenen Fächern wählen. (dürfen)

B Arbeiter in Berlin. Ergänzen Sie die Sätze mit den richtigen Formen der Modalverben **müssen** und **dürfen** im Imperfekt.

Vor hundert Jahren war Berlin eine große Arbeiterstadt. Viele Menschen, die früher auf dem Land lebten, _____[1] jetzt in Fabriken arbeiten. Die Familien wohnten in kleinen, dunklen Arbeiterwohnungen. Kinder _____[2] zwischen den Gebäuden in den Höfen spielen. Natürlich _____[3] sie nicht in den Straßen spielen. Während der Industrialisierung _____[4] Arbeiter viele Stunden in den Fabriken verbringen. Sie _____[5] keinen richtigen Urlaub machen. Deshalb gab der Kleingarten den Arbeiterfamilien ein Stück Natur und Erholung mitten in der Stadt. Erst um die Jahrhundertwende _____[6] man nicht immer auf der Arbeit sein, wie früher.

DA- AND WO-COMPOUNDS
REFERRING TO THINGS AND IDEAS

In German, nouns generally follow prepositions. A personal pronoun also follows a preposition if that pronoun refers to a person or other being.

Ich denke oft an unsere Freunde.	*I often think about our friends.*
Denkst du auch **an sie**?	*Do you think about them, too?*

Personal pronouns do not follow prepositions when the pronoun refers to a thing or an idea. Instead, a **da**-compound replaces the combination of preposition and pronoun.

Ich interessiere mich sehr für Museen.	*I'm very interested in museums.*
Interessiert ihr euch auch **dafür**?	*Are you also interested in them?*

When the preposition begins with a vowel, **da-** becomes **dar-**.

Ich denke oft an die Zukunft.   *I often think about the future.*
Meine Freunde denken auch   *My friends think about it, too.*
   daran.

In questions, **wo-**compounds replace the combination of preposition plus **was.** When the preposition begins with a vowel, **wo-** becomes **wor-**.

Sie denkt an ihren Urlaub.   *She's thinking about her vacation.*

Woran denkt sie?   *What is she thinking about?*

Wo-compounds occur in indirect questions in the same way.

Wovon spricht er?   *What is he speaking of?*
Ich weiß nicht, **wovon** er   *I don't know what he's*
spricht.   *speaking of.*

Übungen

A Lieblingsinteressen. Die Leute im Video erzählen, was sie gerne in der Freizeit machen. Ergänzen Sie die Sätze mit **da-**Verbindungen.

KLAUS: Mein Hauptinteresse ist die Musik. In meiner Freizeit beschäftige ich mich oft _____.[1]

DER PROFESSOR: Theater und Museen machen sehr viel Spaß. Ich interessiere mich sehr _____.[2]

FRAU VOGTLÄNDER: Obwohl unser Malkurs sehr beliebt ist, habe ich persönlich noch nicht _____[3] teilgenommen.

SUSANNE: Für mich ist es wichtig, andere Sprachen und Kulturen kennen zu lernen. Ich lege viel Wert _____.[4]

KURSTEILNEHMERIN: Vor meinem Kurs wusste ich nicht viel von Computern und solchen Geräten, aber jetzt weiß ich ziemlich viel _____.[5]

B Freizeit und Urlaub. Stellen Sie Fragen mit Personalpronomen oder mit **wo-**Verbindungen.

MODELL: Dirk denkt an seine Freunde in Spanien. →
An wen denkt er?

1. Claudia denkt an ihre Freundin Bärbel.
2. Bärbel denkt an ihre Sommerferien.
3. Stefan interessiert sich für Musik.
4. Susanne geht gern mit ihrer Schwester Sabine aus.
5. Daniela beschäftigt sich mit Computern.
6. Stefan trifft sich gern mit seinen Freunden.
7. Grace freut sich auf die Schulferien.
8. Grace wartet auf ihre Freunde.

A. **1.** damit **2.** dafür **3.** daran **4.** darauf
5. davon

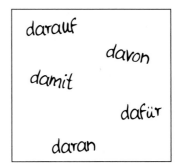

darauf
davon
damit
dafür
daran

Klaus.

B. **1.** An wen denkt sie? **2.** Woran denkt sie?
3. Wofür interessiert er sich? **4.** Mit wem geht sie gern aus? **5.** Womit beschäftigt sich Daniela? **6.** Mit wem trifft er sich gern?
7. Worauf freut sich Grace? **8.** Auf wen wartet Grace?

PERSPEKTIVEN

HÖREN SIE ZU!
FRAGEN SIE PROFESSOR CATO!

vierbeinig	four-legged
die Katze	cat
abgewöhnen	to cure someone of something
die Ursache	cause
die Aufmerksamkeit	attention
stubenrein	housebroken
das muss ich mir verbitten	I won't put up with that
bezüglich	in reference to
die Raststätte	rest area
die Leine	leash
Felidae	cat (scientific term)

A. Answers will vary.

IPP ZUM HÖREN

In der Radiosendung hören Sie das folgende Sprichwort: „Was Hänschen nicht lernt, lernt Hans nimmermehr." Was ist der Unterschied zwischen Hänschen und Hans? Was bedeutet das Sprichwort? Was sagt es Ihrer Meinung nach über die Kultur? Was meinen Ihre Mitschüler und Mitschülerinnen? Gibt es ein Sprichwort auf Englisch, das eine ähnliche Bedeutung hat?

B. Answers will vary.

Die live gesendete Radiosendung „Fragen Sie Professor Cato!" erfreut sich immer größerer Beliebtheit. Hier hören Sie Auszüge interessanter Fragen und Antworten.

Bei einer deutschen Radiosendung.

A Professor Cato. Hören Sie die Radiosendung, und beantworten Sie danach die folgenden Fragen.

1. Wer ist Professor Cato?
2. Was haben die zwei Anrufer gemeinsam?
3. Welches Problem hat der erste Anrufer?
4. Welche Fragen stellt der Professor an den Anrufer?
5. Welche Frage hat die Anruferin?
6. Wie antwortet der Professor darauf?
7. Was wissen Sie über Julia und Nelly?
8. Wie reagieren die Anrufer auf Professor Catos Antworten?
9. An welchem Wochentag wird diese Radiosendung gesendet?

B Was möchten Sie den Professor fragen? Hören Sie der Radiosendung noch einmal gut zu. Formulieren Sie dann Fragen über Katzen oder andere Vierbeiner, die Sie selbst an Herrn Professor Cato stellen möchten. Welche Antworten erwarten Sie auf Ihre Fragen?

LESEN SIE!

Zum Thema

Answers will vary.

● Tiere. Tiere symbolisieren gewisse Eigenschaften oder erinnern uns oft an bestimmte Feiertage. Welche Assoziationen haben Sie mit diesen Tieren? Denken Sie an Märchen oder andere Texte, die Sie kennen, aber auch an Ihre Familientraditionen. Vielleicht sind in Ihrer Kultur ganz andere Tiere wichtig? Ergänzen Sie dann die Liste.

> die Katze   der Hase   der Frosch   der Esel[a]
>
> die Schnecke[c]   der Fuchs   der Hund[b]
>
> der Löwe   die Ameise[d]   die Maus   das Schaf

MODELLE:
- Der Fuchs wird in Fabeln oft als „der schlaue Fuchs" gesehen, er kann also Schlauheit symbolisieren.
- Am Ostersonntag bringt er als Osterhase in deutschsprachigen Ländern Schokoladeneier für die Kinder.

[a]*donkey* [b]*dog* [c]*snail* [d]*ant*

Die erste Begegnung

Er war noch nie in einem Wohnzimmer gewesen und besah sich alles ganz genau. Zuerst klärte er mögliche Gefahren ab: gab es Hühner mit scharfen Schnäbeln? Einen Hund? Jemanden, der einen
5 Pantoffel nach ihm werfen würde? Das Zimmer war leer und still bis auf das leise knisternde Kaminfeuer. Im Nebenzimmer gab es Geräusche, dort schien sich jemand an Schränken zu schaffen zu machen, aber hier im großen Wohnraum
10 herrschte eine schöne Ruhe. Nero schritt zum erstenmal in seinem Katerleben über einen Teppich, einen weichen, rosa Teppich mit kleinen grünen Ranken. Vorsichtig setzte er die Pfoten, sank ein wenig ein, streckte sich, machte sich gaaaaanz
15 lang und wetzte ratsch, ratsch, ratsch seine Krallen

in der Wolle. Dabei zog er ein paar Teppichfäden heraus—das gefiel ihm, und er kratzte sich den ganzen Teppichrand entlang ritscheratsche bis zum Sofa. Es war ein grünes Sofa mit dicken rosa Kissen.
20 Nero stellte sich auf die Hinterbeine und testete mit den Vorderpfoten: gut, sehr gut, das war sehr schön weich, fast so weich wie das Heu drüben auf dem Hof und nicht so pieksig. Mit einem Satz war er oben, drehte sich ein paarmal und rollte sich in die
25 Polster.

Dazu muß man bedenken, wie hoch so ein Sofa und wie klein so eine Katze ist. Es ist etwa so, als würde ein Mensch aus dem Stand und ohne Anlauf mal eben so auf das Dach seines Hauses springen
30 oder doch wenigstens auf den Balkon im ersten

Stock. Eine Katze ist ein Wunder – nicht nur wegen solcher Sprünge. Eine Katze kann auch im Schlaf alles hören, das leiseste Mäusefiepen. Sie kann im Stockdunkeln sehen und wird nie eine Brille
35 brauchen. Sie geht völlig lautlos und trägt einen dicken, weichen Pelz, mit dem sie auch in der Sonne nicht schwitzt. Ihre Pfoten sind zart und weich, und doch läuft sie damit über spitze Steine, heißes Pflaster und gefrorene Felder, ohne sich
40 weh zu tun, und wenn es sein muß, sausen wie Klappmesser vorn die schärfsten Krallen heraus, die man sich vorstellen kann. Eine Katze kann in den Schlamm fallen und schon nach zehn Minuten wieder so adrett und sauber aussehen, als sei sie in
45 der Städtischen Badeanstalt gewesen. Eine Katze kann senkrecht an einem Baum hochgehen, und dann landet sie mit zwei, drei Sprüngen wieder unten, als wäre nichts gewesen, und wenn sie sich wohlfühlt, kann sie ein unbeschreibliches Geräusch
50 in ihrer Kehle rollen lassen – etwas zwischen einem fernen, leisen Gewittergrummeln, einem kleinen Güterzug, der weit weg in der Nacht über eine Holzbrücke fährt und einem Wasserkessel, der gerade zu summen anfängt, kurz ehe das Wasser
55 kocht. Es ist eines der schönsten Geräusche auf der Welt, und man nennt es Schnurren.

Nero schnurrte.

Er lag in den grünen Polstern, hingelehnt an die rosa Kissen und schnurrte. Und er hörte sehr wohl,
60 daß sich aus dem Nebenzimmer jemand näherte, aber er hatte keine Lust, diesen paradiesischen Platz wieder aufzugeben, aufzuspringen und wegzusausen. Er vertraute auf seine schon andernorts bewiesene Überzeugungskraft. Er war
65 sicher, daß er ein Recht hatte, hier zu liegen, und wenn nicht – dann hatte er ja immer noch seine gefährlichen, blitzschnellen Krallen.

Aus kleinen Augenschlitzen beobachtete Nero eine blonde Frau, die einen Stapel Wäsche in eine
70 Kommodenschublade packte. Sie strich sich eine Haarsträhne aus dem Gesicht und faßte sich mit der Hand auf den schmerzenden Rücken, als sie sich wieder aufrichtete und –

"JETZT!" dachte Nero, "jetzt sieht sie sich um, nur
75 jetzt nicht rühren. Wachsam sein! AUFGEPASST!"

Die Frau sah ihn an, aber, fand Nero sofort heraus, nicht unfreundlich. Sie war nur halb so dick wie die Bäuerin vom Hof, sie hatte blaue Augen und schaute sehr verwundert und, wie Nero
80 registrierte, auch bewundernd auf den schwarzen kleinen Besuch da in ihren Kissen. Nero setzte sich ruckartig auf, bereit das „Wer-bist-du-denn"-Spiel mitzuspielen. Er machte seine grünen Augen erschrocken rund, starrte in die blauen Augen der
85 Frau und öffnete sein niedliches rosa Schnäuzchen, um ein klägliches, an langweiligen Nachmittagen sorgfältig eingeübtes, zu Herzen gehendes MIAUOUOUOUAUO! ertönen zu lassen. Es verfehlte seine Wirkung nicht. "Wer bist du denn?" fragte die
90 blonde Frau gerührt und kam vorsichtig näher. "Du liebe Güte", dachte Nero, "wer bin ich denn, wer bin ich denn, das sieht man doch, ich bin ein schwarzer Kater." Und er streckte ihr zutraulich sein Köpfchen entgegen. Die Frau kniete sich vors Sofa
95 und streichelte ihn.

"Du bist ja ein süßes Kerlchen", sagte sie, "wo kommst du denn auf einmal her?"

"Wahrscheinlich bin ich durchs Fenster hereingeflogen", sagte Nero, schmiegte seinen
100 kleinen schwarzen Kopf an ihren Arm, in ihre Hand und maunzte laut.

"Hast du Hunger?" fragte die Frau und stand auf.

"Jajaja!" krähte Nero, denn Hunger, oder sagen wir: Appetit hatte er eigentlich immer, und er wußte
105 sofort: diese blonde Puppe kann ich um die Pfote wickeln.

Die Frau ging in die Küche. Gleich sprang Nero vom Sofa, trippelte hinter ihr her, rieb sich an ihrem Bein und maunzte noch einmal, so rührend er nur
110 konnte. Die Frau öffnete den Kühlschrank, holte eine kleine Dose heraus und schüttete ein wenig Milch auf einen Teller. Sie ließ ein bißchen warmes Leitungswasser dazu, verrührte alles mit dem Zeigefinger und sagte: "So ist es nicht zu kalt für
115 dein Bäuchlein."

"Bäuchlein, pah!" dachte Nero, "was weißt denn du von meinem Bäuchlein, nun mal endlich runter mit dem blöden Teller!" Und er stellte sich auf die Hinterbeine, machte sich ganz lang und angelte mit
120 den Vorderpfoten so kräftig nach dem Teller, mit

dem die blonde Frau sich ihm entgegenbückte, daß ein paar Tropfen Milch verschüttet wurden. Noch ehe der Teller ganz auf den Küchenfliesen stand, hatte Nero schon seine rosa Zunge
125 eingetaucht und schlappte und trank.

„Du bist aber stürmisch!" lachte die Frau, und Nero dachte: „Was meinst du denn, wen du hier vor dir hast, den heiligen Antonius?" und leckte den Teller blitzeblank.

130 Die blonde Frau ging zur Wohnzimmertür und rief: „Robert, komm mal gucken, was für einen niedlichen Besuch wir haben!"

„Robert?" dachte Nero, „aufgepaßt, wer ist denn nun wieder Robert?" und er mußte rasch an den
135 Bauern denken, der wütend seine Gummischuhe nach ihm warf.

Robert war ein baumlanger Mensch mit einer dicken Brille und einer Zigarre im Mund. Er näherte sich der Küche, und Nero sicherte sich aus den
140 Augenwinkeln rasch einen Fluchtweg.

„Wo kommt der denn her?" brummte der Mann. „Er lag auf dem Sofa", sagte sie, „und der arme kleine Kerl hatte Hunger, ich hab ihm ein bißchen Milch gegeben."

145 „Wenn er Hunger hat, mußt du ihm was Richtiges zu essen geben", sagte Robert, „ist denn von den Wurstbroten nichts mehr da?"

„Robert, du bist in Ordnung", dachte Nero vergnügt, und die Frau sagte: „Wurstbrote! Eine
150 Katze frißt doch keine Wurstbrote!"

„Die Brote könnt ihr euch schenken", dachte Nero, „aber nur immer her mit der Wurst!" Und er stieß einen langen, äußerst kläglichen Jammerlaut aus.

155 „Siehst du, er hat Hunger", sagte Robert. „Versuch's mal mit einem Wurstbrot."

„Wieso er?" fragte sie, und wühlte in einer Reisetasche, die noch unausgepackt auf dem Küchentisch stand.

160 „Das ist ein Kater", sagte Robert, „das seh ich." Er bückte sich, blies Nero ekelhaften Zigarrenrauch ins Gesicht und sah ihm unter den Schwanz. „Kater", nickte er, und Nero quäkte empört.

Die Frau hatte inzwischen ein Butterbrot aus
165 einem knisternden Papier gewickelt und fing an, es in den Milchteller zu brocken. Nero schnupperte gute deutsche Fleischwurst. Mit der rechten Vorderpfote, der weißen, räumte er die Brotbröckchen beiseite, leckte höchstens etwas
170 Butter da ab, wo es Butter abzulecken gab, und machte sich über die kleinen, runden rosa Fleischwurstscheibchen her. Schwapp, die erste, happ, die zweite, schwupp, die dritte, schmatz, die vierte – „Meine Güte, kann der futtern!" freute sich
175 die blonde Frau, kniete nieder und streichelte ihn, und Robert brummte düster: „Den wirst du nicht mehr los."

Elke Heidenreich

Possible answers are: **1.** Nero hat vor seinem Besuch im Wohnzimmer auf einem Bauernhof gewohnt. Er geht zum ersten Mal in seinem Leben über einen Teppich und legt sich zum ersten Mal auf ein weiches Sofa. **2.** In dem Text kommen eine blonde Frau mit blauen Augen und Robert vor. Außerdem wird noch der Bauer erwähnt. **3.** Katzen sind ein Wunder, weil sie aus dem Stand sehr hoch springen können, weil sie auch im Schlaf alles hören und weil sie in der Dunkelheit alles sehen können. Sie können lautlos gehen und schwitzen nie in ihrem Pelz. (*etc.*) **4.** *Answers will vary.*

Zum Text

● Neros Abenteuer. Beantworten Sie die Fragen.

1. „Er war noch nie in einem Wohnzimmer gewesen . . ." erfahren wir im ersten Satz. Wo hat Nero vor seinem Besuch im Wohnzimmer gewohnt? Was ist alles neu für ihn?
2. Welche Menschen kommen in diesem Text vor? Was erfahren wir über sie? Wie werden sie beschrieben?
3. Warum ist eine Katze „ein Wunder"? Welche Fähigkeiten von Katzen beschreibt der Erzähler? Was von Neros Verhalten ist typisch für eine Katze?
4. Nero erzählt seiner Freundin Rosa von seinem ersten Besuch bei Isolde und Robert. Beschreiben Sie seine Erlebnisse aus seiner Perspektive.

KULTURSPIEGEL

Elke Heidenreich ist eine bekannte deutsche Kolumnistin. Ihre Kolumnen erscheinen regelmäßig in der Frauenzeitschrift „Brigitte". Sie ist auch engagierte Tierschützerin und Autorin des Bestsellers „Nero Corleone".

TIPP ZUM LESEN

Animal body parts often have different names than those of humans. For example, a cat has paws, not hands and feet. Look for other words and expressions in the text that are specific for animals, particularly for cats.

Zur Interpretation

● Verstehen Sie Neros Ironie? Erklären Sie, was er in den kursiv gedruckten Sätzen meint.

1. „Wer bist du denn?" fragte die blonde Frau gerührt und kam vorsichtig näher. „Du liebe Güte", dachte Nero, *„wer bin ich denn, wer bin ich denn, das sieht man doch, ich bin ein schwarzer Kater"*.

2. „Du bist ja ein süßes Kerlchen", sagte sie, „wo kommst du denn auf einmal her?" *„Wahrscheinlich bin ich durchs Fenster hereingeflogen"*, sagte Nero, schmiegte seinen kleinen schwarzen Kopf an ihren Arm, in ihre Hand und maunzte laut.

3. „Hast du Hunger?" fragte die Frau und stand auf. „Jajaja!" krähte Nero, denn Hunger, oder sagen wir: Appetit hatte er eigentlich immer, und er wußte sofort: *diese blonde Puppe kann ich um die Pfote wickeln.* Possible answers are: **1.** Es ist offensichtlich, dass Nero eine schwarze Katze ist. Diese rhetorische Frage findet er überflüssig und lächerlich. **2.** Noch eine überflüssige Frage. Katzen können nicht fliegen, also wird er wohl hineingelaufen sein. **3.** Nero verändert eine Redensart: „jemanden um den Finger wickeln", was meint, dass man jemanden leicht beeinflussen kann. Weil er keine Finger hat, sagt er „Pfoten".

INTERAKTION

Answers will vary.

● Was ist das ideale Haustier? Diskutieren Sie mit Ihren Mitschülern/ Mitschülerinnen, welche Tiere sich als Haustiere am besten eignen. Was denken Sie? Was sind die Vor- und Nachteile?

TIPP ZUM SCHREIBEN

In advertising, grabbing the audience's attention is just as important as relaying factual information. Comedy, action, drama, music, special effects, or other devices help get the listener's attention. Clever, entertaining messages are remembered better than long, factual ones. Short, simple slogans also stick in the mind. Pay attention to the devices used in ads and announcements before trying to write your own.

SCHREIBEN SIE!

Texts will vary.

Ein Werbespot für das Radio

● Ihr Klub hat vor, eine große Abendveranstaltung zu organisieren und gibt Ihnen den Auftrag, die Werbung dafür zu gestalten. Ihre Aufgabe ist, den Text für einen 60-Sekunden-langen Radiowerbe-Spot zu schreiben und danach eine Aufnahme davon zu machen.

Purpose:	To write and produce a radio ad
Audience:	Radio listeners
Subject:	A public event
Structure:	A radio commercial

Schreibmodell

The authors specify the music and mood they want, telling the producer how to use it.

The commercial grabs the listener's attention by switching to rock music and a younger, informal tone.

Date, time, place, and price of the event are mentioned without elaborate detail.

By using **du,** modals and imperatives, the writer personalizes the message.

The **da**-compound refers to information elsewhere in the commercial.

> **Werbespot für den**
> **Musikverein Rostock**
>
> (*Mozarts „Eine kleine Nachmusik" einblenden*)
> Lieben Sie klassische Musik? Verlieren Sie sich gern in der anmutigen Ruhe der Klassiker?
>
> (*Mozart mit Platten-Kratzergeräusch unterbrechen; Rockmusik laut einblenden*)
> Damit haben **w i r** gar nichts zu tun! Der Musikverein Rockstock – uh, Verzeihung, Rostock – lädt ein: zu einem langen lauten Abend der neusten Popmusik auf dieser Seite der Republik.
> Sänger, Bands, Rocker, Rapper und Klangkünstler aller Art bringen ihr Bestes auf die Bühne. Diesen Freitag um 19 Uhr 30 in der Großen Aula des Hanseaten-Gymnasiums. Eintritt: für Schüler und Studenten E[a] 5,50 / DM 10,75; für Erwachsene E 15,50 / DM 30,32 – denn sie können's sich leisten.
> Aber **d u** kannst es dir nicht leisten, dieses Konzert zu verpassen!
> Also denk daran: Freitag um 19 Uhr 30, die neuste Popmusik auf dieser Seite der Republik! Rostock rockt wie noch nie! Für weitere Infos, wähle 894 17.
> Eine Veranstaltung des Musikvereins Rostock e.V.

[a]*Euro*

Schreibstrategien

Vor dem Schreiben

- First, decide for what organization you are writing the advertisement and think about the types of events such a group would sponsor. Pick one event to advertise and write down the facts: title of the event, date, time, place, price, etc.

- Specify your audience: by age, gender, interests, and any other important criteria. Now brainstorm: What are people's interests? Their senses of humor? What entertains them?

- Start generating ideas that are funny and appealing, or will otherwise grab your audience's attention. Include music, sound effects, imagery, and other special effects as you brainstorm. If a good slogan comes to mind, jot it down.

KULTURSPIEGEL

€ is the symbol of the Euro—the new currency of the eleven member nations of the European Union. The Euro was introduced as an accounting currency in January 1999. As of January 2002, it will be the legal currency of the participating member nations and will replace their national currencies.

Werbespot für
das Oktoberfest der
Newburyport High-School

~~Sag mal~~ *Sagen Sie*: wann haben Sie zum letzten Mal ein deutsch~~er~~ *s* Lied gehört? Oder eine richtige Bratwurst gegessen? All das und *noch* mehr finden Sie auf ~~das~~ *dem* Deutsche *n* Oktoberfest der Newburyport High-School!

(*Lachende Leute und Geräusche mit Tellern und Gläsern einblenden*)

Der Deutsche Klub lädt ~~Ihnen~~ *Sie* zu unserem Deutschen Fest am kommenden Samstag, den einundzwanzigsten Oktober *ein.* Was bieten wir? Deutsche Küche und deutsche Unterhaltung. Für deutsche Musik sorg *en* die Sänger vom Concert Choir. Wir haben auch tolle Spiele und ~~viel~~ *noch* viel mehr.

~~Sind~~ *Seien* Sie dabei und kommen Sie zu uns, diesen Samstag, von 9 bis 15 Uhr in Newburyport High School, in der High Straße. Wir freuen uns auf Ihren Besuch!

- Now read through your ideas and select the ones that will be the most effective. Think about the tone you want to create and the devices that will help you achieve it.

Beim Schreiben

- Keep all factual information close at hand—date, time, place, price, etc.—along with your notes for the text. Decide how long the spoken text should be. Remember you are writing the script for a 60-second commercial.

- Think about whether complete sentences are necessary for your ad. What would your audience expect? What would it find entertaining?

- Decide which information is most important, and be sure to repeat it in the body of the text.

- Would sound effects, music, or using more than one narrator make your commercial more effective?

- Don't be afraid to write several different versions. If you don't like your text, chances are your audience won't either.

- Read your ad aloud, timing yourself as you do so. Have you written too much or do you need more text? If you are including music or sound effects, allow time for it.

Nach dem Schreiben

- Compare your draft text with the list of factual information and make sure you've included all of it in your message.

- Trade papers with a peer editor and edit each other's work. Correct misspellings, grammar errors, etc. If you have suggestions for improvement, note them on the draft. Return the paper to its author.

- Read through your first draft again and review your peer editor's comments. Write your second draft.

Stimmt alles?

- Read the final product one more time and correct any undetected problems.

- Gather all the additional material you may need for your finished product: music, musicians, sound effects, additional narrators, etc. Be sure you have a blank cassette, a microphone, and a cassette recorder. Record your commercial with all special effects.

- Play the recording for your class. You may also want to distribute copies of your script and let classmates read along as they listen.

WORTSCHATZ

Substantive	Nouns
die **Anregung**	stimulation
die **Erholung**	rest; recuperation
die **Gartenarbeit**	gardening
die **Gestaltung, -en**	organization; shape; design
die **Industrialisierung**	industrialization
die **Volkshochschule, -n**	extension school, adult education center
der **Hof, ⸚e**	yard; courtyard
der **Kleingarten**, *pl.* **Kleingärten**	small garden
der **Leiter, -** / die **Leiterin, -nen**	leader; director; supervisor; head
der **Nachweis, -e**	proof
das **Gefühl, -e**	feeling
das **Gerät, -e**	device; appliance
das **Hobby, -s**	hobby
das **Lagerfeuer, -**	campfire
das **Mal, -e**	point in time
das **Verhalten**	attitude

Verben	Verbs
an•fassen	to touch; to grasp
an•regen	to stimulate
bedenken, bedachte, bedacht	to consider
bieten, bot, geboten	to offer
bummeln, ist gebummelt	to stroll; to idle
sich entspannen	to relax
erwachsen (erwächst), erwuchs, ist erwachsen	to arise
erwähnen	to mention
grillen	to grill
sich langweilen	to be bored
musizieren	to play music
pflegen	to look after

rühren	to move; to stir
teilen	to divide; to share
töpfern	to make pottery
sich weiter•bilden	to continue one's education

Adjektive und Adverbien	Adjectives and adverbs
draußen	outside
hauptsächlich	mainly, primarily
im Freien	in the open air; outdoors
preisgünstig	fairly priced
sorgfältig	careful
unbeschreiblich	indescribable
unersetzlich	irreplaceable
vorsichtig	cautious(ly)
im Wesentlichen	essentially; fundamentally

Sie wissen schon	You already know
die **Freizeit**	free time
der **Feiertag**	holiday
an•fangen (fängt an), fing an, angefangen	to start
belegen	to take (a class)
gefallen (gefällt), gefiel, gefallen (+ *dat.*)	to be pleasing to, to like
sich interessieren für	to be interested in
unternehmen (unternimmt), unternahm, unternommen	to undertake; to do
verbringen, verbrachte, verbracht	to spend (time)
zelten	to camp
ziehen, zog, gezogen	to pull

PLANNING GUIDE • CLASSROOM MANAGEMENT

OBJECTIVES

Communication
- Talk about travel, now and in the past, pp. 164–165.
- Talk about vacations, pp. 166–167.

Grammar
- Review the present perfect tense, pp. 168, 170.
- Use modal verbs in the past tense, p. 172.

Culture
- Learn about paid vacation time in Germany, p. 165.
- Learn about Wolfgang Hildesheimer, p. 175.

Recycling
- Review vocabulary related to sports, pp. 166–167.
- Go over the present perfect tense, pp. 168–171.

STRATEGIES

Listening Strategies
- Listen for information about nature travel tours, pp. 174–175.

Speaking Strategies
- Talk about the pros and cons of demanding sports, p. 165.
- Talk about dream vacations, pp. 165, 178.
- Recount a recent trip, p. 169.
- Describe childhood sports experiences, p. 173.

Reading Strategies
- Read and interpret a short story, pp. 176–178.

Writing Strategies
- Write testimonials about your hometown for German-speaking tourists, pp. 178–180.

Connecting Cultures Strategies
- Compare travel experiences for East vs. West Germans, pp. 164–165.
- Reflect on the attraction of your town to a German tourist, pp. 178–180.

PROGRAM RESOURCES

Print
- *Arbeitsheft* (Workbook), pp. 115–128
- *Arbeitsheft* (Workbook), Teacher's Edition, pp. 115–128

Audiovisual
- Overhead Transparencies 32.1–32.G2
- Audio Program, Cassette 4B, 7B/CD 5, 9
- Audioscript, pp. 53–60

Technology
- Annenberg *Fokus Deutsch* Video Series, *Folge 32*
- www.mcdougallittell.com

Assessment Program Options
- *Prüfung, Kapitel 32,* Assessment Program, pp. 94–103
- Audio Program, Cassette 8B/CD 10
- Audioscript, p. 112
- Teacher's Resource CD-ROM

DAY 1

Note: (1) Please see TE, pp. 162E–162J, for other suggestions not referenced in these plans. (2) Not all homework options need be assigned.

CHAPTER OPENER

- Quick Start Review: Dative objects (TE, p. 162E). 5 MIN
- Use the photos on pp. 162–163 as a basis for class discussion (TE, p. 162E). 4 MIN

VIDEOTHEK

- Review *Wortschatz zum Video* and then watch *Folge I: Urlaub gestern und heute* (TE, p. 162F). 7 MIN
- Do *Akt. A,* p. 164, as a class. Include the follow-up activity in the Teaching Suggestions (TE, p. 162F). 8 MIN
- Do *Akt. B,* p. 164, in small groups (TE, p. 162F). 8 MIN
- Do *Akt. C,* pp. 164–165, silently, then check answers as a class (TE, p. 162F). 9 MIN
- Watch *Folge II: Abenteuerurlaub* (TE, p. 162F) after reading the introduction to the episode and looking over *Akt. A,* p. 165. Immediately do *Akt. A,* p. 165, as a class. 9 MIN

Homework Options:

- Interdisciplinary connection (TE, p. 162F)

DAY 2

VIDEOTHEK

- Quick Start Review 1: Ordering activity (TE, p. 162E). 5 MIN
- Have students do *Akt. B,* p. 165, and then break into pairs to do *Akt. C,* p. 165 (TE, p. 162F). 15 MIN
- *Arbeitsheft,* p. 117, audio *Akt. F–G.* 14 MIN

VOKABELN

- Present the vocabulary on p. 166 using the picture on p. 166 (TE, p. 162G). 8 MIN
- Do *Akt. B,* p. 167, and the follow-up activity in the Teaching Suggestions (TE, p. 162G). 8 MIN

Homework Options:

- *Arbeitsheft,* p. 119, *Vokabeln, Akt. C–D*

DAY 3

VOKABELN

- Quick Start Review 1: Sports (TE, p. 162G). 5 MIN
- *Arbeitsheft,* p. 118, audio *Akt. A–B.* 14 MIN
- Do *Akt. A,* pp. 166–167, silently, then check the answers as a class (TE, p. 162G). 13 MIN
- Do *Akt. C,* p. 167, silently, then check their answers as a class (TE, p. 162G). 8 MIN
- Do *Akt. D,* p. 167, in small groups. Encourage students to discuss all aspects of the various activities. 10 MIN

Homework Options:

- *Arbeitsheft,* p. 120, *Vokabeln, Akt. E–F*

DAY 4

VOKABELN

- Quick Start Review 2: Vocabulary review (TE, p. 162G). 5 MIN

STRUKTUREN

- Review the present perfect tense I on p. 168 using OHT 32.G1 and the Teaching Suggestions (TE, p. 162H). 8 MIN
- Do *Übung A,* p. 169, silently, then check the answers as a class. 14 MIN
- Do *Übung B,* p. 169, on the board as a class (TE, p. 162H). 7 MIN
- Have students do *Übung C,* p. 169, and then summarize their partners' responses for the class. 8 MIN
- Present the present perfect tense II on p. 170 using OHT 32.G1. Follow the Teaching Suggestions (TE, p. 162H). 8 MIN

Homework Options:

- *Übung B,* p. 171
- *Arbeitsheft,* pp. 122–123 *Strukturen, Akt. F–G*

PACING GUIDE • SAMPLE LESSON PLAN, 50-MINUTE SCHEDULE

PACING GUIDE: KAPITEL 32 **162B**

DAY 5

STRUKTUREN

- Quick Start Review 1: Modal verbs (TE, p. 162G). 4 MIN
- Do *Übung A,* p. 171, as a class and the follow-up activity in the Teaching Suggestions (TE, p. 162H). 8 MIN
- Have students do *Übung C,* p. 171, with a partner (TE, p. 162H). 12 MIN
- Present modal verbs in the perfect tense on p. 172 using OHT 32.G2. 8 MIN
- Do *Übung A,* p. 173, as a class (TE, p. 162H). 8 MIN
- *Übung B, Schritt 1,* p. 173 (TE, p. 162H). 10 MIN

Homework Options:

- *Arbeitsheft,* p. 124, *Strukturen, Akt. J–K*

DAY 6

STRUKTUREN

- Quick Start Review 2: Time expressions (TE, p. 162H). 5 MIN
- Have students do *Übung B, Schritt 2,* p. 173, and then share some answers with the class (TE, p. 162H). 10 MIN

PERSPEKTIVEN

- After reviewing *Wortschatz zum Hörtext* and cues for *Hören Sie zu!, Akt. A,* p. 174, play the recording once. Have students do the activity while they listen. 12 MIN
- Do *Hören Sie zu!, Akt. B,* p. 175, as a class. Write the categories on the board (TE, p. 162I). 6 MIN
- Discuss *Zum Thema,* p. 175, as a class (TE, p. 162I). 5 MIN
- Follow the Teaching Suggestions for reading the text. Encourage students to help each other understand it (TE, p. 162I). 12 MIN

Homework Options:

- *Zum Text, Akt. A–B,* pp. 177–178
- *Arbeitsheft,* pp. 126–127, *Perspektiven, Akt. C–D*

DAY 7

PERSPEKTIVEN

- Quick Start Review 1: Vocabulary (TE, p. 162I). 5 MIN
- Check the answers to *Zum Text, Akt. A–B,* pp. 177–178 as a class. 7 MIN
- Discuss the questions in *Zur Interpretation* p. 178 as a class (TE, p. 162J). 5 MIN
- *Interaktion,* p. 178. Have some students share their ideas with the class. 10 MIN
- Begin *Schreiben Sie!* by discussing the assignment, *Tipp zum Schreiben,* and *Schreibmodell* (TE, p. 162J). 8 MIN
- Do as much of *Vor dem Schreiben* as possible, then begin *Beim Schreiben,* p. 180 (TE, p. 162J). 15 MIN

Homework Options:

- Finish *Vor dem Schreiben,* pp. 179–180, and write the first draft of the brochure
- *Arbeitsheft,* p. 128, *Perspektiven, Akt. E*

DAY 8

PERSPEKTIVEN

- Quick Start Review 2: Simple past (TE, p. 162I). 5 MIN
- Do *Nach dem Schreiben,* p. 180, and begin the final draft of the brochure. 10 MIN
- Questions and review. 5 MIN
- *Prüfung, Kapitel 32.* 30 MIN

Homework Options:

- Complete the final draft of your brochure
- *Arbeitsheft,* p. 128, *Perspektiven, Akt. F*

DAY 1

Note: (1) Please see TE, pp. 162E–162J, for other suggestions not referenced in these plans. (2) Not all homework options need be assigned.

CHAPTER OPENER

- Quick Start Review: Dative objects (TE, p. 162E). 5 MIN
- Discuss the photos on pp. 162–163 (TE, p. 162E). 5 MIN

VIDEOTHEK

- Review the *Wortschatz* and then watch *Folge I* (TE, p. 162F). 7 MIN
- Do *Akt. A–C*, pp. 164–165 (TE, p. 162F). 28 MIN
- Watch *Folge II* after reading the introduction to the episode. Do *Akt. A*, p. 165. 10 MIN
- Block Schedule activity: Variety (TE, p. 162F). 10 MIN
- Do *Akt. B*, p. 165, then do *Akt. C*, p. 165 in pairs. Discuss. 15 MIN
- *Arbeitsheft*, p. 115, audio *Akt. A–B*. 10 MIN

Homework Options:

- Interdisciplinary connection (TE, p. 162F)

DAY 2

VOKABELN

- Quick Start Review 1: Sports (TE, p. 162G). 5 MIN
- Present the vocabulary on p. 166 (TE, p. 162G). 8 MIN
- Do *Akt. A*, pp. 166–167, silently, then check answers (TE, p. 162G). 14 MIN
- Do *Akt. B*, p. 167, (TE, p. 162G). 8 MIN
- Do *Akt. C*, p. 167, silently, then check answers as a class (TE, p. 162G). 10 MIN
- Do *Akt. D*, p. 167, in small groups. 10 MIN
- Block Schedule activity: Peer Teaching (TE, p. 162G). 15 MIN

STRUKTUREN

- Review the present perfect tense I on p. 168 (TE, p. 162H). 8 MIN
- Do *Übung A*, p. 169, silently, then check answers as a class. 12 MIN

Homework Options:

- *Arbeitsheft*, pp. 119–120, *Vokabeln, Akt. C–F*

DAY 3

STRUKTUREN

- Quick Start Review 1: Modal verbs (TE, p. 162H). 5 MIN
- Do *Übung B*, p. 169, as a class (TE, p. 162H). 6 MIN
- Do *Übung C*, p. 169, then summarize partners' responses. 8 MIN
- Present the present perfect tense II on p. 170 (TE, p. 162G). 7 MIN
- Do *Übung A*, p. 171, as a class (TE, p. 162H). 7 MIN
- Do *Übung C*, p. 171, with a partner (TE, p. 162H). 12 MIN
- Block Schedule activity: Fun Break (TE, p. 162H). 10 MIN
- Present modal verbs in the perfect tense on p. 172. 8 MIN
- Do *Übung A*, p. 173, as a class (TE, p. 162H). 8 MIN
- Do *Übung A–B*, p. 173 (TE, p. 162H). 19 MIN

Homework Options:

- *Übung B*, p. 171
- *Arbeitsheft*, pp. 122–124 *Akt. F–G, Akt. J–K*

DAY 4

PERSPEKTIVEN

- Quick Start Review 1: Vocabulary (TE, p. 162I). 5 MIN
- Review *Wortschatz* and cues for *Hören Sie zu!, Akt. A*, p. 174. Play the recording and do the activity. 14 MIN
- Do *Hören Sie zu!, Akt. B*, p. 175, as a class. (TE, p. 162I). 8 MIN
- Discuss *Zum Thema*, p. 175, then read the text, pp. 176–177. (TE, p. 162I). 18 MIN
- Do *Zum Text, Akt. A–B*, pp. 177–178 in pairs and check answers. 15 MIN
- Do *Zur Interpretation* and *Interaktion*, p. 178. 15 MIN
- Begin *Schreiben Sie!* by discussing the assignment. (TE, p. 162J). 7 MIN
- Start *Vor dem Schreiben*, pp. 179–180 and begin *Beim Schreiben*. (TE, p. 162J). 8 MIN

Homework Options:

- Finish *Vor dem Schreiben* and write the first draft
- *Arbeitsheft*, pp. 126–127, *Akt. C–D*

DAY 5

PERSPEKTIVEN

- Quick Start Review 2: Simple past (TE, p. 162I). 5 MIN
- *Arbeitsheft*, p. 125, audio *Akt. A–B*. 15 MIN
- Do *Nach dem Schreiben*, p. 180, and begin the final draft of the brochure. 20 MIN
- Block Schedule activity: Expansion (TE, p. 162J). 15 MIN
- Questions and review. 5 MIN
- *Prüfung, Kapitel 32*. 30 MIN

Homework Options:

- Complete the final draft of the brochure
- *Arbeitsheft*, p. 128, *Perspektiven, Akt. F*

Chapter Opener, pp. 162–163

PROGRAM RESOURCES

- Overhead Transparency 32.1

Quick Start Review

♻ Dative objects

Ergänzen Sie die Sätze mit den Wörtern in Klammern.

1. San Francisko hat _____ Sabine sehr gut gefallen. (unsere Freundin)
2. Sie ist vier Tage bei _____ geblieben. (wir)
3. Wir sind an einem Tag mit _____ nach Chinatown gefahren. (sie, sing.)
4. Sabine und ich fanden das Essen lecker, aber _____ hat es nicht geschmeckt. (mein Mann)
5. _____ ging es nach dem Essen gar nicht gut. (er)
6. Dann wurde er richtig krank. Er tat _____ so leid! (ich)
7. Wir mussten _____ helfen, zurück zum Auto zu kommen. (der Arme)
8. Wir sagten _____, dass es bestimmt eine Lebensmittel-vergiftung ist. (der Arzt) Aber er sagte: „Nein, es ist eine Grippe."

Answers: 1. unserer Freundin 2. uns 3. ihr 4. meinem Mann 5. Ihm 6. mir 7. dem Armen 8. dem Arzt

TEACHING SUGGESTIONS

- Introduce the topic of vacation and holidays by talking about where you like to go on vacations and what you like to do. Ask students what their favorite travel destinations are. Ask how many of them have been to countries abroad. Also introduce the notion of *Abenteuerurlaub* or *Aktivurlaub*.

- Photos, pp. 162–163

Have students look at the photos and describe the action in each one. Supply the following vocabulary: *der Drachenflieger, starten, Wind surfen, das Windsurfbrett.* Finally, have them look again at the black-and-white photo and comment on what vacations might have been like for tourists 100 years ago.

TEACHING ALL STUDENTS

Multiple Intelligences Intrapersonal: *Wandern, Drachenfliegen oder Windsurfen?* Give students 4 minutes to write a positive or negative reaction to 1 of these activities. Prompt them with the question *Würden Sie lieber Wind surfen, Drachen fliegen oder wandern? Warum?*

CLASSROOM COMMUNITY

Challenge Write *Drachenfliegen* and *Windsurfen* on the board. Give students 1 minute to brainstorm for associations. Encourage them to come up with various parts of speech.

Videothek, pp. 164–165

PROGRAM RESOURCES

- Videocassette, *Folge 32*
- *Arbeitsheft,* pp. 115–117
- Audio Program, Cassette 4B/CD 5
- Audioscript, pp. 53–55

Quick Start Review 1

♻ Ordering activity

Bringen Sie die Sätze in die richtige Reihenfolge.

Im Reisebüro

_____ Aber, fliegen möchte ich gar nicht. Ich mache Urlaub hier in Europa und fahre also lieber mit der Bahn.

_____ Guten Tag! Wie kann ich Ihnen helfen?

_____ Ja, dann würde ich Griechen-land oder Spanien vorschlagen. Hier sind ein paar Prospekte.

_____ Wir haben ja ein großes Angebot an Reisen. Wann möchten Sie fahren?

_____ Ich möchte mich ein bisschen über die Urlaubsreisen informieren, die Sie hier anbieten.

__1__ Guten Tag!

_____ Alles klar. Die Zugverbindungen sind selten ein Problem. Und was suchen Sie im Urlaub?

_____ Ja, wahrscheinlich Ende dieses Monats, aber vielleicht erst in der ersten Augustwoche.

_____ Gut, dann müssen Sie sich schnell entscheiden. Im Sommer werden die Flüge sehr schnell ausgebucht.

_____ Vor allem will ich schönes Wetter. Und relativ billig.

Answers: 7, 2, 10, 4, 3, 1, 8, 5, 6, 9

Quick Start Review 2

♻ Geography

Wie heißen die Länder?

1. Der Rhein fließt durch diese vier Länder.

2. Das EU-Land mit den meisten Einwohnern.
3. Deutschlands Nachbarland im Norden.
4. Die fünf Nachbarländer der Schweiz.
5. Die Insel Mallorca ist ein Teil von diesem Land.
6. Die sechs Länder um das Schwarze Meer herum.
7. Die Hauptstadt von diesem Land ist Oslo.

Answers: 1. die Schweiz, Frankreich, Deutschland, die Niederlande
2. Deutschland   3. Dänemark
4. Österreich, Liechtenstein, Italien, Frankreich, Deutschland   5. Spanien
6. die Türkei, Bulgarien, Rumänien, Ukraine, Russland, Georgien
7. Norwegen

TEACHING SUGGESTIONS

• *Folge I: Urlaub gestern und heute,* pp. 164–165

Ask students to highlight one particular fact or aspect of the video they find most interesting and tell why.

• *Aktivität A,* p. 164

Follow-up: Review the answers to the activity, then discuss the differences between German and American vacations. Write the points made by students on the board under the headings *In Deutschland* and *Bei uns.*

• *Aktivität B,* p. 164

Follow-up: Bring in wall maps or make OHTs showing the places referred to in the video. Point out both the countries and natural landmarks mentioned.

• *Aktivität C,* pp. 164–165

Expansion: Have students close their books. Show a transparency of the words in the box on p. 165. Ask students to make statements about the video, beginning each with an expression from the transparency.

• *Folge II: Abenteuerurlaub,* p. 165

Use an anecdote to illustrate *Abenteuer* before viewing this section. Then have the class do an *Assoziogramm* on the word *Abenteuerurlaub.*

• *Aktivität C,* p. 165

Have students report to the class any "extreme" or unusual experiences their partners have had.

TEACHING ALL STUDENTS

Multiple Intelligences Naturalist: *Die Natur: Spielplatz der Menschen?* Have students reflect on the potentially detrimental effects on nature of such activities as canyoning, mountain biking, and mountain climbing. Should access to remote areas be limited? Are there any positive consequences of the growing popularity of these *Extremsportarten* in terms of the environment? After discussing different points of view in class, have students summarize their ideas in writing as homework.

CLASSROOM COMMUNITY

Group Activity Introduce the following *Sportarten: Fallschirmspringen, Freiklettern, Skifahren, Gleitschirmfliegen, Joggen, Schnorcheln, Bungee-Springen, Wasserskifahren, Canyoning* (*Schluchtwandern*), *River-Rafting,* *Snowboarden, Mountainbike fahren, Tauchen, Trekken, Radwandern.* Have students form groups of 4 and rate the sports as *nicht extrem, extrem,* or *ganz extrem.*

LANGUAGE NOTE

Point out the high frequency of words borrowed from English in the category of adventure sports. Have students speculate why there are so many.

CULTURE HIGHLIGHTS

Talk about stereotypes of German tourists in this country or of Americans abroad. Ask students whether these stereotypes are well founded according to their experiences.

INTERDISCIPLINARY CONNECTION

Have students research the geography of a region where one could pursue an adventure sport. Have them write a short description of their findings.

BLOCK SCHEDULE

Variety Replay the scene from the video of Birgit's visit to the travel agency and have students jot down useful vocabulary. In pairs, have students prepare a dialogue called *Im Reisebüro.* Encourage the integration of more unusual vacation options into the dialogues. Choose a few pairs of students to perform their dialogues.

Vokabeln, pp. 166–167

PROGRAM RESOURCES

• *Arbeitsheft,* pp. 118–120
• Audio Program, Cassette 4B/CD 5
• Audioscript, pp. 55–56

Quick Start Review 1

♻ Sports

Verbinden Sie die Sportart mit der passenden Definition.

1. _____ Man muss gut Schlittschuh laufen können.
2. _____ Ohne ein Pferd geht es nicht.
3. _____ Dazu braucht man viel Schnee.
4. _____ 18 mal muss man den Ball ins Loch bringen.
5. _____ Es ist von Vorteil, möglichst groß zu sein.
6. _____ Der Ball ist klein, weiß und aus Plastik, die Schläger sind aus Holz und Gummi.
7. _____ Man braucht ein Boot, aber ohne Segel.
8. _____ Den Ball darf man nicht mit der Hand berühren, mit dem Kopf aber schon.

  a. Rudern   e. Eishockey
  b. Golf   f. Tischtennis
  c. Fußball   g. Basketball
  d. Reiten   h. Schilaufen

Answers: 1. e   2. d   3. h   4. b
5. g   6. f   7. a   8. c

Quick Start Review 2

♻ Vocabulary review

Ergänzen Sie die Sätze mit den Wörtern aus der Liste.

WÖRTER: mieten, Sache, verbringen, Meer, klettern, Mannschaften, wenig, spannend

1. Das Hockeyspiel war bis zum Ende ganz _____.
2. Beide _____ haben wirklich gut gespielt.
3. Im Sommer werden wir drei Wochen auf Kreta _____.
4. Vielleicht sollten wir ein Ferienhaus _____.
5. Gut, aber es muss direkt am _____ liegen.
6. Nichts ist schöner, als auf große Felsen zu _____!
7. Ja, Extremsport ist wirklich eine tolle _____!
8. Meint ihr? Ich habe _____ Interesse daran.

Answers: 1. spannend
2. Mannschaften   3. verbringen
4. mieten   5. Meer   6. klettern
7. Sache   8. wenig

TEACHING SUGGESTIONS

• Photo, p. 166

Point out the difference between a *Gleitschirmflieger* (p. 166), a *Drachenflieger* (pp. 162–163), and a *Fallschirmspringer.*

• *Aktivität A,* pp. 166–167

Ask content questions, such as *Was ist ein Vorteil von Wandern? Wie bleibt man fit?*

• *Aktivität B,* p. 167

Follow-up: Have students work in pairs to rewrite the sentences in a different word order, for example, *4. Vor hundert Jahren konnten sich nur wenige Menschen eine richtige Urlaubsreise leisten.*

• *Aktivität C,* p. 167

Write the 5 *Begriffe* from the activity on the board and elicit further associations from the class.

TEACHING ALL STUDENTS

Multiple Intelligences Visual: Describe a detailed scene involving one of the vacation activities from the chapter and have students draw the scene. In pairs, have students compare their drawings and point out differences.

CLASSROOM COMMUNITY

Group Activity Divide the class into groups of 3. Divide up roles in each group: (1) *eine Person, die sich für einen Urlaub entscheiden muss,* (2) *eine abenteuerlustige Person und* (3) *eine konservative Person.* Give students 3 minutes to come up with 3 different vacation ideas and arguments supporting them.

BLOCK SCHEDULE

Peer Teaching Have each student choose a sports activity and research the equipment needed to pursue it. Using their dictionaries, students will compile lists of the necessary *Ausrüstung.* If possible, supply students with photos of people engaging in the activities or have students bring in their own photos or drawings. Students then present their vocabulary to the class.

Strukturen, pp. 168–173

PROGRAM RESOURCES

• Overhead Transparencies 32.G1–32.G2
• *Arbeitsheft,* pp. 121–124
• Audio Program, Cassette 4B/CD 5
• Audioscript, pp. 57–59

Quick Start Review 1

♻ Modal verbs

Bilden Sie Sätze.

1. ich / müssen / aufstehen / montags / früh

2. du / sonntags / nicht / sollen / ins Bett gehen / so spät
3. wollen / kommen / ihr / zu meiner Party / ?
4. leider / nicht / wir / kommen / können
5. dürfen / mit meinen Freunden / ich / fahren / in Urlaub / ?
6. du / sein / ein paar Jahre älter / müssen / erst
7. mit uns / sie (*sing.*) / möchten / Tennis spielen / ?

Answers: 1. Ich muss montags früh aufstehen.   2. Du sollst sonntags nicht so spät ins Bett gehen.   3. Wollt ihr zu meiner Party kommen?   4. Leider können wir nicht kommen.   5. Darf ich mit meinen Freunden in Urlaub fahren? 6. Du musst erst ein paar Jahre älter sein.   7. Möchte sie mit uns Tennis spielen?

Quick Start Review 2

♻ Time expressions
Verbinden Sie die Definitionen mit den passenden Zeitangaben.
1. _____ Heute ist Mittwoch, und man spricht von Dienstag.
2. _____ Man spricht von einer Zeit, die nicht gekommen ist.
3. _____ Es ist 2000, und man spricht von 1999.
4. _____ Vor zwei Tagen.
5. _____ Vor sieben Tagen.
6. _____ Es ist Donnerstag, und man spricht von Mittwoch zwischen 18 und 22 Uhr.
7. _____ Es ist März, und man spricht von Februar.
8. _____ Seit relativ kurzer Zeit.
a. vorgestern
b. neuerdings

c. letzte Woche
d. gestern Abend
e. letzten Monat
f. noch nie
g. gestern
h. letztes Jahr

Answers: 1. g   2. f   3. h   4. a   5. c 6. d   7. e   8. b

....

TEACHING SUGGESTIONS

• The present perfect tense I, pp. 168–169

Explain the uses of the present perfect in German. Point out that even though the form is similar in English, the use is not the same. Remind students that the present perfect is the predominant past-tense form in spoken German.

• *Übung B,* p. 169

Expansion: Have students create similarly constructed sentences concerning *Reisevorbereitungen.* For example, *Ich habe meine Koffer schon gepackt.*

• The present perfect tense II, pp. 170–171

Remind students that although some patterns are easy to see, it is best to memorize irregular participles. This will facilitate their use in further activities.

• *Übung A,* p. 171

Follow-up: Have students close their books. Write the infinitive form of the verbs in each sentence on the board and see if students can recall the answers.

• *Übung C,* p. 171

Expansion: Have students make up their own questions. *Sind Sie schon*

einmal in Berlin gewesen? Sind Sie schon ein mit dem Zug gereist? Haben Sie schon ein in einem See gebadet?

• *Übung B,* p. 173

Remind students that modals in the perfect tense are highly colloquial. Have students formulate alternate answers using simple past forms.

TEACHING ALL STUDENTS

Challenge Give students a choice of topics, such as *Urlaub, Vor drei Jahren,* or *Kindheit,* and ask them to think of 5–7 sentences about the topic. Their narration must be in the present perfect tense. Give them 4 minutes to formulate sentences, then call on individuals to read their sentences.

CLASSROOM COMMUNITY

Group Activity *Eine Kettengeschichte:* Tell your class about your unfortunate friend "Peter Pechvogel," for whom nothing ever seems to work out. Then start a story: *Letzten Sommer ist Peter Pechvogel mit seinem Hund in Urlaub gefahren.* Point out the tense you used in the sentence and ask *Wie ist die Geschichte weitergegangen?* Choose a student to formulate the next sentence in the present perfect tense. Have each student contribute a sentence. If a student gets stumped, help out with questions such as: *Musste Peter ein Hotelzimmer suchen?* or *Interessiert sich Peter für Extremsportarten?*

BLOCK SCHEDULE

Fun Break Ask students to bring in magazines and use the images they find to make travel posters. Introduce typical catch phrases, such as *Mit*

Swissair dem Winter entfliegen! Paris: Metropole der Romantik und der Lichter. Stellen Sie sich vor, Sie wären in Indien . . . and encourage students to coin their own phrases.

Perspektiven, pp. 174–181

PROGRAM RESOURCES

- *Arbeitsheft,* pp. 124–128
- Audio Program, Cassette 4B, 7B/CD 5, 9
- Audioscript, pp. 59–60
- www.mcdougallittell.com

. . . .

Quick Start Review 1

♻ Vocabulary

Verbinden Sie die Wörter mit den Definitionen oder Synonymen.

   1. _____ draußen
   2. _____ vorsichtig
   3. _____ bedenken
   4. _____ sich entspannen
   5. _____ teilen
   6. _____ unersetzlich
   7. _____ preisgünstig
   a. aus Einem, zwei oder mehr machen
   b. nicht sehr teuer
   c. im Freien
   d. sorgfältig
   e. sich etwas fragen
   f. findet man kein zweites Mal
   g. relaxen

Answers: 1. c 2. d 3. e 4. g 5. a 6. f 7. b

Quick Start Review 2

♻ Simple past

Formulieren Sie Sätze im Imperfekt.

MODELL: eine Urlaubsreise planen → *Ich plante eine Urlaubsreise.*

1. ins Reisebüro gehen
2. mit der Angestellten sprechen
3. einen Flug nach Helsinki buchen
4. nach Hause fahren
5. die Wohnung aufräumen
6. die Koffer packen
7. um drei Uhr am Flughafen sein

Answers: 1. Ich ging ins Reisebüro. 2. Ich sprach mit der Angestellten. 3. Ich buchte einen Flug nach Helsinki. 4. Ich fuhr nach Hause.   5. Ich räumte die Wohnung auf.   6. Ich packte die Koffer.   7. Ich war um drei Uhr am Flughafen.

. . . .

TEACHING SUGGESTIONS

- *Aktivität B,* p. 175

Give students time to read through the activity and to figure out the meaning of unfamiliar vocabulary before listening to the audio text. Follow-up by asking *Für welche dieser Exkursionen interessieren Sie sich am meisten?*

- *Zum Thema,* p. 175

Discuss *Reiselust* with the class. Ask students to describe the situations in which their desire to take a trip is the strongest. Have students tell where they would go. Finally, ask what factors hold them back.

- *Der hellgraue Frühjahrsmantel,* pp. 176–177

Have students review the *Wortschatz zum Lesen* in small groups before reading the story. Preview the text with students by having them read down to line 21 silently, then answer *wer, wo, was, wann* questions. Ask them to speculate what will happen next.

- *Zum Text, Aktivität A,* p. 177

As you review the correct order of the sentences, ask for further clarification of the story. For example, *Wo wohnt Eduard? Wie lange schon? Warum will Eduard das Taschenbuch nicht haben?* Expansion: Elicit the names of the characters in the story and write them on the board. Ask students what they know about each character. Jot down words and phrases as you create an *Assoziogramm* for each character.

- *Zur Interpretation,* p. 178

Ask *Worin liegt der Humor dieser Geschichte? Kann man etwas von der Geschichte lernen?* Have students work in pairs on more extensive answers to question 1. Have students share their theories.

- *Schreiben Sie!,* pp. 178–180

Introduce the topic by talking about your hometown. Tell about experiences you have had hosting visitors from other countries. What were the things about your town that most impressed them? Have students relate experiences they have had with foreign visitors.

- *Schreibmodell,* p. 179

Point out to students the inclusion of the short introduction in the *Schreibmodell.* After students have read the text, have them find the words and phrases that express the speaker's enthusiasm for Laconia. Write them on the board and then brainstorm more ways of expressing enthusiasm.

- *Vor dem Schreiben,* p. 179

Once students have created the 5 persona, have them introduce one of them to the class. Elicit 1–2 additional questions about the person from the class and have students improvise answers.

• *Tipp zum Schreiben*, p. 180

Make a recording of "typical citizens" commenting on your town. Have students take notes and tell you who and how old the people are and what they like about the town.

• *Beim Schreiben*, p. 180

Write the categories *Kinder, Teenager, Erwachsene, Rentner* on the board. Give students a minute to think of interests typical of these different groups.

• *Nach dem Schreiben*, p. 180

Have students share their work with the class before they turn it in. You may want to post student work on a bulletin board and give students time to peruse it.

TEACHING ALL STUDENTS

Multiple Intelligences
Musical/Rhythmic: Read aloud one of the statements from the *Schreibmodell* or one you have written yourself and concentrate on its rhythm and intonation. Emphasize the enthusiasm of the speaker. Then have students choose a quote from their own *Schreiben Sie!* assignment and practice reading it with appropriate enthusiasm to a partner.

CLASSROOM COMMUNITY

Group Activity Obtain a video camera and have students use their completed *Schreiben Sie!* quotes to produce a promotional piece for your town or city to be shown on German TV. Divide class into groups of 5. Have each member choose a quote from his or her work. The group then should combine the 5 quotes into a smooth advertisement. Encourage students to bring in props to enhance their production. Have them tape their ad. Use the following rubric to grade their videos.

RUBRIC **A** = 13–15 pts. **B** = 10–12 pts. **C** = 7–9 pts. **D** = 4–6 pts. **F** < 4 pts.

Writing Criteria	Scale				
Content	1	2	3	4	5
Grammatical accuracy, vocabulary	1	2	3	4	5
Fluency and pronunciation	1	2	3	4	5

CULTURE HIGHLIGHTS

Tell students about the long history of German *Reiselust*. Have students read Goethe's famous poem *Wanderers Nachtlied* or one of the many German Romantic poems on the subject. Discuss the factors that might contribute to this enduring love for travel.

BLOCK SCHEDULE

Expansion Have students come up with their own *Fachexkursion* for "Club Natura" and write an advertisement for it. Then have them read their ads to the class and students choose which excursion they find most interesting.

PORTFOLIO

Have students write an essay about staying healthy throughout the course of their lives. They should reflect on the potential challenges associated with growing old. Work, nutrition, exercise, attitude, medicine, and so on, are factors to be addressed.

RUBRIC **A** = 13–15 pts. **B** = 10–12 pts. **C** = 7–9 pts. **D** = 4–6 pts. **F** < 4 pts.

Writing Criteria	Scale				
Grammar	1	2	3	4	5
Range of vocabulary	1	2	3	4	5
Creativity	1	2	3	4	5

PROJECT

Have students research and plan a vacation using the Internet. They should start with a search using the words *Urlaub, Tourismus,* or *Reiseziele.* Or they can search for a specific city or region. Each student writes a full itinerary, including *Daten, Übernachtung (mit Zimmerbeschreibung und Preisen), Mietwagen, Zug- oder Flugverbindungen,* and *Ausflüge/Aktivitäten.* Have students include a written description of their planned trip. Use the following rubric to grade their projects.

RUBRIC **A** = 13–15 pts. **B** = 10–12 pts. **C** = 7–9 pts. **D** = 4–6 pts. **F** < 4 pts.

Writing Criteria	Scale				
Organization	1	2	3	4	5
Grammar	1	2	3	4	5
Creativity	1	2	3	4	5

KAPITEL 32

FERIEN UND URLAUB

In diesem Kapitel

- lernen Sie, wie die heutige Reiseindustrie in Deutschland begonnen hat.
- erfahren Sie, was die beliebtesten Reiseziele von heute sind.
- lernen Sie Menschen kennen, die mehr Abenteuer im Urlaub suchen.

Sie werden auch

- wiederholen, wie man über die Vergangenheit spricht.
- lernen, wie man Modalverben im Perfekt gebraucht.
- eine Geschichte über einen hellgrauen Mantel lesen.
- einen Prospekt für Ihre Stadt schreiben.

So sah Reisen damals aus – eine Wanderung in Bayern.

Drachenflieger vor dem Sprung in die Luft.

Jetzt will man mehr als nur Erholung.

Freizeit hat man nach der Arbeit, am Wochenende und auch an Feiertagen – aber man braucht auch Urlaub. Woran denken Sie, wenn Sie das Wort „Urlaub" hören? Reisen Sie gern ins Ausland, oder machen Sie lieber Urlaub zu Hause? Was sind ihre Lieblingsbeschäftigungen, wenn Sie Urlaub haben?

I: Urlaub gestern und heute

Bevor es eine Reiseindustrie gab, hatte man natürlich ab und zu Urlaub gemacht. Aber wie machte man damals Urlaub? Wer konnte einen richtigen Urlaub machen?

A Persönliche Meinungen. Susanne erzählt von Ferien und Urlaub. Beantworten Sie die Fragen.

1. Welche Ferien haben Schüler und Schülerinnen in Deutschland?
2. Welche Ferien haben Sie?
3. Wie viele Tage Urlaub haben Susannes Eltern?
4. Wissen Sie, wie viele Tage Urlaub die meisten Berufstätigen in Ihrem Land haben?

B Mein schönster Urlaub

SCHRITT 1: Wer fährt wohin? Die Personen im Video erzählen, wo sie ihren Urlaub gern verbringen. Wer sagt das, Gürkan, Anett, Susanne, Erika oder Stefan?

1. „Ich war im Dezember dort und, als es in Europa geschneit hat, . . . war ich im schönen Sommerwetter."
2. „Dann waren wir irgendwo angekommen bei einem Strandabschnitt, da haben wir unser Zelt aufgeschlagen und da sind wir auch geblieben."
3. „Wir sind in Norwegen gewesen, Schweden und Finnland, und wir sind ans Nordkap gefahren."
4. „In den Winterferien verbringen wir unseren Urlaub immer in Deutschland, im Schwarzwald, wo sehr viel Schnee liegt."
5. „In den Urlaub fahre ich gerne nach Jamaika."

SCHRITT 2: Welche dieser Reisen finden Sie am schönsten? Erklären Sie Ihre Wahl.

C Urlaub gestern. In den letzten hundert Jahren haben sich die Reisegewohnheiten in Deutschland geändert. Wann sind die folgenden Ereignisse passiert?

A. 1. Sommer-, Winter-, Herbst- und Osterferien. 2. *Answers will vary.* 3. Susannes Eltern haben um die dreißig Tage Urlaub. 4. *Answers will vary.*

Damals konnten sich nur die reichen Leute eine Schiffsreise leisten.

WORTSCHATZ ZUM VIDEO

die Hütte	*hut*
der Ostblock	*Eastern bloc countries*
das Schwarze Meer	*the Black Sea*
die Schlucht	*ravine, gulch*
begehbar	*passable*
der Bergführer	*mountain guide*

B. Schritt 1: 1. Stefan 2. Gürkan 3. Anett 4. Susanne 5. Erika
Schritt 2: *Answers will vary.*

C. 1. zu Beginn der dreißiger Jahre 2. in den fünfziger Jahren 3. in der Nazizeit 4. nach dem Zweiten Weltkrieg 5. in den siebziger Jahren 6. ab 1920 7. vor hundert Jahren

1. Arbeitslosigkeit war ein großes Problem. In diesem Jahrzehnt kamen dann die Nationalsozialisten zur Macht.
2. Reisen wurde zum Hobby der Westdeutschen.
3. Der Staat organisierte Schiffsreisen für Erwachsene und Ferienlager für die Kinder.
4. Die DDR-Bürger durften nur in andere Ostblockländer reisen.
5. Eine große und wichtige Tourismusindustrie ist entstanden.
6. Die deutschen Arbeiter und Arbeiterinnen bekamen erst jetzt eine Woche Urlaub im Jahr.
7. Man fand Spaß und Erholung an Badeseen in der Nähe, denn nur wenige Menschen konnten sich eine richtige Urlaubsreise leisten.

in den siebziger Jahren
in den fünfziger Jahren
zu Beginn der dreißiger Jahre   in der Nazizeit
vor hundert Jahren
nach dem Zweiten Weltkrieg   ab 1920

II: Abenteuerurlaub

A. Birgit sucht im Urlaub Abwechslung, Nervenkitzel und Gefahr.

Erholung ist vielen Urlaubern nicht mehr genug. Man interessiert sich jetzt mehr für „Extremsportarten" – aber was heißt das? Welche Sportarten würden Sie als „extrem" bezeichnen?

A Birgits idealer Urlaub. Birgit will im Urlaub etwas Besonderes erleben. Was sucht sie?

Abwechslung	Erholung	Gefahr
Natur	Nervenkitzel	Ruhe
Sonne	Strand	Wärme

B Ein tolles Erlebnis? Was Birgit sagt, klingt beim ersten Hören eher negativ. Aber Canyoning hat Birgit eigentlich sehr gut gefallen. Was sind die Vor- und Nachteile von Extremsportarten? Machen Sie eine Liste, und diskutieren Sie mit Ihren Mitschülern/Mitschülerinnen darüber.

VORTEILE	NACHTEILE
spannend	gefährlich
man erlebt, was nicht jeder erlebt	die Ausrüstung kostet manchmal viel Geld

C Traumurlaub. Manche suchen Abenteuer im Urlaub, manche nur Ruhe. Arbeiten Sie mit einem Partner / einer Partnerin, und stellen Sie einander die folgenden Fragen.

1. Was machst du normalerweise im Urlaub?
2. Wo verbringst du deine Ferien?
3. Was machst du dort?
4. Was suchst du im Urlaub – Abenteuer, Erholung oder beides?
5. Würdest du jemals eine Extremsportart wählen?

C. Answers will vary.

Birgit.
B. Lists will vary.

KULTURSPIEGEL

In Deutschland hatte man natürlich immer Freizeit, aber den staatlich anerkannten jährlichen Urlaub (den sogenannten dreißig-Tage-Urlaub von heute) gibt es erst seit dem zwanzigsten Jahrhundert. Heute bekommen Berufstätige bis zu sechs Wochen bezahlten Urlaub im Jahr. Deutsche geben im Durchschnitt fünfzehn Prozent ihres Einkommens für Urlaub aus.

VOKABELN

die Abwechslung	*change; variety*
die Ausrüstung	*outfitting; equipment*
die Entspannung	*relaxation*
die Extremsportart	*adventure sport*
die Gefahr	*danger*
die Reiselust	*desire to travel*
die Schiffsreise	*voyage, cruise*
die Vorbereitung	*preparation*
der Luxus	*luxury*
der Nervenkitzel	*excitement*
das Ferienlager	*vacation camp*
die Ferien (*pl.*)	*vacation*
baden	*to bathe*
sich bräunen	*to tan*
sich leisten	*to afford*
nutzen	*to use*
springen	*to jump*
überwachen	*to supervise*
aktiv	*active(ly)*
gespannt	*excited*
herrlich	*wonderful(ly)*
irre	*crazy; wild*
wenig	*little; few*

Extremsportarten werden in Europa immer beliebter.

Sie wissen schon
die Mannschaft, die Sportart, der Urlaub, das Abenteuer, besteigen, sich fit halten, gewinnen, klettern, reiten, rudern, Sport treiben, wandern, spannend

Abwechslung
Vorbereitungen wenig
bräunen nutzen
Ausrüstung
baden Luxus
sich fit halten
verreisen

Aktivitäten

A. 1. nutzen 2. verreisen 3. Ausrüstung
4. Vorbereitungen 5. wenig 6. bräunen
7. baden 8. sich fit halten 9. Abwechslung
10. Luxus

A Urlaub durch das Jahr. Ergänzen Sie die Sätze 1–10 mit den Wörtern im Kasten.

1. Deutsche ＿＿＿ ihren Urlaub, um in die ganze Welt zu reisen.
2. Manche Deutsche ＿＿＿ mehrmals im Jahr.
3. Diejenigen, die keine eigene ＿＿＿ zum Skilaufen haben, können solche Sachen leihen.
4. Aber wenn man einfach wandern will, braucht man keine großen ＿＿＿ zu treffen.
5. Für manche Sportarten muss man nur ＿＿＿ Geld ausgeben.
6. Im Sommer will man lieber am Strand liegen und sich ＿＿＿.

7. Wenn das Wasser nicht zu kalt ist, kann man natürlich auch im Meer _____.
8. Wer _____ will, muss das ganze Jahr Sport treiben, nicht nur wenn das Wetter schön ist.
9. Zur _____ suchen manche Menschen mehr Spannung in ihrer Freizeit.
10. Weil Extremsportarten oft sehr teuer sind, bleiben sie für viele ein _____.

B Definitionen. Lesen Sie die Sätze links und suchen Sie aus der rechten Spalte die passenden Definitionen für die kursiv gedruckten Wörter.

1. Im Urlaub suche ich beides, *Abenteuer* aber auch Ruhe.
2. Und das war mein schönster Urlaub, weil es einfach *herrlich* da war.
3. Wir werden sehen, wann und wie die *Reiselust* der Deutschen begonnen hat.
4. Eine richtige Urlaubsreise konnten *sich* vor hundert Jahren nur wenige Menschen *leisten*.
5. Für Jungen und Mädchen gab es *Ferienlager*.
6. Im Urlaub versuche ich erstmal *Entspannung* zu finden.
7. Canyoning ist eine Mischung zwischen *Klettern*, Schwimmen, Springen und Wandern.
8. Ich bin ganz schön *gespannt*, wie es wird.
9. Insgesamt war es eine tolle *Erfahrung*.

a. Relaxen
b. ein Erlebnis
c. Campingplätze mit organisierten Aktivitäten
d. voller Erwartung
e. fantastisch, super
f. Bergsteigen
g. starker Wunsch zum Reisen
h. genug Geld dafür haben
i. gefahrvolle Situation, erregendes Erlebnis

B. 1. i 2. e 3. g 4. h 5. c 6. a 7. f 8. d 9. b

C. 1. e 2. d 3. b 4. a 5. c

C Assoziationen. Welche Begriffe aus der rechten Spalte assoziiert man mit den Wörten links?

MODELL: Man assoziiert Familienfeste und Dekorationen mit Feiertagen.

1. Extremsportarten
2. Schiffsreise
3. Vorbereitungen
4. Urlaub
5. Ferienlager

a. Reiselust und ein Wunsch nach Abwechslung
b. Ausrüstung und feste Pläne
c. Jugendliche und organisierte Aktivitäten
d. Luxus und Entspannung
e. Gefahr und Nervenkitzel

D. *Answers will vary.*

D Was möchten Sie gern im Urlaub machen? Für welche der folgenden Freizeitaktivitäten interessieren Sie sich am meisten? Warum? Was erwarten Sie von solchen Sportarten oder Aktivitäten? Für welche interessieren Sie sich gar nicht? Warum? Was assoziieren Sie mit diesen Beschäftigungen?

1. Schluchtwandern
2. in den Alpen wandern
3. Mountainbiken
4. Klettertouren
5. River-Rafting
6. eine Schiffsreise
7. Snowboarden
8. ___?___

Schluchtwanderer.

STRUKTUREN

REVIEW OF THE PRESENT PERFECT TENSE I
TALKING ABOUT THE PAST

Use the present perfect tense to talk about past events in German. As you recall, this tense consists of the present-tense form of **haben** or **sein** as the auxiliary verb plus the past participle of the main verb at the end of the clause or sentence.

Das Mädchen **hat** in Bremen eine Fahrkarte **gekauft.**	*The girl bought a ticket in Bremen.*
Sie **ist** nach Italien **gereist.**	*She traveled to Italy.*

Most past participles combine the verb stem with the prefix **ge-** and the ending **-(e)t,** as in the following examples. Such verbs are called weak verbs.

INFINITIVE	STEM	AUXILIARY + PAST PARTICIPLE
arbeiten	arbeit-	hat **ge**arbeit**et**
fragen	frag-	hat **ge**frag**t**
haben	hab-	hat **ge**hab**t**
lernen	lern-	hat **ge**lern**t**
machen	mach-	hat **ge**mach**t**
wohnen	wohn-	hat **ge**wohn**t**
wandern	wander-	ist **ge**wander**t**

Some weak verbs show irregular stem changes in the past participle. These verbs are called irregular weak verbs.

INFINITIVE	STEM	AUXILIARY + PAST PARTICIPLE
bringen	br**ach**-	hat gebr**ach**t
denken	d**ach**-	hat ged**ach**t
verbringen	verbr**ach**-	hat verbr**ach**t
kennen	k**ann**-	hat gek**ann**t
wissen	w**uss**-	hat gew**uss**t
rennen	r**ann**-	ist ger**ann**t

Verbs that begin with **be-** or end with **-ieren** do not add the prefix **ge-.**

INFINITIVE	STEM	AUXILIARY + PAST PARTICIPLE
besuchen	besuch-	hat besucht
studieren	studier-	hat studiert

Übungen

A Susannes Kindheit. Susanne erzählt, wie sie als Kind ihre Ferien verbracht hat. Schreiben Sie ihre Sätze im Perfekt um.

MODELL: Wir reisen jedes Jahr nach Mallorca. →
Wir sind jedes Jahr nach Mallorca gereist.

1. Auf Mallorca lerne ich ein bisschen Spanisch.
2. Wir machen Ausflüge auf die anderen Inseln.
3. Ich bade im Meer.
4. Meine Eltern bummeln durch kleine Städte.
5. Wir wohnen in unserem eigenen Ferienhaus.
6. Wir verbringen die Winterferien in Deutschland.
7. Meine Schwester baut Schneemänner.
8. Wir denken immer an die Ferien.

B Sie wollen auf eine Party gehen. Sie dürfen aber nur gehen, wenn Sie zuerst einiges erledigt haben. Sagen Sie, dass Sie das alles schon gemacht haben.

MODELL: die Hausaufgaben machen →
Ich habe die Hausaufgaben schon gemacht.

1. den Rasen mähen
2. die Großeltern besuchen
3. die Katze füttern
4. für die Matheprüfung lernen
5. das Zimmer in Ordnung bringen

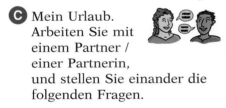

C Mein Urlaub. Arbeiten Sie mit einem Partner / einer Partnerin, und stellen Sie einander die folgenden Fragen.

1. Wann hast du zum letzten Mal Urlaub gemacht?
2. Wohin bist du gereist?
3. Wo hast du da gewohnt?
4. Was hast du da alles gemacht?
5. Wie viele Tage hast du da verbracht?

Winterferien mit der Familie Dyrchs.

A. **1.** Auf Mallorca habe ich ein bisschen Spanisch gelernt. **2.** Wir haben Ausflüge auf die anderen Inseln gemacht. **3.** Ich habe im Meer gebadet. **4.** Meine Eltern sind durch kleine Städte gebummelt. **5.** Wir haben in unserem eigenen Ferienhaus gewohnt. **6.** Wir haben die Winterferien in Deutschland verbracht. **7.** Meine Schwester hat Schneemänner gebaut. **8.** Wir haben immer an die Ferien gedacht.

B. **1.** Ich habe den Rasen schon gemäht. **2.** Ich habe die Großeltern schon besucht. **3.** Ich habe die Katze schon gefüttert. **4.** Ich habe für die Matheprüfung schon gelernt. **5.** Ich habe das Zimmer schon in Ordnung gebracht.

C. *Answers will vary.*

Urlaub am Strand.

REVIEW OF THE PRESENT PERFECT TENSE II
MORE ON TALKING ABOUT THE PAST

SIND SIE WORTSCHLAU?

In German, verbs that share the same stem form their past participles in the same way.

kommen	ge**komm**en
an•**komm**en	ange**komm**en
be**komm**en	be**komm**en
mit•**komm**en	mitge**komm**en
vorbei•**komm**en	vorbeige**komm**en
zurück•**komm**en	zurückge**komm**en

Most German verbs form the past participle by combining the verb stem with the prefix **ge-** and the suffix **-(e)t.** These are the so-called weak verbs; irregular weak verbs (mixed verbs) have changes within the verb stem. Some verbs form the past participle with the prefix **ge-** and the ending **-en;** these are the so-called strong verbs.

INFINITIVE	STEM	AUXILIARY + PAST PARTICIPLE
fahren	fahr-	ist **ge**fahr**en**
geben	geb-	hat **ge**geb**en**
kommen	komm-	ist **ge**komm**en**
laufen	lauf-	ist **ge**lauf**en**
lesen	les-	hat **ge**les**en**
schlafen	schlaf-	hat **ge**schlaf**en**
sehen	seh-	hat **ge**seh**en**

In addition, some verbs show a stem change in the past participle.

INFINITIVE	STEM	AUXILIARY + PAST PARTICIPLE
bleiben	bl**ieb**-	ist gebl**ie**ben
finden	f**und**-	hat gef**u**nden
fliegen	fl**og**-	ist gefl**o**gen
nehmen	n**omm**-	hat gen**omm**en
schreiben	schr**ieb**-	hat geschr**ie**ben
sitzen	s**ess**-	hat ges**ess**en
sprechen	spr**och**-	hat gespr**o**chen
werden	w**ord**-	ist gew**o**rden
wissen	w**uss**-	hat gew**u**sst

KURZ NOTIERT

Verbs that take **sein** in the present perfect tense are typically verbs of motion or change: **gehen, (mit•, vorbei•, zurück•)kommen, reisen, wandern, werden.** In addition, the verbs **ankommen, bleiben,** and **sein** also take **sein** in the present perfect tense.

The past participle of **sein** is **(ist) gewesen.** The past participle of two-part verbs, is a single word with **-ge-** between the prefix and the stem plus the **-(e)t** or **-en** ending.

INFINITIVE	STEM	AUXILIARY + PAST PARTICIPLE
an•rufen	ruf-	hat angerufen
auf•hören	hör-	hat aufgehört
auf•passen	pass-	hat aufgepasst
auf•schlagen	schlag-	hat aufgeschlagen
auf•stehen	st**and**-	ist aufgest**and**en
ein•laden	lad-	hat eingeladen
ein•steigen	st**ieg**-	ist eingest**ie**gen

Verbs that begin with the unstressed prefixes **be-, emp-, ent-, er-, ge-, ver-,** and **zer-** do not add the prefix **ge-: gefallen > hat gefallen; genießen > hat genossen; vergessen > hat vergessen.**

Übungen

A Gürkans schönster Urlaub. Gürkan erzählt von seiner Reise in die Türkei. Bilden Sie Sätze im Perfekt.

1. Wir fahren in die Türkei.
2. Wir nehmen einen Rucksack mit.
3. Wir steigen in den Bus ein.
4. Ich schlage das Zelt auf.
5. Meine Freundin sitzt am Strand.
6. Wir bleiben da einige Tage.
7. Ich schreibe Postkarten an meine Familie.
8. Die Reise gefällt mir sehr.
9. Ich vergesse diese schönen Tage nie.

B Alles über Canyoning. Birgit ist gerade von ihrer Canyoning-Reise zurückgekommen, und Sie haben viele Fragen für sie. Ergänzen Sie die Verben im Perfekt.

Gürkan.

A. 1. Wir sind in die Türkei gefahren. 2. Wir haben einen Rucksack mitgenommen. 3. Wir sind in den Bus eingestiegen. 4. Wir haben das Zelt aufgeschlagen. 5. Meine Freundin hat am Strand gesessen. 6. Wir sind da einige Tage geblieben. 7. Ich habe Postkarten an meine Familie geschrieben. 8. Die Reise hat mir sehr gefallen. 9. Ich habe diese schönen Tage nie vergessen.

B. 2. Hast . . . gelesen? 3. bist . . . gekommen? 4. Hast . . . geschlafen? 5. seid . . . aufgestanden? 6. Bist . . . gewesen? 7. Hast . . . gefunden? 8. Hast . . . mitgenommen? 9. Hast . . . ausgegeben? 10. Haben . . . genossen?

> ausgeben
> mitnehmen
> kommen
> genießen
> schlafen
> sein
> aufstehen
> finden
> lesen
> werden

1. Wie _hast_ du die Reise _gefunden_?
2. _____ du vor der Reise Zeitschriftenartikel über Canyoning _____?
3. Wie _____ du zum Startort _____?
4. _____ du in einem Schlafsack _____?
5. Wie früh _____ ihr morgens _____?
6. _____ du nicht ziemlich müde _____?
7. _____ du die anderen Teilnehmer nett _____?
8. _____ du viel Gepäck _____?
9. _____ du viel Geld für deine Reise _____?
10. _____ alle Teilnehmer das Erlebnis _____?

C Reiseerlebnisse. Sagen Sie, ob Sie das alles gemacht haben.

MODELL: nach Mallorca fahren →
Ja, ich bin schon nach Mallorca gefahren.
oder: Nein, ich bin noch nie nach Mallorca gefahren.

1. in die Türkei reisen
2. in einem Luxushotel übernachten
3. in einem Flugzeug fliegen
4. auf einen hohen Berg klettern
5. in den Alpen wandern
6. Schlittschuh laufen
7. Snowboard fahren
8. einen Schneemann bauen

C. 1. Ja, ich bin schon in die Türkei gereist. oder: Nein, ich bin noch nie in die Türkei gereist. 2. Ja, ich habe schon in einem Luxushotel übernachtet. oder: Nein, ich habe noch nie in einem Luxushotel übernachtet. 3. Ja, ich bin schon in einem Flugzeug geflogen. oder: Nein, ich bin noch nie in einem Flugzeug geflogen. 4. Ja, ich bin schon auf einen hohen Berg geklettert. oder: Nein ich bin noch nie auf einen hohen Berg geklettert. 5. Ja, ich bin schon in den Alpen gewandert. oder: Nein, ich bin noch nie in den Alpen gewandert. 6. Ja, ich bin schon Schlittschuh gelaufen. oder: Nein, ich bin noch nie Schlittschuh gelaufen. 7. Ja, ich bin schon Snowboard gefahren. oder: Nein, ich bin noch nie Snowboard gefahren. 8. Ja, ich habe schon einen Schneemann gebaut. oder: Nein, ich habe noch nie einen Schneemann gebaut.

MODAL VERBS IN THE PERFECT TENSE
EXPRESSING DESIRES, TALENTS, AND OBLIGATIONS IN THE PAST

Whereas German speakers use the present perfect tense in conversation or to write about unrelated events in the past, they still use the simple past tense—even in speaking—for **haben, sein, wissen,** and the modal verbs.

Wir **konnten** uns die Reise nicht **leisten.**	*We weren't able to afford the trip.*
Hunde **durften** nicht in manche Hotels **gehen.**	*Dogs weren't allowed to go inside some hotels.*
Wir **wollten** einen schönen Urlaub.	*We wanted a nice vacation.*

However, these verbs all have past participles and do occasionally occur in the present perfect tense. You have already seen these constructions: **ist gewesen, hat gehabt, hat gewusst.** Modal verbs also take the auxiliary **haben** and form the past participle with the **ge-**prefix, no umlaut in the stem, and the ending **-(e)t: hat gedurft.** The past participle appears only when the infinitive of the main verb is not present. The construction with past participle only is a characteristic of conversational rather than written German.

Wir **haben** es nicht **gekonnt.**	*We weren't able (to do it).*
Hunde **haben** nicht in manche Hotels **gedurft.**	*Dogs weren't allowed in some hotels.*

However, when the infinitive of the main verb is present, modal verbs may still appear in the present perfect tense but in a double infinitive construction. The present-tense form of the auxiliary **haben** appears in second position, and the infinitive of the modal verb follows that of the main verb.

Wir **haben** uns die Reise nicht **leisten können.**	*We weren't able to afford the trip.*
Hunde **haben** nicht in manche Hotels **gehen dürfen.**	*Dogs weren't allowed to go inside some hotels.*

When such constructions stand in dependent clauses, the conjugated verb *precedes* the double infinitive construction.

Sie weiß, dass wir uns die Reise nicht **haben leisten können.**	*She knows that we weren't able to afford the trip.*
Es war früher so, dass Hunde nicht in manche Hotels **haben gehen dürfen.**	*It used to be that dogs weren't allowed to go inside some hotels.*

Übungen

A So war es früher. Schreiben Sie die Sätze im Imperfekt.[a]

> MODELL: Die meisten Deutschen können nicht verreisen. →
> Die meisten Deutschen konnten nicht verreisen.

1. Man darf nur ein Paar Tage im Jahr Urlaub machen.
2. DDR-Bürger dürfen nur in Länder des Ostblocks reisen.
3. Der Staat muss Ferienheime für die Arbeiter bauen.
4. Erwachsene wollen Ruhe und Erholung haben.
5. Man muss nicht viel Geld für Ausrüstung ausgeben.
6. Die Reiseindustrie soll den Touristen größere Reisemöglichkeiten anbieten.

[a]*simple past*

B Frühanfänger

SCHRITT 1: Viele beginnen schon als kleine Kinder mit manchen Sportarten. Und Sie? Arbeiten Sie mit einem Partner / einer Partnerin, und stellen Sie einander die folgenden Fragen.

> MODELL: Konntest du schon als Kind Ski laufen? →
> Ja, das habe ich gekonnt.
> *oder:* Nein, das habe ich nicht gekonnt.

1. Konntest du schon als Kind Fahrrad fahren?
2. Durftest du als Kind Fußball spielen?
3. Wolltest du als Kind Sportler/Sportlerin werden?
4. Durftest du als Kind allein wandern?
5. Musstest du als Kind Sport treiben?
6. Wolltest du als Kind die Fußball-Weltmeisterschaft gewinnen?

SCHRITT 2: Anders gesagt. Schreiben Sie Ihre Antworten jetzt im Perfekt mit zwei Infinitivformen.

> MODELL: Konntest du schon als Kind Ski laufen? →
> Als Kind habe ich schon Ski laufen können.
> *oder:* Als Kind habe ich nicht Ski laufen können.

Ein staatliches Ferienheim aus DDR-Zeiten.

A. 1. Man durfte nur ein paar Tage im Jahr Urlaub machen. 2. DDR-Bürger durften nur in Länder des Ostblocks reisen. 3. Der Staat musste Ferienheime für die Arbeiter bauen. 4. Erwachsene wollten Ruhe und Erholung haben. 5. Man musste nicht viel Geld für Ausrüstung ausgeben. 6. Die Reiseindustrie sollte den Touristen größere Reisemöglichkeiten anbieten.

B. Schritt 1: 1. Ja, das habe ich gekonnt. *oder:* Nein, das habe ich nicht gekonnt. 2. Ja, das habe ich gedurft. *oder:* Nein, das habe ich nicht gedurft. 3. Ja, das habe ich gewollt. *oder:* Nein, das habe ich nicht gewollt. 4. Ja, das habe ich gedurft. *oder:* Nein, das habe ich nicht gedurft. 5. Ja, das habe ich gemusst. *oder:* Nein, das habe ich nicht gemusst. 6. Ja, das habe ich gewollt. *oder:* Nein, das habe ich nicht gewollt. **Schritt 2: 1.** Als Kind habe ich schon Fahrrad fahren können. *oder:* Als Kind habe ich nicht Fahrrad fahren können. **2.** Als Kind habe ich schon Fußball spielen dürfen. *oder:* Als Kind habe ich nicht Fußball spielen dürfen. **3.** Als Kind habe ich schon Sportler/in werden wollen. *oder:* Als Kind habe ich nicht Sportler/in werden wollen. **4.** Als Kind habe ich schon allein wandern dürfen. *oder:* Als Kind habe ich nicht alleine wandern dürfen. **5.** Als Kind habe ich schon Sport treiben müssen. *oder:* Als Kind habe ich keinen Sport treiben müssen. **6.** Als Kind habe ich schon die Fußball-Weltmeisterschaft gewinnen wollen. *oder:* Als Kind habe ich nicht die Fußball-Weltmeisterschaft gewinnen wollen.

PERSPEKTIVEN

HÖREN SIE ZU!
CLUB NATURA

WORTSCHATZ ZUM HÖRTEXT

fade	stale; dull
sich betätigen	to engage oneself
die Anlage	facility
vermeiden	to avoid
begleitend	accompanying
das Ausflugsprogramm	excursion list
der Vordergrund	foreground
die Annehmlichkeit	comfort
die Verpflegung	board; provisions
die Vollpension	full room and board

A. 1. b **2.** a **3.** b **4.** b **5.** a **6.** b **7.** b

Informieren Sie sich in den aktuellen Katalogen!

Sie hören jetzt einen Informationstext des Reiseunternehmens Dr. Koch.

A Was haben Sie über Club Natura gelernt?

1. Club Natura
   a. ist ein reiner Badeurlaub.
   b. ist eine Verbindung von Studienreise und Badeurlaub.
2. Im Club Natura
   a. können Sie sich aktiv betätigen.
   b. zieht man ständig von Hotel zu Hotel um.
3. Im Club Natura
   a. können Sie alle fünfzehn Tage anreisen.
   b. können Sie an jedem Wochenende anreisen.
4. Ein weiterer Vorteil von Club Natura ist,
   a. dass alle Teilnehmer im gleichen Alter sind.
   b. dass sich die Teilnehmer schnell kennen lernen.
5. Die Anlagen von Club Natura
   a. liegen am Strand.
   b. liegen in kleinen Städten.
6. Die Größe der Reisegruppen
   a. liegt bei siebzig bis achtzig.
   b. liegt bei sieben bis achtzehn.

Wandern weckt die Liebe zur Natur.

7. Die Verpflegung im Club Natura
   a. ist wie die klassische Art von Vollpension.
   b. ist eine neuartige Art der Vollverpflegung.

B Dr. Kochs Fachexkursionen sind in verschiedene Themen gruppiert. Welche der Reiseangebote passen am besten zu den folgenden Themen?   B. Geschichte und Kultur: 1, 5, 7; Naturkundliches Wandern: 3, 10; Ornithologisch-landschaftliche Exkursionen: 9; Bergwandern: 6, 8; Botanische Studienreisen: 2, 4

Geschichte und Kultur

Naturkundliches Wandern

Ornithologisch-landschaftliche Exkursionen

Bergwandern

Botanische Studienreisen

---

1. durch die Syrische Wüste zum Euphrat
2. Siziliens Flora
3. Sardinien – ein Naturerlebnis erwartet Sie!
4. Pflanzensammeln in Südspanien
5. Persepolis und Geschichte des Perserreiches
6. im Apennin – Bergwandern im romantischen Zentralitalien
7. faszinierendes Istanbul
8. durch unbekannte Teile der Rocky Mountains
9. Italiens interessante Vogelwelt
10. Naturparadies Donaudelta

LESEN SIE!

Zum Thema

● Die Reiselust. Haben Sie öfters Lust, plötzlich zu verreisen? Möchten Sie ab und zu irgendwohin gehen, wo alles anders ist – halt die Tapeten wechseln?[a] Warum (nicht)?   *Answers will vary.*

[a]literally: *to change the wallpaper;* figuratively: *to have a change of scenery or surroundings*

KULTURSPIEGEL

Wolfgang Hildesheimer wurde 1916 in Hamburg geboren. 1933, als er sechzehn Jahre alt war, flüchtete er mit seinen Eltern nach England und dann nach Palästina. Er lernte Tischler und nahm Unterricht im Zeichnen, in Möbeltechnik und Innenarchitektur. 1946–1948 arbeitete er als Dolmetscher bei den Nürnberger Kriegsverbrecher-Prozessen. Seit den fünfziger Jahren arbeitete er als Schriftsteller. „Der hellgraue Frühjahrsmantel" erschien 1952 in *Lieblose Legenden*, eine Sammlung von Kurzgeschichten. Er starb 1991 in der Schweiz.

Der hellgraue Frühjahrsmantel

Vor zwei Monaten – wir saßen gerade beim Frühstück – kam ein Brief von meinem Vetter Eduard. Mein Vetter Eduard hatte an einem Frühlingsabend vor zwölf Jahren das Haus

5 verlassen, um, wie er behauptete, einen Brief in den Kasten zu stecken, und war nicht zurückgekehrt. Seitdem hatte niemand etwas von ihm gehört. Der Brief kam aus Sydney in Australien. Ich öffnete ihn und las:

10   Lieber Paul!
  Könntest Du mir meinen hellgrauen Frühjahrsmantel nachschicken? Ich kann ihn nämlich brauchen, da es hier oft empfindlich kalt ist, vor allem nachts. In der linken
15 Tasche ist ein *Taschenbuch für Pilzsammler.* Das kannst Du herausnehmen und behalten. Eßbare Pilze gibt es hier nämlich nicht. Im voraus vielen Dank.

        Herzlichst Dein Eduard

20   Ich sagte zu meiner Frau: „Ich habe einen Brief von meinem Vetter Eduard aus Australien bekommen." Sie war gerade dabei, den Tauchsieder in die Blumenvase zu stecken, um Eier darin zu kochen, und fragte: „So? Was schreibt er?"

25   „Daß er seinen hellgrauen Mantel braucht und daß es in Australien keine eßbaren Pilze gibt." – „Dann soll er doch etwas anderes essen", sagte sie. – „Da hast Du recht", sagte ich.

  Später kam der Klavierstimmer. Er war ein
30 etwas schüchterner und zerstreuter Mann, ein wenig weltfremd sogar, aber er war sehr nett, und natürlich sehr musikalisch. Er stimmte nicht nur Klaviere, sondern reparierte auch Saiteninstrumente und erteilte Blockflötenunterricht. Er hieß Kolhaas.
35 Als ich vom Tisch aufstand, hörte ich ihn schon im Nebenzimmer Akkorde anschlagen.

  In der Garderobe sah ich den hellgrauen Mantel hängen. Meine Frau hatte ihn also schon vom Speicher geholt. Das wunderte mich, denn
40 gewöhnlich tut meine Frau die Dinge erst dann,

wenn es gleichgültig geworden ist, ob sie getan sind oder nicht. Ich packte den Mantel sorgfältig ein, trug das Paket zur Post und schickte es ab. Erst dann fiel mir ein, daß ich vergessen hatte, das
45 Pilzbuch herauszunehmen. Aber ich bin kein Pilzsammler.

  Ich ging noch ein wenig spazieren, und als ich nach Hause kam, irrten der Klavierstimmer und meine Frau in der Wohnung umher und schauten in
50 die Schränke und unter die Tische.

  „Kann ich helfen?" fragte ich.

  „Wir suchen Herrn Kolhaas' Mantel", sagte meine Frau.

  „Ach so", sagte ich, meines Irrtums bewußt, „den
55 habe ich soeben nach Australien geschickt," –
„Warum nach Australien?" fragte meine Frau. „Aus Versehen", sagte ich. „Dann will ich nicht weiter stören", sagte Herr Kolhaas, etwas betreten, wenn auch nicht besonders erstaunt, und wollte sich
60 entschuldigen, aber ich sagte: „Warten Sie, Sie können dafür den Mantel von meinem Vetter bekommen."

  Ich ging auf den Speicher und fand dort in einem verstaubten Koffer den hellgrauen Mantel
65 meines Vetters. Er war etwas zerknittert – schließlich hatte er zwölf Jahre im Koffer gelegen – aber sonst in gutem Zustand.

  Meine Frau bügelte ihn noch ein wenig auf, während Herr Kolhaas mir von einigen Klavieren
70 erzählte, die er gestimmt hatte. Dann zog er ihn an, verabschiedete sich und ging.

  Wenige Tage später erhielten wir ein Paket. Darin waren Steinpilze, etwa ein Kilo. Auf den Pilzen lagen zwei Briefe. Ich öffnete den ersten und las:

75   Lieber Herr Holle, (so heiße ich)
  da Sie so liebenswürdig waren, mir ein Taschenbuch für Pilzsammler in die Tasche zu stecken, möchte ich Ihnen als Dank das Resultat meiner ersten Pilzsuche zuschicken
80 und hoffe, daß es Ihnen schmecken wird.

Außerdem fand ich in der anderen Tasche einen Brief, den Sie mir wohl irrtümlich mitgegeben haben. Ich schicke ihn hiermit zurück.

85   Ergebenst Ihr A. M. Kolhaas

Der Brief, um den es sich hier handelte, war also wohl der, den mein Vetter damals in den Kasten stecken wollte. Offenbar hatte er ihn dann mitsamt dem Mantel zu Hause vergessen. Er war an Herrn
90 Bernhard Haase gerichtet, der, wie ich mich erinnerte, ein Freund meines Vetters gewesen war. Ich öffnete den Umschlag. Eine Theaterkarte und ein Zettel fielen heraus. Auf dem Zettel stand:

Lieber Bernhard!
95 Ich schicke Dir eine Karte zu *Tannhäuser* nächsten Montag, von der ich keinen Gebrauch machen werde, da ich verreisen möchte, um ein wenig auszuspannen. Vielleicht hast Du Lust, hinzugehen. Die
100 Schmidt-Hohlweg singt die Elisabeth. Du schwärmst doch immer so von ihrem hohen Gis.
                    Herzliche Grüße, Dein Eduard

Zum Mittagessen gab es Steinpilze. „Die Pilze
105 habe ich hier auf dem Tisch gefunden. Wo kommen sie eigentlich her?" fragte meine Frau. „Herr Kolhaas hat sie geschickt." – „Wie nett von ihm. Es wäre doch gar nicht nötig gewesen."

„Nötig nicht", sagte ich, „aber er ist eben sehr
110 nett."
„Hoffentlich sind sie nicht giftig. – Übrigens habe ich auch eine Theaterkarte gefunden. Was wird denn gespielt?"
„Die Karte, die du gefunden hast", sagte ich, „ist
115 zu einer Aufführung von *Tannhäuser*, aber die war vor zwölf Jahren!" – „Na ja", sagte meine Frau, „zu *Tannhäuser* hätte ich ohnehin keine große Lust gehabt."
Heute morgen kam wieder ein Brief von Eduard
120 mit der Bitte, ihm eine Tenorblockflöte zu schicken. Er habe nämlich in dem Mantel (der übrigens seltsamerweise länger geworden sei, es sei denn, er selbst sei kürzer geworden) ein Buch zur Erlernung des Blockflötenspiels gefunden und gedenke, davon
125 Gebrauch zu machen. Aber Blockflöten seien in Australien nicht erhältlich.
„Wieder ein Brief von Eduard", sagte ich zu meiner Frau. Sie war gerade dabei, die Kaffeemühle auseinanderzunehmen und fragte:
130 „Was schreibt er?" – „Daß es in Australien keine Blockflöten gibt." – „Dann soll er doch ein anderes Instrument spielen", sagte sie.
„Das finde ich auch", meinte ich.
Meine Frau ist von erfrischender, entwaffnender
135 Sachlichkeit. Ihre Repliken sind zwar nüchtern aber erschöpfend.

Wolfgang Hildesheimer (1916–1991)

Zum Text

A Ordnen Sie folgende Sätze in der richtigen Reihenfolge.

a. Paul bekommt ein Paket mit Pilzen von Herrn Kohlhaas.
b. Paul bringt das Paket mit dem Mantel zur Post.
c. Herr Kolhaas kommt an, um das Klavier zu stimmen.
d. Paul bekommt einen Brief von seinem Vetter Eduard.
e. Herr Kolhaas verlässt das Haus mit dem Mantel von Eduard.
f. Paul bekommt einen Brief von Eduard, in dem er um eine Blockflöte bittet.
g. Frau Holle und Herr Kolhaas suchen den Mantel von Herrn Kolhaas.
h. Paul packt den Mantel ein.

A. 1. d 2. j 3. c 4. i 5. h 6. b 7. g
8. e 9. a 10. f

i. Frau Holle hat den hellgrauen Mantel von Herrn Kolhaas in den Schrank gehängt.

j. Eduard will, dass Paul ihm seinen hellgrauen Mantel, ohne das *Taschenbuch für Pilzsammler*, schickt.

B Manteltaschen. Was steckte in den Taschen von Eduards Mantel? Was steckte in der Tasche des Mantels von Herrn Kolhaas?

B. Possible answers are: In Eduards Mantel steckte ein Buch über Pilze. Im Mantel von Herrn Kolhaas steckte ein Buch mit Anleitungen zum Flötenspiel.

Zur Interpretation

● Was denken Sie?

1. Warum ging Eduard vor zwölf Jahren weg? Warum kam er nicht zurück? Was für ein Mensch ist er?
2. Was für ein Leben führen Herr und Frau Holle?
3. Was haben Eduard und Herr Kolhaas gemeinsam?

1. Answers will vary. *2. Possible answers are:* Herr und Frau Holle führen ein beständiges Leben. Wir wissen, dass sie seit zwölf Jahren nicht umgezogen sind, weil der Brief sie ohne Umwege erreicht hat. *3. Possible answers are:* Beide Männer haben den selben Geschmack in Kleidern. Beide mögen Pilze und sind musikalisch.

INTERAKTION

Discussions will vary.

● Geld ist kein Problem. Planen Sie Ihren Traumurlaub mit einem Partner / einer Partnerin. Einigen Sie sich über folgende Details: das Reiseziel, die Reisezeit und die Dauer der Reise, die Transportmittel, die Übernachtung, die Urlaubsaktivitäten und so weiter.

Texts will vary.

TIPP ZUM SCHREIBEN

Customer comments are used to create a positive message through association. Customers representing different segments of society—by gender, age, race, economic background—are interviewed and their statements are recorded. Advertising pieces reproduce these comments for people in a target market audience. Readers can then associate with the individuals most like themselves and form an opinion based on the messages they see.

SCHREIBEN SIE!

Empfehlungen von glücklichen Kunden

● Um Touristen aus deutschsprachigen Ländern anzuziehen, will das Fremdenverkehrsbüro Ihrer Heimat einen Prospekt auf Deutsch produzieren. Darin sollen viele Zitate von glücklichen Besuchern aus Europa stehen. Was könnten Besucher wohl Positives über das Freizeitangebot Ihrer Stadt sagen? Schreiben Sie die Aussagen von fünf Leuten zu vier unterschiedlichen Themen.

Purpose:	To create a positive image of your hometown
Audience:	German-speaking tourists coming to the United States
Subject:	Reasons to visit your hometown, area, state
Structure:	Testimonials from German-speaking tourists

Schreibmodell

Erleben auch Sie Laconia/ New Hampshire! Lesen Sie die Meinungen von verschiedenen Besuchern aus Mitteleuropa über die Gastfreundschaft und die Freizeitsmöglichkeiten rund um den Winnipesaukee-See:

„Wir waren erstaunt, dass es hier so viele schöne Unterkunftsmöglichkeiten gibt. Alte Gasthäuser mit Antiquitäten, Luxushotels mit erstklassigem Komfort und Spitzenrestaurants, Motels mit Schwimmbad und Fitnessstudios – und alles nicht zu teuer!"
— *Anke und Moritz Schnitzler,*
45-jähriges Lehrer-Ehepaar aus Wien

„Die Kinder freuen sich über den Kabelanschluss im Zimmer, das Schwimmbad und die vielen Amusement-Parks in der Nähe. Und dann haben wir einen tollen Ausblick auf den Winnipesaukee-See."
— *Frau Solothurnmann aus Bern*

„Wir haben ja wenig Geld und sind mit Zelt und Schlafsack losgezogen, aber sofort haben wir einen tollen Campingplatz finden können, ganz nah am Wasser, mit Warmwasserduschen und einem Platz für ein Lagerfeuer. Es gefällt uns total gut!"
— *Tobias, Günther und Mischa,*
drei 20-jährige Studenten aus Bochum

„Mir gefällt das Minigolf am Besten. Mein Papa und ich gehen jeden Abend spielen. Ich kann jetzt auch schwimmen! Das Wasser ist ganz warm."
— *Nathan Solothurnmann, 5 Jahre*

A short introduction establishes the topic and frames the comments. Since this is a formal brochure aimed at unknown potential customers, the **Sie**-form is used.

The verb **los•ziehen** is a verb of motion so it takes **sein** in the present perfect tense.

Can you find the double infinitive in this quotation?

Vor dem Schreiben

- Select the four topics about your hometown that you feel most qualified and interested in writing about.

- Decide on four fictional characters who will produce your "quotations." Make it a diverse group—not all the same age. Create personae for these characters: give them names, ages, professions, home addresses, then determine their interests. Determine why they would come to your hometown, and what they would do once there.

TIPP ZUM SCHREIBEN

mögliche Sprecher: Rentner-Ehepaar, 68 J. • 30-jähriger Angesteller • Studentin, 22 J. • 45-jähriges Lehrer-Ehepaar • 7-jähriger Junge • 53-jähriger Manager auf Geschäftsreise • 14-jährige Schülerin • 17-jähriger Schüler • Student, 20 J., in den Semesterferien
mögliche Themen: Transport • Unterkunft/Hotel • Sehenswürdigkeiten • Verpflegung/Essen • Sport • Kultur • Einkaufsmöglichkeiten • Unterhaltung • Natur • Feste • Geschichte

---

Entdecken Sie die Kunst, Kultur und Geschichte von Santa Fe/New Mexiko! Das sagen unsere Besucher.

„Verrückt! Hier in der Wüste gibt es eine Oper mit erstklassigen Aufführungen von Klassikern und von modernen Komponisten. Wahnsinn!" — Martina Nowak, Opernfan, Wien

„Wir sind zu den Pueblos gefahren und haben richtige Indianertänze auf den Straßen sehen können. Das war toll." — Oliver Beck, 10 Jahre, Frankfurt

---

- Contact your local Chamber of Commerce, tourist-information center, or state tourism office to obtain tourist information on your hometown, area, or state, and see what attractions are featured.

- As you prepare to write, you may choose to write all the characters' comments about one topic or to write all of one character's comments about all four topics. You may also simply jot down main ideas and flesh them out later. Decide how you want to proceed.

Beim Schreiben

- Remember that these "quotations" need to sound as conversational and informal as possible. Vary them in length and tone.

- People being interviewed are likely to refer to things they are doing as well as things they have done. A mix of present and past tenses is natural and realistic.

Nach dem Schreiben

- Read through your "quotations," looking for misspellings and mistakes in word order and grammar. Also check to see that they sound conversational—would someone really say this?

- Exchange papers with a peer editor. Check this person's paper for mistakes, then read it again for content and tone. Do the "quotations" sound conversational or stilted? Would a person of this age say something like this? Make comments on the paper, then return it to the author and get your own paper back.

Stimmt alles?

- Read through the corrections and comments of your peer editor. Prepare a revised draft.

- Consider using pictures from your hometown and surrounding area to make your work more visually effective.

- Decide whether you'd rather make an actual-size brochure or a larger poster. Position the title, the introduction, the "quotations," and illustrations on the paper in the most appealing and effective manner.

- Check your layout against the final draft to make sure you've included everything.

- Hand in your finished product with a copy of the final draft of your text.

WORTSCHATZ

Substantive	Nouns
die **Abwechslung, -en**	change; variety
die **Ausrüstung**	outfitting; equipment
die **Entspannung**	relaxation
die **Extremsportart, -en**	adventure sport
die **Gefahr, -en**	danger
die **Reiselust**	desire to travel
die **Schiffsreise, -n**	voyage, cruise
die **Vorbereitung, -en**	preparation
der **Luxus**	luxury
der **Nervenkitzel**	excitement
das **Ferienheim, -e**	vacation home
das **Ferienlager, -**	vacation camp
die **Ferien** (*pl.*)	vacation

Verben	Verbs
an•**gucken** (*coll.*)	to have a look at
baden	to bathe
sich **bräunen**	to tan
geschehen (geschieht), geschah, ist geschehen	to happen
auf etwas an•**kommen, kam an, ist angekommen**	to depend upon
sich **leisten**	to afford
marschieren, ist marschiert	to march
nutzen	to use
springen, sprang, ist gesprungen	to jump
überwachen	to supervise
verreisen	to go on a trip

Adjektive und Adverbien	Adjectives and adverbs
aktiv	active(ly)
gespannt	excited

herrlich	wonderful(ly)
irre (*coll.*)	crazy; wild
jeweils	respectively; for each
normalerweise	normally; usually
persönlich	personal(ly)
ratlos	helpless(ly)
sogar	as well; indeed; even
sowieso	in any case; anyway
wenig	little; few

Sie wissen schon	You already know
die **Mannschaft, -en**	team
die **Sportart, -en**	type of sport
die **Verspätung, -en**	delay
der **Rucksack, ⁻e**	backpack
der **Urlaub, -e**	vacation
das **Abenteuer, -**	adventure
besteigen, bestieg, bestiegen	to climb
sich **fit halten (hält), hielt, gehalten**	to keep fit
gewinnen, gewann, gewonnen	to win
klettern	to climb
reiten, ritt, ist geritten	to ride (*an animal*)
rudern	to row (*a boat*)
Sport treiben, trieb, getrieben	to play a sport
wandern	to hike
spannend	exciting; tense

PLANNING GUIDE • CLASSROOM MANAGEMENT

OBJECTIVES

Communication
- Talk about health and fitness, pp. 186–187.
- Describe your morning routine, p. 189.

Grammar
- Practice reflexive verbs and pronouns, pp. 188–189.
- Use two-way prepositions, p. 190.
- Learn about verbs of direction or location, p. 192.

Culture
- Learn about German health spas, pp. 184, 194.
- Learn about German health insurance, p. 185.
- Learn about sports clubs, p. 195.

Recycling
- Review the use of reflexive verbs and pronouns, pp. 188–190.
- Review food vocabulary, p. 185.

STRATEGIES

Listening Strategies
- Listen to a health spa director speak, p. 194.

Speaking Strategies
- Discuss health and stress, p. 190.
- Describe vacation preferences, p. 191.
- Share knowledge of German health spas, p. 194.
- Discuss sports and fitness, p. 198.

Reading Strategies
- Read a guide to getting started jogging, pp. 195–197.

Writing Strategies
- Write a personal health and fitness program, pp. 198–200.

Connecting Cultures Strategies
- Compare the health care systems in the U.S. and Europe, p. 185.

PROGRAM RESOURCES

Print
- *Arbeitsheft* (Workbook), pp. 129–142
- *Arbeitsheft* (Workbook), Teacher's Edition, pp. 129–142

Audiovisual
- Overhead Transparencies 33.1–33.G2
- Audio Program, Cassette 5A, 7B/CD 6, 9
- Audioscript, pp. 61–68

Technology
- Annenberg *Fokus Deutsch* Video Series, *Folge 33*
- www.mcdougallittell.com

Assessment Program Options
- *Prüfung, Kapitel 33,* Assessment Program, pp. 104–115
- Audio Program, Cassette 8B/CD 10
- Audioscript, pp. 112–113
- Teacher's Resource CD-ROM

Note: (1) Please see TE, pp. 182E–182J, for other suggestions not referenced in these plans. (2) Not all homework options need be assigned.

CHAPTER OPENER

- Quick Start Review: Present perfect (TE, p. 182E). 5 MIN
- Use the photos on p. 182 as a basis for class discussion (TE, p. 182E). 5 MIN

VIDEOTHEK

- After reviewing the *Wortschatz zum Video*, have students watch *Folge I: Ein Kurort*. Encourage them to take notes as they watch (TE, p. 182F). 9 MIN
- Do *Akt. A*, p. 184, as a class and then do the expansion activity in the Teaching Suggestions (TE, p. 182F). 7 MIN
- Have students do *Akt. B–C*, p. 184, silently, then play the video again so they can check their answers (TE, p. 182F). 14 MIN
- *Arbeitsheft*, p. 129, audio *Akt. A.* 4 MIN
- Play *Folge II: Ein Arztbesuch* and encourage students to take notes for later use (TE, p. 182F). 6 MIN

Homework Options:

- *Arbeitsheft*, p. 131, *Videothek, Akt. G*

VIDEOTHEK

- Quick Start Review 1: Foods (TE, p. 182E). 5 MIN
- Have students do *Akt. A*, p. 185 silently and then watch *Folge II: Ein Arztbesuch* again to check their answers. 7 MIN
- Have students do *Akt. B*, p. 185, in writing (TE, p. 182F), then share their answers with the class. 8 MIN
- Do *Akt. C*, p. 185, in small groups, then end with a class discussion (TE, p. 182F). 10 MIN
- *Arbeitsheft*, p. 130, audio *Akt. E.* 7 MIN

VOKABELN

- Present the vocabulary on p. 186. 8 MIN
- *Arbeitsheft*, p. 132, audio *Akt. B.* 5 MIN

Homework Options:

- *Vokabeln, Akt. B*, p. 187

VOKABELN

- Quick Start Review 1: Adjective endings (TE, p. 182G). 5 MIN
- Discuss the answers to *Akt. B*, p. 187, and do the follow-up activity in the Teaching Suggestions (TE, p. 182G). 8 MIN
- Have students do *Akt. A*, pp. 186–187, in pairs. 12 MIN
- Do *Akt. C*, p. 187, as outlined in the Teaching Suggestions (TE, p. 182G). 10 MIN
- Have students do *Akt. D, Schritt 1*, p. 187, silently, then discuss their answers as a class. 7 MIN
- Do *Akt. D, Schritt 2*, p. 187, with a partner, then end with a class discussion (TE, p. 182H). 8 MIN

Homework Options:

- *Arbeitsheft*, pp. 132–133, *Vokabeln, Akt. D–E*

VOKABELN

- Quick Start Review 2: Pronouns (TE, p. 182G). 4 MIN
- *Arbeitsheft*, p. 132, audio *Akt. C.* 6 MIN

STRUKTUREN

- Present reflexive verbs and pronouns on pp. 188–189 using OHT 32.G1 (TE, p. 182I). 7 MIN
- *Arbeitsheft*, p. 134, audio *Akt. B.* 5 MIN
- Do *Übung A*, p. 189, silently. Check answers as a class and then ask comprehension questions (TE, p. 182I). 10 MIN
- Do *Übung B*, p. 189, with a partner. Have several students share the morning routines of their partners with the class (TE, p. 182I). 8 MIN
- *Übung C*, p. 190. 10 MIN

Homework Options:

- *Arbeitsheft*, pp. 135–136, *Strukturen, Akt. F–G*

DAY 5

STRUKTUREN

- Quick Start Review 1: Past participles (TE, p. 182H). 5 MIN
- Present two-way prepositions on p. 190 using OHT 33.2 and 33.G1 and the Teaching Suggestions (TE, p. 182H). 7 MIN
- Do *Übung A,* p. 191, silently. Check answers as a class and follow the Teaching Suggestions for follow-up questions (TE, p. 182H). 10 MIN
- Do *Übung C,* p. 191, including the follow-up activity. 10 MIN
- Present verbs on p. 192 using OHT 33.G2 (TE, p. 182H). 8 MIN
- Have students do *Übung A,* p. 193, with a partner. 10 MIN

Homework Options:

- *Übung B,* p. 191
- *Arbeitsheft,* p. 137, *Strukturen, Akt. J*

DAY 6

STRUKTUREN

- Quick Start Review 2: Question words (TE, p. 182H). 5 MIN
- Do *Übung B,* p. 193, as a class. Check answers as a class and do the follow-up activity (TE, p. 182I). 8 MIN
- Have students do *Übung C,* p. 193, in pairs. Do the follow-up activity on (TE, p. 182I). End with a brief class discussion. 12 MIN

PERSPEKTIVEN

- Review *Wortschatz zum Hörtext,* read through *Hören Sie zu!, Akt. A,* p. 194, listen to the recording once, and then do the activity. Discuss the answers to the activity in pairs and then do follow-up activity on (TE, p. 182J). 8 MIN
- Do *Hören Sie zu!, Akt. B,* p. 194, in pairs. 4 MIN
- Do *Zum Thema,* pp. 194–195. 9 MIN
- Review *Wortschatz zum Lesen* and have students begin reading *Das neue Lauf-Einmaleins*

Homework Options:

- *Arbeitsheft,* p. 138, *Strukturen, Akt. K*
- Finish reading the text on pp. 195–197

DAY 7

PERSPEKTIVEN

- Quick Start Review 1: Time expressions of frequency (TE, p. 182I). 4 MIN
- Do *Zum Text, Akt. A,* p. 197, silently. 10 MIN
- Have students do *Zum Text, Akt. B,* p. 197, in small groups. Then have groups share their answers with the class. 13 MIN
- Do *Zur Interpretation,* p. 198, as a class (TE, p. 182J). 10 MIN
- *Interaktion,* p. 198 (TE, p. 182J). 6 MIN
- Begin *Schreiben Sie!* by discussing the assignment, *Tipp zum Schreiben,* and *Schreibmodell.* 7 MIN

Homework Options:

- Do *Vor dem Schreiben* and *Beim Schreiben,* p. 200, and write the first draft of the fitness plan
- *Arbeitsheft,* p. 141, *Perspektiven, Akt. C–D*

DAY 8

PERSPEKTIVEN

- Quick Start Review 2: Reflexive verbs (TE, p. 182I). 4 MIN
- Have students do *Nach dem Schreiben,* p. 200, and then begin writing the final draft of the fitness plan. 11 MIN
- Questions and review. 5 MIN
- *Prüfung, Kapitel 33.* 30 MIN

Homework Options:

- Complete the final draft of the fitness plan
- *Arbeitsheft,* p. 142, *Perspektiven, Akt. E*

DAY 1

Note: (1) Please see TE, pp. 182E–182J, for other suggestions not referenced in these plans. (2) Not all homework options need be assigned.

CHAPTER OPENER

- Quick Start Review: Present perfect (TE, p. 182E). 5 MIN
- Discuss photos on p. 183 (TE, p. 182E). 5 MIN

VIDEOTHEK

- Watch *Folge I* (TE, p. 182F). 9 MIN
- Do *Akt. A–C*, p. 184 (TE, p. 182F). 21 MIN
- *Arbeitsheft*, p. 129, audio *Akt. A*. 4 MIN
- Block Schedule activity: Survey (TE, p. 182F). 10 MIN
- Play *Folge II and* (TE, p. 182F). 6 MIN
- Do *Akt. A*, p. 185, then watch *Folge II.* 7 MIN
- Do *Akt. B*, p. 185, in writing. 8 MIN
- Do *Akt. C*, p. 185, in small groups (TE, p. 182F). 10 MIN
- *Arbeitsheft*, p. 130, audio *Akt. E*. 5 MIN

Homework Options:

- *Arbeitsheft*, p. 131, *Videothek*, *Akt. F–G*

DAY 2

VOKABELN

- Quick Start Review 1: Adjective endings (TE, p. 182G). 5 MIN
- Present the vocabulary on p. 186. 10 MIN
- *Arbeitsheft*, p. 132, audio *Akt. B*. 7 MIN
- Do *Akt. A–C*, pp. 186–187, (TE, p. 182G). 32 MIN
- Block Schedule activity: Fun Break (TE, p. 182G). 10 MIN
- Do *Akt. D, Schritt 1*, p. 187, silently. Do *Schritt 2*, p. 187, with a partner, then discuss (TE, p. 182G). 10 MIN

STRUKTUREN

- Present reflexive verbs and pronouns on pp. 188–189 using the OHT 33.G1 (TE, p. 182H). 7 MIN
- Do *Übung B*, p. 189, with a partner. (TE, p. 182H). 9 MIN

Homework Options:

- *Arbeitsheft*, pp. 132–133, *Akt. D–E*, pp. 135–136, *F–G*

DAY 3

STRUKTUREN

- Quick Start Review 1: Past participles (TE, p. 182H). 4 MIN
- Do *Übung A*, p. 189, silently. (TE, p. 182H). 10 MIN
- *Übung C*, p. 190. 9 MIN
- Present prepositions on p. 190 (TE, p. 182H). 6 MIN
- Do *Übung A and C*, p. 191, silently. (TE, p. 182H). 15 MIN
- Block Schedule activity: Expansion (TE, p. 182I). 10 MIN
- Present verbs on pp. 192–193 (TE, p. 182H). 8 MIN
- Do *Übung A–C*, p. 193 (TE, p. 182I). 28 MIN

Homework Options:

- *Übung B*, p. 191
- *Arbeitsheft*, pp. 137–138, *Akt. J–K*

DAY 4

PERSPEKTIVEN

- Quick Start Review 1: Time expressions of frequency (TE, p. 182J). 4 MIN
- Do *Akt. A*, p. 194, while listening to the recording. (TE, p. 182J). 8 MIN
- Do *Hören Sie zu!, Akt. B*, p. 194, in pairs. 5 MIN
- Do *Zum Thema*, pp. 194–195 (TE, p. 182J). 8 MIN
- Begin *Das neue Lauf-Einmaleins*, p. 195. 10 MIN
- Do *Zum Text, Akt. A–B*, p. 197. 23 MIN
- Block Schedule activity: Fun Break (TE, p. 182J). 10 MIN
- Do *Zur Interpretation* and *Interaktion*, p. 198 (TE, p. 182J). 16 MIN
- Begin *Schreiben Sie!* by discussing the assignment. 6 MIN

Homework Options:

- *Vor dem Schreiben* and *Beim Schreiben*, p. 200, and write the first draft
- Finish the sports update from Block Schedule activity
- *Arbeitsheft*, p. 141, *Akt. C–D*

DAY 5

PERSPEKTIVEN

- Quick Start Review 2: Reflexive verbs (TE, p. 182I). 5 MIN
- Have scheduled students share their sports reports that were started Day 4 during the Block Schedule activity: Fun Break (TE, p. 182J). 15 MIN
- Do *Nach dem Schreiben*, p. 200, then begin writing the final draft of the fitness plan. 15 MIN
- Block Schedule activity: Peer Teaching (TE, p. 182J). 10 MIN
- *Arbeitsheft*, p. 139, audio *Akt. A–B*. 10 MIN
- Questions and review. 5 MIN
- *Prüfung, Kapitel 33*. 30 MIN

Homework Options:

- Complete the final draft of the fitness plan if necessary
- *Arbeitsheft*, p. 142, *Perspektiven*, *Akt. E*

Chapter Opener, pp. 182–183

PROGRAM RESOURCES

• Overhead Transparency 33.1

Quick Start Review

♻ Present perfect

Wählen Sie das passende Hilfsverb.

1. Wie weit _____ ihr bis zum Bahnhof gelaufen? (sind / habt / hat / seid / ist)

2. Wir _____ beim Kaufhaus gewartet. (haben / ist / sind / hast / habe)

3. Um wie viel Uhr _____ Sie von der Stadt gekommen? (hat / bin / ist / sind / haben)

4. Peter _____ mir nichts gesagt. (ist / haben / sein / hast / hat)

5. _____ du ihm deinen Kuli gegeben? (Haben / Bist / Hat / Habe / Hast)

6. Sie _____ gestern Abend zu Hause geblieben. (hat / sind / seid / haben / bist)

7. Um wie viel Uhr _____ du eingeschlafen? (hat / hast / ist / bist / haben)

Answers: 1. seid 2. haben 3. sind 4. hat 5. Hast 6. sind 7. bist

TEACHING SUGGESTIONS

• Introduce the topic of *Gesundheit und Krankheit* by using an *Assoziogramm* (web diagram). Preview other topics in the chapter by asking students to make statements on what they do to stay healthy and keep fit.

• Photos, p. 183

Look at the photos closely and explain the concept of *Kur* and its tradition in Germany. Ask students if they know of any similar concepts.

TEACHING ALL STUDENTS

Challenge After you have introduced the concept of *Kur,* ask students to write down as many sentences as they can about possible rules at a *Kurort.* For example, *Man darf nicht rauchen. Man muss gesund essen.*

CLASSROOM COMMUNITY

Dictation Introduce the concept of *Kur* with a dictation. *Wenn Deutsche gesundheitliche Probleme oder einfach zu viel Stress haben, können sie zu einem Kurort gehen. Dort bleiben sie ein paar Wochen, um wieder gesund zu werden. Wasser ist oft ein wichtiger Teil der Kur. Viele Kurorte haben natürliches Quellwasser, das man trinkt und in dem man baden kann. Gesundes Essen, Spaziergänge und Vergnügen gehören auch zur Kur.*

Videothek, pp. 184–185

PROGRAM RESOURCES

• Videocassette, *Folge 33*
• *Arbeitsheft,* pp. 129–131
• Audio Program, Cassette 5A/CD 6
• Audioscript, pp. 61–63

Quick Start Review 1

♻ Foods

Verbinden Sie die Wörter mit den Definitionen.

1. die Kartoffel   5. die Eier
2. der Spinat   6. das Fleisch
3. der Zucker   7. der Käse
4. die Milch   8. der Pfirsich

a. gesunde grüne Blätter, die viel Eisen enthalten
b. wächst in der Erde; man macht Pommes frites daraus
c. eine süße Frucht
d. ein Milchprodukt; die Schweizer Sorte hat Löcher drin
e. ein weißes Getränk mit viel Kalzium
f. macht alles süßer
g. werden von Hühnern gelegt; damit machst du ein Omelette
h. Vegetarier essen es nicht

Answers: 1. b 2. a 3. f 4. e 5. g 6. h 7. d 8. c

Quick Start Review 2

♻ Modal verbs

Ergänzen Sie die passende Form des Modalverbs, erst im Präsens und dann im Imperfekt.

MODELL: Du _____ gesünder essen. (müssen) → Du *musst gesünder essen. Du musstest gesünder essen.*

1. _____ ihr um drei Uhr kommen? (dürfen)

2. Die Jungen _____ nicht so laut singen. (sollen)

3. Er _____ die Arbeit machen. (müssen)

4. Petra _____ heute nicht zur Schule kommen. (können)

5. Am Sonntag _____ wir ins Kino gehen. (wollen)

Answers: 1. Dürft/Durftet 2. sollen/sollten 3. muss/musste 4. kann/konnte 5. wollen/wollten

TEACHING SUGGESTIONS

• *Folge I: Ein Kurort,* p. 184

The video presents a short history of Bad Ems. Ask students if they know the names of any other *Kurorte* in Germany.

• *Aktivität A,* p. 184

Expansion: Give students 5 minutes to write pairs of sentences comparing Bad Ems past and present. Remind them to use appropriate tenses. Write responses on the board.

• *Aktivität B,* p. 184

Have students reflect on the positive and negative aspects of life in a *Kurort.*

• *Aktivität C,* p. 184

Ask students to say which statements apply to their own habits. Discuss what other ways there are of staying fit.

• *Folge II: Ein Arztbesuch,* p. 185

Before watching the video, ask questions like *Wie oft gehen Sie zum Arzt? Wie oft gehen Sie zum Zahnarzt?* and *Gehen Sie gern zum Arzt?*

• *Aktivität C,* p. 185

Ask students to relate stories about their own experiences in a hospital. Remain sensitive to the possibility that some students will not want to talk about their health.

TEACHING ALL STUDENTS

Multiple Intelligences Interpersonal: Ask students to write *Frühstück, Mittagessen,* and *Abendessen* on a piece of paper and what foods eat at these meals.

CLASSROOM COMMUNITY

Group Activity Discuss briefly the famous clients of the spa mentioned in the video: Kaiser Wilhelm I, Dostoyevski, Richard Wagner, Clara Schumann, Czar Alexander. Assign students the identities of various famous people from the nineteenth century. Have them imagine that they are all at the spa together and what they might say to each other. (Have them prepare their roles the night before.) Have students mill around the room and converse with each other. Have the class guess who is who.

CULTURE HIGHLIGHTS

Read through the *Kulturspiegel* on p. 185 with students. Discuss the advantages and disadvantages of socialized medicine. Using the Internet or other sources, find out how many people are without health insurance in the U.S. versus Canada and Germany and the average cost of health insurance to the consumer in the 3 countries. Ask questions about socialized medicine in the U.S. such as *Sollten alle amerikanischen Staatsbürger eine staatliche Krankenversicherung haben? Sind Sie bereit, dafür höhere Steuern zu zahlen?*

INTERDISCIPLINARY CONNECTION

See if any of the students are currently enrolled in a health and nutrition class. If so, have them obtain information about proper nutrition and present it to the class.

BLOCK SCHEDULE

Survey Develop a survey to discover the class's health history and habits. Include questions such as *Haben Sie Sich je den Arm oder das Bein gebrochen? Sind Sie gegen etwas allergisch? Haben Sie Angst vor Spritzen? Essen Sie Fleisch?* Have students question each other and write their findings. Have a pair of students compile the results, calculate percentages, and share their findings with the class.

PROJECT

Have students learn about another spa via the Internet. Assign different spas to different students to research, or have them identify German spas on their own. Have them give a short presentation. Use the following rubric to evaluate their presentations.

RUBRIC **A** = 13–15 pts. **B** = 10–12 pts. **C** = 7–9 pts. **D** = 4–6 pts. **F** < 4 pts.

Presentation Criteria	Scale				
Grammar and vocabulary	1	2	3	4	5
Content	1	2	3	4	5
Presentation	1	2	3	4	5

Vokabeln, pp. 186–187

PROGRAM RESOURCES

• *Arbeitsheft,* pp. 132–133
• Audio Program, Cassette 5A/CD 6
• Audioscript, pp. 63–64

Quick Start Review 1

♻ Adjective endings

Geben Sie die richtigen Adjektivendungenan.

1. Der _____ Amerikaner isst ein ganz anderes Frühstück als der _____ Deutsche. (typisch)
2. Ja, es gibt einen _____ Unterschied. (groß)
3. In Deutschland isst man oft ein _____ Brötchen mit Butter und Marmelade zum Frühstück. (frisch)
4. Das _____ Brötchen ist manchmal noch warm, wenn es gerade vom Bäcker geholt wurde. (frisch)
5. Eine _____ Tasse Kaffee trinkt man oft dazu. (schön)
6. Der Geschmack des _____ Kaffees ist ganz toll. (schwarz)
7. Manchmal gibt es auch ein _____ Ei. (gekocht)
8. _____ Eier isst man mit einem Löffel. (gekocht)

Answers: 1. typische, typische
2. großen 3. frisches 4. frische
5. schöne 6. schwarzen
7. gekochtes 8. Gekochte

Quick Start Review 2

♻ Pronouns

Wählen Sie die passenden Pronomen. Achten Sie dabei auf die Wortstellung.

1. Hast du Peter das Buch gegeben? Ja, ich habe _____ gegeben.
   a) es ihm   b) ihm es   c) ihn sie
2. Schreibt Susanne ihren Eltern heute einen Brief? Nein, _____ hat _____ gestern schon geschrieben.

a) sich . . . ihr   b) es . . . sie
c) sie . . . ihnen

3. Rolf kauft Angelika eine neue Halskette. Ja, er kauft _____ viele Dinge.
   a) sie   b) ihr   c) euch
4. Bringst du uns den Koffer? Ja, ich bringe _____ sofort!
   a) uns er   b) ihn euch
   c) euch ihm
5. Hat die Frau dir die Stadt gezeigt? Nein, sie hat sie _____ nicht gezeigt.
   a) mir   b) ihr   c) mich
6. Wem soll ich die Hausaufgaben erklären? Du sollst _____erklären.
   a) sie mir   b) den den Schülern
   c) uns die Schülern

Answers: 1. a   2. c   3. b   4. b
5. a   6. a

TEACHING SUGGESTIONS

• Photo, p. 186

Provide a few vocabulary terms such as *die Untersuchung, die Kinderärztin,* and *der Patient,* and have students write 2 or 3 sentences describing the picture.

• *Aktivität B,* p. 187

Follow-up: Ask students to write the definition of one of the vocabulary terms on p. 186 on a slip of paper. Call on students to give the definition they have written. The class must find the word in the vocabulary list that matches the definition.

• *Aktivität C,* p. 187

Give students 30 seconds per vocabulary item to come up with all the related vocabulary they can. Have them write the related words on a sheet of paper and compare them with those of a partner when the activity is finished. Discuss the results as a class and keep track of students' responses on the board or on an OHT.

• *Aktivität D,* p. 187

Ask students if they go to the gym or a health club. Have them explain why and how often they go. Discuss the advantages and disadvantages of such clubs.

TEACHING ALL STUDENTS

Multiple Intelligences Intrapersonal: Read through Erika's response once more (activity D, p. 187) to the question about how she stays physically fit. Emphasize her preference for a natural setting when physically active. Have students reflect on her preference and write a paragraph about the advantages of exercising in a natural setting.

CLASSROOM COMMUNITY

Group Activity Divide students into groups of 2 or 3 and have each group write a short dialogue for one of the following situations: *im Wartezimmer, bei der Untersuchung, in der Apotheke.* Encourage students to use the vocabulary on p. 186. Select groups to perform their dialogues for the class.

BLOCK SCHEDULE

Fun Break Read aloud the poem *"fünfter sein"* by Ernst Jandl (*Der künstliche Baum,* Darmstadt: Luchterhand, 1970), but leave out the final line ('tagherrdoktor'). Have students try to guess the ending from context, then write their own final line.

fünfter sein

tür auf	tür auf
einer raus	einer raus
einer rein	einer rein
vierter sein	nächster sein
tür auf	tür auf
einer raus	einer raus
einer rein	selber rein
dritter sein	[tagherrdoktor]

tür auf
einer raus
einer rein
zweiter sein

Have students share their final lines with the class. When all have been given, read the author's final line: *tagherrdoktor.*

Strukturen, pp. 188–193

PROGRAM RESOURCES

- Overhead Transparencies 33.2–33.G2
- *Arbeitsheft,* pp. 134–138
- Audio Program, Cassette 5A/CD 6
- Audioscript, pp. 65–67

Quick Start Review 1

Past participles
Ergänzen Sie mit dem Partizip des Verbs in Klammern.

1. Das Wetter ist gestern sehr schön _____. (sein)
2. Hast du den Lehrer _____? (fragen)
3. Der Schüler hat die Aufgabe sehr gut _____. (verstehen)
4. Wir sind zu Fuß _____. (gehen)
5. Die Touristen haben gut Deutsch _____. (sprechen)
6. Habt ihr bei Herrn Blumberg Pizza _____? (essen)

7. Ich bin gestern um sechs _____. (aufstehen)
8. Es tut mir leid! Ich habe mich _____. (verrechnen)

Answers: 1. gewesen   2. gefragt
3. verstanden   4. gegangen
5. gesprochen   6. gegessen
7. aufgestanden   8. verrechnet

Quick Start Review 2

Question words
Ergänzen Sie mit *was, wer, wen, wem* oder *wessen.*

1. Mit _____ hast du in der Disko getanzt?
2. _____ Zelt hast du auf die Reise mitgebracht?
3. _____ ist der neue Schüler?
4. _____ habt ihr gestern gesehen?
5. _____ hat die freundliche Dame geholfen?
6. _____ hat er im Kaufhaus gekauft?
7. _____ kaufte der Junge die Blumen?
8. Nach _____ Haus gingen sie nach der Schule?
9. _____ hat dir geschrieben?

Answers: 1. wem   2. Wessen   3. Wer
4. Wen/Was   5. Wem   6. Was
7. Wem   8. wessem   9. Wer

TEACHING SUGGESTIONS

- Reflexive verbs and pronouns, pp. 188–189

Ask students which reflexive verbs they already know and to form sentences with these verbs. Review the distinction between accusative and dative reflexive pronouns: *Ich wasche **mich**. Ich wasche **mir** die Haare.*

- *Übung A,* p. 189

Follow-up: Ask comprehension questions, for example, *Mit wem hat sich Sabine heute in der Stadt getroffen? Wofür hat sich Melanie interessiert? Was hat Melanie sich anders überlegt?*

- *Übung B,* p. 189

Additional verbs: *sich abtrocken, sich die Beine rasieren,* or *sich beeilen.* Not every sentence needs to contain a reflexive verb.Have students share the morning routines of their partners with the class.

- Two-way prepositions, p. 190

Point out the distinction between direction and location, as well as the transivity and intransivity, of positional verbs (*setzen, stellen, legen* versus *sitzen, stehen, liegen*). Also explain that time expressions after two-way prepositions are always in the dative case. *Ich sah ihn vor einer Stunde. In einem Monat bin ich fertig mit dem Projekt.*

- *Übung A,* p. 191

Follow-up: Ask students about their personal experiences during a vacation day. Ask questions such as *Was machen Sie gern an einem freien Tag? Was haben Sie das letzte Mal gemacht, als Sie einen freien Tag hatten? Wann haben Sie das letzte Mal ein Picknick gemacht?*

- Verbs with two-way prepositions, p. 192

Explain the difference between *Wir fahren morgen in die Stadt* and *Wir fuhren drei Stunden überall in der*

Stadt herum. Introduce the concept of crossing (accusative) or staying within (dative) boundaries.

• *Übung B,* p. 193

Follow-up: Choose a few students to act out the actions described.

• *Übung C,* p. 193

Follow-up: Have students write a continuation of the *Diebstahl* story. Ask *Wohin stellen sie das Bild? Wohin fahren sie jetzt? An wen versuchen sie, das Bild zu verkaufen?*

TEACHING ALL STUDENTS

Multiple Intelligences Visual: Draw a simple picture of a room with approximately 5 recognizable objects in locations on, next to, or under various pieces of furniture. This will be the "before" picture. On another OHT or the board, draw an "after" picture of the same room, but with the locations of numerous objects changed. Show the "before" picture and ask students to describe the locations of the objects. Then show the "after" picture and ask *Was habe ich gemacht?* Variation: Have students prepare "before" and "after" drawings of their own rooms and describe them to a partner.

CLASSROOM COMMUNITY

Group Activity Introduce the character Kirstin Chaot and have the class narrate her morning routine. Provide prompts such as *Also, zuerst steht Kirstin auf. Und dann? Was macht sie dann?* Make it clear that humorous or illogically ordered answers are acceptable.

BLOCK SCHEDULE

Expansion Ask students to choose 5 reflexive verbs and use them in a poem.

MODELL: ***Wer ich bin →***
*Ich **interessiere mich** für nichts und für alles.*
Mit allen **unterhalte** ich **mich** gern.
Ich **rege mich** über viel **auf,** besonders wenn ich gestresst bin.
Ich **entspanne mich,** wo und wann ich kann.
Ich **stelle mir vor,** ich bin glücklich . . . oder nicht?

Perspektiven, pp. 194–201

PROGRAM RESOURCES

• *Arbeitsheft,* pp. 139–142
• Audio Program, Cassette 5A, 7B/CD 6, 9
• Audioscript, pp. 67–68
• www.mcdougallittell.com

Quick Start Review 1

Time expressions of frequency
Verbinden Sie die Beispiele mit den Zeitausdrücken.

1. Montag, Mittwoch, Freitag, Sonntag
2. am ersten und am fünfzehnten
3. einmal im Januar, einmal im April, einmal im Juli
4. Montag – Sonntag
5. um 9 Uhr morgens und um 3 Uhr nachmittags
6. 7 Uhr, 7 Uhr 30, 8 Uhr, 8 Uhr 30, 9 Uhr
7. am 8. September 2000
a. alle dreißig Minuten
b. jeden Tag

c. zweimal im Monat
d. einmal im Jahr
e. alle drei Monate
f. zweimal am Tag
g. jeden zweiten Tag

Answers: 1. g 2. c 3. e 4. b 5. f
6. a 7. d

Quick Start Review 2

Reflexive verbs
Wählen Sie das passende Reflexivpronomen.

1. Ich putze _____ die Zähne zweimal am Tag.
   a) sich b) mich c) mir
   d) uns
2. Du musst _____ aber noch die Haare kämmen.
   a) dir b) sich c) euch
   d) dich
3. Wir freuen _____ auf die Ferien.
   a) euch b) sich c) mich
   d) uns
4. Um wie viel Uhr trefft ihr _____?
   a) euch b) sich c) mich
   d) uns
5. Setzen Sie _____, bitte!
   a) uns b) euch c) sich
   d) mir
6. Du musst _____ beeilen.
   a) mir b) dir c) sich
   d) dich
7. Meine Frau hat _____ vor der Party geschminkt.
   a) mir b) dir c) sich
   d) dich
8. Die Basketballspieler duschen _____ nach dem Spiel.
   a) mir b) dir c) sich
   d) dich

9. Morgen ziehe ich _____ das neue Hemd an.
   a) dich   b) sich   c) mich
   d) mir

Answers: 1. c   2. a   3. d   4. a   5. c
6. d   7. c   8. c   9. d

TEACHING SUGGESTIONS

• *Hören Sie zu!*, p. 194

Follow-up: Have students give one fact about *Oberstaufen*. Then ask several students to summarize the listening passage orally using the facts listed.

• *Zum Thema*, pp. 194–195

After students have done the activity, choose 4 students to sit with you and participate in a discussion group. Encourage students in the "audience" to interject additional questions and ask for clarifications.

• *Zur Interpretation*, p. 198

Ask students to describe associations they have with jogging and make them into an *Assoziogramm* on the board. Then have students find examples in the text of the author's argumentative strategies. Have students read aloud the passages they have found, isolate the technique being used, and say how effective it is. List the techniques on the board under the headings *überzeugend* or *nicht überzeugend*. Next, have students find the problems addressed in the text. Write them under the heading *Probleme*. Write the heading *Lösungen* next to *Probleme* and have students comment on the solutions offered. Finally, have students write their sentences on the board and vote for the best ones.

• *Interaktion*, p. 198

Refer students to the list of topics in *Zum Text, Aktivität A*, p. 197 for ideas. Once students have decided what information they would like to include in a continuation, have them write it as a homework assignment.

• *Schreiben Sie!*, pp. 198–200

Discuss other situations in which making a resolution and formulating a program would be useful. Brainstorm for conditions that would have to be met for the resolution to be successful, for example: *Man muss Disziplin haben. Man muss sich realistische Ziele setzen.*

• *Tipp zum Schreiben*, p. 198

Assign students to look through newspapers and magazines for relevant information as homework. Have them give brief reports the next day.

• *Nach dem Schreiben*, p. 200

Go over the student model before the peer review. Make copies of 2–3 examples of students' work on OHTs once you have collected the writing assignments. Make sure the students' names are not visible.

TEACHING ALL STUDENTS

Multiple Intelligences Kinesthetic: Tell students to go on a jog, bike ride, swim, or hike after school or over the weekend. Tell them to try their best to think in German while exercising. Mention that athletes sometimes use mantras to focus their thinking and maintain a steady rhythm while exercising. Have them jot down their thoughts after exercising and discuss them in class the following day with a partner.

CLASSROOM COMMUNITY

TPR Discuss with students the different muscles and body parts referred to in the *5 empfehlenswerte Dehnübungen* on pp. 196–197. Using the pictures as a reference, perform the 5 stretches with students in class.

LANGUAGE NOTE

Joggen, Rollerbladen, Skateboard fahren, Mountainbike fahren. Point out the origin of these words in American English. Have students speculate why there are so many borrowed words in the area of physical fitness.

CULTURE HIGHLIGHTS

Read the *Kulturspiegel* on p. 195 with students. Explain that sports in German-speaking countries are not associated with schools, but rather with municipal and regional sports clubs.

INTERDISCIPLINARY CONNECTION

Physical Education Encourage students to consult their gym teachers about the fitness programs they formulated.

BLOCK SCHEDULE

Fun Break Have students sign up to give 5-minute talks on any sport. Encourage them to bring in pictures and to formulate their own headlines.
Peer Teaching Have students think of a piece of good advice related to physical fitness, diet, stress reduction, or athletic performance and share it.

33 GESUNDHEIT UND KRANKHEIT

In diesem Kapitel

- lernen Sie einiges über die Stadt Bad Ems, einen berühmten Kurort in Rheinland-Pfalz.

- begleiten Sie Sven Schüder beim Arztbesuch.

- diskutieren Sie, wie man sich fit und gesund hält.

Sie werden auch

- wiederholen, wie man Reflexivpronomen gebraucht.

- wiederholen, wie man zwischen Ziel und Ort unterscheidet.

- etwas über die Stadt Oberstaufen lernen.

- einen Artikel über Joggen lesen.

- Ihr persönliches Gesundheits- und Fitnessprogramm beschreiben.

VIDEOTHEK

In diesem Kapitel erfahren Sie, wie man sich in Europa traditionell gesund hält. Sie erfahren auch, wie das Gesundheitswesen in Deutschland funktioniert. Was machen Sie, um fit und gesund zu bleiben? Was wissen Sie über das Gesundheitswesen in Ihrem Land?

I: Ein Kurort

Kurorte und Bäder haben eine lange Geschichte in Deutschland. In dieser Folge lernen Sie den historischen Kurort Bad Ems kennen.

A Bad Ems. Was haben Sie im Video über Bad Ems gelernt?

1. Welche Leute reisten im neunzehnten Jahrhundert nach Bad Ems? Wissen Sie etwas über einige dieser Leute?
2. Warum ist der 13. Juli 1870 um zehn Minuten nach neun Uhr besonders wichtig in Bad Ems? Wer hat sich dort getroffen? Welche Konsequenzen hatte diese Begegnung?
3. Wer wurde gleich nach dem Ersten Weltkrieg in den Hotels in Bad Ems untergebracht?
4. Wer macht heutzutage Kur in Bad Ems?

In Bad Ems wurde auch Politik gemacht.

B. 1. Das stimmt. 2. Das stimmt nicht. 3. Das stimmt. 4. Das stimmt nicht. 5. Das stimmt.

B Die Kur. „Ich gehe zur Kur", sagt man, wenn man in einen Kurort fährt. Sie hören die Meinungen von Susanne und Erika zum Thema Kur. Was stimmt? Was stimmt nicht?

1. Susanne kennt nur ältere Leute, die zur Kur gehen.
2. Susanne geht persönlich gern zur Kur.
3. Erikas Tante findet es schön, zur Kur zu gehen.
4. In Kuren darf man machen, was man will.
5. Kuren sind für Erika etwas langweilig.

C Gesund leben. Welche Person im Video macht das?

Diese Person . . . / Diese Leute . . .

1. ist etwas faul und macht nicht jeden Tag Sport.
2. schwimmen gern.
3. gehen in einen Fitnessclub.
4. treiben regelmäßig Sport.
5. fahren Rad.
6. geht jeden Tag mit dem Hund spazieren.
7. spielt Handball mit dem Bruder.
8. versucht, joggen zu gehen.
9. ging früher in einen Fitnessclub.
10. macht Aerobic.

WORTSCHATZ ZUM VIDEO

die Spielbank	casino
der/die Adlige	aristocrat
das Parteimitglied	party member
jedermann	everyone
die Nebenhöhlen	sinuses
der Weiher	fishpond
kneten	to knead
die Versichertenkarte	insurance card
die Behandlung	treatment
die Faust	fist
der Imbiss	snack

C. 1. Daniela   2. Claudia und Daniela
3. Claudia und Gürkan   4. Claudia, Anett und Dirk   5. Claudia und Anett   6. Erika
7. Dirk   8. Stefan   9. Erika   10. Claudia

A. *Possible answers are:* 1. Adlige, Künstler und Politiker aus ganz Europa reisen nach Bad Ems, zum Beispiel der deutsche Kaiser Wilhelm II, der russische Schriftsteller Dostojewski, der Komponist Richard Wagner, der russische Zar Alexander, Clara Schumann und Jacques Offenbach.   2. Am 13. Juli 1870 trafen sich der französische Botschafter und der deutsche Kaiser auf der Kurpromenade in Bad Ems. Sie gerieten in einen Streit miteinander, der zum Krieg zwischen Deutschland und Frankreich führte.
3. Gleich nach dem Ersten Weltkrieg wurden französische Truppen in den Hotels in Bad Ems untergebracht.
4. Heutzutage machen Arbeiter und Angestellte Kur in Bad Ems.

II: Ein Arztbesuch

In dieser Folge geht Sven Schüder zur Vorsorgeuntersuchung. Wie oft gehen Sie zum Arzt? Waren Sie sogar schon mal im Krankenhaus? Warum?

A Bei der Vorsorgeuntersuchung. Was stimmt? Was stimmt nicht? Wenn ein Satz nicht stimmt, schreiben Sie ihn neu mit der richtigen Information.

1. Svens Arzt ist der einzige Arzt, der in diesem Haus arbeitet.
2. Sven muss die Vorsorgeuntersuchung selber bezahlen.
3. Sven wird sofort vom Arzt untersucht.
4. Sven hat hohen Blutdruck.
5. Sven bekommt das Medikament beim Arzt.

Warum geht Sven zum Arzt?

A. **1.** Das stimmt nicht. **2.** Das stimmt nicht. **3.** Das stimmt nicht. **4.** Das stimmt. **5.** Das stimmt nicht.

B Gesundes Essen. Das Essen spielt eine wichtige Rolle, wenn man sich fit halten will. Was essen Sie, um gesund zu bleiben? Wie sollen Sie essen, um gesünder zu werden?

B. *Answers will vary.*

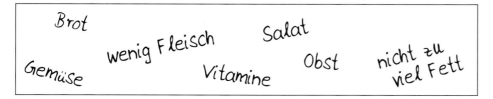

Brot
Gemüse
wenig Fleisch
Salat
Vitamine
Obst
nicht zu viel Fett

C. *Answers will vary.*

C Meinungen zur Gesundheitspflege. Lesen Sie zuerst die folgenden Erfahrungen von Gürkan, Daniela und Stefan. Beantworten Sie dann diese Fragen: Welche persönlichen Erfahrungen haben Sie mit dem Gesundheitswesen in Ihrem Land gehabt? Waren diese Erfahrungen positiv oder negativ? Warum?

GÜRKAN: Arztbesuch? Vielleicht mal alle zwei, drei Jahre, aber . . . ja, jedes Jahr gehe ich einmal zum Arzt, Zahnarzt. Das muss man bei uns tun.

DANIELA: Ich war einmal im Krankenhaus, weil ich mich sehr schlecht gefühlt habe. Ich hatte sehr hohes Fieber, und ich war alleine, und ich wusste nicht, wie ich das Fieber bekämpfen kann, und deswegen bin ich ins Spital gegangen.

STEFAN: Die Krankenkasse in der Schweiz ist sehr, sehr teuer. Es gibt leider zu wenig Leute, die dafür zahlen können. Aber die Krankenhäuser sind alle sehr, sehr gut und dementsprechend hoch sind auch die Kosten für die Gesundheitspflege.

KULTURSPIEGEL

Neunzig Prozent der Einwohner Deutschlands sind Mitglieder einer staatlichen Krankenversicherung. Die Krankenkasse bezahlt für die ärztliche Behandlung. Die Kosten der Krankenkasse werden auf den Arbeitgeber und den Arbeitnehmer verteilt: Jeder bezahlt die Hälfte des monatlichen Beitrags. Zur Zeit liegen diese Versicherungsbeiträge bei ungefähr vierzehn Prozent des Einkommens.

VOKABELN

die Gesundheitspflege	health care
die Körperpflege	personal hygiene
die Krankenkasse	wellness fund
die Kur	health spa; course of treatment
die Übung	exercise
die Untersuchung	examination
die Versicherung	insurance
die Vorsorge	preventive medicine
der Arztbesuch	visit to the doctor
der Blutdruck	blood pressure
der Umstand	circumstance
das Ergebnis	result, outcome
das Fett	fat
das Heilmittel	remedy
das Wartezimmer	waiting room
atmen	to breathe
erhöhen	to raise, increase
geraten	to come upon
mahnen	to urge
messen	to measure
sich verrechnen	to miscalculate
verschreiben	to prescribe
regelmäßig	regular(ly)

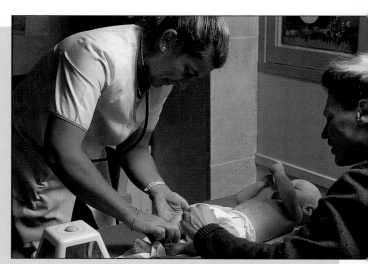

Ärztliche Behandlungen können ziemlich teuer sein – wie bezahlt man das?

sinnvoll	sensible; meaningful
vegetarisch	vegetarian

Sie wissen schon

das Fieber, das Krankenhaus, das Labor, das Medikament, das Rezept, gesund

---

Aktivitäten

A Wie heißt das? Beantworten Sie die Fragen 1–10. Benutzen Sie die Vokabeln aus der Liste.

1. Was soll man täglich machen, um sich fit zu halten?
2. Was tut man, wenn man jemanden an etwas erinnert?
3. Was macht man, wenn man nicht richtig addiert?
4. Welches Verb bedeutet „höher machen"?
5. Wie ist man, wenn man nicht krank ist?
6. Wie kann man feststellen, wie hoch oder wie lang etwas ist?
7. Wie beschreibt man etwas, was Sinn (Bedeutung) hat?
8. Wie beschreibt man eine Form oder eine Aktivität, die eine bestimmte Ordnung hat?

A. *Possible answers are:* **1.** Man soll täglich Übungen machen. **2.** Man mahnt jemanden. **3.** Man verrechnet sich. **4.** „Erhöhen" bedeutet „höher machen". **5.** Wenn man nicht krank ist, ist man gesund. **6.** Man misst, um festzustellen, wie hoch oder wie lang etwas ist. **7.** Etwas, das Sinn hat, beschreibt man als sinnvoll. **8.** Das beschreibt man als regelmäßig. **9.** Man isst vegetarisch. **10.** Im Krankenhaus.

9. Wie isst man, wenn man kein Fleisch isst?
10. Wo bekommen kranke Menschen Gesundheitspflege, Therapie oder Chirurgie (Operationen)?

B Definitionen: Lesen Sie die Sätze links und suchen Sie die passende Definition für die kursiv gedruckten Wörter aus der rechten Spalte.

B. 1. c 2. i 3. b 4. h 5. f 6. d 7. a
8. g 9. e

1. Ich weiß ja von meiner Tante, die immer zur *Kur* geht.
2. Jetzt *atmen* Sie ganz tief für zwei Stunden.
3. Die Vorsorgeuntersuchung wird von der *Krankenkasse* bezahlt.
4. Nehmen Sie bitte im *Wartezimmer* Platz.
5. Sven wartet auf die *Untersuchung* durch den Arzt.
6. Ich *verschreibe* Ihnen ein Blutdruckmittel.
7. Das *Rezept* können Sie vorne an der Anmeldung abholen.
8. Die Krankenkasse bezahlt das *Medikament*.
9. Ich hatte sehr hohes *Fieber* und war allein.

a. schriftliche Anweisung eines Arztes an den Apotheker für Medikamente
b. Institution, bei der man sich gegen die Kosten der Krankheit versichert
c. Aufenthalt unter ärztlicher Aufsicht, damit man wieder gesund wird
d. ein Rezept geben
e. hohe Körpertemperatur
f. Feststellung der Gesundheit einer Person durch einen Arzt
g. Mittel für die Heilung von Krankheiten
h. Zimmer, wo man wartet
i. Luft in die Lungen einziehen und ausstoßen

C Verwandte Wörter. Kennen Sie Wörter, die mit den folgenden Wörtern verwandt sind? Machen Sie eine Liste.

MODELL: der Arzt →
die Ärztin, ärztlich, Arztbesuch, Tierarzt, Zahnarzt

1. üben
2. sorgen
3. krank
4. pflegen
5. suchen
6. drücken
7. sicher

D Fitnessclubs

SCHRITT 1: Was halten Claudia, Gürkan und Erika von Fitnessclubs? Lesen Sie ihre Meinungen dazu.

CLAUDIA: Um fit zu bleiben, gehe ich jetzt regelmäßig seit einem Jahr in einen Fitnessclub, „Swiss Training". Ich mach dort manchmal Aerobic, manchmal Geräte, im Wechsel.

GÜRKAN: Ich habe mich jetzt im letzten Jahr in einem Fitnessclub eingeschrieben. Den habe ich pro Woche einmal, zweimal besucht.

ERIKA: Um fit zu bleiben, mache ich jetzt etwas mit meinem kleinen Hund, den ich mir gerade angeschafft habe. Früher bin ich zu einem Fitnessclub gegangen, aber jetzt ist es viel schöner, in der Natur mit dem kleinen Hund um den See zu rennen.

SCHRITT 2: Was halten Sie davon? Was kann man machen, um fit zu bleiben? Diskutieren Sie darüber mit einem Partner / einer Partnerin. Denken Sie auch an die folgenden Fragen.

1. Gehen Sie regelmäßig in einen Fitnessclub?
2. Welche Übungen machen Sie?
3. Welchen Sport treiben Sie?

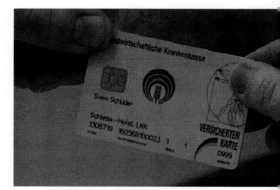

Beim Arztbesuch muss man die Versichertenkarte zeigen.

C. *Possible answers are:* 1. üben, Übung
2. sorgen, Sorge, Vorsorge, besorgen, vorsorgen, versorgen 3. krank, der/die Kranke, Krankheit, Krankenhaus, Krankenkasse 4. pflegen, Pflege, Gesundheitspflege, Körperpflege, verpflegen, Verpflegung 5. suchen, Suche, untersuchen, Untersuchung, besuchen, Besuch 6. drücken, Druck, Blutdruck 7. sicher, versichern, Versicherung, Krankenversicherung

D. *Answers will vary.*

STRUKTUREN

REVIEW OF REFLEXIVE VERBS AND PRONOUNS
DOING SOMETHING FOR ONESELF

As you recall, some verbs have reflexive pronouns that refer back to the subject. Note the objects in the following sentences.

Ich ziehe **mich** an.	*I'm getting dressed.*
Ich ziehe **mir** eine Jacke an.	*I'm putting on a jacket.*

Reflexive pronouns occur in the accusative or dative case. The only distinctly different case forms are **mich/mir** and **dich/dir.** All other reflexive pronouns are identical in the accusative and dative cases.

KURZ NOTIERT

Some German verbs are always reflexive, although their English counterparts may not be.

sich erinnern an (+ *acc.*)	*to remember*
sich interessieren für	*to be interested in*
sich unterhalten	*to have a conversation*
sich überlegen	*to decide*
sich aufregen	*to get excited*
sich entspannen	*to relax*
sich freuen auf (+ *acc.*)	*to look forward to*
sich freuen über (+ *acc.*)	*to be glad about*
sich vorstellen	*to imagine; to introduce*
sich schminken	*to put on makeup*

SINGULAR				PLURAL		
ACCUSATIVE		DATIVE		ACCUSATIVE		DATIVE
mich	*myself*	mir		uns	*ourselves*	uns
dich	*yourself*	dir		euch	*yourselves*	euch
sich	*yourself*	sich		sich	*yourselves*	sich
sich	*herself himself itself*	sich		sich	*themselves*	sich

Note that the verbs **legen** and **setzen** require accusative reflexive pronouns to describe the process of lying or sitting down.

Ich **lege mich** ins Bett.	*I'm going to lie down in bed. (I'm going to put myself to bed.)*
Du **hast dich** an den Tisch **gesetzt.**	*You sat down at the table. (You seated yourself at the table.)*

If a sentence with a reflexive verb contains a direct object, the reflexive pronoun will be in the dative case.

Du ziehst **dich** an.   *You're getting dressed.*
Du ziehst **dir** die Jacke an.   *You're putting on your jacket.*

German has a number of reflexive verbs that refer to daily routines and that take articles of clothing or parts of the body as direct objects. In these instances, the reflexive pronoun appears in the dative case.

Übungen

A. 1. dich   2. uns   3. sich   4. mich   5. sich
6. mir   7. mich   8. dich

A Alte Freunde. Susanne trifft sich mit Sabine im Fitnessclub. Sabine hat gerade eine alte Freundin gesehen, die vor einiger Zeit ein Zimmer bei Familie Dyrchs mieten wollte.

SABINE: Erinnerst du _____[1] an Melanie Schmidt? Wir haben _____[2] heute in der Stadt getroffen.

SUSANNE: Ja, sie war doch mal hier, weil sie _____[3] für ein Zimmer bei uns interessiert hat.

SABINE: Ich hatte _____[4] schon gefreut, dass sie bei uns einziehen würde.

SUSANNE: Ja, aber sie hat es _____[5] dann doch anders überlegt.

SABINE: Schade, ich könnte es _____[6] wirklich gut vorstellen, sie bei uns als Mitbewohnerin zu haben.

SUSANNE: Ja, ich erinnere _____[7] noch, dass du _____[8] vorher lange mit ihr unterhalten hast.

Susanne und ihre Schwester Sabine im Fitnessclub.

B Morgentoilette. Was machen Sie morgens und in welcher Reihenfolge? Erklären Sie Ihre Routine.

MODELL: Erst stehe ich auf, dann mache ich Tee, dann . . .

B. *Possible answers are:* Erst stehe ich auf, dann mache ich Tee, dann dusche ich mich und wasche mir die Haare, dann kämme ich mir die Haare, dann ziehe ich mich an, dann putze ich mir die Zähne, dann schminke ich mich.

sich die Haare waschen

sich die Zähne putzen

sich duschen

sich anziehen

sich rasieren

sich die Haare kämmen

sich schminken

In Bad Ems kann man sich gut erholen.

C. *Answers will vary.*

C Gesundheit und Stress. Arbeiten Sie mit einem Partner / einer Partnerin, und stellen Sie einander die folgenden Fragen.

1. Wie hältst du dich fit?
2. Interessierst du dich für Fitness-Training?
3. Was solltest du essen, um gesund zu bleiben?
4. Was machst du, wenn du dich krank fühlst?
5. Wie viele Stunden in der Woche arbeitest du?
6. Regst du dich auf, wenn die Schule zu stressig ist?
7. Ärgerst du dich, wenn du zu viel zu tun hast?
8. Wie kannst du dich in der Freizeit am besten entspannen?

REVIEW OF TWO-WAY PREPOSITIONS
TALKING ABOUT DIRECTION AND LOCATION

German has groups of prepositions that always require objects in just one case: the accusative, dative, or genitive. However, German has also another group—called two-way prepositions—that takes either an accusative or a dative object, depending on whether the preposition refers to location or destination. This set includes the following prepositions.

an	*at, near*	über	*above, over*
auf	*on, on top of, at*	unter	*below, under, among*
hinter	*behind, in back of*	vor	*in front of*
in	*in, into*	zwischen	*between*
neben	*next to*		

In sentences that answer the question **wo** (*where*), these prepositions require the dative case to indicate location.

WO?	**LOCATION**
Wo ist Sabine?	Sie ist **auf dem** Flughafen.
Wo ist Susanne?	Sie ist **im** Fitnessclub.

In sentences that answer the question **wohin** (*where to*), they require the accusative case to indicate destination.

WOHIN?	**DESTINATION**
Wohin geht Susanne?	Sie geht **in den** Fitnessclub.
Wohin steckt Sabine ihren Reisepass?	Sie steckt ihren Reisepass **in die** Tasche.

Contractions commonly occur with the following combinations.

an dem → am		in dem → im
an das → ans		in das → ins

Übungen

A Urlaub auf Mallorca. Sie erinnern sich an eine schöne Reise. Ergänzen Sie die Lücken mit Hilfe des Wortkastens.

Letzten Sommer sind wir nach Mallorca gefahren. Wir haben da in einem Hotel gewohnt. Als wir am ersten Tag _____¹ Hotel gingen, haben wir einen Freund getroffen. Wir sind zusammen _____² Strand gegangen. Es war so schön da! Wir haben ganz schön _____³ Meer gebadet und in der Sonne gelegen. Am zweiten Tag haben wir ein Auto gemietet, und wir sind _____⁴ andere Seite der Insel gefahren. Wir haben das Auto _____⁵ sehr alten Ferienheim geparkt. Dann sind wir _____⁶ kleinen Hügel geklettert, um die ganze Insel zu sehen. Ich habe mich richtig _____⁷ tolle Reise gefreut.

```
über diese
              auf die
       ins
              auf einen
       im
              vor einem
   an den
```

B Wo? Wohin? Die Eltern fahren bald zur Kur ab. Sie regen sich auf, weil sie so viel in so kurzer Zeit zu tun haben. Die Tochter hilft ihnen. Wie antwortet sie auf ihre Fragen?

MODELL: Wo ist meine Sonnenbrille? (in / die Schublade)ᵃ
In der Schublade.

1. Wo ist Vatis Brieftasche?ᵇ (in / seine Tasche)
2. Wo sind meine Sandalen? (vor / die Tür)
3. Wo ist unser Reiseführer? (auf / der Bücherschrank)
4. Wo ist meine liebe Katze? (unter / das Bett)
5. Wohin geht der Hund jetzt? (unter / das Bett)
6. Wohin sollen wir unser Gepäck stellen? (in / der Kofferraum)
7. Wohin wirst du unsere Post legen? (neben / der Computer)
8. Wohin fährst du uns jetzt? (auf / der Bahnhof)
9. Woran denkst du? (an / eure Abfahrt)

ᵃdrawer ᵇwallet

Vor einer Reise hat man viel zu erledigen!

C Mein Lieblingsurlaub. Arbeiten Sie mit einem Partner / einer Partnerin, und stellen Sie einander die folgenden Fragen.

1. Was möchtest du lieber im Urlaub machen, an den Strand gehen oder ins Museum?
2. Möchtest du auf einer tropischen Insel Urlaub machen?
3. Möchtest du in einen deutschen Kurort reisen? Warum (nicht)?
4. Gehst du gern in die Disko, wenn du im Urlaub bist?
5. Reist du lieber mit Freunden oder mit der Familie?
6. Unterhältst du dich gern mit neuen Leuten, wenn du im Urlaub bist?
7. Übernachtest du lieber in einem Hotel oder auf einem Campingplatz?
8. Möchtest du lieber in den Bergen wandern oder am Meer segeln?

REVIEW OF VERBS OF DIRECTION AND LOCATION
MORE ON CONTRASTING DIRECTION AND LOCATION

KURZ NOTIERT

You will recall also these verbs that indicate direction and location.

Direction

setzen, setzte, gesetzt
to set, put in position

stecken, steckte, gesteckt
to stick; to hide, put in a concealed place

Location

sitzen, saß, gesessen
to sit, be in a sitting position

stecken, steckte, gesteckt
to stick; to be in a concealed place

In addition to two-way prepositions, verbs also indicate direction or location. For example, you know that **gehen** and **fahren** indicate direction *toward* a place; whereas **sein, liegen,** and **treffen** designate location *at* a place. The following verbs combine with the two-way prepositions to describe an exact direction or location.

DIRECTION	LOCATION
stellen, stellte, hat gestellt *to stand, place in an upright position*	stehen, stand, hat gestanden *to stand, be in an upright position*
hängen, hängte, hat gehängt *to hang onto a vertical surface*	hängen, hing, hat gehangen *to hang on a vertical surface*
legen, legte, hat gelegt *to lay, place in a horizontal position*	liegen, lag, hat gelegen *to lie in a horizontal position*
sich legen, legte, hat gelegt *to lie (oneself) down*	

Note that the past forms of the verbs that indicate direction are regular, while the verbs that indicate location form their past tense with a stem change and their participles with **-en.**

Er hat seine Bücher auf den Tisch **gelegt.**	*He put his books on the table.*
Seine Bücher haben auf dem Tisch **gelegen.**	*His books were lying on the table.*

Always use reflexive pronouns to say that someone is seating himself or herself down or is lying down:

Ich **lege mich** ins Bett.	*I'm going to bed.*
Wir haben **uns** an den Tisch **gesetzt.**	*We seated ourselves at the table.*

Übungen

A Ein freier Tag. Sie haben einen schönen Tag in Bad Ems verbracht. Wählen Sie die richtige Verbform.

1. Wir _____ uns auf eine Bank. (saßen, setzten)
2. Wir _____ gemütlich da und redeten miteinander. (saßen, setzten)
3. Meine Schwester _____ sich auf den Rasen und las ein Buch. (lag, legte)
4. Dann haben wir uns alle auf den Rasen _____. (gelegen, gelegt)
5. Als wir auf dem Rasen _____, kamen unsere Freunde vorbei. (lagen, legten)
6. Sie haben da einige Minuten _____, weil sie auf den Tennisplatz gehen wollten. (gestanden, gestellt)
7. Endlich _____ sie sich aber auch neben uns. (lagen, legten)
8. Wir haben alle da den ganzen Nachmittag in der Sonne _____. (gelegen, gelegt)

B Beim Arztbesuch. Die Arzthelferin erklärt Sven, was er während der Untersuchung machen muss. Ergänzen Sie die Sätze mit Hilfe der Wörter in Klammern.

1. Herr Schüder, bitte gehen Sie (in / das Labor).
2. Sie dürfen Ihre Jacke hier (auf / dieser Haken) hängen.
3. Stellen Sie Ihre Sachen (unter / der Tisch).
4. Legen Sie Ihren Arm (auf / der Tisch), und machen Sie eine Faust.
5. Gehen Sie jetzt (in / das Sprechzimmer), und warten Sie bitte auf den Arzt.
6. Ich schreibe die Ergebnisse (auf / der Zettel).

C Diebstahl im Museum. Jemand hat ein berühmtes Bild aus dem Museum gestohlen – aber wie ist es passiert? Schreiben Sie die Sätze im Imperfekt.

1. Das wertvolle Bild hängt im Museum.
2. Die Diebe liegen hinter den Bäumen, bis es dunkel ist.
3. Sie stellen eine Leiter vor das Fenster.
4. Sie klettern auf die Leiter und kommen ins Museum.
5. Der Wachmann sitzt in einem Sessel und schläft.
6. Sie hängen ein falsches Bild an die Stelle des echten.
7. Sie stecken das echte Bild in den Sack.
8. Sie fahren mit dem Bild weg.

A. 1. setzten 2. saßen 3. legte 4. gelegt
5. lagen 6. gestanden 7. legten 8. gelegen

B. 1. in das 2. auf diesen Haken 3. unter den Tisch 4. auf den Tisch 5. in das Sprechzimmer 6. auf den Zettel

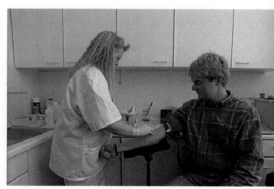

Sven mit der Arzthelferin.

C. 1. Das wertvolle Bild hing im Museum.
2. Die Diebe lagen hinter den Bäumen, bis es dunkel war. 3. Sie stellten eine Leiter vor das Fenster. 4. Sie kletterten auf die Leiter und kamen ins Museum. 5. Der Wachmann saß in einem Sessel und schlief. 6. Sie hängten ein falsches Bild an die Stelle des echten.
7. Sie steckten das echte Bild in den Sack.
8. Sie fuhren mit dem Bild weg.

PERSPEKTIVEN

HÖREN SIE ZU!
LIEBER GAST

Sie hören jetzt eine Begrüßung des Kurdirektors. Er beschreibt das umfangreiche Angebot der Stadt Oberstaufen.

A Was wissen Sie jetzt über Oberstaufen? Beantworten Sie die Fragen.

1. Warum sagt der Kurdirektor, „von Umweltschutz reden wir schon lange nicht mehr"?
2. Wie ist die Luftqualität in Oberstaufen? Warum ist das so?
3. Was kann man mit einer Kurkarte machen?
4. Wo liegt Oberstaufen?

B Wie ist es bei Ihnen? Gibt es solche Kur- oder Erholungsorte in Ihrem Land? Was sind die Hauptattraktionen solcher Kurorte? Arbeiten Sie mit einem Partner / einer Partnerin, und besprechen Sie, was Sie jetzt alles über „Kur" und Kurorte in Deutschland wissen.

A. *Possible answers are:* **1.** Der Kurdirektor sagt das, weil Oberstaufen Umweltschutz in allen Bereichen des täglichen Lebens praktiziert. **2.** Die Luftqualität in Oberstaufen ist erstklassig, weil der Ortskern eine Fußgängerzone mit viel Grün hat, weil die Seitentäler und Alpenwege für den Autoverkehr gesperrt sind und weil der Ort frei vo Nebel ist und windgeschützt liegt. **3.** Mit der Kurkarte kann man kostenfrei mit dem Bus zwisc Oberstaufen, Steibis, der Skiarena und der Hochgratbahn hin- und herfahren Außerdem erhält r mit der Kurkarte einen einmaligen kostenfreien Eintritt für eine Stunde in das Panorama-Erlebnisbad „Aquaria". **4.** Oberstaufen liegt im Allgäu.

LESEN SIE!

Zum Thema

● **Wie halten Sie sich fit?** Halten Sie sich gern fit? Oder machen Ihnen Sport und Bewegung keinen Spaß? Lesen Sie die folgenden Fragen, und diskutieren Sie sie dann mit einem Partner / einer Partnerin.

1. Merken Sie es, wenn Sie sich lange nicht bewegt haben? Wie denn?
2. Wie lockern Sie Ihre Glieder[a] am liebsten? Freuen Sie sich auf die Bewegung?
3. Treiben Sie gern Sport? Warum, oder warum nicht? Wie oft?
4. Haben Sie immer dieselbe Einstellung zum Sport gehabt, oder hat sich das geändert? Warum?
5. Brauchen Sie viel Abwechslung beim Sport, oder konzentrieren Sie sich lieber auf eine Sportart? Oder schauen Sie einfach lieber zu?

[a]*joints, limbs*

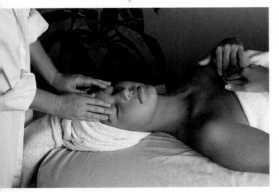

Oberstaufen, ein attraktiver Erholungsort im bayerischen Allgäu.

B. *Answers will vary.*

WORTSCHATZ ZUM HÖRTEXT

anerkannt	*recognized*
das Heilbad	*medicinal bath*
umfangreich	*extensive*
der Bereich	*area; field*
die Luftreinheit	*purity of the air*
gesperrt	*closed*
vorbildlich	*exemplary*

Answers will vary.

Eine natürliche Therapie.

6. Was könnte und sollte man machen, um Erfolg zu garantieren, wenn man sich nach langem Nichtstun wieder fit machen will?

7. Wie gefällt Ihnen das Joggen? Was sind Ihrer Meinung nach die Vor- und Nachteile davon?

Das neue Lauf-Einmaleins
10 erste Schritte für Einsteiger

SCHRITT 1: Sie haben zehn Sekunden Zeit: Was fällt Ihnen spontan zum Stichwort „Joggen" ein? – Die Uhr läuft.

Stopp! Nun antworten Sie ehrlich: War auch nur ein Gedanke aus dem Umfeld „eigentlich müßte ich", „schlechtes Gewissen", „jaja, ich weiß",
5 „Verpflichtung", „wann denn bloß" dabei? Dann heißt der erste Schritt für Sie: Vergessen Sie alles, was Sie bislang über Joggen zu wissen glaubten!

SCHRITT 2: Jetzt folgt der wichtigste dieser zehn Schritte: Betrachten Sie Joggen nicht als eine Verpflichtung, nicht als einen lästigen, zusätzlich abzuhakenden Punkt in Ihrem Tagesablauf, sondern als etwas Lustvolles
10 und Kostbares. Versuchen Sie, das neue „Joggen" in dem Gehirnbereich abzuspeichern, wo Sie bereits „wolkenloser Himmel" und „sternenklare Nacht", „Frühstück im Freien" und „Sauna" angesiedelt haben. Glauben Sie uns einfach: Joggen, jedenfalls das neue Joggen, zu dem wir Sie hier führen wollen, macht Spaß.

15 SCHRITT 3: Lassen Sie Ihre übliche Arbeitswoche in Gedanken Revue passieren: An welchen drei Tagen würden Sie sich am dringlichsten eine Auflockerung der Routine wünschen oder sich selbst etwas Gutes gönnen?

Okay, Ihr Wunsch wird erfüllt: Reservieren Sie sich an diesen drei Tagen eine halbe Stunde Spaß. (Wenn Sie jetzt „keine Zeit" denken,
20 haben Sie Schritt 2 übersprungen.)

SCHRITT 4: Wissen Sie, warum so viele Jogger einfach nicht danach aussehen, als hätten sie gerade Spaß? Weil sie sich unrealistische Ziele gesetzt haben. („10 Kilogramm weniger in drei Wochen"), deshalb zu schnell laufen, deshalb außer Atem kommen, deshalb nur denken: „Wann
25 bin ich endlich wieder am Auto?", deshalb noch schneller laufen . . .

Setzen Sie sich statt dessen ein realistisches Ziel. Das ist das Gegenteil von einem abstrakten Ziel – also alle Vorgaben, die irgendetwas mit Zahlen zu tun haben, mit verlorenen Kilos, mit Minuten-pro-Kilometer, mit Kilometer-pro-Woche. Deshalb jetzt ein Geheimtip. Das beste
30 realistische Ziel, das wir kennen, lautet: Ich will mich nach dem Joggen besser fühlen als vorher. Daraus lassen sich die Antworten auf alle anderen Fragen ableiten, die Sie vielleicht noch haben.

SCHRITT 5: Wählen Sie eine Strecke, auf der Sie sich wohl fühlen. Wenn Ihnen der Gedanke nicht behagt, daß andere Ihnen zuschauen, dann

KULTURSPIEGEL

Wer in den deutschsprachigen Ländern seine sportlichen Talente entwickeln und gegen Mannschaften aus anderen Städten spielen will, wird Mitglied bei einem Sportverein. Diese Sportvereine bieten Spielmöglichkeiten auf verschiedenen Ebenen: sie trainieren Kinder und Jugendliche, bieten Erwachsenen Spiel- und Trainingsprogramme, und in den Großstädten unterstützen sie professionelle Mannschaften.

35 laufen Sie eben nicht den unbefestigten Weg um den nahegelegenen See, auf dem sich morgens und abends Ihre joggenden Freunde und Nachbarn treffen.

SCHRITT **6**: Beinahe jeder Einsteiger glaubt, daß
40 Laufen automatisch schneller sein müsse als Gehen. Vergessen Sie es. Wenn Sie eine Person Ihres Vertrauens finden, die während Ihres ersten Jogging-Versuchs neben Ihnen her geht, können Sie den Gegenbeweis im Wortsinn antreten:
45 Konzentrieren Sie sich darauf, maximal so schnell zu laufen, wie Ihr Begleiter geht. Das wird Ihnen anfangs komisch vorkommen, funktioniert aber und ist obendrein eine ausgezeichnete Übung für die Muskulatur, die sich ja erst einmal an den neuen
50 Bewegungsablauf gewöhnen muß.

SCHRITT **7**: Ein Hinweis, damit Ihnen vor Begeisterung nicht die Luft wegbleibt: Die Puste wird knapp, wenn der Körper nicht genug einatmen kann. Und er kann nicht genug einatmen, wenn wir nicht
55 intensiv genug ausatmen. Hört sich simpel an, ist aber der eigentliche Schlüssel zur richtigen Atmung: Das Einatmen besorgt der Körper selbst, wenn wir ihm nur durch bewußtes, kräftiges Ausatmen die Lungen freimachen. Für den Anfang kann man sich
60 gut damit behelfen, in vier Schüben zeitgleich mit vier Laufschritten die Luft aus Mund und Nase auszustoßen. Wenn Sie nur noch zwei Schritte schaffen, verringern Sie das Tempo oder gehen ein Stück. So haben Sie auch eine gute Kontrolle über
65 Ihre Geschwindigkeit.

SCHRITT **8**: Jetzt sollten Sie sich mit einer schlechten Nachricht vertraut machen: Um den optimalen Nutzen zu erreichen, dürfen Sie Ihrem neuen Hobby nicht uneingeschränkt frönen. Dreimal pro Woche
70 30 Minuten lautet die einfache Regel, die das weltgrößte Fitneß-Forschungsinstitut von Kenneth H. Cooper in Dallas aus einer Flut von Daten als Optimalpensum herausgefiltert hat. Mehr ist weniger (zumindest für die Gesundheit), weniger ist zu
75 wenig. Das heißt keinesfalls, daß Sie 30 Minuten am Stück laufen sollen. Wichtig ist die gleichmäßige Belastung, die Sie am Anfang auch durch einen ständigen Wechsel von Laufen und Gehen erreichen.

80 SCHRITT **9**: Fehlt noch die Ausrüstung. Die Turnschuhe, mit denen Sie im letzten Jahr den Rasen gemäht haben, sollten Sie jetzt nicht zweckentfremden. 30 Minuten sind zwar kein Marathon, aber für eine Blase reicht's. Suchen Sie
85 lieber im Sportgeschäft einen Verkäufer, der sich die Zeit nimmt, Ihren Fuß zu begutachten und Ihnen einige für Sie passende Modelle zu empfehlen. Wenn Sie sich für eines entschieden haben, fragen Sie nach Restposten des Vorläufers aus der
90 vergangenen Saison. Die haben nur grüne statt blaue Dekorstreifen, kosten aber 75 Mark weniger.

SCHRITT **10**: Den letzten Schritt – tja, den können wir Ihnen nicht abnehmen. Den müssen, Entschuldigung, dürfen Sie jetzt selber tun.

Frank Hofmann

5 empfehlenswerte Dehnungsübungen

Dehnung für den Wadenmuskel:
Schrittstellung, Hände stützen in
Schulterhöhe ab, hinteres Knie
wird gestreckt

Dehnung für den Schollenmuskel:
hinterer Fuß zieht nach vorne,
Gesäß wird zurückverlagert,
hinteres Knie gebeugt

Dehnung Oberschenkel-Rückseite: leicht gebeugtes Standbein, gestrecktes Spielbein setzt mit Ferse auf

Dehnung Oberschenkel-Vorderseite: Kniegelenk des liegenden Beins wird so weit gedehnt, bis die Ferse das Gesäß berührt

Dehnung Schienbein: im Kniestand das Gesäß langsam auf Fersen absenken, Spann liegt flach auf dem Boden auf

Zum Text

A Welche Themen werden im Text angesprochen, und welche nicht?

Brainstorming
optimale
   Trainingseinheiten
richtiges Ein- und
   Ausatmen
Ausrüstung
Joggingpartner

Jogging-Vereine
Denktraining
Zeiteinteilung
realistische Ziele
Joggingstrecken
Sportgetränke
Fußblasen

Diät
Jogging-Mode
Gehen vs. Joggen
Tempo
Dehnungsübungen
Marathon

B „10 erste Schritte für Einsteiger." Suchen Sie die Antworten zu diesen Fragen im Text.

1. Was sind normale Reaktionen auf das Wort „Joggen"?
2. Was sollte man über das Joggen denken? Mit was sollte man Joggen assoziieren?
3. Wie oft in der Woche sollte man sich etwas Gutes gönnen bzw. die Routine auflockern? Für wie lange?
4. Was für Ziele soll sich der Jogging-Anfänger setzen? Was wären falsche Ziele?
5. Wo soll der Einsteiger nicht joggen?
6. Was ist das richtige Jogging-Tempo für den Einsteiger?
7. Was sollte man machen, um nicht außer Atem zu kommen?
8. Wie oft und wie lange soll der Einsteiger trainieren?
9. Wie wichtig ist es, dass man das Joggen nicht unterbricht?
10. Was ist das Wichtigste an der Ausrüstung? Wie kann man Geld sparen?

A. Nicht angesprochen werden Denktraining, Diät, Jogging-Mode, Sportgetränke und Jogging-Vereine.

B. *Possible answers are:* **1.** Schlechtes Gewissen und dass man Joggen mit Arbeit in Verbindung bringt. **2.** Man sollte an Spaß denken. **3.** An drei Tagen für etwa eine halbe Stunde. **4.** Realistische Ziele, das heißt man soll sich nicht Ziele mit unrealistischen Zeitangaben, Geschwindigkeiten usw. setzten. **5.** Anfänger sollen nicht da joggen, wo sie sich nicht wohl fühlen. **6.** Schritttempo. **7.** Richtig ausatmen. **8.** Dreimal pro Woche 30 Minuten. **9.** Nicht wichtig, man kann zwischendrin auch gehen. **10.** Gute Schuhe. Man sollte nach Modellen aus der letzten Saison fragen.

Zur Interpretation

● Einstellungen ändern. Der Autor dieses Artikels geht von einer bestimmten weitverbreiteten Einstellung zum Joggen aus und will Sie umstimmen. Von welcher? Mit welchen Mitteln versucht der Autor Sie umzustimmen? Welche Probleme für Jogger spricht er an? Mit einem Satz: was ist die wichtigste Aussage dieses Textes?

INTERAKTION

● Die Fortsetzung. Der Autor der „10 Schritte für Einsteiger" zeigt Ihnen den Text und fragt, wie er den Artikel wohl fortsetzen soll. Welche Themen würden Sie ihm empfehlen? Für welche Informationen würden Sie sich am meisten interessieren? Diskutieren Sie mit einem Partner / einer Partnerin.

SCHREIBEN SIE!

Ein Gesundheits- und Fitnessprogramm

TIPP ZUM SCHREIBEN

Newspapers and magazines are full of information about how to lead a healthy lifestyle. Before you write, spend some time reading about foods to avoid and the reasons for avoiding them. Then think about the kinds of things you like to eat. Compare your diet to the information you gathered in your reading. Do the same for physical activities.

● Sie haben sich endlich dazu entschieden, fit zu werden. Oder Sie sind bereits fit und möchten weiterhin in Form und gesund bleiben. Schreiben Sie für sich selbst ein Gesundheitsprogramm, in dem Sie geeignete Sportarten, Übungen und andere Maßnahmen beschreiben, die Sie an Ihr persönliches Fitnessziel führen sollen.

Purpose:	To write a health and fitness plan
Audience:	Yourself
Subject:	Becoming or remaining physically fit and in good health
Structure:	A resolution

Schreibmodell

The writer clearly states his/her reason for wanting to get fit.

The writer also states his/her goal and, briefly, the activities he/she will do to reach it.

Here the writer outlines his/her plan in detail.

Setzen indicates direction so the two-way preposition **auf** is followed by the accusative case. Watch for other two-way prepositions throughout the model.

Legen requires the accusative reflexive pronoun when it describes the process of lying down.

Ausdauer-Trainingsprogramm fürs Bergwandern

Grund: Ich möchte im Sommer mit Freunden in den Rocky Mountains wandern gehen. Leider habe ich aber überhaupt keine Ausdauer[a] und schon beim Treppensteigen geht mir die Puste aus.

Ziel: Ich möchte so fit werden, dass ich ohne Mühe mit dem Rucksack auf alle Gipfel komme.

Maßnahmen: Ausdauer-Training bestehend aus Schwimmen, Rad fahren, Seilspringen[b] und Dehnungsübungen. Mehr Obst und Gemüse und weniger fette Snacks essen und viel Wasser trinken.

Mein Trainingsprogramm: Als tägliche Übung springe ich mindestens zehn Minuten mit dem Seil. Jeden Tag will ich versuchen, etwas schneller zu springen. Wenn ich aus der Schule nach Hause komme, ziehe ich mir meine Turnschuhe an und übe hinter dem Haus Seilspringen. Jeden Dienstag und Donnerstag setze ich mich auf mein Rad und fahre zum Aussichtspunkt auf dem Chestnut Hill. Bis zum Sommer will ich den ganzen Weg in einem Stück schaffen, ohne abzusteigen. Jeden Samstag und Sonntag Vormittag gehe ich außerdem in das Schwimmbad und schwimme 30 Bahnen.[c] Jeden Abend lege ich mich vor dem Bett auf den Boden und mache Dehnungsübungen. Wenn ich dann im Bett liege, werde ich noch ein bisschen von den Bergen träumen.

[a]*stamina* [b]*jumping rope* [c]*laps*

Schreibstrategien

Vor dem Schreiben

- Do you feel you need to improve your stamina and strengthen your muscles? Begin the writing process by deciding why you are going to undertake a fitness plan or why you are going to change or add to your current fitness activities. Figure out your reason for writing this plan and write it down. You don't have to write in complete sentences at this point. Just make notes that you can refer to later.

- Brainstorm a list in German of things you can do to maintain or improve your level of fitness. If there are specific benefits from doing a particular activity, make a note of those, too.

- What about your eating habits? Are there ways you can improve them—eat more fruits and less junk food, drink more water? Make notes about how you can change your diet and the benefits you hope to gain by doing so.

Beim Schreiben

- With your notes, begin writing your plan. What do you hope to achieve? State your goal or reasons for making the plan.

- Write a sentence or two about the activities you choose. What will you do? How often? When? Where? Mention the benefits of doing these activities.

- Finally, write a sentence or two about the foods you will eat. You might want to mention the ones you are going to try to stop eating.

Nach dem Schreiben

- Review your first draft critically yourself, correcting errors in spelling, punctuation, and grammar. Then exchange your draft with a classmate with whom you feel comfortable. If you don't want to share your plan with a classmate, ask your teacher to read it.

Stimmt alles?

- Revise your plan based on your classmate's or teacher's suggestions and corrections.

- Now comes the difficult part—try following your plan! Keep it handy for reference. But be careful, don't overdo it!

Mein Anti-Stress-Programm

Nach der Schule bin ich immer sehr kaputt: Ich habe schlechte Laune und ich fühle Stress wegen ~~die~~ der vielen Hausaufgaben. Das soll anders werden! Mein neues Anti-Stress-Programm sieht so aus: Im Morgen stehe ich auf und stelle ~~mir~~ mich vor das Bett für eine Yoga-Übung von 10 Minuten. Jeden Tag nach der Schule treffe ich ~~mir~~ mich mit meiner Freundin Claudia. Wir ziehen uns unsere Turnschuhe an und gehen 20 Minuten Joggen. Nach den Hausaufgaben und dem Lernen, stelle ich ~~mich~~ mir die Musik an und ich tanze zu meinen neuen CDs. Außerdem will ich keine Cola mehr mit Koffein trinken und weniger Schokolade essen. Ich will mehr Obst und Nüsse essen. Diese Lebensmittel sind gut für ~~die~~ das Gehirn, hat ~~mich~~ mir meine Tante gesagt.

WORTSCHATZ

Substantive	Nouns
die **Begegnung, -en**	meeting; encounter
die **Gesundheitspflege**	health care
die **Körperpflege**	personal hygiene
die **Krankenkasse**	health insurance; wellness fund
die **Kur, -en**	health spa; course of treatment
die **Übung, -en**	exercise
die **Untersuchung, -en**	examination
die **Versicherung, -en**	insurance
die **Vorsorge**	preventive medicine
der **Arztbesuch, -e**	visit to the doctor
der **Blutdruck**	blood pressure
der **Umstand, ¨e**	circumstance
der **Zettel**	note; piece of paper
das **Bad, ¨er**	bath; spa
das **Ergebnis, -se**	result, outcome
das **Fett, -e**	fat
das **Gesundheitswesen, -**	health care system
das **Heilmittel, -**	remedy
das **Wartezimmer, -**	waiting room

Verben	Verbs
achten	to respect; to take notice
atmen	to breathe
begeben, begab, begeben	to negotiate
ein•treten (tritt ein), trat ein, ist eingetreten	to occur; to enter
erhöhen	to raise, increase
geraten (gerät), geriet, ist geraten	to come upon
mahnen	to urge

messen	to measure
nehmen: Zeit in Anspruch nehmen (nimmt), nahm, genommen	to take up time
riechen nach	to smell like
sich vergnügen	to amuse oneself
sich verrechnen	to miscalculate
verschreiben, verschrieb, verschrieben	to prescribe
sich vor•nehmen (nimmt vor), nahm vor, vorgenommen	to undertake; to carry out

Adjektive und Adverbien	Adjectives and adverbs
gewohnheitsmäßig	in a habitual manner
heimlich	secret(ly)
regelmäßig	regular(ly)
sinnvoll	sensible; meaningful
tief	deep(ly)
unschlüssig	undecided
vegetarisch	vegetarian
verzweifelt	desperate

Sie wissen schon	You already know
das **Fieber**	fever
das **Gemüse**	vegetable
das **Krankenhaus, ¨er**	hospital
das **Labor, -s**	laboratory
das **Medikament, -e**	medication
das **Obst**	fruit
das **Rezept, -e**	prescription
gesund	healthy

PLANNING GUIDE
CLASSROOM MANAGEMENT

OBJECTIVES

Communication
- Talk about leisure-time activities, pp. 203–204, 205.
- Talk about health and fitness, p. 204.

Grammar
- Review modal verbs, p. 204.
- Review reflexive verbs, p. 205.
- Review past participles, p. 205.
- Review two-way prepositions, p. 206.

Culture
- Talk about *Volkshochschulen*, p. 202.
- Talk about German tourism and leisure, pp. 202–203, 206.
- Read the text of a German Romantic song, p. 207.

PROGRAM RESOURCES

Print
- *Arbeitsheft* (Workbook), pp. 143–146
- *Arbeitsheft* (Workbook), Teacher's Edition, pp. 143–146

Audiovisual
- Overhead Transparencies 31.G1–31.G2, 32.1–32.G1, 33.1, and 33.G1
- Audio Program, Cassette 5A/CD 6
- Audioscript, pp. 69–71

Technology
- Annenberg *Fokus Deutsch* Video Series, *Wiederholung 11*
- www.mcdougallittell.com

Assessment Program Options
- *Prüfung, Wiederholung 11,* Assessment Program, pp. 116–125
- Audio Program, Cassette 8B/CD 10
- Audioscript, p. 113
- Teacher's Resource CD-ROM

PACING GUIDE
50-MINUTE SCHEDULE

DAY 1

Note: (1) Please see TE, pp. 202C–202D, for other suggestions not referenced in these plans. (2) Not all homework options need be assigned.

VIDEOTHEK
- Quick Start Review: Vocabulary (TE, p. 202C). 5 MIN
- Watch the first video episode, then discuss *Akt. A,* p. 202, in small groups (TE, p. 202C). 12 MIN
- Watch the second episode, then discuss *Akt. B,* p. 202, as a class. 8 MIN
- Do *Akt. C,* pp. 202–203, then watch the third episode. 8 MIN

VOKABELN
- Do the warm-up activity (TE, p. 202C) before doing *Akt. A,* p. 203, in small groups. Check answers as a class. 10 MIN
- Have students do *Akt. B,* p. 204, silently. 7 MIN

Homework Options:
- *Arbeitsheft,* p. 144, *Vokabeln, Akt. A–B*

DAY 2

VOKABELN
- Quick Start Review: *Da-* and *wo-*compounds (TE, p. 202C). 5 MIN
- *Akt. C,* p. 204. 8 MIN

STRUKTUREN
- Do *Übung A,* p. 204, silently, then check answers as a class. 8 MIN
- Have students do *Übung B,* p. 205, then report their findings to the class. 10 MIN
- Briefly review the present perfect tense of the verbs in the box on p. 205, then do *Übung C,* p. 205, as a class (TE, p. 202D). 9 MIN
- Do *Übung D,* p. 205, silently, then discuss the answers as a class (TE, p. 202D). 10 MIN

Homework Options:
- *Arbeitsheft,* p. 145, *Vokabeln, Akt. C*

PACING GUIDE
50-MINUTE SCHEDULE

DAY 3

STRUKTUREN

- Quick Start Review: Vocabulary (TE, p. 202C). 5 MIN
- Do *Übung E*, p. 205, silently, then discuss the answers. 10 MIN

PERSPEKTIVEN

- Do *Akt. A*, p. 206, as outlined in the Teaching Suggestions (TE, p. 202D). 10 MIN
- Do *Akt. B*, p. 206, as a class (TE, p. 202D). 8 MIN
- Discuss *Akt. C*, p. 206, as a class. 5 MIN
- Do *Akt. D*, p. 207, as a class. 12 MIN

Homework Options:

- *Übung F*, p. 206

DAY 4

PERSPEKTIVEN

- Quick Start Review: Modals in the present perfect tense (TE, p. 202D). 5 MIN
- Do *Arbeitsheft*, p. 145, *Strukturen*, audio *Akt. A–B*. 10 MIN
- Questions and review. 5 MIN
- *Prüfung, Wiederholung 11*. 30 MIN

Homework Options:

- *Arbeitsheft*, p. 146, *Strukturen, Akt. D–E*

PACING GUIDE
90-MINUTE SCHEDULE

DAY 1

Note: (1) Please see TE, pp. 202C–202D, for other suggestions not referenced in these plans. (2) Not all homework options need be assigned.

VIDEOTHEK

- Quick Start Review: Vocabulary (TE, p. 202C). 5 MIN
- Watch the video episodes and then discuss *Akt. A–B*, p. 202 (TE, p. 202C). 21 MIN
- Do *Akt. C*, pp. 202–203, in small groups, then watch the video episode. 9 MIN

VOKABELN

- Do *Akt. A*, p. 203, in small groups. Check answers as a class (TE, p. 202C). 10 MIN
- Do *Akt. B–C*, p. 204. 15 MIN
- Block Schedule activity: Survey (TE, p. 202C). 10 MIN

STRUKTUREN

- Do *Übung A–B*, p. 204–205. 20 MIN

Homework Options:

- *Arbeitsheft*, pp. 144–145, *Vokabeln, Akt. A–C*
- *Übungen E–F*, p. 206

DAY 2

STRUKTUREN

- Quick Start Review: Vocabulary (TE, p. 202D). 5 MIN
- Briefly review the present perfect tense of the verbs in the box on p. 205, then do *Übung C*, p. 205, as a class. 7 MIN
- Do *Übung D*, p. 205, silently, then discuss the answers as a class. 7 MIN
- Block Schedule activity: Peer Teaching (TE, p. 202D). 10 MIN

PERSPEKTIVEN

- Do *Akt. A*, p. 206, (TE, p. 202D). 8 MIN
- Do *Akt. B–C*, p. 206, as a class (TE, p. 202D). 10 MIN
- Do *Akt. D*, p. 207, as a class. 8 MIN
- Questions and review. 5 MIN
- *Prüfung, Wiederholung 11*. 30 MIN

Homework Options:

- *Arbeitsheft*, p. 146, *Strukturen, Akt. E*

TEACHING SUGGESTIONS

Videothek, pp. 202–203

PROGRAM RESOURCES

- Videocassette, *Wiederholung 11*
- *Arbeitsheft*, pp. 143–144
- Audio Program, Cassette 5A/CD 6
- Audioscript, pp. 69–70

Quick Start Review

♻ Vocabulary
Ergänzen Sie die Sätze mit einem der folgenden Wörter.
WÖRTER: Blutdruck, Krankenkasse, Ergebnis, Gesundheitssystem

1. Die neue Regierung will das _____ reformieren.
2. Mein Arzt sagt, mein _____ sei zu hoch.
3. Meine _____ wird die Kosten für die Kur übernehmen.
4. Wie war das _____ deiner gestrigen Untersuchung?

Answers: 1. Gesundheitssystem
2. Blutdruck   3. Krankenkasse
4. Ergebnis

TEACHING SUGGESTIONS

- *Aktivität A*, p. 202

Expansion: Ask *Belegen Sie Kurse in Ihrer Freizeit? Warum? Warum nicht? Wo belegen Sie sie?*

TEACHING ALL STUDENTS

Multiple Intelligences Verbal: After watching the video episodes in chapters 31–33, ask students to choose the 3 episodes they liked the best and write a 5-sentence summary of each.

CLASSROOM COMMUNITY

Group Activity Bring a stuffed animal to class and put it in varied places: Ask *Wohin habe ich das Tier gelegt? Wo liegt das Tier jetzt? Wohin habe ich das Tier gestellt? Wo steht es jetzt? usw.*

BLOCK SCHEDULE

Process Time Have students work in groups to re-create scenes from the video. Possible scenes to re-enact might be *Weiterbilden in der Freizeit* (*Kapitel 31*) or students in a course at the *Volkshochschule* (*Kapitel 31*). Challenge: Have students create and enact a scene that was not in the video but could have been.

Vokabeln, pp. 203–204

PROGRAM RESOURCES

- *Arbeitsheft*, pp. 144–145
- Audio Program, Cassette 5A/CD 6

Quick Start Review

♻ *Da-* and *wo-*compounds
Antworten Sie negativ.
MODELL: Verstehen Sie viel von Musik?
→ *Nein, ich verstehe nicht viel davon.*

1. Interessieren Sie sich für Politik?
2. Denken Sie oft an Ihre Kindheit?
3. Denken Sie oft an Ihren Vater?
4. Beschäftigen Sie sich viel mit Computern?

Answers: 1. Nein, ich interessiere mich nicht dafür.   2. Nein, ich denke nicht oft daran.   3. Nein, ich denke nicht oft an ihn.   4. Nein, ich beschäftige mich nicht damit.

TEACHING SUGGESTIONS

- *Aktivität A*, p. 203

Warm-up: Have students use the vocabulary in the box to create their own sentences.

TEACHING ALL STUDENTS

Extra Help Before doing each of the activities in this section, activate students' memory of vocabulary. With books closed, have the whole class brainstorm vocabulary related to the activity.

CLASSROOM COMMUNITY

Dictation Give the following dictation, then have students work in pairs to correct each other.
In den Winterferien verbringen wir unseren Urlaub immer in Deutschland. Wir fahren in den Schwarzwald, wo viel Schnee liegt. Unsere Freunde wohnen in einer kleinen Stadt mitten in den Bergen. Ihr Haus steht an einem steilen Hang. Es gibt dort auch einen See, auf dem wir Schlittschuh laufen können.

BLOCK SCHEDULE

Survey Have students interview each other about vacations they would choose if they could (if, for example, they had no financial constraints). They should come up with 3–4 reasons why this would be their dream vacation.

PROJECT

Have students write an ad about their home town or region intended to attract German tourists to the area. Where would they take German visitors?

RUBRIC **A** = 13–15 pts.   **B** = 10–12 pts.
C = 7–9 pts.   **D** = 4–6 pts.   **F** < 4 pts.

Writing Criteria	Scale				
Grammar and vocabulary	1	2	3	4	5
Content	1	2	3	4	5
Presentation	1	2	3	4	5

Strukturen, pp. 204–206

PROGRAM RESOURCES

- Overhead Transparencies 31.G1–31.G2, 32.G2, and 33.G1
- *Arbeitsheft,* pp. 157–158
- Audio Program, Cassette 5A/CD 6
- Audioscript, pp. 70–71

Quick Start Review

♻ Vocabulary

Ergänzen Sie die Sätze mit einem der folgenden Wörter.

WÖRTER: bräunen, Vorbereitung, Ausrüstung, Nervenkitzel

1. Wenn man keine _____ zum Skifahren hat, kann man sich die Sachen leihen.
2. Ich fahre am liebsten an den Strand um mich zu _____.
3. Die _____ einer weiten Reise ist oft auch stressig.
4. Viele Extremsportarten sind mit _____ verbunden.

Answers: 1. Ausrüstung 2. bräunen 3. Vorbereitung 4. Nervenkitzel

TEACHING SUGGESTIONS

- *Übung C,* p. 205

Encourage students to visit the Web site of Freiburg, at www.freiburg.de.

- *Übung D,* p. 205

Follow-up: What do students know about their parents' childhoods? Have them answer using modals in the simple past. For example, *Meine Mutter musste viel im Haushalt helfen.*

TEACHING ALL STUDENTS

Multiple Intelligences Musical: Teach students a German song such as *Wenn ich ein Vöglein wär,* or *Grün, grün, grün sind alle meine Kleider.*

CLASSROOM COMMUNITY

Challenge Have students practice the present perfect tense by giving a detailed account of last night's or this morning's activities. *Ich bin um 7.30 Uhr aufgestanden. Dann bin ich . . .*

BLOCK SCHEDULE

Peer Teaching Have students work together in groups or pairs to review the grammar of Chapters 31–33.

Perspektiven, pp. 206–207

PROGRAM RESOURCES

- Overhead Transparencies 32.1 and 33.1
- Audio Program, Cassette 5A/CD 6
- www.mcdougallittell.com

Quick Start Review

♻ Modals in the present perfect tense
Schreiben Sie Ihre Antworten im Perfekt mit zwei Infinitivformen. Antworten Sie positiv oder negativ.

1. Musstest du als Kind auf deine Geschwister aufpassen?
2. Durftest du als Kind abends lange aufbleiben?
3. Konntest du als Kind schon gut malen?
4. Durftest du als Kind viel fernsehen?

Answers: 1. Ich habe als Kind (nicht) auf meine Geschwister aufpassen müssen. 2. Ich habe als Kind abends (nicht) lange aufbleiben dürfen. 3. Ich habe als Kind (noch nicht) gut malen können. 4. Ich habe als Kind (nicht) viel fernsehen dürfen.

TEACHING SUGGESTIONS

- *Aktivität A,* p. 206

Have students interview partners about their favorite activities.

- *Aktivität B,* p. 206

Follow-up: Have students make a poster about leisure activities and how they are portrayed in the media.

- *Aktivität C,* p. 206

Introduce students to 1–2 German hiking songs, for example, *Das Wandern ist des Müller's Lust* or *Wem Gott will rechte Gunst erweisen.*

TEACHING ALL STUDENTS

Multiple Intelligences Intrapersonal: Have students write a poem in German about their favorite leisure-time activity.

CLASSROOM COMMUNITY

Group Activity Have students practice prepositions by asking questions, such as *Wo kann man schwimmen gehen?* (*im Meer, in einem See, im Schwimmbad*) or *Wo kann man etwas essen?* (*in der Cafeteria, in einem Restaurant, bei Freunden*) usw.

BLOCK SCHEDULE

Fun Break Have students play charades using popular movie or book titles. The guessing will have to be all in German.

PORTFOLIO

Have students create vacation ads. Have them look at magazine ads and the Internet to get ideas. They should use magazine pictures or photos to complement their writing.

RUBRIC A = 13–15 pts. B = 10–12 pts. C = 7–9 pts. D = 4–6 pts. F < 4 pts.

Writing Criteria	Scale				
Mechanics	1	2	3	4	5
Content	1	2	3	4	5
Presentation	1	2	3	4	5

A. 1. *Possible answers are:* Das erste Bild zeigt Leute, die lernen, realistisch nach der Natur zu malen. Solch einen Kurs belegt man vor allem, wenn man Spaß am Malen hat. Manche Leute entspannen sich dabei, andere besuchen einen Malkurs, um sich Anregungen von anderen zu holen. Das zweite Bild zeigt, wie Leute in der Volkshochschule lernen, mit dem Computer umzugehen. Einen solchen Kurs besucht man, um sich beruflich fortzubilden. Im dritten Bild lernen Leute Spanisch. Man besucht einen solchen Sprachkurs, um sich beruflich weiterzubilden oder um sich zum Beispiel im Urlaubsland mit den Menschen unterhalten zu können. **2.** *Possible answers are:* Die Volkshochschule hat den Vorteil, dass die Kurse preisgünstig sind. Die Kursteilnehmer müssen nur ein Drittel der Kosten selber zahlen. So kann sich eigentlich jeder einen Kurs an der Volkshochschule leisten. Ausserdem finden viele Kurse am Abend statt. So können auch Berufstätige sich in ihrer Freizeit an der Volkshochschule weiterbilden oder ein Hobby erlernen. **3.** *Answers will vary.*

VIDEOTHEK

A Weiterbilden in der Freizeit. Claudia und Bärbel belegen einen Malkurs an der Volkshochschule in Potsdam. Was wissen Sie noch über Volkshochschulen?

1. Beschreiben Sie, was Sie in jedem Bild sehen. Was macht man in jedem Bild? Warum will man solche Kurse belegen? Wollen Sie auch diese Kurse belegen? Warum? Warum nicht?
2. Welche Vorteile gibt es an einer Volkshochschule? Denken Sie an die Preise, wann die Kurse angeboten werden und welche Kurse man belegen kann.
3. Gibt es auch eine Volkshochschule oder eine Art Volkshochschule, wo Sie wohnen? Was für Kurse kann man an dieser Volkshochschule belegen?

Der Malkurs.

Informatik.

Im Spanischkurs.

B. *Possible answers are:* **1.** Vor hundert Jahren konnten nur wenige, reiche Leute eine Urlaubsreise machen. **2.** Die meisten Leute haben Spaß und Erholung an Badeseen in der Nähe gefunden. **3.** In den zwanziger Jahren bekamen die Arbeiter eine Woche Urlaub im Jahr. **4.** Im Nationalsozialismus war der Urlaub staatlich organisiert. Für Jungen und Mädchen gab es Ferienlager und für Erwachsene wurden Schiffsreisen organisiert. **5.** Nach dem Zweiten Weltkrieg durften die Menschen in der DDR nur in Staaten des Ostblocks fahren, zum Beispiel nach Ungarn, Rumänien oder Bulgarien. Im eigenen Land wurden staatliche Ferienheime gebaut. Im Westen entwickelte sich das Reisen zu einem Hobby. Heute nutzen viele Deutsche ihre dreißig Tage Urlaub im Jahr, um in die ganze Welt zu reisen, aber auch der Urlaub in Deutschland ist immer noch beliebt.

B Urlaub gestern und heute. Beschreiben Sie die Entwicklung der modernen deutschen Tourismusindustrie. Denken Sie an die folgenden Fragen.

1. Wer konnte vor hundert Jahren eine Urlaubsreise machen?
2. Wo haben die meisten Leute Spaß und Erholung gefunden?
3. Was hat sich in den zwanziger Jahren geändert?
4. Wie war der Urlaub im Nationalsozialismus organisiert?
5. Was waren die Unterschiede bezüglich Urlaub im Westen und im Osten nach dem Zweiten Weltkrieg? Wie ist es heute?

C Abenteuerurlaub. Birgit geht Canyoning. Sehen Sie sich die Bilder auf Seite 203 an, und beantworten Sie die Fragen.

a.

b.

c.

1. Beschreiben Sie jedes Bild: Was machen die Leute?
2. Was heißt eigentlich Canyoning?
3. Was sucht Birgit, wenn sie in Urlaub geht?
4. Wie findet Birgit das ganze Abenteuer?
5. Wollen Sie mal Canyoning gehen? Warum? Warum nicht?

C. *Possible answers are:* **1. a.** Die Teilnehmer der Canyoning-Reisegruppe wandern durch den Wald. **b.** Birgit schwimmt durch das eiskalte Wasser im Canyon. **c.** Ein Teilnehmer springt von einem Felsen in das Wasser. **2.** Canyoning heißt „Schluchtwandern" und besteht aus Klettern, Springen, Schwimmen und Wandern. **3.** Wenn Birgit in Urlaub geht, sucht sie das Abenteuer, Abwechslung, Gefahr und Nervenkitzel. Sie will etwas Besonderes erleben, was nicht jeder macht. **4.** Sie findet, das Abenteuer war eine tolle Erfahrung. Es hat ihr Spaß gemacht. Es war anstrengend, aber sie hat sich dabei entspannt und erholt. **5.** *Answers will vary.*

VOKABELN

A Freizeit. Ergänzen Sie die Sätze mit den Wörtern im Kasten.

Erholung   belegen   hauptsächlich
Wirkungen   verbringen   Nachweis
unternehmen   unersetzlich

A. **1.** verbringen **2.** belegen **3.** hauptsächlich **4.** Erholung **5.** Wirkungen **6.** unersetzlich **7.** unternehmen **8.** Nachweis

Wie _____¹ Sie Ihre Freizeit? Manche interessieren sich für Sport, aber andere _____² Kurse wie Malen oder Fremdsprachen. Diese Kurse sind _____³ für Erwachsene gedacht, die etwas Neues lernen wollen. Diese Kurse können schon sehr viel Arbeit machen – wie kann man das denn als _____⁴ betrachten? Weiterbilden muss nicht stressig sein – es hat auch positive _____.⁵ Man übt ein neues Hobby aus und lernt andere Menschen kennen. Für viele ist dieser Kontakt zu anderen Menschen _____.⁶ Sie wollen lieber etwas mit Freunden _____,⁷ als abends allein zu Hause bleiben. Ein wichtiger _____⁸ dafür ist, dass kontaktfreudige Menschen oft einen niedrigeren Blutdruck haben und sich besser entspannen können, also mehr aus ihrer Freizeit machen.

Die Volkshochschule bietet verschiedene Kurse an.

B. 1. i **2.** h **3.** j **4.** a **5.** f **6.** d **7.** c
8. g **9.** e **10.** b

B Ferien und Urlaub. Kombinieren Sie!

1. die Abwechslung	a. passieren
2. vegetarisch	b. auf jeden Fall
3. die Gefahr	c. Luft holen
4. geschehen	d. relaxen
5. sich leisten	e. noch dazu
6. sich entspannen	f. genug Geld oder Zeit haben
7. atmen	g. erwartungsvoll
8. gespannt	h. sich von Gemüse ernähren
9. sogar	i. nicht immer das Gleiche, sondern etwas anderes
10. sowieso	j. die Möglichkeit, dass etwas schlimmes passieren könnte

C Wie ich mich fit und gesund halte. Arbeiten Sie mit
einem Partner / einer Partnerin, und stellen Sie einander
folgende Fragen.

1. Wie oft machst du einen Arztbesuch?
2. Hast du Angst davor, zum Arzt zu gehen?
3. Nimmst du gern natürliche Heilungsmittel?
4. Hältst du dich fit? Wie?
5. Gehst du regelmäßig ins Fitness-Center?
6. Welche Übungen machst du, wenn du ins Fitness-Center gehst?
7. Isst du vegetarisch? Warum? Warum nicht?

**Beim Arztbesuch muss man oft
lange warten.**

C. Answers will vary.

A. 1. konnten **2.** kann **3.** muss **4.** soll
5. mussten **6.** durften **7.** wollten **8.** will

STRUKTUREN

A Arbeit und Freizeit. Ergänzen Sie die Sätze mit den richtigen Formen
der Modalverben im Präsens oder Imperfekt.

1. Im neunzehnten Jahrhundert _____ sich nur die Reichen eine
Schiffsreise leisten. (können)
2. Jetzt _____ fast jeder einen langen Urlaub machen. (können)
3. Man _____ viel Geld sparen, wenn man eine Luxusreise machen
will. (müssen)
4. Die Gesellschaft _____ dafür sorgen, dass jeder Arbeiter / jede
Arbeiterin mindestens ein Paar Wochen im Jahr Urlaub hat.
(sollen)
5. Früher _____ Arbeiter fast die ganze Woche in den Fabriken
arbeiten. (müssen)
6. Sie _____ nicht am Samstag zu Hause bleiben. (dürfen)
7. Die Arbeiter _____ mehr Rechte haben, wie kürzere Arbeitszeiten
und Urlaub (wollen).
8. Jetzt _____ man die Arbeitszeit noch kürzer machen, damit man
mehr Zeit für Freunde und Familie hat. (wollen)

**Eine Schiffsreise um die
Jahrhundertwende.**

B Persönliche Meinungen. Arbeiten Sie mit einem Partner / einer Partnerin, und stellen Sie einander die folgenden Fragen.

1. Interessierst du dich für Extremsportarten?
2. Womit beschäftigst du dich in der Freizeit?
3. Woran denkst du, wenn du das Wort „Freizeit" hörst?
4. Hast du früher Aktivitäten in der Freizeit gemacht, die du jetzt nicht mehr machst? Was für Aktivitäten? Warum machst du sie nicht mehr?
5. Kannst du dir vorstellen, dass du als Erwachsene/Erwachsener einen Abendkurs belegen würdest? Warum? Warum nicht?
6. Was hältst du von organisierten Freizeitaktivitäten?

B. Answers will vary.

C Reisen im Schwarzwald. Ergänzen Sie die Sätze mit den richtigen Formen der Verben im Kasten.

Ich bin gerade von meiner Reise zurück _____.¹ Ich habe meinen ganzen Urlaub mit Freunden im Schwarzwald _____.² Wir sind überall _____.³ Einmal sind wir so gar auf einen hohen Felsen _____.⁴ Das hat Spaß _____.⁵ Danach sind wir zurück ins Hotel _____⁶ und haben uns gemütlich _____.⁷ Die Reise hat uns sehr gut _____.⁸ Nächstes Jahr fahren wir bestimmt wieder hin!

C. 1. gekommen *2.* verbracht *3.* gewandert *4.* geklettert *5.* gemacht *6.* gegangen *7.* entspannt *8.* gefallen

> gefallen
> gehen
> klettern
> verbringen
> wandern
> machen
> entspannen
> kommen

D Meine Kindheit. Beantworten Sie die Fragen.

MODELL: Konntest du als Kind gut zeichnen?
   Ja, ich konnte immer gut zeichnen.
oder: Nein, ich konnte nie gut zeichnen.

1. Musstest du Klavierunterricht nehmen?
2. Musstest du beim Geschirrspülen helfen?
3. Durftest du spät aufbleiben?
4. Konntest du allein dein Zimmer aufräumen?
5. Durften deine Freunde bei dir übernachten?
6. Durftest du viel fernsehen?
7. Wolltest du in die Schule gehen?

D. 1. Ja, ich musste Klavierunterricht nehmen. *oder:* Nein, ich musste keinen Klavierunterricht nehmen. *2.* Ja, ich musste beim Geschirrspülen helfen. *oder:* Nein, ich musste nicht beim Geschirrspülen helfen. *3.* Ja, ich durfte spät aufbleiben. *oder:* Nein, ich durfte nicht spät aufbleiben. *4.* Ja, ich konnte allein mein Zimmer aufräumen. *oder:* Nein, ich konnte nicht allein mein Zimmer aufräumen. *5.* Ja, meine Freunde durften bei mir übernachten. *oder:* Nein, meine Freunde durften nicht bei mir übernachten. *6.* Ja, ich durfte viel fernsehen. *oder:* Nein, ich durfte nicht viel fernsehen. *7.* Ja, ich wollte in die Schule gehen. *oder:* Nein, ich wollte nicht in die Schule gehen.

E Interessen und Pläne. Ergänzen Sie die Sätze mit dem richtigen Reflexivpronomen.

1. Susanne interessiert _____ für Sprachen und will deshalb nach Spanien reisen.
2. Klaus und Stefan beschäftigen _____ gern mit Musik. In der Freizeit gehen beide gern in Konzerte oder in die Oper.
3. Wofür interessierst du _____?
4. Ich überlege _____, was ich während des Sommers machen werde.
5. Ich kann _____ keine Luxusreise leisten, aber ich will trotzdem etwas Schönes unternehmen.
6. Kannst du _____ vorstellen, wie es damals auf den großen Luxusschiffen war?
7. Das habe ich _____ nie vorstellen können.

E. 1. sich *2.* sich *3.* dich *4.* mir *5.* mir *6.* dir *7.* mir

F. Schritt 1: 1. Ich stelle die Bücher auf das Regal. **2.** Martin stellt die sauberen Gläser in den Küchenschrank. **3.** Felicia legt das Besteck in die Schublade. **4.** Ich hänge das Bild wieder an die Wand. **5.** Martin legt die Bettdecke auf sein Bett. **6.** Felicia stellt den Rasenmäher in die Garage. **7.** Martin ruht sich endlich aus. **8.** Ich setze mich auf den Boden. **9.** Felicia legt sich ins Bett.

Schritt 2: 1. Ich habe die Bücher auf das Regal gestellt. **2.** Martin hat die sauberen Gläser in den Küchenschrank gestellt. **3.** Felicia hat das Besteck in die Schublade gelegt. **4.** Ich habe das Bild wieder an die Wand gehängt. **5.** Martin hat die Bettdecke auf sein Bett gelegt. **6.** Felicia hat den Rasenmäher in die Garage gestellt. **7.** Martin hat sich endlich ausgeruht. **8.** Ich habe mich auf den Boden gesetzt. **9.** Felicia hat sich ins Bett gelegt.

A. *Answers will vary.*

B. *Answers will vary.*

C. *Answers will vary.*

F Die Eltern kommen!

SCHRITT 1: Sie und Ihre Geschwister müssen das Haus wieder in Ordnung bringen, bevor Ihre Eltern von der Arbeit nach Hause kommen. Es gibt ziemlich viel zu tun, und alle helfen mit. Aber wohin mit den ganzen Sachen? Schreiben Sie die Sätze im Präsens.

1. ich / stellen / die Bücher / auf / das Regal
2. Martin / stellen / die sauberen Gläser / in / der Küchenschrank
3. Felicia / legen / das Besteck / in / die Schublade
4. ich / hängen / das Bild / wieder / an / die Wand
5. Martin / legen / die Bettdecke / auf / sein Bett
6. Felicia / stellen / der Rasenmäher / in / die Garage
7. Martin / ruhen / sich / endlich / aus
8. ich / setzen / sich / auf / der Boden
9. Felicia / legen / sich / in / das Bett

SCHRITT 2: Alles erledigt! Jetzt schreiben Sie die Sätze im Perfekt.

PERSPEKTIVEN

A Was machen Sie gern in Ihrer Freizeit? Bleiben Sie lieber zu Hause, oder machen Sie lieber einen Ausflug? Sind Sie gern draußen?

B Eine Umfrage. Machen Sie eine Umfrage in der Klasse zum Thema typische Freizeitaktivitäten. Welche Aktivitäten sind beliebt, wo Sie wohnen? Was glauben Sie ist die beliebteste Freizeitaktivität in Ihrem Land?

C Wandern als Freizeitaktivität hat eine lange Tradition in den deutschsprachigen Ländern. Warum wandert man? Wo kann man wandern? Was sieht und hört man auf einer Wanderung?

KULTURSPIEGEL

„Der frohe Wandersmann" ist ein Gedicht der deutschen Romantik. Für viele Dichter dieser Periode war die Natur eine Offenbarung[a] Gottes, ein Bereich, in dem man die verloren gegangene Harmonie finden konnte. Obwohl Eichendorff kein sentimentaler Idylliker oder Vorläufer der Wanderbewegung war, bleibt „Der frohe Wandersmann" heute noch ein beliebtes Wanderlied in Deutschland.

[a]*revelation*

Beim Wandern.

Der frohe Wandersmann

Wem Gott will rechte Gunst erweisen,
Den schickt er in die weite Welt;
Dem will er seine Wunder weisen
In Berg und Wald und Strom und Feld.

5 Die Trägen, die zu Hause liegen,
Erquicket nicht das Morgenrot;
Sie wissen nur von Kinderwiegen,
Von Sorgen, Last und Not und Brot.

Die Bächlein von den Bergen springen,
10 Die Lerchen schwirren hoch vor Lust,
Was sollt' ich nicht mit ihnen singen
Aus voller Kehl und frischer Brust?

Den lieben Gott lass ich nur walten;
Der Bächlein, Lerchen, Wald und Feld
15 Und Erd' und Himmel will erhalten,
Hat auch mein Sach auf's Best' bestellt!

Joseph von Eichendorff (1788–1857)

D Zur Interpretation. Welche Beschreibung passt zu welcher Strophe?

1. Leute, die nicht wandern, kennen kein schönes Leben.
2. Gott schützt die Natur und den Wandersmann.
3. Wenn Gott jemanden mag, lässt er ihn wandern.
4. Der Wandersmann singt mit den Vögeln und Bächlein.

WORTSCHATZ ZUM LESEN

die Gunst	*favor*
erweisen	*to show*
weisen	*here: to point out, show*
der Strom	*stream, river*
die Trägen	*the lazy ones*
die Kinderwiege	*cradle*
die Last	*burden*
die Not	*need*
das Bächlein	*small brook*
die Lerche	*lark*
die Kehle	*throat*
walten	*to reign; to prevail*

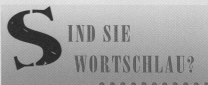

SIND SIE WORTSCHLAU?

The suffixes **-lein** and **-chen** indicate something small and dear. Nouns with these suffixes are neuter.

der Bach	**das** Bäch**lein**
der Tisch	**das** Tisch**lein**
der Mann	**das** Männ**lein**
das Kind	**das** Kind**chen**
der Bruder	**das** Brüder**chen**

D. 1. zweite Strophe **2.** vierte Strophe
3. erste Strophe **4.** dritte Strophe

PLANNING GUIDE • CLASSROOM MANAGEMENT

OBJECTIVES

Communication
- Talk about what it means to be German or Austrian, pp. 210–211.
- Talk about multiculturalism in Germany, pp. 212–213.

Grammar
- Use relative clauses to describe people and things, p. 214.
- Use relative clauses with prepositions, p. 216.
- Use infinitive clauses with *zu*, pp. 218–219.

Culture
- Learn about foreign workers in Germany, p. 211.
- Learn about the German asylum law, p. 213.
- Learn about foreign exchange programs, p. 220.
- Learn about an organization supporting exchange students, p. 223.

Recycling
- Review relative clauses, pp. 214–215.

STRATEGIES

Listening Strategies
- Listen to an interview with 2 foreign students, p. 220.

Speaking Strategies
- Discuss rules and regulations, p. 211.
- Discuss common attitudes toward foreigners, p. 211.
- Discuss the concept of nationality, pp. 215, 220–223.

Reading Strategies
- Read about a Brazilian searching for the "typical" German, pp. 220–223.

Writing Strategies
- Write a multicultural city guide, p. 224.

Connecting Cultures Strategies
- Compare German and American attitudes toward foreigners, p. 213.
- Identify stereotypes of Germans, p. 222.
- Learn about how nationality is determined in different countries, p. 224.

PROGRAM RESOURCES

Print
- *Arbeitsheft* (Workbook), pp. 147–160
- *Arbeitsheft* (Workbook), Teacher's Edition, pp. 147–160

Audiovisual
- Overhead Transparencies 34.1–34.G2
- Audio Program, Cassette 5B, 7B/CD 7, 9
- Audioscript, pp. 72–78

Technology
- Annenberg *Fokus Deutsch* Video Series, *Folge 34*
- www.mcdougallittell.com

Assessment Program Options
- *Prüfung, Kapitel 34,* Assessment Program, pp. 126–136
- Audio Program, Cassette 8B/CD 10
- Audioscript, p. 114
- Teacher's Resource CD-ROM

DAY 1

Note: (1) Please see TE, pp. 208E–208J, for other suggestions not referenced in these plans. (2) Not all homework options need be assigned.

CHAPTER OPENER

- Quick Start Review: Vocabulary (TE, p. 208E). 5 MIN
- Discuss the photos on pp. 208–209 (TE, p. 208E). 5 MIN

VIDEOTHEK

- View the video and do *Akt. B,* pp. 210–211. Discuss *Wortschatz zum Video.* 7 MIN
- Read through *Akt. A, Schritt 1,* p. 210, then play *Folge I: Typisch deutsch?* Have students do *Schritt 1* while watching the video, then discuss *Schritt 2* as a class (TE, p. 208E). 11 MIN
- *Arbeitsheft,* p. 147, audio *Akt. A.* 4 MIN
- Do *Akt. C, Schritt 1,* p. 211, as a class. Make a list on the board. 5 MIN
- Do *Akt. C, Schritt 2,* p. 211, then end with a brief class discussion. 8 MIN
- *Arbeitsheft,* p. 148, audio *Akt. C.* 5 MIN

Homework Options:

- *Arbeitsheft,* p. 147, *Videothek, Akt. B*

DAY 2

VIDEOTHEK

- Quick Start Review 1: Reflexive pronouns (TE, p. 208E). 5 MIN
- Do *Akt. A,* p. 211, as a class and conclude with the follow-up activity in the Teaching Suggestions (TE, p. 208F). 6 MIN
- Read through *Akt. B, Schritt 1,* p. 211, then watch *Folge II: Vom Sauerkraut zur Pizza* (TE, pp. 208E–F). 9 MIN
- Have students do *Akt. B, Schritt 1,* p. 211, silently, then check their answers with a partner. Work with the same partner to do *Schritt 2,* then end with a brief class discussion (TE, p. 208F). 10 MIN
- *Arbeitsheft,* p. 150, audio *Akt. G–H.* 10 MIN

VOKABELN

- Present the vocabulary on p. 212 and discuss the words in the box next to *Akt. A.* 10 MIN

Homework Options:

- *Arbeitsheft,* pp. 148–149, *Videothek, Akt. D–E*
- *Vokabeln, Akt. A,* pp. 212–213
- *Arbeitsheft,* p. 152, *Vokabeln, Akt. E*

DAY 3

VOKABELN

- Quick Start Review 1: Vocabulary (TE, p. 208F). 5 MIN
- As a class, do *Akt. A,* pp. 212–213, and ask comprehension questions about the text (TE, p. 208G). 8 MIN
- Do *Akt. B,* p. 213, silently, then check answers with a partner (TE, p. 208G). 10 MIN
- Read *Akt. C, Schritt 1,* p. 213, silently, then have a brief class discussion about the paragraph. Ask comprehension questions. 10 MIN
- Do *Akt. C, Schritt 2,* p. 213, then do the follow-up activity in the Teaching Suggestions (TE, p. 208G). 12 MIN
- *Arbeitsheft,* p. 151, audio *Akt. D.* 5 MIN

Homework Options:

- *Arbeitsheft,* p. 152, *Vokabeln, Akt. F*

DAY 4

VOKABELN

- Quick Start Review 2: Present perfect (TE, p. 208G). 5 MIN

STRUKTUREN

- Present relative clauses I on p. 214 using OHT 34.G1–34.G2 (TE, p. 208H). 8 MIN
- Have students do *Übung A,* p. 215, with a partner. Have them write their answers on the board, then check them as a class (TE, p. 208H). 10 MIN
- Do *Übung B,* p. 215, silently, then check answers with a partner. Do the follow-up activity in the Teaching Suggestions (TE, p. 208H). 10 MIN
- Present relative clauses II on p. 216. 8 MIN
- *Arbeitsheft,* p. 153, audio *Akt. A–B.* 9 MIN

Homework Options:

- *Übung A,* p. 217
- *Arbeitsheft,* pp. 154–155, *Strukturen, Akt. E–G*

PACING GUIDE • SAMPLE LESSON PLAN, 50-MINUTE SCHEDULE

STRUKTUREN

- Quick Start Review 1: Vocabulary (TE, p. 208H). 4 MIN
- As a class, discuss the answers to *Übung A,* p. 217. 3 MIN
- Have students do *Übung B,* p. 217, silently and then work with a partner to check answers (TE, p. 208H). 12 MIN
- Have students do *Übung C,* p. 217, with the same partner (TE, p. 208H). 5 MIN
- Present infinitive clauses with *zu* on pp. 218–219. 10 MIN
- As an introduction to the concept, do *Arbeitsheft,* p. 156, audio *Akt. H.* 6 MIN
- Have students do *Übung A,* p. 219, silently and then check their answers with a partner. Do the variation in the Teaching Suggestions (TE, p. 208I). 10 MIN

Homework Options:

- *Arbeitsheft,* p. 156, *Strukturen, Akt. I–J*

STRUKTUREN

- Quick Start Review 2: *Da-* and *wo*-compounds (TE, p. 208H). 5 MIN
- *Übung B,* p. 219 (TE, p. 208I). 6 MIN

PERSPEKTIVEN

- Review the *Wortschatz zum Hörtext* and the questions in *Hören Sie zu!, Akt. A,* p. 220, as a class. Then play the recording and encourage students to take notes. 8 MIN
- Have students discuss *Hören Sie zu!, Akt. A,* p. 220, in small groups. Encourage them to use their notes to answer the questions (TE, p. 208I). 8 MIN
- Discuss *Hören Sie zu!, Akt. B,* p. 220, as a class (TE, p. 208J). 6 MIN
- Discuss *Zum Thema, Akt. A,* p. 220, as a class (TE, p. 208I). 5 MIN
- Do *Zum Thema, Akt. B,* p. 221, as a class. List students' ideas on the board (TE, p. 208J). 6 MIN
- Follow the Teaching Suggestions for previewing the text, *Die Suche nach den Deutschen,* p. 221 (TE, p. 208J). 6 MIN

Homework Options:

- Read *Die Suche nach den Deutschen,* pp. 221–223
- *Arbeitsheft,* pp. 158–159, *Perspektiven, Akt. C–D*

PERSPEKTIVEN

- Quick Start Review 1: Vocabulary (TE, p. 208I). 4 MIN
- Do *Zum Text, Akt. A,* p. 224, as a class. Do the follow-up questions in the Teaching Suggestions (TE, p. 208J). 8 MIN
- After reviewing the *Kulturspiegel,* pp. 223 and 224, have students work in small groups on *Zum Text, Akt. B,* p. 223. Conclude by having a class discussion and writing the letter to *DAAD* as a class. 12 MIN
- Do *Zur Interpretation,* p. 223, as a class (TE, p. 208J). 8 MIN
- Have the students do *Interaktion,* p. 224, in small groups (TE, p. 208J). 10 MIN
- Begin *Schreiben Sie!* by discussing the assignment, *Tipp zum Schreiben,* and *Schreibmodell.* 5 MIN
- Begin *Vor dem Schreiben,* p. 225. 3 MIN

Homework Options:

- Finish *Vor dem Schreiben,* p. 225, and do *Beim Schreiben,* p. 226
- Complete the first draft of the guide

PERSPEKTIVEN

- Quick Start Review 2: Present perfect (TE, p. 208J). 5 MIN
- Do *Nach dem Schreiben,* p. 226, and begin working on the final draft of the guide. 10 MIN
- Questions and review. 5 MIN
- *Prüfung, Kapitel 34.* 30 MIN

Homework Options:

- Finish the final draft of the guide
- *Arbeitsheft,* p. 160, *Perspektiven, Akt. E*

Note: (1) Please see TE, pp. 208E–208J, for other suggestions not referenced in these plans. (2) Not all homework options need be assigned.

CHAPTER OPENER

- Quick Start Review: Vocabulary (TE, p. 208E). 5 MIN
- Discuss photos on pp. 208–209. 5 MIN

VIDEOTHEK

- View the video, then do *Akt. B*, pp. 210–211. 7 MIN
- Do *Akt. A*, p. 210, while watching *Folge I*. 11 MIN
- *Arbeitsheft*, pp. 147–148, audio *Akt. A, C*. 9 MIN
- Do *Akt. C*, p. 211, as a class. 13 MIN
- Block Schedule activity: Change of Pace (TE, p. 208F). 10 MIN
- Do *Akt. A*, p. 211, and the follow-up activity on TE, p. 208F. 6 MIN
- Watch *Folge II*. Do *Akt B* (TE, p. 208F). 19 MIN
- *Arbeitsheft*, p. 161, audio *Akt. F*. 5 MIN

Homework Options:

- *Arbeitsheft*, pp.158–159, *Akt. B, D–E*

VIDEOTHEK

- Quick Start Review 1: Reflexive pronouns (TE, p. 208E). 5 MIN
- *Arbeitsheft*, p. 150, audio *Akt. H*. 7 MIN

VOKABELN

- Present the vocabulary on p. 212, then do *Akt. A*, pp. 212–213 (TE, p. 208G). 18 MIN
- Do *Akt. B–C*, p. 213, silently, then check answers and discuss (TE, p. 208G). 31 MIN
- Block Schedule activity: Expansion (TE, p. 208G). 10 MIN

STRUKTUREN

- Present relative clauses on p. 214 using OHT 34.G1–34.G2 (TE, p. 208H). 8 MIN
- Do *Übung A*, p. 215, with a partner, then check answers as a class (TE, p. 208H). 11 MIN

Homework Options:

- *Arbeitsheft*, p. 152, *Vokabeln, Akt. E–F*, and p. 154, *Vokabeln, Akt. E*

STRUKTUREN

- Quick Start Review 1: Vocabulary (TE, p. 208H). 5 MIN
- Do *Übung B*, p. 215, silently, then check answers. Do the follow-up activity on TE page 208H. 10 MIN
- Present relative clauses II on p. 216. 8 MIN
- *Arbeitsheft*, p. 153, audio *Akt. A*. 6 MIN
- Do *Übungen A–B*, p. 217 (TE, p. 208H). 20 MIN
- Do *Übung C*, p. 217, with a partner (TE, p. 208H). 5 MIN
- Block Schedule activity: Recycle (TE, p. 208J). 10 MIN
- Present infinitive clauses with *zu* on pp. 218–219. Do *Arbeitsheft*, p. 156, audio *Akt. H*. 16 MIN
- Do *Übung A*, p. 219, silently, then check answers. Do the variation on TE, p. 208H. 10 MIN

Homework Options:

- *Übung B*, p. 219
- *Arbeitsheft*, p. 155, *Strukturen, Akt. F–G*

PERSPEKTIVEN

- Quick Start Review 1: Vocabulary (TE, p. 208I). 4 MIN
- Do *Hören Sie zu! Akt. A*, p. 220, while playing the recording. Discuss it in small groups (TE, p. 208I). 16 MIN
- Discuss *Hören Sie zu! Akt. B*, p. 220, as a class (TE, p. 208J). 6 MIN
- Do *Zum Thema, Akt. A–B*, pp. 220–221. (TE, p. 208J). 11 MIN
- Do Block Schedule activity: Time Saver in pairs (TE, p. 208J). 10 MIN
- Preview reading on pp. 221–223, then have students read it (TE, p. 208J). 16 MIN
- Do *Zum Text, Akt. A*, p. 223, as a class. Do the follow-up on TE, p. 208J. 8 MIN
- Review *Kulturspiegel*, pp. 223 and 224, and do *Zum Text, Akt. B*, p. 223, in groups. Write the letter as a class. 12 MIN
- Do *Zur Interpretation*, p. 223, as a class (TE, p. 208J). 8 MIN

Homework Options:

- *Arbeitsheft*, pp. 158–159, *Perspektiven, Akt. C–D*

PERSPEKTIVEN

- Quick Start Review 2: Present perfect (TE, p. 208J). 5 MIN
- Do *Interaktion*, p. 224, in small groups (TE, p. 208J). 8 MIN
- Begin *Schreiben Sie!* by discussing the assignment, *Tipp zum Schreiben*, and *Schreibmodell*. 5 MIN
- Have students do *Vor dem Schreiben* and *Beim Schreiben*, pp. 225–226. Have them write the first draft of their guide. 17 MIN
- Do *Nach dem Schreiben*, p. 226, and begin the final draft of the guide. 10 MIN
- Block Schedule activity: Change of Pace (TE, p. 208J). 10 MIN
- Questions and review. 5 MIN
- *Prüfung, Kapitel 34*. 30 MIN

Homework Options:

- *Arbeitsheft*, p. 160, *Perspektiven, Akt. E*
- Finish the final draft of the guide

Chapter Opener, pp. 208–209

PROGRAM RESOURCES

- Overhead Transparency 34.1

Quick Start Review

♻ Vocabulary
Ergänzen Sie die Sätze mit den folgenden Wörtern.

WÖRTER: Blutdruck, Krankenkasse, Kur, mahnen, Medikament, verschreiben

1. Mein Arzt hat mir ein neues _____ gegen Asthma verschrieben.
2. Bei meinem letzten Arztbesuch war mein _____ erhöht.
3. Ich muss mir bei meinem Hausarzt ein Medikament gegen Husten _____ lassen.
4. Die Ärzte _____ uns, nicht zu viel Fett zu essen.
5. Mein Onkel ist nach seiner Herzoperation drei Wochen lang in _____ gegangen.
6. Seine _____ hat die ganzen Kosten für die Kur übernommen.

Answers: 1. Medikament 2. Blutdruck 3. verschreiben 4. mahnen 5. Kur 6. Krankenkasse

TEACHING SUGGESTIONS

- Photos, pp. 208–209

Begin a discussion on what students believe it means to live in a multicultural society and what they believe it means in Germany. Why is a photo of food included?

CLASSROOM COMMUNITY

Group Activity Introduce the topic of multiculturalism by means of an Assoziogramm. Have students brainstorm about multiculturalism. What does it mean to them? Create the Assoziogramm on the board or on an OHT as students add to it.

Videothek, pp. 210–211

PROGRAM RESOURCES

- Videocassette, *Folge 34*
- *Arbeitsheft,* pp. 147–150
- Audio Program, Cassette 5B/CD 7
- Audioscript, pp. 72–73

Quick Start Review 1

♻ Reflexive pronouns
Ergänzen Sie die Pronomen in den Sätzen.

1. Ich muss _____ jetzt duschen.
2. Erinnerst du _____ noch an unsere alten Nachbarn?
3. Sie wollte zuerst nicht mitkommen, aber dann hat sie es _____ doch anders überlegt.
4. Kurt ist erst drei Jahre alt und kann _____ schon alleine anziehen.
5. Hast du _____ auch die Zähne geputzt?
6. Er muss _____ noch rasieren.

Answers: 1. mich 2. dich 3. sich 4. sich 5. dir 6. sich

Quick Start Review 2

♻ Vocabulary
Ergänzen Sie die Sätze mit den folgenden Wörtern.

WÖRTER: angucken, besteigen, bräunen, gewonnen, halten, treiben

1. Meine Freundin will im Urlaub immer Sport _____.
2. Baden und sich am Strand _____ sind der Urlaubstraum vieler Menschen, die im kalten Norden leben.
3. In meinem nächsten Urlaub will ich den Mount McKinley _____.
4. Mein Bruder hat beim Reiten schon viele Preise _____.
5. Sein Ziel ist es, sich auch im Winter fit zu _____.
6. Ich freue mich darauf, dass wir uns im Zoo die Gorillas _____ werden.

Answers: 1. treiben 2. bräunen 3. besteigen 4. gewonnen 5. halten 6. angucken

TEACHING SUGGESTIONS

- *Folge I: Typisch deutsch?,* p. 210

Before watching the video episode, ask students what they believe is typically German. Ask them *Was bedeutet „typisch deutsch"? Was assoziieren Sie mit Deutschland?* Or, have students write their reactions to these questions on a slip of paper. Collect the slips of paper in a box. Have each student draw a slip of paper out of the box and read the comment. While comments are read, 1 or 2 students can stand at the board and write the comments on the board to demonstrate the varied thoughts and opinions about the topic.

- *Folge II: Vom Sauerkraut zur Pizza,* p. 211

Ask students what they know about German cooking. Which foods do they consider typically German? If they have ever visited Germany, what did they eat? Have them comment on the cuisines of different cultures.

- *Aktivität A*, p. 211

Follow-up: Have students make a list of their favorite dishes and have them comment on what they think is the cultural origin of each dish.

- *Aktivität B*, p. 211

Have students react to several of the statements made by Anja, Susanne, or Daniela. List words and phrases for expressing opinions or for disagreeing on the board or on an OHT beforehand. Have students use the following expressions as well:

Eine Meinung ausdrücken

Ich finde . . .
Ich glaube . . .
Meiner Meinung nach . . .
Ich bin der Meinung, dass . . .
Ich bin davon überzeugt, dass . . .

Nichtübereinstimmung ausdrücken

Es stimmt nicht, dass . . .
Ich glaube nicht, dass . . .
Ich stimme damit gar nicht überein.
Ich bin aber ganz anderer Meinung.

TEACHING ALL STUDENTS

Multiple Intelligences Interpersonal: Have students interview each other about their contacts with different cultures at school, in their neighborhoods, in after-school activities, at community events, and so forth. Ask *Wie und wo kommen Sie in Kontakt mit Menschen, die aus anderen Ländern kommen? Was erfahren Sie dabei über andere Kulturen und Gewohnheiten? Sind diese Erfahrungen positiv oder manchmal auch negativ? Was können Sie noch darüber sagen? usw.* Have students report on their interviews

and write the results on the board or on an OHT.

CLASSROOM COMMUNITY

Challenge Divide students into 2 groups. Have groups complete the following sentences.

Group 1: Ich freue mich über . . . Wir freuen uns über . . . Ich freue mich auf . . . Wir freuen uns auf . . .

Group 2: Ich erinnere mich gern an . . . Wir erinnern uns gern an . . . Ich interessiere mich für . . . Wir interessieren uns für . . .

BLOCK SCHEDULE

Change of Pace Have students look through German-language magazines and cut out ads for food and recipes. They can either make a collage or comment in writing on their findings. If they choose to make a collage, they should include the names of the different dishes or foods underneath the pictures.

PORTFOLIO

Have students research an ethnic group and report on its use of language. When do the people speak their native language and when do they speak English? *Wer spricht welche Sprache mit wem? Für wie viele Jahre?* Also research their eating habits after immigrating to the U.S. If possible, have students interview members of 2 different generations, for example, the grandparents and the parents of a friend, all of whom moved to the U.S.

RUBRIC **A** = 13–15 pts. **B** = 10–12 pts.
C = 7–9 pts. **D** = 4–6 pts. **F** <4 pts.

Writing Criteria	Scale				
Grammar and vocabulary	1	2	3	4	5
Detail and accuracy	1	2	3	4	5
Organization	1	2	3	4	5

Vokabeln, pp. 212–213

PROGRAM RESOURCES

- *Arbeitsheft,* pp. 151–152
- Audio Program, Cassette 5B/CD 7
- Audioscript, pp. 73–75

. . . .

Quick Start Review 1

Vocabulary
Bilden Sie ganze Sätze.

1. mich / bei der Gartenarbeit / am besten / entspannen / ich / kann
2. meiner / in / Freizeit / ich / gerne / und / musiziere / töpfere
3. Volkshochschule / kann / an / der / man / weiterbilden / sich / oder / Hobbies / seine / pflegen
4. an den Feiertagen / gehe / wandern / wir / im Frühjahr / ich / mit meinen Freunden
5. samstags / mit meiner Freundin / ich / gerne / durch die Stadt / bummele
6. verbringt / meine Oma / viel Zeit / in / Kleingarten / ihrem

Answers: 1. Ich kann mich bei der Gartenarbeit am besten entspannen. 2. In meiner Freizeit musiziere und töpfere ich gerne. 3. An der Volkshochschule kann man sich weiterbilden oder seine Hobbies pflegen. 4. An den Feiertagen im Frühjahr gehe ich mit meinen Freunden wandern. 5. Samstags bummele ich gerne mit meiner Freundin durch die

Stadt.   6. Meine Oma verbringt viel Zeit in ihrem Kleingarten.

Quick Start Review 2

♻ Present perfect

Ergänzen Sie die Verben im Perfekt.

WÖRTER: aufstehen, ausgeben, mitnehmen, sein, übernachten, werden

1. Wir haben in unserem Urlaub zu viel Geld _____.
2. Er ist am sechsten Januar 75 Jahre alt _____.
3. Ich glaube, meine Freundin hat meinen Rucksack _____.
4. Er ist gestern nicht sehr nett zu mir _____.
5. Wir haben auf Mallorca in einem Luxushotel _____.
6. Ich bin gestern zu spät _____ und deshalb habe ich meinen Bus verpasst.

Answers: 1. ausgegeben   2. geworden
3. mitgenommen   4. gewesen
5. übernachtet   6. aufgestanden

TEACHING SUGGESTIONS

• Photo, p. 212

Ask *Welche Länder oder Kulturen werden durch die Werbung auf dem Bild repräsentiert?*

• *Aktivität A,* pp. 212–213

Warm-up: Have students give the infinitive forms of the verbs in the box on p. 212 (bottom) and encourage them to use those verbs in original sentences.

• *Aktivität B,* p. 213

Follow-up: Ask each student to write the definition of 1 of the vocabulary items on p. 212 on a slip of paper. Call on students to give the definition they have written. The class must find the word in the vocabulary list that matches the definition.

• *Aktivität C,* p. 213

Follow-up: Ask students *Wie ist in den USA die rechtliche Situation für Menschen, die aus anderen Ländern kommen? Stimmen Sie mit Anjas Meinung überein? Haben Sie selber Erfahrungen mit Fremdenfeindlichkeit gemacht oder diese beobachtet?*

TEACHING ALL STUDENTS

Multiple Intelligences Rhythmic: Have students find the simple past and past participle forms of the verbs in the vocabulary list on p. 212. Have students call out the infinitive form and have their partners give the other 2 forms. Do this repeatedly until they can recite some forms automatically or find a rhythm to which to memorize them.

LANGUAGE NOTE

Brauchen replaces *müssen* in a sentence with a negative meaning, indicating "there is no need to do something" as in *Hier braucht man keine Angst zu haben. Du brauchst mir nicht zu helfen.*

CLASSROOM COMMUNITY

Dictation Dictate the following text to the class. Then provide students with the correct version of the dictation on an OHT. Have them exchange their writings with another student and correct each other's papers.
Die fünfziger Jahre waren eine Zeit des Wohlstands in Deutschland und die deutsche Wirtschaft brauchte dringend Arbeitskräfte. Viele junge Menschen, besonders Türken und Griechen, kamen nach Deutschland, um zu arbeiten. Viele von ihnen öffneten später Restaurants. So haben sie die Essgewohnheiten in Deutschland beeinflusst.

CULTURE HIGHLIGHTS

Refer to the *Kulturspiegel* on p. 224 and help students to find some more information on the legal requirements for German citizenship. During the last 10 years there has been a debate in the *Bundestag* about changing the requirements for German citizenship. The Green party and some of the Social Democrats are advocates of dual citizenship.

BLOCK SCHEDULE

Expansion Have students write down the recipe for a dish they especially like. Have them rewrite the recipe in German, using European measurements.

PROJECT

Ask some Germans you know whether they could share a recipe of a favorite German dish they eat at special occasions (Christmas, Easter, birthdays). If they do not remember all the ingredients, do some research on the Internet and try to find the recipe. Find out the time of year and occasion for which the dish is served. Write down the recipe and any cultural information you have obtained. Bonus points: Prepare the dish for your classmates!

Writing Criteria	Scale				
Accuracy	1	2	3	4	5
Grammar, vocabulary	1	2	3	4	5
Creativity	1	2	3	4	5

Strukturen, pp. 214–219

PROGRAM RESOURCES

- Overhead Transparencies 34.G1–34.G2
- *Arbeitsheft,* pp. 153–156
- Audio Program, Cassette 5B/CD 7
- Audioscript, pp. 75–77

Quick Start Review 1

♻ Vocabulary
Bilden Sie Sätze.

1. geraten / mein Freund / in den Bergen / ist / beim Klettern / in große Gefahr
2. vorgenommen, / hat / nicht / allein / dass / er / wird / klettern / danach / er / sich / mehr
3. isst / meine Schwester / seit zehn Jahren / vegetarisch / nur
4. habe / ein Rezept / von meiner ungarischen Freundin / bekommen / für Gulaschsuppe / ich
5. das Kochen / nimmt / Zeit / viel / zu Hause / in Anspruch
6. ist / dünner / auf hohen Bergen / die Luft / das Atmen / schwerer / und / fällt

Answers: 1. Mein Freund ist beim Klettern in den Bergen in große Gefahr geraten. 2. Er hat sich danach vorgenommen, dass er nicht mehr allein klettern wird. 3. Meine Schwester isst seit zehn Jahren nur vegetarisch. 4. Ich habe von meiner ungarischen Freundin ein Rezept für Gulaschsuppe bekommen. 5. Das Kochen zu Hause nimmt viel Zeit in Anspruch. 6. Auf hohen Bergen ist die Luft dünner und das Atmen fällt schwerer.

Quick Start Review 2

♻ *Da-* and *wo*-compounds
Bilden Sie Fragesätze nach dem Modell.
MODELL: Ich interessiere mich für klassische Musik. → *Interessierst du dich auch dafür?*

1. Ich beschäftige mich oft mit alten Photos von meiner Familie.
2. Ich denke oft an unsere Zukunft.
3. Ich freue mich schon auf unseren Ausflug.
4. Ich warte schon auf die Sommerferien.
5. Ich freue mich sehr über das schöne Wetter heute.
6. Ich denke oft an unsere alte Lehrerin.

Answers: 1. Beschäftigst du dich auch damit? 2. Denkst du auch daran? 3. Freust du dich auch darauf? 4. Wartest du auch darauf? 5. Freust du dich auch darüber? 6. Denkst du auch an sie?

TEACHING SUGGESTIONS

- Relative clauses I, pp. 214–215

Explain that relative clauses elaborate on a topic. Relative clauses are used more in writing than in everyday conversation but are used most often in conversation of a particular register. Students should become familiar with their use, especially in writing.

- *Übung A,* p. 215

Follow-up: Have students write 2 sentences each about their hometown or neighborhood, for example, *Ich wohne in einer Gegend, die viele Parks hat. Ich wohne in einer Stadt, die viele schöne Restaurants hat. usw.* Encourage them to use relative pronouns in their sentences. Now have students name the gender, number, and case of the relative pronouns they used.

- *Übung B,* p. 215

Follow-up: Give students some more cues to form into sentences. For example, *Rotkäppchen ist ein Mädchen, . . . Dornröschen ist eine Prinzessin, . . . Rumpelstilzchen ist ein Zwerg, . . . Die Bremer Stadtmusikanten sind Tiere, . . . Tom Sawyer ist ein Junge, . . . usw.*

- *Übung B,* p. 217

To check answers, have one partner read Karin's statement and the other give the resulting question. Have them alternate the roles of Karin and friend. Variation: Have students talk about their own vacations. One student provides a statement, and the next student asks a question with a relative clause. *Wir waren an einem tollen Strand in Kalifornien. Wie heißt der Strand, an dem ihr wart?*

- *Übung C,* p. 217

Narration: Have students focus on a topic of their choice, such as *Studium, Urlaub,* or *Ausländerfeindlichkeit.* Have them write 3 or more statements about the topic, 1 of which must include a relative clause.

- *Übung A*, p. 219

Variation: Have students create their own versions of the examples given, for example, *Ich spare, um mir ein paar neue Schuhe zu kaufen. Ich räume mein Zimmer auf, um mein Biologieheft zu finden. Ich fahre mit dem Bus, um nicht im Stau zu stehen.*

- *Übung B*, p. 219

Follow-up: Encourage students to give advice to their younger siblings, for example, *Anstatt deine Spielsachen kaputt zu machen, könntest du mir aufräumen helfen. Anstatt zu schreien, könntest du dich beruhigen. Anstatt deinen Freund zu ärgern, könntest du ihn in Ruhe lassen. Anstatt über deinen Lehrer zu schimpfen, könntest du deine Matheaufgaben machen.*

TEACHING ALL STUDENTS

Challenge Put the following sentences on the board or on an OHT. Have students rephrase the sentences using *um . . . zu.*

1. Erika trifft sich mit vielen deutschen Freunden, damit sie schneller Deutsch lernt.
2. Ich brauche dringend Urlaub, damit ich mich vom Stress von der Arbeit erhole.
3. Du musst dich beeilen, wenn du noch Theaterkarten bekommen willst.
4. Ich bin in die Stadt gefahren, weil ich einkaufen wollte.

Are there any other ways of expressing these sentences? Where could you use *weil, denn,* or *damit*?

CLASSROOM COMMUNITY

Group Activity Have students work in groups to answer the following questions: *Wenn ich nicht heute leben würde, in welcher Zeit (Zukunft–Vergangenheit) möchte ich gerne leben? Welche Kleider würde ich tragen? Welchen Beruf hätte ich? Wie sähen unsere Häuser aus?* Have the groups each choose a spokesperson who will present their imagined lives to the class.

BLOCK SCHEDULE

Recycle Have students create sentences using relative clauses.
MODELL: Schüler: Mathebuch → *Ich kenne den Schüler, dem das Mathebuch gehört.*

1. Mädchen: Rucksack
2. Lehrer: Auto
3. Leute: Haus
4. Kinder: Hund
5. Junge: Fußball
6. Frau: Katze

Perspektiven, pp. 220–227

PROGRAM RESOURCES

- *Arbeitsheft,* pp. 157–160
- Audio Program, Cassette 5B, 7B/CD 9
- Audioscript, pp. 77–78
- www.mcdougallittell.com

....

Quick Start Review 1

Vocabulary
Ergänzen Sie die Adjektive und Adverbien in den Sätzen.
WÖRTER: gewohnheitsmäßig, heimlich, preisgünstig, sorgfältig, tief, verzweifelt

1. Als Kinder haben wir oft _____ Süßigkeiten gegessen.
2. Er erledigt seine Hausaufgaben immer sehr _____.
3. Ich nehme seit Jahren _____ eine Vitamin-C-Tablette nach dem Frühstück.
4. Nach Weihnachten kann man in den Geschäften sehr _____ einkaufen.
5. Der See ist in der Mitte sehr _____.
6. Nachdem sein Vater gestorben war, war er zunächst ganz _____.

Answers: 1. heimlich   2. sorgfältig   3. gewohnheitsmäßig   4. preisgünstig   5. tief   6. verzweifelt

Quick Start Review 2

Present perfect
Goldilocks und die drei Bären.
Schreiben Sie Fragen.
MODELL: von meinem Teller essen →
Wer hat von meinem Teller gegessen?

1. mit meinem Löffel essen
2. auf meinem Stuhl sitzen
3. meinen Stuhl kaputtmachen
4. in meinem Bett liegen
5. meine Bettdecke herunterwerfen
6. die Haustür öffnen

Answers: 1. Wer hat mit meinem Löffel gegessen?   2. Wer hat auf meinem Stuhl gesessen?   3. Wer hat meinen Stuhl kaputtgemacht?   4. Wer hat in meinem Bett gelegen?   5. Wer hat meine Bettdecke heruntergeworfen? 6. Wer hat die Haustür geöffnet?

....

TEACHING SUGGESTIONS

- *Hören Sie zu!, Aktivität A,* p. 220

Follow-up: Have students summarize as much as they can remember about Sarah and Magnus. Have them look up *Würzburg* on a map.

- *Hören Sie zu!, Aktivität B*, p. 220

Do a survey of the class. Who might be interested in studying abroad? To which countries and cities would they choose to go? You might have students interview each other to discover their preferences.

- *Zum Thema, Aktivität A*, p. 220

Ask *Haben Sie schon einmal bemerkt, dass Sie selbst stereotype Erwartungen haben oder in Stereotypen denken? Haben Sie Ihr Denken geändert?*

- *Zum Thema, Aktivität B*, p. 221

Variation: Have students create a collage with the title *Typisch deutsch?* Provide them with German magazines and newspapers.

- *Die Suche nach den Deutschen*, p. 221

Have students review *Wortschatz zum Lesen*, p. 222, before reading the text. Make sure they limit their use of the dictionary. Preview the text with the students by having them read the first paragraph silently. Ask *wer, was, wo, wann* questions about the paragraph. Alternately, have students close their books. Put the first paragraph of the reading on an OHT without showing the title of the reading and let them read it silently. Then ask *wer, was, wo, wann* questions. Finally, have them come up with a possible title for the reading.

- *Zum Text, Aktivität A*, p. 223

Follow-up: Ask *Warum sagt Dieter: „Ich bin kein Deutscher!"? Was denkt Dieter über die Deutschen? Warum fühlen sich viele Deutsche nicht als Deutsche? Fühlen Sie sich als Amerikaner oder Angehöriger der Nation, die in Ihren Pass eingetragen ist?*

- *Zur Interpretation*, p. 223

Ask *Hat diese Reaktion vielleicht mit der deutschen Geschichte zu tun? Kennen Sie Deutsche? Wie denken Sie über die Geschichte ihres Landes?*

- *Interaktion*, p. 224

Have students work in groups. Ask *Gibt es Schüler in der Klasse, die sich zwei verschiedenen Nationen zugehörig fühlen? Was gefällt Ihnen an der einen oder der anderen Nation? Was gefällt Ihnen nicht?*

TEACHING ALL STUDENTS

Extra Help Ask for a volunteer to tell a short anecdote (which you may wish to prescreen). That student then chooses another student to restate the anecdote using indirect speech. Review *Tipp zum Schreiben*, p. 224, and refer to *Kapitel 30* for a review of Subjunctive I forms if necessary.

CLASSROOM COMMUNITY

Paired Activity Have students work in pairs. One student describes a situation or a person in detail while the other draws a picture of what is being described. Students should use adjectives and comparisons in their descriptions.

INTERDISCIPLINARY CONNECTION

History: Research the concept of German nationalism and how it evolved during the twentieth century. How did German reunification affect the concept of national identity? Students might want to interview their history teacher and some older Germans they know.

BLOCK SCHEDULE

Time Saver Students have 5 minutes to jot down as many German words as they can think of. Have them read their lists to each other. Which words did they think of first?

Change of Pace Have students come up with questions testing each others' knowledge of German culture/history/trivia. Divide the class into 2 groups and have them write a set of 10 questions each. Then have the 2 groups quiz each other. For example, *Was ist der höchste Berg Deutschlands? (Die Zugspitze) Wer hat **Die Blechtrommel** geschrieben? (Günter Grass) Für welches Volksfest ist München bekannt? (Oktoberfest) usw.*

PORTFOLIO

Visit the Web site of a German city of your choice (Tübingen, Freiburg im Breisgau, Frankfurt am Main, Weimar, Göttingen, etc.) and create a 2-day sightseeing plan. Provide a brief introduction to the city: geographic location, history, famous sights. Include a visit to a museum, church or another site of historic interest and give the names of at least 2 restaurants where you would suggest eating. Feel free to be creative.

RUBRIC **A** = 13–15 pts. **B** = 10–12 pts. **C** = 7–9 pts. **D** = 4–6 pts. **F** <4 pts.

Writing Criteria	Scale				
Grammar, vocabulary	1	2	3	4	5
Content	1	2	3	4	5
Creativity	1	2	3	4	5

34 MULTI-KULTI?

In diesem Kapitel

- sehen Sie, was ein junger Türke von Deutschland und den Deutschen hält.

- erfahren Sie, wie Ausländer den Alltag in Deutschland verändert haben.

- besprechen Sie, was eine multikulturelle Gesellschaft bedeutet.

Sie werden auch

- Relativpronomen und den Gebrauch von Relativsätzen wiederholen.

- lernen, wie man Relativpronomen mit Präpositionen benutzt.

- mehr über den Gebrauch von Infinitivsätzen mit **zu** lernen.

- lesen, wie ein Brasilianer nach dem „typischen" Deutschen sucht.

- einen multikulturellen Stadtführer schreiben.

Ist Deutschland wirklich eine multikulturelle Gesellschaft geworden?

In den Supermärkten kauft man Produkte aus aller Welt.

Gab es damals eine „typisch" deutsche Küche?

VIDEOTHEK

Was heißt für Sie „deutsch"? In diesem Kapitel sehen Sie, was ausländische Einwohner von Deutschland und den Deutschen halten und wie Deutsche und Österreicher auf ihre ausländischen Mitbürger reagieren.

I: Typisch deutsch?

In dieser Folge lernen Sie Ergün Çevik kennen, der schon lange in Deutschland lebt. Was heißt für ihn „deutsch"?

A Ergün erwähnt drei Eigenschaften, die ihm einfallen: Sauberkeit, Ordnung und Pünktlichkeit.

Ergün Çevik.

SCHRITT 1: Welche dieser drei Eigenschaften werden in den folgenden Aussagen dargestellt?

1. „Bei Rot stehen, bei Grün gehen."
2. „Wenn du eine Verabredung mit einem Deutschen hast, verspäte dich nie länger als fünf Minuten."
3. „Samstag ist in Deutschland Putztag."
4. „Damit sich alle an die Regeln halten, ist alles beschildert."
5. „Ein Terminkalender ist in Deutschland eine sehr wichtige Sache."
6. „Für mich zeigt sich in einem Schrebergarten die deutsche Seele."

SCHRITT 2: Wie finden Sie die „Regeln", die Ergün beschreibt? Gibt es solche Regeln auch bei Ihnen? Erklären Sie Ihre Antwort.

B Verkehrsschilder. Verbinden Sie jede Beschreibung auf Seite 211 mit dem richtigen Verkehrsschild.

WORTSCHATZ ZUM VIDEO

der Putztag	cleaning day
der Schrebergarten	small allotted garden
der Fahrplan	transit schedule
die Aufführung	performance
die Passkontrolle	passport control
die Flitterwochen	honeymoon

FOKUS INTERNET

For more information on the cultures represented in Germany, visit the **Auf Deutsch!** Web Site at www.mcdougallittell.com.

a.

b.

c.

d.

e.

f.

Schritt 1: *Possible answers are:* Ergün sagt, man muss sich in Deutschland an die Ordnung halten, zum Beispiel an ~~Verk~~ehrsschilder, sonst bekommt man Ärger. Er sagt, ein Terminkalender ist in Deutschland sehr wichtig. Ergün erwähnt ~~au~~ch die Regel, dass man sich nie mehr als fünf Minuten verspäten soll, wenn man mit einem Deutschen verabredet ist. ~~We~~nn Ergün sagt, „Die Ausnahme bestätigt die Regel", dann meint er, dass die Regel trotzdem gilt, auch wenn es ~~ma~~nchmal eine Ausnahme gibt. Das Beispiel über die Pünktlichkeit der Deutschen illustriert diese Aussage.

1. Das Tempolimit ist dreißig Kilometer pro Stunde.
2. Hier darf man Fahrrad fahren.
3. Fußgängerweg: Fahrradfahren verboten.
4. Parkplatz: Hier kann man das Auto parken.
5. Hier geht man über die Straße.
6. Das Ampelmännchen zeigt, dass man jetzt über die Straße gehen darf.

C Regeln und Ausnahmen

SCHRITT 1: Ergün spricht über Deutschland und die Deutschen. Welche Regeln erwähnt er? Er sagt: „In Deutschland sagt man auch, die Ausnahme bestätigt die Regel." Was meint er wohl mit diesem Satz? Welches Beispiel im Video illustriert diese Aussage?

SCHRITT 2: Welche Regeln sind in Ihrem Land wichtig? Arbeiten Sie mit einem Partner / einer Partnerin, und machen Sie eine Liste. Würden Sie auch sagen: „Die Ausnahme bestätigt die Regel?" Warum (nicht)? Geben Sie ein Beispiel.

C. Schritt 2: *Answers will vary.*

A. „typisch deutsch": 2, 3, 5, 7

II: Vom Sauerkraut zur Pizza

In dieser Folge sehen Sie, was Ausländer zur Kultur in Deutschland und Österreich beigetragen haben. Inwiefern haben Minderheiten oder Einwanderer das Leben bei Ihnen bereichert?[a]

[a]*enriched*

A Die deutsche Küche. Welche Lebensmittel sind Ihrer Meinung nach „typisch deutsch"? Welche kommen wohl aus anderen Ländern?

1. Lammfleisch
2. Brathähnchen
3. Schnitzel
4. Zucchini
5. Bratwürste
6. Oliven
7. Schweinshaxe mit Knödeln
8. Knoblauch
9. Artischocken

B Persönliche Meinungen

SCHRITT 1: Aussagen. Drei Frauen sprechen über Ausländer und die multikulturelle Gesellschaft in Deutschland. Wer sagt was? Anja, Susanne oder Daniela?

1. „Die Ausländer nehmen Arbeiten an, die die Österreicher nicht annehmen würden."
2. „Wenn man heute in Berlin lebt und die vielen Ausländer sieht, die ausländische Restaurants eröffnen . . . denke ich, dass unser Leben nur reicher werden kann."
3. „Ich denke schon, dass Deutschland zu einer multikulturellen Gesellschaft geworden ist."
4. „Das ist ein schönes Gefühl für mich, wenn die Klassen international werden und . . . wenn man viele Sprachen hört."

SCHRITT 2: Partnerarbeit. Wählen Sie drei von den Aussagen oben und besprechen Sie sie mit einem Partner / einer Partnerin.

1. Stimmen diese Aussagen auch in Ihrem Land? Wenn ja, inwiefern?
2. Was bedeutet eine multikulturelle Gesellschaft für diese drei Frauen? In welchen Bereichen wirken die Einflüsse am stärksten?

Ausländische Arbeiter in den fünfziger Jahren.

B. Schritt 1: 1. Daniela   2. Anja   3. Susanne   4. Susanne

KULTURSPIEGEL

1973 erreichte die Ausländerbeschäftigung in Deutschland einen Höhepunkt von rund 2,6 Millionen Arbeitnehmern; 1996 gab es in Deutschland, vor allem in den alten Bundesländern, rund 2,1 Millionen. Arbeiter aus der Türkei, Italien, dem ehemaligen Jugoslawien und Griechenland stellen den größten Anteil dieser ausländischen Beschäftigten dar.

Schritt 2: *Answers will vary.*

VOKABELN

die Essgewohnheit	*eating habit*
die Genauigkeit	*accuracy; exactness*
die Nichtakzeptanz	*nonacceptance*
die Ordnung	*order*
die Pünktlichkeit	*promptness; punctuality*
die Regel	*rule*
die Sauberkeit	*cleanliness*
die Verabredung	*appointment; date*
die Verachtung	*contempt*
der Auswanderer / die Auswanderin	*emigrant*
der Einwanderer / die Einwanderin	*immigrant*
das Asyl	*political asylum*
das Bedürfnis	*necessity*
an•nehmen	*to accept, take on*
beachten	*to observe*
bei•tragen zu	*to contribute to*
dar•stellen	*to depict, portray; to present*
duzen	*to address someone with **du***
ein•fallen	*to come to mind*
ein•halten	*to keep (an appointment)*
siezen	*to address someone with **Sie***
vereinbaren	*to arrange*
verfolgen	*to persecute*
sich verspäten	*to be late*

Das Essen in Deutschland ist multikultureller geworden.

deutlich	*clear(ly)*
inzwischen	*in the meantime*
rechtlich	*legal(ly)*
unmittelbar	*direct(ly)*
unweigerlich	*inevitable; inevitably*

Sie wissen schon

die Ausländerfeindlichkeit, der Ausländer, der Schritt, beeinflussen, unbedingt

A. 1. Ausländer 2. inzwischen 3. angenommen 4. Verachtung 5. rechtlich 6. Asyl 7. verfolgt 8. beigetragen 9. beeinflusst

Asyl   rechtlich
Ausländer
inzwischen
Verachtung
beigetragen
beeinflusst
angenommen   verfolgt

Aktivitäten

A Ausländer in der Bundesrepublik. Ergänzen Sie die Sätze mit Wörtern aus dem Kasten.

Die fünfziger Jahre waren eine Zeit des Wohlstands in Deutschland. 1950 gab es wenige _____¹ in der Bundesrepublik, aber _____² ist die Zahl der ausländischen Arbeiter in Deutschland enorm gestiegen. Die deutsche Wirtschaft brauchte dringend Arbeitskräfte. Viele junge Männer, besonders Türken und Griechen, kamen nach Deutschland, um zu arbeiten. Sie haben Arbeiten

_____,[3] die die Deutschen selbst nicht machen wollten. Deswegen wurden sie oft mit _____[4] behandelt.

Obwohl man sie „Gastarbeiter" nannte, blieben viele von diesen Arbeitern ihr ganzes Leben in Deutschland. Obwohl die Kinder dieser Arbeiter in Deutschland geboren und aufgewachsen sind, werden sie _____[5] als Bürger anderer Länder betrachtet.

In den vergangenen Jahren beantragten viele Flüchtlinge in Deutschland _____,[6] weil sie in ihrer Heimat politisch _____[7] wurden.

Ausländer haben zu den Kulturen der deutschsprachigen Länder viel _____.[8] Auch haben ihre Essgewohnheiten die Küche stark _____.[9] Jetzt können Österreicher und Deutsche Gerichte und Lebensmittel aus vielen anderen Ländern genießen.

B Definitionen. Wie kann man das anders sagen? Lesen Sie die Sätze links, und suchen Sie aus der rechten Spalte Synonyme für die kursiv gedruckten Wörter.

1. Das erste, was mir zu Deutschland einfällt, ist: Sauberkeit, Ordnung und *Pünktlichkeit*.
2. Und diese *Genauigkeit*, Verkehrsschilder an einem solchen Ort.
3. Die Schilder muss man unbedingt *beachten*.
4. Alles wird vorher *vereinbart*, zum Beispiel ein Friseurbesuch.
5. Wenn du *eine Verabredung* mit einem Deutschen hast, *verspäte dich nie*.
6. Die ausländische Küche hat auch *die Essgewohnheiten* der Deutschen verändert.
7. Zu Österreich haben Ausländer sehr viel *beigetragen*.
8. Hätten Sie etwas dagegen, mich *zu siezen*?

C Ausländer und Einwanderer

SCHRITT 1: Meinungen. Lesen Sie, was Anja zum Thema Ausländerfeindlichkeit sagt.

ANJA: Die Gründe für die Ausländerfeindlichkeit in Deutschland sehe ich vorrangig in der Nichtakzeptanz, der rechtlichen Nichtakzeptanz von Ausländern. Es kann nicht sein, dass ein Ausländer in Deutschland wohnt, sogar dort geboren ist, und gar kein Ausländer ist, doch aber den Status eines Ausländers hat. Man kann nicht dreißig Jahre in Deutschland wohnen und nicht das Recht haben, zu wählen, oder andere Rechte, die die Deutschen haben.

SCHRITT 2: Und in Ihrem Land? Arbeiten Sie mit einem Partner / einer Partnerin, und versuchen Sie, die Situation in Deutschland mit der Situation in Ihrem Land zu vergleichen. Denken Sie an die folgenden Fragen.

1. Wie bekommt man die Staatsbürgerschaft in Ihrem Land?
2. Woher kommen die meisten Ausländer bei Ihnen? Aus welchen Gründen wandern sie ein? Welche Arbeiten nehmen sie an?
3. Was bedeutet „rechtliche Nichtakzeptanz"?

KULTURSPIEGEL

Während der Nazizeit mussten viele Deutsche ihre Heimat verlassen und im Ausland Asyl suchen. Nach dem Krieg hatte man im deutschen Grundgesetz das Recht auf Asyl festgelegt. „Politisch Verfolgte genießen Asylrecht": So steht es in Artikel 16a des Grundgesetzes. In den Jahren 1989 bis 1992 kamen besonders viele Asylbewerber nach Deutschland (1992: 438 191 Menschen), die Hälfte davon aus Rumänien und dem ehemaligen Jugoslawien.

a. die genaue Einhaltung eines Termins
b. befolgen
c. arrangiert; besprochen
d. mitgeholfen; geleistet
e. komm nie spät an
f. mit „Sie" anzureden
g. das traditionelle Essen
h. einen Termin, ein Meeting
i. Exaktheit

B. 1. a   2. i   3. b   4. c   5. h, e   6. g
7. d   8. f

Anja und Grace diskutieren über Ausländerfeindlichkeit.

C. Schritt 2: *Answers will vary.*

STRUKTUREN

REVIEW OF RELATIVE CLAUSES I
DESCRIBING PEOPLE AND THINGS

Relative clauses add information about a person, place, or thing. In German, the relative pronoun is essential to the relative clause and cannot be omitted, unlike in English.

Die Frage, **die** Sie gestellt haben, ist sehr interessant.	*The question (that) you asked is very interesting.*

Note that the relative clause usually follows the noun it describes and that commas separate it from the rest of the sentence. Note also that the relative pronoun agrees in gender and number with the noun it describes, but takes the case of its function within the relative clause.

Der Lehrer, **den** du gerade gesehen hast, ist bei seinen Schülern beliebt.	*The teacher (whom) you just saw is popular with his students.*

In the preceding example, the relative pronoun is masculine and singular to agree with the noun, **der Lehrer.** However, it is in the accusative case, because it functions as the direct object of the verb within the relative clause (**du hast *den Lehrer* gerade gesehen**). As with all dependent clauses, the conjugated verb appears at the end of the relative clause (**den du gerade gesehen *hast***).

The forms of the relative pronouns are the same as those of the definite article **die, der, das,** except in the dative plural and all forms of the genitive. These forms have an extra **-en: denen, deren, dessen, dessen, deren.**

	FEMININE	MASCULINE	NEUTER	PLURAL
NOMINATIVE	die	der	das	die
ACCUSATIVE	die	den	das	die
DATIVE	der	dem	dem	**denen**
GENITIVE	**deren**	**dessen**	**dessen**	**deren**

Übungen

A Typisch deutsch? Ein Mann schreibt einen Zeitungsartikel über die Deutschen. Er will „typische Deutsche" finden. Suchen Sie in jedem Satz das Relativpronomen, und schreiben Sie das Genus (Feminin, Maskulin, Neutrum), den Numerus (Einzahl oder Mehrzahl) und den Kasus (Nominativ, Akkusativ, Dativ oder Genitiv) des Relativpronomens auf.

MODELL: Der Mann schreibt für eine Zeitung, die sehr berühmt ist.

RELATIVPRONOMEN	GENUS	NUMERUS	KASUS
die	Feminin	Einzahl	Nominativ

1. Der Mann sucht Menschen, die typisch deutsch sind.
2. Er reist mit einem Zug, der direkt von Berlin nach München fährt.
3. Er kommt in München an und übernachtet in einem Hotel, das sehr alt ist.
4. Im Hotel lernt er einige Menschen kennen, die er untypisch findet.
5. Er muss Menschen finden, deren Eigenschaften typisch deutsch sind.
6. Der Mann spricht mit seinem Freund Dieter, den er für einen typischen Deutschen hält.
7. Dieter spricht mit diesem Mann, dem er helfen will.
8. Der Mann, dessen Name in Italien gut bekannt ist, dankt seinem Freund Dieter für die Informationen.

B Transport und Reisen. Hier sind einige Definitionen. Ergänzen Sie sie mit den fehlenden Relativpronomen.

1. Ein Pkw ist ein Fahrzeug, _____ man privat besitzt.
2. Flugreisende sind Menschen, _____ mit dem Flugzeug fliegen.
3. Ein ICE ist ein sehr schneller Zug, _____ bis zu 280 Kilometer in der Stunde fahren kann.
4. Eine Radlerin ist eine Frau, _____ Rad fährt.
5. Ein Führerschein ist eine Lizenz, _____ man zum Fahren braucht.
6. Ein Reisepass ist ein Pass, _____ man auf Auslandsreisen mitnehmen muss.
7. Ein Zollbeamter ist ein Mann, _____ Touristen ihre Reisepässe zeigen müssen.
8. Ein Mofa ist ein Motorrad, _____ Motor sehr klein ist.

Zeigen diese Schrebergärten „typisch" deutsche Eigenschaften?

A. 1. die, Maskulin, Plural, Nominativ **2.** der, Maskulin, Singular, Nominativ **3.** das, Neutrum, Singular, Nominativ **4.** die, Maskulin, Plural, Akkusativ **5.** deren, Maskulin, Plural, Genitiv **6.** den, Maskulin, Singular, Akkusativ **7.** dem, Maskulin, Singular, Dativ **8.** dessen, Maskulin, Singular, Genitiv

B. 1. das **2.** die **3.** der **4.** die **5.** die **6.** den **7.** dem **8.** dessen

RELATIVE CLAUSES II
USING PREPOSITIONS WITH RELATIVE CLAUSES

A relative pronoun may also function as the object of a preposition in a relative clause. As always, the number and gender of the relative pronoun agrees with the noun; and the case of the relative pronoun is that required by the preposition within the clause.

Ich wohne **in einer Stadt.** Sie ist sehr schön.	*I live in a city. It is very beautiful.*
Die Stadt, **in der** ich wohne, ist sehr schön.	*The city I live in is very beautiful. / The city, in which I live, is very beautiful.*
Wir fahren **an den Strand.** Der Strand ist einer der schönsten hier.	*We're going to the beach. The beach is one of the nicest ones here.*
Der Strand, **an den** wir fahren, ist einer der schönsten hier.	*The beach we're going to is one of the nicest ones here. / The beach, to which we're going, is one of the nicest ones here.*

Note that in German the preposition immediately precedes the relative pronoun at the beginning of the relative clause.

A relative clause begins with a **wo**-compound when it describes an indefinite thing or place.

Das ist etwas, **worauf** ich mich seit langem gefreut habe.	*That is something (that) I have looked forward to for a long time.*
Eines Tages werde ich auf einer tropischen Insel leben, **wovon** ich immer geträumt habe.	*One day I'll live on a tropical island, which is something I've always dreamed about.*

Note that in the first example, the relative clause refers to the word **etwas;** in the second example, the relative clause refers to the entire idea expressed in the preceding clause.

KURZ NOTIERT

Recall that **da-** and **wo**-compounds include an **-r-** before prepositions that begin with a vowel.

Ich freue mich **darauf.**
Worauf freust du dich?

Übungen

A Ausländerfeindlichkeit und Politik. Ergänzen Sie die Sätze mit den Wörtern im Kasten.

1. Die Ausländerfeindlichkeit ist ein Thema, _____ _____ wir uns alle beschäftigen.
2. Wir wohnen in einer Gesellschaft, _____ _____ sich viele benachteiligt fühlen.
3. Eine Lösung, _____ _____ jeder einverstanden sein würde, gibt es wohl nicht.
4. Eine Änderung des Asylgesetzes, _____ _____ viele Bürger warten, ist im Moment politisch nicht möglich.
5. Andere meinen, dass die Probleme, _____ _____ so viel geschrieben wird, übertrieben sind.
6. In der Zukunft, _____ _____ wir träumen, braucht kein Mensch Angst vor Gewalt zu haben.

mit der   auf die
   von denen
        in der
  mit dem
         von der

A. **1.** mit dem   **2.** in der   **3.** mit der   **4.** auf die
5. von denen   **6.** von der

B Ihre Freundin Karin erzählt von ihrer Reise nach Rügen. Sie wollen wissen, wie die Orte, in denen Karin war, genau heißen. Bilden Sie Fragen mit Relativsätzen.

MODELL: Ich habe *in einem billigen Hotel* gewohnt. →
Wie heißt das Hotel, in dem du gewohnt hast?

1. Ich bin *an einen tollen Strand* gegangen.
2. Ich bin *auf eine kleine Insel* gefahren.
3. Ich bin *mit einem Zug* nach Sassnitz gefahren.
4. Ich habe da *in einer Jugendherberge* übernachtet.
5. Ich habe *in einem gemütlichen Restaurant* gegessen.
6. Ich habe *mit netten Menschen* geredet.
7. Ich bin *in den alten Dörfern* spazieren gegangen.

Auf der Insel Rügen.

B. *Possible answers are:* **1.** Wo liegt der Strand, an den du gegangen bist?   **2.** Wie heißt die Insel, auf die du gefahren bist?   **3.** Wie heißt der Zug, mit dem du nach Sassnitz gefahren bist?   **4.** Wo ist die Jugendherberge, in der du übernachtet hast?   **5.** Wie heißt das Restaurant, in dem du gegessen hast?   **6.** Wo kamen die netten Menschen her, mit denen du geredet hast?   **7.** Wie groß sind die Dörfer, in denen du spazieren gegangen bist?

C Eine multikulturelle Gesellschaft? Die Personen im Video sagen, was für sie eine multikulturelle Gesellschaft bedeutet. Ergänzen Sie die Sätze mit **wo-**Verbindungen.

1. SUSANNE: Sprachen sind etwas, _____ ich mich immer interessiert habe.
2. DANIELA: Die ausländischen Theater- und Musikaufführungen sind etwas, _____ ich mich sehr freue.
3. GRACE: Die negativen Einstellungen zu Ausländern sind etwas, _____ ich mich ärgere.
4. KLAUS: Die Integration von Ausländern in der Gesellschaft ist etwas, _____ ich mich schon lange beschäftigt habe.
5. ANJA: Die menschliche und rechtliche Akzeptanz von Ausländern ist etwas, _____ ich immer geträumt habe.

C. **1.** wofür   **2.** worüber   **3.** worüber   **4.** womit
5. wovon

INFINITIVE CLAUSES WITH ZU
STATING GOALS AND INTENTIONS

You have learned to use modal verbs with infinitives.

Wir müssen eine Lösung finden.	*We have to find a solution.*
Ausländer wollen mehr soziale Rechte haben.	*Foreigners want to have more social rights.*

As you recall, verbs other than the modal auxiliaries may also take infinitives. However, these infinitives occur in phrases or clauses with the word **zu.**

Ich **hoffe,** nächstes Jahr in die Schweiz **zu reisen.**	*I hope to travel to Switzerland next year.*
Meine Freundin **hilft** mir, Informationen über die Schweiz **zu finden.**	*My girlfriend is helping me find information about Switzerland.*

The verbs **brauchen** and **scheinen** frequently appear with **zu** plus an infinitive. **Brauchen** can replace **müssen** in a sentence with a negative meaning.

Hier **braucht** man keine Angst **zu** haben.	*One doesn't have to be afraid of anything here.*
Nichts **scheint** typisch deutsch **zu** sein.	*Nothing seems to be typically German.*

The combination **zu** plus infinitive may occur in a phrase by itself or in a clause that begins with a preposition such as **(an)statt, ohne,** or **um.** A comma generally sets off clauses that include more words than just **zu** plus infinitive.

Wir finden es schön **zu reisen.**	*We find it nice to travel.*
Wir fahren nach München, **anstatt in Berlin zu bleiben.**	*We're going to Munich instead of staying in Berlin.*
Wir möchten viel erfahren, **ohne viel Geld auszugeben.**	*We want to experience a lot without spending a lot of money.*
Wir versuchen alles Mögliche, **um billige Zugfahrkarten zu finden.**	*We're trying everything possible in order to find cheap train tickets.*

As you have learned, certain verbs often appear in combination with a preposition: **sich beschweren über, denken an, sich engagieren für, sich erinnern an, sich interessieren für, reagieren auf, warten auf, sich wundern über.** An infinitive clause frequently follows the combination of a verb with an "anticipatory" **da**-compound. In such instances, the infinitive clause describes the situation that the **da**-compound anticipates.

Er wartet **darauf,** einen typischen Deutschen kennen zu lernen.

He is waiting to get to know a typical German.

Such anticipatory **da**-compounds have no corresponding forms in English.

Übungen

A Was sind die Gründe dafür? Sagen Sie, warum diese Leute die folgenden Sachen machen. Benutzen Sie dabei **um . . . zu . . .**

MODELL: Heinrich geht jeden Tag zum Sport. Er will sich fit halten. → Heinrich geht jeden Tag zum Sport, um sich fit zu halten.

1. Erika spart. Sie will ein neues Auto kaufen.
2. Richard räumt sein Zimmer auf. Er will seine Armbanduhr finden.
3. Stefan fährt mit der U-Bahn. Er will den dichten Autoverkehr vermeiden.ᵃ
4. Peter liest die Stellenanzeigen. Er will eine Stelle finden.
5. Claudia kauft eine Kinokarte. Sie will den neuen Film sehen.

ᵃto avoid

A. 1. Erika spart, um sich ein neues Auto zu kaufen. 2. Richard räumt sein Zimmer auf, um seine Armbanduhr zu finden. 3. Stefan fährt mit der U-Bahn, um den dichten Autoverkehr zu vermeiden. 4. Peter liest die Stellenanzeigen, um eine Stelle zu finden. 5. Claudia kauft eine Kinokarte, um den neuen Film zu sehen.

B In der Freizeit. Alle müssen entscheiden, was sie in ihrer Freizeit machen wollen oder können. Bilden Sie Sätze mit dem Ausdruck **anstatt . . . zu . . .**

MODELL: Susanne hilft dem Professor. Sie geht abends nicht aus. → Susanne hilft dem Professor, anstatt abends auszugehen.

1. Grace geht abends ins Theater. Sie besucht keine Freunde.
2. Anja fährt nach Spanien. Sie bleibt nicht in Berlin.
3. Der Professor kocht zu Hause. Er geht nicht ins Restaurant.
4. Daniela macht Urlaub in Österreich. Sie reist nicht ins Ausland.
5. Gürkan macht abends einen Sprachkurs. Er bleibt nicht zu Hause.
6. Klaus beschäftigt sich mit seiner Arbeit. Er ruht sich nicht aus.

B. 1. Grace geht abends ins Theater, anstatt Freunde zu besuchen. 2. Anja fährt nach Spanien, anstatt in Berlin zu bleiben. 3. Der Professor kocht zu Hause, anstatt ins Restaurant zu gehen. 4. Daniela macht Urlaub in Österreich, anstatt ins Ausland zu fahren. 5. Gürkan macht abends einen Sprachkurs, anstatt zu Hause zu bleiben. 6. Klaus beschäftigt sich mit seiner Arbeit, anstatt sich auszuruhen.

PERSPEKTIVEN

Die Residenz in Würzburg. Hier finden Vorlesungen der Julius-Maximilians-Universität statt.

HÖREN SIE ZU!
AUSLÄNDISCHE STUDENTEN ZU GAST IN WÜRZBURG

Sie hören ein kurzes Interview mit zwei ausländischen Studenten in Würzburg.

A Sarah und Magnus. Welche Informationen erhalten die Zuhörer? Beantworten Sie die folgenden Fragen. *See answers below.*

1. Woher kommen Sarah und Magnus? Was studieren sie in Würzburg?
2. Arbeiten die beiden auch an der Universität?
3. Welche Fremdsprachen lernt man in den Heimatländern der beiden Studenten? Geben Sie Gründe für diese Sprachwahl an.
4. Ist den beiden Sport in ihrer Freizeit wichtig? Erklären Sie Ihre Antwort.
5. Welche schwedischen Feste feiert Magnus mit seinen Kommilitonen?
6. Warum studieren die beiden in Würzburg?

B Das Auslandsstudium. Möchten Sie im Ausland studieren oder sind Sie vielleicht schon im Ausland zur Schule gegangen? Welche Vor- oder Nachteile kann ein Auslandsstudium mit sich bringen? Was meinen Sie?

A. *Possible answers are:* **1.** Sarah kommt aus Flagstaff, Arizona. Sie studiert Germanistik und Slawistik. Magnus kommt aus Umea in Schweden. Er studiert Germanistik und Naturwissenschaften. **2.** Sarah arbeitet nicht an der Uni, aber Magnus unterrichtet dort Schwedisch. **3.** In Schweden lernt man Englisch, Deutsch, Französisch und Spanisch. In Arizona lernen viele Studenten Spanisch. Deutsch lernen dort nur wenige.

LESEN SIE!

Zum Thema

A. *Examples will vary.*

A Was ist typisch? Oft erwarten wir von Menschen aus anderen Ländern ein anderes Verhalten als unseres, ein anderes Aussehen, andere Kleidung und andere Sitten.[a] Nennen Sie Beispiele Ihrer stereotypischen Erwartungen. Entscheiden Sie zusammen mit Ihren Mitschülern/Mitschülerinnen, welche dieser Gedanken am häufigsten gehört werden.

A (continued). **4.** Sarah spielt in ihrer Freizeit Softball. Aber der Sport selbst ist ihr vielleicht gar
[a]*customs* nicht so wichtig. Sie betont eher, dass es schön ist, mit anderen Nationalitäten zusammen zu spielen. Für Magnus ist Sport in der Freizeit nicht wichtig. Als er gefragt wird, was er in seiner Freizeit macht, erwähnt er Sport nicht einmal. **5.** Im Sommer feiert er manchmal mit seinen Kommilitonen die Mittsommernachtsfeier und am dreizehnten Dezember das Fest der Heiligen Lucia. **6.** Sarah studiert in Würzburg, weil ihr die Stadt gefällt, und Magnus studiert dort, weil die Universität von Würzburg die Partneruniversität der Uni in seiner Heimatstadt Umea ist.

WORTSCHATZ ZUM HÖRTEXT

außerdem	*additionally*
zweisprachig	*bilingual*
der Austauschstudent	*exchange student*
das Fest der Heiligen Lucia	*festival of St. Lucia (a Swedish holiday)*
abbrechen	*to break off*

B. *Answers will vary.*

KULTURSPIEGEL

Viele Universitäten haben eine oder mehrere Partneruniversitäten im Ausland. Oft erhalten Studenten, die an einem Austauschprogramm zwischen Partneruniversitäten teilnehmen, finanzielle oder andere Unterstützung durch das Austauschprogramm.

B Was ist typisch oder stereotypisch deutsch? Welche Wörter und Ausdrücke fallen Ihnen zu den folgenden Themen ein? Machen Sie eine zusätzliche Liste mit anderen Eigenschaften und Verhaltensweisen, die für Sie typisch deutsch sind.

1. Essen
2. Frisur
3. Kleidung

4. Musik
5. Feiern
6. Reisen

B. Answers will vary.

In den fünfziger Jahren kamen viele ausländische Arbeiter nach Deutschland.

Die Suche nach den Deutschen

Am Anfang schien es leicht. Schließlich sind wir in Deutschland, und einen Deutschen zu treffen sollte nicht schwer sein, wir hatten sogar gedacht, wir würden schon eine ganze Reihe kennen. Jetzt nicht mehr. Jetzt wissen wir, daß das so einfach nicht ist, und ich habe gewisse

5 Befürchtungen, daß wir nach Brasilien zurückkehren, ohne einen einzigen Deutschen gesehen zu haben. Das habe ich zufällig entdeckt, als ich mit meinem Freund Dieter sprach, den ich für einen Deutschen gehalten hatte.

„Jetzt bin ich doch wahrhaftig schon ein Jahr in Deutschland, wie die
10 Zeit vergeht", sagte ich, als wir in einer Kneipe am Savignyplatz saßen.

„Ja", sagte er. „Die Zeit vergeht schnell, und du hast Deutschland nun gar nicht kennengelernt."

„Was heißt das, nicht kennengelernt? Ich bin doch die ganze Zeit über kaum fort gewesen."

15 „Na eben. Berlin ist nicht Deutschland. Das hier hat mit dem wirklichen Deutschland überhaupt nichts zu tun."

„Darauf war ich nicht gefaßt. Wenn Berlin nicht Deutschland ist, dann weiß ich nicht mehr, was ich denken soll, dann ist alles, was ich bis heute über Deutschland gelernt habe, falsch."

20 „Glaubst du etwa, daß eine Stadt wie Berlin, voller Menschen aus aller Herren Länder, wo nichts so schwierig ist, wie ein Restaurant zu finden, das nicht italienisch, jugoslawisch, chinesisch oder griechisch ist – alles, nur nicht deutsch –, und wo das Mittagessen für neunzig Prozent der Bevölkerung aus Döner Kebab besteht, wo du dein ganzes
25 Leben zubringen kannst, ohne ein einziges Wort Deutsch zu sprechen, wo alle sich wie Verrückte anziehen und mit Frisuren herumlaufen, die aussehen wie ein Modell der Berliner Philharmonie, da glaubst du, das sei Deutschland?"

„Na ja, also ich dachte immer, ist doch so, oder? Schließlich ist
30 Berlin . . ."

„Da irrst du dich aber gewaltig. Berlin ist nicht Deutschland. Deutschland, das ist zum Beispiel die Gegend, aus der ich komme."

„Vielleicht hast du recht. Schließlich bist du Deutscher und mußt wissen, wovon du redest."

35 „Ich bin kein Deutscher."

WORTSCHATZ ZUM LESEN

düster	gloomy
unbeholfen	helpless
verschlossen	reserved
ähneln	to be similar
die Erfindung	invention
die Entdeckung	discovery
anspielen	to allude to
bescheiden	modestly
enttäuscht	disappointed
bewerkstelligen	to manage
die Schande	shame
geschieden	divorced

KULTURSPIEGEL

João Ubaldo Ribeiro wurde 1941 in Brasilien geboren. 1991 verbrachte er ein Jahr in Berlin und schrieb für die „Frankfurter Rundschau" diese humorvollen Kolumnen über seine Eindrücke und Erlebnisse. Weitere dieser amüsanten Aufsätze erschienen in „Ein Brasilianer in Berlin". Seit 1991 lebt er in Rio de Janeiro.

„Wie bitte? Entweder bin ich verrückt, oder du machst mich erst verrückt. Hast du nicht gerade gesagt, du seist in einer wirklich deutschen Gegend geboren?"

„Ja, aber das will in diesem Fall nichts heißen. Die Gegend ist deutsch, aber ich fühle mich nicht als Deutscher. Ich finde, die Deutschen sind ein düsteres, unbeholfenes, verschlossenes Volk . . . Nein, ich bin kein Deutscher, ich identifiziere mich viel mehr mit Völkern wie deinem, das sind fröhliche, entspannte, lachende Menschen, die offen sind . . . Nein, ich bin kein Deutscher." 40

„Also laß mal gut sein, Dieter, natürlich bist du Deutscher, bist in Deutschland geboren, siehst aus wie ein Deutscher, deine Muttersprache ist Deutsch . . ." 45

„Meine Sprache ist nicht Deutsch. Ich spreche zwar deutsch, aber in Wahrheit ist meine Muttersprache der Dialekt aus meiner Heimat, der ähnelt dem Deutschen, ist aber keins. 50

Obwohl ich jahrelang hier wohne, fühle ich mich wohler, wenn ich meinen Dialekt spreche, das ist viel unmittelbarer. Und wenn ich zu Hause nicht den Dialekt unserer Heimat spreche, dann versteht meine Großmutter kein Wort."

„Halt mal, du bringst mich ja völlig durcheinander. Erst sagst du, deine Heimat sei wirklich deutsch, und jetzt sagst du, dort spricht man nicht die Sprache Deutschlands. Das verstehe ich nicht." 55

„Ganz einfach. Was du die Sprache Deutschlands nennst, ist Hochdeutsch, und das gibt es nicht, es ist eine Erfindung, etwas Abstraktes. Niemand spricht Hochdeutsch, nur im Fernsehen und in den Kursen vom Goethe-Institut, alles gelogen. Der wirkliche Deutsche spricht zu Hause kein Hochdeutsch, die ganze Familie würde denken, er sei verrückt geworden. Nicht einmal die Regierenden sprechen Hochdeutsch, ganz im Gegenteil, du brauchst dir nur ein paar Reden anzuhören. Es wird immer deutlicher, daß du die Deutschen wirklich nicht kennst." 60 65

Nach dieser Entdeckung unternahmen wir verschiedene Versuche, einen Deutschen kennenzulernen, aber alle, auch wenn wir uns noch so anstrengten, schlugen unweigerlich fehl. Unter unseren Freunden in Berlin gibt es nicht einen einzigen Deutschen. In Zahlen ausgedrückt ist das etwa so: 40% halten sich für Berliner und meinen, die Deutschen seien ein exotisches Volk, das weit weg wohnt; 30% fühlen sich durch die Frage beleidigt und wollen wissen, ob wir auf irgend etwas anspielen, und rufen zu einer Versammlung gegen den Nationalismus auf; 15% sind Ex-Ossis, die sich nicht daran gewöhnen können, daß sie keine Ossis mehr sein sollen; und die restlichen 15% fühlen sich nicht als Deutsche, dieses düstere, unbeholfene, verschlossene Volk usw. usw. 70 75

Da uns hier nicht mehr viel Zeit bleibt, wird es langsam ernst. Wir beschlossen also, bescheiden in einige Reisen zu investieren. Zunächst wählten wir München und freuten uns schon alle über die Aussicht, 80

endlich einige Deutsche kennenzulernen, als Dieter uns besuchte und
uns voller Verachtung erklärte, in München würden wir keine Deutschen
finden, sondern Bayern – eine Sache sei Deutschland, eine andere
Bayern, es gebe keine größeren Unterschiede auf dieser Welt. Leicht
85 enttäuscht fuhren wir dennoch hin, es gefiel uns sehr, aber wir kamen
mit diesem dummen Eindruck zurück, daß wir Deutschland nicht
gesehen hatten – es ist nicht leicht, das zu bewerkstelligen. Noch weiß
ich nicht recht, wie ich der Schande entgehen kann, daß wir nach
unserer Rückkehr aus Deutschland in Brasilien gestehen müssen, wir
90 hätten Deutschland nicht kennengelernt. Eins ist jedoch sicher: Ich werde
mich beim DAAD wegen falscher Versprechungen beschweren und
deutlich machen, daß sie mich beim nächsten Mal gefälligst nach
Deutschland bringen sollen, sonst sind wir geschiedene Leute.

João Ubaldo Ribeiro (1941–   )

Zum Text

A Ein Brasilianer in Deutschland. Beantworten Sie die Fragen.

1. Warum denkt der Erzähler, dass sie „nach Brasilien zurückkehren
   werden, ohne einen einzigen Deutschen gesehen zu haben"?
2. Wie erklärt Dieter seine Aussage, dass Berlin nicht Deutschland
   sei? dass er kein Deutscher sei?
3. Wie werden die Deutschen in diesem Text beschrieben?

B Briefwechsel. Was hat der Brasilianer von seinem Aufenthalt in
Deutschland erwartet? Waren diese Erwartungen realistisch oder
unrealistisch? Warum war er am Ende des Aufenthalts enttäuscht?[a]
Was will er nämlich vom DAAD?

1. Schreiben Sie den Brief des Erzählers an den DAAD, in dem er
   sich über die „falschen Versprechungen" beschwert.[b]
2. Ist die Beschwerde des Erzählers begründet[c] oder unbegründet?
   Hat er wirklich keine Deutschen kennen gelernt? Schreiben Sie
   den Antwortbrief der Institution.

[a]*disappointed* [b]*complains* [c]*justified*

Zur Interpretation

● Reaktionen. Diskutieren Sie den folgenden Textauszug.

„Dreißig Prozent fühlen sich durch die Frage beleidigt und wollen
wissen, ob wir auf irgend etwas anspielen, und rufen zu einer
Versammlung gegen den Nationalismus auf."

1. Auf welche Frage haben die Leute vielleicht so reagiert?
2. Warum rufen die Befragten zu einer „Versammlung gegen den
   Nationalismus auf"?

KULTURSPIEGEL

DAAD ist eine Kurzform für den
Deutschen Akademischen
Austauschdienst. Das ist eine
Institution, die deutsche Studenten und
Akademiker im Ausland und umgekehrt,
ausländische Studenten und
Akademiker in Deutschland, finanziell
unterstützt und akademisch betreut.

A. *Answers will vary. Possible answers are:* **1.** Er
denkt das, weil es den typischen Deutschen, der
dem Klischee entspricht, eigentlich nicht gibt und
weil die Deutschen, die sie treffen, sich selbst
nicht als typische Deutsche verstehen. **2.** Berlin
ist nach Dieters Aussage nicht Deutschland, weil
die Menschen dort aus der ganzen Welt kommen, die Küche international ist und man sein
Leben dort zubringen kann, ohne ein einziges
Wort Deutsch zu sprechen. Er selbst bezeichnet
sich nicht als Deutscher, weil er dem Klischee
des Deutschen nicht entsprechen will und weil
er nicht Hochdeutsch spricht, sondern einen
Dialekt. **3.** In dem Text werden die typischen
Deutschen als düster, unbeholfen und
verschlossen beschrieben.

TIPP ZUM SCHREIBEN

Remember that to report in German
what someone else has said you use
Subjunctive I. Use of Subjunctive I
indicates that the writer makes no
claim for the accuracy of the
statements. To review Subjunctive I,
refer to Kapitel 30.

B. *Letters will vary.*

Answers will vary.

INTERAKTION

● **Nationalität.** Warum sagt man, dass eine Person eine Nationalität (Deutscher, Amerikaner, Kanadier, Mexikaner und so weiter) hat? Was muss man haben, um zu einer gewissen Nationalität zu gehören? Was meinen Sie, stimmen folgende Aussagen oder nicht? Besprechen Sie sie mit einem Partner / einer Partnerin und versuchen Sie, Ihre Meinung zu begründen.

Man gehört zu einer gewissen Nationalität,
1. wenn man einen Pass des Landes hat.
2. wenn man sich mit dem Land, der Politik oder dem Volk identifiziert.
3. wenn man die Sprache dieses Landes ohne Akzent spricht.
4. wenn man dort geboren ist.
5. wenn man mindestens einen Dialekt des Landes spricht.
6. wenn man die Kultur versteht.
7. wenn man die Ironie des Landes versteht.

1. Das stimmt. 2. Das stimmt nicht.
3. Das stimmt nicht. 4. *Answers will vary.*
5. Das stimmt nicht. 6. Das stimmt nicht.
7. Das stimmt nicht.

KULTURSPIEGEL

Während zum Beispiel alle in den USA geborene Menschen automatisch Amerikaner sind, bestimmt in Deutschland die Nationalität der Eltern die Staatsbürgerschaft der Kinder. Die Regelung in den USA stützt sich auf das sogenannte *Jus soli* (Latein: das Recht des Bodens). In Deutschland, ebenso wie in Österreich und der Schweiz, gilt das *Jus Sanguinis* (Latein: das Recht des Blutes). Erst seit kurzem gibt es auch die doppelte Staatsbürgerschaft für alle in Deutschland geborenen Kinder ausländischer Eltern.

SCHREIBEN SIE!

Ein multikultureller Stadtführer

● Schreiben Sie (entweder einzeln oder als Team) einen multikulturellen Führer für Ihre Heimatstadt. Listen Sie die Vereine, Kirchen, Restaurants, Geschäfte bzw. Menschen Ihrer Heimat auf, die etwas mit einer besonderen ethnischen Gruppe zu tun haben und beschreiben Sie sie. Versuchen Sie, auch etwas von der Geschichte der Menschen zu erfahren. Wenn möglich, ergänzen Sie den Text mit Bildern oder Visitenkarten.[a]

[a]*business cards*

Purpose:	To research and describe the multicultural aspects of your town
Audience:	Students and adults
Subject:	The ethnic and multicultural resources in your town
Structure:	Descriptive catalogue or guide

Texts will vary.

TIPP ZUM SCHREIBEN

Most towns have organizations, businesses, and individuals with immigrant roots: churches with foreign language services, ethnic restaurants, businesses started by immigrants, special ethnic social clubs, and foreign-born professionals serving the community. Through this project you can get to know your town and its inhabitants better. You may want to expand the range to cover neighboring towns, a larger geographic area, the county, or the state.

Schreibmodell

Headings can indicate categories, nationalities, and/or countries of origin.

Information about key persons and their histories makes for more interesting reading.

To vary the sentence structure, the writer begins the sentence with an infinitive clause with **zu**.

The days of the week are not capitalized when used as adverbs.

Cafés und Restaurants

Österreich

Greta's Café & Bakery

(24 Pleasant St.) wurde 1994 von der Österreicherin Greta Reineke gegründet, die eine reiche Auswahl an vollwertigen Brotwaren, Torten, Getränken und Gebäck anbietet. Um Gäste zum Verweilen anzuregen, bietet Frau Reineke bequeme Stühle und Tische und viele Illustrierten. Frau Reineke spricht gern Deutsch mit ihren Kunden. Montags bis samstags von 6.00 bis 18.00 Uhr geöffnet; sonntags 7.00 bis 15.00 Uhr (Tel. 465-1709)

Kleider nach Maß und Änderungen

Vietnam

Mihn Tailors

(12 Federal St.) ist eine Schneiderei, die die vietnamesische Immigrantin Gabrielle Mihn 1988 gründete. Frau Mihn lernte das Schneidern in ihrer Heimat Cantho. 1986 verließ sie Vietnam. Im November 1988 machte sie ihre Schneiderei in den USA auf. Frau Mihn macht Änderungen aller Art und kann auf Wunsch maßgeschneiderte Kleidung anfertigen. (Tel. 462-5617)

The writer uses relative pronouns and relative clauses to give more detailed information.

Schreibstrategien

Vor dem Schreiben

If you are working individually, you should aim to have a minimum of five entries in your guide; if you are working as a team, there should be five entries per team member.

- Collect the names and addresses of ethnic or immigrant-owned stores, businesses, restaurants, churches, and other organizations. To get ideas, walk through the nearest main business district and notice any

Menschen und Kulturen in unserer Gegend

Italien

Giuseppe's *(257 Walden St.)* ist ein Restaurant, ~~dem~~ (das) frische hausgemachte Nudelgerichte anbietet und das Giuseppe Masia gehört. Herr Masia kommt aus Sardinien und hat von seiner Mutter kochen gelernt. Er und seine amerikanische Frau ~~kommen~~ (kamen) vor fünf Jahren ~~nach~~ (in die) USA, um hier ihr Traum-Restaurant auf(zu)machen. Montags bis samstags von 11.00 bis 20.00 Uhr geöffnet. Sonntag Ruhetag. (Tel. 837-2225)

Multikulturell

Der **International Club** am Fokus College ist ein Treffpunkt für die mehr als 40 ausländischen Studenten, ~~wer~~ (die) auf dem Campus leben und studieren. Mitglieder treffen (sich) einmal in der Woche mit Studenten, mit ~~den~~ (denen) sie über das Leben an einer amerikanischen Hochschule diskutieren und die Feste des Heimatlands feiern können. (Tel. 836-1763)

businesses with foreign or ethnic connections, or look through the phone book. Ask your family and neighbors for additional ideas.

- Now select the resources to include in your guide. Either make a selection that demonstrates the wide range of ethnicity in your area or focus on resources from a specific area or country.

- Phone or visit the establishments you've chosen and talk to the people in charge. Find out about their personal histories: When did they (or their families) immigrate and why? How did they develop their interests and skills? When and why did they start their work? Take detailed notes and try to collect a business card or an ad. Be sure to thank people for their help.

- Think about how you will organize the information—by type of organization, country of origin, language, or some other way.

- Decide on a format. How will you draw the reader's attention to the name and address of each entry? Will you use a simple sentence or longer paragraphs to describe each business or organization?

Beim Schreiben

- Keep notes, business cards, and other material close at hand.

- Make a model of the format you intend to use.

- Start by writing all the entries for one category. Make sure the content of each entry is similar. Then move on to the next category.

- Vary the way you tell stories about individuals. Keep it interesting! Make sure contact information is clear and includes addresses, phone numbers, and the names of contact persons.

Nach dem Schreiben

- Reread your entries for consistency. If important information is missing, add it. Think about a title for your guide and prepare a draft title page. Write an introductory paragraph.

- Exchange drafts with a peer editor and read each other's work critically. Make some positive comments, suggestions for improvement, and return the draft guides.

- Prepare a revised guide that includes all changes and additions.

Stimmt alles?

- Position business cards or other materials you've collected (such as ads) and make your final cover page.

- Hand in your guide, making sure to include the names of all authors.

WORTSCHATZ

Substantive	Nouns
die **Arbeitskraft, ⸚e**	labor force
die **Ausnahme, -n**	exception
die **Befürchtung, -en**	fear
die **Essgewohnheit, -en**	eating habit
die **Genauigkeit**	accuracy; exactness
die **Nichtakzeptanz**	nonacceptance
die **Ordnung**	order
die **Pünktlichkeit**	promptness; punctuality
die **Regel, -n**	rule
die **Sauberkeit**	cleanliness
die **Verabredung, -en**	appointment; date
die **Verachtung**	contempt
die **Versprechung, -en**	promise
der **Akzent, -e**	accent
der **Ärger**	annoyance; anger
der **Auswanderer, -** / die **Auswanderin, -nen**	emigrant
der **Eindruck, ⸚e**	impression
der **Einwanderer, -** / die **Einwanderin, -nen**	immigrant
das **Asyl**	political asylum
das **Bedürfnis, -se**	necessity
das **Gericht, -e**	meal; dish

Verben	Verbs
an•nehmen (nimmt an), nahm an, angenommen	to accept, take on
beachten	to observe
bei•tragen zu (trägt bei), trug bei, beigetragen	to contribute to
bestätigen	to prove
dar•stellen	to depict, portray; to present
duzen	to address someone with **du**
ein•fallen (fällt ein), fiel ein, ist eingefallen	to come to mind

einhalten (hält ein), hielt ein, eingehalten	to keep (*an appointment*)
sich entfernen	to remove oneself
gestehen, gestand, gestanden	to admit
sich halten an (+ *acc.*) **(hält), hielt, gehalten**	to keep to, stick to/with
siezen	to address someone with **Sie**
vereinbaren	to arrange
verfolgen	to persecute
sich verspäten	to be late
willkommen heißen, hieß, geheißen	to welcome

Adjektive und Adverbien	Adjectives and adverbs
aufgeschlossen	open-minded, receptive
beschildert	labeled
deutlich	clear(ly)
dringend	desperate(ly)
gewaltig	powerful(ly); tremendous(ly)
inzwischen	in the meantime
multikulturell	multicultural(ly)
rechtlich	legal(ly)
unmittelbar	direct(ly)
unvoreingenommen	unbiased
unweigerlich	inevitable; inevitably

Sie wissen schon	You already know
die **Ausländerfeindlichkeit**	xenophobia
der **Ausländer, -** / die **Ausländerin, -nen**	foreigner
der **Schritt, -e**	step
beeinflussen	to influence
unbedingt	absolutely, in any case, necessarily

PLANNING GUIDE • CLASSROOM MANAGEMENT

OBJECTIVES

Communication
- Talk about the environment, pp. 230–231.
- Talk about the effects of tourism on the environment, pp. 232–233.

Grammar
- Review use of the passive voice, pp. 234–235.
- Review present perfect and past perfect forms of the passive voice, p. 237.
- Use the future tense, pp. 238–239.

Culture
- Learn about the effects of *Waldsterben* in various parts of Germany, p. 231.
- Learn about different modes of transportation and their effects on the environment, p. 233.
- Get to know the environment near you, p. 242.

Recycling
- Review the passive voice, pp. 234–236.

STRATEGIES

Listening Strategies
- Listen to a story about 3 European environmentalists, p. 240.

Speaking Strategies
- Re-tell a story you have read, pp. 245–246.

Reading Strategies
- Read a short story, pp. 241–242.

Writing Strategies
- Write a short story, pp. 244–246.

Connecting Cultures Strategies
- Compare your relationship with the environment to that of various Germans, pp. 231, 233.

PROGRAM RESOURCES

Print
- *Arbeitsheft* (Workbook), pp. 161–178
- *Arbeitsheft* (Workbook), Teacher's Edition, pp. 161–178

Audiovisual
- Overhead Transparencies 35.1–35.G2
- Audio Program, Cassette 6A, 7B/CD 7, 9
- Audioscript, pp. 79–85

Technology
- Annenberg *Fokus Deutsch* Video Series, *Folge 35*
- www.mcdougallittell.com

Assessment Program Options
- *Prüfung, Kapitel 35*, Assessment Program, pp. 137–146
- Audio Program, Cassette 8B/CD 10
- Audioscript, p. 114
- Teacher's Resource CD-ROM

DAY 1

Note: (1) Please see TE, pp. 228E–228J, for other suggestions not referenced in these plans. (2) Not all homework options need be assigned.

CHAPTER OPENER

- Quick Start Review: Vocabulary (TE, p. 228E). 5 MIN
- Discuss the photos on pp. 228–229 as a class (TE, p. 228E). 5 MIN

VIDEOTHEK

- Do *Akt. A*, p. 230, silently, then check their answers with a partner. Do the follow-up activity in the Teaching Suggestions as a class (TE, p. 228F). 10 MIN
- Read through *Akt. B*, pp. 230–231, then play *Folge I: Auf Kosten der Umwelt.* Have students do the activity with a partner (TE, p. 228F). 13 MIN
- Do the warm-up activity in the Teaching Suggestions for *Folge II: Umweltschutz zu Hause* as a class (TE, p. 228F). 5 MIN
- Read through *Akt. A*, p. 231, then play the episode. Have students do the activity while watching the video, then discuss the answers. 12 MIN

Homework Options:

- *Arbeitsheft*, pp. 161–162, *Videothek, Akt. B–C*

DAY 2

VIDEOTHEK

- Quick Start Review 1: Relative clauses (TE, p. 228E). 5 MIN
- *Arbeitsheft*, p. 161, *Videothek, Akt. A.* 4 MIN
- Do *Akt. B*, p. 231, as a class (TE, p. 228F). 16 MIN
- Do *Akt. C*, p. 231, in small groups. Play the video again so students can check their answers (TE, p. 228F). 10 MIN
- *Arbeitsheft*, p. 163, audio *Akt. D.* 8 MIN
- *Arbeitsheft*, p. 164, *Akt. F.* 7 MIN

Homework Options:

- *Arbeitsheft*, p. 163, *Videothek, Akt. E*
- *Arbeitsheft*, p. 164, *Videothek, Akt. G*

DAY 3

VOKABELN

- Quick Start Review 1: Vocabulary (TE, p. 228G). 5 MIN
- Present the vocabulary on p. 232 (TE, p. 228G). 8 MIN
- Do *Akt. A*, pp. 232–233, silently, then check answers as a class. Conclude with comprehension questions. 8 MIN
- Do *Akt. B*, p. 233, with a partner, then do the follow-up activity in the Teaching Suggestions as a class (TE, p. 228G). 12 MIN
- Do *Akt. C, Schritt 1*, p. 233, in pairs. Move directly to *Schritt 2.* 10 MIN
- Discuss *Akt. C, Schritt 2*, p. 233, as a class. Create a large chart on the board to record all answers (TE, p. 228G). 7 MIN

Homework Options:

- *Arbeitsheft*, pp. 165–166, *Vokabeln, Akt. C–E*

DAY 4

VOKABELN

- Quick Start Review 2: Modal verbs in the perfect tense (TE, p. 228G). 4 MIN
- *Arbeitsheft*, p. 165, audio *Akt. A.* 7 MIN

STRUKTUREN

- Present the passive voice I on pp. 234–235 using OHT 35.G1 (TE, p. 228H). 8 MIN
- Do *Übung A*, p. 236, silently, then check answers as a class by having several students read the text aloud. Conclude by asking a few comprehension questions. 10 MIN
- Do *Übung B*, p. 236, in pairs. Students should take turns asking and answering (TE, p. 228H). 8 MIN
- Present the passive voice II on p. 237 by using OHT 35.G1 (TE, p. 228H). 8 MIN
- Do *Übung A*, p. 238, as a class. 5 MIN

Homework Options:

- *Übung C*, p. 236
- *Arbeitsheft*, pp. 169–170, *Strukturen, Akt. E–G*

PACING GUIDE • SAMPLE LESSON PLAN, 50-MINUTE SCHEDULE

STRUKTUREN

- Quick Start Review 1: Simple past (TE, p. 228H). 4 MIN
- Do *Übung B*, p. 238, silently, then check the answers with partners. Have pairs come up with more examples to share with the class. 10 MIN
- *Arbeitsheft*, p. 169, audio *Akt. C*. 6 MIN
- Present the future tense on pp. 238–239 using OHT 35.2 and 35.G2 (TE, p. 228H). 8 MIN
- Do *Übung A*, p. 239, in small groups (TE, p. 228H). 14 MIN
- Do *Übung B*, p. 239, silently, then share answers as a class. 8 MIN

Homework Options:

- *Arbeitsheft*, pp. 172–173, *Strukturen, Akt. J–K*

STRUKTUREN

- Quick Start Review 2: Vocabulary (TE, p. 228H). 5 MIN
- *Arbeitsheft*, p. 171, audio *Akt. H.* 7 MIN

PERSPEKTIVEN

- Read through *Hören Sie zu!*, p. 240, listen to the recording, and do the activity. Check answers as a class (TE, p. 228I). 10 MIN
- Do *Zum Thema, Akt. A, Schritt 1*, p. 240. End with a class discussion of *Schritt 2* (TE, p. 228I). 10 MIN
- Do *Zum Thema, Akt. B*, p. 240, as a class (TE, p. 228I). 4 MIN
- Start reading the text *Herr Munzel hört das Gras wachsen*, p. 241, in groups. Encourage students to help each other understand the text (TE, p. 228J). 10 MIN
- Do *Zum Text, Akt. A*, p. 242, as a class (TE, p. 228J). 4 MIN

Homework Options:

- Finish reading *Herr Munzel hört das Gras wachsen*, pp. 241–242
- *Zum Text, Akt. B*, p. 245
- *Arbeitsheft*, pp. 175–177, *Perspektiven, Akt. C–D*

PERSPEKTIVEN

- Quick Start Review 1: Vocabulary (TE, p. 228I). 4 MIN
- Briefly discuss the answers to *Zum Text, Akt. B*, p. 243 as a class. 5 MIN
- Discuss *Zur Interpretation*, p. 243, in small groups, then end with a class comparison of these discussions (TE, p. 228J). 12 MIN
- *Interaktion*, p. 243. Ask for volunteers to tell the story to the class. 12 MIN
- Begin *Schreiben Sie!* by discussing the assignment, *Tipp zum Schreiben*, and *Schreibmodell* (TE, p. 228J). 5 MIN
- Do *Vor dem Schreiben*, p. 245 and begin *Beim Schreiben*, p. 246. 12 MIN

Homework Options:

- Complete *Vor dem Schreiben*, p. 245, and *Beim Schreiben*, p. 246, and write the first draft of the short story

PERSPEKTIVEN

- Quick Start Review 2: Prepositions (TE, p. 228I) 4 MIN
- *Nach dem Schreiben*, p. 246. Then begin the final version of the short story. 11 MIN
- Questions and review. 5 MIN
- *Prüfung, Kapitel 35.* 30 MIN

Homework Options:

- Finish the final draft of the story
- *Arbeitsheft*, p. 178, *Perspektiven, Akt. E–F*

DAY 1

Note: (1) Please see TE, pp. 228E–228J, for other suggestions not referenced in these plans. (2) Not all homework options need be assigned.

CHAPTER OPENER

- Quick Start Review: Vocabulary (TE, p. 228E). 5 MIN
- Discuss the photos on pp. 228–229 (TE, p. 228E). 5 MIN

VIDEOTHEK

- Do *Akt. A*, p. 230, silently, then check answers (TE, p. 228F). 6 MIN
- Read through *Akt. B*, pp. 230–231, then play *Folge I.* 16 MIN
- *Arbeitsheft*, p. 161, audio *Akt. A.* 5 MIN
- Block Schedule activity: Expansion (TE, p. 228F). 10 MIN
- Do the warm-up activity (TE, p. 228F) for *Folge II*, then play the episode. Do *Akt. A*, p. 231. 17 MIN
- Do *Akt. B*, p. 231 (TE, p. 228F). 16 MIN
- Do *Akt. C*, p. 231, in small groups (TE, p. 228F). 10 MIN

Homework Options:

- *Arbeitsheft*, pp. 162–163, *Videothek, Akt. B–C, E*

DAY 2

VIDEOTHEK

- Quick Start Review 1: Relative clauses (TE, p. 228E). 5 MIN
- *Arbeitsheft*, p. 164, audio *Akt. F.* 7 MIN

VOKABELN

- Present the vocabulary on p. 232 (TE, p. 228G). 8 MIN
- Do *Akt. A*, pp. 232–233, silently, then check answers. 8 MIN
- Do *Akt. B* and *Akt. C, Schritt 1*, p. 233, in pairs (TE, p. 228G). 22 MIN
- Discuss *Akt. C, Schritt 2*, p. 233 (TE, p. 228G). 7 MIN
- Block Schedule activity: Fun Break (TE, pp. 228F–G). 10 MIN
- *Arbeitsheft*, p. 165, audio *Akt. A.* 7 MIN

STRUKTUREN

- Present the passive voice I on pp. 234–235 using OHT 35.G1 (TE, p. 228H). 8 MIN
- Do *Übung A*, p. 236, silently, then check answers. 8 MIN

Homework Options:

- *Arbeitsheft*, pp. 165–166, *Akt. C–E*, and pp. 169–170, *Akt. E–G*
- *Übung C*, p. 236

DAY 3

STRUKTUREN

- Quick Start Review 1: Simple past (TE, p. 228H). 5 MIN
- Do *Übung B*, p. 236, in pairs. (TE, p. 228H). 8 MIN
- *Arbeitsheft*, p, 167, audio *Akt. A–B.* 10 MIN
- Present the passive voice II on p. 237 by using OHT 35.G1 (TE, p. 228H). 9 MIN
- Do *Übung A*, p. 238, as a class. 6 MIN
- Do *Übung B*, p. 238, silently, then check the answers with partners. 10 MIN
- *Arbeitsheft*, pp. 168–169, audio *Akt. C–D.* 10 MIN
- Block Schedule activity: Expansion, work in small groups. Discuss (TE, p. 228I). 10 MIN
- Present the future tense on pp. 238–239 using OHT 35.2 and 35.G2 (TE, p. 228H). 8 MIN
- Do *Übung A*, p. 239, in small groups (TE, p. 228H). 14 MIN

Homework Options:

- *Arbeitsheft*, pp. 172–173, *Strukturen, Akt. J–K*

DAY 4

STRUKTUREN

- Quick Start Review 2: Vocabulary (TE, p. 228H). 5 MIN
- Do *Übung B*, p. 239, silently, then check answers. 8 MIN
- *Arbeitsheft*, pp. 171–172, audio *Akt. H–I.* 10 MIN

PERSPEKTIVEN

- *Hören Sie zu!*, activity, p. 240 (TE, p. 228I).10 MIN
- *Arbeitsheft*, p. 174, audio *Akt. A.* 5 MIN
- Block Schedule activity: Fun Break (TE, p. 228J). 10 MIN
- Do *Zum Thema, Akt. A–B*, p. 240. (TE, p. 228I). 14 MIN
- Read the text, p. 241, in groups (TE, p. 228J). 13 MIN
- Do *Zum Text, Akt. A–B*, pp. 242–243 (TE, p. 228J). 9 MIN
- Begin *Schreiben Sie!* by discussing the assignment (TE, p. 228J). 5 MIN
- *Vor dem Schreiben*, p. 245. 6 MIN

Homework Options:

- Complete *Vor dem Schreiben* and *Beim Schreiben*, pp. 245–246, and write the first draft
- *Arbeitsheft*, pp.175–177, *Akt. C–D*

DAY 5

PERSPEKTIVEN

- Quick Start Review 2: Prepositions (TE, p. 228I). 5 MIN
- Discuss *Zur Interpretation*, p. 243, in small groups, then end with a class comparison of these discussions (TE, p. 228J). 12 MIN
- *Interaktion*, p. 243. Ask for volunteers to tell the story to the class. 12 MIN
- Do *Nach dem Schreiben*, p. 246, and begin the final version of the short story. 16 MIN
- Block Schedule activity: Peer Teaching (TE, p. 228J). 10 MIN
- Questions and review. 5 MIN
- *Prüfung, Kapitel 35.* 30 MIN

Homework Options:

- Finish the final draft of the story
- *Arbeitsheft*, p. 178, *Perspektiven, Akt. E–F*

Chapter Opener, pp. 228–229

PROGRAM RESOURCES

- Overhead Transparency 35.1

Quick Start Review

♻ Vocabulary
Bilden Sie Sätze.

1. in / sich / an / einem fremden Land / muss / die Regeln / halten / man
2. aufgeschlossen / viele Leute / die Deutschen / seien / sagen / nicht / sehr
3. in Deutschland / sollte / Fremde / nicht / duzen / man
4. beitragen zu / der Kultur / eines Landes / Einwanderer
5. er / seit einem Jahr / erst / in München / und / schon ohne Akzent / Deutsch / lebt / spricht
6. die Essgewohnheiten / eines Volkes / darstellen / einen wichtigen Teil / seiner Kultur

Answers: 1. In einem fremden Land muss man sich an die Regeln halten. 2. Viele Leute sagen, die Deutschen seien nicht sehr aufgeschlossen. 3. In Deutschland sollte man Fremde nicht duzen. 4. Einwanderer tragen zur Kultur eines Landes bei. 5. Er lebt erst seit einem Jahr in München und spricht schon ohne Akzent Deutsch. 6. Die Essgewohnheiten eines Volkes stellen einen wichtigen Teil seiner Kultur dar.

TEACHING SUGGESTIONS

- Photos, pp. 228–229

Have students look at the photos and ask them to describe each. This is a good opportunity to recycle some of the grammar of the previous chapters, such as modals, relative clauses, and adjectives. Ask students how the photos reflect aspects of environmental protection.

TEACHING ALL STUDENTS

Multiple Intelligences Intrapersonal: Have students write down what they personally are doing now or would like to do to protect the environment. Ask *Was machen Sie der Umwelt zuliebe? Was würden Sie gerne in der Zukunft machen?* Let students share their experiences with the class.

CLASSROOM COMMUNITY

Group Activity Have students develop a questionnaire to find out what the class considers today's major environmental concerns. Divide the class into groups of 4. Each group must generate 4 questions for the questionnaire. They must agree on the questions they will present to the class. Each group writes its questions on a sheet of paper and reports them to the class. While the questions are being read, several students write them on the board or on an OHT. The class votes as a group on the questions that should be included on the questionnaire. When it is complete, students break into pairs and poll one another. Their findings are submitted to the teacher, who consolidates them on the board.

Videothek, pp. 230–231

PROGRAM RESOURCES

- Videocassette, *Folge 35*
- *Arbeitsheft*, pp. 161–164
- Audio Program, Cassette 6A/CD 7
- Audioscript, pp. 79–80

Quick Start Review 1

♻ Relative clauses
Ergänzen Sie die Relativpronomen in den Sätzen.

1. Der Brief, _____ du mir geschickt hast, ist nicht angekommen.
2. Die Frau, _____ ich das Geld gegeben habe, ist verschwunden.
3. Die Freunde, mit _____ wir im Urlaub waren, kommen uns morgen besuchen.
4. Der Fluss, _____ die Chemiefirmen in unserer Stadt sehr verschmutzt hatten, ist jetzt sauberer.
5. Der Lehrer, _____ ich am meisten respektierte, unterrichtet immer noch an meiner alten Schule.
6. Die Fußballspieler, _____ am schnellsten laufen, wären gut für unser Team.

Answers: 1. den 2. der 3. denen 4. den 5. den 6. die

Quick Start Review 2

♻ Vocabulary
Ergänzen Sie die Wörter in den Sätzen.
WÖRTER: Arbeitskräfte, Ausnahme, Gerichte, Ordnung, Pünktlichkeit, Verabredungen, verspätet

1. Die _____ bestätigt die Regel.
2. _____ und _____ sollen typisch deutsche Eigenschaften sein.
3. Es ist wichtig, _____ einzuhalten.
4. Einwanderer bringen oft neue _____ mit in ein Land.
5. In den fünfziger Jahren wurden in Deutschland viele _____ gebraucht.

6. Es tut mir leid, dass ich mich _____ habe.

Answers: 1. Ausnahme   2. Ordnung, Pünktlichkeit   3. Verabredungen 4. Gerichte   5. Arbeitskräfte 6. verspätet

TEACHING SUGGESTIONS

• *Folge I: Auf Kosten der Umwelt,* pp. 230–231

Remind students to review the *Wortschatz zum Video* before they watch. Encourage them to take notes during the video so they can ask questions afterwards. Ask students to single out 1–2 facts they found especially interesting while watching the video.

• *Aktivität A,* p. 230

Follow-up: What other associations come to mind when looking at the photos? Ask *Könnte man die gleichen Photos in den USA aufnehmen?*

• *Aktivität B,* pp. 230–231

Warm-up: Ask *Was sind chemische Rohstoffe? Wann und wo benutzen Sie Einweggeschirr? Was ist die Ökobewegung in Deutschland? Gibt es etwas Ähnliches in den USA?*

• *Folge II: Umweltschutz zu Hause,* p. 231

Warm-up: Discuss what students do for the environment. Ask questions like *Was machen Sie, um Energie zu sparen? Was wird bei Ihnen recycelt? Benutzen Sie öffentliche Verkehrsmittel oder fahren Sie mit dem Fahrrad? usw.*

• *Aktivität B,* p. 231

Keep track of students' answers on the board or on an OHT and ask students to write a summary of the class's collective answers. Have them turn this summary into a proposal to do more for the environment.

• *Aktivität C,* p. 231

Follow-up: Have students pretend to interview each other for a TV or radio program. The reporters ask questions such as *Glauben Sie, dass wir die Umwelt schützen müssen? Was tun Sie, um die Umwelt zu schützen? Würden Sie gerne mehr für die Umwelt tun? usw.*

TEACHING ALL STUDENTS

Multiple Intelligences Naturalist: Take students outside. They should take pens and notepads along. Take a walk on the school grounds or in the immediate neighborhood and have them write down ideas on how to clean up or protect certain areas. Collect all their ideas when you get back into the classroom and draw up a list of recommendations for the school administration.

CLASSROOM COMMUNITY

Challenge Give students a list of nouns and have them construct definitions of those nouns using relative clauses. For example, *Campingplatz: Ein Campingplatz ist ein Platz, auf dem man zeltet.*

INTERDISCIPLINARY CONNECTION

Biology: Have students read the *Kulturspiegel,* p. 231, and discuss the notion of *Waldsterben* with them. Ask what they know about environmental problems in this country and what is being done about them. Have students gather more information about environmental issues from their science teacher.

BLOCK SCHEDULE

Expansion Divide students in groups of 4. Each group should come up with 4 ideas for protecting the environment in or around the school. They should present their suggestions to the whole class in writing.

Variety Replay the video without sound, pause after each scene, and have students provide a narration for what they have just seen.

PORTFOLIO

Have students research the environmental agenda of the Green Party in Germany. They could enlist the help of their biology or political science teacher. They will find plenty of information on the Internet. They should name 3 areas that seem to be of major concern to the Greens and give detailed information on what is being suggested to alleviate these problems. Students might need some help with vocabulary for this project. Have them write a summary of their findings and present orally to the class.

RUBRIC   **A** = 13–15 pts.   **B** = 10–12 pts. **C** = 7–9 pts.   **D** = 4–6 pts.   **F** <4 pts.

Writing Criteria	Scale				
Accuracy, organization	1	2	3	4	5
Vocabulary, grammar	1	2	3	4	5
Presentation	1	2	3	4	5

Vokabeln, pp. 232–233

PROGRAM RESOURCES

- *Arbeitsheft*, pp. 165–166
- Audio Program, Cassette 6A/CD 7
- Audioscript, pp. 80–81

Quick Start Review 1

♻ Vocabulary

Ergänzen Sie die Wörter in den Sätzen.

WÖRTER: angenommen, eingefallen, eingehalten, geheißen, gestanden, verspätet

1. Er hat der Polizei _____, dass er das Geld gestohlen hat.
2. Ich konnte dich nicht anrufen, weil mir deine Telefonnummer nicht mehr _____ ist.
3. Sie hat unsere Verabredungen immer _____.
4. Als wir hierher zogen, haben uns alle Nachbarn willkommen _____.
5. Nach seiner Heirat hat er den Namen von seiner Frau _____.
6. Er _____ sich normalerweise nie.

Answers: 1. gestanden   2. eingefallen
3. eingehalten   4. geheißen
5. angenommen   6. verspätet

Quick Start Review 2

♻ Modal verbs in the perfect tense
Bilden Sie Sätze nach dem folgenden Modell.

MODELL: Konntest du schon als Kind Basketball spielen? → *Ja, das habe ich gekonnt.* oder: *Nein, das habe ich nicht gekonnt.*

1. Konntest du schon als Kind Schach spielen?
2. Durftest du als Kind lange aufbleiben?

3. Durftest du als Kind allein einkaufen gehen?
4. Wolltest du als Kind ein Musikinstrument lernen?
5. Wolltest du als Kind an einer Olympiade teilnehmen?
6. Durftest du als Kind deine eigenen Kleider aussuchen?

Answers: 1. Ja, das habe ich gekonnt.
2. Nein, das habe ich nicht gedurft.
3. Ja, das habe ich gedurft.   4. Nein, das habe ich nicht gewollt.   5. Ja, das habe ich gewollt.   6. Ja, das habe ich gedurft.

TEACHING SUGGESTIONS

- Vocabulary, p. 232

Have students ask questions about items on the list. Give example sentences when necessary.

- *Aktivität B*, p. 233

Follow-up: Have each student write a definition of 1 of the vocabulary items on p. 232 on a slip of paper. Call on students to give the definition they have written. The class must guess the word that matches the definition.

- *Aktivität C*, p. 233

Create a large chart on the board to record all answers or have students copy their charts onto poster board and post them in the classroom.

TEACHING ALL STUDENTS

Extra Help Have students write a To Do list for a household. This could include *das Geschirr spülen, die Blumen gießen, die Wäsche waschen, den Müll hinausbringen*. Have them rephrase each item using the passive voice: *Das

Geschirr muss gespült werden. Die Blumen müssen gegossen werden.* If you do not want to teach the passive voice at this point, you could have them use informal imperatives instead.

CLASSROOM COMMUNITY

Dictation Dictate the following text to the class. Put the text on the board or on an OHT when you are done. Have students exchange their dictations and correct them.

Manche Leute sind zu bequem, etwas für die Umwelt zu tun. Es dauert etwas länger, den Müll zu trennen, als einfach alles in einen Abfalleimer zu werfen. Es ist auch nicht immer angenehm, öffentliche Verkehrsmittel zu benutzen. Wenn es regnet, wird man nass und die Busse und Züge sind oft voll, so dass man keinen Sitzplatz bekommt. Aber vielleicht ist das alles besser, als auf der Autobahn im Stau zu stehen.

CULTURE HIGHLIGHTS

Read the *Kulturspiegel* on p. 233 with students and have them comment on the topic of tourism and its implications for the environment. Ask *Warum reist man in andere Länder? Wie ist Reisen am schönsten? Wie umweltfeindlich ist der moderne Massentourismus? usw.*

BLOCK SCHEDULE

Fun Break Play a game called: *Stadt, Land, Fluss, Name, Tier, Beruf*. Have students write the 6 nouns as headings across a piece of paper so that they can fill in columns underneath. The teacher names a letter of the alphabet and students have to fill in 6 nouns with that letter, for example, *N: Nürnberg, Norwegen, Neckar, Nora, Nilpferd, Neurologe.* Whoever finishes first calls out "stop." Go over their choices as a class. Students award themselves 1 point for each correct entry.

Strukturen, pp. 234–239

PROGRAM RESOURCES

- Overhead Transparencies 35.2–35.G2
- *Arbeitsheft,* pp. 167–174
- Audio Program, Cassette 6A/CD 7
- Audioscript, pp. 81–84

Quick Start Review 1

Simple past
Schreiben Sie die Sätze im Imperfekt.
1. Mein Klassenfoto hängt über meinem Schreibtisch.
2. Meine Tasche liegt auf dem Sofa.
3. Der Hund liegt neben dem Bett und schläft.
4. Ich stelle die Leiter an den Baum.
5. Er fährt mit meinem Fahrrad weg.
6. Die Katze sitzt unter meinem Bett.

Answers: 1. Mein Klassenfoto hing über meinem Schreibtisch. 2. Meine Tasche lag auf dem Sofa. 3. Der Hund lag neben dem Bett und schlief. 4. Ich stellte die Leiter an den Baum. 5. Er fuhr mit meinem Fahrrad weg. 6. Die Katze saß unter meinem Bett.

Quick Start Review 2

Vocabulary
Bilden Sie Sätze.
1. haben / sich / in den sechziger Jahren / die Frauenbewegung / die Ökobewegung / organisiert
2. fühlen / sich / manche Minderheiten / von den Abgeordneten / nicht / im Parlament / repräsentiert
3. die Tat / gestanden / dem Richter / er / hat
4. in der DDR / es / gab / viele Kinderkrippen
5. Eltern / allein erziehende / müssen / um vieles / sich / kümmern
6. Manche Leute / die Gleichberechtigung / sei / denken / der Frauen / erreicht

Answers: 1. In den sechziger Jahren haben sich die Frauenbewegung und die Ökobewegung organisiert. 2. Manche Minderheiten fühlen sich von den Abgeordneten im Parlament nicht repräsentiert. 3. Er hat dem Richter die Tat gestanden. 4. In der DDR gab es viele Kinderkrippen. 5. Allein erziehende Eltern müssen sich um vieles kümmern. 6. Manche Leute denken, die Gleichberechtigung der Frauen sei erreicht.

TEACHING SUGGESTIONS

- The passive voice I, pp. 234–235

Remind students of the different uses of *werden* in German and point out that the passive voice is only 1 of its functions. Point out that *man* is much more frequently used in German than is *one* in English. The passive voice in German is also less common than in English. The active voice using *man* is preferred. Look up the functions of *man* in a German dictionary or grammar book and give some examples. For example, *So kann man das wirklich nicht sagen. Von dieser Medizin nehme man täglich dreimal drei Tropfen. Man nehme drei Eier und 100 Gramm Zucker.*

- *Übung B,* p. 236

Expansion: Have students add household chores, yard work, or school activities to the list.

- The passive voice II, p. 237

Point out the necessity of dropping the *ge*-prefix on the *werden* auxiliary in the past perfect passive. Give additional examples.

- The future tense, pp. 238–239

Remind students that the most idiomatic way to talk about the future in German is to use present tense verb forms and to mark the future with temporal adverbs.

- *Übung A,* p. 239

Put students into groups of 4 and have them generate more questions to add to the list. Give groups 10 minutes to come up with as many questions as they can. Have groups report their questions to the class.

TEACHING ALL STUDENTS

Multiple Intelligences Verbal: Have students fill in the correct forms of *werden* in the following sentences.
1. Wann _____ du nach Rom fliegen?
2. Wir _____ morgen unser Auto verkaufen.
3. Der Rasen muss noch gewässert _____.
4. Mein Opa _____ morgen an seinem Herzen operiert.
5. Du _____ erwartet.
6. Deine Haare sollten geschnitten _____.

Answers: 1. wirst   2. werden
3. werden   4. wird   5. wirst
6. werden
Have students create some more
examples for their classmates to
fill in.

LANGUAGE NOTE

Point out that *werden* is used as an
auxiliary for both the future tense and
the passive voice: *Ich **werde** morgen
nach Berlin fahren. Er **wird** morgen von
Dr. Schiller operiert.* Have students
notice that in the future example, the
conjugated form of *werden* is followed
by an infinitive, whereas it is followed
by a past participle in the passive
construction.

CLASSROOM COMMUNITY

Paired Activity Ask students to write
down 5 words that they find hard to
memorize or have learned very recently.
Have them work with a partner to write
a short story using the words from
both their lists.

BLOCK SCHEDULE

Expansion Provide students with a few
interesting photos from a magazine.
Ask *Was passierte in den zwei Minuten
bevor dieses Bild aufgenommen wurde?
Was passierte gleich nach dieser
Aufnahme? Was denken die Leute auf
dem Bild?* This can be done as a whole
class activity or in groups.

Perspektiven, pp. 240–247

PROGRAM RESOURCES

- *Arbeitsheft*, pp. 174–178
- Audio Program, Cassette 6B, 7B/CD 9

- Audioscript, pp. 84–85
- www.mcdougallittell.com

....

Quick Start Review 1

♻ Vocabulary
Ergänzen Sie die Wörter in den Sätzen.
WÖRTER: ausüben, begriffen, eingesetzt,
erlernen, steigern, übertreibt

1. Meine Schwester will nach dem
   Abitur zunächst einmal einen
   Beruf _____.
2. Ich glaube, er hat noch immer
   nicht _____, wie man den
   Konjunktiv benutzt.
3. Ich habe gemerkt, dass dein
   Freund in seinen Geschichten
   gerne _____.
4. Es ist unwahrscheinlich, dass
   man in Zukunft 20 oder 30 Jahre
   lang den selben Beruf _____
   wird.
5. In der Produktion werden mehr
   und mehr Computer _____.
6. Es ist uns gelungen, die
   Produktion durch den Einsatz
   neuer Maschinen zu _____.

Answers: 1. erlernen   2. begriffen
3. übertreibt   4. ausüben   5. eingesetzt
6. steigern

Quick Start Review 2

♻ Prepositions
Ergänzen Sie die Präpositionen in den
Sätzen.

PRÄPOSITIONEN: auf, aus, durch, für, nach,
seit, um

1. Die Katze liegt _____ meinem Bett
   und schläft.
2. Was ist denn das _____ eine
   verrückte Musik?
3. Er kommt _____ Neuseeland und
   lebt _____ einem Jahr hier.

4. Der Hund passt nicht _____ das
   Mauseloch.
5. Sie wachte _____ Mitternacht auf.
6. Ich gehe jetzt _____ Hause.

Answers: 1. auf   2. für   3. aus, seit
4. durch   5. um   6. nach

....

TEACHING SUGGESTIONS

- *Hören Sie zu!*, p. 240

Remind students to look over the
Wortschatz zum Hörtext before they
listen. Encourage them to take notes.
After checking answers, play the
recording again if necessary.

  Expansion: Have students find the
Alps and *Berchtesgaden* on a map.
Have them go to the library or Internet
to find answers to these questions: *Wie
hoch sind die Alpen? Über welche
Länder erstrecken sich die Alpen?
Weshalb sind die Alpen bei Urlaubern
so beliebt? usw.*

- *Zum Thema, Aktivität A,* p. 240

Whether students take their walk as a
class or after school as homework,
they should be required to take their
own notes and not talk to each other
while walking. If there is no time for a
walk or if weather is inclement, have
them imagine a walk they have taken.

- *Zum Thema, Aktivität B,* p. 240

Follow-up: Introduce students to the
following simple folksong:

  *Es war eine Mutter, die hatte vier
Kinder,*
  *den Frühling, den Sommer, den
Herbst und den Winter.*
  *Der Frühling bringt Blumen, der
Sommer bringt Klee,*

der Herbst der bringt Trauben, der Winter bringt Schnee.

- *Herr Munzel hört das Gras wachsen,* p. 241

Have students first review the *Wortschatz zum Lesen* on p. 243 before reading the text. Make sure they use their dictionaries only to look up words that are necessary for comprehension.

- *Zum Text, Aktivität A,* p. 242

Have a student record the class's lists on the board or on an OHT. Ask *Welche Geräusche gefallen Ihnen? Welche hätten Sie anders erwartet? Welche haben Sie überrascht?*

- *Zur Interpretation,* p. 243

Ask *Gefällt Ihnen die Geschichte? Warum oder warum nicht?*

- *Schreibmodell,* p. 244

Have students read the model carefully and write down the gist of the story in a few words.

TEACHING ALL STUDENTS

Extra Help Stereotypes: *In Bayern werden Lederhosen getragen. In den USA werden nur Hamburger gegessen. In Italien wird nur Pizza gegessen.*

Have students come up with other stereotypes according to the model.

CLASSROOM COMMUNITY

Challenge Present students with some German *Sprichwörter* and have them guess and discuss their meanings. Possible proverbs: *Der Apfel fällt nicht weit vom Stamm. Lügen haben kurze Beine. Morgenstund hat Gold im Mund. Was du heute kannst besorgen, das verschiebe nicht auf morgen. Einem geschenkten Gaul schaut man nicht ins Maul.*

INTERDISCIPLINARY CONNECTION

Music: Have students listen to Beethoven's Sixth Symphony (available at most public libraries). Explain that the piece is subtitled "The Pastoral" and was inspired by walks Beethoven enjoyed in the rural areas around Vienna. Ask students to try to imagine what the music is depicting in each of the movements and to write a short reaction to each movement in German.

BLOCK SCHEDULE

Peer Teaching Have students go over the three grammar subsections in the *Strukturen* section of Chapter 35. Have them write 2 examples each of the concepts introduced. They should also write their own rules for the different uses of *werden* on a card. Have them compare their rules with those of a partner.

Fun Break Have students think of 5 questions that they would not like to answer. They should write them down on a piece of paper. Collect the papers in a box and have students draw the papers and read them out loud. Don't have students answer them!

PORTFOLIO

Have students choose a region Germany (*Schwarzwald, Ostsee, Alpen, Allgäu, Taunus*) and research some basic geological facts about it. Then have them research some of the major tourist attractions in the area. Have them find pictures of the region to create a poster and then use it in presenting their findings to the class.

RUBRIC **A** = 13–15 pts. **B** = 10–12 pts. **C** = 7–9 pts. **D** = 4–6 pts. **F** <4 pts.

Writing Criteria	Scale				
Content	1	2	3	4	5
Grammar, vocabulary	1	2	3	4	5
Presentation	1	2	3	4	5

DER UMWELT ZULIEBE

In diesem Kapitel

- lernen Sie, wie sich das Umweltbewusstsein in Deutschland entwickelt hat.
- sehen Sie, wie eine Familie in Hamburg umweltfreundlich lebt.
- besprechen Sie, was man alles für die Umwelt tun kann.

Sie werden auch

- den Gebrauch des Passivs lernen.
- das Futur mit **werden** wiederholen.
- etwas über einen Mann mit einem ungewöhnlichen Talent lesen.
- eine Kurzgeschichte schreiben.

Industrielles Wachstum
führte zu einer
Verschmutzung der
Umwelt.

Die Menschen in
dieser Siedlung
nehmen viel Rücksicht
auf die Umwelt.

Altglas und Altpapier
kann man zur
Sammelstelle bringen.

VIDEOTHEK

Früher hat man nicht so viel Rücksicht auf die Natur genommen wie heute. Was assoziieren Sie mit dem Wort „Umwelt"? Wie wird die Umwelt bei Ihnen geschützt?

A. **1.** d **2.** e **3.** b **4.** f **5.** a **6.** c

I: Auf Kosten der Umwelt

A Deutschland als Industrieland. Das industrielle Wachstum nach dem Zweiten Weltkrieg führte zu einer starken Verschmutzung der Umwelt. Welcher Satz beschreibt welches Bild?

Damals war das industrielle Wachstum wichtiger als der Umweltschutz.

a.   b.   c.

d.   e.   f.

WORTSCHATZ ZUM VIDEO

die Ökowelle	*ecology movement*
gelungen	*successful*
der Rand	*edge*
die Solaranlage	*solar panel*
die Neonröhre	*neon tube*

B. **1.** Anja **2.** Susanne **3.** Tobias
4. Susanne **5.** Anja

1. „Verkehr in den Städten wurde zum Problem."
2. „Das sogenannte Waldsterben alarmierte die Menschen."
3. „Sie demonstrierten gegen das Waldsterben."
4. „Fabriken müssen den Rauch filtern."
5. „Energie wird jetzt umweltfreundlicher produziert."
6. „Immer mehr Menschen tun etwas für den Umweltschutz."

B Persönliche Meinungen. Wer sagt das, Anja, Tobias oder Susanne?

1. „Ich finde es gut, dass wenig chemische Rohstoffe verwendet werden."
2. „Es gab nur mal eine Aktion, dass wir nicht mehr Einweggeschirr am Kiosk haben wollten."

3. „Die Ökobewegung in Deutschland ist viel zu extrem und zu schnell."
4. „Da haben wir schon ein bisschen was geleistet."
5. „Wenn es zum Essen kommt, muss ich sagen, dass ich der Ökowelle nicht angehöre."

II: Umweltschutz zu Hause

A Eine umweltfreundliche Siedlung. Verbinden Sie die Satzteile.

1. Die Häuser hat man so gebaut,
2. Mit Solaranlagen
3. Dächer aus Gras
4. Die Fußböden aus Holz
5. Die ökologische Gestaltung der Siedlung
6. Bärbel Barmbeck macht selbst Jogurt
7. Energiesparlampen
8. Der Abfall

a. wird sorgfältig getrennt.
b. bringt gute Lebensqualität für die Menschen.
c. damit keine Plastikbecher ins Haus kommen.
d. dass viel Energie gespart wird.
e. gewinnt man Energie aus Sonnenlicht.
f. brauchen weniger Strom.
g. bringen Wärme in das Haus.
h. schützen vor Hitze und Kälte.

B Umweltschutz bei Ihnen. Familie Barmbeck lebt besonders umweltfreundlich. Welche dieser Ideen würden Sie auch umsetzen? Welche nicht? Warum?

WAS ICH SCHON MACHE	WAS ICH MACHEN WILL	WAS ICH NICHT MACHEN WILL
den Müll trennen	ein Haus mit einem Grasdach kaufen	Jogurt selbst machen

C Leben diese Leute umweltfreundlich? Sie hören, was Anett, Anja, Claudia und Dirk zum Thema Umwelt sagen. Wer sagt das, Anett, Anja, Claudia oder Dirk?

1. „Für die Umwelt tue ich mein Bestes."
2. „Ich kaufe Umweltpapier, anstatt dieses normalen weißen Chemikalien-Papiers."
3. „Umwelt ist ein großes Thema für meine Tochter . . . "
4. „Ich versuche, nicht so viel Strom und Wasser zu benutzen."
5. „ . . . unsere öffentlichen Verkehrsmittel so perfekt organisiert sind."
6. „Wir in der Familie recyclen . . . also wir sortieren Müll."

KULTURSPIEGEL

Das sogenannte Waldsterben – die Schädigung der Wälder durch die Luftverschmutzung von Industrieanlagen und dem Autoverkehr – betrifft die neuen Bundesländer am stärksten. Die Schädigung ist am größten im Bundesland Thüringen, am wenigsten in Rheinland-Pfalz.

A. 1. d 2. e 3. h 4. g 5. b 6. c 7. f 8. a

Wie finden Sie dieses Haus?

B. *Answers will vary.*

Die Familie Barmbeck wohnt besonders umweltbewusst.

C. 1. Anett 2. Dirk 3. Claudia 4. Anett 5. Anja 6. Dirk

VOKABELN

die Debatte	*debate*
die Einwegflasche	*nonreturnable bottle*
die Pfandflasche	*returnable bottle*
die Rücksicht	*consideration*
die Verschmutzung	*pollution*
der Rohstoff	*raw material*
der Umweltschutz	*environmental protection*
der Verbraucher / die Verbraucherin	*consumer*
der Verkehr	*traffic*
das Einweggeschirr	*disposable utensils*
das Gesetz	*law*
das Gleichgewicht	*ecological balance*
das Umweltbewusstsein	*environmental awareness*
das Verkehrsmittel	*mode of transportation*
das Verpackungsmaterial	*packaging*
das Wachstum	*growth*
das Waldsterben	*dying of the forest*
schädigen	*to damage*
sparen	*to save*
verschmutzen	*to pollute*
verzichten auf (+ *acc.*)	*to renounce*
weg•schmeißen	*to throw away*
wieder verwerten	*to recycle*

Solche Landschaften zeigen die hohen Kosten des industriellen Wachstums deutlich auf. Aber wer soll diese Kosten jetzt bezahlen?

giftfrei	*non-toxic*
öffentlich	*public(ly)*
umweltfeindlich	*hostile to the environment*
zuliebe (+ *dat.*)	*for the sake of*

Sie wissen schon

die Umwelt, der Abfall, der Lärm, der Müll, der Umweltsünder, recyceln, schützen, trennen, organisch, umweltfreundlich

---

Verschmutzung
öffentlichen
Verkehr   *Müll*
Gleichgewicht
verzichten
umweltfreundlicher

Aktivitäten

A. 1. öffentlichen   2. Verkehr   3. Verschmutzung   4. Müll   5. Gleichgewicht
6. umweltfreundlicher   7. verzichten

A Ein „sanfter Tourismus"? Heute kann man überall in der Welt Urlaub machen. Aber wie wirkt dieser Massentourismus auf die Umwelt? Ergänzen Sie die Sätze.

Früher hat man die Natur anders genossen als heute. Man wanderte in den Bergen, oder machte Spaziergänge im Wald. Die meisten fuhren in ihren Urlaub in der Natur nicht mit dem Auto, sondern mit den _____¹ Verkehrsmitteln, vor allem mit dem Zug. Jetzt gibt es in den Ferienmonaten viel _____² auf den Autobahnen. Die _____³ der Luft durch Autoabgase führt zu Waldsterben und Krankheit. Auch wenn man am Urlaubsort angekommen ist, geht die

Umweltzerstörung weiter. Touristen in den berühmten Nationalparks produzieren viel _____,⁴ der irgendwie entfernt werden muss. Auch die hohe Zahl der Touristen in Naturschutzgebieten stört das ökologische _____.⁵ Viele Touristen wollen _____⁶ reisen und deswegen _____⁷ sie auf Hotels und Ressorts und gehen lieber einfach zelten oder wandern, um die Natur selbst besser kennen zu lernen.

B Definitionen. Lesen Sie die Sätze links, und suchen Sie aus der rechten Spalte passende Definitionen für die kursiv gedruckten Wörter.

1. Der organische *Müll*, zum Beispiel Essensreste oder Kartoffelschalen, kommt auf den Komposthaufen.
2. Wir *trennen den Müll*.
3. Wir benutzen keine *Einwegflaschen*.
4. Wir haben darauf geachtet, dass möglichst *giftfreie* umweltfreundliche Farben verwendet worden sind.
5. Wir in der Familie versuchen, alles wieder zu *verwerten*.
6. Ich trage dazu bei, dass die Umwelt in Berlin nicht durch Autos und Abgase *verschmutzt* wird.
7. Energie wird jetzt sehr viel *umweltfreundlicher* produziert.

a. frei von Chemikalien oder anderen Substanzen, die eine schädliche Wirkung auf Menschen, Tiere oder die Umwelt haben
b. Abfall, den man wegwirft
c. Flaschen, die man nicht zurückbringen kann
d. recyceln
e. stecken Papier, Glas, Aluminium und so weiter in verschiedene Tonnen
f. besser (nicht so schädlich) für die Umwelt
g. ganz schmutzig (nicht mehr sauber) gemacht

C Was machen Sie für die Umwelt?

SCHRITT 1: Lesen Sie, was Susanne und Iris für die Umwelt machen.

SUSANNE: Wir trennen den Müll und wir kaufen nur recyceltes Papier und bringen das Papier auch weg. Ich fahre mit dem Bus, anstatt mit dem Auto zu fahren. Und wir benutzen kein Einweggeschirr, sondern wir verzichten darauf und benutzen eher Porzellan.

IRIS: Das Thema Umwelt ist mir sehr wichtig, denn wenn das ökologische Gleichgewicht nicht mehr besteht, dann, glaube ich, können wir auch nicht weiterleben. Und ich persönlich versuche, so wenig wie möglich mit dem Auto zu fahren und so wenig Verpackungsmaterial wie möglich wegzuschmeißen und meinen Müll zu trennen.

SCHRITT 2: Was machen Susanne und Iris für die Umwelt? Was machen Sie der Umwelt zuliebe? Schreiben Sie drei Listen. Machen Sie etwas anderes als Susanne oder Iris?

SUSANNE   IRIS   ICH

Sind Extremsportarten wie Canyoning umweltfreundlich?

B. 1. b 2. e 3. c 4. a 5. d 6. g 7. f

KULTURSPIEGEL

Wie fahren Sie in den Urlaub? Noch in den fünfziger Jahren fuhr die Hälfte der Reisenden mit der Bahn, und ein Viertel mit Bus oder Auto. Heute stellen Zugfahrer nur zehn Prozent aller Reisenden dar. Mehr als die Hälfte fährt mit dem eigenen Pkw, und zwanzig Prozent nehmen das Flugzeug.

FOKUS INTERNET

For more information about environmental protection efforts in Germany, visit the *Auf Deutsch!* Web Site at www.mcdougallittell.com.

C. Schritt 2: SUSANNE: Müll trennen, recyceltes Papier verwenden, Papier zum Recycling bringen, mit dem Bus statt mit dem Auto fahren, kein Einweggeschirr benutzen. IRIS: Müll trennen, so wenig wie möglich Auto fahren, wenig Verpackungsmaterial wegschmeißen. ICH: *Answers will vary.*

STRUKTUREN

REVIEW OF THE PASSIVE VOICE I
FOCUSING ON THE EFFECT OF THE ACTION

The passive voice focuses on the effect of the action, rather than on the person performing the action. The direct object (accusative case) of the active sentence becomes the subject (nominative case) of the passive sentence; and the agent, the one performing the action, follows the preposition **von** (if the agent is a person) or **durch** (if it is a thing). Often the agent remains unnamed, because it is understood, unimportant, or unknown.

ACTIVE VOICE

Susanne trennt **den Müll.** *Susanne is sorting the garbage.*

PASSIVE VOICE

Der Müll wird (von Susanne) getrennt. *The garbage is being sorted (by Susanne).*

The passive voice uses the auxiliary **werden.** In the present or simple past tenses, the conjugated form of **werden** stands in second position and the past participle of the main verb goes at the end of the sentence. In dependent clauses, the conjugated verb follows the past participle.

PRESENT TENSE

Die Bäume **werden** (durch Luftverschmutzung) **beschädigt.** *The trees are being damaged (by air pollution).*

SIMPLE PAST TENSE

Die Bäume **wurden** (durch Luftverschmutzung) **beschädigt.** *The trees were damaged (by air pollution).*

Wissen Sie, wie die Bäume **beschädigt wurden**? *Do you know how the trees were damaged?*

The forms of **werden** in the present and simple past tenses are shown on the next page.

PRESENT STEM: **werd-**		INFINITIVE: **werden**		PAST STEM: **wurd-**	
SINGULAR	PLURAL	SINGULAR	PLURAL		
ich werde	wir werden	ich wurde	wir wurden		
du wirst	ihr werdet	du wurdest	ihr wurdet		
Sie werden	Sie werden	Sie wurden	Sie wurden		
sie/er/es wird	sie werden	sie/er/es wurde	sie wurden		

When a sentence in the passive voice contains a modal verb, the infinitive **werden** appears after the past participle of the main verb at the end of the sentence or clause. This combination of past participle plus **werden** is called the "passive infinitive."

ACTIVE VOICE

Wir **müssen** die Wäsche **waschen.**　　　*We have to do the laundry.*

PASSIVE VOICE

Die Wäsche **muss gewaschen werden.**　　　*The laundry needs to be done.*

As you recall, several German verbs require dative objects: **danken, gefallen, gehören, helfen, passen, schmecken.** The verb **schaden** (*to damage, harm*) also belongs to this category. When one of these verbs appears in a passive sentence, the dative object remains in the dative case but functions as the subject.

ACTIVE VOICE

Die Luftverschmutzung schadet **der Umwelt.**　　　*Air pollution damages the environment.*

PASSIVE VOICE

Der Umwelt wird geschadet.　　　*The environment is being damaged.*

ACTIVE VOICE

Claudia hat **mir** sehr geholfen.　　　*Claudia helped me a lot.*

PASSIVE VOICE

Mir wurde sehr geholfen.　　　*I was helped a lot.*

Wie wurde diese Siedlung gebaut?

A. **1.** gebaut **2.** gespart **3.** gewonnen
4. geschützt **5.** benutzt **6.** verbraucht
7. gesammelt **8.** gebracht

B. **1.** Das Auto muss gewaschen werden.
2. Das Wohnzimmer muss aufgeräumt werden.
3. Die Bücher müssen ins Bücherregal gestellt
werden. **4.** Am Sonntag können die Fahrräder
repariert werden. **5.** Am Sonntag darf der
Rasen nicht gemäht werden. **6.** Der Müll soll
sorgfältig getrennt werden. **7.** Die Katzen
dürfen nicht zu viel gefüttert werden. **8.** Die
andere Hausarbeit kann nächste Woche gemacht
werden.

C. **1.** In Bayern wird viel Schweinefleisch
gegessen. **2.** In Hamburg wird „Labskaus"
gegessen. **3.** In thailändischen Restaurants
wird Pad Thai probiert. **4.** In griechischen
Restaurants wird Moussaka serviert. **5.** Jetzt
wird fast jeden Tag Pizza genossen. **6.** Ein
Hamburger und Pommes werden als typisch
Amerikanisch angesehen. **7.** Sauerkraut und
Bratwurst werden nur selten bestellt.

Übungen

A Eine umweltfreundliche Siedlung. Ergänzen Sie die fehlenden Partizipien.

Die Häuser in dieser Siedlung wurden so _____,[1] dass viel Energie _____[2] wird. Zum Beispiel wird Energie aus Sonnenlicht mit Solaranlagen _____.[3] Die Einwohner werden auch durch das Grasdach von Hitze und Kälte _____.[4] Auch innerhalb der Häuser werden Energiesparlampen _____,[5] damit weniger Strom _____[6] wird. Natürlich werden Problemstoffe wie Neonröhren und Batterien _____[7] und zur Sammelstelle _____.[8] Schon viel, sagt man, aber die Einwohner sagen, dass ihre ökologische Siedlung viel Lebensqualität bringt.

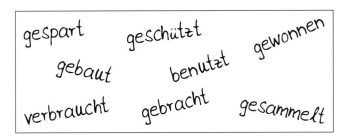

gespart   geschützt   gewonnen
gebaut   benutzt
verbraucht   gebracht   gesammelt

B Haushalt. Heute ist Putztag. Was muss alles für den Haushalt gemacht werden? Bilden Sie Sätze im Passiv.

MODELL: Man muss die Fenster putzen. →
Die Fenster müssen geputzt werden.

1. Man muss das Auto waschen.
2. Man muss das Wohnzimmer aufräumen.
3. Man muss die Bücher ins Bücherregal stellen.
4. Man kann am Sonntag die Fahrräder reparieren.
5. Man darf nicht am Sonntag den Rasen mähen.
6. Man soll den Müll sorgfältig trennen.
7. Man darf die Katzen nicht zu viel füttern.
8. Man kann die andere Hausarbeit nächste Woche machen.

C Essgewohnheiten in Deutschland. Setzen Sie die folgenden Sätze ins Passiv.

1. In Bayern isst man viel Schweinefleisch.
2. In Hamburg isst man „Labskaus".
3. In thailändischen Restaurants probiert man Pad Thai.
4. In griechischen Restaurants serviert man Moussaka.
5. Jetzt genießt man fast jeden Tag Pizza.
6. Man sieht einen Hamburger und Pommes als typisch amerikanisch an.
7. Man bestellt nur selten Sauerkraut und Bratwurst.

THE PASSIVE VOICE II
FOCUSING ON EVENTS IN THE PAST

Like the active voice, the passive voice occurs in the perfect tenses as
well as in the present and simple past tenses, which you have just
reviewed. The present perfect tense of the passive voice uses the present
tense of the auxiliary **sein** as the conjugated verb form. A special passive
participle, **worden,** follows the past participle of the main verb at the
end of the sentence.

PRESENT PERFECT TENSE

ACTIVE VOICE

Susanne hat den Müll schon
  getrennt.

*Susanne has already sorted
  the garbage.*

PASSIVE VOICE

Der Müll **ist** schon **getrennt
  worden.**

*The garbage has already been
  sorted.*

ACTIVE VOICE

Wir haben die Pfandflaschen zur
  Sammelstelle gebracht.

*We brought the disposable
  bottles to the recycling
  center.*

PASSIVE VOICE

Die Pfandpflaschen **sind** zur
  Sammelstelle **gebracht
  worden.**

*The disposable bottles have
  been brought to the
  recycling center.*

Similarly, the past perfect tense of the passive voice has the same
construction. The only difference is that the auxiliary verb **sein** is in the
simple past rather than the present tense.

PAST PERFECT TENSE

ACTIVE VOICE

Wir hatten die Flaschen schon
  zur Sammelstelle gebracht.

*We had already brought the
  bottles to the recycling
  center.*

PASSIVE VOICE

Die Flaschen **waren** schon zur
  Sammelstelle **gebracht
  worden.**

*The bottles had already been
  brought to the recycling
  center.*

As in the active voice, the past perfect tense describes events or
conditions that took place prior to other past events. In general, the
passive voice appears more frequently in the simple past than in the
perfect tenses.

Hamburg – eine Kulturstadt ersten Ranges.

Bei Familie Barmbeck wird der Abfall jeden Tag sortiert.

A. 1. Das erste deutsche Schauspielhaus ist 1678 in Hamburg gebaut worden.   2. Ein Viertel der Stadt ist in einem großen Feuer zerstört worden.   3. Nach dem Zweiten Weltkrieg ist die Stadt wieder aufgebaut worden.   4. Die privaten Museen sind fürs Publikum geöffnet worden. 5. Viele Bücher sind über die Stadt Hamburg geschrieben worden.

B. 1. Der Müll wurde getrennt. Der Müll ist getrennt worden.   2. Es wurden sehr wenig Dosen benutzt. Es sind sehr wenig Dosen benutzt worden.   3. Früher wurde zu viel Papier verbraucht. Früher ist zu viel Papier verbraucht worden.   4. Das Altglas wurde zum Glascontainer gebracht. Das Altglas ist zum Glascontainer gebracht worden.   5. Alle Dosen wurden in einen separaten Container geworfen. Alle Dosen sind in einen separaten Container geworfen worden.

Übungen

A Hamburg damals und heute. Schreiben Sie die Sätze im Perfekt.

MODELL: Das Rathaus wurde im neunzehnten Jahrhundert gebaut →
Das Rathaus ist im neunzehnten Jahrhundert gebaut worden.

1. Das erste deutsche Schauspielhaus wurde 1678 in Hamburg gebaut.
2. Ein Viertel der Stadt wurde in einem großen Feuer zerstört.
3. Nach dem Zweiten Weltkrieg wurde die Stadt wieder aufgebaut.
4. Die privaten Museen wurden fürs Publikum geöffnet.
5. Viele Bücher wurden über die Stadt Hamburg geschrieben.

B Umweltschutz zu Hause. Machen Sie aus den Aktivsätzen Passivsätze im Imperfekt und Perfekt.

MODELL: Man hat den Abfall sortiert. →
Der Abfall wurde sortiert.
Der Abfall ist sortiert worden.

1. Man hat den Müll getrennt.
2. Man hat sehr wenig Dosen benutzt.
3. Früher verbrauchte man zu viel Papier.
4. Man hat das Altglas zum Glascontainer gebracht.
5. Man hat alle Dosen in einen separaten Container geworfen.

REVIEW OF THE FUTURE TENSE
TALKING ABOUT WHAT WILL HAPPEN

In German, it is possible to talk about future events by using the present tense and a word or phrase to indicate time, such as **morgen, nächste Woche, nächstes Jahr,** and so forth.

Nächstes Jahr reisen wir nach Norwegen.   *We're going to Norway next year.*

German also has a future tense, which you can use to talk about future events in general, especially in the absence of time expressions. The future tense uses **werden** as an auxiliary verb, with the meaning *will,* and the infinitive of the main verb.

Wir **werden** eine Lösung **finden.**   *We will find a solution.*

The future tense frequently occurs with the adverb **wohl** to express probability.

Wir werden wohl eine Lösung finden.	*We will probably find a solution.*

You can also use the future tense in the passive voice: Simply place the infinitive **werden** at the end of a passive sentence in the present tense.

ACTIVE VOICE

Die Umwelt wird geschützt.	*The environment is being protected.*

PASSIVE VOICE

Die Umwelt wird geschützt werden.	*The environment will be protected.*

You should now be able to recognize the following uses and meanings of the verb **werden.**

- As a main verb, **werden** means *to get* or *to become.*
- As an auxiliary for the future tense, **werden** means *will.*
- As an auxiliary for the passive voice in all tenses, **werden** helps express the tense of the main verb.

KURZ NOTIERT

Remember, the conjugated form of **werden** goes at the end of a dependent clause.

Ich weiß nicht, was mit der Umwelt geschehen **wird.**
I don't know what will happen to the environment.

A. *Possible answers are:* **1.** Ja, in der Zukunft wird es mehr Arbeitslosigkeit geben. *oder:* Nein, es wird in der Zukunft nicht mehr Arbeitslosigkeit geben. **2.** Ja, wir werden wohl durch Maschinen ersetzt werden. *oder:* Nein, wir werden nicht durch Maschinen ersetzt werden. **3.** Nein, es wird nicht zu viele Menschen auf der Erde geben. *oder:* Ja, es wird zu viele Menschen auf der Erde geben. **4.** Ja, es wird in der Zukunft nur eine Sprache geben. *oder:* Nein, es wird in der Zukunft nicht nur eine Sprache geben. **5.** Ja, wir werden nur elektrische Autos fahren. *oder:* Nein, wir werden nicht nur elektrische Autos fahren. **6.** Ja, wir werden wohl bewohnbare Planeten finden. *oder:* Nein, wir werden keine bewohnbaren Planeten finden. **7.** Ja, wir werden wohl Außerirdische kennen lernen. *oder:* Nein, wir werden wohl keine Außerirdischen kennen lernen.

Übungen

(A) **In der fernen Zukunft.** Wie sehen Sie und Ihre Mitschüler/ Mitschülerinnen die Zukunft? Stellen Sie aneinander die folgenden Fragen, und beantworten Sie sie.

1. Wird es in der Zukunft mehr Arbeitslosigkeit geben?
2. Werden wir durch Maschinen ersetzt werden?
3. Wird es zu viele Menschen auf der Erde geben?
4. Wird es in der Zukunft nur eine Sprache geben?
5. Werden wir nur elektrische Autos fahren?
6. Werden wir bewohnbare[a] Planeten finden?
7. Werden wir Außerirdische[b] kennen lernen?

[a]*inhabitable* [b]*extraterrestrials*

(B) **Pläne.** Ein Freund fragt nach Ihren Zukunftsplänen. Beantworten Sie die Fragen im Futur mit **wohl.**

MODELL: Wann reist du nach Spanien? (nächstes Jahr) →
Ich werde wohl nächstes Jahr nach Spanien reisen.

1. Wann kommst du zu Besuch? (im Sommer)
2. Wann bist du mit der Schule fertig? (in einem Jahr)
3. Wann kaufst du ein Auto? (nach den Sommerferien)
4. Wann spielst du Fußball? (am Samstag)
5. Wann gehst du einkaufen? (erst morgen früh)

Der Arbeitsplatz der Zukunft?

B. **1.** Ich werde wohl im Sommer zu Besuch kommen. **2.** Ich werde wohl in einem Jahr mit der Schule fertig sein. **3.** Ich werde wohl nach den Sommerferien ein Auto kaufen. **4.** Ich werde wohl am Samstag Fußball spielen. **5.** Ich gehe wohl erst morgen früh einkaufen.

PERSPEKTIVEN

HÖREN SIE ZU!
UMWELT KENNT KEINE GRENZEN

1. Russland 2. Bergbauern, Touristen und Geschäftsleute 3. Touristen 4. Hof 5. einfache 6. Österreich 7. Alpen

Tagesausflüger in den bayerischen Alpen.

A. Schritt 1: *Notes will vary.* Schritt 2: *Reports will vary.*

WORTSCHATZ ZUM HÖRTEXT

der Bergbauer	alpine farmer
das Ergebnis	result
die Berglandwirtschaft	alpine farming
die Alm	pasture
die Weide	meadow
der Erhalt	preservation
der Hof	farm
erzeugen	to produce
nebenberuflich	on the side
die Untersuchung	investigation
imponieren	to impress
der Nachwuchsforscher	next-generation researcher
landschaftsprägend	landscape-affecting

B. 1. d 2. a 3. c 4. b

Sie hören einen Text über junge Umweltforscher aus drei europäischen Ländern.

● Interview im Nationalpark Berchtesgaden. Ergänzen Sie die fehlenden Wörter.

1. Swetlana kommt aus _____.
2. Die Nachwuchsforscher interviewten _____.
3. Die Berglandwirtschaft macht die Region für _____ attraktiv.
4. Die meisten Bergbauern können von ihrem _____ nicht leben.
5. Das _____ Leben hat den Nachwuchsforschern vor allem imponiert.
6. Wolfgang kommt aus _____.
7. Wolfgang sagt, dass er die _____ jetzt mit ganz anderen Augen sieht.

LESEN SIE!

Zum Thema

A Ihre eigenen Beobachtungen

SCHRITT 1: Ein Spaziergang. Bevor Sie die Geschichte von Herrn Munzel lesen, machen Sie einen kleinen Spaziergang in der Natur. Nehmen Sie einen Notizblock mit und schreiben Sie folgende Dinge auf: alle Geräusche, die Sie hören; alle Gerüche, die Sie riechen; und alles, was in Ihr Blickfeld kommt.

SCHRITT 2: Ein Bericht. Berichten Sie der Klasse in der nächsten Unterrichtsstunde, was Sie alles gehört, gerochen und gesehen haben.

B Die Jahreszeiten und die Natur. Kombinieren Sie!

1.	Im Sommer	a.	schläft die Natur.
2.	Im Winter	b.	fallen die Blätter von den Bäumen.
3.	Im Frühling	c.	bringen der warme Wind und der Sonnenschein alles zum Blühen.
4.	Im Herbst	d.	blüht und gedeiht[a] die Natur.

[a]*thrives*

Herr Munzel hört das Gras wachsen

Herr Munzel lag wieder mal auf der Wiese. Er sah den Wolken zu und kaute an einem Gänseblümchen. Es war Frühjahr und schon warm in der Sonne, die ersten Sträucher blühten, und Herr
5 Munzel war zufrieden mit sich und der Welt.

Ringsherum war alles ganz still. Ab und zu in der Ferne das Brummen eines Lastwagens, der in die Stadt fuhr. Ganz still also war es nicht, und Herr Munzel strengte sich an, alle Geräusche, die es
10 gab, zu hören.

Und es schien ihm, als höre er etwas, was ihm noch nie aufgefallen war. Ein feines Klinglein, sehr hell und sehr hoch.

Ein angenehmes Geräusch, dachte Herr Munzel
15 und strengte sich noch mehr an, schloss die Augen und lauschte. Das Klingeln wurde lauter, war um ihn herum, unüberhörbar. Und als Herr Munzel die Augen wieder öffnete, wurde das Geräusch schwächer. Als er sich schließlich aufsetzte,
20 verschwand es völlig.

Kein Wunder, dachte Herr Munzel, dass es bei mir klingelt, ich habe schlecht geschlafen. Das wird es sein.

Das war es aber keineswegs, denn es begann
25 wieder zu klingeln, als Herr Munzel sich erneut zurücklegte und die Augen schloss. Es half nichts, dass er die Wiese verließ und sich auf eine andere Rasenfläche dicht beim Wald legte. Das Klingeln änderte nur seine Klangfarbe und blieb.

30 Das alle hätte Herrn Munzel gar nicht weiter beschäftigt, wenn nicht Tage später bei einer Kahnfahrt auf dem kleinen See nahebei der Stadt ein Brummen gewesen wäre, laut und vernehmlich. Und je näher Herr Munzel dem Schiff
35 am Ufer des Sees kam, um so lauter brummte es, so wie eine dicke Hummel im Sommer.

"Verzeihung, brummt es bei Ihnen auch?" hatte er die Leute gefragt, die auf dem Weg um den See herum spazieren gingen, aber die hatten den Kopf
40 geschüttelt und ihm verständnislos nachgesehen.

"Ein klarer Fall", sagte der Arzt von Herrn Munzel und räumte seine Bestecke wieder weg. "Sie hören das Gras wachsen." Herr Munzel hatte sich elend gefühlt, weil die Geräusche, die nur er hörte, sich
45 vermehrten, sobald er das Haus verließ. Seine Blumen hatte er schon vom Balkon genommen, weil er das ständige Klopfen nicht mehr ertrug. Blumen klopfen nämlich leise, während sie wachsen.

Die nächste Zeit wurde schwer für Herrn Munzel.
50 Der Frühling brachte mit warmem Wind und Sonnenschein ringsum alles zum Blühen. Das Klingeln, das Herr Munzel an jenem ersten Tag auf der Wiese gehört hatte, schwoll an zu einem Geläut, wie von drei Kirchen am Samstagabend.
55 Spaziergänge wurden ihm verleidet, und bald mied er auf dem Weg zur Arbeit alle Grünflächen, jede Blume, konnte keinen Baum ertragen, weil es rings um ihn bummerte und schepperte, klingelte und brummte. So blieb Herr Munzel immer öfter zu
60 Hause, verstopfte sich die Ohren mit Watte, und hielt auch bei Sonne die Läden geschlossen.

Eines Morgens schellte das Telefon. Es war Herr Hecke vom Gartenamt der Stadt, der Herrn Munzel sprechen wollte.

65 "Ich habe von Ihren Fähigkeiten gehört", begann er, "und möchte, dass Sie für uns arbeiten." Und bevor Herr Munzel entrüstet ablehnen konnte, fuhr er fort: "Es ist eine gut bezahlte Stelle als Wachstumsprüfer mit Arbeitskleidung, Mittagessen
70 und Ohrenschützern."

Herr Munzel war es leid, zu Hause zu sitzen. Obwohl er die Geräusche fürchtete, die die wachsende Natur verursachte, sagte er für ein paar Probetage zu.

75 Am nächsten Tag wurde er mit einem Auto durch die Stadt gefahren, von der Grünanlage zum nächsten Park und von dort zur Städtischen Gemüseanbauversuchsstelle, um zu hören, ob auch alle Pflanzen ordnungsgemäß wüchsen. Er hatte
80 nichts weiter zu tun, als sich auf den Boden zu legen, dem Klingeln, Pfeifen oder Brummen zu lauschen und seine Ratschläge zu geben. Wo es genügend brummte, ordnete er Bewässerung wie bisher an, und wo das Klingeln des Rasens zu

85 schwach war, empfahl er, Dünger zu streuen.
Zwischendurch konnte er immer wieder seine
Ohrenklappen tragen, die eigens für ihn angefertigt
und völlig schalldicht waren. Er war recht zufrieden.

Herr Munzel verdiente nicht schlecht in dieser
90 Zeit, gewöhnte sich auch an das Tragen der
Ohrenklappen und hatte einige gute
Nebeneinnahmen. So ließ ihn die
Fußballmannschaft der Stadt, die in der höchsten
Liga spielte, vor jedem Spiel rufen und den
95 Zustand des Rasens prüfen. Vor der ehrfürchtig
schweigenden Menge, die ungeduldig auf den
Beginn des Spiels wartete, legte sich Herr Munzel
rücklings auf den Rasen, und wenn er anschließend
mit erhobenem rechten Daumen den guten
100 Zustand der Spielfläche bestätigte, brach im Stadion
ein Jubel aus, als habe die Heimmannschaft ein Tor
geschossen.

Reiche Leute ließen ihn mit großen Autos
kommen und wöchentlich den Zustand der
105 gepflegten Gartenflächen überprüfen. Herr Munzel
befand sie jedesmal für gut, allein schon um den
ängstlich dabeistehenden Gärtnern eine Freude zu
machen.

Aber auch Leute mit finsteren Absichten
110 wollten sich Herrn Munzels Fähigkeiten bedienen.
So erschien eines abends an Herrn Munzels Tür ein
stadtbekannter Dunkelmann und bat ihn, ein Ohr
auf seine Gerichtsakte mit ein paar ihm
angelasteten Fällen zu haben, ob nicht schon
115 wenigstens etwas Gras darüber gewachsen sei.

Herr Munzel sagte dies eine Mal zu, lehnte jedoch
alle weiteren Ansinnen in dieser Richtung ab.

Wochenlang half er durch seine Fähigkeit,
Schonungen zu errichten und morsche Waldflächen
120 abzuholzen, er legte Gärten an und beriet die
Bauern der Umgebung bei der Wahl des richtigen
Zeitpunktes für die Getreideernte. Er gewöhnte sich
an seine neue Aufgabe. Und je mehr der Sommer
heranrückte, desto öfter konnte er seine
125 Ohrenklappen abnehmen. Denn die Geräusche
wurden immer weniger, weil Bäume, Sträucher und
Blumen fast aufgehört hatten, zu wachsen. Immer
seltener wurde Herr Munzel nun in die Gärten
gerufen, die dank seines Rates blühten und
130 gediehen. Fast kam er sich ein wenig überflüssig
vor.

Und als der Herbst kam und die ersten Blätter
von den Bäumen fielen und die grünen und die
grauen Felder abgeerntet dalagen, hörte Herr
135 Munzel nur noch das, was andere Menschen auch
hören. Er verbrachte im frühen Herbst zwei ruhige
Wochen an der See, wo nichts wuchs, außer
uraltem spirrigem Gras. Lange Spaziergänge am
Wasser ließen ihn fast vergessen, was er im Frühjahr
140 und Sommer gehört hatte.

Den Winter über, als draußen nichts wuchs,
arbeitete Herr Munzel in den Treibhäusern der Stadt.
Seine liebsten Pflanzen waren die Tomaten, deren
leises Summen angenehm im Ohr klang.

Achim Bröger / Bernd Küsters

Zum Text

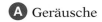

A Geräusche

SCHRITT 1: Die Natur macht viele Geräusche, die Herr Munzel
wahrnimmt. Welche Geräusche machen die folgenden Pflanzen?

1. die Blumen   **2.** das Gras   **3.** die Bäume

SCHRITT 2: Welche anderen Geräusche „hört" Herr Munzel? Machen Sie
eine Liste.

A. **Schritt 1: 1.** Die Blumen klopfen. **2.** Das
Gras klingelt. **3.** Die Bäume bummern,
scheppern, klingeln und brummen.
Schritt 2: *Possible answers are:* Herr Munzel
hört . . . das Brummen eines Lastwagens, . . , ein
Schiff brummen, . . . das Telefon schellen, . . . die
wachsenden Pflanzen klingeln, pfeifen und
brummen, . . . das, was andere Menschen
auch hören, . . . das Summen der Tomaten.

B Umwelt und Beruf. Herr Munzel hat eine Stelle als Wachstumsprüfer beim Gartenamt der Stadt bekommen. Welche der folgenden Aufgaben gehören zu seinem Beruf?

B. 1, 2, 4

1. Er legte sich auf den Boden, lauschte dem Gras und gab Ratschläge.
2. Er ordnete Bewässerung des Rasens an, wo es genug brummte.
3. Er pflanzte Bäume.
4. Er empfahl, Dünger zu streuen, wo das Klingeln des Rasens schwach war.
5. Er beseitigte tote Bäume.

Zur Interpretation

● Was meinen Sie dazu?

1. Welches Talent entwickelte Herr Munzel? Genoss er dieses Talent völlig, oder wurde es ihm zur Last[a]? Erklären Sie Ihre Antwort.
2. Herr Munzel fürchtete die Geräusche. Warum?
3. Was symbolisiert Herrn Munzels Talent, das Gras wachsen hören zu können?

[a]*burden*

WORTSCHATZ ZUM LESEN

kauen	*to chew*
der Strauch	*shrub*
das Brummen	*buzzing*
sich anstrengen	*to make an effort*
das Geräusch	*sound*
das Klinglein	*ringing*
lauschen	*to listen*
die Kahnfahrt	*boat trip*
vernehmlich	*audible; distinct*
elend	*miserable*
meiden	*to avoid*
scheppern	*to rattle*
die Bewässerung	*irrigation*
die Nebeneinnahmen	*supplementary income*
die Absicht	*intention*
der Fall	*(legal) case*
abgeerntet	*harvested*

INTERAKTION

Narrations will vary.

Possible answers are: **1.** Herr Munzel entwickelte die Fähigkeit, die Pflanzen wachsen zu hören. Sein neues Talent wurde ihm bald zur Last. Er fühlte sich elend, weil die Geräusche, die nur er hörte, sich vermehrten, wenn er das Haus verließ. **2.** Herr Munzel fürchtete die Geräusche, weil er nie mehr seine Ruhe hatte. **3.** Herrn Munzels Talent, das Gras wachsen hören zu können, symbolisiert Anderssein. Das Gras wachsen hören bedeutet aus den kleinsten Veränderungen etwas für die Zukunft lesen können. Es ist eine subjektive Erfahrung, andere hören es nicht.

● Lesetheater. Arbeiten Sie mit einem Partner / einer Partnerin. Benutzen Sie das Diagramm, um die Geschichte von Herrn Munzel nachzuerzählen.

ARZT
„Sie hören das Gras wachsen."

HERR MUNZEL
lag auf der Wiese
Frühjahr
zufrieden mit sich und der Welt
strengte sich an und hörte . . .

GARTENAMT DER STADT
Herr Hecke rief . . . an
bot ihm Stelle als . . .
gut bezahlt, mit . . .
gab Ratschläge
ordnete Bewässerung . . .
empfahl . . .

DER WINTER
wuchs . . .
Herr Munzel arbeitete in . . .
Seine liebsten Pflanzen waren . . .

DER HERBST
Blätter fielen von . . .
Herr Munzel hörte
das, was . . .
. . . verbrachte zwei Wochen.

NEBENEINNAHMEN
Fußballmannschaft ließ . . .
Reiche Leute ließen ihn mit großen Autos . . .
Leute mit finsteren Absichten . . .
aber Herr Munzel . . .

Texts will vary.

TIPP ZUM SCHREIBEN

Ecology is a serious topic, but this project lets you to do something imaginative with it. Look around for an everyday object that lends itself to an ecological story, then let your imagination play with the idea. Ecology can play a large role or a small one. The ending may be happy or sad, or maybe there is no ending—only you and your creativity can decide.

SCHREIBEN SIE!

Eine originelle Kurzgeschichte

● Schreiben Sie eine originelle Kurzgeschichte über einen alltäglichen Gegenstand mit einem umweltbezogenen Thema.

Purpose:	To write a creative short story with an ecological theme
Audience:	Readers of short stories
Subject:	An everyday object
Structure:	One-page short story

Schreibmodell

Die tapfere Tragetasche

„Das macht fünfundsiebzig achtzig, bitte." Frau Plogmann schaute kurz auf. Der Einkaufskorb, den sie mitgebracht hatte, war voll, Platz für das Gemüse gab es kaum noch. Die Kassiererin wartete. „Geben Sie mir noch eine Tragetasche, bitte." Sie reichte der Kassiererin vier Zwanziger[a] und packte weiter. Ihr wurde eine bunte billige Plastik-Tragetasche hingelegt.

„Uho, jetzt ist es soweit! Ich bin dran! Ob ich das schaffe?" sagte die Tasche etwas unsicher. Andere Taschen riefen ihr Mut zu: „Das schaffst du schon! . . . Klar, du bist aus gutem Stoff! . . . Lass dich nicht kaputtmachen! . . . Reiß bloß nicht durch! . . . Pass auf, dass du nicht weggeworfen wirst! . . . Tschüss, mach's gut!" Aber dabei mußte die Tasche denken: „Was ist mein Schicksal? Was wird bloß aus mir werden?"

Sie war jung, stark, elastisch, aus bester Polymermischung. Sie war direkt von der Fabrik in das Geschäft gebracht worden, ohne lange im Lagerhaus herumzuliegen. Sie fühlte sich umweltbewusst und wieder verwendbar. Sie wollte lange halten und überall helfen. Sie glaubte an ein Jenseits im Recycling, aber wie konnte man da sicher sein? Jetzt aber war die Probe. Und diese Probe musste bestanden werden.

The action is described in the third-person past tense.

The writer allows the characters to talk in the first-person present tense.

Werden is used in this sentence twice: once for the future tense and once as a dependent infinitive *to become*.

The past perfect tense in the passive voice is used to tell about the shopping bag's earlier life.

[a]*twenty mark bill*

„Und eine Tragetasche, das macht zusammen sechs siebzig." Frau Plogmann nahm das Kleingeld und begann, Gemüse in die Tasche zu stopfen. „Bitte, gehen Sie nicht so grob mit mir um!" rief die Tasche. Frau Plogmann reagierte nicht. Sie hob die Tasche an. „Aua!" schrie die Tasche. Nie zuvor hatte sie soviel Gewicht auf sich gefühlt. Zu ihrem Staunen konnte sie es tragen. „Gut" dachte die Tasche „Aber wo geht es hin?"

Gleich waren sie am Wagen. Der Kofferraum wurde aufgemacht, Korb und Tasche wurden angehoben und hineingelegt, und dann schlug die Tür zum Kofferraum zu. Dunkelheit. Stille. Dann wurde eine zweite Tür zugemacht und ein Motor gestartet. Die Tasche war unterwegs aber sie hatte ein unsicheres Gefühl: War dies das Ende oder nur der Anfang ihres Schicksals?

Passive voice draws attention to the action rather than the person performing it.

Schreibstrategien

Vor dem Schreiben

- The goal of this project is to write a story with a beginning, a middle, and an end. It may be serious or humorous.

- Pick an everyday object that you know well enough so you can describe it and its uses. Decide whether human beings will play a role in your story. If you include people, give them names and determine what they have to do with your chosen object.

- Choose a voice for your narration: tell the story either in the third person or in the first person, from the object's point of view.

- Now mull over a story line. Where did your object come from? Is it mute or can it talk? Consider where it is, what it is doing, and what the humans (if any) are doing around it. What can possibly happen between the object and humans or other objects?

- Decide how to introduce your characters. Create a point of departure. Set the scene with a time, a place, and an activity. If you wish, jot down the main points of your plot or create a rough outline. Don't worry about details now; concentrate on the main gist of your story.

May Schwittchen und die gelben Zwerge

~~Einmal auf einer Zeit~~ es war ein neues *(Es war einmal)*
Produkt im Büro: selbstklebende gelbe Zettel.
Sie ~~waren~~ Haftnotizen[a] genennt. *(wurden)* Wie sie ins
Büro gebracht geworden waren, wusste
niemand. Was sollte man mit ihnen machen? Sie
waren so klein. Sie waren gelb: sie durften nicht
recycelt werden. Und teuer! Für Notizen waren
Papier und Klammer[b] gut genug. Also ~~ließen~~ *(ließ man)*
~~sie~~ die Haftnotizen liegen.

Es war auch einmal eine ungeschickte[c]
Sekretärin namens May Schwittchen. Sie hatte
heute schon ein Fax verloren und ihre Chefin war
böse. Jetzt sollte sie ein Dokument mit wichtigen
Notizen fertigstellen. Sie ~~bekam~~ nervös. *(wurde)* Die
Papiere, die mit Notizen belegt und Klammern
festgemacht geworden waren, lagen vor ihr, als
sie heißen Tee über alles schüttete.[d] Was konnte
sie tun? Sie hatte eine Kopie des Dokuments,
aber Notizen und Klammer waren alle nass.
Dann hörte sie die Haftnotizen rufend: „Frau
Schwittchen, Sie sind die Schönste hier, aber die
nasse Klammer haftet nicht so schön wie wir!"
~~Wenn~~ sie eine Haftnotiz auf das Papier ~~druckt~~, *(Als) (drückte)*
klebte sie wunderbar! Frau Schwittchen schrieb
dann schnell die Notizen mit der Hand. Kurz
vor Mittag war das Dokument fertig. Überall
kleb~~en~~ gelbe Haftnotizen. Sie gab es ~~die~~ Chefin, *(t) (der)*
die sagte: „Schön!"

[a]removable, self-sticking notes   [b]paper clips   [c]clumsy   [d]spilled

Beim Schreiben

- Keep notes, outlines, and any other materials handy. Keep a note pad at hand to jot down ideas that come to you as you write.

- Double-space your draft and leave wide margins so you have plenty of room for corrections and additions. If you are using a word processor, remember to save regularly to avoid losing all your hard work!

- If you get writer's block, get away from your story for awhile. Go for a walk, listen to music, study something else, then come back to it. You'll start again refreshed and will have given yourself time to come up with ideas you can develop.

Nach dem Schreiben

- Read your story again critically. Is the story in a consistent tense? Is the narrative voice consistent? Is the passive voice used effectively? Is your story interesting? Make any necessary changes.

- Exchange papers with a peer editor. First read the whole story, then write notes and suggestions for improvements in the margins or on a separate piece of paper. Return the paper to its author.

- Based on your peer editor's comments and your reactions to them, write a revised draft. Remember to leave room for additions.

- After a break, read the revised draft. If something doesn't sound right or needs to be altered, fix it now.

Stimmt alles?

- Read over your final draft. Make sure you've made all corrections.

- Give your story an appropriate title and hand it in.

WORTSCHATZ

Substantive	Nouns
die **Aktion, -en**	action
die **Debatte, -n**	debate
die **Einwegflasche, -n**	nonreturnable bottle
die **Landwirtschaft**	agriculture
die **Pfandflasche, -n**	returnable bottle
die **Rücksicht**	consideration
die **Siedlung, -en**	settlement; neighborhood
die **Tonne, -n**	bin
die **Verschmutzung**	pollution
der **Anstrich, -e**	paint
der **Komposthaufen, -**	compost heap
der **Plastikbecher, -**	plastic cup
der **Rauch**	smoke
der **Rohstoff, -e**	raw material
der **Strom**	electricity; current
der **Umweltschutz**	environmental protection
der **Verbraucher, -** / die **Verbraucherin, -nen**	consumer
der **Verkehr**	traffic
der **Wäschetrockner, -**	(clothes) dryer
das **Aufsehen**	sensation
das **Einweggeschirr**	disposable utensils
das **Gesetz, -e**	law
das **Gleichgewicht**	balance
das **Umweltbewusstsein**	environmental awareness
das **Verkehrsmittel, -**	mode of transportation
das **Verpackungsmaterial, -ien**	packaging material
das **Wachstum**	growth
das **Waldsterben**	dying of the forest

Verben	Verbs
begehren	to desire
bestehen aus, bestand aus, bestanden aus	to consist of
schädigen	to damage
sparen	to save
in die Praxis um•setzen	to put into practice
verschmutzen	to pollute
weg•schmeißen, schmiss weg, weggeschmissen (*coll.*)	to throw away
wieder verwerten	to recycle

Adjektive und Adverbien	Adjectives and adverbs
extrem	extreme(ly)
giftfrei	nontoxic
umweltfeindlich	hostile to the environment
zuliebe (+ *dat.*)	for the sake of

Sie wissen schon	You already know
die **Fabrik, -en**	factory
die **Umwelt**	environment
der **Abfall, ̈-e**	trash; garbage, waste
der **Container, -**	container; dumpster
der **Lärm**	noise
der **Müll**	trash
der **Umweltsünder, -** / die **Umweltsünderin, -nen**	polluter, litterbug
bestehen, bestand, bestanden	to pass (an exam); to exist
recyceln	to recycle
schützen	to protect
trennen	to separate; to divide
verbrauchen	to consume; to use
vergiften	to poison
verwenden	to apply
verzichten auf (+ *acc.*)	to renounce; to do without
öffentlich	public(ly)
organisch	organic
umweltfreundlich	environmentally friendly

KAPITEL 36 FOKUS AUF KULTUR

pages 248–267

PLANNING GUIDE • CLASSROOM MANAGEMENT

OBJECTIVES

Communication
- Discuss what "culture" means to you, pp. 250–251.
- Talk about German films, pp. 252–253.
- Tell about your childhood, pp. 258–259.

Grammar
- Review the past perfect tense, p. 254.
- Review alternatives to the passive, p. 256.
- Review word order with verbs, pp. 257–258.

Culture
- Learn about a musical production in a Berlin children's theater, p. 250.
- Learn about the history of German film, p. 251.

Recycling
- Review the past perfect tense, pp. 254–255.
- Review German word order, pp. 257–259.

STRATEGIES

Listening Strategies
- Listen to a description of a play, p. 260.

Speaking Strategies
- Talk about a favorite story, p. 261.
- Read a text aloud, p. 261.
- Discuss your performance, p. 263.

Reading Strategies
- Read with an eye to performance, pp. 261–262.

Writing Strategies
- Write a cultural survey, p. 263.
- Write a Top Ten list, p. 264

Connecting Cultures Strategies
- Compare German and American definitions of culture, p. 251.
- Learn about the contributions of German speakers to the American film industry, p. 251.

PROGRAM RESOURCES

Print
- *Arbeitsheft* (Workbook), pp. 179–194
- *Arbeitsheft* (Workbook), Teacher's Edition, pp. 179–194

Audiovisual
- Overhead Transparencies 36.1–36.G2
- Audio Program, Cassette 6B, 7B/ CD 8, 9
- Audioscript, pp. 86–91

Technology
- Annenberg *Fokus Deutsch* Video Series, *Folge 36*
- www.mcdougallittell.com

Assessment Program Options
- *Prüfung, Kapitel 36,* Assessment Program, pp. 147–156
- Audio Program, Cassette 8B/CD 10
- Audioscript, p. 115
- Teacher's Resource CD-ROM

Note: (1) Please see TE, pp. 248E–248J, for other suggestions not referenced in these plans. (2) Not all homework options need be assigned.

CHAPTER OPENER

- Quick Start Review: Future tense (TE, p. 248E). 5 MIN
- Discuss the photos on pp. 248–249 (TE, p. 248E). 4 MIN

VIDEOTHEK

- Discuss the questions on the top of p. 250 as a class. 4 MIN
- Read through the statements in *Akt. A,* p. 250, and do the activity while watching *Folge I: Theater für Jugendliche* (TE, p. 248F). 8 MIN
- Do *Akt. B,* p. 250, in small groups. End with a brief class discussion of the topics discussed (TE, p. 248F). 8 MIN
- Discuss the questions at the top of p. 251 as a class. 4 MIN
- Do *Akt. A,* p. 251, while watching *Folge II: Hundert Jahre deutscher Film* (TE, p. 248F). 11 MIN
- Do the follow-up activity in the Teaching Suggestions for *Akt. A,* p. 251 (TE, p. 248F). 6 MIN

Homework Options:

- *Arbeitsheft,* p. 180, *Videothek, Akt. C–D*

VIDEOTHEK

- Quick Start Review 1: Genitive (TE, p. 248E). 5 MIN
- Have students do *Akt. B, Schritt 1,* p. 251, individually, then check their answers in small groups. Show the video episode again if necessary. Discuss *Akt. B, Schritt 2,* p. 251, in the same small groups. 12 MIN
- *Arbeitsheft,* p. 180, audio *Akt. F.* 6 MIN

VOKABELN

- Present the vocabulary on p. 252. 8 MIN
- Do *Akt. A,* pp. 252–253, as a class. 8 MIN
- Have students do *Akt. B,* pp. 252–253, individually, then check answers as a class. Do the follow-up activity in the Teaching Suggestions (TE, p. 248G). 11 MIN

Homework Options:

- *Arbeitsheft,* p. 182, *Videothek, Akt. H*
- *Arbeitsheft,* p. 184, *Vokabeln, Akt. C–D*

VOKABELN

- Quick Start Review 1: Vocabulary review (TE, p. 248G). 5 MIN
- Have the students discuss *Akt. C,* p. 253, in small groups and then do the follow-up activity (TE, p. 248G). 11 MIN
- *Arbeitsheft,* p. 183, audio *Akt. A–B.* 9 MIN

STRUKTUREN

- Present the past perfect tense on p. 254 using 36.G1. 8 MIN
- Do *Übung A,* pp. 254–255, silently. Check answers as a class and encourage students to form several more compound sentences (TE, p. 248H). 8 MIN
- *Arbeitsheft,* p. 183, audio *Akt. A–B.* 9 MIN

Homework Options:

- *Arbeitsheft,* p. 185, *Vokabeln, Akt. E*
- *Arbeitsheft,* p. 188, *Strukturen, Akt. E*

VOKABELN

- Quick Start Review 2: Passive (TE, p. 248G). 5 MIN

STRUKTUREN

- *Arbeitsheft,* p. 187, audio *Akt. C.* 7 MIN
- Do *Übung B,* p. 255, in small groups (TE, p. 248H). 7 MIN
- Do *Übung C,* p. 255, silently, then check their answers as a class and create a time line. 9 MIN
- Present alternatives to the passive on p. 256 using 36.1 and 36.G2 (TE, p. 248H). 6 MIN
- Do *Übung A,* pp. 256–257, in small groups. Each group should practice acting out the recipe preparation. Choose 1–2 groups to perform for the class, while other groups narrate. 8 MIN
- Do *Übung B,* p. 257, silently, then check the answers with partners (TE, p. 248H). 8 MIN

Homework Options:

- *Arbeitsheft,* pp. 188–189, *Strukturen, Akt. H–I*

PACING GUIDE • SAMPLE LESSON PLAN, 50-MINUTE SCHEDULE

STRUKTUREN

- Quick Start Review 1: Vocabulary review (TE, p. 248H). 5 MIN
- Do *Übung C,* p. 257, as a class. 7 MIN
- Present word order with verbs on pp. 257–258. (TE, p. 248H). 8 MIN
- Do *Übung A,* pp. 258–259, silently, then share the answers in small groups. End with the whole class sharing their sentences. Do the follow-up activity in the Teaching Suggestions as a class (TE, p. 248H). 11 MIN
- *Arbeitsheft,* pp. 189–190, audio, *Akt. J–K.* 9 MIN
- Do *Übung B,* p. 259, silently, then share the sentences in small groups. Follow the Teaching Suggestions for an expansion activity (TE, p. 248H). 10 MIN

Homework Options:

- *Arbeitsheft,* p. 190, *Strukturen, Akt. L–M*

STRUKTUREN

- Quick Start Review 2: Passive/Active (TE, p. 248H). 5 MIN

PERSPEKTIVEN

- After reviewing the *Wortschatz zum Hörtext* and reading through the questions in *Hören Sie zu!,* p. 260, play the recording one time. Have students do the activity as they listen and take notes. Discuss the answers to the activity as a class. 10 MIN
- Model *Zum Thema,* pp. 261–262, then have students do the activity (TE, p. 248I). 8 MIN
- *Zum Text, Schritte 1–2,* p. 261. Allow students time to ask you about the texts or discuss the texts with other class members (TE, p. 248J). 10 MIN
- *Zur Interpretation, Schritt 1,* p. 263. Have students share responses with a partner. 6 MIN
- *Interaktion, Schritt 1,* p. 263 (TE, p. 248J). 11 MIN

Homework Options:

- Prepare to perform a poem from pp. 261–262
- *Arbeitsheft,* pp. 193–194, *Perspektiven, Akt. B–D*

PERSPEKTIVEN

- Quick Start Review 1: Relative clauses (TE, p. 248I). 4 MIN
- Do *Zum Text, Schritt 3,* p. 261, as a class or in small groups. 15 MIN
- *Interaktion, Schritte 2–3,* p. 263. 11 MIN
- Begin *Schreiben Sie!* by discussing the assignment, *Tipp zum Schreiben,* and *Schreibmodell.* 5 MIN
- Begin *Vor dem Schreiben,* p. 265 (TE, p. 248J). 5 MIN

Homework Options:

- Complete *Vor dem Schreiben* and *Beim Schreiben,* pp. 265–266. Finish the first draft of the Top Ten list

PERSPEKTIVEN

- Quick Start Review 2: Infinitive clauses with *zu* (TE, p. 248I). 4 MIN
- *Nach dem Schreiben,* p. 266 (TE, p. 248J). 11 MIN
- Questions and review. 5 MIN
- *Prüfung, Kapitel 36.* 30 MIN

Homework Options:

- Complete the final draft of the Top Ten list

DAY 1

Note: (1) Please see TE, pp. 248E–248J, for other suggestions not referenced in these plans. (2) Not all homework options need be assigned.

CHAPTER OPENER

- Quick Start Review: Future tense (TE, p. 248E). 5 MIN
- Discuss photos on pp. 248–249. 4 MIN

VIDEOTHEK

- Discuss questions on p. 250. 4 MIN
- Do *Akt. A,* p. 250, while watching *Folge I* (TE, p. 248F). 9 MIN
- *Akt. B,* p. 250. Discuss. 8 MIN
- *Arbeitsheft,* p. 179, audio *Akt. A–B.* 8 MIN
- Discuss questions on p. 251. 4 MIN
- Do *Akt. A,* while watching *Folge II.* Do follow-up (TE, p. 248F). 17 MIN
- Block Schedule activity: Change of Pace (TE, pp. 248F–G). 10 MIN
- *Akt. B,* p. 251. 12 MIN
- *Arbeitsheft,* p. 181, *Akt. E–F.* 9 MIN

Homework Options:

- *Arbeitsheft,* pp. 180, 182, *Akt. C–D, H*

DAY 2

VOKABELN

- Quick Start Review 1: Vocabulary review (TE, p. 248G). 5 MIN
- Present the vocabulary on p. 252. 8 MIN
- Do *Akt. A,* pp. 252–253, as a class. 8 MIN
- Do *Akt. B–C,* p. 253, then do the follow-up activities on TE, p. 248G. 22 MIN
- *Arbeitsheft,* p. 183, audio *Akt. B.* 7 MIN
- Block Schedule activity: Fun Break (TE, p. 248G). 10 MIN

STRUKTUREN

- Present the past perfect tense on p. 254 using OHT 36.G1. 8 MIN
- Do *Übung A,* pp. 254–255, silently. Check answers as a class (TE, p. 248H). 8 MIN
- *Arbeitsheft,* p. 184, *Akt. C.* 7 MIN
- Do *Übung B,* p. 255, in small groups (TE, p. 248H). 7 MIN

Homework Options:

- *Arbeitsheft,* pp. 184–185, *Akt. C–E* and p. 188, *Akt. E*

DAY 3

STRUKTUREN

- Quick Start Review 1: Vocabulary review (TE, p. 248H). 5 MIN
- Do *Übung C,* p. 255, silently, check answers, and create a time line. 9 MIN
- Present alternatives to the passive on p. 256 using OHT 36.2 and 36.G2 (TE, p. 248H). 7 MIN
- Do *Übung A,* pp. 256–257, in small groups (TE, p. 248H). 8 MIN
- Do *Übung B,* p. 257, then check answers with a partner (TE, p. 248H). 8 MIN
- *Übung C,* p. 257, as a class. 7 MIN
- Block Schedule activity: Expansion (TE, p. 248I). 10 MIN
- Present word order with verbs on pp. 257–258. (TE, p. 248H). 8 MIN
- Do *Übungen A–B,* pp. 258–259 (TE, p. 248H). 21 MIN
- *Arbeitsheft,* p. 189, audio *Akt. J.* 6 MIN

Homework Options:

- *Arbeitsheft,* pp. 189–190, *Akt. H–I, L–M*

DAY 4

PERSPEKTIVEN

- Quick Start Review 1: Relative clauses (TE, p. 248I). 5 MIN
- Play the recording and have students do the *Hören Sie zu!* activity, p. 260 (TE, p. 248I). 10 MIN
- Do *Zum Thema* activity, p. 260 (TE, p. 248I). 8 MIN
- Do *Zum Text, Schritte 1–2,* p. 261 (TE, p. 248J). 15 MIN
- *Zur Interpretation, Schritt 1,* p. 263. Share responses in pairs. 8 MIN
- *Interaktion, Schritt 1,* p. 263 (TE, p. 248J). 15 MIN
- Block Schedule activity: Change of Pace (TE, p. 248J). 10 MIN
- Begin *Schreiben Sie!* by discussing the assignment. 7 MIN
- *Vor dem Schreiben,* p. 265, and begin *Beim Schreiben* (TE, p. 248J). 12 MIN

Homework Options:

- Complete the first draft of the Top Ten list
- Prepare to perform a poem from pp. 261–262
- *Arbeitsheft,* pp. 193–194, *Akt. B–D*

DAY 5

PERSPEKTIVEN

- Quick Start Review 2: Infinitive clauses with *zu* (TE, p. 248I). 5 MIN
- Do *Zum Text, Schritt 3,* page 261 as a whole class or in small groups. 15 MIN
- *Interaktion, Schritte 2–3,* p. 263. 15 MIN
- *Nach dem Schreiben,* p. 266 (TE, p. 248J). 11 MIN
- Block Schedule activity: Fun Break (TE, p. 248J). 10 MIN
- Questions and review. 5 MIN
- *Prüfung, Kapitel 36.* 30 MIN

Homework Options:

- Complete the final draft of the Top Ten list

TEACHING SUGGESTIONS

Chapter Opener, pp. 248–249

PROGRAM RESOURCES

- Overhead Transparency 36.1

Quick Start Review

Future tense
Schreiben Sie die Sätze ins Futur.
1. Christa und Frank gehen zum Eiscafé.
2. Christa isst eine Portion Erdbeereis.
3. Ihr trinkt Cola.
4. Heute regnet es.
5. Morgen genießen wir das schöne Wetter.

Answers: 1. Christa und Frank werden zum Eiscafé gehen. 2. Christa wird eine Portion Erdbeereis essen. 3. Ihr werdet Cola trinken. 4. Heute wird es regnen. 5. Morgen werden wir das schöne Wetter genießen.

TEACHING SUGGESTIONS

Show pictures of famous Germans, Austrians, and Swiss who are literary figures, famous people in the film industry, artists, musicians, composers, and the like. Ask students to identify as many of them as they can and, if possible, the contributions they made.

- Photos, pp. 248–249

Use the photos to introduce famous cultural figures and the topic of culture in German-speaking countries. Look over the photos and have students discuss their entertainment preferences. Ask questions like *Gehen*

Sie gern in die Oper? Gehen Sie gern ins Theater? Gehen Sie gern ins Konzert? Was für kulturelle Veranstaltungen sind Ihnen am liebsten? usw.

TEACHING ALL STUDENTS

Challenge Give students 5 minutes to write down as many works in the following categories as they can: *Opern, Theaterstücke, Filme, Romane.* Ask *Von wem ist das Werk? Wann hat er/sie es geschaffen?* Have students translate the titles of non-German works into German and have the class try to guess the English title.

CLASSROOM COMMUNITY

Group Activity Twenty questions: Choose a famous German-speaking person and have students try to guess his/her identity by asking yes/no questions in turns. Whoever guesses the person before 20 questions have been asked, wins. Let that student choose the next mystery person, and so on.

INTERDISCIPLINARY CONNECTION

Fine Arts/Literature/Science: Have students ask their teachers about some famous individuals from German-speaking countries and about their contributions to fine arts, literature, or science. Have students report back to class.

Videothek, pp. 250–251

PROGRAM RESOURCES

- Videocassette, *Folge 36*
- *Arbeitsheft*, pp. 179–182

- Audio Program, Cassette 6B/CD 8
- Audioscript, pp. 86–87

Quick Start Review 1

Genitive
Ergänzen Sie die passenden Wörter im Genitiv und die passenden Endungen.
1. Ich fahre das Auto _____ Bruder___.
   a. meinem, -es   b. meiner, -
   c. meines, -s   d. mein, -n
2. Das ist das Haus _____ Eltern___.
   a. seiner, -   b. seines, -es
   c. seinen, -s   d. seine, -en
3. Er bekam die Telefonnummer _____ schönen Frau___.
   a. das, -es   b. der, -   c. des, -s
   d. die, -en
4. Der Titel _____ Buch___ ist *Im Westen nichts Neues.*
   a. dieses, -es   b. diesem, -s
   c. dieser, -   d. diesen, -en
5. Die Uniform _____ Pilot___ war blau.
   a. das, -es   b. der, -s   c. des, -en   d. die, -

Answers: 1. c   2. a   3. b   4. a   5. c

Quick Start Review 2

Relative pronouns
Ergänzen Sie die Relativpronomen.
1. MICHAEL: Kennst du die Musik, _____ wir heute Abend im Konzert hören werden?
2. IRIS: Klar! Das Orchester wird Gustav Mahlers neunte Symphonie spielen, _____ er am Ende seines Lebens geschrieben hat.
   MICHAEL: Mahler kenne ich nicht. Wo hat er gelebt?

3. IRIS: Gustav Mahler war ein Komponist, _____ in Wien gelebt hat. Während der Zeit, _____ er in Wien verbrachte, war er Dirigent der Wiener Philharmoniker.

4. MICHAEL: Ist Wien die Stadt, in _____ auch Sigmund Freud gelebt hat, _____ Bücher über die Psychologie sehr bekannt sind?

5. IRIS: Richtig! Und das sind nur zwei von den vielen berühmten Leuten, _____ in Wien gelebt haben.

   MICHAEL: Wie weißt du so viel über Wien?

6. IRIS: Ich habe zwei Kurse besucht, in _____ wir das kulturelle Leben in Wien diskutiert haben.

7. MICHAEL: War einer der Kurs, _____ Professor Schröder unterrichtet hat?

8. IRIS: Ja, ich glaube, dass er der beste Professor ist, _____ hier an der Uni unterrichtet.

Answers: 1. die   2. die   3. der, die
4. der, dessen   5. die   6. denen
7. den   8. der

TEACHING SUGGESTIONS

• *Aktivität A,* p. 250

Review the following vocabulary items by writing them on the board: *auf der Suche, begegnen* + dative, *bestehen aus, reagieren auf, erforschen.* After completing the activity, view the segment again and have students write down another statement made by one of the interviewees. Have students read the statements they have written and then have the class determine who is speaking.

• *Aktivität B,* p. 250

Point out that the song in the video episode is actually a *Selbstgespräch.* It presents the unspoken thoughts of the singer. Discuss the context of the song and ask students if they have been in similar situations. Have them create and perform a similar inner monologue.

• *Folge II: Hundert Jahre deutscher Film,* p. 251

Before watching this episode, have students brainstorm words associated with film and write them on the board. For example, *der Regisseur, das Filmstudio, die Kameraführung, der Schnitt, der Gruselfilm.*

• *Aktivität A,* p. 251

Follow-up: Have students conjecture about the plots of the films presented. Start by having students describe the photos in this activity. Show the video episode again if necessary.

TEACHING ALL STUDENTS

Extra Help To help students understand some of the major themes running through New German Cinema, discuss the stories of *Die Blechtrommel* and *Die Ehe der Maria Braun* in more detail. Focus on important topics such as *das Wirtschaftswunder, die deutsche Schuld und Vergangenheitsbewältigung,* or *deutsch-amerikanische Beziehungen in der Nachkriegszeit.* You may want to show additional clips from these films.

CLASSROOM COMMUNITY

Dictation Choose 1–2 of the responses made by the interviewees in the video and play them to the class as a dictation. Show each one at least twice.

CULTURE HIGHLIGHTS

Have students read the *Kulturspiegel* on p. 251. Explain that German and Austrian intellectuals and artists from many fields immigrated to the U.S. in the 30s and 40s. Novelists such as Thomas Mann and Lion Feuchtwanger, composers such as Arnold Schoenberg and Kurt Weill, playwrights such as Bertolt Brecht, and painters such as George Grosz all went to America. Have students conjecture about why they left and what factors might have made leaving difficult for them. You may also discuss the concept of the *innere Immigration* practiced by many artists who stayed in Germany and Austria despite the Nazis' attitudes toward their art.

LANGUAGE NOTE

Show the credits of a German-language film and have students jot down the various job titles. Have students try to guess their meanings.

BLOCK SCHEDULE

Change of Pace Using a short sequence from any film, introduce the concept of a story board. Show the sequence several times without sound and use the still function on the VCR or DVD to freeze the various shots. Provide the class with a scenario involving a short sequence of events, for example, *Ein Mann geht in ein Geschäft, um es zu überfallen. Sein Kumpel wartet im Auto. Das Mietshaus brennt, und eine Frau muss aus einem Fenster im fünften Stock springen, um sich zu retten. Unten ist die Feuerwehr.* Have students work in pairs to draw pictures to diagram the sequence. Have them present their storyboards to the class and give detailed descriptions of each shot.

Vokabeln, pp. 252–253

PROGRAM RESOURCES

- *Arbeitsheft*, pp. 183–185
- Audio Program, Cassette 6B/CD 8
- Audioscript, pp. 87–88

Quick Start Review 1

♻ Vocabulary review
Ergänzen Sie die Sätze mit den folgenden Wörtern.
WÖRTER: der Autor, das Gemälde, die Komposition, der Künstler, der Roman, der Schauspieler, die Stimmung

1. Heinrich von Kleist ist _____ berühmter Dramen und Erzählungen.
2. Die intensiven Farben und Formen machen _____ zu einem Meisterwerk der expressionistischen Kunst.
3. _____ Max Schreck hat den Vampir in dem alten Film *Nosferatu* gespielt.
4. *Erwartung* ist _____ des jüdischen Komponisten Arnold Schönbergs.
5. _____ *Der Zauberberg* ist vom Schriftsteller Thomas Mann geschrieben worden.
6. Auf der Party war _____ sehr gut.
7. Franz Marc war _____, dessen Werke oft Tiere als Subjekt hatten.

Answers: 1. der Autor 2. das Gemälde 3. Der Schauspieler 4. die Komposition 5. Der Roman 6. die Stimmung 7. der Künstler

Quick Start Review 2

♻ Passive
Schreiben Sie die Sätze ins Passiv.
MODELL: Der Regisseur dreht den Film. → *Der Film wird von dem Regisseur gedreht.*

1. Die Deutschen synchronisieren oft ausländische Filme.
2. Der Kameramann filmt die Szene.
3. Kurt Weill komponierte die Musik zu diesem Theaterstück.
4. Die Kritiker loben den Film.
5. Max Beckmann malte das Bild im Jahre 1925.

Answers: 1. Ausländische Filme werden von den Deutschen oft synchonisiert. 2. Die Szene wird von dem Kameramann gefilmt. 3. Die Musik zu diesem Theaterstück wurde von Kurt Weill komponiert. 4. Der Film wird von den Kritikern gelobt. 5. Das Bild wurde von Max Beckmann im Jahre 1925 gemalt.

TEACHING SUGGESTIONS

- *Aktivität B*, p. 253

Follow-up: Ask students to write a definition of one of the vocabulary items on p. 252 on a slip of paper. Call on students to give the definition they have written. The class must guess what word matches the definition.

- *Aktivität C*, p. 253

Follow-up: In pairs, have students read the dialogue again and look for points supporting Stefan's and Daniela's film preferences. Give students a few minutes to think of other arguments for both sides. Then have them choose a

side and improvise an argument. Call on pairs to perform their debates in front of the class.

TEACHING ALL STUDENTS

Multiple Intelligences Kinesthetic: Have students form groups of 4–6 and play charades with the words from the vocabulary list on p. 252. Add more words to the list for a greater challenge.

CLASSROOM COMMUNITY

Challenge Give students 10 minutes to work with a partner to write a paragraph using at least 10 of the vocabulary items from p. 252. Suggest topics such as *Was sind die Unterschiede der verschiedenen Filmarten?* or *Was sind die Unterschiede zwischen Film und Theater?*

LANGUAGE NOTE

Visit a German-language Internet site with film listings and print out the titles. Discuss with the class why some non-German titles are translated into German while others are left in their original language.

BLOCK SCHEDULE

Fun Break Play a category game in German. Compile a list of categories such as *Österreichische Komponisten, Vokabeln zum Stichwort „Theater", Berühmte Regisseure, Europäische Schriftsteller.* Draw a letter of the alphabet out of a bag and give students 4 minutes to come up with words for each category starting with the letter drawn. Play in teams and award points for each correct word.

Strukturen, pp. 254–259

PROGRAM RESOURCES

- Overhead Transparencies 36.2, 36.G1–36.2
- *Arbeitsheft,* pp. 186–190
- Audio Program, Cassette 6B/CD 8
- Audioscript, pp. 88–91

Quick Start Review 1

♻ Vocabulary review
Finden Sie das Wort, das nicht zu der Liste passt.

1. das Naturparadies, die Berge, die Wiese, das Nebenzimmer
2. die Kommode, der Neffe, der Kleiderschrank, der Nachttisch
3. die Olive, die Kartoffel, die Ursache, die Zitrone
4. das Gedicht, der Roman, der Brief, der Alptraum
5. der Adler, das Kettenglied, der Affe, der Kampfhund
6. der Vogel, die Wildbiene, die Heuschrecke, die Fliege
7. der Einwohner, der Großvater, der Mitstudent, der Müll

Answers: 1. das Nebenzimmer
2. der Neffe   3. die Ursache   4. der Alptraum   5. das Kettenglied   6. der Vogel   7. der Müll

Quick Start Review 2

♻ Passive/Active
Schreiben Sie die Sätze ins Aktiv um. Benutzen Sie *wir* als Subjekt und achten Sie dabei auf die Zeit.
MODELL: An der Uni wird viel über die Politiker geredet. → *An der Uni reden wir viel über die Politiker.*

1. Freitagabend durfte die Musik laut gespielt werden.

2. Hans und Franz wurden am Wochenende besucht.
3. Dieser Film kann schnell vergessen werden.
4. Auf der Party ist viel getanzt worden.
5. Die Umwelt wird geschützt werden.
6. Der Müll ist schon getrennt worden.
7. Die Pfandflaschen wurden zur Sammelstelle gebracht.
8. Das Auto war schon gewaschen worden.

Answers: 1. Freitagabend durften wir die Musik laut spielen.   2. Wir besuchten Hans und Franz am Wochenende.   3. Wir können diesen Film schnell vergessen.   4. Wir haben auf der Party viel getanzt.   5. Wir werden die Umwelt schützen.   6. Wir haben den Müll schon getrennt. 7. Wir brachten die Pfandflaschen zur Sammelstelle.   8. Wir hatten das Auto schon gewaschen.

TEACHING SUGGESTIONS

- *Übung A,* pp. 254–255

To emphasize the importance of temporal succession, have students create a time line of the events in all of the clauses in *Übung A.* Encourage students to form several more compound sentences. Have students work silently and then share their answers in small groups.

- *Übung B,* p. 255

Encourage students to formulate 1–2 additional compound sentences using the past perfect. Supply them with

additional vocabulary, such as *der Produzent, finanzieren, der Filmstar, der Kassenrekord.*

- Alternatives to the passive, p. 256

Remind students that constructions with *man* are very frequent in German. Point out its various functions, such as giving directions in recipes, telling children what is not allowed, or making suggestions.

- *Übung A,* pp. 256–257

Each group should practice acting out the recipe preparation. Choose 1–2 groups to perform for the class while other groups narrate.

- *Übung B,* p. 257

Follow-up: Introduce the use of *sich lassen* in sentences such as *Ich lasse mir die Haare schneiden* and *Er lässt sich das Auto reparieren.* Point out that the reflexive pronoun in these sentences is in the dative case.

- Word order with verbs, pp. 257–258

Point out the unusual word order in subordinating clauses with a double infinitive: *Jetzt verstand er, warum er das nicht hätte machen sollen.* In such clauses the helping verb precedes the double infinitive.

- *Übung A,* pp. 258–259

End with the whole class sharing their sentences. Follow-up: Start each sentence with the subordinating clause *Als ich ein Kind war . . .*

- *Übung B,* p. 259

Expansion: Have students express differences of opinion and support their points of view.

TEACHING ALL STUDENTS

Multiple Intelligences Logical/ Mathematical: Present students with a few dependent clauses that imply prerequisite actions such as *Bevor Herr Schrupp sein Fahrradgeschäft aufmachte . . .* or *Ehe ich meine Reise nach Indonesien begann . . .* Have students finish the sentences, then write several alternate versions of the completed sentences using the past perfect tense.

CLASSROOM COMMUNITY

Paired Activity Make photocopies of several recipes in German. (If you don't have a German-language cookbook, recipes are accessible on the Internet.) Distribute recipes to pairs of students and have them rewrite the directions using *man* or the passive.

BLOCK SCHEDULE

Expansion Instruct students to state the rules of their school using *man*. Have them write the rules on the board. You could also have students write the rules of a game, a sport, or a club.

Perspektiven, pp. 260–266 ♻

PROGRAM RESOURCES

- Overhead Transparencies 36.3–36.4
- *Arbeitsheft,* pp. 191–194
- Audio Program, Cassette 6B, 7B/ CD 8, 9
- Audioscript, p. 91
- www.mcdougallittell.com

Quick Start Review 1
♻ Relative clauses
Verbinden Sie die Sätze mit einem Relativpronomen.

MODELL: Kennst du die Musik? Wir werden die Musik heute Abend im Konzert hören. → *Kennst du die Musik, die wir heute Abend im Konzert hören werden?*

1. Sie hat eine Kassette. Die Kassette gehört mir.
2. Die Kassette war bei den anderen Sachen. Ich habe dir die Sachen gestern gegeben.
3. Hast du auch den Roman gefunden? Ich wollte den Roman schon lange lesen.
4. Stefan ist ein guter Freund. Ich gehe mit Stefan oft ins Konzert.
5. Stefan ist der musikalische Junge. Seine Mutter ist eine bekannte Sängerin.

Answers: 1. Sie hat eine Kassette, die mir gehört.   2. Die Kassette war bei den anderen Sachen, die ich dir gestern gegeben habe.   3. Hast du auch den Roman gefunden, den ich schon lange lesen wollte?   4. Stefan ist ein guter Freund, mit dem ich oft ins Konzert gehe.   5. Stefan ist der musikalische Junge, dessen Mutter eine bekannte Sängerin ist.

Quick Start Review 2
Infinitive clauses with *zu*
Verbinden Sie die Sätze. Benutzen Sie dabei *um . . . zu.*
MODELL: Gürkan macht abends einen Sprachkurs. Er will besser Deutsch sprechen. → *Gürkan macht abends einen Sprachkurs, um besser Deutsch zu sprechen.*

1. Peter liest die Zeitung. Er will informiert sein.
2. Claudia nimmt ihren Regenschirm mit. Sie will nicht nass werden.
3. Erika übt Klavier. Sie will besser spielen.
4. Richard arbeitet. Er will Geld verdienen.
5. Stefan fährt nach Spanien. Er will dort seine Freundin besuchen.
6. Anja geht zur Telefonzelle. Sie will Peter anrufen.

Answers: 1. Peter liest die Zeitung, um informiert zu sein.   2. Claudia nimmt ihren Regenschirm mit, um nicht nass zu werden.   3. Erika übt Klavier, um besser zu spielen.   4. Richard arbeitet, um Geld zu verdienen.   5. Stefan fährt nach Spanien, um dort seine Freundin zu besuchen.   6. Anja geht zur Telefonzelle, um Peter anzurufen.

TEACHING SUGGESTIONS

- *Hören Sie zu!,* p. 260

Variety: Have students make up their own listening activity based on a current ad for a film or play. Have them include the title, time, date, and subject of the film or play.

- *Lesen Sie!,* pp. 260–263

This section is devoted to the performance of text rather than to reading. You can either assign texts to be performed by certain individuals, pairs, or groups or let students choose the texts they would like to perform. Students may need help with pronunciation and intonation.

- *Zum Thema,* pp. 260–261

Prepare a *Lieblingserzählung* or *Lieblingsgedicht* to model for the students. After telling the story or reciting the poem, reiterate the gist.

- *Zum Text,* p. 261

Once students have chosen their texts, let them ask you questions about them. You may give them time in class to read through the texts while you circulate and answer questions.

- *Zur Interpretation, Schritt 2,* p. 263

Warm-up: Have students use a rubric for peer evaluation of the performances. Students should refer to these when sharing their comments with the performers. Use German versions of the criteria on the rubric: *Aussprache, Rhythmus und Intonation, Vorbereitung.*

- *Interaktion, Schritt 1,* p. 263

Encourage students to write 3–4 questions of their own. You may want to have some of them integrate questions concerning another art form into their questionnaire.

- *Schreiben Sie!,* pp. 264–266

Start with a discussion of the Internet. Ask students what they think are the positive and negative aspects of the Internet. Have them tell you about some of their favorite Web sites and ask if any of them have their own personal sites. Find a few personal sites of German speakers on the Internet and visit them with your class.

- *Schreibmodell,* p. 264

Read through the 2 reviews with students. Point out the footnotes and write the sentences referred to on the board.

- *Vor dem Schreiben,* p. 265

Students who choose movies, TV programs, or books as their genre should use the Internet to search for German versions of the titles.

- *Nach dem Schreiben,* p. 266

Circulate through the classroom as students do peer editing. Encourage students to be rigorous in their editing and answer any questions that arise.

TEACHING ALL STUDENTS

Multiple Intelligences Musical/Rhythmic: Bring in a recording of instrumental music and have students do a free-write while listening. Encourage them to let their thoughts flow, whether they be about the music they are hearing or not. Ask students who are interested to share their free-writes.

CLASSROOM COMMUNITY

Group Activity Have students present their Top Ten lists to the class. Give the class the opportunity to ask questions of the speaker about the works chosen. Ask if other students chose the same or similar works. Make a bulletin board available for students to post their lists.

Change of Pace Watch a feature-length German-language film with your class. Encourage students to listen and not rely on the subtitles. (Some DVDs allow you to turn off the subtitles altogether.) Make a handout with a list of the main characters, useful vocabulary, content questions, and discussion questions. After students have had a chance to complete the worksheet, have a class discussion based on the questions. Have students role-play the film's main characters.

BLOCK SCHEDULE

Fun Break Choose a scene from a German-language film showing people speaking while doing something. Show the scene without sound. Have students in groups of 2–3 invent a script for the scene. Choose groups to read their dialogue as the scene is viewed again. Finally, view the scene with the original sound on dialogue and discuss.

Change of Pace Ask students if they have favorite artists or favorite works of art. Introduce a few of the artists of the German Expressionist period, such as Max Beckmann, George Grosz, Franz Marc, Gabriele Münter, or Otto Dix, and discuss some of the major themes running through their art, for example, industrialization, alienation, abstraction, or war. Show pictures of 1–2 works of art and have students take 3 minutes to write down their reactions. Discuss their reactions as a class.

PORTFOLIO

Have students choose a German-language film to watch at home. (Many video stores have a foreign film section and Goethe Institutes often have German films for rent.) Have them write a review of it. Supply some examples of German movie reviews to use as models.

RUBRIC **A** = 13–15 pts. **B** = 10–12 pts. **C** = 7–9 pts. **D** = 4–6 pts. **F** < 4 pts.

Writing Criteria	Scale				
Vocabulary, usage	1	2	3	4	5
Grammatical accuracy	1	2	3	4	5
Content, originality	1	2	3	4	5

KAPITEL 36 FOKUS AUF KULTUR

In diesem Kapitel

- sehen Sie einen Auszug aus einem Musical in einem Kindertheater in Berlin.
- erfahren Sie, wie sich die deutsche Filmindustrie entwickelt hat.
- besprechen Sie, was für Sie der Begriff „Kultur" bedeutet.

Sie werden auch

- den Gebrauch des Plusquamperfekts wiederholen.
- Alternativen zum Passiv lernen.
- die Wortstellung wiederholen.
- einen Text vor der Klasse aufführen.
- eine Bestenliste schreiben.

Bei einer
Theateraufführung
in Berlin.

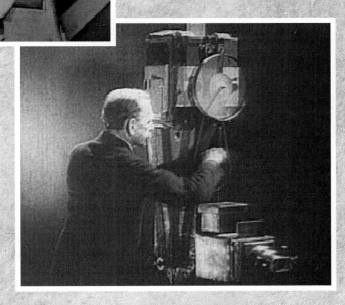

Deutsche Filme haben
eine lange Geschichte.

Straßenkünstler
erfreuen sich großer
Beliebtheit.

VIDEOTHEK

Kultur – dazu gehören Theater, Musik, Film, Literatur und noch mehr. Was assoziieren Sie mit dem Wort „Kultur"? Warum geht man ins Theater oder ins Kino?

I: Theater für Jugendliche

In dieser Folge sehen Sie Auszüge aus dem Musical, „Linie Eins". Ein Mädchen, Sunny, kommt aus Westdeutschland zum ersten Mal nach Berlin.

A Wer sagt das?

Das Grips Theater in Berlin.

a. **Volker Ludwig**

b. **Der Schauspieler**

c. **Die Schauspielerin**

1. „Und auf dieser Suche fährt sie mit der „Linie Eins" – der U-Bahn Linie Eins – und begegnet auf ihrer Fahrt auf den Stationen, den Menschen der Großstadt."
2. „Der Unterschied von einem Publikum, was nur aus Kindern besteht, und einem Erwachsenenpublikum ist tatsächlich der, dass die Kinder ganz direkt auf das reagieren, was sie sehen."
3. „Wir erforschen die Sehnsüchte, Probleme und Fragen unseres Publikums und machen daraus für dieses Publikum Stücke."

B In der U-Bahn. Welchen Eindruck bekommen Sie vom folgenden Lied, das die Fahrgäste singen? Wie würden Sie die Fahrgäste beschreiben? Welche Aspekte des Großstadtlebens stellen sie hier dar?

> Du sitzt mir gegenüber und schaust an mir vorbei
> Ich seh dich jeden Morgen und manchmal auch um drei.
> Du bist mir mal sympathisch und manchmal eine Qual
> Aber meistens egal, total egal.
> Aber meistens egal, total egal.

WORTSCHATZ ZUM VIDEO

die Qual	torture
zurückbleiben	stay back (called out when a train leaves the platform)
der Schmalz	sentimentality
zwinkern	to wink
die Rechenschaft	accountability
betrübt	sad
schwermütig	melancholy
die Geige	violin

B. *Answers will vary.*

II: Hundert Jahre deutscher Film

In dieser Folge sehen Sie einen kurzen Bericht zur deutschen Filmindustrie. Was wissen Sie bereits von der Geschichte der Filmindustrie in Ihrem Land? Haben Sie einen alten Stummfilm gesehen? Kennen Sie die Namen der großen Schauspieler/ Schauspielerinnen in den ersten Jahrzehnten des zwanzigsten Jahrhunderts?

A Deutsche Filme. Welcher Film ist das? Verbinden Sie jeden Titel mit dem passenden Bild.

a.

b.

c.

d.

e.

f.

1. „Die Blechtrommel"
2. „Der blaue Engel"
3. „Die Mörder sind unter uns"
4. „Die Ehe der Maria Braun"
5. „Nosferatu – Eine Symphonie des Grauens"
6. „Das Cabinett des Dr. Caligari"

B Persönliche Meinungen

SCHRITT 1: Wer sagt das? Verbinden Sie jede Person mit dem richtigen Satzteil.

1. _____ hat nicht viel Zeit für längere Bücher neben dem Studium.
2. _____ liest gern Bücher deutscher Autoren, zum Beispiel Heinrich Mann.
3. _____ bevorzugt das Theater, weil das Kino doch manchmal oberflächlich ist.
4. _____ mag klassische Musik, besonders Violinkonzerte.
5. _____ mag alte Filme, weil sie so schön nostalgisch sind.
6. Für _____ ist Kultur etwas Privates.

SCHRITT 2: Und Sie? Wie stehen Sie zum Thema „Kultur"? Lesen Sie gern? Was lesen Sie gern? Sehen Sie lieber Filme oder Theateraufführungen? Was für Filme oder Theaterstücke sehen Sie? Warum? Was für Musik hören Sie gern? Äußern Sie Ihre eigenen Meinungen.

KULTURSPIEGEL

Wegen der politischen Verfolgungen in Deutschland und Österreich in den dreißiger und vierziger Jahren wanderten viele deutsche Schauspieler und Regisseure in die USA aus. Diese Leute haben eine große Rolle in der amerikanischen Filmindustrie gespielt. Der österreichische Regisseur Billy Wilder zum Beispiel ist immer noch wegen seiner Filme „Sunset Boulevard" und „Witness for the Prosecution" berühmt.

A. a. 5 b. 2 c. 1 d. 3 e. 4 f. 6

B. Schritt 1: 1. Tobias 2. Anett 3. Susanne 4. Grace 5. Bob 6. Erika
Schritt 2: Answers will vary.

VOKABELN

die Bühne	stage
die Komödie	comedy
die Romanverfilmung	filming of a novel
die Unterhaltung	entertainment
der Actionfilm	action film
der Film	film
der Höhepunkt	high point, climax
der Humor	humor
der Komponist / die Komponistin	composer
der Liebesfilm	romantic film
der Regisseur / die Regisseurin	director
der Stummfilm	silent film
der Tonfilm	sound film
der Untertitel	subtitle
das Geheimnis	secret
das Publikum	audience
das Schauspiel	play
das Stück	(theater) piece
das Theater	theater
(einen Film) drehen	to film (a movie)
fördern	to promote; to support
komponieren	to compose
synchronisieren	to dub (a film)
verfilmen	to film

In deutschen Kinos kann man sich sehr unterschiedliche Filme ansehen.

aufmerksam	attentive(ly)
bekannt	(well)known
künstlerisch	artistic(ally)
spürbar	traceable
ursprünglich	orginal(ly)

Sie wissen schon
die Stimmung, der Autor, der Künstler, der Schauspieler, oberflächlich

A. 1. Höhepunkt 2. spürbar 3. komponiert
4. gedreht 5. bekannt 6. Romanverfilmung

bekannt

Spürbar

gedreht

Höhepunkt

komponiert

Romanverfilmung

Aktivitäten

A Deutscher Film. Ergänzen Sie die Sätze mit den Wörtern im Kasten.

1. Die Stummfilme der zwanziger Jahre waren ein künstlerischer _____ in der Geschichte des deutschen Films.

2. Die Schrecken des Ersten Weltkrieges sind in Filmen wie „Nosferatu" deutlich _____.

3. In den vierziger Jahren hat Kurt Weill Musik für Theaterstücke sowie für Filme _____.

4. Der erste deutsche Nachkriegsfilm „Die Mörder sind unter uns" wurde 1946 in Berlin _____.

5. Erst in den siebziger Jahren wurden deutsche Filme wieder international _____.

6. Die _____ von Günter Graß' „Die Blechtrommel" hat einen Oscar als bester fremdsprachiger Film gewonnen.

B Definitionen. Lesen Sie die Sätze links und suchen Sie die passende Definition für die kursiv gedruckten Wörter aus der rechten Spalte.

1. Das heißt, eine Person intellektuell *fördern*, anregen, zum Denken animieren.

2. Wir erforschen die Sehnsüchte, Probleme und Fragen unseres *Publikums* und machen daraus für dieses *Publikum* Stücke.

3. Wir verbinden diese Leute mit Hollywood, aber sie kamen *ursprünglich* aus Deutschland und Österreich.

4. Die *Stummfilme* der zwanziger Jahre sind ein erster künstlerischer Höhepunkt in der Geschichte des deutschen Films.

5. In diesen Filmen sind die Schrecken des Ersten Weltkrieges noch *spürbar*.

6. Ja, aber wenn ich *Unterhaltung* will, dann setze ich mich mit meinen Freunden zusammen.

7. Wir gehen alle zwei, drei Wochen in irgendein *Schauspiel*.

8. Also, ich bevorzuge das Theater, weil das Kino manchmal sehr *oberflächlich* ist.

9. Es ist ein bisschen mehr wie ein *Geheimnis* und ich denke mit Büchern ist es dasselbe.

B. 1. b 2. d 3. i 4. g 5. f 6. h 7. e 8. c 9. a

a. etwas mysteriös, was man andere Leute nicht wissen lassen will
b. unterstützen
c. flach, flüchtig, dilettantisch
d. Zuschauer
e. Drama, Theaterstück
f. zu fühlen
g. Filme ohne Ton
h. Amüsement
i. zuerst, am Anfang

C. *Answers will vary.*

C Lieblingsfilme. Stefan und Daniela sprechen über Filme. Lesen Sie ihren Dialog, und beantworten Sie die Fragen.

STEFAN: Welche Kinofilme schaust du dir am liebsten an?

DANIELA: Traurige. Mit einem traurigen Ende, wo ich dann richtig melancholisch bin und in einer betrübten Stimmung. Keine Aktion.

STEFAN: Wieso magst du traurige Filme?

DANIELA: Weil ich glaube, sie sind realitätsnäher als Actionfilme. Die kommen mir immer so surreal vor, nicht richtig.

STEFAN: Ja, Actionfilme sind nur für Unterhaltung. Wenn ich ins Kino gehen will, dann möchte ich zwei Stunden Unterhaltung, nicht Weinen.

1. Mit welcher Meinung stimmen Sie überein?
2. Welche Filme sehen Sie sich am liebsten an?
3. Gehen Sie gern ins Kino? Warum (nicht)?

Stefan und Daniela.

To learn more about film and theater in German-speaking countries, visit the *Auf Deutsch!* Web Site at www.mcdougallittell.com.

STRUKTUREN

REVIEW OF THE PAST PERFECT TENSE
TALKING ABOUT A SEQUENCE OF EVENTS IN THE PAST

KURZ NOTIERT

In German, the present perfect and the simple past tenses have the same meaning. However, German speakers prefer the present perfect tense to relate isolated past events in conversation using the simple past tense to tell a story or to relate a string of past events, particularly in writing.

The past perfect tense in German functions the same way as in English: It points to an event that took place prior to another past event. In German, it is appropriate to use the past perfect in contexts with either the present perfect or the simple past tense.

The past perfect tense describes events that precede other events in the past. To form the past perfect, use the simple past-tense form of **haben (hatte)** or **sein (war)** as the auxiliary verb and place the past participle at the end of the sentence. Note that verbs use the same auxiliary verb in the past perfect as in the present perfect tense.

PRESENT PERFECT	PAST PERFECT
Ich **habe** mir die Bilder **angeschaut.**	Ich **hatte** mir die Bilder schon **angeschaut.**
I (have) looked at the pictures.	*I had already looked at the pictures.*
Die Jungen **sind** ins Kino **gegangen.**	Die Jungen **waren** ins Kino **gegangen.**
The boys went to the movies.	*The boys had gone to the movies.*

Dependent clauses beginning with **bevor** or **nachdem** frequently appear in sentences to clarify the sequence of events: what took place before or after something else. Notice the use of the past perfect tense in the following sentences.

> Karsten **hatte** seine Arbeit schon **geschrieben,** bevor er ins Kino ging.
> *Karsten had already written his paper before he went to the movies.*

> Er hat seine Mutter angerufen, nachdem er den Film **gesehen hatte.**
> *He called his mother after he had seen the film.*

Übungen

A Ein Studentenfilm. Einige Studenten erklären, wie sie einen Film gedreht haben. Kombinieren Sie die Sätze mit der Konjunktion in Klammern.

MODELL: (nachdem) Wir hatten das Drehbuch geschrieben. Wir suchten Schauspieler aus. →
Nachdem wir das Drehbuch geschrieben hatten, suchten wir Schauspieler aus.

1. (nachdem) Wir hatten eine Regisseurin gefunden. Wir konnten mit der Verfilmung anfangen.
2. (bevor) Sie hatte mit uns gearbeitet. Sie war Leiterin eines Studententheaters gewesen.
3. (nachdem) Jeder in der Klasse hatte eine Rolle geübt. Wir fingen mit den Proben an.
4. (nachdem) Unser Film war auf einem Filmfest gezeigt worden. Wir wurden ganz berühmt.
5. (nachdem) Wir hatten den Erfolg eine Weile genossen. Wir wollten einen zweiten Film drehen.

A. 1. Nachdem wir eine Regisseurin gefunden hatten, konnten wir mit der Verfilmung anfangen. **2.** Bevor sie mit uns arbeitete, war sie Leiterin eines Studententheaters gewesen. **3.** Nachdem jeder in der Klasse eine Rolle geübt hatte, fingen wir mit den Proben an. **4.** Nachdem unser Film auf einem Filmfest gezeigt worden war, wurden wir ganz berühmt. **5.** Nachdem wir den Erfolg eine Weile genossen hatten, wollten wir einen zweiten Film drehen.

B Die Wende. Beschreiben diese Sätze das Leben in Deutschland vor oder nach der Wiedervereinigung? Schreiben Sie die Sätze im Plusquamperfekt, und benutzen Sie **vor der Wende** oder **nach der Wende.**

MODELL: Die Deutschen im Osten hatten nur begrenzte Reisefreiheit. →
Vor der Wende hatten die Deutschen im Osten nur begrenzte Reisefreiheit gehabt.

1. Tausende von DDR-Bürgern protestierten in Leipzig.
2. Viele Menschen im Osten verloren ihre Arbeit.
3. Man erwartete die schnelle Wiedervereinigung nicht.
4. Touristen aus der DDR flohen nach Ungarn.
5. Man baute die Berliner Mauer ab.
6. Die ersten gesamtdeutschen Bundestagswahlen fanden statt.

B. 1. Tausende von DDR-Bürgern hatten vor der Wende in Leipzig demonstriert. **2.** Viele Menschen im Osten hatten nach der Wende ihre Arbeit verloren. **3.** Vor der Wende hatte man die schnelle Wiedervereinigung nicht erwartet. **4.** Vor der Wende waren viele Touristen aus der DDR nach Ungarn geflohen. **5.** Nach der Wende hatte man die Berliner Mauer abgebaut. **6.** Nach der Wende hatten die ersten gesamtdeutschen Bundestagswahlen stattgefunden.

C Deutschland in den dreißiger Jahren. Ordnen Sie die passenden Satzteile aus der rechten und linken Spalte einander zu.

C. 1. e **2.** d **3.** b **4.** a **5.** c

1. Als die Nazis 1933 an die Macht kamen,
2. Nachdem Hitler Kanzler geworden war,
3. Bevor die Kabaretts geschlossen worden waren,
4. Nachdem die Verfolgung der Juden begonnen hatte,
5. Als der Zweite Weltkrieg zu Ende war,

a. flohen viele jüdische Künstler in die USA.
b. konnte man alles Mögliche auf der Bühne sehen – Musicals, Revues und auch satirische Stücke.
c. baute man die deutsche Filmindustrie wieder auf.
d. wollte er die kulturelle Vielfalt in Deutschland stark begrenzen.
e. war Berlin als Kulturstadt weltweit berühmt.

Viele bekannte Regisseure flohen vor den Nazis ins Ausland.

REVIEW OF ALTERNATIVES TO THE PASSIVE
FOCUSING ON ACTIONS AND STATES

The passive voice often occurs when the person or force performing the action is unknown. However, there are three different ways of turning a passive sentence into an active one. The most common alternative is to use the impersonal pronoun **man** (meaning *one, you, we, they,* or *people in general*) as the subject of an active sentence. Regardless of its intended meaning, **man** always requires a verb in the third-person' singular.

In der Bibliothek wird nicht gegessen.	*Eating isn't done in the library.*
In der Bibliothek isst **man** nicht.	*People don't eat in the library.*

A second alternative is the active construction **sich lassen** plus infinitive, which replaces a passive construction with **können** plus past participle and **werden**.

Mein Fahrrad kann nicht repariert werden.	*My bike can't be fixed.*
Mein Fahrrad **lässt sich** nicht **reparieren.**	*lit.: My bike doesn't let itself be fixed.*

A third alternative is to use the verb **sein** with **zu** plus infinitive.

Dieses Ziel wird im Moment nicht erreicht.	*This goal isn't being attained right now.*
Dieses Ziel **ist** im Moment nicht **zu erreichen.**	*This goal isn't attainable right now.*

Übungen

A Ein Gericht. Wie wird dieses Gericht zubereitet? Bilden Sie Aktivsätze mit **man.**

MODELL: Zuerst wird das Rezept im Kochbuch durchgelesen. →
Zuerst liest man das Rezept im Kochbuch durch.

A. 1. Zuerst kauft man die Schnitzel ein.
2. Dann paniert man die Schnitzel mit Ei und Paniermehl. 3. Dann brät man die Schnitzel in heißem Fett. 4. Dann serviert man sie knusprig. 5. Man garniert die Schnitzel mit Zitronenscheiben.

1. Zuerst werden die Schnitzel eingekauft.
2. Dann werden die Schnitzel mit Ei und Paniermehl paniert.[a]
3. Dann werden die Schnitzel in heißem Fett gebraten.
4. Dann werden sie knusprig[b] serviert.
5. Die Schnitzel werden mit Zitronenscheiben[c] garniert.

[a]breaded   [b]crunchy   [c]lemon slices

B Sabine in Hamburg. Sabine beschreibt ihre Reise nach Hamburg. Schreiben Sie ihre Aussagen mit dem Verb **sich lassen** um.

MODELL: Hamburg kann nicht an einem Tag besichtigt werden. →
          Hamburg lässt sich nicht an einem Tag besichtigen.

1. Vom Hotelfenster kann das „Thalia" Theater gesehen werden.
2. Der plattdeutsche Dialekt kann nur schwer verstanden werden.
3. Der Fischmarkt kann nicht leicht gefunden werden.
4. Das Essen auf dem Fischmarkt kann nicht gegessen werden, weil es nicht so gut schmeckt.
5. In Hamburg wird gut gelebt.

C Meinungen zur modernen Kultur. Bilden Sie neue Sätze mit **sein** und **zu** plus **Infinitiv.**

MODELL: Moderne Musik wird nicht oft gehört. →
          Moderne Musik ist nicht oft zu hören.

1. Moderne Theaterstücke werden oft nur schwer verstanden.
2. Dieser Autor wird nicht leicht verstanden.
3. Im neuen Theatersaal wird fast nichts gehört.
4. Hinten im Theatersaal wird nichts gesehen.
5. Die neue Skulptur wird leicht gefunden.

Können Sie Wiener Schnitzel machen?

Das „Thalia" Theater in Hamburg.

B. 1. Von meinem Hotelzimmer lässt sich das „Thalia" Theater sehen.   2. Der plattdeutsche Dialekt lässt sich nur schwer verstehen.   3. Der Fischmarkt lässt sich nicht leicht finden.   4. Das Essen auf dem Fischmarkt lässt sich nicht essen, weil es nicht so gut schmeckt.   5. In Hamburg lässt es sich gut leben.

C. 1. Moderne Theaterstücke sind oft nur schwer zu verstehen.   2. Dieser Autor ist schwer zu verstehen.   3. Im neuen Theatersaal ist fast nichts zu hören.   4. Hinten im Theatersaal ist nichts zu sehen.   5. Die neue Skulptur ist nicht zu finden.

REVIEW OF WORD ORDER WITH VERBS EXPRESSING ACTION

The verb is the only element in a German sentence that has a fixed position. The position of the verb depends on the type of sentence. In a simple declarative sentence, the conjugated verb occupies the second position. The first element is often the subject, but another expression, such as one of time or place, can also come first. When this happens, the subject takes the third position, immediately following the conjugated verb. The verb is also in second position after question words such as **wann, warum, was, wie, wo, woher, wohin,** and so forth.

Der Mensch **braucht** Unterhaltung.	*People need entertainment.*
In Berlin **kann** man abends viel machen.	*One can do a lot in Berlin in the evenings.*
Am Wochenende **geht** man ins Kino oder ins Theater.	*One can go to the movies or to the theater on weekends.*
Wann **reist** du nach Berlin?	*When are you going to Berlin?*

The verb appears in first position in yes/no questions.

Braucht der Mensch Unterhaltung?	*Do people need entertainment?*
Kann man abends viel in Berlin machen?	*Can one do a lot in Berlin in the evenings?*

The conjugated verb appears at the end of dependent clauses, such as relative clauses and clauses introduced by subordinating conjunctions.

Die deutschen Künstler, die nach Los Angeles **kamen,** haben zum Erfolg der amerikanischen Filmindustrie sehr viel beigetragen.	*The German artists who came to Los Angeles contributed much to the success of the American film industry.*
Weil sie von den Nazis politisch verfolgt **wurden,** mussten sie ihre Heimat verlassen.	*Because they were politically persecuted by the Nazis, they had to leave their homeland.*

Notice in the first example that the relative clause modifies the subject. Therefore, the subject and relative clause function together as the first element; and the conjugated verb of the main clause (**haben**) takes the second position in the sentence as a whole. In the second example, the dependent clause beginning with **weil** occupies the first position of the sentence, the verb of the main clause (**mussten**) occupies the second position of the sentence.

Übungen

A Kindheit. Erzählen Sie, was Sie als Kind **oft, manchmal** oder **nie** gemacht haben. Die Wörter im Kasten auf Seite 259 stehen Ihnen zur Hilfe.

MODELL: In meiner Kindheit habe ich oft Sandburgen gebaut.

die Eltern ärgern   Kuchen backen   Geld verlieren

Schmetterlinge suchen   Schneemänner bauen

Videospiele spielen

andere Kinder ärgern   mit Buntstiften schreiben

B Meine Meinungen. Was meinen Sie zu den folgenden Aussagen? Bilden Sie Sätze mit der Konjunktion **dass** und den angegeben Ausdrücken.

Ich meine,
Ich finde,
Ich glaube (nicht),
Ich habe immer gedacht,
Ich bin (nicht) der Meinung,
Es ist sicher,

1. Tonfilme sind interessanter als Stummfilme.
2. man sollte fremdsprachige Filme nicht synchronisieren.
3. Actionfilme sind meistens oberflächlich.
4. Kino soll nur Unterhaltung sein.
5. Theaterstücke sind wichtiger als Kinofilme.
6. der Roman ist immer besser als die Romanverfilmung.
7. traurige Filme sind für schwermütige Leute.

B. *Possible answers are:* **1.** Ich habe immer gedacht, dass Tonfilme interessanter sind als Stummfilme. **2.** Ich finde, dass man fremdsprachige Filme nicht synchronisieren sollte. **3.** Ich bin der Meinung, dass Actionfilme meistens oberflächlich sind. **4.** Ich glaube (nicht), dass Kino nur Unterhaltung sein soll. **5.** Ich meine, dass Theaterstücke wichtiger sind als Kinofilme. **6.** Es ist sicher, dass der Roman immer besser ist als die Romanverfilmung. **7.** Ich finde, dass traurige Filme für schwermütige Leute sind.

PERSPEKTIVEN

HÖREN SIE ZU!
BIEDERMANN UND DIE BRANDSTIFTER

Sie hören jetzt eine kurze Beschreibung eines Theaterstücks. Hören Sie gut zu und beantworten Sie dann die Fragen.

1. Wovor hat Herr Biedermann Angst?
2. Warum gewährt er den zwei Obdachlosen in seiner Dachkammer Unterschlupf?
3. Was haben die zwei Männer in der Dachkammer gelagert?
4. Was hat Herr Biedermann den zwei Männern gegeben? Warum hat er das gemacht?
5. Was, glauben Sie, wird dann passieren? Erzählen Sie die Geschichte weiter.

WORTSCHATZ ZUM HÖRTEXT

ständig	continual
der Dachkammerbrand	fire in the attic
gewähren	to allow
der Unterschlupf	accommodation
die Feigheit	cowardice
die Zündschnur	fuse
das Streichholz	match

Possible answers are: **1.** Herr Biedermann hat Angst vor Dachkammerbränden. **2.** Er gewährt den beiden Obdachlosen Unterschlupf aus Feigheit, Unentschlossenheit und einem schlechten Gewissen. **3.** Die Männer haben Benzinkanister und Zündschnüre in der Dachkammer gelagert. **4.** Herr Biedermann hat ihnen Streichhölzer gegeben. Er will nicht glauben, was er hört und sieht. **5.** *Answers will vary.*

LESEN SIE!

Zum Thema

Straßenkünstler erfreuen sich großer Beliebtheit.

● Haben Sie eine Lieblingserzählung oder ein Lieblingsgedicht? Wie heißt dieser Text? Wovon handelt der Text? Finden Sie einen Partner / eine Partnerin, und erzählen Sie ihm/ihr, worum es in dem Text geht.

Favorite stories and poems will vary.

Zum Text

Performances will vary.

● Sie haben in Ihrem Deutschkurs schon mehrere Texte gelesen und besprochen. In diesem Kapitel werden Sie einen Text selber aufführen.

SCHRITT 1: Unten stehen einige Texte. Wählen Sie einen davon aus, den Sie vor der Klasse aufführen möchten. Bevor Sie Ihren Text aussuchen, denken Sie an folgende Fragen:

1. Wollen Sie den Text allein aufführen?
2. Möchten Sie einen ernsthaften oder einen lustigen Text aufführen?

SCHRITT 2: Wählen Sie Ihren Text. Denken Sie daran, wie der Text inszeniert werden kann. Brauchen Sie für Ihre Aufführung Kostüme, Möbel oder andere Dinge?

SCHRITT 3: Führen Sie den Text vor der Klasse auf.

Der Tiberbiber

ein Biber
saß im Tiber
und biberte
vor Fieber
und sprach
ach wär doch lieber
mein Fieber
schon vorieber

doch kaum
war es vorieber
das Fieber
von dem Biber
da ging
der Biber lieber
doch wieder
korrekt zum Umlaut über

Nach Ihnen!

Disposition: Zwei Teilnehmer – A und B – liefern sich ein Höflichkeitsduell: Jeder will dem anderen den Vortritt lassen, etwa beim Eintreten durch eine imaginäre Tür.

A   Bitte . . .
B   Nein, bitte . . .
A   Nach Ihnen, bitte . . .
B   Nein bitte, nach Ihnen . . .
A   Aber ich bitte Sie . . .
B   Aber nicht doch, bitte . . .
A   So gehen Sie doch, bitte . . .
B   Bitte, Sie zuerst . . .
A   Warum diese Umstände . . .
B   Eben. Das muss doch nicht sein!
A   Haben wir das etwas nötig?
B   Natürlich nicht!
A   Na also! Dann – bitte!
B   Nein, bitte . . .
A   Nach Ihnen, bitte . . .

und so weiter . . .

Wer wird das Höflichkeitsduell gewinnen?

Von wo zieht es?

Von wo zieht's . . . ?

Drei Personen

Eins   Ich finde, es zieht.

Zwei   Das finde ich nicht.

Drei   Ich bin mir nicht sicher.

Eins   Und zwar zieht es von da.

Zwei   Also von da kann es gar nicht ziehen.

Drei   Das glaube ich auch. Wenn es zieht, dann zieht es eher von dort.

Eins   Nein, von dort zieht es ganz sicher nicht.

Drei   Von wo denn sonst?

Zwei   Jedenfalls nicht von oben – so viel ist sicher.

Drei   Auch nicht von unten – das steht fest.

Eins   Also zieht es von der Seite her – genau das sage ich. Und zwar von da her, also von rechts.

Zwei   Rechts? Für mich wäre das links.

Drei   Und für mich geradeaus.

Eins   Meinetwegen. Jedenfalls – ich finde, es zieht.

Zwei   Das finde ich nicht.

Drei   Ich bin mir nicht sicher.

und so weiter . . .

Der verdrehte Schmetterling

Ein Metterschling
mit flauen Blügeln
log durch die Fluft.
Er war einem Computer
entnommen, dem war was
durcheinandergekommen,
Irgendein Drähtchen
Irgendein Rädchen.
Und als man es merkte, da
war's schon zu spätchen.
da war der Metterschling
schon feit wort,
wanz geit.
Mir lut er teid.

WORTSCHATZ ZUM LESEN

vorüber	over with
kaum	barely
das Höflichkeitsduell	politeness duel
der Vortritt	precedence
Es zieht.	There's a draft.
verdreht	distorted; turned around
der Schmetterling	butterfly

Zur Interpretation

● Innere Bedeutung

Answers will vary.

SCHRITT 1: Welche Bedeutung hat der Text, den Sie ausgewählt haben? Gibt es eine versteckte Bedeutung? In welchen Zeilen wird diese Bedeutung klar gemacht?

SCHRITT 2: Schreiben Sie zwei oder drei Sätze auf, die Ihren Text beschreiben. Dann fragen Sie Ihre Mitschüler/Mitschülerinnen, was sie von Ihrer Aufführung halten.

INTERAKTION

Questionnaires and reports will vary.

● Eine Umfrage über Film und Literatur. Um die kulturellen Interessen Ihrer Mitschüler und Mitschülerinnen herauszufinden, machen Sie mit einem Partner / einer Partnerin eine Umfrage in der Klasse.

SCHRITT 1: Zuerst schreiben Sie mit Ihrem Partner / Ihrer Partnerin einen Fragebogen mit allen Fragen, die Sie an Ihre Mitschüler/ Mitschülerinnen stellen wollen und auf den Sie ihre Antworten notieren.

1. Fragen Sie Ihre Mitschüler/Mitschülerinnen, was für Filme sie gern sehen, welche Schauspieler/Schauspielerinnen sie besonders gern haben, welche fremdsprachigen Filme sie gesehen haben und wie sie ihnen gefielen.
2. Fragen Sie sie auch, was für Bücher sie gern lesen, welche Autoren/Autorinnen sie besonders gern haben und ob sie lieber ein Buch lesen oder die Verfilmung eines Buches sehen.

SCHRITT 2: Werten Sie gemeinsam mit Ihrem Partner / Ihrer Partnerin die Antworten zu Ihrer Umfrage aus. Gibt es Antworten, die immer wieder vorkommen? Bereiten Sie einen kurzen mündlichen[a] Bericht vor. Wenn es den Zuhörern helfen könnte, Ihrem Vortrag besser zu folgen, dann benutzen Sie Tabellen oder Bilder für Ihren Bericht.

SCHRITT 3: Berichten Sie die Klasse über die Ergebnisse Ihrer Umfrage.

[a]*oral*

SCHREIBEN SIE! *Texts will vary.*

Meine Bestenliste

Für Ihre Webseite wollen Sie eine Liste Ihrer zehn Lieblingsfilme (bzw. die zehn besten Fernsehprogramme, Bücher, CDs u.a.) zusammenstellen. Treffen Sie Ihre Auswahl, erzählen Sie in Kurzform deren Inhalt oder Thema, bestimmen Sie die Rangordnung und erteilen Sie zum Schluss Ihr Prädikat.

Purpose:	To create a personal Top Ten list of creative works
Audience:	Visitors to your web site
Subject:	Ten personal favorites
Structure:	Critical review and ordered list of ten creative works

Schreibmodell

Here you see the fifth and sixth choices of the Top Ten.

The past perfect and the simple past show which of two events happened first.

This film was given four stars, along with the comment that it has historical value.

The verb **sein** with **zu** + an infinitive is an alternative to passive voice.

Meine zehn Lieblingsfilme

5. Schindler's List. <u>Zusammenfassung:</u> Der Film erzählt die wahre Geschichte von Oskar Schindler, einem deutschen Industriellen während der Nazizeit, der zuerst von den jüdischen Zwangsarbeitern profitiert hatte, dann aber seine Verantwortung für ihr Schicksal erkannte. Er riskierte sein Leben, um die „Schindler-Juden" vor dem Tod im Konzentrationslager zu retten. <u>Bewertung:</u> Dieser moderne Schwarzweißfilm vermittelt die Atmosphäre von Angst, Hass und Gefahr, die im Dritten Reich überall zu finden war. <u>Prädikat:</u> ★★★★ wertvoll, von historischem Interesse

6. The Wizard of Oz. <u>Zusammenfassung:</u> Bei einem Wirbelsturm in Kansas werden Dorothy und ihr kleiner Hund Toto in das magische Land von Oz versetzt. Dorothy muss selber den Weg nach Hause finden und glaubt, ihr sei nur durch den Zauberer von Oz zu helfen. Auf dem Weg helfen ihr eine Vogelscheuche ohne Gehirn, ein Zinnmann ohne Herz und ein Löwe ohne Mut. Sie folgen dem gelben Backsteinweg und suchen das Schloss des Zauberers. Unterwegs werden sie vielen Gefahren ausgesetzt, aber sie halten zusammen und halten durch, bis ihre Wünsche in Erfüllung gehen. <u>Bewertung:</u> Viele halten dies für einen Kinderfilm, aber ich liebe die unglaubliche Phantasie, die in der Geschichte steckt, die kindliche Naivität der Figuren und besonders die tollen Bühnenbilder und Kostüme. <u>Prädikat:</u> ★★★ gut, sehenswert

Schreibstrategien

Vor dem Schreiben

- Putting together a personal Top Ten list can be fun. Pick a genre for your list: movies, TV programs, books, CDs, music videos, video games, or some other area of creative endeavor. Be prepared to explain each of your choices, what you like about it, and why you gave it the ranking you did.

- Develop a rating system. Think about differences between good and bad creative works within your genre. Write down your criteria and explain each one in a word or two.

- Write down any and all of your favorite works. Don't rank them yet. If you have trouble coming up with ten entries, talk to someone working on the same topic and trade notes.

- Once you have the names of all your favorites on paper, look them over and decide which are your top ten favorites. Delete the rest.

- Refresh your memory about each entry on your list. Reread notes or descriptions of the work, look up information about its creator, or take time to watch or listen to a brief selection.

- Order your entries from number 1 (your most favorite) to number 10 (your least favorite of the ten).

Beim Schreiben

- Remember: In describing each work, your writing must be *objective*. In explaining your reactions to a work, your writing will be *subjective*.

- Start by writing a description of each work on your list. Give a brief synopsis (**Zusammenfassung**) of the plot where appropriate or describe the central themes of musical or artistic works. Keep your descriptions short and to the point.

- Write a critical evaluation (**Bewertung**) of each work from your personal point of view. Explain what you think makes it one of the top ten best works of its type (as well as any weaknesses it has). This part of the assignment is purely subjective—only you know why you selected this work. First-person (**ich**) sentences are appropriate. You can consult references, but be sure to restate information in your own words. If you use quotations, identify your sources.

TIPP ZUM SCHREIBEN

A rating scale provides a quick way of evaluating a creative work. A common rating system uses stars; for example, a movie receiving four or five stars is considered terrific and a movie with only one star is considered not very good or not worth seeing. Here is an example scale in German. You may use it or make up your own.

★★★★★	ausgezeichnet, hervorragend
★★★★	sehr gut, wertvoll
★★★	gut, sehenswert (hörenswert, lesenswert)
★★	anständig, überdurchschnittlich, unterhaltsam
★	tolerabel, mittelmässig
keine Sterne	langweilig, nicht empfehlenswert

Beatles: *White Album.*
<u>Zusammenfassung:</u> Nachdem die Beatles zur populärsten Band der sechziger Jahre geworden ~~sind~~ waren, hörten sie auf, leichte Popmusik zu machen. Mit dem *White Album* bewegten sich die Beatles in eine neue kreative Richtung. Das Ergebnis ist ein Meisterwerk: ein Doppelalbum mit Kompositionen von allen vier Beatles über die wichtigen Themen der Zeit: Sozialkritik, Selbstverwirklichung und Liebe. Jeder Beatle singt die Leitstimme für die eigene Komposition. <u>Bewertung:</u> Mit diesem kontroversen Doppelalbum riskierten die Beatles ihre Popularität, und komponierten einige ihre besten Lieder: „Ob-La-Di, Ob-La-Da" und „Blackbird". Ein einmaliges Tondokument einer turbulenten Zeit! <u>Prädikat:</u> ★★★★★ das Beste der Besten

Nach dem Schreiben

- Read over your work. Make sure each entry on your list includes a description, and an evaluation. Reassess your rankings. If you need to reorder the list, do it now.

- Read your paper again and correct obvious errors in grammar, syntax, and word choice.

- Exchange papers with a peer editor. Read each other's work twice, the first time reading for content, and the second time correcting errors in grammar, word choice, and word order. After writing down three positive comments and three suggestions for improvement, return your papers.

Stimmt alles?

- Evaluate your list based on your peer editor's comments and revise it as appropriate.

- Hand in the finished product. If you have your own web page, post your list.

WORTSCHATZ

Substantive	Nouns
die **Bühne, -n**	stage
die **Komödie, -n**	comedy
die **Kultur, -en**	culture
die **Pantomime, -n**	pantomime
die **Romanverfilmung, -en**	filming of a novel
die **Unterhaltung, -en**	entertainment
der **Actionfilm, -e**	action film
der **Film, -e**	film
der **Höhepunkt, -e**	high point, climax
der **Humor**	humor
der **Komponist (-en** *masc.***) /**	composer
die **Komponistin, -nen**	
der **Liebesfilm, -e**	romantic film
der **Regisseur, -e /** die	director (*of a film*
Regisseurin, -nen	*or play*)
der **Stummfilm, -e**	silent film
der **Tanz, ⸚e**	dance
der **Tonfilm, -e**	sound film
der **Untertitel, -**	subtitle
der **Zweck, -e**	purpose
das **Geheimnis, -se**	secret
das **Publikum**	audience
das **Schauspiel, -e**	play
das **Stück, -e**	(theater) piece
das **Theater, -**	theater

Verben	Verbs
beobachten	to observe
beziehen, bezog, bezogen	to take up
(einen Film) drehen	to film (*a movie*)
faszinieren	to fascinate
fördern	to promote; support

inszenieren	to stage
komponieren	to compose
locken	to attract, entice
mit•teilen	to convey; to tell
synchronisieren	to dub (*a film*)
verfilmen	to film

Adjektive und Adverbien	Adjectives and adverbs
aufmerksam	attentive(ly)
bekannt	(well-)known
fähig	capable; capably
geschickt	clever(ly)
imaginär	imaginary
intellektuell	intellectual(ly)
kulturell	cultural(ly)
künstlerisch	artistic(ally)
spürbar	traceable
ursprünglich	original(ly)

Sie wissen schon	You already know
die **Kunst, ⸚e**	art
die **Literatur, -en**	literature
die **Musik**	music
die **Stimmung, -en**	mood, atmosphere
der **Autor, -en /** die	author
Autorin, -nen	
der **Künstler, -** / die	artist
Künstlerin, -nen	
der **Schauspieler, -** / die	actor
Schauspielerin, -nen	
oberflächlich	superficial(ly)

WIEDERHOLUNG 12

PLANNING GUIDE
CLASSROOM MANAGEMENT

OBJECTIVES

Communication
- Talk about foreign films, p. 270.
- Talk about your hometown, p. 272.

Grammar
- Review relative pronouns, p. 270.
- Review infinitive clauses with *zu*, p. 270.
- Review uses of *werden*, p. 271.

Culture
- Discuss multiculturalism in Germany, p. 268.
- Discuss environmentalism, p. 268.
- Learn about Expressionist poet Georg Heym, p. 272.

PROGRAM RESOURCES

 Print
- *Arbeitsheft* (Workbook), pp. 195–198
- *Arbeitsheft* (Workbook), Teacher's Edition, pp. 195–198

 Audiovisual
- Overhead Transparencies 34.G1–34.G2, 35.G1, and 36.G2
- Audio Program, Cassette 6B/CD 8
- Audioscript, pp. 92–93

 Technology
- Annenberg *Fokus Deutsch* Video Series, *Wiederholung 12*
- www.mcdougallittell.com

 Assessment Program Options
- *Prüfung, Wiederholung 12,* Assessment Program, pp. 157–166
- Audio Program, Cassette 8B/CD 10
- Audioscript, p. 115
- Teacher's Resource CD-ROM

PACING GUIDE
50-MINUTE SCHEDULE

DAY 1

Note: (1) See TE, pp. 268C–268D, for other suggestions not referenced in these plans. (2) Not all homework options need be assigned.

VIDEOTHEK
- Quick Start Review: Vocabulary (TE, p. 268C). 5 MIN
- View the first video episode, then do *Akt. A,* p. 268. (TE, p. 268C.) 7 MIN
- Do *Akt. B,* p. 268, then view the second video episode. Discuss. 9 MIN
- View the third video episode, then do *Akt. C,* p. 268, as a class. 6 MIN
- View the final video episode, then do *Akt. D,* p. 269. 6 MIN

VOKABELN
- Do the warm-up and *Akt. A,* p. 269 (TE, p. 268C). 10 MIN
- Do *Akt. B,* p. 269, and warm-up activity on page TE, p. 268C. 7 MIN

Homework Options:
- *Arbeitsheft,* p. 195, *Akt. C* and p. 196, *Akt. B*

DAY 2

VOKABELN
- Quick Start Review: Relative clauses (TE, p. 268C). 5 MIN
- Do the warm-up activity in the Teaching Suggestions for *Akt. C,* p. 270, as a class, then do the activity in pairs. Discuss (TE, p. 268C). 13 MIN

STRUKTUREN
- Review relative pronouns and clauses using OHT 34.G1–34.G2. Do *Übung A,* p. 270, silently, then check answers with partners (TE, p. 268D). 10 MIN
- Quickly review the *zu* + infinitive construction. Do *Übung B,* p. 270, as a class. Do follow-up activity on page TE, p. 268D. 12 MIN
- Do *Übung C,* p. 271, silently. Discuss answers. 10 MIN

Homework Options:
- *Arbeitsheft,* p. 197, *Vokabeln, Akt. C*
- *Arbeitsheft,* p. 198, *Strukturen, Akt. C*

268A PLANNING GUIDE: WIEDERHOLUNG 12

PACING GUIDE
50-MINUTE SCHEDULE

DAY 3

STRUKTUREN

- Quick Start Review: Passive voice (TE, p. 268D). 5 MIN
- Do *Übung D,* p. 271, in pairs. Check answers as a class and review the passive voice as necessary using OHT 35.G1 and 36.G2. 10 MIN
- Do *Übung E,* p. 271, silently, then compare the answers in small groups. 11 MIN

PERSPEKTIVEN

- Do the warm-up activity in the Teaching Suggestions, then discuss *Akt. A,* p. 272 (TE, p. 268D). 8 MIN
- Read *Der Gott der Stadt* on p. 272, in small groups. Encourage them to help each other understand the meaning of the text. 9 MIN
- Do *Akt. B,* p. 273, in small groups. Compare the groups' work as a class. 7 MIN

Homework Options:

- *Arbeitsheft,* p. 198, *Strukturen, Akt. D*

DAY 4

PERSPEKTIVEN

- Quick Start Review: Vocabulary (TE, p. 268D). 4 MIN
- Do *Akt. C,* p. 273, in pairs. 8 MIN
- As a class, discuss *Akt. D,* p. 273 (TE, p. 268D). 3 MIN
- Questions and review. 5 MIN
- *Prüfung, Wiederholung 12.* 30 MIN

PACING GUIDE
90-MINUTE SCHEDULE

DAY 1

Note: (1) See TE, pp. 268C–268D, for other suggestions not referenced in these plans. (2) Not all homework options need be assigned.

VIDEOTHEK

- Quick Start Review: Vocabulary (TE, p. 268C). 5 MIN
- View first episode then do *Akt. A,* p. 268. 7 MIN
- Do *Akt. B,* then view second episode. 9 MIN
- View the third and fourth episodes, then do *Akt. C–D,* pp. 268–269. 12 MIN
- Block Schedule activity: Process Time (TE, p. 268C). 10 MIN

VOKABELN

- Warm-up and *Akt. A–B,* p. 269, (TE, p. 268C). 16 MIN
- *Akt. C,* p. 270. 10 MIN

STRUKTUREN

- *Übung A,* p. 270. 10 MIN
- *Übung B,* p. 270 and follow-up (TE, p. 268D). 11 MIN

Homework Options:

- *Arbeitsheft,* p. 195, *Akt. C;* pp. 196–197, *Akt. B–C*

DAY 2

STRUKTUREN

- Quick Start Review: Passive voice (TE, p. 268D). 4 MIN
- Do *Übung C,* p. 271, silently. Discuss. 6 MIN
- Do *Übung D,* p. 271, in pairs. Check answers as a class and review passive voice as necessary. 8 MIN
- Do *Übung E,* p. 271, silently, then compare answers in groups. 8 MIN

PERSPEKTIVEN

- Discuss *Akt. A,* p. 272, as a class. 5 MIN
- Read *Der Gott der Stadt* on p. 272 in groups. 8 MIN
- Block Schedule activity: Fun Break (TE, p. 268D). 10 MIN
- Do *Akt. B,* p. 273, in small groups. Compare the groups' work. 6 MIN
- Questions and review. 5 MIN
- *Prüfung, Wiederholung 12.* 30 MIN

Homework Options:

- *Arbeitsheft,* p. 198, *Strukturen, Akt. C–D*

TEACHING SUGGESTIONS

Videothek, pp. 268–269

PROGRAM RESOURCES

- Videocassette, *Folge 12*
- *Arbeitsheft,* p. 195
- Audio Program, Cassette 6B/CD 8
- Audioscript, p. 92

Quick Start Review

♻ Vocabulary

Ergänzen Sie die Sätze mit den folgenden Wörtern.

WÖRTER: inszeniert, komponiert, locken, verfilmt

1. An der Schaubühne wurde der Hamlet ganz modern _____.
2. Bertolt Brecht hat viele seiner Lieder in seinen Theaterstücken selbst _____.
3. Die Romane von Günter Grass sind fast alle _____ worden.
4. Viele Firmen _____ ihre Kunden mit faszinierenden Werbefilmen.

Answers: 1. inszeniert   2. komponiert
3. verfilmt   4. locken

TEACHING SUGGESTIONS

- *Aktivität A,* p. 268

Have students give an oral summary of the video episode.

- *Aktivität B,* p. 268

Have students give an oral summary of the episode. Ask *Welche Essgewohnheiten haben die Menschen im Video?*

TEACHING ALL STUDENTS

Multiple Intelligences Verbal: Have students practice relative pronouns by playing a guessing game. Have them guess the name of a famous person.

CLASSROOM COMMUNITY

Dictation Dictate the following text to the class, then write it on an OHT or on the board. Have students exchange their dictations and correct each other's writing. *Deutsche halten sich sehr streng an Regeln: „Bei Rot stehen, bei Grün gehen." Damit sich alle an die Regeln halten, ist alles beschildert. Die Schilder sind manchmal sehr lustig. Samstag ist Putztag. Autos werden gewaschen, Straßen werden gekehrt, Fenster werden geputzt.*

BLOCK SCHEDULE

Process Time Have students work in groups to re-create scenes from the video.

Vokabeln, pp. 269–270

PROGRAM RESOURCES

- *Arbeitsheft,* pp. 196–197
- Audio Program, Cassette 6B/CD 8
- Audioscript, pp. 92–93

Quick Start Review

♻ Relative clauses

Ergänzen Sie mit Relativpronomen.

1. Der Mann, _____ neben uns wohnt, fährt einen Mercedes.
2. Ich habe mein Buch der Studentin geliehen, _____ in der Vorlesung neben mir saß.
3. Der Roman, von _____ ich dir gestern erzählt habe, hat 420 Seiten.
4. Der Strand, an _____ wir fahren wollen, liegt weit im Süden.
5. Die Stadt, in _____ ich studiert habe, hatte 50.000 Einwohner.

Answers: 1. der   2. die   3. dem
4. den   5. der

TEACHING SUGGESTIONS

- *Aktivität B,* p. 269

Warm-up: Have students brainstorm a list of things they can do to protect the environment. Ask *Was kann jeder von uns ohne große Mühe tun?*

- *Aktivität C,* p. 270

Warm-up: Have students discuss their movie preferences. Ask *Was erwarten Sie von einem wirklich guten Film? Sehen Sie sich traurige Filme lieber an, wenn Sie selbst traurig sind? usw.*

TEACHING ALL STUDENTS

Extra Help Activate students' memory of vocabulary. With books closed, have the class brainstorm vocabulary pertinent to an activity.

CLASSROOM COMMUNITY

Storytelling Show students an everyday object, such as your wallet, a special pen, or a scarf and tell a story about it. Encourage students to ask questions about your object and then tell stories of their own.

CULTURE HIGHLIGHTS

Show students some videos of children's television in Germany, such as the German version of *Sesame Street. Die Sendung mit der Maus* is an excellent program that viewers of all ages find fascinating; it also has a Web site.

BLOCK SCHEDULE

Peer Teaching Have students review the structures taught in Chapter 35. Ask them to write a brief summary of the different uses of the verb *werden*: as a main verb, as an auxiliary for the passive voice, and as an auxiliary for the future tense.

Strukturen, pp. 270–271

PROGRAM RESOURCES

- Overhead Transparencies 34.G1–34.G2, 35.G1, and 36.G2
- *Arbeitsheft,* pp. 197–198
- Audio Program, Cassette 6B/CD 8
- Audioscript, p. 93

Quick Start Review

♻ Passive voice
Ehe wir in Urlaub fahren, gibt es noch viel zu tun. Bilden Sie Sätze im Passiv.

1. Zeitung abbestellen 2. Nachbarn informieren 3. Rasen wässern
4. Koffer packen 5. Briefe zur Post bringen

Answers: 1. Die Zeitung muss abbestellt werden. 2. Die Nachbarn müssen informiert werden. 3. Der Rasen muss gewässert werden. 4. Die Koffer müssen gepackt werden. 5. Die Briefe müssen zur Post gebracht werden.

TEACHING SUGGESTIONS

- *Übung B,* p. 270

Follow-up: A student makes a statement about food or health, such as *Mein Bruder sitzt immer nur auf der Couch.* Next student follows up with an infinitive construction: *Es ist ungesund immer nur auf der Couch zu sitzen.*

TEACHING ALL STUDENTS

Multiple Intelligences Naturalist: Take students outside for a walk if possible. Have them take notes on anything they see that impacts the environment in a positive or negative way.

CLASSROOM COMMUNITY

Challenge Have students complete the following sentences: 1. Nachdem wir gegessen hatten, . . . 2. Nachdem wir schlafen gegangen waren, . . . 3. Nachdem der Hund aus dem Haus gerannt war, . . .

PROJECT

Have students research music that is popular in the German-speaking countries now. Have students prepare a written report of their findings. Encourage them to include recordings of the music they will be talking about.

RUBRIC **A** = 13–15 pts. **B** = 10–12 pts.
C = 7–9 pts. **D** = 4–6 pts. **F** <4 pts.

Criteria	Scale				
Vocabulary	1	2	3	4	5
Grammar	1	2	3	4	5
Presentation	1	2	3	4	5

BLOCK SCHEDULE

Peer Teaching Have students work together in groups or pairs to review and help each other with grammar from chapters 35–36.

Perspektiven, pp. 272–273

PROGRAM RESOURCES

- Audio Program, Cassette 6B/CD 8
- www.mcdougallittell.com

Quick Start Review

♻ Vocabulary
Ergänzen Sie die Sätze mit den Wörtern.
WÖRTER: Pfandflaschen, Umweltbewusstsein, Umweltschutz, Verkehrsmittel, Verpackungsmaterial, Waldsterben

1. Öffentliche _____ sind umweltfreundlicher als Privatautos.
2. Das _____ ist besonders im Schwarzwald und im Fichtelgebirge zu einem Problem geworden.
3. Es ist oft sinnvoll, am _____ zu sparen.
4. Ich kaufe meine Milch jetzt immer in _____.
5. Manche Leute halten nicht viel vom _____.

Answers: 1. Verkehrsmittel
2. Waldsterben   3. Verpackungsmaterial
4. Pfandflaschen   5. Umweltschutz

TEACHING SUGGESTIONS

- *Aktivität A,* p. 272

Warm-up: Have students describe their hometown for a German visitor.

TEACHING ALL STUDENTS

Multiple Intelligences Intrapersonal: Have students write a poem or a short prose piece on a city of their choice.

BLOCK SCHEDULE

Fun Break Tell students to pack a suitcase for a trip. The first student says *Ich packe in meinen Koffer . . .* The next student repeats what has been said and adds one new item, such as *Ich packe . . . und . . . in meinen Koffer.* When the chain breaks down, start over.

PORTFOLIO

Have students research an expressionist poet or painter, such as Gottfried Benn, Else Lasker-Schüler, or Wassily Kandinsky. Have students write their findings, then present them, including visual or audio material if possible.

RUBRIC **A** = 13–15 pts. **B** = 10–12 pts.
C = 7–9 pts. **D** = 4–6 pts. **F** <4 pts.

Writing Criteria	Scale				
Vocabulary	1	2	3	4	5
Style, organization	1	2	3	4	5
Grammar	1	2	3	4	5

VIDEOTHEK

A. *Possible answers are:* **1.** Ein Schrebergarten in Deutschland sieht immer ordentlich und sauber aus. **2.** Am Samstag ist in Deutschland Putztag. Alles wird sauber und ordentlich gemacht, und auch regelmäßig, d.h. pünktlich.

B. *Possible answers are:* Auf dem ersten Bild kommen Leute mit dem Zug auf einem deutschen Bahnhof an. Es sind Gastarbeiter. In den sechziger Jahren kamen Hunderttausende Arbeiter aus Italien, Griechenland, Spanien und der Türkei nach Deutschland, um dort zu arbeiten. Das zweite Bild zeigt eine Pizzeria. Die Arbeiter aus anderen Ländern haben ihre Kultur und ihr Essen mit nach Deutschland gebracht. Sie haben die deutsche Küche beeinflusst und verändert. Heute gibt es viele verschiedene Restaurants in Deutschland, wo man essen kann wie in anderen Ländern.

C. *Possible answers are:* **1.** Die Leute in dieser Siedlung wohnen umweltfreundlicher als die meisten Deutschen, weil die Häuser energiesparend gebaut sind. Die Dächer aus Gras schützen zum Beispiel vor Hitze und Kälte. Ausserdem produzieren Solaranlagen auf den Dächern Strom aus Sonnenlicht. **2.** Bärbel Barmbecks Waschmaschine ist umweltfreundlich, weil sie wenig Wasser verbraucht. Ihr Wäschetrockner ist umweltfreundlich, weil er ohne Strom und nur mit warmer Raumluft funktioniert. Ihre Lampen sind umweltfreundlich, weil sie Strom sparen. **3.** *Answers will vary.*

Eine umweltfreundliche Siedlung.

Ⓐ Typisch deutsch? Ergün Çevik sagt: „Für mich zeigt sich in einem Schrebergarten die deutsche Seele." Sehen Sie sich die Bilder genau an. Welche „typisch" deutsche Eigenschaften sehen Sie in diesen Bildern?

1.

2.

Ⓑ Vom Sauerkraut zur Pizza. Beschreiben Sie, was Sie in diesen Bildern sehen. Wer sind diese Menschen? Was machen sie? Was haben diese Bilder mit dem Thema „multikulturelle Gesellschaft" zu tun?

1.   2.

Ⓒ Umweltschutz zu Hause. Schauen Sie sich das Bild an und beantworten Sie die Fragen.

1. Wie wohnen die Leute in dieser Wohnsiedlung? Inwiefern wohnen sie umweltfreundlicher als die meisten Deutschen?
2. Warum ist Bärbel Barmbecks Waschmaschine umweltfreundlich? ihr Wäschetrockner? ihre Lampen?
3. „Viele Menschen in dieser Siedlung nehmen Rücksicht auf die Umwelt. Dadurch verbessert sich die Lebensqualität für alle." Was meinen Sie? Wie kann sich die Lebensqualität für alle in einer solchen Siedlung verbessern?

D Theater für Jugendliche. Wie heißt dieses Theater? Was für Stücke werden da aufgeführt? Was wissen Sie über die künstlerischen Ziele des Ensembles?   See answers below.

Ein Theater, das „gebraucht" wird.

VOKABELN

A Deutsche, Ausländer und Einwanderer. Ergänzen Sie die Lücken mit den Wörtern im Kasten.

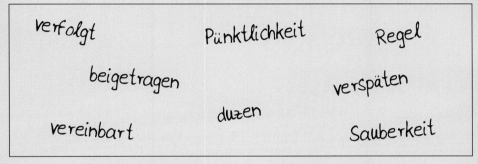

> verfolgt   Pünktlichkeit   Regel
>
> beigetragen   verspäten
>
>   duzen
> vereinbart   Sauberkeit

1. Ausländer haben kulturell sehr viel _____.
2. Die Liebe zur _____ hat natürlich Vorteile; beispielsweise werden die Fahrpläne eingehalten.
3. In Deutschland sagt man, die Ausnahme bestätigt die _____.
4. Leute, die politisch _____ werden, genießen in Deutschland das Asylrecht.
5. Wenn man eine Verabredung hat, sollte man sich nie _____.
6. Amerikaner in Deutschland wissen oft nicht, ob man jemanden _____ darf, wenn man ihn nicht kennt.
7. In Deutschland wird alles vorher _____.
8. Der wöchentliche Putztag zeigt die Liebe zur _____.

Ein Termin wird vereinbart.

A. 1. beigetragen   2. Pünktlichkeit   3. Regel
4. verfolgt   5. verspäten   6. duzen
7. vereinbart   8. Sauberkeit

B Probleme und Lösungen. Verbinden Sie jedes Umweltproblem in der linken Spalte mit der möglichen Lösung in der rechten Spalte.

B. 1. b   2. e   3. d   4. a   5. f   6. c

1. Wir verbrauchen zu viel Strom.
2. Die Wälder werden abgeholzt.
3. Kohlekraftwerke vergiften die Umwelt.
4. Abgase verschmutzen die Luft.
5. Plastik und andere Verpackungsmaterialien lassen sich nur schwer recyceln.
6. Wir verbrauchen zu viel Wasser.

a. Man sollte so wenig wie möglich mit dem Auto fahren.
b. Man sollte das Licht ausmachen, wenn man aus dem Zimmer geht.
c. Man soll im Sommer den Rasen nicht so oft wässern.
d. Man sollte Energie umweltfreundlicher produzieren – zum Beispiel mit Windkraft- oder Solaranlagen.
e. Man soll recyceltes Papier kaufen.
f. Man sollte Produkte mit umweltfreundlicherem Verpackungsmaterial kaufen.

D. *Possible answers are:* Das Theater heißt GRIPS Theater. Dort werden Stücke für Kinder, Jugendliche und Erwachsene aufgeführt, die Bedürfnisse, Probleme und Sehnsüchte des Publikums behandeln. Zu den künstlerischen Zielen des Theaters gehört es, dass die Zuschauer sich in den Stücken wiedererkennen sollen und die Stücke den Zuschauern helfen, ihre Umwelt besser zu durchschauen und zu verändern.

Eine Szene aus Volker Schlöndorffs Film „Die Blechtrommel".

C. *Answers will vary.*

Im Reisebüro.

A. 1. Für den ersten August suchen wir eine Verkäuferin, die mindestens zehn Jahre Erfahrung im Schuhverkauf hat.
2. Kinderreiche Familie sucht ein Einfamilienhaus, das mindestens fünf Zimmer hat.
3. Älteres Ehepaar sucht jungen Mann, der im Haushalt helfen und den Garten pflegen soll.
4. Für die Sommerreisesaison suchen wir Studenten, die als Reisebegleiter arbeiten sollen.

B. 1. Karin vergisst oft, ihren Hund zu füttern.
2. Aber wir haben keine Lust, jetzt Tennis zu spielen. 3. Es macht uns Spaß, in den Fitness-club zu gehen. 4. Ich finde, es ist wirklich schwer, gut Russisch zu sprechen. 5. Es ist leicht, auf Spanisch zu zählen. 6. Es ist immer schön, etwas Zeit mit Freunden zu verbringen.

C Sind Sie Filmkenner/Filmkennerin? Arbeiten Sie mit einem Partner / einer Partnerin, und stellen Sie einander die folgenden Fragen.

1. Siehst du gern ausländische Filme?
2. Welche ausländischen Filme hast du gesehen?
3. Sollen ausländische Filme deiner Meinung nach synchronisiert oder untertitelt werden? Warum?
4. Was ist für dich ein „typisch" amerikanischer Film? ein „typisch" deutscher Film?
5. Sind traurige Filme eigentlich realitätsnäher als Actionfilme? Was meinst du?

STRUKTUREN

A Anzeigen. Verbinden Sie die Sätze durch Relativpronomen.

MODELL: Für unser Reisebüro suchen wir Mitarbeiter. Sie müssen über Extremsportarten gut informiert sein. →
Für unser Reisebüro suchen wir Mitarbeiter, die über Extremsportarten gut informiert sind.

1. Für den ersten August suchen wir eine Verkäuferin. Sie soll mindestens zehn Jahre Erfahrung im Schuhverkauf haben.
2. Kinderreiche Familie sucht ein Einfamilienhaus. Es muss mindestens fünf Zimmer haben.
3. Älteres Ehepaar sucht jungen Mann. Er soll im Haushalt helfen und den Garten pflegen.
4. Für die Sommerreisesaison suchen wir Studenten. Sie sollen als Reisebegleiter arbeiten.

B Bemerkungen. Ergänzen Sie die Sätze mit **zu** plus **Infinitiv**.

MODELL: Jens isst viel Fleisch. Es ist ungesund, . . . →
Es ist ungesund, viel Fleisch zu essen.

1. Karin füttert ihren Hund. Karin vergisst oft, . . .
2. Thomas und Klara spielen jetzt Tennis. Aber wir haben keine Lust, . . .
3. Wir gehen in den Fitnessclub. Es macht uns Spaß, . . .
4. Ihr sprecht gut Russisch. Ich finde, es ist wirklich schwer, . . .
5. Kannst du auf Spanisch zählen? Es ist leicht, . . .
6. Ich verbringe gern etwas Zeit mit Freunden. Es ist immer schön, . . .

C Festspiele in Österreich. Ergänzen Sie die Sätze mit der richtigen Form von **werden.**

1. In vielen Teilen Österreichs sind Festspiele zu einer beliebten Tradition _____.
2. Dieses Jahr _____ wir zu den Salzburger Festspielen fahren.
3. In Salzburg _____ auch Mozart geboren.
4. Vor dem Salzburger Dom _____ jedes Jahr das Drama „Jedermann" aufgeführt.
5. Dieses Drama erinnert an eine Geschichte aus dem Mittelalter, es _____ jedoch erst in unserem Jahrhundert geschrieben.
6. Obwohl das Stück auf Deutsch gespielt _____, sind doch viele nicht deutschsprechende Besucher unter den Zuschauern.
7. Nach der Aufführung _____ wir noch ein bisschen in der Stadt bummeln.

D Musizieren. Schreiben Sie die Sätze ins Passiv um.

MODELL: Man singt Händels „Messias" oft zu Weihnachten. →
          Händels „Messias" wird oft zu Weihnachten gesungen.

1. Viele Musiker spielen die Trompete.
2. Der Berliner Rundfunk überträgt heute Abend die „Brandenburgischen Konzerte".
3. Man führt diese Woche in Salzburg „Die Zauberflöte" auf.
4. Heute bevorzugen viele Jugendliche Technomusik.
5. In unserem Laden verkauft man CD-Anlagen und Videorecorder.

E Nach München oder nach Hamburg? Sie wissen nicht, ob Sie nach München oder nach Hamburg reisen wollen. Ergänzen Sie die Satzteile in der linken Spalte mit einem passenden Satz aus der rechten Spalte. Für jeden Satzteil gibt es mehrere mögliche Ergänzungssätze.

MODELL: Ich glaube, dass . . . →
          Ich glaube, dass der Hamburger Akzent leichter zu verstehen ist.

1. Ich sollte vielleicht Hamburg besuchen, weil
2. München soll interessante Museen haben und
3. Ich will aber nicht nur Museen und Galerien besuchen, sondern
4. Man sagt, dass
5. Ich möchte gern wissen, ob
6. Ich glaube, dass
7. Ich könnte von München aus in die Alpen fahren, oder

a. Hamburg hat ausgezeichnete Theater.
b. Ich will (auch) etwas Zeit an der Nordseeküste verbringen.
c. Der Hamburger Akzent ist leichter zu verstehen.
d. Ich will mir gern Kunstwerke ansehen.
e. Die Münchner sollen sehr gastfreundlich sein.
f. Ich könnte auf der Alster segeln.
g. Ich will (auch) Spaziergänge in der Natur machen.

KULTURSPIEGEL

Georg Heym, 1887 in Hirschberg (Schlesien) geboren, lebte ab 1900 in Berlin. Er studierte Jura und promovierte 1911 in Rostock. 1912, ein Jahr nach Erscheinen seines ersten Gedichtbandes, ertrank er beim Eislaufen in der Havel. Er gehörte zum Kreis junger Lyriker, die als Ausdruck des Protests den Expressionismus schufen.

A. *Descriptions will vary.*

WORTSCHATZ ZUM LESEN

lagern	to camp
die Stirn	forehead
die Wut	anger
die Einsamkeit	loneliness
verirren	to get lost
die Kirchenglocken	church bells
wogen	to surge up
Korybanten	mythological dancing figures
dröhnen	to drone
die Schlote	factory chimneys
der Weihrauch	incense
betäuben	to anesthetize
der Geier	vulture
der Zorn	anger
schütteln	to shake
jagen	to hunt
der Glutqualm	fiery smoke
fressen	to eat, consume (as animals do)

PERSPEKTIVEN

A Zum Thema. Beschreiben Sie Ihre eigene Stadt.

1. Was tut man in Ihrer Stadt für die Umwelt?
2. Was tun Sie selbst für die Umwelt?
3. Welche Unterschiede gibt es zwischen einer Großstadt und einer Kleinstadt? Wo lebt man umweltfreundlicher? Warum?

Der Gott der Stadt

Auf einem Häuserblocke sitzt er breit.
Die Winde lagern schwarz um seine Stirn.
Er schaut voll Wut, wo fern in Einsamkeit
Die letzten Häuser in das Land verirrn.

5 Vom Abend glänzt der rote Bauch dem Baal.
Die großen Städte knien um ihn her.
Der Kirchenglocken ungeheure Zahl
Wogt auf ihn aus schwarzer Türme Meer.

Wie Korybanten-Tanz dröhnt die Musik
10 Der Millionen durch die Straßen laut.
Der Schlote Rauch, die Wolken der Fabrik
Ziehn auf zu ihm, wie Duft von Weihrauch blaut.

Das Wetter schwelt in seinen Augenbrauen.
Der dunkle Abend wird in Nacht betäubt.
15 Die Stürme flattern, die wie Geier schauen
Von seinem Haupthaar, das im Zorne sträubt.

Er streckt ins Dunkel seine Fleischerfaust.
Er schüttelt sie. Ein Meer von Feuer jagt
Durch eine Straße. Und der Glutqualm braust
20 Und frisst sie auf, bis spät der Morgen tagt.

Georg Heym (1887–1912)

B Zum Text. Welche Wörter im Gedicht passen zu den folgenden Kategorien? Passen Sie auf – manche Vokabeln passen vielleicht zu mehreren Kategorien.

    KRIEG   RELIGION   TIERE   MENSCHLICHE EIGENSCHAFTEN

C Zur Interpretation. In einem Gedicht werden Bilder mit Wörtern „gemalt". Lesen Sie jede Strophe noch einmal genau, und versuchen Sie, einzelne Bildelemente grafisch darzustellen. Ihre Bilder können abstrakt sein, oder Sie können eine Collage erstellen.

D Die Stadt. Wie erfährt man „die Stadt" in diesem Gedicht? Ist diese Beschreibung auch Ihre Erfahrung?

B. KRIEG: rot, schwelt, Feuer, Glutqualm
RELIGION: Baal, knien, Kirchenglocken, Korybanten, Weihrauch   TIERE: Geier, frisst
MENSCHLICHE EIGENSCHAFTEN: Wut, Einsamkeit, Zorn

C. *Pictures will vary.*

D. *Answers will vary.*

APPENDIX A

Grammar Tables

1. Personal Pronouns

	SINGULAR					PLURAL		
NOMINATIVE	ich	du / Sie	sie	er	es	wir	ihr / Sie	sie
ACCUSATIVE	mich	dich / Sie	sie	ihn	es	uns	euch / Sie	sie
DATIVE	mir	dir / Ihnen	ihr	ihm	ihm	uns	euch / Ihnen	ihnen

2. Definite Articles and *der*-Words

	SINGULAR			PLURAL
	FEMININE	MASCULINE	NEUTER	
NOMINATIVE	die	der	das	die
ACCUSATIVE	die	den	das	die
DATIVE	der	dem	dem	den
GENITIVE	der	des	des	der

Words declined like the definite article: **jeder, dieser, welcher**

3. Indefinite Articles and *ein*-Words

	SINGULAR			PLURAL
	FEMININE	MASCULINE	NEUTER	
NOMINATIVE	(k)eine	(k)ein	(k)ein	keine
ACCUSATIVE	(k)eine	(k)einen	(k)ein	keine
DATIVE	(k)einer	(k)einem	(k)einem	keinen
GENITIVE	(k)einer	(k)eines	(k)eines	keiner

Words declined like the indefinite article: all possessive adjectives (**mein, dein, sein, ihr, unser, euer, Ihr**).

4. Question Pronouns

	PEOPLE	THINGS AND CONCEPTS
NOMINATIVE	wer	was
ACCUSATIVE	wen	was
DATIVE	wem	
GENITIVE	wessen	

5. Attributive Adjectives without Articles

	SINGULAR			PLURAL
	FEMININE	MASCULINE	NEUTER	
NOMINATIVE	gute	guter	gutes	gute
ACCUSATIVE	gute	guten	gutes	gute
DATIVE	guter	gutem	gutem	guten
GENITIVE	guter	guten	guten	guter

6. Attributive Adjectives with *der*-Words

	SINGULAR			PLURAL
	FEMININE	MASCULINE	NEUTER	
NOMINATIVE	die gute	der gute	das gute	die guten
ACCUSATIVE	die gute	den guten	das gute	die guten
DATIVE	der guten	dem guten	dem guten	den guten
GENITIVE	der guten	des guten	des guten	der guten

7. Attributive Adjectives with *ein*-Words

	SINGULAR			PLURAL
	FEMININE	MASCULINE	NEUTER	
NOMINATIVE	eine gute	ein guter	ein gutes	keine guten
ACCUSATIVE	eine gute	einen guten	ein gutes	keine guten
DATIVE	einer guten	einem guten	einem guten	keinen guten
GENITIVE	einer guten	eines guten	eines guten	keiner guten

8. Prepositions

ACCUSATIVE	DATIVE	ACCUSATIVE/DATIVE	GENITIVE
durch	aus	an	außerhalb
für	außer	auf	innerhalb
gegen	bei	hinter	trotz
ohne	mit	in	während
um (. . . herum)	nach	neben	wegen
	seit	über	
	von	unter	
	zu	vor	
		zwischen	

9. Relative and Demonstrative Pronouns

	SINGULAR			PLURAL
	FEMININE	MASCULINE	NEUTER	
NOMINATIVE	die	der	das	die
ACCUSATIVE	die	den	das	die
DATIVE	der	dem	dem	denen
GENITIVE	deren	dessen	dessen	deren

10. Weak Masculine Nouns

These nouns add **-(e)n** in the accusative, dative, and genitive.
A. *International nouns ending in **-t** denoting male persons:* Komponist, Patient, Polizist, Präsident, Soldat, Student, Tourist
B. *Nouns ending in **-e** denoting male persons or animals:* Drache, Junge, Neffe, Riese
C. *The following nouns:* Elefant, Herr, Mensch, Nachbar, Name

	SINGULAR	PLURAL
NOMINATIVE	der Student der Junge	die Studenten die Jungen
ACCUSATIVE	den Studenten den Jungen	die Studenten die Jungen
DATIVE	dem Studenten dem Jungen	den Studenten den Jungen
GENITIVE	des Studenten des Jungen	der Studenten der Jungen

11. Principal Parts of Irregular Verbs

The following is a list of the most important strong and mixed verbs that are used in this book. Included in this list are the modal auxiliaries. Since the principal parts of two-part verbs follow the forms of the base verb, two-part verbs are generally not included, except for a few high-frequency verbs whose base verb is not commonly used. Thus you will find **einladen** listed, but not **zurückkommen.**

INFINITIVE	(3RD PERS. SG. PRESENT)	SIMPLE PAST	PAST PARTICIPLE	MEANING
anbieten		bot an	angeboten	*to offer*
anfangen	(fängt an)	fing an	angefangen	*to begin*
backen		backte	gebacken	*to bake*
beginnen		begann	begonnen	*to begin*
begreifen		begriff	begriffen	*to comprehend*
beißen		biss	gebissen	*to bite*
bitten		bat	gebeten	*to ask, beg*
bleiben		blieb	(ist) geblieben	*to stay*
brennen		brannte	gebrannt	*to burn*
bringen		brachte	gebracht	*to bring*
denken		dachte	gedacht	*to think*

INFINITIVE	(3RD PERS. SG. PRESENT)	SIMPLE PAST	PAST PARTICIPLE	MEANING
dürfen	(darf)	durfte	gedurft	to be allowed
einladen	(lädt ein)	lud ein	eingeladen	to invite
empfehlen	(empfiehlt)	empfahl	empfohlen	to recommend
entscheiden		entschied	entschieden	to decide
essen	(isst)	aß	gegessen	to eat
fahren	(fährt)	fuhr	(ist) gefahren	to drive
fallen	(fällt)	fiel	(ist) gefallen	to fall
finden		fand	gefunden	to find
fliegen		flog	(ist) geflogen	to fly
geben	(gibt)	gab	gegeben	to give
gefallen	(gefällt)	gefiel	gefallen	to like; to please
gehen		ging	(ist) gegangen	to go
genießen		genoss	genossen	to enjoy
geschehen	(geschieht)	geschah	(ist) geschehen	to happen
gewinnen		gewann	gewonnen	to win
haben	(hat)	hatte	gehabt	to have
halten	(hält)	hielt	gehalten	to hold; to stop
hängen		hing	gehangen	to hang
heißen		hieß	geheißen	to be called
helfen	(hilft)	half	geholfen	to help
kennen		kannte	gekannt	to know
kommen		kam	(ist) gekommen	to come
können	(kann)	konnte	gekonnt	can; to be able
lassen	(lässt)	ließ	gelassen	to let; to allow
laufen	(läuft)	lief	(ist) gelaufen	to run
leihen		lieh	geliehen	to lend; to borrow
lesen	(liest)	las	gelesen	to read
liegen		lag	gelegen	to lie
mögen	(mag)	mochte	gemocht	to like
müssen	(muss)	musste	gemusst	must; to have to
nehmen	(nimmt)	nahm	genommen	to take
nennen		nannte	genannt	to name
raten	(rät)	riet	geraten	to advise
reiten		ritt	(ist) geritten	to ride
rennen		rannte	gerannt	to run
scheinen		schien	geschienen	to seem; to shine
schlafen	(schläft)	schlief	geschlafen	to sleep
schließen		schloss	geschlossen	to close
schreiben		schrieb	geschrieben	to write
schwimmen		schwamm	(ist) geschwommen	to swim
sehen	(sieht)	sah	gesehen	to see
sein	(ist)	war	(ist) gewesen	to be
singen		sang	gesungen	to sing
sitzen		saß	gesessen	to sit

INFINITIVE	(3RD PERS. SG. PRESENT)	SIMPLE PAST	PAST PARTICIPLE	MEANING
sollen	(soll)	sollte	gesollt	*should, ought; to be supposed*
sprechen	(spricht)	sprach	gesprochen	*to speak*
stehen		stand	gestanden	*to stand*
steigen		stieg	(ist) gestiegen	*to rise; to climb*
sterben	(stirbt)	starb	(ist) gestorben	*to die*
tragen	(trägt)	trug	getragen	*to carry; to wear*
treffen	(trifft)	traf	getroffen	*to meet*
trinken		trank	getrunken	*to drink*
tun		tat	getan	*to do*
umsteigen		stieg um	(ist) umgestiegen	*to change; to transfer*
vergessen	(vergisst)	vergaß	vergessen	*to forget*
vergleichen		verglich	verglichen	*to compare*
verlieren		verlor	verloren	*to lose*
wachsen	(wächst)	wuchs	(ist) gewachsen	*to grow*
waschen	(wäscht)	wusch	gewaschen	*to wash*
werden	(wird)	wurde	(ist) geworden	*to become*
wissen	(weiß)	wusste	gewusst	*to know*
wollen	(will)	wollte	gewollt	*to want*
ziehen		zog	(ist/hat) gezogen	*to move; to pull*

12. Common Inseparable Prefixes of Verbs

be-   besichtigen, besuchen, bezahlen
er-   erleben, erlösen
ver-   vergessen, vermieten, versprechen

13. Conjugation of Verbs

Present Tense
Auxiliary Verbs

	sein	**haben**	**werden**
ich	bin	habe	werde
du	bist	hast	wirst
Sie	sind	haben	werden
sie/er/es	ist	hat	wird
wir	sind	haben	werden
ihr	seid	habt	werdet
sie	sind	haben	werden
Sie	sind	haben	werden

Regular Verbs, Strong Verbs, Mixed (or Irregular Weak) Verbs

	REGULAR		STRONG		MIXED
	fragen	**arbeiten**	**geben**	**fahren**	**wissen**
ich	frage	arbeite	gebe	fahre	weiß
du	fragst	arbeitest	gibst	fährst	weißt
Sie	fragen	arbeiten	geben	fahren	wissen
sie/er/es	fragt	arbeitet	gibt	fährt	weiß
wir	fragen	arbeiten	geben	fahren	wissen
ihr	fragt	arbeitet	gebt	fahrt	wisst
sie	fragen	arbeiten	geben	fahren	wissen
Sie	fragen	arbeiten	geben	fahren	wissen

Simple Past Tense

Auxiliary Verbs

	sein	**haben**	**werden**
ich	war	hatte	wurde
du	warst	hattest	wurdest
Sie	waren	hatten	wurden
sie/er/es	war	hatte	wurde
wir	waren	hatten	wurden
ihr	wart	hattet	wurdet
sie	waren	hatten	wurden
Sie	waren	hatten	wurden

Regular Verbs, Strong Verbs, Mixed (or Irregular Weak) Verbs

	REGULAR	STRONG		MIXED
	fragen	**geben**	**fahren**	**wissen**
ich	fragte	gab	fuhr	wusste
du	fragtest	gabst	fuhrst	wusstest
Sie	fragten	gaben	fuhren	wussten
sie/er/es	fragte	gab	fuhr	wusste
wir	fragten	gaben	fuhren	wussten
ihr	fragtet	gabt	fuhrt	wusstet
sie	fragten	gaben	fuhren	wussten
Sie	fragten	gaben	fuhren	wussten

Wissen *and the Modal Verbs*

	MODAL VERBS						
	wissen	**dürfen**	**können**	**müssen**	**sollen**	**wollen**	**mögen**
ich	wusste	durfte	konnte	musste	sollte	wollte	mochte
du	wusstest	durftest	konntest	musstest	solltest	wolltest	mochtest
Sie	wussten	durften	konnten	mussten	sollten	wollten	mochten
sie/er/es	wusste	durfte	konnte	musste	sollte	wollte	mochte
wir	wussten	durften	konnten	mussten	sollten	wollten	mochten
ihr	wusstet	durftet	konntet	musstet	solltet	wolltet	mochtet
sie	wussten	durften	konnten	mussten	sollten	wollten	mochten
Sie	wussten	durften	konnten	mussten	sollten	wollten	mochten

Present Perfect Tense

	sein		**haben**		**geben**		**fahren**	
ich	bin		habe		habe		bin	
du	bist		hast		hast		bist	
Sie	sind		haben		haben		sind	
sie/er/es	ist	} gewesen	hat	} gehabt	hat	} gegeben	ist	} gefahren
wir	sind		haben		haben		sind	
ihr	seid		habt		habt		seid	
sie	sind		haben		haben		sind	
Sie	sind		haben		haben		sind	

Past Perfect Tense

	sein		**haben**		**geben**		**fahren**	
ich	war		hatte		hatte		war	
du	warst		hattest		hattest		warst	
Sie	waren		hatten		hatten		waren	
sie/er/es	war	} gewesen	hatte	} gehabt	hatte	} gegeben	war	} gefahren
wir	waren		hatten		hatten		waren	
ihr	wart		hattet		hattet		wart	
sie	waren		hatten		hatten		waren	
Sie	waren		hatten		hatten		waren	

Subjunctive

Present Tense: Subjunctive I (Indirect Discourse Subjunctive)

	sein	haben	werden	fahren	wissen
ich	sei	—	—	—	wisse
du	sei(e)st	habest	—	—	—
Sie	seien	—	—	—	—
sie/er/es	sei	habe	werde	fahre	wisse
wir	seien	—	—	—	—
ihr	sei(e)t	habet	—	—	—
sie	seien	—	—	—	—
Sie	seien	—	—	—	—

For the forms left blank, the subjunctive II forms are preferred in indirect discourse.

Present Tense: Subjunctive II

	fragen	sein	haben	werden	fahren	wissen
ich	fragte	wäre	hätte	würde	führe	wüsste
du	fragtest	wär(e)st	hättest	würdest	führ(e)st	wüsstest
Sie	fragten	wären	hätten	würden	führen	wüssten
sie/er/es	fragte	wäre	hätte	würde	führe	wüsste
wir	fragten	wären	hätten	würden	führen	wüssten
ihr	fragtet	wär(e)t	hättet	würdet	führ(e)t	wüsstet
sie	fragten	wären	hätten	würden	führen	wüssten
Sie	fragten	wären	hätten	würden	führen	wüssten

Past Tense: Subjunctive I (Indirect Discourse)

	fahren	wissen
ich	sei	—
du	sei(e)st	habest
Sie	sei(e)n	—
sie/er/es	sei	habe
wir	seien } gefahren	— } gewusst
ihr	sei(e)t	habet
sie	sei(e)n	—
Sie	sei(e)n	—

Past Tense: Subjunctive II

	sein		geben		fahren	
ich	wäre		hätte		wäre	
du	wär(e)st		hättest		wär(e)st	
Sie	wären		hätten		wären	
sie/er/es	wäre	gewesen	hätte	gegeben	wäre	gefahren
wir	wären		hätten		wären	
ihr	wär(e)t		hättet		wär(e)t	
sie	wären		hätten		wären	
Sie	wären		hätten		wären	

Passive Voice

	einladen					
	Present		*Simple Past*		*Present Perfect*	
ich	werde		wurde		bin	
du	wirst		wurdest		bist	
Sie	werden		wurden		sind	
sie/er/es	wird	eingeladen	wurde	eingeladen	ist	eingeladen worden
wir	werden		wurden		sind	
ihr	werdet		wurdet		seid	
sie	werden		wurden		sind	
Sie	werden		wurden		sind	

Imperative

	sein	geben	fahren	arbeiten
FAMILIAR SINGULAR	sei	gib	fahr	arbeite
FAMILIAR PLURAL	seid	gebt	fahrt	arbeitet
FORMAL	seien Sie	geben Sie	fahren Sie	arbeiten Sie

APPENDIX B

Alternate Spelling and Capitalization

With the German spelling reform, some words now have an alternate old spelling along with a new one. The vocabulary lists at the end of each chapter in this text present the new spelling. Listed here are some common words that are affected by the spelling reform, along with their traditional alternate spellings. This list is not a complete list of words affected by the spelling reform.

NEW	ALTERNATE
Abschluss (⸚e)	Abschluß (Abschlüsse)
auf Deutsch	auf deutsch
dass	daß
Erdgeschoss (-e)	Erdgeschoß (Erdgeschosse)
essen (isst), aß, gegessen	essen (ißt), aß, gegessen
Esszimmer (-)	Eßzimmer (-)
Fitness	Fitneß
Fluss (⸚e)	Fluß (Flüsse)
heute Abend / . . . Mittag / . . . Morgen / . . . Nachmittag / . . . Vormittag	heute abend / . . . mittag / . . . morgen / . . . nachmittag / . . . vormittag
lassen (lässt), ließ, gelassen Lass uns doch . . .	lassen (läßt), ließ, gelassen Laß uns doch . . .
morgen Abend / . . . Mittag / . . . Nachmittag / . . . Vormittag	morgen abend / . . . mittag / . . . nachmittag / . . . vormittag
müssen (muss), musste, gemusst	müssen (muß), mußte, gemußt
passen (passt), gepasst	passen (paßt), gepaßt
Rad fahren (fährt Rad), fuhr Rad, ist Rad gefahren	radfahren (fährt Rad), fuhr Rad, ist radgefahren
Samstagabend / -mittag / -morgen / -nachmittag / -vormittag	Samstag abend / . . . mittag / . . . morgen / . . . nachmittag / . . . vormittag
Schloss (⸚er)	Schloß (Schlösser)
spazieren gehen (geht spazieren), ging spazieren, ist spazieren gegangen	spazierengehen (geht spazieren), ging spazieren, ist spazierengegangen
Stress	Streß
vergessen (vergisst), vergaß, vergessen	vergessen (vergißt), vergaß, vergessen
wie viel	wieviel

VOCABULARY

GERMAN-ENGLISH

This cumulative vocabulary list contains nearly all the German words that appear in the textbook for *Auf Deutsch! 3 Drei.* Exceptions include identical or very close cognates with English that are not part of the active vocabulary. It also contains German words that appeared in *Auf Deutsch! 1 Eins* and *Auf Deutsch! 2 Zwei.* Chapter numbers indicate active vocabulary items from the end-of-chapter **Wortschatz** lists. For **Sie wissen schon** vocabulary, the chapter in *1 Eins* or *2 Zwei* in which the item originally appeared is provided as well. Words in the **Wortschatz** list in the **Einführung** chapter are designated by the book number. For example, "11/3E" indicates that the word appears in the **Wortschatz** list of *Kapitel 11* in *Auf Deutsch! 1 Eins* and the **Einführung** of *3 Drei.*

Entries for strong and mixed verbs include all principal parts, including the third-person singular of the present tense if it is irregular: **fahren (fährt), fuhr, ist gefahren; trinken, trank, getrunken.**

The vocabulary list also includes the following abbreviations.

acc.	accusative
adj.	adjective
adv.	adverb
coll.	colloquial
coord. conj.	coordinating conjunction
dat.	dative
decl. adj.	declined adjective
fig.	figurative
form.	formal
gen.	genitive
indef. pron.	indefinite pronoun
inform.	informal
(**-n** *masc.*) / (**-en** *masc.*)	masculine noun ending in **-n** or **-en** in all cases but the nominative singular
pl.	plural
sg.	singular
subord. conj.	subordinating conjunction

A

ab (+ *dat.*) from; from . . . on; beginning, **Fahrverbindungen ab Kloster** connections from the monastery; **für die Kids ab zehn** for kids age ten and older; **ab 1850** from 1850 on; **ab und zu** from time to time

der Abbau reduction; **Abbau der Aggression** stress reduction

abbauen (baut ab) to dismantle; to decompose; to reduce

abbiegen (biegt ab), bog ab, abgebogen to turn (22)

abbrechen (bricht ab), brach ab, abgebrochen to break up; to end

das Abc alphabet

der Abend (-e) evening; **am Abend** in the evening; **gestern Abend** last night; **guten Abend!** good evening!; **heute Abend** this evening; **jeden Abend** every night; **morgen Abend** tomorrow evening

das Abendessen (-) dinner; **nach dem Abendessen** after dinner; **zum Abendessen** for dinner (19)

das Abendkleid (-er) evening gown

abends (in the) evenings

die Abendveranstaltung (-en) evening event

das Abenteuer (-) adventure (9/32)

abenteurlich adventurous

der Abenteuerurlaub (-e) adventure vacation

aber (*coord. conj.*) but, however

abernten (erntet ab) to harvest

abfahren (fährt ab), fuhr ab, ist abgefahren to depart

die Abfahrt (-en) departure (24)

der Abfall (¨-e) trash (20/35)

die Abfallberatung waste management

die Abfallmenge volume of waste

abfliegen (fliegt ab), flog ab, ist abgeflogen to take off, to depart by plane (24)

abfließen (fließt ab), floss ab, ist abgeflossen to drain

der Abflug (¨-e) departure

abführen (führt ab) to remove

das Abgas (-e) exhaust

abgeben (gibt ab), gab ab, abgegeben to give up; to pass on; to drop off (19)

abgefahren (*adj.*) departed

abgelehnt (*adj.*) declined

der/die Abgeordnete (*decl. adj.*) delegate; member of parliament (30)

abgeschlossen (*adj.*) completed, closed

abgeschnitten (*adj.*) cut

abgeschrieben (*adj.*) copied

abgezogen (*adj.*) skinned, peeled, blanched

die Abgrenzung (-en) separation

abhacken (hackt ab) to check off; to chop off

abhängen (hängt ab) to hang up (*telephone*)

abhängig dependent(ly) (13)

die Abhängigkeit dependence

abhauen: hau ab! (*slang*) beat it!

abholen (holt ab) to pick up (23)

abholzen (holzt ab) to deforest

das Abi = Abitur

die Abifete (-n) graduation party (celebrating the *Abitur*)

das Abitur (-e) *exam at the end of secondary school* (*Gymnasium*) (10)

der Abiturient (-en *masc.***) / die Abiturientin (-nen)** *person who has passed the Abitur*

abkaufen (kauft ab) to buy

abkriegen (kriegt ab): (*coll.*) to get, to be hurt

abladen (lädt ab), lud ab, abgeladen to unload

der Ablauf (Abläufe) course; order of events

ablehnen (lehnt ab) to decline, reject

die Ablehnung (-en) rejection

ableiten (leitet ab) to derive

abliefern (liefert ab) to deliver

abnehmen (nimmt ab), nahm ab, abgenommen to take off; to lose weight

abonnieren to subscribe to (21)

abraten (rät ab), riet ab, abgeraten to advise against

(sich) abreagieren (reagiert ab) to unwind, relax; **zum Abreagieren** for relaxation

abreisen (reist ab), ist abgereist to depart (8)

abreißen, riss ab, abgerissen to tear down (*a building*)

abrunden (rundet ab) to round up; to complete

die Absage (-n) rejection

der Absatz (¨-e) heel (*of a shoe*) (21); paragraph, section (*in a text*)

abschaffen (schafft ab) to get rid of (20)

der Abschaum scum, dregs of society

der Abschied (-e) farewell

abschließen (schließt ab), schloss ab, abgeschlossen to finish, conclude

der Abschluss (¨-e) completion of studies, degree

abschmecken (schmeckt ab) to taste

abschneiden (schneidet ab), schnitt ab, abgeschnitten to cut

der Abschnitt (-e) cut; segment (28); paragraph in a text

abschreiben (schreibt ab), schrieb ab, abgeschrieben to copy (*in writing*)

absenken (senkt ab) to lower

die Absicht (-en) intention

absolut absolute(ly)

absolvieren to complete (*a degree*) **die Schule absolvieren** to complete school education

abspeichern (speichert ab) to store (*data*)

absprechen (spricht ab), sprach ab, abgesprochen to agree; to make arrangements

die Abstammung (-en) descent, origin

absteigen (steigt ab), stieg ab, ist abgestiegen to get off, dismount

absterben (stirbt ab), starb ab, ist abgestorben to die off

abstrakt abstract(ly)

abstützen to support; to prop up

absuchen (sucht ab) to search

die Abteilung (-en) department

abträglich (+ *dat.*) detrimental

das Abwasser (-) sewage

sich abwechseln (wechselt ab) to take turns, alternate

abwechselnd alternately

die Abwechslung (-en) change; variety (32)

abwechslungsreich variable, changeable (14)

die Abwesenheit (-en) absence

abziehen (zieht ab), zog ab, abgezogen to skin, peel

ach! oh!; **ach ja!** oh right!; **ach so!** I see!; **ach, was!** come on!, **ach wo!** not at all!

acht eight; **es ist acht Uhr** it's eight o'clock (1E)

die Acht (-) attention; **Acht geben (gibt Acht), gab Acht, Acht gegeben: auf den Lehrer Acht geben** to pay attention to the teacher

achten to respect; to take notice (33); **achten auf** (+ *acc.*) to pay attention to

die Achterbahn (-en) roller coaster

achtzehn eighteen (1E)

achtzehnte eighteenth; **der achtzehnte Januar** January eighteenth

achtzig eighty (1E); **die achtziger Jahre** the eighties

der Ackerbau agriculture

der Actionfilm (-e) action film (36)

der ADAC = Allgemeiner Deutscher Automobil Club

addieren to add

adelig noble, of noble birth

das Adjektiv (-e) adjective

die Adjektivendung (-en) adjective ending

der Adler (-) eagle

die Adresse (-n) address

adrett neat(ly)

das Adverb (Adverbien) adverb

die Aerobikübung (-en) aerobic exercise, aerobics

der Affe (-n *masc.***)** ape, monkey

(das) Afrika Africa

der Afrikaner (-) / die Afrikanerin (-nen) African (*person*) (18)

der Agent (-en *masc.***) / die Agentin (-nen)** secret agent, spy

die Agentur (-en) agency

die Aggression (-en) aggression

(das) Ägypten Egypt

ägyptisch (*adj.*) Egyptian

aha! I see!

ähneln (+ *dat.*) to resemble

ahnen to foresee, know

ähnlich similar(ly); **etwas**

Ähnliches something similar

Ahnung: keine Ahnung! I have no idea!

ahoi! ahoy!

der Ahornsirup maple syrup

das Airbrushing airbrushing

die Akademie (-n) academy

der Akademiker (-) / die Akademikerin (-nen) academic; college graduate

akademisch academic(ally)

der Akkusativ accusative case

die Akkusativpräposition (-en) accusative preposition

das Akkusativpronomen (-) pronoun in the accusative case

die Aktion (-en) action (35)

aktiv active(ly) (32)

das Aktiv active voice

die Aktivität (-en) activity

aktuell current, topical (21)

der Akzent (-e) accent (34)

die Akzeptanz (-en) acceptance

akzeptieren to accept

alarmieren to alarm; to call

albern silly

das Alibi (-s) alibi

der Alkohol alcohol

all, all- all; **all das** all that; **all das Zeug** all that stuff; **all ihr jungen Leute** all you young people; **vor allem, vor allen Dingen** above all

alle (*pl.*) all, everyone; **alle zusammen!** everybody!, all together! (1E); **ein Drittel aller Schüler** a third of all students

die Allee (-n) avenue

die Allegorie (-n) allegory

allein(e) alone (4)

allein erziehend single parenting (30)

allein stehend single

aller-: am aller- (+ *superlative*) the very most; **am allerschönsten** the most beautiful of all

allerdings indeed; though; however; to be sure

die Allergie (-n) allergic reaction, allergy

das Allergiepotential (-e) potential for allergies

allergisch allergic

der Allergologe (-n *masc.***) / die Allergologin (-nen)** allergy specialist

alles everything; **alles Gute!** best wishes!, all the best!; **alles klar!** everything ok!; **alles Liebe** love (*closing in letters*); **das ist alles!** that's all!

allgemein general(ly); **Allgemeiner Deutscher Automobil Club** *German automobile association*; **im Allgemeinen** in general, generally

alljährlich annual(ly), every year

die Allmacht omnipotence

der Allmächtige (*decl. adj.*) Almighty One

allmählich gradual(ly) (28)

der Alltag everyday life (27)

alltäglich daily, ordinary, commonplace

das Alltagsleben everyday life

allzu all too; **allzu menschlich** all too human; **allzu viel** far too much; **allzu wenig** all too few

die Alm (-en) alpine pasture

der Almanach almanac

die Alpen (*pl.*) the Alps (17); **der Alpengipfel (-)** alpine peak; **die Alpenlandschaft** landscape in the Alps

das Alphabet (-e) alphabet

alpin alpine

der Alptraum (-träume) nightmare (27)

als (*subord. conj.*) when; than; as; **als ich jung war** when I was young; **länger als** longer than; **als Gast** as a guest

also well; thus; therefore; so (12); **also, bis dann!** all right then, see you later; **na also!** there we go!

alt (älter, ältest-) old (1)

der Altar (-̈e) altar

die Altbatterie (-n) empty battery

der Altbaubezirk (-e) historic district (*of a city*)

die Altbauwohnung (-en) pre-1945 building (4)

der/die Alte (*decl. adj.*) the old one

**der Altenpfleger (-) / die
Altenpflegerin (-nen)** old people's
nurse
das Alter (-) age
alternativ alternative(ly)
die Alternative (-n) alternative
der Altersgenosse (-n *masc.***) / die
Altersgenossin (-nen)** person of
the same age
das Altersheim (-e) home for the
elderly
das Altglas recyclable glass
die Altkleidersammlung (-en)
collection of old clothes
altmodisch old-fashioned
das Altpapier recyclable paper
die Altstadt ("e) old part of town
am = an dem: am achten Mai on
May eighth; **am allerschönsten**
the most beautiful; **am Montag**
on Monday
der Amazonas Amazon river
die Ameise (-n) ant
(das) Amerika America
die Amerikafahrt (-en) trip to
America
der Amerikafan (-s) America nut,
*person who likes everything about
America*
**der Amerikaner (-) / die
Amerikanerin (-nen)** American
(*person*) (18)
amerikanisch (*adj.*) American
die Ampel (-n) traffic lights
das Amt ("er) bureau, agency
das Amtsgeschäft (-e) business
matter, transaction
die Amtstätigkeit (-en) job
responsibility
amüsant amusing(ly)
amüsieren to amuse
an (+ *acc./dat.*) at; near; up to; to;
on (11); **am Internet surfen** to
surf the internet (18); **an _____
vorbei** past _____ (22)
analysieren to analyze
die Ananas (-) pineapple
der Anbau cultivation, growing;
kontrolliert biologischer Anbau
organic cultivation / growing
anbei enclosed (*in letters*)

**anbieten (bietet an), bot an,
angeboten** to offer
**der Anbieter (-) / die Anbieterin
(-nen)** supplier
der Anblick (-e) sight
**anbringen (bringt an), brachte an,
angebracht** to install; to put
forward
anbrüllen (brüllt an) to yell at
ander- other; **alles andere**
everything else; **eins nach dem
anderen** one thing at at time;
etwas anderes something else;
unter anderem among other
things
der/die/das andere (*decl. adj.*) other
(one), different (one)
andererseits on the other hand (26)
(sich) ändern to change
andernorts somewhere else
anders different(ly); **anders herum**
the other way around; **ganz
anders** totally different
andersartig of a different kind
anderswohin in a different place
anderthalb one and a half
die Änderung (-en) change,
alteration
aneinander to each other, to one
another
die Anekdote (-n) anecdote
die Anerkennung (-en) recognition
anfällig prone
der Anfang ("e) beginning, start;
am Anfang in the beginning; **von
Anfang an** from the beginning;
**Anfang des zwanzigsten
Jahrhunderts** at the beginning of
the twentieth century
**anfangen (fängt an), fing an,
angefangen** to start (23/31)
anfangs at first (30)
der Anfangsbuchstabe (-n *masc.***)**
initial
anfassen (fasst an) to touch; to
grasp (31)
die Anfeindung (-en) hostility
anfertigen (fertigt an) to make; to
do; to prepare, draw up
anfordern (fordert an) to request,
ask for

das Anführungszeichen (-)
quotation mark
die Angabe (-n) information
**angeben (gibt an), gab an,
angegeben** to indicate; to give; to
name, cite
das Angebot (-e) offer (23)
angeboten (*adj.*) offered
angebracht (*adj.*) attached; suitable
**angehen (geht an), ging an,
angegangen** to concern; **was die
Frauen angeht** as far as the
women are concerned
angehören (gehört an) to belong
to; to be associated with
der/die Angeklagte (*decl. adj.*)
defendant (30)
die Angelegenheit (-en) matter
angeln to fish (8)
angemessen appropriate(ly)
angenehm pleasant(ly) (10)
angepasst conformist (26)
angestellt employed (1)
der/die Angestellte (*decl. adj.*)
employee
angestrebt desired, sought after
**angetan: von jemandem angetan
sein** to be attracted to someone
angewandt (*adj.*) applied
**angreifen (greift an), griff an,
angegriffen** to attack
der Angriff (-e) attack; **bereit zum
Angriff** ready to attack
die Angst ("e) fear (20); **Angst
haben** to be afraid; **keine Angst!**
don't be afraid!
ängstlich timid(ly), anxious(ly)
angucken (guckt an) (*coll.*) to have
a look at (32)
**anhalten (hält an), hielt an,
angehalten** to stop
der Anhänger (-) trailer
anheben, hob an, angehoben to
lift up
anhören (hört an) to listen to
animieren to stimulate
anklagen (klagt an) to accuse
**ankommen (kommt an), kam an,
ist angekommen** to arrive (24);
auf etwas ankommen to depend
upon (32)

ankreuzen (kreuzt an) to cross, check off
ankündigen (kündigt an) to announce
die Ankunft (¨e) arrival
die Anlage (-n) facility
anlasten (lastet an) to accuse
anlegen (legt an) dock (a boat)
das Anliegen (-) concern, matter, request
anmachen (macht an) to turn on; **Licht anmachen** turn on a light
anmalen (malt an) to paint on; **ein Clowngesicht anmalen** to paint on a clown's face
das Anmeldeformular (-e) registration form
(sich) anmelden (meldet an) to register (19)
die Anmeldung (-en) registration
anmütig (adj) charming; graceful
annähernd approximately
die Annalen (pl.) annals, history
annehmen (nimmt an), nahm an, angenommen to accept, take on (34)
die Annehmlichkeiten (pl.) comforts, convenience
die Anonymität anonymity
der Anorak (-s) parka, winter jacket (7)
anorganisch inorganic
(sich) anpassen (passt an) (+ dat.) to adapt (to); to conform (to) (26)
anprobieren (probiert an) to try on (clothes) (7)
anrechnen (rechnet an) to count; to take into account
anreden (redet an) to address
anregen (regt an) to stimulate (31)
die Anregung (-en) stimulation (31)
die Anreise (-n) arrival
anreisen (reist an), reiste an, ist angereist to arrive
der Anruf (-e) phone call
anrufen (ruft an), rief an, angerufen to call up (on the phone) (7/3E)

der Anrufer (-) / die Anruferin (-nen) caller
ans = an das
(sich) ansammeln (sammelt an) to accumulate
anschaffen (schafft an) to aquire, purchase
anschauen (schaut an) to look at; to watch (21)
anschaulich vivid(ly), clear(ly)
anschlagen (schlägt an), schlug an, angeschlagen to strike
anschließend immediately following
der Anschluss (¨e) entry, connection, annexation
sich anschmiegen (schmiegt an) to cuddle, snuggle
sich anschnallen (schnallt an) to fasten (20)
das Anschreiben (-) letter
sich ansehen (sieht an), sah an, angesehen to look at; to watch (21)
das Ansehen reputation, recognition
ansiedeln (siedelt an) to settle
ansonsten otherwise
ansprechen (spricht an), sprach an, angesprochen to address, speak to
der Ansprechpartner (-) / die Ansprechpartnerin (-nen) contact person
der Anspruch (¨e) claim, right; **in Anspruch nehmen** to claim; to take advantage of
anständig decent
anstarren (starrt an) to stare at
anstatt (+ gen.) instead of
ansteigen (steigt an), stieg an, ist angestiegen to rise, increase
anstellen (stellt an) to hire
anstoßen (stößt an), stieß an, angestoßen to touch; to push, shove
anstreben (strebt an) to strive for something
anstrengend strenuous (23)
die Anstrengung (-en) strain, effort
der Anstrich (-e) paint (35)

der Anteil (-e) part, share, portion
der Anthropologe (-n masc.) / die Anthropologin (-nen) anthropologist
die Antike antiquity
die Antikensammlung (-en) collection of classical antiquities
antiquarisch antique (22)
die Antiquität (-en) antique
antisemitisch anti-Semitic
der Antisemitismus anti-Semitism
der Antrag (¨e) application, request
das Antragsformular (-e) application form
antun: (jemandem etwas) antun (tut an), tat an, angetan to do (something to someone)
die Antwort (-en) answer
der Antwortbrief (-e) letter of response
antworten to answer
der Anwalt (¨e) / die Anwältin (-nen) lawyer (13)
die Anweisung (-en) instruction
die Anwendung (-en) application
anwinkeln (winkelt an) to bend
die Anzeige (-n) advertisement (14)
anzeigen (zeigt an) to sue
(sich) anziehen (zieht an), zog an, angezogen to put on (clothes) (7); to attract
der Anzug (¨e) dress suit
anzünden (zündet an) to light (17)
apart distinctive(ly), unusual(ly)
der Apfel (¨) apple
der Apfelsaft (¨e) apple juice
der Apfelstrudel (-) apple strudel (15)
der Apostel (-) apostle
die Apotheke (-n) drugstore (for prescription drugs) (16)
der Apothekenhelfer (-) / die Apothekenhelferin (-nen) pharmaceutical assistant
der Apotheker (-) / die Apothekerin (-nen) pharmacist
der Apparat (-e) apparatus, appliance, gadget; (phone) **am Apparat!** speaking!
das Appartement (-s) apartment
der Appetit appetite

der April April (5); **am dreizehnten April** on April thirteenth; **im April** in April

das Aquarium (*pl.* **Aquarien**) aquarium

die Arbeit (-en) work; exam; **an die Arbeit!** back to work!

arbeiten to work

der Arbeiter (-) / die Arbeiterin (-nen) blue collar worker

die Arbeiterfamilie (-n) blue collar family

die Arbeiterstadt (-städte) working class city

der Arbeitgeber (-) / die Arbeitgeberin (-nen) employer (14)

der Arbeitnehmer (-) / die Arbeitnehmerin (-nen) employee (14)

das Arbeitsamt (-er) department of labor, employment office

die Arbeitsatmosphäre (-n) work atmosphere

die Arbeitsbedingungen (*pl.*) working conditions

die Arbeitserfahrung (-en) work experience (14)

die Arbeitsgemeinschaft (-en) association, agency, society

die Arbeitsgruppe (-n) team, workshop

die Arbeitskraft labor force (34)

die Arbeitslage employment situation (*in a society*)

das Arbeitsleben work life, professional life

arbeitslos unemployed (1)

der/die Arbeitslose (*decl. adj.*) unemployed (person)

das Arbeitslosengeld (-er) unemployment benefit

die Arbeitslosenzahl (-en) number of unemployed (29)

die Arbeitslosigkeit unemployment (20)

der Arbeitsmarkt (-e) job market

die Arbeitsmoral work ethic

der Arbeitsplatz (-e) workplace (13/29)

die Arbeitssituation (-en) employment situation

die Arbeitsstelle (-n) job, position

die Arbeitsstunde (-n) work hour

die Arbeitssuche job search; **auf Arbeitssuche sein** to be looking for a job

der/die Arbeitssuchende (*decl. adj.*) person looking for employment

der Arbeitstag (-e) work day

Arbeits- und Studienaufenthalte in Afrika *organization for work and study exchange programs to Africa*

der Arbeitsvermittler (-) / die Arbeitsvermittlerin (-nen) employment agent (29)

der Arbeitsvertrag (-e) employment contract

die Arbeitswelt (-en) professional world, professional environment (13)

die Arbeitswoche (-n) workweek

die Arbeitszeit (-en) work schedule

das Arbeitszimmer (-) (home) office, study

der Architekt (-en *masc.***) / die Architektin (-nen)** architect (13)

die Architektur (-en) architecture

(das) Argentinien Argentina

der Ärger annoyance; anger (34); **aus Ärger** out of anger

ärgern to annoy, make angry (10); **sich ärgern (über)** (+ *acc.*) to be / get upset, annoyed / angry (about) (16)

das Argument (-e) argument

arm (ärmer, ärmst-) poor

der Arm (-e) arm (16)

die Armbanduhr (-en) wristwatch

der/die Arme (*decl. adj.*) poor person; **den Armen helfen** to help the poor

die Armee (-n) army

armenisch (*adj.*) Armenian

die Armenküche (-n) soup kitchen (*for the homeless*)

ärmlich poor, shabby, meager

die Armut poverty (20)

arrangieren to arrange

die Art (-en) type, sort (26)

der Artikel (-) article (*in a newspaper*) (10)

die Artischocke (-n) artichoke

der Arzt (-e) / die Ärztin (-nen) doctor, physician (6); **zum Arzt gehen** to see a doctor

der Arztbesuch (-e) visit to the doctor (33)

der Arzthelfer (-) / die Arzthelferin (-nen) medical assistant

ärztlich medical

ASA = Arbeits- und Studienaufenthalte in Afrika

die Asche (-n) ash

(das) Aschenputtel Cinderella (12)

der Asiat (-en *masc.***) / die Asiatin (-nen)** Asian (*person*) (18)

(das) Asien Asia

der/die Asoziale (*decl. adj.*) social outcast

der Aspekt (-e) aspect

der Asphalt asphalt

der Assistent (-en *masc.***) / die Assistentin (-nen)** assistant

die Assoziation (-en) association (*cognitive process*)

assoziieren to associate

der Ast (-e) branch (*of a tree*)

die Ästhetik aesthetics

ästhetisch aesthetic(ally)

das Asthma asthma

der Astronaut (-en *masc.***) / die Astronautin (-nen)** astronaut

der Astronom (-en *masc.***) / die Astronomin (-nen)** astronomer

das Asyl political asylum (34)

der Asylbewerber (-) / die Asylbewerberin (-nen) asylum seeker

das Asylgesetz (-e) asylum law

das Asylrecht right to asylum

der Atem breath; **den Atem anhalten** to hold one's breath

(das) Athen Athens (Greece)

der Athlet (-en *masc.***) / die Athletin (-nen)** athlete

athletisch athletic

der Atlantik Atlantic (Ocean)

der Atlas (*pl.* **Atlanten**) atlas
atmen to breathe (33)
die Atmosphäre (-n) atmosphere
die Atmung breathing
die Atomkraft nuclear power
der Atommüll nuclear waste
die Attraktion (-en) attraction
attraktiv attractive(ly)
das Attraktive (*decl. adj.*) attractive (thing)
auch also, as well, too
auf (+ *acc./dat.*) on, upon; onto, to; at; in, into; **auf bald** see you soon; **auf das Gewicht achten** to watch one's figure; **(sich) auf den Weg machen** to get underway, leave; **auf der Straße** in the street; **auf Deutsch** in German; **auf die Frage antworten** to answer the question; **auf die Reise gehen** to travel; **auf eine Idee kommen** to have an idea; **auf einmal** suddenly, at once (12); **auf etwas achten** to pay attention to something; **auf jemanden zukommen** to approach someone; **auf jeden Fall** in any case; **auf nach Köln!** on to Cologne!; **auf Rezept** by prescription; **auf Urlaub** on vacation; **auf Widerruf** without commitment; **auf Wiedersehen!** good-bye!
aufatmen (atmet auf) to take a deep breath, be relieved
aufbauen (baut auf) to build; to set up (29)
das Aufbauen the process of building
aufbauend auf based on
aufbleiben (bleibt auf), blieb auf, ist aufgeblieben to stay up
aufbügeln (bügelt auf) to iron out (*clothing*)
aufdecken (deckt auf) to uncover
der Aufenthalt (-e) stay (7); visit; layover
der Aufenthaltsort (-e) residence, whereabouts
der Aufenthaltsraum (-̈e) club room (10)

auffallen (fällt auf), fiel auf, ist aufgefallen (+ *dat.*) to stand out; **mir ist aufgefallen** I have noticed
auffällig conspicuous(ly)
auffangen (fängt auf), fing auf, aufgefangen to catch hold of
die Auffassung (-en) opinion, view, conception
die Auffassungsgabe intelligence
aufflattern (flattert auf) to flutter (up)
aufführen (führt auf) to put on, perform
die Aufführung (-en) performance
die Aufgabe (-n) task, job, responsibility, assignment (10)
aufgeben (gibt auf), gab auf, aufgegeben to give up (18/25)
aufgeregt (*adj.*) agitated, upset (24)
aufgeschlossen open-minded, receptive (34)
aufgrund (+ *gen.*) because of, due to
aufhalten (hält auf), hielt auf, aufgehalten to hold up; **ich bin aufgehalten worden** I was held up
aufhören (hört auf) to stop (7/3E)
der Aufkleber (-) sticker
aufknallen (knallt auf) to bang
auflegen (legt auf) to put down
auflockern (lockert auf) to loosen up
(sich) auflösen (löst auf) to dissolve; to disintegrate
aufmachen (macht auf) to open (6); **macht die Bücher auf** open your books (1E)
aufmerksam attentive(ly) (36)
die Aufmerksamkeit attention
die Aufnahme (-n) exposure; reception; recording
die Aufnahmeprüfung (-en) entrance exam
aufnehmen (nimmt auf), nahm auf, aufgenommen to start, take up (28); to record (video) (21)
aufpassen (passt auf) to watch out, pay attention; to be careful (9/3E); **auf jemanden aufpassen** to keep an eye on someone (23)

aufräumen (räumt auf) to clean up, organize (23/3E)
(sich) aufregen (regt auf) to be upset; to worry
aufregend exciting
die Aufregung (-en) excitement, agitation
(sich) aufrichten (richtet auf) to straighten up; to erect; to restore
aufs = auf das
der Aufsatz (-̈e) essay, paper
aufschauen (schaut auf) (*coll.*) to look up
aufscheuchen (scheucht auf) to startle
aufschlagen (schlägt auf) to open; to set up; to increase (prices)
aufschließen (schließt auf), schloss auf, aufgeschlossen to unlock
der Aufschnitt (-e) cold cuts
aufschreiben (schreibt auf), schrieb auf, aufgeschrieben to write down
der Aufschwung (-̈e) upswing (29)
das Aufsehen sensation (35); **Aufsehen erregen** to cause a stir
die Aufsicht supervision
aufspringen (springt auf), sprang auf, ist aufgesprungen to jump up
aufstehen (steht auf), stand auf, ist aufgestanden to get up (7)
aufsteigen (steigt auf), stieg auf, ist aufgestiegen to climb up, advance, rise
aufstellen (stellt auf) to put up (*right side up/in a vertical position*)
der Aufstieg (-e) advancement, ascent, rise
die Aufstiegschance (-n) career opportunity
die Aufstiegsmöglichkeit (-en) opportunity for advancement
auftauchen (taucht auf) to appear; to surface
auftauen (taut auf) to thaw, melt
der Auftrag (-̈e) task; order, instructions; **im Auftrag** on behalf of

das Auftreten appearance, manner

der Auftritt (-e) performance, appearance (*on stage*)

aufwachen (wacht auf), wachte auf, ist aufgewacht to wake up (12)

aufwachsen (wächst auf), wuchs auf, ist aufgewachsen to grow up (25)

aufweichen (weicht auf) to make soft, soften

aufzählen (zählt auf) to list, count

aufzehren (zehrt auf) to eat up

der Aufzug (ǟe) elevator (8)

das Auge (-n) eye (6)

der Augenarzt (ǟe) / die Augenärztin (-nen) optometrist

der Augenblick (-e) moment; **im Augenblick** at the moment

die Augenbraue (-n) eyebrow

der Augenschlitz (-e) opening of the eye

der Augenwinkel (-) corner of the eye

der August August (5)

der Augustinermönch (-e) Augustine monk

das Au Pair (-s) au pair

aus (+ *dat.*) out; out of; of; from (12); **aus Liebe** out of love; **von (Paris) aus** from (Paris) (*with a destination*); **aus vollem Herzen lachen** to laugh out loud; **es ist aus!** it's over!; **die Kirche ist aus** church is out

ausarten (artet aus) to degenerate

ausatmen (atmet aus) to exhale

ausbilden (bildet aus) to train, educate

die Ausbildung (-en) education, training

der Ausbildungsgang (-gänge) educational background (14)

der Ausbildungsplatz (ǟe) position as trainee, apprenticeship

die Ausbildungsstelle (-n) training position (13)

der Ausblick (-e) view

ausbrechen (bricht aus), brach aus, ist ausgebrochen to break out

die Ausdauer endurance, stamina

(sich) ausdenken (denkt aus), dachte aus, ausgedacht to think up, invent

der Ausdruck (ǟe) expression (26)

(sich) ausdrücken (drückt aus) to express (oneself) (21)

ausdrücklich explicitly

auseinander apart

auseinander brechen (bricht auseinander), brach auseinander, ist auseinander gebrochen to break apart

die Auseinandersetzung (-en) dispute, argument (26)

ausfahren (fährt aus), fuhr aus, ist ausgefahren to go out (*in a boat*)

ausflippen (flippt aus) to flip out

der Ausflug (ǟe) trip, outing (10)

das Ausflugsprogramm (-e) schedule of trips, outings

ausführen (führt aus) to carry out, perform

ausfüllen (füllt aus) to fill out (8)

die Ausgabe (-n) edition

der Ausgangspunkt (-e) point of departure

ausgeben (gibt aus), gab aus, ausgegeben to spend (*money*)

ausgedacht (*adj.*) invented

ausgeflippt (*adj.*) flipped out, crazy

ausgehen (geht aus), ging aus, ist ausgegangen to go out; **ausgehen von** to start out from; to assume; **wie ist die Geschichte ausgegangen?** how did the story end?

ausgeklügelt sophisticated, refined

ausgesprochen extremely

ausgestattet equipped; **mit Dusche und W.C. ausgestattet** equipped with shower and toilet

ausgezeichnet excellent(ly), exceptional(ly)

aushalten (hält aus), hielt aus, ausgehalten to put up with (24)

aushelfen (hilft aus), half aus, ausgeholfen to help out

die Aushilfe (-n) help, temp, substitute

(sich) auskennen (kennt aus), kannte aus, ausgekannt to know one's way around

ausklügeln to think up, design

(mit jemandem) auskommen (kommt aus), kam aus, ist ausgekommen to get along (with someone)

die Auskunft (ǟe) information (7)

auslachen (lacht aus) to ridicule, to laugh (*about someone*)

das Ausland foreign country; **im Ausland** abroad

der Ausländer (-) / die Ausländerin (-nen) foreigner (20/34)

die Ausländerfeindlichkeit xenophobia (20/34)

der Ausländerhass xenophobia

ausländisch foreign

das Auslandsamt (ǟer) immigration services

das Auslandspraktikum (-praktika) internship abroad

die Auslandsreise (-n) travel abroad

das Auslandsstudium (-studien) study abroad program

auslassen (lässt aus), ließ aus, ausgelassen to leave out

die Auslastung utilization at full capacity

auslegen (legt aus) to lay out

ausleihen (leiht aus), lieh aus, ausgeliehen to lend; to borrow

ausliefern (liefert aus) to subject to, expose to

ausmachen (macht aus) to turn off; **(mit jemandem) ausmachen** to make plans (with someone); (*visual*) to make out, to be able to see; **die Fischschwärme ausmachen** to locate the fish

das Ausmaß (-e) size, measure, degree

ausmessen (misst aus), maß aus, ausgemessen to measure up

ausmisten (mistet aus) to clean animal cages

die Ausnahme (-n) exception (34)

auspacken (packt aus) to unpack

ausprägen (prägt aus) to mark, impress (25)
ausprobieren (probiert aus) to try out
ausräumen (räumt aus) to clean out
die Ausrede (-n) excuse
ausreichen (reicht aus) to be enough; to suffice
ausreichend enough, sufficient(ly)
der Ausruf (-e) exclamation
sich ausruhen (ruht aus) to rest; to relax
die Ausrüstung (-en) outfitting; equipment (32)
die Aussage (-n) statement
ausschlafen (schläft aus), schlief aus, ausgeschlafen to sleep in
ausschließlich only, exclusive(ly)
ausschreiten (schreitet aus), schritt aus, ist ausgeschritten to stride out, step out
aussehen (sieht aus), sah aus, ausgesehen to look, appear (3E)
der Außenseiter (-) outsider
außer (+ dat.) except (for), besides (12)
außerdem besides that, moreover, on top of that
außergewöhnlich exceptional(ly)
außerhalb (+ gen.) outside of
außerirdisch extraterrestrial
(sich) äußern to express (oneself) (10)
äußerst extremely
aussetzen (setzt aus) (+ dat.) to expose (to)
die Aussicht (-en) view
der Aussichtspunkt (-e) observation point
der Aussiedler (-) / die Aussiedlerin (-nen) emigrant
sich ausspannen (spannt aus) to unwind, relax
die Aussprache (-n) pronunciation
aussprechen (spricht aus), sprach aus, ausgesprochen to pronounce; to express verbally
ausstatten (stattet aus) to equip with, to furnish
die Ausstattung (-en) equipment

aussteigen (steigt aus), stieg aus, ist ausgestiegen to get off / out of (a train, car, etc.) (7)
die Ausstellung (-en) exhibition, fair, show
das Ausstellungsstück (-e) show piece
ausstoßen (stieß aus), ausgestoßen to expel (breath)
die Ausstrahlung aura, charisma
aussuchen (sucht aus) to pick out
sich etwas aussuchen (sucht aus) to choose something for oneself (21)
der Austausch exchange, interaction
der Austauschdienst (-e) exchange service
das Austauschprogramm (-e) exchange program
der Austauschschüler (-) / die Austauschschülerin (-nen) exchange student
der Austauschstudent (-en masc.) / die Austauschstudentin (-nen) exchange student
(das) Australien Australia
austreten (tritt aus), trat aus, ist ausgetreten to leave (an organization or the like)
ausüben (übt aus) to practice, exercise; **einen Beruf ausüben** to practice a profession; **Gewalt ausüben** to exercise power
die Auswahl choice; range; selection
auswählen (wählt aus) to select, choose
der Auswanderer (-) / die Auswandererin (-nen) emigrant (34)
auswandern (wandert aus) to emigrate
sich ausweinen (weint aus) to cry (until one feels better)
der Ausweis (-e) identification, ID card
auswendig (lernen) (to learn) by heart (27)
sich auswirken auf (+ acc.) **(wirkt aus)** to have an effect on, influence

auswringen (wringt aus) to wring out
ausziehen (zieht aus), zog aus, ist ausgezogen to move out
die Ausziehtusche (-n) drawing ink
der/die Auszubildende (decl. adj.) trainee (13)
der Auszug (¨e) excerpt, extract
das Auto (-s) car (7); **Auto fahren** to drive a car
die Autoabgas (-e) car exhaust; exhaust fumes
die Autobahn (-en) freeway
die Autobahnraststätte (-n) freeway rest area
der Autofahrer (-) / die Autofahrerin (-nen) driver
die Autofahrt (-en) car trip
die Autofirma (-firmen) automobile shop/company
autofrei no cars allowed
der Automat (-en masc.) vending machine
automatisch automatic(ally)
der Automechaniker (-), die Automechanikerin (-nen) car mechanic
die Automobilindustrie (-n) automobile industry
die Autonummer (-n) license plate number
die Autopanne (-n) automobile breakdown
der Autor (-en) / die Autorin (-nen) author, writer (13/36)
autoritär authoritarian
die Autorität authority
der Autounfall (¨e) car accident
der Autoverkehr traffic
die Autoversicherung (-en) car insurance
die Autowerkstatt (¨en) machine shop
die Avocado (-s) avocado
der/die Azubi = Auszubildende

B

das Baby (-s) baby
der Babybrei (-e) baby food
babylonisch (adj.) Babylonian
das Babysitten babysitting

der Bach (¨e) creek, brook
das Bächlein (-) little brook
die Backe (-n) cheek
backen (bäckt), backte, gebacken to bake
der Bäcker (-) / die Bäckerin (-nen) baker
die Bäckerei (-en) bakery (16)
der Background (-s) background
das Backpulver (-) baking powder
der Backsteinweg (-e) brick path
die Backwaren (*pl.*) baked goods
das Bad (¨er) bath; bathroom; spa (33)
die Badeanstalt (-en) spa, bath
der Badeanzug (¨e) swimsuit, bathing suit (7)
der Badeaufenthalt (-e) stay at a spa
das Badebecken (-) pool
die Badehose (-n) swim trunks (7)
baden to bathe (32); to swim (*for recreation*)
der Badespaß fun of bathing/swimming
das Badetuch (¨er) bath towel
der Badeurlaub (-e) beach vacation
die Badewanne (-n) bathtub (3)
das Badezimmer (-) bathroom (3)
das BAföG = Bundesausbildungs-förderungsgesetz
die Bahn (-en) rail (7); train; **mit der Bahn** by train
der Bahnhof (¨e) train station (7); **am Bahnhof** at the station
die Bahnkarte (-n) train ticket
der Bahnsteig (-e) platform (7)
bald soon (12/3E); **bis bald!** see you soon!
der Balken (-) beam
der Balkon (-s) balcony
der Ball (¨e) ball (17)
ballen: die Faust ballen to make a fist
die Banane (-n) banana (16)
das Band (¨er) ribbon, band; assembly line; **vom Band rollen** to roll off the assembly line
der Band (¨e) volume (*of a book*)
die Band (-s) band, rock group

die Bank (-en) bank (*financial institution*); **auf die Bank** to the bank (4)
die Bank (¨e) bench
die Bankkaufmann (-leute) / die Bankkauffrau (-en) bank clerk
die Bar (-s) bar
die Baseballkappe (-n) baseball cap
die Basis basis
der Basketball (¨e) basketball
das Basketballspiel (-e) basketball game
basteln to tinker, build things (*as a hobby*)
das Basteln crafts
das Batikkleid (-er) tie-dyed dress
die Batterie (-n) battery
der Bau building, process of building
der Bauarbeiter (-) / die Bauarbeiterin (-nen) construction worker
die Baubranche construction business
der Bauch (¨e) abdomen (6)
der Bauchredner (-) / die Bauchrednerin (-nen) ventriloquist
die Bauchschmerzen (*pl.*) stomachache
bauen to build, construct
der Bauer (-n *masc.*) / die Bäuerin (-nen) farmer
das Bauernhaus (¨er) farmhouse (4)
der Bauernhof (¨e) farm
baufällig run-down, dilapidated
der Bauingenieur (-e) / die Bauingenieurin (-nen) civil engineer
das Bauland development area
der Baum (¨e) tree
baumlang very tall
die Baumreihe (-n) row of trees
die Baumwurzel (-n) tree root
die Baustelle (-n) construction site
der Bauzeichner (-) / die Bauzeichnerin (-nen) building-plan artist

bayerisch (*adj.*) Bavarian
(das) Bayern Bavaria (17)
beachten to observe (34)
der Beamte (-n *masc.*) / die Beamtin (-nen) civil servant, government employee
beantworten to answer
bearbeiten to work on, develop
der Becher (-) mug
bedauern to regret (20)
bedenken, bedachte, bedacht to consider (31)
bedeuten to mean, signify (17)
bedeutend important, distinguished, eminent
die Bedeutung (-en) meaning
bedienen to serve (*someone*); to operate (*something*)
die Bedienung (-en) service (15)
die Bedingung (-en) condition (29)
bedürfen (bedarf), bedurfte, bedurft to need, require
das Bedürfnis (-se) necessity (34)
sich beeilen to hurry
beeindrucken to impress
beeindruckend impressive
beeinflussen to influence (21/34)
beenden to end
die Beere (-n) berry
der Befehl (-e) order, command
sich befinden, befand, befunden to be located (28)
befolgen to follow, observe, comply with
befragen to question, interrogate
die Befreiung (-en) liberation
befreundet friends with someone (25)
die Befürchtung (-en) fear (34)
begabt talented
sich begegnen to meet (27)
die Begegnung (-en) meeting; encounter (33)
begehbar accessible
begehren to desire (35)
begeistern to inspire (26)
begeistert (*adj.*) amazed, excited
die Begeisterung enthusiasm
der Beginn beginning
beginnen, begann, begonnen to begin (29)

begleichen, beglich, beglichen to settle, pay

begleiten to accompany

der Begleiter (-) / die Begleiterin (-nen) companion

begreifen, begriff, begriffen to understand, grasp (29)

begreiflich comprehensible

begrenzen to limit, restrict

begrenzt (*adj.*) limited

der Begriff (-e) concept, idea (28)

begründen to give reasons for, justify

der Begründer (-) / die Begründerin (-nen) founder

begrüßen to greet (24); to welcome

die Begrüßung (-en) greeting (24), welcoming

behalten (behält), behielt, behalten to keep, hold (16)

behandeln to treat (30)

die Behandlung (-en) treatment

beharrlich persistent

behaupten to claim, make a statement

behelfen (behilft), behalf, beholfen to manage

beherrschen to dominate

behindert handicapped

der/die Behinderte (*decl. adj.*) handicapped person

der/die Behörde (*decl. adj.*) government office (18); official

behüten to protect (30)

bei (+ *dat.*) at, at the place of; for; by; near; with; when (12)

das Beiboot (-e) small boat

beide, beides both; **die beiden** the two of them

beige beige, tan (2)

beigeben (gibt bei), gab bei, beigegeben to add

die Beilage (-n) side dish (15)

beim = bei dem

das Bein (-e) leg (6)

beinahe almost

der Beinbruch: Hals- und Beinbruch! good luck!, break a leg!

beiseite aside

das Beispiel (-e) example; **zum Beispiel** for example, for instance

beispielsweise for example, for instance

beißen, biss, gebissen to bite

beistehen (steht bei), stand bei, beigestanden (+ *dat.*) to support (*someone*) (3E)

der Beitrag (¨e) contribution (30)

beitragen (trägt bei), trug bei, beigetragen to contribute to (34)

beitreten (tritt bei), trat bei, ist beigetreten to join

bekämpfen to fight, combat

bekannt (well-)known (36)

der/die Bekannte (*decl. adj.*) acquaintance

die Bekanntmachung announcement

die Bekanntschaft (-en) acquaintance

(sich) beklagen to complain; **ich kann mich nicht beklagen** I can't complain

die Bekleidung clothing

bekommen, bekam, bekommen to receive, get (15/28)

bekümmert worried, sad

beladen (belädt), belud, beladen to load

belegen to cover; to take (*a course*) (11/3E); **einen Kurs belegen** to take a course

belehren to instruct, advise, teach

beleidigen to insult (10/28)

(das) Belgien Belgium (9)

beliebt popular; famous (28)

bellen to bark

bemerken to notice; to remark

die Bemerkung (-en) observation; remark, comment (24/28)

sich bemühen um to make an effort, try to do

benachbart neighboring

benachrichtigen to notify

die Benachrichtigung (-en) notification

benachteiligen to place at a disadvantage (30)

die Benachteiligung (-en) putting at a disadvantage

sich benehmen (benimmt), benahm, benommen to behave

beneiden to envy

benennen, benannte, benannt to name, call

benoten to grade

benötigen to need, require

benutzen to use

das Benzin gasoline, fuel

der Benzinkanister (-) gas can

beobachten to observe (36)

bequem comfortable, convenient

beraten (berät), beriet, beraten to advise

der Berater (-) / die Beraterin (-nen) consultant

die Beratung counseling, consulting

das Beratungsangebot (-e) range of advisory services

der Beratungsbedarf demand for consulting, counseling

die Beratungsstelle (-n) counseling office

der Beratungstermin (-e) appointment for counseling

berechnen to calculate

der Bereich (-e) area, field

bereit ready

bereiten to prepare; **Probleme bereiten** to cause problems

bereits already

die Bereitschaft readiness, willingness

bereitwillig eager(ly), willing(ly)

der Berg (-e) mountain (4); **in die Berge fahren** to go to the mountains

der Bergbauer (-n *masc.*) / die Bergbäuerin (-nen) farmer in the mountains

der Bergführer (-) / die Bergführerin (-nen) mountain guide

die Berglandschaft (-en) alpine landscape

die Berglandwirtschaft alpine farming

bergsteigen: bergsteigen gehen, ging, ist gegangen to go mountain climbing

das **Bergsteigen** mountain climbing
der **Bergwanderer (-)** person who hikes in the mountains
das **Bergwandern** mountain hiking
der **Bericht (-e)** report, statement (21)
berichten to report (21)
der **Berliner (-)** / die **Berlinerin (-nen)** Berliner (*person*)
die **Berliner Mauer** Berlin Wall (18)
der **Bernstein** amber
der **Beruf (-e)** job (29); profession, occupation (13); **einen Beruf ausüben** to practice a profession (13/29)
beruflich occupational(ly); professional(ly) (18); **was machen Sie beruflich?** what do you do for a living?
die **Berufsausbildung (-en)** professional training
der **Berufsberater (-)** / die **Berufsberaterin (-nen)** career counselor
die **Berufsberatung** career counseling
das **Berufsbild (-er)** job outline
die **Berufserfahrung** work experience (29)
die **Berufsfachschule (-n)** trade school (11)
das **Berufsfeld (-er)** career field (29)
das **Berufsleben** professional life
die **Berufsmöglichkeit (-en)** career opportunity
die **Berufspraxis** practical job experience
die **Berufsschule (-n)** professional school
berufstätig employed (23/25)
die **Berufswahl** choice of profession
der **Berufswechsel (-)** career change
der **Berufswunsch (¨e)** preferred choice of profession
das **Berufsziel (-e)** professional goal
die **Berufung** vocation (28)

beruhigen to comfort; **sich beruhigen** to calm oneself, relax
beruhigend calming
berühmt famous, popular
berühren to touch
die **Besatzung (-en)** military occupation; crew (*on a ship*)
die **Besatzungstruppe (-n)** troop of the occupying army
beschädigt (*adj.*) damaged (22/27)
sich beschäftigen mit to be occupied with (13/27)
die **Beschäftigung (-en)** occupation
Bescheid: Bescheid geben to notify
bescheiden modest(ly)
die **Bescheidenheit** modesty (26)
beschildern to label, put up signs
beschildert (*adj.*) labeled (34)
beschimpfen to insult (30)
beschließen, beschloss, beschlossen to decide, resolve
der **Beschluss (¨e)** resolution, decision, order
beschränken to limit, restrict
beschreiben, beschrieb, beschrieben to describe
die **Beschreibung (-en)** description
beschuldigen to accuse (30)
beschützen to protect
die **Beschwerde (-n)** complaint
sich beschweren (über + *acc.*) to complain (about) (22)
besehen (besieht), besah, besehen to scrutinize
beseitigen to remove
die **Beseitigung (-en)** removal
besetzen to occupy (27)
besetzt (*adj.*) occupied; **hier ist besetzt** this seat is taken (15)
besichtigen to visit (*as a sightseer*) (8)
die **Besichtigung (-en)** guided tour
besiedeln to populate
besiegen to defeat
der **Besitz** ownership, possessions
besitzen, besaß, besessen to possess, own (30)
der **Besitzer (-)** / die **Besitzerin (-nen)** owner (14)
das **Besondere** (*decl. adj.*) what is special, special (thing)

besonders especially
besorgen to tend to, get done; to take care of
besorgt (*adj.*) worried
die **Besorgung (-en)** errand
besprechen (bespricht), besprach, besprochen to discuss (18)
besser better
bessern to improve
Besserung: gute Besserung! get well soon!
best-: am besten (the) best
der **Bestandteil (-e)** component
bestätigen to prove (34)
die **Bestätigung (-en)** confirmation
das **Besteck (-e)** silverware (19)
bestehen, bestand, bestanden to pass (*an exam*) (10/27); to overcome (35); **bestehen aus** to consist of (35)
bestehend existing
besteigen, bestieg, bestiegen to climb (23/32)
bestellen to order (15)
bestens: es geht mir bestens I'm doing really well
bestimmen to determine (29)
bestimmt surely, certainly
Bestimmtes: etwas Bestimmtes something specific
die **Bestnote (-n)** highest possible grade
bestrafen to punish (10)
die **Bestrafung (-en)** punishment
bestreichen to spread
der **Bestseller (-)** bestseller
der **Besuch (-e)** visit; **zu Besuch kommen** to come for a visit
besuchen to visit (8); **die Schule besuchen** to go to school
der **Besucher (-)** / die **Besucherin (-nen)** visitor
sich betätigen to be active, involved
betäuben to numb
beteiligt (*adj.*) involved
betonen to emphasize
betrachten to consider; to regard (30); **Kunstwerke betrachten** to look at art objects (8)
betragen (beträgt), betrug, betragen to amount to

betreffen (betrifft), betraf, betroffen to concern, affect (25)

betreffend relevant, in question

betreten (betritt), betrat, betreten to step into, enter

betreuen to look after (30)

der Betreuer (-) / die Betreuerin (-nen) caretaker, person who takes care of someone

die Betreuung (-en) care

der Betrieb (-e) business operation (29)

die Betriebswirtschaft business management

betroffen (*adj.*) upset, dismayed

betrüben to distress

betrübt (*adj.*) distressed, sad

betrügen, betrog, betrogen to betray, deceive

das Bett (-en) bed (3)

die Bettdecke (-n) cover, comforter

betteln to beg

die Bettwäsche bedding, sheets

das Bettzeug bedding

beugen to bend

beunruhigen to worry; to disturb

beurteilen to judge, assess

die Bevölkerung (-en) population

die Bevölkerungsschicht (-en) social class

bevor (*subord. conj.*) before

bevormunden to patronize

bevorzugen to prefer

bewährt proven

bewaldet wooded

bewältigen to cope with, to manage, to get over

die Bewässerung irrigation

bewegen to set into motion (26); **sich bewegen** to move

bewegt eventful; turbulent (27)

die Bewegung (-en) movement (26)

der Beweis (-e) proof

beweisen, bewies, bewiesen to prove (25)

sich bewerben um (bewirbt), bewarb, beworben to apply for (14)

der Bewerber (-) / die Bewerberin (-nen) job applicant (14/29)

die Bewerbung (-en) application (14)

der Bewerbungsbrief (-e) application cover letter

die Bewerbungsunterlagen (*pl.*) application material / portfolio

bewerkstelligen to manage

bewerten to evaluate

die Bewertung assessment, judgement

bewohnbar inhabitable

bewohnen to inhabit

der Bewohner (-) / die Bewohnerin (-nen) inhabitant, resident

bewundern to marvel at, admire

bewusst conscious(ly)

bezahlen to pay (4)

bezeichnen to mark; to indicate; to describe; **bezeichnen als** to call

beziehen, bezog, bezogen to take up (36); **sich beziehen auf** to refer to, relate to

die Beziehung (-en) relationship, relation

beziehungsweise or, respective(ly) (28)

der Bezirk (-e) area, district

Bezug: in Bezug auf (+ *acc.*) in relation to; concerning, regarding, as to

bezüglich regarding

die Bezugsperson (-en) support person

bezuschussen to subsidize

bezweifeln to doubt

die Bibelübersetzung (-en) translation of the Bible

die Bibliothek (-en) library (10)

der Bibliothekar (-e) / die Bibliothekarin (-nen) librarian (13)

bieder conventional, conservative

die Biene (-n) bee

das Biest (-er) beast

bieten, bot, geboten to offer (31)

das Bild (-er) picture

das Bildelement (-e) component of an image

bilden to build, form

bildhaft pictorial, like an image

bildlich pictorial

der Bildschirm (-e) screen, display; **Bildschirmseiten im Internet** pages on the Internet

die Bildung education (11/28); formation, derivation; **die Allgemeinbildung** general education

das Billard billiards (8); **Billard spielen** to play billiards (8)

billig cheap, inexpensive (2)

das Bindewort (¨er) conjunction

Bio = Biologie

die Biografie (-n) biography

der Bioladen (¨) health food store

die Biologie biology (11)

der Biologieprofessor (-en) / die Biologieprofessorin (-nen) biology professor

die Biologievorlesung (-en) biology lecture

biologisch organic(ally)

der Biomarkt (¨e) organic market

das Bioprodukt (-e) organic product

die Biotonne (-n) container for biodegradable waste

die Birne (-n) pear

bis until, till, to; **bis bald** see you later; **bis dann** see you later; **bis jetzt** until now; **bis morgen** see you tomorrow

der Bischof (¨e) / die Bischöfin (-nen) bishop

bisher until now

bislang so far, until now

ein bisschen a little bit

das Bistum (¨er) diocese

bitte please; **bitte noch einmal!** once more, please! (E)

bitten um (+ *acc.*) to ask for

bitter bitter(ly)

bladen to rollerblade (23)

blasen (bläst), blies, geblasen to blow

das Blatt (¨er) leaf; **ein Blatt Papier** sheet of paper

das Blättchen (-) little leaf, plate
blau blue (2)
der Blaue Reiter *group of Expressionist artists*
blaugekachelt tiled in blue
blaurandig with a blue edge
blauweiß bluish white
das Blechblasinstrument (-e) brass instrument
die Blechtrommel (-n) tin drum
bleiben, blieb, ist geblieben to stay, remain; **zu Hause bleiben** to stay at home
der Bleistift (-e) pencil (E1)
der Blick (-e) look, view, eye contact
blicken to look
das Blickfeld (-er) field of vision
der Blickpunkt (-e) viewpoint
blind blind
blinken to shine
der Blitz (-e) lightning; **es blitzt** it's lightning (5)
blitzeblank spick and span
blitzschnell fast as lightning
der Block (-s) block, unit
die Blockflöte (-n) recorder (*musical instrument*)
blockieren to block
blöd (*coll.*) dumb, stupid
der Blödmann idiot
blond blonde, fair
blondiert (*adj.*) bleached/dyed blonde
bloß only
die Bluejeans (-) jeans
blühen to bloom
die Blume (-n) flower (5)
das Blumengeschäft (-e) flower shop
der Blumenkohl cauliflower (19)
der Blumenladen (¨) flower shop
der Blumentopf (¨e) flowerpot
die Blumenvase (-n) flower vase
blumig flowery
die Bluse (-n) blouse (7)
das Blut blood
der Blutdruck blood pressure (33)
das Blutdruckmittel (-) blood pressure medication
die Blüte (-n) blossom

die Blütezeit (-en) the golden age, heyday
der Bluthochdruck high blood pressure
der Bock (¨e) buck, ram
der Boden (¨) floor
der Bodensee Lake Constance
die Bodenvergiftung (-en) soil contamination
der Bogen (¨) bow
die Bohne (-n) bean (15)
bombardieren to bomb, bombard
das Bonbon (-s) candy, treat
(der) Bonifatius St. Boniface
Bonner: in seiner Bonner Villa in his villa in Bonn
das Boot (-e) boat
der Bootsrand (¨er) edge of the boat
Bord: an Bord on board; **von Bord** off board
der Bordstein (-e) curb
borgen to borrow, lend
böse naughty; evil, mean; angry (1)
botanisch botanical
die Boutique boutique (22)
brach fallow
das Brandenburger Tor Brandenburg Gate
der Brandstifter (-) / die Brandstifterin (-nen) arsonist
(das) Brasilien Brazil
der Brasilianer (-) / die Brasilianerin (-nen) Brazilian (*person*)
der Bratapfel (-äpfel) baked apple
der Braten (-) roast
braten (brät), briet, gebraten to fry (19)
das Brathähnchen (-) baked chicken
die Bratkartoffeln fried potatoes (15)
die Bratwurst (¨e) *type of sausage*
brauchen to need (2/3E)
braun brown (2)
bräunen to tan (32)
brausen to roar, thunder
die Braut (¨e) bride
das Brautpaar (-e) couple, bride and groom
brav obedient, well-behaved (1)

brechen (bricht), brach, gebrochen to break
der Brei (-e) mush, porridge, baby food
breit wide
die Breite (-en) width
brennen, brannte, gebrannt to burn, be on fire
brennend burning
das Brett (-er) board (19); **das schwarze Brett** bulletin board
bretteben as flat as a board
die Brezel (-n) pretzel (15)
der Brief (-e) letter; **Briefe schreiben** to write letters
das Briefchen (-) note
der Brieffreund (-e) / die Brieffreundin (-nen) pen pal
die Briefmarke (-n) stamp
das Briefpapier stationery
die Brieftasche (-n) wallet
der Briefwechsel (-) correspondence
die Brille (-n) pair of glasses
bringen, brachte, gebracht to bring (5)
der Brokkoli broccoli (19)
die Broschüre (-n) brochure
das Brot (-e) bread (16)
das Brotbröckchen (-) bread chunks
das Brötchen (-) roll (16)
der Brotkrümel (-) bread crumb
der Brotteller (-) bread plate
der Bruchteil (-e) fraction
die Brücke (-n) bridge
der Bruder (¨) brother (1/25)
das Brüderchen (-n) little brother
das Bruderherz (-ens, -en) beloved brother
brummen to buzz; to growl; to drone
der Brunnen (-) well
(das) Brüssel Brussels
die Brust (¨e) breast
der Bube (-n *masc.*) boy
das Buch (¨er) book (1E)
buchen to book (7)
das Bücherregal (-e) bookshelf
der Bücherschrank (¨e) bookcase

der Buchhalter (-) / die Buchhalterin (-nen) accountant, bookkeeper
der Buchhändler (-) / die Buchhändlerin (-nen) bookseller
die Buchhandlung (-en) bookstore (16)
der Buchladen (⁻) bookstore
der Buchstabe (-n *masc.***)** letter (of the alphabet)
die Bucht (-en) bay (9)
sich bücken to bend over
die Bude (-n) (*coll.*) room, pad
das Buffet (-s) buffet
bügeln to iron
die Bühne (-n) stage (36)
die Bulette (-n) meat patty
(das) Bulgarien Bulgaria
bummeln, ist gebummelt to stroll; to idle (31)
der Bund (⁻e) federation, federal government
der Bund = die Bundeswehr German army
die Bundesallee street name
das Bundesausbildungs-förderungsgesetz *federal law in Germany that provides financial aid to students*
die Bundeshauptstadt (⁻e) federal capital
der Bundeskanzler (-) / die Bundeskanzlerin (-nen) federal chancellor
das Bundesland (⁻er) federal state (17)
die Bundesliga national league (*soccer*)
der Bundesligafan (-s) soccer fan
das Bundesligaspiel (-e) national league soccer game
die Bundesrepublik Deutschland Federal Republic of Germany (17)
der Bundesstaat (-en) federal state
der Bundestag (Lower House of Parliament)
die Bundestagswahl (-en) federal parliamentary election
die Bundeswehr German army
das Bündnis (-se) confederation
der Bungalow (-s) bungalow

der Bunsenbrenner (-) Bunsen burner
bunt colorful(ly), multicolored
buntblühend blooming in colors
der Buntstift (-e) colored pen
die Burg (-en) castle, fort; **Burgen besichtigen** to visit castles (8)
der Bürger (-) / die Bürgerin (-nen) citizen
der Bürgerkrieg (-e) civil war
der Bürgermeister (-) / die Bürgermeisterin (-nen) mayor
das Büro (-s) office, study (13)
die Büroparty (-s) office party
der Büroschreibtisch (-e) office desk
der Bus (-se) bus (7); **mit dem Bus** by bus
die Busfahrt (-en) bus ride
die Bushaltestelle (-n) bus stop
der Bustransfer (-s) bus transfer
die Busverbindung (-en) bus connection
die Butter butter
das Butterbrot (-e) bread with butter
bzw. = beziehungsweise

C

ca. = circa
das Café (-s) café, coffee shop (4)
die Cafeszene (-n) coffee shop scene
die Cafeteria (Cafeterien) cafeteria (10)
der Campingplatz (Campingplätze) campsite
der Campus campus
das Canyoning canyoning
die CD (-s) (*abbrev.* **Compact Disc**) compact disc
die CD-Sammlung (-en) CD collection
der CD-Spieler (-) CD player
das Center (-) center
der Champignon (-s) mushroom (15)
die Chance (-n) chance
die Chancengleichheit equal opportunities
die Chanukka Hanukkah (5)

das Chaos chaos
chaotisch chaotic(ally)
der Charakter (-e) character, nature
charakterisieren to characterize
chatten to chat (*on the Internet*)
der Chef (-s) / die Chefin (-nen) boss, supervisor (13)
der Chefkoch (⁻e) / die Chefköchin (-nen) master chef
die Chemie chemistry (11/28)
die Chemikalie (-n) chemical substance
der Chemielehrer (-) / die Chemielehrerin (-nen) chemistry teacher
der Chemikant (-en *masc.***) / die Chemikantin (-nen)** chemical technician, lab assistant
der Chemiker (-) / die Chemikerin (-nen) chemist
chemisch chemical(ly)
der Chinese (-n *masc.***) / die Chinesin (-nen)** Chinese person (18)
das Cholesterin cholesterol
der Cholesterinwert (-e) cholesterol level
Christi Himmelfahrt Ascension Day
der Christkindlmarkt (⁻e) Christmas fair (in Bavaria and Austria)
Christus: nach Christus A.D.; **vor Christus** B.C.
circa circa, about, approximately
der Clown (-s) / die Clownin (-nen) clown
das Clowngesicht (-er) clown face
der Club (-s) club
die Cola (-s) coke
die Colaflasche (-n) coke bottle
die Collage (-n) collage
die Comedyserie (-n) sitcom show
der Computer (-) computer
die Computerfirma (-firmen) computer company
die Computerkenntnisse (*pl.*) computer literacy

der Computerkurs (-e) computer class

das Computerspiel (-e) computer game (2)

der Container (-) (large) container, dumpster (20/35)

die Cordjacke (-n) corduroy jacket

die Couch (-s) couch

die Couchgarnitur (-en) living room furniture set

der Cousin (-s) / die Cousine (-n) cousin (1)

der Cowboyhut (-̈e) cowboy hat

das Currypulver (-) curry powder

die Currywurst (-̈e) *a sausage prepared with curry and served with ketchup*

D

da there; **da drüben** over there

DAAD = Deutscher Akademischer Austauschdienst

dabei by it/that; with it/that; **was meinen Sie dabei?** what do you mean by that?; **dabei haben** to have with; **dabei sein** to be a part of; **gerade dabei sein** to be in the process (*of doing something*)

dabeistehen, stand dabei, dabeigestanden to stand by

das Dach (-̈er) roof

der Dachboden (-̈) attic

das Dächermeer (-e) sea of roofs, roofs of a city

die Dachkammer (-n) attic room, garret

der Dachkammerbrand (-̈e) fire in the attic

die Dachrinne (-n) gutter

dadurch through it

dafür instead; in return; for it/them (26)

dagegen against it

daheim at home

daher therefore, thus

dahin there, to it

dahinkommen (kommt dahin), kam dahin, ist dahingekommen to come there

dahinter behind it

daliegen, lag da, dagelegen to lie there

damals back then (25)

die Dame (-n) lady

damit with it/that; (*subord. conj.*) so that, in order that

der Dampf (-̈e) steam

die Dampfmaschine (-n) steam engine

danach after it, afterwards, later; **danach fragen** to ask about it

(das) Dänemark Denmark (9)

dänisch (*adj.*) Danish

der Dank gratitude, thanks; **vielen Dank!** thanks a lot!

dankbar grateful(ly)

die Dankbarkeit gratitude

danke! thanks!

danken to thank

dann then, afterwards, later (12); **also dann!** all right then!; **bis dann!** see you later!

dannen: von dannen (*obsolete*) (from) thence, away

d(a)ran on it, with it, about it; at it; **denken Sie daran** think about it

darauf on it; after it/that; **darauf kommen** to think of (something); **darauf reagieren** to react to it; **es kommt darauf an** it depends

daraus out of it/that

darin in it, within

darstellen (stellt dar) to depict, portray; to present (34); **dramatisch darstellen** to act out

darüber about it/that; **darüber hinaus** moreover, what's more

darüberlegen (legt darüber) to lay over

darübersieben (siebt darüber) to sift over

darum therefore, thus, for this reason

darunter under(neath) it

dass (*subord. conj.*) that

dasselbe the same

dastehen stand da, dagestanden to stand there

die Daten (*pl.*) data

die Datenbank (-en) data base

die Datenflut flood of data, masses of data

der Dativ dative case, case of the indirect object (recipient or benefactive)

die Dativpräposition (-en) dative preposition

das Dativpronomen (-) dative pronoun

das Datum (Daten) date

die Dauer duration

dauerhaft permanent(ly)

dauern to last (7); **wie lange dauert die Fahrt?** how long is the drive?

dauernd constant(ly)

der Daumen (-) thumb; **ich halte dir die Daumen** I'll keep my fingers crossed for you

davon from it, of it

davor in front of it, before it

dazu to it, with it, for it; **und noch dazu** and also, besides

dazugeben (gibt dazu), gab dazu, dazugegeben to add (to it)

DDR = Deutsche Demokratische Republik

die Debatte (-n) debate (35)

das Deck (-s) deck (*on a ship*)

die Decke (-n) cover, blanket; ceiling

decken to cover; **den Tisch decken** to set the table

definieren to define

die Definition (-en) definition

deftig substantial(ly), solid(ly)

(sich) dehnen to stretch; to expand, widen

die Dehnungübung (-en) stretching exercise

dein (*inform. sg.*) your; **dein Michael** yours, Michael (*closing in letters*); **deiner, deine, dein(e)s** (*inform. sg.*) yours (*closing in letters*)

die Dekoration (-en) decoration

dekorieren to decorate, ornate

die Delikatesse (-n) delicacy

der Delphin (-e) dolphin

dementsprechend corresponding(ly), according(ly), respective(ly)
demnächst soon
Demo = Demonstration
die Demokratie (-n) democracy
demokratisch democratic(ally)
demokratisieren to democratize
die Demokratisierung (-en) democratization
der Demonstrant (-en *masc.***) / die Demonstrantin (-nen)** demonstrator
die Demonstration (-en) demonstration (10)
demonstrieren to demonstrate (10)
denken, dachte, gedacht to think (6); **denken an** (+ *acc.*) to think about (26)
das Denkmal (¨er) monument, memorial
denn (*coord. conj.*) because, for
dennoch anyway, still
deponieren to deposit
depressiv depressing
deprimiert depressed
derartig such, of that kind; **der einzige derartige Fall** the only case of that kind
dergleichen of that kind, such, like that
derjenige, diejenige, dasjenige the one (who)
derselbe, dieselbe, dasselbe the same
derzeit at present, at the moment, at that time (past)
derzeitig present, current
deshalb therefore
der Designer (-) / die Designerin (-nen) designer
desillusioniert disillusioned
der Despot (-en *masc.***)** tyrant
desto: je mehr, . . . desto mehr . . . the more, . . . the more . . .
das Detail (-s) detail
der Detektiv (-e) / die Detektivin (-nen) detective
der Detektivroman (-e) detective novel

deuten auf to point to
deutlich clear(ly) (34)
deutsch (*adj.*) German
das Deutsch German (*language*) (11)
das Deutschbuch (¨er) German textbook
der/die Deutsche (*decl. adj.*) German (*person*) (18)
der Deutsche Akademische Austauschdienst German Academic Exchange Service
die Deutsche Demokratische Republik German Democratic Republic
die Deutsche Mark (DM) German mark (*currency*)
der Deutschkurs (-e) German class
(das) Deutschland Germany (9)
die Deutschlandreise (-n) tour of Germany
das Deutschlehren teaching German
der Deutschlehrer (-) / die Deutschlehrerin (-nen) German teacher
deutschsprachig German-speaking
der Deutschstudent (-en *masc.***) / die Deutschstudentin (-nen)** German student, student of German
die Deutschstunde (-n) German class, German hour
der Deutschunterricht German instruction, German class
der Dezember December (5)
das Diagramm (-e) diagram, chart
der Dialekt (-e) dialect
der Dialog (-e) dialogue
der Dialogpartner (-) / die Dialogpartnerin (-nen) dialogue partner
der Diamantring (-e) diamond ring
die Diät (-en) diet (*to lose weight*); **Diät halten** to be on a diet; to diet
die Diätform (-en) diet program
das Diätsystem (-e) dietsystem
dich you (*acc. inform. sg.*) (5); yourself (*refl. pron.*)

dicht tight(ly), dense(ly); heavy; heavily
der Dichter (-) / die Dichterin (-nen) poet
dick fat, thick
der Dieb (-e) / die Diebin (-nen) thief (12)
der Diebstahl (¨e) theft
die Diele (-n) entryway, hall (3)
dienen to serve
der Diener (-) / die Dienerin (-nen) servant
der Dienst (-e) service, duty (14); **zu Diensten** (*archaic*) at your service
der Dienstag (-e) Tuesday (E)
dienstags on Tuesdays
dieser, diese, dies(es) this
der Diesel diesel fuel
dieselbe the same
die Diktatur (-en) dictatorship
das Dilemma (-s) dilemma (23)
das Ding (-e) thing; **vor allen Dingen** above all, most importantly
das Diplom (-e) diploma
die Diplomarbeit (-en) thesis work (28)
die Diplomprüfung (-en) comprehensive exam
das Diplomzeugnis (-se) degree grade report
dir (*inform. sg.*) to you
direkt direct(ly)
der Direktor (-en) / die Direktorin (-nen) director, school principal
der Dirigent (-en) / die Dirigentin (-nen) conductor (*music*)
der Discountladen (¨) discount store
die Disko = Diskothek
die Diskoklamotten (*pl.*) disco outfit
die Diskothek (-en) club, disco
die Diskrepanz (-en) discrepancy
diskriminieren to discriminate
die Diskriminierung (-en) discrimination
die Diskussion (-en) discussion
diskutieren to discuss, debate; **diskutieren über** (+ *acc.*) to discuss (26)

die **Dissertation (-en)** dissertation
die **Distanz (-en)** distance
die **Disziplin (-en)** discipline
divers diverse, various
DM = Deutsche Mark
doch (*coord. conj.*) but, however;
(*particle*) **nimm doch zwei
Aspirin!** why don't you take two
aspirin?; **das ist doch Quatsch!**
that really is nonsense!;
(*affirmative response to negative
question*) **kommst du nicht?
—doch!** aren't you coming?
—yes, I am!
der **Doktor (-en) / die Doktorin
(-nen)** doctor
der **Doktortitel (-)** doctorate
degree, academic title
das **Dokument (-e)** document
dolmetschen to interpret
(*languages*) (28)
der **Dolmetscher (-) / die
Dolmetscherin (-nen)** interpreter
(13)
der **Dom (-e)** cathedral
dominieren to dominate
das **Dominospiel (-e)** domino game
der **Donner (-)** thunder; **es
donnert** it's thundering. (5)
der **Donnerstag (-e)** Thursday (1E)
doof stupid, dumb
das **Doppelhaus ('-er)** duplex (4)
die **Doppelhaushälfte (-n)** part of a
duplex
die **Doppelmonarchie** double
monarchy, Austro-Hungarian
Empire
doppelt double
das **Doppelzimmer (-)** double
room (8)
das **Dorf ('-er)** small town (27),
village (4)
das **Dornröschen** Sleeping Beauty
dort there; **dort drüben** over there
dorthin there
die **Dose (-n)** can (20)
dösen to doze, to nap (16)
dösend dozing
der **Dozent (-en** *masc.*) **/ die
Dozentin (-nen)** instructor (*at a
university*)

der **Drache (-n** *masc.*) dragon (12)
das **Drachenfliegen** hang gliding
das **Drama** (*pl.* **Dramen**) drama
dramatisch dramatic(ally)
der **Dramaturg (-en** *masc.*) **/ die
Dramaturgin (-nen)** literary and
artistic director
dran = daran; dran sein to be
one's turn; **gut dran sein** to be
well-off
drängen to push, press
drauf = darauf; gut drauf sein to
be in a good mood
draußen outside (31)
der **Dreck** dirt, filth
das **Drehbuch ('-er)** film script
drehen: einen Film drehen to film
(a movie) (36)
das **Drehrestaurant (-s)** revolving
restaurant
drei three (E)
dreieinhalb three and a half
die **Dreierarbeit (-en)** (group) work
for three people
die **Dreiergruppe (-n)** group of
three
dreijährig (*adj.*) three-year-old
dreimal three times
das **Dreimannzelt (-e)** three-man
tent
dreimonatig three-month-long
dreißig thirty (E)
dreiwöchig three-week-long
dreizehn thirteen (E)
drin = darin
dringend desperate(ly) (34);
urgent(ly)
drinnen within, in there, inside
dritt- third; **zu dritt** in a group of
three
das **Drittel (-)** third
die **Droge (-n)** drug
die **Drogerie (-n)** drugstore (16)
drohen to threaten
dröhnen to rumble, roar (*engine*)
drüben: dort drüben, da drüben
over there
drüber = darüber
drücken to press; **die Daumen
drücken** to keep one's fingers
crossed (*for good luck*)

du (*inform. sg.*) you (1)
sich ducken to duck
der **Duft ('-e)** scent, fragrance
duften to smell, be fragrant
duftend aromatic
dumm (dümmer, dümmst-) stupid,
dumb
die **Düne (-n)** dune
der **Dünger** fertilizer
dunkel dark (2)
das **Dunkel** darkness; **im Dunkeln**
in the dark
dunkelbraun dark brown
die **Dunkelheit** darkness
dünn thin(ly)
der **Dunst** mist, haze
durch (*+ acc.*) through, by (5);
quer durch all through, all over
durchaus by any means, indeed;
durchaus nicht by no means
der **Durchbruch ('-e)** breakthrough
**durchfallen (fällt durch), fiel
durch, ist durchgefallen** to fail;
beim Examen durchfallen to fail
the exam (10)
durchführbar feasible
durchführen (führt durch) to
perform, lead through, take
through
**durchgeben (gibt durch), gab
durch, durchgegeben** to pass
through, tell, let know
**durchhalten (hält durch), hielt
durch, durchgehalten** to survive;
to see through
durchkauen (kaut durch) to chew;
to plow through
durchkreuzen, (kreuzt durch) to
cross out; **(durchkreuzt)** to cross
(*continent, sea, etc.*)
**durchlesen (liest durch), las
durch, durchgelesen** to read
through
durchmachen (macht durch) to
experience, endure
durchproben (probt durch) to
rehearse
durchqueren to cross, pass
through, traverse
**durchreißen, riss durch,
durchgerissen** to tear

durchs = **durch das** (*coll.*)

durchschneiden, schnitt durch, durchgeschnitten to cut in two, cut in half

der Durchschnitt (-e) average; **im Durchschnitt** on average

durchschnittlich on average

die Durchschnittsnote (-n) average grade

durchsetzen (setzt durch) to carry through, to achieve

die Durchsetzung (-en) carrying through, achievement

dürfen (darf), durfte, gedurft to be allowed to; may; **was darf's sein?** what will you have? (15)

der Durst thirst

die Dusche (-n) shower (3)

duschen to shower

düster gloomy, dismal, murky

das Dutzend (-e) dozen

duzen to address someone with **du** (34)

dynamisch dynamic(ally)

der Dynamo (-s) generator

E

eben (*particle*) **warum eben das?** why that of all things?; (*adj.*) flat, even; (*adv.*) just now

die Ebene (-n) plain; level

ebenfalls as well, likewise

ebenso the same way

echt genuine(ly), real(ly); **echt gut** really good (2); **echt klasse** really great (10)

die Ecke (-n) corner (22)

der Edelstein (-e) gem (22)

das Edelweiß (-e) edelweiss (*alpine flower*)

die EDV = **elektronische Datenverarbeitung**

effektiv effective(ly)

effizient efficient(ly)

egal equal; **das ist mir egal** it's all the same to me (18)

ehe before

die Ehe (-n) marriage (5/23/25)

die Ehefrau (-en) wife

ehelich marital (25)

ehemalig former (18)

der Ehemann (¨er) husband

das Ehepaar (-e) married couple (25)

der Ehepartner (-) / die Ehepartnerin (-nen) spouse

eher rather; sooner (27)

die Ehre (-n) honor

ehrfürchtig reverent(ly)

ehrgeizig ambitious(ly) (26)

ehrlich honest(ly), sincere(ly)

die Ehrlichkeit (-en) honesty (14)

das Ei (-er) egg

der Eierkocher (-) egg boiler

die Eiernudel (-n) egg noodle

die Eifersucht jealousy

eifersüchtig jealous(ly)

der Eiffelturm Eiffel Tower

eifrig eager(ly), keen(ly)

eigen own (4/25)

eigenartig unique(ly) (28)

die Eigeninitiative (-n) self-initiative (14)

eigens: eigens für (ihn) exclusively for (him)

die Eigenschaft (-en) quality, property, characteristic

eigentlich actual(ly), real(ly) (21)

die Eigentumswohnung (-en) condominium (4)

sich eignen als to be suitable as

eilfertig zealous

der Eimer (-) bucket

einander each other, one another

einatmen (atmet ein) to inhale

einbauen (baut ein) to install

einbeziehen (in) (bezieht ein), bezog ein, einbezogen to include (in); to apply (to)

einbiegen (in) (biegt ein), bog ein, eingebogen to turn (drive) in (22)

einblenden (blendet ein) to fade in

der Einblick (-e) insight, view

einbrocken (brockt ein) to crumble

einchecken (checkt ein) to check in

eindeutig clear(ly), definite(ly), unambiguous(ly)

der Eindruck (¨e) impression (34)

eineinhalb one and a half

einerseits on the one hand

eines Tages one day

einfach simple, simply; easy, easily; one-way (24)

einfallen (fällt ein), fiel ein, ist eingefallen (+ *dat.*) to come to mind (34); **sich einfallen lassen** to think (*of something*)

das Einfamilienhaus (¨er) single-family house (4)

einfassen (fasst ein) to set (*a gemstone*)

der Einfluss (¨e) influence (26)

einflussreich influential

einführen (führt ein) to introduce

die Einführung (-en) introduction

der Eingang (¨e) entrance

eingeben (gibt ein), gab ein, eingegeben to put in

eingehen (geht ein), ging ein, ist eingegangen to enter

eingeschult werden to start school, be enrolled in first grade

einhalten (hält ein), hielt ein, eingehalten to keep (*an appointment*) (34)

die Einhaltung (-en) keeping, following, carrying out

einheimisch local, indigenous

die Einheit (-en) unit; unification; unity (18)

einig: sich einig sein to be in agreement

einige some

sich einigen to come to an agreement

einigermaßen relative(ly); reasonable, reasonably

einiges some (things); quite a bit

die Einigung (-en) agreement

der Einkauf (¨e) shopping; **Einkäufe machen** to go shopping

einkaufen (kauft ein) to shop, go shopping

der Einkäufer (-) / die Einkäuferin (-nen) shopper, buyer

der Einkaufsbummel (-s) shopping trip; **einen Einkaufsbummel machen** to go shopping (leisurely)

der Einkaufskorb (Einkaufskörbe) shopping basket

die Einkaufsliste (-n) shopping list
(16)
die Einkaufsstraße (-n) shopping
street, street with lots of shops
die Einkaufstasche (-n) shopping
bag
das Einkaufszentrum (-zentren)
shopping center
Einklang: in Einklang bringen mit
to bring into line with
einkleiden (kleidet ein) to dress
up; to clothe
einklemmen (klemmt ein) to jam,
catch
das Einkommen (-) income (13)
**einladen (lädt ein), lud ein,
eingeladen** to invite (3E)
die Einladung (-en) invitation
**einlassen (lässt ein), ließ ein,
eingelassen** to let in; **sich auf
etwas einlassen** to get involved in
something
sich einleben (lebt ein) to get
accustomed to a place
einmal once; **auf einmal** suddenly,
unexpectedly; **es war einmal . . .**
once upon a time (12); **noch
einmal** once again, one more time
das Einmaleins (multiplication)
tables; basics
einmalig unique, wonderful
**einnehmen (nimmt ein), nahm
ein, eingenommen** to take up
einnehmend likeable
einpacken (packt ein) to pack; to
wrap (7)
der Einpersonenhaushalt (-e)
single household
einquartieren to put up,
accommodate
einrahmen (rahmt ein) to frame
einreichen (reicht ein) to submit
(*a form, application*)
einrichten (richtet ein) to furnish,
decorate (*an apartment or
house*) (4)
die Einrichtung (-en) facility
eins one (E); **er will auch eins** he
wants one, too; **es ist eins** it's one
o'clock
einsam lonely

die Einsamkeit loneliness
der Einsatz (¨e) use
einschätzen (schätzt ein) to
estimate; to assess
**einschlafen (schläft ein), schlief
ein, ist eingeschlafen** to fall
asleep (3)
das Einschlafen: zum Einschlafen
boring
**einschließen (schließt ein),
schloss ein, eingeschlossen** to
include
**sich einschreiben (schreibt ein),
schrieb ein, eingeschrieben** to
enroll, sign up (19)
einschüchtern (schüchtert ein) to
intimidate
einsetzen (setzt ein) to put in
place (29); to use; **sich einsetzen**
to show commitment
einst(ens) once; one day; one time
**einsteigen (steigt ein), stieg ein,
ist eingestiegen** to get in/on (*a
train, car, etc.*) (7)
**der Einsteiger (-) / die
Einsteigerin (-nen)** beginner
einstellen (stellt ein) to appoint,
adjust; to cease
die Einstellung (-en) attitude;
point of view (18)
einstündig hour-long
**eintauchen (taucht ein), tauchte
ein, ist eingetaucht** to dive in
einteilen (teilt ein) to divide
der Eintopf (¨e) stew
**eintragen (trägt ein), trug ein,
eingetragen** to enter, register, put
down (*on a list*)
das Eintreffen arrival
**eintreten (tritt ein), trat ein, ist
eingetreten** to occur; to enter
(33)
der Eintritt (-e) admission
die Eintrittskarte (-n) ticket,
admission
**einverstanden: mit etwas
einverstanden sein** to be in
agreement (18/29)
**der Einwanderer (-) / die
Einwanderin (-nen)** immigrant
(34)

**einwandern (wandert ein),
wanderte ein, ist eingewandert**
to immigrate
das Einwanderungsland (¨er)
country of immigrants
die Einwegflasche (-n)
nonreturnable bottle (35)
das Einweggeschirr disposable
utensils (35), disposable dishes
einwickeln (wickelt ein) to wrap
**der Einwohner (-) / die
Einwohnerin (-nen)** inhabitant,
citizen (17)
das Einwohnermeldeamt (¨er)
residents' registration office
die Einzahl singular
einzeichnen (zeichnet ein) to draw
in; to mark
das Einzelbad (¨er) single bath
die Einzelberatung (-en) individual
counseling
einzeln single, singly; individual(ly)
das Einzelzimmer (-) single room
(8)
**einziehen (zieht ein), zog ein, ist
eingezogen** to move in; to pull in
einzig only (23)
der Einzug (¨e) move, entry
das Eis ice, ice cream (15)
der Eisbecher (-) ice cream sundae
das Eisbein (-e) pork knuckle
die Eisdiele (-n) ice cream parlor
der Eisenstock (¨e) metal club
eisern (*adj.*) iron
das Eishockey ice hockey
das Eislaufen ice skating
das Eiswasser ice water
der Eiszapfen (-) icicle
das Eiweiß egg white; protein
eiweißhaltig containing protein
eklatant sensational, spectacular,
striking
eklig disgusting, repulsive
elastisch elastic; stretchy; flexible
elegant elegant(ly)
die Eleganz elegance
**der Elektriker (-) / die
Elektrikerin (-nen)** electrician
elektrisch electric(ally)
das Elektrogerät (-e) electric
appliance

der Elektromeister (-) / die Elektromeisterin (-nen) electrician (29)

der Elektroniker (-) / die Elektronikerin (-nen) electronic technician, electrical engineer

die elektronische Datenverarbeitung electronic data processing

das Element (-e) element

elend miserable; miserably

elf eleven (1E)

die Eltern (*pl.*) parents (1/25)

das Elternhaus (¨er) parental house, house in which one grew up

das Elternschlafzimmer (-) parents' bedroom, master bedroom

der Elternteil (-e) parent

die E-Mail (-s) e-mail

die Emanzipation emancipation (30)

emanzipieren to emancipate (30)

emanzipiert (*adj.*) emancipated

emigrieren to emigrate

empfangen (empfängt), empfing, empfangen to receive; to conceive

empfehlen (empfiehlt), empfohl, empfohlen to recommend

empfehlenswert to be recommended

die Empfehlung (-en) recommendation

empfinden, empfand, empfunden to feel, perceive

empfindlich sensitive; **empfindlich kalt** bitterly cold

die Empfindung (-en) emotion

das Ende end; **am Ende** in the end; **ohne Ende** never ending; **zu Ende gehen** to come to an end; **zu Ende schreiben** to finish writing

enden to end

endgültig finally

endlich finally (10)

der Endsieg (-e) final victory

die Endung (-en) ending (*grammatical*)

die Energie (-n) energy

die Energiesparlampe (-n) energy-saving lamp

eng narrow(ly), small, tight(ly)

das Engagement (-s) commitment

sich engagieren für to get involved in (26)

engagiert für active(ly) interested (in)

die Enge (-n) narrowing

der Engel (-) angel

(das) England England (9)

der Engländer (-) / die Engländerin (-nen) English person (18)

das Englisch English (*language*) (11); **auf Englisch** in English; **was heißt das auf Englisch?** what does that mean in English?

die Englischkenntnisse (*pl.*) knowledge of English

der Enkel (-) / die Enkelin (-nen) grandson/granddaughter (1/25)

das Enkelkind (-er) grandchild (1)

enorm enormous(ly), tremendous(ly)

das Ensemble (-s) ensemble, cast

entdecken to discover

die Entdeckung (-en) discovery

die Ente (-n) duck

(sich) entfernen to remove (oneself) (34)

entfernt away (from); **der Bahnhof ist nur zehn Minuten entfernt** the station is only ten minutes from here

die Entfernung (-en) distance

sich entfremden to alienate (oneself)

entführen to kidnap, abduct

entgegensetzen (setzt entgegen) to counteract; to set against

entgegenstrecken (streckt entgegen) to hold out

enthalten (enthält), enthielt, enthalten to contain

entkräften to weaken

entlang along(side); **(die Straße) entlang** along (the street) (22)

entlanggehen (geht entlang), ging entlang, ist entlanggegangen to go along (22)

entlarven to unmask; to find out about

entrüstet appalled

(sich) entscheiden, entschied, entschieden to decide (14)

die Entscheidung (-en) decision

sich entschließen, entschloss, entschlossen to decide (19)

(sich) entschuldigen to excuse (oneself); **entschuldigen Sie!** excuse me!

entsenden to send out

entsetzt (*adj.*) shocked

entsorgen to remove

der Entsorger (-) person or authority who removes waste

die Entsorgung (-en) removal, disposal

sich entspannen to relax (31)

die Entspannung (-en) relaxation (32)

entsprechen (entspricht), entsprach, entsprochen (+ *dat.*) to correspond to something

entstehen, entstand, ist entstanden to arise (28)

die Entstehung (-en) development, evolution

enttäuschen to disappoint

enttäuscht (*adj.*) disappointed

entwaffnend (*adj.*) disarming

entweder . . . oder . . . either . . . or . . .

entwerfen (entwirft), entwarf, entworfen to design

entwickeln to develop (20)

die Entwicklung (-en) development (29)

das Entwicklungsland (¨er) developing country

entzwei apart, into pieces

entzweireißen (reißt entzwei), riss entzwei, entzweigerissen to tear into pieces

die Enzyklopädie (-n) encyclopedia

die Epik epic poetry

er he

sich erarbeiten to work for (*something*)

erbauen to build (up)

der Erbprinz (-en *masc.***)** prince, heir to the throne
die Erbse (-n) pea (15)
die Erbsensuppe (-n) pea soup
die Erbswurst *pea-based meal compressed into the shape of a sausage*
die Erde Earth
das Erdgeschoss (-e) ground floor (8)
die Erdkunde geography (11)
die Erdnussbutter peanut butter
der Erdteil (-e) continent
der Erdton (¨e) earth tone
das Ereignis (-se) occurrence, incident, event
erfahren (erfährt), erfuhr, erfahren to learn, hear about; to experience
die Erfahrung (-en) experience (28)
der Erfahrungsaustausch exchange of experience
erfinden, erfand, erfunden to invent (21)
der Erfinder (-) / die Erfinderin (-nen) inventor
die Erfindung (-en) invention
der Erfolg (-e) success (13/26)
erfolgen to follow, ensue, result
erfolgreich successful(ly)
die Erfolgskurve (-n) success rate
das Erfolgsstück (-e) successful production
erforderlich necessary
erfordern to require (29)
erforschen to discover; to explore; to find out
die Erforschung (-en) investigation, research, examination
erfreuen to please, delight; **sich großer Beliebtheit erfreuen** to enjoy popularity, be popular
erfrischend refreshing
erfüllen to fulfill
ergänzen to complete
das Ergebnis (-se) result, outcome (33)
ergreifen, ergriff, ergriffen to seize; to grasp, grip
erhalten (erhält), erhielt, erhalten to receive (29)

erhältlich obtainable, available
die Erhaltung conservation
erheben (erhebt), erhob, erhoben to raise, lift
erhellen to lighten up
erhellend lightening up, brightening
erhitzen to heat (19)
erhoben raised
erhöhen to raise; to increase (33)
sich erholen to recover, recuperate
erholsam relaxing
die Erholung (-en) recreation; rest; recuperation (31)
der Erholungsort (-e) recreational town
die Erholungsreise (-n) recreational vacation
erinnern to remind; **sich erinnern an** (+ *acc.*) to remember (26)
die Erinnerung (-en) memory
erjagen to chase; to hunt down
sich erkälten to catch a cold
erkältet sein to have a cold
die Erkältung (-en) cold, flu (6)
erkämpfen to gain by struggle (26)
erkennen, erkannte, erkannt to recognize
die Erkenntnis (-se) insight, understanding
erklären to explain
die Erklärung (-en) explanation (29)
erkranken to become ill
erkunden to scout, reconnoiter, find out
sich erkundigen (über) to inquire, to ask (about)
erlauben to allow
erlaubt (*adj.*) allowed
erleben to experience (8/26)
das Erlebnis (-se) experience
das Erlebnisbad (¨er) spa, pool
die Erlebnisgastronomie eating as a culinary experience
die Erlebnisreise (-n) adventure trip
erledigen to see to, take care of, do
erledigt (*adj.*) done, taken care of
erleichtern to relieve
erleiden, erlitt, erlitten to suffer
erlernen to learn; to acquire (29)

erlisten to list
erlösen to save (12)
ermitteln to investigate, find out
ermöglichen to make possible, enable
ermüden to get tired
ermüdend tiring (21)
ermuntern to encourage
ermutigen to encourage
ernähren to nourish (25)
die Ernährung (-en) diet
ernst serious(ly) (1); **ist das dein Ernst?** are you serious?
ernsthaft serious(ly)
die Ernte (-n) harvest
das Erntedankfest (-e) Thanksgiving (5)
erobern to conquer (27)
eröffnen to open
erörtern to discuss
erproben to try out
erquicken to revitalize, bring back to life
erraffen to grab
erraten (errät), erriet, erraten to guess
errechnen to calculate
erregen to excite, arouse
die Erregung (-en) excitement, arousal
erreichen to achieve (25); to reach (30)
erscheinen, erschien, ist erschienen to seem, appear
die Erscheinung (-en) appearance
erschöpfen to exhaust
erschrecken (erschrickt), erschrak, erschrocken to startle
ersetzen to replace, substitute
erst not until; only; **erst** first; **erst einmal** first of all
erstarren to stiffen, harden
erstaunt startled, amazed
erst- first; **am ersten Juni** on the first of June; **der erste beste Mann** the first suitable man; **der erste Stock** the second floor (8); **erst seit kurzem** only recently; **zum ersten Mal** for the first time
erstellen to compile; to put together
erstens first (*in a list*)

das Erstgespräch (-e) first interview
erstklassig first class
erstmal first, primarily
erstmals for the first time
der Erstsemestler (-) / die Erstsemestlerin (-nen) first-semester student at a university
ertappen to catch
erteilen to give; to grant; **jemandem eine Lehre erteilen** to teach someone a lesson; **Unterricht erteilen** to teach, give instruction
ertönen to sound
ertragen (erträgt), ertrug, ertragen to bear, cope with
erträglich bearable
ertrinken, ertrank, ist ertrunken to drown
erübrigen: es erübrigt sich it becomes irrelevant, it is no longer an issue
erwachen to awaken
erwachsen (erwächst), erwuchs, ist erwachsen to arise (31)
der/die Erwachsene (*decl. adj.*) adult (25)
das Erwachsenenpublikum adult audience
erwählen to choose
erwähnen to mention (31)
(sich) erwandern to hike, cover ground
sich erwärmen für etwas to warm up to (develop a liking for) something
erwarten to expect (14); **erwarten von** to expect from (25)
die Erwartung (-en) expectation
(sich) erweisen to prove (oneself)
erweitern to expand; to broaden
erweitert (*adj.*) expanded, widened
erwerben (erwirbt), erwarb, erworben to buy; to obtain
erwischen to catch; **erwischt werden** to get caught
das Erz (-e) ore
erzählen to tell, narrate
der Erzähler (-) / die Erzählerin (-nen) narrator

der Erzbischof (¨e) archbishop
erziehen, erzog, erzogen to bring up, educate (20)
der Erzieher (-) / die Erzieherin (-nen) educator, teacher, child care person
die Erziehung (-en) upbringing
das Erziehungsgeld (-er) child benefit
der Erziehungsstil (-e) kind of upbringing, way of bringing up children
der Erziehungsurlaub (-e) family leave (23)
es it; **es gibt** there is/are; **es war einmal . . .** once upon a time . . . (12)
der Esel (-) donkey
der Essay (-s) essay
essbar edible
essen (isst), aß, gegessen to eat (3)
das Essen food, meal, eating
die Essensabfälle (*pl.*) table scraps, garbage
die Essensreste (*pl.*) table scraps
die Essgewohnheit (-en) eating habit (34)
der Esstisch (-e) dinner table (3)
das Esszimmer (-) dining room (3)
sich etablieren to establish oneself
etabliert (*adj.*) established
die Etage (-n) floor (*in a building*)
etwa about, roughly
etwaig possible
etwas something, a little, some
euch (*acc./dat. inform. pl.*) you; **wie geht es euch?** how are you? (5)
euer (*inform. pl.*) your; **liebe Grüße, eu(e)re Marion** best wishes, yours, Marion (*closing in letters*)
die Euphorie (-n) euphoria
der Euro *European currency unit*
(das) Europa Europe
der Europäer (-) / die Europäerin (-nen) European (*person*) (18)
europäisch (*adj.*) European; **die Europäische Union** European Union
eventuell possible; possibly
ewig eternal(ly), forever

die Ewigkeit (-en) eternity
exakt exact(ly)
die Exaktheit (-en) exactness, precision, accuracy
das Examen (-) exam
das Examensergebnis (-se) exam results
das Exemplar (-e) specimen
die Existenz (-en) existence
existieren to exist
die Exkursion (-en) excursion
exotisch exotic(ally)
expandieren to expand
der Experte (-n *masc.***) / die Expertin (-nen)** expert
die Expertenhilfe (-n) expert assistance
explodieren to explode
das Exponat (-e) exhibit
exportieren to export
der Expressionismus Expressionism
expressionistisch expressionist
exquisit exquisite(ly)
extra special(ly), additional(ly), extra
die Extralektion (-en) extra lecture
extrem extreme(ly) (35)
der Extremismus extremism
die Extremsportart (-en) adventure sport (32)
exzellent excellent(ly)

F

die Fabel (-n) fable
die Fabrik (-en) factory (4/35)
der Fabrikationsverkauf (¨e) factory outlet
das Fach (¨er) (school) subject (11/27)
der Fachbereich (-e) subject area
die Fachexkursion (-en) educational excursion
der Fachhändler (-) specialty store
das Fachlehrerstudium (-studien) education program
Fachleute (*pl.*) experts
fachlich technical, specialist, professional
der Fachmediziner (-) / die Fachmedizinerin (-nen) specialist

die Fachoberschule (-en) specialized high school (11)
die Fachrichtung (-en) subject area
das Fachwerkhaus (¨er) half-timbered house
die Fackel (-n) torch
das Fädchen (-) little thread
fad(e) boring
der Faden (¨) thread
fähig capable; capably (36)
die Fähigkeit (-en) capability (29)
die Fahne (-n) flag
die Fahrbahn (-en) lane on a road
fahren (fährt), fuhr, ist gefahren to ride, drive, go (3)
der Fahrer (-) / die Fahrerin (-nen) driver
der Fahrgast (¨e) passenger
die Fahrkarte (-n) ticket
der Fahrkartenschalter (-) ticket counter (7)
der Fahrplan (¨e) schedule (7)
das Fahrrad (¨er) bicycle; **mit dem Fahrrad fahren** to go by bicycle (7)
die Fahrradpanne (-n) bicycle breakdown
die Fahrstunde (-n) driving lesson
die Fahrt (-en) trip, journey; ride, drive (24); **gute Fahrt!** have a good trip! (14)
der Fahrtweg (-e) driving time, distance
die Fahrverbindung (-en) connection
faktisch actual, real
das Faktum (*pl.* **Fakten)** fact
der Fall (¨e) case; **auf jeden Fall** in any case; **auf keinen Fall** under no circumstance
fallen (fällt), fiel, ist gefallen to fall
falls in case
falsch false(ly), wrong(ly), incorrect(ly)
falten to fold
faltenfrei without wrinkles, wrinkle-free
familiär familial; familiar
die Familie (-n) family (1)

der Familienalltag daily family routine
das Familiendokument (-e) family document
das Familienerbstück (-e) family heirloom
das Familienfoto (-s) family photo
der Familienfragebogen (¨) family questionnaire
die Familiengeschichte (-n) family history
das Familienleben family life
das Familienmitglied (-er) family member
der Familienname (-n *masc.***, -ns** *gen.***)** family name
die Familienrolle (-n) family role, role in the family
der Familienstand family status (14/25)
die Familientradition (-en) family tradition
der Fan (-s) fan
der Fang (¨e) catch
fangen (fängt), fing, gefangen to catch
die Fantasie (-n) fantasy (14)
fantasielos unimaginative, uncreative
fantastisch fantastic(ally)
die Farbe (-n) color
färben to dye; to color
der Farbfilm (-e) roll of color film
der Farbstoff (-e) dye, stain
der Fasching Carnival, Mardi Gras (17)
die Fassade (-n) facade, front of a building
fassen to grasp; to believe
fast almost (27)
faszinieren to fascinate (36)
faszinierend fascinating
die Fata Morgana mirage
faul lazy (1)
faulenzen to laze about, be lazy
die Faust (¨e) fist
das Fax (-e) fax
das Faxgerät (-e) fax machine
die Faxmöglichkeit (-en) possibility to fax
FC = Fußballclub soccer club

FDJ = Freie Deutsche Jugend
der Februar February (5)
die Fee (-n) fairy (12)
fegen to sweep
fehlen (+ *dat.***)** to lack; to be missing (21)
fehlend missing
der Fehler (-) error, mistake
der Feierabend (-e) time off (work) (29)
feiern to celebrate (5)
der Feiertag (-e) holiday (5/31)
die Feigheit (-en) cowardliness
fein fine(ly)
feindlich hostile(ly)
feindselig hostile
die Feinheit (-en) fineness, delicateness; (*pl.*) details
die Feinkost delicacies
das Feld (-er) field (9)
der Feldweg (-e) road between fields
das Fell (-e) fur
der Felsen (-) rock
feminin feminine
der Feminismus feminism
das Fenster (-) window (1E)
die Ferien (*pl.***)** vacation (32)
die Ferienanlage (-n) vacation community
das Feriencamp (-s) vacation camp
das Ferienhaus (¨er) vacation home
das Ferienheim (-e) vacation home (32)
das Ferienlager (-) vacation camp (32)
der Ferienmonat (-e) vacation month
der Ferienplatz (¨e) vacation spot, holiday resort
die Ferienregion (-en) holiday region
die Ferienwohnung (-en) vacation apartment (8)
das Ferienzentrum (-zentren) vacation center
fern far, distant
das Fernglas (¨er) binoculars
fernsehen (sieht fern), sah fern, ferngesehen to watch television/TV (2)

das Fernsehen television; **im Fernsehen schauen** to watch on TV
der Fernseher (-) television/TV set (3)
der Fernsehkrimi (-s) detective show on television/TV
das Fernsehprogramm (-e) television/TV program, television/TV channel
die Fernsehsendung (-en) television/TV program
die Fernsehstation (-en) television/TV station
das Fernsehstudio (-s) television/TV production studio
die Fernsehumfrage (-n) television/TV survey
die Ferse (-n) heel
fertig finished (3E)
fertigstellen (stellt fertig) to complete
fest permanent(ly); certain(ly) (13)
das Fest (-e) festival; party (5); celebration; holiday
festlegen (legt fest) to determine, set
festmachen (macht fest) to fasten
festlich festive(ly) (17)
der Festsaal (-säle) great hall, celebration hall
das Festspiel (-e) cultural festival
feststellen (stellt fest) to ascertain, to establish
die Feststellung (-en) observation
der Festtag (-e) holiday
die Festwoche (-n) festival week
das Festzelt (-e) festival tent
die Fete (-n) (coll.) party
fett fat
das Fett (-e) fat (33)
fettgedruckt bold
fetthaltig containing fat, fatty
feucht humid, damp, moist
das Feuer (-) fire
die Feuerbrunst (-e) heat of fire, lust
feuerfarben (adj.) the color of fire
das Feuerwerk (-e) fireworks (5)

das Feuerzeug (-e) lighter
das Fieber (-) fever (6/33)
die Figur (-en) figure, shape
der Film (-e) film (36)
das Filmfest (-e) film festival
die Filmindustrie (-n) film industry
der Filmkenner (-) / die Filmkennerin (-nen) movie buff
filtern to filter
der Filzstift (-e) felt-tip pen, marker
finanziell financial(ly) (13)
finanzieren to finance; to sponsor
das Finanzzentrum (-zentren) financial center
finden, fand, gefunden to find (2)
der Finger (-) finger (6)
der Fingernagel (-) fingernail
der Finne (-n masc.) / die Finnin (-nen) Finnish (person)
(das) Finnland Finland (9)
finster dark
die Firma (Firmen) firm, company (13)
der Firmenwagen (-) company car
der Firmenwechsel (-) change of company
der Fisch (-e) fish (19)
fischen to fish
der Fischer (-) / die Fischerin (-nen) fisherman/fisherwoman
das Fischerboot (-e) fishing boat
die Fischerei fishing, fishing industry
die Fischermütze (-n) fisherman's hat
der Fischmarkt (-e) fish market
das Fischrestaurant (-s) seafood restaurant
der Fischschwarm (-e) swarm of fish
die Fischspezialität (-en) seafood specialty
fit fit; **sich fit halten (hält), hielt, gehalten** to keep fit (23/32)
die Fitness fitness
das Fitnesscenter (-) gym, fitness center
der Fitnessclub (-s) gym, health club

fix und fertig completely exhausted
flach flat
die Fläche (-n) plane, surface
das Fladenbrot (-e) pita bread
das Flair flair
flankieren to flank; to accompany
die Flasche (-n) bottle (20)
flattern to flutter
der Fleck (-e) spot, stain
das Fleisch meat (19)
der Fleischer (-) / die Fleischerin (-nen) butcher
die Fleischwurst kind of sausage
fleißig industrious(ly) (1)
flexibel flexible (18); flexibly
die Fliege (-n) fly
fliegen, flog, ist geflogen to fly (7)
fliehen, floh, ist geflohen to flee, escape
fließen, floss, ist geflossen to flow (17)
flink quick(ly)
das Flinserlkostüm (-e) Austrian Fasching (Karneval) costume
die Flinserlmusik Austrian Fasching (Karneval) music
die Flintenpulverflasche (-n) gunpowder sack
Flitterwochen (pl.) honeymoon
der Floh (-e) flea
der Flohmarkt (-märkte) flea market (22)
die Flora flora
der Florist (-en masc.) / die Floristin (-nen) florist
die Flöte (-n) flute
die Flucht (-en) flight, escape
flüchten, ist geflüchtet to flee; to escape
flüchtig cursory, cursorily; sketchy, sketchily
der Flüchtling (-e) refugee, fugitive
der Fluchtweg (-e) escape route
der Flug (-e) flight (in an airplane)
der Flugbegleiter (-) / die Flugbegleiterin (-nen) flight attendant (13)
das Flugblatt (-er) flyer
der Flughafen (Flughäfen) airport (24)
die Flugkarte (-n) airline ticket (24)

R-37

der/die Flugreisende (*decl. adj.*) air passenger

das Flugzeug (-e) airplane (7); **mit dem Flugzeug fliegen** to fly (by airplane)

der Flur (-e) hallway; corridor

der Fluss (¨e) river (9)

flüstern to whisper

die Flut (-en) flood; incoming tide

föderalistisch federal

der Fokus (-se) focus

die Folge (-n) episode; consequence

folgen (+ *dat.*) to follow (14)

folgend following

die Foltermethode (-n) method of torture

fordern to demand; to ask; to require

fördern to promote; to support (36)

die Forderung (-en) demand

die Förderung support

die Forelle (-n) trout (15)

die Form (-en) form, shape

formal formal(ly)

förmlich formal(ly); literal(ly)

das Formular (-e) form (8)

formulieren to formulate

forschen to research

der Forscher (-) / die Forscherin (-nen) scientist, researcher

die Forschung (-en) research

das Forschungscamp (-s) research camp

das Forschungsinstitut (-e) research institute

(sich) fortbilden (bildet fort) to further educate (oneself)

fortbleiben (bleibt fort), blieb fort, ist fortgeblieben to stay away

fortgehen (geht fort), ging fort, ist fortgegangen to leave

fortgeschritten advanced

der Fortschritt (-e) advance

fortsetzen (setzt fort) to continue

die Fortsetzung continuation

das Foto (-s) photo

der Fotoapparat (-e) camera

der Fotograf (-en *masc.*) / die Fotografin (-nen) photographer (13)

fotografieren to photograph (2)

das Fotografieren photography

fotokopieren to photocopy

das Fotokopiergerät (-e) photocopy machine

der Frachter (-) / die Frachterin (-nen) shipping manager

die Frage (-n) question

der Fragebogen (¨) questionnaire

fragen to ask (8); **fragen nach** to ask about

der Fragenkatalog (-e) battery of questions

die Fragestellung (-en) formulation of a question

das Fragewort (¨er) question word, interrogative pronoun

der Franken (-) franc (*currency in France and Switzerland*)

das Frankenreich Frankish Empire

das Fränkische Reich Frankish Empire

(das) Frankreich France (9)

der Franzose (-n *masc.*) / die Französin (-nen) French (*person*)

französisch (*adj.*) French

das Französisch French (*language*) (11)

die Frau (-en) woman; wife (1)

der/die Frauenbeauftragte (*decl. adj.*) women's spokesperson

die Frauenbewegung (-en) women's movement (30)

die Frauenbildung women's education

der Frauenbuchladen (¨) women's bookstore

frauenfeindlich misogynous(ly), anti-women

die Frauenpower women's power (*feminist motto*)

die Frauenrechtlerin (-nen) feminist

der Frauensakko (-s) women's blazer (7)

das Frauenzimmer (-) (*derogatory*) woman

frech fresh, impudent(ly)

die Frechheit (-en) offensive behavior; **das ist eine Frechheit!** what nerve! (10)

die Fregatte (-n) frigate, type of ship

frei free; **ist hier noch frei?** is this seat taken? (15); **wann sind Sie frei?** when do you have time?

das Freibad (¨er) outdoor pool

die Freibühne (-n) outdoor theater

die Freie Deutsche Jugend (FDJ) *a youth organization of the former GDR*

Freien: im Freien in the open air; outdoors (31)

die Freiheit (-en) freedom, liberty (23)

die Freiheitsstatue Statue of Liberty

das Freiheitssymbol (-e) symbol of freedom

der Freiherr (-en, -n *masc.*) baron

die Freistunde (-n) free hour

der Freitag (-e) Friday (E)

der Freitagabend (-e) Friday evening

freiwillig voluntarily

die Freizeit free time (16/3E)

die Freizeitaktivität (-en) pastime, hobby

der Freizeitbereich (-e) recreation industry

die Freizeitbeschäftigung (-en) pastime, hobby

das Freizeitzentrum (-zentren) recreation center

fremd foreign, strange (24)

der/die Fremde (*decl. adj.*) stranger

das Fremdenverkehrsbüro (-s) tourist office

die Fremdsprache (-n) foreign language

die Fremdsprachenkenntnisse (*pl.*) foreign language skills

fremdsprachig in a foreign language

fressen (frisst), fraß, gefressen (*animals*) to eat up, gobble

die Freude (-n) pleasure, joy (27)

freudig joyful(ly); happy; happily (26)

sich freuen to be happy; **sich freuen auf** (+ *acc.*) to look forward to (18/26); **sich freuen über** (+ *acc.*) to be happy about

der Freund (-e) / die Freundin (-nen) close friend; boyfriend/girlfriend (1)
der Freundeskreis (-e) circle of friends
freundlich friendly (1)
die Freundschaft (-en) friendship
freundschaftlich friendly, as friends
der Frieden peace (26)
die Friedensarbeit (-en) work for peace
die Friedensbewegung peace movement
friedlich peaceful(ly) (26)
frieren, fror, gefroren to freeze, be cold
der Fries (-e) frieze
friesverziert (adj.) decorated with friezes
frisch fresh(ly) (5)
frischgefangen freshly caught
der Friseur (-e) / die Friseurin (-nen), die Friseuse (-n) hairdresser
der Frisör (-e) / die Frisöse (-n) hairdresser
der Frisörbesuch (-e) hair salon appointment
die Frisur (-en) hairstyle
froh glad, happy (1); **frohe Weihnachten!** merry Christmas!
fröhlich happy; happily, cheerful(ly), in good spirits
die Front (-en) front, frontage
die Frontlänge (-n) length of the front
der Frosch (⁻e) frog
das Fröschchen (-) little frog
der Froschkönig (-e) frog king (12)
die Froschprinzessin (-nen) frog princess
die Frucht (⁻e) fruit
fruchtig fruity
das Fruchtkonzentrat (-e) fruit concentrate
der Fruchtsaft (⁻e) fruit juice
früh early (16)
der Frühanfänger (-) / die Frühanfängerin (-nen) early beginner
der Früheinwohner (-) early inhabitant

früher earlier, before, in earlier times
das Frühjahr (-e) spring
der Frühjahrsputz spring cleaning
der Frühling (-e) spring
der Frühlingsmarkt (⁻e) spring market
der Frühlingstag (-e) spring day
der Frühruhestand early retirement
das Frühstück (-e) breakfast
frühstücken to have breakfast
der Frühstückstisch (-e) breakfast table
das Frühstückszimmer (-) breakfast room
die Frühzeit prehistory
die Frustphase (-n) phase of frustration
frustrieren to frustrate
frustriert (adj.) frustrated
fügen to put; to join
fühlen to feel; **sich wohl fühlen** to feel well; to be comfortable
führen to lead; to guide; to manage; **führen zu** to lead to (26)
führend leading
der Führer (-) leader; guide
die Führerhörigkeit obedience to a leader
der Führerschein (-e) driver's license
das Fuhrunternehmen (-) shipping company
die Fülle abundance
fummeln to fumble
fünf five (E)
fünfeinhalb five and a half
fünfte fifth
fünfzehn fifteen (E)
fünfzig fifty (E); **die fünfziger Jahre** the Fifties
Funk: Funk und Fernsehen radio and television; **per Funk** by radio
funkeln to sparkle, shine
die Funktion (-en) function
funktionieren to function
für (+ acc.) for (5)
furchtbar terrible, terribly; awful(ly)
sich fürchten vor (+ dat.) to be afraid of (19/28)
fürs = für das

die Fürsorge support (25)
der Fuß (⁻e) foot (6); **zu Fuß** on foot (4)
der Fußball (⁻e) soccer ball
der Fußball soccer; **Fußball spielen** to play soccer (2)
der Fußballfanatiker (-) / die Fußballfanatikerin (-nen) soccer fanatic, soccer nut
das Fußballländerspiel (-e) European championship soccer game
die Fußballmannschaft (-en) soccer team
das Fußballspiel (-e) soccer game (16)
der Fußboden (⁻) floor
der Fußgängerweg (-e) walkway, pedestrian way
die Fußgängerzone (-n) pedestrian zone (20)
die Fußreise (-n) travels on foot
die Fußspitze (-n) tip of the foot
das Futter feed
füttern to feed
das Futur future tense

G

die Gabe (-n) gift, present
die Gabel (-n) fork (19)
gähnen to yawn
die Galerie (-n) gallery (22)
der Gallier (-) / die Gallierin (-nen) Gaul
der Gang (⁻e) gear; corridor
das Gänseblümchen (-) daisy
ganz whole, complete, very; really; **ganz Deutschland** all of Germany; **ganz am Ende** at the very end; **ganz und gar (nicht)** absolutely (not); **ganz schön schwierig** pretty difficult; **nicht ganz** not quite, not really
ganzjährig through the year
die Ganzpackung (-en) full body treatment
ganztags full-time (work)
gar: gar kein absolutely no; **gar nicht** absolutely not, not at all; **gar nichts** absolutely nothing, nothing at all

die Garage (-n) garage
garantieren to guarantee
die Garderobe (-n) wardrobe; closet
die Gardine (-n) curtain
die Garnele (-n) large shrimp
garnieren to garnish
garstig nasty
der Garten (¨) garden (4)
das Gartenamt (¨er) office of parks and recreation
die Gartenanlage (-n) garden facility
die Gartenarbeit (-en) gardening (31)
das Gartengitter (-) garden fence
die Gartenmauer (-n) garden wall
der Gärtner (-) / die Gärtnerin (-nen) gardener
die Gasse (-n) alley
der Gast (¨e) guest (8)
der Gastarbeiter (-) / die Gastarbeiterin (-nen) guest worker
das Gäste-WC guest bathroom
die Gastfamilie (-n) host family
gastfreundlich hospitable; hospitably
der Gastgeber (-) / die Gastgeberin (-nen) host/hostess
das Gasthaus (¨er) restaurant, inn (15)
der Gasthof (¨e) hotel; restaurant (15)
das Gastland (¨er) host country
das Gastmahl (-e) banquet
die Gastmutter (¨) host mother
der Gastronom (-en masc.) / die Gastronomin (-nen) restaurant owner, restaurateur
die Gaststätte (-n) restaurant, inn (15)
die Gaststube (-n) lounge
der Gastvater (¨) host father
der Gastwirt (-e) restaurant owner
gaukeln to flutter
der Gaumen (-) gums, palate
der Gauner (-) / die Gaunerin (-nen) rogue, scoundrel, rascal
das Gebäck (e) cookies; pastries
das Gebäude (-) building

geben (gibt), gab, gegeben to give (3); **es gibt** there is/are
das Gebet (-e) prayer
das Gebirge mountains, alpine region (9)
die Gebirgshose (-n) pants for the mountains
die Gebirgskette (-n) mountain range
das Gebiss (-e) teeth, dentures
geblümt (adj.) flowered (21)
geboren born (25); **wann sind Sie geboren?** when were you born? (14)
die Geborgenheit security
gebrauchen to use
gebrochen (adj.) broken
die Gebrüder Grimm Brothers Grimm
die Gebühr (-en) fee (3E)
gebührenfrei free of charge
gebunden sein an (+ acc.) to be tied to, bound by
das Geburtsdatum (-daten) date of birth
das Geburtshaus (¨er) birth house
das Geburtsjahr (-e) year of birth
der Geburtsort (-e) place of birth (14)
der Geburtstag (-e) birthday (5)
das Geburtstagsessen (-) birthday meal
die Geburtstagsfeier (-n) birthday party
die Gedächtniskirche war memorial church in Berlin
der Gedanke (-n masc.) thought
die Gedankenfreiheit freedom of thought (30)
die Gedankenwiedergabe (-n) representation of thought, expression of thought
das Gedicht (-e) poem
der Gedichtband (¨e) volume of poetry
die Gedichtsammlung (-en) poetry collection, anthology
die Geduld patience
geehrt: sehr geehrter Herr Gurtler dear Mr. Gurtler
geeignet suitable, appropriate (22)

die Gefahr (-en) danger (32)
gefährlich dangerous(ly) (7)
gefahrvoll dangerous(ly)
gefallen (gefällt), gefiel, gefallen (+ dat.) to be pleasing to; to like (14/31); **die Blumen gefallen mir** I like the flowers
der Gefallen (-) favor
gefangen (adj.) caught, captured
das Gefängnis (-se) jail
gefärbt (adj.) tinted, colored (21)
das Geflügel poultry
die Gefriertruhe (-n) freezer
gefroren (adj.) frozen
das Gefühl (-e) feeling (31)
gefühlsbetont emotional, emotive
gegebenenfalls should the situation arise
gegen (+ acc.) against (5); approximately (27)
der Gegenbeweis (-e) counter-evidence
die Gegend (-en) vicinity, neighborhood
gegeneinander against each other
der Gegensatz (¨e) opposite, contradiction
die Gegenschwimmanlage jet stream pool
der Gegenstand (¨e) thing, inanimate object
das Gegenteil (-e) opposite
gegenüber opposite; **gegenüber von** _____ opposite _____ (22); **jemandem gegenüber** toward someone
gegenübertreten (tritt gegenüber), trat gegenüber, ist gegenübergetreten to face; to step in front of
die Gegenwart present time (27)
gegensätzlich opposite, opposing
gegründet (adj.) founded
das Gehalt (¨er) salary (13)
der Gehaltsvorschlag (¨e) proposed salary
das Geheimnis (-se) secret
geheimnisvoll strange, secretive
gehen, ging, ist gegangen to go, walk (2); **wie geht's?** how are you?; **mir geht's auch gut** I am

well, too; **das geht zu weit!** that's too much!, that pushes it over the top! (10)

das Gehirn (-e) brain

gehören (+ *dat.*) to belong (to) (21)

der Geier (-) vulture

der Geist (-er) spirit; mind

die Geisteswissenschaften (*pl.*) humanities (28)

geistig mental(ly); spiritual(ly)

geistlich spiritual(ly)

geizig miserly, stingy

der/die Gejagte (*decl. adj.*) hunted person

gelb yellow (2)

das Geld (-er) money

der Geldschein (-e) bill, banknote

die Gelegenheit (-en) opportunity (13)

gelegentlich occasional(ly)

gelingen, gelang, gelungen (+ *dat.*) to succeed; **gut gelungen** came out well

gelten (gilt), galt, gegolten to be valid; **gelten als** to be regarded as; **gelten lassen** to approve (of something); to agree (30)

das Gemälde (-) painting (22)

gemäß (+ *dat.*) according to

gemein mean, malicious(ly)

die Gemeinde (-n) community, town

gemeinsam common; together (28)

die Gemeinsamkeit (-en) common ground, things in common

die Gemeinschaftsdienst (-e) community service

gemischt (*adj.*) mixed

das Gemüse vegetable (5/33)

der Gemüseanbauversuch (-e) vegetable growing experiment

die Gemüsesorte (-n) (kind of) vegetable

gemustert (*adj.*) patterned, printed (21)

das Gemüt (-er) mood, soul, mind

gemütlich comfortable; comfortably; cozy, cozily (16)

die Gemütlichkeit informal atmosphere, cozy atmosphere

genau exact(ly), precise(ly)

die Genauigkeit (-en) accuracy, exactness (34)

genauso just as, exactly the same

genehmigen to authorize; to approve

der General (⸚e) general

die Generation (-en) generation

generell general(ly)

(das) Genf Geneva

genial ingenious(ly), brilliant(ly)

das Genie (-s) genius

genießen, genoss, genossen to enjoy (3E)

der Genitiv genitive case

genmanipuliert genetically manipulated

die Gentechnologie genetic engineering

genug enough

genügen to suffice

genügend enough, sufficient(ly)

das Genus (Genera) gender

genussvoll delightful, pleasurable

geöffnet (*adj.*) open

die Geographie geography

geographisch geographical(ly)

geologisch geological(ly)

geordnet ordered, in order

das Gepäck baggage (7)

die Gepäckaufbewahrung (-en) baggage check (7)

gepflegt (*adj.*) cultured; neat; well-kept

geplant (*adj.*) planned

gepunktet polka-dotted (21)

gerade just, at the moment; straight, even; **gerade noch** just barely; **nicht gerade** not really

geradeaus straight ahead (22)

geraspelt (*adj.*) grated, shredded

das Gerät (-e) device; appliance (31)

geraten (gerät), geriet, ist geraten to come upon (33)

das Geräusch (-e) sound, noise

gerecht fair(ly) (10), just(ly)

die Gerechtigkeit (-en) justice (26)

das Gericht (-e) meal; dish (34); court of law

die Gerichtsakte (-n) file

gering small, negligible (29)

geringschätzig contemptuous, disparaging

germanisch Germanic

die Germanistik German studies (28)

gern(e) (lieber, liebst-) gladly; willingly, with pleasure; **ich hätte gern . . .** I'd like . . . (15); **ich schwimme gern** I like swimming; **ja, gern!** yes, please! my pleasure! **was machen Sie gern?** what do you like to do?

der Geruch (⸚e) smell, scent

der Geruchssinn sense of smell

gesammelt (*adj.*) collected

gesamtdeutsch *pertaining to the unified Federal Republic of Germany*

die Gesamtschule (-n) comprehensive school (11/27)

das Gesamtvermögen national savings, assets

das Gesäß (-e) seat, bottom, posterior

das Geschäft (-e) business; store (26)

geschäftig busily

die Geschäftsfrau (-en) businesswoman

der Geschäftsmann (-leute) businessman (13)

geschändet (*adj.*) blemished

geschehen (geschieht), geschah, ist geschehen to happen (32)

das Geschehen (-) event, happening

gescheit intelligent, sensible (21)

das Geschenk (-e) gift (5)

die Geschichte (-n) history; story (11/28)

geschichtlich historical(ly)

der Geschichtslehrer (-) / die Geschichtslehrerin (-nen) history teacher

geschickt clever(ly) (36)

das Geschirr (*sg.*) dishes; **das Geschirr spülen** to wash or do the dishes (3E)

die Geschirrspülmaschine (-n) dishwasher (3)

das Geschlecht (-er) gender, sex

geschlossen (*adj.*) closed (24)
der Geschmack (¨e) taste
die Geschmacksfrage (-n) question of taste
geschockt (*adj.*) shocked
geschwind(e) quickly
die Geschwister (*pl.*) siblings (1/25)
geschwungen (*adj.*) curved
der Geselle (-n *masc.*) journeyman; guy
die Gesellenprüfung (-en) journeyman's examination
die Gesellschaft (-en) company, society, association; **Gesellschaft mit begrenzter Haftung (GmbH)** company with limited liability
das Gesetz (-e) law (35)
gesetzlich legal(ly)
gesichert (*adj.*) secure
das Gesicht (-er) face (6)
der Gesichtsausdruck (¨e) facial expression
gespannt (*adj.*) **(auf)** excited (about) (32)
gesperrt closed
das Gespräch (-e) conversation
gestalten to design; to create; to shape (26)
die Gestaltung (-en) organization; shape; design (31)
gestatten to allow (30)
gestehen, gestand, gestanden to admit (34)
gestern yesterday (8)
gestorben (*adj.*) deceased
gestört (*adj.*) interrupted
gestreift (*adj.*) striped (21)
gestresst (*adj.*) under stress, stressed out
das Gesuch (-e) petition
gesucht (*adj.*) wanted, sought after
die/der/das Gesuchte (*decl. adj.*) person/thing wanted
gesund healthy (1/33)
die Gesundheit health (6)
das Gesundheitskonzept (-e) health concept
die Gesundheitspflege health care (33)

das Gesundheitswesen health care system (33)
geteert (*adj.*) tarred, covered with asphalt
das Getränk (-e) drink, beverage
das Getreide grain, cereals
die Getreideernte (-n) grain harvest
getrennt (*adj.*) separate, separated (25)
das Getue to-do, fuss
die Gewähr für etwas leisten to ensure, guarantee something
die Gewalt (-en) force, violence
gewaltig powerful(ly); tremendous(ly) (34)
gewalttätig violent(ly) (26)
die Gewalttätigkeit (-en) act of violence (20)
das Gewerbe (-) trade
das Gewicht (-e) weight
der Gewinn (-e) gain, profit
gewinnen, gewann, gewonnen to win (23/32)
gewiss sure(ly); certain(ly)
das Gewissen conscience
gewissenhaft conscientious(ly)
das Gewitter (-) thunderstorm
sich gewöhnen an (+ *acc.*) to get used to (24/28)
die Gewohnheit (-en) habit
gewohnheitsmäßig in a habitual manner (33)
gewöhnlich usual(ly), normal(ly)
das Gewürz (-e) spice, seasoning
gewürzt (*adj.*) seasoned
gezwungen (*adj.*) obliged, forced
der Giebel (-) gable, pediment
gießen, goss, gegossen to pour (19)
das Gift (-e) poison
giftfrei nontoxic (35)
gigantisch gigantic
der Gipfel (-) peak, summit (17)
das Gis G sharp (*music*)
die Gitarre (-n) guitar
der Glanz (-e) gleam, shine, glitter, sparkle
glänzen to shine, shimmer, sparkle
das Glas (¨er) glass (19)

der Glascontainer (-) glass recycling bin
gläsern glass(y)
die Glasflasche (-n) glass bottle
glatt even, smooth; **glattstreichen, strich gestrichen** to flatten, smooth out
glauben to believe (14)
gleich immediately; equal, same
gleichaltrig of the same age
die Gleichbehandlung (-en) equal treatment
gleichberechtigt sein to have equal rights (30)
die Gleichberechtigung equality (23/30)
der/die/das Gleiche (*decl. adj.*) same (one/person/thing)
gleichfalls you too, as well
gleichgestellt sein to be at an equal level (30)
das Gleichgewicht (-e) balance (35)
gleichgültig indifferently
gleichmäßig even; steady
die Gleichstellung (-en) equal rights
gleichzeitig simultaneous(ly)
das Gleis (-e) track (7); **auf Gleis 3** on track 3; train station platform
gleiten, glitt, ist geglitten to glide, slide
gleitende Arbeitszeit flextime
der Gletscher (-) glacier (17)
die Gliederung (-en) outline, structure
der Globus globe
die Glocke (-n) bell
das Glück happiness, luck; **viel Glück!** good luck! (5); **zum Glück** luckily
glücken (+ *dat.*) to be a success, be successful
glücklich happy (1)
der Glücksbringer (-) lucky charm
der Glücksstern (-e) lucky star
die Glückszahl (-en) lucky number
der Glückwunsch: herzlichen Glückwunsch! congratulations!
die Glut hot coals (*in the fire*)

der Glutqualm smoke from coals
GmbH = Gesellschaft mit begrenzter Haftung company with limited liability
die Gnade (-n) mercy, grace
gnadenlos merciless
gnädig merciful(ly), gracious(ly); **gnädige Frau** *polite form of address; antiquated, but still used in Austria*
das Goethehaus Goethe's birth house
das Gold gold
golden gold(en)
der Goldschmied (-e) goldsmith
das Golf golf; **Golf spielen** to play Golf (8)
der Golfplatz (⸚e) golf course
gönnen: jemandem etwas gönnen to grant someone something; **ich gönne ihm seinen Erfolg** I'm delighted that he's successful, I don't begrude him his success
sich gönnen to allow oneself (*something*)
der Gott (⸚er) God, god; **grüß Gott!** (*in southern Germany, Austria, and Switzerland*) hello!
gottlob thank God
grad/grade = gerade
das Grafengeschlecht (-er) aristocratic lineage
die Grafik (-en) graph, chart
grafisch graphic(ally)
die Grammatik (-en) grammar
das Gras (⸚er) grass
das Grasdach (⸚er) grass roof
grässlich hideous, horrible
die Grasspitze (-n) tip of grass
gratulieren to congratulate (17); **gratuliere!** congratulations! (5)
grau gray (2)
das Grauen horror
graugewaschen faded, discolored
grausam cruel(ly)
die Grazie grace
greifen, griff, gegriffen to grab; to grasp
der Greifvogel (⸚) bird of prey, raptor
die Grenze (-n) border, limit (17)

grenzen an (+ *acc.*) to border on (17)
der Grenzübergang (⸚e) border crossing (18)
grenzüberschreitend across the borders
der Grieche (-n *masc.*) / **die Griechin (-nen)** Greek (*person*) (18)
(das) Griechenland Greece (9)
griechisch (*adj.*) Greek
(das) Griechisch Greek (*language*)
die Grille (-n) cricket
grillen to grill (31)
das Grillfest (-e) barbecue
die Grippe (-n) cold, flu (6)
der Grips (*coll.*) sense
(das) Grönland Greenland
grob rough
groß (größer, größt-) big, tall (1)
großartig magnificent(ly)
(das) Großbritannien Great Britain (9)
die Größe (-n) size (21)
die Großeltern (*pl.*) grandparents (1/25)
der Größenwahnsinn megalomania
größenwahnsinnig megalomaniac(al)
der Großherzog (⸚e) / die Großherzogin (-nen) grand duke / grand duchess
das Großherzogtum (⸚er) grand duchy
die Großmutter (⸚) grandmother (1)
die Großstadt (⸚e) large city, metropolis (4)
das Großstadtleben big city life
die Großtante (-n) great aunt
die Großtat (-en) great achievement
der/die/das Größte (*decl. adj.*) the biggest, tallest, largest (one)
der Großvater (⸚) grandfather (1)
großzügig generous(ly)
grün green (2)
die Grünanlage (-n) park, recreation area
der Grund (⸚e) reason (18)

gründen to found (27)
das Grundgesetz Basic Law (*German constitution*)
die Grundlage (-n) foundation, basis (27)
der Grundsatz (-sätze) principle
die Grundschule (-n) elementary school (11)
die Gründung founding, setting up
die Grünfläche (-n) green area
grunzen to grunt
die Gruppe (-n) group
das Gruppenangebot (-e) group offer, discount
die Gruppenarbeit (-en) group work
die Gruppenberatung (-en) group counseling
gruppieren to group
die Gruppierung (-en) grouping
der Gruß (⸚e) greeting; **herzliche Grüße! liebe Grüße! schöne Grüße! viele Grüße!** best wishes!
grüßen to greet; **grüß Gott!** (*in southern Germany, Austria, and Switzerland*) hello!
gucken (*coll.*) to watch, to look (14); **guck mal!** watch!, look!
gültig valid
der Gummibär (-en *masc.*) gummi bear
der Gummischuh (-e) rubber boot
die Gunst (⸚e) favor, goodwill
günstig inexpensive, cheap
die Gurke (-n) cucumber (19)
der Gürtel (-) belt (7)
das Gut (⸚er) good, item, property, estate
gut (besser, best-) good, **alles Gute!** all the best!; **gute Besserung!** get well soon!; **gute Fahrt!** have a nice trip! (14); **guten Abend!** good evening!; **guten Morgen!** good morning! (1E); **guten Rutsch ins neue Jahr!** Happy New Year!; **guten Tag!** hello! (1E); **gute Reise!** have a nice trip!
das Gute goodness, the good; **etwas Gutes** something good

der Güterzug (⸚e) freight train
das Gütesiegel (-) stamp of quality
gutgelaunt cheerful, in a good mood
gutmütig good-natured(ly)
der Gymnasiallehrer (-) / **die
Gymnasiallehrerin** (-nen)
teacher at a **Gymnasium**
der Gymnasiast (-en *masc.*) / **die
Gymnasiastin** (-nen) student at a
Gymnasium (26)
das Gymnasium (Gymnasien)
college preparatory high school
(10/27)
die Gymnastik gymnastics

H

ha! ha!
das Haar (-e) hair (6)
das Haarnetz (-e) hair net
die Haarsträhne (-n) strand of hair
haben (hat), hatte, gehabt to
have (2); **ich hätte gern . . .** I'd
like . . . (15)
hacken to chop, to mince; to grind
das Hackfleisch ground meat
der Hafen (⸚) harbor
die Hafenstadt (⸚e) port, harbor city
hager gaunt, thin
der Hahn (⸚e) rooster
halb half; **eine halbe Stunde** half
an hour; **es ist halb sechs** it's
five-thirty
der Halbedelstein (-e) semi-
precious gem
die Halbinsel (-n) peninsula (9)
die Halbkugel (-n) hemisphere
die Hälfte (-n) half
hallo! hello!
hallöchen! hello!
der Hals (⸚e) neck, throat (6)
**der Halsbruch: Hals- und
Beinbruch!** break a leg! good
luck!
die Halsschmerzen (*pl.*) sore
throat (6)
das Halsweh sore throat
halt (*particle*) **dann müsst ihr halt
mit dem Bus fahren** in that case
you'll have to take the bus
halten (hält), hielt, gehalten to
hold (3E); to stop; **sich halten an**

(+ *acc.*) to keep to, stick to/with
(34); **halten für** to consider; to
regard (20); **halten von** to have
an opinion (3E); **was halten Sie
davon?** what do you think about
it?, what's your opinion?; **jemand
auf dem laufenden halten** to
keep someone informed
die Haltung (-en) attitude, opinion
der Hamburger (-) / **die
Hamburgerin** (-nen) person from
Hamburg
der Hamburger Dom festival in
Hamburg
die Hand (⸚e) hand (6)
die Handarbeit (-en) handicraft
der Handball handball
das Handbuch (⸚er) handbook,
reference work
der Handel trade (27)
handeln to act; **handeln von** to
deal with, be about (21)
die Handelsfirma (-firmen) trading
company
die Handelsstadt (⸚e) city of
commerce
das Handelsunternehmen (-)
commercial enterprise
das Händeschütteln handshake
(24)
der Händler (-) / **die Händlerin**
(-nen) trader, retailer, wholesaler
die Handschmerzen (*pl.*) pain in
the hand
die Handschrift (-en) handwriting;
manuscript
der Handschuh (-e) glove (21)
die Handtasche (-n) handbag,
pocketbook, purse
das Handtuch (⸚er) towel
das Handwerk (-e) craft, trade
der Hang inclination; interest
hängen to hang (up)
hängen, hing, gehangen to hang,
be in a hanging position
(das) Hannover Hanover
die Hanse Hanseatic League
die Hansekogge (-n) Hanseatic cog
(*type of ship*)
das Hanseschiff (-e) Hanseatic ship
die Hansestadt (⸚e) Hanseatic city

die Harmonie (-n) harmony
hart hard
hassen to hate
hässlich ugly (1)
hasten to hurry, hasten
haufenweise in heaps
häufig often, frequent(ly) (27)
das Haupt (⸚er) (*antiquated*) head
die Hauptattraktion (-en) main
attraction
der Hauptautor (-en) main author
der Hauptbahnhof (⸚e) main train
station
das Hauptfach (⸚er) major subject
(11/3E)
das Hauptgebäude (-) main
building
das Hauptgericht (-e) entree (15)
das Haupthaar hair on one's head
die Hauptinformation (-en) main
information
das Hauptinteresse (-n) main
interest
die Hauptperson (-en) main
character
die Hauptsache (-n) the main
thing, mainly
hauptsächlich mainly, primarily
(31)
der Hauptschulabschluss (⸚e) *a
general education degree*
die Hauptschule (-n) general
education high school (11)
der Hauptsitz (-e) headquarters
die Hauptstadt (⸚e) capital (17)
das Hauptthema (-themen) main
topic
der Haupttyp (-en) the main kind,
type
das Haus (⸚er) house (4); **nach
Haus(e) gehen** to go home; **zu
Haus(e)** at home
die Hausarbeit (-en) housework,
household chore
die Hausaufgabe (-n) homework
(10)
der Hausbewohner (-) / **die
Hausbewohnerin** (-nen) resident
das Häuschen (-) little house
der Häuserblock (⸚e) block of
houses

die Hausfrau (-en) housewife
der Haushalt (-e) household; **den Haushalt machen** to take care of the household (23/25)
das Haushaltsgerät (-e) household appliance (20)
der Haushaltshelfer (-) / die Haushaltshelferin (-nen) household help
häuslich domestic
der Hausmann (¨er) househusband (23)
das Hausmärchen (-) folk tale
der Hausmeister (-) / die Hausmeisterin (-nen) maintenance person, janitor
die Hausmeisterstelle (-n) position as building maintenance person
der Hausmüll household waste
die Hausnummer (-n) house number
das Haustier (-e) pet
die Haustür (-en) front door
die Haut skin
die Hautfarbe (-n) color of skin
heben, hob, gehoben to lift
das Heft (-e) notebook (E)
heften to clip
heftig hard, intense, strong(ly)
die Heide (-n) heath (9)
die Heidelandschaft (-en) heath landscape
heil whole, healed, in order
das Heilbad (¨er) health spa
heilen to heal
heilig holy; **heilig sprechen (spricht), sprach, gesprochen** to canonize
heilklimatisch with a healthy climate
die Heilung (-en) healing, curing, cure
das Heilmittel (-) remedy (33)
das Heilverfahren (-) treatment, cure
das Heim (-e) home; **trautes Heim** home sweet home
die Heimat (-en) home, sense of belonging
das Heimatgefühl (-e) sense of home

der Heimathafen (¨) home port
das Heimatland (¨er) home country
heimatlich familiar
das Heimatmuseum (-museen) local history museum
die Heimatstadt (¨e) hometown
heimlich secret(ly) (33)
die Heimmannschaft (-en) home team
das Heimweh homesickness
die Heirat (-en) marriage
heiraten to marry (12/25)
der Heiratsantrag (¨e) marriage proposal
heiß hot (5)
heißen, hieß, geheißen to be called (1)
heiter clear (*weather*) (5)
die Heiterkeit (-en) cheerfulness
die Hektik hectic, rush
der Held (-en *masc.*) / die Heldin (-nen) hero, heroine
die Heldentat (-en) heroic deed, feat
helfen (hilft), half, geholfen to help (13)
hell light, bright (2)
hellblau light blue
hellhörig werden to prick up one's ears, pay close attention
das Hemd (-en) shirt (7)
die Hemisphäre (-n) hemisphere
die Hemmung (-en) inhibition
herab downwards
herabfliegen (fliegt herab), flog herab, ist herabgeflogen to fly down
heranziehen (zieht heran), zog heran, herangezogen to involve, consult with
herausfiltern (filtert heraus) to filter out; (*fig.*) to sift out
herausfinden (findet heraus), fand heraus, herausgefunden to find out
die Herausforderung (-en) challenge; provocation
herausgeben (gibt heraus), gab heraus, herausgegeben to publish

der Herausgeber (-) / die Herausgeberin (-nen) publisher
herausragend outstanding
herb sharp, tangy, bitter
herbei hither, here
der Herbst fall, autumn (5); **im Herbst** in the fall
der Herd (-e) stove, hearth (3)
die Herde (-n) herd, flock
herein! come in!
hereinbrechen (bricht herein), brach herein, ist hereingebrochen to break out
hereinrollen (rollt herein) to roll in
hergeben (gibt her), gab her, hergegeben to give away
herkommen (kommt her), kam her, ist hergekommen to come here
die Herkunft (¨e) origin, background
der Herr (-n *masc.*, -en) gentleman; Mr.
herrlich wonderful(ly) (32)
die Herrlichkeit magnificence
herrschen to rule, govern
der Herrscher (-) / die Herrscherin (-nen) ruler, sovereign
herstellen (stellt her) to manufacture; to produce (29)
herum around; **anders herum** the other way around; **um (Köln) herum** around (Cologne)
herumfahren (fährt herum), fuhr herum, ist herumgefahren to drive around
herumliegen, lag herum, herumgelegen to lie around
sich herumprügeln (prügelt herum) to get into fights
herumschaukeln (schaukelt herum) to jiggle around
herunterkurbeln: das Fenster herunterkurbeln (kurbelt herunter) to roll down the window
hervor forth
hervorragend excellent
hervortreten (tritt hervor), trat hervor, ist hervorgetreten to step forward, appear

R-45

das Herz (-en *gen.,* **-en** *pl.***)** heart; **am Herzen liegen** to be very dear; **zu Herzen gehen** to touch the heart

herzaubern (zaubert her) to conjure forth

der Herzinfarkt (-e) heart attack

herzlich warm, kind; **herzliche Grüße!** best wishes!; **herzlichen Glückwunsch!** congratulations!; **herzlichen Glückwunsch zum Geburtstag!** happy birthday! (5); **herzlich Willkommen** welcome (5)

(das) Hessen Hesse (17)

hetzen to chase, race

das Heu hay

die Heuschrecke (-n) grasshopper

heute today (5)

heutig today's (28)

heutzutage these days, nowadays

die Hexe (-n) witch (12)

hier here; **ist hier noch frei?** is this seat taken?

die Hilfe help, assistance; **mit Hilfe** (+ *gen.*) with the help of

das Hilfeangebot (-e) help offer

hilflos helpless

hilfsbereit willing to help, helpful

das Hilfsverb (-en) auxiliary verb

der Himmel sky, heaven (9)

himmlisch heavenly

hin und her back and forth

die Hin- und Rückfahrt (-en) round-trip

hin und zurück (*adv.*) round trip (24)

hinab (*away from speaker*) down

hinabsteigen (steigt hinab), stieg hinab, ist hinabgestiegen (*away from speaker*) to climb down

hinaus out, outside (*away from the speaker*)

hinauslaufen (läuft hinaus), lief hinaus, ist hinausgelaufen to run out(side) (*away from the speaker*)

hinauswollen auf (will hinaus) to imply (30)

hindern to hinder

hindurch through

hineinsehen (sieht hinein), sah hinein, hineingesehen to look in(side) (*away from the speaker*)

hinfahren (fährt hin), fuhr hin, ist hingefahren to go there, drive there

hinkommen (kommt hin), kam hin, ist hingekommen to get there

hinlegen (legt hin) to put down; **sich hinlegen** to lie down (16)

hinlehnen (lehnt hin) to lean against

hinrichten (richtet hin) to execute

hinschmeißen (schmeißt hin), schmiss hin, hingeschmissen to fling down; to quit

sich hinsetzen (setzt hin) to take a seat, sit down

hinstellen (stellt hin) to put

hinten in the back

hinter (+ *acc./dat.*) behind

die Hinterbeine (*pl.*) hind legs

der Hintergrund (¨e) background (30)

das Hinterhaus *living quarters at the back of or behind a house and accessible only through a courtyard*

hinterlassen (hinterlässt), hinterließ, hinterlassen to leave (*something*) behind

der Hinweis (-e) tip; piece of advice

der Hippie (-s) hippie

historisch historical(ly)

die Hitparade hit parade

die Hitze heat

das Hobby (-s) hobby (31)

der Hobbykoch (¨e) hobby chef

hoch (höher, höchst-) high; **bis ins hohe Alter** to old age; **Kopf hoch!** keep your chin up!

die Hochachtung deep respect, admiration

der Hochbahnbogen (¨) bridge construction

das Hochdeutsch standard German, High German

hochgehen (geht hoch), ging hoch, ist hochgegangen to go up

die Hochgratbahn (-en) type of ski lift

das Hochhaus (¨er) skyscraper (4)

hochklettern (klettert hoch) to climb up

hochschlagen (schlägt hoch), schlug hoch, hochgeschlagen to flip up, fold up

der Hochschulabschluss (¨e) university degree

die Hochschule (-n) college, institution of higher education (11)

der Hochschüler (-) / die Hochschülerin (-nen) student

die Hochschulreife (-n) exam for admission to higher education institutions

das Hochschulstudium (-studien) program at an institution of higher education

das Hochschulwissen university knowledge

der Hochspannungsmast (-en) electrical pole

der/die/das Höchste (*decl. adj.*) highest (one)

hochtreiben (treibt hoch), trieb hoch, hochgetrieben to drive up, raise

die Hochzeit (-en) wedding

der Hochzeitsgast (¨e) wedding guest

die Hochzeitsliste (-n) gift registry

der Hochzeitsmarsch (¨e) wedding march

die Hochzeitsreise (-n) honeymoon (trip)

der Hochzeitsservice wedding service

der Hof (¨e) yard; courtyard (31)

hoffen to hope

hoffentlich hopefully

die Hoffnung (-en) hope

hoffnungslos hopeless

hoffnungsvoll hopeful

höfisch courtly

höflich polite(ly), courteous(ly)

die Höflichkeit (-en) courtesy

hoh- high; **hohe Cholesterinwerte** high cholesterol level; **bis ins hohe Alter** into old age
die Höhenlage (-n) elevation
der Höhepunkt (-e) high point, climax (36)
hohl hollow
höhlen to hollow out
holen to get, fetch
der Holocaust holocaust
das Holz (¨er) wood
die Holzbrücke (-n) wooden bridge
die Homöopathie homeopathic medicine
hören to hear (2)
hörenswert worth hearing
der Hörer (-) telephone receiver
der Hörer (-) / die Hörerin (-nen) listener
der Horizont (-e) horizon
der Hörsaal (-säle) auditorium, lecture hall (19)
der Hörtext (-e) listening comprehension text
die Hose (-n) pants, trousers (7)
der Hosenschlitz (-e) fly (*in a pair of pants*)
die Hosentasche (-n) pocket
das Hotel (-s) hotel (8)
die Hotelbar (-s) hotel bar
der Hotelfachmann (¨er) / die Hotelfachfrau (-en) hotel manager
das Hotelfenster (-) hotel window
der Hotelwechsel (-) change of hotel
das Hotelzimmer (-) hotel room
Hrsg. = Herausgeber
hübsch pretty, good-looking
der Hubschrauber (-) helicopter
der Huf (-e) hoof
der Hügel (-) hill (9)
die Hügellandschaft (-en) hills, hilly landscape
die Hummel (-n) bumblebee
der Hummer (-) lobster (15)
der Humor humor (36)
humorvoll humorous(ly)
der Hund (-e) dog
das Hundefutter dog food
hundemüde dead tired

hundert one hundred (1E)
hundertjährig hundred-year-old
hundertprozentig one hundred percent
der Hunger hunger (20); **hast du Hunger?** are you hungry?
die Hungersnot (¨e) famine
hungrig hungry
husten to cough (6)
der Husten (-) cough
der Hut (¨e) hat (7)
das Hütchen (-) little hat
die Hütte (-n) cabin
die Hymne (-n) hymn

I

der ICE = Intercityexpresszug high speed train
ich I (1)
ideal ideal(ly)
das Ideal (-e) ideal (26)
die Idee (-n) idea (10)
(sich) identifizieren (mit) to identify (with)
die Identität (-en) identity (26)
die Identitätskrise (-n) identity crisis
der Idiot (-en *masc.***) / die Idiotin (-nen)** idiot
idyllisch idyllic, picturesque
ihm (*dat.*) to him
ihn (*acc.*) him
Ihnen (*dat.*) you, to you (*form.*)
Ihr (*nom./gen. pl.*) you, your
ihr you; (*gen.*) their; **ihr** (*gen./dat.*) her, to her
ihrerseits on her part, herself; on their part, themselves
illegal illegal(ly)
die Illustration (-en) illustration
die Illustrierte (-n) magazine
imaginär imaginary (36)
der Imbiss (-e) snack, fast food
der Imbissstand (¨e) snack stand (15)
die Imbissstube (-n) hot dog stand
immer always (3E)
der Imperativ (-e) imperative
das Imperfekt imperfect
impliziert implied
imponieren to impress

imposant impressive
die Impression (-en) impression
in (+ *acc./dat.*) in, into; **in der Nähe** in the vicinity (17)
inbrünstig fervent, ardent
indem (*subord. conj.*) in that, by
der Inder (-) / die Inderin (-nen) person from India (18)
indirekt indirect(ly)
individuell individual(ly)
die Industrialisierung industrialization (31)
die Industrie (-n) industry
das Industrieland (¨er) industrial country
die Industrieanlage (-n) industrial facility
die Industriegesellschaft (-en) industrial society
das Industrielabor (-s) industrial lab
industriell industrial(ly)
der Industrielle(r) (*decl. adj.*) industrialist
ineinander in/with each other
die Infektion (-en) infection
der Infinitiv (-e) infinitive
die Inflation (-en) inflation
die Info (-s) info
infolge (+ *gen.*) due to
die Informatik computer science (11)
der Informatiker (-) / die Informatikerin (-nen) computer programmer (13)
die Information (-en) information
das Informationsamt (¨er) information office (22)
der Informationsbroker (-) information broker
informieren to inform; **sich informieren** to get information
die Infrastruktur (-en) infrastructure
der Ingenieur (-e) / die Ingenieurin (-nen) engineer (13)
die Ingenieurswissenschaften mechanical engineering (*as a subject*)
der Inhalt (-e) content
die Initiative (-n) initiative

inklusive including, included
innen within, inside
der Innenarchitekt (-en *masc.***) /
die Innenarchitektin (-nen)**
interior designer
die Innenarchitektur interior
design
die Inneneinrichtung (-en) interior
decoration
die Innenstadt (ˮe) inner city,
downtown area
die Innentemperatur (-en) inside
temperature
die Innentür (-en) interior door
das Innere (*decl. adj.*) interior,
inside
innerhalb (+ *gen.*) within, inside
innovativ innovative
insbesondere in particular
die Insel (-n) island (9)
insgesamt altogether
inspirieren to inspire
das Institut (-e) institute
die Institution (-en) institution
das Instrument (-e) instrument,
device
inszenieren to stage (36)
intakt intact
die Integration (-en) integration
integrieren to integrate
intellektuell intellectual(ly) (36)
intelligent intelligent(ly)
die Intelligenz intelligence
intensiv intensive(ly)
die Interaktion (-en) interaction
der Intercity (*also:* **InterCity**) *train
between major cities*
der Intercityexpresszug *high-speed
train between major cities*
interessant interesting (1)
das Interesse (-n) interest (14);
Interesse haben an (+ *dat.*) to be
interested in, to have interest in
interessieren to interest; **sich
interessieren für** to be interested
in (13/31)
das Internat (-e) boarding school
international international(ly)
das Internet Internet
der Internetanschluss connection
to the Internet

die Interpretation (-en)
interpretation
interpretieren to interpret
das Interview (-s) interview
interviewen to interview
intuitiv intuitive(ly)
investieren to invest
die Investition (-en) investment
inwiefern to what extent, in what
way
inzwischen in the meantime (34)
irgendein(e) some, any
irgendetwas something, anything
irgendwann sometime
irgendwas = irgendetwas
irgendwie somehow, some way
irgendwo somewhere, anywhere
(das) Irland Ireland (9)
die Ironie (-n) irony
ironisch ironic; ironically
ironisieren to treat ironically
irre (*coll.*) crazy; wild (32)
der Irrtum (ˮer) mistake, error
irrtümlich by mistake; in error
der Islam Islam
(das) Island Iceland (9)
(das) Italien Italy (9)
**der Italiener (-) / die Italienerin
(-nen)** Italian (*person*) (18)
italienisch (*adj.*) Italian
der Italienurlaub (-e) vacation in
Italy

J

ja yes; **ja, gern!** yes, please!;
(*particle*) **ist ja echt super**
that's really great; **wir wissen
ja, wie schwer du arbeitest** we
do know, after all, how hard you
work
die Jacke (-n) jacket (7)
das Jackett (-s) jacket (7)
die Jagd (-en) hunt
der Jagdhund (-e) hunting dog
jagen to hunt
der Jäger (-) / die Jägerin (-nen)
hunter
das Jahr (-e) year; **im kommenden
Jahr** next year; **im Jahr(e) 1750**
in 1750; **jedes Jahr** every year;
mit sechs Jahren when (s)he was

six years old; **vor einem Jahr** a
year ago
die Jahreszeit (-en) season (5)
das Jahrhundert (-e) century
(27); **im achtzehnten
Jahrhundert** in the eighteenth
century
die Jahrhundertwende turn of the
century
-jährig: ein 16-jähriger Schüler a
sixteen-year old student (11)
jährlich annual(ly)
der Jahrmarkt (-märkte) fair
das Jahrzehnt (-e) decade (26)
(das) Jamaika Jamaica
der Jammerlaut (-e) wailing
jammern to wail, lament
der Januar January (5)
jauchzen to rejoice, exult
die Jazzmusik jazz
je ever
die Jeans (-) jeans (7)
die Jeanshose (-n) jeans
jeder, jede, jedes each, every, any;
auf jeden Fall in any case
jedenfalls in any case (30)
jedermann everyone
jedesmal every time
jedoch however
jeglicher, jegliche, jegliches any
jemals ever
jemand someone, anyone
jener, jene, jenes that, that one
jenseits on the other side of, beyond
jetzig current, present
jetzt now; **erst jetzt** not until now
jeweilig respective
jeweils respectively; for each (32)
der Job (-s) job
jobben to have a temporary job
das Jobinterview (-s) job interview
joggen to jog (8)
der Jogginganzug (ˮe) jogging
suit (7)
der Jogurt (-s) yogurt
**der Jongleur (-e) / die Jongleurin
(-nen)** juggler
der Journalismus journalism
der Journalist (-en *masc.***) / die
Journalistin (-nen)** journalist
(13)

der Jubel jubilation, cheering
das Jubiläum (Jubiläen) anniversary
der Jude (-n *masc.***) / die Jüdin (-nen)** Jew
jüdisch Jewish
die Jugend (-en) youth (25)
die Jugendbewegung (-en) youth movement
die Jugendforschung (-en) youth research
das Jugendfreizeitheim (-e) youth retreat house
der Jugendfreund (-e) / die Jugendfreundin (-nen) childhood friend
die Jugendgruppe (-n) youth group
die Jugendherberge (-n) youth hostel (8)
jugendlich youthful
der/die Jugendliche (*decl. adj.***)** young person, teenager (26)
das Jugendmagazin (-e) youth magazine
das Jugendmuseum (-museen) youth museum
die Jugendpolitik youth politics
das Jugendporträt (-s) youth portraits
der Jugendreiseveranstalter (-) / die Jugendreiseveranstalterin (-nen) youth travel organizer
die Jugendstudie (-n) youth study
das Jugendtheater (-) youth theater
das Jugendzentrum (-zentren) youth social organization
(das) Jugoslawien Yugoslavia
der Juli July (5)
jung (jünger, jüngst-) young (1)
der Junge (-n *masc.***)** boy
die Jungfrau Virgo
der Jüngling (*antiquated***)** young man
die Jungsozialisten Young Socialist (*youth organization of the German Social Democratic Party*)
der Juni June (5)
der Junker (-) squire
Jura law (studies) (28)

der Juwelier (-e) / die Juwelierin (-nen) jeweler
das Juweliergeschäft (-e) jewelry store (22)

K

das Kabarett (-s) cabaret
das Kabel (-) cable, wire, cord
das Kabelfernsehen cable television/TV
die Kachel (-n) tile
der Kachelofen (¨) tiled stove
der Kaffee (-s) coffee (16); **Kaffee trinken** to drink coffee (2)
die Kaffeemaschine (-n) coffeemaker
die Kaffeemühle (-n) coffee grinder
der Kaffeetopf (¨e) coffeepot
das Kaffeetrinken coffee drinking
das Kaffeewasser water for coffee
die Kahnfahrt (-en) boat ride
der Kaiser (-) / die Kaiserin (-nen) emperor/empress
die Kaiserzeit imperial era
das Kajak (-s) kayak
der Kakao cocoa
das Kalbfleisch veal
der Kalender (-) calendar
(das) Kalifornien California
die Kalkulation (-en) calculation
kalt (kälter, kältest-) cold (5)
die Kamera (-s) camera
der Kamerad (-en *masc.***)** fellow soldier, comrade
(das) Kamerun Cameroon
der Kamillentee (-s) chamomile tea
der Kamin (-e) chimney
das Kaminfeuer (-) fire in the fireplace
sich kämmen to comb
der Kampf (¨e) fight, struggle, combat
kämpfen to struggle; to fight (30)
der Kampfgenosse (-n *masc.***) / die Kampfgenossin (-nen)** fellow soldier
der Kampfhund (-e) attack dog
(das) Kanada Canada
der Kanadier (-) / die Kanadierin (-nen) Canadian (*person*) (18)

kanadisch Canadian
die Kanalisation sewer system
der Kandidat (-en *masc.***) / die Kandidatin (-nen)** candidate
das Kaninchen (-) rabbit
der Kanton (-e) canton
der Kanzler (-) / die Kanzlerin (-nen) chancellor
das Kapital capital
der Kapitän (-e) captain (14)
das Kapitel (-) chapter
kaputt broken, out of order
kaputtmachen (macht kaputt) to break
die Kardinalzahl (-en) cardinal number
der Karfreitag Good Friday
die Karibik Caribbean
kariert checkered (21)
der Karneval carnival (5), Mardi Gras (5)
das Karnevalsfest (-e) traditional festival (related to Mardi Gras)
die Karotte (-n) carrot (19)
die Karriere (-n) career (13)
die Karrierechance (-n) career opportunity
die Karte (-n) card; ticket; menu; map; **Karten spielen** to play cards (2)
der Kartendienst (-e) map service
das Kartenhaus (¨er) house made out of cards
die Kartoffel (-n) potato (15)
die Kartoffelschale (-n) potato skin
die Kartoffelsuppe (-n) potato soup
der Käse cheese (16)
der Käsekuchen (-) cheesecake (15)
das Kasino (-s) casino
die Kasse (-n) cashier, cash register
der Kassierer (-) / die Kassiererin (-nen) cashier
der Kasten (¨) box
der Kasus case (*grammatical*)
die Kasusform (-en) case ending
der Katalog (-e) catalogue
die Kategorie (-n) category
der Kater (-) tomcat
das Katerleben (-) cat's life

der **Katheder** (-) teacher's desk; lectern

katholisch (*adj.*) Catholic

das **Kätzchen** (-) little cat, kitten

die **Katze** (-n) cat

das **Katzenfutter** cat food

die **Katzentoilette** (-n) cat litter box

kauen to chew

kaufen to buy, purchase

das **Kaufhaus** (-̈er) department store (16)

der **Kaufmann** (-leute) / die **Kauffrau** (-en) salesperson, businessperson, manager (13)

kaum hardly; barely

keeken (*dialect*) to look

die **Kegelbahn** (-en) bowling alley

der **Kegler** (-) / die **Keglerin** (-nen) bowler

die **Kehle** (-n) throat

kein no, not a, not any (3)

kein(e)s none

keinesfalls under no circumstances

keineswegs! by no means!

der **Keller** (-) cellar, basement

der **Kellner** (-) / die **Kellnerin** (-nen) waitperson (15)

kennen, kannte, gekannt to know, be acquainted with (8)

kennen lernen (lernt kennen) to get to know

die **Kenntnis** (-se) knowledge (14/29)

das **Kennzeichen** (-) logo, symbol, registration number

der **Kerl** (-e) fellow, guy

das **Kerlchen** (-) little fellow

die **Kerze** (-n) candle (17)

die **Kette** (-n) chain

das **Kettenglied** (-er) link in a chain

die **Kettenreaktion** (-en) chain reaction

kichern to giggle

kicken to kick

die **Kids** (*pl.*) kids

die **Kieler Woche** sailing event in Kiel

der **Kilometer** (-) kilometer

kilometerlang miles long

das **Kind** (-er) child; **als Kind** as a child

das **Kindchen** (-) little child

der **Kinderbetreuer** (-) / die **Kinderbetreuerin** (-nen) child-care worker

die **Kindererziehung** child care, upbringing

der **Kindergarten** (-̈) kindergarten (11)

das **Kindergeld** child benefit

die **Kinderkrippe** (-n) daycare center (30)

kinderreich with many children

die **Kindersachen** (*pl.*) children's clothes and toys

das **Kinder(schlaf)zimmer** (-) child's room (3)

das **Kinderspiel** (-e) child's game

das **Kindertheater** (-) children's theater

der **Kinderwagen** (-) stroller

die **Kindheit** (-en) childhood

das **Kinn** (-e) chin (6)

das **Kino** (-s) movie theater (4); **ins Kino gehen** to go see a movie (2)

der **Kinofilm** (-e) movie

der **Kiosk** (-s) kiosk

die **Kirche** (-n) church (5)

die **Kirchenglocke** (-n) church bell

die **Kirsche** (-n) cherry

die **Kirschtorte** (-n) cherry cake

das **Kirschwasser** (-) cherry liquor

das **Kissen** (-) pillow

das **Kistenbrett** (-er) cheap boards (*from boxes*)

der **Kitsch** junk

klagen to complain

kläglich pitiful, wretched, miserable

Klammern (*pl.*) parentheses

die **Klamotten** (*pl.*) (*slang*) clothes (21)

die **Klangfarbe** (-n) tone color

klappen to work out

das **Klappmesser** (-) flick knife

klar clear; **alles klar?** everything clear?

die **Klarinette** (-n) clarinet

die **Klärung** (-en) clarification

klasse! great!; **echt klasse!** really great! (10)

die **Klasse** (-n) class, grade (10)

die **Klassenarbeit** (-en) exam

der **Klassenkamerad** (-en *masc.*) / die **Klassenkameradin** (-nen) classmate

der **Klassenlehrer** (-) / die **Klassenlehrerin** (-nen) homeroom teacher

das **Klassenprofil** (-e) class profile

die **Klassenumfrage** (-n) class survey

das **Klassenzimmer** (-) classroom (10)

die **Klassik** classicism

klassisch classical, classic

klauen (*coll.*) to steal

die **Klausur** (-en) exam (10)

das **Klavier** (-e) piano (3)

der **Klavierlehrer** (-) / die **Klavierlehrerin** (-nen) piano instructor

kleben to stick

die **Kleckergefahr** (*silly*) danger of spilling

kleckern to spill

der **Klee** clover

das **Kleeblatt** (-̈er) clover leaf

das **Kleid** (-er) dress (7)

der **Kleiderschrank** (-̈e) closet, dresser

der **Kleiderstil** (-e) dress style

die **Kleidung** clothes (21)

das **Kleidungsstück** (-e) piece of clothing (7)

klein small, little (1)

die **Kleinanzeige** (-n) classified ad (*in a paper*) (21)

die **Kleinfamilie** (-n) small family

der **Kleingarten** (-̈) small garden

das **Kleingeld** (small) change

die **Kleingruppe** (-n) small group

die **Kleinigkeit** (-en) small thing, trivial matter

die **Kleinstadt** (-̈e) small town (4)

klettern to climb (8/32)

die **Klettertour** (-en) mountain climbing tour

die **Kletterwand** (-̈e) climbing wall

klicken to klick

das **Klima** climate

der Klimawechsel (-) change of climate
klingeln to ring (23)
klingen to sound
das Klinglein (-) little bell
die Klinik (Kliniken) clinic, infirmary, hospital
das Klinikum clinical internship
klirrend clinking
klopfen to knock, rap (19); to pat
die Klosterpforte (-n) gate to the monastery
der Klub (-s) club
klug (klüger, klügst-) smart
km = der Kilometer
knabbern to nibble
der Knabe (-n *masc.***)** boy
das Knabengesicht (-er) boy's face
das Knabenpensionat (-e) boarding school for boys
knapp short; tight; barely, shy of
die Kneipe (-n) pub (15)
kneten to knead
das Knie (-) knee
das Kniegelenk (-e) knee joint
knistern to crackle, rustle
der Knoblauch garlic (15)
der Knochen (-) bone
der Knödel (-) dumpling
Knopfdruck: per Knopfdruck by pushing a button
knusprig crunchy
der Koch (¨e) / die Köchin (-nen) chef, cook
kochen to cook (2)
die Kochkunst (¨e) art of cooking, cooking skills
der Kochtopf (¨e) pot
der Koffer (-) suitcase
das Kofferpacken packing suitcases
der Kofferraum (¨e) trunk of a car
die Kogge (-n) cog (*type of ship*)
die Kohle (-n) coal
das Kohlekraftwerk (-e) coal power plant
der Kollege (-n *masc.***) / die Kollegin (-nen)** colleague (13)
das Kollegheft (-e) booklet
das Kollegium (-ien) faculty

(das) Köln Cologne; **der Kölner Dom** cathedral in Cologne
(das) Kolumbien Colombia
die Kolumne (-n) column
der Kolumnist (-en *masc.***) / die Kolumnistin (-nen)** columnist
die Kombination (-en) combination
kombinieren to combine
der Komiker (-) / die Komikerin (-nen) comedian
komisch funny, comical, strange (10)
kommen, kam, ist gekommen to come (2)
kommend coming, next; **im kommenden Jahr** in the coming year, next year
der Kommentar (-e) comment; **kein Kommentar!** no comment!
kommentieren to comment
kommerziell commercial(ly)
der Kommilitone (-n *masc.***) / die Kommilitonin (-nen)** classmate (28)
die Kommode (-n) dresser, chest of drawers (3)
die Kommodenschublade (-n) drawer in a chest
kommunal communal, public
die Kommunikation (-nen) communication
die Kommunikationswissen-schaften (*pl.*) mass communication (*as a subject*)
kommunikativ communicative
kommunizieren to communicate
die Komödie (-n) comedy (36)
der Komparativ (-e) comparative
kompetent competent(ly)
komplett complete, whole
die Komplikation (-en) complication
das Kompliment (-e) compliment
kompliziert (*adj.*) complicated
komponieren to compose (36)
der Komponist (-en *masc.***) / die Komponistin (-nen)** composer (36)
die Komposition (-en) composition
der Komposthaufen (-) compost heap (35)

kompostieren to compost (20)
der Kompromiss (-e) compromise
die Konditorei (-en) pastry shop, bakery (16)
die Konfitüre (-n) preserves
der Konflikt (-e) conflict
konfrontieren to confront
der König (-e) / die Königin (-nen) king/queen (12)
das Königspaar (-e) the royal couple
der Königssohn (¨e) prince
die Königstochter (¨) princess
die Konjugation (-en) conjugation
konjugieren to conjugate
die Konjunktion (-en) conjunction
der Konjunktiv subjunctive
konkret concrete
die Konkurrenz competition
konkurrieren to compete
können (kann), konnte, gekonnt to be able to
die Konsequenz (-en) consequence (10)
konservativ conservative(ly)
die Konstruktion (-en) construction
das Konsulat (-e) consulate
konsultieren to consult
der Konsum consumption
das Konsumgut (¨er) consumer item
konsumieren to consume
der Kontakt (-e) contact
kontaktbereit personable, sociable
kontaktieren to contact
der Kontext (-e) context
kontra against; **pro und kontra** pro and con, for and against
der Kontrast (-e) contrast
das Kontrastprogramm (-e) side program, alternative program
kontrollieren to control
kontrovers controversial
die Konversation (-en) conversation
das Konzentrationslager (-) concentration camp
die Konzentrationsschwäche (-n) attention deficit
sich konzentrieren to concentrate

konzentriert (*adj.*) concentrated

das Konzept (-e) concept

das Konzert (-e) concert; ins Konzert gehen to go to a concert (2)

die Kooperative (-n) cooperative

koordinieren to coordinate

der Kopf (ˆe) head (6)

der Kopfhörer (-) headphones

das Kopfkissen (-) pillow (3)

das Kopfnicken nodding

der Kopfsalat (-e) lettuce

die Kopfschmerzen (*pl.*) headache

kopfschüttelnd shaking one's head; der Fremde setzte sich kopfschüttelnd the foreigner sat down shaking his head

das Kopftuch (ˆer) scarf, head cover

das Kopfweh headache

die Kopie (-n) copy

kopieren to copy

das Kopiergerät (-e) copy machine

der Korb (ˆe) basket

die Kordhose (-n) corduroy pants

der Koreakrieg Korean War

das Korn (ˆer) grain

der Körper (-) body (6)

körperlich physical(ly)

die Körperpflege personal hygiene (33)

der Körperteil (-e) body part (6)

die Körpertemperatur (-en) body temperature

korrekt correct(ly)

die Korrespondenz (-en) correspondence

korrespondieren to correspond

korrigieren to correct

kosmopolit cosmopolitan

der Kosmos cosmos

die Kost diet, board

kostbar precious; valuable

kosten to cost

kostenfrei free of charge

köstlich delicious

das Kostüm (-e) costume (5); woman's suit (7)

kotzen (*vulgar*) to vomit

die Krabbe (-n) shrimp

der Krabbencocktail (-s) shrimp cocktail (15)

der Krach noise, racket; mit Ach und Krach (*formulaic*) barely

die Kraft (ˆe) power, strength

kräftig powerful(ly)

der Kragen (ˆ) collar

krähen to crow

die Kralle (-n) claw

krank sick, ill (1)

der Krankenbesuch (-e) visit with a sick person

das Krankenhaus (ˆer) hospital (6/33)

die Krankenkasse (-n) wellness fund

der Krankenpfleger (-) / die Krankenpflegerin (-nen) nurse (6)

die Krankenschwester (-n) nurse (*female*)

die Krankenversicherung (-en) health insurance

der Krankenwagen (-) ambulance (6)

das Krankenzimmer (-) hospital room

die Krankheit (-en) illness, disease (20)

das Krankheitssymptom (-e) symptom of a disease

kratzen to scratch

das Kraut (ˆer) herb

der Kräutertee (-s) herbal tea

die Krawatte (-n) tie (7)

kreativ creative(ly)

die Kreativität creativity

das Krebsforschungszentrum (-zentren) cancer research center

die Kreide chalk (1E)

die Kreidefelsen (*pl.*) chalk cliffs

der Kreis (-e) circle (28)

der Kreislauf circulation

die Kreuzfahrt (-en) cruise

das Kreuzfahrtschiff (-e) cruise ship

die Kreuzung (-en) intersection (22)

kriechen, kroch, ist gekrochen to creep

der Krieg (-e) war (20)

kriegen (*coll.*) to get (20)

das Kriegsende (-n) end of the war

der Kriegsverbrecher (-) war criminal

der Krimi (-s) detective novel or film

der/die Kriminelle (*decl. adj.*) criminal

die Krimiserie (-n) detective story (*on television*)

der Kringel (-) ring

kringelig crinkly, frizzy; sich kringelig lachen to laugh oneself silly

die Krippe (-n) day care center

die Krise (-n) crisis

die Kritik (-en) criticism

der Kritiker (-) / die Kritikerin (-nen) critic

kritisch critical(ly) (29)

kritisieren to criticize

(das) Kroatien Croatia

kroatisch Croatian

die Krone (-n) crown

krumm crooked, bent

(das) Kuba Cuba

die Küche (-n) kitchen (3); cuisine

der Kuchen (-) cake (16)

die Küchenerfindung (-en) kitchen invention

die Küchenfliese (-n) kitchen tile

der Küchenschrank (ˆe) kitchen cabinet

der Küchentisch (-e) kitchen table

kucken (*coll.*) to look

die Kugel (-n) ball

der Kugelschreiber (-) ballpoint pen (1E)

kühl cool (5)

das Kühlhaus (ˆer) walk-in refrigerator

der Kühlschrank (ˆe) refrigerator (3)

kulinarisch culinary

die Kultur (-en) culture (36)

der Kulturbesitz (-e) cultural property

der Kulturbeutel (-) toilet bag

kulturell cultural(ly) (36)

die Kulturgeschichte cultural history

die Kulturgruppe (-n) cultural group

die Kulturhauptstadt (⁻e) cultural capital
das Kulturprojekt (-e) cultural project
der Kulturspiegel (-) culture mirror
die Kulturstadt (⁻e) cultural metropolis
die Kultusbehörde (-n) ministry for culture and education
sich kümmern um to concern oneself with (30)
die Kümmernis (-se) trouble, worry
der Kumpel (-) buddy, friend
der Kunde (-n *masc.*) / die Kundin (-nen) customer (26)
der Kundenberater (-) / die Kundenberaterin (-nen) customer service representative
der Kundendienst (-e) customer service
künftig future (29)
die Kunst (⁻e) art (11/36)
die Kunstausstellung (-en) art exhibit, art show
das Kunstbild (-er) painting
der Kunsthistoriker (-) / die Kunsthistorikerin (-nen) art historian
die Kunsthochschule (-n) art academy
der Künstler (-) / die Künstlerin (-nen) artist (13/36)
künstlerisch artistic(ally) (36)
die Künstlervereinigung (-en) art association
das Künstlerviertel (-) artists' quarter (*in a city*)
künstlich artificial(ly)
der Kunstmarkt (⁻e) art exhibition, auction
das Kunstobjekt (-e) art object
der Kunstsalon (-s) art studio, gallery
das Kunstwerk (-e) work of art; **ein Kunstwerk betrachten** to look at a work of art (8)
die Kuppel (-n) dome, cupola
die Kur (-en) health spa; course of treatment (33); **eine Kur machen** to go to a spa (8)

der Kurarzt (⁻e) / die Kurärztin (-nen) spa physician
der Kurbetrieb (-e) spa therapy organization
der Kurdirektor (-en) / die Kurdirektorin (-nen) spa director
die Kurkarte (-n) ID card for spa therapy participant
der Kurort (-e) health spa, resort (3E)
der Kurpark (-s) park at a health resort
der Kurs (-e) (academic) course; class (11/3E)
kursiv in italics
das Kursprojekt (-e) course project
die Kurstadt (⁻e) town with therapy programs
der Kursteilnehmer (-) / die Kursteilnehmerin (-nen) course participant
kurz (kürzer, kürzest-) short (1)
kurzerhand on the spot, without further ado
die Kurzform (-en) short form
die Kurzgeschichte (-n) short story
das Kurzinterview (-s) short interview
kuscheln to snuggle
die Kusine (-n) (*female*) cousin (25)
der Kuss (⁻e) kiss
küssen to kiss
die Küste (-n) coast (9)
die Kutsche (-n) carriage
der Kutter (-) cutter, boat

L

das Label (-s) label
das Labor (-s) laboratory (10/33)
lächeln to smile
lachen to laugh
lächerlich ridiculous(ly)
der Lachs (-e) salmon (15)
die Lackhose (-n) patent leather pants
lackieren to varnish; to paint
laden (lädt), lud, geladen to load
der Laden (⁻) store (16)
der Ladenschluss store closing time (24)

die Ladenschlusszeit store hours
die Lage (-n) situation; location (18)
das Lagerfeuer (-) campfire (31)
das Lagerhaus (Lagerhäuser) warehouse
lagern to store
die Lakritze licorice
die Lakritzfabrik (-en) licorice factory
das Lakritzprodukt (-e) licorice product
die Lakritzschnecke (-n) licorice (shaped like a spiral)
das Lamm (⁻er) lamb (3)
das Lammfleisch mutton
der Lammrücken (-) rack of lamb
die Lampe (-n) lamp
das Lampenlicht light from a lamp
das Land (⁻er) country, countryside (4); **auf dem Land** in the country (4)
landen, ist gelandet to land (24)
länderspezifisch (*adj.*) specific to a country
das Landesamt state office
das Landesexamen (-) state board exam
die Landesgrenze (-n) national border
die Landeshauptstadt (⁻e) capital
die Landeskunde regional studies
die Landessprache (-n) national language
das Landestheater (-) state theater
die Landfläche (-n) land, space, area
der Landgraf (-en *masc.*) / die Landgräfin (-nen) count/countess
die Landkarte (-n) map
das Landleben life in the country
die Landschaft (-en) countryside, landscape
landschaftlich regional
die Landschaftsform (-en) kind of landscape
die Landschaftspflege environmental preservation
die Landsleute (*pl.*) compatriots
die Landwirtschaft agriculture (35)

lang (länger, längst-) long (1); **lange schlafen** to sleep in; **seit langem** for a long time

langsam slow(ly)

langweilen to bore; **sich langweilen** to be bored (31)

langweilig boring (1/27)

der Lärm noise (20/35)

lassen (lässt), ließ, gelassen to let; to have (*something done*)

lästig tiresome, annoying

der Lastwagen (-) truck

(das) Latein Latin (*language*)

(das) Lateinamerika Latin America

die Lateinstunde (-n) Latin class

die Laterne (-n) lantern

das Laub foliage, leaves

die Laube (-n) garden cabin, gazebo

die Laubenkolonie (-n) area of privately owned gardens with cabins

der Lauf (Läufe) run

laufen (läuft), lief, ist gelaufen to run; to walk (3); **Schi laufen** to ski; **Schlittschuh laufen** to ice skate; **um die Wette laufen** to race; **wie läuft es?** how is it going?

der Laufschritt (-e) run; running pace

die Laune (-n) mood

lauschen to listen

laut loud(ly) (1)

der Laut (-e) sound

lauten to sound; to be; to read; **wie lautet die Frage?** what's the question?

läuten to ring (10)

lauter pure, nothing but

lautlos without a sound

leben to live (12)

das Leben (-) life

lebend(ig) alive, living

die Lebensart (-en) way of life

die Lebensgemeinschaft (-en) lifetime relationship

Lebensgewohnheiten (*pl.*) lifestyle, way of life

die Lebensgröße life-size, actual size

das Lebensjahr (-e) year of one's life

der Lebenslauf (¨-e) résumé, curriculum vitae, CV (14)

das Lebensmittel (-) (*pl.*) groceries (19)

das Lebensmittelgeschäft (-e) grocery store

die Lebensqualität quality of life

der Lebensstil (-e) lifestyle (26)

lebenswert worth living

das Lebenszeichen (-) vital sign, sign of life

die Lebenszeit lifetime

das Lebensziel (-e) lifetime goal

die Leber liver

der Leberkäs(e) Bavarian meat loaf (15)

lebhaft lively

der Lebkuchen (-) gingerbread (17)

lecker (*coll.*) delicious, tasty (19)

das Leder leather (21)

der Lederball (¨-e) leather ball

der Lederhandschuh (-e) leather glove

die Lederhose (-n) leather shorts, lederhosen

die Lederjacke (-n) leather jacket

ledig single, unmarried (14/25)

lediglich only

leer empty

legen to lay (down); **sich ins Bett legen** to lie down, go to bed; **Wert legen auf** (+ *acc.*) to value something (27)

die Legende (-n) legend

legendenhaft legendary

das Lehrangebot (-e) course offerings (*in a school or university*)

der Lehrassistent (-en *masc.*) / **die Lehrassistentin (-nen)** teaching assistant

der Lehrberuf (-e) profession, craft

das Lehrbuch (¨-er) textbook

die Lehre (-n) traineeship, apprenticeship; **eine Lehre erteilen** to teach a lesson

lehren to teach (11/27)

der Lehrer (-) / die Lehrerin (-nen) teacher (1E)

die Lehrergruppe (-n) teacher group

das Lehrerpult (-e) teacher's desk

das Lehrerzimmer (-) teacher's office, staff room

die Lehrkraft (¨-e) teacher, instructor

der Lehrling (-e) apprentice (13)

die Lehrlingsstelle (-n) apprenticeship, position as an apprentice

der Lehrmeister (-) / die Lehrmeisterin (-nen) master

die Lehrstelle (-n) apprenticeship

die Lehrveranstaltung (-en) class, lecture

die Lehrzeit (-en) (period of) apprenticeship

leicht light, easy (2)

das Leid (-en) sorrow, grief; **es tut mir Leid!** I'm sorry!

leiden, litt, gelitten to suffer; **sie konnten ihn nicht leiden** they couldn't stand him

die Leidenschaft (-en) passion

leider unfortunately

leihen, lieh, geliehen (+ *dat.*) to borrow (3E); to lend; **kannst du mir ein bisschen Geld leihen?** can you lend me some money?

der Lein flax

die Leine (-n) leash

das Leinen linen

leise quiet(ly) (26)

leisten to achieve; **sich leisten** to afford (32)

das Leistungsfach (¨-er) main subject

der Leistungskurs (-e) main subject class

die Leistungsübersicht grade report, transcript

der Leitartikel (-) lead article

leiten to lead (30)

leitend leading

der Leiter (-) / die Leiterin (-nen) leader; director; supervisor, head (31)

die Leitstimme (-n) lead voice

die Leitung (-en) wire, line (*telephone*); administration

das Leitungswasser tap water

die Lektion (-en) lesson

lenken to steer, guide
der Lenz (*poetic*) spring (season)
lernen to learn (8); to study (10)
die Lernsoftware instructional software
das Lernziel (-e) learning goal
lesen (liest), las, gelesen to read (3)
lesenswert worth reading
der Leser (-) / die Leserin (-nen) reader
die Leseratte (-n) bookworm
der Leserbrief (-e) letter to the editor (21)
die Leserschaft (-en) readers, audience
das Lesetheater (-) reading theater
letzt- last; **in der letzten Folge . . .** in the last episode . . .
leuchten to shine
die Leute (*pl.*) people
libanesisch Lebanese
das Licht (-er) light
das Lichtbild (-er) photograph
die Lichterkette (-n) chain of lights (*line of people carrying candles*)
lichterloh brennen to burn like wildfire
lieb lovely, nice; **liebe Daniela** dear Daniela; **lieber Lars** dear Lars (*salutation in letters*)
die Liebe (-n) love
lieben to love
lieber rather; preferably
das Liebesdrama (-dramen) romantic drama
das Liebesdreieck (-e) love triangle
der Liebesfilm (-e) romantic movie (36)
das Liebesgedicht (-e) love poem
die Liebesgeschichte (-n) love story
das Liebespaar (-e) couple
der Liebesroman (-e) romantic novel
Lieblings- favorite
liebst: am liebsten best of all; **was machst du am liebsten?** what is your favorite thing to do?

(das) Liechtenstein Liechtenstein (9)
das Lied (-er) song (17)
liegen, lag, hat gelegen to lie, be situated (2); **in der Sonne liegen** to sunbathe
die Liegewiese (-n) lawn for sunbathing
lila purple (2)
die Lilie (-n) lily
die Limo = Limonade
die Limonade (-n) carbonated soft drink (15)
die Linguistik linguistics (11)
die Linie (-n) track, line
link- left
links to the left (8)
der Lippenstift (-e) lipstick
(das) Lissabon Lisbon
die Liste (-n) list
die Litanei (-en) litany
der Liter (-) liter
literarisch literary
die Literatur (-en) literature (11/36)
die Literaturgeschichte (-n) literary history
die Literaturvorlesung (-en) lecture on literature
die Lizenz (-en) license
loben to praise
das Loch (-er) hole
locken to attract, entice (36)
die Lockerheit (-en) informality, relaxed manner (24)
lockern to loosen
der Löffel (-) spoon (19)
logisch logical(ly)
die Logistik logistics
der Logistiker (-) / die Logistikerin (-nen) logistics expert
das Logo (-s) logo
der Lohn (-e) wages
sich lohnen to be worthwhile; to pay off
das Lokal (-e) restaurant
die Lokalnachrichten (*pl.*) local news (21)
die Lorelei *a legendary maiden who lived on a cliff above the Rhine* (17)

los: was ist los? what's up? what's wrong?; **ich muss los** I have to be off
das Löschblatt (-er) blotting paper
lose loose
lösen to loosen (30); to solve
losfahren (fährt los), fuhr los, ist losgefahren to depart (14)
losgehen, ging los, ist losgegangen to leave
die Lösung (-en) solution
die Lösungssuche search for a solution
loswerden (wird los), wurde los, ist losgeworden to get rid of
losziehen, zog los, ist losgezogen to set out
der Lotse (-n *masc.***)** pilot, navigator, guide
die Lotterie (-n) lottery
der Löwe (-n *masc.***)** lion
die Lücke (-n) gap, blank
die Luft air (4)
die Luftkrankheit (-en) air sickness
die Luftqualität air quality
die Luftreinheit purity of the air, air quality
der Luftverkehr air traffic
die Luftverschmutzung air pollution
die Lüge (-n) lie (10)
lügen to lie, tell an untruth
die Lunge (-n) lung
die Lungenentzündung (-en) pneumonia
der Lurch (-e) salamander
die Lust (-e) pleasure; **Lust haben** to feel like
lustig fun(ny); cheerful(ly) (17/27)
das Lustschloss (-er) pleasure castle
der Lutscher (-) lollipop
(das) Luxemburg Luxemburg (9)
der Luxus luxury (32)
das Luxushotel (-s) luxury hotel
die Luxuskreuzfahrt (-en) luxury cruise
die Luxusreise (-n) luxury vacation
das Luxusschiff (-e) luxury ship
der Lyriker (-) / die Lyrikerin (-nen) poet

M

machen to do, make (2)
mächtig strong, mighty
der Machtinstinkt (-e) power instinct
machtlos powerless, helpless
das Mädchen (-) girl
die Made (-n) maggot
der Magen (-:) stomach; **mit leerem Magen** on an empty stomach
magisch magic(al)
mähen to mow; **Rasen mähen** to mow the lawn
die Mahlzeit (-en) meal
mahnen to urge (33)
die Mahnung (-en) warning
der Mai May (5)
der Maifeiertag (-e) May Day
(das) Mailand Milan
der Mais corn
das Make-up makeup
die Makrele (-n) mackerel
mal = einmal; (*particle*) **schreib mal wieder!** come on, write again!; (*adv.*) ever
das Mal (-e) point in time (31); **zum ersten Mal** for the first time
malen to paint
der Maler (-) / die Malerin (-nen) painter
die Malerei (-en) painting
der Malkurs (-e) painting class
die Mama (-s) momma
mancher, manche, manches some, a few
manchmal sometimes
die Mandel (-n) almond
der Mangel (-:) an (+ *dat.*) lack of
mangeln an (+ *dat.*) to lack
mangelnd lacking
die Mango (-s) mango
der Mann (-:er) man; husband (1)
die Männerwelt (-en) man's world
die Mannigfaltigkeit (-en) variety
das Männlein (-) little man
männlich masculine, male (25)
die Mannschaft (-en) team (23/32)
der Mantel (-:) coat (7)
die Manteltasche (-n) coat pocket
das Märchen (-) fairy tale

die Märchenfigur (-en) fairy tale figure (12)
die Margarine margarine
die Mark mark (*German currency*)
das Marketing marketing
der Marketingspezialist (-en *masc.*) / die Marketingspezialistin (-nen) marketing expert
markieren to mark
der Markt (-:e) market
die Marktkaufleute (*pl.*) market vendors
der Marktplatz (-:e) marketplace
das Markttor (-e) market gate
das Markttreiben having a market
die Marktwirtschaft (-en) market economy (18)
die Marmelade (-n) jam (16)
der Marmor marble
(das) Marokko Morocco
marschieren, ist marschiert to march (32)
die Marschkolonne (-n) marching column
die Marschmusik march music
der März March (5)
die Maschine (-n) machine
der Maschinenbau mechanical engineering (11/28)
der Maschinenraum (-:e) engine room
das Maschinenschreiben typing
die Maske (-n) mask
maskulin masculine
das Maß (-e) measure, measurement; **mit Maß** in moderation
der Massageraum (-:e) massage room
der Massentourismus mass tourism
die Massenuniversität (-en) mass university
mäßig moderate(ly)
maßgeschneidert custom made
maßlos immoderate, excessive
die Maßnahme (-n) measure
das Material (Materialien) material
der Materialfluss flow of materials

die Mathe(matik) math(ematics) (11)
die Mathe(matik)arbeit (-en) math(ematics) test
der Mathematiklehrer math teacher
mathematisch mathematical(ly)
die Matrone (-n) matron
der Matrose (-n *masc.*) sailor, seaman
matschig slushy, muddy
die Mauer (-n) wall (18); **die Berliner Mauer** the Berlin Wall
der Mauerstein (-e) brick of a wall
das Maul (-:er) (*animals*) mouth
maunzen to meow
der Maurer (-) / die Maurerin (-nen) bricklayer, mason
die Maus (-:e) mouse
das Mäusefiepen mouse squeak
die Mäusenahrung mouse food
das Mäusetier (-e) rodent
maximal maximal(ly)
der Mechaniker (-) / die Mechanikerin (-nen) mechanic (13)
der Mechanismus (Mechanismen) mechanism
(das) Mecklenburg-Vorpommern Mecklenburg-Western Pomerania (17)
die Medaille (-n) medal
die Medien (*pl.*) media (21)
das Medikament (-e) medication (6/33)
die Medizin medicine (28)
medizinisch medicinal(ly)
der Medizinstudiengang (-:e) medical school, program in medicine
das Meer (-e) ocean, sea (9); **das Schwarze Meer** Black Sea
die Meeresatmosphäre (-n) atmosphere of the ocean
die Meeresbiologie marine biology
die Meeresverschmutzung pollution of the ocean
die Meerschaumpfeife (-n) meerschaum pipe
das Mehl flour

mehr more; **nicht mehr** not anymore
mehren to augment; to increase
mehrere several, various
die Mehrfachbelastung (-en) multiple responsibilities
die Mehrheit (-en) majority
mehrmals several times, often
der Mehrpersonenhaushalt (-e) household with several persons
die Mehrwegflasche (-n) reusable bottle
die Mehrzahl (-en) plural
meiden to avoid
die Meile (-n) mile
der Meilenstein (-e) mile stone
mein my
meinen to think; to mean (3E)
die Meinung (-en) opinion (10)
der Meinungsaustausch exchange of opinions, discussion
die Meinungsforschung public opinion research
die Meinungsfreiheit freedom of speech (18)
meist most(ly)
meisten: am meisten most(ly)
meistens most of the time, most often
der Meister (-) / die Meisterin (-nen) master craftsman
die Meisterprüfung (-en) exam for the master craftsman's certificate
die Meisterschaft (-en) championship (23)
das Meisterwerk (-e) masterpiece
melancholisch melancholic(ally)
sich melden bei to go to, report to
die Meldung (-en) report
die Menge (-n) amount, quantity; **eine Menge** a lot
die Mensa (Mensen) university cafeteria (19)
der Mensch (-en *masc.***)** person; human being (4)
der Menschenauflauf (¨e) crowd
die Menschenhand human hand
das Menschenrecht (-e) human right (30)

menschlich human(ly); **Menschliches** that which is human
merken to notice (20)
merklich noticeable
das Merkmal (-e) characteristic
merkwürdig remarkable; peculiar; odd (24/28)
messbar measurable
messen to measure (33)
das Messer (-) knife (19)
das Messezentrum (-zentren) convention center
der Messias Messiah
das Metall (-e) metal
der Meteorologe (-n *masc.***) / die Meteorologin (-nen)** meteorologist
der/das Meter (-) meter
die Methode (-n) method
die Metropole (-n) metropolis
die Metzgerei (-en) butcher's shop (16)
der Mexikaner (-) / die Mexikanerin (-nen) Mexican (*person*) (18)
mexikanisch (*adj.*) Mexican
(das) Mexiko Mexico
miauen to meow
mich (*acc.*) me (5)
die Mickymaus Mickey Mouse
die Miene (-n) demeanor; facial expression (29)
die Miete (-n) rent (4)
mieten to rent (4)
der Mietpreis (-e) rent
das Mietshaus (¨er) apartment building (4)
die Mikrowelle (-n) microwave (3)
die Milch milk
der Milchteller (-) milk bowl
mild mild(ly)
das Militär military
die Milliarde (-n) billion
die Million (-en) million
die Minderheit (-en) minority (30)
mindestens at least
das Mineralwasser mineral water (15)
das Miniatur-Modell miniature model

die Miniaturtrompete (-n) miniature trumpet
der Minidialog (-e) mini-dialogue
das Minidrama mini-drama
das Minimum minimum
der Minnesänger (-) minnesinger
die Minute (-n) minute
die Minze mint
mir (*dat.*) (to) me
mischen to mix
die Mischung (-en) mixture
miserabel bad, terrible
missmutig depressed, in low spirits
missverstehen, missverstand, missverstanden to misunderstand (21)
der Mist: so ein Mist! (*vulgar*) what a nuisance!
mit (+ *dat.*) with; by; **mit meiner Mutter** with my mother; **mit der Bahn fahren** to go by train; **mit dem Schiff** by ship; **mit dem Auto** by car (7)
mitarbeiten (arbeitet mit) to work together with
der Mitarbeiter (-) / die Mitarbeiterin (-nen) co-worker (13)
mitbestimmen (bestimmt mit) to have a say (27)
die Mitbestimmung codetermination
der Mitbewohner (-) / die Mitbewohnerin (-nen) roommate
mitbringen (bringt mit), brachte mit, mitgebracht (+ *dat.*) to bring along, take along
der Mitbürger (-) / die Mitbürgerin (-nen) fellow citizen
miteinander with each other, together
mitfahren (fährt mit), fuhr mit, ist mitgefahren to ride with, ride together
das Mitglied (-er) member
mithelfen (hilft mit), half mit, mitgeholfen to help out
mitkommen (kommt mit), kam mit, ist mitgekommen to come along (7/3E)

das Mitleid pity, compassion, sympathy
mitmachen (macht mit) to participate
mitnehmen (nimmt mit), nahm mit, mitgenommen to take along (23)
der/die Mitreisende (*decl. adj.*) travel companion
der Mitschüler (-) / die Mitschülerin (-nen) classmate (10)
mitspielen (spielt mit) to participate (*in a game*), play with
der Mitstudent (-en *masc.***) / die Mitstudentin (-nen)** fellow student (*at a university*)
der Mittag (-e) noon; **zu Mittag essen** to have lunch
das Mittagessen (-) lunch
mittags in the afternoon
die Mittagshitze midday heat
die Mitte middle, center (22)
mitteilen (teilt mit) to convey; to tell (36)
die Mittel (*pl.*) means; funds; **ohne künstliche Mittel** without artificial ingredients
das Mittelalter Middle Ages (28)
mittelalterlich medieval
mittelmäßig medium, middling, mediocre
der Mittelpunkt center
mittendrin in the middle
mitten in right in the middle of
die Mitternacht (¨e) midnight
Ein Mittsommernachtstraum *A Midsummer Night's Dream*
mitwirken (wirkt mit) to participate
der Mittwoch Wednesday (1E)
die Möbel (*pl.*) furniture (3)
das Möbelstück (-e) piece of furniture
die Mobilität mobility (18)
möblieren to furnish; **möbliert** furnished (4)
möchten: ich möchte I would like
das Modalverb (-en) modal verb
die Mode (-n) fashion
der Modeexperte (-n *masc.***)** fashion expert

das Modell (-e) model
modellieren to sculpt
das Modellschiff (-e) model ship
die Moderation (-en) mediation, direction
der Moderator (-en) / die Moderatorin (-nen) host of a television or radio show
modern modern
die Modernisierung (-en) modernization
der Modetrend (-s) fashion trend
modisch stylish(ly) (21)
das Mofa (-s) moped
mogeln to cheat
das Mogeln cheating
mögen (mag), mochte, gemocht to like
möglich possible (10)
die Möglichkeit (-en) possibility (29)
möglichst as much as possible; **möglichst viele** as many as possible
moin! (*dialect*) hello!
die Molkerei (-en) dairy
das Molkereiprodukt (-e) dairy product
der Moment (-e) moment; factor (23); **im Moment** at the moment
momentan at the moment
der Monat (-e) month (5)
monatlich monthly (4)
der Mönch (-e) monk
das Mönchsgut (¨er) monastic estate
der Mond (-e) moon
das Monstrum monstrosity, monstrous thing
der Montag (-e) Monday (E)
das Moor (-e) bog, moor
das Moped (-s) moped
morgen tomorrow; **bis morgen** until tomorrow; **morgen Abend** tomorrow evening; **morgen früh** tomorrow morning
der Morgen morning; **am Morgen** in the morning; **guten Morgen!** good morning!; **heute Morgen** this morning; **jeden Morgen** every morning; **eines Morgens** one morning

das Morgenrot dawn
die Morgenroutine (-n) morning routine
morgens in the morning(s)
das Mosaik (-e) mosaic
mosaikartig like a mosaic
die Motivation (-en) motivation
motivieren to motivate
der Motor (-en) engine
das Motorrad (-räder) motorcycle, motorbike (7)
der Motorradstiefel (-) motorcycle boot
der Motorradunfall (¨e) motorcycle accident
der Motorwagen (-) automobile
das Motto (-s) motto
das Mountainbiken mountain biking
die Mozartkugel (-n) *marzipan- and nougat-filled chocolate ball*
müde tired; **todmüde** (*coll.*) dead tired
muffig grumpy
die Mühe (-n) trouble (29)
die Mühle (-n) mill
der Müll trash; garbage, waste (20/35)
die Mülldeponie (-n) landfill
der Mülleimer (-) garbage can
die Müllgebühr (-en) garbage collection fee
die Mülltonne (-n) garbage can
die Mülltrennung garbage sorting
multi-kulti (*coll.*) multicultural
multikulturell multicultural(ly) (34)
(das) München Munich
der Mund (¨er) mouth (6)
mündlich oral(ly)
mundtot machen to silence (*somebody*)
munter lively, bright
die Münze (-n) coin
murmeln to mumble
das Museum (Museen) museum (22)
der Museumsbesucher (-) visitor to a museum
die Musik music (5/36); **Musik hören** to listen to music (2)

musikalisch musical(ly)
der Musikant (-en *masc.***) die Musikantin (-nen)** musician
das Musikantenland *area where music plays an important role*
die Musikaufführung (-en) musical performance
der Musiker (-) / die Musikerin (-nen) (*professional*) musician
das Musikgeschäft (-e) music store
die Musikhochschule (-n) conservatory
die Musikwissenschaft (-en) musicology
musizieren to play music (31)
die Muskulatur muscle system
das Müsli muesli
der Muslim (-e) / die Muslimin (-nen) Muslim
die Muße leisure
müssen (muss), musste, gemusst to have to, must
die Mußestunde (-n) leisure hour
das Musterkind (-er) model child
mustern to scrutinize
der Musterschüler (-) / die Musterschülerin (-nen) model student
der Mut courage
mutig courageous(ly) (20)
Mut machen (macht Mut) to encourage
die Mutter (⁻) mother (1/25)
der Mutterkomplex (-e) mother complex
die Muttersprache (-n) native language
der Muttersprachler (-) / die Muttersprachlerin (-nen) native speaker
der Muttertag (-e) Mother's Day (5)
die Mutti (-s) mommy, mom
die Mütze (-n) cap, hat (7)
der Mythos (Mythen) myth

N

nach (+ *dat.*) after; according to; to (*place*) (12); **nach Hause** (*going*) home; **von . . . nach . . .** from . . . to . . .

der Nachbar (-n *masc.***) / die Nachbarin (-nen)** neighbor (4)
das Nachbarbundesland (⁻er) neighboring state
die Nachbildung (-en) replica
nachdem (*subord. conj.*) after
nachdenken (denkt nach), dachte nach, nachgedacht to reflect, contemplate
nachdenklich pensive(ly), contemplative(ly)
der Nachdruck stress, emphasis
nacheinander after each other
nachforschen (forscht nach) to research into
nachfragen (fragt nach) to inquire, ask
nachhaltig lasting(ly), effective(ly)
nachher afterwards, later
die Nachhilfe tutoring
nachinszenieren (inszeniert nach) to reenact
der Nachkriegsfilm (-e) postwar movie
der Nachkriegsroman (-e) postwar novel
die Nachkriegszeit (-en) postwar era
nachlassen (lässt nach), ließ nach, nachgelassen to recede, drop
der Nachmittag (-e) afternoon; **am Nachmittag** in the afternoon
nachmittags in the afternoon(s)
die Nachricht (-en) news (22)
die Nachrichtensendung (-en) news show
nachschlagen (schlägt nach), schlug nach, nachgeschlagen to look up
nachsehen (sieht nach), sah nach, nachgesehen to look, check into
die Nachspeise (-n) dessert (15)
nachspüren (spürt nach) to track, trace, spy on
nächst- next; **am nächsten Tag** the next day
nachstehen (steht nach) to be second to
nächstfolgend next, following
die Nacht (⁻e) night
der Nachteil (-e) disadvantage

die Nachtigall (-en) nightingale
der Nachtisch (-e) dessert
der Nachtklub (-s) nightclub
das Nachtleben nightlife
der Nachtmusikant (-en *masc.***) / die Nachtmusikantin (-nen)** night musician
nachts at night
der Nachttisch (-e) nightstand (3)
die Nachtwanderung (-en) night walk
der Nachweis (-e) proof (31)
nachweisbar provable
nachweisen (weist nach), wies nach, nachgewiesen to prove
der Nachwuchsforscher (-) / die Nachwuchsforscherin (-nen) junior scientist
nachwürzen (würzt nach) to season to taste, to season again
der Nacken (-) back of the neck
der Nagelschuh (-e) hobnailed boot
nagen to gnaw
nah(e) (näher, nächst-) near, close by (7); **jemandem nah stehen** to be close to someone (25)
die Nähe vicinity (17/27); **in der Nähe von** in the vicinity of (17)
sich nähern to approach, draw near
die Nahrung nourishment (20)
das Nahrungsmittel (-) food
der Nährwert (-e) nutritional value
na ja! well!
der Name (-n *masc.***, -ns** *gen.***)** name
der Namenszug (⁻e) signature
namentlich by name
nämlich namely
narkotisch narcotic
der Narr (-en *masc.***) / die Närrin (-nen)** fool
NASA-mäßig NASA-type (*person*)
die Nase (-n) nose (6)
nass wet
die Nation (-en) nation
national national(ly)
die Nationalgruppe (-n) national group
der Nationalismus nationalism
die Nationalität (-en) nationality
der Nationalpark (-s) national park

der Nationalsozialismus National Socialism

der Nationalsozialist (-en *masc.***) / die Nationalsozialistin (-nen)** National Socialist

die Nationalspeise (-n) national dish

die Natur nature (9)

der Naturarzt (¨e) / die Naturärztin (-nen) physician with a focus on natural medicine

das Naturerlebnis (-se) nature experience

die Naturfaser (-n) natural fiber

die Naturfreunde (*pl.*) *name of nature organization*

die Naturheilkunde natural medicine, homeopathic medicine

das Naturheilverfahren (-) homeopathic treatment

naturkundlich natural-history

natürlich natural(ly)

naturnahe close to nature, nature friendly

das Naturparadies (-e) paradise

das Naturprodukt (-e) organic product

die Naturschönheit (-en) natural beauty

das Naturschutzgebiet (-e) nature reserve

die Naturwissenschaft (-en) natural science

der Nazi = Nationalsozialist

die Nazizeit Nazi era, Third Reich

der Neandertaler (-) Neanderthal Man

der Nebel (-) fog (5)

die Nebelfreiheit lack of fog, no fog

der Nebelmantel (¨) blanket of fog

neben (+ *acc./dat.*) next to

nebenan next door

nebenbei on the side

nebenberuflich on the side

nebeneinander next to each other

das Nebenfach (¨er) minor subject (11/3E)

die Nebenkosten (*pl.*) additional expenses (*such as for utilities*)

das Nebenzimmer (-) side room

neblig foggy (5)

nee! (*coll.*) no!

der Neffe (-n *masc.***)** nephew (1/25)

negativ negative(ly)

das Negativ negative

negieren to negate

nehmen (nimmt), nahm, genommen to take (3); **etwas auf sich** (*acc.*) **nehmen** to take something upon onself; **Rücksicht nehmen auf** to be considerate of; **Zeit in Anspruch nehmen** to take up time (33)

der Neid envy

nein no

nennen, nannte, genannt to name, call, mention

die Neonröhre (-n) neon light

der Nerv (-en) nerve

nerven to get on (someone's) nerves

der Nervenkitzel excitement (32)

die Nervensäge (-n) (*person who is a*) pain in the neck

nervös nervous(ly)

die Nervosität nervousness, tension

nesteln to fiddle with

nett nice(ly) (1)

das Netz (-e) net

neu new (2)

neuartig new

die Neubauwohnung (-en) post-1945 building (4)

neuerdings recently, as of late

neugekauft (*adj.*) newly purchased

die Neugier(de) curiosity

neugierig curious(ly) (1)

der/die Neugierige (*decl. adj.*) curious person

das Neujahr New Year's Day (5)

neulich recently, the other day

neun nine (E)

neunzehn nineteen (E)

neunzig ninety (E); **die neunziger Jahre** the Nineties

(das) Neuseeland New Zealand

neutral neutral

das Neutrum (*grammatical*) neuter

nicht not (3)

die Nichtakzeptanz (-en) nonacceptance (34)

die Nichte (-n) niece (1/25)

nichts nothing

das Nichtstun inactivity

nicken to nod

nie never

nieder low; down

niederknien (kniet nieder) to kneel down

die Niederlande the Netherlands (9)

der Niederländer (-) / die Niederländerin (-nen) Dutch (*person*) (18)

die Niederlassung (-en) branch, subsidiary

(das) Niedersachsen Lower Saxony (17)

niedlich cute

niedrig low

niemals never

niemand nobody, no one

die Niere (-n) kidney

niesen to sneeze (6)

das Niesen sneezing (6)

der Nikolaus Saint Nicolas (17)

das Nikotin nicotine

der Nil Nile River

nimmer (*coll.*) no more, never again

nimmermehr never again

nirgends nowhere

das Niveau (-s) level, niveau

der Nobelpreis (-e) Nobel prize

das Nobelquartier (-e) extravagant accommodations

noch still; **immer noch** still; **ist hier noch frei?** is this seat taken?; **noch dazu** in addition to that; **noch (ein)mal** one more time, once again; **noch nicht** not yet; **noch nie** never; **was noch?** what else?; **weder . . . noch** neither . . . nor; **wissen Sie noch?** do you remember?

der Nomade (-n *masc.***)** nomad

das Nomen (-) noun

der Nominativ nominative

nominieren to nominate

der Nonkonformismus nonconformism

(das) Nordafrika North Africa

(das) Nordamerika North America

nordamerikanisch North American
norddeutsch (*adj.*) northern German
(das) Norddeutschland northern Germany
der Norden north; **im Norden** in the north; **nach Norden** north
das Nordkap North Cape
nördlich (von) north of
der Nordosten northeast
nordöstlich (von) northeast (of)
der Nordpol North Pole
(das) Nordrhein-Westfalen North Rhine-Westphalia (17)
die Nordsee North Sea
die Nordseeküste North Sea coast
die Nordwestküste (-n) northwest coast
die Norm (-en) norm
normal normal
normalerweise normally; usually (32)
(das) Norwegen Norway (9)
nostalgisch nostalgic(ally)
die Not (¨e) despair, misery
die Note (-n) grade (10)
das Notenheft (-e) sheet music
der Notfall (¨e) emergency (6)
notieren to note, write down; **kurz notiert** briefly noted
nötig necessary
das Nötigste most essential (thing)
die Notiz (-en) note (10)
der Notizblock (¨e) notepad
notwendig necessary
die Notwendigkeit (-en) necessity
der November November (5)
nüchtern sober
die Nudel (-n) noodle (19)
null zero (1E)
die Nummer (-n) number
das Nummernschild (-er) license plate (20)
der Numerus (*grammatical*) number
nun now
(das) Nürnberg Nuremberg; **die Nürnberger Bratwurst (¨e)** pork sausage

die Nuss (¨e) nut
nutzen to use (32)
nützlich helpful, practical

O

ob (*subord. conj.*) whether, if
obdachlos homeless
der/die Obdachlose (*decl. adj.*) homeless person (20)
die Obdachlosigkeit homelessness (20)
oben above; upstairs; **da oben** up there; **obendrein** on top of everything; **obengenannt** above-mentioned
die Oberfläche (-n) surface
oberflächlich superficial(ly) (21/36)
oberhalb (+ *gen.*) above
der Oberschenkel (-) thigh
obig above
das Objekt (-e) object
das Objektpronomen (-) object pronoun
das Obst fruit (5/33)
die Obstschale (-n) skin of fruit
obwohl (*subord. conj.*) although (30)
der Ochse (-n *masc.***)** bull, ox
öd(e) dreary; bleak
oder (*coord. conj.*) or
der Ofen (¨) stove, furnace
offen open (16)
die Offenbarung (-en) revelation
öffentlich public(ly) (35); open(ly) (23)
die Öffentlichkeit public
die Öffentlichkeitsarbeit public relations work
offiziell official(ly)
der Offizier (-e) officer (14)
öffnen to open
die Öffnungszeiten (*pl.*) business hours
oft (öfter, öftest-) often (4)
oftmals often
ohne (+ *acc.*) without (5)
ohnehin anyway
das Ohr (-en) ear (6)
die Ohrenklappen (*pl.*) ear covers
die Ohrenschmerzen (*pl.*) earache
die Ohrenschützer (*pl.*) ear muffs

die Ökobewegung environmental movement
ökologisch ecological(ly), environmental(ly)
der Ökonom (-en *masc.***) / die Ökonomin (-nen)** economist
ökonomisch economic(al)
die Ökowelle environmental wave, movement
der Oktober October (5)
das Oktoberfest *autumn festival in southern Germany* (17)
die Olive (-n) olive
der Ölteppich (-e) oil spill
der Ölverbrauch oil consumption
die Oma (-s) (*coll.*) grandma
der Onkel (-) uncle (1/25)
der Opa (-s) (*coll.*) grandpa
die Oper (-n) opera
die Operation (-en) operation, surgery (6)
operieren to operate, perform surgery
der Opernsänger (-) / die Opernsängerin (-nen) opera singer
opfern to sacrifice
optimal optimal(ly)
optimistisch optimistic(ally)
die Option (-en) option
orange orange (2)
die Orange (-n) orange
der Orangensaft orange juice
das Orchester (-) orchestra
die Orchidee (-n) orchid
der Orden (-) (*religious*) order
ordentlich neat, orderly
ordnen to order
die Ordnung (-en) order (34)
ordnungsgemäß in due order, orderly
das Organ (-e) organ
die Organisation (-en) organization
das Organisationstalent (-e) organizational skills
der Organisator (-en) / die Organisatorin (-nen) organizer
organisch organic(ally) (20/35)
(sich) organisieren to organize (oneself) (30)
die Orgel (-n) (*music*) organ

das **Orgelspiel** organ playing
orientalisch Oriental
sich **orientieren an** (+ *dat.*) to orientate oneself; to inform oneself; to adapt to
die **Orientierung (-en)** orientation
die **Orientierungswoche (-n)** orientation week
das **Original (-e)** original
der **Originalschauplatz (¨e)** original location
das **Originalzitat (-e)** direct quote
originell original(ly) (22)
der **Ort (-e)** place, town (4)
der **Ortseingang (¨e)** town entrance
der **Ortskern (-e)** center of town
die **Ortslage (-n)** location
der **Ortsteil (-e)** part of town
die **Ostalgie** (*sarcastic*) nostalgia for the former GDR
der **Ostblock** Eastern Europe
das **Ostblockland (¨er)** Eastern European countries
ostdeutsch East German
(das) **Ostdeutschland** East Germany
der **Osten** east; **im Osten** in the east
die **Osterblume (-n)** Easter lily
das **Osterei (-er)** Easter egg
die **Osterferien** (*pl.*) Easter holidays
das **Osterfest** Easter
der **Osterhase (-n** *masc.*) Easter bunny
der **Ostermontag** Easter Monday
das **Ostern** Easter
(das) **Österreich** Austria (9)
der **Österreicher (-) /** die **Österreicherin (-nen)** Austrian (person) (18)
österreichisch (*adj.*) Austrian
der **Ostersonntag** Easter Sunday
(das) **Osteuropa** eastern Europe
osteuropäisch eastern European
ostfriesisch East Frisian
(das) **Ostfriesland** East Frisia
östlich (von) east (of)
die **Ostsee** Baltic Sea
die **Ostseeküste** Baltic coast
der **Overheadprojektor (-en)** overhead projector (1E)

der **Ozean (-e)** ocean, sea
das **Ozon** ozone
das **Ozonloch** hole in the ozone layer
der **Ozonwert (-e)** ozone level

P

paar: ein paar some, a few, a couple; **ein paar Mal** a few times
das **Paar (-e)** couple
das **Päckchen (-)** package
packen to pack
der **Packen** stack
die **Packung (-en)** pack, packaging, box, bag
der **Pädagoge (-n** *masc.*) / die **Pädagogin (-nen)** teacher, instructor
das **Paddelboot (-e)** paddle boat
paddeln to paddle
das **Paket (-e)** package
der **Palast (¨e)** palace
die **Palme (-n)** palm tree
das **Paniermehl** bread crumbs
paniert breaded, with a batter
die **Panik** panic
das **Panorama (-s)** panorama
der **Panoramablick (-e)** panoramic view
der **Pantoffel (-n)** slipper
die **Pantomime (-n)** pantomime (36)
der **Papa (-s)** daddy
das **Papier (-e)** paper (1E); **Papiere** (*pl.*) documents
das **Papierknäuel (-)** ball of paper
der **Papierkorb (¨e)** wastepaper basket
die **Pappe** cardboard
die **Paprika** bell pepper
der **Paprika** paprika
die **Parade (-n)** parade
das **Paradies (-e)** paradise
paradiesisch heavenly
der **Paragraf (-en** *masc.*) paragraph, section
die **Parallele (-n)** parallel
das **Parfum (-s)** fragrance
der **Park (-s)** park
der **Parkplatz (¨e)** parking space, parking lot

das **Parlament (-e)** parliament
die **Parole (-n)** motto, slogan, password
die **Partei (-en)** (*political*) party
das **Parteimitglied (-er)** party member
der **Partikel (-n)** particle
das **Partizip (-ien)** participle
der **Partner (-) /** die **Partnerin (-nen)** partner
die **Partnerarbeit (-en)** partner work
die **Partneraufgabe (-n)** partner exercise
das **Partnergespräch (-e)** partner conversation
die **Partnerschaft (-en)** partnership
partnerschaftlich as partners
die **Partneruniversität (-en)** partner university
die **Party (-s)** party (24)
die **Partyvorbereitung (-en)** party preparation
der **Pass (¨e)** passport
der **Passagier (-e) /** die **Passagierin (-nen)** passenger
der **Passant (-en** *masc.*) / die **Passantin (-nen)** passerby, bystander
passen (+ *dat.*) to fit (21); **die Hose passt mir nicht** the pants don't fit me
passend matching, fitting, appropriate
passieren, ist passiert to happen (9); **was ist passiert?** what happened?
das **Passiv** passive voice
die **Passivität** passiveness
die **Passkontrolle (-n)** passport control
das **Patentamt (¨er)** patent office
patentieren to patent
der **Patient (-en** *masc.*) / die **Patientin (-nen)** patient (6)
patriotisch patriotic
pauken to cram, study hard (10)
die **Pauschalreise (-n)** package holiday/tour
die **Pause (-n)** break (10)

das Pausenbrot (-e) snack, sandwich (10)
pausenlos constant(ly)
der Pazifik Pacific (Ocean)
der Pazifische Ozean Pacific Ocean
das Pech bad luck
das Pedal (-e) pedal
der Peiniger (-) / die Peinigerin (-nen) torturer, tormentor
peinlich embarrassing
die Pension (-en) bed-and-breakfast inn (8)
der Pensionsinhaber (-) / die Pensionsinhaberin (-nen) innkeeper, owner of a bed and breakfast inn
das Pensum (Pensa or Pensen) workload
die Pepperoni (*pl.*) chilis
perfekt perfect(ly)
das Perfekt present perfect tense
die Peripherie (-n) periphery
permanent permanent(ly)
das Perserreich Persian Empire
die Person (-en) person
die Personalanzeige (-n) personal ad
der Personalchef (-s) personnel manager
die Personenbeschreibung (-en) description of a person
der Personenkraftwagen (-) private car
persönlich personal(ly) (14/32)
die Persönlichkeit (-en) personality
die Perspektive (-n) perspective
pessimistisch pessimistic(ally)
das Pestizid (-e) pesticide
der Pfad (-e) path
der Pfadfinder (-) / die Pfadfinderin (-nen) pathfinder, scout
die Pfalz Palatinate; **das pfälzische Essen** traditional food of the Palatinate
das Pfand (-er) pledge, security, deposit
die Pfandflasche (-n) returnable bottle (35)

die Pfanne (-n) pan (19)
der Pfarrer (-) priest, minister
der Pfeffer pepper (15)
die Pfefferminze peppermint
pfeffrig peppery
die Pfeife (-n) pipe
pfeifen, pfiff, gepfiffen to whistle (20)
der Pfeifenkopf (-e) pipe bowl
der Pfennig (-e) pfennig (*German currency*)
das Pferd (-e) horse (23)
das Pferdefuhrwerk (-e) horse-drawn carriage
die Pferdekutsche (-n) horse-drawn carriage
das Pfingsten Pentecost
der Pfingstmontag day after Pentecost
die Pflanze (-n) plant
pflanzen to plant
die Pflanzenart (-en) plant family
das Pflanzensammeln collecting plants
das Pflaster (-) bandage
die Pflege care, attention
pflegen to look after (31); **Konversation pflegen** to make conversation
die Pflicht (-en) duty (14)
das Pflichtfach (-er) required course (27)
die Pfote (-n) paw
das Pfund (-e) pound (= 500 g)
die Pfütze (-n) puddle
das Phänomen (-e) phenomenon
die Phantasie (-n) imagination, fantasy
phantasiebegabt imaginative
phantastisch fantastic(ally)
die Pharmaindustrie (-n) pharmaceutical industry
der Philosoph (-en *masc.*) / die Philosophin (-nen) philosopher (13)
die Philosophie philosophy
das Photo (-s) photo
der Photoamateur (-e) / die Photoamateurin (-nen) hobby photographer

der Photograph (-en *masc.*) / die Photographin (-nen) photographer
die Physik physics (11/28)
physikalisch physical(ly)
der Physiker (-) / die Physikerin (-nen) physicist (13)
das Physiklehrbuch (-er) physics textbook
der Physiklehrer (-) / die Physiklehrerin (-nen) physics teacher
das Physikstudium university program in physics
die Physikvorlesung (-en) physics lecture
physisch physical(ly)
der Pianist (-en *masc.*) / die Pianistin (-nen) pianist
das Picknick picnic (9)
pieksig prickly
der Pilz (-e) mushroom (9)
der Pionier (-e) / die Pionierin (-nen) pioneer
der Pirat (-en *masc.*) / die Piratin (-nen) pirate
das Piratengesicht (-er) pirate face
die Pizza (-s) pizza
das Pizzabacken pizza baking
die Pizzeria (-s) pizza restaurant
Pkw = Personenkraftwagen
die Plage (-n) plague
das Plakat (-e) poster
der Plan (-e) plan (16)
planen to plan
der Planet (-en *masc.*) planet
die Planung (-en) planning
die Planwirtschaft planned economy (18)
das Plastik plastic
der Plastikbecher (-) plastic cup (35)
der Plastiksack (-e) plastic bag
die Plastiktüte (-n) plastic bag (20)
der Plateauschuh (-e) platform shoe
das Plattdeutsch Low German (*language*)
der Platz (-e) place, space, seat; **viel Platz** lots of space, room
das Plätzchen (-) cookie (16)
platzieren to place

plaudern to chat (10)
plötzlich suddenly (12)
plündern to plunder
das Plusquamperfekt past perfect
das Podium (Podien) podium
die Pointe (-n) point, gist, joke
der Pole (-n *masc.***) / die Polin
  (-nen)** Polish person (18)
(das) Polen Poland
die Politik politics (21)
**der Politiker (-) / die Politikerin
  (-nen)** politician (13)
politisch political(ly)
die Politologie political science
die Polizei police (20)
der Polizist (-en *masc.***) / die
  Polizistin (-nen)** police officer
polnisch (*adj.*) Polish
das Polster (-) cushion, upholstery
die Polymermischung polymer mix
die Pommes frites (*pl.*) french
  fries (15)
populär popular
das Portemonnaie wallet
die Portion (-en) portion
das Porträt (-s) portrait
porträtieren to portray
**der Porträtmaler (-) / die
  Porträtmalerin (-nen)** portrait
  artist
(das) Portugal Portugal (9)
das Porzellan porcelain
die Position (-en) position
positiv positive(ly)
die Posse (-n) trick, joke
die Post post office (4)
das Postamt (¨er) post office
der Postempfang (¨e) receipt of mail
das Poster (-) poster
das Postfach (¨er) post office box
die Postkarte (-n) postcard
die PR-Abteilung (-en) PR (public
  relations) department
das Prädikat rating
(das) Prag Prague
prägen to emboss; to impress; to
  mint
pragmatisch pragmatic(ally)
prahlen to boast
das Praktikum (*pl.* **Praktika)**
  internship (19)

der Praktikumsplatz (¨e) intern
  position
die Praktikumsstelle (-n) intern
  position
praktisch practical(ly)
praktizieren to practice
prall blazing
präparieren to prepare
die Präposition (-en) preposition
das Präsens present tense
die Präsentation (-en) presentation
präsentieren to present
der Präsident (-en *masc.***) / die
  Präsidentin (-nen)** president
das Präteritum preterite, past tense
die Praxis (Praxen) practice; **in die
  Praxis umsetzen** to put into
  practice (35)
der Preis (-e) price
die Preiselbeere (-n) cranberry
die Preiselbeermarmelade (-n)
  cranberry preserves
preisgünstig fairly priced (31)
preiswert economical; inexpensive
  (7)
die Pressefreiheit freedom of the
  press
pressen to press; to squeeze; to cast
das Prestige prestige (14)
(das) Preußen Prussia
preußisch (*adj.*) Prussian
prima (*coll.*) great, excellent (27)
primitiv primitive(ly)
der Prinz (-en *masc.***)** prince (12)
die Prinzessin (-nen) princess
das Prinzip (-ien) principle
die Priorität (-en) priority
privat private(ly)
**der Privatdetektiv (-e) / die
  Privatdetektivin (-nen)** private
  detective
die Privatisierung (-en)
  privatization
das Privatleben private life
pro per; every; for
die Probe (-n) test; rehearsal
der Probetag (-e) trial day
probieren to try, sample (15)
das Problem (-e) problem (20)
problematisch problematic(ally)
problemlos without problem

der Problemstoff (-e) problematic
  substance
das Produkt (-e) product
die Produktionsgesellschaft (-en)
  manufacturing society
die Produktionsmenge (-n)
  output
produktiv productive(ly)
produzieren to produce
professionell professional(ly)
**der Professor (-en) / die
  Professorin (-nen)** professor
profitieren to benefit, profit
das Programm (-e) program,
  station, channel (21)
progressiv progressive(ly)
das Projekt (-e) project
**der Projektleiter (-) / die
  Projektleiterin (-nen)** project
  manager
die Projektwoche (-n) project
  week
die Promenade (-n) promenade
prominent popular, famous
die Promotion (-en) obtainment of
  a doctorate degree
promovieren to get a doctorate
  degree
prompt prompt(ly)
das Pronomen (-) pronoun
das Proseminar (-e) seminar
prosodisch prosodic
der Protest (-e) protest
die Protestaktion (-en) protest
protestantisch (*adj.*) Protestant
protestieren to protest (10)
das Protokoll (-e) transcript,
  record, minutes
**der Protokollführer (-) / die
  Protokollführerin (-nen)**
  secretary, clerk
die Provinz (-en) province
das Prozent (-e) percent
der Prozentanteil (-e) percentage
die Prozession (-en) procession
prüfen to test (28)
die Prüfung (-en) exam (10)
die Prüfungsangst (¨e) anxiety
  before an exam
**der Psychiater (-) / die
  Psychiaterin (-nen)** psychiatrist

der **Psychologe** (**-n** *masc.*) **/ die Psychologin** (**-nen**) psychologist (13)
die **Psychologie** psychology (11)
psychologisch psychological(ly)
die **Psychotherapie** psychotherapy
das **Publikum** audience (36); public
der **Publikumssport** entertainment sport
der **Puck** (**-s**) puck
der **Pulli** (**-s**) sweater
der **Pullover** (**-**) sweater (7)
das **Pulver** (**-**) powder, gunpowder
der **Pulverblitz** (**-e**) gunpowder explosion
pumpen to pump
der **Punkt** (**-e**) point
pünktlich punctual(ly) (14)
die **Pünktlichkeit** promptness, punctuality (34)
die **Puppe** (**-n**) doll, puppet
das **Puppenspiel** (**-e**) puppet show
das **Puppentheater** (**-**) puppet show
die **Pute** (**-n**) turkey
putzen to clean; **die Nase putzen** to blow one's nose (6)
der **Putztag** (**-e**) cleaning day
das **Puzzle** (**-s**) puzzle
die **Pyramide** (**-n**) pyramid

Q

der **Quadratfuß** (**-**) square foot
der **Quadratkilometer** (**-**) square kilometer
quaken to quack
die **Qual** (**-en**) pain, agony
die **Qualifikation** (**-en**) qualification (14)
die **Qualität** (**-en**) quality
das **Quartal** (**-e**) quarter (11)
quasi- quasi-
quasseln to babble
der **Quatsch** nonsense
quatschen to talk, gossip (28)
das **Quecksilber** mercury
die **Quelle** (**-n**) source
die **Quizsendung** (**-en**) quiz show
die **Quotierungsfrage** (**-n**) question of quotation

R

der **Rabe** (**-n** *masc.*) raven
sich rächen to avenge, seek revenge
das **Rad** (**-̈er**) wheel, bicycle; **mit dem Rad fahren** to go by bike; **Rad fahren** to bicycle (4)
radeln to bicycle
der **Radfahrer** (**-**) **/ die Radfahrerin** (**-nen**) bicyclist
radikal radical(ly)
das **Radio** (**-s**) radio
das **Radioprogramm** (**-e**) radio show
die **Radiosendung** (**-en**) radio show
der **Radler** (**-**) **/ die Radlerin** (**-nen**) (*coll.*) cyclist
die **Radtour** (**-en**) bike ride
das **Rafting** rafting
ragen to rise, tower, loom
der **Rahmen** (**-**) frame, context (18)
die **Rahmenbedingung** (**-en**) basic condition
die **Rakete** (**-n**) rocket
der **Rand** (**-̈er**) edge, top rim, brim
der **Rang** (**-̈e**) rank, position
die **Rangliste** (**-n**) ranking, list
die **Rangordnung** hierarchy
die **Ranke** (**-n**) tendril, branch, stalk
rar rare
rasch quick(ly)
der **Rasen** (**-**) lawn (3E); **den Rasen mähen** to mow the lawn (16/3E)
rasend fast, swift
die **Rasenfläche** (**-n**) lawn area
der **Rasierapparat** (**-e**) electric shaver
sich rasieren to shave
der **Rasierpinsel** shaving brush
der **Rassismus** racism
die **Rast** (**-en**) rest
die **Raststätte** (**-n**) rest area, restaurant
der **Rat** advice
raten (**rät**), **riet, geraten** (+ *dat.*) to advise; to guess (13)
das **Ratespiel** (**-e**) guessing game
der **Ratgeber** (**-**) **/ Ratgeberin** (**-nen**) adviser; counsellor; advice column; columnist (21)

das **Rathaus** (**-̈er**) city hall
ratlos helpless(ly) (32)
ratsam advisable
der **Ratschlag** (**-̈e**) advice (27)
der/die Ratsuchende (*decl. adj.*) person who seeks advice
die **Ratte** (**-n**) rat
der **Rattenfänger von Hameln** Pied Piper of Hamelin
der **Rauch** smoke (35)
rauchen to smoke
die **Raucherecke** (**-n**) smoking area
die **Räucherei** (**-en**) smokehouse
räuchern to smoke (*something*)
der **Raum** (**-̈e**) room, space, area
räumlich spacial(ly), physical(ly)
das **Raumschiff** (**-e**) spaceship
rausfinden (**findet raus**), **fand raus, rausgefunden** to find out
rauskommen (**kommt raus**), **kam raus, ist rausgekommen** to come out
reagieren to react; **reagieren auf** (+ *acc.*) to react to (26)
die **Realien** (*pl.*) realities, facts
die **Realisierung** (**-en**) realization
realistisch realistic(ally)
die **Realität** (**-en**) reality
realitätsnah close to reality, realistic
die **Realschule** (**-n**) vocational school (11/27)
die **Rechenmaschine** (**-n**) calculator
die **Rechenschaft** account
recherchieren to research, investigate
rechnen to calculate (27)
der **Rechner** (**-**) computer, calculator
die **Rechnung** (**-en**) bill (15)
das **Recht** (**-e**) right; **das Recht auf Asyl** right to asylum; **Recht haben** to be right
recht right; rather, quite, pretty; **recht sein** (+ *dat.*) to agree; to approve
rechteckig square, rectangular
rechtlich legal(ly) (34)
rechts to the right, on the right (8); **nach rechts** to the right

das Rechtschreiben spelling
rechtsgerichtet right-oriented
die Rechtswissenschaft
    jurisprudence (28)
rechtwinklig right-angled
sich recken to stretch
recyceln to recycle (16/35)
das Recycling recycling
das Recyclingprogramm (-e)
    recycling program
der Redakteur (-e) / die
    Redakteurin (-nen) editor
die Redaktion (-en) editorial board
die Rede (-n) speech
die Redefreiheit freedom of speech
    (30)
reden über (+ *acc.*) **/ von** to talk
    about/of (10)
die Redewendung (-en) figure of
    speech
reduzieren to reduce
das Referat (-e) term paper; **ein**
    Referat halten to present a paper
    (orally)
das Reflexiv (-e) reflexive
    (pronoun)
das Reflexivpronomen (-) reflexive
    pronoun
die Reform (-en) reform
die Reformation Reformation
der Reformator (-en) (*hist.*)
    Reformer
das Reformhaus (ˇer) health food
    store (22)
reformieren to reform
das Regal (-e) shelf (3)
die Regel (-n) rule (34)
regelmäßig regular(ly) (33)
die Regelmäßigkeit (-en)
    regularity
regeln to regulate (25)
die Regelung (en) regulation
(sich) regen to move, stir
der Regen rain (5)
der Regenbogen (ˇ) rainbow
(sich) regenerieren to regenerate,
    revitalize
der Regenmantel (ˇ) raincoat (7)
der Regenschirm (-e) umbrella
der Regentropfen (-) raindrop
der Regenwald (ˇer) rain forest

das Regenwetter rainy weather
die Regierung (-en) government
die Region (-en) region
regional regional(ly)
die Regionalstadt (ˇe) regional
    city
der Regionalzug (ˇe) *short distance*
    train with frequent stops
der Regisseur (-e) / die
    Regisseurin (-nen) director (*of a*
    film or play) (36)
registrieren to register
regnen to rain; **es regnet** it's
    raining (5)
regnerisch rainy
regulär regular(ly)
die Regung (-en) movement, motion
die Rehabilitationsklinik (-en)
    rehab clinic
reiben to rub
reich rich(ly)
das Reich (-e) empire
reichen to suffice, be enough; to
    give; to pass; to hand
der Reichstag Parliament
reif ripe, mature
der Reifen (-) tire
die Reihe (-n) row; series (30)
die Reihenfolge (-n) order,
    sequence
das Reihenhaus (ˇer) row house (4)
rein pure(ly)
die Reinigungskraft (ˇe) cleaning
    power
reinkommen (kommt rein), kam
    rein, ist reingekommen to get in,
    to come in
reinlassen (lässt rein), ließ rein,
    reingelassen to let in
reinlich clean(ly), neat(ly), tidy
der Reis rice (15)
die Reise (-n) trip, journey
das Reiseangebot (-e) travel
    offer
der Reisebegleiter (-) / die
    Reisebegleiterin (-nen) travel
    guide
der Reisebericht (-e) travel
    report
der Reisebrief (-e) letter from a
    trip

das Reisebüro (-s) travel agency
das Reiseerlebnis (-se) travel
    experience
die Reisefamilie (-n) traveling
    family
die Reisefreiheit freedom to travel
    (18)
der Reiseführer (-) / die
    Reiseführerin (-nen) travel
    guide; (*masc.*) guidebook
die Reisegewohnheiten (*pl.*) travel
    habits
die Reisegruppe (-n) tourist group
die Reiseindustrie travel industry,
    tourist industry
die Reiselust desire to travel (32)
die Reisemöglichkeit (-en) travel
    opportunity
reisen to travel (9)
der/die Reisende (*decl. adj.*)
    traveler (24)
der Reisepass (ˇe) passport (24)
die Reisequalität travel quality
die Reisetasche (-n) travel bag
der Reisetipp (-s) travel tip
das Reiseunternehmen (-) travel
    company
die Reisevorbereitung (-en)
    vacation preparation
das Reiseziel (-e) destination
reißen, riss, gerissen to rip, tear;
    an sich reißen to seize
der Reißnagel (ˇ) thumbtack
reiten, ritt, ist geritten to ride (*an*
    animal) (8/32)
der Reitstall (ˇe) horse stables
die Reklame (-n) advertisement
    (21)
rekonstruieren to reconstruct
der Rektor (-en) / die Rektorin
    (-nen) principal
relativ relative(ly)
das Relativpronomen (-) relative
    pronoun
der Relativsatz (ˇe) relative clause
relaxen (*coll.*) to relax
relevant relevant
die Religion (-en) religion (11)
religiös religious(ly)
rennen, rannte, ist gerannt to run
das Rennen (-) race (23)

VOCABULARY

renovieren to renovate, remodel (*a building*)
die Rente (-n) pension (29)
der Rentner (-) / die Rentnerin (-nen) pensioner (29)
reparieren to repair
repetieren to learn by repetition; to repeat (*a grade*)
die Repetitionsstunde (-n) detention
der Reporter (-) / die Reporterin (-nen) reporter
repräsentieren to represent
die Republik (-en) republic
reservieren to reserve
die Reservierung (-en) reservation (8)
die Residenz (-en) residence; (royal) capital
das Resort (-s) resort
der Respekt respect
respektabel respectable
respektieren to respect (25)
respektvoll respectful
die Ressource (-n) resource
der Rest (-e) rest, remnant
das Restaurant (-s) restaurant (4)
der Restaurantbesitzer (-) / die Restaurantbesitzerin (-nen) owner of a restaurant
der Restaurator (-en) / die Restauratorin (-nen) restorer (22)
restaurieren to restore (*historic preservation*)
restlich remaining
der Restposten remaining stock
das Resultat (-e) result
retten to save, rescue
die Rettung (-en) rescue, salvation
das Revier (-e) police station
das Rezept (-e) prescription (6/33); **auf Rezept** by prescription
die Rezeption (-en) reception desk (*in a hotel or office*) (8)
der Rezeptionist (-en masc.) / die Rezeptionistin (-nen) receptionist
die Rezession recession
der Rhein Rhine River
(das) Rheinland-Pfalz Rhineland Palatinate (17)

die Rheinlandschaft (-en) Rhine landscape
das Rheuma rheumatism
richten an (+ *acc.*) to address; to send to (*a letter*)
sich richten nach to orientate oneself
der Richter (-) / die Richterin (-nen) judge (30)
richtig correct, right (24)
die Richtlinie guideline
die Richtung (-en) direction
riechen nach to smell like (33)
der Riese (-n masc.) / die Riesin (-nen) giant
riesengroß enormous (28)
das Riesenrad (¨er) ferris wheel
riesig (*adj.*) giant
das Rind (-er) cow
das Rinderfett beef fat
das Rinderhackfleisch ground beef
der Ring (-e) ring
die Ringeltaube (-n) pigeon
ringsum / ringsherum (all) around
der Rinnstein (-e) gutter
riskieren to risk
der Riss (-e) tear, rip, crevice, fissure
der Ritter (-) knight
der Rittersaal (-säle) knights' hall (in a medieval castle)
der Roboter (-) robot
der Rock (¨e) skirt (7)
der Rock 'n' Roll Rock 'n' Roll
der Rockfan (-s) rock fan
das Rocklied (-er) rock song
roh raw (19)
der Rohstoff (-e) raw material (35)
die Rolle (-n) roll
rollen to roll
das Rollenspiel (-e) role play
der Rollschuh (-e) roller skate; **Rollschuh laufen (läuft), lief, ist gelaufen** to roller skate
das Rollschuhlaufen roller skating (23)
(das) Rom Rome
der Roman (-e) novel
die Romantik Romantic period (*in German art and literature*)

romantisch romantic(ally) (1)
das Romantsch Rhaetian, Rhaeto-Romanic
die Romanverfilmung (-en) filming of a novel (36)
der Römer (-) / die Römerin (-nen) Roman (*person*)
römisch (*adj.*) Roman
rosa pink (2)
der Rosinenbomber *plane during Berlin airlift in 1948*
rot red (2)
rotgolden red gold
das Rotkäppchen Little Red Riding Hood
die Rübe (-n) beet
rüber over here, over there (*destination*); **ich gehe mal zu den Nachbarn rüber** I'm going over to the neighbors
ruckartig jerky
der Rücken (-) back (6)
die Rückfahrkarte (-n) return ticket (24)
die Rückfahrt (-en) return trip
rücklings backwards, from behind
der Rucksack (¨e) backpack (7/32)
die Rücksicht consideration (35); **Rücksicht auf andere Menschen nehmen** to be considerate of other people
rücksichtsvoll considerate (29)
der Rückstand: im Rückstand to be behind
rückwärts backwards
der Rückweg (-e) return trip, way back
rudern to row (*a boat*) (23/32)
der Ruf (-e) call; reputation (28)
rufen, rief, gerufen to call, shout
die Ruhe peace, silence, stillness; **Ruhe jetzt!** quiet now! (4)
ruhen to rest, be still
der Ruhestand retirement
der Ruhetag (-e) *day when restaurant is closed* (15)
ruhig calm, peaceful(ly) still (1/28)
rühren to move; to stir (31)
rührend touching
das Ruhrgebiet Ruhr Basin

R-67

die Ruine (-n) ruin
ruinieren to ruin
rumbummeln (bummelt rum) (*coll.*) to stroll
das Rumpelstilzchen Rumpelstiltskin (12)
rumrennen (rennt rum) (*coll.*) to run around
rund round; around, about
der Rundbogen (¨) arch
der Rundfunk radio
runter down here, downward; **wir sind runter zum Strand gelaufen** we went down to the beach
runterfallen (fällt runter), fiel runter, ist runtergefallen to fall down
der Russe (-n *masc.*) / **die Russin (-nen)** Russian (person) (18)
russisch (*adj.*) Russian
das Russisch Russian (*language*)
(das) Russland Russia
Rutsch: guten Rutsch (ins neue Jahr)! Happy New Year!

S

der Saal (Säle) hall
die Sache (-n) thing, object
sachkundig well-informed
die Sachlichkeit matter of factness; objectivity
(das) Sachsen Saxony (17)
(das) Sachsen-Anhalt Saxony-Anhalt (17)
sächsisch (*adj.*) Saxon
der Sack (¨e) sack, bag
der Saft (¨e) juice (16)
saftig juicy
sagen to say
sagenhaft legendary, fabulous
die Sahne cream (15)
die Saison (-s) season
das Sakko (-s) man's jacket, coat
die Salami (-s) salami
der Salat (-e) salad; head of lettuce (15)
die Salatgurke (-n) cucumber
die Salbe (-n) ointment
der Salon (-s) salon
das Salz salt (15)

salzig salty (19)
sammeln to collect, gather
die Sammelstelle (-n) collecting station (20)
der Sammler (-) collector; gatherer
die Sammlung (-en) collection
der Samstag (-e) Saturday (1E)
der Samstagabend (-e) Saturday evening
samstags on Saturdays
die Sandale (-n) sandal (7)
die Sandburg (-en) sand castle
der Sandstrand (¨e) sandy beach
sanft soft(ly)
der Sänger (-) / **die Sängerin (-nen)** singer (13)
der Sängerkrieg (-e) competition of Minnesingers
satirisch satirical(ly)
der Sattel (¨) saddle
der Satz (¨e) sentence
der Satzanfang (¨e) beginning of a sentence
das Satzelement (-e) sentence element
der Satzteil (-e) part of a sentence
die Satzverknüpfung (-en) combination of sentences
sauber clean (4)
sauber machen (macht sauber) to clean (23)
die Sauberkeit cleanliness (34)
sauer sour (22)
der Sauerbraten (-) braised beef (*marinaded in vinegar*), sauerbraten
die Sauerei (-en) mess, scandal, filth
das Sauerkraut sauerkraut (15)
sauertöpfisch sour, sour-faced
die Säule (-n) pillar, column
die Sauna (-s) sauna; **in die Sauna gehen** to go in a sauna (8)
sausen to buzz, whistle, roar
sauwohl (*coll.*) really good
die S-Bahn (-en) urban train (22)
die Schachtel (-n) (cardboard) box
schade! too bad!
schaden (+ *dat.*) to damage, harm
schädigen to damage (35)
die Schädigung (-en) damage, damaging

das Schaf (-e) sheep
schaffen, schuf, geschaffen to make; to accomplish (28)
schaffen, schaffte, geschafft to manage
der Schaffner (-) / **die Schaffnerin (-nen)** conductor, ticket collector (*on public transportation*)
der Schal (-s) scarf (21)
schalldicht soundproof
die Schallplatte (-n) record
der Schalter (-) counter
scharf (schärfer, schärfst-) spicy, sharp (19); sharp(ly)
schärfen to sharpen
schattenlos without shade
die Schattenseite (-n) shady side; downside
schattig shady
der Schatz (¨e) treasure; **mein Schatz** honey, darling
schauen to look, watch (2)
der Schauplatz (¨e) scene
das Schauspiel (-e) play (36)
der Schauspieler (-) / **die Schauspielerin (-nen)** actor (13/36)
das Schauspielhaus (¨er) theater
der Schausteller (-) / **die Schaustellerin (-nen)** fairground showman
die Scheibe (-n) (window)pane
die Scheibe (-n) slice
sich scheiden lassen (lässt), ließ, gelassen to divorce
die Scheidung (-en) divorce (23/25)
scheinbar apparent(ly), seeming(ly)
scheinen, schien, geschienen to shine; to appear, seem; **die Sonne scheint** the sun is shining (5); **Marion scheint beschäftigt zu sein** Marion seems to be busy
scheitern to fail
schellen to ring
der Schenkel (-) thigh
schenken to give (*as a present*) (5)
scheppern to rattle
die Schere (-n) scissors, shears
scheren to cut, crop
der Scherz (-e) joke
scheu timid, shy (1)

scheußlich horrible, awful (1)

der Schi (-er) ski; **Schi laufen (läuft), lief, ist gelaufen** to ski (8)

schick chic, elegant

schicken to send

das Schicksal (-e) fate, destiny

schieben, schob, geschoben to push

die Schiebermütze (-n) flat cap

schief crooked; **der Schiefe Turm von Pisa** the Leaning Tower of Pisa; **schief gehen** to go wrong; **schief und krumm** crooked; **sich schief lachen** to laugh oneself silly

das Schienbein (-e) shin

schießen, schoss, geschossen to shoot

das Schiff (-e) ship (7)

die Schifffahrt shipping, navigation

das Schifffahrtsmuseum (-museen) naval museum

der Schiffskoch (¨e) cook on a ship

die Schiffsreise (-n) voyage, cruise (32)

der Schiffstyp (-en) type of ship

das Schild (-er) shield, sign (16)

der Schimmer glimmer, gleam

schimmernd shimmering, glimmering

schimpfen to moan, grumble; to scold; **mit jemandem schimpfen** to tell somebody off, scold someone

der Schinken (-) ham

das Schinkenbrot (-e) ham sandwich

der Schiunfall (¨e) skiing accident

der Schiurlaub (-e) skiing trip, vacation

der Schlafanzug (-züge) pajamas (21)

die Schlafcouch (-s) sofa bed

die Schlafdauer duration of sleep

schlafen (schläft), schlief, geschlafen to sleep (3)

schläfrig sleepy

der Schlafsack (¨e) sleeping bag

das Schlafzimmer (-) bedroom (3)

der Schlag (¨e) blow

schlagen (schlägt), schlug, geschlagen to hit, beat (19)

der Schlager (-) hit (song)

die Schlägerei (-en) fist fight

die Schlaghose (-n) bell-bottom pants

die Schlagsahne whipped cream

die Schlagzeile (-n) headline (21)

der Schlamm mud

die Schlange (-n) snake; **Schlange stehen** to stand in line

schlapp worn-out, tired

schlappen to lap

das Schlaraffenland Cockaigne (*legendary land of plenty*)

schlau clever, smart

die Schlauheit (-en) cleverness, smartness

schlecht bad(ly) (1)

schleichen, schlich, ist geschlichen to sneak

schlendern to stroll

schleppen to lug, drag, haul

der Schlepper (-) tugboat

(das) Schlesien Silesia

schlesisch (*adj.*) Silesian

schleudern to hurl, sling, fling

die Schleuse (-n) lock, floodgate

schließen, schloss, geschlossen to lock, shut

schließlich finally, eventually (10)

schlimm bad, grave, severe

der Schlips (-e) tie

der Schlittschuh (-e) ice skate; **Schlittschuh laufen (läuft), lief, ist gelaufen** to ice skate

die Schlittschuhbahn (-en) ice skating rink

das Schlittschuhlaufen ice skating (23)

das Schloss (¨er) castle (12)

das Schlossrestaurant (-s) restaurant in a castle

der Schlot (-e) chimney

die Schlucht (-en) gorge

das Schluchtwandern hiking through a gorge, ravine

schluchzen to sob

schlucken to swallow

der Schlumpf (¨e) smurf

schlurfen to shuffle

der Schluss (¨e) end, conclusion; **am Schluss** in the end, finally

der Schlüssel (-) key (8)

die Schlussrechnung (-en) final calculation

schmackhaft palatable, tasty

schmal narrow

das Schmalz lard

schmatzen to smack

schmecken (+ *dat.*) to taste; **das schmeckt (mir) gut** that tastes good (to me) (15)

schmeißen, schmiss, geschmissen (*coll.*) to throw

das Schmelzwasser melted snow and ice

der Schmerz (-en) pain (6)

schmerzend painful

der Schmetterling (-e) butterfly

schmieden to forge

sich schminken to put on make-up

der Schmuck jewelry (22)

schmücken to decorate (17)

schmutzig dirty, soiled (4)

der Schnabel (¨) beak

schnalzen to click one's tongue

schnattern to chatter, quack

das Schnäuzchen little snout

die Schnecke (-n) snail

der Schnee snow (5)

der Schneemann (¨er) snowman

schneeweiß snow-white

das Schneewittchen Snow White (12)

schneiden, schnitt, geschnitten to cut, slice (19)

die Schneiderei tailor shop; dressmaking shop; tailoring; dressmaking

schneidern to be a tailor/dressmaker

schneien: es schneit it's snowing (5)

schnell quick(ly), fast

der Schnellimbiss (-e) hot dog stand, fast food joint

das Schnellrestaurant (-s) fast-food restaurant

der Schnippel (-) scrap (of paper)

der Schnitt (-e) cut

das Schnitzel (-) cutlet, schnitzel

der Schnupfen (-) (head) cold

schnuppern to sniff

die Schnur (¨e) rope

schnurren to purr
der Schock (-s) shock
die Schokolade (-n) chocolate
das Schokoladenei (-er) chocolate egg
schön beautiful(ly), nice(ly) (1)
schonen to take care of
die Schonung (-en) forest plantation area
der Schoß (ːe) lap
schräg sloping, slanted
der Schrank (ːe) cupboard; closet, wardrobe (3)
die Schranke (-n) barrier
der Schrebergarten (ː) garden plot
der Schreck (-e) fright
der Schrecken (-) horror
schrecklich terrible, horrible
schreiben, schrieb, geschrieben to write (2)
der Schreiber (-) / die Schreiberin (-nen) writer
die Schreibhilfe (-n) writing aid
der Schreibtisch (-e) desk
die Schreibunterlage (-n) writing pad
das Schreibwarengeschäft (-e) stationery store (22)
schreien, schrie, geschrieen to scream, shout
die Schrift (-en) (hand)writing; script
schriftlich written, in writing
der Schriftsteller (-) / die Schriftstellerin (-nen) author, writer
der Schritt (-e) step (13/34); **Schritt halten** to keep up
die Schrothkur Schroth Therapy
der Schrott junk
der Schub (ːe) push; thrust; batch
der Schubkarchler (-) (*dialect*) small tent
der Schubkasten (ː) drawer
die Schublade (-n) drawer
schüchtern shy
der Schuh (-e) shoe (7)
der Schuhverkauf (ːe) shoe sale
der Schulablauf (ːe) school routine
der Schulabschluss degree

der Schulalltag everyday school routine
die Schularbeit (-en) schoolwork
der Schulbus (-se) school bus (10)
der Schulchor (ːe) school choir
die Schuld (-en) guilt, debt
das Schuldgefühl (-e) guilty feeling, bad conscience
der Schuldienst teaching
der Schuldirektor (-en) / die Schuldirektorin (-nen) school principal, headmaster
die Schule (-n) school (10)
der Schüler (-) / die Schülerin (-nen) student (*not in university*) (1E/3E)
die Schülerinitiative (-n) student association
die Schülerzeitung (-en) student newspaper (10)
das Schulfach (ːer) school subject
die Schulferien (*pl.*) school holidays, vacation
das Schulfest (-e) school festival
der Schulfreund (-e) / die Schulfreundin (-nen) schoolmate, school friend
der Schulgang (ːe) professional training program
das Schulhaus (ːer) school building
der Schulhof (ːe) courtyard (10)
schulisch scholastic
das Schuljahr (-e) school year
der Schuljunge (-n *masc.*) schoolboy
der Schulkamerad (-en *masc.*) / die Schulkameradin (-nen) fellow student, school friend
der Schulkiosk school concessions
die Schulklasse (-n) school class
das Schulleben school life
der Schulkamerad (-en *masc.*) / die Schulkamaradin (-nen) fellow student, school friend
die Schulpflicht mandatory school attendance
der Schulpsychologe (-n *masc.*) / die Schulpsychologin (-nen) school psychologist
die Schulreise (-n) school trip

der Schulrektor (-en) / die Schulrektorin (-nen) school principal
die Schulstunde (-n) school lesson
das Schulsystem (-e) school system
der Schultag (-e) school day
die Schulter (-n) shoulder (6)
die Schulterhöhe (-n) shoulder height
das Schulwesen school system, education system
die Schulzeit (-en) time in school
die Schulzeiterinnerung (-en) school memory
die Schulzeitung (-en) school newspaper
die Schürzentasche (-n) apron pocket
schütteln to shake
schütten to pour
der Schutz protection (26)
schützen to protect (20/35)
der Schutzpatron (-e) / die Schutzpatronin (-nen) saint
die Schwäbische Alb Swabian Mountains
schwach (schwächer, schwächst-) weak
der Schwager (ː) brother-in-law (25)
die Schwägerin (-nen) sister-in-law (25)
der Schwamm (ːe) blackboard eraser (1E)
der Schwan (ːe) swan
schwanken to sway, roll, rock
der Schwanz (ːe) tail
schwärmen to swarm
schwärmen von to enthuse about
schwarz black (2); **das schwarze Brett (-er)** bulletin board (19)
der Schwarzwald Black Forest
schwatzen to chat, gossip
(das) Schweden Sweden (9)
schwedisch (*adj.*) Swedish
schweigen (schwieg, geschwiegen) to be silent
die Schweigsamkeit (-en) silence, not speaking
das Schwein (-e) pig
der Schweinebraten (-) pork roast (15)

das Schweinefleisch pork
die Schweinshaxe (-n) pork knuckle
schweißgebadet bathed in sweat
die Schweiz Switzerland (9)
der Schweizer (-) / die Schweizerin (-nen) Swiss (*person*) (18)
schweizerisch (*adj.*) Swiss
schwellen (schwillt), schwoll, ist geschwollen to swell
schwellend swelling, bulging
schwer heavy; difficult, hard (2)
die Schwerindustrie (-n) heavy industry
die Schwerkraft gravity
schwermütig melancholic(ally)
die Schwester (-n) sister (1)
das Schwesterchen (-) little sister
die Schwestersprache (-n) related language
die Schwiegermutter (¨) mother-in-law (25)
der Schwiegervater (¨) father-in-law (25)
schwierig difficult
die Schwierigkeit (-en) difficulty (30)
schwimmen, schwamm, ist geschwommen to swim (2)
die Schwimmhalle (-n) indoor swimming pool
der Schwindel swindle
schwindelig (+ *dat.*) dizzy; **mir ist schwindelig** I'm dizzy
schwirren to buzz, whizz
schwitzen to sweat
sechs six (E)
sechste sixth
sechzehn sixteen (E)
sechzig sixty (E); **die sechziger Jahre** the Sixties
der See (-n) lake (9)
die See ocean, sea (9)
die Seebrücke (-n) bridge over a lake
seegängig seaworthy
seegehend seafaring
die Seele (-n) soul
die Seeluft sea air
das Seemannslied (-er) sailor's song

der Seeräuber (-) pirate
das Segel (-) sail
das Segelboot (-e) sailboat
segeln to sail (2)
das Segeln sailing
die Segelreise (-n) sailing vacation
segensreich beneficial
sehen (sieht), sah, gesehen to see (3)
sehenswert worth seeing
die Sehenswürdigkeit (-en) sight, attraction
die Sehne (-n) ligament
sich sehnen nach to long for (28)
die Sehnsucht (¨e) yearning, longing
die Seife soap
die Seifenoper (-n) soap opera
das Seifenpulver soap powder, detergent
der Seiltänzer (-) / die Seiltänzerin (-nen) tightrope walker
sein (ist), war, ist gewesen to be (1); **was darf's sein?** what will you have? (15)
sein his
seit (+ *dat.*) since, for; **seit dem Abitur** since the Abitur; **seit kurzem** recently; **seit zehn Jahren** for ten years
seitdem since then
die Seite (-n) page; side; **auf Seite 15** on page 15; **zur Seite stehen** to stand by someone
der Seitenflügel (-) side wing (*of a building*)
das Seitental (¨er) side valley
seither since then
der Sekretär (-e) / die Sekretärin (-nen) secretary
das Sekretariat (-e) secretarial office
der Sekt champagne (15)
der Sekundarbereich (-e) secondary school level
die Sekundarschule (-n) secondary school
selber (one)self
(sich) selbst (one)self
das Selbstbildnis self-portrait

selbstklebend self-sticking
selbstständig independent(ly) (13/29); self-employed
der/die Selbstständige (*decl. adj.*) self-employed person (14)
das Selbstbewusstsein self-confidence
das Selbstporträt (-s) self-portrait
selbstverständlich natural(ly), self-evident(ly)
die Selbstverwirklichung ego-fulfillment; self-realization
das Selbstwertgefühl (-e) self-esteem
selektieren to select
der Sellerie celery
selten seldom, rare(ly) (4)
das Selters(wasser) (-) seltzer water
seltsam strange(ly), peculiar(ly)
seltsamerweise strangely enough
das Semester (-) semester (11/3E)
die Semesterarbeit (-en) term paper
die Semesterferien (*pl.*) school recess
das Seminar (-e) seminar
senden, sandte, gesendet to send
die Sendung (-en) broadcast, show (21)
der Senf mustard (15)
der Senior (-en) / die Seniorin (-nen) senior citizen
senkrecht perpendicular; vertical
sensibel sensitive
sentimental sentimental
separat separate
der September September (5)
die Serie (-n) series
der Service service
der Servicetechniker (-) / die Servicetechnikerin (-nen) service technician
servieren to serve (*food*)
die Serviette (-n) napkin
der Sessel (-) recliner, armchair (3)
sesshaft settled, resident
die Sesshaftigkeit settled way of life
setzen to put; **sich setzen** to sit down, to take a seat
seufzen to sigh

der Seufzer (-) sigh
shoppen to go shopping
die Shorts (-) shorts (7)
die Show (-s) show
sich (one)self
sicher secure(ly), safe(ly); sure(ly), certain(ly) (13)
die Sicherheit (-en) security
der Sicherheitsgurt (-e) seat belt (20)
sicherlich surely (29)
sich sichern to secure for oneself
die Sicht visibility, sight; **aus der Sicht** (+ *gen.*) from the point of view of
sichtbar visible; visibly
sieben seven (E)
siebenfach sevenfold
siebte seventh
siebzehn seventeen (1E)
siebzig seventy (1E); **die siebziger Jahre** the Seventies
die Siedlung (-en) settlement; neighborhood (35)
siegen to win, defeat
siehe oben see above
siezen to address someone with **Sie** (34)
das Signal (-e) signal
signalisieren to signal
silbern (*adj.*) silver
das Silvester New Year's Eve (5)
die Sinfonie (-n) symphony
singen, sang, gesungen to sing (5)
single single (25)
der Singular singular
sinken, sank, ist gesunken to sink
der Sinn (-e) sense (29)
das Sinneserlebnis (-se) sense experience
sinnlich sensual
sinnlos senseless, pointless
sinnvoll sensible; meaningful (33)
die Sitte (-n) custom, practice
die Situation (-en) situation
der Sitz (-e) seat; headquarters
sitzen, saß, gesessen to sit (2), be in a sitting position
(das) Sizilien Sicily
der Skandal (-e) scandal

(das) Skandinavien Scandinavia
das Skateboard (-s) skateboard
der Skaterschuh (-e) skating shoe
skeptisch skeptical(ly)
der Ski (-er) ski
die Skiarena (-arenen) ski arena
das Skifahren skiing (23)
der Skikurs (-e) skiing lessons
die Skikurswoche (-n) skiing instruction week
das Skilaufen skiing
das Skiresort (-s) ski resort
die Skizze (-n) sketch, drawing
die Slawistik Slavic language and culture
der Smoking (-s) tuxedo
das Snowboarden snowboarding
so so; as; thus; **sogenannt** so-called
sobald as soon as
die Socke (-n) sock (7)
das Sofa (-s) sofa (3)
die Sofagarnitur (-en) living room furniture
der Sofatisch (-e) coffee table (3)
sofern in so far as, if
sofort immediately (22)
die Softballmannschaft (-en) softball team
sogenannt so-called
sogar as well; indeed; even (32)
sogleich immediately
der Sohn (¨e) son (1/25)
solange as long as
die Solaranlage (-n) solar generator
die Solarberghütte (-n) solar mountain cabin
das Solarium (*pl.* **Solarien**) tanning bed
solcher, solche, solches such
der Soldat (-en *masc.***) / die Soldatin (-nen)** soldier
solidarisch in solidarity
die Solidarität solidarity
der Solidaritätszuschlag solidarity surcharge on income tax (*for the reconstruction of eastern Germany*)
sollen (soll), sollte, gesollt to be supposed to (*do something*), should
somit therefore

der Sommer (-) summer (5); **im Sommer** in the summer
die Sommerferien (*pl.*) summer vacation
die Sommerferiensaison summer vacation season
das Sommersemester (-) summer semester
der Sommerurlaub (-e) summer vacation
das Sommerwetter summer weather
das Sonderangebot (-e) special offer (16)
die Sonderkommission special committee; special commission
der Sondermüll hazardous waste
sondern (*coord. conj.*) but (rather); **nicht nur . . . sondern auch . . .** not only . . . but also . . .
die Sonderschule (-n) special education school
der Sonnabend Saturday
die Sonne (-n) sun (5)
(sich) sonnen to sun, lie in the sun
die Sonnenbrille (-n) sunglasses
das Sonnenlicht sunlight
sonnenlos sunless
der Sonnenschein sunshine
der Sonnenschirm (-e) sunshade; (beach) umbrella
die Sonnenseite (-n) sunny side
der Sonnenstrahl (-en) sun beam
der Sonnenuntergang (¨e) sunset
sonnig sunny
der Sonntag (-e) Sunday (1E)
sonst else, besides that, apart from that; **was brauchen wir sonst noch?** what else do we need?
sonstig miscellaneous, other
die Sorge (-n) worry (24); **sich Sorgen machen (um)** to worry (about)
sorgen für to care for (23/25)
sorgfältig careful(ly) (31)
die Sorte (-n) kind, type
sortieren to sort, organize
soviel so much
soweit is as far as; thus far
sowie as well as
sowieso in any case; anyway (32)

sowohl . . . als auch . . . as well as

sozial social(ly)

die Sozialhilfe social welfare

die Sozialkritik social criticism

die Sozialkunde social science (11)

die Sozialleistung (-en) social support (29)

die Sozialverträglichkeit social acceptability

sozusagen so to speak

die Spaghetti (*pl.*) spaghetti

die Spalte (-n) column (*of written text*)

spalten to split

die Spaltung (-en) splitting, separation

(das) Spanien Spain (9)

das Spanisch Spanish (*language*) (11)

der Spanischkurs (-e) Spanish class

der Spann (-e) instep

spannend exciting; tense (23/32)

das Sparbuch (¨er) savings account book

sparen to save (35)

das Sparkonto (-konten) savings account

der Spaß fun; **Spaß machen** (+ *dat.*) to be fun; **das macht mir Spaß** that is fun (5); **viel Spaß!** have fun! (5)

spät late; **wie spät ist es?** what time is it?

spätestens at the latest

spazieren gehen, ging spazieren, ist spazieren gegangen to go for a walk (2)

der Spaziergang (¨e) walk; **einen Spaziergang machen** to take a walk

die SPD = Sozialdemokratische Partei Deutschlands

der Speck bacon (15)

die Spedition (-en) shipping company, trucking line

die Speditionsabteilung (-en) shipping department

die Speditionsfirma (-firmen) shipping company

der Speditionskaufmann (-leute) / die Speditionskauffrau (-en) shipping agent

der Speicher (-) storage

die Speise (-n) dish

die Speisekarte (-n) menu (15)

spekulieren to speculate

der Sperrmüll bulky garbage (*for special collection*)

der Spezialist (-en *masc.***) / die Spezialistin (-nen)** specialist

die Spezialität (-en) speciality (15)

speziell special(ly); specific(ally)

spezifisch specific(ally)

der Spickzettel (-) cheat sheet

der Spiegel (-) mirror (3)

das Spieglein (-) little mirror

das Spiel (-e) game

das Spielbein (-e) leg bearing no weight

spielen to play (8); **Streiche spielen** (+ *dat.*) to play tricks

der Spieler (-) / die Spielerin (-nen) player

das Spielfeld (-er) playing field

der Spielfilm (-e) movie (on television)

die Spielfläche (-n) playing area

das Spielkasino (-s) casino

das Spielzeug (-e) toy (17)

das Spielzimmer (-) playroom

der Spießer (-) bourgeois, narrow-minded person

spießig (*adj.*) bourgeois

der Spinat spinach

die Spindel (-n) spindle

die Spinne (-n) spider

spinnen to spin; (*fig.*) to be crazy; **der spinnt doch!** he's crazy! (10)

der Spinner (-) crazy person

das Spital (¨er) hospital

spitz pointy, sharp

der Spitzbube (-n *masc.***)** imp, little boy

die Spitze (-n) top, highest point

der Spitzname (-n *masc.***)** nickname

der Splitter (-) splinter, fragment

spontan spontaneous(ly)

der Sport sports, exercise (11); **Sport treiben, trieb Sport, Sport getrieben** to play a sport (23/32)

die Sportart (-en) type of sport (23/32)

die Sporthalle (-n) sport center (16)

die Sporthochschule (-n) sports academy

der Sportlehrer (-) / die Sportlehrerin (-nen) physical education teacher

der Sportler (-) / die Sportlerin (-nen) athlete (23)

sportlich athletic

der Sportplatz (¨e) sports field (10)

der Sportschuh (-e) sneaker (7)

der Sportverein (-e) sports club

die Sportwissenschaft physical education

der Sprachatlas (-atlanten) language atlas

sprachbegabt linguistically talented, good at languages

die Sprache (-n) language; **die Sprache verschlagen** (+ *dat.*) to leave speechless

die Sprachkenntnisse (*pl.*) foreign language skills, language proficiency

der Sprachkurs (-e) language course

das Sprachlabor (-s) language lab (10)

sprachlich linguistic(ally)

der Sprachspiegel (-) language mirror

die Sprachwahl (-en) choice of language

die Sprachwissenschaft linguistics

die Spraydose (-n) spray can

sprechen (spricht), sprach, gesprochen to speak (3)

sprechend speaking; **sprechende Tiere** speaking animals

der Sprecher (-) / die Sprecherin (-nen) speaker, spokesperson, representative

der Sprechfunk radio-telephone system

die Sprechstunde (-n) office hour

die Sprechstundenhilfe (-n) assistant in a doctor's office

das Sprechzimmer (-) office

das Sprichwort (¨er) proverb

springen, sprang, ist gesprungen to jump (32)

die Springform (-en) springform (pan)

die Spritze (-n) vaccine, shot (6)

spröd(e) aloof; austere; rough; recalcitrant

der Spruch (¨e) saying

das Sprudelwasser carbonated water

der Sprung (¨e) crack

das Sprungbrett (-er) springboard

die Spur (-en) trace

spürbar traceable (36)

spüren to feel

der Staat (-en) state

staatlich (*adj.*) state-owned, state-run; **staatlich anerkannt** state-approved

der Staatsbürger (-) / die Staatsbürgerin (-nen) citizen (26)

die Staatsbürgerschaft (-en) citizenship

die Staatsgrenze (-n) state border

stabil stable

das Stadion (Stadien) stadium

das Stadium (Stadien) phase, stage

die Stadt (¨e) city (4)

das Stadtbad (¨er) municipal pool, public swimming pool

stadtbekannt popular

das Städtchen (-) little town

der Städtebund confederation of cities

die Städteerkundung (-en) exploration of a city

der Stadtführer (-) city guidebook

das Stadtgebiet (-e) city area

städtisch municipal

das Stadtleben city life

das Städtlein (-) little town

die Stadtmitte (-n) downtown area, town center

der Stadtmusikant (-en *masc.***) / die Stadtmusikantin (-nen)** musician

der Stadtpark (-s) public park

der Stadtpfarrer (-) city priest

der Stadtplan (¨e) city map

die Stadtrundfahrt (-en) city tour (*by bus*)

der Stadtteil (-e) part of town, neighborhood

das Stadtviertel (-) quarter, neighborhood (4)

das Stadtzentrum (-zentren) downtown

der Stahl steel

der Stahlarbeiter (-) / die Stahlarbeiterin (-nen) steelworker

das Stahlwerk (-e) steel mill

der Stammbaum (¨e) family tree

stammeln to stammer

stammen aus to be from

das Stammlokal (-e) favorite restaurant

der Stammtisch (-e) table for regulars (*at a restaurant or bar*)

der Standard (-s) standard

das Standbein (-e) weight-bearing leg; pivot leg

ständig permanent(ly), constant(ly)

der Standpunkt (-e) viewpoint

die Standuhr (-en) grandfather clock (3)

der Stapel (-) stack (*of something*)

der Star (-s) star

stark (stärker, stärkst-) strong(ly)

starren to stare

der Startort (-e) starting point

die Station (-en) station

die Statistik (-en) statistics

statt (+ *gen.*) instead of

stattfinden (findet statt), fand statt, stattgefunden to take place (17/27)

die Statue (-n) statue

der Status status

der Stau (-s) traffic jam

der Staub dust; **Staub saugen** to vacuum

stauen to dam, stem the flow

staunen to be astonished, amazed

das Staunen astonishment

staunend amazing(ly)

der/die Staunende (*decl. adj.*) amazed person

stechen (sticht), stach, gestochen to stab, pierce, sting

der Steckbrief (-e) personal description, wanted poster

stecken to put; to stick; to be located; to put in a concealed place; **wo steckt der Schlüssel?** where is the key?

der Stefansdom St. Stephen's Cathedral (*in Vienna*)

stehen, stand, gestanden to stand (16); (+ *dat.*) to suit (21)

stehlen (stiehlt), stahl, gestohlen to steal

die Steiermark Styria

steif stiff(ly)

steigen, stieg, ist gestiegen to climb

steigend rising, increasing

steigern to increase; to raise (29)

die Steilküste (-n) steep coast (*with rocks and cliffs*)

der Stein (-e) stone, rock

die Steinzeit Stone Age

die Stelle (-n) place; position (13/29)

stellen to put, place (*upright*)

das Stellenangebot (-e) job offer (14)

die Stellenanzeige (-n) job advertisement

die Stellensuche (-n) job search (14)

stemmen to lift (*weights*)

sterben (stirbt), starb, ist gestorben to die (12)

die Stereoanlage (-n) stereo system (3)

stereotyp stereotypical

der Stern (-e) star

sternenklar starry

das Sternzeichen (-) sign of the zodiac

stet constant, steady

das Steuer (-) steering wheel (*in a car*)

die Steuer (-n) tax (29)

steuerbar controllable, controlled

das Steuerbord starboard

steuern to steer; to direct
das Stichwort (¨er) key word
der Stiefbruder (¨) stepbrother (25)
der Stiefel (-) boot (7)
die Stiefmutter (¨) stepmother (12)
der Stiefsohn (¨e) stepson (12)
die Stieftochter (¨) stepdaughter (12)
der Stiefvater (¨) stepfather (12)
der Stier (-e) bull
der Stierkämpfer (-) bullfighter
der Stift (-e) pen
der Stil (-e) style (27)
still quiet, calm, silent
die Stille silence
die Stimme (-n) voice
stimmen to be correct, be true; **das stimmt** that's correct
die Stimmung (-en) mood, atmosphere (17/36)
stinken, stank, gestunken to stink
stinkig stinky
stinklangweilig deadly boring
stinksauer very angry
die Stirn (-e) forehead
stochern to poke
der Stock (-werke) floor, story (*above the ground floor*) (8); **im dritten Stock** on the fourth floor
stocken to falter; to hesitate
das Stockwerk (-e) floor, level (*in a building*)
der Stoff (-e) material (28)
der Stoffwechsel metabolism
stöhnen to groan
stolpern to trip
stolz proud(ly)
der Stolz pride
stopfen to stuff
das Stoppelfeld (-er) wheatfield after harvest
stoppen to stop
stören to disturb (24)
störend disturbing
(der) Störtebeker *legendary sailor*
störungsfrei undisturbed
die Story (-s) story
stoßen (stößt), stieß, gestoßen to push, shove
stottern to stutter
die Strafe (-n) punishment

der Strahl (-en) ray, beam
der Strand (¨e) beach (4)
der Strandabschnitt (-e) beach section
der Strandkorb (¨e) covered beach chair
strapaziös stressful, exhausting
die Straße (-n) street; **sie wohnt in der Schiller-Straße** she lives on Schiller Street
die Straßenbahn (-en) streetcar (22)
das Straßenfest (-e) street festival
der Straßenköter (-) mutt
der Straßenkünstler (-) / die Straßenkünstlerin (-nen) street artist
das Straßenschild (-er) street sign
das Straßentheater street theater
die Strategie (-n) strategy
strategisch strategic, strategical(ly)
sich sträuben to resist; **die Haare sträuben** to stand on end (*hair, fur*)
der Strauch (¨er) bush, shrub
streben nach to strive for
die Strecke (-n) stretch, distance; course; **auf der Strecke bleiben** to be left behind, get lost
sich strecken to stretch
der Streich (-e) trick, prank (14)
streicheln to stroke, caress
streichen, strich, gestrichen to paint; to strike, cross out
das Streichholz (¨er) match
der Streifen (-) strip; stripe
der Streifenpolizist (-en *masc.***) / die Streifenpolizistin (-nen)** patrol officer, police officer on the beat
der Streifenwagen (-) police car
der Streik (-s) strike
streiken to go on strike
der Streit (-e) argument, confrontation
streiten, stritt, gestritten to argue (23)
streng strict(ly) (20/27)
der Stress stress
stressig stressful(ly)
streuen to scatter; to spread

das Strichmännchen (-) stick figure
stricken to knit
der Strom electricity (35); current
die Strophe (-n) verse, line
der Strudel (-) strudel
die Struktur (-en) structure
die Strumpfhose (-n) tights (21)
die Stube (-n) room
stubenrein housebroken
das Stück (-e) (theater) piece (36); **ein Stück gehen** to walk for a bit
das Stückchen (-) little piece
der Student (-en *masc.***) / die Studentin (-nen)** (university) student (1E)
der Studentenalltag everyday life of a student
der Studentenball (¨e) dance, ball for students
die Studentenbewegung (-en) student movement
der Studentenfilm (-e) student film
das Studentenleben student life
der Studentenprotest (-e) student protest
das Studententheater (-) student theater
das Studentenwerk (-e) student administration
das Studentenwohnheim (-e) dormitory (19/3E)
das Studentenzimmer (-) student room
der Studienablauf (¨e) course of one's studies, program
der Studienabschnitt (-e) part of a program of study
der Studienaufenthalt (-e) study abroad program
die Studienberatung student advising
die Studiendauer length of a university studies program
das Studienfach (¨er) subject of study
die Studiengebühren (*pl.*) tuition (19)
der Studienplatz (¨e) place in a university program
die Studienreise (-n) student excursion, educational excursion

die Studientour (-en) field trip
studieren to study (8); to be a student at a university (11)
der/die Studierende (*decl. adj.*) student
das Studio (-s) studio
das Studium (Studien) course of study (*at a university*) (19/3E)
die Stufe (-n) step
der Stuhl ("e) chair (1E)
der Stummfilm (-e) silent movie (36)
der Stummfilmstar (-s) star in a silent movie
die Stunde (-n) hour (23), lesson
der Stundenplan ("e) lesson plan, schedule (10)
stur stubborn
die Sturheit stubbornness
der Sturm ("e) storm
stürmisch passionate, ardent
stutzen to trim
sich stützen auf (+ *acc.*) to lean on; to be based on
der Stützpunkt (-e) military outpost
das Subjekt (-e) subject
das Substantiv (-e) noun
subtil subtle; subtly
die Suche (-n) search (26)
suchen to search, seek (9)
die Sucht addiction
die Suchterscheinung (-en) symptom of addiction
(das) Südafrika South Africa
(das) Südamerika South America
(das) Südbaden province in South West Germany
der Süden south; **im Süden** in the south
der Südflügel (-) south wing
südlich (von) south (of)
der Südosten southeast
südöstlich (von) southeast (of)
der Südwesten southwest
südwestlich (von) southwest (of)
das Suffix (-e) suffix
sühnen to atone
summen to hum, buzz
super (*coll.*) super; **das ist super!** that's great!

superlang(e) (*coll.*) super long, extremely long
der Superlativ (-e) superlative
die Superlativform (-en) superlative forms
der Supermarkt ("e) supermarket (4)
superschlacksig (*coll.*) uncoordinated, unorthodox in movement
die Suppe (-n) soup (15)
surfen to surf; **im Web surfen** to surf the Web
surreal surreal
süß sweet (19); **etwas Süßes** something sweet
die Süßigkeiten (*pl.*) candy
das Sweatshirt (-s) sweatshirt
der Swimmingpool (-s) swimming pool
das Symbol (-e) symbol (16)
symbolisieren to symbolize
die Symbolwirkung (-en) symbolism
die Sympathie (-n) fondness; sympathy
sympathisch nice, congenial (1)
das Symptom (-e) symptom
die Synagoge (-n) synagogue
synchronisieren to dub (*a film*) (36)
das Synonym (-e) synonym
syrisch Syrian
das System (-e) system (19)
die Szene (-n) scene

T

die Tabelle (-n) table
die Tablette (-n) pill
tabu taboo (26)
die Tafel (-n) blackboard (1E)
der Tag (-e) day (1E); **der Tag der Deutschen Einheit** Day of German Unity (5); **eines Tages** one day, someday
das Tagebuch (Tagebücher) diary
der Tagebucheintrag ("e) diary entry
tagelang for day's

der Tagesablauf (Tagesabläufe) course of the day, daily routine
der Tagesausflügler (-) / die Tagesausflüglerin (-nen) day-tripper
die Tagesetappe (-n) leg of a journey
das Tageslicht daylight
die Tagesschau *German public television news show*
tageweise per day, for a day
täglich daily (21)
tagsüber during the day
das Tal ("er) valley (9)
das Talent (-e) talent
talentiert talented
der Taler (-) thaler (*old unit of currency*)
tanken to pump gas
die Tankstelle (-n) gas station
die Tante (-n) aunt (1/25)
der Tanz ("e) dance (36)
tanzen to dance (2)
die Tanzmusik dance music
der Tanzsaal (-säle) dancing hall
der Tanzschuh (-e) dancing shoe
tapfer brave
die Tasche (-n) bag, pocket (7)
das Taschengeld (-er) pocket money
die Tasse (-n) cup
die Tat (-en) deed, crime; **auf frischer Tat ertappt** caught in the act
der Täter (-) / die Täterin (-nen) culprit, criminal
tätig active; **tätig sein** to work
die Tätigkeit (-en) activity (13)
die Tatsache (-n) fact
tatsächlich really, indeed, as a matter of fact
taub deaf
die Taube (-n) pigeon
der Taubenschwarm ("e) flock of pigeons
der Taubenzuchtverein (-e) pigeon breeders' club
der Tauchsieder (-) immersion coil (*for boiling water*)
taumeln to stagger, sway

tauschen to change, switch, exchange
tausend thousand (1E)
das Taxi taxicab
der Taxifahrer (-) / die Taxifahrerin (-nen) cabdriver
das Team (-s) team (23)
die Teamberatung (-en) team counseling
der Teamwerker (-) team worker
die Technik (-en) technique, technology (11)
der Techniker (-) / die Technikerin (-nen) technician
technisch technical(ly)
die Technologie (-n) technology
technologisch technological(ly)
die Technomusik techno music
der Teddybär (-en *masc.***)** teddy bear
der Tee (-s) tea (2)
das Teeglas (¨er) tea glass
teeren to tar
der Teig dough, batter
der Teil (-e) part; **zum Teil** partly, in part
teilen to divide; to share (31)
die Teilnahme (-n) participation
teilnehmen (nimmt teil), nahm teil, teilgenommen to participate (20); **teilnehmen an** (+ *dat.*) to take part in (26)
der Teilnehmer (-) / die Teilnehmerin (-nen) participant
die Teilung (-en) division, separation
das Telefon (-e) telephone (3)
das Telefonbuch (¨er) phone book
telefonieren (mit) to be on the phone (with), call
telefonisch by phone
die Telefonnummer (-n) phone number
die Telefonsprechstunde (-n) office hours (by phone)
die Telefonzelle (-n) telephone booth
der Teller (-) plate (19)
das Tempolimit (-s) speed limit
die Tendenz (-en) tendency
das Tennis tennis; **Tennis spielen** to play tennis (2)

der Tennisplatz (¨e) tennis court
der Tennisschläger (-) tennis racket
der Teppich (-e) rug, carpet
der Teppichboden (¨) wall-to-wall carpet
der Teppichfaden (¨) carpet thread
der Teppichrand (¨er) edge of the carpet
der Termin (-e) appointment (29)
das Terminal (-s) airline terminal (24)
der Terminkalender (-) date book
die Terrasse (-n) terrace, patio (16)
der Test (-s) test
testen to test
teuer (teurer, teuerst-) expensive (2)
der Text (-e) text
der Textauszug (¨e) excerpt from a text
das Textbeispiel (-e) example from a text
die Textstelle (-n) quote from a text
die Texttafel (-n) text table
thailändisch (*adj.*) Thai
das Theater (-) theater (36); **ins Theater gehen** to go to the theater (2)
die Theateraufführung (-en) theater play, production
die Theaterdekoration (-en) props, stage set, stage background
der Theatersaal (-säle) theater hall
das Theaterstück (-e) play
die Theaterwissenschaften (*pl.*) drama (*as a subject*)
das Thema (Themen) topic; **zum Thema** on the topic (of)
der Themenbereich (-e) topic area
die Theologie theology
der Theoretiker (-) / die Theoretikerin (-nen) theorist
theoretisch theoretical(ly)
die Theorie (-n) theory
die Therapie (-n) therapy
die Therapieform (-en) kind of therapy
das Thermometer (-) thermometer (6)

die These (-n) hypothesis, thesis
der Thunfisch (-e) tuna (15)
(das) Thüringen Thuringia (17)
thüringisch (*adj.*) Thuringian
tief deep(ly) (33)
tiefblau deep blue
die Tiefkühlpizza (-s) frozen pizza
tiefliegend deep-set (*eyes*)
das Tier (-e) animal
der Tierarzt (¨e) / die Tierärztin (-nen) veterinarian
die Tierbeobachtung (-en) animal observation
die Tierbestimmung identification of animals
der Tiergarten (¨) zoo
die Tierhandlung (-en) pet store (22)
die Tierpraxis (-praxen) veterinarian's practice
der Tierschützer (-) / die Tierschützerin (-nen) animal conservationist
der Tiger (-) tiger
die Tinte (-n) ink
das Tintenfass (¨er) ink bottle
der Tipp (-s) tip, hint
der Tisch (-e) table
die Tischdecke (-n) tablecloth
das Tischlein (-) little table
der Tischler (-) / die Tischlerin (-nen) carpenter
das Tischtennis table tennis (8)
der Titel (-) titel
tja well, . . .
der Toast (-s) toast
der Toaster (-) toaster
die Tochter (¨) daughter (1/25)
die Tochterfirma (-firmen) subsidiary
der Tod (-e) death
die Todeszahlen (*pl.*) death statistics
tödlich deadly, fatal
die Toilette (-n) bathroom, toilet bowl (3)
tolerant tolerant
die Toleranz (-en) tolerance
toll (*coll.*) great (2)
die Tomate (-n) tomato (16)
die Tomatensoße (-n) tomato sauce, marinara sauce (19)

der Ton (¨e) sound
der Tonfilm (-e) sound film (36)
die Tonne (-n) container; bin (35); ton
der Topf (¨e) pot (19)
töpfern to make pottery (31)
topfit fit
das Tor (-e) (*sport*) goal; gate (23)
die Torte (-n) fancy cake
die Tortenplatte (-n) cake platter
die Tortur (-en) ordeal
tot dead
total total(ly)
töten to kill (12)
die Tour (-en) tour
der Tourenverlauf (¨e) course of a trip, route
der Tourismus tourism
der Tourist (-en *masc.***) / die Touristin (-nen)** tourist
der Touristenbetreuer (-) / die Touristenbetreuerin (-nen) tourist attendant, guide
das Touristikcamp (-s) tourist camp, resort
touristisch touristic(ally)
die Tradition (-en) tradition
traditionell traditional(ly)
das Traditionsbewusstsein consciousness of traditions
tragen (trägt), trug, getragen to carry; to wear (5)
tragisch tragic(ally)
die Tragetasche (-n) bag for carrying objects, for example, grocery bag
der Trainer (-) / die Trainerin (-nen) coach
trainieren to train; to exercise
das Training training; exercise
der Transport (-e) transport
der Transporter (-) van
transportieren to transport
das Transportmittel (-) means of transportation
das Transportschiff (-e) freight ship
die Traube (-n) grape
der Traubensaft grape juice (15)
die Trauer mourning, grief
traulich cozy
der Traum (¨e) dream

träumen to dream
das Traumhaus (¨er) dream house
die Traumkarriere (-n) dream career, job (14)
der Traumurlaub (-e) dream vacation
traurig sad (1)
traut beloved, familiar; **trautes Heim** home sweet home
der Treff (-s) joint, bar, disco
treffen (trifft), traf, getroffen to meet
treffend fitting
der Treffpunkt (-e) meeting place
treiben, trieb, getrieben: Sport treiben to exercise; to play a sport
das Treibhaus (¨er) hothouse
der Trenchcoat (-s) trenchcoat (7)
der Trend (-s) trend
trendig trendy
trennbar separable
trennen to separate (17/35); to divide
die Trennung (-en) separation (25)
die Treppe (-n) stairs (8)
das Treppenhaus (¨er) staircase
treten (tritt), trat, ist getreten to kick, step
der Trick (-s) trick (14)
der Trickfilm (-e) animated film
der Trimm-dich-Pfad exercise trail
trinken, trank, getrunken to drink (2)
das Trinkgeld (-er) tip
die Trinkkur: eine Trinkkur machen *to drink mineral waters for healing purposes*
das Trinkwasser drinking water
trippeln to toddle
trocken dry
die Trockenkonserve (-n) dried food
trocknen to dry
der Trommler (-) drummer
die Trompete (-n) trumpet
der Tropfen (-) drop
tropisch tropical
trostlos desolate
trotz (+ *gen.*) in spite of
trotzdem anyway, in spite of that

trüb(e) blurry, foggy
trunken (*poetic*) intoxicated
(das) Tschechien Czech Republic
tschechisch (*adj.*) Czech
tschüss! (*inform.*) bye!
das T-Shirt (-s) T-shirt (7)
die Tuba (Tuben) tuba
tüchtig capable, competent
tun, tat, getan to do
die Tür (-en) door (1E)
turbulent turbulent
der Türke (-n *masc.***) / die Türkin (-nen)** Turk (18)
die Türkei Turkey
türkisch (*adj.*) Turkish
der Turm (¨e) tower
der Turmalinsplitter (-) splinter of tormaline
das Turnier (-e) tournament; competition
der Turnschuh (-e) athletic shoe
der Türsteher (-) bouncer
die Tüte (-n) bag
das Tuten: von Tuten und Blasen keine Ahnung haben to have no clue
der Typ (-en *masc.***)** (*coll.*) guy, dude
typisch typical(ly)

U

die U-Bahn (-en) subway (22)
übel bad; **übel dran sein** to have it bad, be in a bad situation
üben to practice
über (+ *acc./dat.*) above; about; over
überall everywhere
der Überblick (-e) overview
überbrücken to bridge
überdurchschnittlich above average
übereinstimmen (stimmt überein) (mit etwas) to agree (with something) (3E)
überfliegen, überflog, überflogen to skim (21)
überflüssig superfluous
überfüllt (*adj.*) crowded
übergeben (übergibt), übergab, übergeben to hand over
überhaupt (nicht) (not) at all
überholt (*adj.*) out-dated

überlassen (überlässt), überließ, überlassen to leave to; **sich selbst über lassen sein** to be left to one's own devices
überlastet (*adj.*) overwhelmed
die Überlastung (-en) burden, overload (27)
überleben to survive (25)
(sich) überlegen to consider (29)
überleiten to lead to
übermorgen day after tomorrow
übernachten to spend the night (3E)
die Übernachtung (-en) overnight stay (8)
übernehmen (übernimmt), übernahm, übernommen to take over
überprüfen to check
überragen to stand out
überraschen to surprise (17)
überrascht (*adj.*) surprised (14)
die Überraschung (-en) surprise (14)
überreden to persuade, convince
übers = über das
die Überschrift (-en) heading
übersetzen to translate (28)
die Übersetzungsarbeit (-en) translation work
übersichtlich clear, clearly laid out
überspringen, sprang über, übersprungen to jump over; to skip
überstehen, überstand, überstanden to overcome
die Überstunde (-n) overtime hour (22)
übertragen (überträgt), übertrug, übertragen to transmit
übertreiben, übertrieb, übertrieben to exaggerate (29)
übertrieben (*adj.*) exaggerated (20)
überwachen to supervise (32)
überwältigen to overwhelm, overpower
überweisen, überwies, überwiesen to transfer, refer

überwinden, überwand, überwunden to overcome
überzeugen to convince
überzeugt sein (von) to be convinced (of)
die Überzeugungskraft (-e) power of persuasion
üblich usual
übrig left over
übrigens by the way (22)
die Übung (-en) exercise (33)
das Ufo (-s) UFO
die Uhr (-en) clock (1E); **um acht Uhr** at eight o'clock; **wie viel Uhr ist es?** what time is it? (1E)
die Uhrzeit (-en) time
um (. . . herum) (+ *acc.*) around; at (*time*); **um die Ecke** around the corner; **um acht Uhr** at eight o'clock; **um . . . herum** around; **um Köln herum** around Cologne (5); **um wieviel Uhr** at what time; **um (. . .) zu . . .** in order to
umarmen to embrace, hug (24)
die Umarmung (-en) hug (24)
umfallen (fällt um), fiel um, ist umgefallen to fall over, collapse
umfangreich extensive
umfassend comprehensive, thorough
das Umfeld surroundings
die Umfrage (-n) survey, opinion poll
der Umgang interaction
die Umgangssprache colloquial language
umgeben von surrounded by
die Umgebung (-en) surroundings, vicinity (4)
umgehen (geht um), ging um, ist umgegangen to go round; **mit etwas umgehen** to deal with, handle (26)
umgehend immediately
umgekehrt vice versa, the other way around
umhegen to care for
der Umkreis surroundings, vicinity
der Umlaut (-e) umlaut
umreißen (reißt um), riss um, umgerissen to tear down

ums = um das
der Umsatz (-e) turnover
die Umsatzdaten turnover data
der Umschlag (-e) envelope
umschreiben (schreibt um), schrieb um, umgeschrieben to rewrite
sich umsehen (sieht um), sah um, umgesehen to look around
umsetzen (setzt um) to convert; **in die Praxis umsetzen** to put into practice (35)
umsonst for nothing, free
der Umstand (-e) circumstance
umsteigen (steigt um), stieg um, ist umgestiegen to change (*trains*) (7)
die Umstellung (-en) adjustment (25)
umstimmen (stimmt um) to retune; to change someone's mind
umwechseln (wechselt um) to change (28)
die Umwelt environment (20/35)
das Umweltamt (-er) environmental agency
umweltbedingt conditioned by the environment
die Umweltbelastung (-en) damage to the environment
die Umweltbeschädigung (-en) environmental damage
umweltbewusst environmentally conscious
das Umweltbewusstsein environmental awareness (35)
umweltbezogen referring to the environment
umweltfeindlich hostile to the environment (35)
der Umweltforscher (-) / die Umweltforscherin (-nen) environmental scientist
die Umweltforschung environmental research
umweltfreundlich environmentally friendly (20/35)
das Umweltpapier (-e) recycled paper
die Umweltpolitik environmental politics

das Umweltproblem (-e) environmental problem

das Umweltprojekt (-e) environmental project

der Umweltschutz environmental protection (35)

die Umweltschutzbewegung (-en) environmental protection movement

der Umweltsünder (-) / die Umweltsünderin (-nen) polluter, litterbug (20/35)

der Umweltverschmutzer (-) polluter

die Umweltverschmutzung environmental pollution

umziehen (zieht um), zog um, ist umgezogen to move (4)

der Umzug (ʺe) parade (17); move

die Umzugsfirma (-firmen) moving company

unabhängig independent(ly) (25)

die Unabhängigkeit (-en) independence (25)

unangebracht inappropriate(ly)

unangenehm unpleasant(ly)

unaufhörlich uninterrupted

unausgepackt unopened

unbedeutend insignificant(ly)

unbändig boisterous

unbedingt absolutely, in any case, no matter what, necessarily (11/20/34)

unbefangen outgoing; uninhibited (1)

unbefestigt open

unbegrenzt unlimited

unbegründet unfounded

unbeholfen clumsy; clumsily

unbekannt unknown

unbequem uncomfortable; uncomfortably

unbeschreiblich indescribable; indescribably (31)

und (*coord. conj.*) and; **und so weiter** and so forth, et cetera

undankbar ungrateful(ly)

unecht fake

uneingeschränkt unrestricted

unendlich never-ending

unentbehrlich essential (29)

unentschlossen undecided

unersetzlich irreplaceable (31)

unerträglich unbearable; unbearably

unfair unfair(ly)

der Unfall (ʺe) accident

unfreundlich unfriendly (1)

ungarisch (*adj.*) Hungarian

(das) Ungarn Hungary

ungeduldig impatient(ly)

ungefähr approximately (11/22/29)

ungeheuer extreme(ly); **es war ungeheuer kalt** it was extremely cold

ungenießbar inedible, undrinkable

ungerecht unfair(ly) (10)

ungesund unhealthy; unhealthily

ungewöhnlich unusual(ly) (14)

unglaublich unbelievable; unbelievably

das Unglück (-e) unhappiness; accident; bad luck

unglücklich unhappy; unhappily

unheilbar incurable; incurably

unheilvoll fateful(ly), ominous(ly), disastrous(ly)

unheimlich scary, spooky, eerie; eerily, uncanny; uncannily

unhöflich impolite(ly)

die Uni (-s) = Universität

der Uniabschluss (ʺe) university degree

die Uniform (-en) uniform

das Unileben student life, life as a student

uninteressant uninteresting

uninteressiert uninterested

universell universal(ly)

die Union (-en) union

die Universität (-en) university (11)

die Universitätsstadt (ʺe) university town

unklar unclear

unkritisch uncritical(ly)

unmenschlich inhuman(ly)

unmittelbar direct(ly) (34)

unmöglich impossible; impossibly

unnötig unnecessary; unnecessarily

die UNO UN (United Nations)

unordentlich untidy; untidily

die Unordnung (-en) mess

unpersönlich impersonal(ly)

unpraktisch impractical(ly)

Unrecht haben to be wrong

unregelmäßig irregular(ly), uneven(ly)

unromantisch unromantic(ally) (1)

die Unruhe restlessness, agitation

unruhig restless(ly)

uns (*acc./dat.*) us, to us

unschätzbar inestimable; inestimably

unschlüssig undecided (33)

unser our

unsicher insecure(ly), uncertain(ly)

die Unsicherheit (-en) insecurity (27)

der Unsinn nonsense

unsympathisch unpleasant; disagreeable (1)

untätig idle, idly

unten below, down there

unter (+ *acc./dat.*) under(neath)

unterbrechen (unterbricht), unterbrach, unterbrochen to interrupt; to stop

unterbreiten to tell, inform, present with

unterbringen (bringt unter), brachte unter, untergebracht to accommodate

unterdrücken to oppress, hold back, restrain, suppress (30)

die Unterdrückung (-en) suppression, oppression

der Untergang decline, demise, downfall, sinking

sich unterhalten (unterhält), unterhielt, unterhalten to entertain (28); **sich unterhalten über** (+ *acc.*) to converse

unterhaltsam entertaining (21)

die Unterhaltung (-en) entertainment (36)

das Unterhemd (-en) undershirt (21)

unterkriegen: lass dich nicht unterkriegen! keep your chin up!

die Unterkunft (ʺe) accommodation

das Unternehmen (-) business enterprise (29)

unternehmen (unternimmt), unternahm, unternommen to undertake, do (9/31)
die Unternehmung (-en) activity
der Unterricht instruction; class
unterrichten to teach (11/27); instruct
der Unterrichtsausfall cancellation of class
die Unterrichtsmethode (-n) teaching method (27)
der Unterrichtsstil (-e) teaching style
die Unterrichtsstunde (-n) lesson
unterrühren (*cooking*) to fold in
unterscheiden to distinguish
sich unterscheiden von, unterschied, unterschieden to differ from (27)
der Unterschied (-e) difference
unterschiedlich various (26)
der Unterschlupf shelter
unterschreiben, unterschrieb, unterschrieben to sign
die Unterschrift (-en) signature, autograph
unterstreichen, unterstrich, unterstrichen to underline
unterstützen to support
die Unterstützung support
untersuchen to examine (6)
die Untersuchung (-en) examination (33)
der Untertitel (-) subtitle (36)
die Unterwäsche underwear (7)
unterwegs underway, on the road
die Unterweisung (-en) instruction
untrennbar inseparable; inseparably
untypisch atypical(ly)
unüberhörbar loud(ly), obvious(ly)
unverdrossen undeterred(ly)
unvergesslich unforgettable; unforgettably
unvergleichbar incomparable, incomparably
unvernünftig unreasonable; unreasonably
unverschämt shameless(ly), unconscionable; unconscionably (10)

die Unverschämtheit (-en) impudence; **das ist eine Unverschämtheit!** that's outrageous! (10)
unverträglich intolerable; intolerably
die Unverträglichkeit (-en) intolerance, allergy
unvollständig incomplete(ly)
unvoreingenommen unbiased (34)
unweigerlich inevitable; inevitably (34)
unwichtig unimportant(ly)
unwillkürlich spontaneous(ly), instinctive(ly)
unzählig countless
unzufrieden unsatisfied (29)
uralt very old
die Urenkel (*pl.*) great-grandchildren (25)
die Urgroßeltern (*pl.*) great-grandparents (25)
die Urgroßmutter (¨) great-grandmother
der Urgroßvater (¨) great-grandfather
der Urlaub (-e) vacation (17/32); **Urlaub machen** to go on vacation (32)
der Urlauber (-) / die Urlauberin (-nen) vacationer
die Urlaubsatmosphäre holiday atmosphere
die Urlaubsfreude (-n) holiday pleasure
der Urlaubsort (-e) vacation spot
die Urlaubsreise (-n) vacation
die Urlaubszeit (-en) vacation time
die Ursache (-n) cause; **keine Ursache!** don't mention it!
der Ursprung (¨e) origin
ursprünglich original(ly) (36)
der Ursprungsort (-e) origin
die USA USA
usw. = und so weiter and so on

V

der Valentinstag Valentine's Day (5)
die Vanille vanilla
der Vanillinzucker vanilla sugar
die Variante (-n) variety, alternative

die Variation (-en) variation
die Vase (-n) vase
der Vater (¨) father (1/25)
das Vaterland (¨er) home country
der Vatertag Father's Day
der Vati (-s) daddy, dad
der Vegetarier (-) / die Vegetarierin (-nen) vegetarian (*person*)
vegetarisch (*adj.*) vegetarian (33)
(das) Venedig Venice (Italy)
die Verabredung (-en) appointment; date (34)
sich verabschieden to take leave (24)
die Verachtung (-en) contempt (34)
sich verändern to change (27)
die Veränderung (-en) change (25)
veranstalten to organize, arrange, produce
die Verantwortung (-en) responsibility (14)
verarbeiten to use, work, finish
verärgert upset, angry
das Verb (-en) verb
der Verband (¨e) union, association
das Verbandsziel (-e) goal of the union
verbannen to banish; to exile
verbessern to improve
die Verbesserung (-en) improvement
die Verbform (-en) verb form
verbieten, verbot, verboten to forbid (20/27)
verbinden, verband, verbunden to unite (29)
die Verbindung (-en) connection, combination
sich verbitten, verbat, verbeten to refuse to tolerate
verblassen to fade, pale
verboten (*adj.*) not allowed; **Rauchen verboten!** no smoking!
verbrauchen to consume (35); to use (20)
der Verbraucher (-) / die Verbraucherin (-nen) consumer (35)
der Verbrecher (-) / die Verbrecherin (-nen) criminal

die Verbrecherjagd (-en) chase after criminals
verbreiten to distribute (20)
verbrennen, verbrannte, verbrannt to burn
verbringen, verbrachte, verbracht to spend (*time*) (5/3E)
verbunden (*adj.*) allied (18)
verdauen to digest
verderben (verdirbt), verdarb, verdorben to spoil, ruin
verdienen to earn (13/25)
verdreckt dirty
verehren to admire
der Verehrer (-) / die Verehrerin (-nen) admirer
verehrt honorable, dear; **verehrtes Brautpaar!** dear bride and groom!
der Verein (-e) organization; association; club
vereinbaren to agree; to arrange (34)
vereinigen to unite, combine
vereinigt (*adj.*) united; **die Vereinigten Staaten von Amerika** United States of America
die Vereinigung (-en) uniting, organization, union
der Vereinsraum (-̈e) club room
das Verfahren (-) trial, process, method
verfassen to write, compose
verfehlen to defeat, miss
verfestigen to reinforce, strengthen
verfilmen to film (36)
die Verfilmung (-en) film adaptation (*of a novel, play, etc.*)
verfolgen to follow; to persecute (34)
die Verfolgung (-en) persecution
Verfügung: jemandem zur Verfügung stehen to be at one's disposal
vergangen past; preceding (26)
die Vergangenheit past (27)
die Vergangenheitsform (-en) past-tense form
vergeben (vergibt), vergab, vergeben to give, assign

vergeblich futile(ly)
vergeistigt cerebral, spiritual
die Vergeistigung (-en) spiritualization
vergessen (vergisst), vergaß, vergessen to forget (9)
vergesslich forgetful(ly)
vergiften to poison (12/35)
vergiftet (*adj.*) poisoned
der Vergleich (-e) comparison, **im Vergleich mit** in comparison with
vergleichen, verglich, verglichen to compare
sich vergnügen to amuse oneself (33)
das Vergnügen pleasure; **mit Vergnügen** with pleasure
vergnügt happy, happily
der Vergnügungspark (-s) amusement park
sich verhalten (verhält), verhielt, verhalten to act, behave
das Verhalten attitude (31)
die Verhaltensweise (-n) behavioral pattern
das Verhältnis (-se) relationship; circumstance; proportion
verharren to pause, remain
sich verheiraten mit to get married to (23)
verheiratet married (25)
verhüllen to veil, to mask, to disguise
sich verirren to get lost
verjüngen rejuvenate
verjüngt (*adj.*) rejuvenated
verkaufen to sell
der Verkäufer (-) / die Verkäuferin (-nen) vendor, salesperson
der Verkaufsingenieur (-e) / die Verkaufsingenieurin (-nen) sales engineer
die Verkaufsunterlagen (*pl.*) sales documents
der Verkehr traffic (35)
der Verkehrsingenieur (-e) / die Verkehrsingenieurin (-nen) traffic engineer
das Verkehrsmittel (-) mode of transportation (35)

das Verkehrsschild (-er) traffic sign
die Verkleidungsparty (-s) costume party
verknüpfen to connect, combine
verkürzen to shorten
verkürzt (*adj.*) shortened
der Verlag (-e) publisher
verlagern to shift; to move
verlangen to demand (14/28)
verlängern to extend, lengthen; to renew
die Verlängerung (-en) extention, lengthening
verlassen (verlässt), verließ, verlassen to leave (14/27)
verlegen (*adj.*) embarrassed
die Verlegenheit (-en) embarrassment (29)
der Verleger (-) / die Verlegerin (-nen) publisher
verleiden, verlitt, verlitten (+ *dat.*) to spoil
verleihen, verlieh, verliehen to lend
verlernen to forget how to
(sich) verletzen to hurt (oneself), to injure (19)
die Verletzung (-en) injury
sich verlieben in (+ *acc.*) to fall in love with
verliebt (*adj.*) in love (25)
verlieren, verlor, verloren to lose
verlobt (*adj.*) engaged (25)
die Verlobung (-en) engagement (25)
verloren gegangen (*adj.*) lost
die Verlosung (-en) raffle
verlustig: etwas (+ *gen.*) **verlustig gehen** to forfeit, to lose
sich vermählen (*antiquated*) to marry, wed
vermehren to multiply
die Vermehrung increase, reproduction, breeding
vermeiden, vermied, vermieden to avoid
vermieten to rent out (4)
der Vermieter (-) / die Vermieterin (-nen) landlord, landlady

vermindern to reduce (20)
vermischen to mix (19)
vermissen to miss, lack
vermitteln to convey, impart (26)
vermittelst (*antiquated*) by means of, with
die Vermittlungsagentur (-en) agency; **Au-Pair-Vermittlungsagentur** au pair agency
vernehmlich clear(ly), audible; audibly
verneinen to negate
die Vernunft reason
vernünftig reasonable; reasonably (10)
veröffentlichen to publish
verpacken to wrap; to package
die Verpackung (-en) packaging (20)
das Verpackungsmaterial (-ien) packaging material (35)
der Verpackungsmüll packaging waste
verpassen to miss
die Verpflegung (-en) catering, full board
die Verpflichtung (-en) duty; obligation; commitment
verraten (verrät), verriet, verraten to tell, reveal
sich verrechnen to miscalculate (33)
verregnet (*adj.*) rainy
verreisen to go on a trip (32)
verrückt crazy, mad (17)
die Verrücktheit (-en) madness, craziness
versagen to fail
die Versagensangst (¨e) fear of failure
versalzen to put too much salt in
versalzen (*adj.*) too salty
(sich) versammeln to assemble, gather together
die Versammlung (-en) meeting
verschenken to give away
verschärfen to increase
verscheuchen to scare away
verschieben, verschob, verschoben to move, change, reschedule

verschieden different(ly) (22)
verschlossen closed
verschlucken to swallow
verschmutzen to pollute (35)
die Verschmutzung (-en) pollution (35)
verschollen lost, missing
verschränken: die Hände verschränken to cross one's hands
verschreiben, verschrieb, verschrieben to prescribe (33)
verschwenden to waste
die Verschwendung (-en) waste, wastefulness
verschwinden, verschwand, verschwunden to disappear (20)
das Versehen (-) mistake; **aus Versehen** by mistake
versetzen to move; to transplant; to transfer (16)
sich versetzen: sich in die Rolle von jemandem versetzen to put oneself in the role of someone
die Versetzung (-en) transfer
versichern to assure
versichert (*adj.*) insured
die Versichertenkarte (-n) insurance card
die Versicherung (-en) insurance (33)
der Versicherungsbeitrag (¨e) insurance premium
versiert (*adj.*) experienced, practiced
die Version (-en) version
versorgen to provide for, support
die Versorgung care, supply
sich verspäten to be late (34)
verspätet belated, late
die Verspätung (-en) delay (24/32)
versperren to block
das Versprechen (-) promise
versprechen (verspricht), versprach, versprochen to promise
die Versprechung (-en) promise (34)
der Verstand reason; common sense
das Verständnis understanding

verständnislos without understanding
verständnisvoll understanding(ly)
verstärken to reinforce
verstaubt dusty
das Versteck (-e) hiding place
verstecken to hide
verstehen, verstand, verstanden to understand; **verstanden?** understood?
verstopfen to stuff
verstreut (*adj.*) scattered
der Versuch (-e) attempt, experiment, try
versuchen to try, attempt
verteilen to distribute
verteufelt tricky, darned
vertiefen to deepen
vertieft in depth
der Vertrag (¨e) contract (25)
sich vertragen (verträgt), vertrug, vertragen to get along
verträglich amicable; amicably; tolerable; tolerably
das Vertrauen trust
verträumt dreamy, dreamily
vertraut sein mit to be aquainted with
vertreten (vertritt), vertrat, vertreten to appear; to represent (27); **vertreten sein** to be represented
der Vertreter (-) / die Vertreterin (-nen) representative
die Vertreterfirma (-firmen) distributor, wholesaler
die Vertretung (-en) substitute
der Vertrieb sales
verursachen to cause (18)
verurteilen to condemn, convict, sentence
verwalten to manage, run
die Verwaltung management; administration
verwandeln (*adj.*) **(in + acc.)** to turn (into)
verwandelt (*adj.*) transformed (12)
verwandt (*adj.*) related
der/die Verwandte (*decl. adj.*) relative, relation

die Verwandtschaft (-en) relatives, relations, family
das Verweilen stay
verwelken to wilt
verwendbar usable
verwenden to apply (35); to use (20)
verwerten to use
verwickelt (*adj.*) entangled
verwirklichen to realize; to fulfill (26)
verwirren to confuse
verwirrt (*adj.*) confused
(sich) verwöhnen to pamper
verwunden to injure, wound
verwunderlich surprising(ly), astonishing(ly)
verwundet (*adj.*) injured
verwünschen to cast a negative spell on (12)
verwünscht (*adj.*) enchanted (12)
verzaubern to cast a spell, do magic
verzeihen, vezieh, verziehen to forgive; **wird Silke ihm verzeihen?** will Silke forgive him?
die Verzeihung (-en) forgiveness, pardon
verzichten (auf + *acc.*) to renounce (35); to do without (21)
verzweifelt desperate(ly) (33)
die Verzweiflung (-en) desperation
der Vetter (-n) (*male*) cousin (25)
das Video (-s) video
der Videorekorder (-) video recorder
das Videospiel (-e) video game
der Videotext videotext
die Videothek (-en) video store
die Videovorstellung (-en) video show
viel (mehr, meist-) a lot, much
viele many
die Vielfalt variety
vielfältig diverse
vielfarbig multicolored
vielleicht perhaps, maybe (11)
vielmehr . . . rather . . .
vielseitig manifold, versatile, diversified, multifaceted
vier four (1E)

der Vierbeiner (-) four-legged animal
vierbeinig four-legged
die Vierergruppe (-n) group of four
die Viererkabine (-n) cabin for four (*on a ship*)
viermal four times
viert: zu viert the four of us
das Viertel (-) quarter
vierzehn fourteen (1E)
vierzig forty (1E); **die vierziger Jahre** the Forties
der Vietnamkrieg Vietnam War
die Villa (Villen) villa
violett violet
das Violinkonzert (-e) violin concerto
visuell visual(ly)
vital vigorous, energetic
das Vitamin (-e) vitamin
der Vogel (¨) bird
der Vogelkundler (-) / die Vogelkundlerin (-nen) ornithologist
die Vogelmutter (¨) bird mother
die Vogelscheuche scarecrow
die Vogelstimme (-n) bird song
die Vogelwelt (-en) world of birds
die Vokabel (-n) vocabulary item
die Vokabelarbeit vocabulary work
die Vokabelliste (-n) vocabulary list
der Vokabeltest (-s) vocabulary test
das Vokabular (-e) vocabulary
das Volk (¨er) people
die Völkerverständigung intercultural communication
das Volksfest (-e) fair
die Volksgruppe (-n) group of peoples
die Volkshochschule (-n) extension school, adult education center (31)
voll full(y) (15); **aus vollem Herzen** wholeheartedly; **aus voller Kehle** at the top of one's lungs
vollenden to complete
voller full of; **voller Hoffnung** full of hope
der Volleyball volleyball

völlig completely
vollkommen perfect(ly), complete(ly)
die Vollpension (-en) full board
vollständig complete(ly), total(ly)
die Vollverpflegung full board
vollwertigt full
vom = von dem
von (+ *dat.*) from, of; by (12)
vor (+ *acc./dat.*) before, in front of; ago; **vor allem** above all, most importantly; **vor allen Dingen** above all, most importantly; **vor drei Jahren** three years ago
voranbringen (bringt voran), brachte voran, vorangebracht to bring forth, promote
voraus ahead
Voraus: im Voraus in advance
voraussetzen (setzt voraus) to presuppose; to require
die Voraussetzung (-en) prerequisite, condition
vorbehalten (behält vor), behielt vor, vorbehalten to reserve
vorbei over
vorbeifahren (fährt vorbei), fuhr vorbei, ist vorbeigefahren to drive past
vorbeikommen (kommt vorbei), kam vorbei, ist vorbeigekommen to drop by (7/3E)
(sich) vorbereiten (bereitet vor) to prepare (27)
die Vorbereitung (-en) preparation (32)
das Vorbild (-er) example, idol, model
vorbildlich exemplary
vorderasiatisch Near Eastern
(das) Vorderasien Near East
der Vordergrund (¨e) foreground
die Vorderpfote (-n) front paw
das Vordiplom (-e) exam, first diploma
vorerst for now, as of now
der Vorfahre (-n *masc.*) / die Vorfahrin (-nen) ancestor
die Vorgabe points allowed (handicap)

vorgefertigt (*adj.*) prefabricated

vorgehen (geht vor), ging vor, ist vorgegangen to go ahead, go first

vorhaben (hat vor), hatte vor, vorgehabt to plan, intend (23)

vorher before, beforehand; **am Abend vorher** the night before

vorherig preceding, prior

vorhin earlier; before; **es tut mir Leid wegen vorhin** I'm sorry about what happened earlier

vorkommen (kommt vor), kam vor, ist vorgekommen to occur, happen

der Vorläufer (-) / die Vorläuferin (-nen) precursor

vorläufig temporary; temporarily

vorlesen (liest vor), las vor, vorgelesen to read (aloud)

die Vorlesung (-en) lecture (19/3E); **Vorlesung halten** to give a lecture

der Vorlesungssaal (-säle) lecture hall

die Vorliebe (-n) liking

der Vorname (-n *masc.*) first name

vorne: von vorne from the beginning

sich vornehmen (nimmt vor), nahm vor, vorgenommen to undertake; to carry out (33)

der Vorort (-e) suburb (4)

vorrangig primarily, as a priority

der Vorrat (-̈e) stock, supply

die Vorrede (-n) preface, prologue

der Vorsatz (-̈e) resolution

der Vorschlag (-̈e) suggestion (14)

vorschlagen (schlägt vor), schlug vor, vorgeschlagen to suggest (22/3E)

vorsichtig cautious(ly) (31)

vorsichtshalber as a precaution

die Vorsorge preventive medicine (33)

die Vorsorgeuntersuchung (-en) medical check-up

vorsortieren (sortiert vor) to presort, preorganize

die Vorspeise (-n) starter, first course (15)

vorspielen (spielt vor) to act out, perform

sich (*dat.*) **etwas vorstellen (stellt vor)** to imagine something; **ich kann es mir nicht vorstellen** I can't imagine it; **sich** (*acc.*) **vorstellen** to interview for a job; to introduce oneself (13)

die Vorstellung (-en) performance; imagination; ideas

das Vorstellungsgespräch (-e) interview (13)

der Vorteil (-e) advantage

vorteilhaft advantageous

der Vortrag (-̈e) lecture, talk; **einen Vortrag halten** to give a lecture (19/3E)

das Vorurteil (-e) prejudice (24)

vorwiegend primarily, predominantly

der Vorwurf (-̈e) reproach, accusation

vorziehen (zieht vor), zog vor, vorgezogen to prefer (20)

der Vorzug (-̈e) advantage

vorzüglich excellent(ly), superb(ly)

W

der Wachdienst (-e) guard (duty)

wachen to wake; to guard

wachsam watchful, vigilant

wachsen (wächst), wuchs, ist gewachsen to grow

das Wachstum growth (35)

der Wachstumsprüfer (-) / die Wachstumsprüferin (-nen) gardener

die Wade (-n) calf (*lower leg*)

die Waffe (-n) weapon

der Wagen (-) car

die Wahl (-en) election (18); choice

wählen to choose; to elect (26)

das Wahlfach (-̈er) elective course (27)

das Wahlrecht right to vote, suffrage (30)

wahnsinnig crazy; crazily

wahr true

wahren to look after, protect

während (+ *gen.*) during

während (*adj.*) lasting

die Wahrheit (-en) truth

wahrnehmen (nimmt wahr), nahm wahr, wahrgenommen to perceive

wahrscheinlich probable; probably

die Währung (-en) currency (18); **die Währungsreform (-en)** monetary reform, currency reform

die Währungsunion monetary union (18)

der Wal (-e) whale

der Wald (-̈er) forest (9)

die Waldarbeit (-en) forestry work

der Waldeinsatz (-̈e) forest clean-up

die Waldfläche (-n) forest area

die Waldlandschaft (-en) forest landscape

das Waldsterben dying of the forests (35)

der Waldweg (-e) forest path (20)

wallen to surge, seethe

das Wallis Valais

walten to prevail, reign, rule

die Walze (-n) roller

sich wälzen to roll

die Wand (-̈e) wall (1E)

der Wandel change (26)

die Wanderbewegung (-en) hiking movement, rambling

der Wanderer (-) / die Wanderin (-nen) hiker

die Wanderkarte (-n) hiking map

das Wanderlied (-er) hiking song

wandern to hike (2/32)

die Wanderreise (-n) hiking vacation

der Wanderschuh (-e) hiking boot

der Wandersmann (-leute) traveler, wayfarer

der Wanderstock (-̈e) walking stick

die Wanderung (-en) hike, walk

der Wanderverein (-e) rambling club

der Wanderweg (-e) hiking trail

das Wandposter (-) wall poster

die Wange (-n) cheek (6)

wann when

die Waren (*pl.*) goods (22)

das Warenhaus (-̈er) warehouse; department store

das Warenzeichen (-) trademark; **das eingetragene Warenzeichen** registered trademark

warm (wärmer, wärmst-) warm (5)

die Wärme warmth

die Warnung (-en) warning

(das) Warschau Warsaw

warten (auf) (+ *acc.*) to wait (for)

der Warteraum (-räume) waiting area (24)

der Wartesaal (-säle) waiting room

die Wartezeit (-en) waiting period

das Wartezimmer (-) waiting room (33)

was what; **was darf's sein?** what will you have? (15)

das Waschbecken (-) sink (3)

die Wäsche laundry (3E)

waschen (wäscht), wusch, gewaschen to wash (16); **sich waschen** to wash oneself (19)

die Waschküche (-n) laundry room

der Wäschetrockner (-) (clothes) dryer (35)

die Waschmaschine (-n) washing machine

der Waschtag (-e) laundry day

das Wasser (-) water (16)

die Wasseranwendung (-en) water treatment

das Wasserglas (-̈er) water glass

der Wasserkessel (-) hot water heater

die Wasserratte (-n) water rat (*person who likes to swim*)

die Wasserwaage (-n) level

die Watte cotton wool, wadding

die Web-Seite (-n) Web page

der Wechsel (-) change

wechseln to exchange, switch

wecken to waken (16)

der Wecker (-) alarm clock

weder . . . noch . . . neither . . . nor . . .

weg away

der Weg (-e) way; **sich auf den Weg machen** to get on one's way (24)

wegbleiben (bleibt weg), blieb weg, ist weggeblieben to stay away

wegbrausen (braust weg) (*coll.*) to zoom away

wegen (+ *gen.*) because of

wegfahren (fährt weg), fuhr weg, ist weggefahren to drive off, leave

weggehen (geht weg), ging weg, ist weggegangen to go away

wegkommen (kommt weg), kam weg, ist weggekommen to get away

weglaufen (läuft weg), lief weg, ist weggelaufen to run away

wegsausen (saust weg), sauste weg, ist weggesaust to buzz off

wegschicken (schickt weg) to send away

wegschmeißen (schmeißt weg), schmiss weg, weggeschmissen (*coll.*) to throw away (35)

wegwerfen (wirft weg), warf weg, weggeworfen to throw away

die Wegwerfflasche (-n) disposable bottle (20)

wegziehen (zieht weg), zog weg, ist weggezogen to move away (4)

wehen to blow in the wind

wehren (+ *dat.*) to fight; **wehret den Anfängen!** nip it in the bud!

sich wehren gegen to defend oneself against (26)

wehtun (+ *dat.*) to hurt; **das tut mir weh** it hurts me (6)

weiblich feminine, female (25)

weich soft(ly)

die Weide (-n) pasture

sich weigern to resist; to refuse

weihen (+ *dat.*) to dedicate (27)

der Weiher (-) pond

(das) Weihnachten Christmas (5)

der Weihnachtsbaum (-̈e) Christmas tree

der Weihnachtsmann Santa Claus

der Weihnachtsmarkt (-̈e) Christmas fair

der Weihnachtstag: zweiter Weihnachtstag Boxing Day (*legal holiday in Canada for giving boxed gifts to service workers*)

der Weihrauch incense

weil (*subord. conj.*) because

die Weile while; **eine Weile** a while (16); **nach einer Weile** after a while

weinen to cry, weep

weise wise(ly)

die Weisheit (-en) wisdom

weiß white (2)

weit far; **das geht zu weit!** that's too much!; that pushes it over the top!

weiter farther, further

sich weiterbilden (bildet weiter) to continue one's education (31)

die Weiterbildung continuing education, further education

die Weiterentwicklung (-en) further development, advancement

weitergeben (gibt weiter), gab weiter, weitergegeben to pass on

weitergehen (geht weiter), ging weiter, ist weitergegangen to go further

weitgehend mostly, for the most part

weiterhin furthermore

weiterleben (lebt weiter) to live on, survive

weitgehend extensive(ly) (27)

weitverbreitet common; widely held

die Weizenlandschaft (-en) wheat land

welche, welcher, welches which

die Welle (-n) wave

der Wellenkamm (-̈e) crest of a wave

die Welt (-en) world; **die Neue Welt** the New World

weltbekannt known all over the world

weltberühmt world-famous

weltfremd awkward; ignorant of the world

die Weltkarte (-n) world map

der Weltkonzern (-e) international corporation

der Weltkrieg (-e) world war

die Weltmeisterschaft (-en) world championship
die Weltreise (-n) world tour
die Weltstadt (¨e) cosmopolitan city
weltweit worldwide
wem (*dat.*) to whom
wen (*acc.*) who, whom
die Wende the change (*in reference to the reunification of Germany in 1989*) (18)
wenden to turn, flip around
wenig little; few (32); **ein wenig** a little
wenige few
wenigstens at least
wenn (*subord. conj.*) whenever, when, if
wer who
die Werbesendung (-en) commercial (21)
der Werbespot (-s) television commercial
der Werbespruch (¨e) slogan
die Werbung (-en) advertising (21)
werden (wird), wurde, ist geworden to become (9)
werfen (wirft), warf, geworfen to throw
das Werk (-e) manufacturing plant (16); work (*in literature, art, music*)
die Werkstatt (¨en) workshop
der Werktag (-e) weekday
das Werkzeug (-e) tool
der Wert (-e) value; **Wert legen auf** (+ *acc.*) to value (*something*) (27)
wert sein to be worth
wertvoll valuable (22)
das Wesen (-) being; creature; essence; nature
im Wesentlichen essentially; fundamentally (31)
die Wespe (-n) wasp
westdeutsch West German
(das) Westdeutschland West Germany
der Westen (-) west; **im Westen** in the west
die Westküste west coast
westlich (von) west (of)
der Westteil (-e) western part

der Wettbewerb (-e) competition (27)
die Wette (-n) bet
wetten to bet
das Wetter (-) weather (5)
die Wetterlage (-n) weather situation
der Wettkampf (¨e) competition
der Wettstreit competition
wetzen to sharpen
WG = Wohngemeinschaft
wichtig important (23)
die Wicke (-n) sweet pea
wickeln to wrap
der Widerruf (-e) revocation, withdrawal, cancellation
widersprechen (widerspricht), widersprach, widersprochen to contradict
der Widerstand resistance
die Widerstandsbewegung (-en) resistance movement
wie how; **um wie viel Uhr?** at what time?; **wie schade!** too bad!; **wie viel** how much; **wie viele** how many
wieder again; **immer wieder** again and again
der Wiederaufbau reconstruction (29)
die Wiederentdeckung (-en) rediscovery
sich wieder erkennen (erkennt wieder), erkannte wieder, wieder erkannt to recognize oneself, identify with
wiederholen to repeat (3E)
die Wiederholung (-en) repetition
das Wiederhören: auf Wiederhören! (*phone*) good-bye!
wiederkommen (kommt wieder), kam wieder, ist wiedergekommen to come again
wiedermal once again
auf Wiedersehen! good-bye!
die Wiedervereinigung (-en) reunification (18)
wieder verwerten to recycle (35)
die Wiege (-n) cradle
(das) Wien Vienna; **die Wiener Festwochen** (*pl.*) arts festival in

Vienna; **das Wiener Schnitzel** veal cutlet (15)
die Wiese (-n) meadow (9)
wieso why
wild wild(ly)
die Wildbiene (-n) wild bee
die Wildblume (-n) wildflower
der Wildreis wild rice
der Wille will
willkommen welcome; **willkommen heißen, hieß willkommen, willkommen geheißen** to welcome (34)
die Willkür arbitrariness, capriciousness, despotism
die Willkürherrschaft (-en) tyranny
willkürlich arbitrary; arbitrarily; random(ly)
der Wind (-e) wind (5)
die Windel (-n) diaper; **Windeln wechseln** to change diapers
windgeschützt (*adj.*) protected from the wind
windig windy (5)
die Windmühle (-n) windmill
die Windstille (-n) calm, absence of wind
der Winkel (-) angle
der Winter (-) winter (5)
die Winterferien (*pl.*) winter holidays
der Wintermantel (¨) winter coat
das Wintersemester (-) winter semester
wir we
der Wirbelsturm (¨e) whirlwind; tornado
wirken to work, have an effect, act
wirklich real(ly) (10)
die Wirklichkeit reality (14)
die Wirkung (-en) result; effect (27)
die Wirtschaft (-en) economics (11); economy (29)
wirtschaftlich economical
der Wirtschaftsingenieur (-e) / die Wirtschaftsingenieurin (-nen) person holding a university degree in engineering and business administration

die Wirtschaftskraft economic power

wirtschaftspolitisch economic-political

die Wirtschaftswissenschaften (*pl.*) economics

das Wirtschaftswunder economic miracle

das Wirtshaus (¨er) inn, restaurant (15)

wissen (weiß), wusste, gewusst to know (*a fact*) (8)

das Wissen knowledge

die Wissenschaft (-en) science (27), scholarship

der Wissenschaftler (-) / die Wissenschaftlerin (-nen) scientist, scholar

wissenschaftlich scientific(ally), scholarly

der Witz (-e) joke

witzig funny, witty

wo where

woanders somewhere else

wobei where, in which

die Woche (-n) week (1E); **nächste Woche** next week; **seit Wochen** for weeks

die Wochenbelastung (-en) weekly stress

die Wochenendaktivität (-en) weekend activity

das Wochenende (-n) weekend; **am Wochenende** on the weekend

die Wochenendehe (-n) weekend marriage

wochenlang for weeks

der Wochentag (-e) weekday (1E)

wöchentlich weekly

wofür for what

wogen to surge, wave

woher from where

wohin (to) where; **wohin?** where to?; **wo wollen Sie denn hin?** where do you want to go?

wohl (*particle*) probably; (*adv.*) well

sich wohl fühlen (fühlt wohl) to feel well (6), be comfortable

wohlgefällig pleasing, well-pleased

der Wohlgeruch (¨e) scent, fragrance

wohlig pleasant(ly), cozy; cozily

wohlriechend fragrant

der Wohlstand prosperity (26)

das Wohlwollen goodwill

wohlwollend benevolent(ly)

wohnen to live (*in a place*) (8)

die Wohngemeinschaft (-en) shared housing, commune

das Wohnhaus (¨er) residential building

das Wohnheim (-e) dormitory

der Wohnheimplatz (¨e) place in a dormitory

das Wohnheimzimmer (-) dorm room

die Wohnkosten (*pl.*) housing costs

die Wohnmöglichkeit (-en) housing option

der Wohnort (-e) place of residence

der Wohnraum (¨e) living space

die Wohnsiedlung (-en) housing development

die Wohnung (-en) apartment; dwelling (3)

die Wohnungssuche (-n) housing search

das Wohnzimmer (-) living room (3)

die Wohnzimmertür (-en) living room door

sich wölben to bulge, swell, vault

die Wolke (-n) cloud (5)

wolkenlos cloudless

der Wolkenkratzer (-) skyscraper

wolkig cloudy (5)

die Wolle wool

wollen (will), wollte, gewollt to want; **auf etwas hinaus wollen** to imply something; to have a certain goal (30)

der Wollmantel (¨) wool coat

womit with what

woran on what; of what

worauf on what

woraus from what; out of what

das Wort (¨er) word

das Wörterbuch (¨er) dictionary

der Wortkasten (¨) word box

wörtlich literal(ly)

die Wortliste (-n) word list

der Wortsalat (-e) word search (puzzle)

der Wortschatz (¨e) vocabulary

wortschlau clever with words

der Wortsinn (-e) meaning of a word

die Wortstellung (-en) word order

worüber about what; above what

worum around what; about what

wovor before what; of what

das Wrack (-s) wreck

wühlen to dig, burrow

die Wunde (-n) wound, injury (6)

das Wunder (-) wonder; miracle

wunderbar wonderful(ly)

sich wundern (über + *acc.*) to be surprised (at) (28)

wunderschön very beautiful(ly)

der Wunsch (¨e) wish

wünschen to wish; **ich wünsche Ihnen einen schönen Urlaub** I wish you a nice vacation; **sich** (*dat.*) **wünschen** (+ *acc.*) to desire; **ich wünsche mir einen Hut zum Geburtstag** I would like a hat for my birthday

wünschenswert desirable

das Wunschgeschenk (-e) desired present

der Wunschsatz (¨e) wish sentence

würdevoll dignified

würdig dignified

der Würfel (-) die, cube

die Wurst (¨e) sausage (15)

das Wurstbrot (-e) sausage sandwich

wurstförmig shaped like a sausage

der Wurstmarkt sausage festival

der Wurstsalat (-e) sausage salad

die Wurstwaren (*pl.*) sausage products

die Wurzel (-n) root

würzen to season

würzig tasty, spicy, tangy

wuschelig fuzzy

die Wüste (-n) desert

die Wut anger

wütend angry; angrily

Y

der Yuppie (-s) yuppie

Z

z.B. = zum Beispiel
die Zacke (-n) point, prong, tooth
zäh tough (19)
die Zahl (-en) number
zahlen to pay for (15)
zählen to count
zahlreich numerous(ly)
das Zahlwort (¨er) word for a number
zahm tame
zähmen to tame
der Zahn (¨e) tooth (6)
der Zahnarzt (¨e) / die Zahnärztin (-nen) dentist (13)
die Zange (-n) pliers
zart tender(ly)
die Zärtlichkeit (-en) tenderness
der Zauberberg *Magic Mountain* (novel by Thomas Mann)
der Zauberer (-) / die Zauberin (-nen) magician
die Zauberflöte *Magic Flute* (opera by Mozart)
die Zauberkraft (¨e) magic power
das Zaubermeer (-e) magic ocean
zaubern to do magic
der Zaun (¨e) fence
zehn ten (1E)
das Zeichen (-) sign, token (26)
die Zeichensprache sign language
die Zeichentrickserie (-n) cartoon
zeichnen to draw (13)
die Zeichnung (-en) drawing
der Zeigefinger (-) index finger
zeigen to show (6)
die Zeile (-n) *(written)* line
die Zeit (-en) time
das Zeitalter (-) era
die Zeitangabe (-n) time expression
die Zeiteinteilung (-en) time management
zeitlich timewise, temporal(ly)
der Zeitpunkt (-e) point in time
der Zeitraum (¨e) time period
die Zeitschrift (-en) magazine, periodical (21)

die Zeitung (-en) newspaper; **in der Zeitung** in the newspaper
der Zeitungsartikel (-) newspaper article
das Zeitungspapier (old) newspaper; newsprint
der Zeitvertreib (-e) pastime
das Zeitwort (¨er) time expression
das Zelt (-e) tent (8)
zelten to camp (9/31)
das Zeltlager (-) camp
der Zement concrete
die Zensur (-en) grade
der Zentimeter (-) centimeter
der Zentner (-) *(metric system)* hundredweight (100 kg)
zentral central(ly) (4)
die Zentralbank (-en) central bank
das Zentralinstitut (-e) central institution
der Zentralrechner (-) main computer in a network
das Zentrum (pl. Zentren) center
die Zeremonie (-n) ceremony
die Zeremonietradition (-en) ceremonial tradition
zerknittert *(adj.)* creased *(clothing)*
zerlegen to dismantle, take apart
zerreißen, zerriss, zerrissen to tear
zerschmettern to shatter; to crush
zersiedeln to spoil by development
die Zersiedelung (-en) spoiling by development
zerstören to destroy (27)
die Zerstörung (-en) destruction
zerstreuen to scatter, disperse; **sich zerstreuen** to take one's mind off things
zerstückeln to cut into pieces
der Zettel (-) note; piece of paper (33)
das Zeug gear, junk, stuff
das Zeugnis (-se) report card (10)
die Zeugniskopie (-n) grade report, transcript
die Zickzacklinie (-n) zigzag line
die Ziege (-n) goat
ziehen, zog, gezogen to pull; to move (4/31)
das Ziel (-e) goal, aim (26)

die Zielgruppe (-n) target group
ziemlich rather, quite (2)
das Zimmer (-) room (3)
die Zimmerpflanze (-n) indoor plant (3)
der Zinnmann tin man
der Zirkuskünstler (-) / die Zirkuskünstlerin (-nen) circus artist
zirpen to chirp
zischen to hiss
das Zitat (-e) quote, quotation
zitieren to quote
die Zitrone (-n) lemon
die Zitronenscheibe (-n) slice of lemon
die Zitrusfrucht (¨e) citrus fruit
der Zivi (-s) = Zivildienstleistender
die Zivilbevölkerung (-en) civilian population
der Zivildienst (-e) social service *(as an alternative to military service)*
der/die Zivildienstleistende *(decl. adj.)* person who chooses to do social service as an alternative to military service
der Zivilist (-en masc.) / die Zivilistin (-nen) civilian
der Zoff *(coll.)* argument, conflict *(between people)*
der Zollbeamte (-n masc.) / die Zollbeamtin (-nen) customs officer
die Zone (-n) zone
der Zoo (-s) zoo
zoologisch zoological(ly)
der Zorn anger
zu closed (16); **zu** *(prep. + dat.)* to (12); **zu** *(adv.)* too; **zu Fuß** on foot; **zu Hause** (at) home
züchtig modest, chaste
zucken to twitch, flinch
der Zucker sugar
zueinander to each other
zuerst first; **zuerst einmal** first of all
die Zuflucht (¨e) refuge, last resort
zufrieden satisfied (19/29)

die Zufriedenheit (-en) contentedness

zufügen (fügt zu) to add

der Zug (⸚e) train (7)

der Zugang (⸚e) entrance

zugänglich available, approachable

zugeben (gibt zu), gab zu, zugegeben to admit

zugehören (gehört zu) to belong to

die Zugfahrkarte (-n) train ticket

das Zugfenster (-) window in a train

der Zugführer (-) / die Zugführerin (-nen) train conductor

zugleich at the same time

zugreifen (greift zu), griff zu, zugegriffen to grab

die Zugspitze *highest mountain in Germany*

zuhören (hört zu) to listen; **hör gut zu!** listen carefully!

die Zukunft (⸚e) future (26)

zukünftig future

zukunftsorientiert future-oriented

die Zukunftsstrategie (-n) strategy for the future

der Zukunftstraum (⸚e) future dream

das Zukunftsziel (-e) future goal

zulassen (lässt zu), ließ zu, zugelassen to allow, admit

die Zulassung (-en) admission

zuletzt finally, in the end

zuliebe (+ *dat.*) for the sake of (35)

die Zulieferfirma (-firmen) supplier

zum = zu dem

zumachen (macht zu) to close (6)

zumindest at least

zunächst first

die Zündschnur (⸚e) fuse

zunehmen (nimmt zu), nahm zu, zugenommen to increase (28); to gain (*weight*)

die Zunge (-n) tongue

zur = zu der

zurecht: du hast dir zurecht Sorgen gemacht your worries were well-founded

zurechtkommen (kommt zurecht), kam zurecht, ist zurechtgekommen to get by; to get along; to cope

sich zurechtmachen (macht zurecht) to prepare, get ready (*by dressing and grooming oneself*)

(das) Zürich Zurich

zurück back; **hin und zurück** round trip (24)

zurückbekommen (bekommt zurück), bekam zurück, zurückbekommen to get back; to stay behind

zurückbleiben (bleibt zurück), blieb zurück, zurückgeblieben to stay behind, remain

zurückbringen (bringt zurück), brachte zurück, zurückgebracht to bring back

sich zurückerinnern an (+ *acc.*) **(erinnert zurück)** to remember

zurückfallen (fällt zurück), fiel zurück, ist zurückgefallen to fall behind

zurückgehen (geht zurück), ging zurück, ist zurückgegangen to go back

zurückgewinnen (gewinnt zurück), gewann zurück, zurückgewonnen to win back

zurückkehren (kehrt zurück), ist zurückgekehrt to return

zurückkommen (kommt zurück), kam zurück, ist zurückgekommen to come back (7/3E)

sich zurücklegen (legt zurück) to lie back

zurückschrecken vor (schreckt zurück) to shy away from

zurückweisen (weist zurück) to reject

(sich) zurückziehen (zieht zurück), zog zurück, zurückgezogen to withdraw, move back

zurufen, rief zu, zugerufen to shout to

die Zusage (-n) acceptance, positive response to a request

zusammen together (4)

die Zusammenarbeit (-en) cooperation

zusammenfassen (fasst zusammen) to summarize

die Zusammenfassung (-en) summary

sich zusammenfinden (findet zusammen) fand zusammen, zusammengefunden to gather, assemble

zusammenhalten (hält zusammen), hielt zusammen, zusammengehalten to keep together (23); to stay together

der Zusammenhang (⸚e) connection, correlation

zusammenklappen (klappt zusammen) to collapse

zusammenleben (lebt zusammen) to cohabitate, live together

zusammenpassen (passt zusammen) to go together

zusammensetzen (setzt zusammen) to put together, assemble

die Zusammensetzung (-en) composition

zusammenstellen (stellt zusammen) to put together

zusätzlich additional(ly)

zuschauen (schaut zu) to watch

der Zuschauer (-) / die Zuschauerin (-nen) spectator (23)

zuschicken (schickt zu) to send

zuschlagen (schlägt zu), schlug zu, zugeschlagen to slam shut

zuschließen (schließt zu), schloss zu, zugeschlossen to close, shut, lock

zusehen (sieht zu), sah zu, zugesehen to watch

zusprechen (spricht zu), sprach zu, zugesprochen to speak to, grant

der Zustand (⸚e) state, condition

zuständig responsible, in charge

zustechen (sticht zu), stach zu, zugestochen to stab, pierce

zustimmen (stimmt zu) (+ *dat.*) to agree with

die Zutat (-en) ingredient

zutraulich friendly, trusting

zuverlässig reliable; reliably (14)

die Zuverlässigkeit reliability (14)

zuvor before, earlier

zwanzig twenty (1E); **die zwanziger Jahre** the Twenties

die Zwangsarbeit forced labor

zwar in fact, actually; **zwar** (*emphatic*) **er braucht zwar Kraft, aber auch Intelligenz** he does need strength, but he also needs intelligence; **zwar sitzt man viel im Stau, aber das Auto hat Vorteile** in spite of the traffic jams, the car has advantages; **und zwar . . .** namely . . .

der Zweck (-e) purpose (36)

zweckentfremden to misuse

zwei two (1E)

das Zweierkajak (-s) kayak for two

der Zweifel (-) doubt

zweifeln an (+ *dat.*) to doubt someone/something

zweimal twice

zweisprachig bilingual

zweit: zu zweit by twos, in pairs

zweit-: der zweite Stock the third floor (8)

zweitrangig secondary

zweiwöchig two-week-long

der Zwerg (-e) dwarf (12)

die Zwiebel (-n) onion (15)

die Zwiebelsuppe (-n) onion soup

der Zwiebelturm (¨e) onion dome

der Zwilling (-e) twin (1)

zwingen, zwang, gezwungen to force (29)

zwinkern to blink

zwischen (+ *acc./dat.*) between

zwischendurch in between

der Zwischenhändler (-) / die Zwischenhändlerin (-nen) middleman

die Zwischenprüfung (-en) mid-diploma exam (19/3E)

zwitschern to chirp

zwölf twelve (E)

der Zynismus cynicism

ENGLISH-GERMAN

This vocabulary list contains all the words from the end-of-chapter **Wortschatz** lists in *Auf Deutsch!* 1, 2, and 3. For each word the chapter number in which the word appears in the **Wortschatz** list is provided. For **Sie wissen schon** vocabulary, the chapter in *Auf Deutsch!* 1 or 2 is also provided. Words in the **Wortschatz** list in the **Einführung** chapter are designated by the book number. For example "11/3E" indicates that the word appears in the **Wortschatz** list of **Kapitel 11** in *Auf Deutsch!* 1 and the **Einführung** in 3. For a list of the abbreviations used, see page R-13.

A

absolutely unbedingt (11/20/34)
accent der Akzent (-e) (34)
to accept annehmen (nimmt an), nahm an, angenommen (34)
to accomplish schaffen (28)
accuracy die Genauigkeit (34)
to accuse beschuldigen (30)
to achieve erreichen (25)
action die Aktion (-en) (35)
action film der Actionfilm (-e) (36)
active(ly) aktiv (32)
activity die Tätigkeit (-en) (13)
act of violence die Gewalttätigkeit (-en) (20)
actor der Schauspieler (-) / die Schauspielerin (-nen) (13/36)
actually eigentlich (21)
to address someone with *du* duzen (34)
to address someone with *Sie* siezen (34)
adjustment die Umstellung (-en) (25)
to admit gestehen, gestand, gestanden (34)
adult der/die Erwachsene (*decl. adj.*) (25)
adult education center die Volkshochschule (-n) (31)
adventure das Abenteuer (9/32)
adventure sport die Extremsportart (-en) (32)
advertisement die Anzeige (-n) (14)
advertising die Reklame, die Werbung (21)

advice der Ratschlag (¨e) (27)
advice columnist der Ratgeber (-) / die Ratgeberin (-nen) (21)
to advise raten (rät), riet, geraten (13)
to affect betreffen (betrifft), betraf, betroffen (25)
to afford sich leisten (32)
to be afraid of sich fürchten vor (+ *dat.*) (19/28)
African (*person*) der Afrikaner (-) / die Afrikanerin (-nen) (18)
against gegen (+ *acc.*) (5)
agent: employment agent der Arbeitsvermittler / die Arbeits-vermittlerin (-nen) (29)
to agree gelten lassen (lässt), ließ, gelassen (30); **to agree (with something)** übereinstimmen (mit etwas) (stimmt überein) (3E)
agreement: to be in agreement with something mit etwas einverstanden sein (18/29)
agriculture die Landwirtschaft (35)
aim das Ziel (-e) (26)
air die Luft (4); **in the open air** im Freien (31)
airline terminal das Terminal (-s) (24)
airline ticket der Flugschein (-e) (24)
airplane das Flugzeug (-e) (7)
airport der Flughafen (¨) (24)
all together! alle zusammen! (1E)
allied verbunden (18)
to allow gestatten (30)
almost fast (27)

alone allein (4)
along _____ entlang (22)
the Alps die Alpen (*pl.*) (17)
although obwohl (30)
always immer (3E)
ambitious(ly) ehrgeizig (26)
ambulance der Krankenwagen (-) (6)
American (*person*) der Amerikaner (-) / die Amerikanerin (-nen) (18)
to amuse onself sich vergnügen (33)
anger der Ärger (34)
angry böse (1); sauer (22)
to annoy ärgern (10)
annoyance der Ärger (34)
antique antiquarisch (22)
apartment die Wohnung (-en) (3)
apartment building das Mietshaus (¨er) (4)
to appear aussehen (sieht aus), sah aus, ausgesehen (7/3E); vertreten (vertritt), vertrat, vertreten (27)
appetizer die Vorspeise (-n) (15)
apple der Apfel (¨) (16)
apple strudel der Apfelstrudel (-) (15)
appliance das Gerät (-e) (31)
applicant (*for a job*) der Bewerber (-) / die Bewerberin (-nen) (14/29)
application die Bewerbung (-en) (14)
to apply verwenden (35)
to apply for sich bewerben um (bewirbt), bewarb, beworben (13)
appointment der Termin (-e) (29); die Verabredung (-en) (34)
apprentice der Lehrling (-e) (13)

to approve gelten lassen (lässt), ließ, gelassen (30)
approximate(ly) gegen (27); ungefähr (11/22/29)
April der April (5)
architect der Architekt (-en *masc.*) / die Architektin (-nen) (13)
to argue streiten, stritt, gestritten (23)
argument die Auseinandersetzung (-en) (26)
to arise entstehen, entstand, ist entstanden (28); erwachsen (erwächst), erwuchs, ist erwachsen (31)
arm der Arm (-e) (6)
around um . . . herum (+ *acc.*) (5)
to arrange vereinbaren (34)
arrival die Ankunft (¨e) (24)
to arrive ankommen (kommt an), kam an, ist angekommen (24)
art die Kunst (¨e) (11/36)
article der Artikel (-) (10)
artist der Künstler (-) / die Künstlerin (-nen) (13/36)
artistic(ally) künstlerisch (36)
as well sogar (32)
Asian (*person*) der Asiat (-en *masc.*) / die Asiatin (-nen) (18)
to ask fragen (8)
assignment die Aufgabe (-n)
asylum: political asylum das Asyl (34)
at first anfangs (30)
at once auf einmal (12)
at that time damals (25)
athlete der Sportler (-) / die Sportlerin (-nen) (23)
attentive(ly) aufmerksam (36)
attitude das Verhalten (31)
attorney der Anwalt (¨e) / die Anwältin (-nen) (13)
to attract locken (36)
August der August (5)
aunt die Tante (-n) (1/25)
Austria (das) Österreich (9)
Austrian (*person*) der Österreicher (-) / die Österreicherin (-nen) (18)
author der Autor (-en) / die Autorin (-nen) (13/36)
awful scheußlich (1)

B

back der Rücken (-) (6)
back then damals (25)
background der Hintergrund (¨e) (30)
backpack der Rucksack (¨e) (7/32)
bacon der Speck (15)
bad schlecht (1)
bag die Tasche (-n) (7)
baggage das Gepäck (7)
baggage check die Gepäckaufbewahrung (7)
bakery die Bäckerei (-en) (16)
balance das Gleichgewicht (35)
ball der Ball (¨e) (17)
ballpoint pen der Kugelschreiber (-) (1E)
banana die Banane (-n) (16)
bank die Bank (-en) (4)
basis die Grundlage (-n) (27)
bath das Bad (¨er) (33)
to bathe baden (32)
bathroom das Badezimmer (-) (3)
bathtub die Badewanne (-n) (3)
Bavaria (das) Bayern (17)
Bavarian meatloaf der Leberkäs (15)
bay Bucht (-en) (9)
to be sein (1); **to be about** handeln von (21); **to be annoyed** sich ärgern (16); **to be afraid of** sich fürchten vor (+ *dat.*) (19/28); **to be at an equal level** gleichberechtigt sein (30); **to be bored** sich langweilen (31); **to be called** heißen (hieß) (1); **to be close to** nah stehen, stand, gestanden (+ *dat.*); **to be crazy** spinnen (der spinnt doch!) (10); **to be in agreement with something** mit etwas einverstanden sein (18/29); **to be interested in** sich interessieren für (13/31); **to be located** sich befinden, befand, befunden (28); **to be missing** fehlen (+ *dat.*) (21); **to be occupied with** sich beschäftigen mit (13/27); **to be pleasing to** gefallen (gefällt), gefiel, gefallen (+ *dat.*) (14/31); **to be right/wrong** Recht/Unrecht haben (10); **to be surprised at** sich wundern über (+ *acc.*) (28)
beach der Strand (¨e) (4)
bean die Bohne (-n) (15)
to beat schlagen (schlägt), schlug, geschlagen (19)
beautiful schön (1)
to become werden (wird), wurde, ist geworden (9)
bed das Bett (-en) (3)
bed and breakfast inn die Pension (-en) (8)
bedroom das Schlafzimmer (3)
to begin beginnen, begann, begonnen (29); anfangen (fängt an), fing an, angefangen (23)
Belgium (das) Belgien (9)
to believe glauben (14)
to belong to gehören (+ *dat.*) (21)
belt der Gürtel (-) (7)
Berlin Wall die Berliner Mauer (18)
bicycle das Fahrrad (¨er) (7); **go by bicycle** mit dem Fahrrad fahren (7)
big groß (1)
bill die Rechnung (-en) (15)
bin die Tonne (-n) (35)
biology die Biologie (11)
birthday der Geburtstag (-e) (5)
black schwarz (2)
blackboard die Tafel (-n) (1E); **blackboard eraser** der Schwamm (¨e) (1E)
blood pressure der Blutdruck (33)
blouse die Bluse (-n) (7)
to blow one's nose sich die Nase putzen (6)
blue blau (2)
board das Brett (-er) (19)
body part der Körperteil (-e) (6)
body der Körper (-) (6)
to book buchen (7)
book das Buch (¨er) (1E)
bookstore die Buchhandlung (-en) (16)
boot der Stiefel (-) (7)
border die Grenze (-n) (17)
border crossing der Grenzübergang (18)
to border on grenzen an (+ *acc.*) (17)

to be bored sich langweilen (31)
boring langweilig (1/27)
born geboren; **when were you born?** geboren: wann sind Sie geboren? (14/25)
to borrow leihen, lieh, geliehen (3E)
boss der Chef (-s) / die Chefin (-nen) (13)
bottle die Flasche (-n) (20); **nonreturnable bottle** die Einwegflasche (-n) (35); **returnable bottle** die Pfandflasche (-n) (35)
boutique die Boutique (-n) (22)
bread das Brot (-e) (16)
break die Pause (-n) (10)
to breathe atmen (33)
bright hell (2)
to bring bringen, brachte, gebracht (5)
to bring up erziehen, erzog, erzogen (20)
broadcast die Sendung (-en) (21)
broccoli der Brokkoli (19)
brother der Bruder (÷) (1/25)
brother-in-law der Schwager (÷) (25)
brown braun (2)
to build aufbauen (baut auf) (29)
building: post-1945 building die Neubauwohnung (-en); **pre-1945 building** die Altbauwohnung (-en) (4)
bulletin board das schwarze Brett (19)
burden die Überlastung (-en) (27)
bus der Bus (-se) (7)
business das Geschäft (-e) (26)
business enterprise das Unternehmen (-) (29)
business operation der Betrieb (-e) (29)
businessman / businesswoman der Geschäftsmann (-leute) / die Geschäftsfrau (-en) (13)
butcher's store die Metzgerei (-en) (16)
to buy kaufen (2E)
by heart auswendig (27)
by the way übrigens (23)

C

café das Café (-s) (4)
cafeteria die Cafeteria (-s) (10)
cake der Kuchen (-) (16)
to calculate rechnen (27)
to call on the phone anrufen, rief an, angerufen (7/3E)
calm ruhig (1/28)
to camp zelten (9/31)
campfire das Lagerfeuer (-) (9/31)
Canadian (*person***)** der Kanadier (-) / die Kanadierin (-nen) (18)
candle die Kerze (-n) (17)
cap die Mütze (-n) (7)
capability die Fähigkeit (-en) (29)
capable; capably fähig (36)
capital city die Hauptstadt (÷e) (17)
captain der Kapitän (-e) (14)
car das Auto (-s) (7)
carbonated soft drink die Limonade (-n) (15)
to care for sorgen für (23/25)
career die Karriere (-n) (13); **career field** das Berufsfeld (-er) (29); **career school** Berufsschule (-n) (13)
to be careful aufpassen (passt auf) (7/3E)
careful(ly) sorgfältig (31)
Carnival der Fasching (17)
carrot die Karotte (-n) (19)
to carry out sich vornehmen (nimmt vor), nahm vor, vorgenommen (33)
to cast a spell on verwünschen (12)
castle die Burg (-en) (8); das Schloss (÷er) (12)
cauliflower der Blumenkohl (19)
to cause verursachen (18)
cautious(ly) vorsichtig (31)
to celebrate feiern (5)
center die Mitte (-n) (22)
central zentral (4)
century das Jahrhundert (-e) (27)
certain(ly) fest (13)
chair der Stuhl (÷e) (E)
chalk die Kreide (1E)
championship die Meisterschaft (-en) (23)

change die Abwechslung (-en) (32); die Veränderung (-en) (25); der Wandel (26)
to change sich verändern (27); umwechseln (wechselt um) (28); ändern (10)
to change (trains) umsteigen (steigt um), stieg um, ist umgestiegen (7)
channel das Programm (-e) (21)
to chat plaudern (10)
cheap billig (2)
checkered kariert (21)
cheek die Wange (-n) (6)
cheerful(ly) lustig (17/27)
cheese der Käse (16)
cheesecake der Käsekuchen (-) (15)
chemistry die Chemie (11/28)
child das Kind (-er) (1)
child's room das Kinderzimmer (-) (3)
chin das Kinn (-e) (6)
Chinese (*person***)** der Chinese (-n *masc.*) / die Chinesin (-nen) (18)
to choose wählen (26)
to choose something for oneself sich etwas aussuchen (21)
Christmas das Weihnachten (-) (5)
Cinderella das Aschenputtel (12)
circle der Kreis (-e) (28)
circumstance der Umstand (÷e) (33)
citizen der Staatsbürger (-) / die Staatsbürgerin (-nen) (26)
city die Stadt (÷e) (4)
class der Kurs (-e) (27); die Klasse (-n) (10)
classified ad die Kleinanzeige (-n) (21)
classmate der Kommilitone (-n *masc.*) / die Kommilitonin (-nen) (28)
classroom das Klassenzimmer (-) (10)
clean sauber (4)
to clean sauber machen (23)
to clean up aufräumen (räumt auf) (23/3E)
cleanliness die Sauberkeit (34)
clear(ly) deutlich (34)
clear (*weather***)** heiter (5)

clever(ly) geschickt (36)
climax der Höhepunkt (-e) (36)
to climb besteigen, bestieg, bestiegen (23/32); klettern (23/32)
clock die Uhr (-en) (1E)
to close zumachen (macht zu) (6); **close your books!** machen Sie die Bücher zu! (1E)
close by nah (7)
to be close to someone jemandem nah stehen, stand, gestanden (25)
closed zu, geschlossen (16)
closet der Schrank (÷e) (3)
clothes (*slang*) die Klamotten (*pl.*) (21)
clothes dryer der Wäschetrockner (-) (35)
clothing die Kleidung (21)
cloud die Wolke (-n) (5)
cloudy wolkig (5)
club room der Vereinsraum (÷e) (10)
coast die Küste (-n) (9)
coat der Mantel (÷) (7)
coffee der Kaffee (2)
coffee table der Sofatisch (-e) (3)
cold die Erkältung (-en) (6)
cold kalt (5)
collection station die Sammelstelle (-n) (20)
colleague der Kollege (-en) / die Kollegin (-nen) (13)
college die Hochschule (-n)
college preparatory high school das Gymnasium (Gymnasien) (10/27)
colored gefärbt (21)
colorful bunt (E)
to come kommen, kam, ist gekommen (2); **to come along** mitkommen, kam mit, ist mitgekommen (7/3E); **to come back** zurückkommen, kam zurück, ist zurückgekommen (7/3E); **to come by** vorbeikommen, kam vorbei, ist vorbeigekommen (7/3E); **to come to mind** einfallen (fällt ein), fiel ein, ist eingefallen (+ *dat.*) (34);

to come upon geraten (gerät), geriet, ist geraten (33)
comedy die Komödie (-n) (36)
comfortable gemütlich (16)
comment die Bemerkung (-en) (24/28)
commercial die Werbesendung (-en) (21)
common gemeinsam (28)
company die Firma (Firmen) (13)
competition der Wettbewerb (-e) (27)
to complain about sich beschweren über (+ *acc.*) (22)
to compose komponieren (36)
composer der Komponist (-en *masc.*) / die Komponistin (-nen) (36)
to compost kompostieren (20)
compost heap der Komposthaufen (-) (35)
comprehensive school die Gesamtschule (-n) (11/27)
computer game das Computerspiel (-e) (2)
computer programmer der Informatiker (-) / die Informatikerin (-nen) (13)
computer science die Informatik (11)
concept der Begriff (-e) (28)
to concern oneself with sich kümmern um (30)
to concern betreffen (betrifft), betraf, betroffen (25)
concert das Konzert (-e) (2)
condition die Bedingung (-en) (29)
condominium die Eigentumswohnung (-en) (4)
to conform anpassen (passt an) (26)
conformist (*adj.*) angepasst (26)
congenial sympathisch (1)
to congratulate gratulieren (17)
to conquer erobern (27)
to consider bedenken, bedachte, bedacht (31); betrachten (30); halten für (hält), hielt, gehalten (20); sich überlegen (29); **to consider something important** Wert legen auf (+ *acc.*) (27)

considerate rücksichtsvoll (29)
consideration die Rücksicht (35)
to consist of bestehen aus, bestand bestanden (35)
to consume verbrauchen (35)
consumer der Verbraucher (-) / die Verbraucherin (-nen) (35)
container der Container (-) (20/35)
contempt die Verachtung (34)
context der Rahmen (-) (18)
to continue one's education weiterbilden (bildet weiter) (31)
contract der Vertrag (÷e) (25)
contribution der Beitrag (÷e) (30)
to contribute to beitragen zu (trägt bei), trug bei, beigetragen (34)
contribution der Beitrag (÷e) (30)
to converse sich unterhalten über (+ *acc.*) (unterhält), unterhielt, unterhalten (28)
to convey mitteilen (teilt mit) (36); vermitteln (26)
to cook kochen (2)
cookie das Plätzchen (-) (16)
cool kühl (5)
corner die Ecke (-n) (22)
correct richtig (24)
cough der Husten (6)
counter der Schalter (-) (24)
country das Land (÷er) (4)
couple: married couple das Ehepaar (-e) (25)
courageous(ly) mutig (20)
course (academic) der Kurs (-e) (11/3E); **elective course** das Wahlfach (÷er) (27); **required course** das Pflichtfach (÷er)
course: course of study (*at a university*) das Studium (Studien) (19/3E); **course of treatment** die Kur (-en) (33)
courtyard der Hof (÷e) (31); der Schulhof (÷e) (10)
cousin (*male*) der Vetter (-n), der Cousin (-s) (1) / (*female*) die Kusine (-n) (25)
coworker der Mitarbeiter (-) / die Mitarbeiterin (-nen) (13)
to cram pauken (10)
crazy verrückt (17); irre (*coll.*) (32)
cream die Sahne (15)

critical(ly) kritisch (29)
crossing die Kreuzung (-en) (22)
cruise die Schiffsreise (-n) (32)
cucumber die Gurke (-n) (19)
cuisine die Küche (-n) (15)
cultural(ly) kulturell (36)
culture die Kultur (-en) (36)
cup: plastic cup der Plastikbecher (-) (35)
curious neugierig (1)
currency union die Währungsunion (18)
currency die Währung (-en) (18)
current aktuell (21)
current der Strom (35)
curriculum vitae (CV) der Lebenslauf (⸚e) (14)
customer der Kunde (-n *masc.*) / die Kundin (-nen) (26)
cut der Abschnitt (-e) (28)
to cut schneiden, schnitt, geschnitten (19)

D

daily täglich (21)
to damage schädigen (35)
damaged beschädigt (22/27)
dance der Tanz (⸚e) (36)
to dance tanzen (2)
danger die Gefahr (-en) (32)
dangerous gefährlich (7)
dark dunkel (2)
date die Verabredung (-en) (34)
date of birth das Geburtsdatum, *pl.* Geburtsdaten (14)
daughter die Tochter (⸚) (1/25)
day der Tag (-e) (1E)
day care center die Kinderkrippe (-n) (30)
to deal with handeln von (21)
to deal with something mit etwas umgehen, ging um, ist umgegangen (26)
debate die Debatte (-n) (35)
decade das Jahrzehnt (-e) (26)
December der Dezember (5)
to decide entscheiden, entschied, entschieden (14); sich entschließen, entschloss, entschlossen (19)
to decorate schmücken (17)

to dedicate weihen (+ *dat.*) (27)
deep(ly) tief (33)
to defend oneself against sich wehren gegen (26)
defendant der/die Angeklagte (*decl. adj.*) (30)
delay die Verspätung (-en) (24/32)
delegate der/die Abgeordnete (*decl. adj.*) (30)
delicious lecker (19)
to demand verlangen (14/28)
demanding anstrengend (23)
demeanor die Miene (-n) (29)
to demonstrate demonstrieren (10)
demonstration die Demonstration (-en) (10)
Denmark (das) Dänemark (9)
dentist der Zahnarzt (⸚e) / die Zahnärztin (-nen) (13)
to depart abreisen (reist ab), ist abgereist (8); losfahren (fährt los), fuhr los, ist losgefahren (14); **to depart by plane** abfliegen (fliegt ab), flog ab, ist abgeflogen
department store das Kaufhaus (⸚er) (16)
departure die Abfahrt (-en), der Abflug (⸚e) (24)
to depend upon auf etwas ankommen, kam an, ist angekommen (32)
dependent(ly) abhängig (13)
to depict darstellen (stellt dar) (34)
to desire begehren (35)
desire to travel die Reiselust (32)
desk der Schreibtisch (-e)
desperate verzweifelt (33)
desperate(ly) dringend (34)
dessert die Nachspeise (-n) (15)
to destroy zerstören (27)
to determine bestimmen (29)
to develop entwickeln (20)
development die Entwicklung (-en) (29)
device das Gerät (-e) (31)
to die sterben (stirbt), starb, ist gestorben (12)
to differ from sich unterscheiden von, unterschied, unterschieden (27)

different verschieden (22)
different(ly) anders (24)
difficult schwer (2)
difficulty die Schwierigkeit (-en) (30)
dilemma das Dilemma (-s) (23)
dining room das Esszimmer (-) (3)
dinner table der Esstisch (-e) (3)
dinner das Abendessen (-) (19)
direct(ly) unmittelbar (34)
director der Leiter (-) / die Leiterin (-nen) (31); der Regisseur (-e) / die Regisseurin (-nen) (36)
dirty schmutzig (4)
to disappear verschwinden, verschwand, verschwunden (20)
to discuss diskutieren (10); besprechen (bespricht), besprach, besprochen (18); diskutieren über (+ *acc.*) (20/26)
dish (meal) das Gericht (-e) (34)
dishes das Geschirr (3E); **to wash the dishes** das Geschirr spülen
dishwasher die Geschirrspülmaschine (-n) (3)
disposable bottle die Wegwerfflasche (-n) (20)
disposable utensils das Einweggeschirr (35)
dispute die Auseinandersetzung (-en) (26)
to distribute verbreiten (20)
to disturb stören (24)
to divide teilen (31); trennen (17/35)
divorce die Scheidung (-en) (23/25)
to do machen (2); unternehmen (unternimmt), unternahm, unternommen (9/31)
to do without verzichten auf (+ *acc.*) (21/35)
doctor der Arzt (⸚e) / die Ärztin (-nen); **visit to the doctor** der Arztbesuch (-e) (33)
door die Tür (-en) (1E)
dormitory das Studentenwohnheim (-e) (19/3E)
double room das Doppelzimmer (-) (8)
to doze dösen (16)
dragon der Drache (-n *masc.*) (12)

to draw zeichnen (13)
dream career, job die Traumkarriere (-n) (14)
dress das Kleid (-er) (7)
dresser die Kommode (-n) (3)
to drive fahren (fährt), fuhr, ist gefahren (3)
to drop by vorbeikommen, kam vorbei, ist vorbeigekommen (7/3E)
drugstore (*for prescription drugs*) die Apotheke (-n); (*for over-the-counter drugs and sundries*) die Drogerie (-n) (16)
dryer (*for clothes*) der Wäschetrockner (-) (35)
to dub (*a film*) synchronisieren (36)
dumb blöd (2)
dumpster der Container (-) (20/35)
duplex das Doppelhaus (-̈er) (4)
Dutch (*person*) der Niederländer (-) / die Niederländerin (-nen) (18)
dwarf der Zwerg (-e) (12)
dying of the forest das Waldsterben (35)

E

ear das Ohr (-en) (6)
earlier damals (25)
early früh
to earn verdienen (13/25)
easy leicht (2)
to eat essen (isst), aß, gegessen (3)
eating habit die Essgewohnheit (-en) (34)
economy die Wirtschaft (11/29)
to educate erziehen, erzog, erzogen (20)
education die Bildung (11/28)
educational background der Ausbildungsgang (-̈e) (14)
effect die Wirkung (-en) (27)
eight acht (1E)
eighteen achtzehn (1E)
eighty achtzig (1E)
to elect wählen (26)
election die Wahl (-en) (18)
elective das Wahlfach (-̈er) (27)
electrician der Elektromeister (-) / die Elektromeisterin (-nen) (29)
electricity der Strom (35)

elementary school die Grundschule (-n) (11)
elevator der Aufzug (-̈e) (8)
to emancipate emanzipieren (30)
emancipation die Emanzipation (30)
embarrassment die Verlegenheit (-en) (29)
emergency der Notfall (-̈e) (6)
emigrant der Auswanderer (-) / die Auswandererin (-nen) (34)
employed angestellt (1); berufstätig (23/25)
employee der Arbeitnehmer (-) / die Arbeitnehmerin (-nen) (14)
employer der Arbeitgeber (-) / die Arbeitgeberin (-nen) (14)
employment agent der Arbeitsvermittler (-) / die Arbeitsvermittlerin (-nen) (29)
enchanted verwünscht (12)
encounter die Begegnung (-en) (33)
engaged verlobt (25)
engagement die Verlobung (-en) (25)
engineer der Ingenieur (-e) / die Ingenieurin (-nen) (13)
engineering: mechanical engineering der Maschinenbau (11/28)
England (das) England (9)
English (*language*) das Englisch (11)
English (*person*) der Engländer (-) / die Engländerin (-nen) (18)
to enjoy genießen, genoss, genossen (3E)
enormous riesengroß (28)
to enroll einschreiben (schreibt ein), schrieb ein, eingeschrieben (19)
to enter eintreten (tritt ein), trat ein, ist eingetreten (33)
enterprise: business enterprise das Unternehmen (29)
to entertain unterhalten (28)
entertaining unterhaltsam (21)
entertainment die Unterhaltung (-en) (36)
to entice locken (36)
entree das Hauptgericht (-e) (15)

environment die Umwelt (20/35); **hostile to the environment** umweltfeindlich (35)
environmental awareness das Umweltbewusstsein (35)
environmental protection der Umweltschutz (35)
environmentally friendly umweltfreundlich (20/35)
to be at an equal level gleichgestellt sein (30)
to have equal rights gleichberchtigt sein (30)
equality die Gleichberechtigung (23/30)
equipment die Ausrüstung (-en) (32)
essential unentbehrlich (29)
essentially im Wesentlichen (31)
European (*person*) der Europäer (-) / die Europäerin (-nen) (18)
even sogar (32)
evil böse (1)
eventful bewegt (27)
everyday life der Alltag (27)
exactness die Genauigkeit (34)
to exaggerate übertreiben, übertrieb, übertrieben (29)
exaggerated übertrieben (20)
exam die Klausur (-en); die Prüfung (-en) (10); **exam after secondary school** das Abitur (10); **mid-diploma exam** die Zwischenprüfung (-en) (19/3E)
examination die Untersuchung (-en) (33)
to examine untersuchen (6)
excellent prima (27)
exception die Ausnahme (-n) (34)
excited aufgeregt (24); gespannt (32)
excitement der Nervenkitzel (32)
exciting aufregend (21); spannend (23/32)
exercise das Training (23); die Übung (-en) (33)
to exercise trainieren (16)
to exist bestehen, bestand, bestanden (35)
to expect (from) erwarten (von) (14/25)

expensive teuer (2)
experience die Erfahrung (-en) (28); **work experience** die Berufserfahrung (-en) (29)
to experience erleben (8/26)
to explain erklären (21)
explanation die Erklärung (-en) (29)
to express ausdrücken (drückt aus) (21)
expression der Ausdruck (¨e) (26); **facial expression** die Miene (-n) (29)
extension school die Volkshochschule (-n) (31)
extensive(ly) weitgehend (27)
extreme sport die Extremsportart (-en) (32)
extreme(ly) extrem (35)
eye das Auge (-n) (6)

F

face das Gesicht (-er) (6)
facial expression die Miene (-n) (29)
factor das Moment (-e) (23)
factory die Fabrik (-en) (4/35)
to fail (an exam) durchfallen (fällt durch), fiel durch, ist durchgefallen (10)
fairly priced preisgünstig (31)
fairy die Fee (-n) (12)
fairy tale das Märchen (-) (12)
fairy tale figure die Märchenfigur (-en) (12)
Fall der Herbst (5)
to fall asleep einschlafen (schläft ein), schlief ein, ist eingeschlafen (16)
family die Familie (1)
family home das Einfamilienhaus (¨er) (4)
family leave der Erziehungsurlaub (-e) (23)
family status der Familienstand (25)
fantasy die Fantasie (-n) (14)
far weit (7)
farmhouse Bauernhaus (¨er) (4)
to fascinate faszinieren (36)
to fasten anschnallen (schnallt an) (20)

fat das Fett (-e) (33)
father der Vater (¨) (1/25)
father-in-law der Schwiegervater (¨) (25)
fear die Angst (¨e) (20); die Befürchtung (-en) (34)
February der Februar (5)
Federal Republic of Germany die Bundesrepublik Deutschland (17)
fee die Gebühr (-en) (E)
to feel well sich wohl fühlen (6)
feeling das Gefühl (-e) (31)
fellow student der Mitschüler (-) / die Mitschülerin (-nen) (10)
female weiblich (25)
feminine weiblich (25)
festival das Fest (-e) (5)
festive festlich (17)
fever das Fieber (6/33)
few wenig (32)
field das Feld (-er) (9)
fifteen fünfzehn (1E)
fifty fünfzig (1E)
to fight kämpfen (30)
to fill out ausfüllen (füllt aus) (8)
film der Film (-e) (36); **action film** der Actionfilm (-e) (36); **romantic film** der Liebesfilm (-e) (36); **silent film** der Stummfilm (-e) (36); **sound film** der Tonfilm (-e) (36)
to film verfilmen (36); **to film (a movie)** (einen Film) drehen (36)
filming of a novel die Romanverfilmung (-en) (36)
finally endlich (10); schließlich (10)
financial(ly) finanziell (13)
to find finden, fand, gefunden (2)
finger der Finger (-) (6)
finished fertig (3E)
Finland (das) Finnland (9)
fireworks das Feuerwerk (-e) (5)
firm die Firma (Firmen) (13)
first: at first anfangs (30)
to fish angeln (8)
fish der Fisch (-e) (19)
to fit passen (+ dat.) (21)
fit: to keep fit sich fit halten (hält), hielt, gehalten (23/32)
five fünf (1E)
flea market der Flohmarkt (¨e) (22)

flexible flexibel (18)
flight attendant der Flugbegleiter (-) / die Flugbegleiterin (-nen) (13)
floor der Stock (Stockwerke) (8); **second floor** der erste Stock
to flow fließen, floss, geflossen (17)
flower die Blume (-n) (5)
flowered geblümt (21)
flu die Grippe (6)
to fly fliegen, flog, ist geflogen (7)
fog der Nebel (5)
foggy neblig (5)
to follow folgen (+ dat.) (14)
food die Lebensmittel (pl.) (19)
foot der Fuß (¨e) (6)
for für (+ acc.) (5)
for it/them dafür (26)
for the sake of zuliebe (+ dat.)
to forbid verbieten, verbot, verboten (20/27)
to force zwingen, zwang, gezwungen (29)
foreign fremd (24)
foreigner der Ausländer (-) / die Ausländerin (-nen) (20/34)
forest der Wald (¨er) (9); **dying of the forest** das Waldsterben (35)
forest path der Waldweg (-e)
to forget vergessen (vergisst), vergaß, vergessen (9)
fork die Gabel (-n) (19)
form das Formular (-e) (8)
former ehemalig (18)
forty vierzig (E)
to found gründen (27)
foundation die Grundlage (-n) (27)
four vier (1E)
fourteen vierzehn (1E)
France (das) Frankreich (9)
free time die Freizeit (16/3E)
freedom die Freiheit (-en) (23)
freedom of opinion die Meinungsfreiheit (18)
freedom of the press die Pressefreiheit (18)
freedom of speech die Redefreiheit (30)
freedom of thought die Gedankenfreiheit (30)
freedom of travel die Reisefreiheit (18)

French fries die Pommes frites
(*pl.*) (15)
French (*language*) das Französisch
(11)
frequent(ly) häufig (27)
fresh frisch (5)
Friday der Freitag (1E)
fried potato die Bratkartoffel
(-n) (15)
friend der Freund (-e) / die
Freundin (-nen) (1)
friendly freundlich (1)
friends with someone befreundet
(25)
frog king der Froschkönig (12)
fruit das Obst (5/33)
to fry braten (brät), briet, gebraten
(19)
to fullfill oneself sich verwirklichen
(26)
full voll; satt (15)
fun(ny) lustig (17/27)
fund: wellness fund die
Krankenkasse (33)
fundamentally im Wesentlichen
(31)
to furnish möblieren (4)
furniture die Möbel (*pl.*) (3)
future (*adj.*) künftig (29)
future die Zukunft (¨e) (26)

G

to gain by struggle erkämpfen (26)
gallery die Galerie (-n) (22)
garbage der Abfall (¨e) (20/35), der
Müll (20)
garden der Garten (¨) (4); **small
garden** der Kleingarten (-gärten)
(31)
gardening die Gartenarbeit (31)
garlic der Knoblauch (15)
gate das Tor (-e) (23)
general education high school die
Gesamtschule (-n); die Hauptschule
(-n); die Realschule (-n) (11)
geography die Erdkunde (11)
German (*language*) das Deutsch (11)
German (*person*) der/die Deutsche
(*decl. adj.*) (18)
German school system das
deutsche Schulsystem (11)

German studies die Germanistik
(28)
German Unity Day der Tag der
deutschen Einheit (5)
to get bekommen, bekam,
bekommen (15/28); kriegen (20)
to get involved in sich engagieren
für (26)
to get off (*a train, car, etc.*)
aussteigen (steigt aus), stieg aus,
ist ausgestiegen (7)
to get on (*a train, car, etc.*)
einsteigen (steigt ein), stieg ein, ist
eingestiegen (7)
to get on one's way sich auf den
Weg machen (24)
to get rid of abschaffen (schafft
ab), schuf ab, abgeschaffen (20)
to get up aufstehen (steht auf),
stand auf, ist aufgestanden (7)
to get used to sich gewöhnen an
(+ *acc.*) (24/28)
gingerbread der Lebkuchen (17)
to give geben (gibt), gab, gegeben
(3); (*as a gift*) schenken (5)
to give a lecture/talk einen Vortrag
halten (19/3E)
to give up aufgeben (gibt auf), gab
auf, aufgegeben (18/25)
glacier der Gletscher (-) (17)
glad froh (1)
glass das Glas (¨er) (19)
glove der Handschuh (-e) (21)
to go gehen, ging, ist gegangen; **to
go to the movies/theater** ins
Kino/Theater gehen; **to go to a
concert** ins Konzert gehen (2); **to
go for a walk** spazieren gehen
(2); fahren (fährt), fuhr, ist
gefahren; **to go by bicycle/bus/
car/motorcycle/ship/train** mit
dem Fahrrad/Bus/Auto/Motorrad/
Schiff/Zug (der Bahn) fahren (7);
to go to a spa Kur machen (8)
to go along entlanggehen (geht
entlang) ging entlang, ist
entlanggegangen (22)
to go on a trip verreisen (32)
goal das Tor (-e) (23); das Ziel (-e)
(26); **to have a certain goal** auf
etwas hinaus wollen (30)

good gut (1); **good morning!** guten
Morgen! (1E)
goods die Waren (*pl.*) (22)
to gossip quatschen (28)
grade die Note (-n) (10)
gradual(ly) allmählich (28)
grandchild das Enkelkind (-er) (1)
granddaughter die Enkelin (-nen)
(1/25)
grandfather der Großvater (¨) (1)
grandfather clock die Standuhr
(-en) (3)
grandmother die Großmutter (¨) (1)
grandparents die Großeltern (*pl.*)
(1/25)
grandson der Enkel (-) (1/25)
grape juice der Traubensaft (15)
to grasp anfassen (fasst an) (31);
begreifen, begriff, begriffen (29)
gray grau (2)
great prima (27); echt Klasse (10);
super (2); toll (2)
Great Britain (das) Großbritannien
(9)
great-grandchildren die Urenkel
(*pl.*) (25)
great-grandparents die
Urgroßeltern (*pl.*) (25)
Greece (das) Griechenland (9)
Greek (*person*) der Grieche (-n
masc.) / die Griechin (-nen) (18)
green grün (2)
to greet begrüßen (24)
greeting die Begrüßung (-en) (24)
to grill grillen (31)
ground level das Erdgeschoss (-e)
(8)
to grow up aufwachsen (wächst
auf), wuchs auf, ist aufgewachsen
(25)
growth das Wachstum (35)
guest der Gast (¨e) (8)

H

habitual: in a habitual manner
gewohnheitsmäßig (33)
hair das Haar (-e) (6)
hallway die Diele (-n) (3)
hand die Hand (¨e) (6)
hand: on the other hand
andererseits (26)

to handle something mit etwas umgehen, ging um, ist umgegangen (26)

handshake das Händeschütteln (-) (24)

Hanukkah die Chanukka (5)

to happen geschehen (geschieht), geschah, geschehen (32); passieren, ist passiert (9)

happy glücklich (1)

hat der Hut (¨e) (7)

to have haben (hat), hatte, gehabt (2)

to have a certain goal auf etwas hinaus wollen (30); **to have a look at** angucken (guckt an) (coll.) (32); **to have a say** mitbestimmen (bestimmt mit) (27); **to have an opinion of** halten von (hält), hielt, gehalten (3E); **to have equal rights** gleichberechtigt sein (30); **to have fun** Spaß machen (5); **have a good trip!** gute Fahrt! (14)

head der Kopf (¨e) (6)

headline die Schlagzeile (-n) (21)

health die Gesundheit (6)

health attendant der Krankenpfleger (-) / die Krankenpflegerin (-nen) (6)

health care die Gesundheitspflege (33)

health care system das Gesundheitswesen (-) (33)

health food store das Reformhaus (-häuser) (22)

health spa der Kurort (-e) (3E); die Kur (-en) (33)

healthy gesund (1/33)

to hear hören (6)

heart: by heart auswendig (27)

to heat erhitzen (19)

heaven der Himmel (9)

heavy schwer (10)

heel der Absatz (¨e) (21)

hello! guten Tag! (1E)

to help helfen (hilft) (13)

helpless(ly) ratlos (32)

Hesse (das) Hessen (17)

high point der Höhepunkt (-e) (36)

high school: general education high school die Gesamtschule (-n); die Hauptschule (-n); die Realschule (-n); **specialized high school** die Fachoberschule, (-n) (11)

to hike wandern, ist gewandert (2/32)

hill der Hügel (-) (9)

him (acc.) ihn (5)

history die Geschichte (-n) (11/28)

hobby das Hobby (-s) (31)

to hold halten (hält), hielt, gehalten (3E); behalten (behält), behielt, behalten (16)

holiday der Feiertag (-e) (5/31); **holidays** die Ferien (pl.) (32)

homeless person der/die Obdachlose (decl. adj.) (20)

homelessness die Obdachlosigkeit (20)

homework die Hausaufgabe (-n) (10)

honesty die Ehrlichkeit (14)

horse das Pferd (-e) (23)

hospital das Krankenhaus (¨er) (6/33)

hostile to the environment umweltfeindlich (35)

hot heiß (5)

hot (spicy) scharf (19)

hotel das Hotel (-s) (8); der Gasthof (¨e) (15)

hour die Stunde (-n) (23)

house das Haus (¨er) (4)

household der Haushalt (-e) (23/25); **to take care of the household** den Haushalt machen (23)

household appliance das Haushaltsgerät (-e) (20)

househusband der Hausmann (¨er) (23)

houseplant die Zimmerpflanze (-n) (23)

hug die Umarmung (-en) (24)

to hug umarmen (24)

human being der Mensch (-en masc.) (4)

human right das Menschenrecht (-e) (30)

humanities die Geisteswissenschaften (pl.) (28)

humor der Humor (36)

hundred hundert (1E)

hunger der Hunger (20)

to hurt wehtun (tut weh), tat weh, wehgetan (6)

I

I ich (1)

ice cream das Eis (15)

ice skating Schlittschuh laufen (läuft), lief, ist gelaufen; **ice skating rink** die Schlittschuhbahn (-en) (23)

Iceland (das) Island (9)

idea die Idee (-n) (10); der Begriff (-e) (28)

ideal das Ideal (-e) (26)

identity die Identität (-en) (26)

to idle bummeln, bummelte, ist gebummelt (31)

illness die Krankheit (-en) (20)

imaginary imaginär (36)

immediately sofort (22)

immigrant der Einwanderer (-) / die Einwanderin (-nen) (34)

to impart vermitteln (26)

to imply something auf etwas hinaus wollen (30)

important wichtig (23); **to consider something important** wert legen auf (+ acc.) (27)

impossible unmöglich (10)

to impress ausprägen (prägt aus) (25)

impression der Eindruck (¨e) (34)

in: in agreement einverstanden (29); **in any case** jedenfalls (30); unbedingt (11/34); **in return** dafür (26); **in the meantime** inzwischen (34) **in the open air** im Freien (31); **in the vicinity** in der Nähe (17)

income das Einkommen (-) (13)

to increase erhöhen (33); steigern (29); zunehmen (nimmt zu), nahm zu, zugenommen (28)

indeed sogar (32)

independence die Unabhängigkeit (25)

independent(ly) unabhängig (25); selbstständig (13/29)
indescribable; indescribably unbeschreiblich (31)
Indian (*person*) der Inder (-) / die Inderin (-nen) (18)
indoor swimming pool die Schwimmhalle (-n) (22)
industrialization die Industrialisierung (31)
industrious fleißig (1)
inevitable; inevitably unweigerlich (34)
influence der Einfluss (⸚e) (26)
to influence beeinflussen (21/34)
informality die Lockerheit (24)
information die Auskunft (⸚e) (7)
inhabitant der Einwohner (-) / die Einwohnerin (-nen) (17)
injection die Spritze (-n) (6)
inn: bed and breakfast inn die Pension (-en) (8)
inn das Gasthaus (⸚er); das Wirtshaus (⸚er) (15)
insecurity die Unsicherheit (-en) (27)
to inspire begeistern (26)
instead dafür (26)
instruction der Unterricht (10)
to insult beleidigen (28); beschimpfen (30)
insurance die Versicherung (-en) (33)
intellectual(ly) intellektuell (36)
intelligent gescheit (21)
to intend vorhaben (hat vor), hatte vor, vorgehabt (23)
interest das Interesse (-n) (14)
to be interested in sich interessieren für (13/31)
interesting interessant (1)
internship das Praktikum (*pl.* Praktika) (19)
to interpret (*languages*) dolmetschen (28)
interpreter der Dolmetscher (-) / die Dolmetscherin (-nen) (13)
intersection die Kreuzung (-en) (22)
to introduce oneself sich vorstellen (13)

to invent erfinden, erfand, erfunden (21)
to invite einladen (lädt ein), lud ein, eingeladen (7/3E)
to get involved in sich engagieren für (26)
Ireland (das) Irland (9)
to iron bügeln (23)
irreplaceable; irreplaceably unersetzlich (31)
island die Insel (-n) (9)
it es (1)
Italian (*person*) der Italiener (-) / die Italienerin (-nen) (18)
Italy (das) Italien (9)

J

jacket; die Jacke (-n) (7); das Jackett (-s) (7); der Sakko (-s); **women's jacket** der Frauensakko (-s) (7)
jam die Marmelade (-n) (16)
January der Januar (5)
jeans die Jeans (*pl.*) (7)
jelly die Marmelade (-n) (16)
jewelry der Schmuck (22)
jewelry store das Juweliergeschäft (-e) (22)
job der Beruf (-e) (13/29)
job applicant der Bewerber (-) / die Bewerberin (-nen) (14/29)
job interview das Vorstellungsgespräch (-e) (13)
job offer das Stellenangebot (-e) (14)
job search die Stellensuche (14)
to jog joggen (8)
jogging suit der Jogginganzug (⸚e) (7)
journalist der Journalist (-en *masc.*) / die Journalistin (-nen) (13)
journey die Fahrt (-en) (24)
joy die Freude (-n) (27)
joyful(ly) freudig (26)
judge der Richter (-) / die Richterin (-nen) (30)
juice der Saft (⸚e) (16)
July der Juli (5)
to jump springen, sprang, ist gesprungen (32)
June der Juni (5)

jurisprudence die Rechtswissenschaft (28)
justice die Gerechtigkeit (-en) (26)

K

to keep behalten (behält), behielt, behalten (16)
to keep (*an appointment*) einhalten (hält ein), hielt ein, eingehalten (34)
to keep fit sich fit halten (hält), hielt, gehalten (23/32)
to keep to sich halten an (+ *acc.*) (hält), hielt, gehalten (34)
to keep together zusammenhalten (hält zusammen), hielt zusammen, zusammengehalten (23)
key der Schlüssel (-) (8)
to kill töten (12)
kindergarten der Kindergarten (⸚) (11)
king der König (-e) (12)
kitchen die Küche (-n) (3)
knife das Messer (-) (19)
to knock klopfen (19)
to know (*a fact*) wissen (weiß), wusste, gewusst; (*be acquainted with*) kennen, kannte, gekannt (8)
knowledge die Kenntnis (-se) (14/29); das Wissen (26)
known: well-known bekannt (36)

L

labeled beschildert (34)
labor force die Arbeitskraft (⸚e) (34)
laboratory das Labor (-s) (10/33)
to lack fehlen (+ *dat.*) (21)
lake der See (-n) (9)
to land landen, ist gelandet (24)
language die Sprache (-n) (11)
language lab das Sprachlabor (-s) (10)
to last dauern (7)
late spät (16)
to be late sich verspäten (34)
laundry die Wäsche (3E)
law das Gesetz (-e) (35)
law (*as field or course of study*) Jura (28)
lawn der Rasen (16/3E)

lawyer der Anwalt (-̈e) / die Anwältin (-nen) (13)
lazy faul (1)
to lead leiten (30); **to lead to** führen zu (26)
leader der Leiter (-) / die Leiterin (-nen) (31)
to learn lernen (8); erlernen (29); **to learn by heart** auswendig lernen (27)
leather das Leder (21)
to leave verlassen (verlässt), verließ, verlassen (14/27)
lecture die Vorlesung (-en) (19/3E); der Vortrag (-̈e) (3E)
lecture hall der Hörsaal (Hörsäle) (19)
left links (8)
leg das Bein (-e) (6)
legal(ly) rechtlich (34)
letter der Brief (-e) (2)
letter to the editor der Leserbrief (-e) (21)
librarian der Bibliothekar (-e) / die Bibliothekarin (-nen) (13)
library die Bibliothek (-en) (10)
license plate das Nummernschild (-er) (20)
lie Lüge (-n) (10)
to lie (*flat*) liegen, lag, gelegen (2)
lifestyle der Lebensstil (-e) (26)
light hell (2)
to like gefallen (gefällt), gefiel, gefallen (+ *dat.*) (14/31)
linguistics die Linguistik (11)
to listen hören (13); **to listen to music** Musik hören (2)
literature die Literatur (-en) (11/36)
litterbug der Umweltsünder (-) / die Umweltsünderin (-nen) (20/35)
little klein (1); wenig (32)
to live (*exist*) leben (12); **to live (*reside*)** wohnen (8)
living room das Wohnzimmer (-) (3)
lobster der Hummer (-) (15)
local news die Lokalnachrichten (*pl.*) (21)
to be located sich befinden, befand, befunden (28)
location die Lage (-n) (18)

long lang (1)
to long for sich sehnen nach (28)
to look after betreuen (30); pflegen (31); **to look at** angucken (guckt an) (*coll.*) (32); anschauen (schaut an); sich ansehen (sieht an), sah an, angesehen (21); **to look at (*art*)** betrachten (8); **to look forward to** sich freuen auf (+ *acc.*) (18/26)
to loosen lösen (30)
loud laut (1)
love: in love verliebt (25)
Lower Saxony (das) Niedersachsen (17)
luxury der Luxus (32)

M

mad verrückt (17)
magazine die Zeitschrift (-en) (21)
major subject das Hauptfach (-̈er) (11/3E)
to make schaffen (28)
to make enthusiastic begeistern (26)
to make music musizieren (31)
to make pottery töpfern (31)
male männlich (25)
man der Mann (-̈er) (1)
manufacturing plant das Werk (-e) (16)
March der März (5)
to march marschieren, marschierte, ist marschiert (32)
Mardi Gras der Karneval (5); der Fasching (17)
marital ehelich (25); **marital status** der Familienstand (14/25)
market economy die Marktwirtschaft (-en) (18)
marriage die Ehe (-n) (5/23/25)
married verheiratet (14), ehelich (25)
married couple das Ehepaar (-e) (25)
to marry heiraten (12/25)
masculine männlich (25)
material der Stoff (-e) (28); **packaging material** das Verpackungsmaterial (-ien) (35); **raw material** der Rohstoff (-e) (35)

math(ematics) die Mathe(matik) (11)
May der Mai (5)
maybe vielleicht (11)
meadow die Wiese (-n) (9)
meal das Gericht (-e) (34)
to mean meinen (3E); bedeuten (17)
meaningful sinnvoll (33)
meantime: in the meantime inzwischen (34)
to measure messen (misst), maß, gemessen (33)
meat das Fleisch (19)
meatloaf, Bavarian der Leberkäs (15)
mechanic der Mechaniker (-) / die Mechanikerin (-nen) (13)
mechanical engineering der Maschinenbau (11/28)
Mecklenburg-Western Pomerania (das) Mecklenburg-Vorpommern (17)
medication das Medikament (-e) (6/33)
medicine die Medizin (28); **preventive medicine** die Vorsorge (33)
to meet sich begegnen (27)
meeting die Begegnung (-en) (33)
member of parliament der/die Abgeordnete (*decl. adj.*) (30)
to mention erwähnen (31)
menu die Speisekarte (-n) (15)
merchant der Kaufmann, *pl.* die Kaufleute (13)
method: teaching method die Unterrichtsmethode (-n) (27)
metropolis die Großstadt (-̈e) (4)
Mexican (*person*) der Mexikaner (-) / die Mexikanerin (-nen) (18)
microwave die Mikrowelle (-n) (3)
mid-diploma exam die Zwischenprüfung (-en) (19/3E)
middle die Mitte (-n) (22)
Middle Ages das Mittelalter (28)
milk die Milch (5)
mineral water das Mineralwasser (15)
minor subject das Nebenfach (-̈er) (11/3E)

minority die Minderheit (-en) (30)
mirror der Spiegel (-) (3)
to miscalculate sich verrechnen (33)
to misunderstand missverstehen, missverstand, missverstanden (21)
to mix vermischen (19)
mode of transportation das Verkehrsmittel (-) (35)
modesty die Bescheidenheit (-en) (26)
moment der Moment (-e) (23)
Monday der Montag (1E)
month der Monat (-e) (5)
monthly monatlich (4)
mood die Stimmung (-en) (17/36)
mother die Mutter (:) (1/25)
mother-in-law die Schwiegermutter (:) (25)
Mother's Day der Muttertag (5)
motion: to set into motion bewegen (26)
motorcycle das Motorrad (:er) (7)
mountain der Berg (-e) (4)
mountains das Gebirge (9)
mouth der Mund (:er) (6)
to move (change place of residence) umziehen (zieht um), zog um, ist umgezogen (4)
to move rühren (31)
to move away wegziehen (zieht weg), zog weg, ist weggezogen (4)
movement die Bewegung (-en) (26); **women's movement** die Frauenbewegung (-en) (30)
movie theater das Kino (-s) (2)
to mow the lawn den Rasen mähen (16/3E)
multicultural(ly) multikulturell (34)
museum das Museum (Museen) (22)
mushroom der Pilz (-e) (9); der Champignon (-s) (15)
music die Musik (11/36); **to play music** musizieren (31)
mustard der Senf (15)

N

to nap dösen (16)
napkin die Serviette (-n) (19)
nature die Natur (9)

near nah (7)
nearly fast (27)
necessarily unbedingt (11/20/34)
necessity das Bedürfnis (-se) (34)
neck der Hals (:e) (6)
to need brauchen (2/3E)
negligible gering (29)
to negotiate begeben, begab, begeben (33)
neighbor der Nachbar (-n *masc.*) / die Nachbarin (-nen) (4)
neighborhood das Stadtviertel (-) (4); die Siedlung (-en) (35)
nephew der Neffe (-n *masc.*) (1/25)
nerve: what nerve! das ist eine Frechheit! (10)
Netherlands die Niederlande (9)
new neu (2)
New Year's Day das Neujahr (5)
New Year's Eve das Silvester (5)
news die Nachricht (-en) (22)
nice nett (1)
niece die Nichte (-n) (1/25)
nightmare der Alptraum (:e) (27)
nightstand der Nachttisch (-e) (3)
nine neun (1E)
nineteen neunzehn (1E)
ninety neunzig (1E)
no kein (3); nein
noise der Lärm (20/35)
nonacceptance die Nichtakzeptanz (34)
nonreturnable bottle die Einwegflasche (-n) (35)
nontoxic giftfrei (35)
noodle die Nudel (-n) (19)
normally normalerweise (32)
North Rhine-Westphalia (das) Nordrhein-Westfalen (17)
Norway (das) Norwegen (9)
nose die Nase (-n) (6)
not nicht; **not a/any** kein (3)
note die Notiz (-en) (10); der Zettel (33)
notebook das Heft (-e) (1E)
to notice merken (20)
to nourish ernähren (25)
nourishment die Nahrung (20)
November der November (5)

number of unemployed die Arbeitslosenzahl (-en) (29)
nurse der Krankenpfleger (-) / die Krankenpflegerin (-nen) (13)

O

observation die Bemerkung (-en) (24/28)
to observe beachten (34); beobachten (36)
occupation der Beruf (-e) (13/29)
occupational(ly) beruflich (18)
to occupy besetzen (27)
to be occupied with sich beschäftigen mit (13/27)
to occur eintreten (tritt ein), trat ein, ist eingetreten (33)
ocean das Meer (-e) (9)
October der Oktober (5)
odd merkwürdig (24/28)
to offend beleidigen (10)
offer das Angebot (-e) (23)
to offer bieten, bot, geboten (31)
office das Büro (-s) (13)
officer der Offizier (-e) (14)
official der/die Behörde (*decl. adj.*) (18)
often oft (4); häufig (27)
old alt (1)
on the other hand andererseits (26)
once more please! bitte noch einmal! (1E)
once upon a time . . . es war einmal . . . (12)
one ein(s) (1E)
one-way einfach (24)
onion die Zwiebel (-n) (15)
only einzig (23)
open offen (16)
to open aufmachen (macht auf), aufgemacht (6); **open your books!** macht die Bücher auf! (1E)
openly öffentlich (23)
open-minded aufgeschlossen (34)
to operate operieren (6)
operation: business operation der Betrieb (-e) (29)
opinion die Meinung (-en) (10)

opportunity die Gelegenheit (-en) (13)

opposite _____ gegenüber von _____ (22)

orange orange (2)

order die Ordnung (34)

to order bestellen (15)

organic(ally) organisch (20/35)

organization die Gestaltung (-en) (31)

to organize (*clean up*) aufräumen (räumt auf) (23/E3)

to organize oneself sich organisieren (30)

original(ly) originell (22); ursprünglich (36)

other: on the other hand andererseits (26)

outdoors im Freien (31)

outcome das Ergebnis (-se) (33)

outfitting die Ausrüstung (32)

outgoing unbefangen (1)

outrage: that's an outrage! das ist eine Unverschämtheit! (10)

outside draußen (31)

to overcome bestehen, bestand, bestanden (35)

overhead projector der Overheadprojektor (-en) (1E)

overload die Überlastung (-en) (27)

overnight stay die Übernachtung (-en) (8)

overtime hour die Überstunde (-n) (22)

own eigen (4/25)

to own besitzen, besaß, besessen (30)

owner der Besitzer (-) / die Besitzerin (-nen) (14)

P

to pack einpacken (packt ein) (7)

packaging die Verpackung (20); das Verpackungsmaterial (-ien) (35)

pain der Schmerz (-en) (6)

paint der Anstrich (-e) (35)

painting das Gemälde (-) (22)

pajamas der Schlafanzug (¨e) (21)

pan die Pfanne (-n) (19)

pantomime die Pantomime (-n) (36)

pants die Hose (-n) (7)

paper das Papier (1E); **piece of paper** der Zettel (33)

parade der Umzug (¨e) (17)

parenting: single parenting alleinerziehend (30)

parents die Eltern (*pl.*) (1/25)

parka der Anorak (-s) (7)

part der Abschnitt (-e) (28); **to take part in** teilnehmen an (+ *dat.*) (nimmt teil), nahm teil, teilgenommen (26)

to participate teilnehmen (nimmt teil), nahm teil, teilgenommen (20)

party die Party (-s) (24)

to pass (*a test or exam*) bestehen, bestand, bestanden (10/27)

to pass on abgeben (gibt ab), gab ab, abgegeben (19)

passenger der Fahrgast (¨e) (7)

passport der Reisepass (¨e) (24)

past (*adj.*) vergangen (26)

past die Vergangenheit (27)

past _____ an _____ vorbei (22)

pastry shop die Konditorei (-en) (16)

patient der Patient (-en *masc.*) / die Patientin (-nen) (6)

patterned gemustert (21)

pay das Gehalt (¨er) (13)

to pay zahlen (15)

to pay (for) bezahlen (4)

to pay attention aufpassen (passt auf) (7/3E)

pea die Erbse (-n) (15)

peace der Frieden (26)

peaceful(ly) friedlich (26); ruhig (1/28)

peculiar merkwürdig (24/28)

pedestrian zone die Fußgängerzone (-n) (20)

pencil der Bleistift (-e) (1E)

peninsula die Halbinsel (-n) (9)

pension die Rente (-n) (29)

pensioner der Rentner (-) / die Rentnerin (-nen) (29)

pepper der Pfeffer (15)

perfect(ly) perfekt (23)

periodical die Zeitschrift (-en) (21)

to persecute verfolgen (34)

personal persönlich (14)

personal hygiene die Körperpflege (33)

personal(ly) persönlich (32)

pet das Haustier (-e) (22)

pet store die Tierhandlung (-en) (22)

philosopher der Philosoph (-en *masc.*) / die Philosophin (-nen) (13)

photographer der Fotograf (-en *masc.*) / die Fotografin (-nen) (13)

physician der Arzt (¨e) / die Ärztin (-nen) (6)

physicist der Physiker (-) / die Physikerin (-nen) (13)

physics die Physik (11/28)

piano das Klavier (-e) (3)

to pick up abholen (holt ab) (23)

picnic das Picknick (-s) (9)

piece: piece of clothing das Kleidungsstück (-e) (7); **piece of paper** der Zettel (33); **theater piece** das Stück (-e) (36)

pillow das Kopfkissen (-) (3)

pink rosa (2)

place der Ort (-e) (4); die Stelle (-n) (13/29)

to place at a disadvantage benachteiligen (30)

place of birth der Geburtsort (14)

to plan vorhaben (hat vor), hatte vor, vorgehabt (23)

planned economy die Planwirtschaft (18)

plastic bag die Plastiktüte (-n) (20)

plastic cup der Plastikbecher (-) (35)

plate der Teller (-) (19)

platform der Bahnsteig (-e) (7)

platform (*in a train station*) das Gleis (-e)

play (*theater*) das Stück (-e) (36), das Schauspiel (-e) (36)

to play spielen (8); **to play cards** Karten spielen (2); **to play golf** Golf spielen; **to play pool** Billard spielen (8); **to play tennis** Tennis spielen (2)

to play: to play music musizieren (31); **to play a sport** Sport treiben, trieb, getrieben (23/32)

to please gefallen (+ *dat.*) (gefällt), gefiel, gefallen (9/31)
pleasure die Freude (-n) (27)
point: high point der Höhepunkt (-e) (36); **point in time** das Mal (-e) (31); **point of view** die Einstellung (-en) (18)
to poison vergiften (12/35)
police die Polizei (20)
Polish (*person*) der Pole (-n *masc.*) / die Polin (-nen) (18)
political asylum das Asyl (34)
politician der Politiker (-) / die Politikerin (-nen) (13)
politics die Politik (21)
polka-dotted gepunktet (21)
to pollute verschmutzen (35)
polluter der Umweltsünder (-) / die Umweltsünderin (-nen) (20/35); der Umweltverschmutzer (-)
pollution die Verschmutzung (35)
popular beliebt (28)
pork roast der Schweinebraten (-) (15)
to portray darstellen (stellt dar) (34)
Portugal (das) Portugal (9)
position die Stelle (-n) (13/29)
to possess besitzen, besaß, besessen (30)
possibility die Möglichkeit (-en) (29)
possible möglich (10)
post office die Post (4); das Postamt (22)
pot der Topf (¨e) (19)
potato die Kartoffel (-n) (15)
pour gießen, goss, gegossen (19)
poverty die Armut (20)
powerful(ly) gewaltig (34)
practice: to put into practice in die Praxis umsetzen (35)
to practice a profession einen Beruf ausüben (übt aus) (13/29)
prank der Streich (-e) (14)
preceding vergangen (26)
to prefer vorziehen (zieht vor), zog vor, vorgezogen (20)
prejudice das Vorurteil (-e) (24)
preparation die Vorbereitung (-en) (32)

to prepare sich vorbereiten (bereitet vor) (27)
to prescribe verschreiben, verschrieb, verschrieben (33)
prescription das Rezept (6/33)
present das Geschenk (-e) (5)
to present darstellen (stellt dar) (34)
present time die Gegenwart (27)
prestige das Prestige (14)
pretzel die Brezel (-n) (15)
preventive medicine die Vorsorge (33)
primarily hauptsächlich (31)
prince der Prinz (-en *masc.*) (12)
princess die Prinzessin (-nen) (12)
printed gemustert (21)
to produce herstellen (stellt her) (29)
profession der Beruf (-e) (13/29); **to practice a profession** einen Beruf ausüben (13/29)
professional(ly) beruflich (18)
to prohibit verbieten, verbot, verboten (20)
promise die Versprechung (-en) (34)
to promise versprechen (verspricht), versprach, versprochen (3)
to promote fördern (36)
promptness die Pünktlichkeit (34)
proof der Nachweis (-e) (31)
prosperity der Wohlstand (26)
to protect behüten (30); schützen (20/35)
protection der Schutz (26)
to protest protestieren (10)
to prove beweisen, bewies, bewiesen (25); bestätigen (34)
psychologist der Psychologe (-n *masc.*) / die Psychologin (-nen) (13)
psychology die Psychologie (11)
pub die Kneipe (-n) (15)
public das Publikum (36)
publicity die Reklame (-n) (21)
public(ly) öffentlich (23/35)
to pull ziehen, zog, gezogen (4/31)
punctual pünktlich (14)
punctuality die Pünktlichkeit (34)
to punish bestrafen (10)

purple lila (2)
purpose der Zweck (-e) (36)
to put in place einsetzen (setzt ein) (29)
to put into practice in die Praxis umsetzen (setzt um) (35)
to put on anziehen, (zieht an), zog an, angezogen (7)
to put up with aushalten (hält aus), hielt aus, ausgehalten (24)

Q
qualification die Qualifikation (-en) (14)
quarter das Quartal (-e) (11)
queen die Königin (-nen) (12)
quiet(ly) leise (26)

R
race das Rennen (-) (23)
racism der Rassismus (20)
rain der Regen (5)
to rain regnen (es regnet) (5)
raincoat der Regenmantel (¨) (7)
to raise erhöhen (33); steigern (29)
rather ziemlich (2); eher (27)
raw roh (19)
raw material der Rohstoff (-e) (35)
to reach erreichen (30)
to react to reagieren auf (+ *acc.*) (26)
to read lesen (liest), las, gelesen (3)
reality die Wirklichkeit (14)
to realize verwirklichen (26)
real(ly) echt (10); **really good** echt gut (2)
really wirklich (10)
reason der Grund (¨e) (18)
to receive bekommen, bekam, bekommen (15/28); erhalten (erhält), erhielt, erhalten (29)
reception die Rezeption (-en) (8)
receptive aufgeschlossen (34)
recliner der Sessel (-) (3)
reconstruction der Wiederaufbau (29)
to record (video) aufnehmen (nimmt auf), nahm auf, aufgenommen (21)
recuperation die Erholung (31)

to recycle wieder verwerten (35); recyceln (16/35)
red rot (2)
to reduce abbauen, vermindern (20)
refrigerator der Kühlschrank (⸚e) (3)
to regard halten für (hält), hielt, gehalten (20); betrachten (30)
to register anmelden (meldet an) (19)
to regret bedauern (20)
regular(ly) regelmäßig (33)
to regulate regeln (25)
to relax sich entspannen (31)
relaxation die Entspannung (32)
relaxed manner die Lockerheit (24)
reliability die Zuverlässigkeit (14)
reliable zuverlässig (14)
religion die Religion (-en) (11)
to remain bleiben, blieb, ist geblieben (2E)
remark die Bemerkung (-en) (24/28)
remarkable merkwürdig (24/28)
remedy das Heilmittel (-) (33)
to remember sich erinnern an (+ acc.) (26)
to remove oneself sich entfernen (34)
to renounce verzichten auf (+ acc.) (35)
rent die Miete (-n) (4)
to rent mieten; **to rent (out)** vermieten (4)
to repeat wiederholen (3E)
report der Bericht (-e) (21)
report card das Zeugnis (-se) (10)
to report berichten (21)
to represent vertreten (vertritt), vertrat, vertreten (27)
reputation der Ruf (-e) (28)
to require erfordern (29)
required course das Pflichtfach (⸚er) (27)
reservation die Reservierung (-en) (8)
to reside wohnen (2E)
resort der Kurort (-e) (3E)
to respect respektieren (25)
to respect achten (33)

respective(ly) beziehungsweise (28) jeweils
responsibility die Verantwortung (-en) (14)
rest die Erholung (-en) (31)
restaurant das Restaurant (-s) (4); die Gaststätte (-n), der Gasthof (⸚e), das Gasthaus (⸚er), das Wirtshaus (⸚er) (15)
restorer der Restaurator (-en) / die Restauratorin (-nen) (22)
restroom die Toilette (-n) (3)
result das Ergebnis (-se) (33); die Wirkung (-en) (27)
résumé der Lebenslauf (⸚e) (14)
return: in return dafür (26)
return ticket die Rückfahrkarte (-n) (24)
returnable bottle die Pfandflasche (-n) (35)
reunification die Wiedervereinigung (18)
Rhineland Palatinate Rheinland-Pfalz (17)
rice der Reis (15)
to ride (an animal) reiten, ritt, geritten (8/32); **to ride a bicycle** Rad fahren (fährt Rad), fuhr Rad, ist Rad gefahren (4)
right richtig (24)
right: human right das Menschenrecht (-e) (30)
right to vote das Wahlrecht (30)
rights: to have equal rights gleichberechtigt sein (30)
to ring klingeln (23)
river der Fluss (⸚e) (9)
roll das Brötchen (-) (16)
roller skating das Rollschuhlaufen (23)
to rollerblade bladen (23)
romantic romantisch (1)
romantic film der Liebesfilm (-e) (36)
room das Zimmer (-) (3)
roughly ungefähr (11/29)
round trip hin und zurück (24)
row house das Reihenhaus (⸚er) (4)
to row (a boat) rudern (23/32)
row die Reihe (-n) (30)
rug der Teppich (-e) (3)

rule die Regel (-n) (34)
Rumpelstiltskin das Rumpelstilzchen (12)
to run laufen (läuft), lief, ist gelaufen (3)
Russian (person) der Russe (-n masc.) / die Russin (-nen) (18)

S

sad traurig (1)
safe(ly) sicher (13)
to sail segeln (2)
sake: for the sake of zuliebe (+ dat.) (35)
salad der Salat (15)
salary das Gehalt (⸚er) (13)
salmon Lachs (-e) (15)
salt das Salz (15)
salty salzig (19)
same egal (18)
sandal die Sandale (-n) (7)
Santa Claus der Weihnachtsmann (17)
satisfied satt (19); zufrieden (29)
Saturday der Samstag (1E)
sauerkraut das Sauerkraut (15)
sauna die Sauna (in die Sauna gehen) (8)
sausage die Wurst (⸚e) (15)
to save erlösen (12); sparen (35)
Saxony (das) Sachsen (17)
Saxony-Anhalt Sachsen-Anhalt (17)
say: to have a say mitbestimmen (bestimmt mit) (27)
scarf der Schal (-s) (21)
schedule (daily) der Stundenplan (⸚e) (10); **(travel)** der Fahrplan (⸚e) (7)
school die Schule (-n) (10)
school bus der Schulbus (-se) (10)
school newspaper die Schülerzeitung (-en) (10)
science die Wissenschaft (-en) (27)
school: college preparatory high school das Gymnasium (Gymnasien) (10/27); **comprehensive school** die Gesamtschule (-n) (11/27); **extension school** die Volkshochschule (-n) (31);

vocational school die Realschule (-n) (11/27)

search die Suche (-n) (26)

to search suchen (19)

season die Jahreszeit (-en) (5)

seatbelt der Sicherheitsgurt (-e) (20)

secret das Geheimnis (-se) (36)

secret(ly) heimlich (33)

secure(ly) sicher (13)

to see sehen (sieht), sah, gesehen (3)

segment der Abschnitt (-e) (28)

seldom selten (4)

self-employed person der/die Selbstständige (*decl. adj.*) (14)

self-initiative die Eigeninitiative (14)

semester das Semester (-) (11/3E)

to send schicken (22)

sensation das Aufsehen (35)

sense der Sinn (-e) (29)

sensible; sensibly gescheit (21); sinnvoll (33)

to separate trennen (35)

separated (*adj.*) getrennt (25)

separation die Trennung (-en) (25)

September der September (5)

series die Reihe (-n) (30)

to set into motion bewegen (26); **to set up** aufbauen (baut auf) (29)

settlement die Siedlung (-en) (35)

seven sieben (1E)

seventeen siebzehn (1E)

seventy siebzig (1E)

service die Bedienung (15)

service, duty der Dienst, (-e) (14)

shameless unverschämt (10)

shape die Gestaltung (-en) (31)

to shape gestalten (26)

to share teilen (31)

she sie (1)

shelf das Regal (-e) (3)

to shine scheinen; **the sun is shining** die Sonne scheint (5)

ship das Schiff (-e) (7)

shirt das Hemd (-en) (7)

shoe der Schuh (-e) (7)

shopping das Einkaufen (16)

shopping list die Einkaufsliste (-n) (16)

short kurz (1)

shorts die Shorts (*pl.*) (7)

shoulder die Schulter (-n) (6)

show die Sendung (-en) (21)

to show zeigen (6)

shower die Dusche (-n) (3)

shy scheu (1)

shrimp cocktail der Krabbencocktail (-s) (15)

siblings die Geschwister (*pl.*) (1/25)

side dish die Beilage (-n) (15)

sign das Schild (-er) (16); das Zeichen (-) (26)

to sign up einschreiben (schreibt ein), schrieb ein, eingeschrieben

to signify bedeuten (17)

silence die Ruhe (4)

silent ruhig (1)

silent film der Stummfilm (-e) (36)

silverware das Besteck (-e) (19)

simple einfach (2)

simply einfach (24)

simultaneous(ly) gleichzeitig (21)

to sing singen, sang, gesungen (5)

singer der Sänger (-) / die Sängerin (-nen) (13)

single ledig; single (14/25); **single parenting** allein erziehend (30)

single room das Einzelzimmer (-) (8)

sink das Waschbecken (-) (3)

sister die Schwester (-n) (1)

sister-in-law die Schwägerin (-nen) (25)

situation die Lage (-n) (18)

six sechs (1E)

sixteen sechzehn (1E)

sixty sechzig (1E)

size die Größe (-n) (21)

to ski Schi laufen (läuft Schi), lief Schi, ist Schi gelaufen (8)

skills die Kenntnisse (*pl.*) (14)

to skim überfliegen, überflog, überflogen (21)

skirt der Rock (¨e) (7)

sky der Himmel (9)

skyscraper das Hochhaus (¨er) (4)

to sleep schlafen (schläft), schlief, geschlafen (3)

to slice schneiden, schnitt, geschnitten (19)

small gering (29); **small garden** der Kleingarten (¨); **small town** die Kleinstadt (¨e) (4); das Dorf (¨er) (27)

to smell like riechen nach, roch, gerochen (33)

smoke der Rauch (35)

snack das Pausenbrot (-e) (10)

snack stand der Imbissstand (¨e) (15)

sneaker der Sportschuh (-e) (7)

to sneeze niesen (6)

to snow schneien; **it's snowing** es schneit (5)

snow der Schnee (5)

Snow White das Schneewittchen (12)

soccer der Fußball (2)

soccer game das Fußballspiel (-e) (16)

social science die Sozialkunde (11)

social support die Sozialleistung (-en) (29)

sock die Socke (-n) (7)

sofa das Sofa (-s) (3)

sole einzig (23)

son der Sohn (¨e) (1/25)

song das Lied (-er) (17)

soon bald (12/3E)

sooner eher (27)

sore throat die Halsschmerzen (*pl.*) (6)

sort die Art (-en) (26)

to sort sortieren (20)

sound film der Tonfilm (-e) (36)

soup die Suppe (-n) (15)

sour sauer (23)

spa das Bad (¨er) (33); **health spa** die Kur (-en) (33)

Spain (das) Spanien (9)

Spanish (*language*) das Spanisch (11)

to speak sprechen (spricht), sprach, gesprochen (3); **speak German, please!** sprecht bitte Deutsch! (1E); **speak more slowly, please!** sprechen Sie bitte langsamer! (1E)

specialized high school die Fachoberschule (-n) (11)

specialty die Spezialität (-en) (15)

spectator der Zuschauer (-) / die Zuschauerin (-nen) (23)

speech: freedom of speech die Redefreiheit (30)

to spend (*time*) verbringen, verbrachte, verbracht (5/3E); **to spend the night** übernachten (3E)

spicy scharf (19)

sponge der Schwamm (ˉe) (1E)

spoon der Löffel (-) (19)

sport: adventure sport die Extremsportart (-en) (32); **sport center** die Sporthalle (-n) (16)

sports der Sport (23); **sports field** der Sportplatz (ˉe) (10); **type of sports** die Sportart (-en) (23/32)

spring der Frühling (-e) (5)

stage die Bühne (-n) (36)

to stage inszenieren (36)

stairs die Treppe (-n) (8)

to stand stehen, stand, gestanden; **to stand in line** Schlange stehen (16)

to start anfangen (fängt an), fing an, angefangen (23/31); aufnehmen (nimmt auf), nahm auf, aufgenommen (28)

station (channel) das Programm (-e) (21)

stationery store das Schreibwarengeschäft (-e) (22)

stay der Aufenthalt (7/33)

to stay bleiben, blieb, ist geblieben (9)

step der Schritt (-e) (13/34)

stepbrother der Stiefbruder (ˉ) (25)

stepdaughter die Stieftochter (ˉ) (12)

stepfather der Stiefvater (ˉ) (12)

stepmother die Stiefmutter (ˉ) (12)

stepson der Stiefsohn (ˉe) (12)

stereo die Stereoanlage (-n) (3)

to stick to/with sich halten an (+ *acc.*) (hält), hielt, gehalten (34)

still ruhig (1/28)

to stimulate anregen (regt an) (31)

stimulation die Anregung (31)

to stir rühren (31)

stomach der Bauch (ˉe) (6)

to stop aufhören (hört auf) (7/3E); anhalten (hält an), hielt an, angehalten (14)

store der Laden (ˉ) (16); das Geschäft (-e) (26)

store closing time der Ladenschluss (24)

story der Stock (-werke) (21)

story die Geschichte (-n) (11/28)

stove der Herd (-e) (3)

straight ahead geradeaus (22)

to straighten up aufräumen (räumt auf) (23)

strange komisch (10); fremd (24)

street die Straße (-n) (5)

streetcar die Straßenbahn (22)

strenuous anstrengend (23)

strict(ly) streng (20/27)

striped gestreift (21)

to stroll bummeln, bummelte, ist gebummelt (31)

to struggle kämpfen (30)

student (*at a Gymnasium*) der Gymnasiast (-en *masc.*) / die Gymnasiastin (-nen) (26); (***not in a university***) der Schüler (-) / die Schülerin (-nen) (1E/3E); (***university***) der Student (-en *masc.*) / die Studentin (-nen) (1E/3E)

student cafeteria die Mensa (*pl.* Mensen) (19)

student dormitory das Studentenwohnheim (-e) (19)

to study studieren (8)

study fees die Studiengebühren (*pl.*) (19)

style der Stil (-e) (27)

stylishly modisch (21)

subject das Fach (ˉer) (11/27); **major subject** das Hauptfach (ˉer) (11/3E); **minor subject** das Nebenfach (ˉer) (11/3E)

to subscribe to abonnieren (21)

subtitle der Untertitel (-) (36)

suburb der Vorort (-e) (4)

subway die U-Bahn (-en) (22)

success der Erfolg (-e) (13/26)

suddenly plötzlich (12)

suffrage das Wahlrecht (30)

to suggest vorschlagen (schlägt vor), schlug vor, vorgeschlagen (22/3E)

suggestion der Vorschlag (ˉe) (14)

suit der Anzug (ˉe) (7)

to suit stehen (+ *dat.*) (21)

suitcase der Koffer (-) (7)

suited geeignet (22)

summer der Sommer (5)

summit der Gipfel (-) (17)

sun die Sonne (-n) (5)

to sunbathe in der Sonne liegen, lag, gelegen (8)

Sunday der Sonntag (1E)

superficial(ly) oberflächlich (21/36)

supermarket der Supermarkt (ˉe) (4)

to supervise überwachen (32)

to support beistehen, stand bei, beigestanden (3E); fördern (36)

support die Fürsorge (-n) (25); **social support** die Sozialleistung (-en) (29)

to suppress unterdrücken (30)

surely sicherlich (29)

surprise die Überraschung (-en) (14)

to surprise überraschen (17)

surprised (*adj.*) überrascht (14)

to be surpised at sich wundern über (+ *acc.*) (28)

surroundings die Umgebung (4)

to survive überleben (25)

sweater der Pullover (-) (7)

Sweden (das) Schweden (9)

sweet süß (19)

to swim schwimmen, schwamm, geschwommen (2)

swimsuit der Badeanzug (ˉe) (7)

swim trunks die Badehose (-n) (7)

Swiss (*person*) der Schweizer (-) / die Schweizerin (-nen) (18)

Switzerland die Schweiz (9)

symbol das Symbol (-e) (16)

system das System (-e) (19)

T

table der Tisch (-e) (3)

table tennis das Tischtennis (8)

taboo tabu (26)

to take nehmen (nimmt), nahm, genommen (3); **to take along**

mitnehmen (nimmt mit), nahm mit, mitgenommen (23); **to take care of** sorgen für (23); **to take care of the household** den Haushalt machen (23); **to take a course** einen Kurs belegen (11/3E); **to take leave** sich verabschieden (24); **to take notice** achten (33); **to take off** abfliegen (fliegt ab), flog ab, ist abgeflogen (24); **to take on** annehmen (nimmt an) nahm an, angenommen (34); **to take part in** teilnehmen an (+ *dat.*) (nimmt teil), nahm teil, teilgenommen (26); **to take place** stattfinden, fand statt, stattgefunden (17/27); **to take up** aufnehmen (nimmt auf), nahm auf, aufgenommen (28), beziehen, bezog, bezogen (36); **to take up time** Zeit in Anspruch nehmen (nimmt), nahm, genommen (33)

taken: this seat is taken besetzt: hier ist besetzt (15)

talk der Vortrag (⸚e) (19/3E); **to give a talk** einen Vortrag halten (19/3E)

to talk (*gossip*) quatschen (28); **to talk about** reden über (+ *acc.*) (10); diskutieren über (+ *acc.*) (26)

to tan sich bräunen (32)

tan beige (2)

to taste: that tastes good (to me) schmecken: das schmeckt (mir) gut (15)

tasty lecker (19)

tax die Steuer (-n) (29)

tea der Tee (-s) (2)

to teach lehren, Unterricht erteilen (20), unterrichten (11/27)

teacher der Lehrer (-) / die Lehrerin (-nen) (1E)

teaching method die Unterrichtsmethode (-n) (27)

team die Mannschaft (-en) (23/32); das Team (-s) (23)

technology die Technik (-en) (11)

teenager der/die Jugendliche (*decl. adj.*) (26)

telephone das Telefon (-e) (3)

television set der Fernseher (-) (3)

to tell mitteilen (teilt mit) (36)

ten zehn (1E)

tense spannend (23/32)

tent das Zelt (-e) (8)

terminal (*airport*) das Terminal (-s) (24)

terrace die Terrasse (-n) (16)

to test prüfen (28)

theater das Theater (-) (2/36)

theater piece das Stück (-e) (36)

then dann (12)

thermometer das Thermometer (-) (6)

thesis work die Diplomarbeit (-en) (28)

they sie (1)

thief der Dieb (-e) (12)

to think denken, dachte, gedacht (6)

to think about denken an (+ *acc.*) dachte, gedacht (26); (***to have an opinion of***) meinen (3E)

thirteen dreizehn (1E)

thirty dreißig (1E)

thousand tausend (1E)

thought: freedom of thought die Gedankenfreiheit (30)

three drei (E)

throat der Hals (⸚e) (6)

through durch (+ *acc.*) (5)

to throw away wegschmeißen, schmiss weg, weggeschmissen (*coll.*) (35)

Thuringia Thüringen (17)

Thursday der Donnerstag (1E)

ticket counter der Fahrkartenschalter (-) (7)

tie die Krawatte (-n) (7)

tights die Strumpfhose (-n) (21)

time: free time die Freizeit (16/3E); **point in time** das Mal (-e) (31); **time off (work)** der Feierabend (29)

tin can die Dose (-n) (20)

tinted gefärbt (21)

tiring ermüdend (21)

to the left/right links/rechts (8)

today heute (5)

today's heutig (28)

together zusammen (4); gemeinsam (28)

token das Zeichen (-) (26)

tomato die Tomate (-n) (16)

tomato sauce die Tomatensoße (-n) (19)

tooth der Zahn (⸚e) (6)

topical aktuell (21)

to touch anfassen (fasst an) (31)

tough zäh (19)

town: small town das Dorf (⸚er) (27)

toy das Spielzeug (-e) (17)

traceable spürbar (36)

track das Gleis (-e) (7)

trade der Handel (27)

trade school die Berufsfachschule (-n) (11)

traffic der Verkehr (35)

train der Zug (⸚e), die Bahn (-en) (7)

to train trainieren (16)

train station der Bahnhof (⸚e) (7)

train station platform das Gleis (-e)

trainee der/die Auszubildende (*decl. adj.*) (13)

training das Training (23)

training position die Ausbildungsstelle (-n) (13)

to transfer versetzen (16)

to translate übersetzen (28)

transportation: mode of transportation das Verkehrsmittel (-) (35)

trash der Abfall (20/35); der Müll (20/35)

to travel reisen, ist gereist (9)

traveler der/die Reisende (*decl. adj.*) (24)

traveling das Reisen (24)

to treat behandeln (30)

treatment: course of treatment die Kur (-en) (33)

tremendous(ly) gewaltig (34)

trenchcoat der Trenchcoat (-s) (7)

trick der Trick (-s) (14)

trip der Ausflug (⸚e) (10); die Fahrt (-en) (24)

trip: to go on a trip verreisen (32)

trouble die Mühe (-n) (29)

trout die Forelle (-n) (15)

to try probieren (15)
to try on anprobieren (probiert an) (7)
T-shirt das T-Shirt (-s) (7)
Tuesday der Dienstag (1E)
tuition die Studiengebühren (19)
tuna der Thunfisch (-e) (15)
turbulent bewegt (27)
Turk der Türke (-n *masc.*) / die Türkin (-nen) (18)
to turn abbiegen (biegt ab), bog ab, abgebogen (22)
to turn (drive) in einbiegen (biegt ein), bog ein, eingebogen (22)
to turn (into) verwandeln (in + *acc.*) (12)
twelve zwölf (1E)
twenty zwanzig (1E)
twin der Zwilling (-e) (1)
two zwei (1E)
type die Art (-en) (26); **type of sport** die Sportart (-en) (23/32)

U

ugly hässlich (1)
unbiased unvoreingenommen (34)
uncertainty die Unsicherheit (-en) (27)
uncle der Onkel (-) (1/25)
uncongenial unsympatisch (1)
undecided(ly) unschlüssig (33)
undershirt das Unterhemd (-en) (21)
to understand begreifen, begriff, begriffen (29)
to undertake unternehmen (unternimmt), unternahm, unternommen (9/31); sich vornehmen (nimmt vor), nahm vor, vorgenommen (33)
underwear die Unterwäsche (7)
unemployed arbeitslos (1); **number of unemployed** die Arbeitslosenzahl (-en) (29)
unemployment die Arbeitslosigkeit (20)
unfriendly unfreundlich (1)
uninterested uninteressiert (1)
uninteresting uninteressant (1)
unique(ly) eigenartig (28)
to unite verbinden, verband, verbunden (29)

unity die Einheit (18)
university die Universität (-en) (11)
university study das Studium (Studien) (19/28)
unromantic unromantisch (1)
unusual ungewöhnlich (14)
unsatisfied unzufrieden (29)
upswing der Aufschwung (¨e) (29)
urban train die S-Bahn (-en) (22)
to urge mahnen (33)
us, to us uns (5)
to use nutzen (32); verbrauchen (20/35); verwenden (20)
usually normalerweise (32)
utensils: disposable utensils das Einweggeschirr (35)
to utter (sich) äußern (10)

V

vacation die Ferien (*pl.*) (32); der Urlaub (-e) (17/32)
vacation apartment die Ferienwohnung (-en) (8)
vacation camp das Ferienlager (-) (32)
vacation home das Ferienheim (-e) (32)
Valentine's Day der Valentinstag (5)
valley das Tal (¨er) (9)
valuable wertvoll (22)
to value something Wert legen auf (+ *acc.*) (27)
variable abwechslungsreich (14)
variety die Abwechslung (-en) (32)
various unterschiedlich (26)
veal cutlet das Wiener Schnitzel (-) (15)
vegetable das Gemüse (19/33)
vegetarian vegetarisch (33)
vicinity die Nähe (17/27); **in the vicinity** in der Nähe (17)
to view works of art Kunstwerke betrachten (8)
village das Dorf (¨er) (4)
violence, act of die Gewalttätigkeit (-en) (20)
violent(ly) gewalttätig (26)
violet violett (2)
visit der Aufenthalt (33); **visit to the doctor** der Artztbesuch (-e) (33)

to visit besuchen; (*as a sightseer*) besichtigen (8)
vocation die Berufung (-en) (28)
vocational school die Realschule (-n) (11/27)
to vote wählen (26)
voyage die Schiffsreise (-n) (32)

W

waiting area der Warteraum (¨e) (24)
waiting room das Wartezimmer (-) (33)
waitperson der Kellner (-) / die Kellnerin (-nen) (15)
to wake up aufwachen (wacht auf), ist aufgewacht (12)
to waken wecken (16)
to walk zu Fuß gehen, ging, ist gegangen (4)
wall die Wand (¨e) (1E); die Mauer (-n) (18)
war der Krieg (-e) (20)
warm warm (5)
warehouse das Warenhaus (¨er) (16)
to wash waschen (wäscht), wusch, gewaschen (16)
to wash the dishes das Geschirr spülen (3E)
waste der Abfall (¨e) (20/35)
to watch anschauen (schaut an); gucken (14); sich ansehen (sieht an), sah an, angesehen (21)
to watch out aufpassen (passt auf) (9/3E)
to watch television fernsehen (sieht fern), sah fern, ferngesehen (2)
water das Wasser (16)
way der Weg (-e) (22)
we wir (1)
to wear tragen (trägt), trug, getragen (5)
weather das Wetter (5)
Wednesday der Mittwoch (1E)
week die Woche (-n) (1E)
weekday der Wochentag (-e) (1E)
weekly wöchentlich (21)
welcome! herzlich willkommen! (24)

to welcome wilkommen heißen, hieß, geheißen (34)
well-behaved brav (1)
well-known bekannt (36)
wellness fund die Krankenkasse (33)
what is _____ in English/German? Wie heißt _____ auf Englisch/Deutsch? (1E)
while die Weile (16)
to whistle pfeifen, pfiff, gepfiffen (20)
white weiß (2)
wild irre (*coll.*) (32)
to win gewinnen, gewann, gewonnen (23/32)
wind der Wind (-e) (5)
window das Fenster (-) (1E)
windy windig (5)
winter der Winter (-) (5)

to wish wünschen (17)
witch die Hexe (-n) (12)
without ohne (+ *acc.*) (5)
woman die Frau (-en) (1)
women's movement die Frauenbewegung (-en) (30)
wonderful(ly) herrlich (32)
to work arbeiten (2)
work experience die Arbeitserfahrung (-en) (14); die Berufserfahrung (-en) (29)
workplace der Arbeitsplatz (¨e) (13/29)
world of work die Arbeitswelt (13)
worry die Sorge (-n) (24)
wound die Wunde (-n) (6)
to write schreiben, schrieb, geschrieben (9)
written exam Klausur (19)

X
xenophobia die Ausländerfeindlichkeit (20/34)

Y
yard der Hof (¨e) (31)
yellow gelb (2)
yesterday gestern (8)
you (*acc.*) dich; (*acc./dat.*) euch (5); (*form.*) Sie; (*inform. sg.*) du (1)
young jung (1)
young person der/die Jugendliche (*decl. adj.*) (26)
youth die Jugend (25)
youth hostel die Jugendherberge (-n) (8)

Z
zero null (1E)

INDEX

This index consists of two parts—Part 1: Grammar; Part 2: Topics. Everything related to grammar—terms, structure, usage, pronunciation, and so forth—appears in the first part. Topical subsections in the second part include Culture, Functions, Reading Strategies, Vocabulary, and Writing Strategies. Page numbers in italics refer to photos.

Part 1: Grammar

Part 2: Topics

Culture

Functions

Reading Strategies

Vocabulary

Writing Strategies

Grateful acknowledgment is made for use of the following:

Photographs: *Page 1* © Owen Franken/Stock Boston; *10* © Edgar Zippel/DAS Fotoarchiv; *14* © Knut Muller/DAS Fotoarchiv; *22* © Culver Pictures, Inc.; *30–31* © Beryl Goldberg Photographer; *34* © Stuart Cohen/The Image Works; *51* (*top*) © Stuart Cohen/The Image Works; *54* © Mike Mazzaschi/Stock Boston/PNI; *62* © California Institute of Technology and courtesy Hebrew University of Jerusalem; *73* © Verlag Jochen Kallhardt/Blue Box; *76–77* © D. & J. Heaton/Stock Boston; *80* © Dave Bartruff/Corbis Images; *88* © Michael & Patricia Fogden/Corbis Images; *90* © Wolfgang Kaehler; *97* (*top*) © Mike Mazzaschi/Stock Boston; *100* © Bundesbildstelle; *117* (*bottom*) © Adam Woolfitt/Corbis Images; *120* © Bundesbildstelle; *121* Culver Pictures, Inc.; *133* (1) © AKG London, (2) © Bildarchiv Preussischer Kulturbesitz, (3) © AKG London; *146* © Stuart Cohen/The Image Works; *154* © Ullstein BilderDienst/Gabriele Fromm; *162–163* © Robert E. Schwerzel/Stock Boston; *166* © Dagmar Fabricius/Stock Boston; *175* © Andreas Riedmiller/DAS Fotoarchiv; *183* (*top*) © M. Granitsas/ The Image Works; *186* © Owen Franken/Stock Boston; *190* © Sven Martson/The Image Works; *194* (*bottom*) © Willie L. Hill/Stock Boston; *208–209* © M. Pawlowski/images.de; *212* © Steve Raymer/Corbis; *220* © Gunter Peschel/Blue Box; *228–229* © D. Konnerth/Lichtblick/ images.de; *232* © Martin Fejer/images.de.; *240* © Sven Martson/The Image Works; *248–249* © Adam Woolfitt/Corbis; *252* © David Simson/Stock Boston; *260* © A. Bastian/CARO/images.de.

Readings: *Page 23* "meine grossmutter hatte kein gesicht" by Annemarie Zornack from *Stolperherz.* © Verlag Eremiten-Presse, 1988; *44* Notgroschen für das Sorgentelefon, JUMA; *63* "Der Stift," by Heinrich Spoerl in *Gesammelte Werke.* © Piper Verlag GmbH, München, 1963; *88* from *World Travel Guide,* http://german.travel-guides.com Copyright © Columbus Press, London; *90* "Die Freiheitspost" by Günther Anders; *108* reprinted with permission of *Leo Freizeitmagazin;* *109* "Der Lacher" by Heinrich Böll from *Erzählungen, Hörspiele, Aufsätze.* © 1994 Verlag Kiepenheuer & Witsch, Köln; *129* "Emanzipation" by Ingeburg Kanstein from *Papa, Charly hat gesagt* (Munich: Langenscheidt 1983); *141* from *Memoiren eines Clowns* by F. J. Bogner (Bern: Zytglogge, 1993), page 140. Reprinted with permission of the author; *154* http://www.yorkie.ch/cats/rat498.htw; *155* from *Nero Corleone* by Elke Heidenreich (Munich, Carl Hanser Verlag, 1995); *174* Ho Ga Tours; *176* "Der hellgraue Frühjahrsmantel," by Wolfgang Hildesheimer in *Lieblose Legenden.* © 1962 by Suhrkamp Verlag, Frankfurt am Main.

195 "Das neue Lauf-Einmaleins: 10 erste Schritte für Einsteiger from *Men's Health Deutschland,* Mai 1998, pp. 50–56; *220* information from *Alma,* 30 October 1998, Würzburg; *221* "Die Suche nach den Deutschen" by João Ubaldo Ribeiro from *Ein Brasilianer in Berlin.* Reprinted with permission of Suhrkamp Verlag; *240 JUMA* 1/98; *241* "Herr Munzel hört das Gras wachsen" by Achim Bröger and Bernd Küsters.

About the Authors

Lida Daves-Schneider received her Ph.D. from Rutgers, the State University of New Jersey. She has taught at the University of Georgia, the University of Arkansas at Little Rock, Rutgers, Riverside Community College, and Washington College where she taught German language and literature, film and teacher education courses, and served as language lab coordinator. She spent a year in Berlin on the Fulbright Teaching Exchange Program. She is presently teaching German at Ayala High School in Chino Hills, California. She has given numerous presentations and workshops, both in the United States and abroad, about foreign language methods and materials. She co-authored ancillary materials for *Deutsch: Na klar!* and was a contributing writer for the main text of the third edition.

Karl Schneider is a native of Germany. He has been a teacher for 22 years in the Chino Valley Unified School District. He has taught Reading, German, and English as a Second Language. From 1985 to 1990 he worked as Curriculum Coordinator for Foreign Languages. He has served several terms as Mentor teacher in his district. Mr. Schneider has participated in several statewide foreign language curriculum development projects. He has reviewed textbooks as well as national exams. Mr. Schneider has also been a presenter at local, state, and national conferences. He was co-founder of the Inland Empire Foreign Language Association and served as President of that organization.

Daniela R. Dosch Fritz is receiving her Ph.D. in German Literature and Culture from the University of California at Berkeley. Her dissertation combines literary studies and second language acquisition research by employing theories of language and culture from both fields. She has taught German language and literature at the University of California at Berkeley, the University of Arizona in Tucson, and the Goethe-Institut in San Francisco.

Stephen L. Newton received his Ph.D. from the University of California at Berkeley in 1992. Since then he has been the Language Program Coordinator in the German Department at Berkeley. He has made contributions to various textbooks and conducted a variety of workshops to language teachers.

About the Chief Academic and Series Developer

Robert Di Donato is professor of German and Chair of the German, Russian, and East Asian Languages Department at Miami University in Oxford, Ohio. He received his Ph.D. from the Ohio State University. He is lead author of *Deutsch: Na klar!*, a first-year German text, and has written articles about foreign language methodology. In addition, he has given numerous keynote speeches, workshops, and presentations, both in the United States and abroad, about foreign language methods and teacher education. He has also been a consultant for a number of college-level textbooks on foreign language pedagogy.